Ford Fusion

Owners Workshop Manual

M R Storey

Models covered

(5566 - 352)

Fusion Hatchback
Petrol: 1.4 litre (1388cc) & 1.6 litre (1596cc) Duratec
Turbo-Diesel: 1.4 litre (1398cc) & 1.6 litre (1560cc) Duratorq TDCi

Includes coverage of Durashift EST transmission
Does NOT cover fully automatic transmission fitted to 1.6 litre petrol models

ABCDE
FGHIJ
KLMNO
PQRST

A book in the **Haynes Owners Workshop Manual Series**

ISBN **978 0 85733 566 1**

British Library Cataloguing in Publication Data
A catalogue record for this book is available from the British Library.

Printed in the USA

Haynes Publishing
Sparkford, Yeovil, Somerset BA22 7JJ, England

Haynes North America, Inc
861 Lawrence Drive, Newbury Park, California 91320, USA

Haynes Publishing Nordiska AB
Box 1504, 751 45 UPPSALA, Sverige

Contents

Contents

REPAIRS AND OVERHAUL

Engine and associated systems

Transmission

Brakes and suspension

Body equipment

REFERENCE

Introduced in August 2002, the Fusion is based on the best-selling Ford Fiesta (Mk 6). The Fusion was Ford's first attempt to enter the mini MPV market and whilst the Fusion lacks some of the crucial features of a mini MPV (such as easily removable individual rear seats) the upright driving position, good visibility and ease of entry guaranteed its popularity.

In the UK the launch models were based around two petrol models (1.4 and 1.6 litre 16 valve 'Duratec' engines) and a 1.4 litre diesel engine. A 1.6 litre diesel variant was introduced in November 2004. The engines are well-proven and reliable; the diesel engines are a product of the Ford/PSA joint venture to produce a range of efficient common rail engines. All engines are mounted transversely at the front of the car.

At the launch, three trim levels were available – these were simply called 1, 2 and 3. A minor face lift in October 2005 introduced a revised facia, lights and bumpers. The trim levels were also renamed and more options were introduced at the same time. These were: Style, Pursuit, Zetec, Plus and Titanium. In July 2010 the trim options were rationalised and reduced to Zetec and Titanium

All models have front-wheel-drive, with a five-speed manual transmission and a new optional Durashift EST automated gearshift system, giving a new kind of automatic operation – 'clutchless' electronic gearchanging, but using near conventional clutch and gearbox major components.

The front suspension is of conventional MacPherson strut type, incorporating lower arms, and an anti-roll bar; at the rear, a semi-independent beam axle is combined with compact underfloor springs to provide a more spacious load area.

The Fusion has a high equipment level, even at the lower end of the model range. All feature driver's and passenger's airbags, central locking, CD radio and power steering – anti-lock brakes, electric windows and air conditioning are among the options available higher up the range.

For the home mechanic, the Ford Fusion is a straightforward car to maintain and repair, since design features have been incorporated to reduce the actual cost of ownership to a minimum, and most of the items requiring frequent attention are easily accessible.

Your Ford Fusion Manual

The aim of this manual is to help you get the best value from your car. It can do so in several ways. It can help you decide what work must be done (even should you choose to get it done by a garage). It will also provide information on routine maintenance and servicing, and give a logical course of action and diagnosis when random faults occur. However, it is hoped that you will use the manual by tackling the work yourself. On simpler jobs it may even be quicker than booking the car into a garage and going there twice, to leave and collect it. Perhaps most important, a lot of money can be saved by avoiding the costs a garage must charge to cover its labour and overheads.

The manual has drawings and descriptions to show the function of the various components so that their layout can be understood. Tasks are described and photographed in a clear step-by-step sequence.

References to the 'left' and 'right' of the car are in the sense of a person in the driver's seat facing forward.

Acknowledgements

Thanks are due to Draper Tools Limited, who provided some of the workshop tools, and to all those people at Sparkford who helped in the production of this manual.

We take great pride in the accuracy of information given in this manual, but car manufacturers make alterations and design changes during the production run of a particular car of which they do not inform us. No liability can be accepted by the authors or publishers for loss, damage or injury caused by any errors in, or omissions from, the information given.

Working on your car can be dangerous. This page shows just some of the potential risks and hazards, with the aim of creating a safety-conscious attitude.

General hazards

Scalding

• Don't remove the radiator or expansion tank cap while the engine is hot.
• Engine oil, transmission fluid or power steering fluid may also be dangerously hot if the engine has recently been running.

Burning

• Beware of burns from the exhaust system and from any part of the engine. Brake discs and drums can also be extremely hot immediately after use.

Crushing

• When working under or near a raised vehicle, always supplement the jack with axle stands, or use drive-on ramps.
Never venture under a car which is only supported by a jack.
• Take care if loosening or tightening high-torque nuts when the vehicle is on stands. Initial loosening and final tightening should be done with the wheels on the ground.

Fire

• Fuel is highly flammable; fuel vapour is explosive.
• Don't let fuel spill onto a hot engine.
• Do not smoke or allow naked lights (including pilot lights) anywhere near a vehicle being worked on. Also beware of creating sparks (electrically or by use of tools).
• Fuel vapour is heavier than air, so don't work on the fuel system with the vehicle over an inspection pit.
• Another cause of fire is an electrical overload or short-circuit. Take care when repairing or modifying the vehicle wiring.
• Keep a fire extinguisher handy, of a type suitable for use on fuel and electrical fires.

Electric shock

• Ignition HT and Xenon headlight voltages can be dangerous, especially to people with heart problems or a pacemaker. Don't work on or near these systems with the engine running or the ignition switched on.
• Mains voltage is also dangerous. Make sure that any mains-operated equipment is correctly earthed. Mains power points should be protected by a residual current device (RCD) circuit breaker.

Fume or gas intoxication

• Exhaust fumes are poisonous; they can contain carbon monoxide, which is rapidly fatal if inhaled. Never run the engine in a confined space such as a garage with the doors shut.
• Fuel vapour is also poisonous, as are the vapours from some cleaning solvents and paint thinners.

Poisonous or irritant substances

• Avoid skin contact with battery acid and with any fuel, fluid or lubricant, especially antifreeze, brake hydraulic fluid and Diesel fuel. Don't syphon them by mouth. If such a substance is swallowed or gets into the eyes, seek medical advice.
• Prolonged contact with used engine oil can cause skin cancer. Wear gloves or use a barrier cream if necessary. Change out of oil-soaked clothes and do not keep oily rags in your pocket.
• Air conditioning refrigerant forms a poisonous gas if exposed to a naked flame (including a cigarette). It can also cause skin burns on contact.

Asbestos

• Asbestos dust can cause cancer if inhaled or swallowed. Asbestos may be found in gaskets and in brake and clutch linings. When dealing with such components it is safest to assume that they contain asbestos.

Special hazards

Hydrofluoric acid

• This extremely corrosive acid is formed when certain types of synthetic rubber, found in some O-rings, oil seals, fuel hoses etc, are exposed to temperatures above 4000C. The rubber changes into a charred or sticky substance containing the acid. *Once formed, the acid remains dangerous for years. If it gets onto the skin, it may be necessary to amputate the limb concerned.*
• When dealing with a vehicle which has suffered a fire, or with components salvaged from such a vehicle, wear protective gloves and discard them after use.

The battery

• Batteries contain sulphuric acid, which attacks clothing, eyes and skin. Take care when topping-up or carrying the battery.
• The hydrogen gas given off by the battery is highly explosive. Never cause a spark or allow a naked light nearby. Be careful when connecting and disconnecting battery chargers or jump leads.

Air bags

• Air bags can cause injury if they go off accidentally. Take care when removing the steering wheel and trim panels. Special storage instructions may apply.

Diesel injection equipment

• Diesel injection pumps supply fuel at very high pressure. Take care when working on the fuel injectors and fuel pipes.

Warning: Never expose the hands, face or any other part of the body to injector spray; the fuel can penetrate the skin with potentially fatal results.

Remember...

DO

• Do use eye protection when using power tools, and when working under the vehicle.

• Do wear gloves or use barrier cream to protect your hands when necessary.

• Do get someone to check periodically that all is well when working alone on the vehicle.

• Do keep loose clothing and long hair well out of the way of moving mechanical parts.

• Do remove rings, wristwatch etc, before working on the vehicle – especially the electrical system.

• Do ensure that any lifting or jacking equipment has a safe working load rating adequate for the job.

DON'T

• Don't attempt to lift a heavy component which may be beyond your capability – get assistance.

• Don't rush to finish a job, or take unverified short cuts.

• Don't use ill-fitting tools which may slip and cause injury.

• Don't leave tools or parts lying around where someone can trip over them. Mop up oil and fuel spills at once.

• Don't allow children or pets to play in or near a vehicle being worked on.

The following pages are intended to help in dealing with common roadside emergencies and breakdowns. You will find more detailed fault finding information at the back of the manual, and repair information in the main chapters.

If your car won't start and the starter motor doesn't turn

- ☐ Open the bonnet and make sure that the battery terminals are clean and tight.
- ☐ Switch on the headlights and try to start the engine. If the headlights go very dim when you're trying to start, the battery is probably flat. Get out of trouble by jump starting (see next page) using a friend's car.
- ☐ If it's a model with Durashift transmission, make sure the gear lever is in the N position and apply the footbrake.

If your car won't start even though the starter motor turns as normal

- ☐ Is there fuel in the tank?
- ☐ Has the engine immobiliser been deactivated? This should happen automatically, on inserting the ignition key. However, if a replacement key has been obtained, it may not contain the transponder chip necessary to deactivate the system.

A Check the security and condition of the battery connections.

B With the ignition off, check the security of the HT leads at the coil (petrol models).

C With the ignition off, check the security of the HT leads at the spark plugs.

Is there moisture on electrical components under the bonnet? Switch off the ignition, then wipe off any obvious dampness with a dry cloth. Spray a water repellent aerosol product (WD-40 or equivalent) on ignition and fuel system electrical connectors like those shown in the photos. Pay special attention to the ignition coil wiring connector and HT leads.

D Check the security of any accessible electrical connectors.

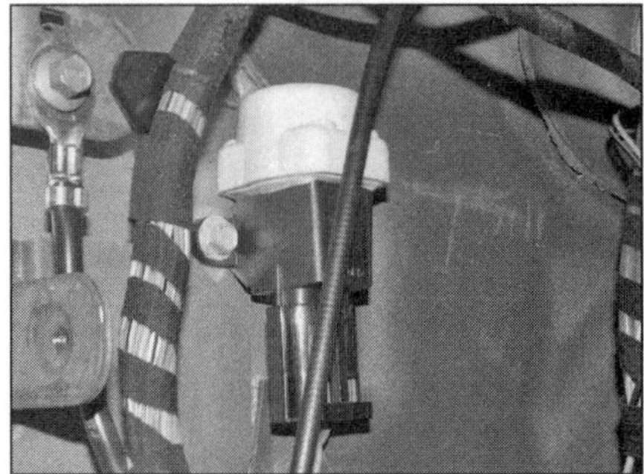

E With the ignition off check that the fuel cut-off switch behind the glovebox has not been activated (petrol models).

Jump starting

Jump starting will get you out of trouble, but you must correct whatever made the battery go flat in the first place. There are three possibilities:

1** **The battery has been drained by repeated attempts to start, or by leaving the lights on.

2** **The charging system is not working properly (alternator drivebelt slack or broken, alternator wiring fault or alternator itself faulty).

3** **The battery itself is at fault (electrolyte low, or battery worn out).

When jump-starting a car, observe the following precautions:

✓ Before connecting the booster battery, make sure that the ignition is switched off.

Caution: Remove the key in case the central locking engages when the jump leads are connected

✓ Ensure that all electrical equipment (lights, heater, wipers, etc) is switched off.

✓ Take note of any special precautions printed on the battery case.

✓ Make sure that the booster battery is the same voltage as the discharged one in the vehicle.

✓ If the battery is being jump-started from the battery in another vehicle, the two vehicles MUST NOT TOUCH each other.

✓ Make sure that the transmission is in neutral (or PARK, in the case of automatic transmission).

Budget jump leads can be a false economy, as they often do not pass enough current to start large capacity or diesel engines. They can also get hot.

1 Connect one end of the red jump lead to the positive (+) terminal of the flat battery

2 Connect the other end of the red lead to the positive (+) terminal of the booster battery.

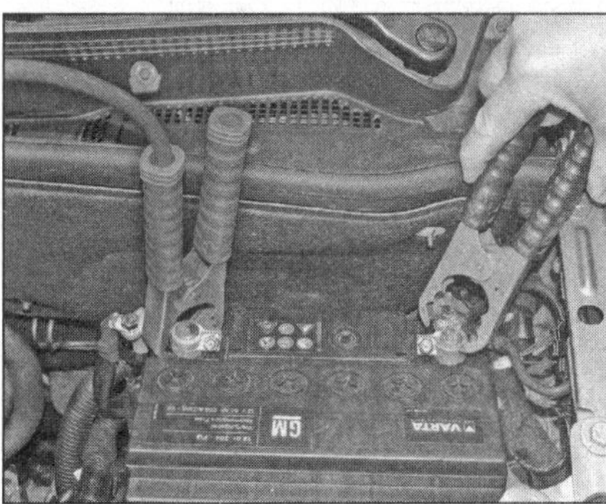

3 Connect one end of the black jump lead to the negative (-) terminal of the booster battery

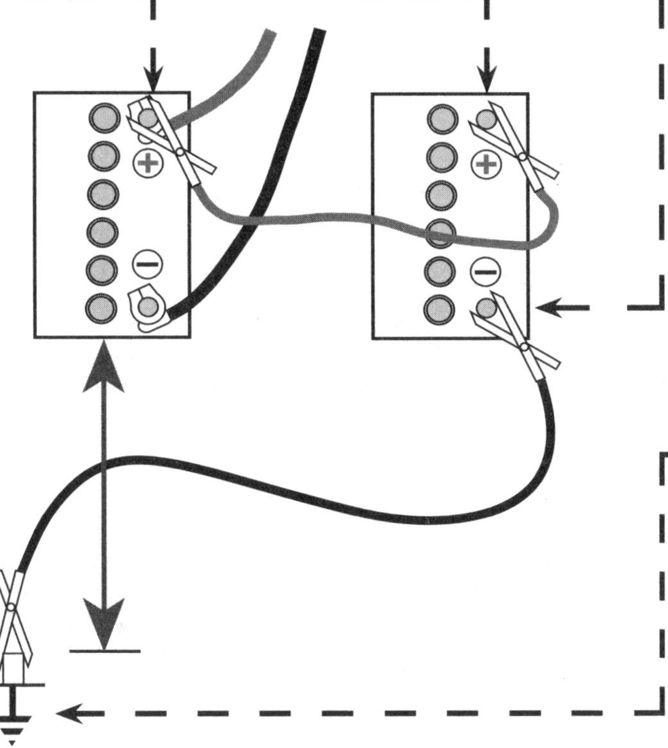

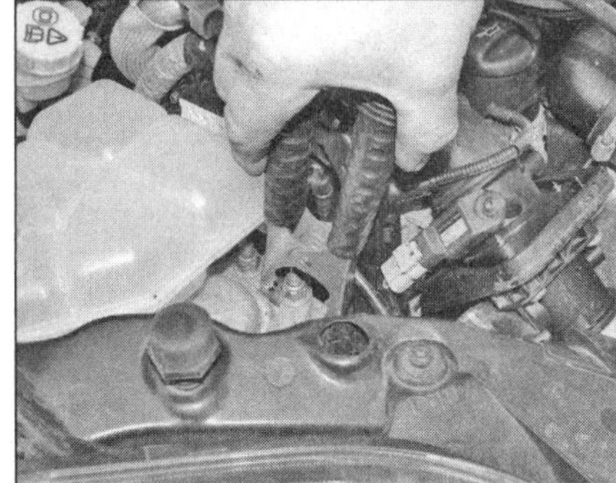

4 Connect the other end of the black jump lead to a bolt or bracket on the engine block, well away from the battery, on the vehicle to be started.

5 Make sure that the jump leads will not come into contact with the fan, drive-belts or other moving parts of the engine.

6 Start the engine using the booster battery and run it at idle speed. Switch on the lights, rear window demister and heater blower motor, then disconnect the jump leads in the reverse order of connection. Turn off the lights etc.

Wheel changing

Warning: Do not change a wheel in a situation where you risk being hit by other traffic. On busy roads, try to stop in a lay-by or a gateway. Be wary of passing traffic while changing the wheel – it is easy to become distracted by the job in hand.

Preparation

- ☐ When a puncture occurs, stop as soon as it is safe to do so.
- ☐ Park on firm level ground, if possible, and well out of the way of other traffic.
- ☐ Use hazard warning lights if necessary.
- ☐ If you have one, use a warning triangle to alert other drivers of your presence.
- ☐ Apply the handbrake and engage first or reverse gear.
- ☐ Chock the wheel diagonally opposite the one being removed – a couple of large stones will do for this.
- ☐ If the ground is soft, use a flat piece of wood to spread the load under the jack.

Changing the wheel

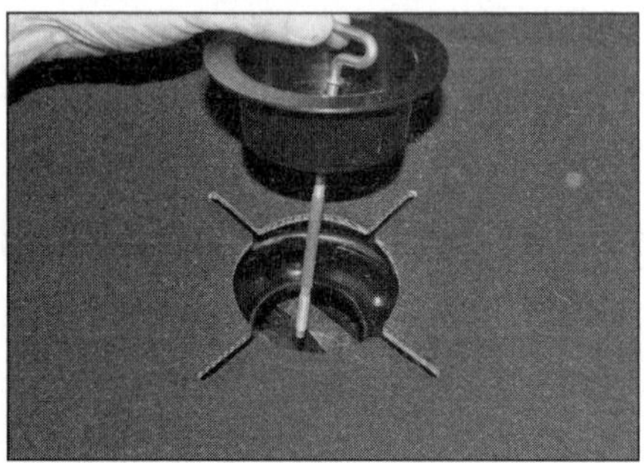

1 The jack and wheel brace are stored beneath the spare wheel (where fitted). Remove the load space cover and unscrew the retaining bolt.

2 Lift out the spare wheel and then remove the jack.

3 Place the spare wheel under the vehicle and then remove the wheel trim (or centre cover on alloy wheels) from the punctured wheel.

4 On models fitted with locking wheel nuts locate and fit the special 'key' socket.

5 Loosen each wheel nut by half a turn. Where locking wheel nuts are fitted, use the special adapter. Where fitted remove the insert from the sill cover.

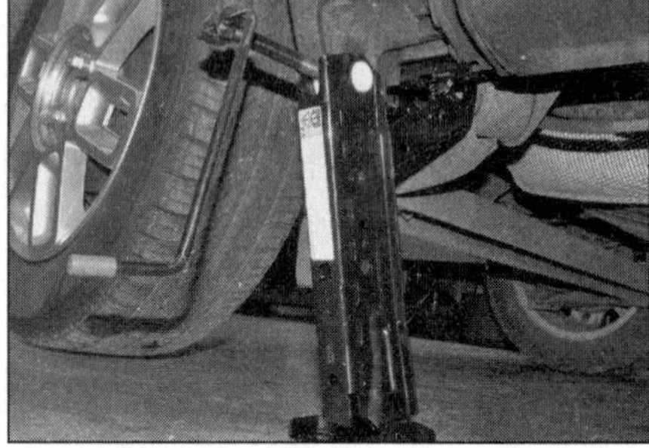

6 Locate the jack head below the reinforced jacking point nearest the wheel to be changed, and with the jack on firm ground, engage the jack head with the cut-out in the jacking point. Turn the handle to raise the wheel clear of the ground.

7 Fully remove the wheel nuts and remove the wheel. Place the wheel under the sill and remove the spare from under the vehicle.

8 Locate the spare wheel on the studs and tighten the nuts moderately with the wheel brace. Lower the vehicle to the ground, and then securely tighten the wheel nuts progressively in diagonal sequence.

Using tyre sealant

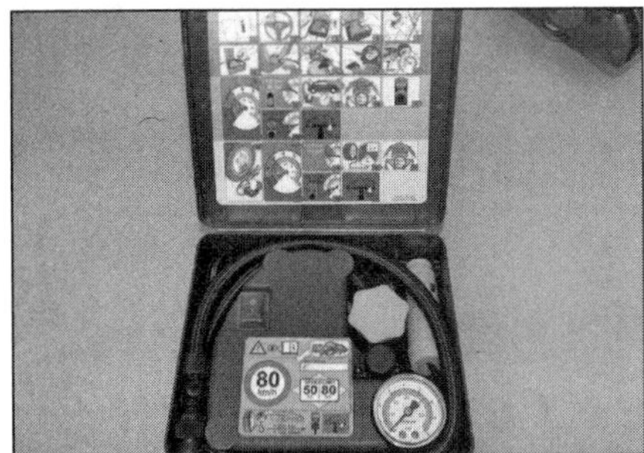

1 Later models may be supplied with a compressor and sealant instead of a spare wheel. Follow the graphic instructions printed on the lid.

2 Install the sealant bottle, following the instructions and inflate the tyre. It should be noted that the sealant is only suitable for repairs in the tyre tread up to a diameter of 6 mm. It is not suitable for repairs to the tyre sidewall.

Finally (all methods) . . .

- ☐ Have the wheel nuts tightened to the specified torque (see Chapter 1A or 1B Specifications) at the earliest possible opportunity.
- ☐ Remove the wheel chocks.
- ☐ Stow the jack, tools and wheel in the luggage compartment.
- ☐ Check the tyre pressure on the wheel just fitted. If it is low, or if you don't have a pressure gauge with you, drive slowly to the nearest garage and inflate the tyre to the right pressure.
- ☐ Have the punctured wheel repaired at the earliest opportunity, or another puncture will leave you stranded.

Towing

When all else fails, you may find yourself having to get a tow home – or of course you may be helping somebody else. Long-distance recovery should only be done by a garage or breakdown service. For shorter distances, DIY towing using another car is easy enough, but observe the following points:

☐Use a proper tow-rope – they are not expensive. The vehicle being towed must display an ON TOW sign in its rear window.

☐Always turn the ignition key to the 'on' position when the vehicle is being towed, so that the steering lock is released, and the direction indicator and brake lights work.

☐The front towing eye is located behind a cover on the front bumper. Use the end of the wheel brace to remove the cover. Fit the towing eye (located with the jack beneath the spare wheel) and fully tighten it with the wheel brace **(see illustration)**. Note that the towing eye has a **left-hand** thread.

☐The rear towing eye is a conventional loop below the rear bumper.

☐Before being towed, release the handbrake and make sure the transmission is in neutral.

☐Note that greater-than-usual pedal pressure will be required to operate the brakes, since the vacuum servo unit is only operational with the engine running.

☐The driver of the car being towed must keep the tow-rope taut at all times to avoid snatching.

☐Make sure that both drivers know the route before setting off.

☐Only drive at moderate speeds and keep the distance towed to a minimum. Drive smoothly and allow plenty of time for slowing down at junctions.

Fit the towing eye and fully tighten it with the wheel brace

Identifying leaks

Puddles on the garage floor or drive, or obvious wetness under the bonnet or underneath the car, suggest a leak that needs investigating. It can sometimes be difficult to decide where the leak is coming from, especially if an engine undershield is fitted. Leaking oil or fluid can also be blown rearwards by the passage of air under the car, giving a false impression of where the problem lies.

Warning: Most automotive oils and fluids are poisonous. Wash them off skin, and change out of contaminated clothing, without delay.

The smell of a fluid leaking from the car may provide a clue to what's leaking. Some fluids are distinctively coloured. It may help to remove the engine undershield, clean the car carefully and to park it over some clean paper overnight as an aid to locating the source of the leak. Remember that some leaks may only occur while the engine is running.

Sump oil

Engine oil may leak from the drain plug...

Oil from filter

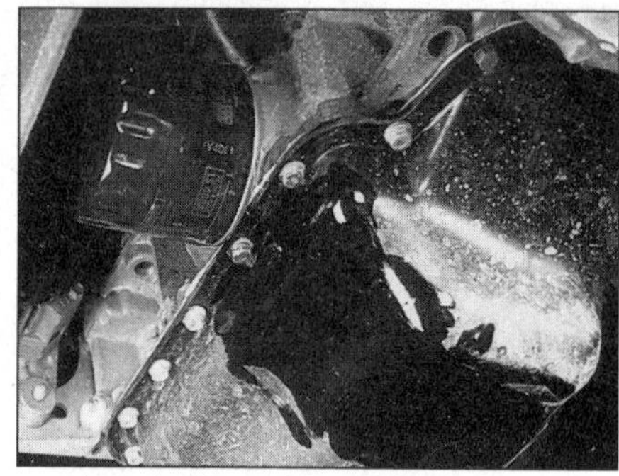

...or from the base of the oil filter.

Gearbox oil

Gearbox oil can leak from the seals at the inboard ends of the driveshafts.

Antifreeze

Leaking antifreeze often leaves a crystalline deposit like this.

Brake fluid

A leak occurring at a wheel is almost certainly brake fluid.

Power steering fluid

Power steering fluid may leak from the pipe connectors on the steering rack.

Introduction

There are some very simple checks which need only take a few minutes to carry out, but which could save you a lot of inconvenience and expense.

These checks require no great skill or special tools, and the small amount of time they take to perform could prove to be very well spent, for example:

☐ Keeping an eye on tyre condition and pressures, will not only help to stop them wearing out prematurely, but could also save your life.

☐ Many breakdowns are caused by electrical problems. Battery-related faults are particularly common, and a quick check on a regular basis will often prevent the majority of these.

☐ If your car develops a brake fluid leak, the first time you might know about it is when your brakes don't work properly. Checking the level regularly will give advance warning of this kind of problem.

☐ If the oil or coolant levels run low, the cost of repairing any engine damage will be far greater than fixing the leak, for example.

Underbonnet check points

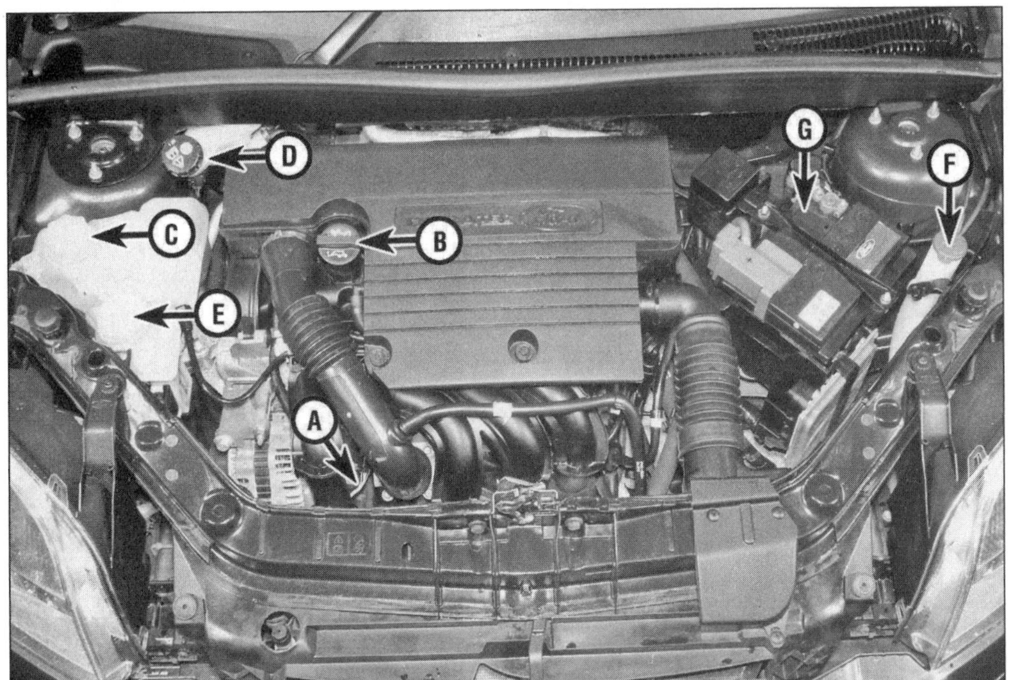

◀ Petrol engine

A *Engine oil level dipstick*
B *Engine oil filler cap*
C *Coolant reservoir (expansion tank)*
D *Brake (and clutch) fluid reservoir*
E *Power steering fluid reservoir*
F *Screen washer fluid reservoir*
G *Battery*

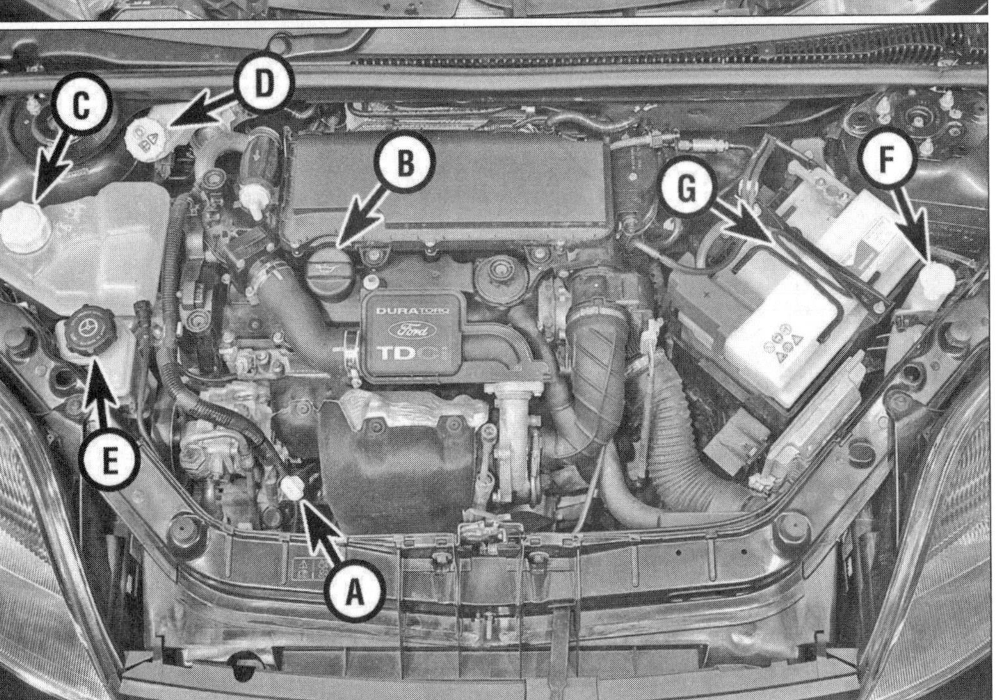

◀ 1.4 litre diesel engine

A *Engine oil level dipstick*
B *Engine oil filler cap*
C *Coolant reservoir (expansion tank)*
D *Brake (and clutch) fluid reservoir*
E *Power steering fluid reservoir*
F *Screen washer fluid reservoir*
G *Battery*

◀ 1.6 litre diesel engine

A *Engine oil level dipstick*
B *Engine oil filler cap*
C *Coolant reservoir (expansion tank)*
D *Brake (and clutch) fluid reservoir*
E *Screen washer fluid reservoir*
F *Battery*

Engine oil level

Before you start

✔ Make sure that your car is on level ground.
✔ Check the oil level before the car is driven, or at least 5 minutes after the engine has been switched off.

If the oil is checked immediately after driving the vehicle, some of the oil will remain in the upper engine components, resulting in an inaccurate reading on the dipstick.

The correct oil

Modern engines place great demands on their oil. It is very important that the correct oil for your car is used (see *Lubricants and fluids*).

Car care

- If you have to add oil frequently, you should check whether you have any oil leaks. Place some clean paper under the car overnight, and check for stains in the morning. If there are no leaks, then the engine may be burning oil.
- Always maintain the level between the upper and lower dipstick marks (see photo 3). If the level is too low, severe engine damage may occur. Oil seal failure may result if the engine is overfilled by adding too much oil.

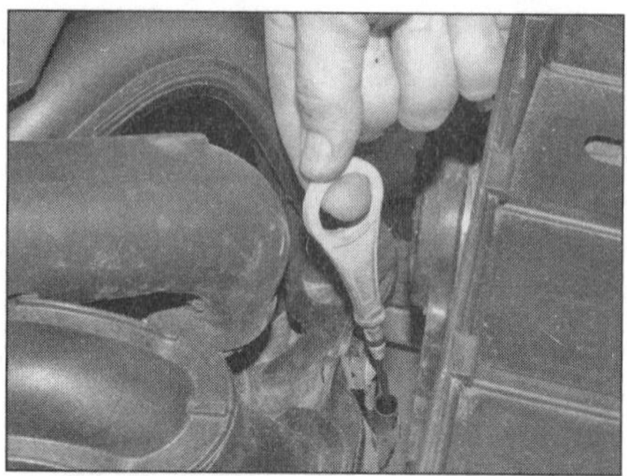

1 The dipstick top is brightly coloured for easy identification (see *Underbonnet check points* for the exact location). Withdraw the dipstick.

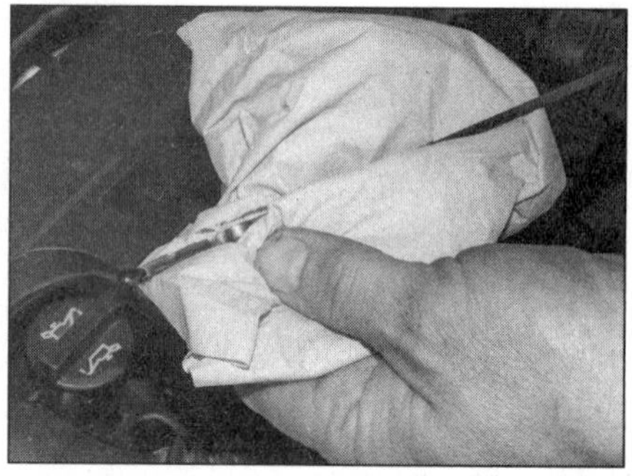

2 Using a clean rag or paper towel wipe all oil from the dipstick. Insert the clean dipstick into the tube as far as it will go, then withdraw it again.

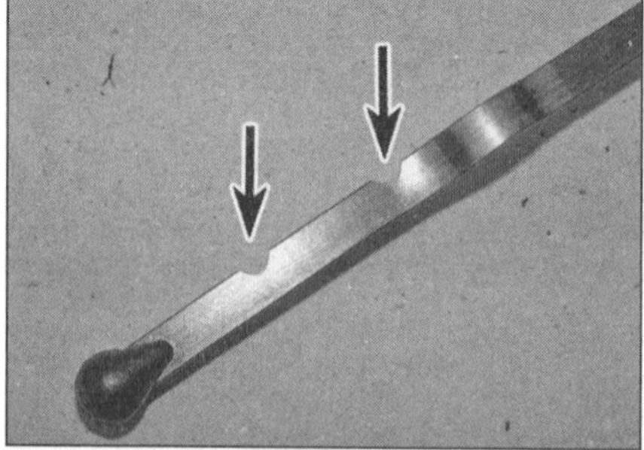

3 Note the oil level on the end of the dipstick, which should be between the upper MAX mark and lower MIN mark. If the oil level is only just above, or below, the MIN mark, topping-up is required. Petrol model shown, but the diesel model is similar.

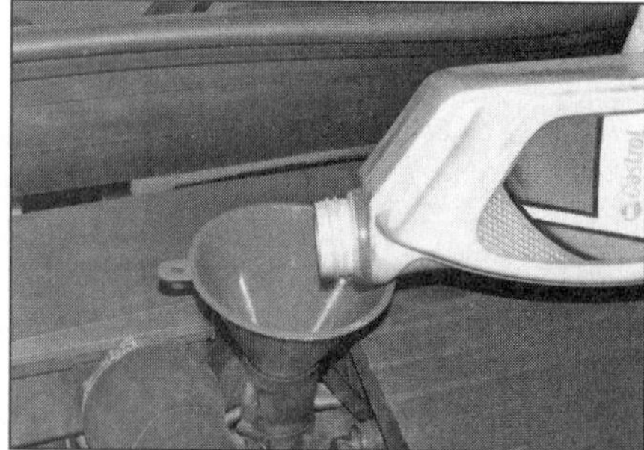

4 Oil is added through the filler cap aperture. Lift off the cap using a twisting motion. Top-up the level taking care not to spill the oil. A funnel may be useful in reducing spillage. Add the oil slowly, checking the level on the dipstick often, and allowing time for the oil to flow to the sump. Add oil until the level is just up to the MAX mark on the dipstick – don't overfill (see *Car care*).

Coolant level

Warning: Do not attempt to remove the expansion tank pressure cap when the engine is hot, as there is a very great risk of scalding. Do not leave open containers of coolant about, as it is poisonous.

Car care

● With a sealed-type cooling system, adding coolant should not be necessary on a regular basis. If frequent topping-up is required, it is likely there is a leak. Check the radiator, all hoses and joint faces for signs of staining or wetness, and rectify as necessary.

● It is important that antifreeze is used in the cooling system all year round, not just during the winter months. Don't top up with water alone, as the antifreeze will become diluted.

1 The coolant level varies with the temperature of the engine. MIN and MAX marks are shown on the side of the tank. When the engine is cold, the coolant level should be between the two marks, but ideally on the MAX mark. When the engine is hot, the level will rise above the MAX mark slightly.

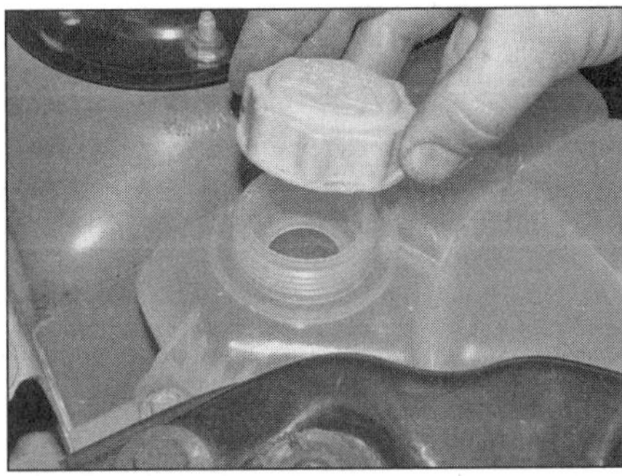

2 If topping up is necessary, **wait until the engine is cold**. Slowly unscrew the expansion tank cap, to release any pressure present in the cooling system, and remove it.

3 Add a mixture of water and antifreeze to the expansion tank until the coolant level is on the MAX mark. Refit the cap and tighten it securely.

Brake and clutch* fluid level

**The brake fluid reservoir also supplies fluid to the clutch master cylinder.*

Warning:

- ***Brake fluid can harm your eyes and damage painted surfaces, so use extreme caution when handling and pouring it.***
- ***Do not use fluid that has been standing open for some time, as it absorbs moisture from the air, which can cause a dangerous loss of braking effectiveness.***

Safety first!

● If the reservoir requires repeated topping-up this is an indication of a fluid leak somewhere in the system, which should be investigated immediately.

● If a leak is suspected, the car should not be driven until the braking system has been checked. Never take any risks where brakes are concerned

1 The MAX and MIN marks are indicated on the side of the reservoir, which is located at the rear right-hand side of the engine compartment. The fluid level must be kept between these two marks.

2 If topping-up is necessary, first wipe the area around the filler cap with a clean rag. When adding fluid, it's a good idea to inspect the reservoir. The fluid should be changed if dirt is visible or if it is more than two years old.

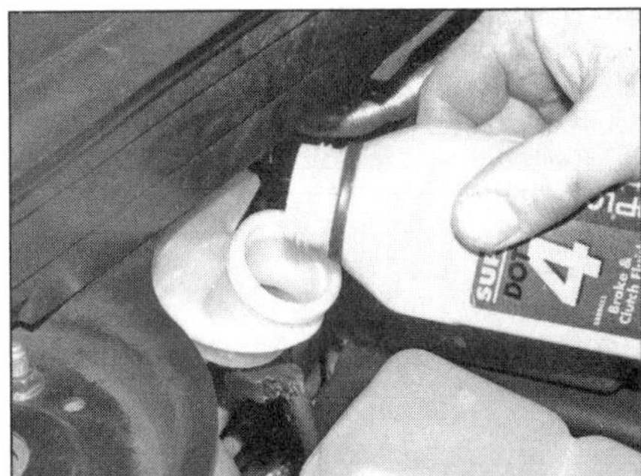

3 Carefully add fluid, avoiding spilling it on surrounding paintwork. Use only the specified hydraulic fluid; mixing different types of fluid can cause damage to the system and/or a loss of braking effectiveness. After filling to the correct level, refit the cap securely. Wipe off any spilt fluid.

Tyre condition and pressure

It is very important that tyres are in good condition, and at the correct pressure - having a tyre failure at any speed is highly dangerous.

Tyre wear is influenced by driving style - harsh braking and acceleration, or fast cornering, will all produce more rapid tyre wear. As a general rule, the front tyres wear out faster than the rears. Interchanging the tyres from front to rear ("rotating" the tyres) may result in more even wear. However, if this is completely effective, you may have the expense of replacing all four tyres at once!

Remove any nails or stones embedded in the tread before they penetrate the tyre to cause deflation. If removal of a nail does reveal that the tyre has been punctured, refit the nail so that its point of penetration is marked. Then immediately change the wheel, and have the tyre repaired by a tyre dealer.

Regularly check the tyres for damage in the form of cuts or bulges, especially in the sidewalls. Periodically remove the wheels, and clean any dirt or mud from the inside and outside surfaces. Examine the wheel rims for signs of rusting, corrosion or other damage. Light alloy wheels are easily damaged by "kerbing" whilst parking; steel wheels may also become dented or buckled. A new wheel is very often the only way to overcome severe damage.

New tyres should be balanced when they are fitted, but it may become necessary to re-balance them as they wear, or if the balance weights fitted to the wheel rim should fall off. Unbalanced tyres will wear more quickly, as will the steering and suspension components. Wheel imbalance is normally signified by vibration, particularly at a certain speed (typically around 50 mph). If this vibration is felt only through the steering, then it is likely that just the front wheels need balancing. If, however, the vibration is felt through the whole car, the rear wheels could be out of balance. Wheel balancing should be carried out by a tyre dealer or garage.

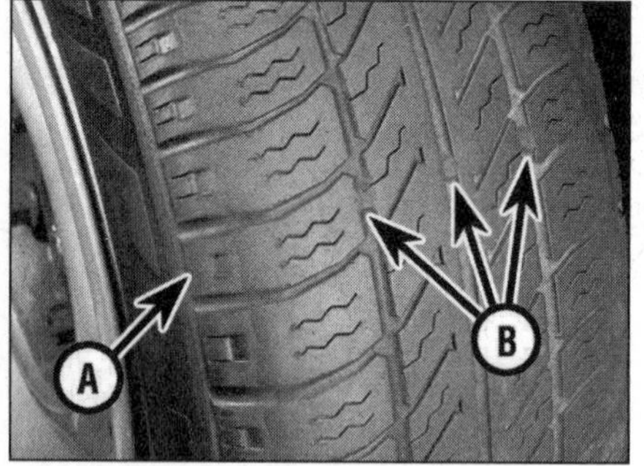

1 ***Tread Depth - visual check***
The original tyres have tread wear safety bands (B), which will appear when the tread depth reaches approximately 1.6 mm. The band positions are indicated by a triangular mark on the tyre sidewall (A).

2 ***Tread Depth - manual check***
Alternatively, tread wear can be monitored with a simple, inexpensive device known as a tread depth indicator gauge.

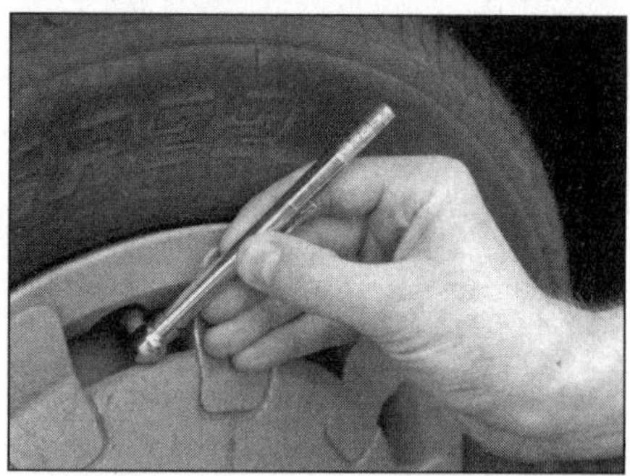

3 ***Tyre Pressure Check***
Check the tyre pressures regularly with the tyres cold. Do not adjust the tyre pressures immediately after the vehicle has been used, or an inaccurate setting will result.

Tyre tread wear patterns

Shoulder Wear

Underinflation (wear on both sides)
Under-inflation will cause overheating of the tyre, because the tyre will flex too much, and the tread will not sit correctly on the road surface. This will cause a loss of grip and excessive wear, not to mention the danger of sudden tyre failure due to heat build-up.
Check and adjust pressures
Incorrect wheel camber (wear on one side)
Repair or renew suspension parts
Hard cornering
Reduce speed!

Centre Wear

Overinflation
Over-inflation will cause rapid wear of the centre part of the tyre tread, coupled with reduced grip, harsher ride, and the danger of shock damage occurring in the tyre casing.
Check and adjust pressures

If you sometimes have to inflate your car's tyres to the higher pressures specified for maximum load or sustained high speed, don't forget to reduce the pressures to normal afterwards.

Uneven Wear

Front tyres may wear unevenly as a result of wheel misalignment. Most tyre dealers and garages can check and adjust the wheel alignment (or "tracking") for a modest charge.
Incorrect camber or castor
Repair or renew suspension parts
Malfunctioning suspension
Repair or renew suspension parts
Unbalanced wheel
Balance tyres
Incorrect toe setting
Adjust front wheel alignment
Note: *The feathered edge of the tread which typifies toe wear is best checked by feel.*

Screen washer fluid level

● Screenwash additives not only keep the windscreen clean during bad weather, they also prevent the washer system freezing in cold weather – which is when you are likely to need it most. Don't top-up using plain water, as the screenwash will become diluted, and will freeze in cold weather.

Warning: On no account use engine coolant antifreeze in the screen washer system – this may damage the paintwork.

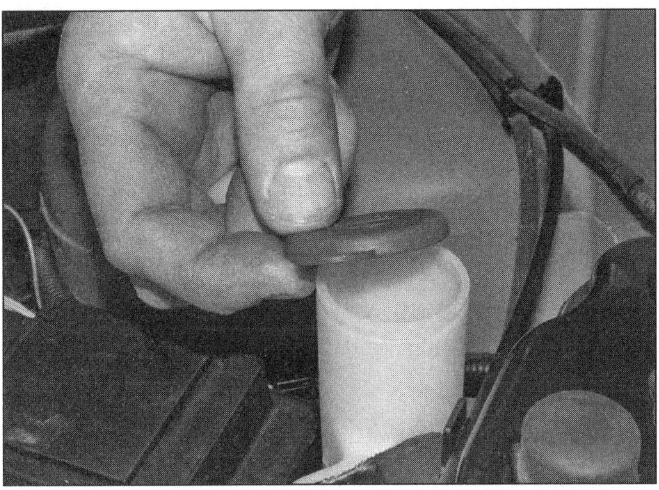

1 The screen/tailgate washer fluid reservoir filler neck is located at the front left-hand side of the engine compartment, adjacent to the battery on all models except the 1.6 litre diesel. On 1.6 litre diesel models the reservoir is located adjacent to the coolant expansion tank. The screen washer level cannot easily be seen. Remove the filler cap, and look down the filler neck – if fluid is not visible, topping-up is required.

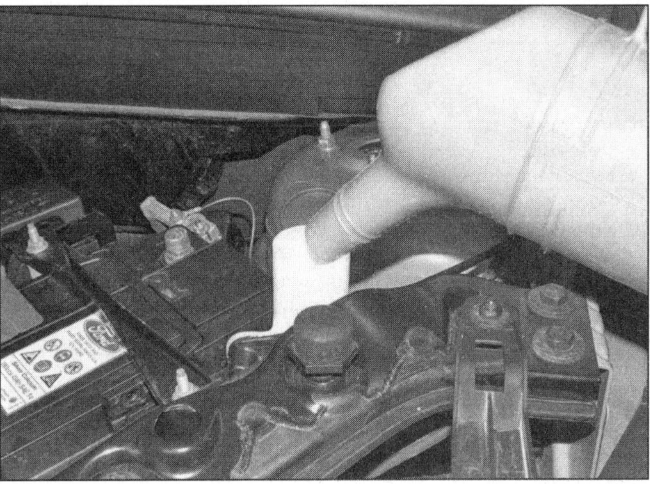

2 When topping-up the reservoir, add a screen wash additive in the quantities recommended on the bottle.

Power steering fluid level

Note: *This section applies to all petrol models and the 1.4 litre diesel models. The reservoir is located beneath the left-hand headlight.*

Note: *1.6 litre diesel models are equipped with an electro-hydraulic power steering system. There is no requirement to carry out a weekly fluid level check on 1.6 litre diesel models.*

✔ Park the vehicle on level ground.

✔ Set the steering wheel straight-ahead.

✔ The engine should be turned off.

Safety first!

● The need for frequent topping-up indicates a leak, which should be investigated immediately.

1 The reservoir is located in front of the coolant expansion tank. The fluid should be checked with the engine stopped. A translucent reservoir is fitted, with MAX and MIN markings on the side of the reservoir.

2 The fluid level should be between the MAX and MIN marks. If topping-up is necessary, wipe clean the area around the cap first

3 Remove the cap and top up to the MAX mark with the correct type of power steering fluid. Refit and tighten the cap. Wipe up any spilt fluid.

Wiper blades

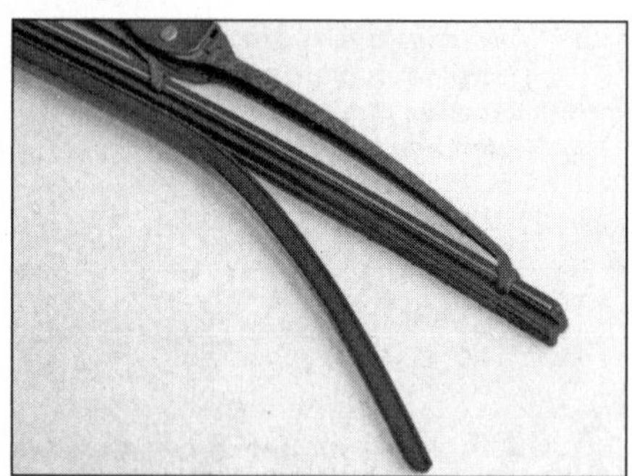

1 Check the condition of the wiper blades; if they are cracked or show any signs of deterioration, or if the glass swept area is smeared, renew them. For maximum clarity of vision, wiper blades should be renewed annually, as a matter of course.

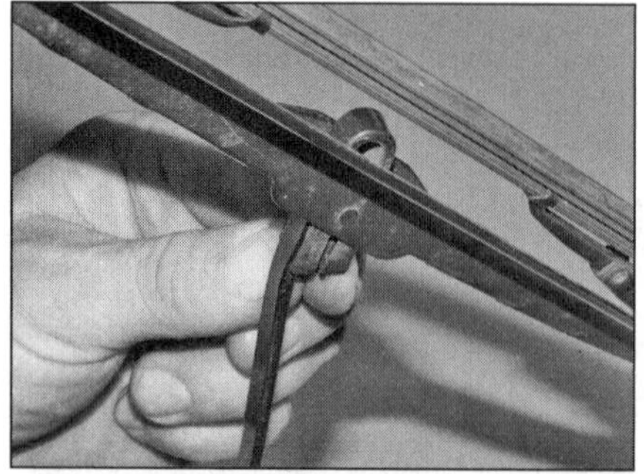

2 To remove a windscreen wiper blade, pull the arm fully away from the screen until it locks. Swivel the blade through 90°, then lift it off the wiper arm. Fit the new blade using a reversal of the removal procedure.

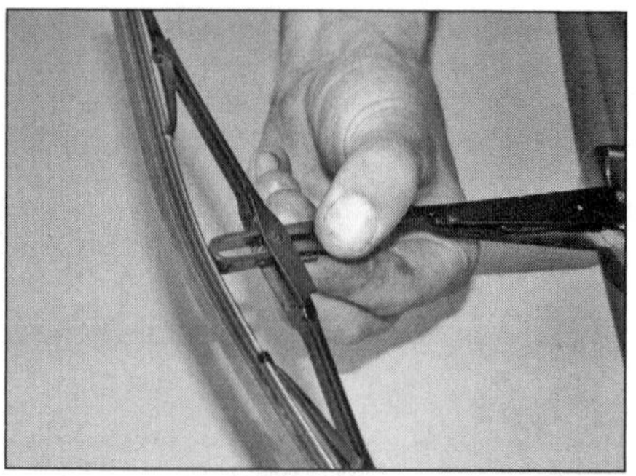

3 Don't forget to check the tailgate wiper blade as well. To remove the tailgate wiper blade, pull the arm away from the window until it locks. Carefully prise the blade from the arm using the fingers only until it is released. Fit the new blade using a reversal of the removal procedure.

Battery

Caution: Before carrying out any work on the vehicle battery, read the precautions given in 'Safety first!' at the start of this manual.

✔ Make sure that the battery tray is in good condition, and that the clamp is tight. Corrosion on the tray, retaining clamp and the battery itself can be removed with a solution of water and baking soda. Thoroughly rinse all cleaned areas with water. Any metal parts damaged by corrosion should be covered with a zinc based primer and then painted.

✔ Periodically (approximately every three months), check the charge condition of the battery as described in Chapter 5A, Section 6.

✔ If the battery is flat, and you need to jump start your vehicle, see *Roadside Repairs*.

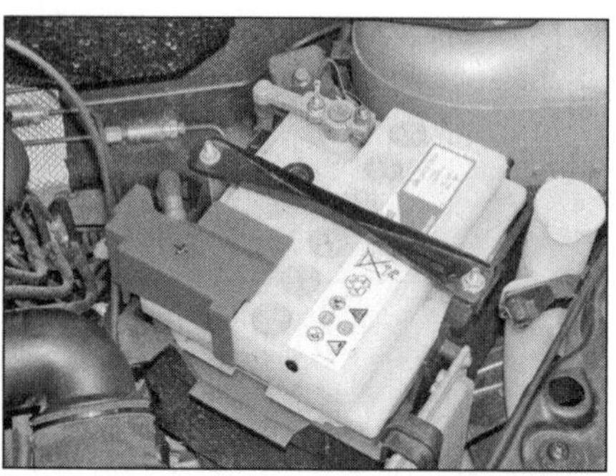

1 The battery is located on the left-hand side of the engine compartment. Periodically inspect the battery for physical damage, such as a cracked case or cover.

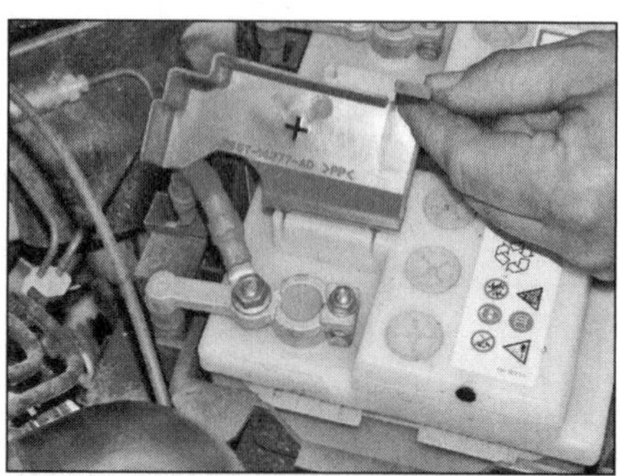

2 Lift the cover from the positive terminal and check the tightness of the battery clamps to ensure good electrical connections. You should not be able to move them. Also check each cable for cracks and frayed conductors.

HAYNES HiNT

Battery corrosion can be kept to a minimum by applying a layer of petroleum jelly to the clamps and terminals after they are reconnected.

3 If corrosion (white, fluffy deposits) is evident, remove the cables from the battery terminals, clean them with a small wire brush, and then refit them. Automotive stores sell a tool for cleaning the battery post ...

4 ... as well as the battery cable clamps.

Electrical systems

✔ Check all external lights and the horn. Refer to the appropriate Sections of Chapter 12 for details if any of the circuits are found to be inoperative.

✔ Visually check all accessible wiring connectors, harnesses and retaining clips for security, and for signs of chafing or damage.

If you need to check your brake lights and indicators unaided, back up to a wall or garage door and operate the lights. The reflected light should show if they are working properly.

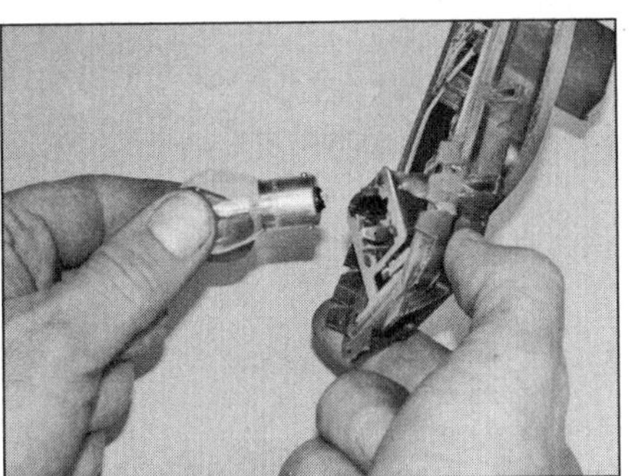

1 If a single indicator light, brake light or headlight has failed, it is likely that a bulb has blown and will need to be renewed. Refer to Chapter 12, Section 5 for details. If both brake lights have failed, it is possible that the switch has failed (see Chapter 9, Section 18).

2 If more than one indicator light or tail light has failed, it is likely that either a fuse has blown or that there is a fault in the circuit (see Chapter 12, Section 3). The main fuses are located in the fusebox, behind the glovebox. Open the glovebox and release the fusebox cover.

3 To renew a blown fuse, use the plastic tool provided to pull the fuse from its location then fit the new one. If the fuse blows again, it is important that you find out why – a complete checking procedure is given in Chapter 12, Section 2.

Lubricants and fluids

Engine	SAE 5W-30 engine oil to Ford specification WSS-M2C913-C
Cooling system	Motorcraft Super Plus antifreeze to Ford specification WSS-M97 B44-D*
Transmission (including EST)	SAE 75W/90 synthetic oil to Ford specification WSD-M2C200-C
Brake (and clutch) hydraulic system	DOT 4 hydraulic fluid to Ford specification WSS-M6C57-A2
Power steering	Hydraulic fluid to Ford specification WSS-M2C204-A2

** Do not mix coolant types, nor top-up with any other type of coolant.*

Tyre pressures

	Front	**Rear**
Normally-laden (up to 3 people):		
All tyre sizes	2.0 bars (29 psi)	1.8 bars (26 psi)
Fully-laden (with more than 3 persons):		
All tyre sizes	2.5 bars (36 psi)	2.8 bars (41 psi)

Note: *Pressures apply to original-equipment tyres, and may vary if any other make of tyre is fitted; check with the tyre manufacturer or supplier for the correct pressures if necessary.*

Chapter 1 Part A: Routine maintenance and servicing – petrol models

Contents

Degrees of difficulty

Easy, suitable for novice with little experience 	**Fairly easy,** suitable for beginner with some experience	**Fairly difficult,** suitable for competent DIY mechanic	**Difficult,** suitable for experienced DIY mechanic 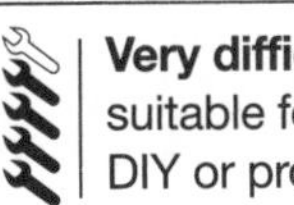	**Very difficult,** suitable for expert DIY or professional

Servicing specifications – petrol models

Lubricants and fluids . . . . Refer to end of *Weekly checks* on page 0•18

Capacities

Engine oil (including oil filter)

1.4 litre engine:	
With Ford EFL500 oil filter	3.75 litres
With Ford EFL10 oil filter	3.80 litres
1.6 litre engine:	
With Ford EFL600 oil filter	4.25 litres
With Ford EFL10 oil filter	4.10 litres

Cooling system (approximate)

All models	5.0 litres

Transmission

All models	2.3 litres

Washer fluid reservoir

All models	2.5 litres

Fuel tank

All models	45.0 litres

Cooling system

Antifreeze mixture:	
50% antifreeze	Protection down to -37°C

Note: *Refer to antifreeze manufacturer for latest recommendations.*

Ignition system

	Type	Gap
Spark plugs:		
All engines	Bosch HR 8 MEV	1.3 mm
	Motorcraft AYFS 22 C	1.3 mm

Brakes

Friction material minimum thickness:	
Front brake pads	1.5 mm
Rear brake shoes	1.0 mm

Tyre pressures

Refer to end of *Weekly checks* on page 0•18

Torque wrench settings

	Nm	lbf ft
Engine oil drain plug	28	21
Roadwheel nuts	110	81
Seat belts:		
Front seat belt height adjuster securing bolts	40	30
Front seat belt sliding rail bolt	40	30
Front seat belt stalk/tensioner assembly securing bolt	47	35
Inertia reel mounting:		
Front seat belt	35	26
Rear centre seat belt	47	35
Rear side seat belt	40	30
Rear seat belt buckle bolts	55	41
Seat belt buckle securing bolt	47	35
Seat belt upper/lower anchor bolts	40	30
Spark plugs	15	11
Transmission filler/level plug	35	26

The maintenance intervals in this manual are provided with the assumption that you, not the dealer, will be carrying out the work. These are the minimum maintenance intervals recommended by us for cars driven daily. If you wish to keep your car in peak condition at all times, you may wish to perform some of these procedures more often. We encourage frequent maintenance, because it enhances the efficiency, performance and resale value of your car.

If the car is driven in dusty areas, used to tow a trailer, or driven frequently at slow speeds (idling in traffic) or on short journeys, more frequent maintenance intervals are recommended.

When the vehicle is new, it should be serviced by a dealer service department (or other workshop recognised by the vehicle manufacturer as providing the same standard of service) in order to preserve the warranty. The vehicle manufacturer may reject warranty claims if you are unable to prove that servicing has been carried out as and when specified, using only original equipment parts or parts certified to be of equivalent quality.

Every 250 miles or weekly

- ☐ Refer to *Weekly checks*

Every 6000 miles or 6 months, whichever comes first

- ☐ Renew the engine oil and filter (Section 3)

Note: *Ford recommend that the engine oil and filter are changed every 12 500 miles or 12 months. However, oil and filter changes are good for the engine, and we recommend that the oil and filter are renewed more frequently, especially if the car is used on a lot of short journeys.*

Every 12 500 miles or 12 months, whichever comes first

- ☐ Renew the pollen filter, where applicable (Section 4)
- ☐ Check all components, pipes and hoses for fluid leaks (Section 5)
- ☐ Check the condition and tension of the auxiliary drivebelt(s) (Section 6)
- ☐ Check and if necessary adjust the handbrake (Section 7)
- ☐ Check the condition and operation of the seat belts (Section 8)
- ☐ Lubricate all hinges and locks (Section 9)
- ☐ Check the front brake pads and discs for wear (Section 10)
- ☐ Check the rear brake shoes and drums for wear (Section 11)
- ☐ Check the steering and suspension components for condition and security (Section 12)
- ☐ Check the condition of the driveshaft gaiters (Section 13)
- ☐ Check the roadwheel nuts are tightened to the specified torque (Section 14)
- ☐ Carry out a road test (Section 15)

Every 37 500 miles or 3 years, whichever comes first

- ☐ Renew the spark plugs (Section 16)
- ☐ Renew the air filter (Section 17)
- ☐ Check the transmission oil level (Section 18)
- ☐ Check the braking system rubber hoses (Section 19)

Every 50 000 miles or 4 years, whichever comes first

- ☐ Renew the timing belt

Note: *Although the normal interval for timing belt renewal is 100 000 miles or 10 years, it is strongly recommended that the interval suggested above is observed, especially on cars which are subjected to intensive use, ie, mainly short journeys or a lot of stop-start driving. The actual belt renewal interval is very much up to the individual owner, but bear in mind that severe engine damage will result if the belt breaks.*

Every 75 000 miles

- ☐ Renew the fuel filter (Section 21)

Every 100 000 miles or 8 years, whichever comes first

- ☐ Adjust the valve clearances
- ☐ Renew the auxiliary drivebelt (Section 23)

Every 2 years, regardless of mileage

- ☐ Renew the brake fluid (Section 24)
- ☐ Renew the remote control battery (Section 25)

Every 4 years, regardless of mileage

- ☐ Renew the coolant and check the condition of the expansion tank pressure cap (Section 26)

Note: *Ford state that, if their purple Super Plus antifreeze is in the system from new, the coolant need only be changed every 10 years. If there is any doubt as to the type or quality of the antifreeze which has been used, we recommend this shorter interval be observed.*

Component location – petrol models

Underbonnet view of a 1.4 litre model (1.6 similar)

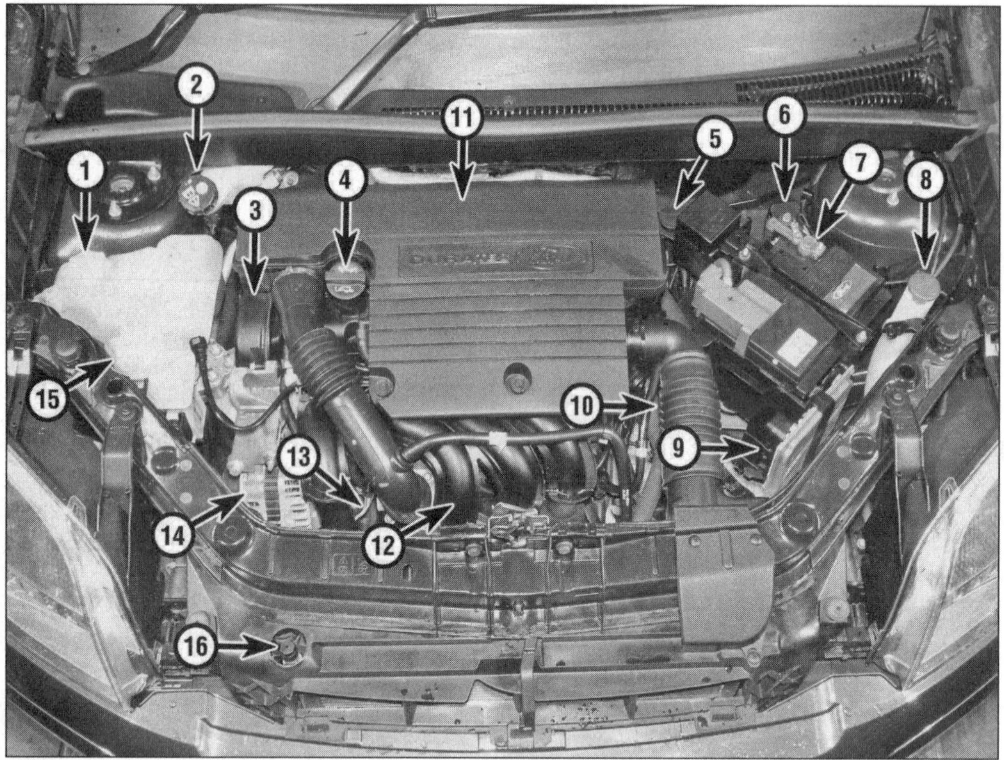

1 Coolant reservoir (expansion tank)
2 Brake and clutch fluid reservoir
3 Timing belt upper cover
4 Engine oil filler cap
5 Ignition coil (under air filter housing)
6 Engine wiring harness connector
7 Battery negative lead
8 Windscreen washer fluid reservoir filler
9 Powertrain control module
10 Air inlet duct
11 Air filter housing
12 Inlet manifold
13 Engine oil level dipstick
14 Alternator
15 Power steering fluid reservoir
16 AC charging connector

Front underbody view of a 1.4 litre model (1.6 similar)

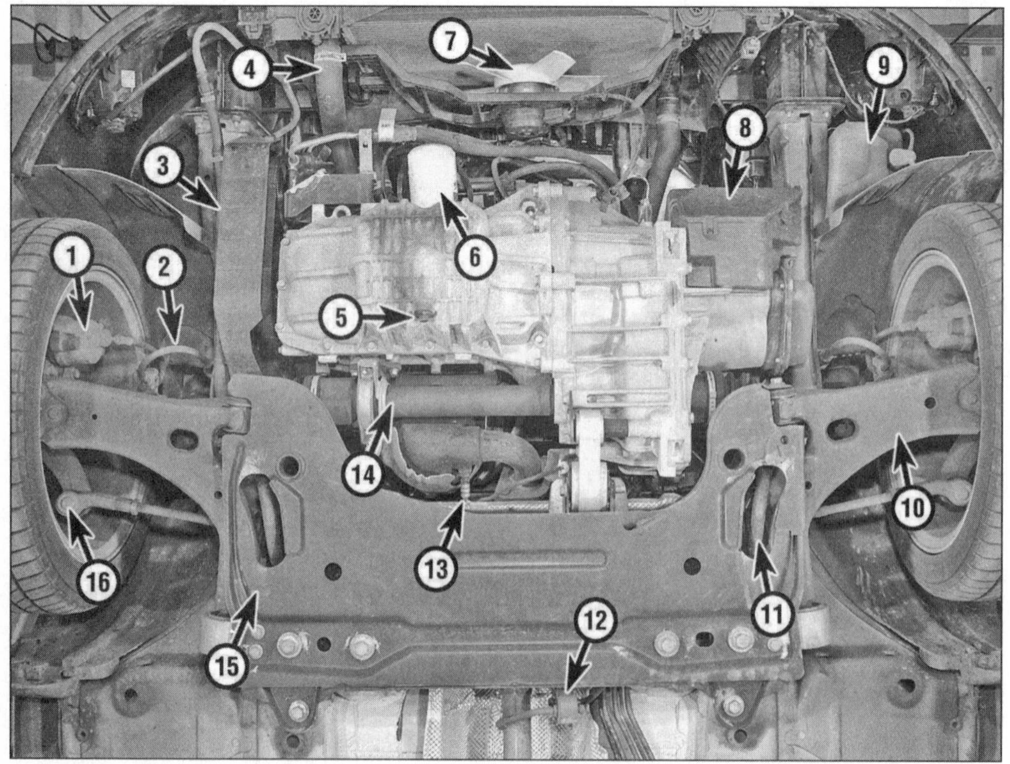

1 Brake caliper
2 Brake hose
3 Auxiliary drivebelt lower cover
4 Radiator bottom hose
5 Engine oil drain plug
6 Engine oil filter
7 Cooling fan
8 Gearchange cable front cover
9 Washer reservoir
10 Suspension lower arm
11 Anti-roll bar
12 Exhaust front mounting
13 Lower oxygen sensor
14 Driveshaft
15 Subframe
16 Track rod end

Rear underbody view

1 *Shock absorber*
2 *Fuel filler pipe*
3 *Rear coil spring*
4 *Rear suspension beam*
5 *Exhaust rear silencer*
6 *Fuel tank*
7 *Handbrake cable*
8 *Fuel filter*

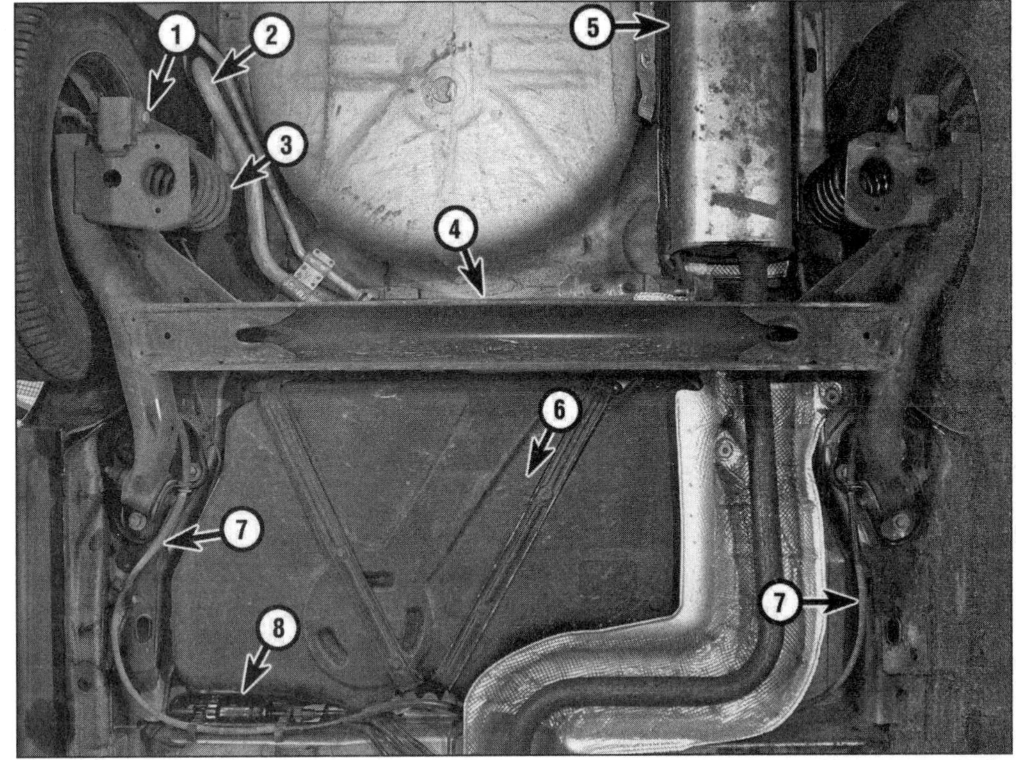

Maintenance procedures

1 General information

1 This Chapter is designed to help the home mechanic maintain his/her car for safety, economy, long life and peak performance.
2 The Chapter contains a master maintenance schedule, followed by Sections dealing specifically with each task in the schedule. Visual checks, adjustments, component renewal and other helpful items are included. Refer to the accompanying illustrations of the engine compartment and the underside of the car for the locations of the various components.
3 Servicing your car in accordance with the mileage/time maintenance schedule and the following Sections will provide a planned maintenance programme, which should result in a long and reliable service life. This is a comprehensive plan, so maintaining some items but not others at the specified service intervals will not produce the same results.
4 As you service your car, you will discover that many of the procedures can – and should – be grouped together, because of the particular procedure being performed, or because of the proximity of two otherwise unrelated components to one another. For example, if the car is raised for any reason, the exhaust can be inspected at the same time as the suspension and steering components.
5 The first step in this maintenance programme is to prepare yourself before the actual work begins. Read through all the Sections relevant to the work to be carried out, then make a list and gather all the parts and tools required. If a problem is encountered, seek advice from a parts specialist, or a dealer service department.

2 Regular maintenance

1 If, from the time the car is new, the routine maintenance schedule is followed closely, and frequent checks are made of fluid levels and high wear items, as suggested throughout this manual, the engine will be kept in relatively good running condition, and the need for additional work will be minimised.
2 It is possible that there will be times when the engine is running poorly due to the lack of regular maintenance. This is even more likely if a used car, which has not received regular and frequent maintenance checks, is purchased. In such cases, additional work may need to be carried out, outside of the regular maintenance intervals.
3 If engine wear is suspected, a compression test (refer to Chapter 2A, Section 2) will provide valuable information regarding the overall performance of the main internal components. Such a test can be used as a basis to decide on the extent of the work to be carried out. If, for example, a compression test indicates serious internal engine wear, conventional maintenance as described in this Chapter will not greatly improve the performance of the engine, and may prove a waste of time and money, unless extensive overhaul work is carried out first.
4 The following series of operations are those most often required to improve the performance of a generally poor running engine:

Primary operations

a) Clean, inspect and test the battery (refer to 'Weekly checks').
b) Check all the engine related fluids (refer to 'Weekly checks').
c) Check the condition and tension of the auxiliary drivebelt (Section 6).

d) Renew the spark plugs (Section 16).

e) Check the condition of the air filter, and renew if necessary (Section 17).

f) Renew the fuel filter (Section 21).

g) Check the condition of all hoses, and check for fluid leaks (Section 5).

5 If the above operations do not prove fully effective, carry out the following secondary operations:

Secondary operations

All items listed under *Primary operations*, plus the following:

a) Check the charging system (Chapter 5A, Section 6).

b) Check the ignition system (Chapter 5B, Section 2).

c) Check the fuel system (Chapter 4A, Section 13).

Every 6000 miles or 6 months

3 Engine oil and filter renewal

1 Frequent oil and filter changes are the most important preventative maintenance procedures which can be undertaken by the DIY owner. As engine oil ages, it becomes diluted and contaminated, which leads to premature engine wear.

2 Before starting this procedure, gather together all the necessary tools and materials. Also make sure that you have plenty of clean rags and newspapers handy, to mop-up any spills. Ideally, the engine oil should be warm, as it will drain more easily, and more built-up sludge will be removed with it. Take care not to touch the exhaust or any other hot parts of the engine when working under the car. To avoid any possibility of scalding, and to protect yourself from possible skin irritants and other harmful contaminants in used engine oils, it is advisable to wear gloves when carrying out this work.

3 Firmly apply the handbrake, then jack up the front of the car and support it on axle stands (see *Jacking and vehicle support*).

4 Remove the oil filler cap **(see illustration)**.

5 Using a spanner, or preferably a socket and bar, slacken the drain plug about half a turn. Position the draining container under the drain plug, then remove the plug completely **(see illustrations)**.

6 Allow some time for the oil to drain, noting that it may be necessary to reposition the container as the oil flow slows to a trickle.

7 After all the oil has drained, wipe the drain plug with a clean rag. Examine the condition of the sealing O-ring, and renew it if it shows signs of damage which may prevent an oil tight seal. Clean the area around the drain plug opening, then refit the plug complete with O-ring and tighten it securely.

8 Move the container into position under the oil filter, which is located on the front of the cylinder block.

9 Use an oil filter removal tool to slacken the filter initially, then unscrew it by hand the rest of the way **(see illustrations)**. Empty the oil from the old filter into the container.

10 Use a clean rag to remove all oil, dirt and sludge from the filter sealing area on the engine.

11 Apply a light coating of clean engine oil to the sealing ring on the new filter, then screw the filter into position on the engine **(see illustrations)**. Tighten the filter firmly by hand only – **do not** use any tools.

3.4 Removing the oil filler cap

3.5a Slacken the oil drain plug on the back of the sump with a socket ...

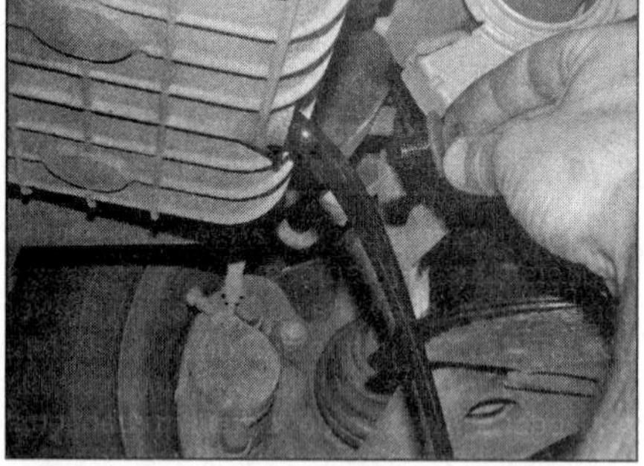

3.5b ... then unscrew it by hand, and allow the oil to drain

3.9a Use an oil filter removal tool to loosen the filter if necessary ...

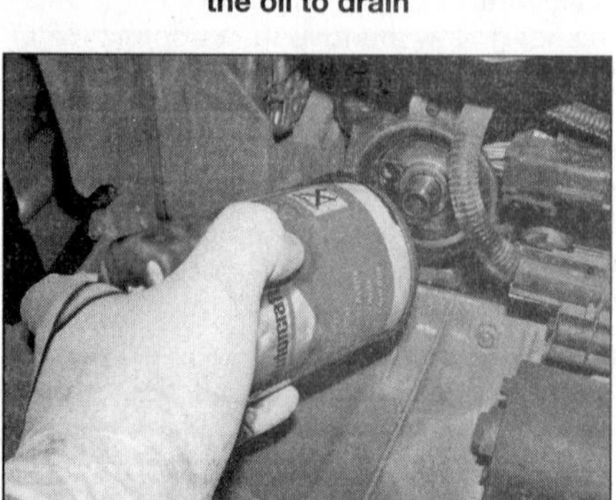

3.9b ... then unscrew it by hand – wear gloves to protect your hands from hot oil

3.11a Apply a light coating of engine oil to the sealing ring on the new filter ...

3.11b ... then screw it firmly in place by hand

12 Remove the old oil and all tools from under the car, then lower the car to the ground.
13 Fill the engine through the filler hole, using the correct grade and type of oil (refer to *Weekly checks* for details of topping-up). Pour in half the specified quantity of oil first, then wait a few minutes for the oil to drain into the sump **(see illustration)**. Continue to add oil, a small quantity at a time, until the level is up to the lower mark on the dipstick. Adding approximately a further 0.5 to 1.0 litre will bring the level up to the upper mark on the dipstick.
14 Start the engine and run it for a few minutes, while checking for leaks around the oil filter seal and the sump drain plug. Note that there may be a delay of a few seconds before the oil pressure warning light goes out when the engine is first started, as the oil circulates through the new oil filter and the engine oil galleries before the pressure builds up.
15 Stop the engine, and wait a few minutes for the oil to settle in the sump once more. With the new oil circulated and the filter now completely full, recheck the level on the dipstick, and add more oil as necessary.
16 Dispose of the used engine oil safely, with reference to *General repair procedures*.

3.13 Fill the engine with oil, wait, then recheck the dipstick

Every 12 500 miles or 12 months

4 Pollen filter renewal

Note: *Models without air conditioning appear not to have been fitted with a pollen filter as standard, although the filter housing IS fitted to all models, meaning that a filter can be added if wished.*
1 For greater access to the filter, remove the glovebox as described in Chapter 11, Section 25, and also the side panel in front of the centre console, which is secured by a single screw at the front, and clips at the rear **(see illustration)**.
2 Working at the very front of the passenger footwell, remove the four screws and take off the cover fitted over the end of the filter housing, in the centre of the car **(see illustrations)**. The housing is almost vertical, and the cover for it should not be confused with the horizontal cover fitted to the side of the heater matrix.
3 Slide out the pollen filter, into the passenger footwell, and remove it.
4 When fitting the new filter, note the direction of flow arrow marked on its top edge – the arrow should point into the car **(see illustration)**.
5 Slide the filter fully into position, secure the cover with the four screws, then refit the glovebox and centre console side panel (if removed).

5 Hose and fluid leak check

Coolant

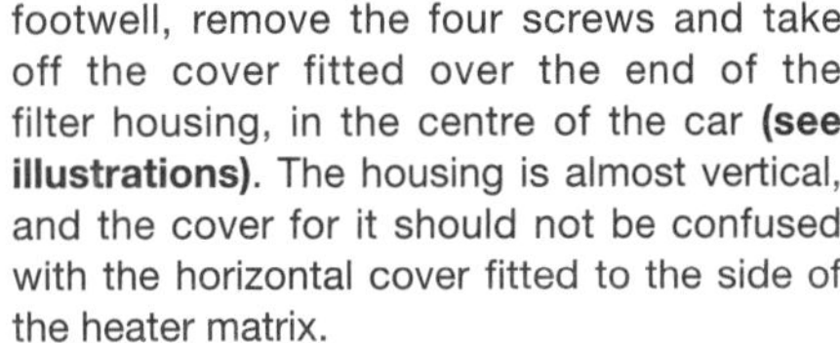

Warning: Refer to the safety information given in 'Safety first!' and Chapter 3, Section 1 before disturbing any of the cooling system components.
1 Carefully check the radiator and heater coolant hoses along their entire length **(see illustration)**. Renew any hose which is cracked, swollen or which shows signs of deterioration. Cracks will show up better if the hose is squeezed. Pay close attention to the clips that secure the hoses to the cooling system components. Hose clips that have been overtightened can pinch and puncture hoses, resulting in cooling system leaks.
2 Inspect all the cooling system components (hoses, joint faces, etc) for leaks. Where any problems of this nature are found on system components, renew the component or gasket with reference to Chapter 3.
3 A leak from the cooling system will usually show up as white- or antifreeze-coloured deposits, on the area surrounding the leak **(see Haynes Hint)**.

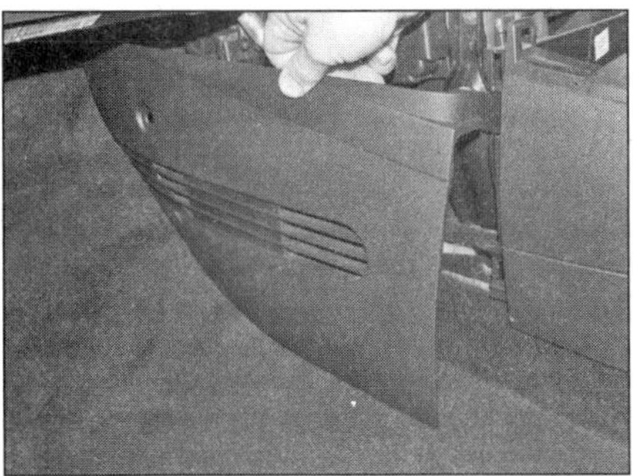

4.1 Removing the centre console side panel

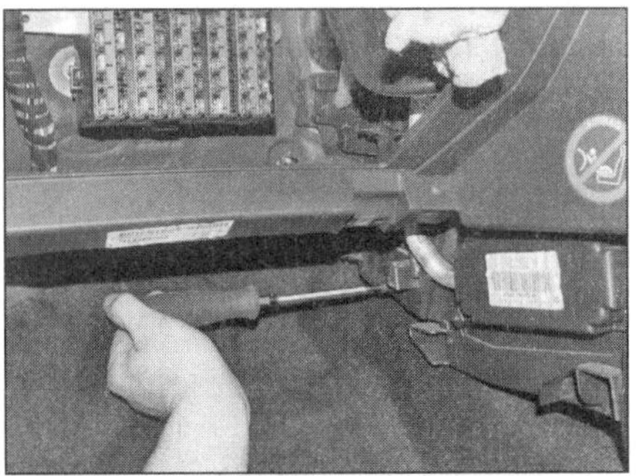

4.2a Remove the four Torx screws ...

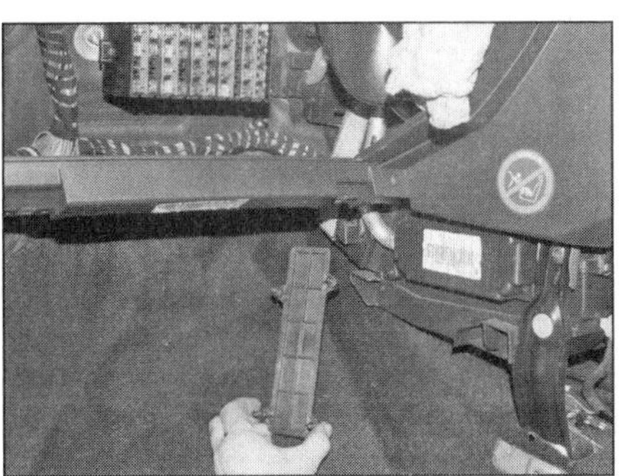

4.2b ... and take off the pollen filter housing end cover

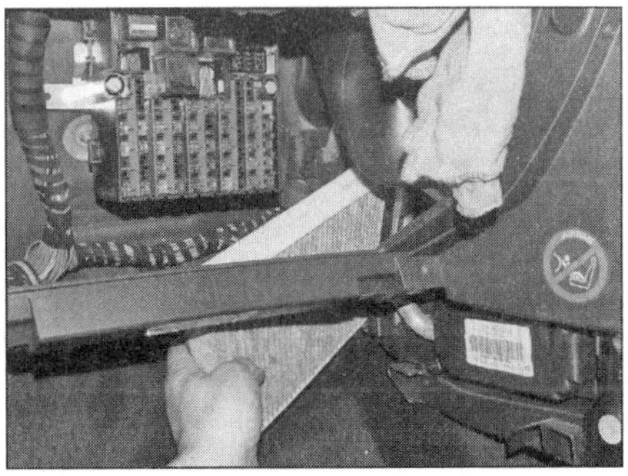

4.4 Fit the new filter, with the arrow marking facing into the car

5.1 Radiator bottom hose connection

A leak in the cooling system will usually show up as white- or antifreeze-coloured deposits on the areas adjoining the leak.

Fuel

Warning: Refer to the safety information given in 'Safety first!' and Chapter 4A, Section 1 before disturbing any of the fuel system components.

4 Check all fuel lines at their connections to the fuel pressure regulator and the fuel rail **(see illustration)**.

5 Examine each fuel hose/pipe along its length for splits or cracks. Check for signs of leakage, which could be anything from a damp hose to an area of bodywork adjacent to the hose which seems especially clean (from being 'washed' by leaking fuel).

6 To identify fuel leaks between the fuel tank and the engine bay, the car should raised and securely supported on axle stands. Inspect the fuel tank and filler neck for punctures, cracks and other damage. The connection between the filler neck and tank is especially critical. Sometimes a rubber filler neck or connecting hose will leak due to loose retaining clamps or deteriorated rubber.

7 Carefully check all rubber hoses and metal fuel lines leading away from the fuel tank. Check for loose connections, deteriorated hoses, kinked lines, and other damage. Pay particular attention to the vent pipes and hoses, which often loop up around the filler neck and can become blocked or kinked, making tank filling difficult. Follow the fuel supply and return lines to the front of the car, carefully inspecting them all the way for signs of damage or corrosion. Renew damaged sections as necessary.

Engine oil

8 Inspect the area around the camshaft cover, cylinder head, oil filter and sump joint faces. Bear in mind that, over a period of time, some very slight seepage from these areas is to be expected – what you are really looking for is any indication of a serious leak caused by gasket failure. Engine oil seeping from the base of the timing belt cover or the transmission bellhousing may be an indication of crankshaft or input shaft oil seal failure. Should a leak be found, renew the failed gasket or oil seal by referring to Chapter 2A, 7A or 7B.

Power steering fluid

9 Examine the hose running between the fluid reservoir and the power steering pump, and the return hose running from the steering rack to the fluid reservoir. Also examine the high-pressure supply hose between the pump and the steering rack.

10 Check the hoses leading to the power steering fluid cooler at the front of the engine bay **(see illustration)**. Look for deterioration caused by corrosion and damage from grounding, or debris thrown up from the road surface.

11 Pay particular attention to crimped unions, and the area surrounding the hoses that are secured with adjustable worm-drive clips.

Air conditioning refrigerant

Warning: Refer to the safety information given in 'Safety first!' and Chapter 3, Section 10, regarding the dangers of disturbing any of the air conditioning system components.

12 The air conditioning system is filled with a liquid refrigerant, which is retained under high pressure. If the air conditioning system is opened and depressurised without the aid of specialised equipment, the refrigerant will immediately turn into gas and escape into the atmosphere. If the liquid comes into contact with your skin, it can cause severe frostbite. In addition, the refrigerant contains substances which are environmentally damaging; for this reason, it should not be allowed to escape into the atmosphere.

13 Any suspected air conditioning system leaks should be immediately referred to a Ford dealer or air conditioning specialist. Leakage will be shown up as a steady drop in the level of refrigerant in the system.

14 Note that water may drip from the condenser drain pipe, underneath the car, immediately after the air conditioning system has been in use. This is normal, and should not be cause for concern.

Brake (and clutch) fluid

Warning: Refer to the safety information given in 'Safety first!' and Chapter 9, Section 1, regarding the dangers of handling brake fluid.

15 With reference to Chapter 9, Section 8, examine the area surrounding the brake pipe unions at the master cylinder for signs of leakage. Check the area around the base of fluid reservoir, for signs of leakage caused by seal failure. Also examine the brake pipe unions at the ABS hydraulic unit, where applicable.

16 If fluid loss is evident, but the leak cannot be pinpointed in the engine bay, the brake calipers and underbody brake lines should be carefully checked with the car raised and supported on axle stands. Leakage of fluid from the braking system is serious fault that must be rectified immediately.

17 Refer to Chapter 6, Section 2 and 3 and check for leakage around the hydraulic fluid line connections to the clutch master cylinder at the bulkhead, and to the clutch slave cylinder on the transmission.

18 Brake/clutch hydraulic fluid is a toxic substance with a watery consistency. New fluid is almost colourless, but it becomes darker with age and use.

Unidentified fluid leaks

19 If there are signs that a fluid of some description is leaking from the car, but you cannot identify the type of fluid or its exact origin, park the car overnight and slide a large piece of card underneath it. Providing that the card is positioned in roughly in the right location, even the smallest leak will show up on the card. Not only will this help you to pinpoint the exact location of the leak, it should be easier to identify the fluid from its colour. Bear in mind, though, that the leak may only be occurring when the engine is running!

Vacuum hoses

20 Although the braking system is hydraulically-operated, the brake servo unit amplifies the effort you apply at the brake pedal, by making use of the vacuum available in the inlet manifold (see Chapter 9, Section 12). Vacuum is ported to the servo by means of a large bore hose. Any leaks that develop in this hose will reduce the effectiveness of the braking system, and may affect engine running.

21 In addition, many of the underbonnet components, particularly the emission control

5.4 Check the fuel line connections

5.10 Power steering fluid cooler hose connections under right-hand wheel arch

components, are driven by vacuum supplied from the vacuum pump via narrow bore hoses. A leak in a vacuum hose means that air is being drawn into the hose (rather than escaping from it) and this makes leakage very difficult to detect. One method is to use an old length of vacuum hose as a kind of stethoscope – hold one end close to (but not in) your ear and use the other end to probe the area around the suspected leak. When the end of the hose is directly over a vacuum leak, a hissing sound will be heard clearly through the hose. Care must be taken to avoid contacting hot or moving components, as the engine must be running when testing in this manner. Renew any vacuum hoses that are found to be defective.

6 Auxiliary drivebelt check

General

1 All models are fitted with 'stretch' type auxiliary drivebelts. If removed they must be renewed, as they are only designed to be stretched and fitted once.

2 Models with air conditioning have two drivebelts, with the second one used to drive the power steering pump – if air conditioning is not fitted, a single belt is used. In either case, a tensioner is not used – the belt is 'elastic' and self-tensioning.

Checking

3 Due to their function and material makeup, drivebelts are prone to failure after a long period of time, and should therefore be inspected regularly.

4 Since the drivebelt is located very close to the right-hand side of the engine compartment, it is possible to gain better access by raising the front of the car and removing the right-hand wheel. Unclip the power steering pipe, then remove the two screws securing the drivebelt lower cover. However, for checking purposes alone, removing the right-hand headlight as described in Chapter 12, Section 7, gives excellent access to the drivebelt **(see illustration)**.

6.4 With the headlight removed, access to the drivebelt is much improved

5 With the engine stopped, inspect the full length of the drivebelt for cracks and separation of the belt plies. It will be necessary to turn the engine (using a spanner or socket and bar on the crankshaft pulley bolt) in order to move the belt from the pulleys so that the belt can be inspected thoroughly. Twist the belt between the pulleys so that both sides can be viewed. Also check for fraying, and glazing which gives the belt a shiny appearance. Check the pulleys for nicks, cracks, distortion and corrosion **(see illustration)**.

6 Small cracks in the belt ribs are not usually serious, but look closely to see whether the crack has extended into the belt plies. If the belt is in any way suspect, or is known to have seen long service, renew it as described in Section 23.

7 If the belt appears to be too slack (or has actually been slipping in service), this indicates that the 'elastic' belt is over stretched or that here is a fault with one of the driven components, such as a failed water pump bearing. Any slipping may also be due to external contamination of the belt (eg, by oil or water).

7 Handbrake check and adjustment

Checking

1 The handbrake should be fully applied (and capable of holding the car on a slope) after approximately four clicks of the ratchet. The operating cables will stretch over time, and adjustment will be needed.

2 The handbrake is a conventional design, having separate cables for the two rear wheels, and a front cable with an equaliser plate which operates both rear cables equally. The handbrake is adjusted by means of a nut attached to the front cable.

3 With the rear of the car raised and supported (see *Jacking and vehicle support*), check that the rear wheels are free to turn with the handbrake fully released.

4 Apply the handbrake one click at a time, and check whether the rear wheels can still be turned. If the handbrake does not appear to be working equally on both wheels, this may indicate a problem with either the rear cable or the brake shoes on the least effective side (see Chapter 9, Section 6 and 20 for more details).

Adjustment

Note: *This procedure is intended only to compensate for stretch in existing cables. If new rear cables have been fitted, a more elaborate adjustment procedure is specified by Ford – see Chapter 9, Section 19 for details.*

Note: *If the travel of the handbrake is excessive it is important that the rear brake self-adjusting mechanism is working correctly before any attempt is made to adjust the cable (see Chapter 9, Section 19 for details).*

5 If the handbrake appears to be working evenly, but requires an excessive amount of lever movement to operate, the front cable should be adjusted as follows. First, unclip and

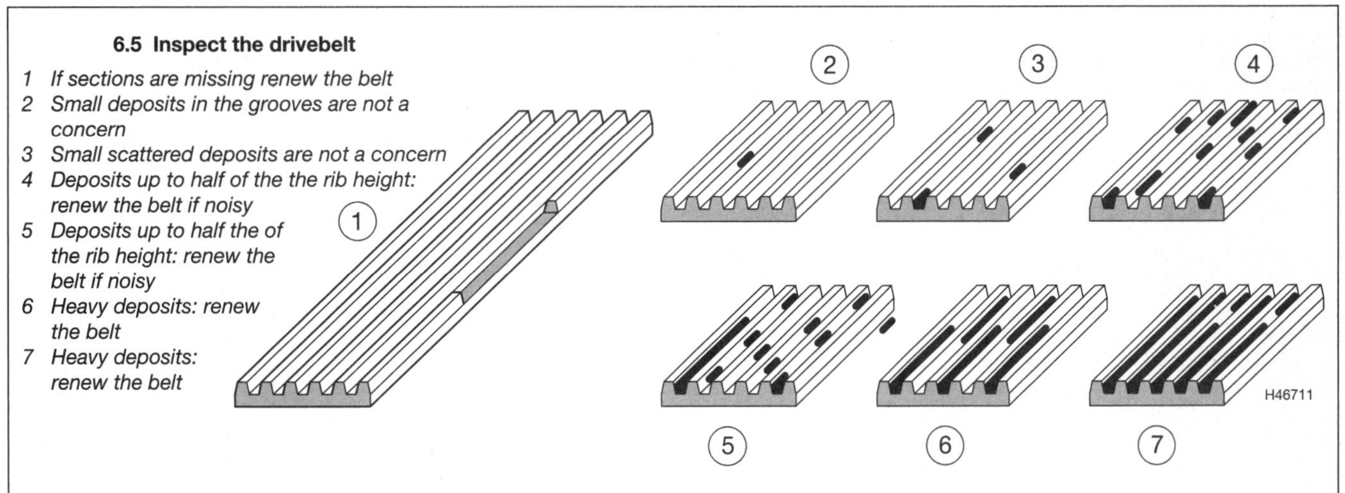

6.5 Inspect the drivebelt

1 *If sections are missing renew the belt*
2 *Small deposits in the grooves are not a concern*
3 *Small scattered deposits are not a concern*
4 *Deposits up to half of the the rib height: renew the belt if noisy*
5 *Deposits up to half the of the rib height: renew the belt if noisy*
6 *Heavy deposits: renew the belt*
7 *Heavy deposits: renew the belt*

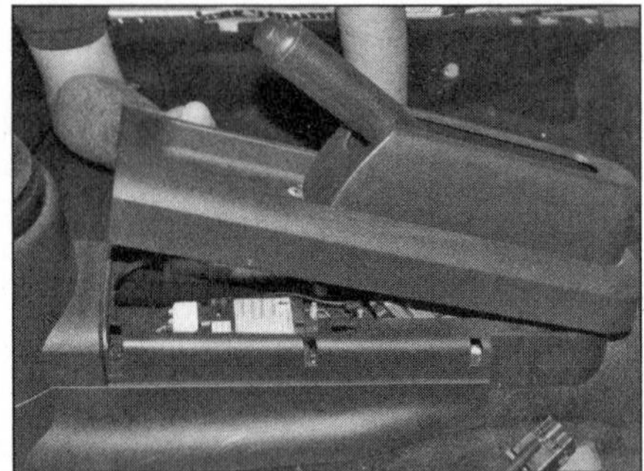

7.5 Unclip the handbrake trim panel, and lift it off

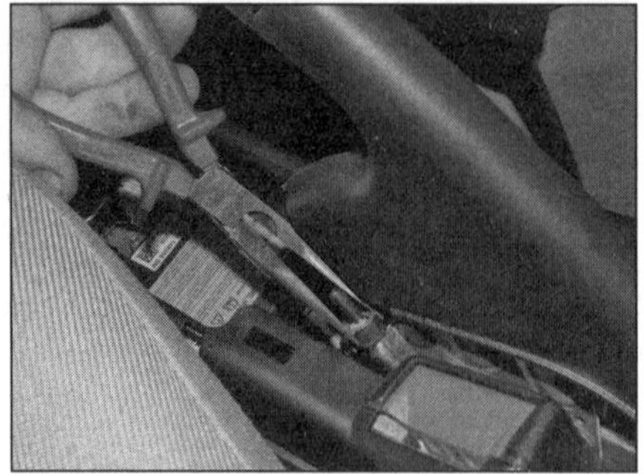

7.6a Remove the locking clip from the handbrake adjuster nut ...

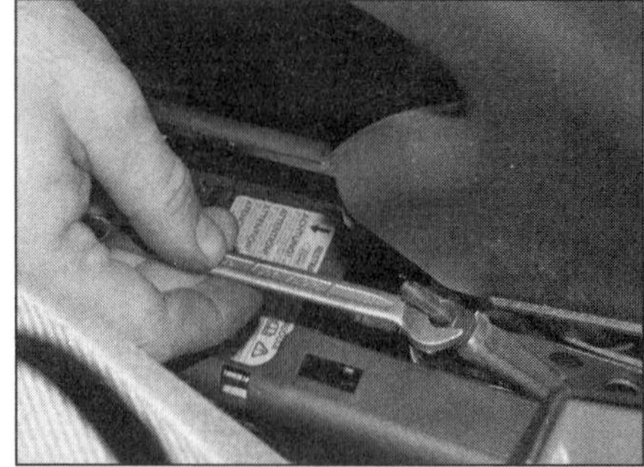

7.6b ... then turn the nut as necessary

remove the trim panel around the handbrake lever **(see illustration)**.

6 Remove the locking clip from the handbrake adjuster nut located directly below the lever. With the lever released, tighten the nut by half a turn, then recheck the operation of the handbrake and repeat if necessary **(see illustrations)**. Do not overadjust, as this may accelerate the stretching of the front cable. When the handbrake operation is satisfactory, check that the rear wheels are free to turn when the handbrake is fully released.

7 On completion, lower the car to the ground. Refit the locking clip to the handbrake adjuster nut (use a new one if the old one is unserviceable), and refit the handbrake lever trim panel.

8 Seat belt check

1 Check the seat belts for satisfactory operation and condition. Pull sharply on the belt to check that the locking mechanism engages correctly. Inspect the webbing for fraying and cuts. Check that they retract smoothly and without binding into their reels.

2 Check that the seat belt mounting bolts are tight, and if necessary tighten them to the specified torque wrench setting.

9 Hinge and lock lubrication

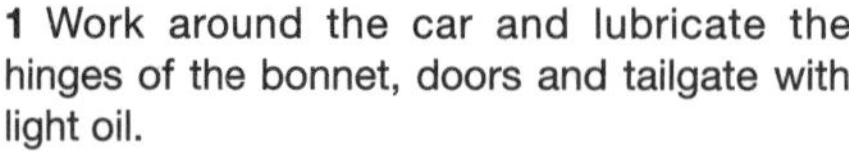

1 Work around the car and lubricate the hinges of the bonnet, doors and tailgate with light oil.

2 Lightly lubricate the bonnet release mechanism with a smear of grease.

3 Check carefully the security and operation of all hinges, latches and locks, adjusting them where required. Check the operation of the central locking system.

4 Check the condition and operation of the tailgate struts, renewing them both if either is leaking or no longer able to support the tailgate securely when raised.

10 Front brake pad and disc wear check

1 Apply the handbrake, then jack up the front of the car and support it securely on axle stands (see *Jacking and vehicle support*). Remove the front roadwheels.

2 The brake pad thickness, and the condition of the disc, can be assessed roughly with just the wheels removed **(see illustration)**. For a comprehensive check, the brake pads should be removed and cleaned. The operation of the caliper can then also be checked, and the condition of the brake disc itself can be fully examined on both sides. Refer to Chapter 9 for further information.

3 On completion, refit the roadwheels and lower the car to the ground.

11 Rear brake shoe and drum wear check

Remove the rear brake drums, and check the brake shoes for signs of wear or contamination. At the same time, also inspect the wheel cylinders for signs of leakage, and the brake drum for signs of wear. Refer to Chapter 9, Section 5 and 7 for further information.

12 Steering and suspension check

Front suspension and steering

1 Raise the front of the car, and securely support it on axle stands (see *Jacking and vehicle support*).

2 Visually inspect the balljoint dust covers and the steering rack-and-pinion gaiters for splits, chafing or deterioration **(see illustration)**. Any

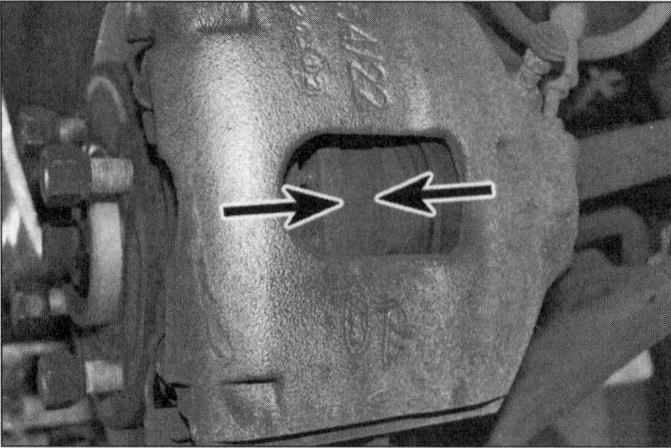

10.2 With the wheel removed, the pad thickness can be seen through the front of the caliper

12.2 Check the steering gaiters for signs of splitting

wear of these components will cause loss of lubricant, together with dirt and water entry, resulting in rapid deterioration of the balljoints or steering gear.

3 Check the power steering fluid hoses for chafing or deterioration, and the pipe and hose unions for fluid leaks. Also check for signs of fluid leakage under pressure from the steering gear rubber gaiters, which would indicate failed fluid seals within the steering gear.

4 Grasp the roadwheel at the 12 o'clock and 6 o'clock positions, and try to rock it **(see illustration)**. Very slight free play may be felt, but if the movement is appreciable, further investigation is necessary to determine the source. Continue rocking the wheel while an assistant depresses the footbrake. If the movement is now eliminated or significantly reduced, it is likely that the hub bearings are at fault. If the free play is still evident with the footbrake depressed, then there is wear in the suspension joints or mountings.

5 Now grasp the wheel at the 9 o'clock and 3 o'clock positions, and try to rock it as before. Any movement felt now may again be caused by wear in the hub bearings or the steering track rod balljoints. If the outer balljoint is worn, the visual movement will be obvious. If the inner joint is suspect, it can be felt by placing a hand over the rack-and-pinion rubber gaiter and gripping the track rod. If the wheel is now rocked, movement will be felt at the inner joint if wear has taken place.

6 Using a large screwdriver or flat bar, check for wear in the suspension mounting bushes by levering between the relevant suspension component and its attachment point. Some movement is to be expected, as the mountings are made of rubber, but excessive wear should be obvious. Also check the condition of any visible rubber bushes, looking for splits, cracks or contamination of the rubber.

7 With the car standing on its wheels, have an assistant turn the steering wheel back and forth, about an eighth of a turn each way. There should be very little, if any, lost movement between the steering wheel and roadwheels. If this is not the case, closely observe the joints and mountings previously described. In addition, check the steering column universal joints for wear, and also check the rack-and-pinion steering gear itself.

Rear suspension

8 Chock the front wheels, then jack up the rear of the car and support securely on axle stands (see *Jacking and vehicle support*).

9 Working as described previously for the front suspension, check the rear hub bearings, the suspension bushes and the shock absorber mountings for wear.

Shock absorber

10 Check for any signs of fluid leakage around the shock absorber body, or from the rubber gaiter around the piston rod **(see illustration)**. Should any fluid be noticed, the

12.4 Check for wear in the front suspension and hub bearings

shock absorber is defective internally, and should be renewed. **Note:** *Shock absorbers should always be renewed in pairs on the same axle.*

11 The efficiency of the shock absorber may be checked by bouncing the car at each corner. Generally speaking, the body will return to its normal position and stop after being depressed. If it rises and returns on a rebound, the shock absorber is probably suspect. Also examine the shock absorber upper and lower mountings for any signs of wear.

13 Driveshaft gaiter check

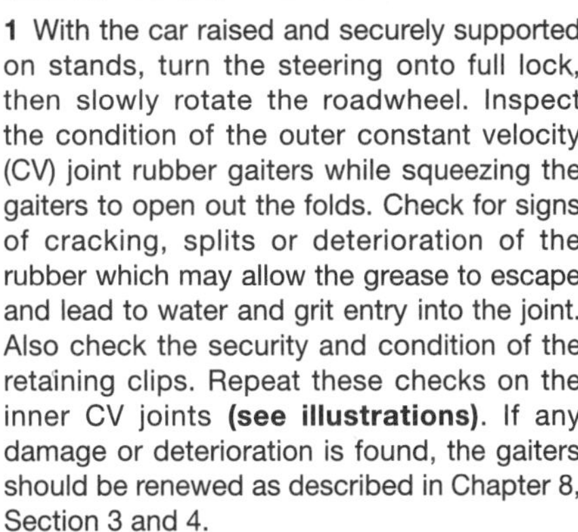

1 With the car raised and securely supported on stands, turn the steering onto full lock, then slowly rotate the roadwheel. Inspect the condition of the outer constant velocity (CV) joint rubber gaiters while squeezing the gaiters to open out the folds. Check for signs of cracking, splits or deterioration of the rubber which may allow the grease to escape and lead to water and grit entry into the joint. Also check the security and condition of the retaining clips. Repeat these checks on the inner CV joints **(see illustrations)**. If any damage or deterioration is found, the gaiters should be renewed as described in Chapter 8, Section 3 and 4.

2 At the same time, check the general condition of the CV joints themselves by first holding the driveshaft and attempting

13.1a Check the outer constant velocity (CV) joint gaiters ...

12.10 Check for signs of fluid leakage from the shock absorbers

to rotate the wheel. Repeat this check by holding the inner joint and attempting to rotate the driveshaft. Any appreciable movement indicates wear in the joints, wear in the driveshaft splines, or a loose driveshaft retaining nut.

14 Roadwheel nut tightness check

1 Remove the wheel trims or alloy wheel centre covers, and slacken the roadwheel nuts slightly.

2 Tighten the nuts to the specified torque, using a torque wrench.

15 Road test

Instruments and electrical equipment

1 Check the operation of all instruments and electrical equipment.

2 Make sure that all instruments read correctly, and switch on all electrical equipment in turn, to check that they function properly.

Steering and suspension

3 Check for any abnormalities in the steering, suspension, handling or road 'feel'.

4 Drive the car, and check that there are no unusual vibrations or noises.

5 Check that the steering feels positive, with

13.1b ... and, though less prone to wear, check the inner gaiters too

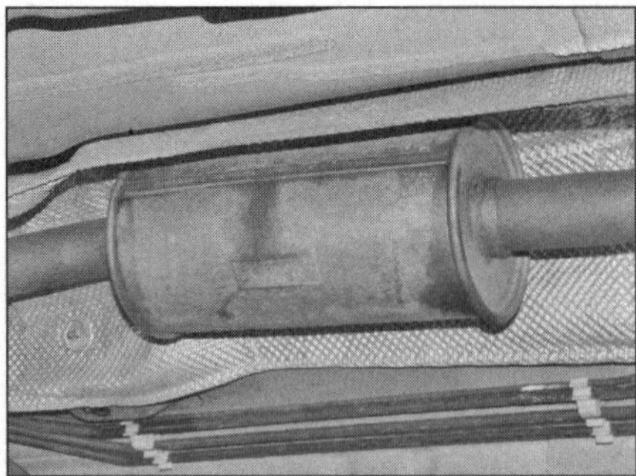

15.17a Check the silencer boxes carefully for signs of leakage

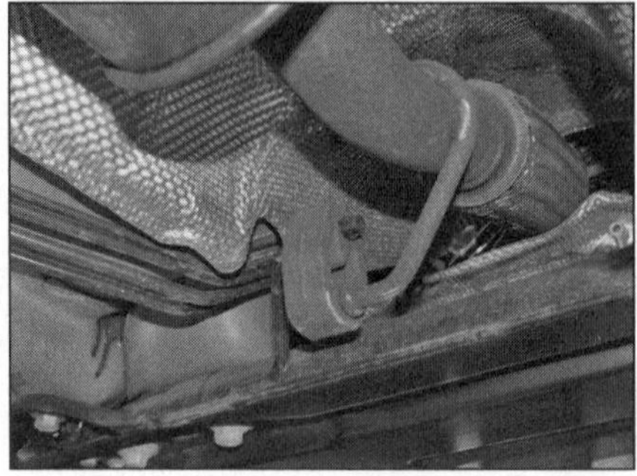

15.17b If the rubber mountings are in poor condition, fit new ones

no excessive 'sloppiness', or roughness, and check for any suspension noises when cornering and driving over bumps.

Drivetrain

6 Check the performance of the engine, clutch, transmission and driveshafts.

7 Listen for any unusual noises from the engine, clutch and transmission.

8 Make sure that the engine runs smoothly when idling, and that there is no hesitation when accelerating.

9 Check that, where applicable, the clutch action is smooth and progressive, that the drive is taken up smoothly, and that the pedal travel is not excessive. Also listen for any noises when the clutch pedal is depressed.

10 Check that all gears can be engaged smoothly without noise, and that the gear lever action is smooth and not abnormally vague or 'notchy'.

11 Listen for a metallic clicking sound from the front of the car, as the car is driven slowly in a circle with the steering on full lock. Carry out this check in both directions. If a clicking noise is heard, this indicates wear in a driveshaft joint (see Chapter 8, Section 5).

Braking system

12 Make sure that the car does not pull to one side when braking, and that the wheels do not lock prematurely when braking hard. They should not lock at all on models with ABS.

13 Check that there is no vibration through the steering when braking.

14 Check that the handbrake operates correctly, without excessive movement of the lever, and that it holds the car stationary on a slope.

15 Test the operation of the brake servo unit as follows. Depress the footbrake four or five times to exhaust the vacuum, then start the engine. As the engine starts, there should be a noticeable 'give' in the brake pedal as vacuum builds up. Allow the engine to run for at least two minutes, and then switch it off. If the brake pedal is now depressed again, it should be possible to detect a hiss from the servo as the pedal is depressed. After about four or five applications, no further hissing should be heard, and the pedal should feel considerably harder.

Exhaust system

16 Listen carefully for any unusual noises from the system, which might indicate that it has started blowing, or that the mountings may be deteriorated, allowing the system to hit the underside of the car.

17 If any noises are detected, inspect the system with the car raised and supported on axle stands (see *Jacking and vehicle support*). Leaks are often accompanied by sooty stains, and are most common at the joints, and at welded sections, where pipes enter silencer boxes. Check the condition of the rubber mountings – if they are cracked or perished, fit new ones **(see illustrations)**.

Every 37 500 miles or 3 years

16 Spark plug renewal and ignition system check

Spark plug renewal

1 The correct functioning of the spark plugs is vital for the correct running and efficiency of the engine. It is essential that the plugs fitted are appropriate for the engine; suitable types are specified at the beginning of this Chapter and on the Vehicle Emissions Control Information (VECI) label located on the underside of the bonnet (only on models sold in some areas). If the correct type is used and the engine is in good condition, the spark plugs should not need attention between scheduled renewal intervals. Do not attempt to clean the spark plugs. If their condition is suspect they should be renewed.

2 Remove the air cleaner as described in Chapter 4A, Section 5 for access to the top of the engine.

3 If the marks on the original equipment spark plug (HT) leads cannot be seen, mark the leads to correspond to the cylinder the lead serves (No 4 spark plug is at the transmission end). Pull the leads from the plugs by gripping the end fitting, not the lead, otherwise the lead connection may be fractured **(see illustration)**. The spark plugs are in the centre of the head.

16.3 Pull off the HT leads

16.5 Unscrew the spark plugs using a suitable socket

4 It is advisable (if possible) to remove any dirt from the spark plug recesses using a clean brush, vacuum cleaner or compressed air before removing the plugs, to prevent dirt dropping into the cylinders.

5 Unscrew the plugs from the cylinder head using a spark plug spanner, suitable box spanner or a deep socket and extension bar **(see illustration)**. Keep the socket aligned with the spark plug – if it is forcibly moved to one side, the ceramic insulator may be broken off. As each plug is removed, examine it as follows.

6 Observation of the spark plugs will give a good indication of the condition of the engine. If the insulator nose of the spark plug is clean and white, with no deposits, this is indicative of a weak mixture or too hot a plug (a hot plug transfers heat away from the electrode slowly, a cold plug transfers heat away quickly).

7 If the tip and insulator nose are covered with hard black looking deposits, then this is indicative that the mixture is too rich. Should the plug be black and oily, then it is likely that the engine is fairly worn, as well as the mixture being too rich.

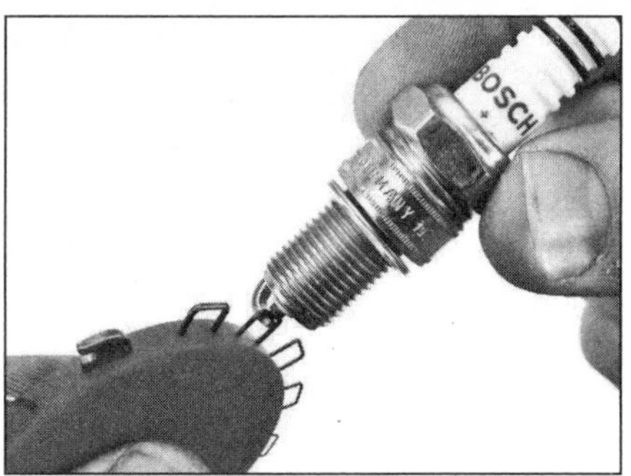

16.10a Using a wire-type gauge when checking the gap

8 If the insulator nose is covered with light tan to greyish brown deposits, then the mixture is correct and it is likely that the engine is in good condition.
9 The spark plug electrode gap is of considerable importance as, if it is too large or too small, the size of the spark and its efficiency will be seriously impaired. The gap should be set to the value given in the Specifications at the beginning of this Chapter.
10 To check the gap, measure it with a feeler blade. The gap is correct when the appropriate size blade is a firm sliding fit **(see illustrations)**.
11 Do not attempt to adjust the spark plug gap. If the gap is outside the specifications given at the beginning of this Chapter the spark plugs must be renewed.
12 Before fitting the spark plugs, check that the threaded connector sleeves are tight, and that the plug exterior surfaces and threads are clean **(see Haynes Hint)**.
13 Remove the rubber/plastic hose (if used), and tighten the plug to the specified torque using the spark plug socket and a torque wrench. Refit the remaining spark plugs in the same manner.
14 Connect the HT leads in their correct order, and clip them back in place, where applicable. **Note:** *Before reconnecting the HT leads to the plugs, Ford recommend lightly coating the insides of the HT lead connectors with silicone grease.*

Ignition system check

Warning: Voltages produced by an electronic ignition system are considerably higher than those produced by conventional ignition systems. Extreme care must be taken when working on the system with the ignition switched on. Persons with surgically implanted cardiac pacemaker devices should keep well clear of the ignition circuits, components and test equipment.

15 The spark plug (HT) leads should be checked whenever new spark plugs are fitted.
16 Ensure that the leads are numbered before removing them, to avoid confusion when refitting. With the plastic top cover removed, pull the leads from the plugs by gripping the end fitting, not the lead, otherwise the lead connection may be fractured.

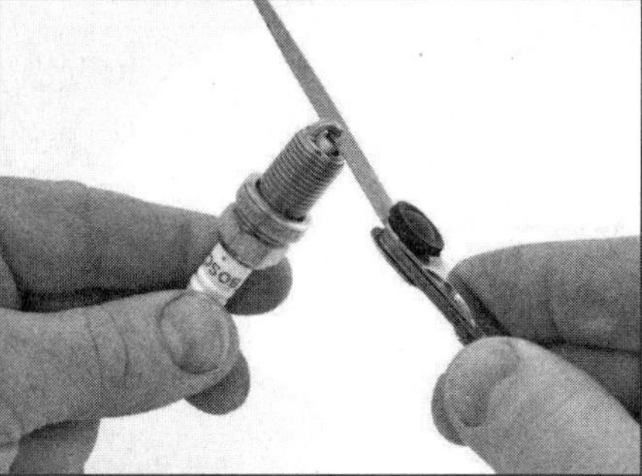

16.10b Measuring a spark plug gap with a feeler blade

17 Check inside the end fitting for signs of corrosion, which will look like a white crusty powder. Push the end fitting back onto the spark plug, ensuring that it is a tight fit on the plug. If not, remove the lead again, and use pliers to carefully crimp the metal connector inside the end fitting until it fits securely on the end of the spark plug.
18 Using a clean rag, wipe the entire length of the lead to remove any built up dirt and grease. Once the lead is clean, check for burns, cracks and other damage. Do not bend the lead excessively, nor pull the lead lengthwise – the conductor inside might break.
19 Disconnect the other end of the lead from the ignition coil **(see illustration)**. Check for corrosion and a tight fit in the same manner as the spark plug end. If an ohmmeter is available, check the resistance of the lead by connecting the meter between each end of the lead. Refit the lead securely on completion. No resistance figures are provide for the HT leads, but they will all show some resistance. With the meter firmly connected to each end of the lead it is always worth flexing the lead to highlight any change in resistance. If there is any doubt about the integrity of the HT leads they should be renewed.
20 Check the remaining leads one at a time, in the same way.
21 If new spark plug (HT) leads are required, purchase a set for your specific car and engine.
22 Even with the ignition system in first class condition, some engines may still occasionally experience poor starting attributable to damp ignition components. To disperse moisture, a water dispersant aerosol can be very effective.
23 On completion, refit the air cleaner, referring to Chapter 4A, Section 5 if necessary.

16.19 Check the HT lead connections at the ignition coil

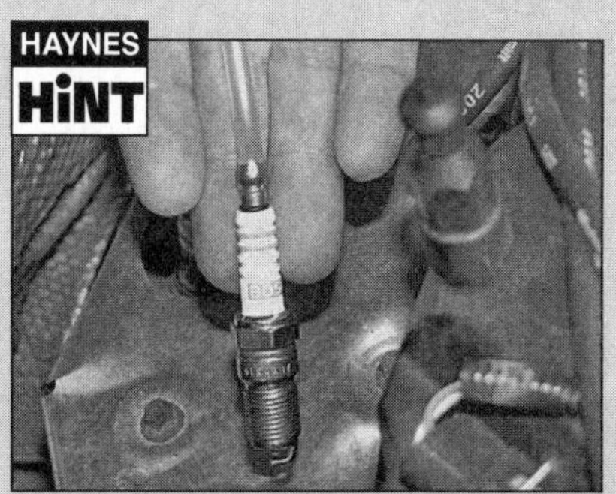

It's often difficult to insert spark plugs into their holes without cross-threading them. To avoid this possibility, fit a short length of rubber or plastic hose over the end of the spark plug. The flexible hose acts as a universal joint, to help align the plug with the plug hole. Should the plug begin to cross thread, the hose will slip on the spark plug, preventing thread damage to the aluminium cylinder head.

17 Air filter element renewal

1 The air cleaner is located on top of the engine.
2 Remove the air cleaner housing as described in Chapter 4A, Section 5. Turn the housing over, and remove ten Torx screws to release the air cleaner cover **(see illustrations)**.
3 Remove the filter element, noting which way round it is fitted **(see illustrations)**.
4 Wipe clean the interior surfaces of the cover and base.
5 Insert the new element, making sure that it is seated correctly in the base.
6 Check the condition of the crankcase breather filter **(see illustration)**. If the foam

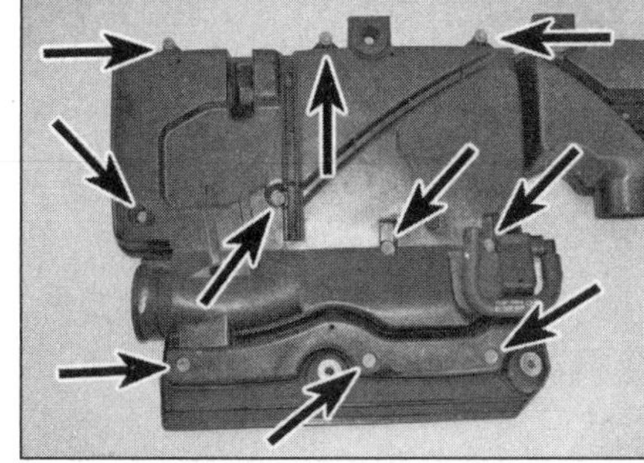

17.2a Locate the ten Torx screws in the underside of the air cleaner (arrowed) ...

17.2b ... and remove them for access to the filter

17.3a Separate the filter housing ...

17.3b ... and remove the engine air filter

filter appears to be particularly dirty, it may be possible to clean it by washing it – if not, or if the filter has otherwise deteriorated, a new filter should be fitted. Some brands of new air filter may be supplied with a breather filter.

7 Refit the cover and secure with the retaining clips and bolts/screws.

18 Transmission oil level check

Note: *This check applies equally to models with Durashift, as the main transmission unit is the same.*

1 Position the car over an inspection pit, on car ramps, or jack it up, but make sure that it is level.

2 Unclip the plastic cover fitted over the gearchange cables at the front of the transmission **(see illustration)**.

3 Remove all traces of dirt, then unscrew the filler/level plug from the front face of the transmission. This will probably be very tight, and a large Allen key or bit will be needed – access is made awkward by the plastic shroud around the gearchange cables **(see illustration)**.

4 The level must be just below the bottom edge of the filler/level plug hole (use a cranked tool such as an Allen key to check the level). If necessary, top-up the level with the specified grade of oil (see *Lubricants and fluids*) until the oil just starts to run out. Allow any excess oil to flow out until the level stabilises **(see illustrations)**.

5 When the level is correct, clean and refit the filler/level plug (check the condition of the O-ring seal, and renew if necessary), then tighten it to the specified torque.

6 Lower the car to the ground.

19 Braking system rubber hose check

1 Position the car over an inspection pit, on car ramps, or jack it up one wheel at a time (see *Jacking and vehicle support*).

2 Inspect the braking system rubber hoses fitted to each front caliper, and on each side of the rear axle **(see illustration)**. Look for perished, swollen or hardened rubber, and any signs of cracking, especially at the metal end fittings. If there's any doubt as to the condition of any hose, renew it as described in Chapter 9, Section 10.

17.6 The breather filter is next to the air filter

18.2 Unclip the plastic cover from the front of the transmission

18.3 Unscrew and remove the filler/level plug

18.4a Top-up the oil level ...

18.4b ... then allow any excess to flow out before refitting the plug

19.2 Rubber brake hose fitted to the front caliper

Every 50 000 miles or 4 years

20 Timing belt renewal

Refer to Chapter 2A, Section 8.

Every 75 000 miles

21 Fuel filter renewal

1 The fuel filter is located just in front of the fuel tank, on the left-hand side **(see illustration)**. First, chock the front roadwheels, then jack up the rear of the car and support on axle stands.

2 Unclip the filter from the mounting clips on the car. Squeeze the tabs and disconnect the quick-release fittings from each end of the filter **(see illustration)**. Plug the fuel lines to prevent loss of fuel.

3 Note the fuel flow arrow on the filter, then remove the filter from the mounting brackets attached to the fuel tank.

4 Fit the new filter using a reversal of the removal procedure – make sure the filter is fitted the correct way round, with the directional arrow pointing towards the fuel line leading to the engine compartment **(see illustration)**.

5 The quick-release fittings should be pushed fully onto the inlet and outlet stubs, and the filter clipped securely back into place **(see illustration)**. On completion, run the engine and check for leaks from the disturbed connections.

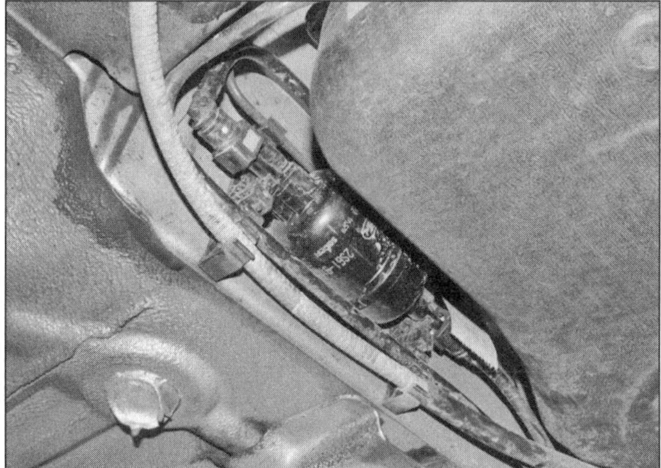

21.1 The fuel filter is under the car, in front of the fuel tank

21.2 Squeeze the quick-release fittings at each end to remove the fuel pipes

21.4 Make sure the fuel flow arrow is pointing the right way

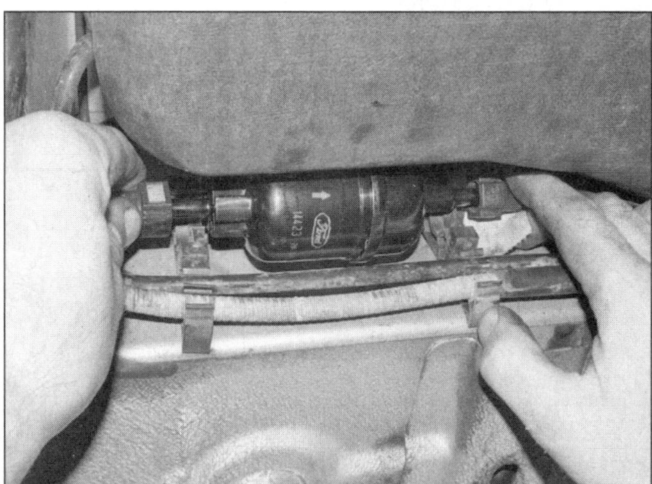

21.5 Refit the fuel lines, and clip the filter back in place

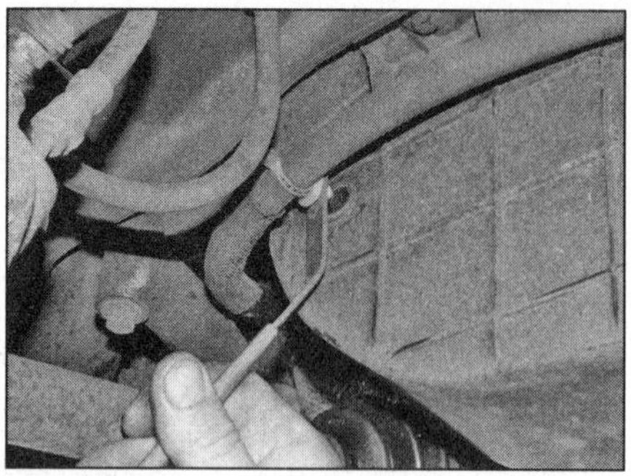

23.3a Prise off the power steering pipe to release the clips ...

23.3b ... then remove the screws ...

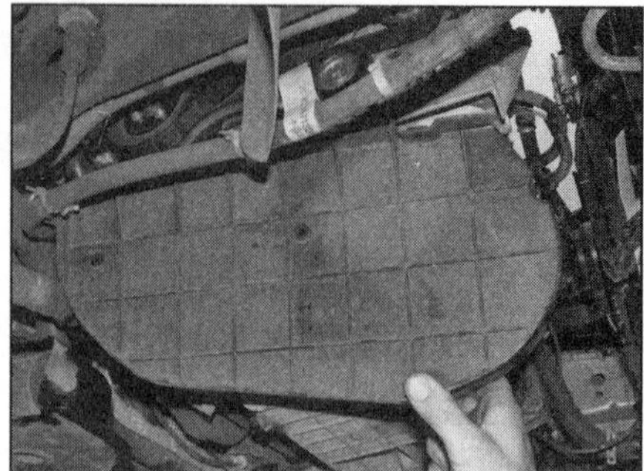

23.3c ... and take off the drivebelt lower cover

Every 100 000 miles or 8 years

22 Valve clearance check and adjustment

Refer to Chapter 2A, Section 5.

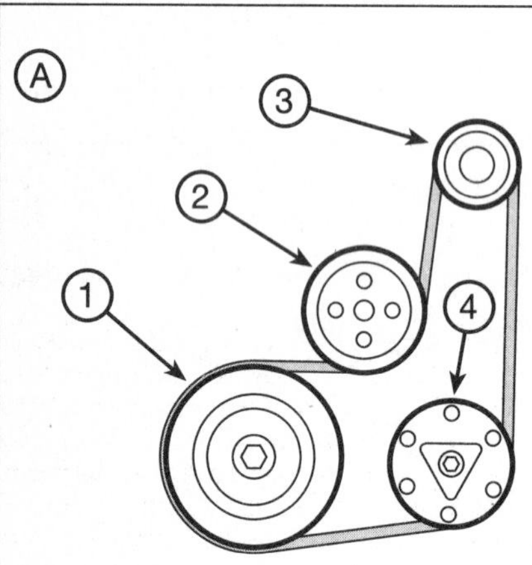

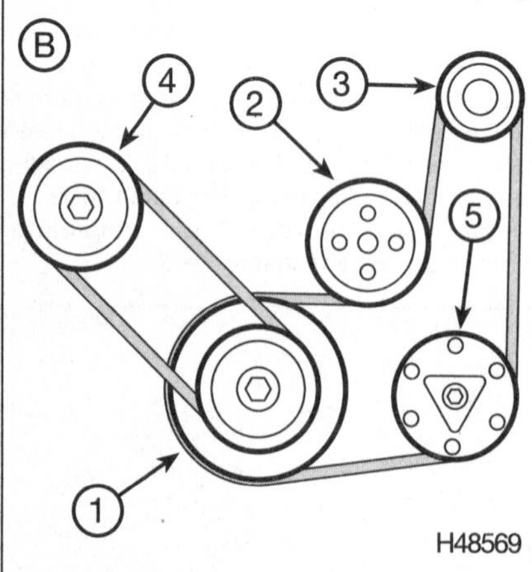

23.8 Auxiliary belt routing without air conditioning (A) and with (B)

1 *Crankshaft*
2 *Coolant pump*
3 *Alternator*
4 *Power steering pump*
5 *AC compressor*

23 Auxiliary drivebelt renewal

Removal

1 Loosen the right-hand front wheel nuts. Raise the front of the car, and support it on axle stands (see *Jacking and vehicle* support). Remove the right-hand front wheel.

2 Access to the drivebelt can be further improved by removing the right-hand headlight, as described in Chapter 12, Section 7.

3 Unclip the power steering pipe, then remove the two screws securing the drivebelt lower cover **(see illustrations)**.

4 All engines feature a 'stretch' type belt. No tensioner is fitted. The only way to remove an old belt is to cut it off. Even if the old belt could be prised off without damaging it or the pulleys, a belt which has already been fitted has stretched, and may slip if re-used.

5 Cut off the old drivebelt – take care that no damage is caused to surrounding components as this is done. Note that models with air conditioning have two drivebelts – both are of 'elastic' type – and the one for the power steering pump must be cut off first.

6 Due to the fitting method required for this unusual type of belt, it is essential that all the belt pulleys are as clean as possible before installing the new belt.

7 Wipe all the pulleys over with a suitable solvent, to ensure any traces of oil are removed. It's important that the new belt doesn't slip round the pulleys as it is stretched into place.

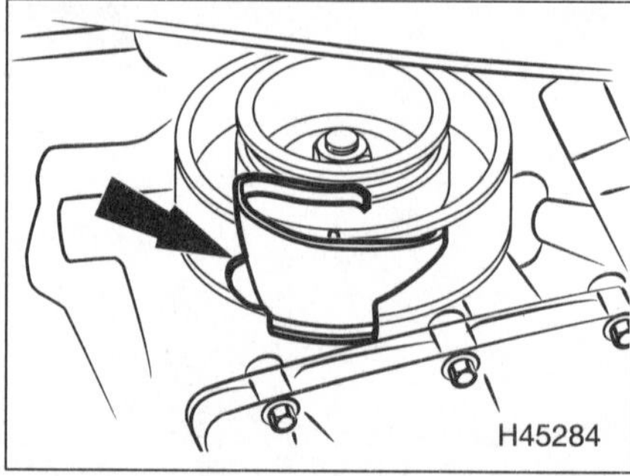

23.12 Fit the first installation tool, centrally on the pulley mark

Refitting

8 On models with air conditioning, two belts are fitted. The power steering pump drivebelt on these models is separate, and is fitted after the main drivebelt **(see illustration)**.

9 Special tools are required to fit the new belt(s). These should be provided with a new, Ford belt.

Main drivebelt

10 The fitting procedure for the 'elastic' drivebelt is quite lengthy, and involves the use of several plastic tools. Ford state that if the fitting procedure is not followed, a new belt may suffer premature failure.

11 Using a dab of paint or typist's correction fluid, mark the crankshaft pulley at the 6 o'clock position. It doesn't matter where the engine is aligned (ie, relative to TDC) before starting.

12 Fit the first installation tool to the crankshaft pulley, fitted centrally on the pulley mark you just made **(see illustration)**.

13 Fit the new belt around the alternator pulley, then the air conditioning or power steering pump pulley (as applicable), the water pump pulley, and finally, around the plastic installation tool. Make sure the drivebelt is seated properly in the pulley grooves.

14 Turn the engine slowly in the normal direction of rotation (clockwise, as seen from the pulley itself). The engine should only be turned so that the mark made earlier moves from the 6 o'clock to the 8 o'clock position. As the engine is turned, guide the belt onto the crankshaft pulley, with the help of the plastic tool.

15 Now fit the second plastic tool to the alternator mounting bracket. The tool clips round the bracket and the new belt, and keeps the belt on the pulley as it is stretched fully over the crankshaft pulley **(see illustration)**.

16 Start turning the engine slowly again, as before. Guide the belt gradually onto the crankshaft pulley, keeping an eye on the other pulleys as this is done. Make sure that the belt goes in to its grooves properly – 'help' it into place if necessary, using a blunt tool.

17 Once the pulley mark comes round to the 3 o'clock position, the belt should be fully fitted onto the crankshaft pulley, and the belt guide tools can be removed.

18 Turn the engine through a full 360°, and check that the belt is sitting correctly in the pulley grooves.

19 On models without air conditioning, refit the crankshaft pulley lower cover, clip the power steering pipe back into place, then refit the wheel and lower the car to the ground. Refit the headlight as described in Chapter 12, Section 7.

Power steering pump drivebelt

Note: *This procedure only applies to models with air conditioning, with a separate power steering pump drivebelt.*

20 Fit the power steering drivebelt plastic fitting tool to the crankshaft pulley, at the 12 o'clock position **(see illustration)**. Again, it doesn't matter where the engine is aligned (either relative to TDC, or to the mark made previously on the crankshaft pulley) before starting.

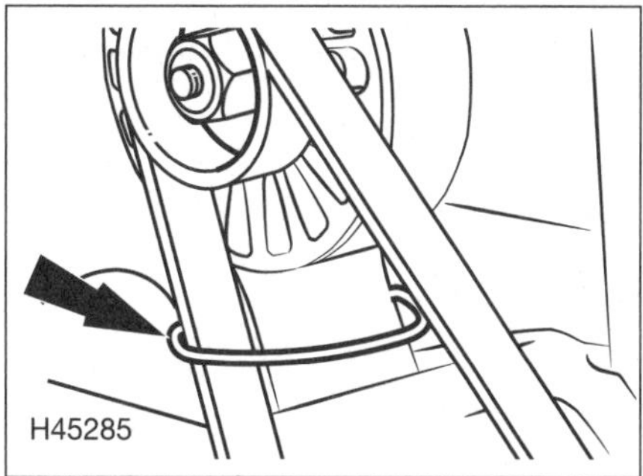

23.15 The second tool fits round the belt and alternator mounting bracket

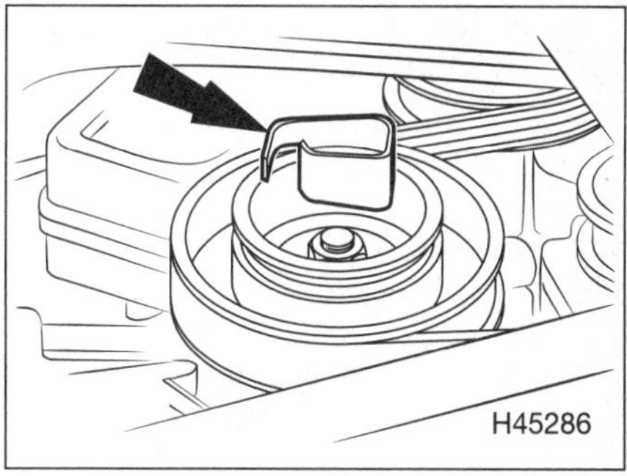

23.20 Fit the power steering belt tool at the 12 o'clock position

21 Fit the new drivebelt around the power steering pump pulley, and around the top of the crankshaft pulley, over the plastic fitting tool. Make sure the belt is sitting properly in the pulley grooves.

22 Turn the engine slowly in the normal direction of rotation (clockwise, as seen from the pulley itself). As the engine is turned, guide the belt onto the crankshaft pulley, with the help of the plastic tool.

23 Once the tool has reached the 9 o'clock position, the belt should be fully located on the crankshaft pulley, and the tool can be removed.

24 Turn the engine through a full 360°, and check that the belt is running true on the pulleys.

25 Refit the crankshaft pulley lower cover, clip the power steering pipe back into place, then refit the wheel and lower the car to the ground. Refit the headlight as described in Chapter 12, Section 7.

Every 2 years, regardless of mileage

24 Brake fluid renewal

⚠ ***Warning: Brake hydraulic fluid can harm your eyes and damage painted surfaces, so use extreme caution when handling and pouring it. Do not use fluid that has been standing open for some time, as it absorbs moisture from the air. Excess moisture can cause a dangerous loss of braking effectiveness.***

1 The procedure is similar to that for bleeding the hydraulic system as described in Chapter 9, Section 11, except that allowance should be made for the old fluid to be expelled when bleeding each section of the circuit.

2 Working as described in Chapter 9, Section 11, open the first bleed screw in the sequence, and pump the brake pedal gently until the level in the reservoir is approaching the MIN mark. Top-up to the MAX level with new fluid, and continue pumping until only new fluid remains in the reservoir, and new fluid can be seen emerging from the bleed screw. Tighten the screw, and top the reservoir level up to the MAX level line.

3 Work through all the remaining bleed screws in the sequence until new fluid can be seen at all of them. Be careful to keep the master cylinder reservoir topped-up above the MIN level at all times, or air may enter the system. If this happens, further bleeding will be required, to remove the air.

4 When the operation is complete, check that all bleed screws are securely tightened, and that their dust caps are refitted. Wash off all traces of spilt fluid, and recheck the master cylinder reservoir fluid level.

5 Check the operation of the brakes before taking the car on the road.

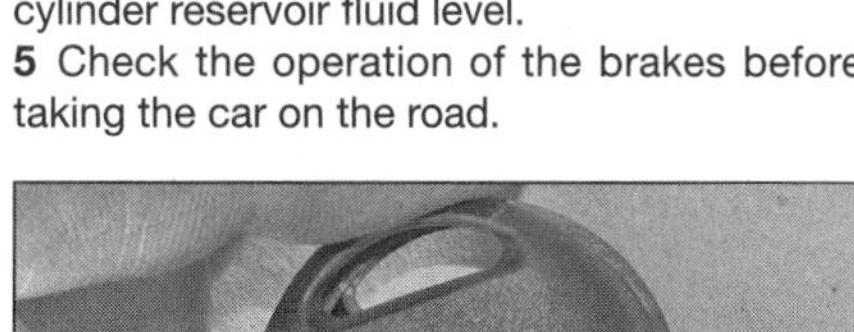

25 Remote control battery renewal

1 Although not in the Ford maintenance schedule, we recommend that the battery is changed every 2 years. However, if the door locks repeatedly fail to respond to signals from the remote, change the battery in the remote control before attempting to troubleshoot any of the vehicle's other systems.

2 Insert a small flat-bladed screwdriver into the slot provided and slide the transmitter unit from the key **(see illustration)**.

3 Use the screwdriver to release the clip each side and open the unit **(see illustration)**.

4 Note the fitted position of the battery (+ve side up), then prise the battery from place, and insert the new one **(see illustration)**. Avoid touching the battery or the terminals with bare fingers.

5 Snap the 2 halves of the transmitter together, and re-attach it to the key.

25.2 Insert a screwdriver into the slot

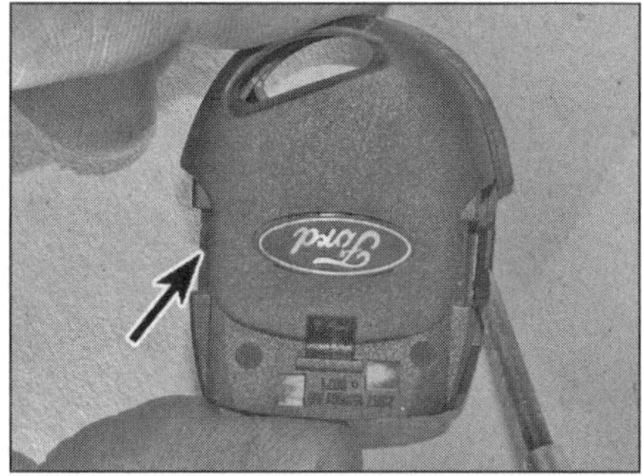

25.3 Release the clip each side (arrowed)

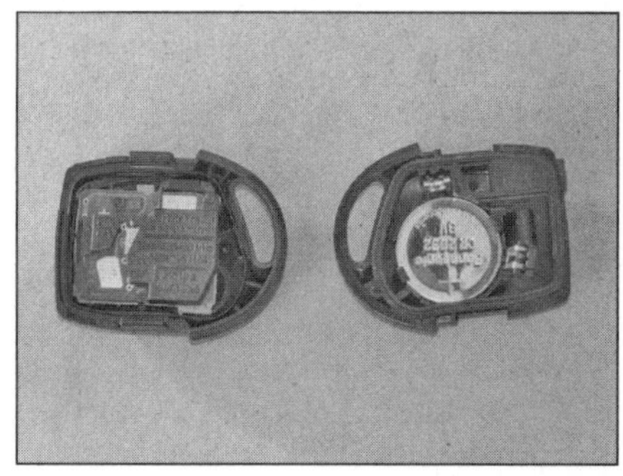

25.4 The battery fits positive side up

Every 4 years, regardless of mileage

26 Coolant renewal and pressure cap check

Warning: Wait until the engine is cold before starting this procedure. Do not allow antifreeze to come in contact with your skin, or with the painted surfaces of the car. Rinse off spills immediately with plenty of water. Never leave antifreeze lying around in an open container, or in a puddle in the driveway or on the garage floor. Children and pets are attracted by its sweet smell, but antifreeze can be fatal if ingested.

Cooling system draining

1 With the engine completely cold, remove the expansion tank filler cap. Turn the cap anti-clockwise, wait until any pressure remaining in the system is released, then unscrew it and lift it off.

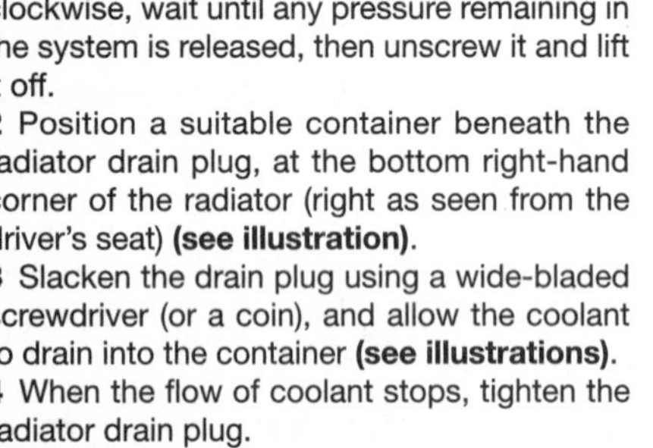

2 Position a suitable container beneath the radiator drain plug, at the bottom right-hand corner of the radiator (right as seen from the driver's seat) **(see illustration)**.

3 Slacken the drain plug using a wide-bladed screwdriver (or a coin), and allow the coolant to drain into the container **(see illustrations)**.

4 When the flow of coolant stops, tighten the radiator drain plug.

5 If the coolant has been drained for a reason other than renewal, then provided it is clean and less than four years old, it can be re-used, though this is not recommended.

Cooling system flushing

6 If coolant renewal has been neglected, or if the antifreeze mixture has become diluted, then in time, the cooling system may gradually lose efficiency, as the coolant passages become restricted due to rust, scale deposits, and other sediment. The cooling system efficiency can be restored by flushing the system clean.

7 The radiator should be flushed independently of the engine, to avoid unnecessary contamination.

Radiator flushing

8 Disconnect the top and bottom hoses and any other relevant hoses from the radiator, with reference to Chapter 3, Section 3.

9 Insert a garden hose into the radiator top inlet. Direct a flow of clean water through the radiator, and continue flushing until clean water emerges from the radiator bottom outlet.

10 If after a reasonable period the water still does not run clear, the radiator can be flushed with a good proprietary cleaning agent. It is important that the manufacturer's instructions are followed carefully. If the contamination is particularly bad, insert the hose in the radiator bottom outlet, and reverse flush the radiator.

Engine flushing

11 Remove the thermostat as described in Chapter 3, Section 4 then, if the radiator top hose has been disconnected from the engine, temporarily reconnect the hose.

12 With the top and bottom hoses disconnected from the radiator, insert a garden hose into the radiator top hose. Direct a clean flow of water through the engine, and continue flushing until clean water emerges from the radiator bottom hose.

13 On completion of flushing, refit the thermostat and reconnect the hoses with reference to Chapter 3, Section 3 and 4.

26.2 The drain plug is at the bottom right-hand corner of the radiator

26.3a Unscrew the radiator drain plug ...

26.3b ... and allow the coolant to drain

26.33 Check the condition of the expansion tank cap rubber seal

Antifreeze mixture

14 The antifreeze should always be renewed at the specified intervals. This is necessary not only to maintain the antifreeze properties, but also to prevent corrosion which would otherwise occur as the corrosion inhibitors become progressively less effective.

15 Always use an ethylene-glycol based antifreeze which is suitable for use in mixed-metal cooling systems. The quantity of antifreeze and levels of protection are given in the Specifications.

16 The antifreeze recommended by Ford at the time of writing is their purple coloured Super Plus antifreeze, which, if it is not mixed with any other antifreeze, can be left in the system for 10 years. Owners may wish to change their antifreeze more frequently, especially if the type and quality in the system is unknown.

17 Before adding antifreeze, the cooling system should be completely drained, preferably flushed, and all hoses checked for condition and security.

18 After filling with antifreeze, a label should be attached to the expansion tank, stating the type and concentration of antifreeze used, and the date installed. Any subsequent topping-up should be made with the same type and concentration of antifreeze.

Caution: Do not use engine antifreeze in the windscreen/tailgate washer system, as it will cause damage to the paintwork. A screenwash additive should be added to the washer system in the quantities stated on the bottle.

Cooling system filling

19 Before attempting to fill the cooling system, make sure that all hoses and clips are in good condition, and that the clips are tight. Note that an antifreeze mixture must be used all year round, to prevent corrosion of the engine components.

20 Locate and unscrew the radiator bleed plug, which looks similar to the drain plug, and is situated at the top left-hand or right-hand corner of the radiator (depending on model).

21 Remove the expansion tank filler cap. If a funnel is available for filling the cooling system, use it to reduce the risk of spillage onto the paintwork under the bonnet.

22 Slowly fill the system until coolant emerges

from the radiator bleed hole, or until the level settles at the MAX mark on the side of the expansion tank.

23 Refit and tighten the radiator bleed plug.

24 If necessary, top-up the coolant level to the MAX mark, and refit the expansion tank cap.

25 Start the engine, run it at approximately 3000 rpm for two minutes, then switch off.

26 Recheck the coolant level in the expansion tank, and top-up if necessary. Although the system should still be some way off full operating temperature at this point, take precautions against scalding if the expansion tank cap has to be removed.

27 With the expansion tank cap refitted, start the engine once more, and run it at 3000 rpm for another two minutes. Switch the engine off on completion, and allow it to cool. When the engine has cooled (preferably overnight), recheck the level once more, and top-up if necessary.

Airlocks

28 If, after draining and refilling the system, symptoms of overheating are found which did not occur previously, then the fault is almost certainly due to trapped air at some point in the system, causing an airlock and restricting the flow of coolant; usually, the air is trapped because the system was refilled too quickly.

29 If an airlock is suspected, first try gently squeezing all visible coolant hoses. A coolant hose which is full of air feels quite different to one full of coolant when squeezed. After refilling the system, most airlocks will clear once the system has cooled, and been topped-up.

30 While the engine is running at operating temperature, switch on the heater and heater fan, and check for heat output. Provided there is sufficient coolant in the system, any lack of heat output could be due to an airlock in the system.

31 Airlocks can have more serious effects than simply reducing heater output – a severe airlock could reduce coolant flow around the engine. Check that the radiator top hose is hot when the engine is at operating temperature – a top hose which stays cold could be the result of an airlock (or a non-opening thermostat).

32 If the problem persists, stop the engine and allow it to cool down **completely**, before unscrewing the expansion tank filler cap or loosening the hose clips and squeezing the hoses to bleed out the trapped air. In the worst case, the system will have to be at least partially drained (this time, the coolant can be saved for re-use) and flushed to clear the problem.

Expansion tank cap check

33 Clean the pressure cap, and inspect the seal inside the cap for damage or deterioration **(see illustration)**. If there is any sign of damage or deterioration to the seal, fit a new pressure cap.

 Notes

Chapter 1 Part B:
Routine maintenance and servicing – diesel models

Contents

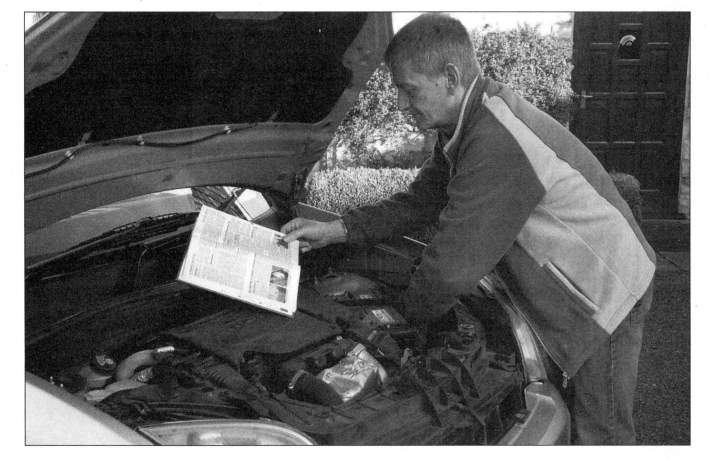

Degrees of difficulty

Easy, suitable for novice with little experience 

Fairly easy, suitable for beginner with some experience

Fairly difficult, suitable for competent DIY mechanic

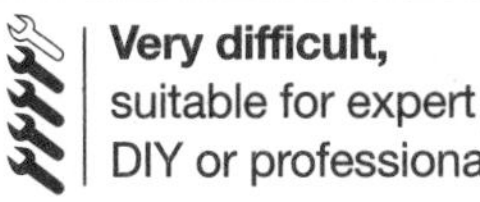

Difficult, suitable for experienced DIY mechanic

Very difficult, suitable for expert DIY or professional 

Lubricants and fluids

Lubricants and fluids	Refer to end of *Weekly checks* on page 0•18

Capacities

Engine oil (including oil filter)

1.4 litre engine	3.8 litres
1.6 litre engine	3.85 litres

Cooling system (approximate)

1.4 litre engine	5.5 litres
1.6 litre engine	6.0 litres

Transmission

All models	2.3 litres

Washer fluid reservoir

All models	2.5 litres

Fuel tank

All models	43 litres

Cooling system

Antifreeze mixture:	
50% antifreeze	Protection down to -37°C

Note: *Refer to antifreeze manufacturer for latest recommendations.*

Brakes

Friction material minimum thickness:	
Front brake pads	1.5 mm
Rear brake shoes	1.0 mm

Tyre pressures

Tyre pressures	Refer to end of *Weekly checks* on page 0•18

Torque wrench settings

Torque wrench settings	Nm	lbf ft
Engine oil drain plug:		
1.4 litre engine	25	18
1.6 litre engine	34	25
Engine oil filter cover	25	18
Roadwheel nuts	110	81
Seat belts:		
Front seat belt height adjuster securing bolts	40	30
Front seat belt sliding rail bolt	40	30
Front seat belt stalk/tensioner assembly securing bolt	47	35
Inertia reel mounting:		
Front seat belt	35	26
Rear centre seat belt	47	35
Rear side seat belt	40	30
Rear seat belt buckle bolts	55	41
Seat belt buckle securing bolt	47	35
Seat belt upper/lower anchor bolts	40	30
Transmission filler/level plug	35	26

The maintenance intervals in this manual are provided with the assumption that you, not the dealer, will be carrying out the work. These are the minimum maintenance intervals recommended by us for cars driven daily. If you wish to keep your car in peak condition at all times, you may wish to perform some of these procedures more often. We encourage frequent maintenance, because it enhances the efficiency, performance and resale value of your car.

If the car is driven in dusty areas, used to tow a trailer, or driven frequently at slow speeds (idling in traffic) or on short journeys, more frequent maintenance intervals are recommended.

When the vehicle is new, it should be serviced by a dealer service department (or other workshop recognised by the vehicle manufacturer as providing the same standard of service) in order to preserve the warranty. The vehicle manufacturer may reject warranty claims if you are unable to prove that servicing has been carried out as and when specified, using only original equipment parts or parts certified to be of equivalent quality.

Every 250 miles or weekly

- ☐ Refer to *Weekly checks*

Every 6000 miles or 6 months, whichever comes first

- ☐ Renew the engine oil and filter (Section 3)

Note: *Ford recommend that the engine oil and filter are changed every 12 500 miles or 12 months. However, oil and filter changes are good for the engine, and we recommend that the oil and filter are renewed more frequently, especially if the car is used on a lot of short journeys.*

Every 12 500 miles or 12 months, whichever comes first

- ☐ Renew the pollen filter, where applicable (Section 4)
- ☐ Drain any water from the fuel filter (Section 5)
- ☐ Check all components, pipes and hoses for fluid leaks (Section 6)
- ☐ Check the condition and tension of the auxiliary drivebelt (Section 7)
- ☐ Check and if necessary adjust the handbrake (Section 8)
- ☐ Check the condition and operation of the seat belts (Section 9)
- ☐ Lubricate all hinges and locks (Section 10)
- ☐ Check the front brake pads and discs for wear (Section 11)
- ☐ Check the rear brake shoes and drums for wear (Section 12)
- ☐ Check the steering and suspension components for condition and security (Section 13)
- ☐ Check the condition of the driveshaft gaiters (Section 14)
- ☐ Check the roadwheel nuts are tightened to the specified torque (Section 15)
- ☐ Carry out a road test (Section 16)

Every 37 500 miles or 3 years, whichever comes first

- ☐ Renew the fuel filter (Section 17)
- ☐ Renew the air filter (Section 18)
- ☐ Check the transmission oil level (Section 19)
- ☐ Check the braking system rubber hoses (Section 20)

Every 50 000 miles or 4 years, whichever comes first

- ☐ Renew the timing belt (Section 21)

Note: *Although the normal interval for timing belt renewal is 150 000 miles or 10 years, it is strongly recommended that the interval suggested above is observed, especially on cars which are subjected to intensive use, ie, mainly short journeys or a lot of stop-start driving. The actual belt renewal interval is very much up to the individual owner, but bear in mind that severe engine damage will result if the belt breaks.*

Every 150 000 miles or 10 years, whichever comes first

- ☐ Renew the auxiliary drivebelt (Section 22)

Every 2 years, regardless of mileage

- ☐ Renew the brake fluid (Section 23)
- ☐ Renew the remote control battery (Section 24)

Every 4 years, regardless of mileage

- ☐ Renew the coolant and check the condition of the expansion tank pressure cap (Section 25)

Note: *Ford state that, if their purple Super Plus antifreeze is in the system from new, the coolant need only be changed every 10 years. If there is any doubt as to the type or quality of the antifreeze which has been used, we recommend this shorter interval be observed.*

Component location – diesel models

Underbonnet view of a 1.4 litre model

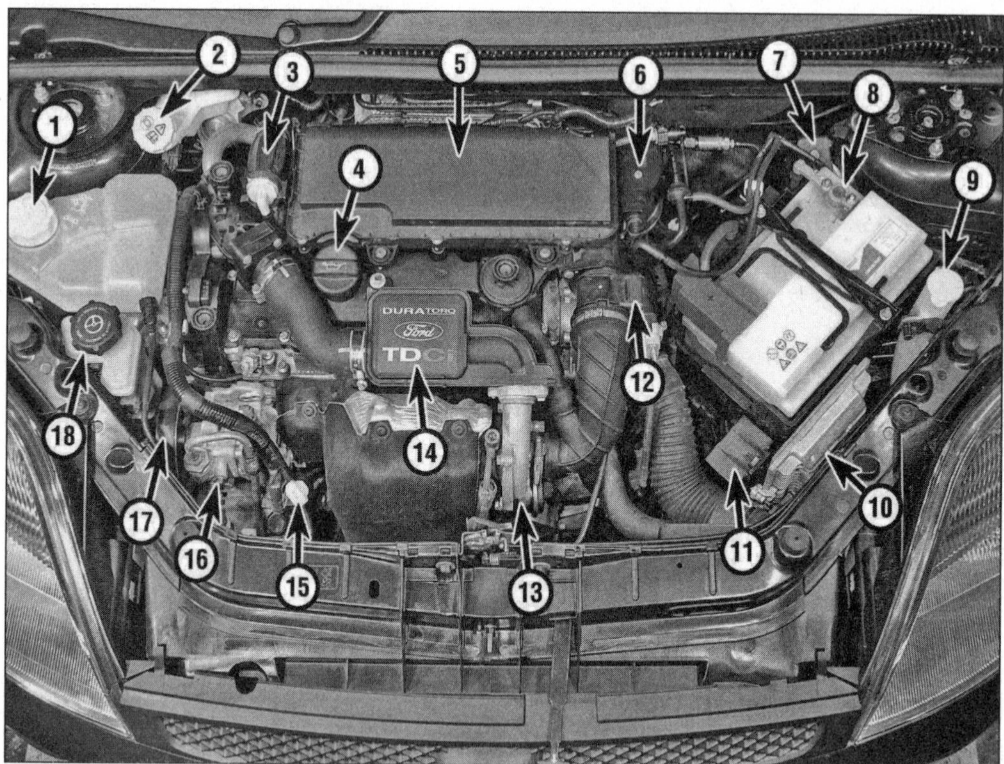

1. Coolant reservoir (expansion tank)
2. Brake and clutch fluid reservoir
3. Fuel system hand-priming bulb
4. Engine oil filler cap
5. Air cleaner
6. Fuel filter
7. Engine wiring harness connector
8. Battery negative lead
9. Windscreen washer fluid reservoir filler
10. Powertrain control module
11. Auxiliary fuse/relay box
12. Airflow sensor
13. Turbocharger
14. Intake air resonator
15. Engine oil level dipstick
16. Power steering pump
17. Auxiliary drivebelt
18. Power steering fluid reservoir

Underbonnet view of a 1.6 litre model

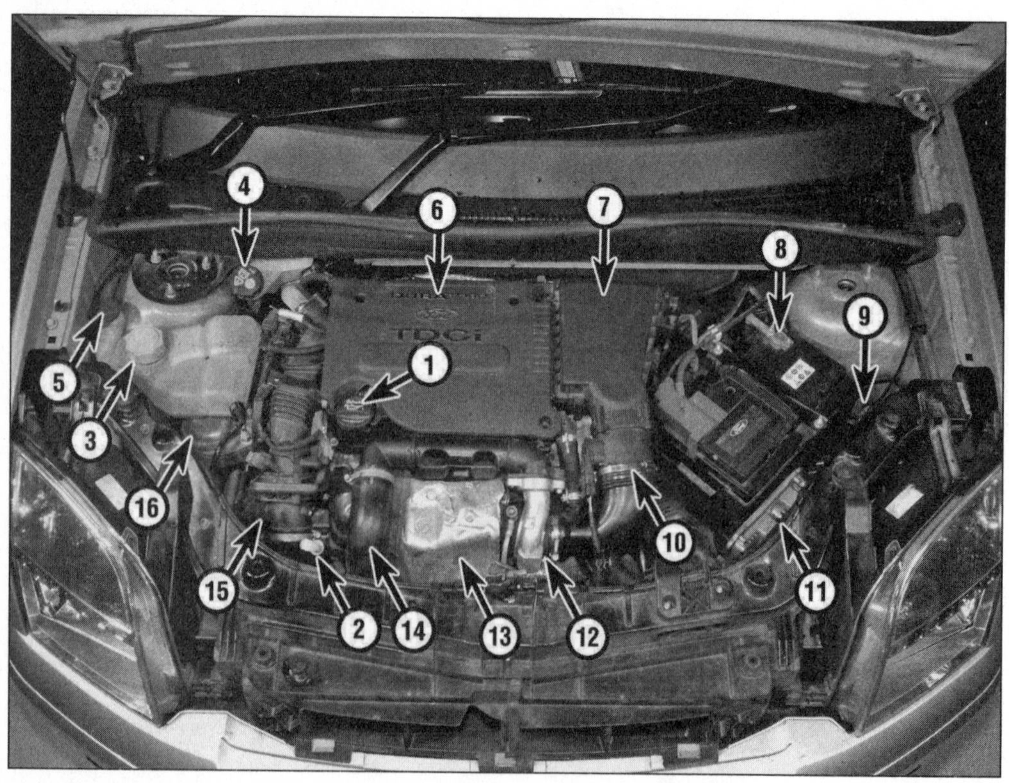

1. Engine oil filler cap
2. Engine oil level dipstick
3. Coolant reservoir (expansion tank)
4. Brake and clutch fluid reservoir
5. Windscreen washer fluid reservoir filler
6. Engine top cover including air cleaner
7. Air cleaner cover
8. Battery negative lead
9. Electro-hydraulic power steering fluid reservoir (hidden)
10. Mass airflow sensor
11. Powertrain control module
12. Turbocharger
13. Turbocharger/exhaust manifold heat shields
14. Air hose from turbocharger to intercooler
15. Intake air shutoff throttle body
16. Right-hand engine mounting

Front underbody view

1 *Brake caliper*
2 *Brake hose*
3 *Auxiliary drivebelt cover*
4 *AC compressor*
5 *Engine oil drain plug*
6 *Exhaust system*
7 *Cooling fan*
8 *Radiator bottom hose*
9 *Gearchange cable cover*
10 *Screen washer pump*
11 *Suspension lower arm*
12 *Engine rear (pendulum) mounting*
13 *Subframe*
14 *Ant-roll bar*
15 *Track rod end*
16 *Driveshaft*

Rear underbody view

1 *Shock absorber*
2 *Fuel filler pipe*
3 *Rear coil spring*
4 *Rear suspension beam*
5 *Exhaust rear silencer*
6 *Fuel tank*
7 *Handbrake cable*
8 *Heat shield*

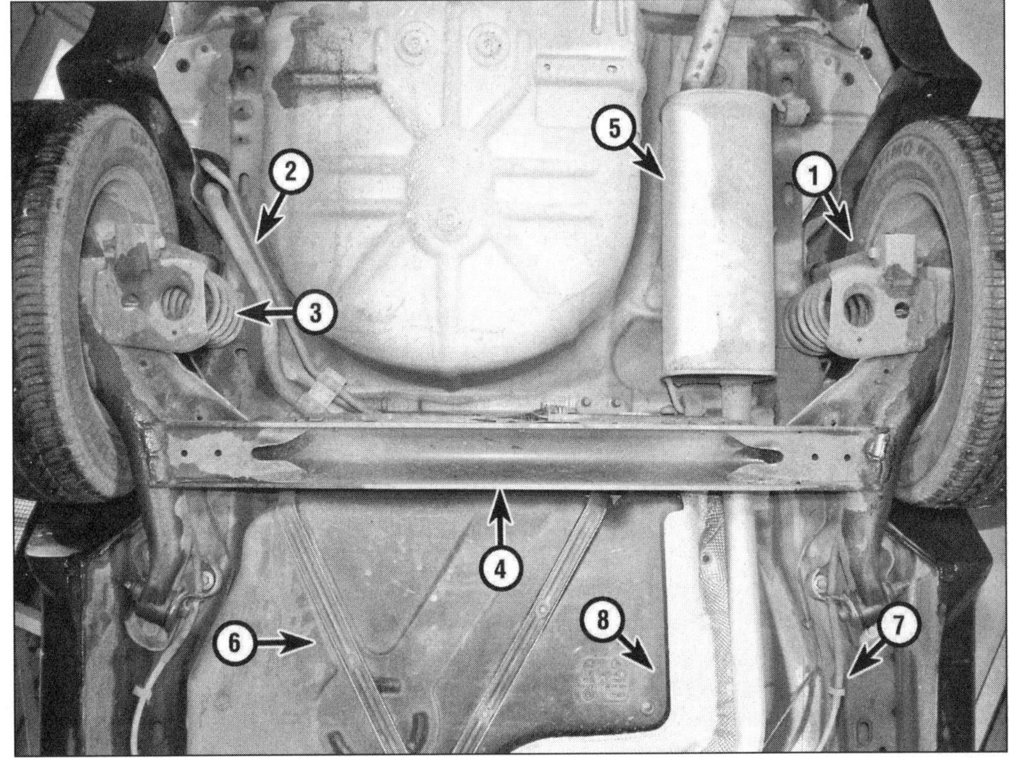

Maintenance procedures

1 General information

1 This Chapter is designed to help the home mechanic maintain his/her car for safety, economy, long life and peak performance.
2 The Chapter contains a master maintenance schedule, followed by Sections dealing specifically with each task in the schedule. Visual checks, adjustments, component renewal and other helpful items are included. Refer to the accompanying illustrations of the engine compartment and the underside of the car for the locations of the various components.
3 Servicing your car in accordance with the mileage/time maintenance schedule and the following Sections will provide a planned maintenance programme, which should result in a long and reliable service life. This is a comprehensive plan, so maintaining some items but not others at the specified service intervals, will not produce the same results.
4 As you service your car, you will discover that many of the procedures can – and should – be grouped together, because of the particular procedure being performed, or because of the proximity of two otherwise unrelated components to one another. For example, if the car is raised for any reason, the exhaust can be inspected at the same time as the suspension and steering components.
5 The first step in this maintenance programme is to prepare yourself before the actual work begins. Read through all the Sections relevant to the work to be carried out, then make a list and gather all the parts and tools required. If a problem is encountered, seek advice from a parts specialist, or a dealer service department.

2 Regular maintenance

1 If, from the time the car is new, the routine maintenance schedule is followed closely, and frequent checks are made of fluid levels and high wear items, as suggested throughout this manual, the engine will be kept in relatively good running condition, and the need for additional work will be minimised.
2 It is possible that there will be times when the engine is running poorly due to the lack of regular maintenance. This is even more likely if a used car which has not received regular and frequent maintenance checks, is purchased. In such cases, additional work may need to be carried out, outside of the regular maintenance intervals.
3 If engine wear is suspected, a compression test (refer to the relevant section of Chapter 2B, Section 2 or Chapter 2C, Section 2) will provide valuable information regarding the overall performance of the main internal components. Such a test can be used as a basis to decide on the extent of the work to be carried out. If, for example, a compression test indicates serious internal engine wear, conventional maintenance as described in this Chapter will not greatly improve the performance of the engine, and may prove a waste of time and money, unless extensive overhaul work is carried out first.
4 The following series of operations are those most often required to improve the performance of a generally poor running engine:

Primary operations

a) Clean, inspect and test the battery (refer to 'Weekly checks').
b) Check all the engine related fluids (refer to 'Weekly checks').
c) Check the condition of all hoses, and check for fluid leaks (Section 6).
d) Check the condition and tension of the auxiliary drivebelt (Section 7).
e) Renew the fuel filter (Section 17).
f) Check the condition of the air filter, and renew if necessary (Section 18).

5 If the above operations do not prove fully effective, carry out the following secondary operations:

Secondary operations

All items listed under *Primary operations*, plus the following:

a) Check the charging system (refer to Chapter 5A, Section 6).
b) Check the preheating system (refer to Chapter 5C, Section 1).
c) Check the fuel system (refer to Chapter 4B, Section 13).

Every 6000 miles or 6 months

3 Engine oil and filter renewal

1 Frequent oil and filter changes are the most important preventative maintenance procedures which can be undertaken by the DIY owner. As engine oil ages, it becomes diluted and contaminated, which leads to premature engine wear.

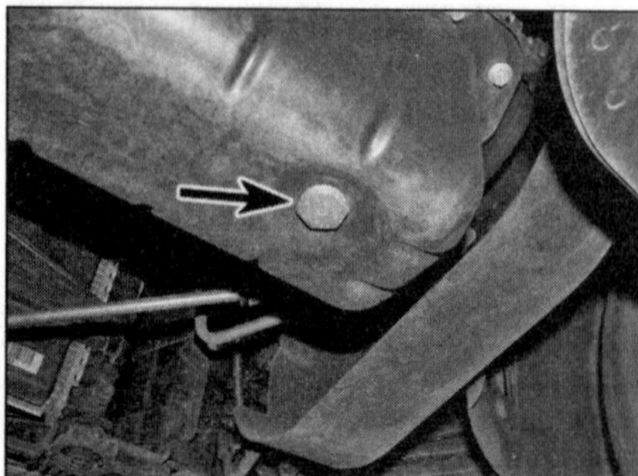

3.3 Unscrew the drain plug from the base of the sump

2 Before starting this procedure, gather together all the necessary tools and materials. Also make sure that you have plenty of clean rags and newspapers handy, to mop-up any spills. Ideally, the engine oil should be warm, as it will drain better, and more built-up sludge will be removed with it. Take care, however, not to touch the exhaust or any other hot parts of the engine when working under the vehicle. To avoid any possibility of scalding, and to protect yourself from possible skin irritants and other harmful contaminants in used engine oils, it is advisable to wear gloves when carrying out this work. Access to the underside of the vehicle will be greatly improved if it can be raised on a lift, driven onto ramps, or jacked up and supported on axle stands. Whichever method is chosen, make sure that the vehicle remains level, or if it is at an angle, that the drain plug is at the lowest point.
3 Slacken the drain plug about half a turn, position the draining container under the drain plug, then remove the plug completely **(see illustration)**. If possible, try to keep the plug pressed into the sump while unscrewing it by hand the last couple of turns **(see Haynes Hint)**. Recover the sealing ring from the drain plug.
4 Allow some time for the old oil to drain, noting that it may be necessary to reposition the container as the oil flow slows to a trickle.
5 After all the oil has drained, wipe off the drain plug with a clean rag, and fit a new sealing washer. Clean the area around the

HAYNES HiNT

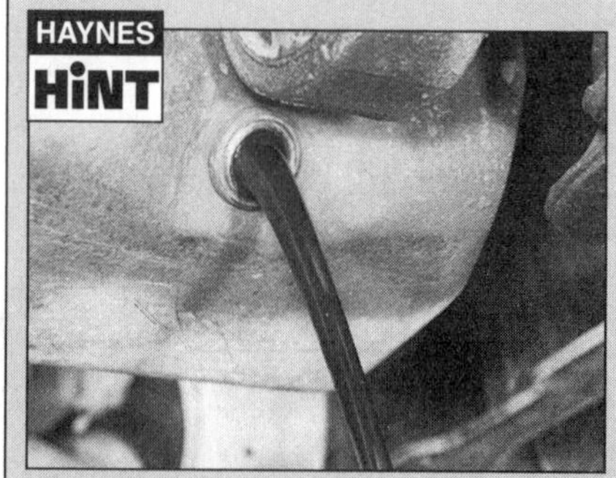

As the drain plug releases from the threads, move it away sharply so the stream of oil issuing from the sump runs into the container, not up your sleeve.

3.7 Engine oil filter cover (arrowed)

3.10a Fit the new O-ring to the cover

3.10b Ensure the filter locating peg (arrowed) locates into the corresponding hole in the housing (arrowed)

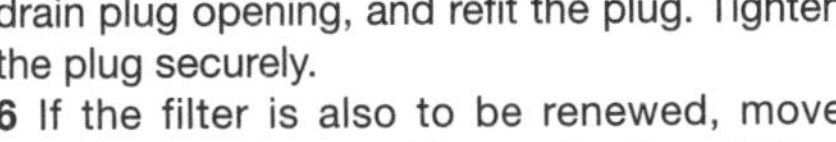

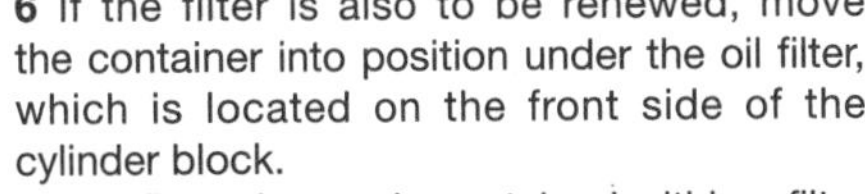

drain plug opening, and refit the plug. Tighten the plug securely.

6 If the filter is also to be renewed, move the container into position under the oil filter, which is located on the front side of the cylinder block.

7 The filter element is contained within a filter cover. Using a socket or spanner, slacken and remove the filter cover from above **(see illustration)**. Be prepared for oil spillage, and recover the O-ring seal from the cover.

8 Pull the filter element from the filter housing.

9 Use a clean rag to remove all oil, dirt and sludge from the inside and outside of the filter cover.

10 Fit the new O-ring to the filter cover, then insert the new filter element into the housing, ensuring that the element locating peg engages correctly with the corresponding hole in the housing **(see illustrations)**.

11 Apply a little clean engine oil to the O-ring seal, then refit the filter/cover to the housing and tighten the cover to the specified torque.

12 Remove the old oil and all tools from under the car, then lower the car to the ground (if applicable).

13 Remove the dipstick, then unscrew the

3.13a Remove the oil filler cap ...

3.13b ... and start filling the engine with oil

oil filler cap. Fill the engine, using the correct grade and type of oil (see *Lubricants and fluids*). An oil can spout or funnel may help to reduce spillage **(see illustrations)**. Pour in half the specified quantity of oil first, then wait a few minutes for the oil to run to the sump. Continue adding oil a small quantity at a time until the level is up to the lower mark on the dipstick. Adding approximately 1.0 litre will bring the level up to the upper mark on the dipstick. Refit the filler cap.

14 Start the engine and run it for a few minutes; check for leaks around the oil filter seal and the sump drain plug. Note that there may be a delay of a few seconds before the oil pressure warning light goes out when the engine is first started, as the oil circulates through the engine oil galleries and the new oil filter before the pressure builds up.

15 Switch off the engine, and wait a few minutes for the oil to settle in the sump once more. With the new oil circulated and the filter completely full, recheck the level on the dipstick, and add more oil as necessary.

16 Dispose of the used engine oil safely, with reference to *General repair procedures*.

Every 12 500 miles or 12 months

4 Pollen filter renewal

Note: *Models without air conditioning appear not to have been fitted with a pollen filter as standard, although the filter housing IS fitted to all models, meaning that a filter can be added if wished.*

1 For greater access to the filter, remove the glovebox as described in Chapter 11, Section 25, and also the side panel in front of the centre console, which is secured by a single screw at the front, and clips at the rear **(see illustration)**.

2 Working at the very front of the passenger footwell, remove the four screws and take off the cover fitted over the end of the filter housing, in the centre of the car **(see illustrations)**. The housing is almost vertical, and the cover for it should not be confused with the horizontal cover fitted to the side of the heater matrix.

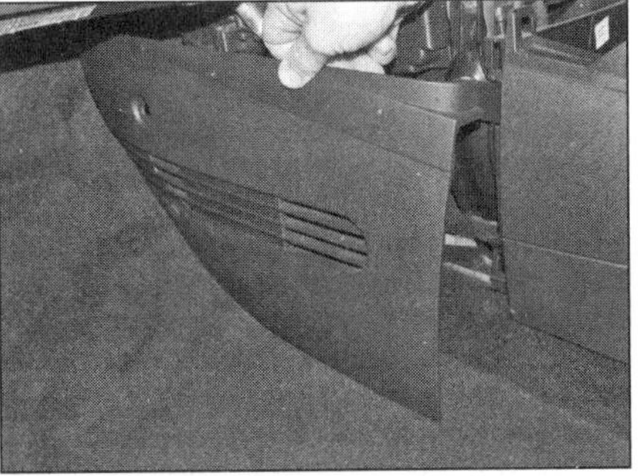

4.1 Removing the centre console side panel

3 Slide out the pollen filter, into the passenger footwell, and remove it.

4 When fitting the new filter, note the direction of flow arrow marked on its top edge –

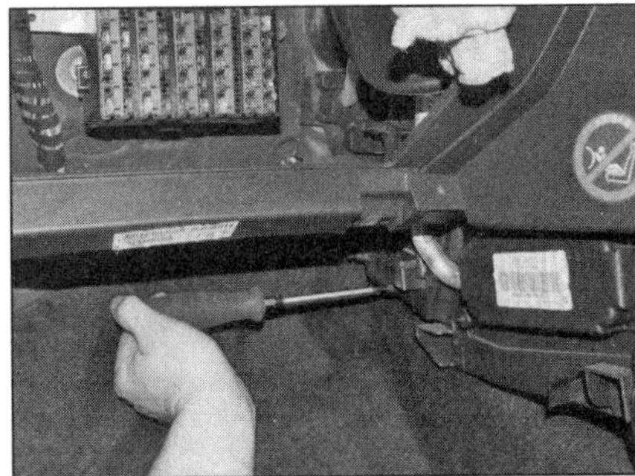

4.2a Remove the four Torx screws ...

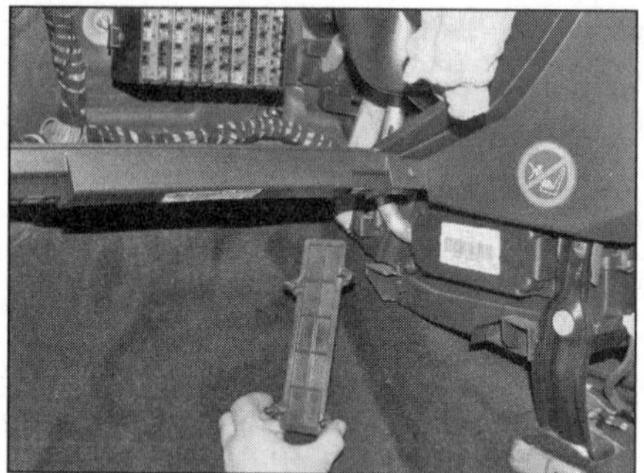

4.2b ... and take off the pollen filter housing end cover

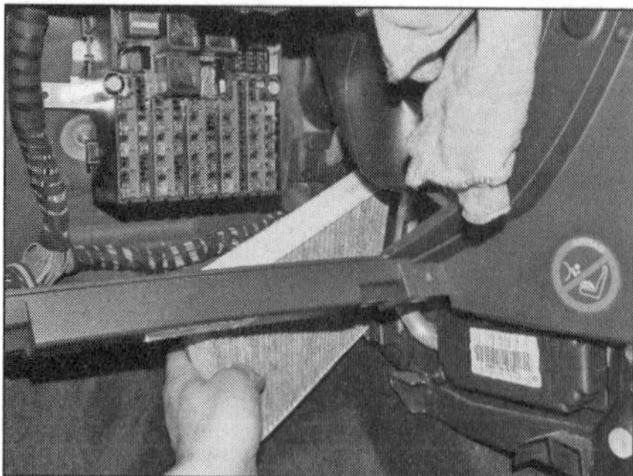

4.4 Fit the new filter, with the arrow marking facing into the car

5.1 The fuel filter is at the rear of the engine, on the passenger side

5.4 Fit a tube to the drain plug, then unscrew the plug

the arrow should point into the car **(see illustration)**.

5 Slide the filter fully into position, secure the cover with the four screws, then refit the glovebox and centre console side panel (if removed).

5 Fuel filter water draining

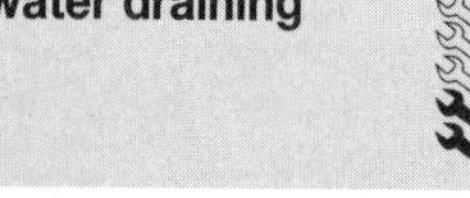

1 The fuel filter is located at the rear of the engine compartment. On 1.4 litre models, it is between the air filter housing and the battery **(see illustration)**. On 1.6 litre models, it is beneath the air cleaner. Where fitted, a water drain outlet is provided at the base of the fuel filter housing, to which a suitable piece of tubing may be fitted. **Note:** *A water drain facility is not provided on later models – if an air purge screw is located on top of the fuel filter, there is no water drain facility.*

6.1 Radiator bottom hose connection

2 On 1.6 litre models, remove the air cleaner assembly as described in Chapter 4B, Section 4.

3 Place a suitable container beneath the drain tube, and cover the surrounding area with rags.

4 Open the drain plug, and allow fuel and water to drain until water free fuel emerges from the end of the tube (see illustration). Close the drain plug.

5 On 1.6 litre models, refit the air cleaner assembly.

6 Dispose of the drained fuel safely.

7 Start the engine. If difficulty is experienced, bleed the fuel system (Chapter 4B, Section 3).

HAYNES HiNT

A leak in the cooling system will usually show up as white- or antifreeze-coloured deposits on the areas adjoining the leak.

6 Hose and fluid leak check

Coolant

Warning: Refer to the safety information given in 'Safety first!' and Chapter 3, Section 1 before disturbing any of the cooling system components.

1 Carefully check the radiator and heater coolant hoses along their entire length **(see illustration)**. Renew any hose which is cracked, swollen or which shows signs of deterioration. Cracks will show up better if the hose is squeezed. Pay close attention to the clips that secure the hoses to the cooling system components. Hose clips that have been overtightened can pinch and puncture hoses, resulting in cooling system leaks.

2 Inspect all the cooling system components (hoses, joint faces, etc) for leaks. Where any problems of this nature are found on system components, renew the component or gasket with reference to Chapter 3.

3 A leak from the cooling system will usually show up as white- or antifreeze-coloured deposits, on the area surrounding the leak **(see Haynes Hint)**.

Fuel

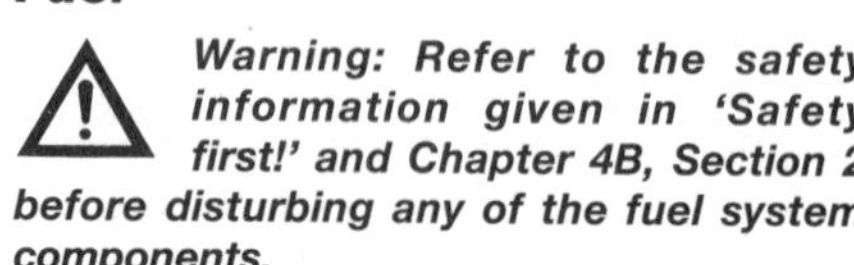

Warning: Refer to the safety information given in 'Safety first!' and Chapter 4B, Section 2 before disturbing any of the fuel system components.

4 Check all fuel lines at their connections to the injection pump, injectors and fuel filter housing.

5 Examine each fuel hose/pipe along its length for splits or cracks. Check for leakage from the union nuts and examine the unions between the metal fuel lines and the fuel filter housing. Also check the area around the fuel injectors for signs of leakage.

6 To identify fuel leaks between the fuel tank and the engine bay, the vehicle should raised and securely supported on axle stands. Inspect the fuel tank and filler neck for punctures, cracks and other damage. The connection between the filler neck and tank is especially critical. Sometimes a rubber filler neck or connecting hose will leak due to loose retaining clamps or deteriorated rubber.

7 Carefully check all rubber hoses and metal fuel lines leading away from the fuel tank. Check for loose connections, deteriorated hoses, kinked lines, and other damage. Pay particular attention to the vent pipes and hoses, which often loop up around the filler neck and can become blocked or kinked, making tank filling difficult. Follow the fuel supply and return lines to the front of the vehicle, carefully inspecting them all the way for signs of damage or corrosion. Renew damaged sections as necessary.

Engine oil

8 Inspect the area around the camshaft cover, cylinder head, oil filter and sump joint faces. Bear in mind that, over a period of time, some very slight seepage from these areas is to be expected – what you are really looking for is any indication of a serious leak caused by gasket failure. Engine oil seeping from the base of the timing belt cover or the transmission bellhousing may be an indication of crankshaft or input shaft oil seal failure. Should a leak be found, renew the failed gasket or oil seal by referring to Chapter 2B, 2C, 7A or 7B.

Power steering fluid

Note: *On 1.6 litre models, the electric power steering pump and reservoir are integral as one unit located beneath the left-hand headlight.*

9 Examine the hose running between the fluid reservoir and the power steering pump, and the return hose running from the steering rack to the fluid reservoir. Also examine the high-pressure supply hose between the pump and the steering rack.

10 Check the hoses leading to the power steering fluid cooler at the front of the engine bay **(see illustration)**. Look for deterioration caused by corrosion and damage from grounding, or debris thrown up from the road surface.

11 Pay particular attention to crimped unions, and the area surrounding the hoses that are secured with adjustable worm-drive clips.

Air conditioning refrigerant

Warning: Refer to the safety information given in 'Safety first!' and Chapter 3, Section 10, regarding the dangers of disturbing any of the air conditioning system components.

12 The air conditioning system is filled with a liquid refrigerant, which is retained under high pressure. If the air conditioning system is opened and depressurised without the aid of specialised equipment, the refrigerant will immediately turn into gas and escape into the atmosphere. If the liquid comes into contact with your skin, it can cause severe frostbite. In addition, the refrigerant contains substances which are environmentally damaging; for this reason, it should not be allowed to escape into the atmosphere.

13 Any suspected air conditioning system leaks should be immediately referred to a Ford dealer or air conditioning specialist. Leakage will be shown up as a steady drop in the level of refrigerant in the system.

14 Note that water may drip from the condenser drain pipe, underneath the car, immediately after the air conditioning system has been in use. This is normal, and should not be cause for concern.

Brake (and clutch) fluid

Warning: Refer to the safety information given in 'Safety first!' and Chapter 9, Section 1, regarding the dangers of handling brake fluid.

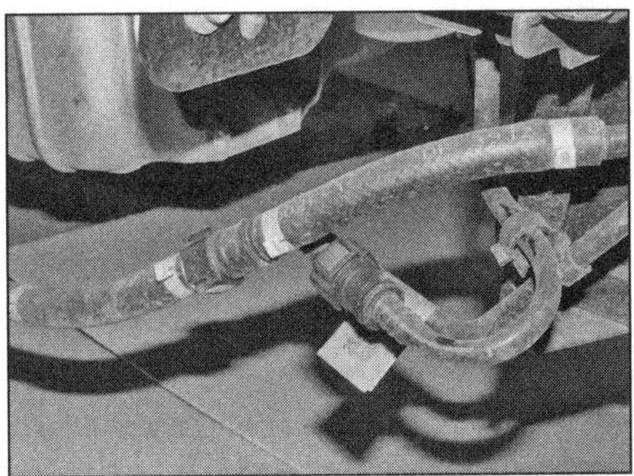

6.10 Power steering fluid cooler hose connections under right-hand wheel arch

15 With reference to Chapter 9, Section 8, examine the area surrounding the brake pipe unions at the master cylinder for signs of leakage. Check the area around the base of fluid reservoir, for signs of leakage caused by seal failure. Also examine the brake pipe unions at the ABS hydraulic unit.

16 If fluid loss is evident, but the leak cannot be pinpointed in the engine bay, the brake calipers and underbody brake lines should be carefully checked with the vehicle raised and supported on axle stands. Leakage of fluid from the braking system is serious fault that must be rectified immediately.

17 Refer to Chapter 6, Section 2 and 3 and check for leakage around the hydraulic fluid line connections to the clutch master cylinder at the bulkhead, and to the clutch slave cylinder, bolted to the side of the transmission bellhousing.

18 Brake/clutch hydraulic fluid is a toxic substance with a watery consistency. New fluid is almost colourless, but it becomes darker with age and use.

Unidentified fluid leaks

19 If there are signs that a fluid of some description is leaking from the vehicle, but you cannot identify the type of fluid or its exact origin, park the vehicle overnight and slide a large piece of card underneath it. Providing that the card is positioned in roughly in the right location, even the smallest leak will show up on the card. Not only will this help you to pinpoint the exact location of the leak, it should be easier to identify the fluid from its colour. Bear in mind, though, that the leak may only be occurring when the engine is running!

7.3 With the headlight removed, access to the drivebelt is much improved

Vacuum hoses

20 Although the braking system is hydraulically operated, the brake servo unit amplifies the effort you apply at the brake pedal, by making use of the vacuum created by the pump (see Chapter 9, Section 12 and 21). Vacuum is ported to the servo by means of a large bore hose. Any leaks that develop in this hose will reduce the effectiveness of the braking system.

21 In addition, many of the underbonnet components, particularly the emission control components, are driven by vacuum supplied from the vacuum pump via narrow bore hoses. A leak in a vacuum hose means that air is being drawn into the hose (rather than escaping from it) and this makes leakage very difficult to detect. One method is to use an old length of vacuum hose as a kind of stethoscope – hold one end close to (but not in) your ear and use the other end to probe the area around the suspected leak. When the end of the hose is directly over a vacuum leak, a hissing sound will be heard clearly through the hose. Care must be taken to avoid contacting hot or moving components, as the engine must be running when testing in this manner. Renew any vacuum hoses that are found to be defective.

7 Auxiliary drivebelt check

General

1 A single auxiliary drivebelt is fitted at the right-hand side of the engine. The length of the drivebelt varies according to whether air conditioning is fitted. An automatic tensioner is fitted, so setting the drivebelt tension is unnecessary.

Checking

2 Due to their function and material makeup, drivebelts are prone to failure after a long period of time, and should therefore be inspected regularly.

3 Since the drivebelt is located very close to the right-hand side of the engine compartment, it is possible to gain better access by raising the front of the car and removing the right-hand wheel. On 1.4 litre models only, unclip the power steering pipe, then remove the two screws securing the drivebelt lower cover. However, for checking purposes alone, removing the right-hand headlight as described in Chapter 12, Section 7, gives excellent access to the drivebelt **(see illustration)**.

4 With the engine stopped, inspect the full length of the drivebelt for cracks and separation of the belt plies. It will be necessary to turn the engine (using a spanner or socket and bar on the crankshaft pulley bolt) in order to move the belt from the pulleys so that the belt can be inspected thoroughly. Twist the

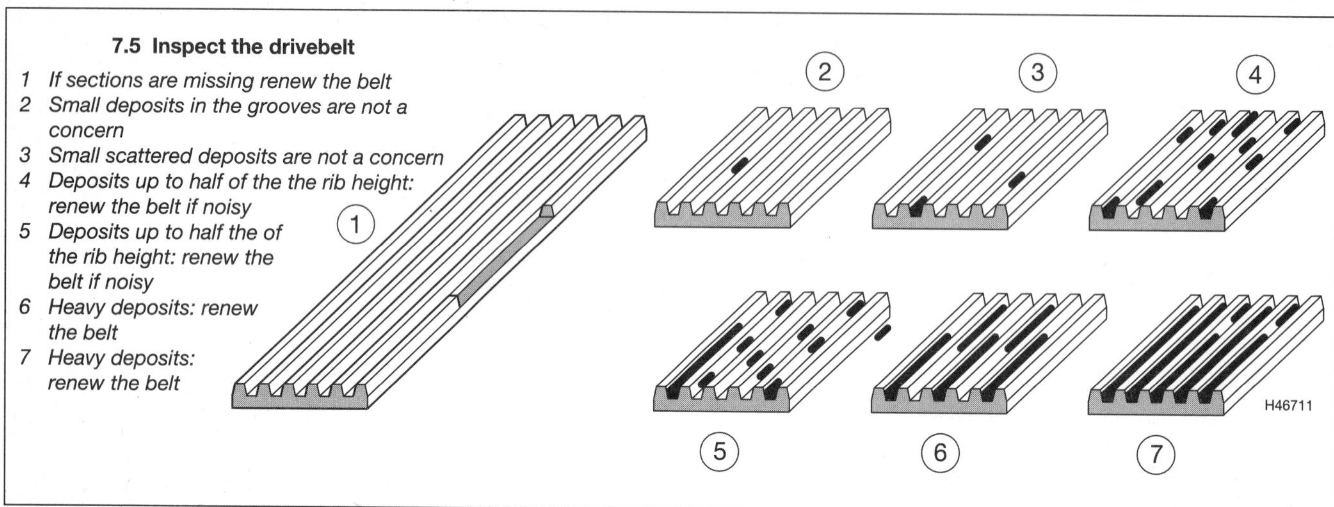

7.5 Inspect the drivebelt

1 If sections are missing renew the belt
2 Small deposits in the grooves are not a concern
3 Small scattered deposits are not a concern
4 Deposits up to half of the the rib height: renew the belt if noisy
5 Deposits up to half the of the rib height: renew the belt if noisy
6 Heavy deposits: renew the belt
7 Heavy deposits: renew the belt

belt between the pulleys so that both sides can be viewed. Also check for fraying, and glazing which gives the belt a shiny appearance. Check the pulleys for nicks, cracks, distortion and corrosion.

5 Small cracks in the belt ribs are not usually serious, but look closely to see whether the crack has extended into the belt plies **(see illustration)**. If the belt is in any way suspect, or is known to have seen long service, renew it as described in Section 22.

6 If the belt appears to be too slack (or has actually been slipping in service), this may indicate a problem with the belt tensioner, or external contamination of the belt (eg, by oil or water).

8 Handbrake check and adjustment

Checking

1 The handbrake should be fully applied (and capable of holding the car on a slope) after approximately four clicks of the ratchet. The operating cables will stretch over time, and adjustment will be needed.

2 The handbrake is a conventional design, having separate cables for the two rear wheels, and a front cable with an equaliser plate which operates both rear cables equally. The handbrake is adjusted by means of a nut attached to the front cable.

3 With the rear of the car raised and supported (see Jacking and vehicle support), check that the rear wheels are free to turn with the handbrake fully released.

4 Apply the handbrake one click at a time, and check whether the rear wheels can still be turned. If the handbrake does not appear to be working equally on both wheels, this may indicate a problem with either the rear cable or the brake shoes on the least effective side (see Chapter 9, Section 6 and 20 for more details).

Adjustment

Note: *This procedure is intended only to compensate for stretch in existing cables. If new rear cables have been fitted, a more elaborate adjustment procedure is specified by Ford – see Chapter 9, Section 19 for details.*

Note: *If the travel of the handbrake is excessive it is important that the rear brake self-adjusting mechanism is working correctly before any attempt is made to adjust the cable (see Chapter 9, Section 19 for details).*

5 If the handbrake appears to be working evenly, but requires an excessive amount of lever movement to operate, the front cable should be adjusted as follows. First, unclip and remove the trim panel around the handbrake lever **(see illustration)**.

6 Remove the locking clip from the handbrake adjuster nut located directly below the lever. With the lever released, tighten the nut by half a turn, then recheck the operation of the handbrake and repeat if necessary **(see illustrations)**. Do not overadjust, as this may accelerate the stretching of the front cable. When the handbrake operation is satisfactory, check that the rear wheels are free to turn when the handbrake is fully released.

7 On completion, lower the car to the ground. Refit the locking clip to the handbrake adjuster nut (use a new one if the old one is unserviceable), and refit the handbrake lever trim panel.

9 Seat belt check

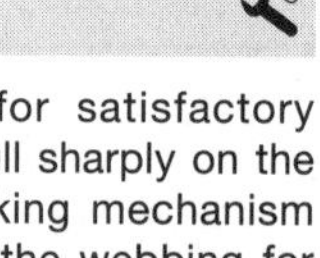

1 Check the seat belts for satisfactory operation and condition. Pull sharply on the belt to check that the locking mechanism engages correctly. Inspect the webbing for fraying and cuts. Check that they retract smoothly and without binding into their reels.

2 Check that the seat belt mounting bolts are tight, and if necessary tighten them to the specified torque wrench setting.

8.5 Unclip the handbrake trim panel, and lift it off

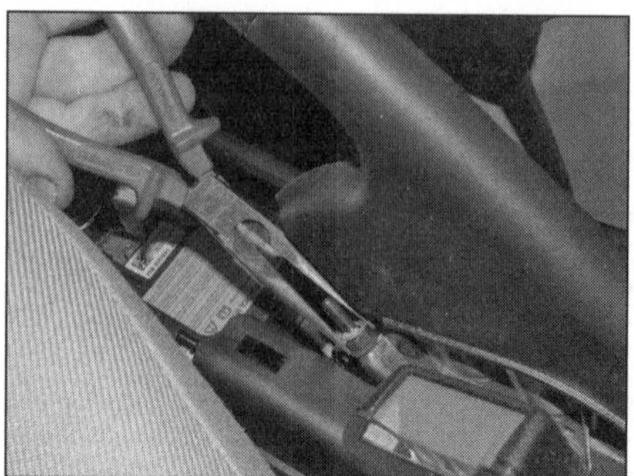

8.6a Remove the locking clip from the handbrake adjuster nut ...

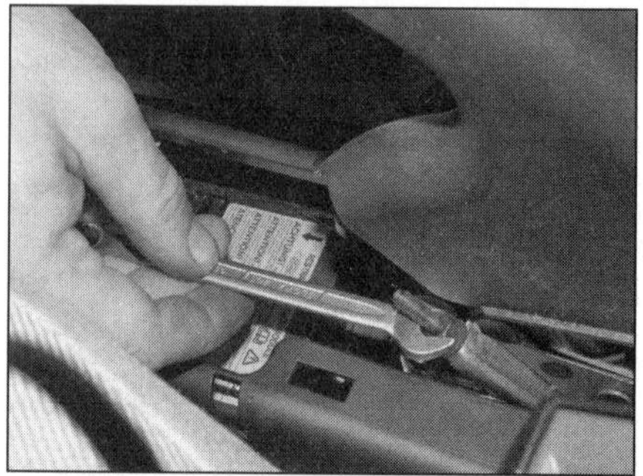

8.6b ... then turn the nut as necessary

10 Hinge and lock lubrication

1 Work around the car and lubricate the hinges of the bonnet, doors and tailgate with light oil.
2 Lightly lubricate the bonnet release mechanism with a smear of grease.
3 Check carefully the security and operation of all hinges, latches and locks, adjusting them where required. Check the operation of the central locking system.
4 Check the condition and operation of the tailgate struts, renewing them both if either is leaking or no longer able to support the tailgate securely when raised.

11 Front brake pad and disc wear check

1 Apply the handbrake, then jack up the front of the car and support it securely on axle stands (see *Jacking and vehicle support*). Remove the front roadwheels.
2 The brake pad thickness, and the condition of the disc, can be assessed roughly with just the wheels removed **(see illustration)**. For a comprehensive check, the brake pads should be removed and cleaned. The operation of the caliper can then also be checked, and the condition of the brake disc itself can be fully examined on both sides. Refer to Chapter 9 for further information.
3 On completion, refit the roadwheels and lower the car to the ground.

12 Rear brake shoe and drum wear check

1 Remove the rear brake drums, and check the brake shoes for signs of wear or contamination. At the same time, also inspect the wheel cylinders for signs of leakage, and the brake drum for signs of wear. Refer to Chapter 9, Section 5 and 7 for further information.

11.2 With the wheel removed, the pad thickness can be seen through the front of the caliper

13 Steering and suspension check

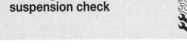

Front suspension and steering

1 Raise the front of the car, and securely support it on axle stands (see *Jacking and vehicle support*).
2 Visually inspect the balljoint dust covers and the steering rack-and-pinion gaiters for splits, chafing or deterioration **(see illustration)**. Any wear of these components will cause loss of lubricant, together with dirt and water entry, resulting in rapid deterioration of the balljoints or steering gear.
3 Check the power steering fluid hoses for chafing or deterioration, and the pipe and hose unions for fluid leaks. Also check for signs of fluid leakage under pressure from the steering gear rubber gaiters, which would indicate failed fluid seals within the steering gear.
4 Grasp the roadwheel at the 12 o'clock and 6 o'clock positions, and try to rock it **(see illustration)**. Very slight free play may be felt, but if the movement is appreciable, further investigation is necessary to determine the source. Continue rocking the wheel while an assistant depresses the footbrake. If the movement is now eliminated or significantly reduced, it is likely that the hub bearings are at fault. If the free play is still evident with the footbrake depressed, then there is wear in the suspension joints or mountings.
5 Now grasp the wheel at the 9 o'clock and 3 o'clock positions, and try to rock it as before. Any movement felt now may again be caused by wear in the hub bearings or the steering track rod balljoints. If the outer balljoint is worn, the visual movement will be obvious. If the inner joint is suspect, it can be felt by placing a hand over the rack-and-pinion rubber gaiter and gripping the track rod. If the wheel is now rocked, movement will be felt at the inner joint if wear has taken place.
6 Using a large screwdriver or flat bar, check for wear in the suspension mounting bushes by levering between the relevant suspension component and its attachment point. Some movement is to be expected, as the mountings are made of rubber, but excessive wear should be obvious. Also check the condition of any visible rubber bushes, looking for splits, cracks or contamination of the rubber.
7 With the car standing on its wheels, have an assistant turn the steering wheel back and forth, about an eighth of a turn each way. There should be very little, if any, lost movement between the steering wheel and roadwheels. If this is not the case, closely observe the joints and mountings previously described. In addition, check the steering column universal joints for wear, and also check the rack-and-pinion steering gear itself.

Rear suspension

8 Chock the front wheels, then jack up the rear of the car and support securely on axle stands (see *Jacking and vehicle support*).
9 Working as described previously for the front suspension, check the rear hub bearings, the suspension bushes and the shock absorber mountings for wear.

Shock absorber

10 Check for any signs of fluid leakage around the shock absorber body, or from the rubber gaiter around the piston rod **(see illustration)**. Should any fluid be noticed, the shock absorber is defective internally, and should be renewed. **Note:** *Shock absorbers should always be renewed in pairs on the same axle.*
11 The efficiency of the shock absorber may be checked by bouncing the car at each corner. Generally speaking, the body will

13.2 Check the steering gaiters for signs of splitting

13.4 Check for wear in the front suspension and hub bearings

13.10 Check for signs of fluid leakage from the shock absorbers

14.1a Check the outer constant velocity (CV) joint gaiters ...

return to its normal position and stop after being depressed. If it rises and returns on a rebound, the shock absorber is probably suspect. Also examine the shock absorber upper and lower mountings for any signs of wear.

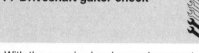

14 Driveshaft gaiter check

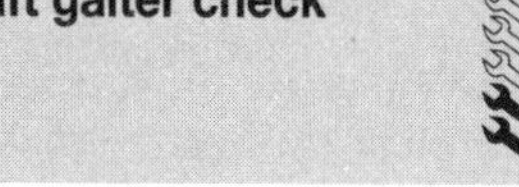

1 With the car raised and securely supported on stands, turn the steering onto full lock, then slowly rotate the roadwheel. Inspect the condition of the outer constant velocity (CV) joint rubber gaiters while squeezing the gaiters to open out the folds. Check for signs of cracking, splits or deterioration of the rubber which may allow the grease to escape and lead to water and grit entry into the joint. Also check the security and condition of the retaining clips. Repeat these checks on the inner CV joints **(see illustrations)**. If any damage or deterioration is found, the gaiters should be renewed as described in Chapter 8, Section 3 and 4.

2 At the same time, check the general condition of the CV joints themselves by first holding the driveshaft and attempting to rotate the wheel. Repeat this check by holding the inner joint and attempting to rotate the driveshaft. Any appreciable movement indicates wear in the joints, wear in the driveshaft splines, or a loose driveshaft retaining nut.

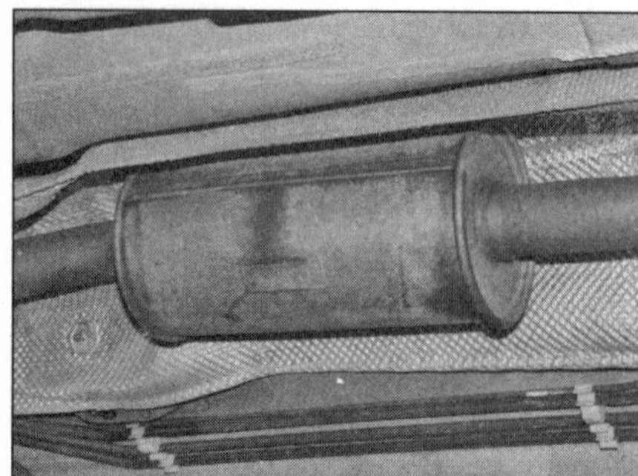

16.17a Check the silencer boxes carefully for signs of leakage

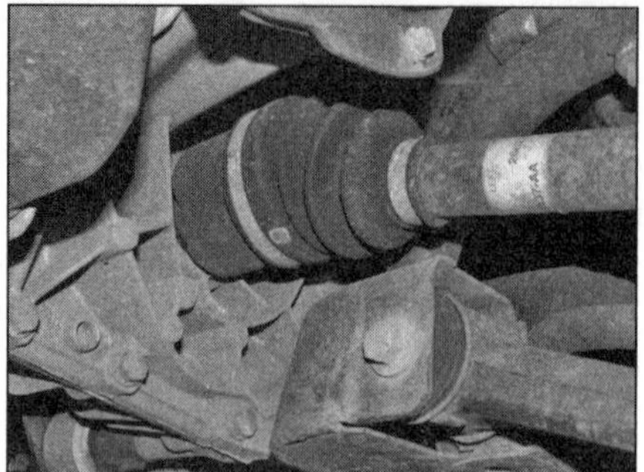

14.1b ... and, though less prone to wear, check the inner gaiters too

15 Roadwheel nut tightness check

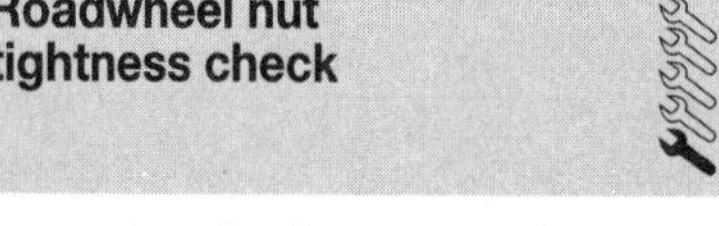

1 Remove the wheel trims or alloy wheel centre covers, and slacken the roadwheel nuts slightly.

2 Tighten the nuts to the specified torque, using a torque wrench.

16 Road test

Instruments and electrical equipment

1 Check the operation of all instruments and electrical equipment.

2 Make sure that all instruments read correctly, and switch on all electrical equipment in turn, to check that they function properly.

Steering and suspension

3 Check for any abnormalities in the steering, suspension, handling or road 'feel'.

4 Drive the car, and check that there are no unusual vibrations or noises.

5 Check that the steering feels positive, with no excessive 'sloppiness', or roughness, and check for any suspension noises when cornering and driving over bumps.

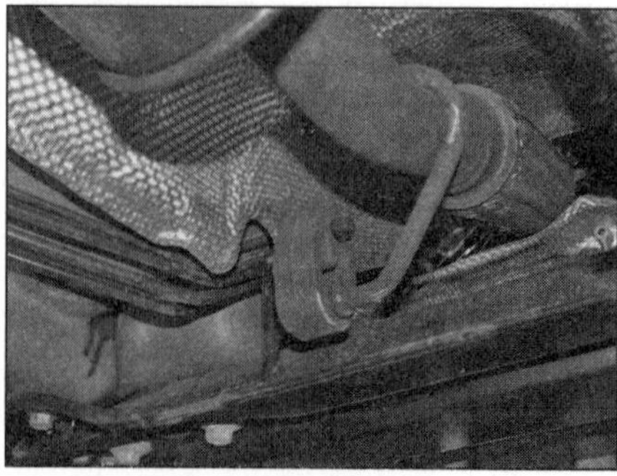

16.17b If the rubber mountings are in poor condition, fit new ones

Drivetrain

6 Check the performance of the engine, clutch, transmission and driveshafts.

7 Listen for any unusual noises from the engine, clutch and transmission.

8 Make sure that the engine runs smoothly when idling, and that there is no hesitation when accelerating.

9 Check that, where applicable, the clutch action is smooth and progressive, that the drive is taken up smoothly, and that the pedal travel is not excessive. Also listen for any noises when the clutch pedal is depressed.

10 Check that all gears can be engaged smoothly without noise, and that the gear lever action is smooth and not abnormally vague or 'notchy'.

11 Listen for a metallic clicking sound from the front of the car, as the car is driven slowly in a circle with the steering on full lock. Carry out this check in both directions. If a clicking noise is heard, this indicates wear in a driveshaft joint (see Chapter 8, Section 5).

Braking system

12 Make sure that the car does not pull to one side when braking, and that the wheels do not lock prematurely when braking hard. They should not lock at all on models with ABS.

13 Check that there is no vibration through the steering when braking.

14 Check that the handbrake operates correctly, without excessive movement of the lever, and that it holds the car stationary on a slope.

15 Test the operation of the brake servo unit as follows. Depress the footbrake four or five times to exhaust the vacuum, then start the engine. As the engine starts, there should be a noticeable 'give' in the brake pedal as vacuum builds-up. Allow the engine to run for at least two minutes, and then switch it off. If the brake pedal is now depressed again, it should be possible to detect a hiss from the servo as the pedal is depressed. After about four or five applications, no further hissing should be heard, and the pedal should feel considerably harder.

Exhaust system

16 Listen carefully for any unusual noises from the system, which might indicate that it has started blowing, or that the mountings may be deteriorated, allowing the system to hit the underside of the car.

17 If any noises are detected, inspect the system with the car raised and supported on axle stands (see *Jacking and vehicle support*). Leaks are often accompanied by sooty stains, and are most common at the joints, and at welded sections, where pipes enter silencer boxes. Check the condition of the rubber mountings – if they are cracked or perished, fit new ones **(see illustrations)**.

17.3 Remove the bolt from the airflow sensor, and unclip the lower air duct

17.6a Remove the two bolts on top ...

17.6b ... then work the cover out between the hoses

Every 37 500 miles or 3 years

17 Fuel filter renewal

1.4 litre engine

1 The fuel filter is located at the rear of the engine compartment, between the air filter housing and the battery.

2 Owing to the extreme difficulty which may be experienced removing the filter, we found it was far easier to remove the air cleaner first, as described in Chapter 4B, Section 4.

3 If the air cleaner is not removed, create more room to remove the filter by removing the bolt securing the airflow sensor to the air inlet duct, then pull the duct off the base of the air cleaner at the rear **(see illustration)**.

4 Place a suitable container beneath the drain screw, and cover the surrounding area with rags. Take care not to allow fuel to enter the transmission bellhousing which is just below. If available, fit a length of hose over the drain screw.

5 Open the drain plug by turning it anti-clockwise. Allow fuel and water to drain, then close the drain plug.

6 Remove the two bolts securing the fuel filter metal cover, then hold the fuel and brake servo vacuum hoses out of the way, and manoeuvre the cover out of position **(see illustrations)**.

7 Squeeze the quick-release fittings and disconnect the fuel feed and return pipes from the filter – one on the front, and one at the rear **(see illustrations)**. Plug or tape over the pipes to prevent dirt ingress and fuel loss.

8 Undo the single filter retaining screw, and manoeuvre the filter from the bracket – this may prove to be quite tricky, as there is very limited room. The filter will only lift up so far, as there is a wiring plug for the fuel heater and water detector at the base **(see illustrations)**. This plug is difficult to disconnect if the air cleaner has not been removed.

9 Unscrew the fuel heater and water detector (where fitted) from the filter. Discard the O-ring seals – new ones must be fitted.

10 Fitting a new filter is a reversal of removal, noting the following points:

a) Ensure that the fuel hose connections are securely remade.
b) On completion, pump the fuel system priming bulb several times to fill the new filter with fuel. Note that, even if this is done, it may take several attempts to start the engine as the system bleeds itself of air.
c) When the engine is running, check for any sign of leakage from the disturbed pipes.

1.6 litre engine

11 The fuel filter is located beneath the air cleaner, between the left-hand end of the cylinder head and the battery. Position a cloth rag below the filter to catch spilled fuel.

12 Remove the engine top cover and air cleaner as follows:

a) Disconnect the vacuum line from the one-way valve on the left-hand side of the air cleaner body and position to one side.
b) Disconnect the air cleaner inlet hose from the inlet duct at the front of the engine compartment.
c) Disconnect the wiring from the mass airflow sensor.
d) Loosen the clip and separate the mass airflow sensor from the turbocharger inlet duct. Alternatively, the top cover and air cleaner may be removed together with the inlet duct by loosening the clip on the turbocharger and also disconnecting the crankcase ventilation hose from the engine valve cover.
e) Lift the top cover and air cleaner directly upwards from the three mounting

17.7a Squeeze the quick-release connectors, and pull off the fuel hose on the front ...

17.7b ... and the one at the rear of the filter

17.8a Undo the filter retaining screw in front ...

17.8b ... then lift the filter, and disconnect the wiring plug (arrows) underneath

17.13 Disconnect the fuel heater wiring plug

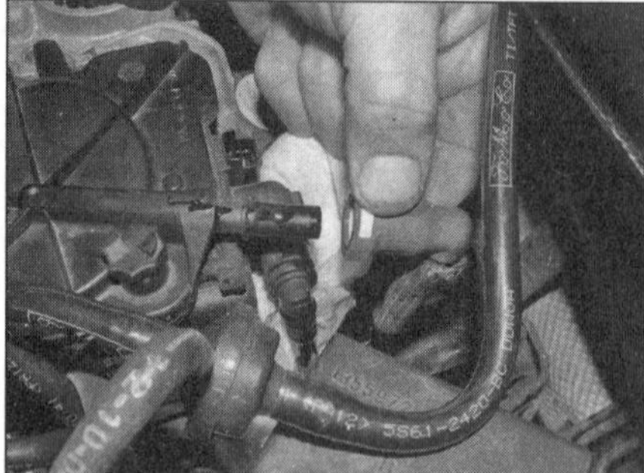
17.14a Disconnect the fuel inlet...

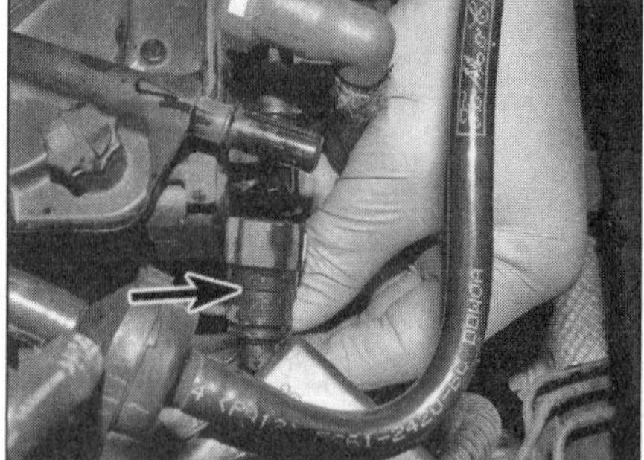
17.14b ... and outlet pipes from the fuel filter

17.15a Release the plastic clip ...

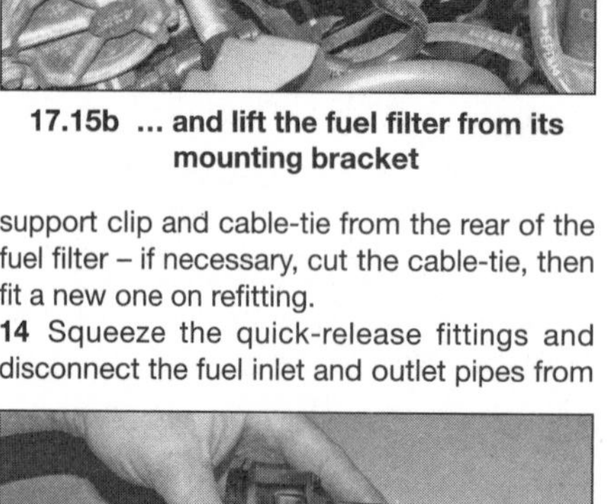
17.15b ... and lift the fuel filter from its mounting bracket

rubbers and withdraw. The mountings are very tight and will require releasing separately.

13 Disconnect the fuel heater wiring plug **(see illustration)**. Also release the wiring support clip and cable-tie from the rear of the fuel filter – if necessary, cut the cable-tie, then fit a new one on refitting.

14 Squeeze the quick-release fittings and disconnect the fuel inlet and outlet pipes from the filter – they are both located on one corner of the filter **(see illustrations)**.

15 Release the plastic clip (using a screwdriver if necessary), and lift the fuel filter from its mounting bracket **(see illustrations)**.

16 New fuel filters are not supplied with fuel heaters, therefore it is necessary to transfer the heater from the old filter to the new filter. To do this, use a screwdriver to lever out the connecting stub while at the same time releasing the clips **(see illustrations)**. Clean the heater and check the O-ring seals for damage, before transferring to the new filter. Smear a little fuel on the O-rings before pressing the heater into the new fuel filter, making sure that the retaining clips are fully engaged.

17 Where fitted transfer the water sensor over to the new filter.

18 Fitting the new filter is a reversal of removal, noting the following points:

a) Ensure that the fuel hose connections are securely remade.

b) On completion, prime the fuel system as described in Chapter 4B, Section 3. Note that it may take several attempts to start the engine.

c) When the engine is running, check for any sign of leakage from the disturbed pipes.

17.16a Use a screwdriver to lever out the fuel heater ...

17.16b ... and remove it from the filter body

17.16c Fuel filter removed from the filter body

18.2a On 1.4 litre models, undo the three Torx screws along the front ...

18 Air filter element renewal

1.4 litre engine

1 The air cleaner is located on top of the engine.

2 Undo the three screws at the front of the filter cover, then lift the cover and withdraw the filter element. Note which way up the element was fitted **(see illustrations)**.

3 Position the new element in the filter housing and refit the filter cover. Note the three lugs at the rear of the cover which engage with the housing. Tighten the retaining screws securely.

1.6 litre engine

4 The air cleaner is integral with the engine top cover, and is located on the left-hand end of the cover, next to the battery.

18.2b ... then lift the cover at the front, unhook at the back ...

18.2c ... and remove the air filter element

18.5a Air cleaner cover retaining screws

18.5b Removing the air cleaner cover and mass airflow sensor from the turbocharger inlet duct

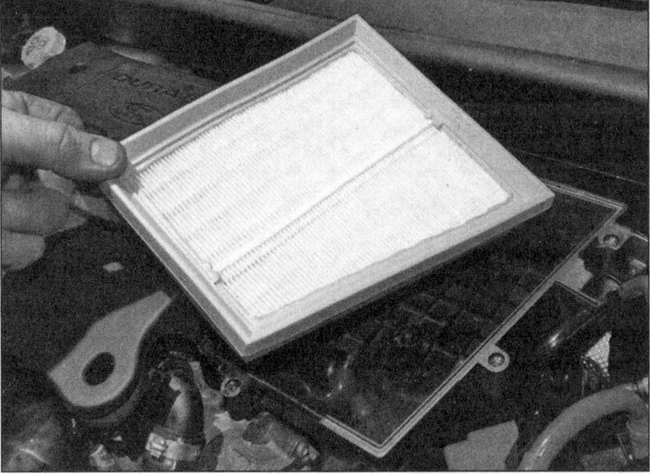

18.5c Removing the air filter element

5 Undo the four screws and lift the cover from the air cleaner body sufficiently to withdraw the filter element. Note which way up the element is fitted. For improved access, disconnect the wiring from the mass airflow sensor, then loosen the hose clip and remove the sensor together with the air cleaner cover from the turbocharger inlet duct **(see illustrations)**.

6 Position the new element in the air cleaner body and refit the cover. Tighten the retaining screws securely. Where applicable, refit the mass airflow sensor to the inlet duct and reconnect the wiring.

19 Transmission oil level check

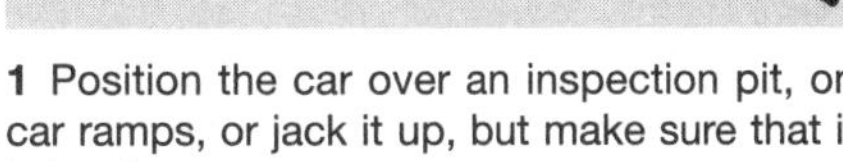

1 Position the car over an inspection pit, on car ramps, or jack it up, but make sure that it is level.

2 Unclip the plastic cover fitted over the gearchange cables at the front of the transmission **(see illustration)**.

3 Remove all traces of dirt, then unscrew the filler/level plug from the front face of the transmission. This will probably be very tight, and a large Allen key or bit will be needed – access is made awkward by the plastic shroud around the gearchange cables **(see illustration)**.

4 The level must be just below the bottom edge of the filler/level plug hole (use a cranked tool such as an Allen key to check the level). If necessary, top-up the level with the specified grade of oil (see *Lubricants and fluids*) until the oil just starts to run out. Allow any excess oil to flow out until the level stabilises **(see illustrations)**.

19.2 Unclip the plastic cover from the front of the transmission

19.3 Unscrew and remove the filler/level plug

19.4a Top-up the oil level ...

5 When the level is correct, clean and refit the filler/level plug (check the condition of the O-ring seal, and renew if necessary), then tighten it to the specified torque.
6 Lower the car to the ground.

19.4b ... then allow any excess to flow out before refitting the plug

20 Braking system rubber hose check

1 Position the car over an inspection pit, on car ramps, or jack it up one wheel at a time.
2 Inspect the braking system rubber hoses fitted to each front caliper, and on each side of the rear axle **(see illustration)**. Look for perished, swollen or hardened rubber, and any signs of cracking, especially at the metal end fittings. If there's any doubt as to the condition of any hose, renew it as described in Chapter 9, Section 10.

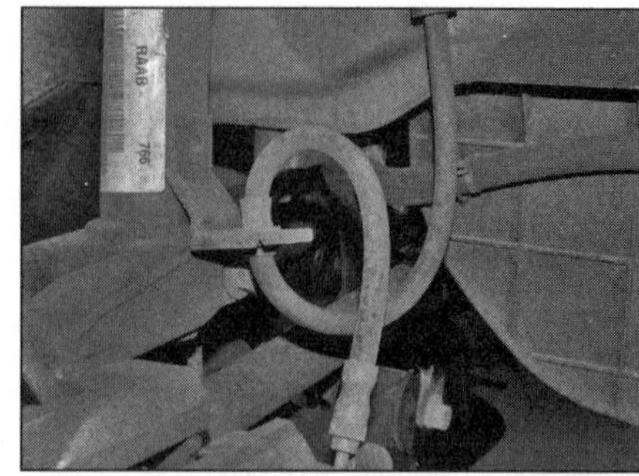

20.2 Rubber brake hose fitted to the front caliper

Every 50 000 miles or 4 years

21 Timing belt renewal

Refer to Chapter 2B, Section 7 or Chapter 2C, Section 7.

Every 150 000 miles or 10 years

22 Auxiliary drivebelt renewal

Removal

1 To gain access to the drivebelt on 1.4 litre models, first remove the right-hand headlight as described in Chapter 12, Section 7.
2 Raise the front of the car and remove the right-hand wheel; unclip the power steering pipe on 1.4 litre models only, then unbolt the crankshaft pulley lower cover from the underbody.
3 On 1.4 litre models, using a spanner on the tensioner centre bolt, turn the tensioner clockwise to release the drivebelt tension. On 1.6 litre models, using a 34 mm spanner on the lower lug of the tensioner, turn the tensioner clockwise to release the drivebelt tension, and lock it in this position by inserting a 5 mm diameter rod or drill in the hole provided at the top of the tensioner body. Note how the drivebelt is routed, then remove the belt from the pulleys **(see illustrations)**.

22.3a On 1.6 litre models, turn the tensioner clockwise and lock it with a 5 mm diameter drill inserted into the hole provided

22.3b Removing the auxiliary drivebelt on the 1.6 litre engine

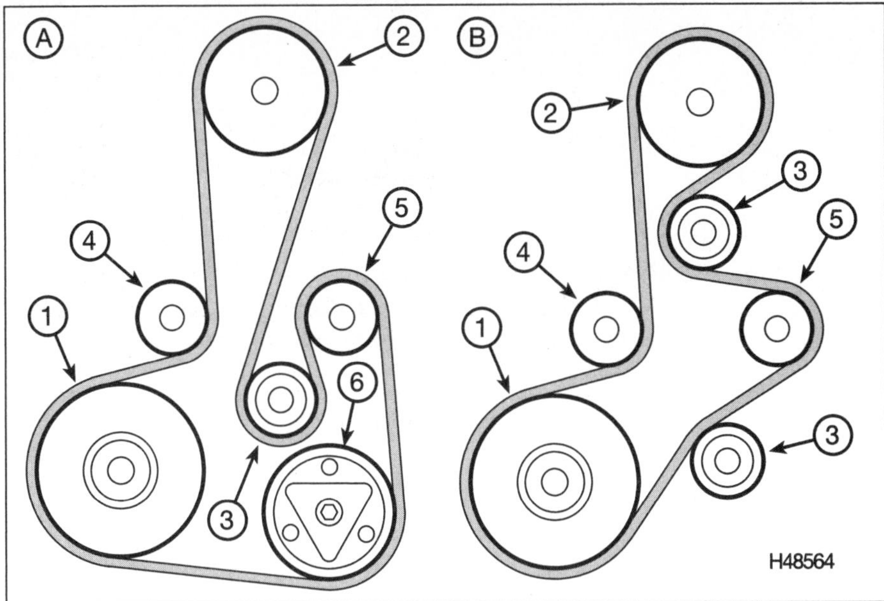

22.4a Auxiliary belt routing 1.4 litre with air conditioning (A) and without (B)

1 Crankshaft
2 Power steering pump
3 Idler
4 Tensioner
5 Alternator
6 AC compressor

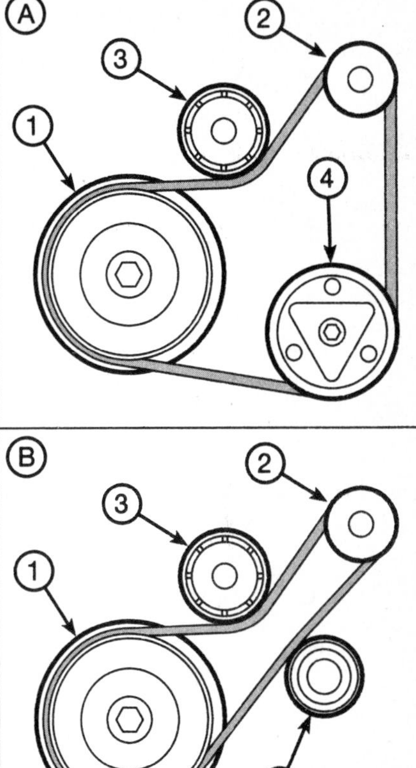

22.4b Auxiliary belt routing 1.6 litre with air conditioning (A) and without (B)

1 Crankshaft
2 Alternator
3 Tensioner
4 AC compressor
5 Idler

Refitting

4 Fitting the new belt is a direct reversal of removing the old one. Feed the belt onto as many pulleys as possible, then turn the tensioner clockwise and fit the belt round the tensioner and remaining pulleys **(see illustrations)**. On 1.6 litre models, remove the rod or drill. Release the tensioner, and make sure the belt is aligned properly – ie, that it is seated properly in the grooved pulleys.

5 Refit the crankshaft pulley lower cover, clip the power steering pipe back into place on 1.4 litre models only, then refit the wheel and lower the car to the ground. Refit the headlight on 1.4 litre models as described in Chapter 12, Section 7.

Every 2 years, regardless of mileage

23 Brake fluid renewal

Warning: Brake hydraulic fluid can harm your eyes and damage painted surfaces, so use extreme caution when handling and pouring it. Do not use fluid that has been standing open for some time, as it absorbs moisture from the air. Excess moisture can cause a dangerous loss of braking effectiveness.

1 The procedure is similar to that for bleeding the hydraulic system as described in Chapter 9, Section 11, except that allowance should be made for the old fluid to be expelled when bleeding each section of the circuit.

2 Working as described in Chapter 9, Section 11, open the first bleed screw in the sequence, and pump the brake pedal gently until the level in the reservoir is approaching the MIN mark. Top-up to the MAX level with new fluid, and continue pumping until only new fluid remains in the reservoir, and new fluid can be seen emerging from the bleed screw. Tighten the screw, and top the reservoir level up to the MAX level line.

3 Work through all the remaining bleed screws in the sequence until new fluid can be seen at all of them. Be careful to keep the master cylinder reservoir topped-up above the MIN level at all times, or air may enter the system. If this happens, further bleeding will be required, to remove the air.

4 When the operation is complete, check that all bleed screws are securely tightened, and that their dust caps are refitted. Wash off all traces of spilt fluid, and recheck the master cylinder reservoir fluid level.

5 Check the operation of the brakes before taking the car on the road.

24 Remote control battery renewal

1 Although not in the Ford maintenance schedule, we recommend that the battery is changed every 2 years, regardless of the mileage. However, if the door locks repeatedly fail to respond to signals from the remote control at the normal distance, change the battery in the remote control before attempting

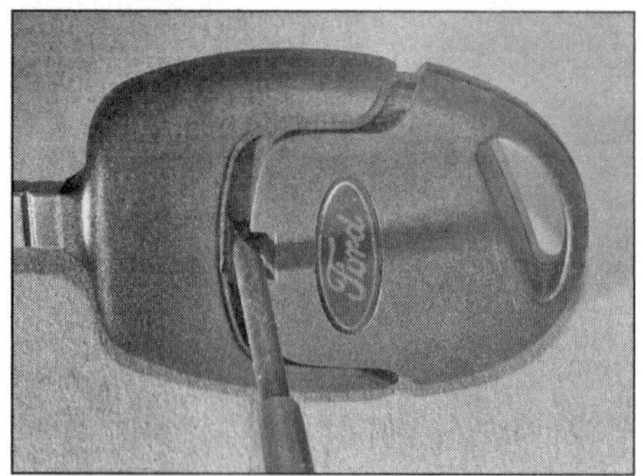

24.2 Insert a screwdriver into the slot

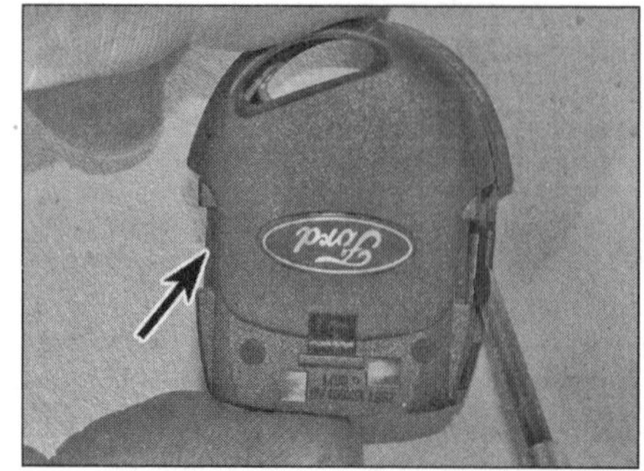

24.3 Release the clip each side (arrowed)

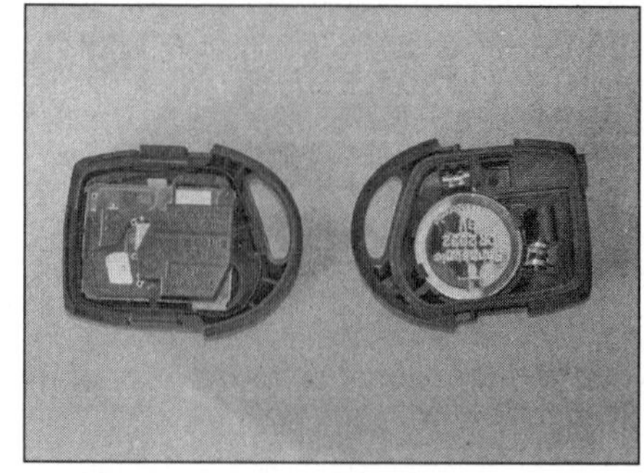

24.4 The battery fits positive side up

to troubleshoot any of the vehicle's other systems.

2 Insert a small flat-bladed screwdriver into the slot provided and slide the transmitter unit from the key **(see illustration)**.

3 Use the screwdriver to release the clip each side and open the transmitter unit **(see illustration)**.

4 Note the fitted position of the battery (positive side up), then prise the battery from place, and insert the new one **(see illustration)**. Avoid touching the battery or the terminals with bare fingers.

5 Snap the 2 halves of the transmitter together, and re-attach it to the key.

Every 4 years, regardless of mileage

25 Coolant renewal and pressure cap check

Warning: Wait until the engine is cold before starting this procedure. Do not allow antifreeze to come in contact with your skin, or with the painted surfaces of the car. Rinse off spills immediately with plenty of water. Never leave antifreeze lying around in an open container, or in a puddle in the driveway or on the garage floor. Children and pets are attracted by its sweet smell, but antifreeze can be fatal if ingested.

Cooling system draining

1 With the engine completely cold, remove the expansion tank filler cap. Turn the cap anti-clockwise, wait until any pressure remaining in the system is released, then unscrew it and lift it off.

2 Position a suitable container beneath the radiator drain plug, at the bottom left-hand corner of the radiator (left as seen from the driver's seat) **(see illustration)**.

3 Slacken the drain plug using a wide-bladed screwdriver, and allow the coolant to drain into the container **(see illustrations)**.

4 When the flow of coolant stops, tighten the radiator drain plug.

5 If the coolant has been drained for a reason other than renewal, then provided it is clean and less than four years old, it can be re-used, though this is not recommended.

Cooling system flushing

6 If coolant renewal has been neglected, or if the antifreeze mixture has become diluted, then in time, the cooling system may gradually lose efficiency, as the coolant passages become restricted due to rust, scale deposits, and other sediment. The cooling system efficiency can be restored by flushing the system clean.

7 The radiator should be flushed independently of the engine, to avoid unnecessary contamination.

Radiator flushing

8 Disconnect the top and bottom hoses and any other relevant hoses from the radiator, with reference to Chapter 3, Section 3.

9 Insert a garden hose into the radiator top inlet. Direct a flow of clean water through the radiator, and continue flushing until clean water emerges from the radiator bottom outlet.

10 If after a reasonable period the water still does not run clear, the radiator can be flushed with a good proprietary cleaning agent. It is important that the manufacturer's instructions are followed carefully. If the contamination is particularly bad, insert the hose in the radiator bottom outlet, and reverse flush the radiator.

Engine flushing

11 Remove the thermostat as described in Chapter 3, Section 4 then, if the radiator top hose has been disconnected from the engine, temporarily reconnect the hose.

12 With the top and bottom hoses disconnected from the radiator, insert a garden hose into the radiator top hose. Direct a clean flow of water through the engine, and continue flushing until clean water emerges from the radiator bottom hose.

13 On completion of flushing, refit the thermostat and reconnect the hoses with reference to Chapter 3, Section 3 and 4.

25.2 The drain plug is at the bottom right-hand corner of the radiator

25.3a Unscrew the radiator drain plug ...

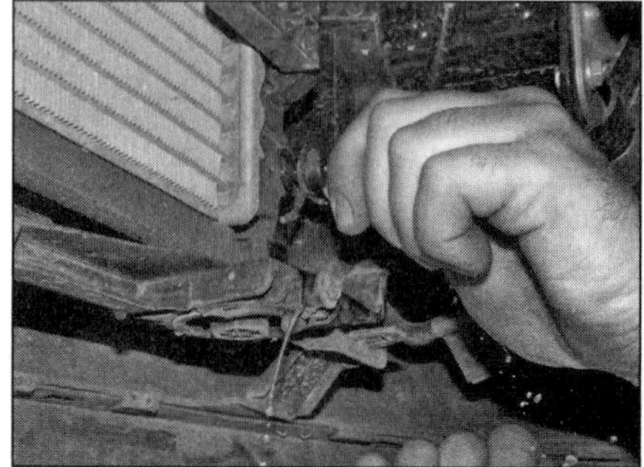

25.3b ... and allow the coolant to drain

Antifreeze mixture

14 The antifreeze should always be renewed at the specified intervals. This is necessary not only to maintain the antifreeze properties, but also to prevent corrosion which would otherwise occur as the corrosion inhibitors become progressively less effective.

15 Always use an ethylene-glycol based antifreeze which is suitable for use in mixed-metal cooling systems. The quantity of antifreeze and levels of protection are given in the Specifications. The antifreeze recommended by Ford at the time of writing is their purple coloured Super Plus antifreeze, which, if it is not mixed with any other antifreeze, can be left in the system for 10 years. Owners may wish to change their antifreeze more frequently, especially if the type and quality in the system is unknown.

16 Before adding antifreeze, the cooling system should be completely drained, preferably flushed, and all hoses checked for condition and security.

17 After filling with antifreeze, a label should be attached to the expansion tank, stating the type and concentration of antifreeze used, and the date installed.

18 Any subsequent topping-up should be made with the same type and concentration of antifreeze.

Caution: Do not use engine antifreeze in the windscreen/tailgate washer system, as it will cause damage to the paintwork. A screen wash additive should be added to the washer system in the quantities stated on the bottle.

Cooling system filling

19 Before attempting to fill the cooling system, make sure that all hoses and clips are in good condition, and that the clips are tight. Note that an antifreeze mixture must be used all year round, to prevent corrosion of the engine components.

20 Locate and unscrew the radiator bleed plug, which looks similar to the drain plug, and is situated at the top left-hand or right-hand corner of the radiator (depending on model).

21 Remove the expansion tank filler cap. If a funnel is available for filling the cooling system, use it to reduce the risk of spillage onto the paintwork under the bonnet.

22 Slowly fill the system until coolant emerges from the radiator bleed hole, or until the level settles at the MAX mark on the side of the expansion tank.

23 Refit and tighten the radiator bleed plug.

24 If necessary, top-up the coolant level to the MAX mark, and refit the expansion tank cap.

25 Start the engine, run it at approximately 3000 rpm for two minutes, then switch off.

26 Recheck the coolant level in the expansion tank, and top-up if necessary. Although the system should still be some way off full operating temperature at this point, take precautions against scalding if the expansion tank cap has to be removed.

27 With the expansion tank cap refitted, start the engine once more, and run it at 3000 rpm for another two minutes. Switch the engine off on completion, and allow it to cool. When the engine has cooled (preferably overnight), recheck the level once more, and top-up if necessary.

Airlocks

28 If, after draining and refilling the system, symptoms of overheating are found which did not occur previously, then the fault is almost certainly due to trapped air at some point in the system, causing an airlock and restricting the flow of coolant; usually, the air is trapped because the system was refilled too quickly.

29 If an airlock is suspected, first try gently squeezing all visible coolant hoses. A coolant hose which is full of air feels quite different to one full of coolant when squeezed. After refilling the system, most airlocks will clear once the system has cooled, and been topped-up.

25.33 Check the condition of the expansion tank cap rubber seal

30 While the engine is running at operating temperature, switch on the heater and heater fan, and check for heat output. Provided there is sufficient coolant in the system, any lack of heat output could be due to an airlock in the system.

31 Airlocks can have more serious effects than simply reducing heater output – a severe airlock could reduce coolant flow around the engine. Check that the radiator top hose is hot when the engine is at operating temperature – a top hose which stays cold could be the result of an airlock (or a non-opening thermostat).

32 If the problem persists, stop the engine and allow it to cool down completely, before unscrewing the expansion tank filler cap or loosening the hose clips and squeezing the hoses to bleed out the trapped air. In the worst case, the system will have to be at least partially drained (this time, the coolant can be saved for re-use) and flushed to clear the problem.

Expansion tank cap check

33 Clean the pressure cap, and inspect the seal inside the cap for damage or deterioration **(see illustration)**. If there is any sign of damage or deterioration to the seal, fit a new pressure cap.

Chapter 2 Part A: Petrol engine in-car repair procedures

Contents

Degrees of difficulty

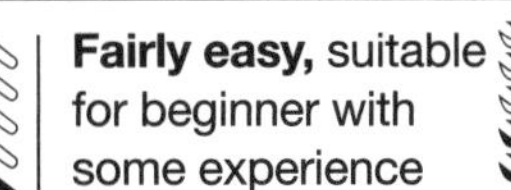

Easy, suitable for novice with little experience	**Fairly easy,** suitable for beginner with some experience	**Fairly difficult,** suitable for competent DIY mechanic	**Difficult,** suitable for experienced DIY mechanic	**Very difficult,** suitable for expert DIY or professional

Specifications

General

Engine type	Four-cylinder, in-line, double overhead camshafts, 16-valve
Designation	Duratec 16V
Engine codes:	
1.4 litre engine	FXJA or FXJB
1.6 litre engine	FYJA or FYJB
Capacity:	
1.4 litre engine	1388 cc
1.6 litre engine	1596 cc
Bore:	
1.4 litre engine	75.9 mm
1.6 litre engine	79.0 mm
Stroke:	
1.4 litre engine	76.5 mm
1.6 litre engine	81.4 mm
Compression ratio (all engines)	11.0:1
Firing order	1-3-4-2 (No 1 cylinder at timing belt end)
Direction of crankshaft rotation	Clockwise (seen from right-hand side of car)

Valves

	Inlet	**Exhaust**
Valve clearances (cold):		
1.4 litre engine	0.17 to 0.23 mm	0.27 to 0.33 mm
1.6 litre engine	0.17 to 0.23 mm	0.31 to 0.37 mm
Valve length:		
1.4 litre engine	97.35 mm	99.40 mm
1.6 litre engine	96.95 mm	99.40 mm

Valve springs

Free length	53.2 mm

Cylinder head

Maximum permissible gasket surface distortion	0.05 mm

Cylinder block

Cylinder bore diameter:	
1.4 litre engine:	
Class 1	76.000 to 76.010 mm
Class 2	76.010 to 76.020 mm
Class 3	76.020 to 76.030 mm
1.6 litre engine:	
Class 1	79.000 to 79.010 mm
Class 2	79.010 to 79.020 mm
Class 3	79.020 to 79.030 mm

Pistons and piston rings

Piston diameter:	
1.4 litre engine:	
Class 1	75.960 to 75.970 mm
Class 2	75.970 to 75.980 mm
Class 3	75.980 to 75.990 mm
1.6 litre engine:	
Class 1	78.975 to 79.005 mm
Class 2	79.005 to 79.015 mm
Class 3	79.015 to 79.025 mm
Oversizes – all engines	None available
Piston-to-cylinder bore clearance	Not specified
Piston ring end gaps – installed:	
Top compression ring	0.170 to 0.270 mm
Second compression ring	0.700 to 0.900 mm
Oil control ring	0.150 to 0.650 mm

Crankshaft

Note: *The crankshaft cannot be removed from the cylinder block (see Section 1).*

Crankshaft endfloat	0.300 to 0.800 mm

Camshafts

Camshaft bearing journal diameter	Unavailable at time of writing
Camshaft bearing journal-to-cylinder head running clearance	Unavailable at time of writing
Camshaft endfloat (typical)	0.05 to 0.13 mm

Lubrication

Oil pressure (minimum, warm engine):	
Idling (800 rpm)	1.0 bar
At 2000 rpm	2.5 bars
Pressure relief valve opens at	4.0 bars
Oil pump clearances	Not specified

Torque wrench settings

	Nm	lbf ft
Air conditioning compressor mounting bolts	25	18
Alternator mounting bracket bolts	42	31
Big-end bearing cap:		
Stage 1	8	6
Stage 2	Angle-tighten a further 90°	
Camshaft bearing cap:		
Stage 1	7	5
Stage 2	Angle-tighten a further 45°	
Camshaft pulley bolt	60	44
Coolant outlet to cylinder head	20	15
Crankcase breather to cylinder block	9	7
Crankshaft pulley/vibration damper:*		
Stage 1	45	33
Stage 2	Angle-tighten a further 90°	
Crankshaft oil seal carrier	9	7
Cylinder head:		
Stage 1	15	11
Stage 2	30	22
Stage 3	Angle-tighten a further 90°	
Cylinder head cover	10	7

Torque wrench settings (continued)	Nm	lbf ft
Engine mountings:		
Right-hand mounting bracket to block	55	41
Right-hand mounting nuts*/bolts	48	35
Left-hand mounting centre nut	90	66
Left-hand mounting outer nuts	48	35
Lower mounting nuts	48	35
Exhaust flexible section-to-catalytic converter nuts	44	32
Exhaust manifold nuts/bolts	54	40
Exhaust manifold heat shield bolts	25	18
Flywheel bolts	85	63
Inlet manifold-to-block bolt	18	13
Oil baffle to cylinder block	9	7
Oil dipstick tube	9	7
Oil drain plug	28	21
Oil filter connector	45	33
Oil intake pipe to oil baffle	9	7
Oil pressure switch	15	11
Oil pump to cylinder block	9	7
Power steering fluid hose support bracket bolt	25	18
Sump bolts:		
Sump-to-block bolts:		
Stage 1	10	7
Stage 2	20	15
Sump-to-transmission bolts	47	35
TDC pin hole blanking plug	20	15
Timing belt cover bolts	9	7
Timing belt tensioner bolts	20	15
Water pump pulley bolts	24	18

** Use new fasteners*

1 General information

How to use this Chapter

This Chapter is devoted to in-car repair procedures on the 1.4 and 1.6 litre Duratec 16V petrol engine. All procedures concerning engine removal and refitting, and engine block/cylinder head overhaul can be found in Chapter 2D.

Refer to *Vehicle identification numbers* at the end of this manual for details of engine code locations.

Most of the operations included in this Chapter are based on the assumption that the engine is still installed in the car. Therefore, if this information is being used during a complete engine overhaul, with the engine already removed, many of the steps included here will not apply.

Engine description

The Duratec engine (formerly the Zetec-SE), is a sixteen-valve, double overhead camshaft (DOHC), four cylinder, in-line unit, mounted transversely at the front of the car, with the transmission on its left-hand end.

Apart from the plastic timing belt covers, plastic cylinder head cover, plastic inlet manifold, and the cast iron cylinder liners, the main engine components (including the sump) are manufactured entirely of aluminium alloy.

Caution: When tightening bolts into aluminium castings, it is important to adhere to the specified torque wrench settings, to avoid stripping threads.

The crankshaft runs in five main bearings, the centre main bearing's upper half incorporating thrustwashers to control crankshaft endfloat. Due to the very fine bearing clearances and bearing shell tolerances incorporated during manufacture, it is not possible to renew the crankshaft without the cylinder block; in fact it is not possible to remove and refit the crankshaft accurately using conventional tooling. This means that if the crankshaft is worn excessively, it must be renewed together with the cylinder block.

Caution: Do not unbolt the main bearing cap/ladder from the cylinder block, as it is not possible to refit it accurately using conventional tooling. Additionally, the manufacturers do not supply torque settings for the main bearing cap/ladder retaining bolts.

The connecting rods rotate on horizontally-split bearing shells at their big-ends, however the big-ends are of unusual design in that the caps are sheared from the rods during manufacture thus making each cap individually matched to its own connecting rod. The big-end bearing shells are also unusual in that they do not have any locating tabs and must be accurately positioned during refitting. The pistons are attached to the connecting rods by gudgeon pins which are an interference fit in the connecting rod small-end eyes. The aluminium alloy pistons are fitted with three piston rings: two compression rings and an oil control ring. After manufacture, the cylinder bores and pistons are measured and classified into three grades, which must be carefully matched together, to ensure the correct piston/cylinder clearance; no oversizes are available to permit reboring.

The inlet and exhaust valves are each closed by coil springs; they operate in guides which are shrink-fitted into the cylinder head, as are the valve seat inserts.

Both camshafts are driven by the same toothed timing belt, each operating eight valves via bucket tappets and shims. Each camshaft rotates in five bearings that are line-bored directly in the cylinder head and the (bolted-on) bearing caps; this means that the bearing caps are not available separately from the cylinder head, and must not be interchanged with caps from another engine.

The water pump is bolted to the right-hand end of the cylinder block, beneath the front run of the timing belt, and is driven by the auxiliary drivebelt from the crankshaft pulley.

Lubrication is by means of an eccentric rotor trochoidal pump, which is mounted on the crankshaft right-hand end, and draws oil through a strainer located in the sump. The pump forces oil through an externally mounted full-flow cartridge type filter.

Operations with engine in car

The following work can be carried out with the engine in the car:

a) Cylinder head cover – removal and refitting.
b) Timing belt – renewal.
c) Timing belt tensioner and sprockets – removal and refitting.
d) Camshaft oil seals – renewal.
e) Camshafts, tappets and shims – removal and refitting.
f) Cylinder head – removal and refitting.

3.7a Unscrewing the blanking plug from the right-hand rear side of the cylinder block

g) Sump – removal and refitting.
h) Crankshaft oil seals – renewal.
i) Oil pump – removal and refitting.
j) Flywheel – removal and refitting.
k) Engine/transmission mountings – removal and refitting.

Note: *It is possible to remove the pistons and connecting rods (after removing the cylinder head and sump) without removing the engine. However, this is not recommended. Work of this nature is more easily and thoroughly completed with the engine on the bench, as described in Chapter 2D, Section 10.*

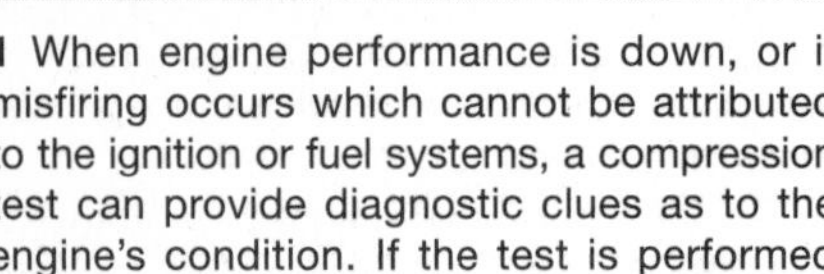

2 Compression test – description and interpretation

1 When engine performance is down, or if misfiring occurs which cannot be attributed to the ignition or fuel systems, a compression test can provide diagnostic clues as to the engine's condition. If the test is performed regularly, it can give warning of trouble before any other symptoms become apparent.

2 The engine must be fully warmed-up to operating temperature, the oil level must be correct and the battery must be fully charged. The help of an assistant will also be required.

3 Refer to Chapter 12, Section 3 and remove the fuel pump fuse from the fusebox. Now start the engine and allow it to run until it stalls.

4 Refer to Chapter 4A, Section 5 and remove the air cleaner for access to the spark plugs.

5 Disable the ignition system by disconnecting the multiplug from the DIS ignition coil. Remove all the spark plugs with reference to Chapter 1A, Section 16.

6 Fit a compression tester to the No 1 cylinder spark plug hole – the type of tester which screws into the spark plug thread is preferable.

7 Arrange for an assistant to hold the accelerator pedal fully depressed to the floor, while at the same time cranking the engine over for several seconds on the starter motor. Observe the compression gauge reading. The compression will build-up fairly quickly in a healthy engine. Low compression on the first stroke, followed by gradually increasing pressure on successive strokes, indicates worn piston rings. A low compression on the first stroke which does not rise on successive strokes, indicates leaking valves or a blown head gasket (a cracked cylinder head could also be the cause). Deposits on the underside of the valve heads can also cause low compression. Record the highest gauge reading obtained, then repeat the procedure for the remaining cylinders.

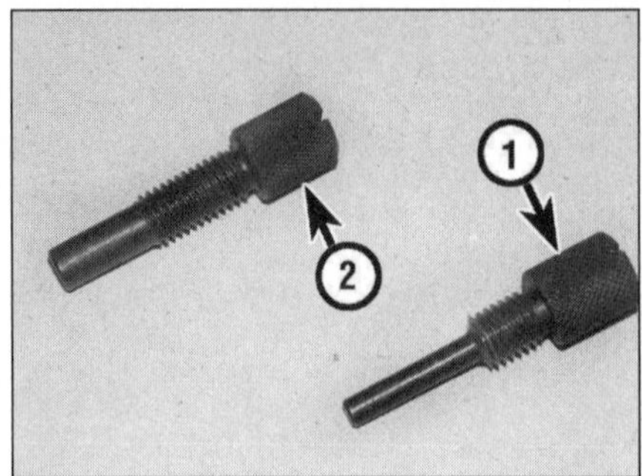

3.7b Ford timing pin (1) and locking tool (2)

8 Due to the variety of testers available, and the fluctuation in starter motor speed when cranking the engine, different readings are often obtained when carrying out the compression test. For this reason, actual compression pressure figures are not quoted by Ford. However, the most important factor is that the compression pressures are uniform in all cylinders, and that is what this test is mainly concerned with.

9 Add some engine oil (about three squirts from a plunger type oil can) to each cylinder through the spark plug holes, and then repeat the test.

10 If the compression increases after the oil is added, the piston rings are probably worn. If the compression does not increase significantly, the leakage is occurring at the valves or the head gasket. Leakage past the valves may be caused by burned valve seats and/or faces, or warped, cracked or bent valves.

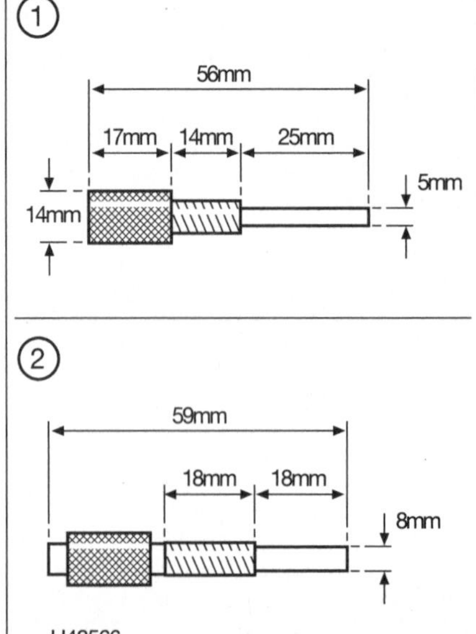

3.7c Timing pin (1) and locking pin (2) dimensions

11 If two adjacent cylinders have equally low compressions, it is most likely that the head gasket has blown between them. The appearance of coolant in the combustion chambers or on the engine oil dipstick would verify this condition.

12 If one cylinder is about 20 percent lower than the other, and the engine has a slightly rough idle, a worn lobe on the camshaft could be the cause.

13 On completion of the checks, refit the spark plugs and reconnect the HT leads and the DIS ignition coil plug. Refit the fuel pump fuse to the fusebox.

3 Top Dead Centre (TDC) for No 1 piston – locating

Note: *A timing pin and camshaft setting bar are required for this procedure (see text).*

1 Top dead centre (TDC) is the highest point of the cylinder that each piston reaches as the crankshaft turns. Each piston reaches its TDC position at the end of its compression stroke, and then again at the end of its exhaust stroke. For the purpose of engine timing, TDC on the compression stroke for No 1 piston is used. No 1 cylinder is at the timing belt end of the engine. Proceed as follows.

2 Disconnect the battery negative (earth) lead (see Disconnecting the battery in Chapter 5A, Section 2). Remove the spark plugs as described in Chapter 1A, Section 16.

3 Apply the handbrake, then jack up the front of the vehicle and support it on axle stands (see Jacking and vehicle support). If the engine is to be turned using the right-hand front roadwheel with 4th gear engaged, it is only necessary to raise the right-hand front roadwheel off the ground.

4 Where necessary, remove the engine undershield, then remove the auxiliary drivebelt lower cover for access to the crankshaft pulley and bolt.

5 Remove the cylinder head cover as described in Section 4.

6 The piston of No 1 cylinder must now be positioned just before top dead centre (TDC). To do this, have an assistant turn the crankshaft until the slots in the left-hand ends of the camshafts are parallel with the upper surface of the cylinder head. Note that the slots are slightly offset so make sure that the lower edges of the slots are aligned with the cylinder head. Turn the crankshaft slightly anti-clockwise (viewed from the right-hand end of the engine).

7 Unscrew the blanking plug from the right-hand rear side of the engine cylinder block **(see illustration)**. A TDC timing pin must now be inserted and tightened into the hole. It is highly recommended that the special Ford timing pin 303-507 (21-210) is obtained, or alternatively, a timing pin from a reputable tool manufacturer. **Note:** *Ford also supply a **locking** pin in addition to the **timing** pin, for use in the same hole when tightening the* *crankshaft pulley bolt;* ***do not*** *use the* ***timing pin*** *as a locking tool, as it is easily broken.* The dimensions of the timing pin are as shown **(see illustration)**. The diameter of the pin is critical as it determines the TDC point where the machined flat on the crankshaft web contacts the *shank* of the tool – note that the web does **not** contact the *end* of the tool.

8 With the timing pin in position, turn the crankshaft slowly clockwise until the specially machined surface on the crank web just touches the timing pin. No 1 piston is now at TDC on its compression stroke. To confirm this, check that the camshaft lobes for No 4 cylinder are 'rocking' (ie, exhaust valves closing and inlet valves opening).

9 It should now be possible to insert the camshaft setting bar into the slots in the left-hand ends of the camshafts. If the Ford setting tool 303-376 (21-162B) is unavailable, a home-made tool can be fabricated out of a length of flat metal bar 5.00 mm thick. The bar must be a good fit in the slots and should be approximately 180 to 230 mm long by 20 to 30 mm wide **(see illustration)**.

10 If the bar cannot be inserted in the slots with the crankshaft at TDC, the valve timing must be adjusted as described in Section 8 of this Chapter.

11 Once the work requiring the TDC setting has been completed, remove the metal bar from the camshaft slots then unscrew the timing pin and refit the blanking plug. Refit the spark plugs (Chapter 1A, Section 16), cylinder head cover (Chapter 1A, Section 4), auxiliary drivebelt lower cover, and where necessary the engine undershield. Lower the vehicle to the ground and reconnect the battery negative lead.

4 Cylinder head cover – removal and refitting

Removal

1 Disconnect the battery negative (earth) lead (see *Disconnecting the battery* in Chapter 5A, Section 2).

2 Remove the air cleaner as described in Chapter 4A, Section 5.

3 Disconnect the HT leads from the spark plugs, unclip them from the cover, and position them to the left-hand side of the engine compartment.

4 The cylinder head cover is secured by a total of twelve bolts, two of which (in the centre at the rear) have sections on top for mounting the air cleaner – note their positions for refitting. Also loosen the timing belt upper cover bolts – the cover has to be pulled back to remove the cylinder head cover **(see illustrations)**.

5 Carefully lift the cover from the top of the cylinder head, unclipping any wiring as necessary **(see illustration)**. Recover the gasket – this may be re-used if it is not damaged.

Refitting

6 Clean the mating surfaces of the cylinder head and the cover gasket.

7 Lower the cover onto the cylinder head, ensuring that the gasket stays in place. Fit the two special bolts to the locations noted on removal.

8 Progressively tighten all bolts to the specified torque.

9 Tighten the timing belt upper cover bolts.

10 Reconnect the HT leads to the spark plugs, and clip them back to the cover.

11 Refit the air cleaner, referring to Chapter 4A, Section 5 if necessary.

12 Reconnect the battery negative lead.

5 Valve clearances – checking and adjustment

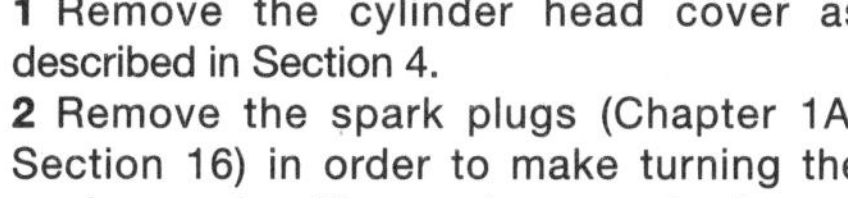

1 Remove the cylinder head cover as described in Section 4.

2 Remove the spark plugs (Chapter 1A, Section 16) in order to make turning the engine easier. The engine may be turned using a spanner on the crankshaft pulley bolt or by raising the front right-hand roadwheel clear of the ground, engaging 4th gear and turning the wheel. If the former method is used, jack up and support the front of the car (see *Jacking and vehicle support*) then unbolt the lower cover for access to the pulley bolt; if the latter method is used, apply the handbrake then jack up the front right-hand side of the car until the roadwheel is clear of the ground and support with an axle stand.

3.9 Home-made camshaft setting bar located in the camshaft slots

3 Draw the valve positions on a piece of paper, numbering them 1 to 8 inlet and exhaust, from the timing belt (right-hand) end of the engine (ie, 1E, 1I, 2E, 2I and so on). As there are two inlet and two exhaust valves for each cylinder, draw the cylinders as large circles and the four valves as smaller circles. The inlet valves are at the front of the cylinder head, and the exhaust valves are at the rear. As the valve clearances are adjusted, cross them off.

4 Turn the engine in a clockwise direction until both inlet valves of No 1 cylinder are fully shut and the apex of the camshaft lobes are pointing upwards away from the valve positions.

5 Insert a feeler blade of the correct thickness (see *Specifications*) between the heel of the camshaft lobe and the shim on the tappet **(see illustration)**. It should be a firm sliding fit.

4.4a Unscrew the twelve cover bolts ...

4.4b ... and loosen the three timing belt upper cover bolts

4.5 Removing the cylinder head cover

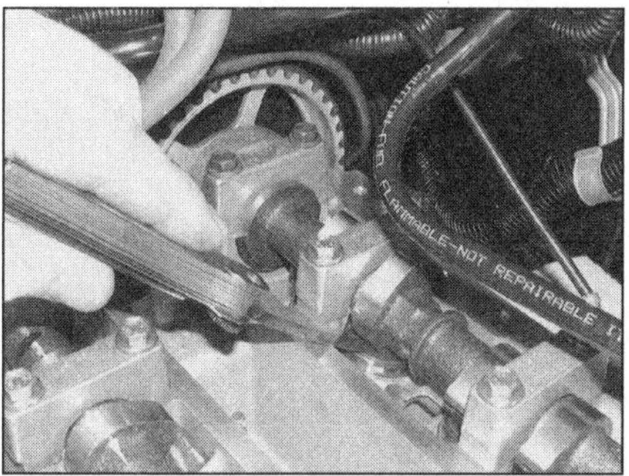

5.5 Checking a valve clearance with a feeler blade

6.3 Loosening the crankshaft pulley bolt while holding the pulley with a home-made tool

If this is the case, the clearance is correct and the valve position can be crossed off. If the clearance is not correct, use feeler blades to determine the exact clearance and record this on the drawing. From this clearance it will be possible to calculate the thickness of the new shim to be fitted.

6 Check the clearance of the second inlet valve for No 1 cylinder, and if necessary record the existing clearance on the drawing.

7 Now turn the engine until the inlet valves of No 2 cylinder are fully shut and the camshaft lobes pointing away from the valve positions. Check the clearances as described previously, and record any that are incorrect.

8 After checking all of the inlet valve clearances, check the exhaust valve clearances in the same way, but note that the clearances are different.

9 Where adjustment is required, the procedure is to remove the shim from the top of the tappet and fit a new shim to provide the correct clearance. Ford technicians use a special tool (21-218) consisting of a bar bolted to the left- and right-hand camshaft bearing caps. A sliding lever on the bar is used, together with a pushrod, to depress the relevant tappet in order to remove the old shim and fit the new one. Use of this tool (or a similar tool) will save a considerable amount of time, as the alternative is to remove the camshafts with the additional time of disconnecting the timing belt and resetting the valve timing. However, if TDC setting tools are available (see Section 3) removal of the camshafts is to be preferred to using an ill-fitting tool to depress the tappets.

10 If the recorded clearance was too small, a thinner shim must be fitted, and conversely if the clearance was too large, a thicker shim must be fitted. To calculate the thickness of the new shim, first use a micrometer to measure the thickness of the existing shim (C) and add this to the measured clearance (B). Deduct the desired clearance (A) to provide the thickness (D) of the new shim. The thickness of the shim should be etched on the downward facing surface, however use the micrometer to verify this. The formula is as follows.

D (new shim thickness) =
C (existing shim thickness)
+ B (measured clearance)
– A (desired clearance)

Sample calculation – clearance too small

Desired clearance (A) = *0.20*
Measured clearance (B) = *0.15*
Existing shim thickness (C) = *2.725*
Shim thickness reqd. (D) = *C+B-A = 2.675*

Sample calculation – clearance too large

Desired clearance (A) = *0.30*
Measured clearance (B) = *0.40*
Existing shim thickness (C) = *2.550*
Shim thickness reqd. (D) = *C+B-A = 2.650*

All measurements in mm.

11 The shims are available in thicknesses from 2.000 mm to 3.300 mm in increments of 0.025 mm. If the Ford tool (or similar) is being used to remove the shims without removing the camshafts, turn the tappets so that the slot is facing towards the centre of the engine. It will then be possible to use a small screwdriver to lift out the old shim. Fit the new shim then release the tool.

12 When fitting the new shim, make sure that the etched thickness is facing downwards onto the tappet.

13 It will be helpful for future adjustment if a record is kept of the thickness of shim fitted at each position. The shims required can be purchased in advance once the clearances and the existing shim thicknesses are known.

HAYNES HiNT ***It is permissible to interchange shims between tappets to achieve the correct clearances, but it is not advisable to turn the camshaft with any shims removed, since there is a risk that the cam lobe will jam in the empty tappet.***

14 When all the clearances have been checked and adjusted, refit the lower cover (where removed), lower the car to the ground and refit the cylinder head cover as described in Section 4.

6 Crankshaft pulley/ vibration damper – removal and refitting

Caution: Removal of the crankshaft pulley effectively loses the valve timing setting, and it will be necessary to reset the timing using the procedure and tools described in Section 3 and 8.

Note: *The vibration damper retaining bolt may only be used once. Obtain a new bolt for the refitting procedure.*

Removal

1 Remove the auxiliary drivebelt as described in Chapter 1A, Section 23.

2 Set the engine to the top dead centre (TDC) position as described in Section 3, then remove the camshaft position bar and the crankshaft timing pin. Do not leave the tools in position while the crankshaft pulley bolt is being loosened.

3 Hold the crankshaft pulley stationary **(see illustration)**. The bolt ends locate in the pulley holes, and an extension bar and socket can then be used to loosen the bolt. Do not turn the crankshaft, otherwise it will be more difficult to reset the valve timing – also, with the bolt loose, the crankshaft sprocket may not turn with the crankshaft, and the pistons may touch the valves.

4 With the bolt loosened several turns and only if necessary use a suitable puller to free the pulley from the end of the crankshaft. Fully unscrew the bolt and withdraw the pulley **(see illustration)**.

5 Clean the end of the crankshaft and the pulley.

Refitting

6 Fit the crankshaft locking tool **(see illustration 3.7c)** and rotate the crankshaft until it is locked in position.

7 Locate the pulley on the end of the crankshaft. Make sure the correct new bolt is used by measuring the depth of the hole (from the end of the crankshaft to the centre of the hole) with Vernier calipers. If it is 42 mm use a M12x29 mm bolt, but if it is 52 mm use a M12x44.5 mm bolt.

8 Insert the new bolt and tighten it to the specified Stage 1 torque setting **(see illustration)**.

9 Now angle-tighten the bolt through the specified Stage 2 angle. An angle gauge is useful for this, but 90° is a right-angle, which is quite easily judged by eye.

10 The valve timing must now be set and the camshaft sprocket bolts tightened as described in Section 8.

11 Refit the timing belt upper cover.

12 Fit a new auxiliary drivebelt as described in Chapter 1A, Section 23.

6.4 Withdraw the pulley from the end of the crankshaft

6.8 Inserting the new crankshaft pulley retaining bolt

7.2 Unscrewing the timing cover upper retaining bolt

7.7a Undo the bolts...

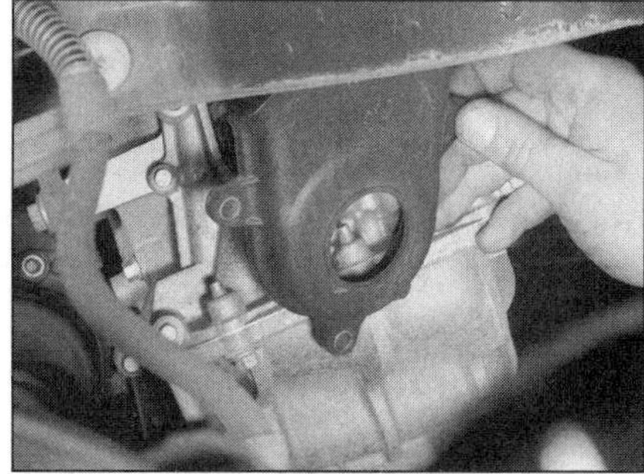

7.7b ... and remove the lower timing cover

7 Timing belt covers – removal and refitting

Upper cover

Removal

1 Remove the auxiliary drivebelt as described in Chapter 1A, Section 23.

2 Unscrew the single upper bolt securing the upper timing cover to the cylinder head cover **(see illustration)**.

3 Unscrew the five remaining cover retaining screws.

4 Manoeuvre the timing cover rearwards, and withdraw it from the engine compartment.

Refitting

5 Refitting is a reversal of removal. Fit a new auxiliary drivebelt as described in Chapter 1A, Section 23.

Lower cover

Removal

6 The timing belt lower cover is located around the crankshaft. First remove the crankshaft pulley/vibration damper as described in Section 6.

7 Working beneath the right-hand wheel arch, unscrew the retaining bolts and withdraw the timing cover **(see illustrations)**.

Refitting

8 Refitting is a reversal of removal.

8 Timing belt – removal and refitting

Caution: Unlike the previous Zetec-SE engine, the Duratec 16V features camshaft sprockets made from a type of plastic. Care must be taken to avoid damage to the sprockets during the following procedure.

Removal

1 Loosen the four bolts securing the water pump pulley.

2 Remove the crankshaft pulley/vibration damper as described in Section 6. This work includes removing the cylinder head cover and upper timing belt cover, and setting the engine at top dead centre (TDC).

3 Remove the water pump pulley.

4 With the camshaft timing bar removed, loosen the camshaft sprocket bolts several turns while holding the sprockets with a suitable tool **(see illustration)**. Bearing in mind the caution at the start of this Section, release the sprockets from the tapers on the ends of the camshafts so that they are free to rotate.

5 Remove the timing belt covers as described in Section 7.

6 Where fitted, remove the timing belt guide disc from the end of the crankshaft. Note which way round the disc is fitted – the concave side faces inwards **(see illustration)**.

7 Disconnect the small hose from the front of the expansion tank by squeezing the quick-release connector. Remove the single bolt securing the coolant expansion tank to the inner wing bracket, lift the tank off its rear locating lug, and move the tank to one side without disconnecting any further hoses **(see illustrations)**.

8 Lift out the power steering fluid reservoir from the mounting clips on the inner wing, and move it to one side without disconnecting the hoses **(see illustration)**.

9 Remove the alternator as described in Chapter 5A, Section 8.

10 The engine must now be supported, as the right-hand mounting (right as seen from the driver's seat) must be removed. Supporting the engine should ideally be done from above, using an engine crane or a special engine lifting beam. However, in the absence of

8.4 Loosening the camshaft sprocket retaining bolts while holding the sprockets with a home-made tool

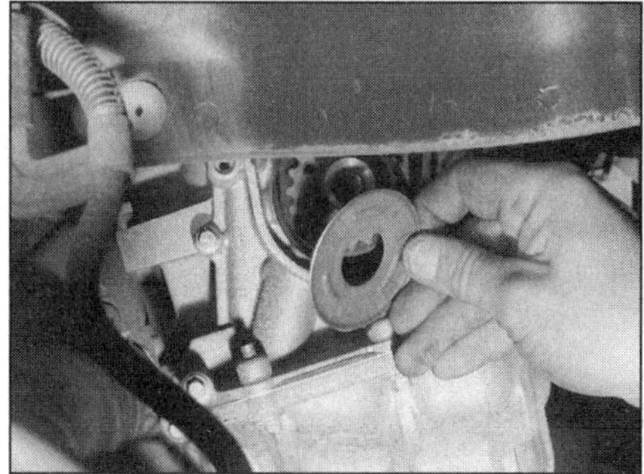

8.6 Removing the timing belt guide disc

8.7a Disconnect the degas hose from the expansion tank ...

8.7b ... then remove the single bolt, and lift the tank away

8.8 Lift out the power steering fluid reservoir

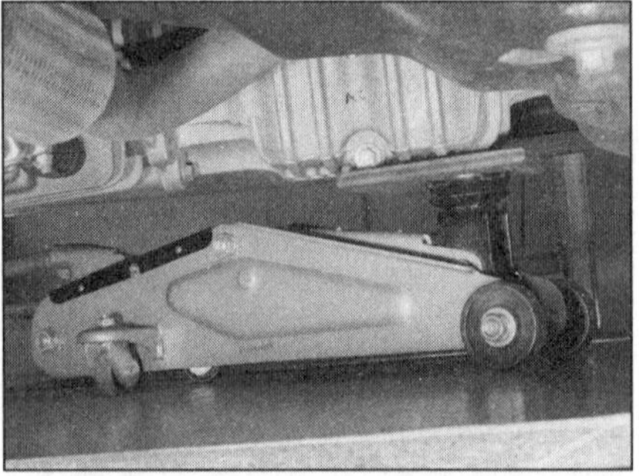

8.10 Supporting the engine with a trolley jack and block of wood under the sump

8.11 Remove the three nuts and three bolts, and lift off the upper half of the engine right-hand mounting

these tools, the engine can be supported from below, on the cast aluminium sump, providing a piece of wood is used to spread the load **(see illustration)**.

11 With the engine securely supported, remove the three nuts and three bolts securing the right-hand mounting, and lift it off **(see illustration)**. Three new nuts should be obtained for refitting the mounting.

12 Unbolt the lower half of the engine right-hand mounting bracket from the engine (four bolts).

13 One of four different types of timing belt tensioner may be fitted:

1. *The tensioner pulley is mounted on an eccentric, and the belt is tensioned by manually rotating the pulley hub.*
2. *The tensioner has a fixed pulley, with the belt being tensioned by manually pivoting the tensioner body's slotted bracket.*
3. *The tensioner is similar to type 1 but is tensioned by an internal spring (09/2003 to 03/2005).*
4. *The tensioner has an internal spring as in type 3, but is mounted on the water pump body (04/2005 on).*

14 Release the tensioner as follows, according to type:

1. *Loosen the centre bolt, then move the tensioner away from the belt, and tighten the bolt to hold the tensioner temporarily in this position.*
2. *Loosen the two tensioner mounting bolts, then rotate the tensioner anti-clockwise away from the belt, and tighten the bolts to hold the tensioner temporarily in this position.*
3. *Turn the tensioner body clockwise and insert a suitable rod or drill through the hole in the hub to temporarily lock the tensioner away from the belt.*
4. *Push on the front section of the belt to cause the tensioner pulley to move to its released position, then lock it in this position by inserting a suitable rod or drill through the hole in the body extension.*

15 If the timing belt is to be re-used (this is not recommended), use white paint or similar to mark its direction of rotation, and note from the manufacturer's markings which way round it is fitted. Withdraw the belt from the sprockets and from over the tensioner **(see illustrations)**. *Do not* attempt to turn the crankshaft or camshafts until the timing belt is refitted.

Inspection

16 If the belt is being removed for reasons other than renewal, check it carefully for any signs of uneven wear, splitting, cracks (especially at the roots of the belt teeth) or contamination with oil or coolant. Renew the belt if there is the slightest doubt about its condition. As a safety measure, the belt should be renewed irrespective of its apparent condition whenever the engine is overhauled.

17 Check the sprockets for signs of wear or damage, and ensure that the tensioner pulley rotates smoothly on its bearings; renew any worn or damaged components. Ford dealers (and many motor factors) now supply 'cambelt kits', consisting of the belt itself and a new tensioner – for peace of mind, it is recommended that one of these is purchased.

18 If signs of oil or coolant contamination are found on the old belt, trace the source of the leak and rectify it, then wash down the engine timing belt area and related components, to remove all traces of oil or coolant.

Refitting

19 Ensure that the engine is still set to TDC, with the crankshaft setting pin and camshaft setting bar temporarily removed. Slightly loosen the camshaft sprocket bolts until they are just finger-tight, so that the sprockets are free to rotate on their shafts.

20 Locate the timing belt on the crankshaft sprocket, then feed it over the tensioner pulley and finally over the two camshaft sprockets. If the original belt is being refitted, make sure that it is the correct way round as noted during removal.

21 Where applicable, refit the timing belt guide disc on the end of the crankshaft, making sure that the concave side faces inwards.

22 Refit the timing belt lower cover, and tighten the bolts to the specified torque.

23 Fit the special crankshaft **locking** tool and then locate the crankshaft pulley/vibration damper on the end of the crankshaft. Insert the new bolt and tighten it to the specified Stage 1 torque setting.

24 Now tighten the bolt crankshaft pulley bolt through the specified Stage 2 angle.

25 Position No 1 piston at TDC as described in Section 3, turning the crankshaft as little as possible to do so. Set the camshafts at TDC, and insert the setting bar in the slots.

26 On engines with the eccentric type

8.15a Showing the manufacturer's markings on the timing belt

8.15b Removing the timing belt from the camshaft sprockets ...

8.15c ... and crankshaft sprocket

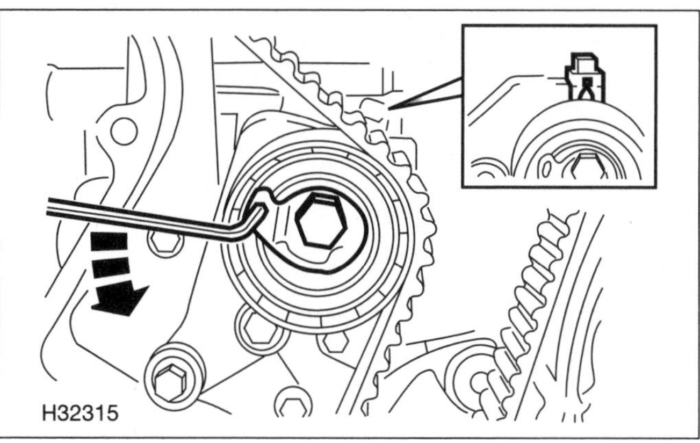

8.26 Setting the timing belt tension on the eccentric-type timing belt tensioner

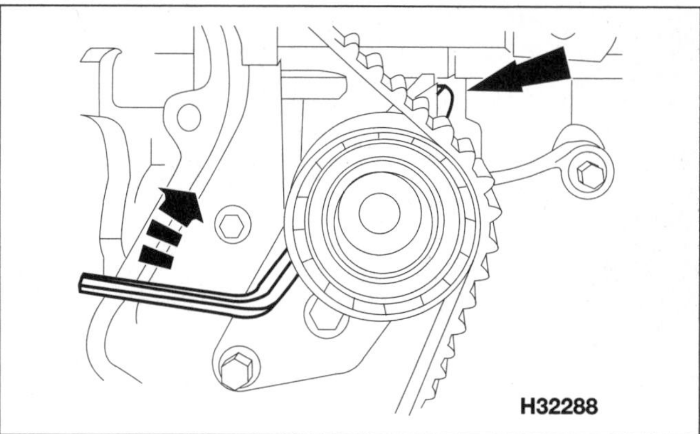

8.27 Setting the timing belt tension on the slotted-bracket timing belt tensioner

tensioner, loosen the centre bolt, then using a 6 mm Allen key in the hole provided, turn the tensioner roller anti-clockwise to tension the belt. The correct tension is indicated by the pointer being exactly central in the rectangular window above and behind the tensioner roller **(see illustration)**. Hold the tensioner in this position, and tighten the centre bolt to the specified torque.

27 On the slotted bracket tensioner, loosen the two bolts so that the tensioner is free to pivot. Using an 8 mm Allen key in the hole provided, turn the tensioner and bracket clockwise to tension the belt. The correct tension is indicated by the pointer being exactly central between the two marks behind the tensioner roller **(see illustration)**. Hold the tensioner in this position, and tighten the two bolts to the specified torque.

28 On models manufactured from 09/2003 onwards, make sure the timing belt is correctly located, then push on the front section of the belt and pull out the locking rod or drill to release the tensioner.

Warning: Keep your fingers clear of the pulley and belt to avoid personal injury

29 Moderately tighten the bolts retaining the camshaft sprockets to the camshafts, then remove the setting bar and timing pin, and fully-tighten the bolts while holding the sprockets using the tool described in Section 6 or using a spanner on the hexagon flats provided **(see illustration)**.

30 Refit the engine right-hand mounting bracket, and tighten the bolts to the specified torque.

31 Refit the top section of the engine right-hand mounting bracket, using new nuts, and tightening the nuts and bolts to the specified torque. Now whatever means of engine support was used (engine support beam, engine crane, trolley jack) can be removed from the car.

32 Remove the TDC setting tools from the engine, and turn the crankshaft two complete turns in its normal direction. Refit the TDC timing pin and position the crankshaft at TDC, then see whether the setting bar will fit in the camshaft slots. If necessary, loosen the camshaft sprocket bolts, turn the **camshafts** slightly (without moving the timing belt) so the setting bar can be fitted, then retighten the camshaft sprocket bolts. On completion, remove the timing pin and bar and refit the blanking plug.

33 Refit the timing belt upper cover, and the alternator. Refit the water pump pulley, and tighten the bolts as far as possible for now – once the auxiliary drivebelt has been fitted it will be easier to tighten the bolts to the specified torque.

34 Fit a new auxiliary drivebelt as described in Chapter 1A, Section 23.

35 Tighten the water pump pulley bolts to the specified torque.

36 Refit the auxiliary drivebelt lower cover and tighten the retaining bolts.

37 Refit the wheel arch liner, then lower the car to the ground.

38 Refit the power steering reservoir and the coolant expansion tank.

39 Reconnect the battery negative lead.

9 Timing belt tensioner and sprockets – removal, inspection and refitting

Tensioner pulley

Removal

1 Remove the auxiliary drivebelt as described in Chapter 1A, Section 23.

8.29 Tightening the camshaft sprocket retaining bolts

2 Remove the timing belt upper cover as described in Section 7.

3 As a precaution against losing the valve timing, use string to tie the front and rear runs of the timing belt together. This will ensure that the belt remains engaged with the camshaft sprockets while the tensioner and pulley are removed.

4 Different types of timing belt tensioner may be fitted:

1. *The tensioner pulley is mounted on an eccentric, and the belt is tensioned by manually rotating the pulley hub.*
2. *The tensioner has a fixed pulley, with the belt being tensioned by manually pivoting the tensioner body's slotted bracket.*
3. *The tensioner is similar to type 1 but is tensioned by an internal spring (09/2003 to 03/2005).*
4. *The tensioner has an internal spring as in type 3, but is mounted on the water pump body (04/2005 on).*

5 Loosen the eccentric type tensioner centre bolt, or the two tensioner mounting bolts (slotted bracket type), then move the tensioner away from the belt to release the belt tension.

6 Remove the two tensioner mounting bolts, and withdraw the tensioner from the engine.

7 While the tensioner and pulley are removed, make sure that the timing belt remains fully engaged with the camshaft and crankshaft sprockets.

Inspection

8 Spin the tensioner pulley, and check that it turns freely without any roughness or tightness. Do not attempt to clean the pulley by immersing in any cleaning fluid. **Note:** *It is recommended that a new tensioner is fitted, regardless of the apparent condition of the old one. If the tensioner were to seize or break up in service, the resulting damage to the timing belt could lead to serious engine damage.*

Refitting

9 Clean the cylinder block in the area of the tensioner.

10 Locate the tensioner pulley on the block, and insert the two mounting bolts. On the eccentric type tensioner, these two bolts

9.18 Using a spanner to hold the camshafts stationary

9.26a Unscrew the bolt ...

9.26b ... and remove the camshaft sprocket

should be tightened to the specified torque, but on the slotted bracket type, leave the bolts hand-tight so that the tensioner is free to pivot.

11 Tension the timing belt using the information in Section 8.

12 Provided that the timing belt has remained fully engaged with the camshaft and crankshaft sprockets, it should not be necessary to check the valve timing. However, if there is any doubt, check the valve timing as described in Section 3.

13 Refit the timing belt upper cover as described in Section 7.

14 Fit a new auxiliary drivebelt as described in Chapter 1A, Section 23.

Camshaft sprockets

Caution: Unlike the previous Zetec-SE engine, the Duratec 16V features camshaft sprockets made from a type of plastic. Care must be taken to avoid damage to the sprockets during the following procedure.

Removal

15 Loosen the four bolts securing the water pump pulley.

16 Remove the crankshaft pulley/vibration damper as described in Section 6. This work includes removing the cylinder head cover and upper timing belt cover, and setting the engine at top dead centre (TDC).

17 Remove the water pump pulley.

18 With the camshaft timing bar removed, loosen the camshaft sprocket bolts several turns while holding the sprockets with a suitable tool. Alternatively, hold the camshafts stationary using a spanner on the hex flats provided **(see illustration)**. Bearing in mind the caution at the start of this sub-Section, release the sprockets from the tapers on the ends of the camshafts so that they are free to rotate.

9.40 Slide the sprocket from the end of the crankshaft

19 Remove the timing belt upper cover as described in Section 7.

20 Remove the single bolt securing the coolant expansion tank to the inner wing bracket, lift the tank off its rear locating lug, and move the tank to one side without disconnecting any hoses.

21 Lift out the power steering fluid reservoir from the mounting clips on the inner wing, and move it to one side without disconnecting the hoses.

22 The engine must now be supported, as the right-hand mounting (right as seen from the driver's seat) must be removed. Supporting the engine should ideally be done from above, using an engine crane or a special engine lifting beam. However, in the absence of these tools, the engine can be supported from below, on the cast aluminium sump, providing a piece of wood is used to spread the load.

23 With the engine securely supported, remove the three nuts and three bolts securing the right-hand mounting, and lift it off. Three new nuts should be obtained for refitting the mounting.

24 Unbolt the engine right-hand mounting bracket from the engine (four bolts).

25 Refer to Section 8 and release the timing belt tension, then remove the belt from the sprockets, taking care not to bend it sharply. The belt will probably remain engaged with the crankshaft sprocket, but as a precaution, keep a little upward pressure on the belt by tying it to the side of the engine compartment.

26 Unscrew the bolts and remove the sprockets from the camshafts. If necessary, carefully use a soft-metal drift to release the sprockets from the taper on the camshafts **(see illustrations)**.

Inspection

27 Examine the teeth of the sprockets for wear and damage, and renew them if necessary.

Refitting

28 Locate the sprockets on the camshafts, and screw in the retaining bolts loosely.

29 Engage the timing belt with the camshaft sprockets, then tension the belt using the information in Section 8.

30 Refit the engine right-hand mounting lower bracket, and tighten the bolts to the specified torque.

31 Refit the top section of the engine right-hand mounting bracket, using new nuts, and tightening the nuts and bolts to the specified torque. Now whatever means of engine support was used (engine support beam, engine crane, trolley jack) can be removed from the car.

32 Remove the TDC setting tools from the engine, and turn the crankshaft two complete turns in its normal direction. Refit the TDC timing pin and position the crankshaft at TDC, then see whether the setting bar will fit in the camshaft slots. If necessary, loosen the camshaft sprocket bolts, turn the camshafts slightly (without moving the timing belt) so the setting bar can be fitted, then retighten the camshaft sprocket bolts. On completion, remove the timing pin and bar, and refit the blanking plug.

33 Refit the timing belt upper cover. Refit the water pump pulley, and tighten the bolts as far as possible for now – once the auxiliary drivebelt has been fitted, it will be easier to tighten the bolts to the specified torque.

34 Fit a new auxiliary drivebelt as described in Chapter 1A, Section 23.

35 Tighten the water pump pulley bolts to the specified torque.

36 Refit the auxiliary drivebelt lower cover and tighten the retaining bolts.

37 Refit the wheel arch liner and where fitted the engine undershield, then lower the car to the ground.

38 Refit the power steering reservoir to its bracket, and bolt the coolant expansion tank back into position.

Crankshaft sprocket

Removal

39 Remove the timing belt as described in Section 8.

40 Slide the sprocket off the end of the crankshaft **(see illustration)**.

Inspection

41 Examine the teeth of the sprocket for wear and damage, and renew if necessary.

Refitting

42 Wipe clean the end of the crankshaft, then slide on the sprocket.

43 Refit the timing belt as described in Section 8.

10 Camshaft oil seals – renewal

1 Remove the camshaft sprockets as described in Section 9.

2 Note the fitted depths of the oil seals as a guide for fitting the new ones.

3 Using a screwdriver or similar tool, carefully prise the oil seals from the cylinder head/ camshaft bearing caps. Take care not to damage the oil seal contact surfaces on the ends of the camshafts or the oil seal seats. An alternative method of removing the seals is to drill a small hole, then insert a self-tapping screw and use pliers to pull out the seal **(see illustrations)**.

4 Wipe clean the oil seal seats and also the ends of the camshafts.

5 Dip each new oil seal in fresh oil, then locate it over the camshaft and into the cylinder head/camshaft bearing cap. Make sure that the closed end of the oil seal faces outwards **(see illustration)**.

6 Using a socket or length of metal tubing, drive the oil seals squarely into position to the previously noted depths. Wipe away any excess oil **(see illustration)**.

7 Refit the camshaft sprockets as described in Section 9.

11 Camshafts and tappets – removal, inspection and refitting

Removal

1 Before removing the camshafts, it may be useful to check and record the valve clearances as described in Section 5. If any clearance is not within limits, new shims can be obtained and fitted.

2 Remove the camshaft sprockets as described in Section 9.

3 The camshaft bearing caps are marked for position – the inlet caps have the letter I and exhaust caps have the letter E. On the project car these were not very clear, and if this is the case, mark them using paint or a marker pen. Make sure they are identified for inlet and exhaust camshafts **(see illustrations)**.

4 Position the crankshaft so that No 1 piston is approximately 25 mm before TDC. This can be done by starting from the TDC position; carefully insert a large screwdriver down No 1 cylinder spark plug hole until the tip touches the top of the piston, and turn the engine anti-clockwise until the screwdriver shaft has descended 25 mm.

5 Position the camshafts so that none of the valves are at full lift (ie, not fully open and being heavily pressed down by the cam lobes). To do this, turn each camshaft using a spanner on the hexagon flats provided.

6 Progressively loosen the camshaft bearing cap retaining bolts, working in the same sequence shown for tightening **(see illustration 11.20)**. Work only as described, to gradually and evenly release the pressure of the valve springs on the caps **(see illustration)**.

7 Withdraw the caps, keeping them in order

10.3a Drill a small hole and insert a self-tapping screw ...

10.3b ... then pull out the oil seal using a pair of pliers

10.5 Locating the new oil seal into the cylinder head/camshaft bearing cap

10.6 Driving the new oil seal into position with a socket

11.3a No 3 inlet camshaft bearing cap

11.3b No 3 exhaust camshaft bearing cap

11.3c Number the camshaft bearing caps with paint if they are not marked

11.6 Unscrew the camshaft bearing cap bolts ...

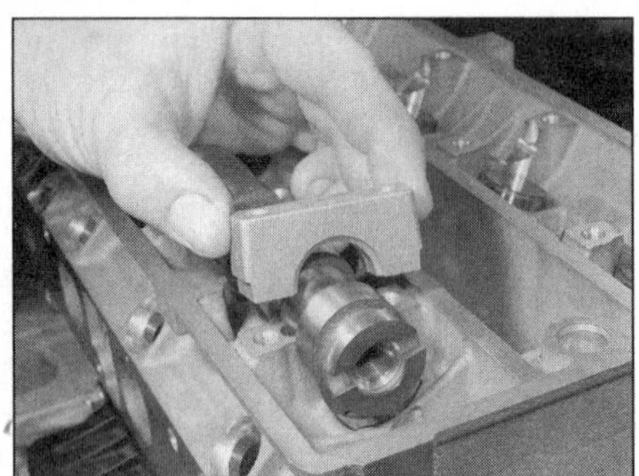
11.7a ... withdraw the caps ...

11.7b ... then remove the camshafts

11.8 Removing the bucket tappets

to aid refitting, then lift the camshafts from the cylinder head and withdraw their oil seals. The exhaust camshaft can be identified by the reference lobe for the camshaft position sensor; therefore, there is no need to mark the camshafts **(see illustrations)**.

8 Obtain sixteen small, clean containers, and number them 1 to 8 for both the inlet and exhaust camshafts. Lift the tappets one by one from the cylinder head, keeping the shims with the respective tappets **(see illustration)**.

Inspection

9 With the camshafts and tappets removed, check each for signs of obvious wear (scoring, pitting, etc) and for ovality, and renew if necessary.

10 If possible, use a micrometer to measure the outside diameter of each tappet – take measurements at the top and bottom of each tappet, then a second set at right-angles to the first; if any measurement is significantly different from the others, the tappet is tapered or oval (as applicable) and must be renewed. If the tappets or the cylinder head bores are excessively worn, new tappets and/or a new cylinder head will be required.

11 Visually examine the camshaft lobes for score marks, pitting, and evidence of overheating (blue, discoloured areas). Look for flaking away of the hardened surface layer of each lobe. If any such signs are evident, renew the component concerned.

12 Examine the camshaft bearing journals and the cylinder head bearing surfaces for signs of obvious wear or pitting. If any such signs are evident, renew the component concerned.

13 To check camshaft endfloat, remove the tappets, clean the bearing surfaces carefully, and refit the camshafts and bearing caps. Tighten the bearing cap bolts to the specified torque wrench setting, then measure the endfloat using a dial gauge mounted on the cylinder head so that its tip bears on the camshaft right-hand end.

14 Tap the camshaft fully towards the gauge, zero the gauge, then tap the camshaft fully away from the gauge, and note the gauge reading. If the endfloat measured is found to be more than the typical value given, fit a new camshaft and repeat the check; if the clearance is still excessive, the cylinder head must be renewed.

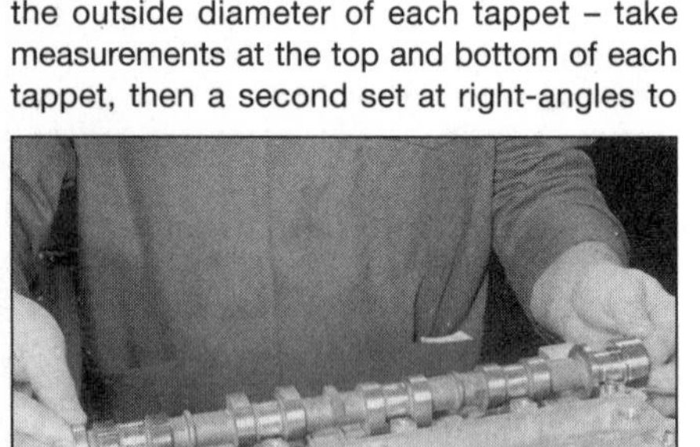
11.16 Locating the camshafts in the cylinder head

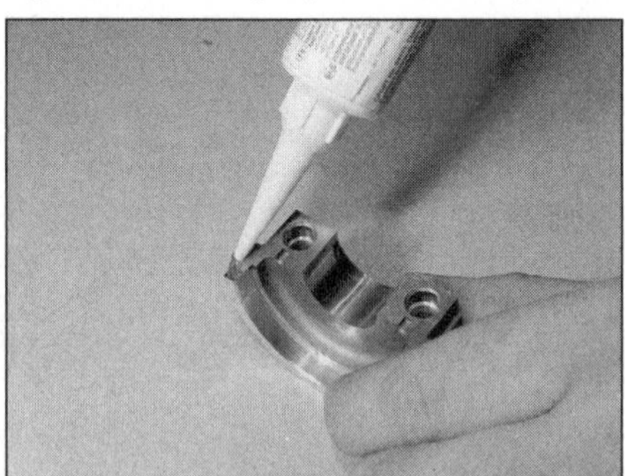
11.18 Apply sealant to the No 1 camshaft bearing caps

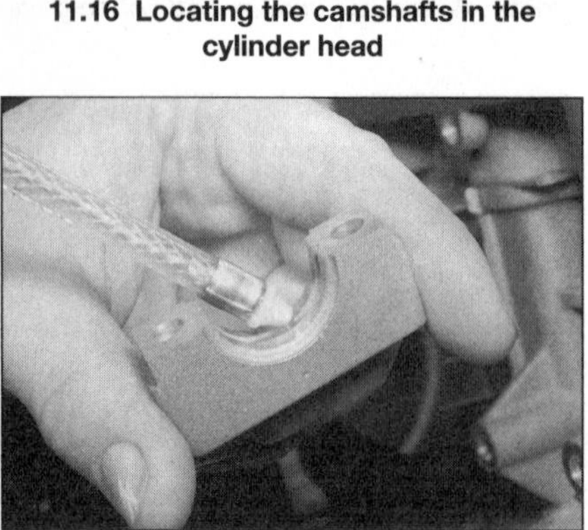
11.19a Oil the bearing surfaces ...

11.19b ... then refit the camshaft bearing caps

Refitting

15 Lubricate the cylinder head tappet bores and the tappets with engine oil. Carefully refit the tappets (together with their respective shims) to the cylinder head, ensuring each tappet is refitted to its original bore. Some care will be needed to enter the tappets squarely into their bores.

16 Liberally oil the camshaft bearings and lobes. Ensuring that each camshaft is in its original location, refit the camshafts, locating each so that the slot in its left-hand end is approximately parallel to, and just above, the cylinder head mating surface. At this stage, position the camshafts so that none of the valves are at full lift – see paragraph 5 **(see illustration)**.

17 Clean the mating faces of the cylinder head and camshaft bearing caps, and ensure that the locating dowels are firmly in place.

18 Apply a 2 to 3 mm diameter bead of suitable sealant (Ford recommend WSK-M2G348-A5) to the No 1 camshaft bearing caps at the oil seal ends only **(see illustration)**. If preferred, the oil seals can be located at this stage, otherwise fit them later.

19 Oil the bearing surfaces, then locate the camshaft bearing caps on the camshafts and insert the retaining bolts loosely. Make sure that each cap is located in its previously noted position **(see illustrations)**.

20 Ensuring each cap is kept square to the cylinder head as it is tightened down, and working in sequence **(see illustration)**, tighten the camshaft bearing cap bolts slowly and by one turn at a time, until each cap touches the cylinder head. Next, go round again in the same sequence, tightening the bolts to the specified Stage 1 torque wrench setting specified.

21 Finally, still working in the tightening sequence, tightening the bolts further to the Stage 2 angle. It is recommended that an angle gauge is used for this, to ensure accuracy.

22 Wipe off all surplus sealant, and if not already done, fit new camshaft oil seals with reference to Section 10.

23 Refit the camshaft sprockets (Section 9).

24 Check the valve clearances as described in Section 5 on completion.

12 Cylinder head – removal, inspection and refitting

Note: *The following paragraphs assume that the cylinder head will be removed together with the inlet manifold attached. This simplifies the procedure, but makes it a bulky and heavy assembly to handle (having an assistant to help is recommended). If it is wished first to remove the inlet manifold, refer to Chapter 4A, Section 15, then amend the following procedure accordingly.*

Removal

1 Depressurise the fuel system as described in Chapter 4A, Section 2, then drain the cooling system as described in Chapter 1A, Section 26.

2 Ensure that the exhaust system is fully cool, then unscrew and remove the two nuts securing the exhaust flexible section to the catalytic converter. Separate the joint and recover the gasket – a new one will obviously be required for refitting.

3 Raise the front of the car, and support it on axle stands (see *Jacking and vehicle support*).

4 To prevent damage to the exhaust flexible section, support it by attaching a pair of splints either side (two scrap strips of wood, plant canes, etc) using some cable-ties.

5 Remove the exhaust manifold lower heat shield, which is secured by a total of six bolts.

6 Remove the inlet manifold support bolt from the front of the engine, at the timing belt end. Lower the car to the ground.

7 Remove the camshafts as described in Section 11.

8 Disconnect the vacuum hoses from the fuel pressure regulator on the fuel rail, and from the EVAP valve just below it. Also disconnect the brake servo vacuum hose from the inlet manifold.

9 Disconnect the following wiring plugs:

a) Alternator main plug.
b) EVAP valve multiplug ***(see illustration)****.*
c) Engine harness multiplug (grey, next to the EVAP valve).
d) Engine coolant temperature sensor wiring plug (on the thermostat housing).
e) Ignition coil wiring plug ***(see illustration)****.*
f) Oxygen sensor wiring plug (on a bracket just behind the ignition coil).

10 Disconnect the fuel supply and return line quick-release connectors from opposite ends of the fuel rail **(see illustration)**. Anticipate some fuel spillage by wrapping the joint with clean rag to soak up any fuel. Ensure that the fuel lines cannot become mixed up – attach labels if necessary.

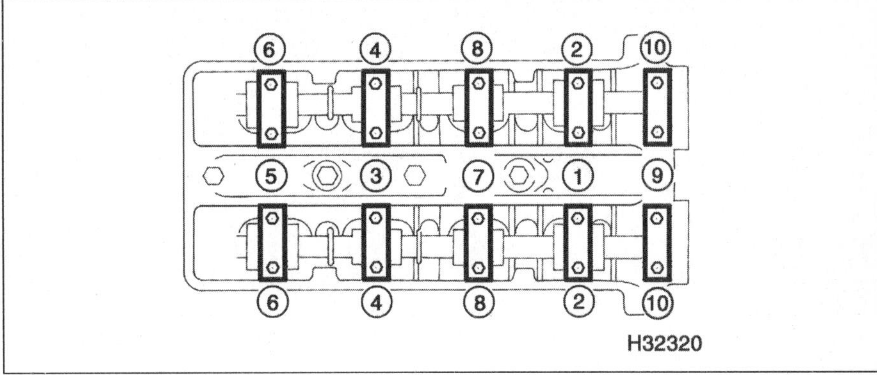

11.20 Camshaft bearing cap bolt loosening and tightening sequence

11 Release the spring-type clips and remove the two large coolant hoses from the thermostat housing. Also disconnect the degas hose (smaller hose leading back to the coolant expansion tank) from the cylinder head.

12 Unbolt the power steering fluid hose support bracket from the rear of the cylinder head.

13 Remove the exhaust manifold upper heat shield, which is secured by four bolts.

14 The exhaust manifold must now be removed. This is secured to the head and block by a total of four nuts and three bolts. Once free, move the manifold to the rear to slide it off the locating studs, and withdraw it. Take care not to damage the oxygen sensor or its wiring as the manifold is removed.

15 Unbolt the timing belt rear cover, which is secured by three bolts.

16 Remove the single bolt securing the dipstick tube to the inlet manifold, and move the tube clear as far as possible. If preferred, the dipstick tube can be pulled out of its location in the block – recover the O-ring seal from the base of the tube, and obtain a new one for reassembly **(see illustrations)**.

17 Make a last check round the cylinder head, to ensure that nothing remains connected or attached which would prevent the head and inlet manifold being lifted off. Prepare a clean surface to lay the head and manifold down on, once it has been removed.

12.9a Disconnect the EVAP valve multiplug ...

12.9b ... and the ignition coil wiring plug

12.10 Disconnect the fuel line quick-release connectors from the fuel rail

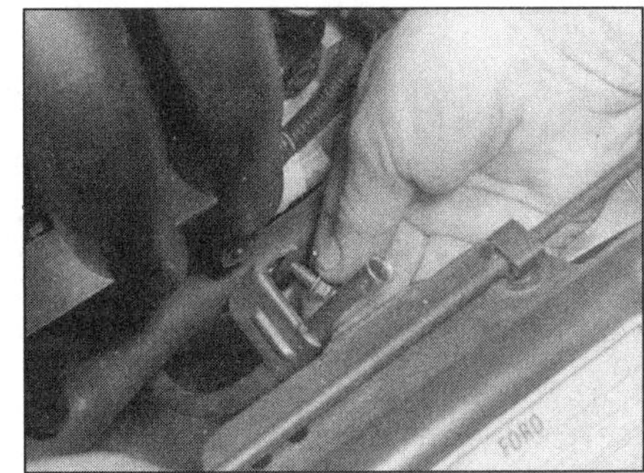

12.16a Unscrew the upper mounting bolt ...

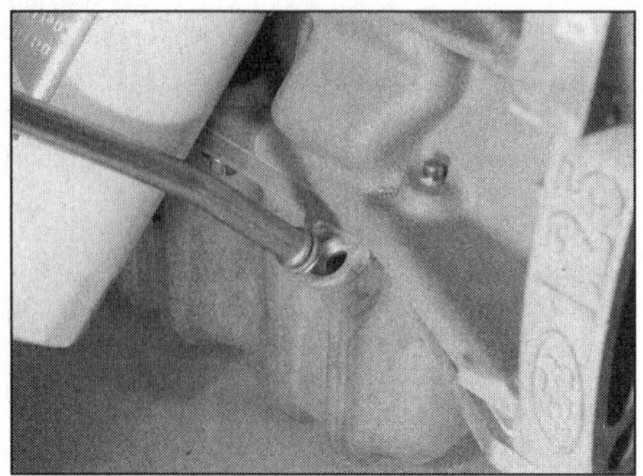
12.16b ... remove the dipstick tube from the cylinder block ...

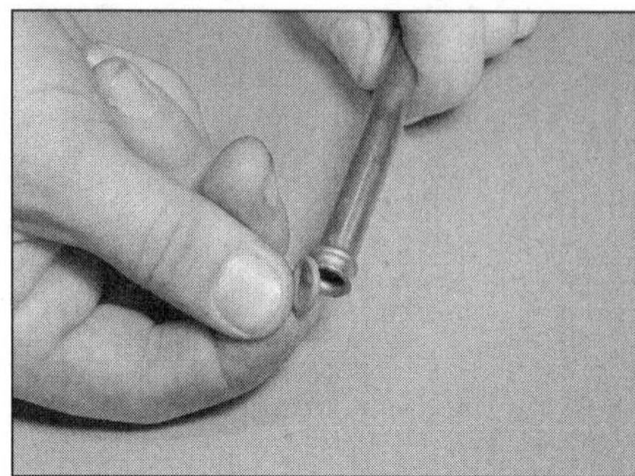
12.16c ... then remove the O-ring

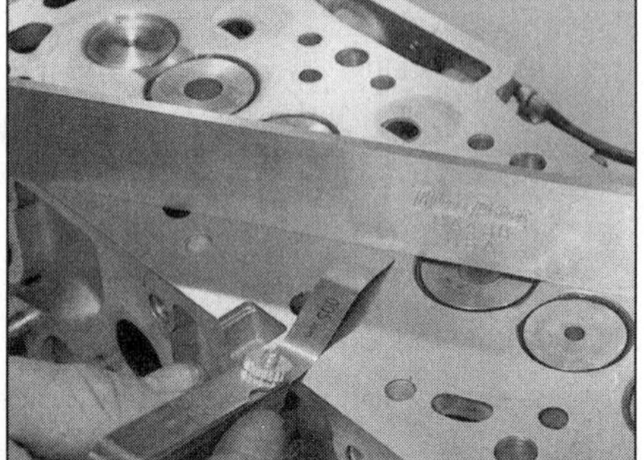
12.23 A straight-edge and feeler blades can be used to check for distortion

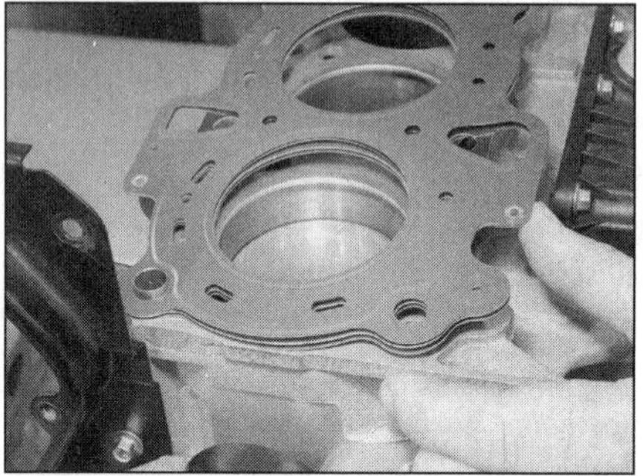
12.29 Locating the new cylinder head gasket on the cylinder block dowels

18 Working in the **reverse** of the tightening sequence **(see illustration 12.32a)**, slacken the ten cylinder head bolts progressively and by half a turn at a time; a Torx key (TX 55 size) will be required. Remove all the bolts.

19 Lift the cylinder head away; use assistance if possible, as it is a heavy assembly. Remove the gasket, noting the two dowels. Although the gasket cannot be re-used, it is advisable to retain it for comparison with the new one, to confirm that the right part has been supplied.

Inspection

20 The mating faces of the cylinder head and cylinder block must be perfectly clean before refitting the head. Use a hard plastic or wood scraper to remove all traces of gasket and carbon; also clean the piston crowns. Take particular care during the cleaning operations, as aluminium alloy is easily damaged.

21 Make sure that the carbon is not allowed to enter the oil and water passages – this is particularly important for the lubrication system, as carbon could block the oil supply to the engine's components. Using adhesive tape and paper, seal the water, oil and bolt holes in the cylinder block. To prevent carbon entering the gap between the pistons and bores, smear a little grease in the gap. After cleaning each piston, use a small brush to remove all traces of grease and carbon from the gap, then wipe away the remainder with a clean rag.

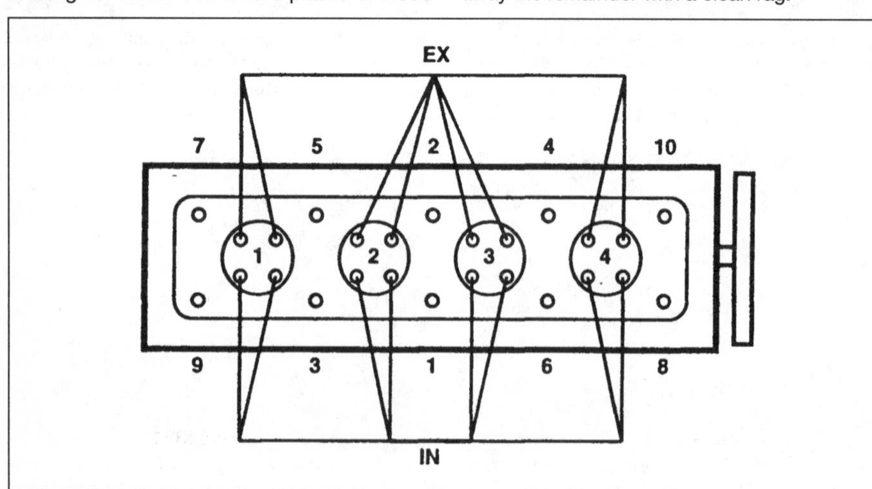

12.32a Cylinder head bolt tightening sequence

22 Check the mating surfaces of the cylinder block and the cylinder head for nicks, deep scratches and other damage. If slight, they may be removed carefully with a file, but if excessive, renewal is necessary as it is not permissible to machine the surfaces.

23 If warpage of the cylinder head gasket surface is suspected, use a straight-edge to check it for distortion **(see illustration)**. Refer to Chapter 2D, Section 8 if necessary.

24 If possible, clean out the bolt holes in the block using compressed air, to ensure no oil or water is present. Screwing a bolt into an oil or water filled hole can (in extreme cases) cause the block to fracture, due to the hydraulic pressure created.

25 Although not essential, if a suitable tap-and-die set is available, it's worth running the correct size tap down the bolt threads in the cylinder block. This will clean the threads of any debris, and go some way to restoring any damaged threads. Make absolutely sure the tap is the right size and thread pitch, and lightly oil the tap before starting.

26 Ford do not state that new head bolts are required when refitting, but re-using the old ones isn't worth the risk – if the bolts or their threads 'let go' when they're tightened, the bottom half of the engine could be reduced to scrap very quickly. We don't advise using bolts which have already been tightened twice. If you are going to re-use the old bolts, at least clean them thoroughly, and check that their threads aren't damaged.

Refitting

27 Wipe clean the mating surfaces of the cylinder head and cylinder block, and check that the two locating dowels are in position in the block.

28 Turn the crankshaft anti-clockwise so that pistons 1 and 4 are approximately 25 mm before TDC, in order to avoid the risk of valve/piston contact. Turn the crankshaft using a spanner on the pulley bolt.

29 If the old gasket is still available, check that it is identical to the new one – for instance, there are several different thicknesses of gasket, indicated by the number of small holes on one side. Position the new gasket over the dowels on the cylinder block surface. It can only be fitted one way round – check carefully that the holes in the gasket align with the holes in the block surface, and that none are blocked **(see illustration)**.

30 It is useful when refitting a cylinder head to have an assistant on hand, to help guide the head onto the dowels. Take care that the gasket does not get moved as the head is lowered into position. To confirm that the head is aligned correctly, once it is in place, temporarily slide in two or more of the head bolts, and check that they fit into the block holes.

31 Though it is not required by Ford, there is no harm in lightly oiling the threads of the head bolts before fitting them. This is particularly recommended if the old bolts are

12.32b Tighten the bolts to the specified torques ...

12.34 ... then angle-tighten them further

13.3 Sump seen from below, showing the engine and transmission bolts

being re-used, or if the block threads have not been cleaned with a tap-and-die set. Fit the head bolts carefully, and screw them in by hand only until finger-tight.

32 Working progressively and in sequence, tighten the cylinder head bolts to their Stage 1 torque setting **(see illustrations)**.

33 Next, go around again in the same sequence, and tighten the bolts to the Stage 2 setting.

34 Finally, the bolts should be angle-tightened further, by the specified Stage 3 amount. This means simply that each bolt in the sequence must be turned through the stated angle. Special 'angle gauges' are available from tool suppliers for measuring this, but since 90° is a right-angle, it is possible to judge reasonably accurately by assessing the start and finish positions of the socket handle **(see illustration)**.

35 The remainder of refitting is a reversal of removal, noting the following points:

a) Refit the camshafts as described in Section 11, and the timing belt as described in Section 8.

b) Tighten all fasteners to the specified torque, where given.

c) Ensure that all hoses and wiring are correctly routed, and that hose clips and wiring connectors are securely refitted.

d) Refill the cooling system as described in Chapter 1A, Section 26.

e) Check all disturbed joints for signs of oil or coolant leakage once the engine has been restarted and warmed-up to normal operating temperature.

13 Sump – removal and refitting

Removal

1 Apply the handbrake, then jack up the front of the car and support it on axle stands (see *Jacking and vehicle support*).

2 Drain the engine oil, then check the drain plug sealing washer and renew if necessary. Clean and refit the engine oil drain plug together with the washer, and tighten it to the specified torque wrench setting. Although not strictly necessary, as the oil is being drained, it makes sense to fit a new oil filter at the same time (see Chapter 1A, Section 3).

3 Unscrew the bolts securing the transmission to the sump, then progressively unscrew the sump-to-block bolts **(see illustration)**.

4 On these models, a sump gasket is not used, and sealant is used instead. Unfortunately, the use of sealant makes removal of the sump more difficult. If care is taken not to damage the surfaces, the sealant can be cut around using a sharp knife.

5 On no account lever between the mating faces, as this will almost certainly damage them, resulting in leaks when finished. Ford technicians have a tool comprising a metal rod which is inserted through the sump drain hole, and a handle to pull the sump downwards. Providing care is taken not to damage the threads, a large screwdriver could be used in the drain hole to prise down the sump.

6 While the sump is removed, take the opportunity to remove the oil pump pick-up/strainer pipe, and clean it with reference to Section 14.

Refitting

7 Thoroughly clean the contact surfaces of the sump and crankcase. Take care not to damage the oil pump gasket or the crankshaft oil seal, both of which are partially exposed when the sump is removed. If necessary, use a cloth rag to clean inside the sump and crankcase. If the oil pump pick-up/strainer pipe was removed, fit a new O-ring and refit the pipe with reference to Section 14.

8 Ford state that, to refit the sump, five M8x20 studs must be screwed into the base of the engine **(see illustration)**. This not only helps to align the sump, ensuring that the bead of sealant is not displaced as the sump is fitted, but also ensures that the sealant does not enter the blind holes. Cut a slot across the end of each stud, to make removal easier when the sump is in place.

9 Apply a 3 to 4 mm diameter bead of sealant (Ford recommend WSE M4G323-A4, or equivalent) to the sump pan, to the inside of the bolt holes **(see illustration)**. The sump bolts must be fitted and tightened within 10 minutes of applying the sealant.

10 Offer the sump up into position over the studs, and fully refit the remaining bolts by hand. Unscrew the studs, and refit the sump

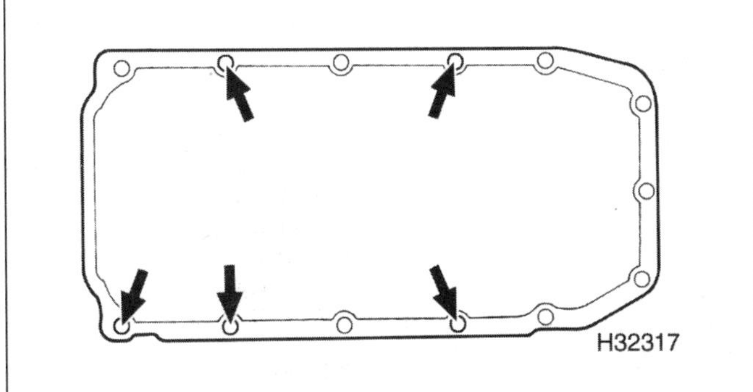

13.8 Sump alignment stud positions (arrowed)

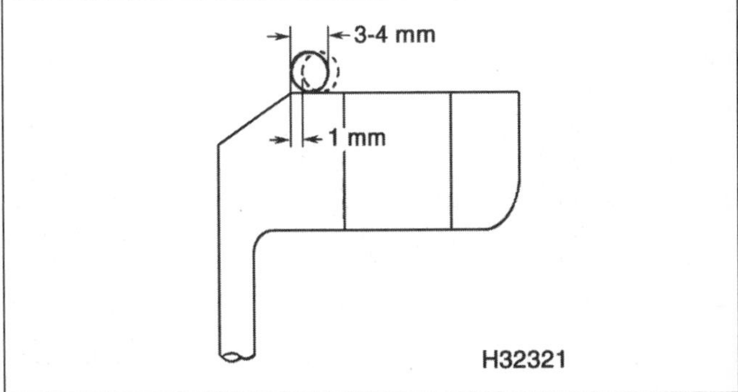

13.9 Showing how the bead of sealant is to be applied to the sump mating surface

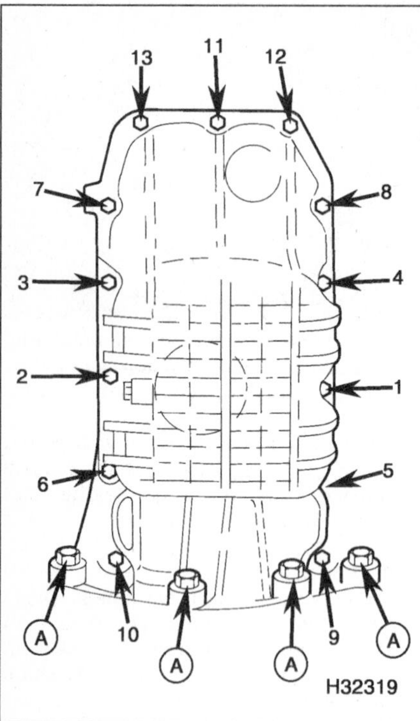

13.12 Sump bolt tightening sequence. Also shows sump-to-transmission bolts (A)

bolts in their place. The sump should be fitted flush with the block at the transmission end.

11 Insert the four sump-to-transmission bolts and tighten them to the specified torque.

12 The sump-to-crankcase bolts are tightened in two stages. Working in sequence **(see illustration)**, tighten all the sump bolts to the specified Stage 1 torque, then go around again in sequence, and tighten them to the Stage 2 setting.

13 Lower the car to the ground. To be on the safe side, wait a further 30 minutes for the sealant to cure before filling the sump with fresh oil, as described in Chapter 1A, Section 3.

14 Finally start the engine and check for signs of oil leaks.

14 Oil pump – removal, inspection and refitting

Removal

1 Remove the timing belt as described in Section 8.

2 Remove the crankshaft sprocket as described in Section 9.

3 If a trolley jack was used to support the engine from below, refit the engine right-hand mounting upper section and mounting bracket, and tighten the mounting bolts/nuts securely. Remove the trolley jack from under the sump.

4 Remove the sump as described in Section 13.

5 On models with air conditioning, remove the four bolts securing the air conditioning compressor, and tie it up clear of the engine without disconnecting any of the hoses.

6 Unscrew the bolts securing the oil pump pick-up/strainer pipe to the baffle plate/main bearing cap.

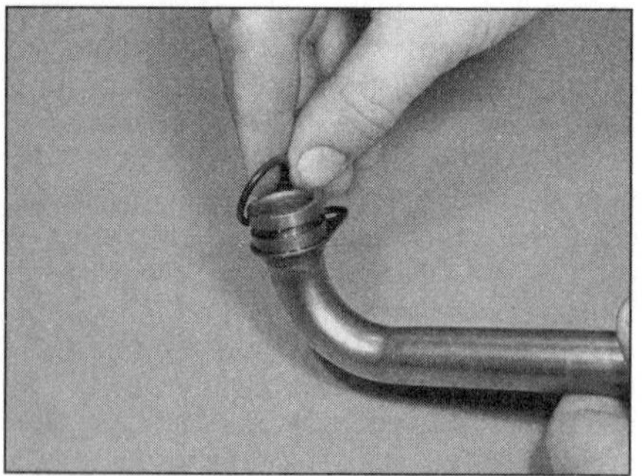

14.7 Removing the O-ring from the oil pump pick-up/strainer pipe

14.8 Removing the oil pump mounting bolts

14.9 Removing the oil pump gasket

14.11 Unbolting the baffle plate from the main bearing cap/ladder

7 Unscrew the bolt securing the oil pump pick-up/strainer pipe to the oil pump, then withdraw the pipe and recover the sealing O-ring **(see illustration)**. Discard the O-ring.

8 Unscrew the bolts securing the oil pump to the cylinder block/crankcase **(see illustration)**. Withdraw the pump over the nose of the crankshaft.

9 Recover then discard the gasket **(see illustration)**.

10 Support the oil pump on wooden blocks, then use a screwdriver to hook or drive out the crankshaft oil seal.

11 If necessary, unbolt and remove the baffle plate from the main bearing cap/ladder **(see illustration)**. Thoroughly clean all components, particularly the mating surfaces of the pump, the sump, and the cylinder block/crankcase.

Inspection

12 It is not possible to obtain individual components of the oil pump, furthermore, there are no torque settings available for tightening the pump cover plate bolts. However, the following procedure is provided for owners wishing to dismantle the oil pump for examination.

13 Take out the screws, and remove the pump cover plate; noting any identification marks on the rotors, withdraw the rotors.

14 Inspect the rotors for obvious signs of wear or damage, and renew if necessary; if either rotor, the pump body, or its cover plate are scored or damaged, the complete oil pump assembly must be renewed.

15 The oil pressure relief valve can be dismantled as follows.

16 Unscrew the threaded plug, and recover the valve spring and plunger. If the plug's sealing O-ring is worn or damaged, a new one must be obtained, to be fitted on reassembly.

17 Reassembly is the reverse of the dismantling procedure; ensure the spring and valve are refitted the correct way round, and tighten the threaded plug securely.

Refitting

18 If removed, refit the oil baffle plate to the crankcase and tighten the bolts.

19 The oil pump must be primed on installation, by pouring clean engine oil into it, and rotating its inner rotor a few turns.

20 Use a little grease to stick the new gasket in place on the cylinder block/crankcase.

21 Offer the oil pump over the nose of the crankshaft, and turn the inner rotor as necessary to align its flats with the flats on the crankshaft. Locate the pump on the dowels, then insert the retaining bolts and progressively tighten them to the specified torque.

22 Fit a new crankshaft oil seal (Section 16).

23 Locate a new O-ring (dipped in oil) on the pick-up/strainer pipe, then locate the pipe in the oil pump and insert the retaining bolts. Insert the bolts retaining the pipe on the baffle plate/main bearing cap. Tighten the bolts to the specified torque.

24 Where removed, refit the air conditioning compressor, tightening the bolts to the specified torque.
25 Refit the sump as described in Section 13.
26 If the engine was previously being supported using a trolley jack and wood block beneath the sump, reposition the jack, then unscrew the nuts and bolts and remove the engine right-hand mounting upper section and mounting bracket.
27 Refit the crankshaft sprocket with reference to Section 9.
28 Refit the timing belt with reference to Section 8.

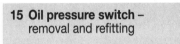

15 Oil pressure switch – removal and refitting

1 The oil pressure switch is a vital early warning of low oil pressure. The switch operates the oil warning light on the instrument panel – the light should come on with the ignition, and go out almost immediately when the engine starts.
2 If the light does not come on, there could be a fault on the instrument panel, the switch wiring, or the switch itself. If the light does not go out, low oil level, worn oil pump (or sump pick-up blocked), blocked oil filter, or worn main bearings could be to blame – or again, the switch may be faulty.
3 If the light comes on while driving, the best advice is to turn the engine off immediately, and not to drive the car until the problem has been investigated – ignoring the light could mean expensive engine damage.

Removal

4 The oil pressure switch is located on the front face of the engine, above the oil filter.
5 Disconnect the wiring plug from the switch.
6 Unscrew the switch from the block, and remove it. There should only be a very slight loss of oil when this is done.

Inspection

7 Examine the switch for signs of cracking or splits. If the top part of the switch is loose, this is an early indication of impending failure.
8 Check that the wiring terminals at the switch are not loose, then trace the wire from the switch connector until it enters the main loom – any wiring defects will give rise to apparent oil pressure problems.

Refitting

9 Refitting is the reverse of the removal procedure, noting the following points:
- *a) Tighten the switch securely.*
- *b) Reconnect the switch connector, making sure it clicks home properly. Ensure that the wiring is routed away from any hot or moving parts.*
- *c) Check the engine oil level and top-up if necessary (see 'Weekly checks').*
- *d) Check for signs of oil leaks once the engine has been restarted and warmed-up to normal operating temperature.*

16.7 Locating the new right-hand oil seal over the crankshaft

16 Crankshaft oil seals – renewal

Right-hand oil seal

1 Remove the timing belt as described in Section 8.
2 Remove the crankshaft sprocket as described in Section 9.
3 As a safety precaution, refit the engine right-hand mounting upper section and mounting bracket, and tighten the mounting bolts/nuts.
4 Note the fitted depth of the oil seal as a guide for fitting the new one.
5 Using a screwdriver, prise the old oil seal from the oil pump housing. Take care not to damage the seal contact surface on the nose of the crankshaft, or the seating in the housing.
6 Wipe clean the seating and the nose of the crankshaft.
7 Dip the new oil seal in fresh oil, then locate it over the crankshaft and into the oil pump housing. Make sure that the closed end of the oil seal faces outwards **(see illustration)**.
8 Using a socket or length of metal tubing, drive the oil seal squarely into position to the previously noted depth. The Ford installation tool (303-395) is used together with an old crankshaft pulley bolt to press the oil seal into position. The same idea may be used with metal tubing and a large washer – do not use a new crankshaft pulley bolt, as it is only permissible to use the bolt once. With the oil seal in position, wipe away any excess oil.
9 With the weight of the engine once more supported, unscrew the nuts and bolts and remove the engine right-hand mounting upper section and mounting bracket.
10 Refit the crankshaft sprocket with reference to Section 9.
11 Refit the timing belt with reference to Section 8.

16.19 With the oil seal housing bolted in position, remove the fitting ring

16.17 Locating the new left-hand oil seal housing (complete with fitting ring) over the end of the crankshaft

Left-hand oil seal

12 Remove the transmission as described in Chapter 7A, Section 7 or Chapter 7B, Section 7, and the clutch as described in Chapter 6, Section 7.
13 Remove the flywheel as described in Section 17.
14 Unscrew the six bolts and withdraw the oil seal carrier from the end of the crankshaft. Note that the seal and carrier are made as one unit – it is not possible to obtain the seal separately.
15 Clean the carrier contact surface on the cylinder block, and the end of the crankshaft.
16 The new oil seal carrier is supplied complete with a fitting sleeve, which ensures that the oil seal lips are correctly located on the crankshaft. Ford state that neither the crankshaft nor the new oil seal should be lubricated before fitting.
17 Locate the oil seal carrier and fitting sleeve over the end of the crankshaft. Press the carrier into position, noting that the centre bolt holes are formed into locating dowels **(see illustration)**.
18 Insert the retaining bolts and progressively tighten them to the specified torque.
19 Remove the fitting sleeve and check that the oil seal lips are correctly located **(see illustration)**.
20 Refit the flywheel as described in Section 17.
21 Refit the clutch as described in Chapter 6, Section 7, and the transmission as described in Chapter 7A, Section 7 or Chapter 7B, Section 7.

17.2 Home-made tool for holding the flywheel stationary while loosening the bolts

17.3 Removing the flywheel retaining bolts (note the location dowel in the crankshaft)

17.6 Crankshaft speed/position sensor mounting and retaining bolt

17 Flywheel – removal, inspection and refitting

Removal

1 Remove the transmission as described in Chapter 7A, Section 7 or Chapter 7B, Section 7, and the clutch as described in Chapter 6, Section 7.

2 Hold the flywheel stationary using one of the following methods:

a) *If an assistant is available, insert one of the transmission mounting bolts into the cylinder block and have the assistant engage a wide-bladed screwdriver with the starter ring gear teeth while the bolts are loosened. Alternatively, a piece of angle-iron can be engaged with the ring gear and located against the transmission mounting bolt.*

b) *A further method is to fabricate a piece of flat metal bar with a pointed end to engage the ring gear – fit the tool to the transmission bolt and use washers and packing to align it with the ring gear, then tighten the bolt to hold it in position **(see illustration)**.*

3 Unscrew and remove the bolts, then lift the flywheel off the locating dowel on the crankshaft **(see illustration)**.

Inspection

4 Clean the flywheel to remove grease and oil. Inspect the surface for cracks, rivet grooves, burned areas and score marks. Light scoring can be removed with emery cloth. Check for cracked and broken ring gear teeth. Lay the flywheel on a flat surface, and use a straight-edge to check for warpage.

5 Clean and inspect the mating surfaces of the flywheel and the crankshaft. If the crankshaft oil seal is leaking, renew it (see Section 16) before refitting the flywheel. In fact, given the large amount of work needed to remove the flywheel, it's probably worth fitting a new seal anyway, as a precaution.

6 While the flywheel is removed, clean carefully its inner face, particularly the recesses which serve as the reference points for the crankshaft speed/position sensor. Clean the sensor's tip, and check that the sensor is securely fastened. The sensor mounting may be removed if necessary by first removing the sensor, then unscrewing the bolt and withdrawing the mounting from the cylinder block **(see illustration)**.

Refitting

7 Make sure that the mating faces of the flywheel and crankshaft are clean, then locate the flywheel on the crankshaft and engage it with the locating dowel.

8 Insert the retaining bolts finger-tight.

9 Lock the flywheel (see paragraph 2), then tighten the bolts in a diagonal sequence to the specified torque.

10 Refit the clutch with reference to Chapter 6, Section 7, and the transmission as described in Chapter 7A, Section 7 or Chapter 7B, Section 7.

18 Engine/transmission mountings – inspection and renewal

Inspection

1 The engine/transmission mountings seldom require attention, but broken or deteriorated mountings should be renewed immediately, or the added strain placed on the driveline components may cause damage or wear.

2 During the check, the engine/transmission must be raised slightly, to remove its weight from the mountings.

3 Apply the handbrake, then jack up the front of the car and support it on axle stands (see *Jacking and vehicle support*). Position a jack under the sump, with a large block of wood between the jack head and the sump, then carefully raise the engine just enough to take the weight off the mountings.

18.9a Remove the three nuts and three bolts ...

4 Check the mountings to see if the rubber is cracked, hardened or separated from the metal components. Sometimes, the rubber will split right down the centre.

5 Check for relative movement between each mounting's brackets and the engine or body (use a large screwdriver or lever to attempt to move the mountings). If movement is noted, lower the engine and check the mounting nuts and bolts for tightness.

Renewal

6 The engine mountings can be removed if the weight of the engine is supported by one of the following alternative methods.

7 Either support the weight of the assembly from underneath, using a jack and a suitable piece of wood between the jack and the sump (to prevent damage), or from above by attaching a hoist to the engine. A third method is to use a suitable support bar, with end pieces which will engage in the water channel each side of the bonnet lid aperture. Using an adjustable hook and chain connected to the engine, the weight of the engine and transmission can then be taken from the mountings.

8 Once the weight of the engine and transmission is suitably supported, any of the mountings can be unbolted and removed. **Note:** *All references to left and right are as seen from the driver's seat.*

9 To remove the engine right-hand mounting, unscrew the three nuts and three bolts, and lift off the upper section. If required, unscrew the bolts and remove the lower section from the cylinder head/block **(see illustrations)**.

10 To remove the left-hand mounting, first remove the battery and battery tray as described in Chapter 5A, Section 4. Unscrew the three mounting nuts from the engine left-hand mounting, then remove the upper bracket **(see illustrations)**.

11 To remove the engine rear mounting/support link, apply the handbrake, then jack up the front of the car and support it on axle

18.9b ... then lift off the upper half of the engine right-hand mounting

18.9c Remove the bolts ...

18.9d ... and take off the lower half of the right-hand mounting

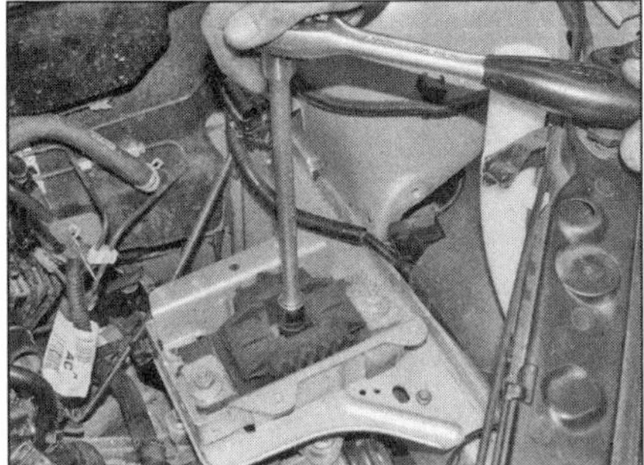
18.10a Unscrew the nuts from the left-hand mounting ...

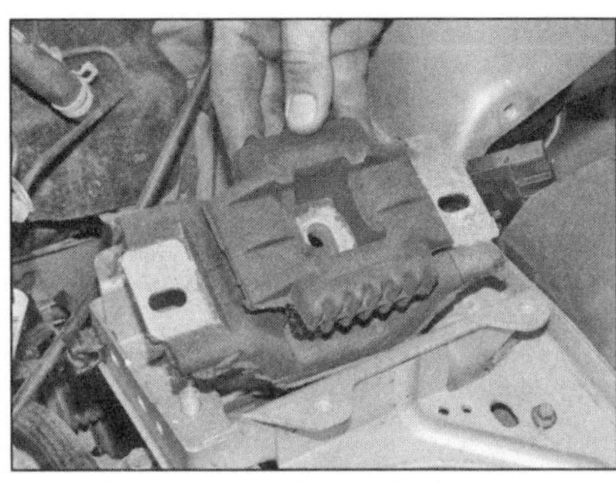
18.10b ... and lift off the bracket

18.11 Unscrew the through-bolts and remove the lower mounting link

stands (see *Jacking and vehicle support*). Unscrew the through-bolts and remove the engine rear mounting link from the bracket on the transmission and from the bracket on the subframe **(see illustration)**. Hold the engine stationary while the bolts are being removed, since the link will be under tension.

12 Refitting of all mountings is a reversal of the removal procedure. Where nuts are used for any mounting, new ones must be fitted. Do not fully-tighten the mounting nuts/bolts until all of the mountings are in position. Check that the mounting rubbers do not twist or distort as the mounting bolts and nuts are tightened to their specified torques.

Notes

Chapter 2 Part B: 1.4 litre diesel engine in-car repair procedures

Contents

Degrees of difficulty

Easy, suitable for novice with little experience	**Fairly easy,** suitable for beginner with some experience	**Fairly difficult,** suitable for competent DIY mechanic	**Difficult,** suitable for experienced DIY mechanic	**Very difficult,** suitable for expert DIY or professional

Specifications

General

Engine type	Four-cylinder, in-line, single overhead camshaft, 8-valves
Designation	Duratorq TDCi
Engine code	F6JA, F6JB or F6JC
Capacity	1398 cc
Bore	73.7 mm
Stroke	82.0 mm
Compression ratio	18.0:1
Firing order	1-3-4-2
Direction of crankshaft rotation	Clockwise (seen from right-hand side of car)
No 1 cylinder location	Timing belt end

Compression pressures (engine hot, at cranking speed)

Normal	25 to 30 bar (363 to 435 psi)
Minimum	18 bar (261 psi)
Maximum difference between any two cylinders	5 bar (73 psi)

Cylinder head

Maximum permissible gasket surface distortion	0.025 mm

Cylinder block

Main bearing radial clearance	0.017 to 0.043 mm

Pistons and piston rings

Piston diameter	73.520 to 73.536 mm
Piston-to-bore clearance	0.164 to 0.196 mm
Piston ring end gaps – installed:	
Top compression ring	0.200 to 0.350 mm
Second compression ring	0.200 to 0.400 mm
Oil control ring	0.800 to 1.000 mm
Piston ring gap arrangement	120° to each other

Connecting rods

Big-end bore diameter	48.655 to 48.671 mm
Small-end bore diameter	25.000 mm
Connecting rod bearing clearance	0.024 to 0.070 mm
Gudgeon pin length	59.700 to 60.000 mm
Gudgeon pin diameter	24.995 to 25.000 mm

Camshaft

Endfloat	0.195 to 0.300 mm
Bearing journal diameter	23.959 to 23.980 mm

Crankshaft

Endfloat	0.100 to 0.300 mm
Main bearing journal diameter	49.962 to 49.981 mm
Connecting rod journal diameter	44.975 to 44.991 mm

Lubrication system

Oil pump type	Gear type, driven directly by the right-hand end of the crankshaft, by two flats machined along the crankshaft journal
Oil pressure	1.0 to 2.0 bar @ idle 2.3 to 3.7 bar @ 2000 rpm
Oil pressure warning switch operating pressure	0.8 bar

Torque wrench settings

	Nm	lbf ft
Auxiliary drivebelt tensioner roller	20	15
Big-end bolts:*		
Stage 1	10	7
Stage 2	Slacken 180°	
Stage 3	10	7
Stage 4	Angle-tighten a further 130°	
Camshaft bearing upper and lower housings	10	7
Camshaft position sensor bolt	5	4
Camshaft sprocket	45	33
Coolant outlet housing bolts	10	7
Crankshaft position/speed sensor bolt	5	4
Crankshaft pulley/sprocket bolt:		
Stage 1	32	24
Stage 2	Angle-tighten a further 190°	
Cylinder head bolts:*		
Stage 1	20	15
Stage 2	40	30
Stage 3	Angle-tighten a further 260°	
Cylinder head cover bolts	10	7
Engine-to-transmission fixing bolts	45	33
Engine mountings:		
Right-hand mounting bracket to block	55	41
Right-hand mounting nuts*/bolts	48	35
Left-hand mounting centre nut	90	66
Left-hand mounting outer nuts	48	35
Lower mounting nuts	48	35
Flywheel bolts:*		
Models with dual mass flywheel:		
Stage 1	30	22
Stage 2	Angle-tighten a further 90°	
Models without dual mass flywheel:		
Stage 1	17	13
Stage 2	Angle-tighten a further 75°	
Fuel pump sprocket nut	50	37
Intermediate shaft centre bearing cap locknuts	25	18
Main bearing ladder outer (smaller) bolts	8	6
Main bearing ladder to cylinder block (M11 bolts):*		
Stage 1	10	7
Stage 2	Slacken 180°	
Stage 3	30	22
Stage 4	Angle-tighten a further 140°	
Piston oil jet spray tube bolt	20	15
Oil drain plug	34	25
Oil filter housing	10	7
Oil pressure switch	30	22
Oil pump to cylinder block:		
Stage 1	3	2
Stage 2	9	6
Sump:		
Studs	8	6
Nuts	10	7
Bolts	12	9
Timing belt idler pulley	35	26
Timing belt tensioner pulley	30	22
Vacuum pump mounting bolts	20	15

** Use new fasteners*

1 General information

How to use this Chapter

This Chapter describes the repair procedures that can reasonably be carried out on the engine while it remains in the car. If the engine has been removed from the car and is being dismantled as described in Chapter 2D, any preliminary dismantling procedures can be ignored.

Note that, while it may be possible physically to overhaul items such as the piston/connecting rod assemblies while the engine is in the car, such tasks are not usually carried out as separate operations. Usually, several additional procedures are required (not to mention the cleaning of components and oilways); for this reason, all such tasks are classed as major overhaul procedures, and are described in Chapter 2D.

Chapter 2D describes the removal of the engine/transmission from the car, and the full overhaul procedures that can then be carried out.

Engine description

The Duratorq TDCi turbo-diesel engine was developed jointly by Ford and the Peugeot/Citroën group, and appears in several of the latest small Peugeot and Citroën models, where it is known as the 1.4 HDi engine. The engine is a single overhead camshaft eight-valve design, with four cylinders in-line, mounted transversely in the car, with the transmission on the left-hand side.

A toothed timing belt drives the camshaft, high-pressure fuel pump and water pump. The camshaft operates the inlet and exhaust valves via rocker arms, which are supported at their pivot ends by hydraulic self-adjusting tappets. The camshaft is supported by bearings machined directly in the cylinder head and camshaft bearing housing.

The high-pressure fuel pump supplies fuel to the fuel rail, and subsequently to the electronically controlled injectors which inject the fuel directly into the combustion chambers. This 'common-rail' design differs from previous diesel engines, where an injection pump supplies the fuel at high pressure to each injector. The earlier, conventional type injection pump required fine calibration and timing, and these functions are now undertaken by the high-pressure pump, electronic injectors and engine management ECU.

The crankshaft runs in five main bearings of the usual shell type. Endfloat is controlled by thrustwashers either side of No 2 main bearing.

The pistons are selected to be of matching weight, and incorporate fully-floating gudgeon pins retained by circlips.

The gear-type oil pump is fitted over the end of the crankshaft, and is driven by interlocking machined flats on the crankshaft and pump gear.

Precautions

The engine is a complex unit, with numerous accessories and ancillary components. The design of the engine compartment is such that every conceivable space has been utilised, and access to virtually all of the engine components is extremely limited. In many cases, ancillary components will have to be removed, or moved to one side, and wiring, pipes and hoses will have to be disconnected or removed from various cable clips and support brackets.

When working on this engine, read through the entire procedure first, look at the car and engine at the same time, and establish whether you have the necessary tools, equipment, skill and patience to proceed. Allow considerable time for any operation, and be prepared for the unexpected. Any major work on these engines is not for the faint hearted!

Because of the limited access, many of the engine photographs appearing in this Chapter were, by necessity, taken with the engine removed from the car.

Warning: It is essential to observe strict precautions when working on the fuel system components of the engine, particularly the high-pressure side of the system. Before carrying out any engine operations that entail working on, or near, any part of the fuel system, refer to the special information given in Chapter 4B, Section 2.

Operations with engine in car

a) Compression pressure – testing.
b) Cylinder head cover – removal and refitting.
c) Crankshaft pulley – removal and refitting.
d) Timing belt covers – removal and refitting.
e) Timing belt – removal, refitting and adjustment.
f) Timing belt tensioner and sprockets – removal and refitting.
g) Camshaft oil seal – renewal.
h) Camshaft, rocker arms and hydraulic tappets – removal, inspection and refitting.
i) Sump – removal and refitting.
j) Oil pump – removal and refitting.
k) Crankshaft oil seals – renewal.
l) Engine/transmission mountings – inspection and renewal.
m) Flywheel – removal, inspection and refitting.

2 Compression and leakdown tests – description and interpretation

Compression test

Note: *A compression tester specifically designed for diesel engines must be used for this test.*

1 When engine performance is down, or if misfiring occurs which cannot be attributed to the fuel system, a compression test can provide diagnostic clues as to the engine's condition. If the test is performed regularly, it can give warning of trouble before any other symptoms become apparent.

2 A compression tester specifically intended for diesel engines must be used, because of the higher pressures involved. On these engines, an adapter suitable for use in the glow plug holes will be required, so as not to disturb the fuel system components. It is unlikely to be worthwhile buying such a tester for occasional use, but it may be possible to borrow or hire one – if not, have the test performed by a garage.

3 Unless specific instructions to the contrary are supplied with the tester, observe the following points:

a) The battery must be in a good state of charge, the air filter must be clean, and the engine should be at normal operating temperature.
b) All the glow plugs should be removed as described in Chapter 5C, Section 2 before starting the test.
c) The wiring connector on the engine management system ECU (located in the plastic box behind the battery) must be disconnected.

4 The compression pressures measured are not so important as the balance between cylinders. Values are given in the Specifications.

5 The cause of poor compression is less easy to establish on a diesel engine than on a petrol one. The effect of introducing oil into the cylinders ('wet' testing) is not conclusive, because there is a risk that the oil will sit in the swirl chamber or in the recess on the piston crown instead of passing to the rings. However, the following can be used as a rough guide to diagnosis.

6 All cylinders should produce very similar pressures; any difference greater than that specified indicates the existence of a fault. Note that the compression should build-up quickly in a healthy engine; low compression on the first stroke, followed by gradually increasing pressure on successive strokes, indicates worn piston rings. A low compression reading on the first stroke, which does not build-up during successive strokes, indicates leaking valves or a blown head gasket (a cracked head could also be the cause). Deposits on the undersides of the valve heads can also cause low compression.

7 A low reading from two adjacent cylinders is almost certainly due to the head gasket having blown between them; the presence of coolant in the engine oil will confirm this.

8 If the compression reading is unusually high, the cylinder head surfaces, valves and pistons are probably coated with carbon deposits. If this is the case, the cylinder head should be removed and decarbonised (see Chapter 2D, Section 8).

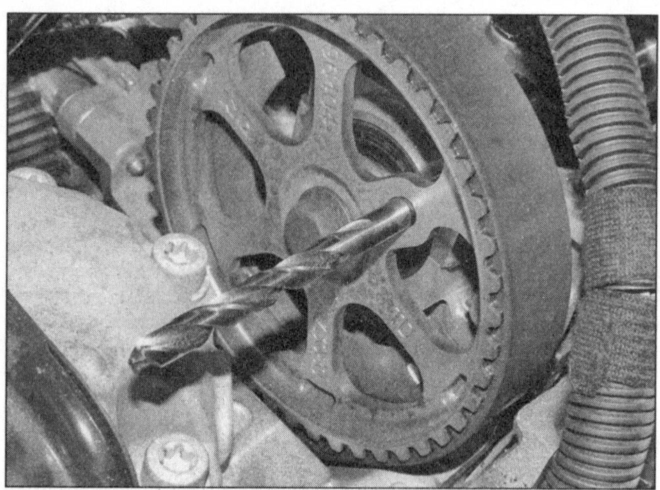

3.8 Insert an 8 mm drill through the camshaft sprocket hole, into the corresponding hole in the cylinder head

3.10 Insert a 5 mm drill through the crankshaft sprocket flange hole, into the corresponding oil pump hole

Leakdown test

9 A leakdown test measures the rate at which compressed air fed into the cylinder is lost. It is an alternative to a compression test, and in many ways it is better, since the escaping air provides easy identification of where pressure loss is occurring (piston rings, valves or head gasket).

10 The equipment needed for leakdown testing is unlikely to be available to the home mechanic. If poor compression is suspected, have the test performed by a suitably-equipped garage.

3 Engine assembly/ valve timing holes – general information and usage

Note: *Do not attempt to rotate the engine whilst the crankshaft and camshaft are locked in position. If the engine is to be left in this state for a long period of time, it is a good idea to place suitable warning notices inside the car, and in the engine compartment. This will reduce the possibility of the engine being accidentally cranked on the starter motor, which is likely to cause damage with the locking pins in place.*

1 Timing holes are located in the crankshaft sprocket flange, and in the camshaft sprocket hub. The holes are used to align the crankshaft and camshaft with the pistons halfway up the cylinder bores. This ensures that the valve timing is maintained during operations that require removal and refitting of the timing belt. When the holes are aligned with their corresponding holes in the cylinder block/ head and flywheel, suitable diameter bolts/ pins can be inserted to lock the crankshaft and camshaft in position, preventing rotation.

2 Note that the fuel system on these engines uses a high-pressure fuel pump that does not have to be timed. The alignment of the fuel pump sprocket (and hence the fuel pump itself) with respect to crankshaft and camshaft position, is therefore less critical than on a conventional diesel engine.

3 To align the engine assembly/valve timing holes, proceed as follows.

4 Apply the handbrake, then jack up the front of the car and support it on axle stands (see *Jacking and vehicle support*). Remove the right-hand front roadwheel.

5 To gain access to the crankshaft pulley, to enable the engine to be turned, the wheel arch plastic liner must be removed. The liner is secured by several plastic expanding rivets. To remove the rivets, push in the centre pins a little, then prise the clips from place. Remove the liner from under the front wing. Where necessary, unclip the coolant hoses from under the wing to improve access further. The crankshaft can then be turned using a suitable socket and extension bar fitted to the pulley bolt.

6 Remove the timing belt upper and lower covers as described in Section 6.

7 Turn the crankshaft until the timing hole in the camshaft sprocket hub is aligned with the corresponding hole in the cylinder head (at approximately the 2 o'clock position). The crankshaft must always be turned in a clockwise direction (viewed from the right-hand side of car). When the hole is aligned with the corresponding hole in the cylinder head, the camshaft is positioned correctly.

8 Insert an 8 mm bolt, rod or drill through the hole in the camshaft sprocket hub and into engagement with the cylinder head **(see illustration)**.

9 Remove the crankshaft drivebelt pulley as described in Section 5.

10 Insert a 5 mm diameter bolt, rod or drill through the hole in crankshaft sprocket flange and into the corresponding hole in the oil pump **(see illustration)**, if necessary, carefully turn the crankshaft either way until the rod enters the timing hole in the block.

11 The crankshaft and camshaft are now locked in position, preventing unnecessary rotation.

4 Cylinder head cover/inlet manifold – removal and refitting

Removal

1 Remove the timing belt upper cover, as described in Section 6.

2 The cylinder head cover is integral with the inlet manifold and oil separator. Disconnect the mass airflow meter wiring plug **(see illustration)**.

3 Slacken the retaining clip, and remove the turbocharger outlet elbow **(see illustration)**.

4.2 Disconnect the mass airflow meter wiring plug

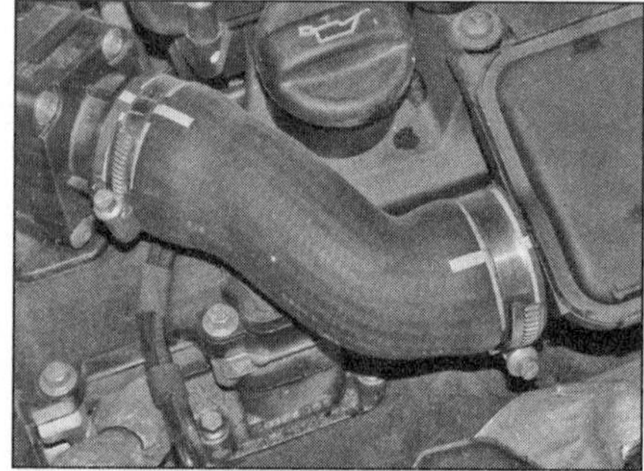

4.3 Slacken the retaining clamps and disconnect the turbo outlet hose

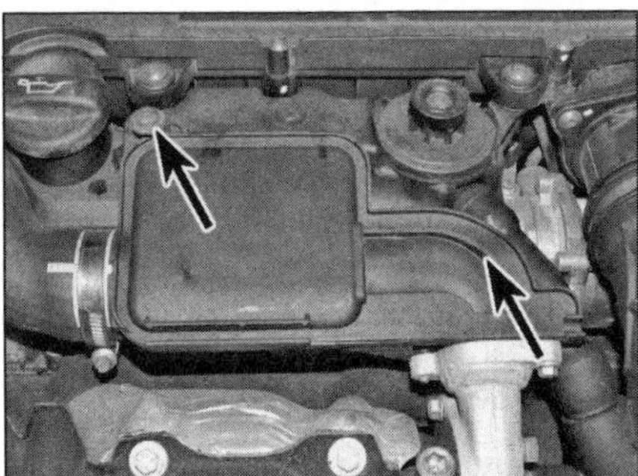

4.4a Undo the bolts (arrowed) and lift up the right-hand end ...

4.4b ... to disengage the resonator box from the turbocharger

4.6 Undo the two bolts (arrowed) and pull the air filter housing up from its place

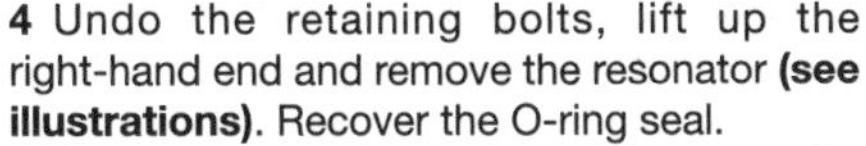

4.10 Depress the locking buttons (arrowed) and disconnect the fuel feed and return hoses

4.12 Undo the bolt securing the EGR pipe to the rear of the block (arrowed)

4.14a Undo the 8 bolts (arrowed) at the front ...

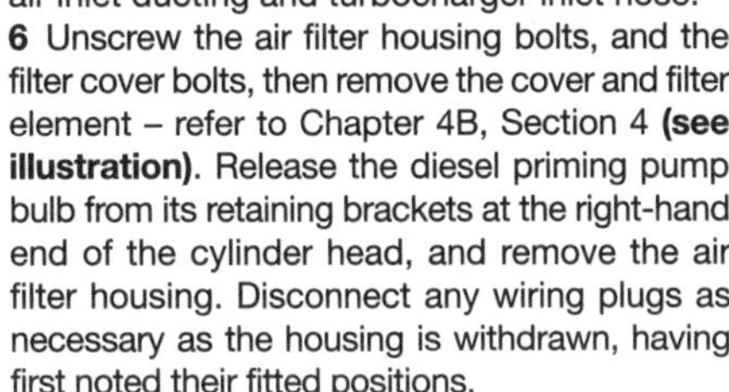

4 Undo the retaining bolts, lift up the right-hand end and remove the resonator **(see illustrations)**. Recover the O-ring seal.

5 Slacken the retaining clips and remove the air inlet ducting and turbocharger inlet hose.

6 Unscrew the air filter housing bolts, and the filter cover bolts, then remove the cover and filter element – refer to Chapter 4B, Section 4 **(see illustration)**. Release the diesel priming pump bulb from its retaining brackets at the right-hand end of the cylinder head, and remove the air filter housing. Disconnect any wiring plugs as necessary as the housing is withdrawn, having first noted their fitted positions.

7 Remove the diesel fuel filter as described in Chapter 1B, Section 17, then undo the three bolts securing the diesel filter support bracket.

8 Disconnect the wiring plugs from the top of each injector, then make sure all wiring harnesses are freed from any retaining brackets on the cylinder head cover/inlet manifold. Disconnect any vacuum pipes as necessary, having first noted their fitted positions.

9 Prise out the retaining clips and disconnect the fuel return pipes from the injectors. Plug the openings to prevent dirt ingress.

10 Disconnect the fuel feed and return pipes at the right-hand end of the cylinder head cover **(see illustration)**. Undo the Torx screw securing the fuel pipes bracket.

11 Unclip the fuel temperature sensor from the retaining bracket and move the pipe/priming bulb assembly to the rear.

12 Undo the two screws securing the EGR pipe to the cylinder head cover, and the bolt securing the pipe to the rear of the cylinder head **(see illustration)**.

13 Undo the two bolts securing the EGR valve to the left-hand end of the cylinder head, disconnect the vacuum hose, then remove the valve along with the EGR pipe. Recover the O-ring seal from the pipe.

14 Undo the eight bolts securing the cylinder head cover and inlet manifold at the front, and the two retaining bolts along the rear edge of the cover. Lift the assembly away **(see illustrations)**. Recover the manifold rubber seals.

Refitting

15 Refitting is a reversal of removal, bearing in mind the following points:

a) *Examine the cover seal(s) for signs of damage and deterioration, and renew if necessary. Smear a little clean engine oil on the manifold seals.*

b) *Tighten the cylinder head cover bolts to the specified torque, in order* ***(see illustration)****.*

4.14b ... and the two bolts (arrowed) at the rear

4.15 Cylinder head cover tightening sequence

5.1 Insert a drill or pin to lock the auxiliary drivebelt tensioner in position

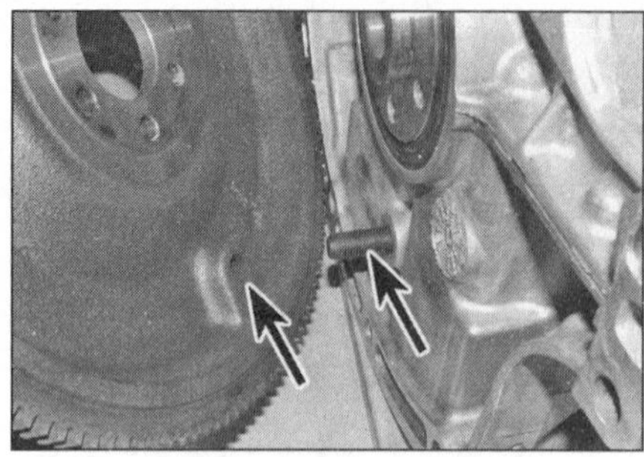

5.2 The locking pin/bolt (arrowed) must locate in the hole in the flywheel (arrowed) to prevent rotation

5.3 Undo the crankshaft pulley retaining bolt

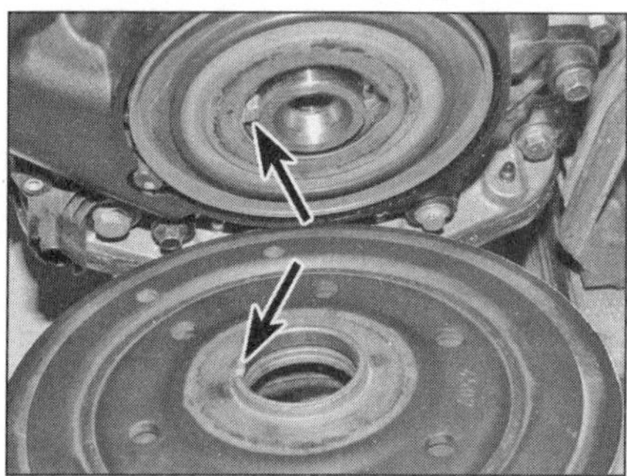

5.4 The notch in the pulley (arrowed) must align with the key in the sprocket (arrowed)

5 Crankshaft pulley – removal and refitting

Removal

1 Remove the auxiliary drivebelt as described in Chapter 1B, Section 22. Turn the tensioner anti-clockwise, and insert a pin or drill to hold it away from the drivebelt **(see illustration)**.

2 To lock the crankshaft, working underneath the engine, insert a 12 mm rod or drill bit into the hole in the right-hand face of the engine block casting over the lower section of the flywheel. Rotate the crankshaft until the tool engages in the corresponding hole in the flywheel **(see illustration)**. **Note:** *The hole in the casting and the hole in the flywheel are provided purely to lock the crankshaft whilst the pulley bolt is undone. It does **not** position the crankshaft at TDC.*

3 Using a suitable socket and extension bar, unscrew the retaining bolt, remove the washer, then slide the pulley off the end of the crankshaft **(see illustration)**. If the pulley is tight fit, it can be drawn off the crankshaft using a suitable puller. If a puller is being used, refit the pulley retaining bolt without the washer, to avoid damaging the crankshaft as the puller is tightened.

Caution: Do not touch the outer magnetic sensor ring of the sprocket with your fingers, or allow metallic particles to come into contact with it.

Refitting

4 Refit the pulley onto the crankshaft sprocket face, ensuring that the notch on the back of the pulley aligns with the key on the sprocket **(see illustration)**.

5 Thoroughly clean the threads of the pulley retaining bolt, then apply a coat of locking compound to the bolt threads.

6 Refit the crankshaft pulley retaining bolt and washer. Tighten the bolt to the specified torque, then through the specified angle, preventing the crankshaft using the locking rod method employed on removal.

7 Refit and tension the auxiliary drivebelt as described in Chapter 1B, Section 22.

6 Timing belt covers – removal and refitting

Caution: Refer to the precautions in Section 1 before proceeding.

Removal

Upper cover

1 Release the wiring harness and fuel pipes from the upper cover – cut any cable-ties used **(see illustration)**.

2 Undo the five screws and remove the timing belt upper cover **(see illustration)**.

Lower cover

3 Remove the upper cover as described previously.

4 Remove the crankshaft pulley as described in Section 5.

5 Undo the five bolts and remove the lower cover **(see illustration)**. Detach the wiring harness from the cover as necessary.

Refitting

6 Refitting is a reversal of removal, ensuring that each cover section is correctly located, and that the cover retaining bolts are securely tightened. Ensure that all disturbed hoses are reconnected and retained by their relevant clips.

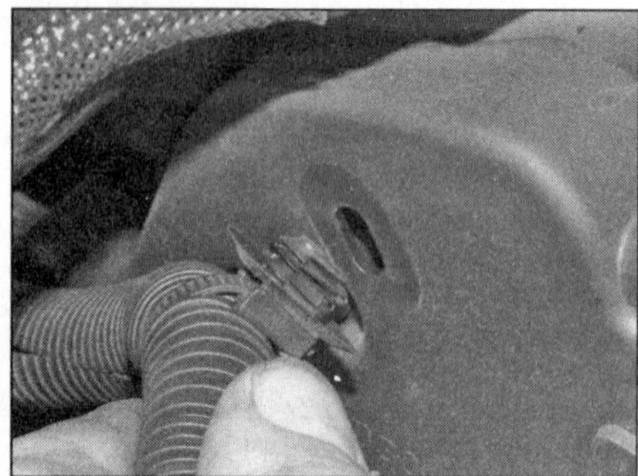

6.1 Release the wiring harness from the timing belt upper cover

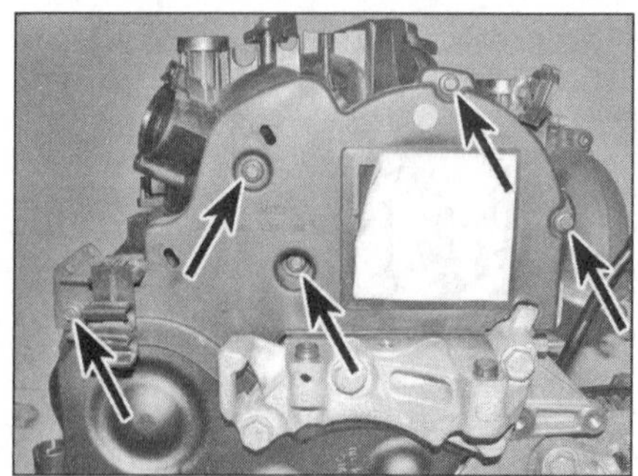

6.2 Undo the five screws (arrowed) and remove the upper timing belt cover

6.5 Lower cover retaining bolts (arrowed)

7 Timing belt – removal and refitting

General

1 The timing belt drives the camshaft, high-pressure fuel pump and water pump from a toothed sprocket on the end of the crankshaft. If the belt breaks or slips in service, the pistons are likely to hit the valve heads, resulting in expensive damage.

2 The timing belt should be renewed at the specified intervals, or earlier if it is contaminated with oil, or at all noisy in operation (a 'scraping' noise due to uneven wear).

3 If the timing belt is being removed, it is a wise precaution to check the condition of the water pump at the same time (check for signs of coolant leakage). This may avoid the need to remove the timing belt again at a later stage, should the water pump fail.

Removal

4 Disconnect the battery negative lead, and position the lead away from the battery (also see *Disconnecting the battery* in Chapter 5A, Section 2).

5 Drain the cooling system as described in Chapter 1B, Section 25.

6 Disconnect the small return hose from the coolant expansion tank, then remove the tank mounting bolt, and position the tank to one side.

7 Remove the timing belt upper cover as described in Section 6.

8 Remove the auxiliary drivebelt as described in Chapter 1B, Section 22.

9 Apply the handbrake, then jack up the front of the car and support it on axle stands (see *Jacking and vehicle support*). Remove the front right-hand roadwheel, wheel arch liner (to expose the crankshaft pulley) and the engine undershield.

10 Remove the crankshaft pulley as described in Section 5.

11 Remove the timing belt lower cover as described in Section 6, then refit the crankshaft pulley bolt.

12 Lock the crankshaft and camshaft in the correct position as described in Section 3.

13 Insert a hexagon key into belt tensioner pulley centre, slacken the pulley bolt, and allow the tensioner to rotate, relieving the belt tension **(see illustration)**. With the belt slack, temporarily tighten the pulley bolt. If the tensioner is being renewed with the belt, it can be removed completely.

14 Undo the retaining screw and remove the timing belt guide, again adjacent to the crankshaft sprocket flange **(see illustration)**.

15 Undo the crankshaft pulley bolt, and remove the crankshaft sprocket, recovering the Woodruff key.

Caution: Do not touch the outer magnetic sensor ring of the sprocket with your fingers, or allow metallic particles to come into contact with it.

7.13 Insert an Allen key into the hole (arrowed), slacken the pulley bolt and allow the tensioner to rotate

16 Position a trolley jack under the engine, and using a block of wood on the jack head, take the weight of the engine.

17 Lift the power steering fluid reservoir off its mounting bracket, and move it to one side, without disconnecting any hoses.

18 Remove the locking tool from the camshaft sprocket.

19 With the engine securely supported, remove the three nuts and three bolts securing the right-hand mounting, and lift it off. Three new nuts should be obtained for refitting the mounting.

20 Unbolt the engine right-hand mounting bracket from the engine (four bolts).

21 Note its routing, then remove the timing belt from the sprockets.

Inspection

22 Renew the belt as a matter of course, regardless of its apparent condition. The cost of a new belt is nothing compared with the cost of repairs should the belt break in service.

23 Check the old belt for signs of oil or coolant contamination – if any are found, trace the source of the leak and rectify it, then wash down the engine timing belt area and related components, to remove all traces of oil or coolant.

24 Check the sprockets for signs of wear or damage, and ensure that the tensioner and idler pulleys rotate smoothly; renew any worn or damaged components. Ford dealers (and many motor factors) now supply 'cambelt kits', consisting of the belt itself, a new tensioner and a new idler pulley – for peace of mind, it is recommended that one of these is purchased.

25 As stated previously, since the water pump is also driven by the timing belt, it pays to check its condition while the belt is off. If the pump pulley does not rotate freely and quietly, if there is the slightest sign of coolant leakage, or simply if the pump is known to have seen long service, it would make sense to fit a new pump at the same time (see Chapter 3, Section 7).

7.14 Timing belt protection bracket retaining bolt (arrowed)

Refitting

26 Refit the Woodruff key to the crankshaft nose, then fit the crankshaft sprocket. Ensure that the crankshaft and camshaft timing holes are aligned, and refit the locking pins.

27 Turn the fuel pump sprocket so that the two holes at the centre of the hub are aligned vertically.

28 Locate the timing belt on the crankshaft sprocket then, keeping it taut, locate it around the idler pulley, camshaft sprocket, fuel pump sprocket, water pump sprocket, and the tensioner pulley **(see illustration)**.

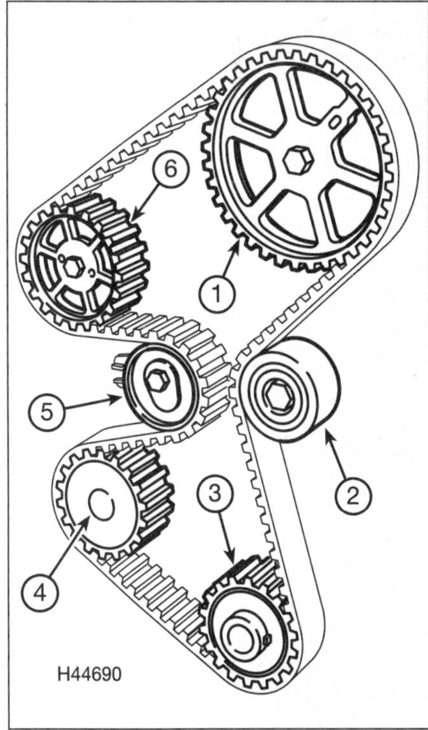

7.28 Timing belt routing

1 *Camshaft sprocket*
2 *Idler pulley*
3 *Crankshaft sprocket*
4 *Coolant pump sprocket*
5 *Tensioner pulley*
6 *High-pressure fuel pump sprocket*

7.30 Align the index arm (A) with the locating stud (B)

29 Refit the timing belt guide below the crankshaft sprocket, and tighten the retaining bolt securely.

30 Slacken the tensioner pulley bolt and, using an Allen key, rotate the tensioner anti-clockwise to tension the belt. As the belt is tensioned in this way, the tensioner's index arm will move clockwise, until the index arm is aligned **(see illustration)**.

31 Refit the engine right-hand mounting bracket, and tighten the bolts to the specified torque.

32 Refit the top section of the engine right-hand mounting bracket, using new nuts, and tightening the nuts and bolts to the specified torque. Now the trolley jack can be removed from under the car.

TOOL TIP

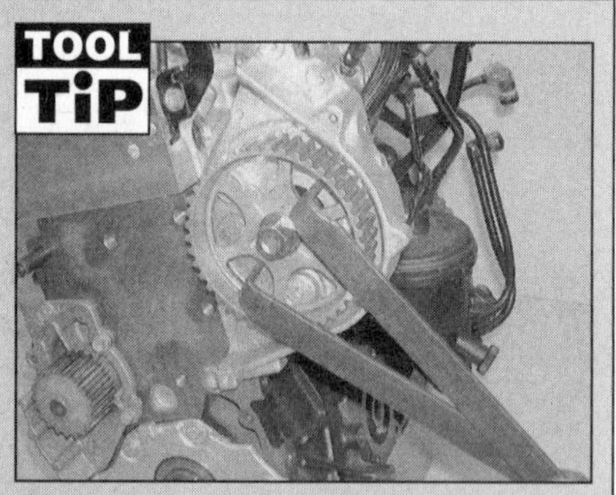

A sprocket holding tool can be made from two lengths of steel strip bolted together to form a forked end. Bend the end of the strip through 90° to form the fork 'prongs'.

33 Remove the camshaft and crankshaft timing pins and, using a socket on the crankshaft pulley bolt, rotate the engine clockwise ten complete revolutions. Refit the crankshaft and camshaft locking pins, and check that the fuel pump sprocket holes are aligned as described in paragraph 27.

34 Check that the tensioner index arm is still aligned between the sides of the 'window' behind it, and in line with the locating stud. If it is not, reset the tension as necessary, then repeat paragraph 33.

35 Lock the engine against rotation as described in Section 5, then remove the crankshaft pulley bolt.

36 Fit the crankshaft pulley and bolt, and tighten to the specified torque.

37 Refit the timing belt lower cover, re-attaching the crankshaft position sensor wiring harness as necessary.

38 Remove the locking tool from the flywheel, and lower the car to the ground.

39 The remainder of refitting is a reversal of removal. Tighten all fasteners to the specified torque where given.

8 Timing belt sprockets and tensioner – removal and refitting

Camshaft sprocket

Removal

1 Remove the timing belt as described in Section 7.

2 Remove the locking tool from the camshaft sprocket. Slacken the sprocket retaining bolt – to prevent the camshaft rotating as the bolt is slackened, a sprocket holding tool will be required **(see Tool Tip)**. *Do not* try to use the tool in the timing hole to prevent the sprocket from rotating while the bolt is slackened.

3 Remove the sprocket retaining bolt, then slide the sprocket off the end of the camshaft **(see illustration)**. Examine the camshaft oil seal for signs of oil leakage and, if necessary, renew it as described in Section 14.

4 Clean the camshaft sprocket thoroughly, and renew it if there are any signs of wear, damage or cracks.

Refitting

5 Refit the camshaft sprocket, aligning the lug on the back of the sprocket with the notch in the camshaft **(see illustration)**.

6 Refit the sprocket retaining bolt, and tighten it to the specified torque, preventing the camshaft from turning as during removal.

7 Align the engine assembly/valve timing hole in the camshaft sprocket with the hole in the cylinder head, and refit the timing pin to lock the camshaft in position.

8 Fit the timing belt as described in Section 7.

Crankshaft sprocket

Removal

9 Remove the timing belt as described in Section 7.

10 Check that the engine assembly/valve timing holes are still aligned as described in Section 3.

11 Slide the sprocket off the end of the crankshaft, and recover the Woodruff key if it is loose.

12 Examine the crankshaft oil seal for signs of oil leakage and, if necessary, renew it as described in Section 14.

13 Clean the crankshaft sprocket thoroughly, and renew it if there are any signs of wear, damage or cracks.

Refitting

14 Refit the crankshaft sprocket, locating it over the Woodruff key.

15 Fit the timing belt as described in Section 7.

Fuel pump sprocket

Removal

16 Remove the timing belt as described in Section 7.

17 Using a suitable socket, undo the pump sprocket retaining nut. The sprocket can be held stationary by inserting a suitably sized locking pin, drill or rod through the hole in the sprocket, and into the corresponding hole in the backplate **(see illustration)**, or by using a suitable forked tool engaged with the holes in the sprocket **(see Tool Tip in paragraph 2)**.

18 The pump sprocket is a taper fit on the pump shaft, and it will be necessary to make

8.3 Undo the retaining bolt and remove the camshaft sprocket

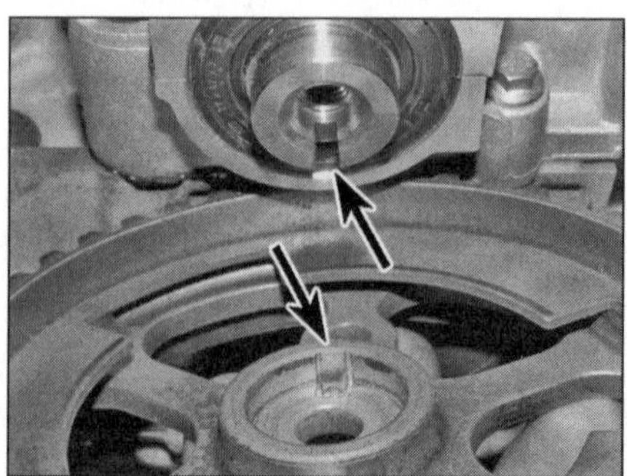

8.5 Align the sprocket lug with the notch in the end of the camshaft (arrowed)

8.17 Insert a suitable drill bit through the sprocket into the hole in the backplate

up another tool to release it from the taper **(see Tool Tip)**.

19 Partially unscrew the sprocket retaining nut, fit the home-made tool, and secure it to the sprocket with two suitable bolts. Prevent the sprocket from rotating as before, and unscrew the sprocket retaining nut. The nut will bear against the tool as it is undone, forcing the sprocket off the shaft taper. Once the taper is released, remove the tool, unscrew the nut fully, and remove the sprocket from the pump shaft.

20 Clean the sprocket thoroughly, and renew it if there are any signs of wear, damage or cracks.

Refitting

21 Refit the pump sprocket and retaining nut, and tighten the nut to the specified torque. Prevent the sprocket rotating using the sprocket holding tool as the nut is tightened.

22 Fit the timing belt as described in Section 7.

Water pump sprocket

23 The water pump sprocket is integral with the pump, and cannot be removed. Water pump removal is described in Chapter 3, Section 7.

Tensioner pulley

Removal

24 Remove the timing belt as described in Section 7.

25 Remove the tensioner pulley retaining bolt, and slide the pulley off its mounting stud.

26 Clean the tensioner pulley, but do not use any strong solvent which may enter the pulley bearings. Check that the pulley rotates freely, with no sign of stiffness or free play. Renew the pulley if there is any doubt about its condition, or if there are any obvious signs of wear or damage.

27 Examine the pulley mounting stud for signs of damage and if necessary, renew it.

Refitting

28 Refit the tensioner pulley to its mounting stud, and fit the retaining bolt.

29 Refit the timing belt as described in Section 7.

Idler pulley

Removal

30 Remove the timing belt as described in Section 7.

31 Undo the retaining bolt/nut and withdraw the idler pulley from the engine.

32 Clean the idler pulley, but do not use any strong solvent which may enter the bearings. Check that the pulley rotates freely, with no sign of stiffness or free play. Renew the idler pulley if there is any doubt about its condition, or if there are any obvious signs of wear or damage.

Refitting

33 Locate the idler pulley on the engine, and fit the retaining bolt/nut. Tighten the bolt/nut to the specified torque.

34 Refit the timing belt as described in Section 7.

Make a sprocket releasing tool from a short strip of steel. Drill two holes in the strip to correspond with the two holes in the sprocket. Drill a third hole just large enough to accept the flats of the sprocket retaining nut.

9 Camshaft, rocker arms and hydraulic tappets – removal, inspection and refitting

Removal

1 Drain the cooling system as described in Chapter 1B, Section 25.

2 Remove the cylinder head cover as described in Section 4.

3 Remove the camshaft sprocket as described in Section 8.

4 Refit the right-hand engine mounting, but only tighten the bolts moderately; this will keep the engine supported during the camshaft removal.

5 Undo the bolts and remove the vacuum pump. Recover the pump O-ring seals **(see illustration)**.

6 Protect the alternator against the risk of coolant being splashed onto it (a plastic bag of some kind will do), then unbolt and completely remove the coolant expansion tank from the inner wing.

7 Disconnect the wiring plug, unscrew the retaining bolt, and remove the camshaft position sensor from the cylinder head.

8 Working in a spiral pattern, progressively and evenly unscrew the twelve camshaft upper bearing housing bolts **(see illustration)**. Carefully lift the housing away.

9 Note the orientation of the camshaft, then lift it upwards from the housing and slide off and discard the oil seal.

10 To remove the rocker arms and hydraulic tappets, undo the thirteen bolts and remove the lower half of the camshaft bearing housing.

11 Obtain eight small, clean plastic containers, and number them 1 to 8; alternatively, divide a larger container into eight compartments.

12 Lift out each rocker arm. Place the rocker arms in their respective positions in the box or containers **(see illustration)**.

13 A compartmentalised container filled with engine oil is now required to retain the hydraulic tappets while they are removed from the cylinder head (plastic egg boxes might be suitable). Withdraw each hydraulic follower and place it in the container, keeping them each identified for correct refitting. The tappets must be totally submerged in the oil to prevent air entering them **(see illustration)**.

9.5 Undo the vacuum pump bolts (arrowed)

9.8 Upper camshaft bearing housing bolts (arrowed)

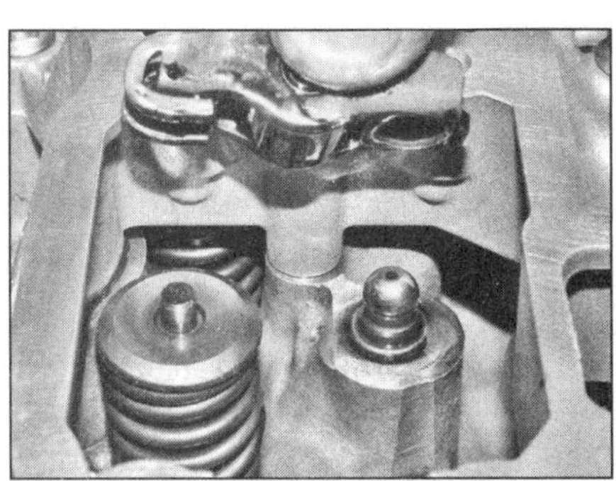

9.12 Remove the rocker arms

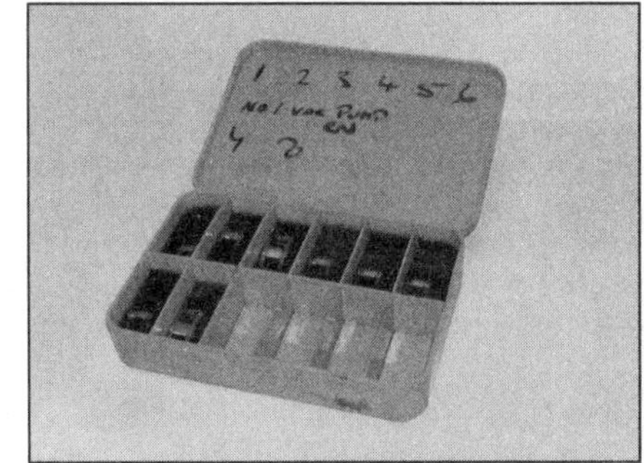

9.13 Place all the components in the respective positions in a box

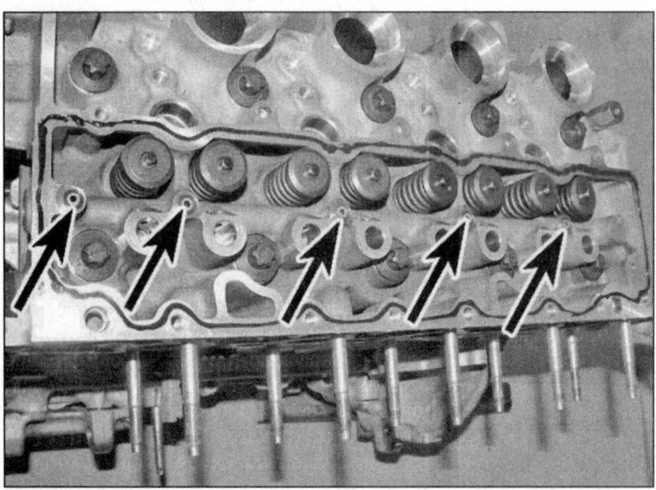

9.24 **Apply a bead of sealant, and fit the new O-rings (arrowed)**

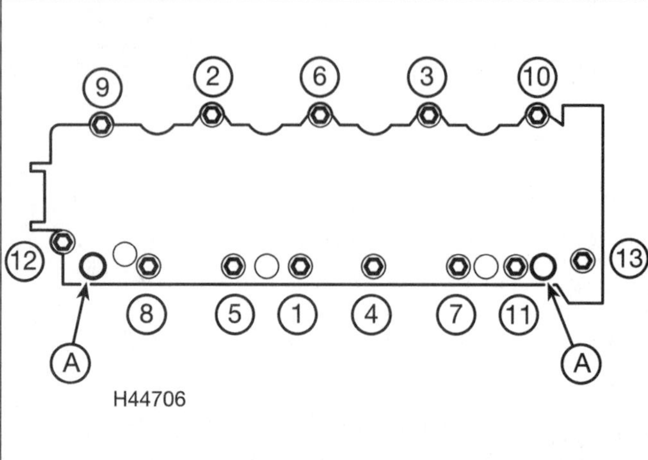

9.25 **Insert guide pins/rods into the guide holes (A), fit the housing and tighten the bolts in sequence**

14 Recover the five O-ring seals between the housing and the cylinder head.

Inspection

15 Inspect the cam lobes and the camshaft bearing journals for scoring or other visible evidence of wear. Once the surface hardening of the cam lobes has been eroded, wear will occur at an accelerated rate. **Note:** *If these symptoms are visible on the tips of the camshaft lobes, check the corresponding rocker arm, as it will probably be worn as well.*

16 Examine the condition of the bearing surfaces in the cylinder head and camshaft bearing housing. If wear is evident, the cylinder head and bearing housing will both have to be renewed, as they are a matched assembly.

17 Inspect the rocker arms and tappets for scuffing, cracking or other damage and renew any components as necessary. Also check the condition of the tappet bores in the cylinder head. As with the camshafts, any wear in this area will necessitate cylinder head renewal.

Refitting

18 Thoroughly clean the sealant from the mating surfaces of the cylinder head and camshaft bearing housing. Use a suitable liquid gasket dissolving agent (available from motor factors) together with a soft putty knife; do not use a metal scraper, or the faces will be damaged. As there is no conventional gasket used, the cleanliness of the mating faces is of the utmost importance.

19 Clean off any oil, dirt or grease from both components and dry with a clean lint-free cloth. Ensure that all the oilways are completely clean.

20 Ensure that the timing marks are aligned as described in Section 3 – in this position, the pistons are halfway down the cylinder bores.

21 Liberally lubricate the hydraulic tappet bores in the cylinder head with clean engine oil.

22 Insert the hydraulic tappets into their original bores in the cylinder head unless they have been renewed.

23 Lubricate the rocker arms, and place them over their respective tappets and valve stems.

24 Sparingly apply a bead of RTV sealant (such as Ford sealant WSE-M4G323-A4) to the mating face of the cylinder head-to-camshaft lower bearing housing, and position the five new O-ring seals **(see illustration)**. Make sure the sealant does not enter the blind holes in the cylinder head and housing, or damage may result. The housing should be fitted within four minutes of applying the sealant.

25 Insert two 12 mm rods or drill bits into the locating holes in the cylinder head to guide the bearing housing into position (Ford special tool number 303-034). Refit the lower bearing housing over the tools, insert the bolts and finger-tighten them in order **(see illustration)**.

26 Remove the guide pins/rods, and tighten the housing bolts in sequence to the specified torque.

27 Lubricate the camshaft bearing journals with clean engine oil, and lay the camshaft in position.

28 Sparingly apply a bead of RTV sealant to the mating face of the camshaft lower bearing housing **(see illustration)**.

29 Insert two 12 mm rods or drill bits into the locating holes in the lower camshaft bearing housing to guide the upper housing into position.

30 Lower the upper housing over the guide pins/rods, and finger-tighten the bolts gradually and evenly, in sequence, until the housing makes firm contact with the lower housing **(see illustration)**.

31 Remove the guides pins/rods, and tighten the housing to the specified torque in sequence.

32 Fit a new camshaft oil seal as described in Section 14.

33 Refit the camshaft sprocket to the camshaft, and tighten the bolt to the specified torque.

9.28 **Lay the camshaft in position, and apply a bead of sealant to the housing mating face**

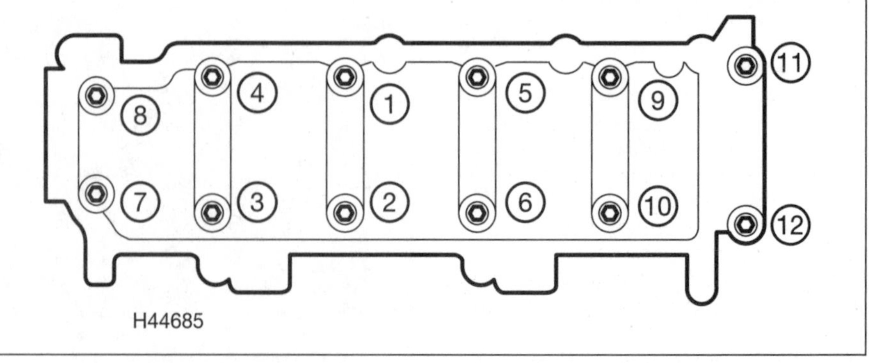

9.30 **Upper camshaft housing bolts tightening sequence**

34 Refit the camshaft position sensor to the camshaft housing. If necessary, turn the camshaft so that the sensor tip aligns with one of the three webs on the signal ring. Position the sensor so that the gap between the sprocket signal ring and the sensor end is 1.2 mm for a used sensor. If fitting a new sensor, the small tip of the sensor must be just touching one of the three webs of the signal ring **(see illustration)**. Tighten the bolt to the specified torque.
35 Turn the camshaft sprocket to the position where the timing tool can be inserted, then refit the timing belt as described in Section 7.
36 The remainder of refitting is a reversal of removal.

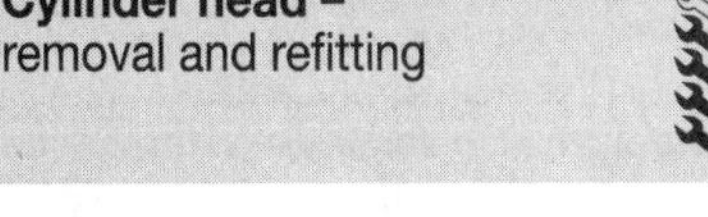

10 Cylinder head – removal and refitting

Note: *This is an involved procedure, and it is suggested that the Section is read thoroughly before starting work. To aid refitting, make notes on the locations of all relevant brackets and the routing of hoses and cables before removal.*

Removal

1 Apply the handbrake, then jack up the front of the car and support it on axle stands (see *Jacking and vehicle support*). Remove the front right-hand roadwheel, the engine undershield, and the front wheel arch liner. The undershield is secured by several screws, and the wheel arch liner is secured by several plastic expanding rivets. Push the centre pins in a little, then prise the rivet from place.
2 Remove the battery (see Chapter 5A, Section 4).
3 Drain the cooling system as described in Chapter 1B, Section 25. For improved general access, remove the bonnet as described in Chapter 11, Section 8.
4 Remove the cylinder head cover as described in Section 4.
5 Remove the timing belt as described in Section 7.
6 Disconnect the vacuum pipe from the brake vacuum pump.
7 Protect the alternator against the risk of coolant being splashed onto it (a plastic bag of some kind will do), then unbolt and completely remove the coolant expansion tank from the inner wing.
8 Unbolt and remove the heat shield from the catalytic converter – do not remove the two screws either side of the circular cut-outs.
9 Remove the turbocharger heat shield, which is secured by two bolts.
10 Remove the camshaft, rocker arms and hydraulic tappets as described in Section 9.
11 Disconnect either the vacuum hose or wiring plug from the EGR valve, as applicable.
12 Take out the four bolts securing the thermostat housing to the cylinder head, and remove the housing **(see illustration)**.

9.34 When fitting a used sensor, the gap between the sensor end and the sensor ring web should be 1.2 mm

13 Remove the rear retaining bolt from the power steering pump, then remove the two further bolts securing the pump to its mounting bracket. Move the pump away without disconnecting the hoses, and support it by tying it up.
14 Unbolt the power steering pump mounting bracket from the cylinder head.
15 Undo the union bolts and remove the oil feed pipe from the engine block and the turbocharger. Recover the union sealing washers.
16 Slacken the retaining clamp and disconnect the turbocharger oil return hose from the engine block.
17 Working from underneath, remove the four bolts securing the catalytic converter to the turbocharger, and separate the joint. **Note:** *Do not allow any strain to be placed on the flexible section of the exhaust pipe, as damage will result. Support the system using axle stands, bricks, etc.*
18 Remove the injectors as described in Chapter 4B, Section 12.
19 Working in the **reverse** of the tightening sequence **(see illustration 10.36)**, undo the cylinder head bolts by half a turn at a time, until they are all loose and can be removed. Discard the bolts once they're removed – new ones should be used when refitting.
20 Release the cylinder head from the cylinder block and location dowels by rocking it. Do not prise between the mating faces of the cylinder head and block, as this may damage the gasket faces – if the head is stuck, try rocking it upwards using a blunt instrument (eg, a suitable piece of wood) inserted into the inlet ports at the rear of the head.

10.12 Thermostat housing bolts (arrowed)

21 Lift the cylinder head from the block, and recover the gasket. Although the gasket cannot be re-used, it should be retained so that a new one of identical type can be obtained for refitting.

Inspection

22 The mating faces of the cylinder head and cylinder block must be perfectly clean before refitting the head. Use a hard plastic or wood scraper to remove all traces of gasket and carbon; also clean the piston crowns. Take particular care during the cleaning operations, as aluminium alloy is easily damaged.
23 Make sure that the carbon is not allowed to enter the oil and water passages – this is particularly important for the lubrication system, as carbon could block the oil supply to the engine's components. Using adhesive tape and paper, seal the water, oil and bolt holes in the cylinder block. To prevent carbon entering the gap between the pistons and bores, smear a little grease in the gap. After cleaning each piston, use a small brush to remove all traces of grease and carbon from the gap, then wipe away the remainder with a clean rag.
24 Check the mating surfaces of the cylinder block and the cylinder head for nicks, deep scratches and other damage. If slight, they may be removed carefully with a file, but if excessive, renewal is necessary as it is not permissible to machine the surfaces.
25 If warpage of the cylinder head gasket surface is suspected, use a straight-edge to check it for distortion. Refer to Chapter 2D, Section 8 if necessary.
26 If possible, clean out the bolt holes in the block using compressed air, to ensure no oil or water is present. Screwing a bolt into an oil or water-filled hole can (in extreme cases) cause the block to fracture, due to the hydraulic pressure created.
27 Although not essential, if a suitable tap and die set is available, it's worth running the correct size tap down the bolt threads in the cylinder block. This will clean the threads of any debris, and go some way to restoring any damaged threads. Make absolutely sure the tap is the right size and thread pitch, and lightly oil the tap before starting.
28 New head bolts must be used when refitting – re-using the old ones isn't worth the risk. If the bolts or their threads 'let go' when they're tightened, the bottom half of the engine could be reduced to scrap very quickly.
29 The head gasket has a series of notches along one edge, which denote its thickness **(see illustration)**. Ford state that the new gasket should have the same number of notches as the old one.

Refitting

30 Before fitting the head, make sure that the crankshaft sprocket timing holes are still aligned (check that the timing pin can be fitted). In this

10.29 Cylinder head gasket thickness identification notches (arrowed)

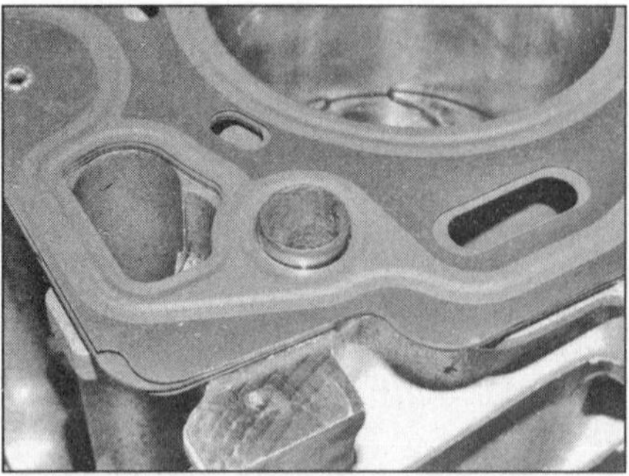
10.32 Ensure the gasket fits correctly over the locating dowels

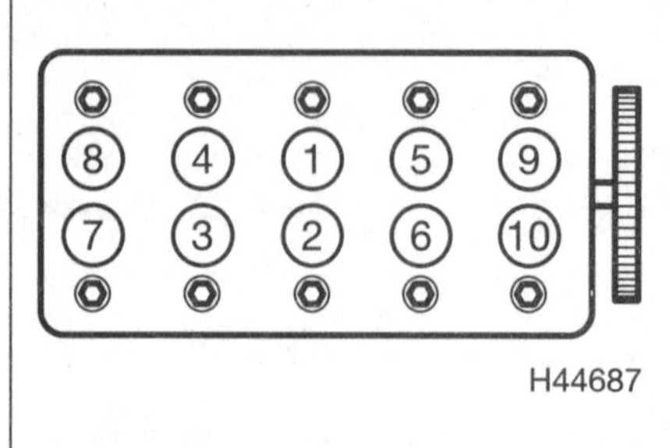

10.36 Cylinder head bolt tightening sequence

position, the pistons are halfway down the bores, which avoids the possibility of piston-to-valve contact when the head is fitted.

31 Wipe clean the mating surfaces of the cylinder head and cylinder block, and check that the two locating dowels are in position in the block.

32 Fit the new head gasket the right way round on the cylinder block **(see illustration)**.

33 Carefully lower the cylinder head onto the gasket and block, making sure that it locates correctly onto the dowels.

34 It is useful when refitting a cylinder head to have an assistant on hand, to help guide the head onto the dowels. Take care that the gasket does not get moved as the head is lowered into position. To confirm that the head is aligned correctly, once it is in place, temporarily slide in two or more of the head bolts, and check that they fit into the block holes.

35 Though it is not required by Ford, there is no harm in lightly oiling the threads of the head bolts before fitting them. This is particularly recommended if the block threads have not been cleaned with a tap and die set. Fit the head bolts carefully, and screw them in by hand only until finger-tight.

36 Working progressively and in sequence, tighten the cylinder head bolts to their Stage 1 torque setting, using a torque wrench and suitable socket **(see illustration)**.

37 Once all the bolts have been tightened to their Stage 1 torque setting, working again in the specified sequence, tighten each bolt to the specified Stage 2 setting. Finally, angle-tighten the bolts through the specified Stage 3 angle. It is recommended that an angle-measuring gauge is used during this stage of tightening, to ensure accuracy. **Note:** *Retightening of the cylinder head bolts after running the engine is not required.*

38 Refit the hydraulic tappets, rocker arms, and camshaft housing (complete with camshaft) as described in Section 9.

39 Refit the timing belt as described in Section 7.

40 The remainder of refitting is a reversal of removal, noting the following points:

a) Use new sealing washers when refitting the turbocharger oil feed pipe, and make sure the pipe is routed so that it is at least 15 mm away from the turbocharger housing.

b) When refitting a cylinder head, it is good practice to renew the thermostat.

c) Refit the camshaft position sensor and set the air gap with reference to Section 9.

d) Tighten all fasteners to the specified torque where given.

e) Refill the cooling system as described in Chapter 1B, Section 25.

f) The engine may run erratically for the first few miles, until the engine management ECU relearns its stored values.

11 Sump – removal and refitting

Removal

1 Drain the engine oil, then clean and refit the engine oil drain plug, tightening it securely. If the engine is nearing its service interval when the oil and filter are due for renewal, it is recommended that the filter is also removed, and a new one fitted. After reassembly, the engine can then be refilled with fresh oil. Refer to Chapter 1B, Section 3 for further information.

2 Apply the handbrake, then jack up the front of the car and support it on axle stands (see *Jacking and vehicle support*). Undo the screws and remove the engine undershield.

3 To improve access, remove the exhaust front pipe as described in Chapter 4B, Section 19.

4 Progressively slacken and remove the sixteen sump retaining bolts, and two nuts. Since the sump bolts vary in length, remove each bolt in turn, and store it in its correct fitted order by pushing it through a clearly marked cardboard template. This will avoid the possibility of installing the bolts in the wrong locations on refitting.

5 Try to break the joint by striking the sump with the palm of your hand, then lower and withdraw the sump from under the car. If the sump is stuck (which is quite likely) use a putty knife, or similar, carefully inserted between the sump and block. Ease the knife along the joint until the sump is released, taking care not to damage the mating faces.

6 While the sump is removed, take the opportunity to check the oil pump pick-up/strainer for signs of clogging or splitting. If necessary, remove the pump as described in Section 12, and clean or renew the strainer.

Refitting

7 Clean all traces of sealant from the mating surfaces of the cylinder block/crankcase and sump, then use a clean rag to wipe out the sump and the engine's interior.

8 Ensure that the sump mating surfaces are clean and dry, then apply a thin coating of suitable RTV sealant (such as Ford WSE-M4G323-A4) to the sump or crankcase mating surface **(see illustration)**. The sump should be fitted within four minutes of applying the sealant.

9 Offer up the sump to the cylinder block/crankcase. Refit its retaining nuts and bolts, ensuring that each bolt is screwed into its original location. Tighten the nuts and bolts evenly and progressively to the specified torque setting **(see illustration)**.

10 Lower the car to the ground, then refill the engine with oil as described in Chapter 1B, Section 3.

11.8 Apply a bead of sealant to the sump of crankcase mating surface

11.9 Refit the sump and tighten the bolts

12.5 Undo the three Allen bolts (arrowed) and remove the oil pick-up tube

12.6 Undo the eight bolts (arrowed) and remove the oil pump

12 Oil pump - removal, inspection and refitting

Removal

1 Remove the sump as described in Section 11.

2 Unscrew and remove the sump stud nearest the crankshaft sprocket end of the engine.

3 Remove the crankshaft sprocket as described in Section 8. Make sure the Woodruff key is removed from its slot in the crankshaft nose.

4 Disconnect the wiring plug, undo the bolts and remove the crankshaft position sensor, located on the right-hand end of the cylinder block.

5 Undo the three Allen bolts and remove the oil pump pick-up tube from the pump/block, complete with the dipstick guide tube **(see illustration)**. Discard the oil seal, a new one must be fitted.

6 Undo the eight bolts, and remove the oil pump **(see illustration)**.

Inspection

7 Undo and remove the Torx screws securing the cover to the oil pump **(see illustration)**. Examine the pump rotors and body for signs of wear and damage. If worn, the complete pump must be renewed.

8 Remove the circlip, and extract the cap, spring and valve piston, noting which way around they are fitted **(see illustrations)**. The condition of the relief valve spring can only be measured by comparing it with a new one; if there is any doubt about its condition, it should also be renewed.

9 Refit the relief valve piston, spring and cap, then secure them in place with the circlip.

10 Refit the cover to the oil pump, and tighten the Torx screws securely.

Refitting

11 Remove all traces of sealant, and thoroughly clean the mating surfaces of the oil pump and cylinder block.

12 Apply a 4 mm wide bead of RTV sealant (such as Ford WSE-M4G323-A4) to the mating face of the cylinder block **(see illustration)**. Ensure that no sealant enters any of the holes in the block. The pump should be fitted within four minutes of applying the sealant.

13 With a new oil seal fitted, refit the oil pump over the end of the crankshaft, aligning the flats

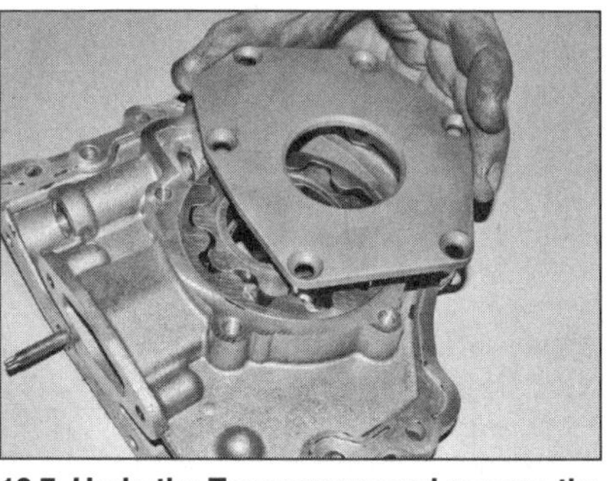
12.7 Undo the Torx screws and remove the pump cover

12.8a Remove the circlip ...

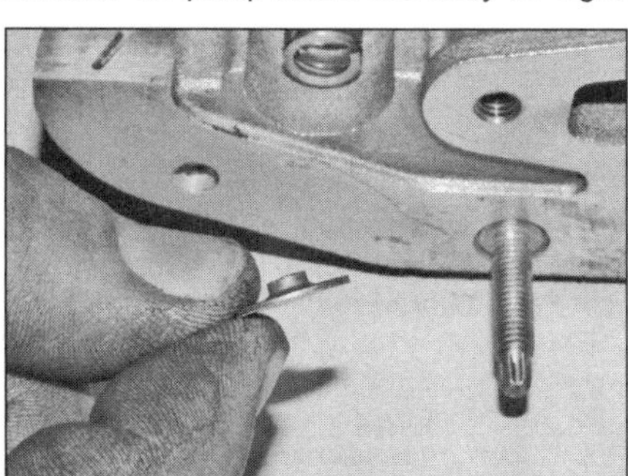
12.8b ... cap ...

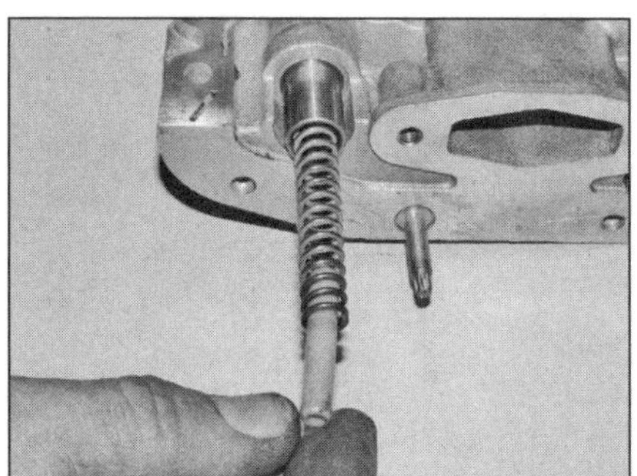
12.8c ... spring ...

12.8d ... and piston

12.12 Apply a bead of sealant to the cylinder block mating surface

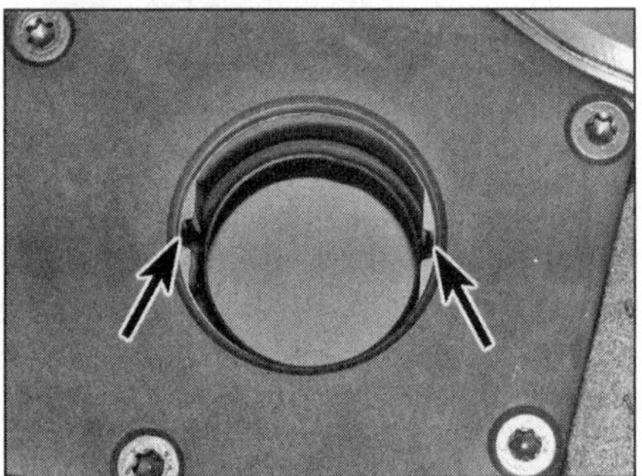

12.13b ... align the pump gear flats (arrowed) ...

in the pump drivegear with the flats machined in the crankshaft **(see illustrations)**. Note that new oil pumps are supplied with the oil seal already fitted, and a seal protector sleeve. The sleeve fits over the end of the crankshaft, to protect the seal as the pump is fitted.

13.4a Undo the bolts (arrowed), remove the oil cooler ...

13.4b ... and recover the O-ring seals

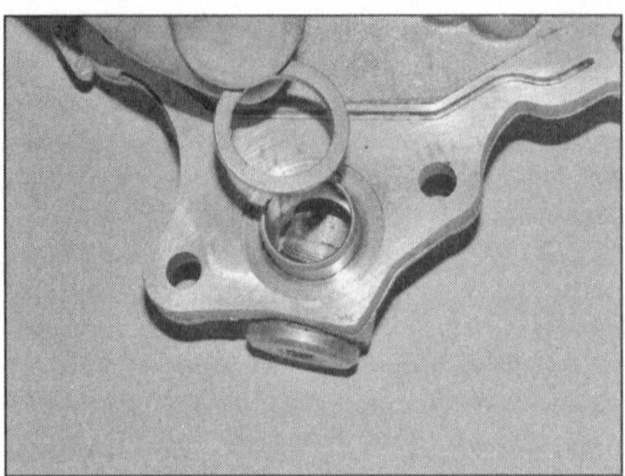

12.13a Fit a new oil seal ...

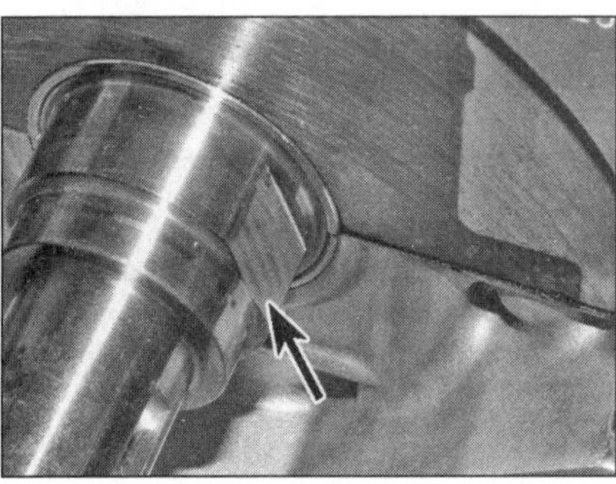

12.13c ... with those of the crankshaft (arrowed)

14 Install the oil pump bolts, and tighten them to the specified torque.

15 Refit the oil pick-up tube to the pump/cylinder block using a new O-ring seal. Ensure the oil dipstick guide tube is correctly refitted.

16 Refit the Woodruff key to the crankshaft, and slide the crankshaft sprocket into place.

17 The remainder of refitting is a reversal of removal.

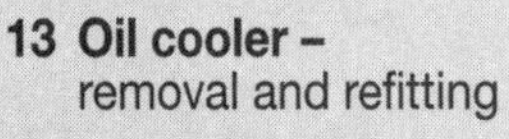

13 Oil cooler – removal and refitting

Removal

1 Apply the handbrake, then jack up the front of the car and support it on axle stands (see *Jacking and vehicle support*). Undo the screws and remove the engine undershield.

2 The oil cooler is fitted to the front of the oil filter housing. Drain the coolant as described in Chapter 1B, Section 25.

3 Drain the engine oil as described in Chapter 1B, Section 3, or be prepared for fluid spillage.

4 Undo the bolts and remove the oil cooler. Recover the O-ring seals **(see illustrations)**.

Refitting

5 Fit new O-ring seals into the recesses in the oil filter housing, and refit the cooler. Tighten the bolts securely.

6 Refill or top-up the cooling system and engine oil level as described in Chapter 1B, Section 3 and 25 or Weekly checks (as applicable). Start the engine, and check the oil cooler for signs of leakage.

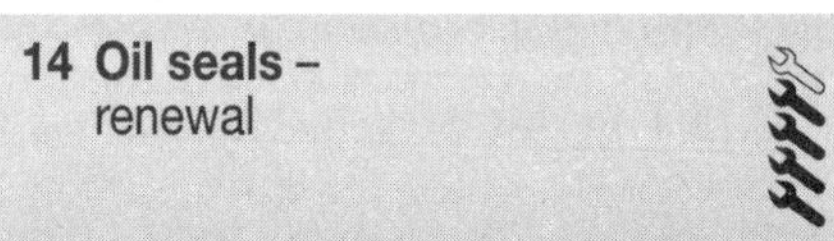

14 Oil seals – renewal

Crankshaft right-hand oil seal

1 Remove the crankshaft sprocket as described in Section 8.

2 Measure and note the fitted depth of the oil seal.

3 Pull the oil seal from the housing using a hooked instrument. Alternatively, drill a small hole in the oil seal, and use a self-tapping screw and a pair of pliers to remove it **(see illustration)**.

4 Clean the oil seal housing and the crankshaft sealing surface.

5 The new seal has a Teflon lip, and must not be oiled or marked. The new seal should be supplied with a protector sleeve, which fits over the end of the crankshaft to prevent any damage to the seal lip. With the sleeve in place, press the seal (open end first) into the pump to the previously-noted depth, using a suitable tube or socket.

6 Refit the crankshaft sprocket as described in Section 8.

Crankshaft left-hand oil seal

7 Remove the flywheel as described in Section 16.

8 Measure and note the fitted depth of the oil seal.

9 Pull the oil seal from the housing using a hooked instrument. Alternatively, drill a small hole in the oil seal, and use a self-tapping screw and a pair of pliers to remove it **(see illustration 14.3)**.

10 Clean the oil seal housing and the crankshaft sealing surface.

11 The new seal has a Teflon lip, and must not be oiled or marked. The new seal should be supplied with a protector sleeve, which fits over the end of the crankshaft to prevent any damage to the seal lip **(see illustration)**. With the sleeve in place, press the seal (open end first) into the housing to the previously-noted depth, using a suitable tube or socket.

12 Refit the flywheel as described in Section 16.

14.3 Drill a hole then use a self-tapping screw and pliers to extract the oil seal

Camshaft oil seal

13 Remove the camshaft sprocket as described in Section 8. In principle, there is no need to remove the timing belt completely, but remember that if the belt has been contaminated with oil from a leaking seal, it must be renewed.

14 Pull the oil seal from the housing using a hooked instrument. Alternatively, drill a small hole in the oil seal and use a self-tapping screw and a pair of pliers to remove it **(see illustration 14.3)**.

15 Clean the oil seal housing and the camshaft sealing surface.

16 The seal has a Teflon lip, and must not be oiled or marked. The new seal should be supplied with a protector sleeve. which fits over the end of the camshaft to prevent any damage to the seal lip **(see illustration)**. With the sleeve in place, press the seal (open end first) into the housing to the previously-noted depth, using a suitable tube or socket which bears only of the outer edge of the seal.

17 Refit the camshaft sprocket as described in Section 8.

18 Where necessary, fit a new timing belt with reference to Section 7.

15 Oil pressure switch – removal and refitting

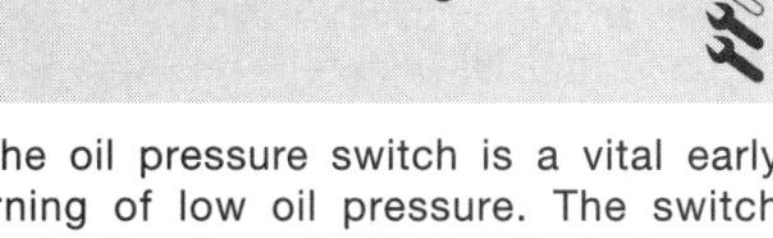

1 The oil pressure switch is a vital early warning of low oil pressure. The switch operates the oil warning light on the instrument panel – the light should come on with the ignition, and go out almost immediately when the engine starts.

2 If the light does not come on, there could be a fault on the instrument panel, the switch wiring, or the switch itself. If the light does not go out, low oil level, worn oil pump (or sump pick-up blocked), blocked oil filter, or worn main bearings could be to blame – or again, the switch may be faulty.

3 If the light comes on while driving, the best advice is to turn the engine off immediately, and not to drive the car until the problem has been investigated – ignoring the light could mean expensive engine damage.

Removal

4 The oil pressure switch is located at the front of the cylinder block, adjacent to the oil dipstick guide tube. If preferred, access to the switch may be gained from below, with the car jacked up and the engine undershield removed (see *Jacking and vehicle support*).

5 Remove the protective sleeve from the wiring plug (where applicable), then disconnect the wiring from the switch.

6 Unscrew the switch from the cylinder block, and recover the sealing washer **(see illustration)**. Be prepared for oil spillage (as the switch is well above the oil level in the sump, this should be virtually nil). If the switch is to be left removed from the engine for any

14.11 The new oil seal comes with a protective sleeve (arrowed) which fits over the end of the crankshaft

length of time, plug the hole in the cylinder block.

Inspection

7 Examine the switch for signs of cracking or splits. If the top part of the switch is loose, this is an early indication of impending failure.

8 Check that the wiring terminals at the switch are not loose, then trace the wire from the switch connector until it enters the main loom – any wiring defects will give rise to apparent oil pressure problems.

Refitting

9 Refitting is the reverse of the removal procedure, noting the following points:

a) Use a new sealing washer, and tighten the switch securely.

b) Reconnect the switch connector, making sure it clicks home properly. Ensure that the wiring is routed away from any hot or moving parts.

c) Check the engine oil level and top-up if necessary (see 'Weekly checks').

d) Check for signs of oil leaks once the engine has been restarted and warmed up to normal operating temperature.

16 Flywheel – removal, inspection and refitting

Removal

1 Remove the transmission as described in Chapter 7A, Section 7, then remove the clutch assembly as described in Chapter 6, Section 7.

15.6 The oil pressure switch is on the front face of the cylinder block

14.16 The new oil seal comes with a protective sleeve (arrowed) which fits over the end of the camshaft

2 To lock the crankshaft and stop the flywheel turning as the bolts are undone, working underneath the engine, insert a 12 mm rod or drill bit into the hole in the right-hand face of the engine block casting over the lower section of the flywheel. Rotate the crankshaft until the tool engages in the corresponding hole in the flywheel **(see illustration 5.2)**.

3 Make alignment marks between the flywheel and crankshaft to aid refitment. Slacken and remove the flywheel retaining bolts, and remove the flywheel from the end of the crankshaft. Be careful not to drop it; it is heavy. If the flywheel locating dowel (where fitted) is a loose fit in the crankshaft end, remove it and store it with the flywheel for safe keeping. Discard the flywheel bolts; new ones must be used on refitting.

Inspection

4 Examine the flywheel for scoring of the clutch face, and for wear or chipping of the ring gear teeth. If the clutch face is scored, the flywheel may be surface-ground, but renewal is preferable. Seek the advice of a Ford dealer or engine reconditioning specialist to see if machining is possible. If the ring gear is worn or damaged, the flywheel must be renewed, as it is not possible to renew the ring gear separately.

5 Where a dual mass flywheel is fitted it must be renewed if there is any evidence of fluid or grease on the flywheel or clutch components. The following procedures are given for guidance only. If in doubt as to the condition of the flywheel a professional inspection is recommended. If the assembly passes all the checks listed and there was no juddering from the clutch when taking up the drive, the flywheel can be refitted. However if the vehicle has covered a high mileage and especially if the vehicle is on its second new clutch, then it would be prudent to renew the dual mass flywheel.

Warpage

Check the drive surface for any signs of warpage or damage **(see illustration)**. The flywheel will normally warp like a bowl – ie, higher at the circumference. If the warpage

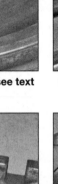

16.5a Flywheel warpage check – see text

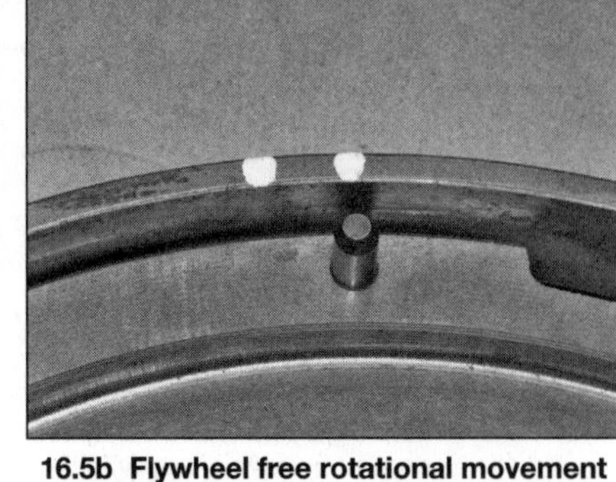

16.5b Flywheel free rotational movement check alignment marks – see text

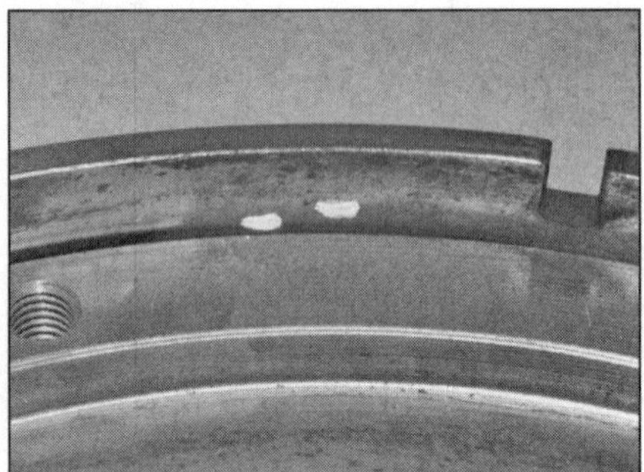

16.5c Flywheel lateral movement check marks – see text

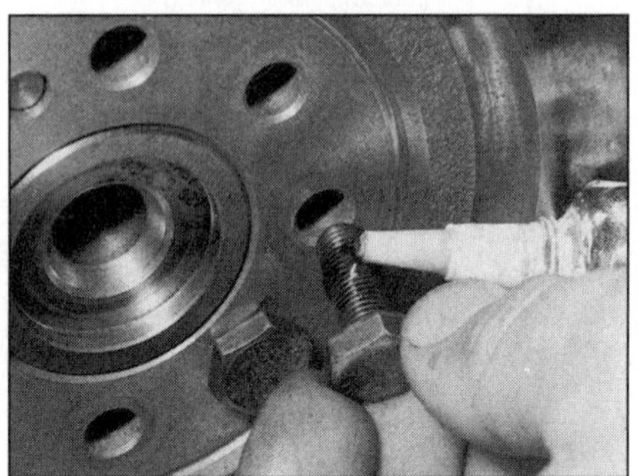

16.7 If the new bolts are not supplied with their threads precoated, apply thread-locking compound

is more than 4.0 mm consider renewing the flywheel.

Free rotational movement

This is the distance the drive surface of the flywheel can be turned independently of the flywheel primary element, using finger pressure only. Move the drive surface in one direction and make a mark where the locating pin aligns with the flywheel edge. Move the drive surface in the other direction (finger pressure only) and make another mark **(see illustration)**. The total of free movement should not exceed 10 mm. If it is more consider renewing the flywheel.

Total rotational movement

This is the total distance the drive surface can be turned independently of the flywheel primary elements. Insert two bolts into the clutch pressure/plate damper unit mounting holes and with the crankshaft flywheel held stationary user a pry bar between the bolts and use some effort to move the drive surface fully in one direction. Make a mark where the locating pin aligns with the flywheel edge. Now force the drive surface fully in the opposite direction, and make another mark. The total rotational movement should not exceed 44.0 mm. If it does have the flywheel professionally inspected.

Lateral movement

The lateral movement (up and down) of the drive surface in relation to the primary element of the flywheel should not exceed 2.0 mm, if it does the flywheel may need renewing. This can be checked by pressing the drive surface down on one side into the flywheel (flywheel horizontal) and making an alignment mark between the drive surface and the inner edge of the primary elements. Now press down on the opposite side of the drive surface and make another mark above the original one. The difference between the two marks is the lateral movement **(see illustration)**.

Refitting

6 Clean the mating surfaces of the flywheel and crankshaft. Remove any remaining locking compound from the threads of the crankshaft holes, using the correct size tap, if available.

7 If the new flywheel retaining bolts are not supplied with precoated threads, apply a suitable thread-locking compound to the threads of each bolt **(see illustration)**.

8 Ensure that the locating dowel is in position. Offer up the flywheel, locating it on the dowel (where fitted) and fit the new retaining bolts. Where no locating dowel is fitted, align the previously-made marks to ensure the flywheel is refitted in its original position.

9 Lock the flywheel using the method employed on dismantling, and tighten the retaining bolts to the specified torque.

10 Refit the clutch as described in Chapter 6, Section 7. Remove the flywheel locking tool, and refit the transmission as described in Chapter 7A, Section 7.

17 Engine/transmission mountings – inspection and renewal

Refer to Chapter 2A, Section 18.

Chapter 2 Part C:
1.6 litre diesel engine in-car repair procedures

Contents

Degrees of difficulty

Easy, suitable for novice with little experience	**Fairly easy,** suitable for beginner with some experience	**Fairly difficult,** suitable for competent DIY mechanic	**Difficult,** suitable for experienced DIY mechanic	**Very difficult,** suitable for expert DIY or professional 

Specifications

Note: *At the time of writing, some specifications were not available. Where the relevant specifications are not given here, refer to your Ford dealer for further information.*

General

Designation	Duratorq
Engine codes:*	
Emission level 3	HHJA
Emission level 4	HHJB
Capacity	1560 cc
Bore	75.0 mm
Stroke	88.3 mm
Direction of crankshaft rotation	Clockwise (viewed from the right-hand side of vehicle)
No 1cylinder location	At the transmission end of block
Maximum power output	66 kW @ 4000 rpm
Maximum torque output	195 Nm @ 2000 rpm
Compression ratio	18.0 :1

* *The engine code is stamped on a plate attached to the front of the cylinder block, next to the oil filter*

Compression pressures (engine hot, at cranking speed)

Normal	20 ± 5 bar
Minimum	15 bar
Maximum difference between any two cylinders	5 bar

Camshafts

Drive:	
Inlet camshaft	Toothed belt from crankshaft
Exhaust camshaft	Chain-drive from inlet camshaft
Endfloat	0.195 to 0.300 mm

Cylinder head

Maximum gasket face distortion	0.025 mm
Cylinder head height:	
Nominal	124 ± 0.05 mm
Minimum (after grinding)	Not available

Valves

	Inlet	Exhaust
Valve stem diameter	5.485 +0.0 -0.015 mm	5.475 +0.0 -0.015 mm
Overall length	96.43 ± 0.25 mm	96.65 ± 0.2 mm

Cylinder block

Cylinder bore diameter (reboring not possible)	75.000 to 75.018 mm

Pistons

Clearance in bores	0.164 to 0.196 mm

Piston rings

End gaps:	
Top compression ring	0.20 to 0.35 mm
Second compression ring	0.20 to 0.40 mm
Oil control ring	0.85 to 1.00 mm

Crankshaft

Endfloat	0.10 to 0.3 mm
Big end radial clearance	0.024 to 0.070 mm
Main bearing radial clearance	0.017 to 0.043 mm

Lubrication system

Oil pump type	Gear-type, driven directly by the right-hand end of the crankshaft, by two flats machined along the crankshaft journal.
Minimum oil pressure at 80°C:	
1000 rpm	1.3 bar
4000 rpm	3.5 bar

Torque wrench settings

	Nm	lbf ft
Auxiliary drivebelt tensioner	25	18
Big-end bolts:*		
Stage 1	10	7
Stage 2	Slacken 180°	
Stage 3	10	7
Stage 4	Angle-tighten a further 130°	
Camshaft bearing caps	10	7
Camshaft cover/bearing ladder:		
Studs	10	7
Bolts	10	7
Camshaft position sensor bolt	5	4
Camshaft sprocket	43	32
Coolant outlet housing bolts	7	6
Crankshaft position/speed sensor bolt	5	4
Crankshaft pulley/sprocket bolt:*		
Stage 1	30	22
Stage 2	Angle-tighten a further 180 °	
Cylinder head bolts:*		
Stage 1	20	15
Stage 2	40	30
Stage 3	Angle-tighten a further 260°	
Cylinder head cover/inlet manifold	10	7
EGR valve	10	7
Engine mountings:		
Rear engine/transmission mounting:		
Connecting link to mounting assembly	48	35
Connecting link-to-subframe nut/bolt	48	35
Mounting to engine	48	35
Right-hand engine mounting:		
Mounting to body	48	35
Mounting to support bracket	48	35
Support bracket to engine	55	41
Left-hand engine/transmission mounting:		
Mounting bracket to transmission	48	35
Mounting to bracket	90	66
Engine-to-transmission fixing bolts	47	35
Flywheel bolts:*		
Vehicles with a dual mass flywheel:		
Stage 1	30	22
Stage 2	Angle-tighten a further 90°	
Vehicles without a dual mass flywheel:		
Stage 1	17	13
Stage 2	Angle-tighten a further 75°	

Torque wrench settings (continued)	Nm	lbf ft
Fuel pump sprocket	50	37
Main bearing ladder outer seam bolts:		
Stage 1	5	4
Stage 2	10	7
Main bearing ladder to cylinder block:		
Stage 1	10	7
Stage 2	Slacken 180°	
Stage 3	30	22
Stage 4	Angle-tighten a further 140°	
Oil filter cover	25	18
Oil pick-up pipe	10	7
Oil pressure switch	30	22
Oil pump to cylinder block	10	7
Piston oil jet spray tube bolt	20	15
Sump bolts/nuts	10	7
Sump drain plug	34	25
Timing belt idler pulley	37	27
Timing belt tensioner pulley	30	22
Timing chain tensioner	10	7
Vacuum pump mounting bolts	18	13

* *Do not re-use*

1 General information

How to use this Chapter

This Chapter describes the repair procedures that can reasonably be carried out on the engine while it remains in the vehicle. If the engine has been removed from the vehicle and is being dismantled as described in Chapter 2D, any preliminary dismantling procedures can be ignored.

Note that, while it may be possible physically to overhaul items such as the piston/connecting rod assemblies while the engine is in the car, such tasks are not usually carried out as separate operations. Usually, several additional procedures are required (not to mention the cleaning of components and oilways); for this reason, all such tasks are classed as major overhaul procedures, and are described in Chapter 2D.

Chapter 2D describes the removal of the engine/transmission from the car, and the full overhaul procedures that can then be carried out.

Engine description

The 1.6 litre Duratorq engine is the result of development collaboration between Ford and Citroën/Peugeot. The engine is of double overhead camshaft (DOHC) 16-valve design. The direct injection, turbocharged, four-cylinder engine is mounted transversely, with the transmission mounted on the left-hand side.

A toothed timing belt drives the inlet camshaft, high-pressure fuel pump and coolant pump. The inlet camshaft drives the exhaust camshaft via a chain. The camshafts operate the inlet and exhaust valves via rocker arms which are supported at their pivot ends by hydraulic self-adjusting tappets. The camshafts are supported by bearings machined directly in the cylinder head and camshaft bearing housing.

The high-pressure fuel pump supplies fuel to the fuel rail, and subsequently to the electronically controlled injectors which inject the fuel direct into the combustion chambers. This design differs from the previous type where an injection pump supplies the fuel at high-pressure to each injector. The earlier, conventional type injection pump required fine calibration and timing, and these functions are now completed by the high-pressure pump, electronic injectors and engine management ECM.

The crankshaft runs in five main bearings of the usual shell type. Endfloat is controlled by thrustwashers either side of No 2 main bearing.

The pistons are selected to be of matching weight, and incorporate fully-floating gudgeon pins retained by circlips.

Repair operations precaution

The engine is a complex unit with numerous accessories and ancillary components. The design of the engine compartment is such that every conceivable space has been utilised, and access to virtually all of the engine components is extremely limited. In many cases, ancillary components will have to be removed, or moved to one side, and wiring, pipes and hoses will have to be disconnected or removed from various cable clips and support brackets.

When working on this engine, read through the entire procedure first, look at the car and engine at the same time, and establish whether you have the necessary tools, equipment, skill and patience to proceed. Allow considerable time for any operation, and be prepared for the unexpected.

Because of the limited access, many of the engine photographs appearing in this Chapter were, by necessity, taken with the engine removed from the vehicle.

Warning: It is essential to observe strict precautions when working on the fuel system components of the engine, particularly the high-pressure side of the system. Before carrying out any engine operations that entail working on, or near, any part of the fuel system, refer to the special information given in Chapter 4B, Section 2.

Operations with engine in car

a) Compression pressure – testing.
b) Cylinder head cover/inlet manifold – removal and refitting.
c) Crankshaft pulley – removal and refitting.
d) Timing belt covers – removal and refitting.
e) Timing belt – removal, refitting and adjustment.
f) Timing belt tensioner and sprockets – removal and refitting.
g) Camshaft oil seal – renewal.
h) Camshafts, rocker arms and hydraulic tappets – removal, inspection and refitting.
i) Sump – removal and refitting.
j) Oil pump – removal and refitting.
k) Crankshaft oil seals – renewal.
l) Engine/transmission mountings – inspection and renewal.
m) Flywheel – removal, inspection and refitting.

3.9 Insert a 5.0 mm drill bit/bolt through the round hole in the sprocket flange, into the hole in the oil pump housing (lower timing belt cover removed for clarity)

3.10 Insert an 8.0 mm drill bit/bolt through the hole in the camshaft sprocket into the corresponding hole in the cylinder head

2 Compression and leakdown tests – description and interpretation

Compression test

Note: *A compression tester specifically designed for diesel engines must be used for this test.*

1 When engine performance is down, or if misfiring occurs which cannot be attributed to the fuel system, a compression test can provide diagnostic clues as to the engine's condition. If the test is performed regularly, it can give warning of trouble before any other symptoms become apparent.

2 A compression tester specifically intended for diesel engines must be used, because of the higher pressures involved. On this engine, an adapter suitable for use in the glow plug holes will be required, so as not to disturb the fuel system components. It is unlikely to be worthwhile buying such a tester for occasional use, but it may be possible to borrow or hire one – if not, have the test performed by a garage.

3 Unless specific instructions to the contrary are supplied with the tester, observe the following points:

a) The battery must be in a good state of charge, the air filter must be clean, and the engine should be at normal operating temperature.

b) All the glow plugs should be removed as described in Chapter 5C, Section 2 before starting the test.

c) The wiring connectors on the engine management system PCM (located behind the front left-hand headlight) must be disconnected.

4 The compression pressures measured are not so important as the balance between cylinders. Values are given in the Specifications.

5 The cause of poor compression is less easy to establish on a diesel engine than on a petrol one. The effect of introducing oil into the cylinders ('wet' testing) is not conclusive, because there is a risk that the oil will sit in the swirl chamber or in the recess on the piston crown instead of passing to the rings. However, the following can be used as a rough guide to diagnosis.

6 All cylinders should produce very similar pressures; any difference greater than that specified indicates the existence of a fault. Note that the compression should build-up quickly in a healthy engine; low compression on the first stroke, followed by gradually increasing pressure on successive strokes, indicates worn piston rings. A low compression reading on the first stroke, which does not build-up during successive strokes, indicates leaking valves or a blown head gasket (a cracked head could also be the cause). Deposits on the undersides of the valve heads can also cause low compression.

7 A low reading from two adjacent cylinders is almost certainly due to the head gasket having blown between them; the presence of coolant in the engine oil will confirm this.

8 If the compression reading is unusually high, the cylinder head surfaces, valves and pistons are probably coated with carbon deposits. If this is the case, the cylinder head should be removed and decarbonised (see Chapter 2D, Section 8).

Leakdown test

9 A leakdown test measures the rate at which compressed air fed into the cylinder is lost. It is an alternative to a compression test, and in many ways it is better, since the escaping air provides easy identification of where pressure loss is occurring (piston rings, valves or head gasket).

10 The equipment needed for leakdown testing is unlikely to be available to the home mechanic. If poor compression is suspected, have the test performed by a suitably-equipped garage.

3 Engine assembly/valve timing holes – general information and usage

Note: *Do not attempt to rotate the engine whilst the crankshaft and camshaft are locked in position. If the engine is to be left in this state for a long period of time, it is a good idea to place suitable warning notices inside the vehicle, and in the engine compartment. This will reduce the possibility of the engine being accidentally cranked on the starter motor, which is likely to cause damage with the locking pins in place.*

General

1 Timing holes or slots are located in the crankshaft pulley flange, camshaft sprocket hub and high-pressure fuel pump sprocket. The holes/slots are used to position the pistons halfway up the cylinder bores. This will ensure that the valve timing is maintained during operations that require removal and refitting of the timing belt. When the holes/slots are aligned with their corresponding holes in the cylinder block and cylinder head, suitable diameter bolts/pins can be inserted to lock the crankshaft and camshaft in position, preventing rotation.

2 Note that the type of fuel system used on these engines does not have a conventional diesel injection pump, but instead uses a high-pressure fuel pump. Although it may be argued that timing of the fuel pump is irrelevant because it merely pressurises the fuel in the fuel rail, Ford include this procedure using the same timing rod/pin used for crankshaft sprocket timing. In addition, note that the hole in the fuel pump sprocket only aligns correctly with the hole in the mounting bracket every 12 revolutions of the crankshaft (or every 6 revolutions of the camshaft sprocket).

3 To align the engine assembly/valve timing holes, proceed as follows.

4 Apply the handbrake, then jack up the front of the vehicle and support it on axle stands (see *Jacking and vehicle support*). Remove the right-hand front roadwheel.

5 To gain access to the crankshaft pulley, to enable the engine to be turned, the lower wheel arch plastic liner must be removed. The liner is secured by several plastic expanding rivets/nut/screws. To remove the rivets, push in the centre pins a little, then prise the clips from place. Remove the liner from under the front wing. The crankshaft can then be turned using a suitable socket and extension bar fitted to the pulley bolt.

6 Remove the upper and lower timing belt covers as described in Section 6.

7 Temporarily refit the crankshaft pulley bolt, remove the crankshaft locking tool, then turn the crankshaft until the timing hole in the camshaft sprocket hub is aligned with the corresponding hole in the cylinder head. Note that the crankshaft must always be turned in a clockwise direction (viewed from the right-hand side of vehicle). Use a small mirror so that the position of the sprocket hub timing slot can be observed. When the slot is aligned with the corresponding hole in the cylinder head, the camshaft is positioned correctly.

8 Remove the crankshaft drive belt pulley as described in Section 5.

9 Insert a 5 mm diameter bolt, rod or drill through the hole in crankshaft sprocket flange and into the corresponding hole in the oil pump **(see illustration)**, if necessary, carefully turn the crankshaft either way until the rod enters the timing hole in the block.

10 Insert an 8 mm bolt, rod or drill through the hole in the camshaft sprocket hub and into engagement with the cylinder head **(see illustration)**.

11 Insert a 5 mm diameter bolt, rod or drill through the hole in the fuel pump sprocket and into the corresponding hole in the cylinder head **(see illustration)**. **Note:** *On some engines, a hole is provided at the 5 o'clock position for locking purposes only, however, the timing hole is at the 12 o'clock position.* Note the comment in paragraph 2 – if the fuel pump sprocket holes are not aligned during removal of the timing belt, it is of no consequence, however, it is important to align the holes during the refitting procedure. If timing alignment is only being *checked* and the holes do not align at this stage, rotate the crankshaft one turn at a time (max 12 turns) until the holes do align.

12 The crankshaft and camshaft are now locked in position, preventing unnecessary rotation while working on the engine.

4 Cylinder head cover/ inlet manifold – removal and refitting

Removal

1 Remove the engine top cover together with the integral air cleaner as follows:

a) Disconnect the vacuum line from the one-way valve on the left-hand side of the air cleaner body and position to one side.

b) Disconnect the air cleaner inlet hose from the inlet duct at the front of the engine compartment.

c) Disconnect the wiring from the mass airflow sensor.

*d) Loosen the clip and separate the mass airflow sensor from the turbocharger inlet duct. Alternatively, the top cover and air cleaner may be removed together with the inlet duct by loosening the clip on the turbocharger and also disconnecting the crankcase ventilation hose from the engine valve cover **(see illustration)**.*

*e) Lift the top cover and air cleaner directly upwards from the three mounting rubbers and withdraw **(see illustration)**. The mountings are very tight and will require releasing separately.*

3.11 Insert a 5.0 mm drill bit/bolt through the round hole in the fuel pump sprocket into the cylinder head

2 Disconnect the wiring plugs from the top of each injector, undo the guide bolts, then make sure all wiring harnesses are freed from any retaining brackets on the cylinder head cover/ inlet manifold.

3 Unscrew the two bolts securing the EGR pipe to the right-hand end of the cylinder head cover/inlet manifold **(see illustration)**.

4 Disconnect the wiring from the camshaft position sensor and the fuel temperature sensor **(see illustration)**.

5 Disconnect the quick-release fuel inlet hose from the fuel filter. Also, unclip the in-line fuel filter from the top of the engine, and the feed and return lines from the right-hand end of the engine, and position to one side with the fuel lines **(see illustrations)**.

6 Prise out the retaining clips and disconnect the fuel return pipes from the injectors, then undo the unions and remove the high-pressure fuel pipes from the injectors and the common fuel rail at the rear of the cylinder head – counterhold the unions with a second spanner **(see illustrations)**. Plug the openings to prevent dirt ingress.

7 Unscrew the throttle body retaining bolts, then unbolt and remove the turbocharger outlet pipe and disconnect it from the intercooler hose **(see illustrations)**.

8 Remove the inlet manifold wiring harness trunking from the right-hand end of the engine.

9 Disconnect the wiring from the MAP sensor.

10 Undo the retaining bolts and remove the

4.1a Disconnecting the turbocharger inlet hose

4.1b Pull the plastic cover upwards to release it from the rubber mountings

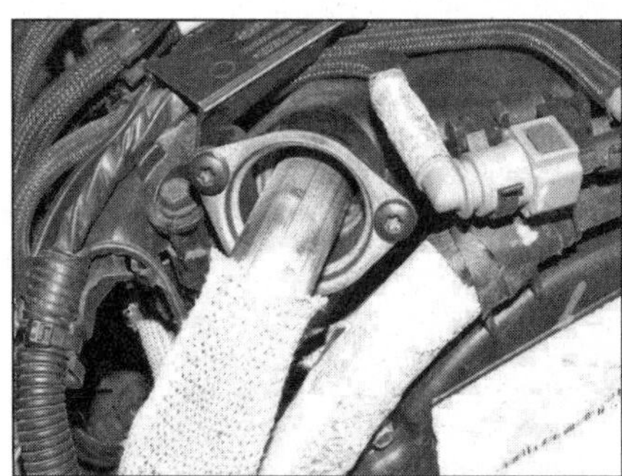

4.3 EGR pipe connection to the inlet manifold/cylinder head cover

4.4 Disconnect the fuel temperature sensor wiring plug (arrowed)

4.5a In-line fuel filter located on the top of the engine

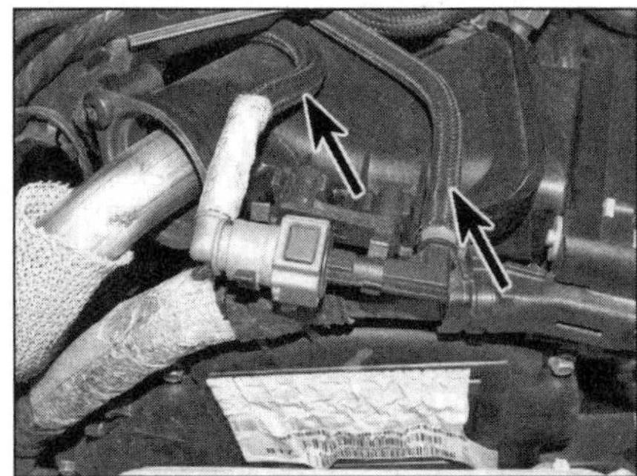

4.5b Fuel lines on the right-hand end of the engine

4.6a Prise out the clip and pull the return hose from the top of each injector

4.6b Use a second spanner to hold the injector port whilst slackening the fuel pipe unions

4.7a Unbolt the turbocharger outlet pipe ...

4.7b ... and disconnect it from the intercooler hose

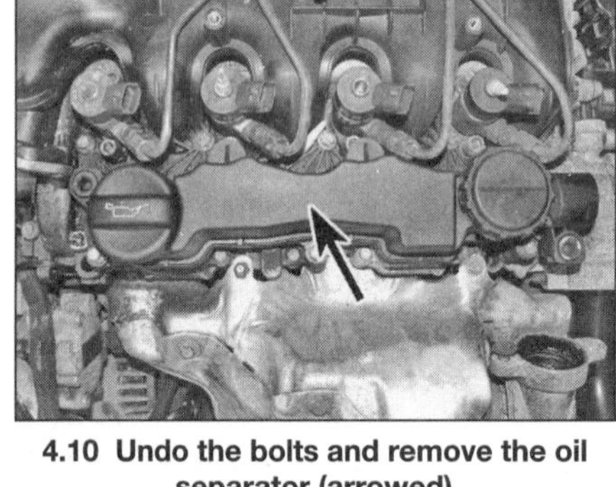

4.10 Undo the bolts and remove the oil separator (arrowed)

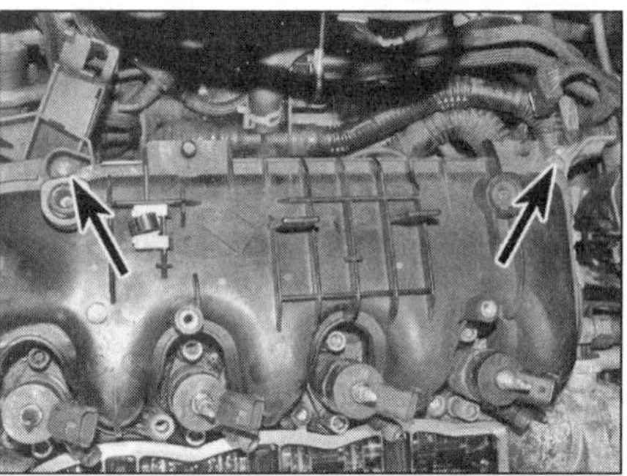

4.11 Undo the 2 remaining bolts (arrowed) and pull the cover/manifold upwards

oil separator from the top of the cylinder head **(see illustration)**. Recover the rubber seal.

11 Undo the bolts securing the cylinder head cover/inlet manifold. Lift the assembly away **(see illustration)**. Recover the manifold rubber seals.

Refitting

12 Refitting is a reversal of removal, bearing in mind the following points:

a) *Examine the seals for signs of damage and deterioration, and renew if necessary. Smear a little clean engine oil on the manifold seals.*

b) *Renew the fuel injector high-pressure pipes – see Chapter 4B, Section 12.*

5 Crankshaft pulley – removal and refitting

Removal

1 Remove the auxiliary drivebelt as described in Chapter 1B, Section 22.

2 To lock the crankshaft, working underneath the engine, insert a 12 mm rod or drill into the hole in the right-hand face of the engine block casting over the lower section of the flywheel **(see illustration)**. **Note:** *The hole in the casting and the hole in the flywheel are provided purely to lock the crankshaft whilst the pulley bolt is undone, it does* ***not*** *position the crankshaft at TDC.* Rotate the crankshaft until the tool engages in the corresponding hole in the flywheel.

3 Using a suitable socket and extension bar, unscrew the retaining bolt, remove the washer, then slide the pulley off the end of the crankshaft. If the pulley is a tight fit, it can be drawn off the crankshaft using a suitable puller. If a puller is being used, refit the pulley retaining bolt without the washer, to avoid damaging the crankshaft as the puller is tightened. With the pulley removed, note the cut-out which engages the tab on the nose of the crankshaft **(see illustrations)**.

Caution: Do not touch the outer magnetic

5.2 The locking pin/bolt (arrowed) must locate in the hole in the flywheel (arrowed) to prevent rotation

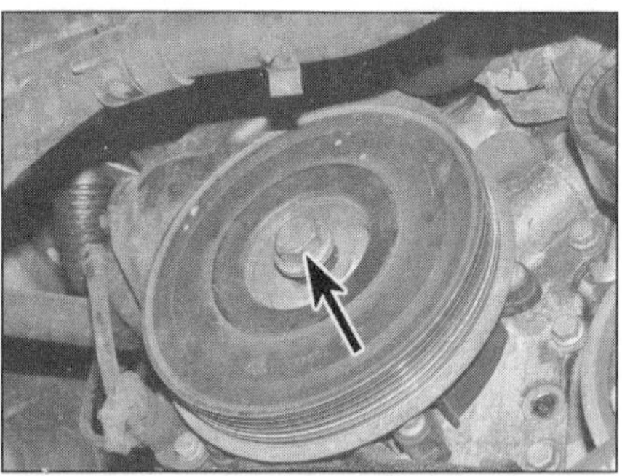

5.3a Undo the crankshaft pulley retaining bolt (arrowed)

5.3b Removing the crankshaft pulley – note the location cut-out and tab

5.3c Location cut-out on the inner side of the crankshaft pulley

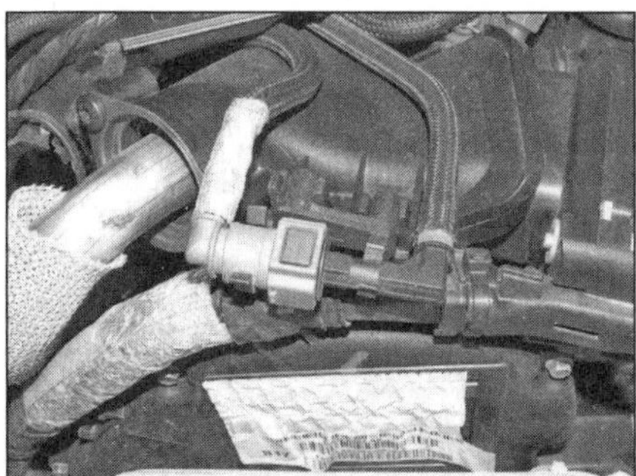

6.2 Unclip the fuel pipes and the wiring harness from above the upper cover

6.3a Undo the screws (arrowed) ...

6.3b ... and remove the timing belt upper cover

sensor ring of the crankshaft sprocket with your fingers, or allow metallic particles to come into contact with it.

Refitting

4 Refit the pulley to the end of the crankshaft, making sure the cut-out engages with the tab on the nose of the crankshaft.

5 Thoroughly clean the threads of the pulley retaining bolt, then apply a coat of locking compound to the bolt threads using Loctite (available from your Ford dealer); in the absence of this, any good quality locking compound may be used. **Note:** *Ford recommend that a new bolt is fitted.*

6 Refit the crankshaft pulley retaining bolt and washer. Tighten the bolt to the specified torque, then through the specified angle, preventing the crankshaft from turning using the method employed on removal.

7 Refit and tension the auxiliary drivebelt as described in Chapter 1B, Section 22.

6 Timing belt covers – removal and refitting

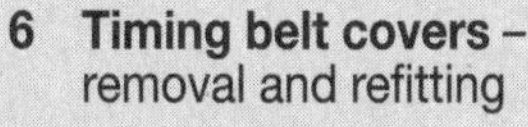

Warning: Refer to the precautionary information contained in Section 1 before proceeding.

Removal

Upper cover

1 With the engine cold, unscrew the filler cap from the coolant expansion tank, then siphon the coolant into a suitable container. Remove the expansion tank as follows **(see illustrations 17.5a to 17.5e)**:

a) Unscrew the mounting bolt and lift the expansion tank for access to the lower hoses.

b) Disconnect the thermostat housing degas (by-pass) hose from the top of the tank by squeezing the connector.

c) Disconnect the radiator purge (degas) hose from the side of the tank (near the level marks).

d) Disconnect the water pump by-pass hose from the bottom of the tank.

e) Remove the expansion tank, and plug the coolant hoses.

2 Release the wiring harness and fuel pipes above the upper cover **(see illustration)**.

3 Undo the five screws and remove the timing belt upper cover **(see illustrations)**.

Lower cover

4 Remove the upper cover as described previously.

5 Remove the crankshaft pulley as described in Section 5.

6 Unbolt and remove the auxiliary drivebelt tensioner, then undo the five bolts and remove the lower cover **(see illustrations)**.

Refitting

7 Refitting of all the covers is a reversal of the relevant removal procedure, ensuring that each cover section is correctly located, and that the cover retaining bolts are securely tightened. Ensure that all disturbed hoses are reconnected and retained by their relevant clips.

7 Timing belt – removal, inspection, refitting and tensioning

General

1 The timing belt drives the camshaft(s), high-pressure fuel pump and coolant pump from a toothed sprocket on the end of the crankshaft. If the belt breaks or slips in service, the pistons are likely to hit the valve heads, resulting in expensive damage.

2 The timing belt should be renewed at the specified intervals, or earlier if it is contaminated with oil, or at all noisy in operation (a 'scraping' noise due to uneven wear).

3 If the timing belt is being removed, it is a wise precaution to check the condition of the coolant pump at the same time (check for signs of coolant leakage). This may avoid the need to remove the timing belt again at a later stage, should the coolant pump fail.

Removal

4 Apply the handbrake, then jack up the front of the vehicle and support it on axle stands (see *Jacking and vehicle support*). Remove the front right-hand roadwheel, lower wheel arch liner (to expose the crankshaft pulley), and the engine undershield (where fitted). The wheel arch liner is secured by several plastic expanding rivets/nuts/plastic clips.

5 Remove the auxiliary drivebelt as described in Chapter 1B, Section 22.

6 Remove the upper and lower timing belt covers, as described in Section 6.

6.6a Auxiliary drivebelt tensioner removed from the engine

6.6b Lower timing belt cover screws (arrowed)

6.6c Removing the lower timing belt cover

7.8 Support the engine with a trolley jack

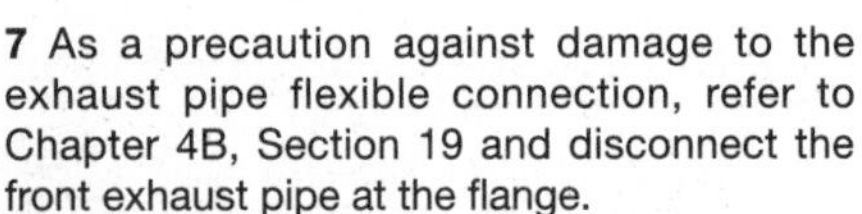

7.9a Removing the right-hand engine mounting ...

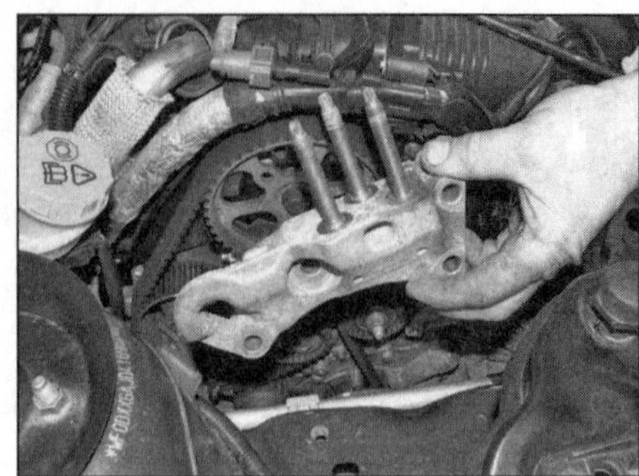

7.9b ... and support bracket

7 As a precaution against damage to the exhaust pipe flexible connection, refer to Chapter 4B, Section 19 and disconnect the front exhaust pipe at the flange.

8 Position a trolley jack under the engine, and using a block of wood on the jack head, take the weight of the engine **(see illustration)**.

9 Undo the bolts/nut and remove the right hand engine mounting – see Section 17. Also, unbolt and remove the mounting support bracket **(see illustrations)**.

10 As a precaution against damage, undo the screw and remove the crankshaft position sensor adjacent to the crankshaft sprocket flange, and move it to one side **(see illustration)**.

11 Undo the retaining screw and remove the timing belt protection bracket, again, adjacent to the crankshaft sprocket flange.

12 Lock the crankshaft and camshaft sprockets in their correct timing positions as described in Section 3. If necessary, temporarily refit the crankshaft pulley bolt to enable the crankshaft to be rotated. At this stage, it is of no consequence that the fuel pump sprocket aligns correctly with the hole in the pump mounting bracket.

13 Insert a hexagon key into the belt tensioner pulley centre, slacken the pulley bolt, and allow the tensioner to rotate, relieving the belt tension **(see illustration)**. With the belt slack, temporarily tighten the pulley bolt.

14 Note its routing, then remove the timing belt from the sprockets.

Inspection

15 Renew the belt as a matter of course, regardless of its apparent condition. The cost of a new belt is nothing compared with the cost of repairs, should the belt break in service. If signs of oil contamination are found, trace the source of the oil leak and rectify it. Wash down the engine timing belt area and all related components, to remove all traces of oil. Check that the tensioner and idler pulleys rotate freely without any sign of roughness, and also check that the coolant pump pulley rotates freely. If necessary, renew these items.

Refitting and tensioning

16 Commence refitting by ensuring that the crankshaft and camshaft timing pins are still in position correctly. Also, locate and lock the fuel pump sprocket in its correct position as described in Section 3.

17 Locate the timing belt on the crankshaft sprocket, then keeping it taut, locate it around the idler pulley, camshaft sprocket, high-pressure pump sprocket, coolant pump sprocket, and the tensioner pulley **(see illustration)**. If the timing belt has directional arrows on it, make sure that they point in the direction of normal engine rotation.

18 Refit the timing belt protection bracket and tighten the retaining bolt securely.

19 Slacken the tensioner pulley bolt, and using a hexagonal key, rotate the tensioner anti-clockwise, which moves the index arm clockwise, until the index arm is aligned as shown **(see illustration)**.

20 Remove the camshaft, crankshaft and fuel pump timing pins and, using a socket on the crankshaft pulley bolt, turn the crankshaft clockwise 10 complete revolutions. Align the camshaft and crankshaft timing holes and check that the timing pins can be inserted, then remove them. There is no requirement to check the fuel pump sprocket alignment, as it will only be aligned after 12 complete revolutions.

21 Check that the tensioner index arm is still aligned between the edges of the area shown **(see illustration 7.19)**. If it is not, remove and belt and begin the refitting process again, starting at Paragraph 19.

22 The remainder of refitting is a reversal of removal. Tighten all fasteners to the specified torque where given.

7.10 Undo the bolt (arrowed) and remove the crankshaft position sensor

7.13 Slacken the bolt and allow the tensioner to rotate, relieving the tension on the belt

7.17 Timing belt routing

7.19 The index arm must align with the lug (arrowed)

TOOL TiP

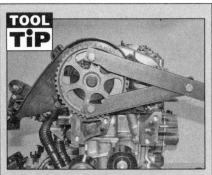

A sprocket holding tool can be made from two lengths of steel strip bolted together to form a forked end. Drill holes and insert bolts in the ends of the fork to engage with the sprocket spokes.

8 Timing belt sprockets and tensioner – removal and refitting

Camshaft sprocket

Removal

1 Remove the timing belt as described in Section 7.

2 Remove the locking tool from the camshaft sprocket/hub. Slacken the sprocket hub retaining bolt. To prevent the camshaft rotating as the bolt is slackened, a sprocket holding tool will be required. In the absence of a special tool, an acceptable substitute can be fabricated at home **(see Tool Tip)**. *Do not* attempt to use the engine assembly/ valve timing locking tool to prevent the sprocket from rotating whilst the bolt is slackened.

3 Remove the sprocket hub retaining bolt, and slide the sprocket and hub off the end of the camshaft.

4 Clean the camshaft sprocket thoroughly, and renew it if there are any signs of wear, damage or cracks.

Refitting

5 Refit the camshaft sprocket to the camshaft **(see illustration)**.

6 Refit the sprocket hub retaining bolt. Tighten the bolt to the specified torque, preventing the camshaft from turning as during removal.

7 Align the engine assembly/valve timing slot in the camshaft sprocket hub with the hole in the cylinder head and refit the timing pin to lock the camshaft in position.

8 Fit the timing belt around the pump sprocket and camshaft sprocket, and tension the timing belt as described in Section 7.

Crankshaft sprocket

Caution: Do not touch the outer magnetic sensor ring of the crankshaft sprocket with your fingers, or allow metallic particles to come into contact with it.

8.5 Ensure the lug on the sprocket hub engages with the slot on the end of the camshaft (arrowed)

8.11a Slide the sprocket from the crankshaft ...

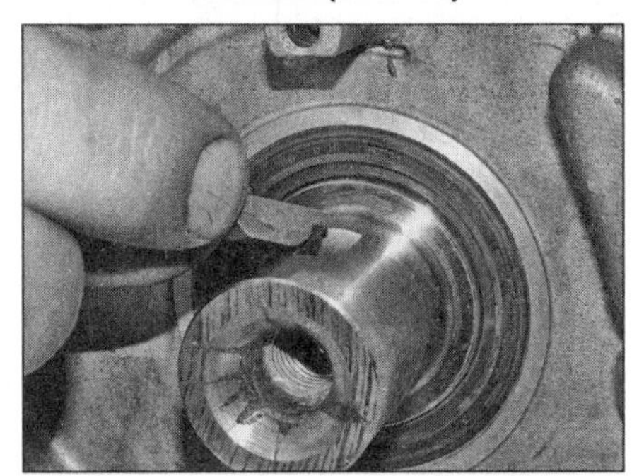

8.11b ... and recover the Woodruff key

8.17 Insert a suitable drill bit through the sprocket into the hole in the backplate

Removal

9 Remove the crankshaft pulley and timing belt as described in Sections 5 and 7.

10 Check that the engine assembly/valve timing holes are still aligned as described in Section 3, and the camshaft sprocket and flywheel are locked in position.

11 Slide the sprocket off the end of the crankshaft and collect the Woodruff key **(see illustrations)**.

12 Examine the crankshaft oil seal for signs of oil leakage and, if necessary, renew it as described in Section 14.

13 Clean the crankshaft sprocket thoroughly, and renew it if there are any signs of wear, damage or cracks. Recover the crankshaft locating key.

Refitting

14 Refit the key to the end of the crankshaft, then refit the crankshaft sprocket (with the flange facing the crankshaft pulley).

15 Refit the crankshaft pulley as described in Section 5, then fit the timing belt around the crankshaft sprocket, and tension the timing belt as described in Section 7.

Fuel pump sprocket

Removal

16 Remove the timing belt as described in Section 7.

17 Using a suitable socket, undo the pump sprocket retaining nut. The sprocket can be held stationary by inserting a suitably sized locking pin, drill or rod through the hole in the sprocket, and into the corresponding hole in the backplate **(see illustration)**, or by using a suitable forked tool engaged with the holes in the sprocket **(see Tool Tip in paragraph 2)**. **Note:** *On some engines, a hole is provided at the 5 o'clock position for locking purposes only, however, the timing position hole is at the 12 o'clock position.*

18 The pump sprocket is a taper fit on the pump shaft and it will be necessary to make up another tool to release it from the taper **(see Tool Tip)**.

19 Partially unscrew the sprocket retaining nut, fit the home-made tool, and secure it to the sprocket with two suitable bolts. Prevent

Make a sprocket releasing tool from a short strip of steel. Drill two holes in the strip to correspond with the two holes in the sprocket. Drill a third hole just large enough to accept the flats of the sprocket retaining nut.

8.31 Timing belt idler pulley retaining nut (arrowed)

the sprocket from rotating as before, and unscrew the sprocket retaining nut. The nut will bear against the tool as it is undone, forcing the sprocket off the shaft taper. Once the taper is released, remove the tool, unscrew the nut fully, and remove the sprocket from the pump shaft. Note that although the sprocket is on a taper, it incorporates a key so that it will only locate in one position.

20 Clean the sprocket thoroughly, and renew it if there are any signs of wear, damage or cracks.

Refitting

21 Refit the pump sprocket and retaining nut, and tighten the nut to the specified torque. Prevent the sprocket rotating as the nut is tightened using the sprocket holding tool.

22 Fit the timing belt around the pump sprocket, and tension the timing belt as described in Section 7.

Coolant pump sprocket

23 The coolant pump sprocket is integral with the pump, and cannot be removed. Coolant pump removal is described in Chapter 3, Section 7.

Tensioner pulley

Removal

24 Remove the timing belt as described in Section 7.

9.5 Vacuum pump bolts (arrowed)

25 Remove the tensioner pulley retaining bolt, and slide the pulley off its mounting stud.

26 Clean the tensioner pulley, but do not use any strong solvent which may enter the pulley bearings. Check that the pulley rotates freely, with no sign of stiffness or free play. Renew the pulley if there is any doubt about its condition, or if there are any obvious signs of wear or damage.

27 Examine the pulley mounting stud for signs of damage and if necessary, renew it.

Refitting

28 Refit the tensioner pulley to its mounting stud, and fit the retaining bolt.

29 Refit the timing belt as described in Section 7.

Idler pulley

Removal

30 Remove the timing belt as described in Section 7.

31 Undo the retaining bolt/nut and withdraw the idler pulley from the engine **(see illustration)**.

32 Clean the idler pulley, but do not use any strong solvent which may enter the bearings. Check that the pulley rotates freely, with no sign of stiffness or free play. Renew the idler pulley if there is any doubt about its condition, or if there are any obvious signs of wear or damage.

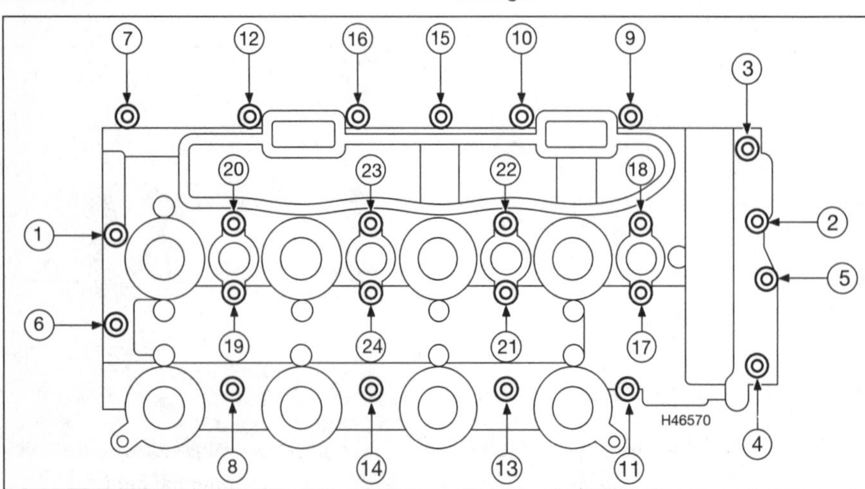

9.9 Camshaft cover/bearing ladder bolt slackening sequence

9.7 Timing belt inner, upper cover bolts (arrowed)

Refitting

33 Locate the idler pulley on the engine, and fit the retaining bolt/nut. Tighten the bolt/nut to the specified torque.

34 Refit the timing belt as described in Section 7.

9 Camshafts, rocker arms and hydraulic tappets – removal, inspection and refitting

Removal

1 Remove the cylinder head cover/inlet manifold as described in Section 4.

2 Remove the injectors as described in Chapter 4B, Section 12.

3 Remove the camshaft sprocket as described in Section 8.

4 Refit the right-hand engine mounting, but only tighten the bolts moderately; this will keep the engine supported during the camshaft removal.

5 Undo the bolts and remove the vacuum pump. Recover the pump O-ring seals **(see illustration)**.

6 Remove the fuel filter (see Chapter 1B, Section 17), then undo the bolts and remove the fuel filter mounting bracket.

7 Release the wiring harness clips, then undo the 3 bolts and remove the timing belt inner, upper cover **(see illustration)**.

8 Disconnect the wiring plug, unscrew the retaining bolt, and remove the camshaft position sensor from the camshaft cover/bearing ladder.

9 Unbolt the turbocharger heat shields, then working gradually and evenly, slacken and remove the bolts securing the camshaft cover/bearing ladder to the cylinder head in the sequence shown **(see illustration)**. Lift the cover/ladder from position complete with the camshafts.

10 Undo the retaining bolts and remove the bearing caps. Note their fitted positions, as they must be refitted into their original positions **(see illustration)**. Note that the bearing caps are marked A for inlet, and E for exhaust, and 1 to 4 from the flywheel end of the cylinder head.

11 Undo the bolts securing the chain tensioner assembly to the camshaft cover/

bearing ladder, then lift the camshafts, chain and tensioner from the housing **(see illustrations)**. Discard the camshaft oil seal.

12 Obtain 16 small, clean plastic containers, and number them 1 to 8 inlet and 1 to 8 exhaust ; alternatively, divide a larger container into 16 compartments.

13 Lift out each rocker arm. Place the rocker arms in their respective positions in the box or containers.

14 A compartmentalised container filled with engine oil is now required to retain the hydraulic tappets while they are removed from the cylinder head. Withdraw each hydraulic follower and place it in the container, keeping them each identified for correct refitting. The tappets must be totally submerged in the oil to prevent air entering them.

Inspection

15 Inspect the cam lobes and the camshaft bearing journals for scoring or other visible evidence of wear. Once the surface hardening of the cam lobes has been eroded, wear will occur at an accelerated rate. **Note:** *If these symptoms are visible on the tips of the camshaft lobes, check the corresponding rocker arm, as it will probably be worn as well.*

16 Examine the condition of the bearing surfaces in the cylinder head and camshaft bearing housing. If wear is evident, the cylinder head and bearing housing will both have to be renewed, as they are a matched assembly.

17 Inspect the rocker arms and tappets for scuffing, cracking or other damage and renew any components as necessary. Also check the condition of the tappet bores in the cylinder head. As with the camshafts, any wear in this area will necessitate cylinder head renewal.

Refitting

18 Thoroughly clean the sealant from the mating surfaces of the cylinder head and camshaft bearing housing. Use a suitable liquid gasket dissolving agent (available from

9.10 The camshaft bearing caps are numbered 1 to 4 from the flywheel end – A for inlet, and E for exhaust (arrowed)

9.11b ... then lift the camshafts, chain and tensioner from the housing

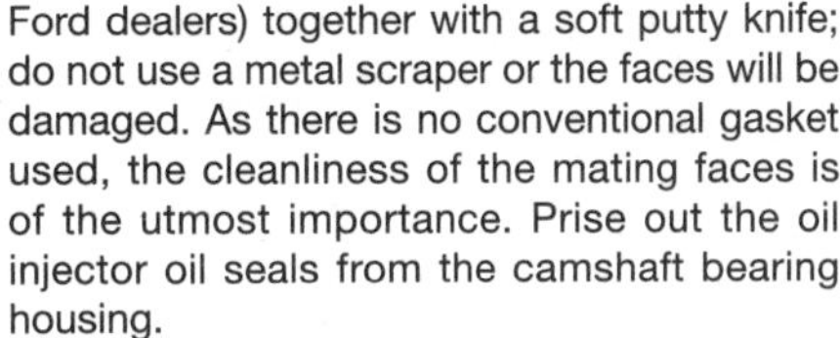

Ford dealers) together with a soft putty knife; do not use a metal scraper or the faces will be damaged. As there is no conventional gasket used, the cleanliness of the mating faces is of the utmost importance. Prise out the oil injector oil seals from the camshaft bearing housing.

19 Clean off any oil, dirt or grease from both components and dry with a clean lint-free cloth. Ensure that all the oilways are completely clean.

20 Liberally lubricate the hydraulic tappet bores in the cylinder head with clean engine oil.

9.11a Undo the tensioner bolts (arrowed) ...

9.21 Refit the hydraulic tappets ...

21 Insert the hydraulic tappets into their original bores in the cylinder head unless they have been renewed **(see illustration)**.

22 Lubricate the rocker arms and place them over their respective tappets and valve stems **(see illustration)**.

23 Engage the timing chain around the camshaft sprockets, aligning the black-coloured links with the marked teeth on the camshaft sprockets **(see illustration)**. If the black colouring has been lost, there must be 12 chain link pins between the marks on the sprockets.

24 Fit the chain tensioner between the upper

9.22 ... and rocker arms to their original locations

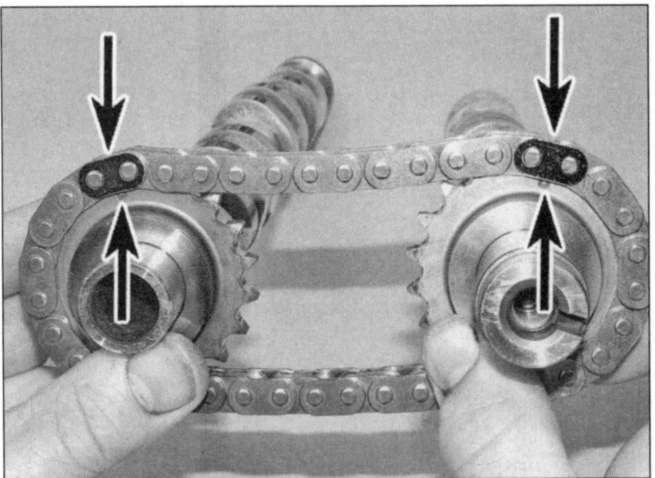

9.23 Align the marks on the sprockets with the centre of the black coloured chain links (arrowed). There must be 12 link pins between the sprocket marks

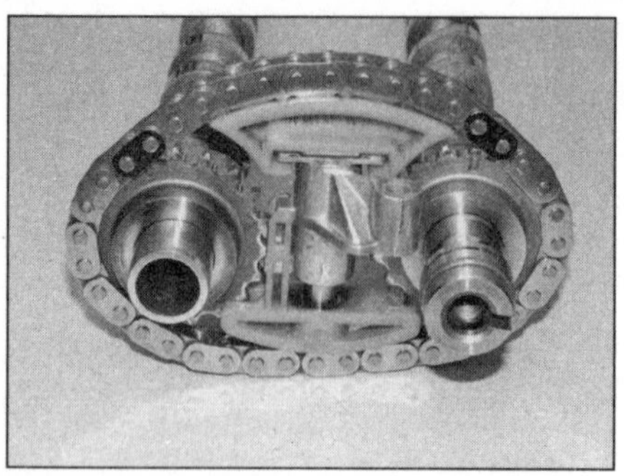

9.24a Assemble the chain tensioner between the upper and lower runs of the chain ...

9.24b ... and lower the camshafts, chain and tensioner into position

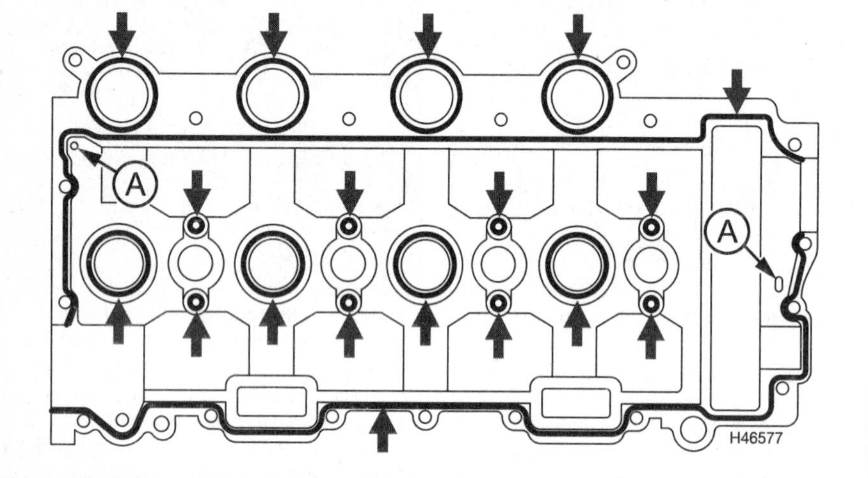

9.25 Apply sealant to the camshaft cover/bearing ladder as indicated by the heavy black lines. Ensure sealant does not enter the tensioner oil holes – marked A

and lower runs of the chain, then lubricate the bearing surfaces with clean engine oil, and fit the camshafts into position on the underside of the camshaft cover/bearing ladder. Refit the bearing caps to their original positions and tighten the retaining bolts to the specified torque **(see illustrations)**. Tighten the tensioner retaining bolts to the specified torque.

25 Apply a thin bead of sealant to the mating surface of the camshaft cover/bearing ladder as shown. Ford recommend the use of silicone sealant WSE-M4G323-A4 **(see illustration)**. Do not allow the sealant to obstruct the oil channels for the hydraulic chain tensioner.

26 Check that the black-coloured links on the chain are still aligned with the marks on the camshaft sprockets, then refit the camshaft cover/bearing ladder, and gradually and evenly tighten the retaining bolts until the cover/ladder is in contact with the cylinder head, then tighten the bolts to the specified torque in the sequence shown **(see illustration)**. **Note:** *Ensure the cover/ladder is correctly located by checking the bores of the vacuum pump and camshaft oil seal at each end of the cover/ladder.*

27 Fit a new camshaft oil seal as described in Section 14.

28 Refit the camshaft sprocket, and tighten the retaining bolt finger-tight.

29 Using a spanner on the camshaft sprocket bolt, rotate the camshafts approximately 40 complete revolutions clockwise. Check the black-coloured links on the chain still align with the marks on the camshaft sprockets.

30 If the marks still align, refit the camshaft sprocket as described in Section 8.

31 Refit and adjust the camshaft position sensor as described in Chapter 4B, Section 13.

32 Press the new oil seals into the bearing housing, using a tube/socket of approximately 20 mm outside diameter, ensuring the inner lip of the seal fits around the injector guide tube **(see illustrations)**. Refit the injectors as described in Chapter 4B, Section 12.

33 Refit the cylinder head cover/inlet manifold as described in Section 4.

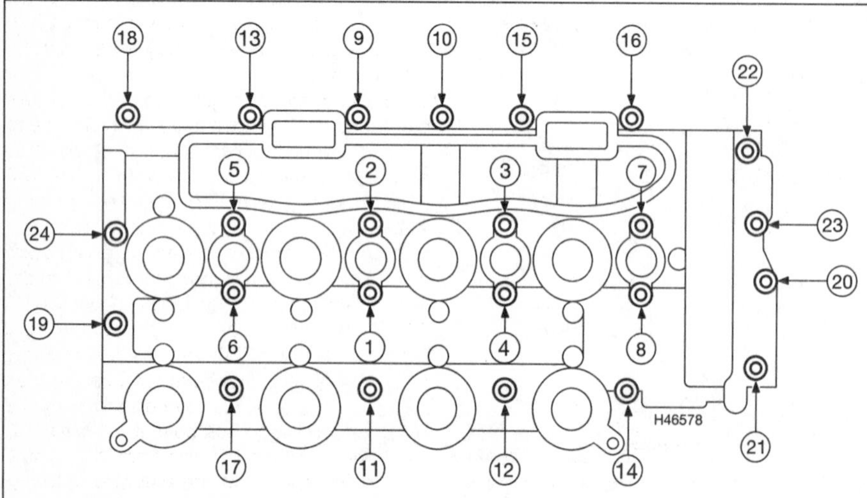

9.26 Camshaft cover/bearing ladder bolt tightening sequence

9.32a Fit the new seal around a 20 mm outside diameter socket ...

9.32b ... and push it into place

10.8 The engine oil level dipstick is secured to the alternator bracket by a Torx bolt (arrowed)

10.9 Undo the bolts (arrowed) and pull the coolant outlet housing from the left-hand end of the cylinder head

10.10a Remove the high-pressure pipe (arrowed) ...

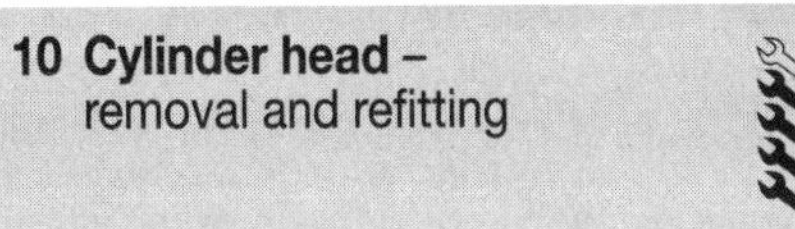

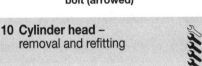

10 Cylinder head – removal and refitting

Removal

1 Apply the handbrake, then jack up the front of the vehicle and support it on axle stands (see *Jacking and vehicle support*). Remove the front right-hand roadwheel, the engine undershield, and the front wheel arch liner. The undershield is secured by several screws, and the wheel arch liner is secured by several plastic expanding rivets/nuts/plastic clips. Push the centre pins in a little, then prise the rivet from place.

2 Disconnect the battery negative lead as described in Chapter 5A, Section 2.

3 Drain the cooling system as described in Chapter 1B, Section 25.

4 Remove the camshafts, rocker arms and hydraulic tappets as described in Section 9.

5 Remove the turbocharger as described in Chapter 4B, Section 17.

6 Remove the glow plugs as described in Chapter 5C, Section 2.

7 Remove the inlet manifold as described in Section 4.

8 Undo the upper mounting bolts, and pivot the alternator away from the engine, undo the oil dipstick guide tube bolt, then undo the bolts securing the alternator mounting bracket to the cylinder head/block **(see illustration)**.

9 Undo the coolant outlet housing (left-hand end of the cylinder head) retaining bolts, slacken the two bolts securing the housing support bracket to the top of the transmission bellhousing, and move the outlet housing away from the cylinder head a little **(see illustration)**. There is no need to disconnect the hoses.

10 Disconnect the high-pressure fuel pipe from the common rail to the pump, and disconnect the fuel supply and return hoses. Remove the bracket at the rear of the pump, then undo the bolt/nut and remove the pump and mounting bracket as an assembly **(see illustrations)**.

11 Working in the **reverse** of the sequence shown **(see illustration 10.32)** undo the cylinder head bolts.

10.10b ... and the bracket (arrowed)

10.10c Pump mounting bracket upper nut and lower mounting bolt (arrowed)

12 Release the cylinder head from the cylinder block and location dowels by rocking it. A suitable tool for doing this consists simply of two metal rods with 90-degree angled ends **(see illustration)**. Do not prise between the mating faces of the cylinder head and block, as this may damage the gasket faces.

13 Lift the cylinder head from the block, and recover the gasket.

14 If necessary, remove the exhaust manifold with reference to Chapter 4B, Section 15.

Preparation for refitting

15 The mating faces of the cylinder head and cylinder block must be perfectly clean before refitting the head. The use of a scouring agent is recommended for this purpose, but acceptable results can be achieved by using a hard plastic or wood scraper to remove all traces of gasket and carbon. The same method can be used to clean the piston crowns. Take particular care to avoid scoring or gouging the cylinder head/cylinder block mating surfaces during the cleaning operations, as aluminium alloy is easily damaged. Make sure that the carbon is not allowed to enter the oil and water passages – this is particularly important for the lubrication system, as carbon could block the oil supply to the engine's components. Using adhesive tape and paper, seal the water, oil and bolt holes in the cylinder block. To prevent carbon entering the gap between the pistons and bores, smear a little grease in the gap. After cleaning each piston, use a small brush to remove all traces of grease and carbon from the gap, then wipe away the remainder with a clean rag.

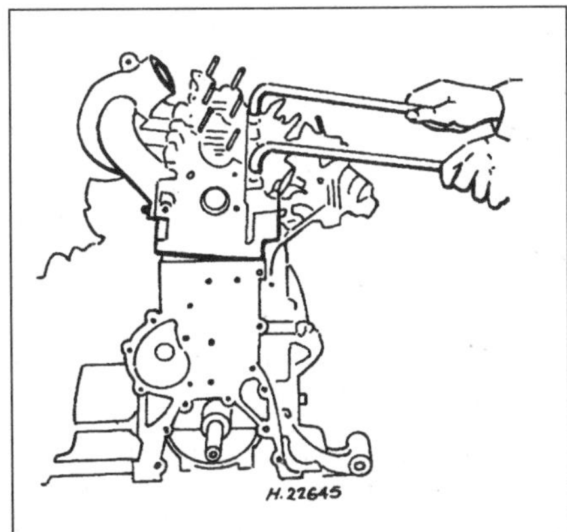

10.12 Free the cylinder head using angled rods

16 Check the mating surfaces of the cylinder block and the cylinder head for nicks, deep scratches and other damage. If slight, they may be removed carefully with a file, but if excessive, machining may be the only alternative to renewal. If warpage of the cylinder head gasket surface is suspected, use a straight-edge to check it for distortion. Refer to Chapter 2D, Section 8 if necessary.

17 Thoroughly clean the threads of the cylinder head bolt holes in the cylinder block. Ensure that the bolts run freely in their threads, and that all traces of oil and water are removed from each bolt hole. If required, pull the oil feed non-return valve from the cylinder head, and check that the ball moves freely. Push a new valve into place if necessary **(see illustrations)**.

10.17a Pull the non-return valve from the cylinder head ...

Gasket selection

18 Remove the crankshaft timing pin, then turn the crankshaft until pistons 1 and 4 are at TDC (Top Dead Centre). Position a dial test indicator (dial gauge) on the cylinder block adjacent to the rear of No 1 piston, and zero it on the block face. Transfer the probe to the crown of No 1 piston (10.0 mm in from the rear edge), then slowly turn the crankshaft back-and-forth past TDC, noting the highest reading on the indicator. Record this reading as protrusion A.

19 Repeat the check described in paragraph 18, this time 10.0 mm in from the front edge of the No 1 piston crown. Record this reading as protrusion B.

20 Add protrusion A to protrusion B, then divide the result by 2 to obtain an average reading for piston No 1.

21 Repeat the procedure described in paragraphs 18 to 20 on piston 4, then turn the crankshaft through 180° and carry out

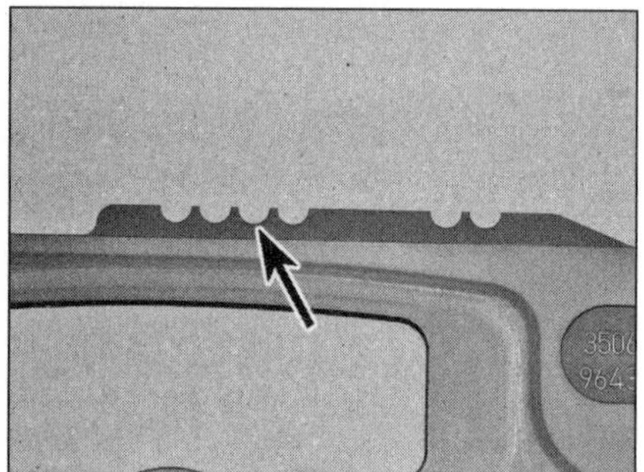

10.23 Cylinder head gasket thickness identification notches (arrowed)

10.27 Ensure the gasket locates over the dowels (arrowed)

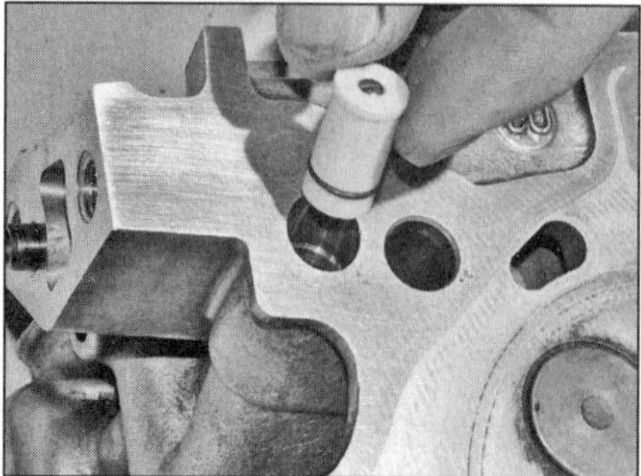

10.17b ... and push a new one into place

the procedure on the piston Nos 2 and 3 **(see illustration)**. Check that there is a maximum difference of 0.07 mm protrusion between any two pistons.

22 If a dial test indicator is not available, piston protrusion may be measured using a straight-edge and feeler blades or Vernier calipers. However, this is much less accurate, and cannot therefore be recommended.

23 Note the greatest piston protrusion measurement, and use this to determine the correct cylinder head gasket from the following table. The series of notches/holes on the side of the gasket are used for thickness identification **(see illustration)**.

Piston protrusion	Gasket identification
0.6115 to 0.720 mm	*2 notches*
0.721 to 0.770 mm	*3 notches*
0.771 to 0.820 mm	*1 notches*
0.821 to 0.870 mm	*4 notches*
0.871 to 0.977 mm	*5 notches*

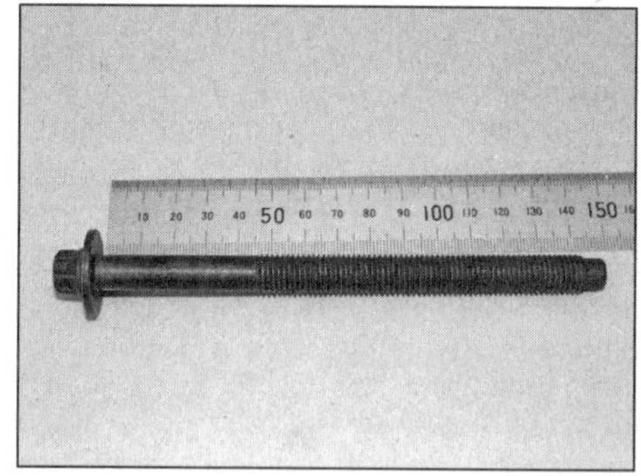

10.24 Measure the length from under the bolt head to its end

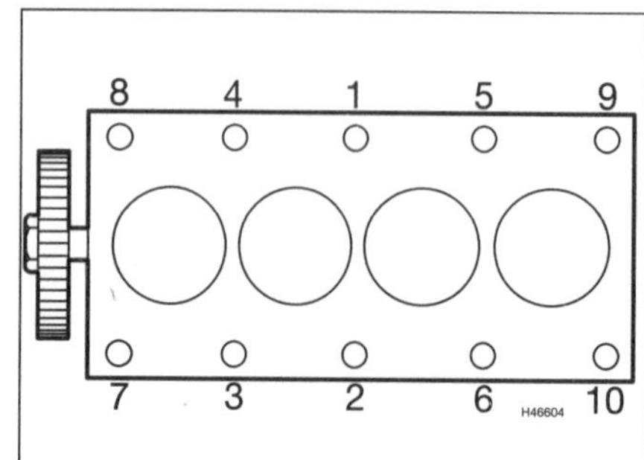

10.32 Cylinder head bolt tightening sequence

10.21 Measure the piston protrusion using a DTI gauge

Head bolt examination

24 Carefully examine the cylinder head bolts for signs of damage to the threads or head, and for any sign of corrosion. If the bolts are in a satisfactory condition, measure the length of each bolt from the underside of the head, to the end of the shank. According to the Citroën information for the identical engine, the bolts may be re-used providing that the measured length does not exceed 149.0 mm **(see illustration)**, however, Ford stipulate that they must be discarded and new ones fitted regardless of length. **Note:** *Considering the stress to which the cylinder head bolts are subjected, it is highly recommended that they are all renewed, regardless of their apparent condition.*

Refitting

25 Turn the crankshaft and position Nos 1 and 4 pistons at TDC, then turn the crankshaft a quarter turn (90°) anti-clockwise.

26 Thoroughly clean the surfaces of the cylinder head and block.

27 Make sure that the locating dowels are in place, then fit the correct gasket the right way round on the cylinder block **(see illustration)**.

28 If necessary, refit the exhaust manifold to the cylinder head as described in Chapter 4B, Section 15.

29 Carefully lower the cylinder head onto the gasket and block, making sure that it locates correctly onto the dowels.

30 Apply a smear of high melting-point grease to the threads, and to the underside of the heads, of the cylinder head bolts.

31 Carefully insert the cylinder head bolts into their holes (*do not drop them in*) and initially finger-tighten them.

32 Working progressively and in the sequence shown, tighten the cylinder head bolts to their Stage 1 torque setting, using a torque wrench and suitable socket **(see illustration)**.

33 Once all the bolts have been tightened to their Stage 1 torque setting, working again in the specified sequence, tighten each bolt to the specified Stage 2 setting. Finally, angle-tighten the bolts through the specified Stage 3 angle. It is recommended that an angle-measuring gauge is used during this stage of tightening, to ensure accuracy. **Note:** *Retightening of the cylinder head bolts after running the engine is not required.*

11.8 Apply a bead of sealant to the sump or crankcase mating surface. Ensure the sealant is applied on the inside of the retaining bolt holes

11.9 Refit the sump and tighten the bolts

34 Refit the hydraulic tappets, rocker arms, and camshaft housing (complete with camshafts) as described in Section 9.

35 Refit the timing belt as described in Section 7.

36 The remainder of refitting is a reversal of removal, noting the following points.

a) Use a new seal when refitting the coolant outlet housing.

b) When refitting a cylinder head, it is good practice to renew the thermostat.

c) Refit the camshaft position sensor and set the air gap with reference to Chapter 4B, Section 13.

d) Tighten all fasteners to the specified torque where given.

e) Refill the cooling system as described in Chapter 1B, Section 25.

f) The engine may run erratically for the first few miles, until the engine management PCM relearns its stored values.

11 Sump - removal and refitting

Removal

1 Drain the engine oil, then clean and refit the engine oil drain plug, tightening it securely. If the engine is nearing its service interval when the oil and filter are due for renewal, it is recommended that the filter is also removed, and a new one fitted. After reassembly, the engine can then be refilled with fresh oil. Refer to Chapter 1B, Section 3 for further information.

2 Apply the handbrake, then jack up the front of the vehicle and support it on axle stands (see *Jacking and vehicle support*).

3 Undo the screws and remove the engine undershield.

4 Remove the exhaust front pipe as described in Chapter 4B, Section 19.

5 Progressively slacken and remove all the sump retaining bolts/nuts. Since the sump bolts vary in length, remove each bolt in turn, and store it in its correct fitted order by pushing it through a clearly marked cardboard template. This will avoid the possibility of installing the bolts in the wrong locations on refitting.

6 Try to break the joint by striking the sump with the palm of your hand, then lower and withdraw the sump from under the car. If the sump is stuck (which is quite likely) use a putty knife or similar, carefully inserted between the sump and block. Ease the knife along the joint until the sump is released. While the sump is removed, take the opportunity to check the oil pump pick-up/strainer for signs of clogging or splitting. If necessary, remove the pump as described in Section 12, and clean or renew the strainer.

Refitting

7 Clean all traces of sealant from the mating surfaces of the cylinder block/crankcase and sump, then use a clean rag to wipe out the sump and the engine's interior.

8 On engines where the sump was fitted without a gasket, ensure that the sump mating surfaces are clean and dry, then apply a thin coating of suitable sealant to the sump or crankcase mating surface **(see illustration)**.

9 Offer up the sump to the cylinder block/ crankcase. Refit its retaining bolts/nuts, ensuring that each bolt is screwed into its original location. Tighten the bolts evenly and progressively to the specified torque setting **(see illustration)**.

10 Where necessary, align the air conditioning compressor with its mountings on the sump, and insert the retaining bolts. Securely tighten the compressor retaining bolts, then refit the drivebelt as described in Chapter 1B, Section 22.

11 Lower the vehicle to the ground, then refill the engine with oil as described in Chapter 1B, Section 3.

12 Oil pump - removal, inspection and refitting

Removal

1 Remove the crankshaft sprocket as described in Section 8. Recover the locating key from the crankshaft.

2 Temporarily refit the right-hand engine mounting and support bracket, and remove the trolley jack, then remove the sump as described in Section 11.

3 Disconnect the wiring plug, undo the bolts and remove the crankshaft position sensor, located on the right-hand end of the cylinder block.

4 Undo the three Allen bolts and remove the oil pump pick-up tube from the pump/block **(see illustration)**. Discard the oil seal, a new one must be fitted.

5 Undo the 8 bolts, and remove the oil pump **(see illustration)**.

Inspection

6 Undo and remove the Torx screws securing the cover to the oil pump **(see illustration)**.

12.4 Oil pick-up tube Allen bolts (arrowed)

12.5 Oil pump retaining bolts (arrowed)

12.6 Undo the Torx screws and remove the pump cover

12.7a Remove the circlip ...

12.7b ... cap ...

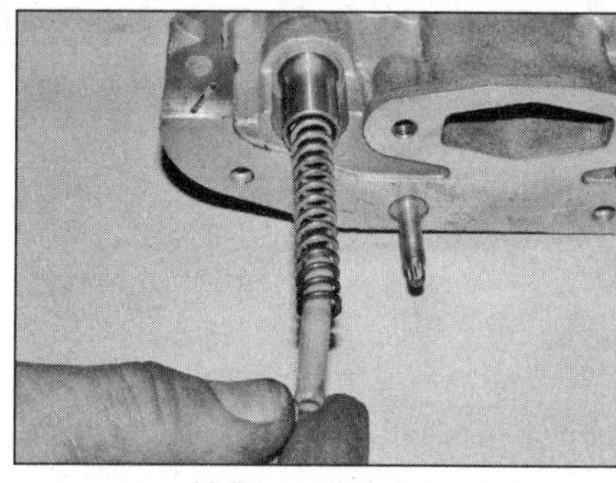
12.7c ... spring ...

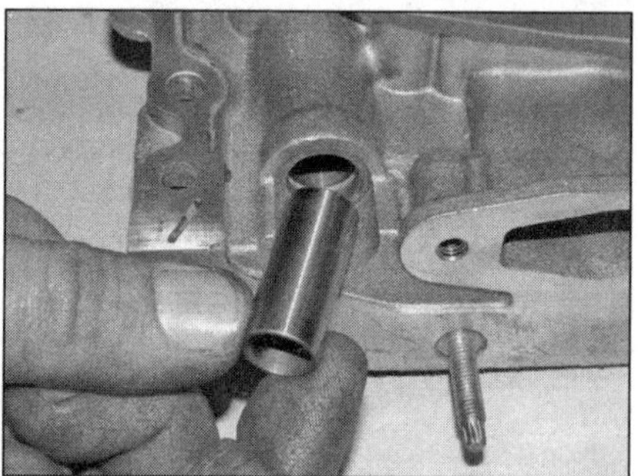
12.7d ... and piston

Examine the pump rotors and body for signs of wear and damage. If worn, the complete pump must be renewed.

7 Remove the circlip, and extract the cap, spring and valve piston, noting which way around they are fitted **(see illustrations)**. The condition of the relief valve spring can only be measured by comparing it with a new one; if there is any doubt about its condition, it should also be renewed.

8 Refit the relief valve piston, spring and cap, then secure them in place with the circlip.

12.11 Apply a bead of sealant to the cylinder block mating surface

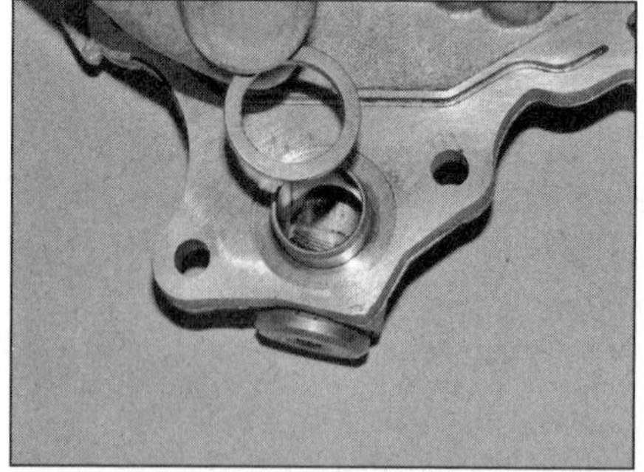
12.12a Fit a new seal ...

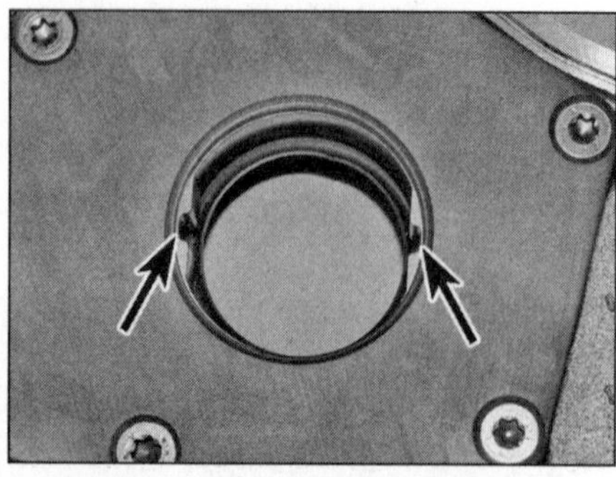
12.12b ... align the pump gear flats (arrowed) ...

12.12c ... with those of the crankshaft (arrowed)

9 Refit the cover to the oil pump, and tighten the Torx screws securely.

Refitting

10 Remove all traces of sealant, and thoroughly clean the mating surfaces of the oil pump and cylinder block.

11 Apply a 4 mm wide bead of silicone sealant to the mating face of the cylinder block **(see illustration)**. Ensure that no sealant enters any of the holes in the block.

12 With a new oil seal fitted, refit the oil pump over the end of the crankshaft, aligning the flats in the pump drivegear with the flats machined in the crankshaft **(see illustrations)**. Note that new oil pumps are supplied with the oil seal already fitted, and a seal protector sleeve. The sleeve fits over the end of the crankshaft to protect the seal as the pump is fitted.

13 Install the oil pump bolts and tighten them to the specified torque.

14 Refit the oil pick-up tube to the pump/cylinder block using a new O-ring seal. Ensure the oil dipstick guide tube is correctly refitted.

15 Refit the Woodruff key to the crankshaft, and slide the crankshaft sprocket into place.

16 The remainder of refitting is a reversal of removal.

13 Oil cooler – removal and refitting

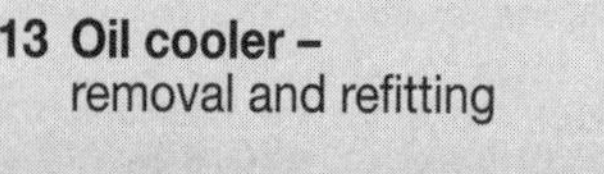

Removal

1 Apply the handbrake, then jack up the front of the vehicle and support it on axle stands

13.4a Undo the oil cooler bolts/stud (arrowed)

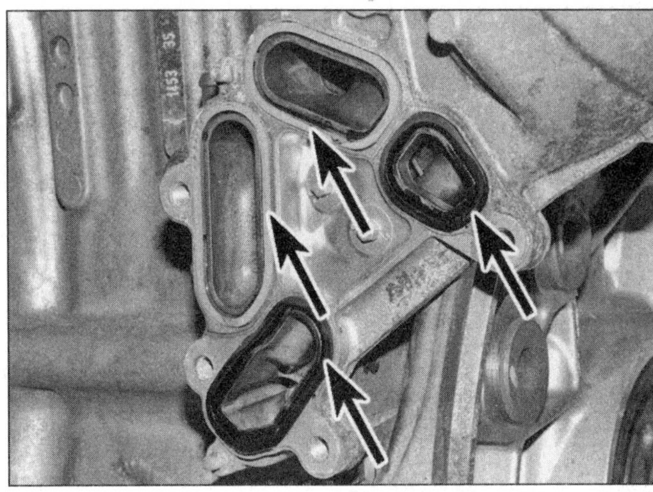

13.4b Renew the O-ring seals (arrowed)

(see *Jacking and vehicle support*). Undo the screws and remove the engine undershield.

2 The oil cooler is fitted to the front of the oil filter housing. Drain the coolant as described in Chapter 1B, Section 25.

3 Drain the engine oil as described in Chapter 1B, Section 3, or be prepared for fluid spillage.

4 Undo the 5 bolts/stud and remove the oil cooler. Recover the O-ring seals **(see illustrations)**.

Refitting

5 Fit new O-ring seals into the recesses in the oil filter housing, and refit the cooler. Tighten the bolts securely.

6 Refill or top-up the cooling system and engine oil level as described in Chapter 1B, Section 3 and 25 or *Weekly checks* (as applicable). Start the engine, and check the oil cooler for signs of leakage.

14 Oil seals – renewal

Crankshaft

Right-hand oil seal

1 Remove the crankshaft sprocket and Woodruff key as described in Section 8.

2 Measure and note the fitted depth of the oil seal.

3 Pull the oil seal from the housing using a screwdriver. Alternatively, drill a small hole in the oil seal, and use a self-tapping screw and a pair of pliers to remove it **(see illustration)**.

4 Clean the oil seal housing and the crankshaft sealing surface.

5 The seal has a Teflon lip and must not be oiled or marked. The new seal should be supplied with a protector sleeve, which fits over the end of the crankshaft to prevent any damage to the seal lip. With the sleeve in place, press the seal (open end first) into the pump to the previously-noted depth, using a suitable tube or socket **(see illustrations)**.

6 Where applicable, remove the plastic sleeve from the end of the crankshaft.

7 Refit the timing belt crankshaft sprocket as described in Section 8.

Left-hand oil seal

8 Remove the flywheel, as described in Section 16.

9 Measure and note the fitted depth of the seal.

10 Pull the oil seal from the housing using a screwdriver. Alternatively, drill a small hole in the oil seal, and use a self-tapping screw and a pair of pliers to remove it **(see illustration 14.3)**.

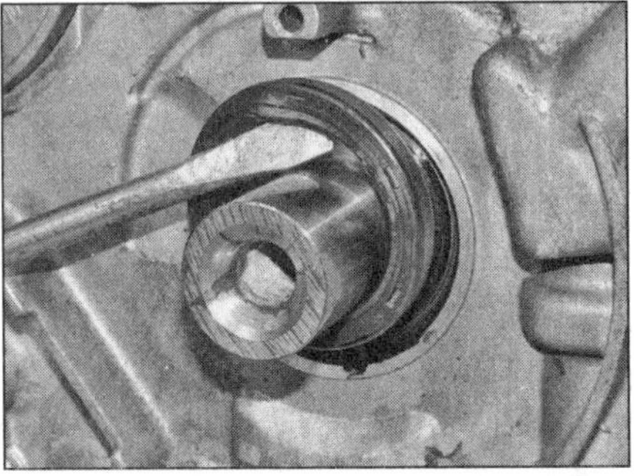

14.3 Take great care not to mark the crankshaft whilst levering out the oil seal

14.5b ... and press the seal into place

11 Clean the oil seal housing and the crankshaft sealing surface.

12 The seal has a Teflon lip and must not be oiled or marked. The new seal should be supplied with a protector sleeve, which fits over the end of the crankshaft to prevent any damage to the seal lip **(see illustration)**. With the sleeve in place, press the seal (open end first) into the housing to the previously-noted depth, using a suitable tube or socket.

13 Where applicable, remove the plastic sleeve from the end of the crankshaft.

14 Refit the flywheel, as described in Section 15.

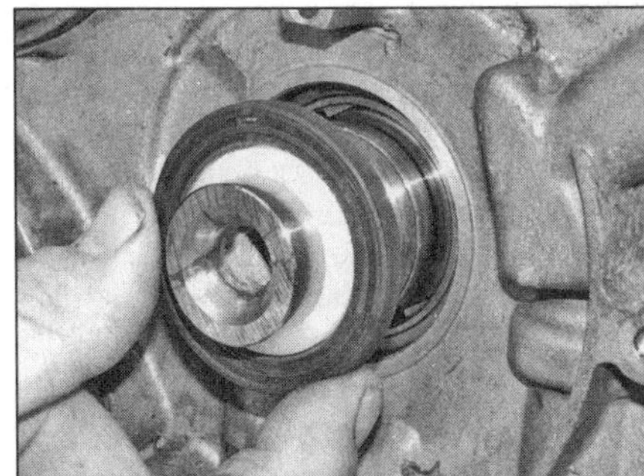

14.5a Slide the seal and protective sleeve over the end of the crankshaft ...

14.12 Slide the seal and protective sleeve over the left-hand end of the crankshaft

14.16 Drill a hole, insert a self-tapping screw, and pull the seal from place using pliers

14.18 Fit the protective sleeve and seal over the end of the camshaft

Camshaft

15 Remove the camshaft sprocket as described in Section 8. In principle there is no need to remove the timing belt completely, but remember that if the belt has been contaminated with oil, it must be renewed.

16 Pull the oil seal from the housing using a hooked instrument. Alternatively, drill a small hole in the oil seal and use a self-tapping screw and a pair of pliers to remove it **(see illustration)**.

17 Clean the oil seal housing and the camshaft sealing surface.

18 The seal has a Teflon lip and must not be oiled or marked. The new seal should be supplied with a protector sleeve. which fits over the end of the camshaft to prevent any damage to the seal lip **(see illustration)**. With the sleeve in place, press the seal (open end first) into the housing to the previously-noted depth, using a suitable tube or socket which bears only of the outer edge of the seal.

19 Refit the camshaft sprocket as described in Section 8.

20 Where necessary, fit a new timing belt with reference to Section 7.

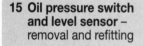

15 Oil pressure switch and level sensor – removal and refitting

Removal

Oil pressure switch

1 The oil pressure switch is located at the front of the cylinder block, adjacent to the oil dipstick guide tube. Note that on some models, access to the switch may be improved if the vehicle is jacked up and supported on axle stands, then undo the screws and remove the engine undershield so that the switch can be reached from underneath (see *Jacking and vehicle support*).

2 Remove the protective sleeve from the wiring plug (where applicable), then disconnect the wiring from the switch.

3 Unscrew the switch from the cylinder block, and recover the sealing washer **(see illustration)**. Be prepared for oil spillage, and if the switch is to be left removed from the engine for any length of time, plug the hole in the cylinder block.

Oil level sensor

4 The oil level sensor (where fitted) is located at the rear of the cylinder block. Jack up the front of the vehicle and support it securely on axle stands (see *Jacking and vehicle support*). Undo the screws and remove the engine undershield.

5 Reach up between the driveshaft and the cylinder block and disconnect the sensor wiring plug **(see illustration)**.

6 Using an open-ended spanner, unscrew the sensor and withdraw it from position.

Refitting

Oil pressure switch

7 Examine the sealing washer for any signs of damage or deterioration, and if necessary renew.

8 Refit the switch, complete with washer, and tighten it to the specified torque.

15.3 The oil pressure switch is located on the front face of the cylinder block (arrowed)

15.5 The oil level sensor is located on the rear face of the cylinder block (arrowed)

9 Refit the engine undershield, and lower the vehicle to the ground.

Oil level sensor

10 Smear a little silicone sealant on the threads and refit the sensor to the cylinder block, tightening it securely.

11 Reconnect the sensor wiring plug.

12 Refit the engine undershield, and lower the vehicle to the ground.

16 Flywheel – removal, inspection and refitting

Removal

1 Remove the transmission as described in Chapter 7A, Section 7, then remove the clutch assembly as described in Chapter 6, Section 7.

2 Prevent the flywheel from turning by locking the ring gear teeth **(see illustration 5.2)**. Alternatively, bolt a strap between the flywheel and the cylinder block/crankcase. *Do not* attempt to lock the flywheel in position using the crankshaft pulley locking tool described in Section 3. Insert a 12 mm diameter rod or drill bit through the hole in the flywheel cover casting, and into a slot in the flywheel **(see illustration 5.3)**

3 Make alignment marks between the flywheel and crankshaft to aid refitment. Slacken and remove the flywheel retaining bolts, and remove the flywheel from the end of the crankshaft. Be careful not to drop it; it is heavy. If the flywheel locating dowel (where fitted) is a loose fit in the crankshaft end, remove it and store it with the flywheel for safe-keeping. Discard the flywheel bolts; new ones must be used on refitting.

Inspection

4 Examine the flywheel for scoring of the clutch face, and for wear or chipping of the ring gear teeth. If the clutch face is scored, the flywheel may be surface-ground, but renewal is preferable. Seek the advice of a Ford dealer or engine reconditioning specialist to see if machining is possible. If the ring gear is worn or damaged, the flywheel must be renewed, as it is not possible to renew the ring gear separately.

Refitting

5 Clean the mating surfaces of the flywheel and crankshaft. Remove any remaining locking compound from the threads of the crankshaft holes, using the correct size of tap, if available.

6 If the new flywheel retaining bolts are not supplied with their threads already pre-coated, apply a suitable thread-locking compound to the threads of each bolt.

7 Ensure that the locating dowel is in position. Offer up the flywheel, locating it on the dowel (where fitted), and fit the new retaining bolts. Where no locating dowel is fitted, align the previously-made marks to ensure the flywheel is refitted in its original position.

8 Lock the flywheel using the method employed on dismantling, and tighten the retaining bolts to the specified torque **(see illustration)**.

9 Refit the clutch as described in Chapter 6, Section 7. Remove the flywheel locking tool, and refit the transmission as described in Chapter 7A, Section 7.

16.8 Flywheel retaining Torx bolts

17 Engine/transmission mountings – inspection and renewal

Inspection

1 If improved access is required, firmly apply the handbrake, then jack up the front of the car and support it on axle stands (see *Jacking and vehicle support*). Undo the screws and remove the engine undershield (if fitted).

2 Check the mounting rubbers to see if they are cracked, hardened or separated from the metal at any point; renew the mounting if any such damage or deterioration is evident.

3 Check that all the mountings' fasteners are securely tightened; use a torque wrench to check if possible.

4 Using a large screwdriver or a crowbar, check for wear in each mounting by carefully levering against it to check for free play. Where this is not possible, enlist the aid of an assistant to move the engine/transmission back-and-forth, or from side-to-side, while you watch the mounting. While some free play is to be expected even from new components, excessive wear should be obvious. If excessive free play is found, check first that the fasteners are correctly secured, then renew any worn components as described below.

Renewal

Right-hand mounting

5 With the engine cold, unscrew the filler cap from the coolant expansion tank, then siphon the coolant into a suitable container. Remove the expansion tank as follows **(see illustrations)**:

a) Unscrew the mounting bolt and lift the expansion tank for access to the lower hoses.
b) Disconnect the thermostat housing degas (by-pass) hose from the top of the tank by squeezing the connector.
c) Disconnect the radiator purge (degas) hose from the side of the tank (near the level marks).
d) Disconnect the water pump by-pass hose from the bottom of the tank.
e) Remove the expansion tank, and plug the coolant hoses.

6 Place a jack beneath the engine, with a block of wood on the jack head. Raise the jack until it is supporting the weight of the engine.

7 Undo the bolts/nut securing the engine mounting to the body and the support bracket **(see illustration)**.

8 If required, undo the bolts/nuts securing the support bracket to the engine.

9 Check all components carefully for signs of wear or damage, and renew as necessary.

10 Where removed, refit the support bracket and tighten the bolts to the specified torque.

11 Refit the mount to the body and support bracket, then tighten the bolts to the specified torque.

12 Remove the jack from underneath the engine.

Left-hand mounting

13 Remove the battery and battery tray (Chapter 5A, Section 4) then unbolt and remove the battery mounting plate **(see illustration)**.

14 Undo the screws and remove the engine undershield (if fitted).

15 Place a jack beneath the transmission, with a block of wood on the jack head. Raise the jack until it is supporting the weight of the transmission.

17.5a Unscrew the mounting bolt ...

17.5b ... lift the coolant expansion tank ...

17.5c ... then disconnect the thermostat housing degas hose ...

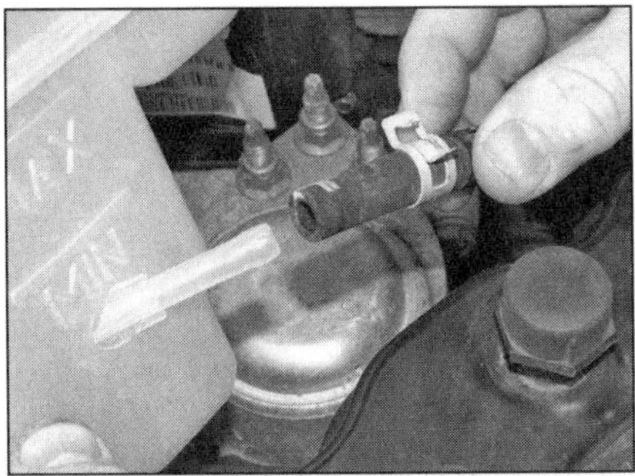

17.5d ... the radiator purge hose ...

17.5e ... and the water pump by-pass hose

17.7 Unscrew the right-hand engine mounting bolts/nuts (arrowed)

17.13 Removing the battery mounting plate

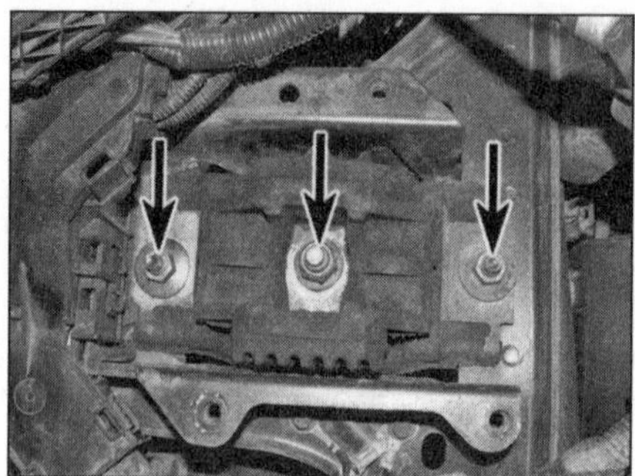
17.16 Left-hand engine/transmission mounting bolts/nut (arrowed), shown with battery mounting plate removed

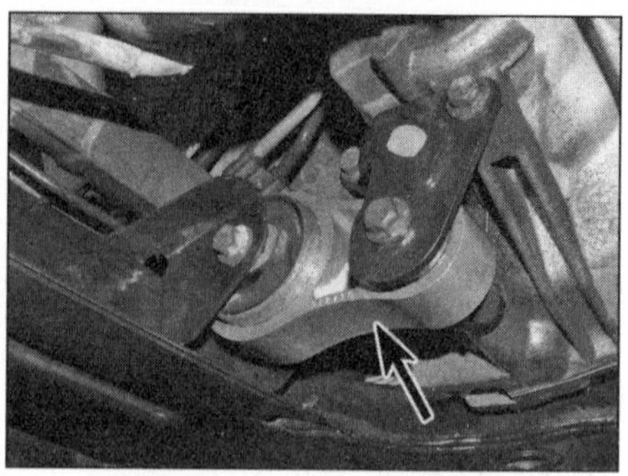
17.20 Lower engine torque rod

16 Slacken and remove the bolts securing the mounting to the support bracket and vehicle body. If required, undo the bolts/nut and remove the support bracket **(see illustration)**.
17 Check all components carefully for signs of wear or damage, and renew as necessary.
18 Refit the mounting, tighten the bolts to the specified torque settings, and remove the jack from underneath the transmission. Refit the battery and mounting plate.

Lower engine torque rod

19 If not already done, chock the rear wheels, then jack up the front of the vehicle and support it securely on axle stands (see *Jacking and vehicle support*). Undo the screws and remove the engine undershield (if fitted).
20 Unscrew and remove the bolt securing the movement limiter link to the driveshaft intermediate bearing housing **(see illustration)**.
21 Remove the bolt securing the link to the subframe. Withdraw the link.
22 To remove the intermediate bearing housing assembly it will first be necessary to remove the right-hand driveshaft as described in Chapter 8, Section 2.
23 With the driveshaft removed, undo the retaining bolts and remove the bearing housing from the rear of the cylinder block.
24 Check carefully for signs of wear or damage on all components, and renew them where necessary. The rubber bush fitted to the bearing housing is available as a separate item (at the time of writing), and can be pressed out of and back into place.
25 On reassembly, fit the bearing housing assembly to the rear of the cylinder block, and tighten its retaining bolts securely. Refit the driveshaft as described in Chapter 8, Section 2.
26 Refit the movement limiter link, and tighten both its bolts to their specified torque settings. Refit the engine undershield.
27 Lower the vehicle to the ground.

Chapter 2 Part D:
Engine removal and overhaul procedures

Contents

Degrees of difficulty

Easy, suitable for novice with little experience 	**Fairly easy,** suitable for beginner with some experience	**Fairly difficult,** suitable for competent DIY mechanic 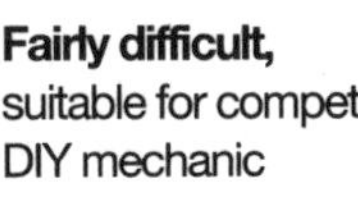	**Difficult,** suitable for experienced DIY mechanic	**Very difficult,** suitable for expert DIY or professional 

Specifications

Engine overhaul data and torque wrench settings

Petrol engine

Refer to Chapter 2A Specifications.

1.4 litre diesel engine

Refer to Chapter 2B Specifications.

1.6 litre litre diesel engine

Refer to Chapter 2C Specifications.

1 General information

Included in this Chapter are details of removing the engine/transmission from the car and general overhaul procedures for the cylinder head, cylinder block/crankcase and internal engine components.

The information given ranges from advice concerning preparation for an overhaul and the purchase of new parts, to detailed step-by-step procedures covering removal, inspection, renovation and refitting of internal engine parts.

The following Sections have been compiled based on the assumption that the engine has been removed from the car. For information concerning in-car engine repair, as well as the removal and refitting of the external components necessary for the overhaul, refer to Chapter 2A (petrol engine), Chapter 2B (1.4 litre diesel engine) or Chapter 2C (1.6 litre diesel engine). Also refer to Section 4 and Section 5 of this Chapter.

2 Engine overhaul – general information

It is not always easy to determine when, or if, an engine should be completely overhauled, as a number of factors must be considered.

High mileage is not necessarily an indication that an overhaul is needed, while low mileage does not preclude the need for an overhaul. Frequency of servicing is probably the most important consideration. An engine which has had regular and frequent oil and filter changes, as well as other required maintenance, will most likely give many thousands of miles of reliable service. Conversely, a neglected engine may require an overhaul very early in its life.

Excessive oil consumption is an indication that piston rings, valve stem oil seals and/ or valves and valve guides are in need of attention. Make sure that oil leaks are not responsible before deciding that the rings and/or guides are to blame. Perform a cylinder compression check to determine the likely cause of the problem.

Check the oil pressure with a gauge fitted in place of the oil pressure switch, and compare it with the value given in the Specifications. If it is extremely low, the main and big-end bearings and/or the oil pump are probably worn out.

Loss of power, rough running, knocking or metallic engine noises, excessive valve gear noise and high fuel consumption may also point to the need for an overhaul, especially if they are all present at the same time. If a complete tune-up does not remedy the situation, major mechanical work is the only solution.

An engine overhaul involves restoring the internal parts to the specifications of a new engine. During an overhaul, the pistons and rings are renewed, and the cylinder bores are reconditioned. New main bearings, connecting rod bearings and camshaft bearings are generally fitted, and if necessary, the crankshaft may be reground to restore the journals (note however that some of this work is not possible on the petrol engine). The valves are also serviced as well, since they are usually in less-than-perfect condition at this point. While the engine is being overhauled, other components, such as the starter and alternator, can be overhauled as well. The end result should be a like-new engine that will give many trouble-free miles. **Note:** *Critical cooling system components such as the hoses, drivebelts, thermostat and water pump should be renewed when an engine is overhauled. The radiator should be checked carefully, to ensure that it is not clogged or leaking. Also, it is a good idea to renew the oil pump whenever the engine is overhauled.*

Before beginning the engine overhaul, read through the entire procedure to familiarise yourself with the scope and requirements of the job. Overhauling an engine is not difficult if you follow all of the instructions carefully, have the necessary tools and equipment, and pay close attention to all specifications; however, it can be time-consuming. Plan on the car being tied up for a minimum of two weeks, especially if parts must be taken to an engineering works for repair or reconditioning. Check on the availability of parts, and make sure that any necessary special tools and equipment are obtained in advance. Most work can be done with typical hand tools, although a number of precision measuring tools are required for inspecting parts to determine if they must be renewed. Often the engineering works will handle the inspection of parts, and offer advice concerning reconditioning and renewal.

Always wait until the engine has been completely dismantled, and all components, especially the engine block, have been inspected before deciding what service and repair operations must be performed by an engineering works. Since the condition of the block will be the major factor to consider when determining whether to overhaul the original engine or buy a reconditioned unit, do not purchase parts or have overhaul work done on other components until the block has been thoroughly inspected. As a general rule, time is the primary cost of an overhaul, so it does not pay to fit worn or substandard parts.

As a final note, to ensure maximum life and minimum trouble from a reconditioned engine, everything must be assembled with care, and in a spotlessly-clean environment.

4.2 Remove the battery support tray

3 Engine removal – methods and precautions

If you have decided that an engine must be removed for overhaul or major repair work, several preliminary steps should be taken.

Locating a suitable place to work is extremely important. Adequate work space, along with storage space for the car, will be needed. If a garage is not available, at the very least a flat, level, clean work surface is required.

Cleaning the engine compartment and engine before beginning the removal procedure will help keep tools clean and organised.

The engine is removed complete with the transmission by lowering it out of the car; the car's body must be raised and supported securely sufficiently high that the engine/transmission can be unbolted as a single unit and lowered to the ground. An engine hoist will therefore be necessary. Make sure the equipment is rated in excess of the combined weight of the engine and transmission. Safety is of primary importance, considering the potential hazards involved in lifting the engine out of the car.

If the engine is being removed by a novice, an assistant should be available. Advice and aid from someone more experienced would also be helpful. There are many instances when one person cannot simultaneously perform all of the operations required when removing the engine from the car.

Plan the operation ahead of time. Arrange for, or obtain, all of the tools and equipment you will need, prior to beginning the job. Some of the equipment necessary to perform engine removal and installation safely and with relative ease are (in addition to an engine hoist) a heavy-duty trolley jack, complete sets of spanners and sockets as described at the end of this manual, wooden blocks, and plenty of rags and cleaning solvent for mopping-up spilled oil, coolant and fuel. If the hoist must be hired, make sure that you arrange for it in advance, and perform all of the operations possible without it beforehand. This will save you money and time.

Plan for the car to be out of use for quite a while. An engineering works will be required to perform some of the work which the home mechanic cannot accomplish without special equipment. These places often have a busy schedule, so it would be a good idea to consult them before removing the engine, in order to accurately estimate the amount of time required to rebuild or repair components that may need work.

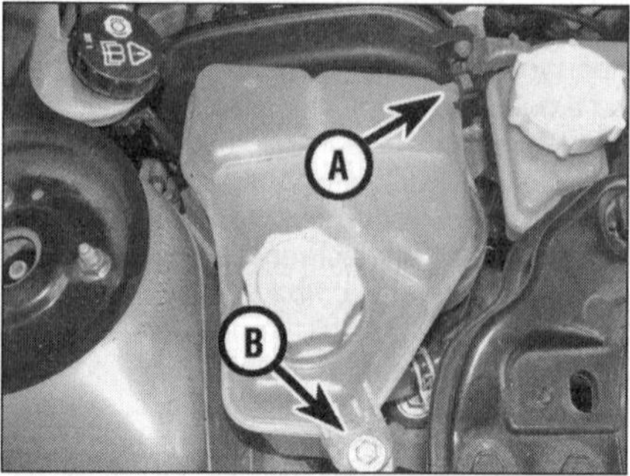

4.8 Remove the hose (A) and remove the bolt (B)

During the engine/transmission removal procedure, it is advisable to make notes of the locations of all brackets, cable-ties, earthing points, etc, as well as how the wiring harnesses, hoses and electrical connections are attached and routed around the engine and engine compartment. An effective way of doing this is to take a series of photographs of the various components before they are disconnected or removed; the resulting photographs will prove invaluable when the engine/transmission is refitted. **Note:** *Such is the complexity of the power unit arrangement on these vehicles, and the variations that may be encountered according to model and optional equipment fitted, that the procedures given in Sections 4, 5 and 6 should be regarded as a guide to the work involved, rather than an accurate step-by-step procedure. Where differences are encountered, or additional component disconnection or removal is necessary, make notes of the work involved as an aid to refitting.*

Warning: Always be extremely careful when removing and refitting the engine. Serious injury can result from careless actions. Plan ahead, take your time, and you will find that a job of this nature, although major, can be accomplished successfully.

4 Petrol engine – removal, separation and refitting

1 Depressurise the fuel system with reference to Chapter 4A, Section 2.

2 Remove the battery and the battery tray as described in Chapter 5A, Section 4 **(see illustration)**. Also unbolt and remove the battery tray support bracket, which is secured by three bolts.

3 Drain the cooling system as described in Chapter 1A, Section 26.

4 If the engine is being dismantled, drain the engine oil with reference to Chapter 1A, Section 3.

5 Remove the air cleaner as described in Chapter 4A, Section 5, then disconnect the fuel supply and return line quick-release connections from the fuel rail at the front of the engine.

6 Loosen the three upper mounting nuts on both front suspension struts by three turns.

7 Disconnect the engine management ECU wiring plug next to the battery location, by sliding the locking clip upwards to separate the plug.

8 Disconnect the small upper hose from the coolant expansion tank, then unbolt the tank from the inner wing and move it to one side, without removing any further hoses **(see illustration)**.

4.10 Unclip the power steering reservoir

4.12 Remove the two front coolant hoses

4.13 Disconnect the wiring plug from the coil pack

9 Cut the cable-tie securing the small-bore coolant hose and the fuel lines to the top of the inlet manifold. Trace the coolant hose along to its connection to the cylinder head, and disconnect it.

10 Lift the power steering fluid reservoir off its mounting clips **(see illustration)** and move it to one side without disconnecting the hoses from it.

11 Disconnect the hose from the EVAP valve just below the fuel pressure regulator on the fuel rail. Also disconnect the brake servo vacuum hose from the inlet manifold.

12 Disconnect the two coolant hoses from the outlet elbow on the left-hand side of the engine, and also the two hoses from the thermostat housing on the front **(see illustration)**.

13 Disconnect the following wiring plugs:

a) Oxygen sensor wiring plug, located just behind the ignition coil, and the catalyst monitor wiring plug below it.

b) Power steering pressure switch, which is located in the fluid line, at the rear of the engine bay.

c) Engine wiring harness main connector, and the EVAP valve wiring plug, both located below the fuel pressure regulator.

d) Camshaft position sensor wiring plug, which is located on the rear of the cylinder head, at the timing belt end.

e) Knock sensor wiring plug, located underneath the inlet manifold.

f) Alternator and starter motor wiring (refer to Chapter 5A if necessary).

g) Where applicable, the following air conditioning wiring plugs – low-pressure switch (behind the right-hand headlight), high-pressure switch (near the battery tray location), and the main compressor wiring plug.

h) Oil pressure switch, next to the oil filter.

i) Crankshaft position switch, on the front of the engine, at the transmission end.

j) Reversing light switch, on the front of the transmission.

k) Coolant temperature sensor, below the ignition coil.

l) Ignition coil main wiring plug ***(see illustration).***

14 Unbolt the engine earth strap just below the ignition coil, and the engine wiring harness support bracket just in front.

15 Working at the rear of the engine, unbolt the exhaust flexible section from the catalytic converter, and separate the joint.

16 Remove the single bolt securing the power steering fluid hose support bracket to the rear of the cylinder head.

17 Remove the auxiliary drivebelt as described in Chapter 1A, Section 23.

18 Where applicable, remove the four bolts securing the air conditioning compressor to the block, and secure the compressor to one side – do not disconnect any of the hoses.

19 Remove the single bolt securing the power steering fluid hose support bracket to the steering gear, a further bolt holding a similar bracket to the power steering pump, and finally, the bolt securing the power steering fluid hose to the inlet manifold.

20 Using a suitable spanner, loosen and disconnect the fluid union at the base of the power steering pump, and allow the fluid to drain into a container.

21 Remove the radiator cooling fan and shroud – refer to Chapter 3, Section 5 if necessary.

22 Jack up the front of the car, and support it on axle stands (see *Jacking and vehicle support*). Although not essential immediately, it would pay at this stage to raise the car sufficiently to allow the engine and transmission to be withdrawn from underneath.

23 Where applicable, unclip the cover from the gear shift cables on the front of the transmission. Unclip the cable end fittings, then twist the cables clockwise to release them from their mounting brackets **(see illustration)**.

24 On both sides of the car, remove the lower arm balljoint clamp bolt from the swivel hub, and lever down the lower arm to separate it. Unclip the balljoint heat shields, and retain them for refitting.

25 Using the information in Chapter 8, Section 2, disconnect both driveshafts from the transmission, and also remove the intermediate shaft. There is no need to remove the driveshafts from the hubs, providing they can be supported clear so that the engine/transmission can drop down. The inner and outer joints should not be bent through more than 18° and 45° respectively.

26 To prevent damage to the exhaust flexible section, support it by attaching a pair of splints either side (two scrap strips of wood, plant canes, etc) using some cable-ties. Undo the nuts securing the flexible section to the exhaust manifold, and separate the joint. Recover the gasket, and discard it.

27 Unbolt the engine rear mounting from under the car **(see illustration)** referring to Chapter 2A, Section 18 if necessary.

28 Taking precautions against fluid spillage, prise up the spring clip and disconnect the clutch slave cylinder fluid pipe from on top of the transmission. Unclip the pipe, and tie it up to the bulkhead to reduce further fluid spillage **(see illustrations)**.

29 Make a final check round the engine and transmission, to make sure nothing (apart from

4.23 Disconnect the gearchange cables

4.27 Remove the rear pendulum mounting

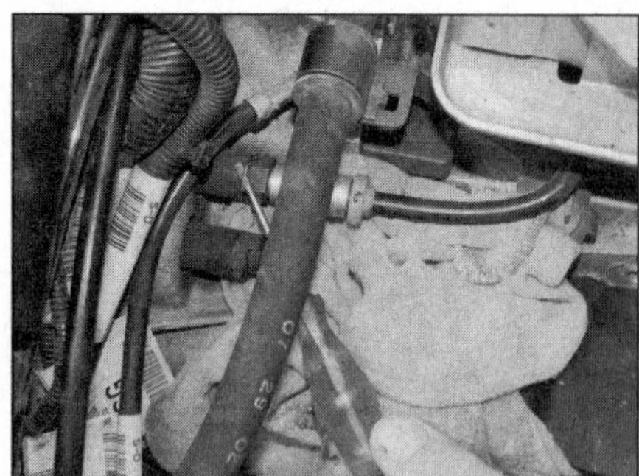

4.28a Use a small screwdriver to prise up the spring clip ...

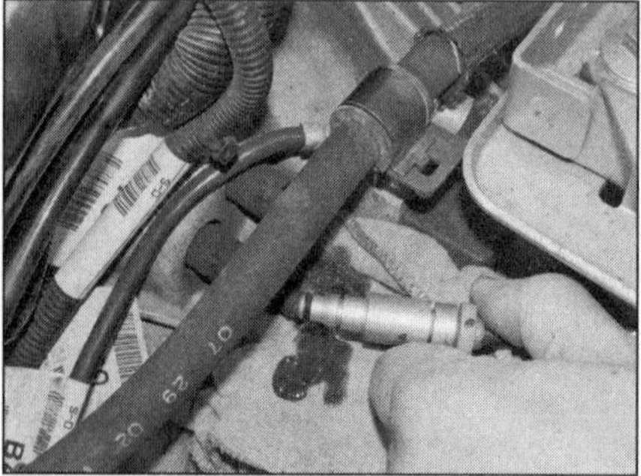

4.28b ... then pull out the clutch supply pipe

the left- and right-hand mountings) remains attached or in the way which will prevent it from being lowered out. Also make sure there is enough room under the front of the car for the engine/transmission to be lowered out and withdrawn.

30 Securely attach the engine/transmission unit to a suitable engine crane or hoist, and raise it so that the weight is just taken off the two remaining engine mountings. It is helpful at this stage to have an assistant available, either to work the crane or to guide the engine out.

31 With the engine securely supported, remove the three nuts from the engine left-hand mounting **(see illustration)**.

32 Similarly, remove the three nuts and bolts from the engine right-hand mounting, on the driver's side of the engine compartment **(see illustration)**.

33 With the help of an assistant, carefully lower the assembly from the engine compartment, making sure it clears the surrounding components and bodywork. Be prepared to steady the engine when it touches down, to stop it toppling over. Withdraw the assembly from under the car, and remove it to wherever it will be worked on.

Separation

34 To separate the transmission from the engine, first remove the starter motor with reference to Chapter 5A, Section 11.

35 Progressively unscrew and remove the transmission-to-engine bolts (eight in total), noting where each one goes, as they are of different lengths.

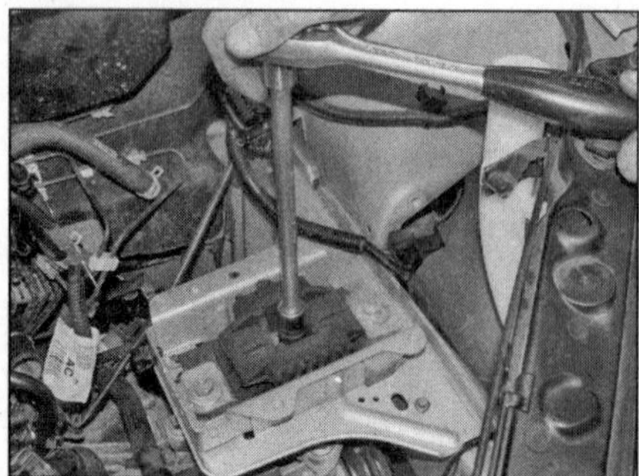

4.31 Unscrew the left-hand mounting nuts

36 With the help of an assistant, withdraw the transmission directly from the engine, making sure that its weight is not allowed to bear on the clutch friction disc.

Refitting

37 Refitting is a reversal of removal, noting the following additional points:

a) *Make sure that all mating faces are clean, and use new gaskets where necessary.*
b) *Tighten all nuts and bolts to the specified torque setting, where given.*
c) *Lightly oil the splines of the transmission input shaft. Do not apply too much, otherwise there is the possibility of the oil contaminating the clutch friction disc.*
d) *Make sure that the clutch release bearing is correctly located in the slave cylinder inside the transmission bellhousing.*
e) *Use new nuts on the engine left- and right-hand mountings, but do not fully-tighten them until the car is resting on its wheels.*
f) *Use a new centre bearing cap and locknuts when refitting the intermediate shaft.*
g) *Fit new circlips to the grooves in the inner end of each driveshaft CV joint, and ensure that they fully engage as they are fitted into the transmission.*
h) *Check and if necessary adjust the gearchange cables as described in Chapter 7A, Section 2.*
i) *Use a new O-ring when refitting the power steering fluid union.*
j) *Replenish the transmission oil, and check the level with reference to Chapter 1A, Section 18.*
k) *Top-up and bleed the clutch hydraulic system as described in Chapter 6, Section 5.*
l) *Refill the cooling system as described in Chapter 1A, Section 26.*
m) *Tighten the suspension strut upper mounting nuts to the specified torque on completion (see Chapter 10, Specifications).*

4.32 Remove the right-hand engine mounting

5 Diesel engine – removal, separation and refitting

Warning: The diesel injection system operates at extremely high pressures when the pump is running. Wait at least one minute after stopping the engine before working on the fuel injection system components.

Removal

1 Remove the battery and the battery tray as described in Chapter 5A, Section 4.

2 Drain the cooling system as described in Chapter 1B, Section 25.

3 If the engine is being dismantled, drain the engine oil with reference to Chapter 1B, Section 3.

4 Loosen the three upper mounting nuts on both front suspension struts by three turns.

5 Where applicable, disconnect the wiring plug for the EGR solenoid valve from behind the screen wash filler neck, then remove the two screws securing the valve to the battery tray mounting bracket, and move the valve to one side.

6 Unbolt the engine earth strap from the inner wing next to the screen wash filler neck. Also, unbolt the earth strap from the top of the transmission.

7 Disconnect the following wiring (all in the battery tray area):

a) *Remove the two plugs from the fuse/relay holder next to the battery.*
b) *Release the three wiring plugs from the engine management ECU by turning their locking collars anti-clockwise, then pulling towards you.*
c) *Disconnect the multiplug from the glow plug relay.*
d) *Unbolt the two glow plug relay power supply cables.*

8 Unbolt and remove the battery tray support bracket (four bolts).

9 Remove the radiator cooling fan and shroud – refer to Chapter 3, Section 5 if necessary.

10 Disconnect the hoses from the coolant expansion tank, then unbolt and remove it from the inner wing.

11 Remove the air cleaner as described in Chapter 4B, Section 4.

12 Disconnect the three coolant hoses from the thermostat housing at the front of the engine, and the two hoses from the heater matrix on the bulkhead.

1.4 litre engine

13 Lift the power steering fluid reservoir off its mounting clips on the engine compartment front panel. The reservoir must now be completely removed, so either siphon the fluid out, pour it out (if possible), or be ready to catch the fluid in a container when the reservoir supply hose at the base is disconnected .

14 Cover the alternator (for instance, with a plastic bag) to protect it from power steering fluid during subsequent operations. Release the spring clip and pull off the power steering fluid reservoir supply hose. Remove the reservoir from the engine compartment.

15 Remove the single bolt securing the power steering fluid hose support bracket to the power steering pump.

16 Using a suitable spanner, loosen and disconnect the fluid union at the top of the power steering pump, and allow the fluid to drain into a container. Discard the union's O-ring seal – a new one should be used when refitting.

17 Trace the engine wiring harness from the transmission end of the engine, and cut any cable-ties securing it to parts of the engine.

18 Disconnect the vacuum hose from the brake vacuum pump, located at the transmission end of the cylinder head (refer to Chapter 9, Section 21 for more details if necessary).

19 At the rear of the engine, disconnect either the vacuum hose from the base of the EGR valve, or disconnect the wiring plug near the EGR pipe elbow.

20 Release the hose clip and disconnect the heater return hose from the rear of the engine.

21 Disconnect the wiring plug for the heater electric control valve.

22 On models with air conditioning, remove the single bolt securing the pressure hose bracket to the transmission, and also disconnect the low-pressure switch wiring plug behind the right-hand headlight (right as seen from the driver's seat).

23 Depress the locking clip and disconnect the quick-release fitting on the fuel return line above the fuel filter.

24 Remove the two bolts securing the fuel filter shield, and remove the shield **(see illustration)**.

25 Clean carefully around the fuel filter connections and lines – it is vitally important that no dirt enters the fuel system. Have ready some caps or plugs (or some tape) to cover any open fuel lines.

26 Disconnect the fuel supply line from the fuel filter, by depressing the locking clip on the quick-release fitting **(see illustration)**. Cover the open end of the fuel line, to prevent further fuel loss, and particularly to prevent dirt entry into the system.

27 Unplug the power steering pressure switch wiring connector, located in the power steering fluid hose under the car.

1.6 litre engine

28 Remove the intercooler as described in Chapter 4B, Section 18.

29 Remove the left-hand headlight assembly as described in Chapter 12, Section 7.

30 Remove the fuel line quick-release coupling located at the left-hand rear corner of the engine compartment.

31 Disconnect the wiring plug next to the left-hand suspension tower.

32 Disconnect the vacuum hose from the brake vacuum servo unit.

33 Remove the turbocharger-to-intercooler hose, then remove the intercooler-to-inlet manifold hose.

34 Remove the powertrain control module (PCM) as described in Chapter 4B, Section 13.

35 On models with air conditioning, remove the single bolt securing the pressure hose bracket to the transmission, and also disconnect the low-pressure switch wiring plug behind the right-hand headlight (right as seen from the driver's seat).

36 Remove the EGR vacuum lines from the left-hand side of the engine compartment.

37 Working through the left-hand headlight aperture, disconnect the wiring from the electro-hydraulic power steering pump.

All engines

38 Jack up the front of the car, and support it on axle stands (see *Jacking and vehicle support*). Although not essential immediately, it would pay at this stage to raise the car sufficiently to allow the engine and transmission to be withdrawn from underneath. Remove both front roadwheels, and also remove the left-hand wheel arch liner.

39 To prevent damage to the exhaust flexible section, support it by attaching a pair of splints either side (two scrap strips of wood, plant canes, etc) using some cable-ties.

40 Unbolt the exhaust flexible section from the catalytic converter, then unhook the front pipe from the mounting. If necessary, support the exhaust system while it is disconnected, using either axle stands or, possibly, cable-ties.

41 Remove the auxiliary drivebelt as described in Chapter 1B, Section 22.

42 Where applicable, disconnect the air conditioning compressor wiring plug, then remove the four mounting bolts and secure the compressor to one side – do not disconnect any of the hoses.

43 Unclip the cover from the gear shift cables on the front of the transmission. Unclip the cable end fittings, then twist the cables clockwise to release them from their mounting brackets. If necessary, unbolt and remove the brackets.

44 On both sides of the car, remove the lower arm balljoint clamp bolt from the swivel hub, and lever down the lower arm to separate it. Unclip the balljoint heat shields, and retain them for refitting.

45 Using the information in Chapter 8, Section 2, disconnect both driveshafts from the transmission, and also remove the intermediate shaft. There is no need to remove the driveshafts from the hubs, providing they can be supported clear so that the engine/transmission can drop down. The inner and outer joints should not be bent through more than 18° and 45° respectively.

5.24 Remove the fuel filter cover

46 Unbolt the engine rear mounting from under the car, referring to Chapter 2B or 2C if necessary.

47 Taking precautions against fluid spillage, remove the spring clip and disconnect the clutch slave cylinder fluid pipe from on top of the transmission.

48 Make a final check round the engine and transmission, to make sure nothing (apart from the left- and right-hand mountings) remains attached or in the way which will prevent it from being lowered out. Also make sure there is enough room under the front of the car for the engine/transmission to be lowered out and withdrawn.

49 Securely attach the engine/transmission unit to a suitable engine crane or hoist, and raise it so that the weight is just taken off the two remaining engine mountings. It is helpful at this stage to have an assistant available, either to work the crane or to guide the engine out.

50 With the engine securely supported, remove the three nuts from the engine left-hand mounting (on top of the transmission).

51 Similarly, remove the three nuts from the engine right-hand mounting, on the driver's side of the engine compartment.

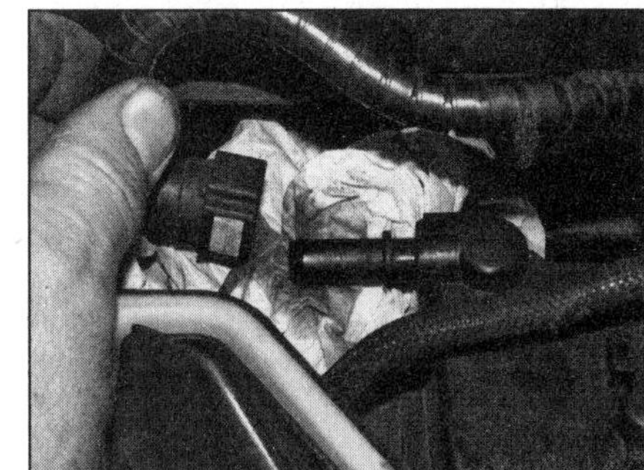

5.26 Release the fuel line from the filter

52 With the help of an assistant, carefully lower the assembly from the engine compartment, making sure it clears the surrounding components and bodywork. Be prepared to steady the engine when it touches down, to stop it toppling over. Withdraw the assembly from under the car, and remove it to wherever it will be worked on. Take care not to damage the fuel pressure sensor wiring plug when moving the assembly.

Separation

53 To separate the transmission from the engine, first remove the starter motor with reference to Chapter 5A, Section 11.

54 Progressively unscrew and remove the transmission-to-engine bolts, noting where each one goes, as they are of different lengths.

55 With the help of an assistant, withdraw the transmission directly from the engine, making sure that its weight is not allowed to bear on the clutch friction disc. Note that there are two locating dowels used.

Refitting

56 Refitting is a reversal of removal, noting the following additional points:

a) Make sure that all mating faces are clean, and use new gaskets where necessary.
b) Tighten all nuts and bolts to the specified torque setting, where given.
c) Lightly oil the splines of the transmission input shaft. Do not apply too much, otherwise there is the possibility of the oil contaminating the clutch friction disc.
d) Make sure that the clutch release bearing is correctly located in the slave cylinder inside the transmission bellhousing.
e) Use new nuts on the engine left and right-hand mountings, but do not fully-tighten them until the car is resting on its wheels.
f) Use a new centre bearing cap and locknuts when refitting the intermediate shaft.
g) Fit new circlips to the grooves in the inner end of each driveshaft CV joint, and ensure that they fully engage as they are fitted into the transmission.
h) Check and if necessary adjust the gearchange cables as described in Chapter 7A, Section 2.
i) On 1.4 litre models, use a new O-ring when refitting the power steering fluid union.
j) Replenish the transmission oil, and check the level with reference to Chapter 1B, Section 19.
k) Top-up and bleed the clutch hydraulic system as described in Chapter 6, Section 5.
l) Refill the cooling system as described in Chapter 1B, Section 25.
m) Tighten the suspension strut upper mounting nuts to the specified torque on completion (see Chapter 10, Specifications).

6 Engine overhaul – dismantling sequence

1 It is much easier to dismantle and work on the engine if it is mounted on a portable engine stand. These stands can often be hired from a tool hire shop. Before the engine is mounted on a stand, the flywheel should be removed from the engine, so that the engine stand bolts can be tightened into the end of the cylinder block.

2 If a stand is not available, it is possible to dismantle the engine with it blocked up on a sturdy workbench or on the floor. Be extra careful not to tip or drop the engine when working without a stand.

Caution: DO NOT attempt to remove the crankshaft or main bearing cap/ladder on petrol engines, as it is not possible to refit it accurately using conventional tooling. The manufacturers do not supply torque settings for the main bearing cap/ladder retaining bolts. If the crankshaft is worn excessively, it will be necessary to obtain a new short motor comprising the cylinder block together with the pistons and crankshaft.

3 If you're going to obtain a reconditioned ('recon') engine, all external components must be removed first, to be transferred to the new engine (just as they will if you are doing a complete engine overhaul yourself). **Note:** *When removing the external components from the engine, pay close attention to details that may be helpful or important during refitting. Note the fitted position of gaskets, seals, spacers, pins, washers, bolts and other small items. These external components include the following:*

Petrol engine

a) Alternator and brackets.
b) DIS ignition coil, HT leads and spark plugs.
c) Thermostat housing.
d) Fuel injection equipment.
e) Inlet and exhaust manifolds.
f) Oil filter.
g) Engine mountings and lifting brackets.
h) Ancillary brackets (power steering pump, air conditioning compressor).
i) Oil filler tube and dipstick.
j) Coolant pipes and hoses.
k) Flywheel.

Diesel engine

a) Alternator mounting bracket.
b) Fuel injection pump and mounting bracket, and fuel injectors and glow plugs.
c) Thermostat housing.
d) Inlet and exhaust manifolds.
e) Oil cooler.
f) Engine lifting brackets, hose brackets and wiring brackets.
g) Ancillary brackets (power steering pump on 1.4 litre, air conditioning compressor).
h) Oil pressure warning light switch and oil level sensor (where applicable).
i) Coolant temperature sensors.
j) Wiring harnesses and brackets.
k) Coolant pipes and hoses.
l) Oil filler tube and dipstick.
m) Clutch.
n) Flywheel.

All engines

4 If you are obtaining a 'short' motor (which, when available, consists of the engine cylinder block, crankshaft, pistons and connecting rods all assembled) then the cylinder head, sump, oil pump, and timing belt will have to be removed also.

5 If you are planning a complete overhaul, the engine can be disassembled and the internal components removed in the following order:

a) Engine external components (including inlet and exhaust manifolds).
b) Timing sprockets and belt.
c) Cylinder head.
d) Flywheel.
e) Sump.
f) Oil pump.
g) Pistons and connecting rods.
h) Crankshaft and main bearings.

6 Before beginning the disassembly and overhaul procedures, make sure that you have all of the correct tools necessary. Refer to *Tools and working facilities* at the end of this manual for further information.

7 Cylinder head – dismantling

Note: *New and reconditioned cylinder heads are available from the manufacturers and from engine overhaul specialists. Due to the fact that some specialist tools are required for the dismantling and inspection procedures, and new components may not be readily available, it may be more practical and economical for the home mechanic to purchase a reconditioned head rather than dismantle, inspect and recondition the original head.*

1 Remove the cylinder head as described in Chapter 2A, 2B or 2C (as applicable).

2 If not already done, remove the inlet and exhaust manifolds with reference to Chapter 4A or 4B. Also remove all external brackets and elbows.

3 Proceed as follows according to engine type.

Petrol engine

4 Remove the camshafts and tappets as described in Chapter 2A, being careful to store the components as described.

5 Using a valve spring compressor, compress each valve spring in turn until the split collets can be removed. A special valve spring compressor will be required, to reach into the deep wells in the cylinder head without risk of damaging the tappet bores; such compressors are now widely available from

most good motor accessory shops. Release the compressor, and lift off the spring upper seat and spring **(see illustration)**.

6 If, when the valve spring compressor is screwed down, the spring upper seat refuses to free and expose the split collets, gently tap the top of the tool, directly over the upper seat, with a light hammer. This will free the seat.

7 Withdraw the valve through the combustion chamber. If it binds in the guide (won't pull through), push it back in, and de-burr the area around the collet groove with a fine file; take care not to mark the tappet bores.

8 Pull the valve stem seals from the valve guides using a pair of pliers. As the seals are removed, note whether they are of different colours for the inlet and exhaust valves – compare with the new parts, and note this for refitting. As a guide, the inlet valve seals are green, and the exhaust seals are red.

9 It is essential that the valves are kept together with their collets, spring seats and springs, and in their correct sequence (unless they are so badly worn that they are to be renewed). If they are going to be kept and used again, place them in a labelled polythene bag or similar small container **(see illustration)**. Note that No 1 valve is nearest to the timing belt end of the engine.

Diesel engine

10 Remove the turbocharger, which is secured by four nuts – discard the nuts once removed, as new ones should be used on reassembly.

11 Remove the nuts securing the exhaust manifold, and withdraw the manifold from the head. Discard the nuts (and the gasket). Ford also state that the manifold studs should be removed, and new ones obtained for reassembly.

12 Take off the glow plug wiring harness, noting how it is routed, then remove the glow plugs.

13 Unbolt and remove the EGR valve and recover the gasket.

14 Remove the oil pressure relief valve, which is located at the transmission end of the head.

15 Take off the fuel filter support nut (at the rear of the head, on the transmission end).

16 Lift out the hydraulic tappets and, on the 1.6 litre engine, the rocker arms – these must all be kept in their fitted order. There is no requirement by Ford to keep the hydraulic tappets in an oil bath while they're removed, but there's no harm in doing so. The most important thing is that the tappets are stored (or marked) so they can be refitted to their original locations.

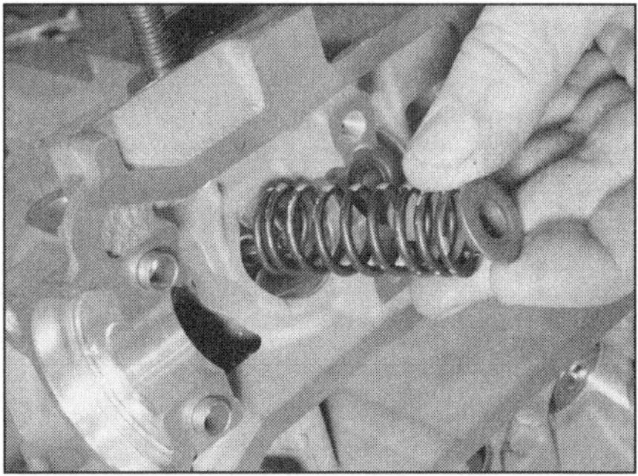

7.5 Removing the valve spring and upper seat

17 To remove the valve springs and valves from the cylinder head, a standard valve spring compressor will be required. Fit the spring compressor to the first valve and spring to be removed. Assuming that all of the valves and springs are to be removed, start by compressing the No 1 valve (nearest the timing cover end) spring. Take care not to damage the valve stem with the compressor, and do not over-compress the spring, or the valve stem may bend.

18 When tightening the compressor, it may be found that the spring retainer does not release and the collets are then difficult to remove. In this instance, remove the compressor, then press a piece of tube (or a socket of suitable diameter) so that it does not interfere with the removal of the collets, against the retainer's outer rim. Tap the tube (or socket) with a hammer to unsettle the components.

19 Refit the compressor, and wind it in to enable the collets to be extracted.

20 Loosen off the compressor, and remove the retainer and spring. Withdraw the valve from the cylinder head.

21 Pull the valve stem seals from the valve guides using a pair of pliers. The valve stem oil seal also forms the spring seat and is deeply recessed in the cylinder head. It is also a tight fit on the valve guide making it difficult to remove with pliers or a conventional valve stem oil seal removal tool. It can be easily removed, however, using a self-locking nut of suitable diameter screwed onto the end of a bolt and locked with a second nut. Push the nut down onto the top of the seal; the locking portion of the nut will grip the seal allowing it to be withdrawn from the top of the valve guide. Access to the valves is limited, and it may be necessary to make up an adapter out of metal tube – cut out a 'window' so that the valve collets can be removed **(see illustrations)**.

7.9 Use a labelled plastic bag to store and identify valve components

22 Repeat the removal procedure with each of the remaining valve assemblies in turn. As they are removed, keep the individual valves and their components together, and in their respective order of fitting, by placing them in a separate labelled bag **(see illustration 7.9)**.

8 Cylinder head and valves – cleaning, inspection and renovation

1 Thorough cleaning of the cylinder head and valve components, followed by a detailed inspection, will enable you to decide how much valve service work must be carried out during the engine overhaul.

Cleaning

2 Scrape away all traces of old gasket material and sealing compound from the cylinder head. Take care not to damage the cylinder head surfaces.

7.21a Use a pair of pliers to remove the valve stem oil seal

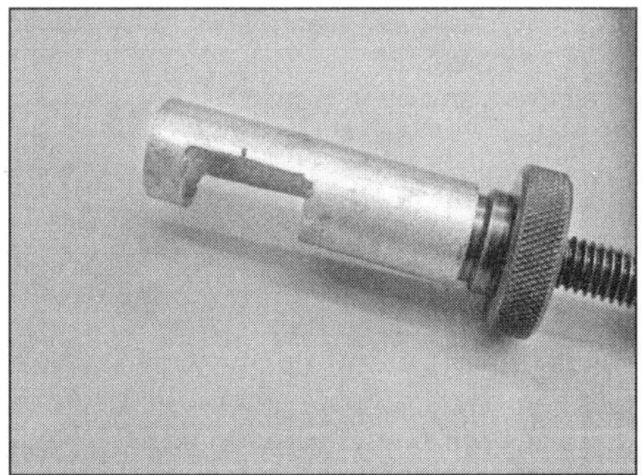

7.21b Metal tube adapter for access to the valve collets

7.21c Secure a self-locking nut of suitable diameter to a long bolt, then use the tool to remove the valve stem oil seal

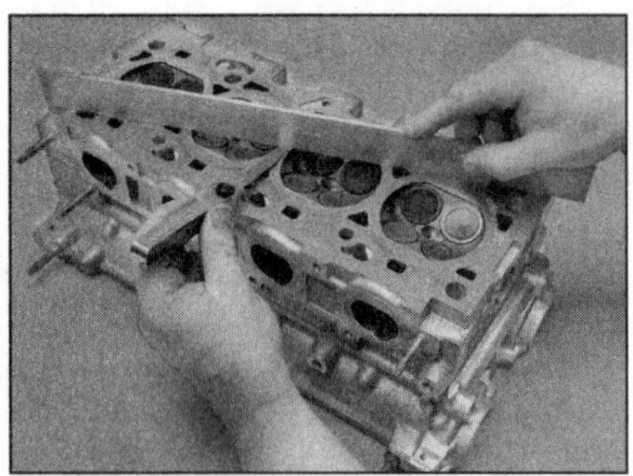

8.7 Check the head for warpage using a straight-edge and feeler blades

8.13 Measuring the diameter of a valve stem

8.19 Checking the valve spring free length

3 Scrape away the carbon from the combustion chambers and ports, then wash the cylinder head thoroughly with paraffin or a suitable solvent.

4 Scrape off any heavy carbon deposits that may have formed on the valves, then use a power-operated wire brush to remove deposits from the valve heads and stems.

5 If the head is extremely dirty, it should be steam cleaned. On completion, make sure that all oil holes and oil galleries are cleaned.

Inspection and renovation

Note: *Be sure to perform all the following inspection procedures before concluding that the services of an engine overhaul specialist are required. Make a list of all items that require attention.*

Cylinder head

6 Inspect the head very carefully for cracks, evidence of coolant leakage and other damage. If cracks are found, a new cylinder head should be obtained.

7 Use a straight-edge and feeler blade to check that the cylinder head surface is not distorted **(see illustration)**. If the specified distortion limit is exceeded, machining of the gasket face is not recommended by the manufacturers, so the only course of action is to renew the cylinder head.

8 Examine the valve seats in each of the combustion chambers. If they are severely pitted, cracked or burned, then they will need to be renewed or recut by an engine overhaul specialist. If they are only slightly pitted, this can be removed by grinding the valve heads and seats together with coarse, then fine, grinding paste as described below.

9.1 Using a special tool to fit the valve stem oil seals

9 If the valve guides are worn, indicated by a side-to-side motion of the valve in the guide, new guides must be fitted. If necessary, insert a new valve in the guides to determine if the wear is on the guide or valve. If new guides are to be fitted, the valves must be renewed as a matter of course. Valve guides may be renewed using a press and a suitable mandrel, however, the work is best carried out by an engine overhaul specialist, since if it is not done skilfully, there is a risk of damaging the cylinder head.

10 Check the tappet bores in the cylinder head for wear. If excessive wear is evident, the cylinder head must be renewed.

11 Examine the camshaft bearing surfaces in the cylinder head as described in Chapter 2A, 2B or 2C.

Valves

12 Examine the head of each valve for pitting, burning, cracks and general wear, and check the valve stem for scoring and wear ridges. Rotate the valve, and check for any obvious indication that it is bent. Look for pits and excessive wear on the end of each valve stem.

13 If the valve appears satisfactory at this stage, measure the valve stem diameter at several points using a micrometer **(see illustration)**. Any significant difference in the readings obtained indicates wear of the valve stem. Should any of these conditions be apparent, the valve(s) must be renewed.

14 If the valves are in satisfactory condition, or if new valves are being fitted, they should be ground (lapped) into their respective seats to ensure a smooth gas-tight seal.

15 Valve grinding is carried out as follows. Place the cylinder head upside-down on a bench, with a block of wood at each end to give clearance for the valve stems. On the 1.6 litre diesel engine, take care to protect the camshaft bearing surfaces.

16 Smear a trace of coarse carborundum paste on the seat face, and press a suction grinding tool onto the valve head. With a semi-rotary action, grind the valve head to its seat, lifting the valve occasionally to redistribute the grinding paste.

17 When a dull-matt even surface is produced on both the valve seat and the valve, wipe off the paste and repeat the process with fine carborundum paste. A light spring placed under the valve head will greatly ease this operation.

18 When a smooth unbroken ring of light grey matt finish is produced on both the valve and seat, the grinding operation is complete. Be sure to remove all traces of grinding paste, using paraffin or a suitable solvent, before reassembly of the cylinder head.

Valve components

19 Examine the valve springs for signs of damage and discoloration, and also measure their free length using Vernier calipers or a steel rule **(see illustration)** or by comparing the existing spring with a new component.

20 Stand each spring on a flat surface, and check it for squareness. If any of the springs are damaged, distorted or have lost their tension, obtain a complete new set of springs. It is normal to renew the springs as a matter of course during a major overhaul.

21 On petrol engines, inspect the tappet buckets and their shims for scoring, pitting (especially on the shims), and wear ridges. Renew any components as necessary. Note that some scuffing is to be expected, and is acceptable provided that the tappets are not scored.

Cam followers – 1.6 litre diesel engine

22 Check the cam follower contact surfaces for pits, wear, score marks or any indication that the surface-hardening has worn through. Given that the followers feature moving parts (the rollers), it may be wise to fit new followers as a matter of course if the engine has completed a very significant mileage.

Valve stem oil seals

23 The valve stem oil seals should be renewed as a matter of course.

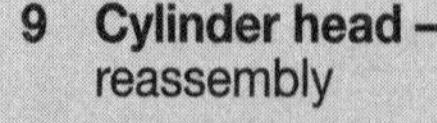

9 Cylinder head – reassembly

1 Lubricate the valve stem oil seals with clean engine oil, then fit them by pushing into position in the cylinder head using a suitable socket or special tool **(see illustration)**. Ensure that the seals are fully engaged with the valve guide. Note that the inlet and exhaust seals are usually different colours – green for the inlet valves, red for the exhaust valves.

2 Lubricate the valve stems, then insert the valves into their original locations. If new valves are being fitted, insert them into the locations to which they have been ground. Take care not to damage the valve stem oil seal as each valve is fitted **(see illustrations)**.

3 Locate the spring seat over the guide. The seat is incorporated in the valve stem seal. Fit the spring and cap.

4 Compress the valve spring and locate the split collets in the recess in the valve stem **(see illustrations)**. Release the compressor, then repeat the procedure on the remaining valves.

5 With all the valves installed, place the cylinder head flat on the bench and, using a hammer and interposed block of wood, tap the end of each valve stem to settle the components.

6 The previously-removed components can now be refitted with reference to Section 7.

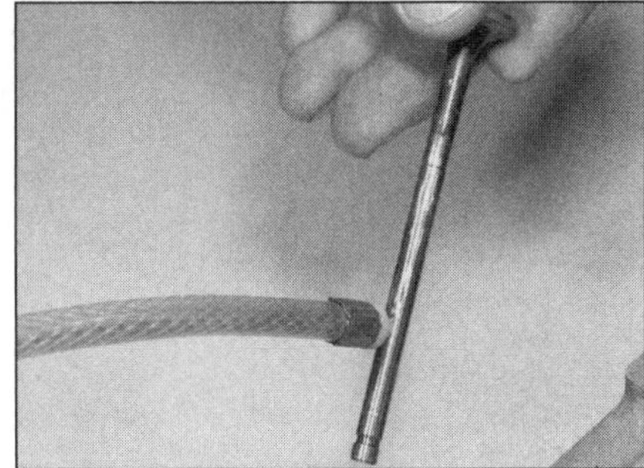

9.2a Oil the valve stems ...

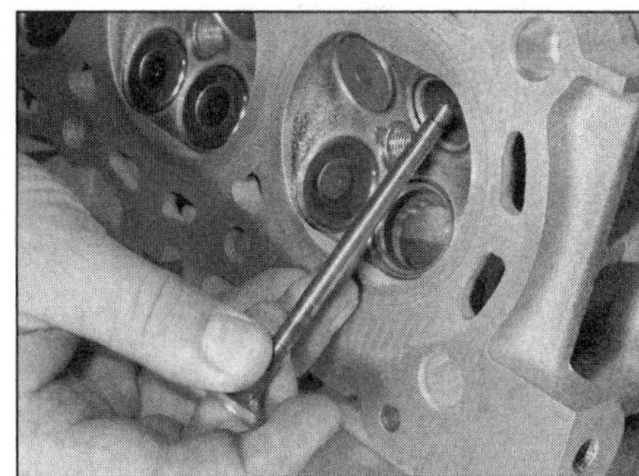

9.2b ... then insert the valves in their guides

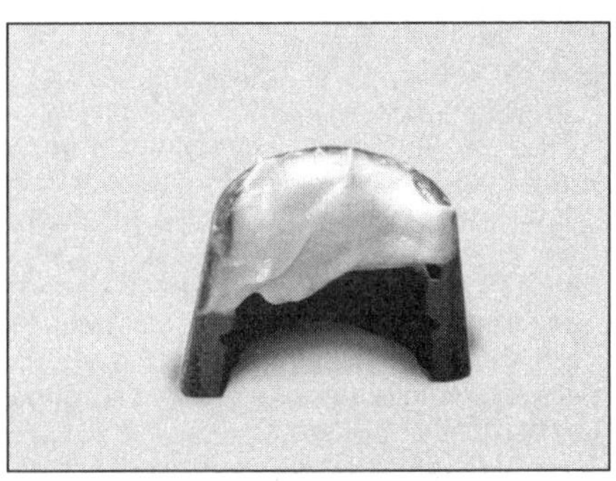

9.4a Apply a small dab of grease to each collet before installation – it will hold them in place on the valve stem

9.4b A dab of grease on a screwdriver will help to fit the collets

10 Piston/connecting rod assemblies – removal

1 Remove the cylinder head, sump, oil pump pick-up tube and baffle plate, as applicable, with reference to Chapter 2A, 2B or 2C.

2 Rotate the crankshaft so that No 1 big-end cap (timing end of the engine) is at the lowest point of its travel. If the big-end cap and rod are not already numbered, mark them with a marker pen **(see illustration)**. Mark both cap and rod to identify the cylinder they operate in.

3 On diesel engines, remove the main bearing ladder as described in Section 11.

4 Unscrew and remove the big-end bearing cap bolts, and withdraw the cap complete with shell bearing from the connecting rod. Make sure that the shell remains in the cap and if necessary identify it for position **(see illustrations)**.

5 If only the bearing shells are being attended to, push the connecting rod up and off the crankpin, and remove the upper bearing shell. Keep the bearing shells and cap together in their correct sequence if they are to be refitted.

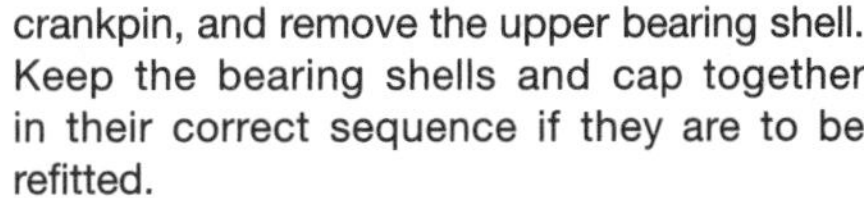

6 If the piston is being removed, push the connecting rod up, and remove the piston and rod from the top of the bore. Note that if there is a pronounced wear ridge at the top of the bore, there is a risk of damaging the piston as the rings foul the ridge. However, it is reasonable to assume that a rebore and new pistons will be required in any case if the ridge is so pronounced.

7 Repeat the procedure for the remaining piston/connecting rod assemblies. Ensure that the caps and rods are marked before removal, as described previously, and keep all components in order.

11 Crankshaft (diesel engine) – removal

Caution: Do not attempt to remove the crankshaft or main bearing cap/ladder on petrol engines, as it is not possible to refit it accurately using conventional tooling. The manufacturers do not supply torque settings for the main bearing cap/ladder retaining bolts. If the crankshaft is worn excessively on the petrol engine, it will be necessary to obtain a new 'short' motor, comprising the cylinder block together with the pistons and crankshaft.

1 Remove the timing belt, crankshaft sprocket, sump, oil pick-up tube, flywheel and

10.2 The big-end caps and connecting rods are normally marked with their cylinder number

10.4a Removing the bolts ...

10.4b ... and big-end bearing caps

11.2 Checking the crankshaft endfloat with a dial gauge

11.4 Crankshaft endfloat can also be checked with feeler blades

11.6 Prise up the two caps to expose the main bearing bolts at the flywheel end

left-hand/flywheel end oil seal housing. The pistons/connecting rods must be free of the crankshaft journals, however it is not essential to remove them completely from the cylinder block.

2 Before the crankshaft is removed, check the endfloat. Mount a dial gauge with the probe in line with the crankshaft and just touching the crankshaft **(see illustration)**.

3 Push the crankshaft fully away from the gauge, and zero it. Next, lever the crankshaft towards the gauge as far as possible, and check the reading obtained. The distance that the crankshaft moved is its endfloat; if it is greater than specified, new thrustwashers will be required (see Chapter 2B or 2C Specifications).

4 If no dial gauge is available, feeler blades can be used. Gently lever or push the crankshaft in one direction, then insert feeler blades between the crankshaft web and the main bearing with the thrustwashers to determine the clearance **(see illustration)**.

5 Work around the outside of the cylinder block, and unscrew all the small bolts securing the main bearing ladder to the base of the cylinder block. Note the correct fitted depth of the left-hand crankshaft oil seal in the cylinder block/main bearing ladder.

6 Working in a diagonal sequence, evenly and progressively slacken the large main bearing ladder retaining bolts by a turn at a time. Once all the bolts are loose, remove them from the ladder. **Note:** *Prise up the two caps at the flywheel end of the ladder to expose the two end main bearing bolts* ***(see illustration)***. The larger (M11) bolts should be discarded, and new bolts obtained for reassembly.

7 With all the retaining bolts removed, carefully lift the main bearing ladder casting away from the base of the cylinder block. Recover the lower main bearing shells, and tape them to their respective locations in the casting. If the two locating dowels are a loose fit, remove them and store them with the casting for safe-keeping. Undo the big-end bolts and remove the pistons/connecting rods as described in Section 10.

8 Lift out the crankshaft, and discard both the oil seals.

9 Recover the upper main bearing shells, and store them along with the relevant lower bearing shell. Also recover the two thrustwashers (one fitted either side of No 2 main bearing) from the cylinder block.

12 Cylinder block/crankcase and bores - cleaning and inspection

Cleaning

Caution: If cleaning the cylinder block (with fitted crankshaft) on the petrol engine, it is recommended that only the external surfaces are cleaned, as otherwise the internal oilways and channels may become contaminated, leading to premature wear of the crankshaft and main bearings.

1 For complete cleaning, the core plugs should be removed. Drill a small hole in them, then insert a self-tapping screw and pull out the plugs using pliers or a slide-hammer. Also remove all external components and senders (if not already done), noting their locations. Where applicable, remove the oil sprayers from the bottom of each bore **(see illustrations)**.

2 Scrape all traces of gasket or sealant from the cylinder block, taking care not to damage the head and sump mating faces.

3 If the block is extremely dirty, it should be steam-cleaned.

4 After the block has been steam-cleaned, clean all oil holes and oil galleries one more time. Flush all internal passages with warm water until the water runs clear, dry the block thoroughly and wipe all machined surfaces with a light rust-preventative oil. If you have access to compressed air, use it to speed up the drying process and to blow out all the oil holes and galleries.

Warning: Wear eye protection when using compressed air.

5 If the block is not very dirty, you can do an adequate cleaning job with hot soapy water and a stiff brush. Take plenty of time, and do a thorough job. Regardless of the cleaning method used, be sure to clean all oil holes and galleries very thoroughly, dry the block completely and coat all machined surfaces with light oil.

6 The threaded holes in the block must be clean to ensure accurate torque wrench readings during reassembly. Run the proper-size tap into each of the holes to remove rust, corrosion, thread sealant or sludge, and to restore damaged threads **(see illustration)**. If possible, use compressed air to clear the holes of debris produced by this operation. Now is a good time to clean the threads on the head bolts and the main bearing cap bolts as well.

7 Where applicable, refit the main bearing caps, and tighten the bolts finger-tight.

8 After coating the mating surfaces of the new core plugs with suitable sealant, refit them in the cylinder block. Make sure that they are driven in straight and seated properly, or leakage could result. Special tools are available for this purpose, but a large socket, with an outside diameter that will just slip

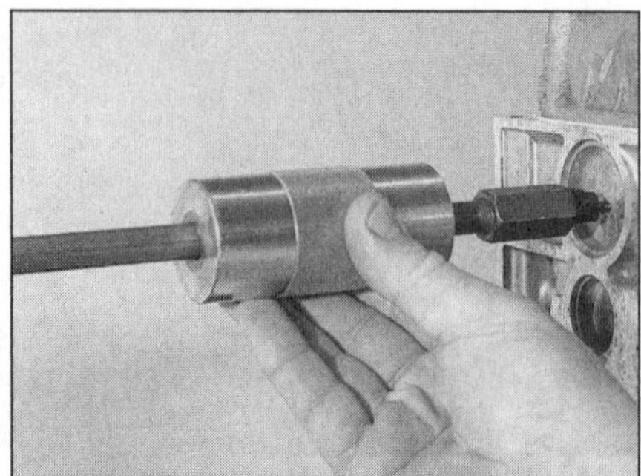
12.1 The core plugs should be removed with a puller - don't drive them inwards

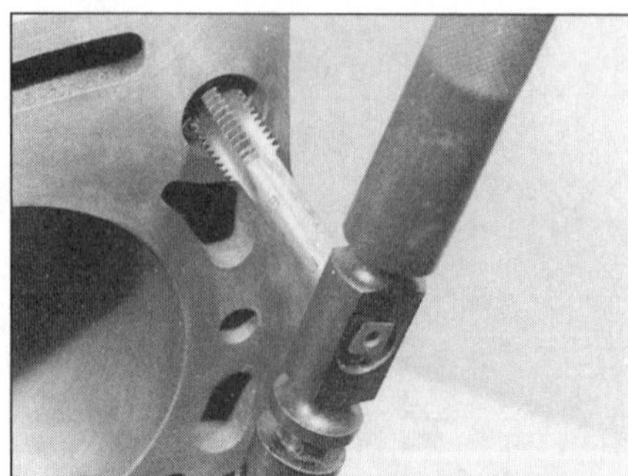
12.6 All bolt holes in the block should be cleaned and restored with a tap

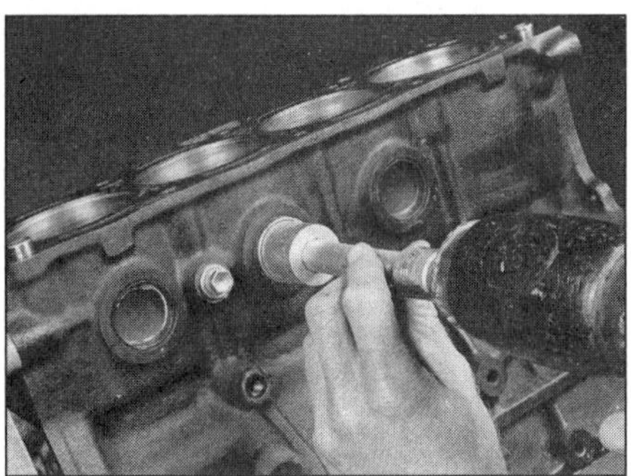

12.8 A large socket on an extension can be used to drive in new core plugs

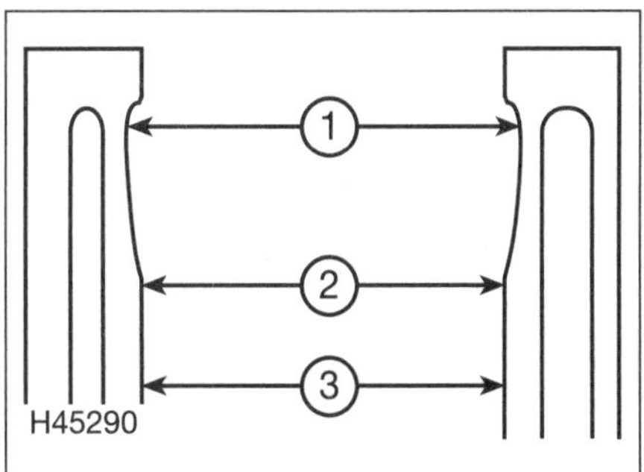

12.13 Measure the diameter of each cylinder just under the wear ridge (1), at the centre (2) and the base (3)

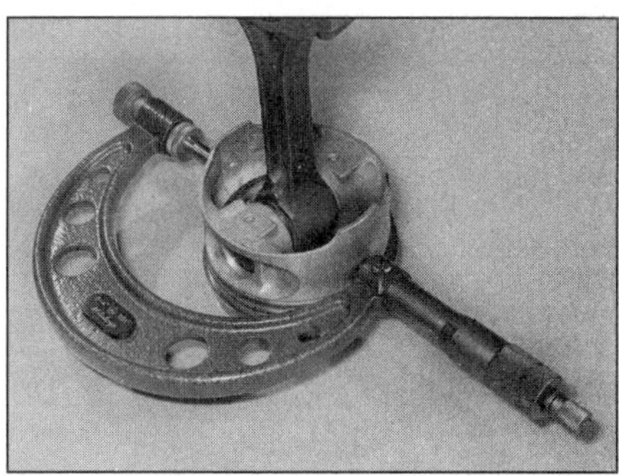

12.15 Measure the piston skirt diameter at right-angles to the gudgeon pin axis, just above the base of the skirt

into the core plug, will work just as well **(see illustration)**.

9 Where applicable, remove the oil jets from their locations in the crankcase and clean them. After cleaning the cylinder block, refit the jets.

10 If the engine is not going to be reassembled right away, cover it with a large plastic bag to keep it clean and prevent it rusting.

Inspection

11 Visually check the block for cracks, rust and corrosion. Look for stripped threads in the threaded holes. If there has been any history of internal water leakage, it may be worthwhile having an engine overhaul specialist check the block with special equipment. If defects are found, have the block repaired, if possible, or renewed.

12 Check the cylinder bores for scuffing and scoring. Normally, bore wear will be evident in the form of a wear ridge at the top of the bore. This ridge marks the limit of piston travel.

13 Measure the diameter of each cylinder at the top (just under the ridge area), centre and base of the cylinder bore, parallel to the crankshaft axis **(see illustration)**.

14 Next measure each cylinder's diameter at the same three locations across the crankshaft axis. If the difference between any of the measurements is greater than 0.20 mm, indicating that the cylinder is excessively out-of-round or tapered, then remedial action must be considered.

15 Repeat this procedure for the remaining cylinders, then measure the diameter of each piston at right-angles to the gudgeon pin axis, and compare the result with the information given in the Specifications **(see illustration)**. By comparing the piston diameters with the bore diameters, an idea can be obtained of the clearances.

16 If the cylinder walls are badly scuffed or scored, or if they are excessively out-of-round or tapered, have the cylinder block rebored (where possible) by an engine overhaul specialist. New pistons (oversize in the case of a rebore) will also be required.

17 If the cylinders are in reasonably good condition, then it may only be necessary to renew the piston rings.

18 If this is the case, the bores should be honed in order to allow the new rings to bed in correctly and provide the best possible seal. The conventional type of hone has spring-loaded stones, and is used with a power drill. You will also need some paraffin or honing oil and rags. The hone should be moved up-and-down the cylinder to produce a crosshatch pattern, and plenty of honing oil should be used.

19 Ideally, the crosshatch lines should intersect at approximately a 60° angle. Do not take off more material than is necessary to produce the required finish. If new pistons are being fitted, the piston manufacturers may specify a finish with a different angle, so their instructions should be followed. Do not withdraw the hone from the cylinder while it is still being turned, but stop it first (keep the hone moving up-and-down the bore while it slows down).

20 After honing a cylinder, wipe out all traces of the honing oil. If equipment of this type is not available, or if you are not sure whether you are competent to undertake the task yourself, an engine overhaul specialist will carry out the work.

21 Refit all external components and senders in their correct locations, as noted before removal.

13 Piston/connecting rod assemblies – inspection and reassembly

Inspection

1 Before the inspection process can begin, the piston/connecting rod assemblies must be cleaned, and the original piston rings removed from the pistons.

2 Carefully expand the old rings over the top of the pistons. The use of two or three old feeler blades will be helpful in preventing the rings dropping into empty grooves **(see illustration)**. Note that the oil control scraper ring is in two sections.

3 Scrape away all traces of carbon from the top of the piston. A hand-held wire brush or a piece of fine emery cloth can be used once the majority of the deposits have been scraped away.

4 Remove the carbon from the ring grooves in the piston by cleaning them using an old ring. Break the ring in half to do this. Be very careful to remove only the carbon deposits; do not remove any metal, or scratch the sides of the ring grooves. Protect your fingers – piston rings are sharp.

5 Once the deposits have been removed, clean the piston/connecting rod assembly with paraffin or a suitable solvent, and dry thoroughly. Make sure the oil return holes in the ring grooves are clear.

6 If the pistons and cylinder bores are not damaged or worn excessively, and if the cylinder block does not need to be rebored, the original pistons can be re-used. Normal piston wear appears as even vertical wear on the piston thrust surfaces, and slight looseness of the top ring in its groove. New piston rings, however, should always be used when the engine is reassembled.

7 Carefully inspect each piston for cracks around the skirt, at the gudgeon pin bosses, and at the piston ring lands (between the piston ring grooves).

8 Look for scoring and scuffing on the sides of the skirt, holes in the piston crown, and burned areas at the edge of the crown. If the skirt is scored or scuffed, the engine may have been suffering from overheating and/or abnormal combustion, which caused excessively-high operating temperatures. The cooling and lubricating systems should be checked thoroughly.

9 Scorch marks on the sides of the pistons show that blow-by has occurred and the

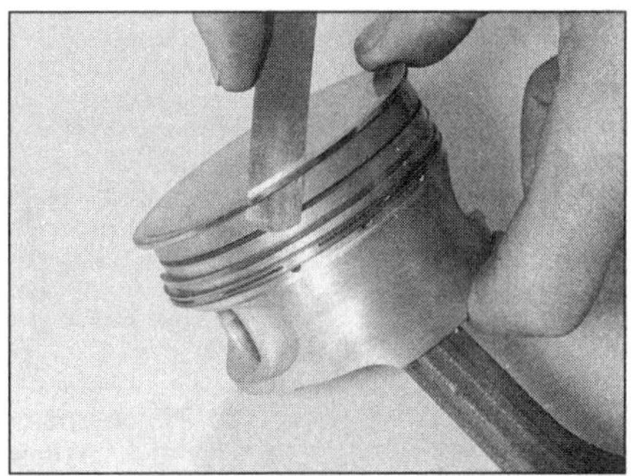

13.2 Using feeler blades to remove piston rings

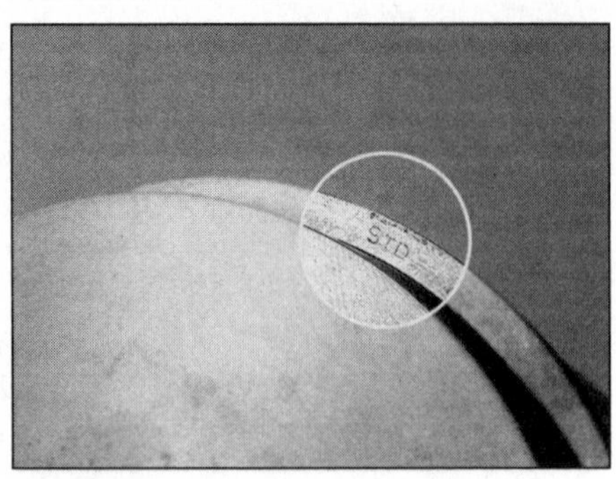

13.15a Look for etched markings identifying the piston ring top surface

rings are not sealing correctly. A hole in the piston crown is an indication that abnormal combustion (pre-ignition, knocking or detonation) has been occurring. If any of the above problems exist, the causes must be corrected, or the damage will occur again. On petrol engines, the causes may include inlet air leaks, incorrect fuel/air mixture or incorrect ignition timing. On diesel engines, incorrect injection pump timing or a faulty injector may be the cause.

10 Corrosion of the piston, in the form of small pits, indicates that coolant is leaking into the combustion chamber and/or the crankcase. Again, the cause must be corrected, or the problem may persist in the rebuilt engine.

11 If new rings are being fitted to old pistons, measure the piston ring-to-groove clearance by placing a new piston ring in each ring groove and measuring the clearance with a feeler blade. Check the clearance at three or four places around each groove. Where no values are specified, if the measured clearance is excessive – say greater than 0.10 mm – new pistons will be required. If the new ring is excessively tight, the most likely cause is dirt remaining in the groove.

12 Check the piston-to-bore clearance by measuring the cylinder bore (see Section 12) and the piston diameter. Measure the piston across the skirt, at a 90° angle to the gudgeon pin, approximately half-way down the skirt. Subtract the piston diameter from the bore diameter to obtain the clearance. If this is greater than the figures given in the Specifications, the block will have to be rebored and new pistons and rings fitted.

13 Check the fit of the gudgeon pin by twisting the piston and connecting rod in opposite directions. Any noticeable play indicates excessive wear, which must be corrected. If the pistons or connecting rods are to be renewed on petrol engines, the work should be carried out by a Ford garage or engine overhaul specialist. Note in the case of the diesel engines, the gudgeon pins are secured by circlips, so the pistons and connecting rods can be separated without difficulty. Note the position of the piston relative to the rod before dismantling, and use new circlips on reassembly.

14 Before refitting the rings to the pistons, check their end gaps by inserting each of them in their cylinder bores. Use the piston to make sure that they are square. Using feeler blades, check that the gaps are within the tolerances given in the Specifications. Genuine rings are supplied pre-gapped; no attempt should be made to adjust the gaps by filing.

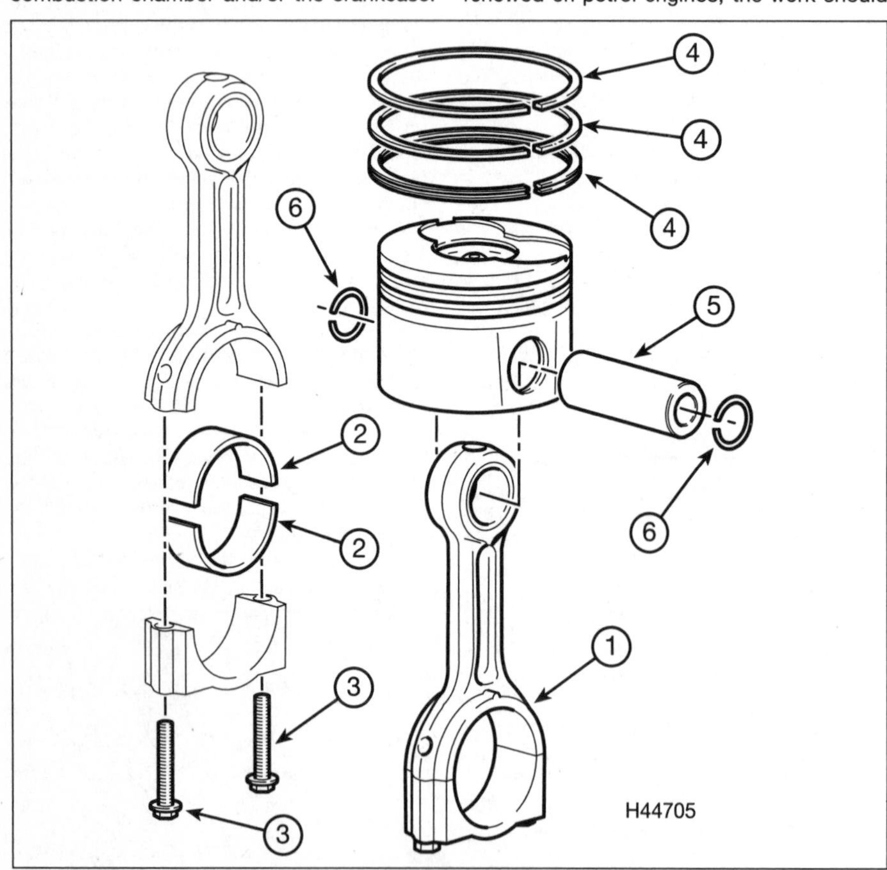

13.15b Piston and connecting rod assembly – diesel engine

1 Connecting rod
2 Big-end shells
3 Big-end bolt
4 Piston rings
5 Gudgeon pin
6 Circlips

Reassembly

15 Install the new rings by fitting them over the top of the piston, starting with the oil control scraper ring sections. Use feeler blades in the same way as when removing the old rings. New rings generally have their top surfaces identified, and must be fitted the correct way round **(see illustrations)**. Note that the first and second compression rings have different sections. Be careful when handling the compression rings; they will break if they are handled roughly or expanded too far. With all the rings in position, space the ring gaps at 120° to each other (unless otherwise specified). The oil control scraper ring expander must also be positioned opposite to the actual ring.

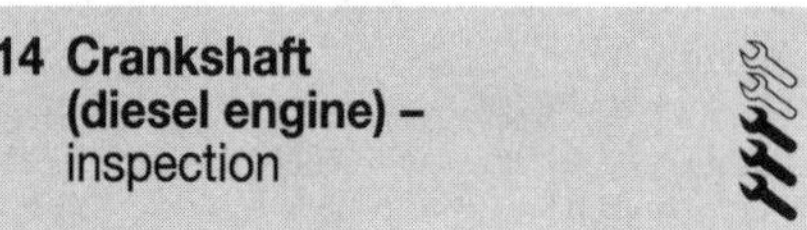

14 Crankshaft (diesel engine) – inspection

1 Clean the crankshaft and dry it with compressed air if available. Be sure to clean the oil holes with a cotton bud or similar probe.

Warning: Wear eye protection when using compressed air.

2 Check the main and big-end bearing journals for uneven wear, scoring, pitting and cracking.

3 If the crankshaft has been reground, check for burrs around the crankshaft oil holes (the holes are usually chamfered, so burrs should not be a problem unless regrinding has been carried out carelessly). Remove any burrs with a fine file or scraper, and thoroughly clean the oil holes as described previously.

4 Using a micrometer, measure the diameter of the main bearing and connecting rod journals, and compare the results with the Specifications **(see illustration)**. By measuring the diameter at a number of points around each journal's circumference, you will be able to determine whether or not the journal is out-of-round. Take the measurement at each end of the journal, near the webs, to determine if the journal is tapered. If any of the measurements vary by more than 0.025 mm, the crankshaft will have to be reground, and undersize bearings fitted.

5 Check the oil seal contact surfaces at each end of the crankshaft for wear and damage. If an excessive groove is evident in the surface of the crankshaft, consult an engine overhaul specialist who will be able to advise whether a repair is possible or if a new crankshaft is necessary.

15 Main and big-end bearings - inspection

1 Even though the main and big-end bearings should be renewed during the engine overhaul, the old bearings should be retained for close examination, as they may reveal valuable information about the condition of the engine. The size of the bearing shells is stamped on the back metal, and this information should be given to the supplier of the new shells.

2 Bearing failure occurs because of lack of lubrication, the presence of dirt or other foreign particles, overloading the engine, and corrosion. Regardless of the cause of bearing failure, it must be corrected before the engine is reassembled, to prevent it from happening again **(see illustration)**.

3 When examining the bearings, remove them from the engine block, the main bearing caps, the connecting rods and the rod caps, and lay them out on a clean surface in the same general position as their location in the engine. This will enable you to match any bearing problems with the corresponding crankshaft journal.

4 Dirt and other foreign particles get into the engine in a variety of ways. Dirt may be left in the engine during assembly, or it may pass through filters or the crankcase ventilation system. It may get into the oil, and from there into the bearings. Metal chips from machining operations and normal engine wear are often present. Abrasives are sometimes left in engine components after reconditioning, especially when parts are not thoroughly cleaned using the proper cleaning methods.

5 Whatever the source, these foreign objects often end up embedded in the soft bearing material, and are easily recognised. Large particles will not embed in the bearing, and will score or gouge the bearing and journal. The best prevention for this cause of bearing failure is to clean all parts thoroughly, and keep everything spotlessly-clean during engine assembly. Frequent and regular engine oil and filter changes are also recommended.

6 Lack of lubrication (or lubrication breakdown) has a number of interrelated causes. Excessive heat (which thins the oil), overloading (which squeezes the oil from the bearing face) and oil leakage (from excessive bearing clearances, worn oil pump or high engine speeds) all contribute to lubrication breakdown. Blocked oil passages, which usually are the result of misaligned oil holes in a bearing shell, will also oil-starve a bearing and destroy it. When lack of lubrication is the cause of bearing failure, the bearing material is wiped or extruded from the steel backing of the bearing. Temperatures may increase to the point where the steel backing turns blue from overheating.

14.4 Measure the diameter of each crankshaft journal at several points, to detect taper and out-of round conditions

7 Driving habits can have a definite effect on bearing life. Full-throttle, low-speed operation (labouring the engine) puts very high loads on bearings, which tends to squeeze out the oil film. These loads cause the bearings to flex, which produces fine cracks in the bearing face (fatigue failure). Eventually, the bearing material will loosen in pieces and tear away from the steel backing. Short-trip driving leads to corrosion of bearings, because insufficient engine heat is produced to drive off the condensed water and corrosive gases. These products collect in the engine oil, forming acid and sludge. As the oil is carried to the engine bearings, the acid attacks and corrodes the bearing material.

8 Incorrect bearing installation during engine assembly will lead to bearing failure as well. Tight-fitting bearings leave insufficient bearing oil clearance, and will result in oil starvation. Dirt or foreign particles trapped behind a bearing shell result in high spots on the bearing which lead to failure.

9 Do not touch any shell's bearing surface with your fingers during reassembly; there is a risk of scratching the delicate surface, or of depositing particles of dirt on it.

10 As mentioned at the beginning of this Section, the bearing shells should be renewed as a matter of course during engine overhaul; to do otherwise is false economy.

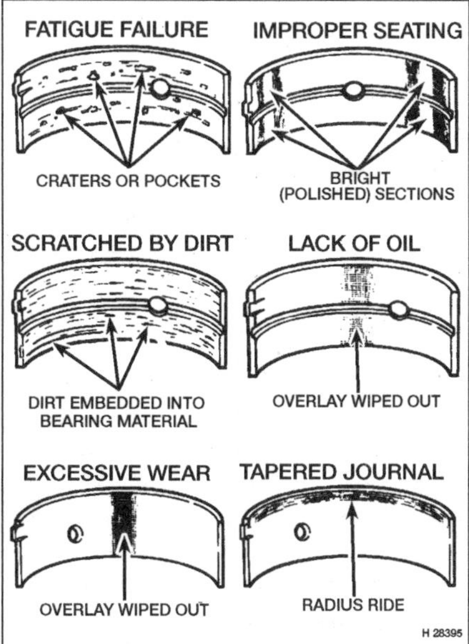

15.2 Typical bearing failures

16 Engine overhaul - reassembly sequence

1 Before reassembly begins, ensure that all new parts have been obtained and that all necessary tools are available. Read through the entire procedure to familiarise yourself with the work involved, and to ensure that all items necessary for reassembly of the engine are at hand. In addition to all normal tools and materials, jointing and thread-locking compound will be needed during engine reassembly. Do not use any kind of silicone-based sealant on any part of the fuel system or inlet manifold, and never use exhaust sealants upstream (on the engine side) of the catalytic converter.

2 In order to save time and avoid problems, engine reassembly can be carried out in the following order.

- *a) Crankshaft and main bearing caps (where applicable).*
- *b) Pistons and connecting rods, and main bearing ladder (where applicable).*
- *c) Oil pump.*
- *d) Sump.*
- *e) Flywheel.*
- *f) Cylinder head.*
- *g) Timing sprockets and belt.*
- *h) Engine external components (including inlet and exhaust manifolds).*

3 Ensure that everything is clean prior to reassembly. As mentioned previously, dirt and metal particles can quickly destroy bearings and result in major engine damage. Use clean engine oil to lubricate during reassembly.

17 Crankshaft (diesel engine) - refitting

Selection of new bearing shells

1 Have the crankshaft inspected and measured by a Ford dealer or engine reconditioning specialist. They will be able to carry out any regrinding/repairs, and supply suitable main and big-end bearing shells.

Refitting

2 It is assumed at this point that the cylinder block/crankcase and crankshaft have been

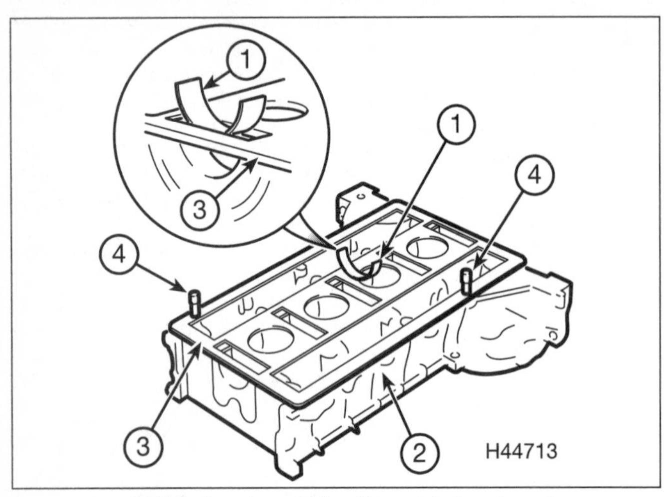

17.4 Main bearing shell refitment – diesel engine

1 Bearing shell
2 Main bearing ladder
3 Special tool
4 Aligning pins

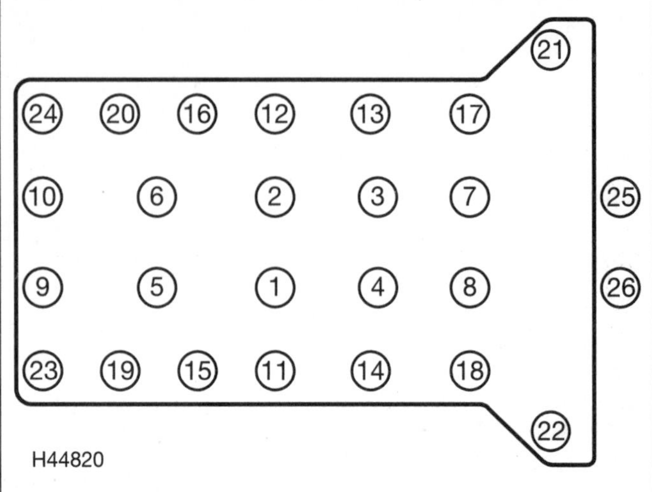

17.11 Main bearing ladder bolts tightening sequence – diesel engine

cleaned and repaired or reconditioned as necessary. Position the engine upside-down.

3 Clean the backs of the bearing shells in both the cylinder block/crankcase and the main bearing ladder. If new shells are being fitted, ensure that all traces of protective grease are cleaned off using paraffin. Wipe dry the shells with a lint-free cloth.

4 Press the bearing shells into their locations, ensuring that the tab on each shell engages in the notch in the cylinder block/crankcase and bearing ladder. Take care not to touch any shell's bearing surface with your fingers. Note that the upper bearing shells all have a grooved surface, whereas the lower shells have a plain bearing surface. It is essential that the lower bearing shell halves are centrally located in the ladder. To ensure this, a Ford special tool (303-737) is positioned over the ladder, and the bearing shells inserted through the slots in the tool **(see illustration)**. If this tool is not available, use a tape-measure or ruler to ensure the shells are perfectly central on their bearings.

5 Liberally lubricate each bearing shell in the cylinder block with clean engine oil, then lower the crankshaft into position.

6 Insert the thrustwashers to either side of No 2 main bearing upper location, and push them around the bearing journal until their edges are horizontal. Ensure that the oilway grooves on each thrustwasher face outwards (they should be visible).

7 Refit the piston and connecting rod assemblies as described in Section 18.

8 Thoroughly degrease the mating surfaces of the cylinder block and the crankshaft bearing cap housing/main bearing ladder. Apply a thin bead of RTV sealant to the bearing cap housing mating surface. Ford recommend the use of their WSE-M4G323-A4 sealant for this purpose. Use two aligning pins inserted into the main bearing ladder, to ensure the correct positioning of the assembly. Make sure the sealant does not enter the blind holes in the cylinder block or ladder, or damage may result. The ladder should be fitted within four minutes of applying the sealant.

9 Lubricate the lower bearing shells with clean engine oil, then refit the bearing cap ladder, ensuring that the shells are not displaced, and that the locating dowels engage correctly. Remove the aligning pins from the bearing ladder.

10 Install the large and small crankshaft bearing cap housing/ladder retaining bolts, and screw them in until they are just making contact with the housing. Note that the larger (M11) bolts must not be re-used – a new set should be obtained.

11 Tighten all the main bearing ladder bolts to their Stage 1 setting in sequence **(see illustration)**.

12 Slacken (Stage 2) the larger bolts half a turn (180°), then tighten them in sequence to the Stage 3 torque setting, followed by the Stage 4 angle-tightening setting. Apply sealant to the two new bearing ladder bolt caps, and tap them into place over the two flywheel end bolts.

13 Finally, tighten the smaller bearing ladder bolts to their Stage 2 setting.

14 Rotate the crankshaft a number of times by hand, to check for any obvious binding.

15 Check the crankshaft endfloat (refer to Section 11).

16 Fit new crankshaft oil seals as described in Chapter 2B or 2C (as applicable).

17 Refit the components removed in Section 11.

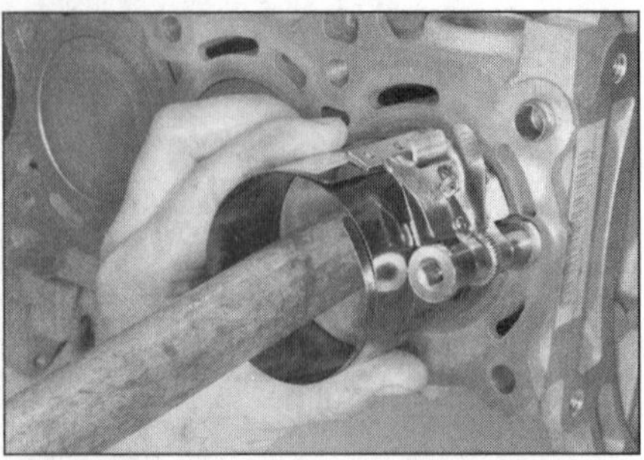

18.3a With the compressor fitted, use the handle of a hammer to gently drive the piston into the cylinder

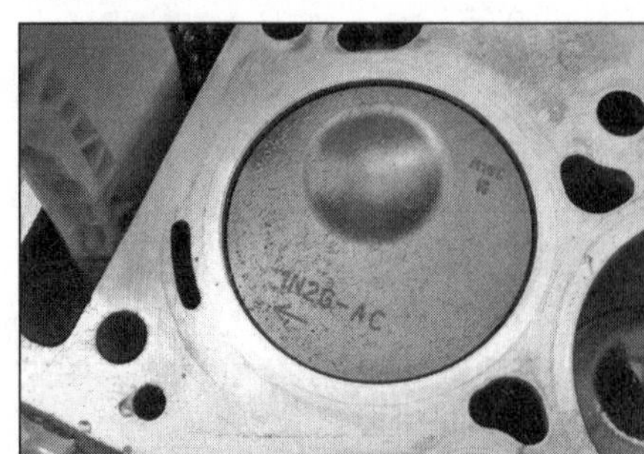

18.3b Make sure that the arrow on the piston crown is facing the timing end of the engine

18 Pistons/connecting rods – refitting

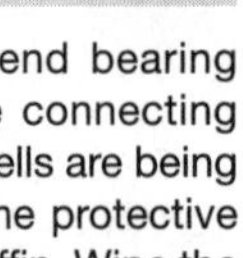

1 Clean the backs of the big-end bearing shells, and the recesses in the connecting rods and big-end caps. If new shells are being fitted, ensure that all traces of the protective grease are cleaned off using paraffin. Wipe the shells and connecting rods dry with a lint-free cloth.

2 Lubricate No 1 piston and piston rings, and check that the ring gaps are spaced at 120° intervals to each other.

3 Fit a ring compressor to No 1 piston, then insert the piston and connecting rod into No 1 cylinder. Make sure that the 'DIST' mark or arrow on the piston crown is facing the timing end of the engine. With No 1 crankpin at its lowest point, drive the piston carefully into the cylinder with the wooden handle of a hammer, at the same time guiding the connecting rod onto the crankpin **(see illustrations)**.

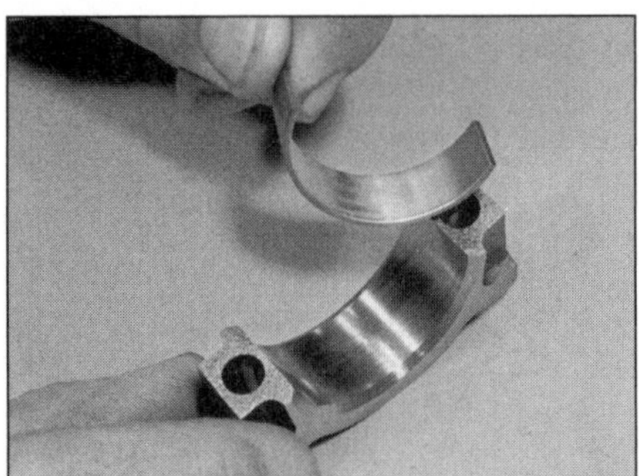

18.4 Make sure that the shells are located centrally and aligned with the split faces of the connecting rod and cap

Petrol engine

4 Press the big-end bearing shells into the connecting rods and caps in their correct positions. Make sure that the shells are located centrally and aligned with the split faces of the connecting rod and cap – the shells are finally held in position when the big-end cap bolts are tightened to the specified torque **(see illustration)**.

5 Liberally lubricate the crankpin journals and big-end bearing shells. Refit the bearing caps, ensuring correct positioning as previously described. Tighten the bearing cap bolts to the specified torque and angles, and turn the crankshaft each time to make sure that it is free before moving on to the next assembly **(see illustration)**.

Diesel engine

6 On these engines, the connecting rod is made in one piece, then the big-end bearing cap is 'cracked' off. This ensures that the cap fits onto the connecting rod only in one position, and with maximum rigidity. Consequently, there are no locating notches for the bearing shells to fit into.

7 To ensure that the big-end bearing shells are centrally located in the connecting rod and cap, two special tools are available from Ford (303-736). These half-moon shaped tools are pressed in from either side of the rod/cap, and locate the shell exactly in the centre **(see illustration)**. Fit the shells into the connecting rods and big-end caps, and lubricate them with plenty of clean engine oil.

8 Tighten the bolts to the Stage 1 torque setting, then slacken them 180° (Stage 2). Tighten the bolts to the Stage 3 setting, followed by the Stage 4 angle-tightening setting.

9 Continue refitting the main bearing shells and ladder as described in Section 17.

All engines

10 On completion, refit the oil pump pick-up tube (and baffle plate on the petrol engine), sump and cylinder head as described in Chapter 2A, 2B or 2C.

18.5 Angle-tightening the big-end bearing cap bolts

19 Engine – initial start-up after overhaul

1 With the engine refitted in the car, double-check the engine oil and coolant levels (see *Weekly checks*). Make a final check that everything has been reconnected, and that there are no tools or rags left in the engine compartment.

Petrol engine models

2 With the ignition and fuel injection systems disabled by disconnecting the ignition coil wiring plug (Chapter 5B, Section 3) and removing the fuel pump fuse (Chapter 12, Section 3), crank the engine on the starter motor until the oil pressure light goes out.

3 Reconnect the ignition coil, and refit the fuel pump fuse.

4 Start the engine, noting that this may take a little longer than usual.

5 While the engine is idling, check for fuel, water and oil leaks. Check the power steering pipe/hose unions for leakage. Do not be alarmed if there are some odd smells and smoke from parts getting hot and burning off oil deposits.

6 Keep the engine idling until hot water is felt circulating through the top hose, then switch it off.

7 After a few minutes, recheck the oil and coolant levels, and top-up as necessary (see *Weekly checks*).

8 If new pistons, rings or crankshaft bearings have been fitted, the engine must be run-in for the first 500 miles. Do not operate the engine at full-throttle, nor allow it to labour in any gear during this period. It is recommended that the oil and filter be changed at the end of this period.

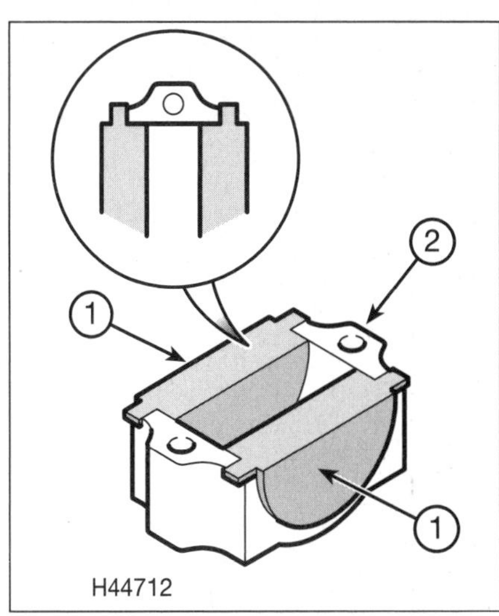

18.7 Big-end bearing shell positioning – diesel engine

1 Special tool *2 Bearing shell*

Diesel engine models

9 Prime the fuel system as described in Chapter 4B, Section 3.

10 Turn the ignition key and turn the engine over immediately, without waiting for the preheating warning light to go out. Continue cranking the engine until the oil pressure warning light goes out.

11 Start the engine as normal. Additional cranking may still be necessary to completely bleed the fuel system before the engine starts.

12 Once started, keep the engine running at fast tickover. Check that there are no leaks of oil, fuel and coolant. Where applicable, check the power steering pipe/hose unions for leakage. Do not be alarmed if there are some odd smells and smoke from parts getting hot and burning off oil deposits.

13 Keep the engine idling until hot coolant is felt circulating through the radiator top hose, indicating that the engine is at normal operating temperature, then stop the engine and allow it to cool.

14 Recheck the oil and coolant levels, and top-up if necessary (see *Weekly checks*).

15 If new pistons, rings or bearings have been fitted, the engine must be run-in at reduced speeds and loads for the first 500 miles or so. Do not operate the engine at full throttle, or allow it to labour in any gear during this period. It is recommended that the engine oil and filter be changed at the end of this period.

Chapter 3
Cooling, heating and air conditioning systems

Contents

Degrees of difficulty

Easy, suitable for novice with little experience	**Fairly easy,** suitable for beginner with some experience 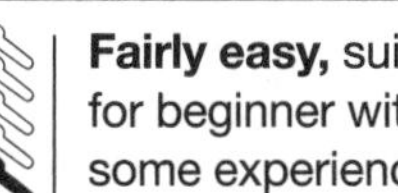	**Fairly difficult,** suitable for competent DIY mechanic	**Difficult,** suitable for experienced DIY mechanic	**Very difficult,** suitable for expert DIY or professional 

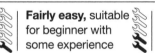

Specifications

General

Maximum system pressure	1.4 bars
Engine coolant temperature sensor resistance (approx):	
Petrol engines:	
20°C	6100 ohms
80°C	620 ohms
Diesel engines:	
60°C	1266 ohms
80°C	642 ohms
Thermostat start of opening temperature	88°C

Torque wrench settings

Torque wrench settings	Nm	lbf ft
Air conditioning compressor mounting bolts	20	15
Radiator mountings	10	7
Thermostat cover bolts	10	7
Thermostat housing bolts:		
Petrol engines	18	13
Diesel engines:		
Stage 1	4	3
Stage 2	7	5
Timing belt tensioner to water pump (petrol engines after 04/2005)	25	18
Water pump bolts:		
Petrol engines	10	7
Diesel engines:		
Stage 1	3	2
Stage 2	10	7
Water pump pulley bolts (petrol engine)	24	18

2.3 Most of the coolant hoses are of the spring clamp type, which need large pliers to remove

2.4a On the radiator top hose, lift the spring clip with a screwdriver ...

2.4b ... then pull the hose fitting off the radiator

1 General information and precautions

The cooling system is of pressurised type, comprising a pump driven by the auxiliary drivebelt (all petrol engines) or the timing belt (diesel engine), an aluminium crossflow radiator, electric cooling fan, and a thermostat. The system functions as follows. Cold coolant from the radiator passes through the hose to the water pump, where it is pumped around the cylinder block and head passages. After cooling the cylinder bores, combustion surfaces and valve seats, the coolant reaches the underside of the thermostat, which is initially closed. The coolant passes through the heater, and is returned via the cylinder block to the water pump. On models fitted with an engine oil cooler, the coolant is also passed through the oil cooler.

When the engine is cold, the thermostat is shut, and the coolant circulates only through the cylinder block, cylinder head and heater. When the coolant reaches a predetermined temperature, the thermostat opens and the coolant passes through to the radiator. As the coolant circulates through the radiator, it is cooled by the inrush of air when the car is in forward motion. Airflow is supplemented by the action of the electric cooling fan when necessary. Once the coolant has passed through the radiator, and has cooled, the cycle is repeated.

The electric cooling fan, mounted on the rear of the radiator, is controlled by a thermostatic switch. At a predetermined coolant temperature, the switch actuates the fan.

An expansion tank is fitted to allow for the expansion of the coolant when hot.

Refer to Section 10 for information on the air conditioning system.

Warning: Do not attempt to remove the expansion tank filler cap, or disturb any part of the cooling system, while the engine is hot; there is a high risk of scalding. If the expansion tank filler cap must be removed before the engine and radiator have fully cooled (even though this is not recommended) the pressure in the cooling system must first be relieved. Cover the cap with a thick layer of cloth, to avoid scalding, and slowly unscrew the filler cap until a hissing sound can be heard. When the hissing has stopped, indicating that the pressure has reduced, slowly unscrew the filler cap until it can be removed; if more hissing sounds are heard, wait until they have stopped before unscrewing the cap completely. At all times, keep well away from the filler cap opening and protect your hands.

Warning: Do not allow antifreeze to come into contact with skin, or with the painted surfaces of the car. Rinse off spills immediately, with plenty of water. Never leave antifreeze lying around in an open container, or in a puddle on the driveway or garage floor. Children and pets are attracted by its sweet smell, but antifreeze can be fatal if ingested.

Warning: If the engine is hot, the electric cooling fan may start rotating even if the engine is not running; be careful to keep hands, hair and loose clothing well clear when working in the engine compartment.

Warning: Refer to Section 10 for precautions to be observed when working on models equipped with air conditioning.

2 Cooling system hoses – disconnection and renewal

Note: *Refer to the warnings given in Section 1 of this Chapter before proceeding. Do not attempt to disconnect any hose while the system is still hot.*

1 If the checks described in Chapter 1A, Section 5 or Chapter 1B, Section 6 reveal a faulty hose, it must be renewed as follows.

2 First drain the cooling system (see Chapter 1A, Section 26 or Chapter 1B, Section 25). If the coolant is not due for renewal, it may be re-used if it is collected in a clean container.

3 Before disconnecting a hose, first note its routing in the engine compartment, and whether it is secured by any clips or ties. Use a pair of pliers to release the spring clamps (or a screwdriver to slacken screw-type clamps) then move them along the hose, clear of the relevant inlet/outlet union. Carefully work the hose free **(see illustration)**.

4 The radiator top hose connection is an unusual combination of conventional spring clamp and quick-release fitting, and can be removed in either of two ways. The spring clamp may be removed as normal. The quick-release connection is removed by lifting up the spring clip with a small screwdriver, after which the hose, still with its spring clamp undisturbed, can be pulled off the radiator. To refit, push the hose back on, and make sure the spring clip clicks into place **(see illustrations)**.

5 Note that the coolant unions are fragile (most are made of plastic); do not use excessive force when attempting to remove the hoses. If a hose proves to be difficult to remove, try to release it by rotating the hose ends before attempting to free it – if this fails, try gently prising up the end of the hose with a small screwdriver to 'break' the seal.

6 When fitting a hose, first slide the clamps onto the hose, then work the hose into position. If spring-type clamps were originally fitted, it is a good idea to use screw-type clamps when refitting the hose (if only to make removal easier next time). If the hose is stiff, use a little soapy water (washing-up liquid is ideal) as a lubricant, or soften the hose by soaking it in hot water.

7 Work the hose into position, checking that it is correctly routed and secured. Slide each clamp along the hose until it passes over the flared end of the relevant inlet/outlet union, before tightening the clamps securely.

8 Refill the cooling system with reference to Chapter 1A, Section 26 or Chapter 1B, Section 25.

9 Check thoroughly for leaks as soon as possible after disturbing any part of the cooling system.

3 Radiator – removal, inspection and refitting

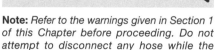

Note: *If leakage is the reason for removing the radiator, bear in mind that minor leaks can often be cured using a radiator sealant with the radiator in situ.*

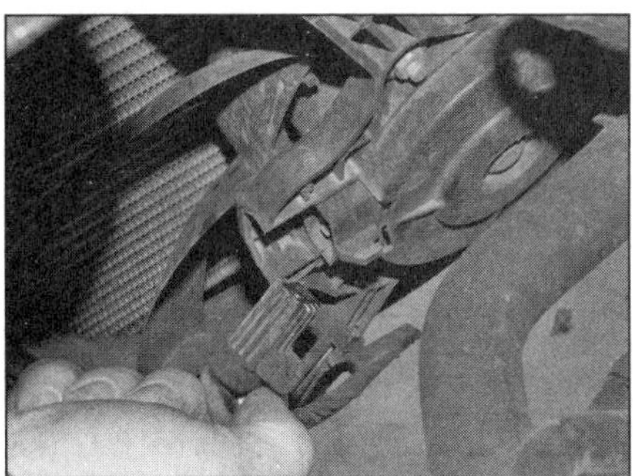
3.4 Disconnect the cooling fan wiring plug

3.5a Release the cooling fan mounting frame catches either side (arrowed) ...

3.5b ... then remove the frame and fan as an assembly

Removal

1 Drain the cooling system as described in Chapter 1A, Section 26 or Chapter 1B, Section 25.

2 Apply the handbrake, then jack up the front of the car and support securely on axle stands (see *Jacking and vehicle support*).

3 On 1.6 litre diesel models, remove the intercooler as described in Chapter 4B, Section 18. Note this work includes removal of the front bumper.

4 Disconnect the cooling fan wiring plug, and unclip the wiring harness as necessary **(see illustration)**.

5 Remove the cooling fan motor and mounting frame by releasing the two plastic catches either side at the top, then lift the motor and frame up to disengage the lower slide-in clips. Once released, the motor and frame can be removed **(see illustrations)**. On some models, it is easier to lower the assembly.

6 On diesel models, disconnect the small purge hose from the top of the radiator. To do this, squeeze together the locking tangs, and pull off the hose.

7 Bearing in mind the advice given in Section 2, disconnect the upper and lower hoses from the radiator. The upper hose is secured by a spring clip, which can be removed as normal. However, if preferred, the additional quick-fit connection may be released instead, by lifting the wire clip with a small screwdriver; when refitting, just press the wire clip back down and push on the hose.

8 Unscrew the small locking bolt used to locate the plastic plug in place, then unscrew the large plastic plug under the radiator on either side. Recover the rubber mounting **(see illustrations)**.

9 Lift the radiator slightly to free it from the mounting frame, and lower it out **(see illustration)**. On models with air conditioning, carefully release the radiator from the condenser – ensure that the condenser remains supported once the radiator is removed. If the radiator is being removed as part of the engine removal procedure (for example), use thick card or a sheet of wood to protect the condenser from damage during subsequent work. **Note:** *On later models, release the clip to free the radiator from the condenser.*

Inspection

10 If the radiator has been removed due to suspected blockage, reverse-flush it as described in Chapter 1A, Section 26 or Chapter 1B, Section 25. Clean dirt and debris from the radiator fins, using an airline (in which case, wear eye protection) or a soft brush. Be careful, as the fins are easily damaged, and are sharp.

11 If necessary, a radiator specialist can perform a 'flow test' on the radiator, to establish whether an internal blockage exists.

12 A leaking radiator must be referred to a specialist for permanent repair. Do not attempt to weld or solder a leaking radiator, as damage may result.

Refitting

13 Refitting is a reversal of removal, bearing in mind the following points:

a) *Ensure that all hoses are correctly reconnected, and their retaining clips securely refitted (or tightened).*

3.8a Unscrew the locking bolt (arrowed) ...

3.8b ... which then allows the plastic plug to be turned ...

3.8c ... and removed ...

3.8d ... together with the rubber mounting

3.9 Lift the radiator slightly, then lower it out

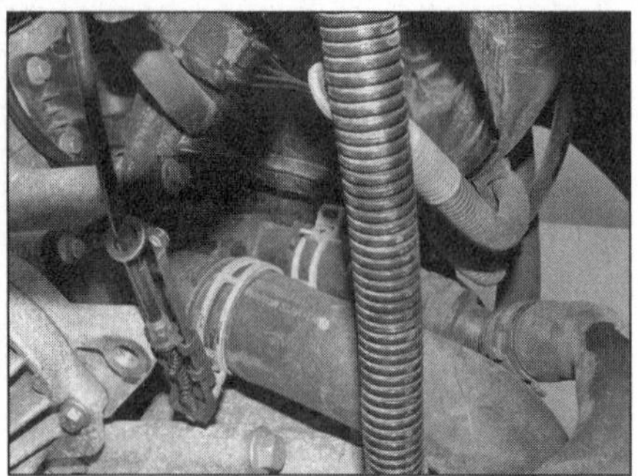

4.13 Remove the coolant hoses

4.14b The housing removed showing the position of the bolts

b) Reconnect the radiator fan wiring, and ensure the harness is routed clear of the fan blades or hot components.

c) On completion, refill the cooling system as described in Chapter 1A, Section 26 or Chapter 1B, Section 25.

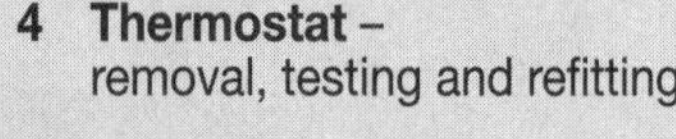

4 Thermostat – removal, testing and refitting

1 As the thermostat ages, it will become slower to react to changes in water temperature ('lazy'). Ultimately, the unit may stick in the open or closed position, and this causes problems. A thermostat which is stuck open will result in a very slow warm-up; a thermostat which is stuck shut will lead to rapid overheating.

2 Before assuming the thermostat is to blame for a cooling system problem, check the coolant level. If the system is draining due to a leak, or has not been properly filled, there may be an airlock in the system (refer to the coolant renewal procedure in Chapter 1A, Section 26 or Chapter 1B, Section 25).

3 If the engine seems to be taking a long time to warm up (based on heater output), the thermostat could be stuck open. Don't necessarily believe the temperature gauge reading – some gauges never seem to register very high in normal driving.

4 A lengthy warm-up period might suggest that the thermostat is missing – it may have been removed or inadvertently omitted by a previous owner or mechanic. Don't drive

4.14a Remove the bolts

4.15 Note the position of the jiggle pin (arrowed)

the car without a thermostat – the engine management system's ECU will then stay in warm-up mode for longer than necessary, causing emissions and fuel economy to suffer.

5 If the engine runs hot, use your hand to check the temperature of the radiator top hose. If the hose isn't hot, but the engine clearly is, the thermostat is probably stuck closed, preventing the coolant inside the engine from escaping to the radiator – renew the thermostat. Again, this problem may also be due to an airlock (refer to the coolant renewal procedure in Chapter 1A, Section 26 or Chapter 1B, Section 25).

6 If the radiator top hose is hot, it means that the coolant is flowing (at least as far as the radiator) and the thermostat is open. Consult the *Fault finding* section at the end of this manual to assist in tracing possible cooling system faults, but a lack of heater output

4.18a Disconnect the wiring plug ...

would now definitely suggest an airlock or a blockage.

7 To gain a rough idea of whether the thermostat is working properly when the engine is warming up, without dismantling the system, proceed as follows.

8 With the engine completely cold, start the engine and let it idle, while checking the temperature of the radiator top hose. Periodically check the temperature indicated on the coolant temperature gauge – if overheating is indicated, switch the engine off immediately.

9 The top hose should feel cold for some time as the engine warms up, and should then get warm quite quickly as the thermostat opens.

10 The above is not a precise or definitive test of thermostat operation, but if the system does not perform as described, remove and test the thermostat as described below. Note that it is not possible to test the thermostat fitted to the diesel engine.

Petrol engine

Removal

11 Remove the alternator as described in Chapter 5A, Section 8.

12 Drain the cooling system as described in Chapter 1A, Section 26.

13 Loosen the clamps, and disconnect the two coolant hoses from the thermostat housing **(see illustration)**, located on the front of the engine, above the oil filter.

14 Unscrew the four securing bolts, and remove the thermostat housing from the engine **(see illustrations)**. Recover the gasket.

15 Lift out the thermostat **(see illustration)** and recover the sealing ring.

Refitting

16 Refitting is a reversal of removal, noting the following points:

a) Thoroughly clean the mating faces of the thermostat housing and the engine.

b) Use a new sealing ring when refitting the thermostat, and make sure the 'jiggle pin' (air bleed valve) is at the top.

c) Use a new gasket when refitting the housing, and tighten the bolts to the specified torque.

d) Refit the alternator as described in Chapter 5A, Section 8.

e) On completion, refill the cooling system as described in Chapter 1A, Section 26.

Diesel engine

Removal

17 Drain the cooling system as described in Chapter 1B, Section 25.

18 Disconnect the MAF sensor wiring plug and then remove the air cleaner intake pipe **(see illustrations)** referring to Chapter 4B, Section 4 if necessary.

19 Remove the battery and battery tray as described in Chapter 5A, Section 4.

20 Disconnect the coolant temperature

4.18b ... and then remove the intake pipe

4.20 Disconnect the wiring plug

4.23 Thermostat housing (arrowed)

sensor wiring plug from the thermostat housing **(see illustration)**.

21 Disconnect the four coolant hoses from the thermostat housing, noting their locations. Note that some of the hoses are disconnected after pressing down on the white-coloured release button.

22 At the base of the housing, loosen the screw and detach the mounting bracket for the bypass tube.

23 Remove the four mounting bolts and take off the thermostat housing **(see illustration)**.

Refitting

24 Refitting is a reversal of removal, noting the following points:

a) Thoroughly clean the mating faces of the thermostat housing and the engine.

b) Use a new gasket when refitting the housing, and tighten the bolts to the specified torque.

c) On completion, refill the cooling system as described in Chapter 1B, Section 25.

Testing

Note: *DIY testing of the thermostat is not possible on the diesel engine, as the thermostat is an integral part of its housing. If there is good reason to suspect the thermostat is not working properly (read the introductory paragraphs in this Section), a new housing will have to be obtained.*

25 If the thermostat remains in the open position at room temperature, it is faulty, and must be renewed as a matter of course.

26 Check to see if there's a open temperature marking stamped on the thermostat.

27 Using a thermometer and container of water, heat the water until the temperature corresponds with the temperature marking stamped on the thermostat. If no marking is found, start the test with the water hot, and heat slowly until it boils.

28 Suspend the (closed) thermostat on a length of string in the water, and check that maximum opening occurs within two minutes, or before the water boils.

29 Remove the thermostat and allow it to cool down; check that it closes fully.

30 If the thermostat does not open and close as described, or if it sticks in either position, it must be renewed. Frankly, if there is any question about the operation of the thermostat, renew it – they are not expensive items.

5 Radiator cooling fan – testing, removal and refitting

Testing

1 On all models, the cooling fan is controlled by the engine management ECU, using signals provided by the engine coolant temperature sensor.

2 The fan operation can be checked by connecting the fan motor directly to a 12 volt power supply. Disconnect the motor wiring plug, and apply 12 volts across the motor terminals (the black wire is the earth) – take great care not to short out the power supply wires.

3 If the fan fails to operate, the fan motor is almost certainly at fault.

4 Testing of the fan motor control circuit must be entrusted to a Ford dealer (or a suitably-equipped specialist) who will have the necessary specialist diagnostic equipment to test the system – do not attempt to test the system using conventional test equipment, as the ECU may be damaged.

Removal

5 Disconnect the battery negative lead with reference to Chapter 5A, Section 2.

6 Apply the handbrake, then jack up the front of the car and support securely on axle stands (see *Jacking and vehicle support*).

5.9 Remove the nuts (arrowed)

7 Disconnect the cooling fan wiring plug from the fan motor and resistor, and unclip the wiring harness as necessary **(see illustration 3.4)**.

8 Remove the cooling fan motor and mounting frame by releasing the two plastic catches either side at the top, then lift the motor and frame up to disengage the lower slide-in clips. Once released, the motor and frame can be removed **(see illustrations 3.5a and 3.5b)**.

9 If desired, the fan motor can be removed from the frame after unscrewing the three securing nuts **(see illustration)**.

Refitting

10 Refitting is a reversal of removal. Reconnect the radiator fan wiring securely, and ensure the harness is routed clear of the fan blades or hot components.

6 Coolant temperature sensor – removal and refitting

Warning: Do not attempt to remove the sensor while the cooling system is hot and/or pressurised, as there is a great risk of scalding.

1 Allow the engine to cool, then slowly remove the cap from the coolant expansion tank to depressurise the cooling system. To avoid any chance of coolant spillage, the system can be drained as described in Chapter 1A, Section 26 or Chapter 1B, Section 25, but this is not essential if a new sensor is being fitted, and can quickly be substituted for the old one. Otherwise, if the system is not drained and the sensor will be left out for some time, a plug of some kind should be inserted to reduce coolant loss.

Petrol engine

Removal

2 On early models the sensor is screwed into the coolant outlet housing, beneath the ignition coil, at the transmission end of the cylinder head. On later models it is secured in position with a clip. To improve access, remove the air cleaner as described in Chapter 4A, Section 5. In order to get a spanner on the sensor, it may also be necessary to remove the four ignition coil mounting bolts, and move the coil to one side (the wiring can be left attached).

6.3 Remove the coolant temperature sensor

6.6 Coolant temperature sensor location – diesel engine

3 Disconnect the sensor wiring plug, then unscrew it or release the clip and pull it from the housing from the outlet housing **(see illustration)**.

4 On the bench the resistance of the sensor can be checked and compared to the figures given in the specifications. It is also possible to warm the sensor with a hot air gun or by immersing it in water to check that the resistance changes with the temperature.

Refitting

5 Refitting is a reversal of removal. Lightly coat the sensor threads with sealant, and tighten it securely to prevent leaks. On models retained by a clip, examine the condition of the O-ring, renewing it if necessary **(see illustration)**. Either refill or top-up the cooling system as described in Chapter 1A, Section 26 or *Weekly checks*.

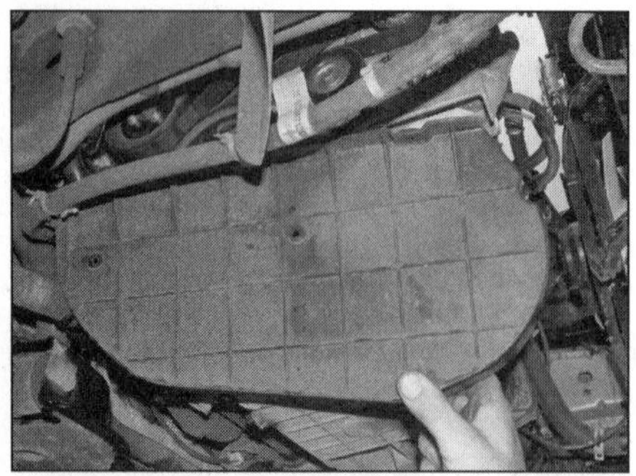

7.4 Remove the drivebelt lower cover

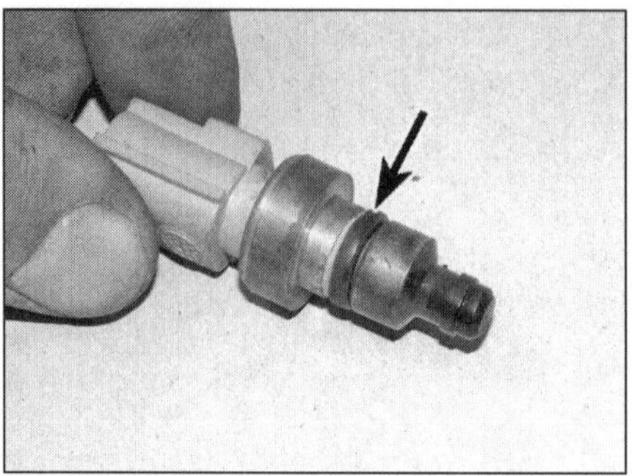

6.5 Check the condition of the O-ring (arrowed)

6.7 Testing the sensor

Diesel engine

Removal

6 The sensor is clipped into the top of the thermostat housing, which is located at the transmission end of the engine **(see illustration)**. If necessary, to improve access, remove the air cleaner and turbocharger air ducting as described in Chapter 4B, Section 4.

7 Disconnect the wiring plug. The resistance of the sensor can be checked with the sensor *in situ* **(see illustration)**. We tested the sensor with a warm engine and watched the resistance change as the engine cooled down.

8 Pull out the spring clip used to retain the sensor and remove the sensor from the housing.

Refitting

9 Refitting is a reversal of removal. If the old sensor is being refitted, check the condition of its sealing ring. Push the sensor fully home, then retain it with the spring clip. Reconnect the wiring plug. Either refill or top-up the cooling system as described in Chapter 1B, Section 25 or *Weekly checks*.

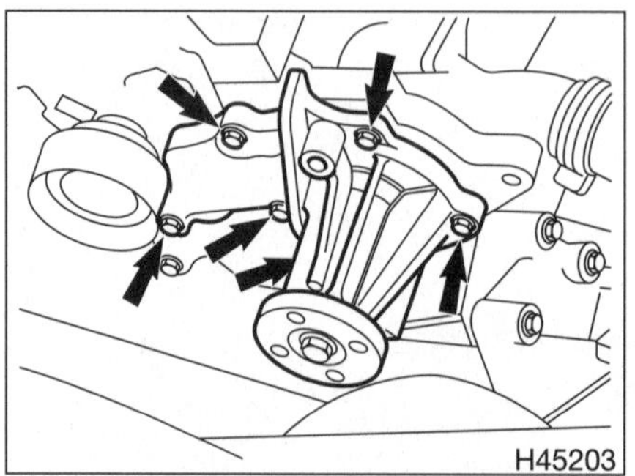

7.11 Water pump bolts (arrowed) – petrol engine

7 Water pump – removal and refitting

Petrol engine before 04/2005

Removal

1 Remove the air cleaner as described in Chapter 4A, Section 5.

2 Drain the cooling system as described in Chapter 1A, Section 26.

3 Loosen the right-hand front wheel nuts, then raise and support the front of the car, and support it on axle stands (see *Jacking and vehicle support*). To improve access, remove the right-hand front wheel.

4 Release the two clips securing the power steering pipe, then remove the two bolts securing the crankshaft pulley lower cover under the wheel arch **(see illustration)**.

5 Before removing the drivebelt, loosen the four water pump pulley bolts.

Warning: Just loosen the pulley bolts – don't remove them at this stage, as the pulley will still be under considerable tension from the drivebelt.

6 Remove the coolant expansion tank upper hose, which has a quick-release fitting, released by squeezing the sides together. Unbolt the tank from the inner wing, and move it to one side without disconnecting the lower hose.

7 Remove the alternator as described in Chapter 5A, Section 8.

8 Remove the water pump pulley.

9 Referring to Chapter 2A, Section 7 if necessary, remove the timing belt upper cover.

10 Protect the timing belt and lower cover area from being splashed with coolant as the water pump is removed (even with the system drained, some residual coolant will remain).

11 Unscrew the six securing bolts, then withdraw the water pump **(see illustration)**. Recover the gasket.

Refitting

12 Commence refitting by thoroughly cleaning the mating faces of the water pump and the cylinder block.

13 Refit the water pump, using a new gasket, and tighten the securing bolts to the specified torque.

14 Further refitting is a reversal of removal, bearing in mind the following points:

a) Refit the timing belt cover (Chapter 2A, Section 7).

b) Tighten all fixings to the specified torque (where given).

c) Fit a new auxiliary drivebelt (Chapter 1A, Section 23).
d) On completion, refill the cooling system (Chapter 1A, Section 26).

Petrol engine after 04/2005

Removal

15 On models manufactured from 04/2005-onwards, the timing belt tensioner is combined with the water pump. First, remove the timing belt as described in Chapter 2A, Section 8. Note that the tensioner will be locked in its tensioned position away from the timing belt, so take care not to release it.
16 Drain the cooling system as described in Chapter 1A, Section 25.
17 Unscrew the bolts and remove the water pump and tensioner assembly from the cylinder block **(see illustration)**. Remove and discard the gasket.
18 If necessary, release the tension and unbolt the tensioner from the water pump.

Warning: Take care when releasing the tension to prevent personal injury.

Refitting

19 If removed, refit the tensioner to the water pump and tighten the bolt to the specified torque.
20 Commence refitting by thoroughly cleaning the mating faces of the water pump and the cylinder block.
21 Refit the water pump/tensioner, using a new gasket, and tighten the securing bolts to the specified torque.
22 Refit the timing belt as described in Chapter 2A, Section 8, then refill the cooling system (Chapter 1A, Section 26).

Diesel engine

Removal

23 Remove the timing belt as described in Chapter 2B, Section 7 or Chapter 2C, Section 7.
24 Remove the seven bolts securing the water pump to the engine, and remove it **(see illustration)**. Recover the sealing ring, if it is loose.

Refitting

25 Commence refitting by thoroughly cleaning the mating faces of the water pump

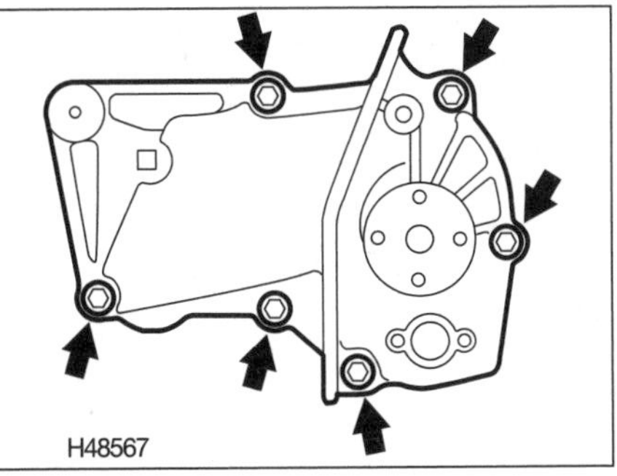

7.17 Water pump bolts – later petrol engine

and the cylinder block. If the old water pump is being refitted, check the condition of the sealing ring. Obtain a new one if possible, but it appears that it may not be available separately.
26 Refit the water pump, and tighten the securing bolts to the specified torque, in two stages. The pump body is made of plastic, so care is required. The first stage of tightening is a very low torque, which in reality approximates to doing the bolts just up to the surface.
27 Further refitting is a reversal of removal. Refit the timing belt as described in Chapter 2B or 2C.

8 Heating and ventilation system – general information

The heater/ventilation system consists of a four-speed blower motor (housed behind the facia), face-level vents in the centre and at each end of the facia, and air ducts to the front footwells.

The control unit is located in the facia, and the controls operate flap valves, to deflect and mix the air flowing through the various parts of the heater/ventilation system. The flap valves are contained in the air distribution housing, which acts as a central distribution unit, passing air to the various ducts and vents.

Cold air enters the system through the grille at the rear of the engine compartment.

The air (boosted by the blower fan if required) then flows through the various ducts,

7.24 Water pump bolts (arrowed) – diesel engine

according to the settings of the controls. Stale air is expelled through ducts at the rear of the car. If warm air is required, the cold air is passed through the heater matrix, which is heated by the engine coolant.

On models with air conditioning, a recirculation switch enables the outside air supply to be closed off, while the air inside the car is recirculated. This can be useful to prevent unpleasant odours entering from outside the car, but should only be used briefly, as the recirculated air inside the car will soon deteriorate.

9 Heater/ventilation system components – removal and refitting

Heater/ventilation control panel

Models built before 10/2005

1 Open the driver's side storage compartment, and remove the two screws inside at the top **(see illustration)**.
2 Remove the driver's lower facia panel from under the steering column – the panel is secured by three screws along its bottom edge, and one clip at the top left (pull the panel towards you to release) **(see illustration)**.
3 Remove the two screws situated below the heater control panel **(see illustration)**.
4 Open the upper storage compartment and remove the tray to access two screws. Remove the screws **(see illustration)**.
5 Carefully prise out the four switches on the side of the panel – these come out as a single

9.1 Remove the two screws inside the driver's storage compartment

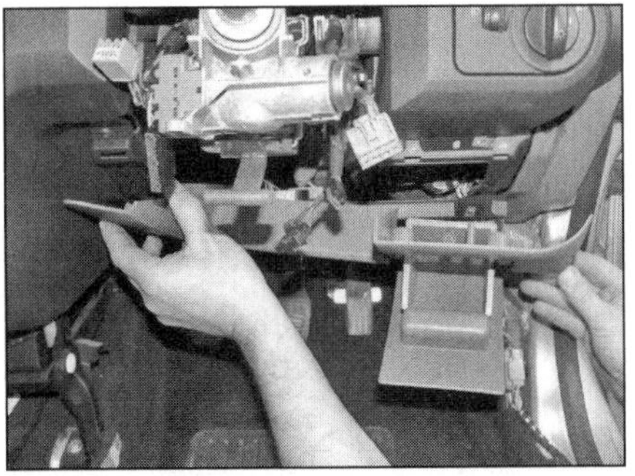

9.2 Remove the three lower screws, and pull out the driver's side lower facia panel

9.3 Remove the two cross-head screws at the base of the panel

9.4 Remove the screws

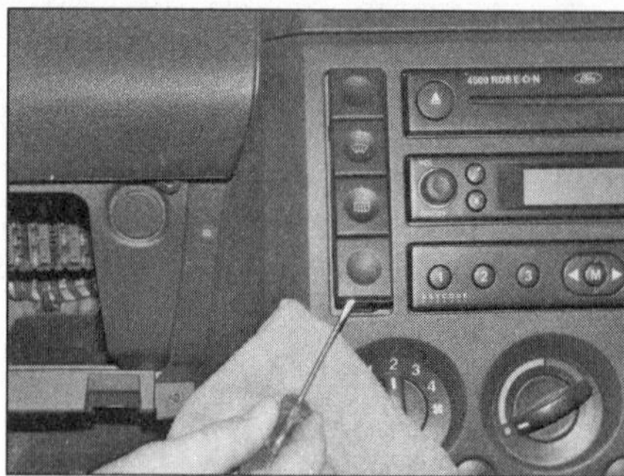
9.5a Prise out the switch panel next to the radio, taking care to protect the facia ...

9.5b ... and disconnect the wiring plug

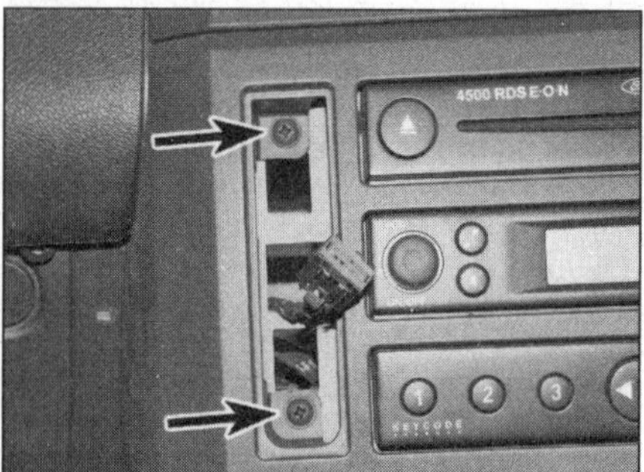
9.6 Remove the two cross-head screws behind the switch panel

9.7 Disconnect the temperature control cable end fitting

9.10 Disconnect the air distribution control cable

unit. Take care to protect the facia from damage as this is done – place a piece of card behind the tool used to prise the switch assembly out. When the switches are free, disconnect the wiring plug and remove the assembly **(see illustrations)**.

6 Remove the two screws located behind the switch panel just removed **(see illustration)**.

7 Now the temperature control cable must be released. Working in the driver's footwell, reach up at the side of the heater box and disconnect the cable at the operating flap – this means unhooking the cable end fitting, then releasing the outer cable from the clip **(see illustration)**.

8 As a precaution, place some masking tape over the three visible panels of the radio/CD unit, to avoid the possibility of scratching it as the heater control panel is removed.

9 Carefully pull the heater control panel surround away from the facia, releasing the two clips at the top. The panel will not come away completely, but will move sufficiently to access the heater/ventilation controls.

10 Disconnect the air distribution flap operating shaft behind the panel – turn the air distribution knob and gently pull the panel out, to release it **(see illustration)**.

11 The control panel can now be withdrawn further from the facia. Disconnect the wiring plugs from the back of the panel, noting their fitted positions **(see illustration)**.

12 Withdraw the heater control panel surround fully, feeding the temperature control cable through.

13 The heater control panel is now fully accessible for component renewal. If required, the panel itself can be separated from the surround by removing the four screws on the back of the panel.

14 Refitting is a reversal of removal.

Models built after 10/2005

15 Remove the audio unit as described in Chapter 12, Section 17.

16 Remove the panel below the steering column **(see illustrations 9.1 and 9.2)**.

17 Push out the heated screen switches and the cabin temperature sensor housing **(see illustrations)**.

18 Remove the panel retaining screws **(see illustration)**.

19 Working in the driver's footwell, reach up at the side of the heater box and disconnect the cable at the operating flap – this means unhooking the cable end fitting, then releasing the outer cable from the clip **(see illustration 9.7)**.

20 Pull forward the panel, disconnect the air distribution cable and unplug the wiring connectors **(see illustrations 9.10 and 9.11)**.

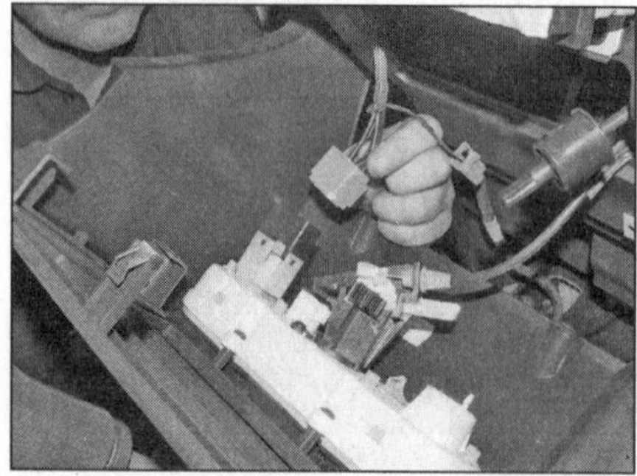
9.11 Disconnect the wiring plugs from the back of the panel

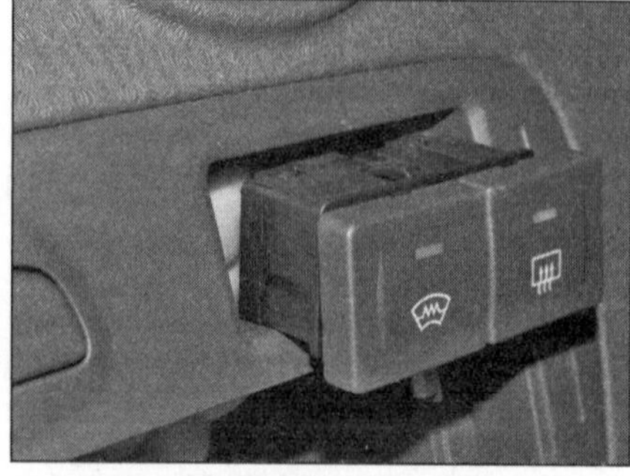
9.17a Remove the heated screen switches ...

9.17b ... and the cabin temperature sensor

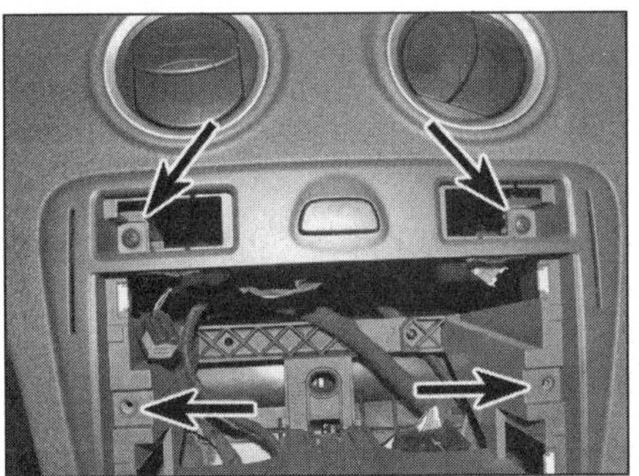
9.18 Remove the panel screws (arrowed)

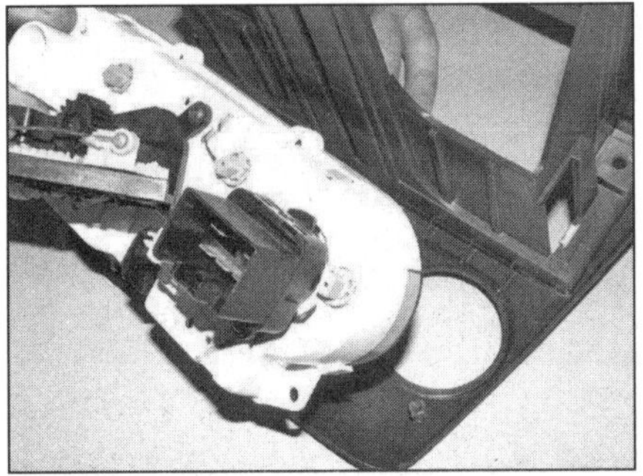
9.22b ... and remove the control panel

21 Completely remove the panel. Note the route of the temperature control cable through the facia **(see illustration)**.
22 If required remove the control panel from the trim panel **(see illustrations)**.
23 Refitting is a reversal of removal.

Heater blower motor switch

24 Remove the heater control panel as described earlier in this Section.
25 Disconnect the wiring plug from the back of the switch. Remove the single screw at the base of the switch, then twist the switch and remove it from the panel **(see illustrations)**.
26 Refitting is a reversal of removal.

Temperature control cable

27 Remove the heater control panel as described earlier in this Section.
28 Remove the single screw securing the cable end assembly to the control panel, then twist the assembly and pull it out of the control panel **(see illustrations)**. It appears that the cable assembly must be bought as a complete unit – a separate cable is not available.
29 Refitting is a reversal of removal.

Air distribution cable

30 Remove the heater control panel as described earlier in this Section.
31 Working in the driver's footwell, trace the cable up the right-hand side of the heater box. Use a screwdriver to prise down the plastic catch that secures the cable end to the operating lever, and withdraw the cable **(see illustration)**. Take care – the plastic catch is surprisingly fragile.
32 Refitting is a reversal of removal.

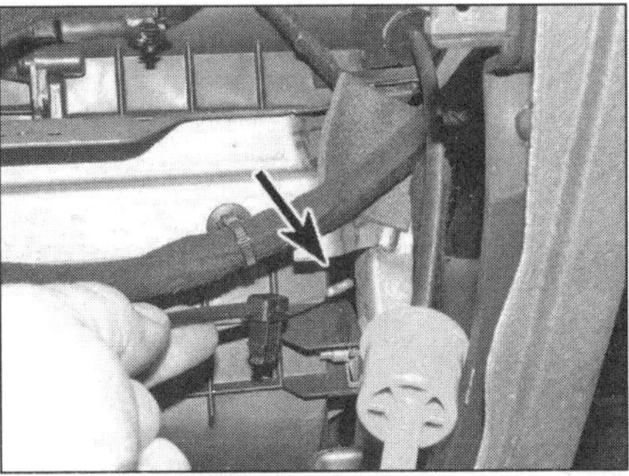
9.21 Note the route of the cable (arrowed)

9.25a Remove the screw above the switch ...

Heater blower motor

Models built before 10/2005

33 Remove the screw from each hinge at the base of the glovebox, then open the glovebox and slide the assembly out of the facia.

9.28a Remove the single screw ...

9.31 Carefully press down the retaining catch, and pull out the cable (seen with facia removed)

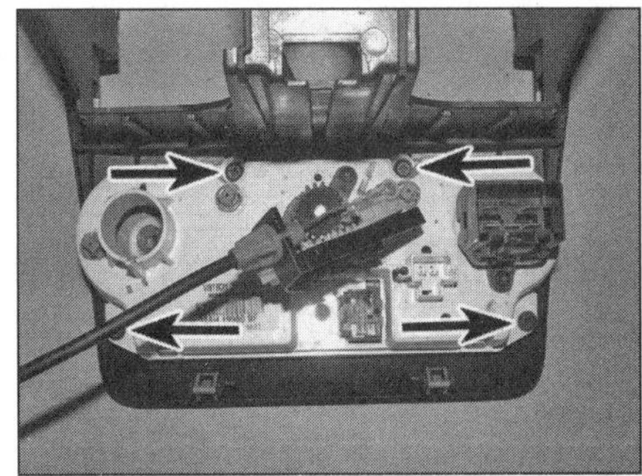
9.22a Remove the screws (arrowed) ...

9.25b ... then twist and remove the switch from the panel

34 Reach in behind the heater unit on the left-hand side, and disconnect the blower motor wiring plug, which is at the bottom of the blower motor, just above the heater pipes **(see illustration)**.
35 Behind the glovebox location, remove

9.28b ... and twist out the cable end assembly

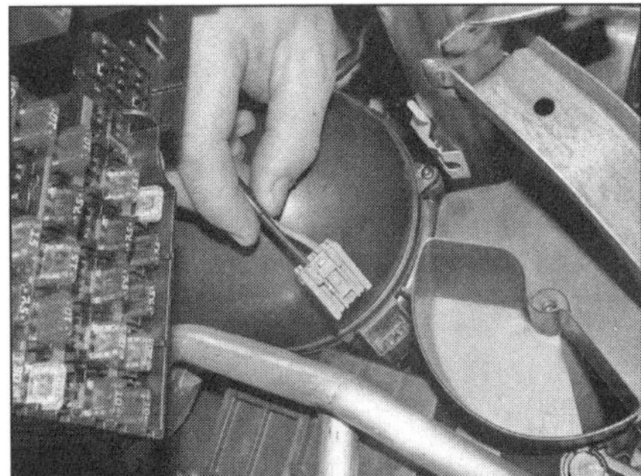
9.34 Disconnect the blower motor wiring plug

9.35a Remove the two screws ...

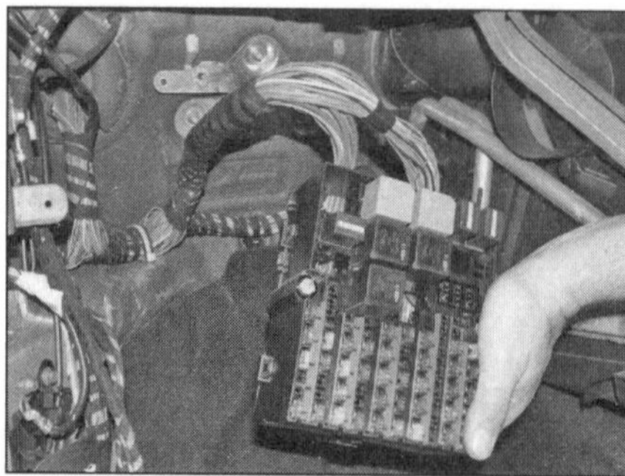
9.35b ... and move the fusebox to one side

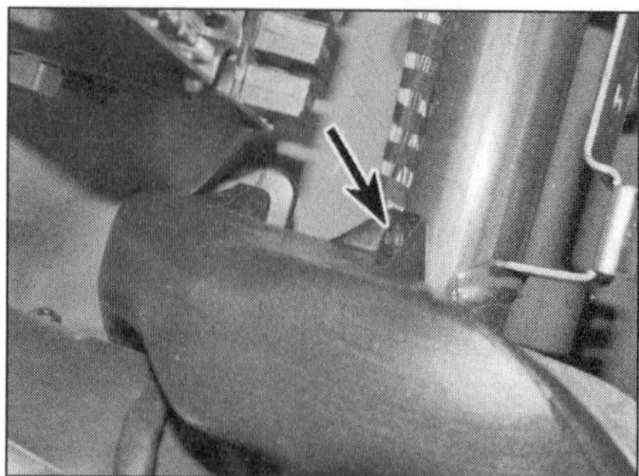
9.36 Remove the screw securing the vent to the crossmember

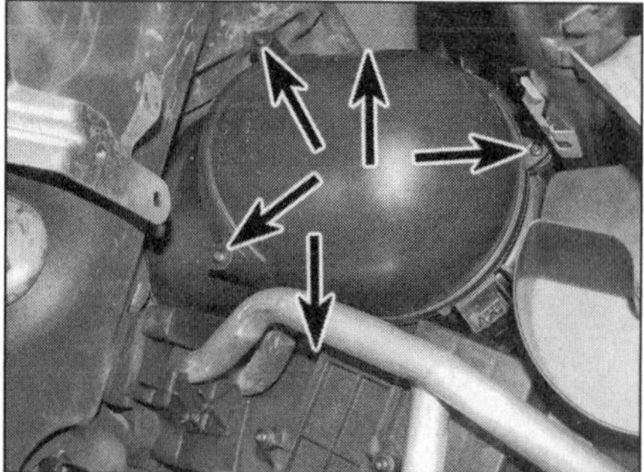
9.37 Remove the five screws from the blower motor cover

9.38a Twist the blower motor round so the lug clears the heater pipes ...

9.38b ... and withdraw it into the footwell

the two screws securing the fusebox to the bulkhead, then lay the fusebox to the side without disconnecting any wiring **(see illustrations)**.

36 Looking directly upwards from the passenger footwell, remove the single screw securing the windscreen left-hand vent duct to the facia crossmember **(see illustration)**. Lower the duct from the facia.

37 Disconnect the air intake control cable. Remove a total of five screws, and take off the blower motor cover **(see illustration)**.

38 The blower motor can now be pulled out into the passenger footwell. However, it's not quite as easy as that – the motor must be twisted round and manipulated so that the mounting lug on the blower passes in front of the heater pipes **(see illustrations)**.

39 Refitting is a reversal of removal.

Models built after 10/2005

40 Remove the facia as described in Chapter 11, Section 27.

41 Disconnect the control cable and unplug the wiring connector.

42 Remove the air intake housing **(see illustration)**.

43 Twist the blower motor and remove it from the housing **(see illustration)**.

44 Refitting is a reversal of removal.

Heater blower motor resistor

45 Remove the driver's side lower facia panel. The panel is secured by five screws (two inside the small storage compartment) and one clip (at the top left – pull the panel towards you to release it).

46 Unclip the right-hand trim panel in the passenger's footwell, which is secured by a screw and push-in clip at the front, and is clipped to the centre console at the rear. The blower motor resistor pack is now accessible, up at the front by the bulkhead.

47 Disconnect the resistor pack wiring plug.

48 Unscrew the two securing screws, and withdraw the resistor pack from the heater assembly **(see illustration)**.

49 Refitting is a reversal of removal.

Air recirculation control motor

50 Unclip the right-hand trim panel in the passenger's footwell, which is secured by a screw and push-in clip at the front, and is clipped to the centre console at the rear. The air recirculation motor is now accessible, up at the front by the bulkhead.

51 Disconnect the control motor wiring plug.

52 Unscrew the securing screws **(see**

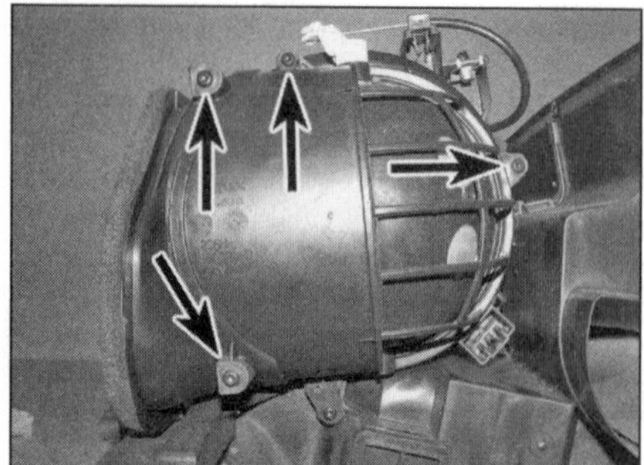
9.42 Remove the screws (arrowed)

9.43 Remove the blower motor

9.48 Withdraw the resistor pack into the driver's footwell

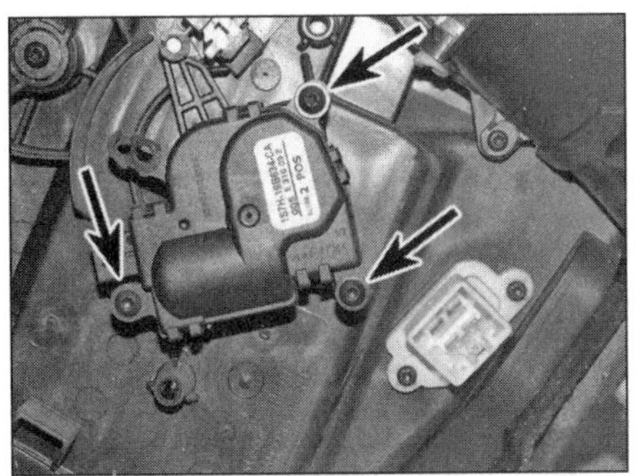

9.52 Remove the screws (arrowed)

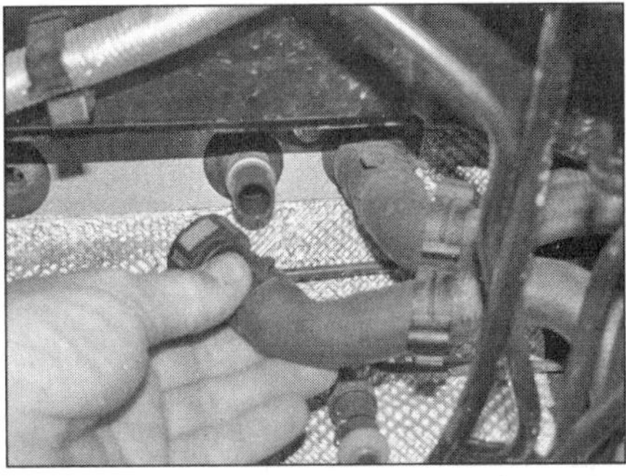

9.57a Disconnect the two heater hoses at the bulkhead

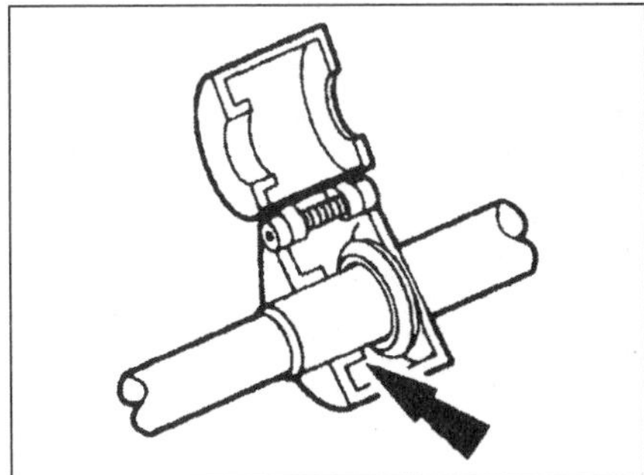

9.57b A special spring lock tool will be required to disconnect the refrigerant pipes

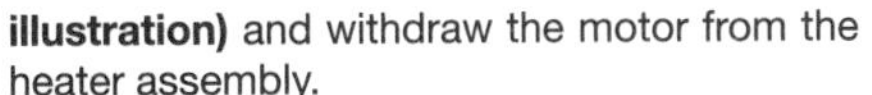

9.57c Plug and seal the refrigerant pipes as soon as they are disconnected

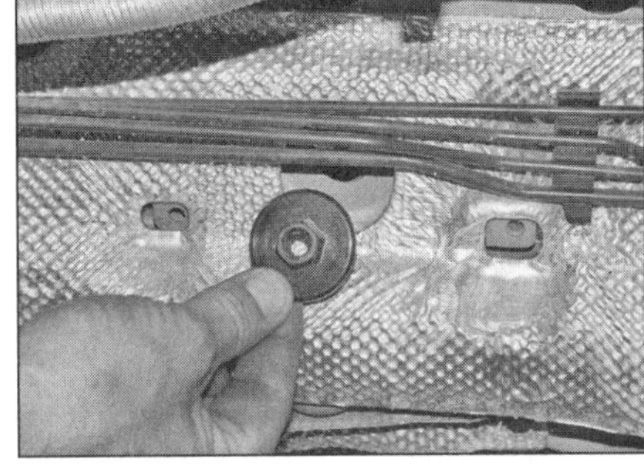

9.60 Unscrew the large plastic securing nut for the heater assembly

9.61 Withdraw the heater assembly into the car

illustration) and withdraw the motor from the heater assembly.

53 Refitting is a reversal of removal.

Heater matrix

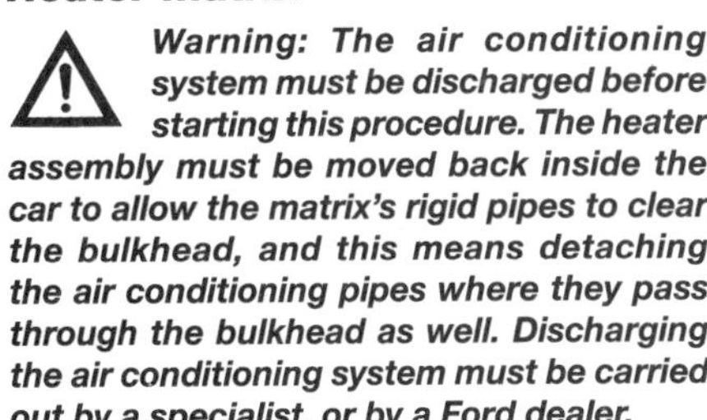

Warning: The air conditioning system must be discharged before starting this procedure. The heater assembly must be moved back inside the car to allow the matrix's rigid pipes to clear the bulkhead, and this means detaching the air conditioning pipes where they pass through the bulkhead as well. Discharging the air conditioning system must be carried out by a specialist, or by a Ford dealer.

54 Have the air conditioning system professionally discharged, on models so equipped.

55 Drain the cooling system as described in Chapter 1A, Section 26 or Chapter 1B, Section 25.

56 Remove the air cleaner as described in Chapter 4A, Section 5 or Chapter 4B, Section 4.

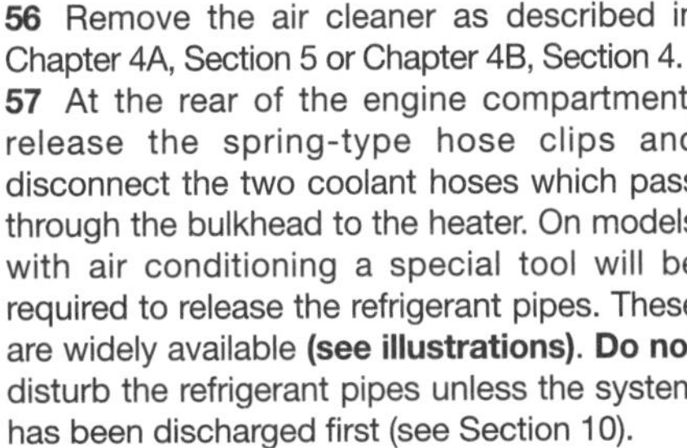

57 At the rear of the engine compartment, release the spring-type hose clips and disconnect the two coolant hoses which pass through the bulkhead to the heater. On models with air conditioning a special tool will be required to release the refrigerant pipes. These are widely available **(see illustrations)**. **Do not** disturb the refrigerant pipes unless the system has been discharged first (see Section 10).

58 Remove the facia panel as described in Chapter 11, Section 27, including removal of the facia crossmember.

59 On models so equipped, remove the two mounting bolts and remove the auxiliary heater from the side of the main heater assembly. Lay the auxiliary heater to one side, without disconnecting any wiring.

60 Have an assistant support the heater housing inside the car. In the engine compartment, unscrew the large plastic mounting nut in the centre of the bulkhead **(see illustration)**.

61 Carefully withdraw the heater housing into the car, disconnecting any wiring from it as necessary **(see illustration)**. On models with an auxiliary heater, pass the heater wiring through into the car as the heater is drawn back. Also ensure that the water drain tube on the base of the housing is not damaged, either when removing the heater assembly or when storing it.

62 Remove the foam gasket from the front of the heater housing, taking care not to damage it **(see illustration)**.

63 Remove the Torx screw which secures the heater pipe bracket to the heater housing **(see illustration)**.

64 Remove the two screws securing the cover on the side of the heater matrix **(see illustration)**.

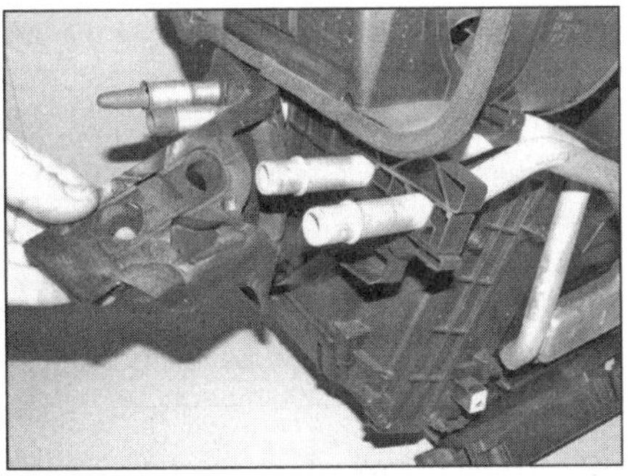

9.62 Remove the heater assembly foam gasket at the front

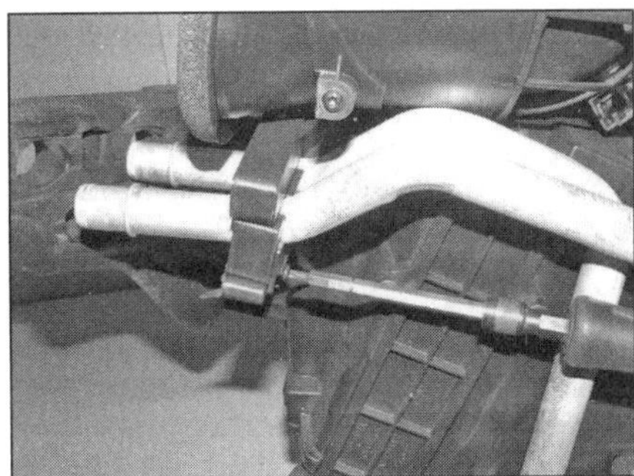

9.63 Disconnect the heater pipe bracket from the housing

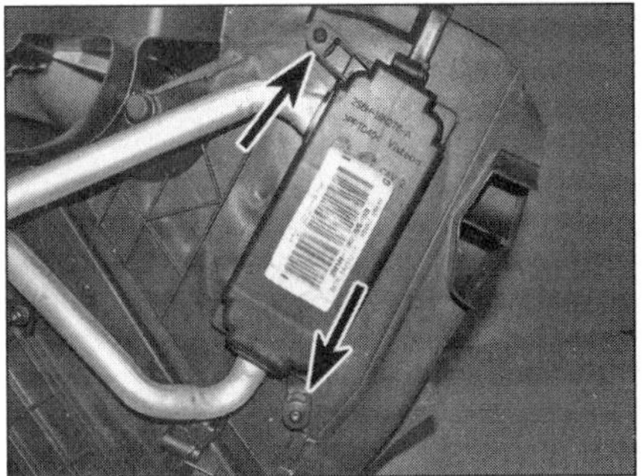

9.64 Remove the screws (arrowed)

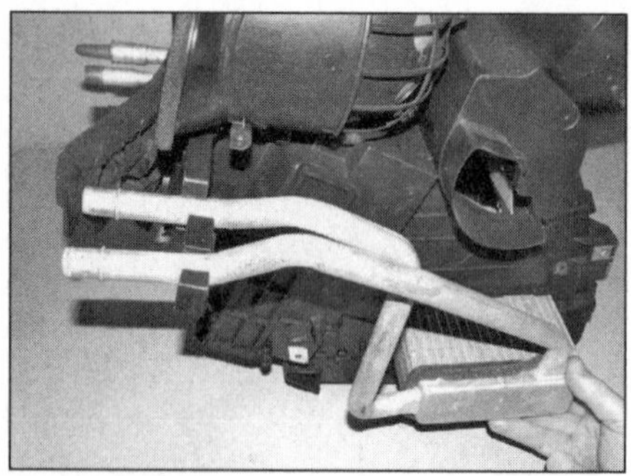

9.65 Carefully slide out the heater matrix

65 Carefully slide out the heater matrix from the side of the heater housing, and remove it **(see illustration)**.

66 Refitting is a reversal of removal, noting the following points:

a) *Before offering the heater housing back into position, make sure that the adjustment nut on the front of the assembly is free to turn. Tighten it fully, then unscrew it one turn* ***(see illustration)****. When the housing is refitted, and the large plastic nut on the engine side of the bulkhead is tightened, the nut inside will also tighten up to the bulkhead.*

b) *Do not forget to refit the foam gasket to the front of the housing. If the gasket is in poor condition, fit a new one.*

c) *The rubber grommet for the water drain tube must be correctly located in the car floor, and the tube correctly fitted into it during refitting* ***(see illustration)****.*

9.69a Remove the mounting screws ...

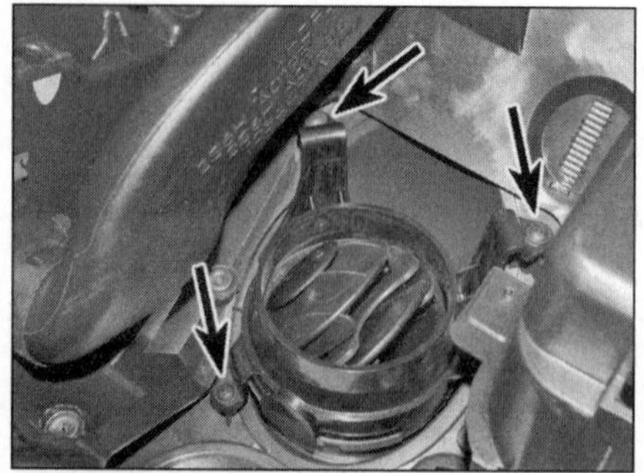

9.70a Remove the screws from the rear ...

9.66a Fully tighten the inner nut, then loosen it one turn

d) *On models with an auxiliary heater, ensure that the heater wiring harness grommet is correctly located in the bulkhead.*

e) *On completion, fill and bleed the cooling system as described in Chapter 1A, Section 26 or Chapter 1B, Section 25.*

f) *On models with air conditioning, have the refrigerant pipes reconnected (using new O-ring seals) and the system recharged by a specialist or a Ford dealer.*

Heater assembly

Warning: On models with air conditioning, read the precautions given in Section 10, and have the system discharged by a Ford dealer or an air conditioning specialist. Do not carry out the following work unless the system had been discharged.

67 Removal and refitting of the heater assembly are as previously described in this Section for the heater matrix.

9.69b ... and detach the vent supply duct

9.70b ... and lift off the vent

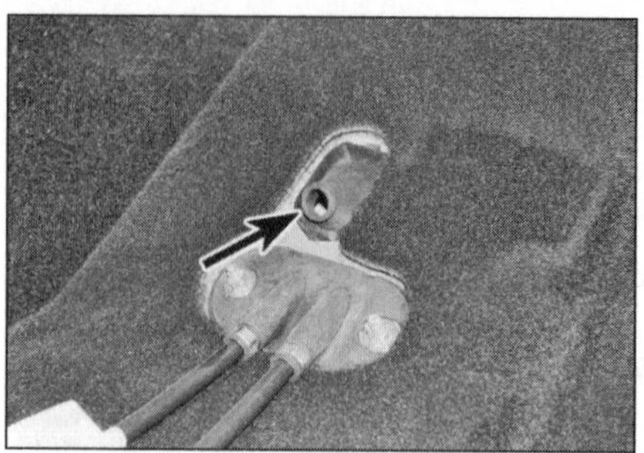

9.66b Check that the heater assembly's water drain tube enters the rubber pipe on the car floor

Facia vents

68 The facia vents can only be removed after the facia panel has been removed, as described in Chapter 11, Section 27. In this case, removing the facia crossmember is not necessary.

69 Remove the mounting screws, and detach the relevant vent supply duct from the rear of the facia. Unclip the duct from the back of the vent, and remove it **(see illustrations)**.

70 Each vent is secured to the rear of the facia panel by a number of screws – remove the screws, and withdraw the vent **(see illustrations)**.

71 Refitting is a reversal of removal. Refit the facia panel as described in Chapter 11, Section 27.

10 Air conditioning system – general information and precautions

1 Air conditioning is available on most models. It is fitted as standard on the earlier Fusion 2 and Fusion 3 models and on the later Zetec and Titanium models. Full climate control was offered as an option on the later Titanium models. It enables the temperature of incoming air to be lowered, and also dehumidifies the air, which makes for rapid demisting and increased comfort.

2 The cooling side of the system works in the same way as a domestic refrigerator. Refrigerant gas is drawn into a belt-driven compressor, and passes into a condenser mounted in front of the radiator, where it loses heat and becomes liquid. The liquid passes through an expansion valve to an evaporator, where it changes from liquid under high pressure to gas under low pressure. This change is accompanied by a drop in temperature, which cools the evaporator. The refrigerant returns to the compressor, and the cycle begins again.

3 Air blown through the evaporator passes to the heater assembly, where it is mixed with hot air blown through the heater matrix, to achieve the desired temperature in the passenger compartment.

4 The heating side of the system works in the same way as on models without air conditioning (see Section 8).

5 The operation of the system is controlled electronically. Any problems with the system should be referred to a Ford dealer or an air conditioning specialist.

Precautions

Warning: The air conditioning system is under high pressure. Do not loosen any fittings or remove any components until after the system has been discharged. Air conditioning refrigerant should be properly discharged at a dealer service department or an automotive air conditioning repair facility capable of handling R134a refrigerant. Always wear eye protection when disconnecting air conditioning system fittings.

6 When an air conditioning system is fitted, it is necessary to observe the following special precautions whenever dealing with any part of the system, its associated components, and any items which necessitate disconnection of the system:

a) While the refrigerant used – R134a – is less damaging to the environment than the previously-used R12, it is still a very dangerous substance. It must not be allowed into contact with the skin or eyes, or there is a risk of frostbite. It must also not be discharged in an enclosed space – while it is not toxic, there is a risk of suffocation. The refrigerant is heavier than air, and so must never be discharged over a pit.

b) The refrigerant must not be allowed to come in contact with a naked flame, otherwise a poisonous gas will be created – under certain circumstances, this can form an explosive mixture with air. For similar reasons, smoking in the presence of refrigerant is highly dangerous, particularly if the vapour is inhaled through a lighted cigarette.

c) Never discharge the system to the atmosphere – R134a is not an ozone-depleting ChloroFluoroCarbon (CFC) like R12, but is instead a hydrofluorocarbon, which causes environmental damage by contributing to the 'greenhouse effect' if released into the atmosphere.

d) R134a refrigerant must not be mixed with R12; the system uses different seals (now green-coloured, previously black) and has different fittings requiring different tools, so that there is no chance of the two types of refrigerant becoming mixed accidentally.

e) If for any reason the system must be disconnected, entrust this task to your Ford dealer or air conditioning specialist.

f) It is essential that the system be professionally discharged prior to using any form of heat – welding, soldering, brazing, etc – in the vicinity of the system, before having the car oven-dried at a temperature exceeding 70°C after repainting, and before disconnecting any part of the system.

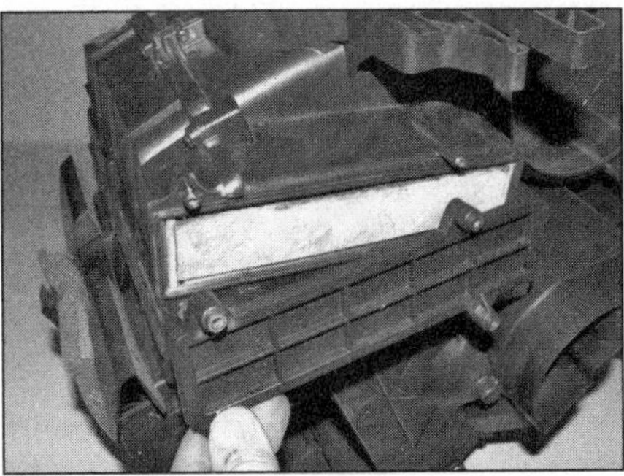

11.8a Remove the pollen filter cover ...

11.8b ... and pull out the filter

11 Air conditioning system components – removal and refitting

Warning: Read the precautions given in Section 10, and have the system discharged by a Ford dealer or an air conditioning specialist. Do not carry out the following work unless the system had been discharged.

Compressor

Note: *If the compressor is being removed as part of another procedure, it may not be necessary to have the system discharged. Usually, the compressor can be unbolted and tied to one side without the need to disturb the refrigerant lines.*

Removal

1 Remove the auxiliary drivebelt as described in Chapter 1A, Section 23 or Chapter 1B, Section 22.

2 Disconnect the compressor wiring plug.

3 With the system discharged, disconnect the refrigerant lines from the compressor. Discard the O-ring seals – new ones must be used when refitting.

4 Support the compressor, then remove the four mounting bolts and lower the compressor out of the engine bay.

Refitting

5 Refitting is a reversal of removal, noting the following points:

a) Use new O-rings, coated with refrigerant oil, when reconnecting the refrigerant lines.

b) Tighten the compressor mounting bolts to the specified torque.

c) Have the system professionally recharged and tested on completion.

Evaporator

Removal

6 The evaporator is fitted inside the heater unit.

7 Remove the facia and the support bar as described in Chapter 11, Section 27 and then remove the heater unit as described in Section 9 of this Chapter.

8 Remove the heater matrix, blower motor and pollen filter **(see illustrations)** as described in Section 9.

9 Remove the foam insulation and remove the evaporator support bracket **(see illustrations)**.

10 The various sections of the heater distribution box must now be separated **(see illustrations)**.

11 Finally, remove the evaporator core from the heater box **(see illustration)**.

Refitting

12 Refitting is a reversal of removal, but remember to use new O-rings (coated with refrigerant oil) when reconnecting the refrigerant lines.

Condenser

Removal

13 Disconnect the battery negative lead with reference to Chapter 5A, Section 2.

11.9a Remove the insulation ...

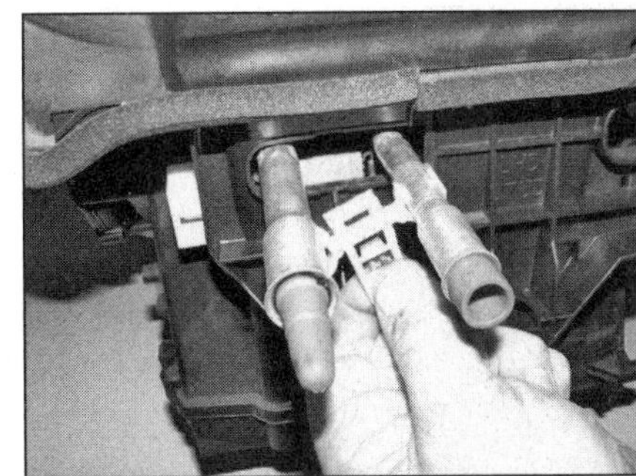

11.9b ... and the bracket

11.10a Remove the air intake section ...

11.10b ... and the base section

11.10c Unscrew and unclip the two main sections ...

11.10d ... and separate them

11.11 Remove the core

11.26 Disconnect the refrigerant pipes (arrowed)

14 Apply the handbrake, then jack up the front of the car and support securely on axle stands (see *Jacking and vehicle support*).

15 Disconnect the cooling fan wiring plugs from the fan motor and resistor, and unclip the wiring harness as necessary.

16 Remove the cooling fan motor and shroud by releasing the two plastic catches each side at the top, then lift the motor and shroud up to disengage the lower slide-in clips. Once released, the motor and shroud can be lowered out.

17 Unscrew the radiator lower mounting bolt and support rubber on either side (as described in Section 3).

18 With the system discharged, disconnect the refrigerant lines from the condenser. Discard the O-rings – new ones must be used when refitting.

19 Lift the radiator slightly to free it from the lower crossmember, and support it in the raised position.

20 Carefully slide the condenser sideways to unclip it from the radiator, and lower it out. A simpler solution is to remove both the radiator and condenser as a single unit (assuming the coolant has been drained first). Once the condenser has been removed, the radiator can be lowered back onto the lower crossmember.

Refitting

21 Refitting is a reversal of removal, noting the following points:

a) Use new O-rings, coated with refrigerant oil, when reconnecting the refrigerant lines.

b) Reconnect the radiator fan wiring, and ensure the harness is routed clear of the fan blades or hot components.

c) Have the system professionally recharged and tested on completion.

Dehydrator

Removal

22 The dehydrator is located at the right-hand front corner of the engine compartment.

23 Disconnect the battery negative lead with reference to Chapter 5A, Section 2.

24 Remove the right-hand headlight (right as seen from the driver's seat) as described in Chapter 12, Section 7.

25 Disconnect the wiring plug from the low-pressure switch. **Note:** *If the switch alone is being removed, it is still strongly recommended that the system is discharged beforehand, since it cannot be assumed the switch valve will be shut.*

26 Disconnect the refrigerant lines from the dehydrator **(see illustration)**. Discard the O-ring seals – new ones must be used when refitting.

27 Remove the two bolts securing the dehydrator mounting bracket to the inner wing, and remove it – one bolt in particular may have to be accessed from below.

Refitting

28 Refitting is a reversal of removal, noting the following points:

a) Use new O-rings, coated with refrigerant oil, when reconnecting the refrigerant lines.

b) Refit the right-hand headlight as described in Chapter 12, Section 7.

c) Have the system professionally recharged and tested on completion.

Chapter 4 Part A:
Fuel and exhaust systems – petrol models

Contents

Degrees of difficulty

Easy, suitable for novice with little experience	**Fairly easy,** suitable for beginner with some experience 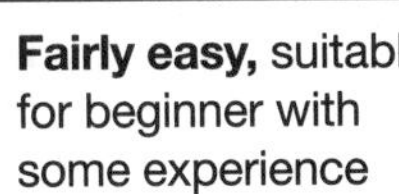	**Fairly difficult,** suitable for competent DIY mechanic	**Difficult,** suitable for experienced DIY mechanic	**Very difficult,** suitable for expert DIY or professional 

Specifications

General

System type	Sequential multi-port fuel injection (SFI)
Fuel octane requirement	95 RON unleaded
Regulated fuel pressure (nominal)	55 psi

Torque wrench settings

	Nm	lbf ft
Engine rear mounting through-bolt	48	35
Engine right-hand mounting nuts/bolts	48	35
Exhaust heat shield bolts	12	9
Exhaust manifold:		
Manifold nuts (to cylinder head):		
Stage 1	20	15
Stage 2	55	41
To engine block	47	35
Manifold to exhaust flexible section	44	32
Fuel pressure regulator mounting bolts	10	7
Fuel rail mounting bolts	15	11
Fuel tank strap retaining bolts	25	18
Inlet manifold nuts/bolts	18	13

1 General information and precautions

The fuel system consists of a fuel tank (mounted under the floor, beneath the rear seats), fuel hoses, an electric fuel pump mounted in the fuel tank, and a sequential electronic fuel injection system controlled by an engine management electronic control unit (powertrain control module).

The electric fuel pump supplies fuel under pressure to the fuel rail, which distributes fuel to the injectors. A pressure regulator controls the system pressure in relation to inlet tract depression. From the fuel rail, fuel is injected into the inlet ports, just above the inlet valves, by four fuel injectors. The fuel rail is mounted to the cylinder head, just above the plastic inlet manifold.

The amount of fuel supplied by the injectors is precisely controlled by the powertrain control module (PCM). The module uses the signals from the crankshaft position sensor and the camshaft position sensor to trigger each injector separately in cylinder firing order (sequential injection), with benefits in terms of better fuel economy and leaner exhaust emissions.

The powertrain control module is the heart of the entire engine management system, controlling the fuel injection, ignition and emissions control systems. The module receives information from various sensors which is then computed and compared with preset values stored in its memory, to determine the required period of injection.

Information on crankshaft position and engine speed is generated by a crankshaft position sensor. The inductive head of the sensor runs just above the engine flywheel and scans a series of protrusions on the flywheel periphery. As the crankshaft rotates, the sensor transmits a pulse to the system's ignition module every time a protrusion passes it. There is one missing protrusion in the flywheel periphery at a point corresponding to 90° BTDC. The ignition module recognises the absence of a pulse from the crankshaft position sensor at this point to establish a reference mark for crankshaft position. Similarly, the time interval between absent pulses is used to determine engine speed. This information is then fed to the powertrain control module for further processing.

The camshaft position sensor is located in the cylinder head so that it registers with a lobe on the camshaft. The camshaft position sensor functions in the same way as the crankshaft position sensor, producing a series of pulses; this gives the powertrain control module a reference point, to enable it to determine the firing order, and operate the injectors in the appropriate sequence.

Engine temperature information is supplied by the coolant temperature sensor. The sensor is an NTC (negative temperature coefficient) thermistor – that is, a semi-conductor whose electrical resistance decreases as its temperature increases. The sensor provides the powertrain control module with a constantly-varying (analogue) voltage signal, corresponding to the temperature of the engine coolant. This is used to refine the calculations made by the module, when determining the correct amount of fuel required to achieve the ideal air/fuel mixture ratio.

Inlet air temperature and density information for air/fuel mixture ratio calculations is provided by a temperature and manifold absolute pressure (TMAP) sensor. The TMAP sensor is located on the inlet manifold or throttle housing, and consists of a pressure transducer and a temperature sensor which directly supersedes the mass airflow and inlet air temperature sensors. The TMAP sensor provides information to the powertrain control module relating to inlet manifold vacuum and barometric pressure, and the temperature of the air in the inlet manifold. When the ignition is switched on with the engine stopped, the sensor calculates barometric pressure and, when the engine is running, the sensor calculates inlet manifold vacuum.

The throttle valve inside the throttle housing is controlled by the driver, through the accelerator pedal. As the valve opens, the amount of air that can pass through the system increases. As the throttle valve opens further, the TMAP sensor signal alters, and the powertrain control module opens each injector for a longer duration, to increase the amount of fuel delivered to the inlet ports.

An idle air control valve allows the powertrain control module to adjust the idle speed as necessary, to aid driveability, and to provide an anti-stall function determined by engine temperature, and the load caused by engine-driven accessories.

The engine features a throttle which is electronically-controlled – an accelerator cable is not fitted. Instead, a throttle position sensor fitted to the accelerator pedal provides the powertrain control module with the throttle opening signal, and this is relayed to a motor-driven throttle valve. This system also enables the PCM to control the engine idle speed, varying the throttle opening as required by changes in engine temperature and load.

On models without ABS, roadspeed is monitored by the vehicle speed sensor. This component is a Hall-effect generator, mounted on the transmission, in place of the old speedometer drive. It supplies the module with a series of pulses corresponding to the car's roadspeed, enabling the module to control features such as the fuel shut-off on overrun. If ABS is fitted, roadspeed information is provided by the ABS wheel sensors, and the vehicle speed sensor is not fitted.

The clutch pedal position is monitored by a switch fitted to the pedal bracket. This sends a signal to the powertrain control module.

A pressure-operated switch is screwed into the power steering system's high-pressure pipe. The switch sends a signal to the powertrain control module to increase engine speed to maintain idle speed as pressure in the system rises – typically, when the steering is near full-lock.

An oxygen sensor in the exhaust system provides the module with constant feedback – 'closed-loop' control – which enables it to adjust the mixture to provide the best possible operating conditions for the catalytic converter. A further sensor is fitted, downstream of the converter, to monitor the converter's operation and its efficiency. The post catalytic convertor sensor allows and even finer degree of emission control.

The air inlet side of the system consists of an air cleaner housing, the TMAP sensor, an inlet hose and duct, and a throttle housing.

Both the idle speed and mixture are under the control of the powertrain control module, and cannot be adjusted.

Warning: Many of the procedures in this Chapter require the removal of fuel lines and connections, which may result in some fuel spillage. Before carrying out any operation on the fuel system, refer to the precautions given in 'Safety first!' at the beginning of this manual, and follow them implicitly. Petrol is a highly-dangerous and volatile liquid, and the precautions necessary when handling it cannot be overstressed.

- ***Residual pressure will remain in the fuel lines long after the car was last used. When disconnecting any fuel line, first depressurise the fuel system as described in Section 2.***
- ***Before disconnecting any of the fuel injection system sensor wiring plugs, ensure at least that the ignition is switched off (ideally, disconnect the battery). If this is not done, it could result in a fault code being logged in the system memory, and may even cause damage to the component concerned.***

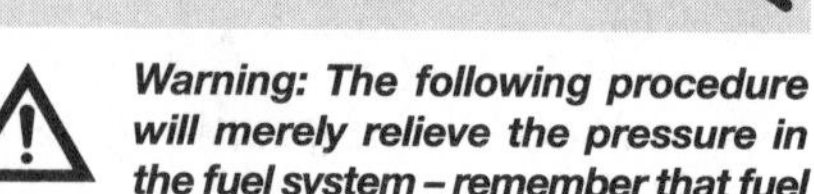

2 Fuel system – depressurisation

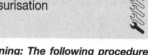

Warning: The following procedure will merely relieve the pressure in the fuel system – remember that fuel will still be present in the system components, and take precautions accordingly before disconnecting any of them.

Note: *Refer to the warning note in Section 1 before proceeding.*

1 The fuel system referred to in this Chapter is defined as the fuel tank and tank-mounted fuel pump/fuel gauge sender unit, the fuel filter, the fuel injectors, fuel pressure regulator, and the metal pipes and flexible hoses of the fuel lines between these components. All these contain fuel, which will be under pressure while the engine is running and/or while the ignition is switched on.

2 The pressure will remain for some time after the ignition has been switched off, and must be relieved before any of these components is disturbed for servicing work.

3 The simplest depressurisation method is to disconnect the fuel pump electrical supply by removing the fuel pump fuse (refer to the wiring diagrams or the label on the relevant fusebox for exact location) and starting the engine; allow the engine to idle until it stops through lack of fuel. Turn the engine over once or twice on the starter to ensure that all pressure is released, then switch off the ignition; do not forget to refit the fuse when work is complete.

4 If an adapter is available to fit the Schrader-type valve on the fuel rail pressure test/release fitting (identifiable by its blue plastic cap, and located on the union of the fuel feed line and the fuel rail), this may be used to release the fuel pressure. The Ford adapter (tool number 23-033) operates similar to a drain tap – turning the tap clockwise releases the pressure. If the adapter is not available, place cloth rags around the valve, then remove the cap and allow the fuel pressure to dissipate. Refit the cap on completion.

5 Note that, once the fuel system has been depressurised and drained (even partially), it will take significantly longer to restart the engine – perhaps several seconds of cranking – before the system is refilled and pressure restored.

3 Unleaded petrol – general information and usage

All petrol models are designed to run on fuel with a minimum octane rating of 95 (RON). All models have a catalytic converter, and so must be run on unleaded fuel **only**. Under no circumstances should leaded fuel (UK '4-star' or LRP) be used, as this will damage the converter.

Super unleaded petrol (98 octane) can also be used in all models if wished, though there is no advantage in doing so.

4 Fuel lines and fittings – general information

Note: *Refer to the warning note in Section 1 before proceeding.*

Quick-release couplings

1 Quick-release couplings are employed at many of the unions in the fuel feed and return lines.

2 Before disconnecting any fuel system component, relieve the residual pressure in the system (see Section 2), and equalise tank pressure by removing the fuel filler cap.

Warning: This procedure will merely relieve the increased pressure necessary for the engine to run – remember that fuel will still be present in the system components, and take precautions accordingly before disconnecting any of them.

3 Release the protruding locking lugs on each union, by squeezing them together and carefully pulling the coupling apart **(see illustration)**. Use rag to soak up any spilt fuel. Where the unions are colour-coded, the pipes cannot be confused. Where both unions are the same colour, note carefully which pipe is connected to which, and ensure that they are correctly reconnected on refitting.

4 To reconnect one of these couplings, press them firmly together. Switch the ignition on and off five times to pressurise the system, and check for any sign of fuel leakage around the disturbed coupling before attempting to start the engine.

Checking fuel lines

5 Checking procedures for the fuel lines are included in Chapter 1A, Section 5.

Component renewal

6 If any damaged sections are to be renewed, use original equipment hoses or pipes, constructed from exactly the same material as the section being renewed. Do not install substitutes constructed from inferior or inappropriate material; this could cause a fuel leak or a fire.

7 Before detaching or disconnecting any part of the fuel system, note the routing of all hoses and pipes, and the orientation of all clamps and clips. New sections must be installed in exactly the same manner.

8 Before disconnecting any part of the fuel system, be sure to relieve the fuel system pressure (see Section 2), and equalise tank pressure by removing the fuel filler cap. Also disconnect the battery negative (earth) lead – see Chapter 5A, Section 2. Cover the fitting being disconnected with a rag, to absorb any fuel that may spray out.

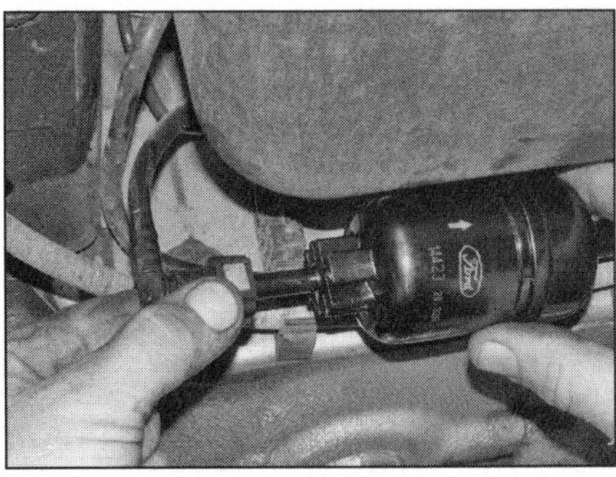

4.3 Squeeze the quick-release connectors to release them

5 Air cleaner assembly – removal and refitting

1 Disconnect the clip near the oil filler cap securing the throttle body air inlet duct to the air cleaner, and also pull out the crankcase breather hose **(see illustrations)**. Note that the clips used on the large-diameter hoses are often difficult to refit successfully – have some large Jubilee clips on hand to use when refitting.

2 Twist the front panel air inlet duct off the side of the air cleaner to release it **(see illustration)**.

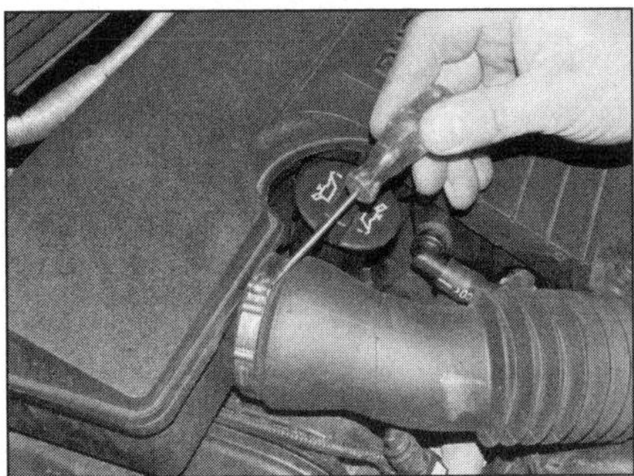

5.1a Release the hose clip near the oil filler cap using a screwdriver ...

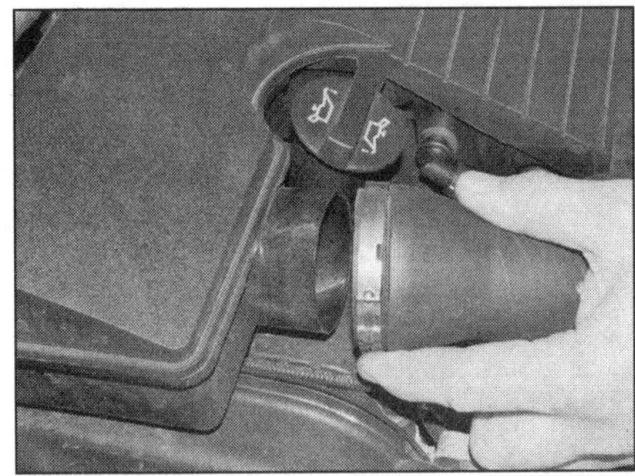

5.1b ... and take off the throttle body air inlet duct

5.1c With the duct removed, also pull off the crankcase breather hose

5.2 Twist the front panel air duct to the rear to disconnect it from the air cleaner

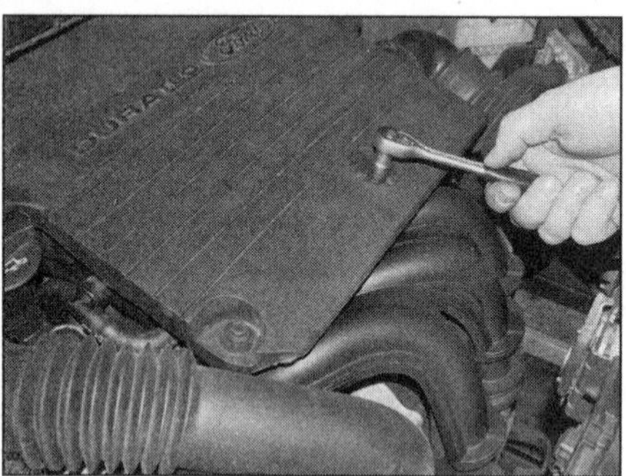

5.3a Remove the two front mounting bolts ...

3 Remove the two bolts securing the air cleaner to the cylinder head cover, then lift the unit upwards to detach the two mounting pegs at the rear **(see illustrations)**.

4 If required, the throttle body air inlet duct can be removed completely by releasing the other clip at the throttle body end. Again, however, it may not be possible to re-use the clip.

5 The air duct on the front panel may be removed if required by removing the three screws and the plastic locating plugs. To access the third screw/plug, unclip and remove the radiator grille, which is secured by a plastic lug either end.

6 When refitting, locate the air cleaner rear pegs first, then secure with the two bolts. Make sure the air cleaner duct clips are securely refitted/tightened, to prevent air leaks.

6 Accelerator pedal – removal and refitting

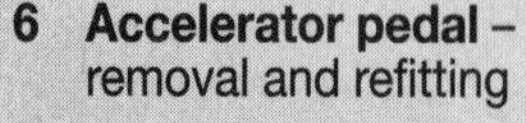

Removal

1 Remove the driver's side facia lower panel, which is secured by a total of five screws, and one clip at the top left (pull the panel towards you to release it).

2 Make sure the ignition is switched off (take out the key). Disconnect the wiring plug from the throttle position sensor, then unscrew the mounting nuts and remove the pedal/sensor assembly from the bulkhead studs **(see illustration)**.

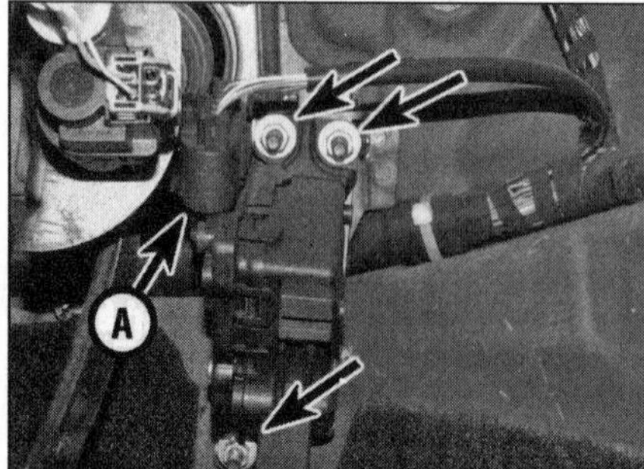

6.2 Remove the wiring plug (A) and then the mounting nuts (arrowed)

5.3b ... then lift the air cleaner to detach the rear pegs

Refitting

3 Refit in the reverse order of removal. On completion, check the action of the pedal to ensure that the throttle has full unrestricted movement, and fully returns when released.

7 Fuel pump/fuel pressure – checking

Note: *Refer to the warning note in Section 1 before proceeding.*

Fuel pump

1 Switch on the ignition, and listen for the fuel pump (the sound of an electric motor running, audible from beneath the rear seats). Assuming there is sufficient fuel in the tank, the pump should start and run for approximately one or two seconds, then stop, each time the ignition is switched on. **Note:** *If the pump runs continuously all the time the ignition is switched on, the electronic control system is running in the backup (or 'limp-home') mode referred to by Ford as 'Limited Operation Strategy' (LOS). This almost certainly indicates a fault in the engine management system. This may be a fault with the powertrain control module (PCM) itself or any one of the engine management components. The car should therefore be taken to a Ford dealer or suitably-equipped specialist for a full test of the complete system, using the correct diagnostic equipment.*

2 Listen for fuel return noises from the fuel pressure regulator. It should be possible to feel the fuel pulsing in the regulator and in the feed hose from the fuel filter.

3 If the pump does not run at all, check the fuse, relay and wiring (see Chapter 12, Section 2 and 3). Check also that the fuel injection system shut-off switch has not been activated and if so, reset it (Section 12).

Fuel pressure

4 A fuel pressure gauge will be required for this check, and should be connected in the fuel line between the fuel filter and the fuel rail, in accordance with the gauge maker's instructions. Ideally, obtain a gauge that has an adapter to suit the Schrader-type valve on the fuel rail pressure test/release fitting (identifiable by its blue plastic cap, and located on the union of the fuel feed line and the fuel rail). If the Ford special tool 29-033 is available, the tool can be attached to the valve, and a conventional-type pressure gauge attached to the tool.

5 If using the service tool, ensure that its tap is turned fully anti-clockwise, then attach it to the valve. Connect the pressure gauge to the service tool. If using a fuel pressure gauge with its own adapter, connect it in accordance with its maker's instructions.

6 Start the engine and allow it to idle. Note the gauge reading as soon as the pressure stabilises, and compare it with the regulated fuel pressure figure listed in the Specifications.

a) *If the pressure is high, check for a restricted fuel return line. If the line is clear, renew the fuel pressure regulator.*

b) *If the pressure is low, pinch the fuel return line. If the pressure now goes up, renew the fuel pressure regulator. If the pressure does not increase, check the fuel feed line, the fuel pump and the fuel filter.*

7 Detach the vacuum hose from the fuel pressure regulator; the pressure shown on the gauge should increase. If the pressure does not increase, check the vacuum hose and pressure regulator.

8 Reconnect the regulator vacuum hose, and switch off the engine. Verify that a significant pressure remains for five minutes after the engine is turned off.

9 Carefully disconnect the fuel pressure gauge, depressurising the system first as described in Section 2. Be sure to cover the fitting with a rag before slackening it. Mop up any spilt petrol.

10 Run the engine, and check that there are no fuel leaks.

8 Fuel tank – removal, inspection and refitting

Note: *Refer to the warning note in Section 1 before proceeding.*

Removal

1 Run the fuel level as low as possible prior to removing the tank. There is no drain plug fitted (and siphoning may prove difficult) but it may be possible to partially drain the tank on petrol models by removing the fuel filter as described in Chapter 1A, Section 21, and letting the fuel drain into a suitable container. On diesel models, it is preferable to keep as much fuel in the pipes as possible, to reduce the need for bleeding the system when restarting the engine.

2 Relieve the residual pressure in the fuel system (see Section 2), and equalise tank pressure by removing the fuel filler cap.

3 Disconnect the battery negative (earth) lead (see Chapter 5A, Section 2).

4 Chock the front wheels, then jack up the

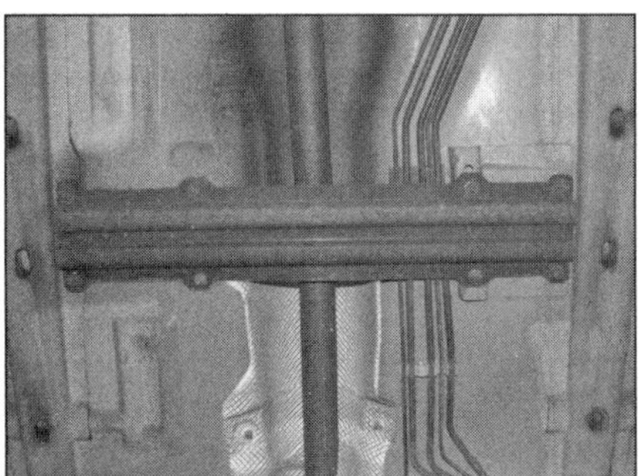

8.5 Remove the crossmember

8.6 Rest the exhaust system on the rear suspension

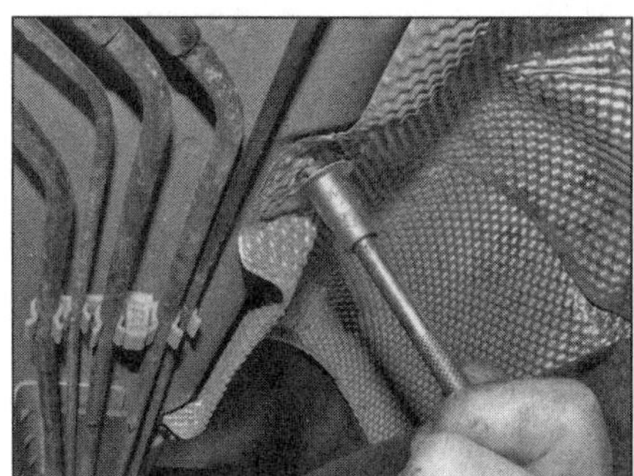

8.7 Remove the heat shield

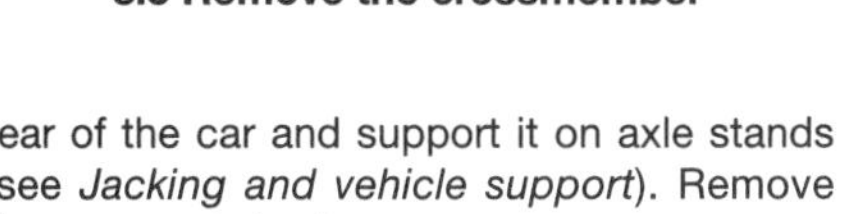

rear of the car and support it on axle stands (see *Jacking and vehicle support*). Remove the rear roadwheels.

5 Remove the floorpan crossmember from under the car – it is secured by eight bolts **(see illustration)**.

6 Unhook the exhaust system mounting rubbers from the centre and rear hangers, and allow the exhaust system to rest on the rear suspension crossmember **(see illustration)**.

7 Unscrew the nuts and remove the centre exhaust heat shield from the underbody **(see illustration)**.

8 Release the clips and disconnect the fuel tank filler and vent pipes **(see illustrations)**. Do not use any sharp-edged tools to release the pipes from their stubs, as the pipes are easily damaged. Discard the pipe clips and obtain some Jubilee clips for refitting.

9 Support the tank using a trolley jack and a large sheet of wood to spread the load.

10 Note exactly how the fuel tank retaining straps are arranged, to make refitting easier. In particular, note their fitted order under the retaining bolt heads, where applicable.

11 Unbolt and remove the fuel tank retaining straps **(see illustration)**, but do not lower the tank at this stage.

12 Squeeze the quick-release fitting, and disconnect the fuel tank vent pipe from the evaporative emissions canister at the side of the tank.

13 Partially lower the tank on the jack, taking care that no strain is placed on any fuel lines or wiring. As soon as the wiring connector for the fuel pump/gauge sender on top of the tank is accessible, reach in and disconnect it **(see illustration)**.

14 Disconnect the fuel supply and return lines from the top of the tank, squeezing the quick-release connectors and pulling off the lines. As each one is removed, note its location – the fuel supply line connector is colour-coded white, and the return line is red.

15 Squeeze the quick-release fitting, and disconnect the remaining pipe from the evaporative emissions canister. Remove the mounting bolt and detach the canister from its recess in the side of the tank.

16 Lower the fuel tank to the ground, checking all the way down that no pipes or wiring are under any strain. Remove the tank from under the car.

Inspection

17 Whilst removed, the fuel tank can be inspected for damage or deterioration. Removal of the fuel pump/fuel gauge sender unit (see Section 9) will allow a partial inspection of the interior. If the tank is contaminated with sediment or water, swill it out with clean fuel. Do not under any circumstances undertake any repairs on a leaking or damaged fuel tank; this work must be carried out by a professional who has experience in this critical and potentially-dangerous work.

18 Whilst the fuel tank is removed from the car, it should be placed in a safe area where sparks or open flames cannot ignite the fumes coming out of the tank. Be especially careful inside garages where a natural-gas type appliance is located, because the pilot light could cause an explosion.

19 Check the condition of the lower filler pipe and renew it if necessary.

Refitting

20 Refitting is a reversal of the removal procedure, noting the following points:

a) Ensure that all pipe and wiring connections are securely fitted.

b) When refitting the quick-release couplings, press them together until the locking lugs snap into their groove.

c) Tighten the tank strap retaining bolts to the specified torque.

d) If evidence of contamination was found, do not return any previously-drained fuel to the tank unless it is carefully filtered first.

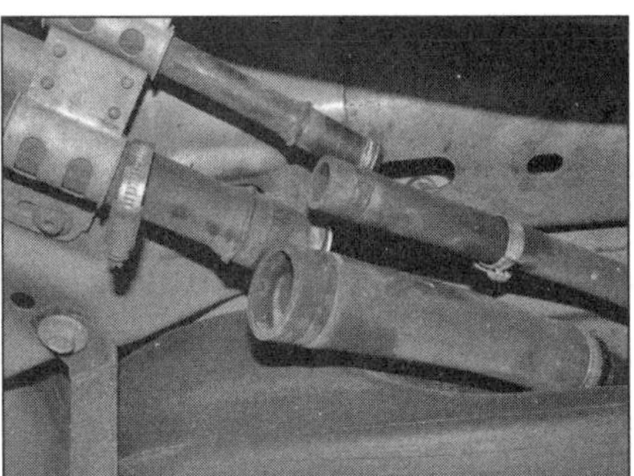

8.8a Disconnect the fuel tank filler and vent pipes ...

8.8b ... and immediately seal them

8.11 Remove the fuel tank retaining strap bolts

8.13 Disconnect the wiring plug

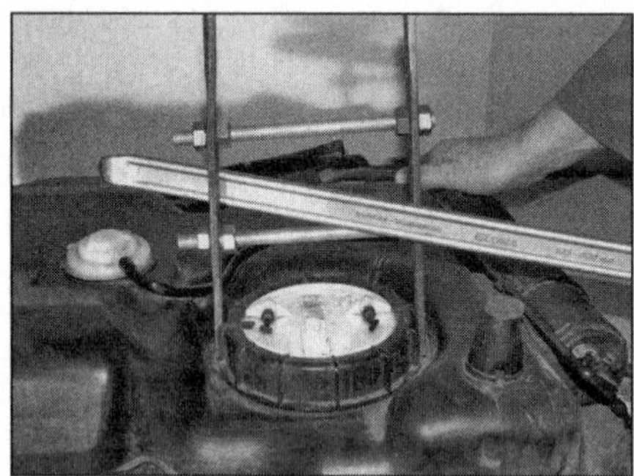

9.3a Use a fabricated tool to remove the locking ring ...

9.4a Remove the assembly with care ...

9 Fuel pump/ fuel gauge sender unit – removal and refitting

Note: *Refer to the warning note in Section 1 before proceeding. Ford specify the use of their service tool 310-069 (a large socket with projecting teeth to engage the fuel pump/ sender unit retaining ring's raised edges) for this task. In practice, it was found that the ring could be loosened with conventional tools.*

Removal

1 A combined fuel pump and fuel gauge sender unit is located in the top face of the fuel tank. The combined unit can only be detached and withdrawn from the tank after the tank is released and lowered from under the car. Refer to Section 8 and remove the fuel tank, then proceed as follows.

9.6 Check the operation of the fuel gauge

9.3b ... or a purpose-made tool

9.4b ... and recover the seal

2 With the fuel tank removed, disconnect the fuel supply pipe (if still attached to the tank) from the inlet stub by squeezing the quick-release lugs. Note that the fuel supply pipe connector is identified by a white band.

3 Unscrew and remove the special retaining ring, either by unscrewing it with the Ford tool, or by carefully tapping it round until it can be unscrewed by hand **(see illustrations)**. If care is taken, the ring could also be loosened using an oil filter removal chain- or strap-wrench.

4 Carefully lift out the fuel pump/gauge sender unit from the tank and then recover the rubber seal **(see illustrations)**. Take care that the sender unit float and arm are not damaged as the unit is removed.

5 If the pump and sender assembly are to be removed for any length of time, refit the old seal and locking ring. This will avoid any possibility of the aperture in the tank distorting.

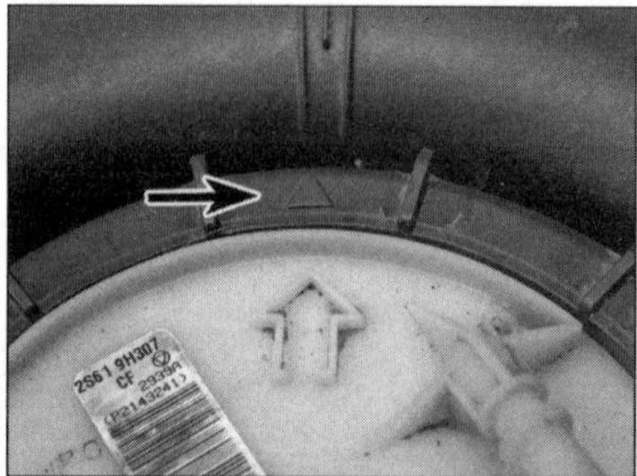

9.7 The pump/gauge assembly, lock-ring and indentation in the tank should all align

6 With the assembly removed the operation of the fuel level gauge can be checked with a multimeter. Identify the correct wires coming from the gauge resister track (green and orange on our vehicle) and connect the multimeter. Operate the float arm and check for a smooth change in resistance as the arm is moved through the full range of travel **(see illustration)**.

Refitting

7 Refitting is a reversal of removal, but fit a new rubber seal and tighten the retaining ring securely **(see illustration)**. Refit the fuel tank as described in Section 8.

10 Fuel tank roll-over valve – removal and refitting

Note: *Refer to the warning note in Section 1 before proceeding.*

Removal

1 Where fitted the roll-over valve is located in a rubber grommet in the top of the fuel tank, in the hose leading rearwards to the carbon canister. Its purpose is to prevent fuel loss if the car becomes inverted in a crash.

2 Remove the fuel tank as described in Section 8.

3 Release the vent hose from the clip on the top of the tank.

4 Carefully prise the roll-over valve from the rubber grommet and remove it together with the hose.

5 Check the condition of the rubber grommet and renew it if necessary.

Refitting

6 Refitting is a reversal of removal, but apply a light smear of clean engine oil to the rubber grommet, to ease fitting.

11 Fuel tank filler neck – removal and refitting

Note: *Refer to the warning note in Section 1 before proceeding.*

Removal

1 Loosen the left-hand rear wheel nuts, then raise and support the rear of the car, and support it on axle stands (see *Jacking and vehicle support*). Remove the left-hand rear wheel.

2 Remove the left-hand rear wheel arch liner, which is secured by a combination of screws and push-in clips.

3 Remove the single bolt securing the filler neck and vent pipe support bracket to the wheel arch **(see illustration)**.

4 At the lower end of the filler neck, release the clips securing the flexible filler and vent

pipes which lead to the tank. Discard the pipe clips and obtain some Jubilee clips for refitting. Release the pipes from their stubs, but do not use any sharp-edged tools, as the pipes are easily damaged.
5 Unscrew the single bolt securing the pipe lower support bracket **(see illustration)**, and remove the filler neck from under the car.
6 Check the condition of the filler neck and vent pipe, and renew if necessary.

Refitting

7 Refitting is a reversal of removal.

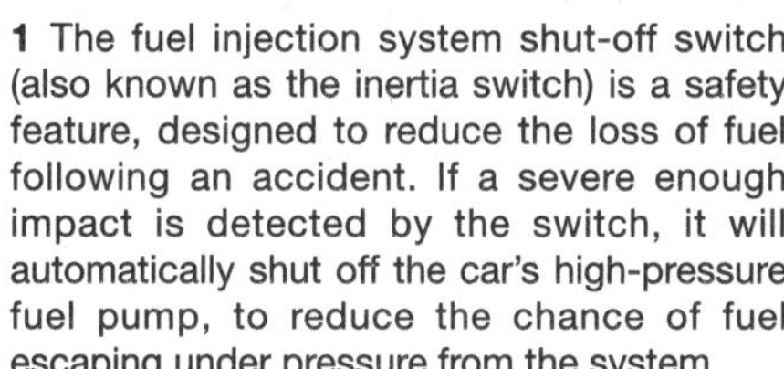

12 Fuel injection system shut-off (inertia) switch – removal and refitting

1 The fuel injection system shut-off switch (also known as the inertia switch) is a safety feature, designed to reduce the loss of fuel following an accident. If a severe enough impact is detected by the switch, it will automatically shut off the car's high-pressure fuel pump, to reduce the chance of fuel escaping under pressure from the system.
2 It has been known for these switches to be triggered by non-life-threatening events, such as minor car parking bumps, or travelling over rough roads or potholes.
3 To reset the switch, pull off the yellow cap and depress the button on top of the switch. **Do not** reset the switch after an accident if fuel has escaped from the fuel system.

Removal

4 The fuel cut-off switch is located behind the glovebox. First disconnect the battery negative (earth) lead (see Chapter 5A, Section 2).
5 Open the glovebox, and press the sides inwards to release the stops, which allows the glovebox to be opened further than normal. The shut-off switch will now be visible inside, on the left **(see illustration)**. For improved access, remove the glovebox completely, as described in Chapter 11, Section 25.
6 Unscrew and remove the switch retaining bolt, then disconnect the wiring plug and remove the switch.

Refitting

7 Refitting is a reversal of removal, but make sure that the switch is reset. Start the engine to prove this.

13 Fuel injection system – checking

Note: *Refer to the warning note in Section 1 before proceeding.*
1 If a fault appears in the fuel injection system, first ensure that all the system wiring connectors are securely connected and free of corrosion – also refer to paragraphs 6 to 9 below. Check that the inertia switch has not been triggered (Section 12). Then ensure that

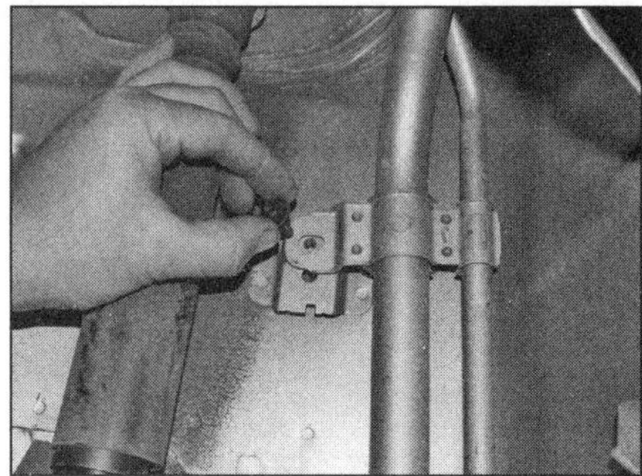

11.3 Removing the filler neck/vent pipe support bracket bolt

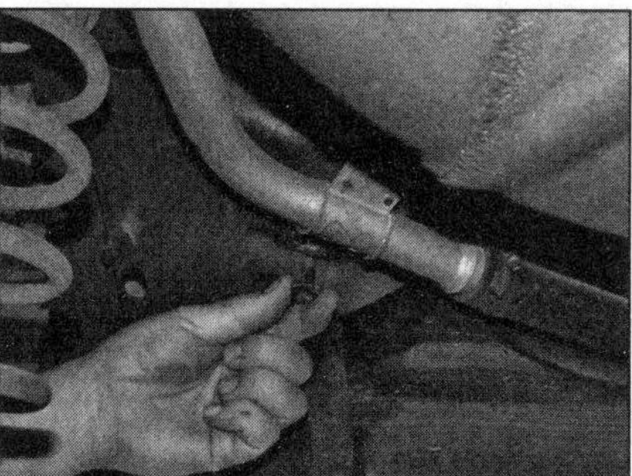

11.5 Unbolt the pipe lower support bracket

the fault is not due to poor maintenance; ie, check that the air cleaner filter element is clean, the spark plugs are in good condition and correctly gapped, the cylinder compression pressures are correct, the ignition system wiring is in good condition and securely connected, and the engine breather hoses are clear and undamaged, referring to Chapter 1A, 2A and 5B.
2 If these checks fail to reveal the cause of the problem, the car should be taken to a Ford dealer or suitably-equipped specialist for testing. A data link connector (DLC) is fitted below the steering column, into which dedicated test equipment can be plugged **(see illustration)**. The test equipment is capable of 'interrogating' the engine management system PCM (powertrain control module) and accessing any stored fault codes.
3 A Ford dealer will obviously have such a reader, but they are also available from other suppliers. Low cost diagnostic equipment is available to the home mechanic, but these 'code readers' often have a limited ability to access any stored fault codes. They are usually limited to accessing the mandatory EOBD (European onboard diagnostic) emissions related fault codes. It is unlikely to be cost-effective for the private owner to purchase a sophisticated fault code reader, but a well-equipped local garage or auto-electrical specialist will have one.
4 Using this equipment, faults can be pinpointed quickly and simply, even if their occurrence is intermittent. Testing all the system components individually in an attempt to locate the fault by elimination is a time-consuming operation that is unlikely to be fruitful (particularly if the fault occurs dynamically), and carries a high risk of damage to the ECU's internal components.
5 Experienced home mechanics equipped with an accurate tachometer and a carefully-calibrated exhaust gas analyser may be able to check the exhaust gas CO content and the engine idle speed; if these are found to be out of specification, then the car must be taken to a suitably-equipped Ford dealer for assessment. Neither the air/fuel mixture (exhaust gas CO content) nor the engine idle speed are manually adjustable; incorrect test results indicate the need for maintenance (possibly, injector cleaning) or a fault within the fuel injection system.

Limited operation strategy

6 Certain faults, such as failure of one of the engine management system sensors, will cause the system will revert to a backup (or 'limp-home') mode, referred to by Ford as 'Limited Operation Strategy' (LOS). This is intended to be a 'get-you-home' facility only – the engine management warning light will come on when this mode is in operation.
7 In this mode, the signal from the defective sensor is substituted with a fixed value (it would normally vary), which may lead to loss of power, poor idling, and generally-poor running, especially when the engine is cold.
8 However, the engine may in fact run quite well in this situation, and the only clue (other than the warning light) would be that the

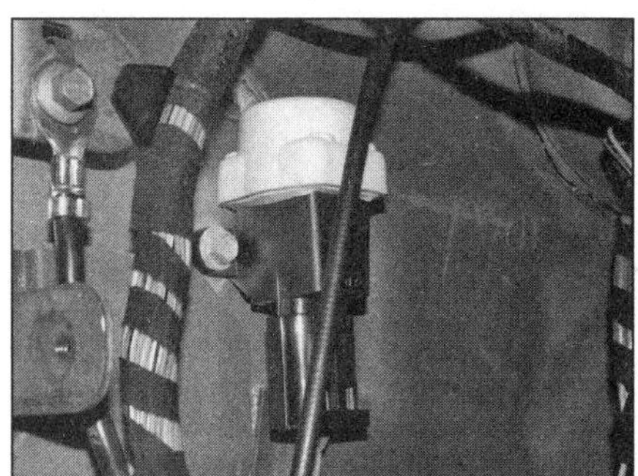

12.5 With the glovebox removed, the inertia switch is visible on the left

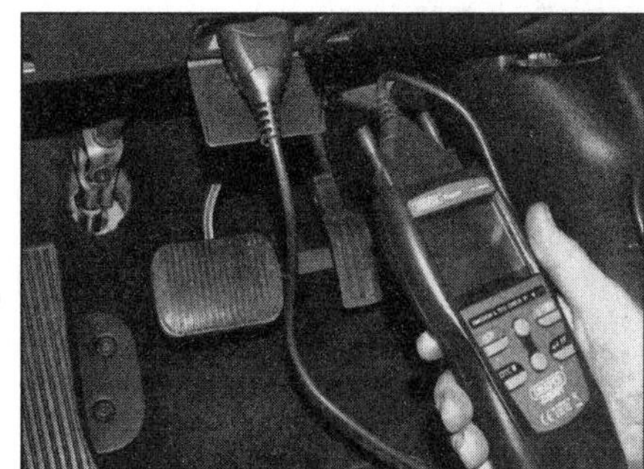

13.2 Checking for stored fault codes

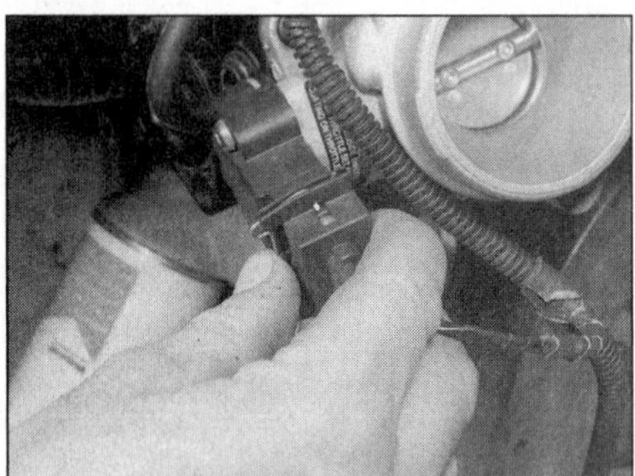
14.2a Disconnect the wiring plugs ...

14.2b ... then unscrew the mounting bolts ...

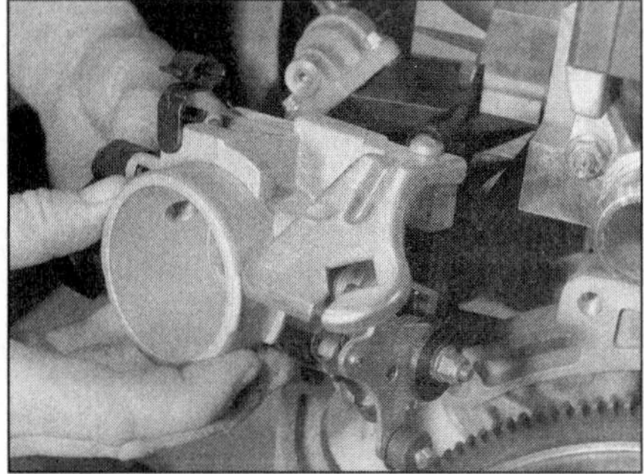
14.2c ... and remove the throttle body ...

14.2d ... recovering the gasket from the inlet manifold

exhaust CO emissions (for example) will be higher than they should be.

9 Bear in mind that, even if the defective sensor is correctly identified and renewed, the engine will not return to normal running until the fault code is erased, taking the system out of LOS. This also applies even if the cause of the fault was a loose connection or damaged piece of wire – until the fault code is erased, the system will continue in LOS.

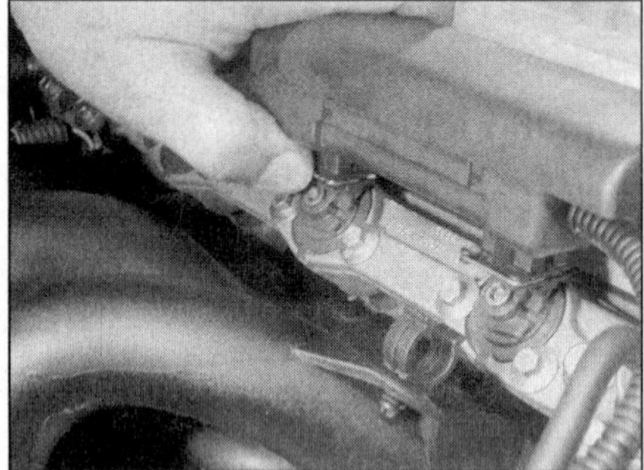
14.9a Depress the wire clips on the injectors ...

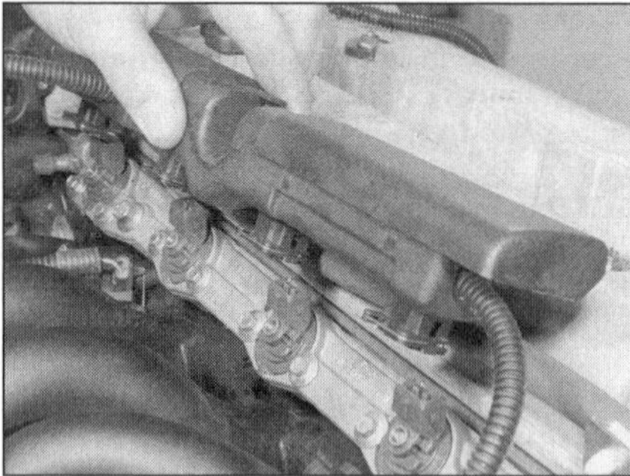
14.9b ... and disconnect the wiring loom adapter

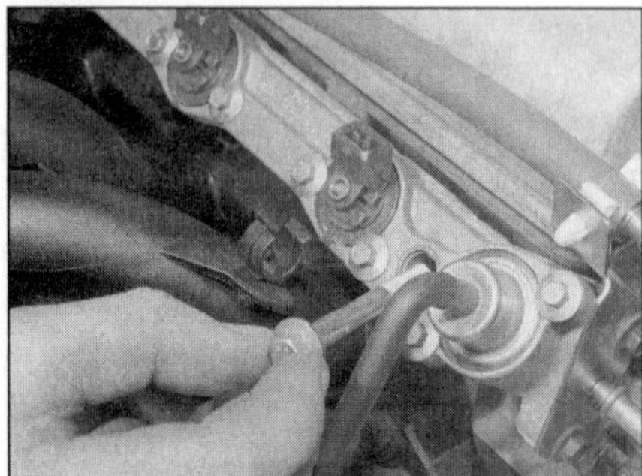
14.12a Unscrew the mounting bolts ...

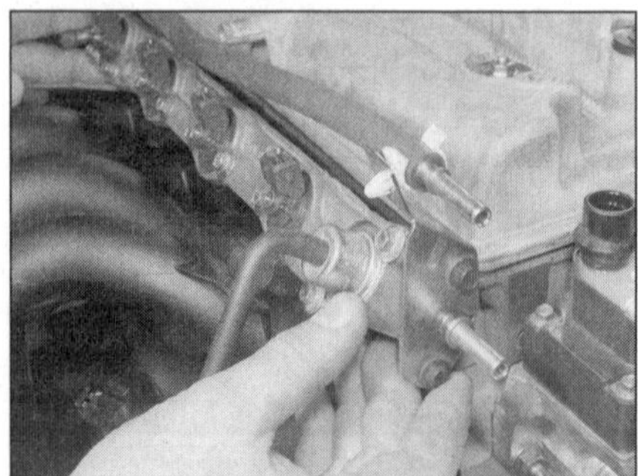
14.12b ... and lift the fuel rail from the cylinder head

14 Fuel injection system components – removal and refitting

Note: *Refer to the precautions in Section 1 before proceeding.*

Throttle body

1 Release the clip securing the air cleaner inlet duct to the top of the throttle body. Note that the clips used are often difficult to refit successfully – have some large Jubilee clips on hand to use when refitting.

2 Remove the four mounting bolts, then disconnect the throttle control motor and TMAP sensor wiring plugs, and remove the throttle body. Recover the seal – a new one should be used when refitting **(see illustrations)**.

3 Do not attempt to clean the inside of the throttle body. The inner surfaces are specially coated during manufacture, and this coating should not be removed.

4 Refitting is a reversal of removal. Use a new seal, and tighten the mounting bolts securely, to prevent air leaks.

Fuel rail and injectors

5 Relieve the residual pressure in the fuel system (see Section 2), and equalise tank pressure by removing the fuel filler cap.

Warning: This procedure will merely relieve the increased pressure necessary for the engine to run – remember that fuel will still be present in the system components, and take precautions accordingly before disconnecting any of them.

6 Disconnect the battery negative (earth) lead (see Chapter 5A, Section 2).

7 Remove the air cleaner as described in Section 5.

8 Disconnect the crankcase breather hose from the cylinder head cover.

9 The wiring loom adapter must now be disconnected from the injectors. To do this, depress two of the injector clips and lift the adapter up a little until it releases from the injectors. Now depress the remaining two clips and lift the complete adapter from the injectors **(see illustrations)**. Position the adapter to one side.

10 Disconnect the vacuum pipe from the fuel pressure regulator.

11 Disconnect the fuel supply and return pipes from opposite ends of the fuel rail by squeezing the lugs on the special quick-release fittings. Note their positions for refitting – the supply line connector is colour-coded white, while the return line connector is red.

12 Unscrew the mounting bolts, then lift the fuel rail from the cylinder head – there will be some resistance from the injector O-ring seals **(see illustrations)**.

13 To remove the injectors, first lift the retaining clips at the top, then slide them off sideways. Now pull the injectors out of the fuel rail.

14 Refitting is the reverse of the removal procedure, noting the following points:

a) Fit new injector O-rings, and lubricate them with clean engine oil to aid refitting.
b) Tighten the fuel rail mounting bolts to the specified torque.
c) Ensure that the hoses and wiring are routed correctly, and secured on reconnection by any clips or ties provided.
d) On completion, switch the ignition on to activate the fuel pump and pressurise the system, without cranking the engine. Check for signs of fuel leaks around all disturbed unions and joints before attempting to start the engine.

Fuel pressure regulator

15 Relieve the residual pressure in the fuel system (see Section 2), and equalise tank pressure by removing the fuel filler cap.

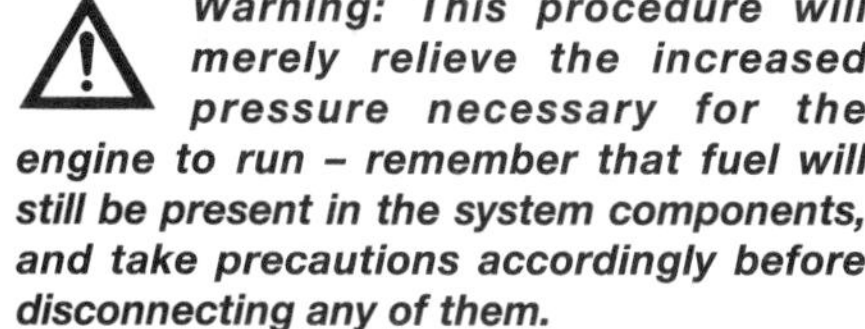

Warning: This procedure will merely relieve the increased pressure necessary for the engine to run – remember that fuel will still be present in the system components, and take precautions accordingly before disconnecting any of them.

16 Disconnect the battery negative (earth) lead (see Chapter 5A, Section 2).

17 Remove the air cleaner as described in Section 5.

18 Disconnect the vacuum pipe from the fuel pressure regulator.

19 The regulator is secured to the fuel rail using two bolts – remove them, then pull the regulator from the fuel rail. Discard the regulator O-ring seal.

20 Refitting is a reversal of removal. Use a new O-ring, lubricated with a little engine oil, when refitting the regulator, and tighten the mounting bolts to the specified torque.

TMAP sensor

21 The valve is located on the throttle body.

22 To improve access, remove the air cleaner and the air inlet duct from the throttle body as described in Section 5.

23 With the ignition switched off, disconnect the sensor wiring plug, then remove the two mounting bolts and withdraw it from the throttle body. Check the condition of the sensor O-ring seal, and obtain a new one if necessary.

24 Refitting is a reversal of removal. Use a new seal if necessary, and tighten the mounting bolts securely, to prevent air leaks.

Powertrain control module

Note: *The module is fragile. Take care not to drop it, or subject it to any other kind of impact. Do not subject it to extremes of temperature, or allow it to get wet.*

25 Remove the battery and battery tray as described in Chapter 5A, Section 4. It is essential that the battery is disconnected before separating the module wiring plug, or the module itself could be damaged.

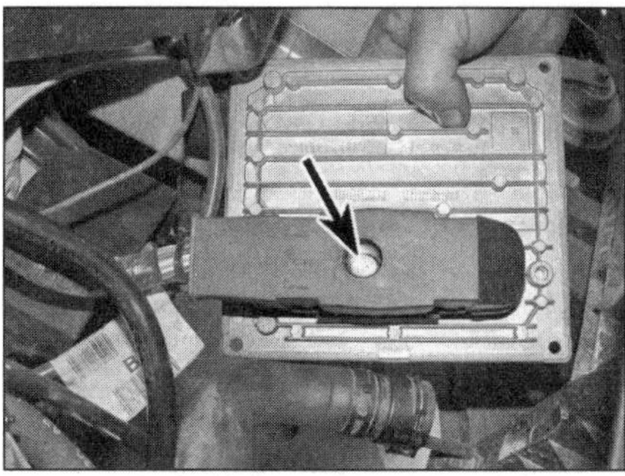

14.26 Powertrain control module wiring connector shear-bolt

26 Place the module squarely on the battery tray support bracket, and drill out the shear-bolt securing the module wiring connector **(see illustration)**. A 6 mm drill bit will be required, and the hole must be drilled centrally, to avoid damaging the module – Ford dealers use a special guide tool (418-537) to ensure this, which is a short tube with a 6 mm hole down the centre. Alternatively, use a centre-punch to mark the centre of the bolt, and drill a smaller pilot hole first.

27 Once the module connector starts to come free, indicating that the shear-bolt has been released, clean up all the swarf from the drilling operations before removing the connector completely.

28 Remove the module connector, and extract the remains of the shear-bolt with some grips. The module itself can now be removed from the car.

29 Refitting is a reversal of removal. Strictly speaking, a new shear-bolt should be obtained for refitting, and tightened until the head shears off. However, as this is only a deterrent to 'chipping' the module, an ordinary bolt can be used instead.

Crankshaft position sensor

30 The sensor is located on the front left-hand side of the engine, close to the transmission. For improved access, apply the handbrake, then jack up the front of the car and support it on axle stands (see *Jacking and vehicle support*).

31 With the ignition switched off, disconnect the wiring plug, then unscrew the mounting bolt and withdraw the sensor **(see illustration)**.

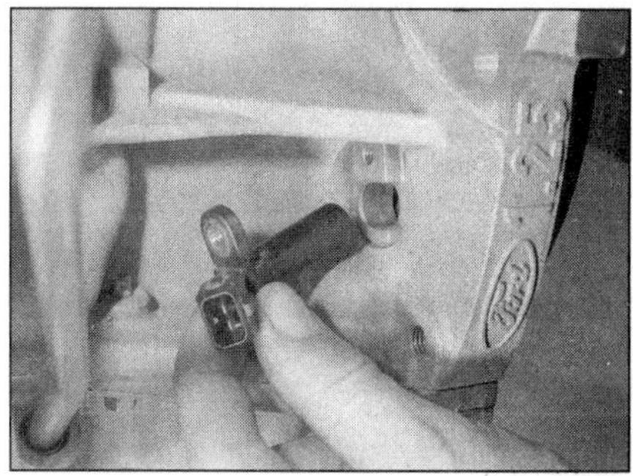

14.31 Removing the crankshaft position sensor

32 Refitting is a reversal of removal. Ensure that the sensor is clean when refitting, and tighten the bolt securely.

Camshaft position sensor

33 The sensor is located is located on the right-hand rear of the cylinder head (right as seen from the driver's seat).

34 Remove the air cleaner as described in Section 5.

35 With the ignition switched off, disconnect the wiring from the camshaft position sensor **(see illustration)**.

36 Unscrew the mounting bolt and withdraw the sensor from the cylinder head or cylinder head cover (as applicable) **(see illustrations)**.

37 Refitting is a reversal of removal, but use a new seal. Smear a little engine oil on the seal before fitting the sensor, and tighten the bolt securely.

Coolant temperature sensor

38 See Chapter 3, Section 6.

Throttle position sensor

39 The throttle position sensor is part of the electronic throttle control system. The sensor is an integral part of the accelerator pedal (refer to Section 6), and the control motor is a part of the throttle body. Before renewing either component, it is recommended that the advice of a Ford dealer is sought to verify the fault, and possibly to programme-in any new components which need to be fitted.

Clutch pedal position switch

40 Remove the driver's side facia lower panel,

14.35 The plug is at the back of the cylinder head

14.36 Removing the sensor

14.41a Disconnect the clutch pedal switch wiring plug ...

14.41b ... then twist the switch and remove it from the bracket above the pedal

14.46a Pull off the wiring plug ...

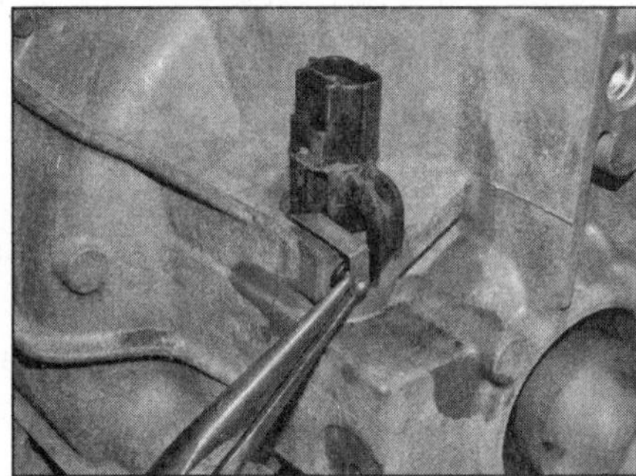

14.46b ... then pull out the retaining pin to remove the sensor

which is secured by a total of five screws, and one clip at the top left (pull the panel towards you to release it).

41 With the ignition switched off, disconnect the wiring from the clutch switch, then twist the switch and remove it from the pedal bracket **(see illustrations)**.

42 Refitting is a reversal of removal.

Power steering pressure switch

43 Refer to Chapter 10, Section 21.

Oxygen sensor

44 Refer to Chapter 4C, Section 2.

Vehicle speed sensor

Note: *On models with ABS, vehicle speed information is derived from the ABS wheel sensors, and a vehicle speed sensor is not fitted. For more information on the ABS wheel sensors, refer to Chapter 9, Section 17.*

45 The sensor is mounted on top of the transmission, above the left-hand driveshaft (where the speedometer cable would otherwise be fitted).

46 With the ignition switched off, disconnect the sensor wiring plug, then pull the sensor retaining pin (at the base) out sideways, and lift the sensor out of the transmission **(see illustrations)**.

47 Refitting is a reversal of removal. Check the condition of the O-ring seal, and fit a new one if necessary. Ensure the sensor is fully seated, and held securely by the retaining pin.

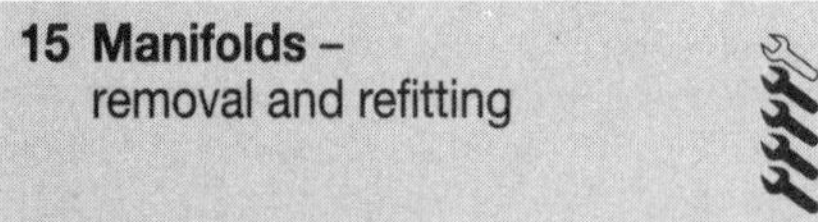

15 Manifolds – removal and refitting

Note: *Refer to the warning note in Section 1 before proceeding.*

Inlet manifold

1 Depressurise the fuel system as described in Section 2. On completion, disconnect the battery negative lead (refer to Chapter 5A, Section 2).

2 Remove the air cleaner as described in Section 5.

3 Lift the power steering fluid reservoir off its mounting lugs on the inner wing, and place it to one side, without disconnecting any of the hoses.

4 Remove the auxiliary drivebelt as described in Chapter 1A, Section 23.

5 Remove the inlet manifold lower retaining bolt.

6 Unbolt the dipstick tube from the front of the manifold.

7 Disconnect the following around the manifold:

- *a) Crankcase breather hose at the base of the manifold.*
- *b) Brake servo vacuum pipe from the manifold.*
- *c) Engine wiring harness main connector, and the EVAP valve hose, both located below the fuel pressure regulator.*
- *d) Knock sensor wiring plug, underneath the inlet manifold.*
- *e) TMAP and throttle control motor wiring plugs, from the throttle housing.*

8 Remove the alternator as described in Chapter 5A, Section 8.

9 Remove the fuel rail and injectors as described in Section 14.

10 Unplug the coolant temperature sensor, on the coolant outlet elbow at the transmission end of the cylinder head.

11 Check carefully around the manifold, unclipping any remaining wiring or pipework which may still be attached to it.

12 Remove the five upper retaining bolts, and withdraw the manifold from the front of the engine. Recover the gaskets **(see illustrations)**.

13 Refitting is a reversal of removal, noting the following points:

- *a) Ensure that the mating faces are clean, and use new manifold gaskets if necessary.*
- *b) Tighten all fixings to the specified torque.*
- *c) On completion, switch the ignition on to activate the fuel pump and pressurise*

15.12a Unscrew the mounting bolts ...

15.12b ... and withdraw the inlet manifold from the cylinder head

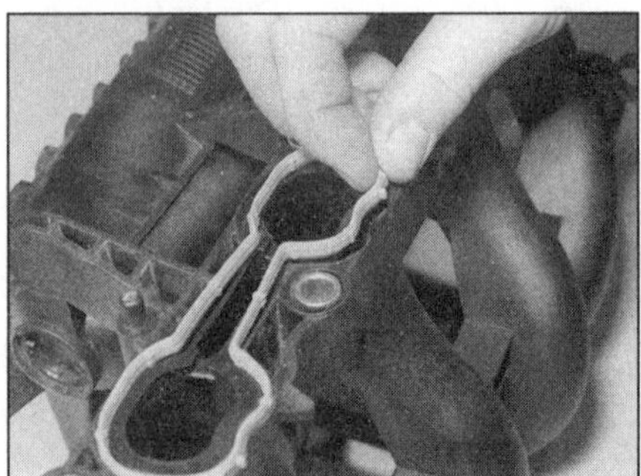

15.12c Recover the gasket from the manifold groove

the system, without cranking the engine. Check for signs of fuel leaks around all disturbed unions and joints before attempting to start the engine.

Exhaust manifold

14 Disconnect the battery negative lead as described in Chapter 5A, Section 2.

15 Remove the air cleaner as described in Section 5.

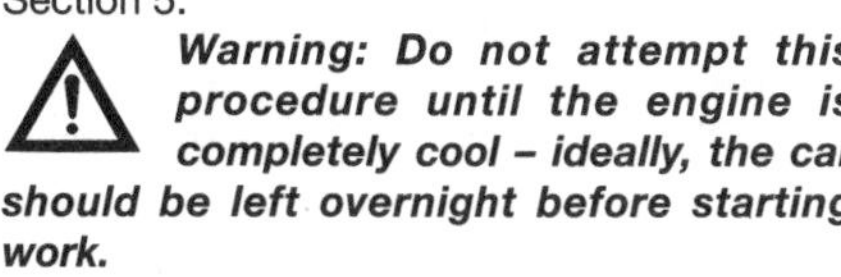

Warning: Do not attempt this procedure until the engine is completely cool – ideally, the car should be left overnight before starting work.

16 Jack up the front of the car, and support it on axle stands (see *Jacking and vehicle support*).

17 To prevent damage to the exhaust flexible section, support it by attaching a pair of splints either side (two scrap strips of wood, plant canes, etc) using some cable-ties **(see illustration)**.

18 Working from the engine compartment, unbolt the exhaust flexible section from the base of the manifold.

19 Back under the car, unhook the exhaust front section rubber mountings.

20 Referring to Chapter 2A, Section 18 if necessary, unbolt the engine lower mounting from the subframe.

21 Remove a total of six bolts and take off the manifold lower heat shield.

22 Disconnect the oxygen sensor and the catalyst monitor sensor wiring connectors behind the ignition coil.

23 Unbolt the power steering fluid hose bracket from the cylinder head.

24 Unbolt the coolant expansion tank from the inner wing, and lift it out without disconnecting the hoses.

25 Lift the power steering fluid reservoir off its mounting lugs on the inner wing, and place it to one side, without disconnecting any of the hoses.

26 The engine must now be supported, as the right-hand mounting (right as seen from the driver's seat) must be removed. Supporting the engine should ideally be done from above, using an engine crane or a special engine lifting beam. However, in the absence of these tools, the engine can be supported from below, using a trolley jack on the cast-aluminium sump, providing a piece of wood is used to spread the load. Whatever method is chosen, it must be possible to lower the engine once the mounting is removed.

27 With the engine securely supported, remove the three nuts and three bolts securing the right-hand mounting, and lift it off. Three new nuts should be obtained for refitting the mounting.

28 Lower the engine as far as the support method will allow, without straining any other components, wiring, hoses, etc.

29 Remove the four bolts securing the exhaust manifold upper heat shield.

30 Undo the exhaust manifold mounting nuts and bolts (seven in total), then slide the manifold off the cylinder head studs and lower it down to remove it. Take care not to damage the sensors or their wiring. Recover the gasket and discard it (see illustrations).

15.17 Exhaust system flexible section must be supported to prevent possible damage

31 Refitting is a reversal of removal, noting the following points:

a) Ensure that the mating faces are clean, and use a new manifold gasket.

b) Tighten all fixings to the specified torque.

16 Exhaust system – general information, removal and refitting

Caution: Any work on the exhaust system should only be attempted once the system is completely cool – this may take several hours, especially in the case of the forward sections, such as the manifold and catalytic converter.

General information

1 The original factory exhaust system consists of the exhaust manifold with integral catalytic converter and a single pipe with a rear silencer. At the front, where the centre section joins the manifold, a flexible ('mesh') section is fitted, to allow for engine movement.

2 The system is suspended throughout its entire length by rubber mountings.

Removal

3 To remove a part of the system, first jack up the front or rear of the car, and support it on axle stands (see *Jacking and vehicle support*). Alternatively, position the car over an inspection pit, or on car ramps.

Manifold and catalytic converter

4 Refer to Section 15.

Centre section

5 To prevent damage to the exhaust flexible section, support it by attaching a pair of splints either side (two scrap strips of wood, plant canes, etc) using some cable-ties. If a new centre section is being fitted, this precaution only applies to the new section of exhaust.

6 Unscrew the nuts securing the centre section to the exhaust manifold, and separate the joint. Recover the gasket **(see illustration)**.

7 Even if just the centre section is being removed, it still has to be separated from the rear silencer. Unbolt the clamp where the centre section joins the silencer, and separate the pipes (bear in mind that a corroded rear silencer may be damaged during removal – see paragraph 9).

15.30a Unscrew the mounting bolts ...

15.30b ... and nuts ...

15.30c ... and withdraw the exhaust manifold from the cylinder head

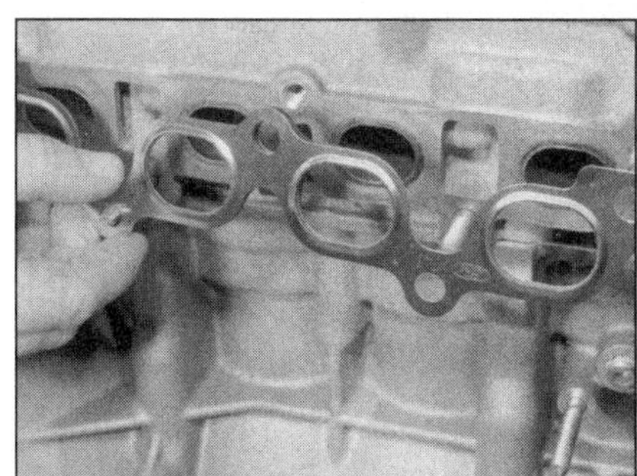

15.30d Recover the gasket from the studs on the cylinder head

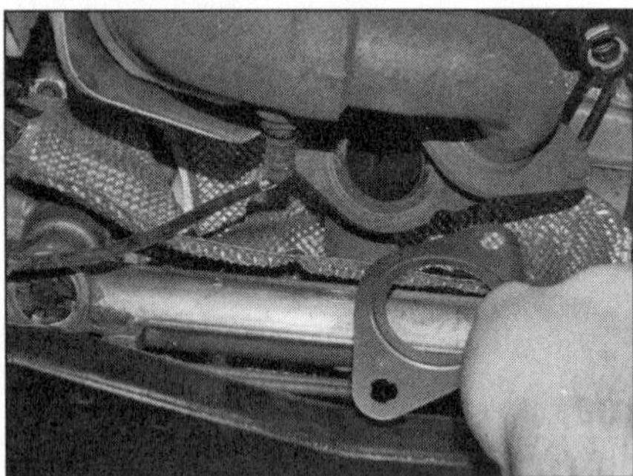

16.6 Separate the centre section from the manifold, and recover the gasket

16.8 Unhook the rubber mountings and remove the centre section

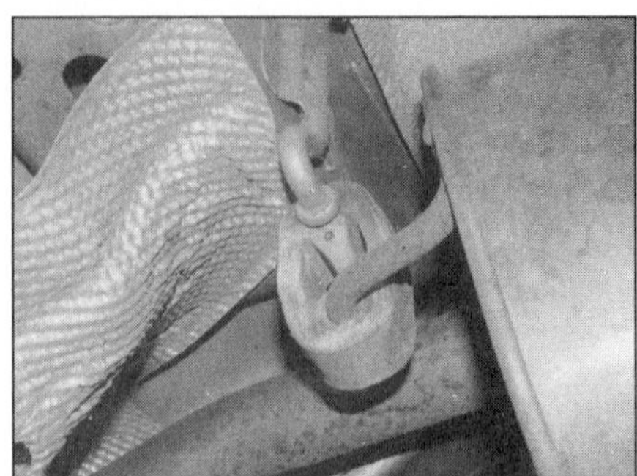

16.11 Rear silencer rubber mounting

8 Unhook the centre section's two rubber mountings, and remove it from under the car **(see illustration)**.

Rear silencer

9 If renewing the original factory fitted system then a separate rear silencer can be fitted. This requires cutting of the exhaust pipe in front of the rear silencer. Obtain a new rear silencer and offer it up to the exhaust system. Mark the cutting point on the old system and then cut of the rear silencer with a hacksaw. This of course assumes that it is the rear silencer that requires renewal.

10 Where the original system has previously been renewed, unbolt the clamp securing the silencer to the centre section, and separate the pipes. Usually, this will require some effort – the most successful method involves twisting the silencer from side to side to break the joint. Unfortunately, if the pipe at the rear of the centre section has suffered from corrosion, it's very likely that the centre section will be damaged beyond repair in removing the silencer. A less-destructive method of removal involves heating the two pipes, but this carries the risk of damaging the underbody components, and even a risk of fire from the fuel tank and lines.

11 Unhook the silencer rubber mountings, and remove it from under the car **(see illustration)**.

Heat shields

12 The heat shields are secured to the underside of the body by special nuts. Each shield can be removed separately, but note that they may overlap, making it necessary to loosen another section first. If a shield is being removed to gain access to a component located behind it, it may prove sufficient in some cases to remove the retaining nuts and/or bolts, and simply lower the shield, without disturbing the exhaust system. Otherwise, remove the exhaust section as described earlier.

Refitting

13 In all cases, refitting is a reversal of removal, but note the following points:

a) Always use new gaskets, nuts and clamps (as applicable), and coat all threads with copper grease. Make sure any new clamps are the same size as the original – overtightening a clamp which is too big will not seal the joint.

b) On a sleeved joint (such as that between the centre section and rear silencer), use a smear of exhaust jointing paste to achieve a gas-tight seal.

c) If any of the exhaust mounting rubbers are in poor condition, fit new ones.

d) Make sure that the exhaust is suspended properly on its mountings, and will not come into contact with the floor or any suspension parts. The rear silencer especially must be aligned correctly before tightening the clamp nuts.

e) Tighten all nuts/bolts to the specified torque, where given.

Chapter 4 Part B:
Fuel and exhaust systems – diesel models

Contents

Degrees of difficulty

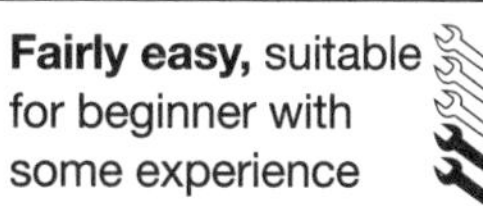

Easy, suitable for novice with little experience	**Fairly easy,** suitable for beginner with some experience	**Fairly difficult,** suitable for competent DIY mechanic	**Difficult,** suitable for experienced DIY mechanic	**Very difficult,** suitable for expert DIY or professional

Specifications

General

System type	TDCi (Turbo-Diesel Common-rail injection) with full electronic control, direct injection and turbocharger. Intercooler on the 1.6 litre engine
System designation	Siemens common rail
Firing order	1-3-4-2 (No 1 at flywheel end)
Fuel system operating pressure	200 to 1350 bars (according to engine speed)
Idle speed:	
1.4 litre engine	800 ± 20 rpm (controlled by PCM)
1.6 litre engine	750 rpm (controlled by PCM)
Engine cut-off speed	5000 rpm (controlled by PCM)

High-pressure fuel pump

Type	Bosch CP3.2
Direction of rotation	Clockwise, viewed from sprocket end

Injectors

Type	Electromagnetic

Turbocharger

Type	KKK
Boost pressure (approximate)	1 bar at 3000 rpm

Torque wrench settings

	Nm	lbf ft
Accumulator rail mounting bolts:		
1.4 litre engine	23	17
1.6 litre engine	22	16
Accumulator rail-to-fuel injector fuel pipe unions:*		
1.4 litre engine:		
Stage 1	17	13
Stage 2	22	16
1.6 litre engine:		
Stage 1	20	15
Stage 2	25	18
Camshaft position sensor bolt	5	4
Catalytic converter mounting nuts	25	18
Exhaust front clamp nut	47	35
Exhaust manifold nuts	25	18
Exhaust manifold studs	8	6
Fuel injector:		
1.4 litre engine:		
Fuel injector clamp bolt:		
Stage 1	15	11
Stage 2	Angle-tighten a further 70°	
1.6 litre engine:		
Fuel injector retaining bracket nuts:		
Stage 1	4	3
Stage 2	Angle-tighten a further 75°	
Fuel pressure sensor to accumulator rail	45	33
Fuel pump-to-accumulator rail fuel pipe unions:*		
Stage 1	20	15
Stage 2	25	18
Fuel pump front mounting bolts/nuts:		
1.4 litre engine	22	16
1.6 litre engine	20	15
Fuel pump rear mounting bolts/nut (8 mm):		
1.4 litre engine	17	13
1.6 litre engine	10	7
Fuel pump sprocket nut	50	37
Turbocharger mounting bolts/nuts	25	18
Turbocharger oil feed pipe banjo bolts:	30	22

** These torque settings are using special crow's-foot adapters – see Section 2*

1 General information and system operation

The fuel system consists of a rear-mounted fuel tank and fuel lift pump, a fuel filter with integral water separator and fuel heater (to avoid fuel waxing in cold conditions), and an electronically-controlled high-pressure diesel injection system, together with a turbocharger.

The exhaust system is conventional, but to meet the latest emission levels, an unregulated catalytic converter and an exhaust gas recirculation system are fitted to all models.

The high-pressure diesel injection system (generally known as a 'common rail' system) derives its name from the fact that a common rail (referred to as an accumulator rail), or fuel reservoir, is used to supply fuel to all the fuel injectors. Instead of an in-line or distributor type injection pump, which distributes the fuel directly to each injector, a high-pressure pump is used, which generates a very high fuel pressure (1500 bars at high engine speed) in the accumulator rail. The accumulator rail stores fuel, and maintains a constant fuel pressure with the aid of a pressure control valve. Each injector is supplied with high-pressure fuel from the accumulator rail, and the injectors are individually controlled via signals from the system electronic control unit (powertrain control module, or PCM). The injectors are electromagnetically-operated.

In addition to the various sensors used on previous diesel engines with a conventional fuel injection pump, common-rail systems also have a fuel pressure sensor. The fuel pressure sensor allows the PCM to maintain the required fuel pressure, via the pressure control valve.

System operation

For the purposes of describing the operation of a common rail injection system, the components can be divided into three sub-systems; the low-pressure fuel system, the high-pressure fuel system, and the electronic control system.

Low-pressure fuel system

The low-pressure fuel system consists of the following components:

a) Fuel tank.
b) Fuel lift pump.
c) Fuel filter/water trap/heater.
d) Low-pressure fuel lines.

The low-pressure system (fuel supply system) is responsible for supplying clean fuel to the high-pressure fuel system.

High-pressure fuel system

The high-pressure fuel system consists of the following components:

a) High-pressure fuel pump with pressure control valve.
b) High-pressure fuel accumulator rail.
c) Fuel injectors.
d) High-pressure fuel lines.

After passing through the fuel filter, the fuel reaches the high-pressure pump, which forces it into the accumulator rail. As diesel fuel has a certain elasticity, the pressure in the accumulator rail remains constant, even though fuel leaves the rail each time one of the injectors operates. Additionally, a pressure control valve mounted on the high-pressure pump ensures that the fuel pressure is maintained within preset limits.

The pressure control valve is operated by the PCM. When the valve is opened, fuel is returned from the high-pressure pump to the tank, via the fuel return lines, and the pressure in the accumulator rail falls. To enable the PCM to trigger the pressure control valve correctly, the pressure in the accumulator rail is measured by a fuel pressure sensor.

The electromagnetically-controlled fuel injectors are operated individually, via signals from the PCM, and each injector injects fuel directly into the relevant combustion chamber. The fact that high fuel pressure is always available allows very precise and highly flexible injection in comparison to a conventional injection pump: for example combustion during the main injection process can be improved considerably by the pre-injection of a very small quantity of fuel.

Electronic control system

The electronic control system consists of the following components:

a) Electronic control unit (powertrain control module or PCM).
b) Crankshaft speed/position sensor.
c) Camshaft position sensor.
d) Accelerator pedal position sensor.
e) Coolant temperature sensor.
f) Fuel temperature sensor.
g) Air mass meter.
h) Fuel pressure sensor.
i) Fuel injectors.
j) Fuel pressure control valve.
k) Preheating control unit.
l) EGR solenoid valve.
m) Vehicle speed sensor (or ABS wheel sensors).
n) Inlet air shutoff throttle body (1.6 litre engine)
o) Inlet manifold absolute pressure sensor (1.6 litre engine)
p) Brake and clutch pedal position switches

The information from the various sensors is passed to the PCM, which evaluates the signals. The PCM contains electronic 'maps' which enable it to calculate the optimum quantity of fuel to inject, the appropriate start of injection, and even pre- and post-injection fuel quantities, for each individual engine cylinder under any given condition of engine operation.

Additionally, the PCM carries out monitoring and self-diagnostic functions. Any faults in the system are stored in the PCM memory, which enables quick and accurate fault diagnosis using appropriate diagnostic equipment (such as a suitable fault code reader).

System components

Fuel lift pump

The fuel lift pump and integral fuel gauge sender unit is electrically-operated, and is mounted in the fuel tank.

High-pressure pump

The high-pressure pump is mounted on the engine in the position normally occupied by the conventional distributor fuel injection pump. The pump is driven at half engine speed by the timing belt, and is lubricated by the fuel which it pumps.

The fuel lift pump forces the fuel into the high-pressure pump chamber, via a safety valve.

The high-pressure pump consists of three radially-mounted pistons and cylinders. The pistons are operated by an eccentric cam mounted on the pump drive spindle. As a piston moves down, fuel enters the cylinder through an inlet valve. When the piston reaches bottom dead centre (BDC), the inlet valve closes, and as the piston moves back up the cylinder, the fuel is compressed. When the pressure in the cylinder reaches the pressure in the accumulator rail, an outlet valve opens, and fuel is forced into the accumulator rail. When the piston reaches top dead centre (TDC), the outlet valve closes, due to the pressure drop, and the pumping cycle is repeated. The use of multiple cylinders provides a steady flow of fuel, minimising pulses and pressure fluctuations.

As the pump needs to be able to supply sufficient fuel under full-load conditions, it will supply excess fuel during idle and part-load conditions. This excess fuel is returned from the high-pressure circuit to the low-pressure circuit (to the tank) via the pressure control valve.

The pump incorporates a facility to effectively switch off one of the cylinders to improve efficiency and reduce fuel consumption when maximum pumping capacity is not required. When this facility is operated, a solenoid-operated needle holds the inlet valve in the relevant cylinder open during the delivery stroke, preventing the fuel from being compressed.

Accumulator rail

As its name suggests, the accumulator rail acts as an accumulator, storing fuel and preventing pressure fluctuations. Fuel enters the rail from the high-pressure pump, and each injector has its own connection to the rail. The fuel pressure sensor is mounted in the rail, and the rail also has a connection to the fuel pressure control valve on the pump.

Pressure control valve

The pressure control valve is operated by the PCM, and controls the system pressure. The valve is integral with the high-pressure pump and cannot be separated.

If the fuel pressure is excessive, the valve opens, and fuel flows back to the tank. If the pressure is too low, the valve closes, enabling the high-pressure pump to increase the pressure.

The valve is an electromagnetically-operated ball valve. The ball is forced against its seat, against the fuel pressure, by a powerful spring, and also by the force provided by the electromagnet. The force generated by the electromagnet is directly proportional to the current applied to it by the PCM. The desired pressure can therefore be set by varying the current applied to the electromagnet. Any pressure fluctuations are damped by the spring.

Fuel pressure sensor

The fuel pressure sensor is mounted in the accumulator rail, and provides very precise information on the fuel pressure to the PCM.

Fuel injector

The injectors are mounted on the engine in a similar manner to conventional diesel fuel injectors. The injectors are electromagnetically-operated via signals from the PCM, and fuel is injected at the pressure existing in the accumulator rail. The injectors are high-precision instruments and are manufactured to very high tolerances.

Fuel flows into the injector from the accumulator rail, via an inlet valve and an inlet throttle, and an electromagnet causes the injector nozzle to lift from its seat, allowing injection. Excess fuel is returned from the injectors to the tank via a return line. The injector operates on a hydraulic servo principle: the forces resulting inside the injector due to the fuel pressure effectively amplify the effects of the electromagnet, which does not provide sufficient force to open the injector nozzle directly. The injector functions as follows. Five separate forces are essential to the operation of the injector:

a) A nozzle spring forces the nozzle needle against the nozzle seat at the bottom of the injector, preventing fuel from entering the combustion chamber.
b) In the valve at the top of the injector, the valve spring forces the valve ball against the opening to the valve control chamber. The fuel in the chamber is unable to escape through the fuel return.
c) When triggered, the electromagnet exerts a force which overcomes the valve spring force, and moves the valve ball away from its seat. This is the triggering force for the start of injection. When the valve ball moves off its seat, fuel enters the valve control chamber.
d) The pressure of the fuel in the valve control chamber exerts a force on the valve control plunger, which is added to the nozzle spring force.
e) A slight chamfer towards the lower end of the nozzle needle causes the fuel in the control chamber to exert a force on the nozzle needle.

When these forces are in equilibrium, the injector is in its rest (idle) state, but when a voltage is applied to the electromagnet, the forces work to lift the nozzle needle, injecting fuel into the combustion chamber. There are four phases of injector operation as follows:

a) Rest (idle) state – all forces are in equilibrium. The nozzle needle closes off the nozzle opening, and the valve spring forces the valve ball against its seat.
b) Opening – the electromagnet is triggered which opens the nozzle and triggers the injection process. The force from the electromagnet allows the valve ball to leave its seat. The fuel from the valve

2.4 Typical plastic plug and cap set for sealing disconnected fuel pipes and components

control chamber flows back to the tank via the fuel return line. When the valve opens, the pressure in the valve control chamber drops, and the force on the valve plunger is reduced. However, due to the effect of the input throttle, the pressure on the nozzle needle remains unchanged. The resulting force in the valve control chamber is sufficient to lift the nozzle from its seat, and the injection process begins.

c) *Injection – within a few milliseconds, the triggering current in the electromagnet is reduced to a lower holding current. The nozzle is now fully open, and fuel is injected into the combustion chamber at the pressure present in the accumulator rail.*

d) *Closing – the electromagnet is switched off, at which point the valve spring forces the valve ball firmly against its seat, and in the valve control chamber, the pressure is the same as that at the nozzle needle. The force at the valve plunger increases, and the nozzle needle closes the nozzle opening. The forces are now in equilibrium once more, and the injector is once more in the idle state, awaiting the next injection sequence.*

PCM and sensors

The PCM and sensors are described earlier in this Section – see *Electronic control system*.

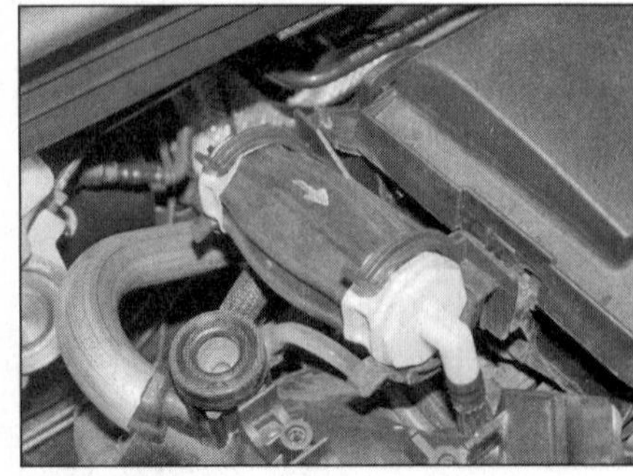

3.1a On early models, operate the hand priming pump until fuel free of bubbles appears in the clear fuel pipe

2.7 Two crow's-foot adapters will be necessary for tightening the fuel pipe unions

Air inlet sensor and turbocharger

An airflow sensor is fitted downstream of the air filter to monitor the quantity of air supplied to the turbocharger. The turbocharger itself is a variable-nozzle geometry type.

Inlet air shutoff throttle body

The inlet air shutoff throttle body controls the volume of air drawn into the engine according to driving conditions, and thus influences the composition of the recirculated exhaust gases. It is activated by the PCM. In addition, the unit ensures that the engine does not run-on after switching off the ignition.

2 High-pressure diesel injection system – special information

Warnings and precautions

1 It is essential to observe strict precautions when working on the fuel system components, particularly the high-pressure side of the system. Before carrying out any operations on the fuel system, refer to the precautions given in *Safety first!* at the beginning of this manual, and to the following additional information.

- Do not carry out any repair work on the high-pressure fuel system unless you are competent to do so, have all the necessary tools and equipment required, and are aware of the safety implications involved.
- Before starting any repair work on the fuel system, wait at least 30 seconds after switching off the engine to allow the fuel circuit pressure to reduce.
- Never work on the high-pressure fuel system with the engine running.
- Keep well clear of any possible source of fuel leakage, particularly when starting the engine after carrying out repair work. A leak in the system could cause an extremely high-pressure jet of fuel to escape, which could result in severe personal injury.
- Never place your hands or any part of your body near to a leak in the high-pressure fuel system.
- Do not use steam-cleaning equipment or compressed air to clean the engine or any of the fuel system components.

Procedures and information

2 Strict cleanliness must be observed at all times when working on any part of the fuel system. This applies to the working area in general, the person doing the work, and the components being worked on.

3 Before working on the fuel system components, they must be thoroughly cleaned with a suitable degreasing fluid. Specific cleaning products may be obtained from dealers. Alternatively, a suitable brake cleaning fluid may be used. Cleanliness is particularly important when working on the fuel system connections at the following components:

a) *Fuel filter.*
b) *High-pressure fuel pump.*
c) *Accumulator rail.*
d) *Fuel injectors.*
e) *High-pressure fuel pipes.*

4 After disconnecting any fuel pipes or components, the open union or orifice must be immediately sealed to prevent the entry of dirt or foreign material. Plastic plugs and caps in various sizes are available in packs from motor factors and accessory outlets, and are particularly suitable for this application **(see illustration)**. Fingers cut from disposable rubber gloves should be used to protect components such as fuel pipes, fuel injectors and wiring connectors, and can be secured in place using elastic bands.

5 Whenever any of the high-pressure fuel pipes are disconnected or removed, new pipes must be obtained for refitting.

6 On the completion of any repair on the high-pressure fuel system, the use of a leak-detecting compound is recommended. This is a powder which is applied to the fuel pipe unions and connections, which is white when dry. Any leak in the system will cause the product to darken, indicating the source of the leak.

7 The torque wrench settings given in the Specifications must be strictly observed when tightening component mountings and connections. This is particularly important when tightening the high-pressure fuel pipe unions. To use a torque wrench on the fuel pipe unions, two crow's-foot adapters are required – these are available from motor factors and accessory outlets **(see illustration)**.

3 Fuel system – priming and bleeding

1 Should the fuel supply system be disconnected between the fuel tank and high-pressure pump, it is necessary to prime the fuel system. On early models, a hand priming pump is fitted as original equipment to the fuel supply line **(see illustration)**, however, no pump is fitted on later models. On the later models it will be necessary to obtain the special Ford hose kit No 310-110 or a suitable alternative with a hand-priming function, and temporarily connect it into the fuel supply line to the fuel filter **(see illustration)**.

2 On some models, a clear plastic fuel pipe is fitted in the fuel return line in the engine compartment, and the pump should be operated until fuel appears in the pipe – on other models, operate the pump until the fuel reaches the pump. Continue to squeeze the pump until it becomes firm, then squeeze and hold the pump for a further 10 seconds. Release the pump, then squeeze and hold it a further 10 seconds.

3 Where applicable, disconnect the temporary hand priming pump, and reconnect the supply pipe to the fuel filter.

4 Operate the starter until the engine starts.

4 Air cleaner assembly – removal and refitting

1.4 litre engine

Air cleaner

1 Unplug the wiring connector from the airflow sensor **(see illustration)**.

2 Undo the air inlet duct retaining bolt near the battery, and unclip the upper pipe from the lower one **(see illustration)**.

3 Loosen the Jubilee clip at the base of the inlet air duct where it joins the turbo, and prise the duct off **(see illustration)**.

3.1b On later models use a hand-priming kit

4 Prise off the breather pipe from the connection on the camshaft cover **(see illustration)**.

5 Release the diesel priming bulb from its holding clips at the right-hand end of the air cleaner, sliding it out to the side – care is needed, as the plastic clips are quite fragile **(see illustration)**.

6 Undo the two air cleaner mounting screws at the front (not to be confused with the three screws securing the air filter lid), then pull up the air cleaner at the rear to release its mounting pegs. As the air cleaner is lifted, detach the wiring harness and the air inlet duct at the rear **(see illustrations)**.

7 To remove the air inlet ducting, release the retaining clips and remove the relevant section of ducting.

8 Refitting is a reversal of removal.

4.1 Disconnect the airflow sensor wiring plug

Inlet air resonator

9 To remove the resonator, first make a note of the fitted position of the outlet ducting clip (it must be refitted into its original position). Loosen the clip, and separate the duct from the resonator box.

10 Undo the Torx bolt at the rear of the resonator box, and the bolt securing the turbocharger outlet pipe to the box. Pivot the right-hand side of the box upwards, and separate the box from the turbocharger **(see illustrations)**. Recover the O-ring seal.

11 Refitting is a reversal of removal. Fit a new O-ring seal to the turbocharger end of the box if the old one is in poor condition.

1.6 litre engine

12 Disconnect the vacuum line from the one-way valve on the left-hand side of the air

4.2 Remove the air inlet duct bolt near the battery

4.3 Slacken the hose clip and disconnect the turbo outlet duct

4.4 Prise off the breather pipe on top of the engine

4.5 Slide the hand-priming bulb out of its retaining clips

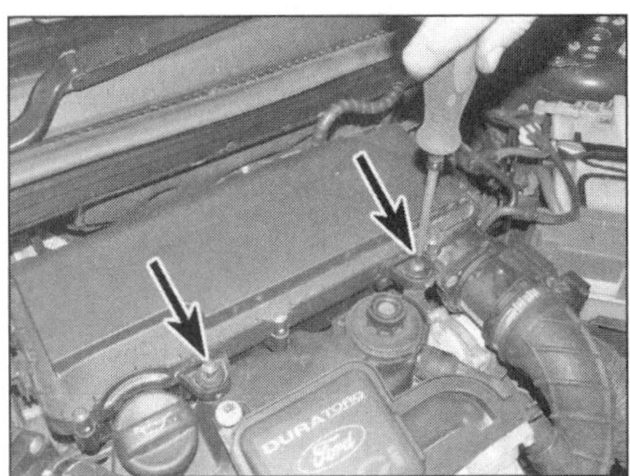

4.6a Unscrew the two mounting screws ...

4.6b ... then lift the air cleaner off the engine, detaching the wiring harness and duct at the rear

4.10a Slacken the clip and disconnect the turbo outlet hose ...

4.10b ... then undo the retaining bolts ...

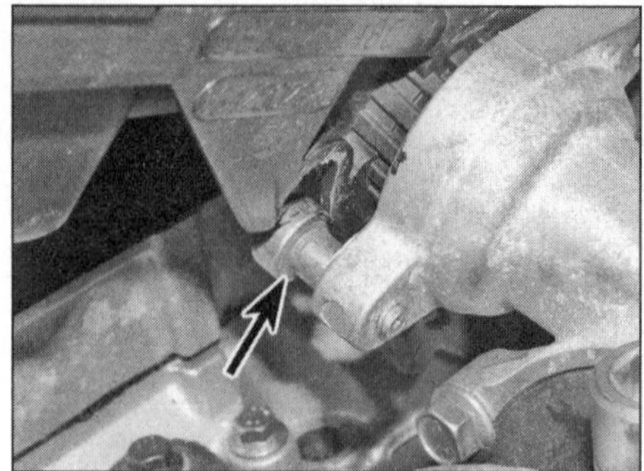

4.10c ... pivot the right-hand end of the box up and disengage it from the turbo outlet stud

cleaner body and position to one side **(see illustration)**.

13 Disconnect the air cleaner inlet hose from the duct at the front of the engine compartment. If necessary, the duct may be unbolted from the engine compartment front crossmember **(see illustrations)**.

14 Disconnect the crankcase ventilation hose from the engine valve cover **(see illustrations)**.

15 Loosen the clip and disconnect the inlet duct from the turbocharger.

16 Lift the air cleaner and engine top cover directly upwards from the three mounting rubbers and withdraw **(see illustration)**. The mountings are very tight.

17 Remove the air filter element together with the mass airflow sensor and air cleaner cover with reference to Chapter 1B, Section 18.

18 Refitting is a reversal of removal.

5 Accelerator pedal – removal and refitting

Removal

1 Remove the driver's lower facia trim panel, which is secured by five screws (two inside the small storage compartment) and one clip (at the top left – pull the panel towards you to release it).

2 Make sure the ignition is switched off (take out the key). Disconnect the wiring plug from the pedal position sensor, then unscrew the two mounting nuts and remove the pedal/sensor assembly from the bulkhead studs.

Refitting

3 Refit in the reverse order of removal. On completion, check the action of the pedal to ensure that the throttle has full unrestricted movement, and fully returns when released.

6 Fuel tank – removal, inspection and refitting

Note: *Refer to the warnings and precautions in Section 2 before proceeding.*

Refer to Chapter 4A, Section 8. Fuel tank removal and refitting is the same as for petrol models, with the exception that an evaporative emissions canister is not fitted to diesel models.

4.12 Disconnect the vacuum line from the one-way valve

4.13a Disconnect the air cleaner inlet hose from the front air inlet duct

4.13b If necessary, remove the air inlet duct

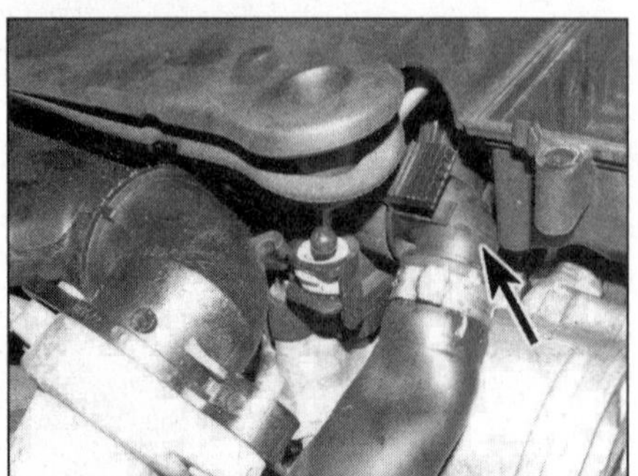

4.14a Crankcase ventilation hose connection to the valve cover...

4.14b ... and turbocharger inlet duct

4.16 Lift the air cleaner upwards from the mounting rubbers/posts

10.6 Depress the release buttons and disconnect the fuel supply and return hoses from the pump

7 Fuel pump/ fuel gauge sender unit – removal and refitting

Note: *Refer to the warnings and precautions in Section 2 before proceeding.*

Refer to Chapter 4A, Section 9.

8 Fuel tank roll-over valve – removal and refitting

Note: *Refer to the warnings and precautions in Section 2 before proceeding.*

Refer to Chapter 4A, Section 10.

9 Fuel tank filler neck – removal and refitting

Note: *Refer to the warnings and precautions in Section 2 before proceeding.*

Refer to Chapter 4A, Section 11.

10 High-pressure fuel pump – removal and refitting

Warning: Refer to the information contained in Section 2 before proceeding.

Note: *A new fuel pump-to-accumulator rail high-pressure fuel pipe will be required.*

10.15a Undo the pump rear support bracket bolts and nut ...

Removal

1 Disconnect the battery as described in Chapter 5A, Section 2.

2 Remove the air cleaner as described in Section 4.

3 Remove the timing belt as described in Chapter 2B or 2C. After removing the timing belt, temporarily refit the right-hand engine mounting.

1.4 litre engine

4 Remove the two screws from the EGR pipe elbow, then remove the clamp and mounting bolt, and take off the EGR pipe.

5 Disconnect the fuel temperature sensor wiring plug.

6 Depress the quick-release clip buttons and disconnect the fuel supply and return hoses from the pump **(see illustration)**. Plug the end of the hoses to prevent dirt ingress.

7 Disconnect the wiring plugs from the fuel flow and pressure control valves, noting their locations for refitting. Detach the wiring loom as necessary.

1.6 litre engine

8 Unscrew the bolts securing the injector wiring harness conduit to the top of the engine, then disconnect the wiring from the injectors.

9 Disconnect the injector fuel return line.

10 Disconnect the wiring from the camshaft position sensor and fuel temperature sensor.

11 Disconnect the glow plug wiring harness, and detach the wiring from the mounting bracket. Disconnect the wiring from the glow plugs.

12 Release the fuel line retaining clips.

10.15b ... and the bolts securing the bracket to the cylinder head

13 Disconnect the wiring from the high-pressure fuel pump.

14 Depress the quick-release clip buttons and disconnect the fuel supply and return hoses from the pump. Also disconnect the fuel tank return hose and the fuel filter supply hose. Plug the end of the hoses to prevent dirt ingress.

All engines

15 Remove the two bolts securing the fuel pump support bracket, and remove the bracket from the engine **(see illustrations)**.

16 Clean carefully around the unions at either end of the pump-to-accumulator rail metal pipe – it is very important that no dirt enters the system. Counterhold the pump union with a second spanner – the union screwed into the pump must not be allowed to unscrew **(see illustration)**. Keep the pipe in place until both unions have been fully loosened, and the pipe can be removed – this reduces the chance of dirt getting in. Plug the open ends on the pump and accumulator rail – this is most important. Discard the pipe – a new one must be fitted.

17 Hold the pump sprocket stationary, and loosen the centre nut securing it to the pump shaft. The manufacturers recommend using an 8 mm pin inserted through the pulley and into the pump support **(see illustration)**. Alternatively, use a home-made tool like the one shown **(see Tool Tip)**.

TOOL TiP

A sprocket holding tool can be made from two lengths of steel strip bolted together to form a forked end. Drill holes and insert bolts in the ends of the fork to engage with the sprocket spokes

10.16 Counterhold the pump union with a second spanner whilst slackening the accumulator-to-pump pipe union

10.17 Stop the fuel pump sprocket from rotating by inserting an 8 mm drill bit or pin through the sprocket into the backplate

Make a sprocket releasing tool from a short strip of steel. Drill two holes in the strip to correspond with the two holes in the sprocket. Drill a third hole just large enough to accept the flats of the sprocket retaining nut.

18 The fuel pump sprocket is a taper fit on the pump shaft, and it will be necessary to make up a tool to release it from the taper **(see Tool Tip)**. Partially unscrew the sprocket retaining nut, fit the home-made tool, and secure it to the sprocket with two 7.0 mm bolts and nuts. Prevent the sprocket from rotating as before, and screw down the nuts, forcing the sprocket off the shaft taper. Once the taper is released, remove the tool, unscrew the nut fully, and remove the sprocket from the pump shaft.

19 Support the pump, then undo the three bolts, and remove the pump **(see illustration)**.

Caution: The high-pressure fuel pump is manufactured to extremely close tolerances, and must not be dismantled in any way. Do not unscrew the fuel pipe male union on the rear of the pump, or attempt to remove the sensor, piston de-activator switch, or the seal on the pump shaft. No parts for the pump are available separately, and if the unit is in any way suspect, it must be renewed.

Refitting

20 Locate the pump in the mounting bracket, and refit the three mounting bolts, hand-tight. Refit the pump rear support bracket, tightening the bolts/nut to the specified torque. Now tighten the three pump mounting bolts to the specified torque.

10.19 Unscrew the three bolts and remove the pump

21 Refit the sprocket to the pump shaft, and tighten the retaining nut to the specified torque, holding the sprocket by the same method used on removal.

22 Fit a new metal fuel pipe between the pump and the accumulator rail. The unions at each end of the pipe must be tightened to the specified torque in two stages. Use a second spanner to counterhold the union screwed into the pump. Do not allow the union to move.

23 The remainder of refitting is a reversal of removal.

24 With everything reassembled and reconnected, prime the fuel system as described in Section 3. Observing the precautions listed in Section 2, start the engine and allow it to idle. Check for leaks at the high-pressure fuel pipe unions with the engine idling. If satisfactory, increase the engine speed to 4000 rpm and check again for leaks.

25 Take the car for a short road test, and check for leaks once again on return. If any leaks are detected, obtain and fit another new high-pressure fuel pipe. Do not attempt to cure even the slightest leak by further tightening of the pipe unions.

11 Accumulator rail – removal and refitting

Warning: Refer to the information contained in Section 2 before proceeding.

Note: *A complete new set of high-pressure fuel pipes will be required for refitting.*

Removal

1 Disconnect the battery as described in Chapter 5A, Section 2.

1.4 litre engine

2 Remove the cylinder head cover as described in Chapter 2B, Section 4.

3 Noting how it is routed, disconnect the glow plug wiring and move it to one side.

1.6 litre engine

4 Remove the exhaust manifold-to-EGR valve tube.

5 Drain the cooling system as described in Chapter 1B, Section 25.

6 Unscrew the bolts securing the injector wiring harness conduit to the top of the engine, then disconnect the wiring from the injectors located on the rear of the cylinder head.

7 Disconnect the injector fuel return line.

8 Disconnect the wiring from the camshaft position sensor and fuel temperature sensor.

9 Disconnect the glow plug wiring harness, and detach the wiring from the mounting bracket. Disconnect the wiring from the glow plugs.

10 Release the fuel line retaining clips.

11 Disconnect the wiring from the high-pressure fuel pump.

12 Disconnect the wiring from the starter motor.

13 Unbolt the coolant transfer pipe from the rear of the cylinder block, withdraw the pipe from the rear of the water pump and recover the O-ring seal.

All engines

14 Clean the area around the high-pressure fuel pipes to and from the accumulator rail, then unscrew the pump-to-accumulator rail pipe unions. Use a second spanner to counterhold the union screwed in to the pump body as described in Section 10. The screwed-in union must not be allowed to move. Remove the pipe.

15 Repeat the procedure on the accumulator rail-to-injector fuel pipes. Use a second spanner to counterhold the unions screwed into the injectors **(see illustration)** – these unions must not be allowed to move. Note their fitted locations and remove the pipes.

16 Plug the openings in the accumulator rail and fuel pump to prevent dirt ingress.

17 Disconnect the pressure sensor wiring plug from the accumulator rail **(see illustration)**.

18 Disconnect the fuel return pipe from the rail **(see illustration)**.

19 Unscrew the two rail mounting bolts, and manoeuvre it out **(see illustration)**. **Note:** *The fuel pressure sensor on the accumulator rail must not be removed.*

Refitting

20 Locate the accumulator rail in position, refit and finger-tighten the mounting bolts.

21 Reconnect the accumulator pressure sensor wiring plug.

22 Fit the new pump-to-rail high-pressure

11.15 Use a second spanner to counterhold the fuel injector unions whilst slackening the pipe unions

11.17 Disconnect the accumulator rail pressure sensor wiring plug

pipe, and only finger-tighten the unions at first, then tighten the unions to the Stage 1 torque setting, followed by the Stage 2 torque setting. Use a second spanner to counterhold the union screwed into the pump body.

23 Fit the new set of rail-to-injector high-pressure pipes, and finger-tighten the unions. If it's not possible to fit the new pipes to the injector unions, remove and refit the injectors as described in Section 12, and try again.

24 Tighten the accumulator mounting bolts to the specified torque.

25 Tighten the rail-to-injector pipe unions to the Stage 1 torque setting, followed by the Stage 2 setting. Use a second spanner to counterhold the injector unions.

26 The remainder of refitting is a reversal of removal, noting the following points:

a) Ensure all wiring connectors and harnesses are correctly refitting and secured.

b) Prime the fuel system as described in Section 3.

c) On the 1.6 litre engine, refill the cooling system with reference to Chapter 1B, Section 25.

d) Observing the precautions listed in Section 2, start the engine and allow it to idle. Check for leaks at the high-pressure fuel pipe unions with the engine idling. If satisfactory, increase the engine speed to 4000 rpm and check again for leaks. Take the car for a short road test, and check for leaks once again on return. If any leaks are detected, obtain and fit additional new high-pressure fuel pipes as required. ***Do not*** *attempt to cure even the slightest leak by further tightening of the pipe unions. During the road test, initialise the engine management PCM as follows – engage third gear and stabilise the engine at 1000 rpm, then accelerate fully up to 3500 rpm.*

12 Fuel injectors – removal and refitting

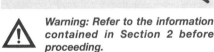

Warning: Refer to the information contained in Section 2 before proceeding.

Note: *The following procedure describes the removal and refitting of the injectors as a complete set. However, each injector may be removed individually if required. New copper washers, upper seals, injector clamp retaining nuts and a high-pressure fuel pipe will be required for each disturbed injector when refitting.*

11.18 Depress the release button and disconnect the fuel return hose

11.19 Remove the accumulator rail mounting bolts

1.4 litre engine

Removal

1 Remove the cylinder head cover as described in Chapter 2B, Section 4.

2 Clean the area around the high-pressure fuel pipes between the injectors and the accumulator rail, then unscrew the pipe unions. Use a second spanner to counterhold the union screwed in to the injector body **(see illustration 11.15)**. The injectors' screwed-in unions must not be allowed to move. Remove the pipes. Plug the openings in the accumulator rail and injectors to prevent dirt ingress.

3 Extract the retaining circlip and disconnect the leak-off pipe from each fuel injector **(see illustration)**.

4 Unscrew the injector retaining bolt, and remove the clamp. If loose, recover the clamp's locating dowel from the cylinder head **(see illustrations)**.

5 Carefully pull or lever the injector out. Do not lever against or pull on the solenoid housing at the top of the injector. Store the injectors in a suitable rack **(see illustration)**. Try to keep the injectors vertical (and full of fuel) at all times whilst they are removed from the engine.

6 Remove the copper washer and the upper seal from each injector, or from the cylinder head if they stayed in place **(see illustration)**. New copper washers and upper seals will be required for refitting. Cover the injector hole in the cylinder head, to prevent dirt ingress.

7 Examine each injector visually for any signs

12.3 Prise out the circlip and disconnect the fuel leak-off pipe

12.4a Undo the injector clamp bolt ...

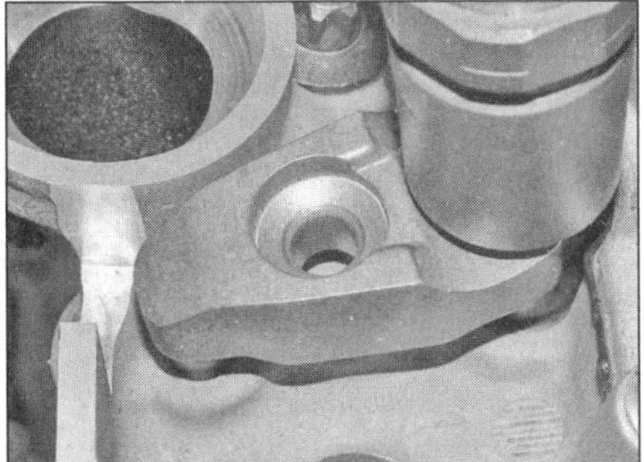

12.4b ... and remove the clamp

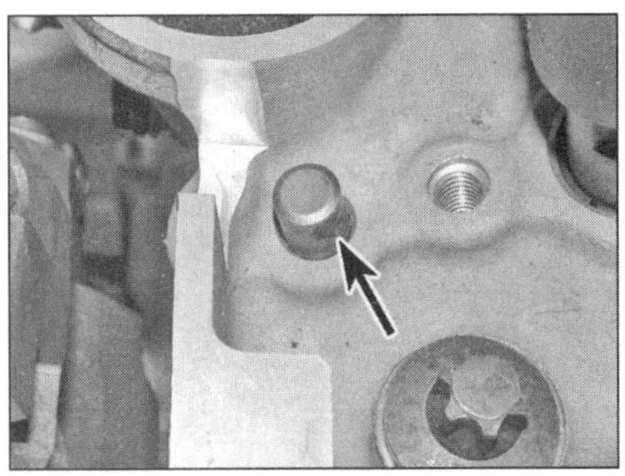

12.4c If it's loose, remove the locating dowel

12.5 Construct a simple storage rack to store the injectors

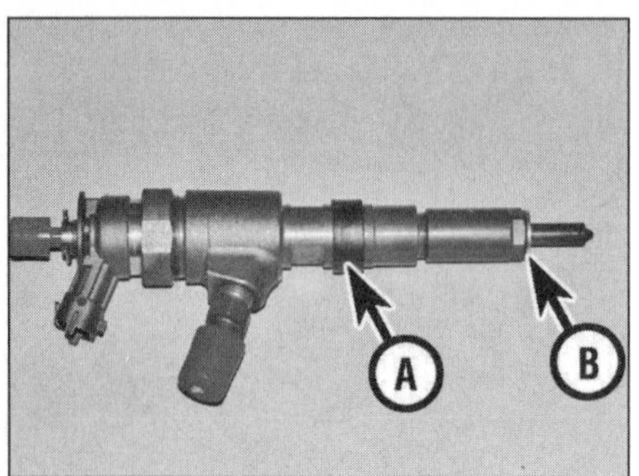

12.6 Fuel injector upper seal (A) and copper washer (B)

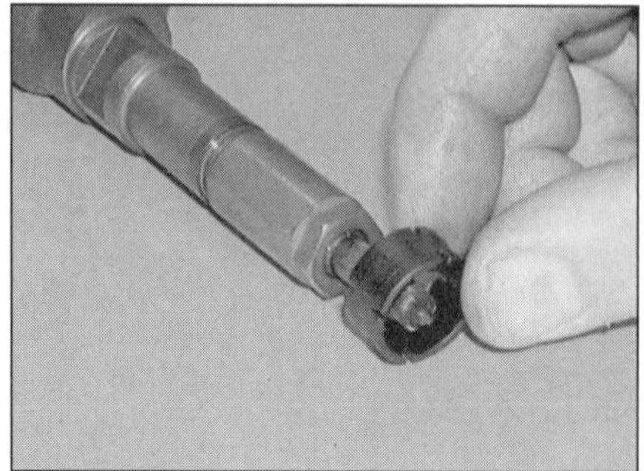
12.8a Locate a new upper seal on the body of each injector ...

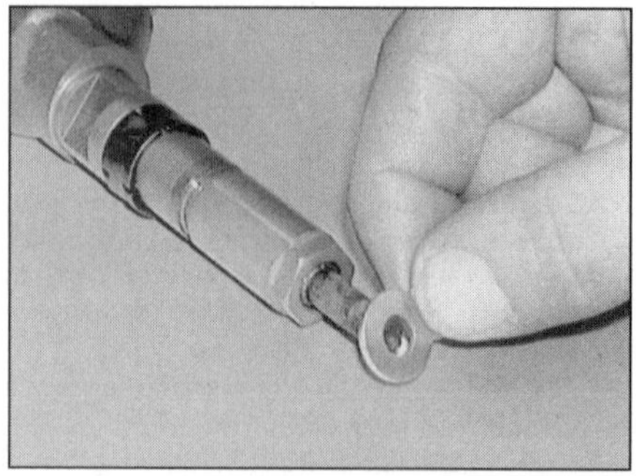
12.8b ... and place a new copper washer on the injector nozzle

of obvious damage or deterioration. If any defects are apparent, renew the injector(s).

Caution: The injectors are manufactured to extremely close tolerances, and must not be dismantled in any way. Do not unscrew the fuel pipe union on the side of the injector, or separate any parts of the injector body. Do not attempt to clean carbon deposits from the injector nozzle or carry out any form of ultrasonic or pressure testing.

Refitting

8 Locate a new upper seal on the body of each injector, and place a new copper washer on the injector nozzle **(see illustrations)**.

9 Refit the injector clamp locating dowels to the cylinder head, if removed.

10 Place the injector clamp in the slot on each injector body, and refit the injectors to the cylinder head. Guide the clamp onto the locating dowel as each injector is inserted. Ensure the upper injector seals are correctly located in the cylinder head.

11 Fit the new injector clamp retaining bolts. Tighten the bolts finger-tight only at this stage.

12 Working on one fuel injector at a time, remove the blanking plugs from the fuel pipe unions on the accumulator rail and the relevant injector. Locate a new high-pressure fuel pipe over the unions, and screw on the union nuts. Take care not to cross-thread the nuts or strain the fuel pipes as they are fitted. Once the union nut threads have started, finger-tighten the nuts only at this stage.

13 When all the fuel pipes are in place, tighten the injector clamp retaining bolts to the specified torque.

14 Using an open-ended spanner, hold each fuel pipe union in turn, and tighten the union nut to the specified torque using a torque wrench and crow's-foot adapter **(see illustration)**. Tighten all the disturbed union nuts in the same way.

15 The remainder of refitting is a reversal of removal, following the points listed in paragraph 26 of Section 11.

1.6 litre engine

Removal

16 Disconnect the battery negative terminal as described in Chapter 5A, Section 2.

17 Remove the air cleaner as described in Section 4.

18 Note the position of the EGR valve tube in its retaining clamp, then unscrew the mounting bolt and release the clamp. Where a crimped clamp is fitted, cut the crimp lug to release it – where a conventional clamp is fitted, unscrew the bolt. Remove the tube from the exhaust manifold and EGR valve. Recover the O-ring seal.

19 Unscrew the bolts securing the injector wiring harness conduit to the top of the engine, then disconnect the wiring from the injectors.

20 Disconnect the injector fuel return line.

21 Disconnect the wiring from the camshaft position sensor and fuel temperature sensor.

22 Disconnect the glow plug wiring harness, and detach the wiring from the mounting bracket. Disconnect the wiring from the glow plugs.

23 Release the fuel line retaining clips **(see illustration)**.

24 Disconnect the wiring from the high-pressure fuel pump.

25 Depress the quick-release clip buttons and disconnect the fuel supply and return hoses from the pump. Also disconnect the fuel tank return hose and the fuel filter supply hose. Plug the end of the hoses to prevent dirt ingress.

26 Clean the area around the high-pressure fuel pipes to and from the accumulator rail, then unscrew the pump-to-accumulator rail pipe unions. Use a second spanner to counterhold the union screwed in to the pump body as described in Section 10. The screwed-in union must not be allowed to move. Remove the pipe.

27 Repeat the procedure on the accumulator rail-to-injector fuel pipes. Use a second spanner to counterhold the unions screwed into the injectors – these unions must not be allowed to move. Note their fitted locations and remove the pipes.

28 Plug the openings in the accumulator rail and fuel pump to prevent dirt ingress.

29 Unscrew the injector retaining nuts, and carefully pull or lever the injector from place. If necessary, use an open-ended spanner and twist the injector to free it from position **(see illustrations)**. Do not lever against or pull on the solenoid housing at the top of the injector. Note down the injectors position – if the injectors are to be refitted, they must be refitted to their original locations. If improved access is required, undo the bolts and remove

12.14 Using a torque wrench and crow's-foot adapter, tighten the fuel pipe union nuts

12.23 Prise out the clip and pull the return pipe from each injector

12.29a Injector retaining nuts (arrowed)

the oil separator housing from the front of the cylinder head cover.

30 Remove the copper washer and the upper seal from each injector, or from the cylinder head if they remained in place during injector removal. New copper washers and upper seals will be required for refitting. Store the injectors vertically in the correct order **(see illustration 12.5)**. Cover the injector hole in the cylinder head to prevent dirt ingress.

31 Examine each injector visually for any signs of obvious damage or deterioration. If any defects are apparent, renew the injector(s). Note down the 8-digit injector classification number – this may be needed during the refitting procedure if the PCM has been renewed **(see illustration)**.

Caution: The injectors are manufactured to extremely close tolerances and must not be dismantled in any way. Do not unscrew the fuel pipe union on the side of the injector, or separate any parts of the injector body. Do not attempt to clean carbon deposits from the injector nozzle or carry out any form of ultrasonic or pressure testing.

Refitting

32 Ensure the injector clamps are in place over their respective circlips on the injector bodies, the fit the injectors into place in the cylinder head. If the original injectors are being refitted, ensure they are fitted into their original positions **(see illustration)**.

33 Fit the injector retaining bolts/nuts, but only finger-tighten them at this stage. When tightening the nuts/bolts, ensure the clamps stay horizontal.

34 Working on one fuel injector at a time, remove the blanking plugs from the fuel pipe unions on the accumulator rail and the relevant injector. Locate a new high-pressure fuel pipe over the unions and screw on the union nuts. Take care not to cross-thread the nuts or strain the fuel pipes as they are fitted. Once the union nut threads have started, finger-tighten the nuts only at this stage, to the ends of the threads.

35 When all the fuel pipes are in place, tighten the injector clamp retaining nuts/bolts to the specified torque and angle.

36 Using an open-ended spanner, hold each fuel pipe union in turn and tighten the union nut to the specified torque using a torque wrench and crow-foot adapter **(see illustration)**. Tighten all the union nuts in the same way.

37 If new injectors have been fitted, their classification numbers must be programmed into the engine management PCM using dedicated diagnostic equipment. If this equipment is not available, entrust this task to a Ford dealer or suitably-equipped specialist. Note that it should be possible to drive the vehicle, albeit with reduced performance/increased emissions, to a repairer for the numbers to be programmed.

38 The remainder of refitting is a reversal of removal, following the points a, b and d listed in paragraph 26 of Section 11. When refitting

12.29b Use a spanner to twist the injector and free it from position

the EGR tube to the EGR valve, locate as noted during removal, and where necessary use a new clamp. If fitting a new crimp-type clamp, tighten the clamp by squeezing together the crimp lug using pincers.

13 Electronic control system components – testing, removal and refitting

Testing

1 If a fault is suspected in the electronic control side of the system, first ensure that all the wiring connectors are securely connected and free of corrosion. Ensure that the suspected problem is not of a mechanical nature, or due to poor maintenance; ie, check that the air cleaner filter element is clean, the engine breather hoses are clear and undamaged, and that the cylinder compression pressures are correct, referring to Chapter 1B and 2B or 2C for further information.

2 If these checks fail to reveal the cause of the problem, the car should be taken to a Ford dealer or suitably-equipped garage for testing.

3 A diagnostic socket is located underneath the steering column, to which a fault code reader or other suitable test equipment can be connected. By using the code reader or test equipment, the engine management PCM (and the various other vehicle system control units) can be interrogated, and any stored fault codes can be retrieved. This will allow the fault to be quickly and simply traced, alleviating

12.31 Note the injector classification number

the need to test all the system components individually, which is a time-consuming operation that carries a risk of damaging the PCM.

Powertrain control module

Note: *If a new PCM is to be fitted, this work must be entrusted to a Ford dealer or suitably-equipped specialist. It is necessary to initialise the new PCM after installation, which requires the use of dedicated Ford diagnostic equipment.*

4 The PCM is located on the left-hand inner wing, behind the left-hand headlight unit.

5 Disconnect the battery negative lead before proceeding as described in Chapter 5A, Section 2 – if this is not done, the module could be damaged when the wiring plugs are disconnected.

6 Remove the left-hand headlight as described in Chapter 12, Section 7.

7 The PCM is retained by two nuts and two bolts – remove these, and pivot the module down from its inner wing location. On later models, a security shield is fitted over the module and onto the wiring. It is retained with a shear bolt/nut. To remove the bolt/nut, file a flat on its edge, then drill a 2 mm diameter hole through it. Follow this with a 5 mm diameter hole to remove it.

8 Disconnect the three wiring plugs from the base of the module, starting with the one nearest the rear of the car when the module was in its fitted position. The plugs each have a locking catch, which is released by turning it anti-clockwise (or towards the rear of the car).

9 Refitting is a reversal of removal. Where

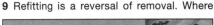

12.32 Fit the injectors into their original locations

12.36 Tighten the high-pressure pipe union nuts using a 'crow-foot' adapter

13.10 Crankshaft position sensor (1.6 litre model)

a security shield is fitted, locate it onto the wiring before reconnecting the wires. Secure the shield with a new shear bolt/nut.

Crankshaft speed/position sensor

Note: *Before carrying out the following procedure, disconnect the battery as described in Chapter 5A, Section 2. Reconnect the battery on completion of refitting.*

10 The crankshaft position sensor is located adjacent to the crankshaft pulley on the right-hand end of the engine **(see illustration)**.

11 Squeeze the sides of the quick-release connector on the coolant expansion tank hose at the top, and pull off the hose. Unbolt the expansion tank from the wing, and lift out the tank, placing it to one side without disconnecting the lower hose. On the 1.6 litre engine, it will be necessary to siphon the coolant from the tank and disconnect the degas hose.

12 Remove the timing belt upper cover as described in Chapter 2B or 2C.

13 Disconnect the wiring plug from the crankshaft sensor, located just above the sump.

14 Remove the crankshaft pulley as described in Chapter 2B or 2C.

15 Remove the timing belt lower cover as described in Chapter 2B or 2C.

16 Unbolt and remove the crankshaft sensor from the engine.

17 Refitting is a reversal of removal. Ensure that the sensor is clean when refitting, and tighten its mounting bolt securely. Refit the crankshaft pulley as described in Chapter 2B or 2C.

Camshaft position sensor

Note: *Before carrying out the following procedure, disconnect the battery as described in Chapter 5A, Section 2. Reconnect the battery on completion of refitting.*

18 The camshaft position sensor is mounted on the right-hand end of the cylinder head cover, directly behind the camshaft sprocket.

19 Remove the coolant expansion tank as described in paragraph 11, then remove the upper timing belt cover as described in Chapter 2B or 2C.

20 Unplug the sensor wiring connector **(see illustration)**.

21 Undo the bolt and pull the sensor from position **(see illustration)**.

22 Upon refitting, position the sensor so that the air gap between the sensor end and the webs of the signal wheel is 1.2 mm, measured with feeler gauges, for a used sensor. If fitting a new sensor, the small tip of the sensor must be just touching one of the three webs of the signal wheel. Tighten the sensor retaining bolt to the specified torque **(see illustration)**.

23 The remainder of refitting is a reversal of removal.

Accelerator pedal position sensor

24 The sensor is integral with the accelerator pedal assembly. Refer to Section 5 for the pedal removal procedure.

Coolant temperature sensor

25 Refer to Chapter 3, Section 6.

Fuel temperature sensor

Warning: Refer to the information contained in Section 2 before proceeding.

Note: *Before carrying out the following procedure, disconnect the battery as described in Chapter 5A, Section 2. Reconnect the battery on completion of refitting.*

26 The sensor is clipped in to the plastic fuel manifold at the right-hand rear end of the cylinder head. To remove the sensor, disconnect the wiring plug, then unclip the sensor from the manifold. Be prepared for fuel spillage **(see illustration)**.

27 Refitting is a reversal of removal.

28 Observing the precautions listed in Section 2, start the engine and allow it to idle. Check for leaks at the fuel temperature sensor with the engine idling. If satisfactory, increase the engine speed to 4000 rpm and check again for leaks. Take the car for a short road test and check for leaks once again on return. If any leaks are detected, obtain and fit a new sensor.

Airflow sensor

Note: *Before carrying out the following procedure, disconnect the battery as described in Chapter 5A, Section 2. Reconnect the battery on completion of refitting.*

29 On the 1.4 litre engine, the airflow sensor is located in the inlet ducting from the air cleaner housing. On the 1.6 litre engine, it is bolted to the air cleaner cover outlet, and an outlet elbow connects it to the turbocharger **(see illustration)**.

13.20 Disconnect the camshaft position sensor wiring plug (1.4 litre model)

13.21 Undo the camshaft position sensor retaining bolt (1.6 litre model)

13.22 The gap between the end of the sensor and the webs of the signal wheel must be 1.2 mm (used sensor only)

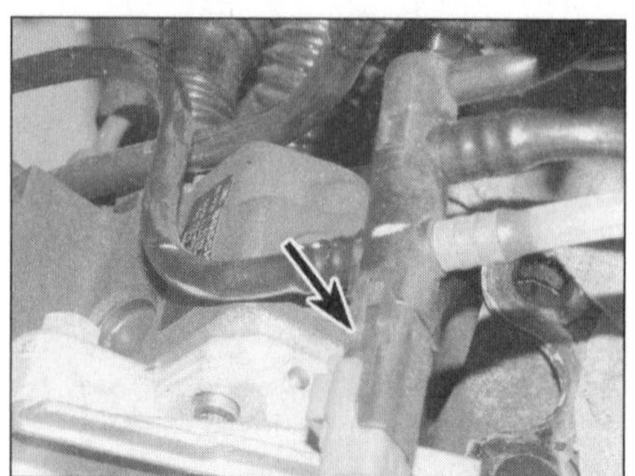

13.26 Fuel temperature sensor

13.29 On the 1.6 litre engine, the mass airflow sensor is bolted to the air cleaner cover outlet

13.30 Air mass meter wiring plug (1.4 litre model)

13.32 Disconnect the wiring from the airflow sensor

13.34 Mass airflow sensor

1.4 litre engine

30 Disconnect the sensor wiring plug **(see illustration).**

31 Slacken the retaining clip, and remove the two bolts securing the air inlet ducting either side of the airflow sensor.

1.6 litre engine

32 Unplug the wiring connector from the airflow sensor **(see illustration)**.

33 Undo the screws and release the cover from the top of the air cleaner.

34 Loosen the clip and remove the airflow sensor from the outlet elbow duct leading to the turbocharger **(see illustration)**. Move the assembly onto the workbench, then undo the screws and separate the airflow sensor from the cover. Recover the O-ring seal.

All engines

35 Suitably plug or cover the turbocharger rigid inlet duct, using clean rag to prevent any dirt or foreign material from entering.

36 Refitting is a reverse of the removal procedure. On the 1.6 litre engine, check the condition of the O-ring seal, and fit a new one if necessary.

Fuel pressure sensor

37 The fuel pressure sensor is integral with the accumulator rail, and is not available separately. The sensor must not be removed from the rail.

Fuel pressure control valve

38 The fuel pressure control valve is integral with the high-pressure fuel pump, and cannot be separated.

Preheating system control unit

39 This is controlled by the PCM, see paragraphs 4 to 9.

EGR solenoid valve

40 Refer to Chapter 4C, Section 3.

Vehicle speed sensor

Note: *On models with ABS, vehicle speed information is derived from the ABS wheel sensors, and a vehicle speed sensor is not fitted. For more information on the ABS wheel sensors, refer to Chapter 9, Section 17.*

41 The sensor is mounted on top of the transmission, above the left-hand driveshaft (where the speedometer cable would otherwise be fitted).

42 With the ignition switched off, disconnect the sensor wiring plug, then pull the sensor retaining pin (at the base) out sideways, and lift the sensor out of the transmission.

43 Refitting is a reversal of removal. Check the condition of the O-ring seal, and fit a new one if necessary. Ensure the sensor is fully seated, and held securely by the retaining pin.

Inlet air shutoff throttle

Note: *The inlet air shutoff throttle is only fitted to models with the 1.6 litre engine. When fitting a new unit, note that its base value must be set by a Ford dealer or suitably-equipped specialist using dedicated diagnostic equipment.*

44 The inlet air shutoff throttle is located on the right-hand front of the cylinder head, in the inlet air duct between the intercooler and inlet manifold **(see illustration)**. Its purpose is to prevent engine run-on when switching off, and to vary the volume air drawn into the engine in order to control the composition of recirculated exhaust gas.

45 Disconnect the wiring from the unit at the connector.

46 Loosen the clip and disconnect the intercooler hose from the unit.

47 Undo the screws and remove the inlet air shutoff throttle from the ducting flange leading to the inlet manifold.

48 Refitting is a reversal of removal, however, check the condition of the O-ring seal, and fit a new one if necessary. Clean any oil residue from inside the intercooler hose to ensure secure refitting.

Manifold absolute pressure (MAP) sensor

Note: *The MAP sensor is only fitted to models with the 1.6 litre engine.*

49 The MAP sensor is located on the inlet manifold inlet duct on the right-hand front of the cylinder head **(see illustration)**.

50 Disconnect the wiring from the sensor.

51 Unscrew the Torx mounting bolt and remove the sensor.

52 Refitting is a reversal of removal.

14 Inlet manifold – removal and refitting

The inlet manifold is integral with the cylinder head cover. Refer to Chapter 2B, Section 4 or Chapter 2C, Section 4.

15 Exhaust manifold – removal and refitting

Removal

1 Remove the turbocharger as described in Section 17.

2 Undo the retaining nuts, recover the spacers, and remove the manifold. Recover the gasket **(see illustrations)**.

13.44 Inlet air shutoff throttle

13.49 Manifold absolute pressure (MAP) sensor

15.2a Undo the exhaust manifold nuts, recover the spacers, and remove the manifold

15.2b Recover the manifold gasket

Refitting

3 Refitting is a reverse of the removal procedure, bearing in mind the following points:

a) *Ensure that the manifold and cylinder head mating faces are clean, with all traces of old gasket removed.*
b) *Use a new gasket when refitting the manifold to the cylinder head.*
c) *Tighten the exhaust manifold retaining nuts to the specified torque.*
d) *Refit the turbocharger as described in Section 17.*

16 Turbocharger – description and precautions

Description

1 A turbocharger is fitted to increase engine efficiency by raising the pressure in the inlet manifold above atmospheric pressure. Instead of the air simply being sucked into the cylinders, it is forced in.

2 Energy for the operation of the turbocharger comes from the exhaust gas. The gas flows through a specially-shaped housing (the turbine housing) and, in so doing, spins the turbine wheel. The turbine wheel is attached to a shaft, at the end of which is another vaned wheel known as the compressor wheel. The compressor wheel spins in its own housing, and compresses the inlet air on the way to the inlet manifold.

3 Boost pressure (the pressure in the inlet manifold) is limited by a wastegate, which diverts the exhaust gas away from the turbine wheel in response to a pressure-sensitive actuator. The turbocharger incorporates a variable intake nozzle to improve boost pressure at low engine speeds.

4 The turbo shaft is pressure-lubricated by an oil feed pipe from the main oil gallery. The shaft 'floats' on a cushion of oil. A drain pipe returns the oil to the sump.

Precautions

5 The turbocharger operates at extremely high speeds and temperatures. Certain precautions must be observed, to avoid premature failure of the turbo, or injury to the operator.

- Do not operate the turbo with any of its parts exposed, or with any of its hoses removed. Foreign objects falling onto the rotating vanes could cause excessive damage, and (if ejected) personal injury.
- Do not race the engine immediately after start-up, especially if it is cold. Give the oil a few seconds to circulate.
- Always allow the engine to return to idle speed before switching it off – do not blip the throttle and switch off, as this will leave the turbo spinning without lubrication.
- Allow the engine to idle for several minutes before switching off after a high-speed run.
- Observe the recommended intervals for oil and filter changing, and use a reputable oil of the specified quality. Neglect of oil changing, or use of inferior oil, can cause carbon formation on the turbo shaft, leading to subsequent failure.

17 Turbocharger – removal, inspection and refitting

Removal

1.4 litre engine

1 Remove the inlet air resonator as described in Section 4.

2 Remove the three upper screws securing the turbo heat shield, and the two bolts inside the circular cut-outs at the front. **Note:** *Do not remove the two screws either side of the circular cut-outs, as this will damage the heat shield.* Lift off the heat shield.

3 Remove the two bolts securing the exhaust manifold heat shield, and take off the shield.

4 Release the hose clips, and remove the air duct from the airflow sensor, air cleaner and turbocharger inlet.

5 Undo the oil supply pipe banjo bolts and recover the sealing washers **(see illustrations)**.

6 Slacken the retaining clip and disconnect the oil return pipe from the turbocharger **(see illustration)**.

7 Remove the four nuts/bolts securing the turbocharger to the catalytic converter.

8 Remove the two pairs of nuts securing the turbocharger to the exhaust manifold **(see illustrations)**, and remove the unit.

1.6 litre engine

9 Place a sheet of thick cardboard over the rear of the radiator to protect it from accidental damage.

17.5a Undo the turbocharger oil supply pipe banjo bolts from the cylinder block ...

17.5b ... and the turbocharger (1.4 litre model)

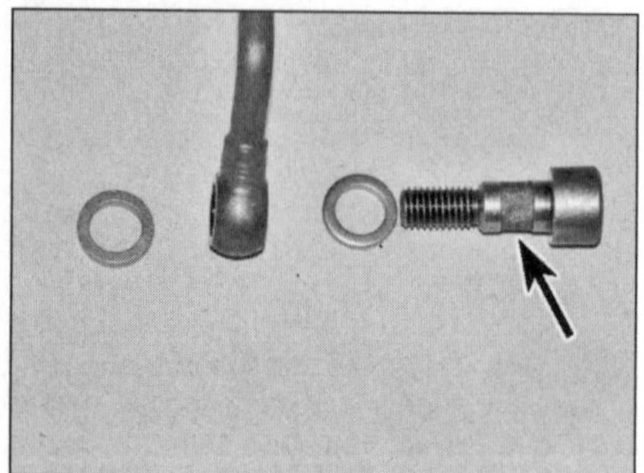

17.5c Note the filter incorporated into the banjo bolt

17.6 Slacken the oil return hose clip

10 Loosen the clips and disconnect the air hose from the intercooler and inlet manifold air duct.

11 Loosen the clips and disconnect the air hose from the intercooler and turbocharger air outlet pipe.

12 Undo the screws and remove the front heat shield from the turbocharger **(see illustration)**.

13 Unbolt the turbocharger air outlet pipe from the turbocharger flange, and remove the pipe.

14 Remove the turbocharger rear heat shield.

15 Unscrew the oil supply pipe banjo bolts and remove the pipe from the turbocharger and cylinder block. Recover the sealing washers.

16 Loosen the clips and remove the oil return hose from the turbocharger and cylinder block.

17 Disconnect the vacuum hose from the turbocharger wastegate capsule.

18 Unbolt the intercooler inlet pipe from the catalytic converter and tie it to one side.

19 Unscrew the bolt securing the catalytic converter to the front of the cylinder block.

20 Note the position of the clamp securing the catalytic converter to the turbocharger as a reference for refitting, then loosen the clamp and move the catalytic converter to one side.

21 Unscrew the four nuts, and remove the turbocharger from the exhaust manifold **(see illustration)**.

Inspection

22 With the turbocharger removed, inspect the housing for cracks or other visible damage.

23 Spin the turbine or the compressor wheel, to verify that the shaft is intact and to feel for excessive shake or roughness. Some play is normal, since in use the shaft is 'floating' on a film of oil. Check that the wheel vanes are undamaged.

24 If oil contamination of the exhaust or induction passages is apparent, it is likely that turbo shaft oil seals have failed.

25 No DIY repair of the turbo is possible, and none of the internal or external parts are available separately. If the turbocharger is suspect in any way, a complete new (or reconditioned) unit must be obtained.

Refitting

26 Refitting is a reverse of the removal procedure, bearing in mind the following points:

- a) *Renew the turbocharger retaining nuts and gaskets.*
- b) *If a new turbocharger is being fitted, follow the fitting instructions precisely. Due to the high failure rate of the turbocharger on the 1.6 litre engine most aftermarket suppliers will require the renewal of the oil supply pipe, the banjo bolts, the oil pump pick-up pipe and the oil return pipe. Additionally several oil and filter changes may be required.*

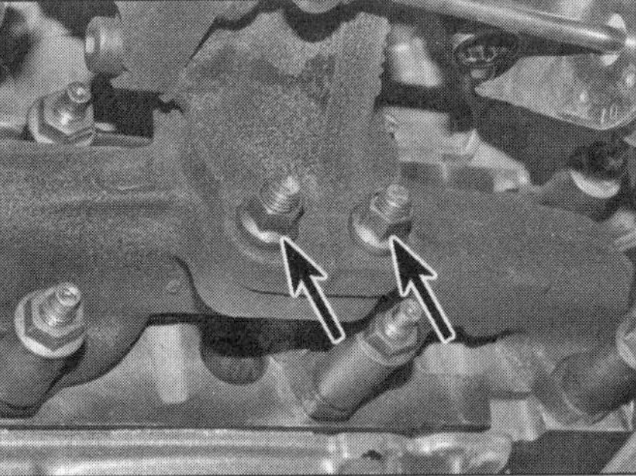

17.8a Undo the lower nuts ...

17.8b ... and upper nuts securing the turbocharger

17.12 Turbocharger heat shields (1.6 litre model)

17.21 Unscrew the support bracket bolt (arrowed), then undo the 3 nuts (arrowed – one hidden) and remove the turbocharger

- c) *If you are refitting the old turbocharger clean or renew the filter in the oil feed pipe.*
- d) *Prime the turbocharger by injecting clean engine oil through the oil feed pipe union before reconnecting the union.*
- e) *When connecting the oil feed pipe at the block, ensure there is a clearance of 65 mm between the pipe and the wastegate. At the top end of the pipe, there must be a clearance of 15 mm between the pipe and the turbocharger body.*

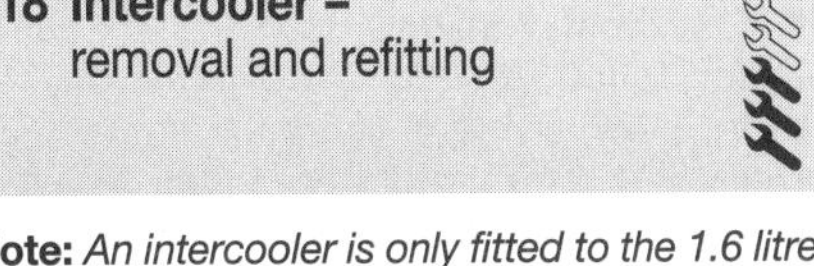

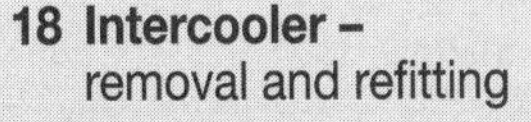

18 Intercooler – removal and refitting

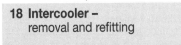

Note: *An intercooler is only fitted to the 1.6 litre engine.*

18.1 Intercooler (viewed with front bumper removed)

Removal

1 The intercooler is located behind the front bumper, in front of the air conditioning condenser **(see illustration)**. It incorporates two lower support legs which locate in slots on the front of the radiator, and, additionally, it has two upper brackets which extend around the air conditioning condenser with securing bolts on the radiator. First apply the handbrake, then jack up the front of the vehicle and support it on axle stands (see *Jacking and vehicle support*).

2 Remove the front bumper as described in Chapter 11, Section 6.

3 Undo the screws and remove the engine undershield (if fitted), at the same time releasing the rear washer hose.

4 Use cable-ties on the radiator grille panel opening to form two support straps around the condenser, radiator and cooling fan motor/shroud, so that when their mountings are released, the units will be approximately 10 cm below their original position.

5 Release the rear washer hose from the clips on the radiator mounting bracket.

6 Unscrew the radiator support bracket upper mounting bolts, lower the radiator, condenser and shroud into the support straps, and remove the bracket. Take care not to strain the refrigerant pipes connected to the condenser.

7 Loosen the clips and disconnect the inlet and outlet hoses from the intercooler **(see illustration)**.

8 Unscrew the intercooler mounting bolts and slide the unit upwards to remove it.

18.7 Intercooler outlet hose

9 Unbolt the air deflectors from the intercooler.

Refitting

10 Refitting is a reversal of removal.

19 Exhaust system – general information and component renewal

Caution: Any work on the exhaust system should only be attempted once the system is completely cool – this may take several hours, especially in the case of the forward sections, such as the catalytic converter.

General information

1 The exhaust system consists of four sections (after the turbocharger): a catalytic converter, a flexible section, a centre section, and a rear silencer. **Note:** *On the original factory-fitted system the centre section and the rear silencer are a single item. On later models, the flexible section and catalytic converter are one-piece.*

2 The catalytic converter is supported by two engine-mounted brackets, but the rest of the system is suspended on rubber mountings.

3 Each exhaust section can be removed individually, or alternatively, the complete system can be removed as a unit. Even if only one part of the system needs attention, it is often easier to remove the whole system and separate the sections on the floor.

Removal

4 To remove the system or part of the system, first jack up the front or rear of the car, and support it on axle stands (see *Jacking and vehicle support*). Alternatively, position the car over an inspection pit, or on car ramps.

Catalytic converter

5 To prevent damage to the exhaust flexible section, support it by attaching a pair of splints either side (two scrap strips of wood, plant canes, etc) using some cable-ties. If a new flexible section is also being fitted, this precaution only applies to the new section of exhaust. On later models with a one-piece converter/flexible section, cut the catalytic converter pipe near the flexible section to leave a 10 mm stub; the new converter can then be connected to the flexible section with a standard clamp.

6 Remove the three upper screws securing the turbo heat shield, and the two bolts inside the circular cut-outs at the front. **Note:** *Do not remove the two screws either side of the circular cut-outs, as this will damage the heat shield.* Lift off the heat shield.

7 Unscrew the nut from the clamp at the front of the flexible section – a new nut should be used when refitting.

8 Undo the two catalytic converter mounting bolts from the brackets on the front of the engine.

9 Remove the four nuts/bolts securing the converter to the turbocharger, and lower the converter carefully from the engine compartment, separating it from the flexible section as it is removed.

Flexible section

10 To prevent damage to the exhaust flexible section, support it by attaching a pair of splints either side (two scrap strips of wood, plant canes, etc) using some cable-ties. If a new flexible section is being fitted, this precaution only applies to the new section of exhaust. On later models with a one-piece converter/flexible section, cut the catalytic converter pipe near the flexible section to leave a 10 mm stub; the converter can then be connected to the new flexible section with a standard clamp.

11 Unscrew the nut from the clamp at the front of the flexible section – a new nut should be used when refitting.

12 Unhook the flexible section's rubber mounting from the hanger on the car floor.

13 Unscrew the two nuts from the centre section front flange, and remove the flexible section from under the car.

Centre section

14 To prevent damage to the exhaust flexible section, support it by attaching a pair of splints either side (two scrap strips of wood, plant canes, etc) using some cable-ties. If a new flexible section is also being fitted, this precaution only applies to the new section of exhaust.

15 Unscrew the nuts securing the centre section front flange to the flexible section, and separate the joint.

16 Even if just the centre section is being removed, it still has to be separated from the rear silencer. Unbolt the clamp where the centre section joins the silencer, and separate the pipes (bear in mind that a corroded rear silencer may be damaged during removal – see paragraph 19).

17 Unhook the centre section's rubber mounting, and remove it from under the car.

Rear silencer

18 If the original factory system is still in use it will be necessary to cut the centre pipe at the appropriate point to fit the new rear silencer. Offer up the new silencer to the exhaust pipe and mark the cutting point.

19 Unbolt the clamp securing the silencer to the centre section, and separate the pipes. Usually, this will require some effort – the most successful method involves twisting the silencer from side to side, to break the joint. Unfortunately, if the pipe at the rear of the centre section has suffered from corrosion, it's very likely that the centre section will be damaged beyond repair in removing the silencer. A less-destructive method of removal involves heating the two pipes, but this carries the risk of damaging the underbody components, and even a risk of fire from the fuel tank and lines.

20 Unhook the silencer rubber mountings, and remove it from under the car.

Heat shields

21 The heat shields are secured to the underside of the body by special nuts. Each shield can be removed separately, but note that they may overlap, making it necessary to loosen another section first. If a shield is being removed to gain access to a component located behind it, it may prove sufficient in some cases to remove the retaining nuts and/or bolts, and simply lower the shield, without disturbing the exhaust system. Otherwise, remove the exhaust section as described earlier.

Refitting

22 In all cases, refitting is a reversal of removal, but note the following points:

a) *Always use new gaskets, nuts and clamps (as applicable), and coat all threads with copper grease. Make sure any new clamps are the same size as the original – overtightening a clamp which is too big will not seal the joint.*
b) *On a sleeved joint (such as that between the centre section and rear silencer), use a smear of exhaust jointing paste to achieve a gas-tight seal.*
c) *If any of the exhaust mounting rubbers are in poor condition, fit new ones.*
d) *Make sure that the exhaust is suspended properly on its mountings, and will not come into contact with the floor or any suspension parts. The rear silencer especially must be aligned correctly before tightening the clamp nuts.*
e) *Tighten all nuts/bolts to the specified torque, where given.*

Chapter 4 Part C: Emission control systems

Contents

Degrees of difficulty

Easy, suitable for novice with little experience 	**Fairly easy,** suitable for beginner with some experience 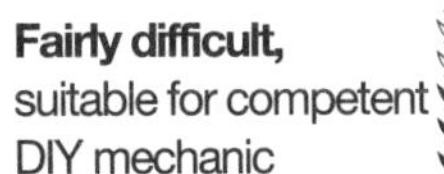	**Fairly difficult,** suitable for competent DIY mechanic	**Difficult,** suitable for experienced DIY mechanic	**Very difficult,** suitable for expert DIY or professional 

Specifications

Torque wrench settings	**Nm**	**lbf ft**
Petrol engines		
Oxygen (lambda) sensors	47	35
Diesel engines		
EGR valve mounting bolts:		
1.4 litre engine	10	7
1.6 litre engine	8	6
EGR solenoid valve mounting bolts (1.4 litre engine)	11	8

1 General information and precautions

Petrol models

Crankcase emission control

1 To reduce the emission of unburned hydrocarbons from the crankcase into the atmosphere, the engine is sealed and the blow-by gases and oil vapour are drawn from inside the crankcase, through an oil separator and regulating (PCV – positive crankcase ventilation) valve, into the inlet manifold to be burned by the engine during normal combustion.

2 Under all conditions the gases are forced out of the crankcase by the (relatively) higher crankcase pressure.

Exhaust emission control

3 To minimise the amount of pollutants which escape into the atmosphere, all models are fitted with a catalytic converter in the exhaust system. The system is of the closed-loop type, in which an oxygen (lambda) sensor in the exhaust manifold provides the fuel injection/ignition system powertrain control module (PCM) with constant feedback, enabling the PCM to adjust the mixture to provide the best possible conditions for the converter to operate.

4 The oxygen sensor has a heating element built-in that is controlled by the PCM through a relay to quickly bring the sensor's tip to an efficient operating temperature. The sensor's tip is sensitive to oxygen and sends the PCM a varying voltage depending on the amount of oxygen in the exhaust gases; if the inlet air/fuel mixture is too rich, the exhaust gases are low in oxygen so the sensor sends a low-voltage signal, the voltage rising as the mixture weakens and the amount of oxygen rises in the exhaust gases.

5 Peak conversion efficiency of all major pollutants occurs if the inlet air/fuel mixture is maintained at the chemically-correct ratio for the complete combustion of petrol of 14.7 parts (by weight) of air to 1 part of fuel (the 'stoichiometric' ratio). The sensor output voltage alters in a large step at this point, the PCM using the signal change as a reference point and correcting the inlet air/fuel mixture accordingly by altering the fuel injector pulse width.

6 A second sensor is fitted downstream of the catalytic converter, to monitor the converter's efficiency, and to fine-tune the information being sent back to the PCM, so that emissions are kept even more tightly under control.

Evaporative emission control

7 To minimise the escape into the atmosphere of unburned hydrocarbons, an evaporative emissions control system is also fitted to all models. The fuel tank filler cap is sealed, and a charcoal canister is mounted on the side of the fuel tank. The canister collects the petrol vapours generated in the tank when the car is parked, and stores them until they can be cleared from the canister (under the control of the fuel injection/ignition system PCM) via the purge valve into the inlet tract to be burned by the engine during normal combustion. The purge (or EVAP) valve is located on the inlet manifold.

8 To ensure that the engine runs correctly when it is cold and/or idling and to protect the catalytic converter from the effects of an over-rich mixture, the EVAP valve is not opened by the PCM until the engine has warmed-up, and the engine is under load; the valve solenoid is then modulated on and off to allow the stored vapour to pass into the inlet tract.

Diesel models

Crankcase emission control

9 To reduce the emission of unburned hydrocarbons from the crankcase into the atmosphere, the engine is sealed and the blow-by gases and oil vapour are drawn from inside the crankcase, through an oil separator and regulating (PCV – positive crankcase ventilation) valve, into the inlet manifold to be burned by the engine during normal combustion.

Exhaust emission control

10 To minimise the level of exhaust pollutants released into the atmosphere, a catalytic converter is fitted in the exhaust system of all models.

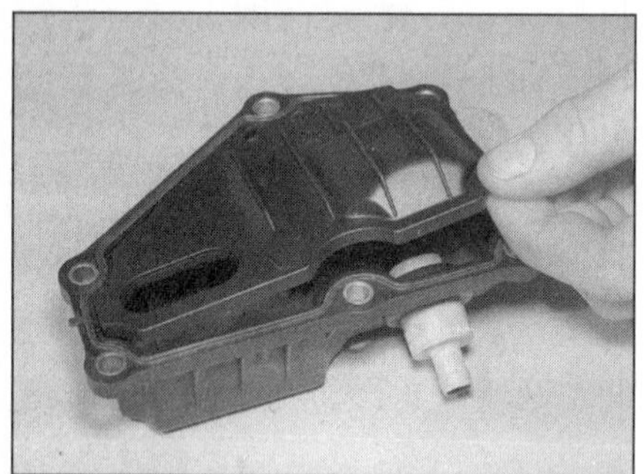
2.1 Always fit a new gasket if the oil separator housing is removed

11 The catalytic converter consists of a canister containing a fine mesh impregnated with a catalyst material, over which the hot exhaust gases pass. The catalyst speeds up the oxidation of harmful carbon monoxide, unburnt hydrocarbons and soot, effectively reducing the quantity of harmful products released into the atmosphere via the exhaust gases.

Exhaust gas recirculation system

12 This system is designed to recirculate small quantities of exhaust gas into the inlet tract, and therefore into the combustion process. This process reduces the level of oxides of nitrogen present in the final exhaust gas which is released into the atmosphere.

13 The volume of exhaust gas recirculated is controlled by the system electronic control unit.

14 On 1.4 litre models, a vacuum-operated valve is fitted to the exhaust manifold, to regulate the quantity of exhaust gas recirculated, and the valve is operated by the vacuum supplied by a solenoid valve. On 1.6 litre models, the EGR valve is mounted on the rear of the cylinder head, and is connected by an internal channel to the exhaust manifold on the front of the engine. It incorporates a stepper motor to regulate the quantity of exhaust gas recirculated, and the valve is controlled directly by the engine management PCM.

Catalytic converter precautions

15 For long life and satisfactory operation of the catalytic converter, certain precautions must be observed. These are as follows.

16 For petrol engines, only use unleaded fuel. Leaded fuel will damage the catalyst and the oxygen sensor.

17 Do not run the engine for long periods if it is misfiring. Unburnt fuel entering the catalytic converter can cause it to overheat, resulting in permanent damage. For the same reason, do not try to start the engine by pushing or towing the car, nor crank it on the starter motor for long periods.

18 Do not strike or drop the catalytic converter. The ceramic honeycomb which forms part of its internal structure may be damaged.

19 Always renew seals and gaskets upstream of the catalytic converter (between the engine and converter) whenever they are disturbed.

2.3 The charcoal canister is mounted on the side of the fuel tank

2 Petrol engine emission control systems – testing and component renewal

Crankcase emission control

1 The components of this system require no attention, other than to check that the hoses are clear and undamaged at regular intervals. The system contains a foam filter in the air cleaner, which should be checked regularly – see Chapter 1A, Section 18. If the hoses are blocked, the oil separator housing should be removed from the front of the cylinder block and cleaned (remove the inlet manifold as described in Chapter 4A, Section 15 first); when refitting the housing, fit a new gasket **(see illustration)**.

Evaporative emission control

Testing

2 If the system is thought to be faulty, disconnect the hoses from the charcoal canister and purge control (EVAP) valve and check that they are clear by blowing through them. If the purge control valve or charcoal canister are thought to be faulty, they must be renewed.

Charcoal canister renewal

3 The charcoal canister is located under the rear of the car, in a recess in the side of the fuel tank **(see illustration)**. Referring to Chapter 4A, Section 8, remove the fuel tank as far as necessary for access to the canister.

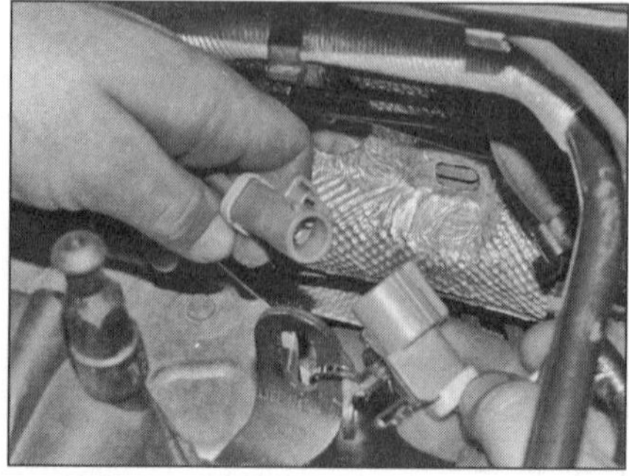
2.14 Disconnect the oxygen sensor wiring connector

2.7 Disconnect the EVAP valve wiring plug

4 Disconnect the hoses and back-pressure valve from the canister, then unscrew the mounting bolt and remove it from the recess in the tank.

5 Fit the new canister using a reversal of the removal procedure.

EVAP valve renewal

6 The EVAP valve is mounted on the inlet manifold.

7 To renew the valve, first disconnect the wiring plug **(see illustration)**.

8 Disconnect the hoses from the valve noting their locations, then detach the valve from its mounting bracket.

9 Fit the new valve using a reversal of the removal procedure.

Exhaust emission control

Testing

10 The performance of the catalytic converter can be checked only by measuring the exhaust gases using a good-quality, carefully-calibrated exhaust gas analyser.

11 If the CO level at the tailpipe is too high, the car should be taken to a Ford dealer so that the complete fuel injection and ignition systems, including the oxygen sensor, can be thoroughly checked using the special diagnostic equipment. Once these have been checked and are known to be free from faults, the fault must be in the catalytic converter, which must be renewed.

Catalytic converter renewal

12 The converter is part of the exhaust manifold – refer to Chapter 4A, Section 16 for details.

Oxygen (lambda) sensor renewal

Note: *The oxygen sensor is delicate and will not work if it is dropped or knocked, if its power supply is disrupted, or if any cleaning materials are used on it.*

13 Remove the air cleaner as described in Chapter 4A, Section 5, and the ignition coil as described in Chapter 5B, Section 3.

14 Trace the wiring back from the oxygen sensor to the connector and disconnect the wiring – this is typically behind the ignition coil location **(see illustration)**.

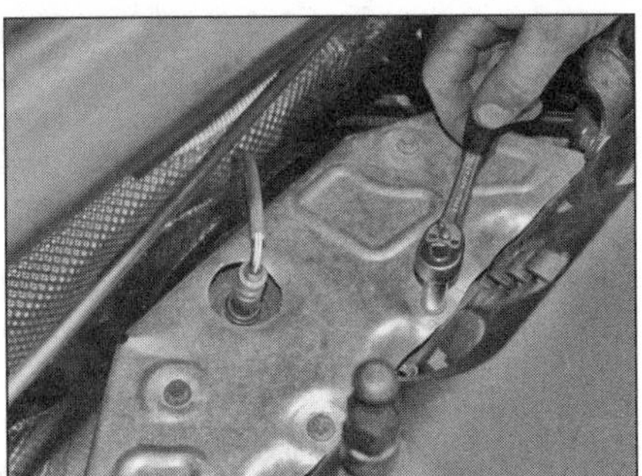
2.15a Remove the four bolts ...

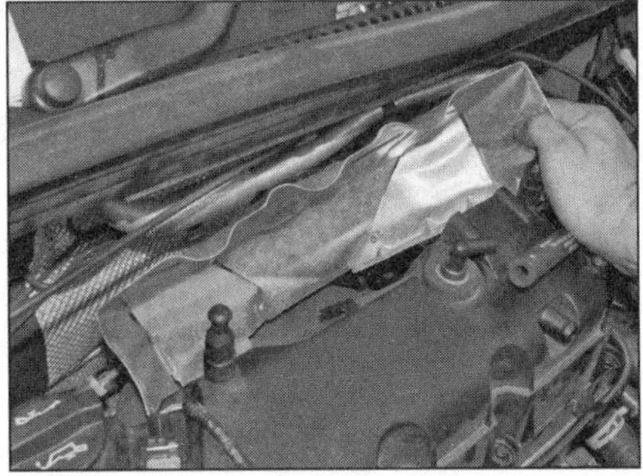
2.15b ... and take off the exhaust manifold heat shield

2.16 The oxygen sensor can now be unscrewed from the manifold

15 Remove the manifold shroud components as necessary for access **(see illustrations)**.

16 Unscrew the sensor and remove it from the exhaust manifold **(see illustration)**. A special slotted socket may be needed (if a spanner cannot be used), to make allowance for the sensor's wiring.

17 Clean the threads of the sensor and the threads in the exhaust manifold.

18 Insert the sensor in the manifold and tighten to the specified torque.

19 Refit the manifold shrouds where removed.

20 Reconnect the wiring, making sure that it is in no danger of contacting the exhaust manifold.

Converter monitor sensor renewal

21 This sensor is very similar to the oxygen sensor, and renewal details are virtually identical. Since the sensor is fitted further down the exhaust manifold than the oxygen sensor, access to the sensor itself will be easier from below **(see illustrations)**.

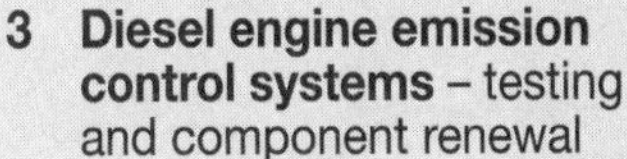

3 Diesel engine emission control systems – testing and component renewal

Crankcase emission control

1 The components of this system require no attention, other than to check that the hoses are clear and undamaged at regular intervals.

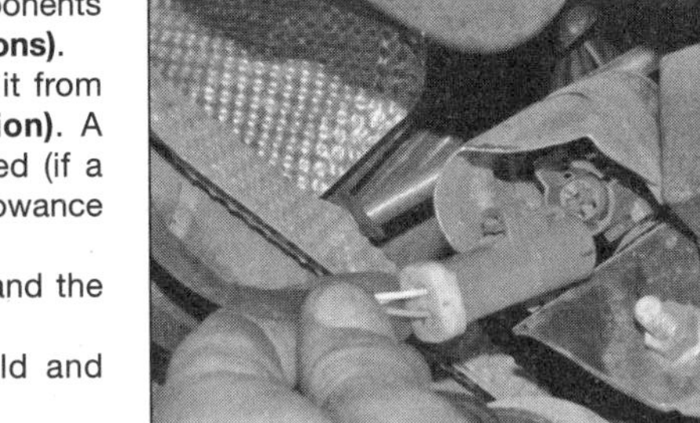
2.21a Disconnecting the converter monitor sensor wiring plug

2.21b Converter monitor sensor

Exhaust emission control

Testing

2 The performance of the catalytic converter can be checked only by measuring the exhaust gases using a good-quality, carefully-calibrated exhaust gas analyser.

3 Before assuming that the catalytic converter is faulty, it is worth checking the problem is not due to a faulty injector. Refer to your Ford dealer for further information.

Catalytic converter renewal

4 Refer to Chapter 4B, Section 19.

Exhaust gas recirculation

Testing

5 Testing of the system should be entrusted to a Ford dealer.

EGR valve renewal (1.4 litre engine)

6 Remove the air cleaner as described in Chapter 4B, Section 4, and the fuel filter as described in Chapter 1B, Section 17.

7 Disconnect the vacuum pipe from the valve.

8 Remove the two screws securing the EGR pipe elbow **(see illustration)**.

9 Remove the EGR pipe clamp, and the single bolt securing the pipe to the engine. Take off the pipe, complete with the valve. Recover the O-ring from the pipe end **(see illustrations)**.

10 Undo the two bolts securing the EGR valve, and take it off. Recover the gasket – a new one must be used when refitting.

11 Refitting is a reversal of removal. Use a new gasket, and tighten the valve mounting bolts to the specified torque.

3.8 The EGR pipe is secured to the manifold by two screws ...

3.9a ... and to the cylinder block by one bolt

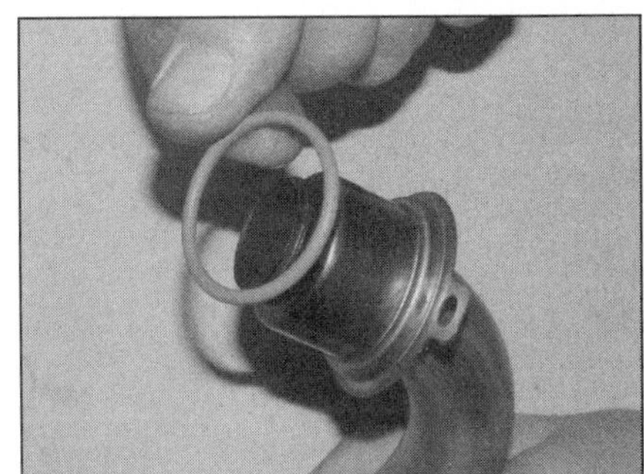
3.9b A new EGR pipe-to-manifold O-ring seal must be fitted

3.15 EGR solenoid valve retaining bolts (arrowed)

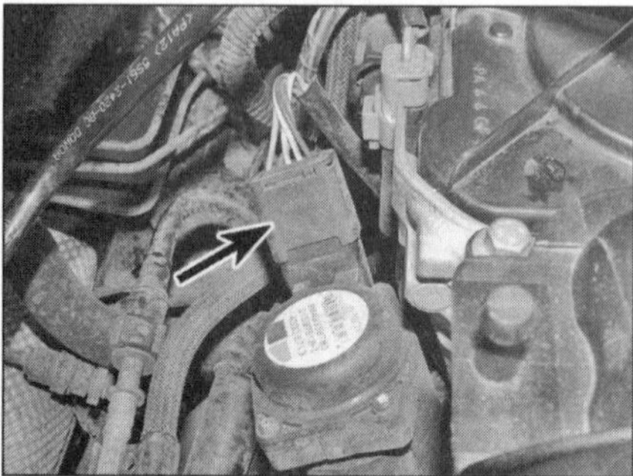
3.25 Disconnect the wiring from the EGR valve (1.6 litre engine)

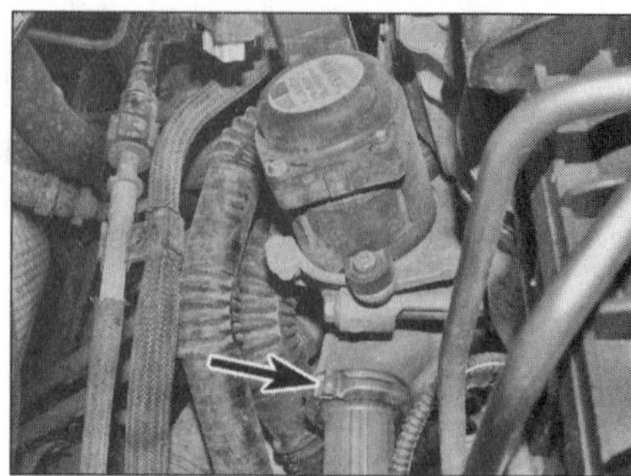
3.27 EGR valve cooler tube connection to the EGR valve (1.6 litre engine)

Solenoid valve renewal (1.4 litre engine)

12 Remove the air cleaner as described in Chapter 4B, Section 4.
13 Remove the clamp securing the EGR cooler to the solenoid valve, and discard it – a new clamp should be used when refitting.
14 Disconnect the solenoid valve wiring plug.
15 Undo the two mounting bolts and take off the valve **(see illustration)**. Recover the gasket – a new one must be used when refitting.
16 Refitting is a reversal of removal. Use a new gasket and clamp, and tighten the valve mounting bolts to the specified torque.

EGR cooler renewal (1.4 litre engine)

17 Drain the cooling system as described in Chapter 1B, Section 25.
18 Remove the air cleaner as described in Chapter 4B, Section 4.
19 Remove the two screws securing the EGR pipe elbow.
20 Release the hose clips, and disconnect the two coolant hoses from the cooler – note their locations for refitting.
21 Remove the clamp securing the EGR cooler to the solenoid valve, and discard it – a new clamp should be used when refitting.
22 Undo the single bolt securing the assembly, then remove the EGR cooler and pipe. If required, the cooler can be separated from the pipe after removing the clamp.
23 Refitting is a reversal of removal. Use new clamps, and on completion, refill the cooling system as described in Chapter 1B, Section 25.

EGR valve renewal (1.6 litre engine)

Note: *If a new EGR valve is being fitted, it must be initialised by a Ford dealer (or suitably-equipped garage) before using the car on the road.*
24 The EGR valve is mounted on the left-hand rear of the cylinder head. First, remove the air cleaner and integral engine top cover as described in Chapter 4B, Section 4.
25 Disconnect the wiring from the EGR valve **(see illustration)**.
26 Release the fuel supply and return lines from the retaining clips.
27 Note the position of the clamp on the EGR valve cooler tube, then remove the clamp and disconnect the tube **(see illustration)**. Discard the clamp as a new one must be used on refitting.
28 Unscrew the mounting bolts and remove the EGR valve from the rear of the cylinder head. Remove and discard the gasket.
29 Using a new gasket, locate the EGR valve on the cylinder head and tighten the mounting bolts finger-tight.
30 Refit the EGR valve tube and tighten the new clamp, making sure it is in the same position as noted during removal.
31 Fully tighten the EGR valve mounting bolts to the specified torque.
32 Reposition the fuel lines in their clips.
33 Reconnect the EGR valve wiring, then refit the air cleaner and integral engine top cover.

EGR valve cooler tube renewal (1.6 litre engine)

34 The EGR valve cooler tube is mounted on the rear of the engine and connects the EGR valve to the inlet manifold. First, remove the air cleaner and integral engine top cover as described in Chapter 4B, Section 4.
35 Note the position of the clamp connecting the cooler tube to the EGR valve, then remove the clamp and discard it as a new one must be used on refitting.
36 Unscrew the bolts securing the upper end of the tube to the inlet manifold flange.
37 Unscrew the mounting bolt and remove the EGR valve cooler tube from the valve and inlet manifold. Recover the O-ring seal.
38 Examine the O-ring seal and obtain a new one if necessary.
39 Refitting is a reversal of removal, but delay tightening the tube mounting bolt until after tightening the clamp and flange bolts.

4 Catalytic converter – general information and precautions

General information

1 The catalytic converter reduces harmful exhaust emissions by chemically converting the more poisonous gases to ones which (in theory at least) are less harmful. The chemical reaction is known as an 'oxidising' reaction, or one where oxygen is 'added'.
2 Inside the converter is a honeycomb structure, made of ceramic material and coated with the precious metals palladium, platinum and rhodium (the 'catalyst' which promotes the chemical reaction). The chemical reaction generates heat, which itself promotes the reaction – therefore, once the car has been driven several miles, the body of the converter will be very hot.
3 The ceramic structure contained within the converter is understandably fragile, and will not withstand rough treatment. Since the converter runs at a high temperature, driving through deep standing water (in flood conditions, for example) is to be avoided, since the thermal stresses imposed when plunging the hot converter into cold water may well cause the ceramic internals to fracture, resulting in a 'blocked' converter – a common cause of failure. A converter which has been damaged in this way can be checked by shaking it (do not strike it) – if a rattling noise is heard, this indicates probable failure.

Precautions

4 The catalytic converter is a reliable and simple device which needs no maintenance in itself, but there are some facts of which an owner should be aware if the converter is to function properly for its full service life:

Petrol models

a) DO NOT use leaded petrol (or lead-replacement petrol, LRP) in a car equipped with a catalytic converter – the lead (or other additives) will coat the precious metals, reducing their converting efficiency and will eventually destroy the converter.
b) Always keep the ignition and fuel systems well-maintained in accordance with the manufacturer's schedule (see Chapter 1A, Section 16).
c) If the engine develops a misfire, do not drive the car at all (or at least as little as possible) until the fault is cured.
d) DO NOT push- or tow-start the car – this will soak the catalytic converter in unburned fuel, causing it to overheat when the engine does start.
e) DO NOT switch off the ignition at high engine speeds – ie, do not 'blip' the throttle immediately before switching off the engine.
f) DO NOT use fuel or engine oil additives –

these may contain substances harmful to the catalytic converter.

g) DO NOT continue to use the car if the engine burns oil to the extent of leaving a visible trail of blue smoke.

h) Remember that the catalytic converter operates at very high temperatures. DO NOT, therefore, park the car in dry undergrowth, over long grass or piles of dead leaves after a long run.

i) As mentioned above, driving through deep water should be avoided if possible. The sudden cooling effect may fracture the ceramic honeycomb, damaging it beyond repair.

j) Remember that the catalytic converter is FRAGILE – do not strike it with tools during servicing work, and take care handling it when removing it from the car for any reason.

k) In some cases, a sulphurous smell (like that of rotten eggs) may be noticed from the exhaust. This is common to many catalytic converter-equipped cars, and has more to do with the sulphur content of the brand of fuel being used than the converter itself.

l) If a substantial loss of power is experienced, remember that this could be due to the converter being blocked. This can occur simply as a result of high mileage, but may be due to the ceramic element having fractured and collapsed internally (see paragraph 3). A new converter is the only cure in this instance.

m) The catalytic converter, used on a well-maintained and well-driven car, should last at least 100 000 miles – if the converter is no longer effective, it must be renewed.

Diesel models

5 The catalytic converter fitted to diesel models is simpler than that fitted to petrol models, but it still needs to be treated with respect to avoid problems:

a) DO NOT use fuel or engine oil additives – these may contain substances harmful to the catalytic converter.

b) DO NOT continue to use the car if the engine burns (engine) oil to the extent of leaving a visible trail of blue smoke.

c) Remember that the catalytic converter operates at very high temperatures. DO NOT, therefore, park the car in dry undergrowth, over long grass or piles of dead leaves after a long run.

d) As mentioned above, driving through deep water should be avoided if possible. The sudden cooling effect will fracture the ceramic honeycomb, damaging it beyond repair.

e) Remember that the catalytic converter is FRAGILE – do not strike it with tools during servicing work, and take care handling it when removing it from the car for any reason.

f) If a substantial loss of power is experienced, remember that this could be due to the converter being blocked. This can occur simply as a result of high mileage, but may be due to the ceramic element having fractured and collapsed internally (see paragraph 3). A new converter is the only cure in this instance.

g) The catalytic converter, used on a well-maintained and well-driven car, should last at least 100 000 miles – if the converter is no longer effective, it must be renewed.

Notes

Chapter 5 Part A:
Starting and charging systems

Contents

Degrees of difficulty

Easy, suitable for novice with little experience	**Fairly easy,** suitable for beginner with some experience	**Fairly difficult,** suitable for competent DIY mechanic	**Difficult,** suitable for experienced DIY mechanic	**Very difficult,** suitable for expert DIY or professional 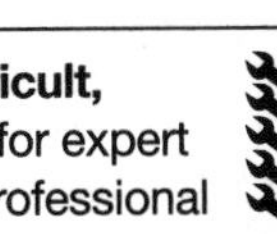

Specifications

System type	12 volt, negative earth

Battery

Type	Lead-acid, low-maintenance or 'maintenance-free'
Charge condition:	
Poor	11.5 volts
Normal	12.0 volts
Good	12.5 volts

Alternator

Type	Bosch, Magneti Marelli, Mitsubishi, or Visteon
Output (typical)	70, 80 or 90 amps
Regulated voltage	13.5 to 14.8 volts

Starter motor

Type	Bosch, Magneti Marelli or Motorcraft

Torque wrench settings	Nm	lbf ft
Air conditioning compressor mounting bolts (diesel engine)	25	18
Alternator bracket-to-engine bolts	30	22
Alternator mounting bolts	45	33
Starter motor mounting bolts:		
Petrol engines	35	26
Diesel engines	25	18

1 General information

The engine electrical system consists mainly of the charging and starting systems. Because of their engine-related functions, these components are covered separately from the body electrical devices such as the lights, instruments, etc (which are covered in Chapter 12). Information on the ignition system is covered in Chapter 5B, Section 1.

The electrical system is of 12 volt negative earth type.

The battery is of the low-maintenance or 'maintenance-free' (sealed for life) type and is charged by the alternator, which is belt-driven from the crankshaft pulley.

The starter motor is of the pre-engaged type incorporating an integral solenoid. On starting, the solenoid moves the drive pinion into engagement with the flywheel ring gear before the starter motor is energised. Once the engine has started, a one-way clutch prevents the motor armature being driven by the engine until the pinion disengages from the flywheel.

Precautions

It is necessary to take extra care when working on the electrical system to avoid damage to semi-conductor devices (diodes and transistors), and to avoid the risk of personal injury. In addition to the precautions given in *Safety first!* at the beginning of this manual, observe the following when working on the system:

- *Always remove rings, watches, etc, before working on the electrical system.* Even with the battery disconnected, capacitive discharge could occur if a component's live terminal is earthed through a metal object. This could cause a shock or nasty burn.
- *Do not reverse the battery connections.* Components such as the alternator, electronic control units, or any other components having semi-conductor circuitry could be irreparably damaged.
- If the engine is being started using jump leads and a slave battery, connect the batteries *positive-to-positive* and *negative-to-negative* (see *Jump starting*). This also applies when connecting a battery charger.
- Never disconnect the battery terminals, the alternator, any electrical wiring or any test instruments when the engine is running.
- Do not allow the engine to turn the alternator when the alternator is not connected.
- Never 'test' for alternator output by 'flashing' the output lead to earth.
- Never use an ohmmeter of the type incorporating a hand-cranked generator for circuit or continuity testing.
- Always ensure that the battery negative lead is disconnected when working on the electrical system.
- Before using electric-arc welding equipment on the car, disconnect the battery, alternator and components such as the fuel injection/ignition electronic control unit to protect them from the risk of damage.

2 Battery - general information, disconnecting and reconnecting

General information

1 Several systems fitted to the car require battery power to be available at all times, either to ensure that their continued operation (such as the clock) or to maintain control unit memories (such as that in the engine management system's ECU/PCM) which would be wiped if the battery were to be disconnected. Whenever the battery is to be disconnected therefore, first note the following, to ensure that there are no unforeseen consequences of this action:

a) *First, on any vehicle with central locking, it is a wise precaution to remove the key from the ignition, and to keep it with you, so that it does not get locked in if the central locking should engage accidentally when the battery is reconnected.*

b) *On cars equipped with an engine management system, the system's ECU will lose the information stored in its memory – referred to by Ford as the 'KAM' (Keep-Alive Memory) – when the battery is disconnected. This includes idling and operating values, and any fault codes detected – in the case of the fault codes, if it is thought likely that the system has developed a fault for which the corresponding code has been logged, the car must be taken to a Ford dealer for the codes to be read, using the special diagnostic equipment necessary for this. Whenever the battery is disconnected, the information relating to idle speed control and other operating values will have to be re-programmed into the unit's memory. The ECU does this by itself, but until then, there may be surging, hesitation, erratic idle and a generally inferior level of performance. To allow the ECU to relearn these values, start the engine and run it as close to idle speed as possible until it reaches its normal operating temperature, then run it for approximately two minutes at 1200 rpm. Next, drive the car as far as necessary – approximately 5 miles of varied driving conditions is usually sufficient – to complete the relearning process.*

c) *If the battery is disconnected while the alarm system is armed or activated, the alarm will remain in the same state when the battery is reconnected. The same applies to the engine immobiliser system.*

d) *If a Ford 'Keycode' audio unit is fitted, and the unit and/or the battery is disconnected, the unit will not function again on reconnection until the correct security code is entered. Details of this procedure, which varies according to the unit and model year, are given in the 'Ford Audio Systems Operating Guide' supplied with the car when new, with the code itself being given in a 'Radio Passport' and/or a 'Keycode Label' at the same time. Ensure you have the correct code before you disconnect the battery.*

2 Devices known as 'memory-savers' (or 'code-savers') can be used to avoid some of the above problems. Precise details vary according to the device used. Typically, it is plugged into the cigarette lighter, and is connected by its own wires to a spare battery; the car's own battery is then disconnected from the electrical system, leaving the 'memory-saver' to pass sufficient current to maintain audio unit security codes and ECU memory values, and also to run permanently-live circuits such as the clock, all the while isolating the battery in the event of a short-circuit occurring while work is carried out.

Warning: Some of these devices allow a considerable amount of current to pass, which can mean that many of the car's systems are still operational when the main battery is disconnected. If a 'memory-saver' is used, ensure that the circuit concerned is actually 'dead' before carrying out any work on it!

Disconnecting

3 Open the bonnet. The battery is located on the left-hand side of the engine compartment, on a platform above the transmission.

4 Remove the ignition key and where possible lower the driver's door window.

5 Loosen the clamp nut, then detach the earth lead from the battery negative (earth) terminal post **(see illustration 4.2)**. This is the terminal to disconnect before working on, or disconnecting, any electrical component on the car. Position the lead away from the battery. To ensure that the earth lead does not make contact with the earth terminal at any time, consider insulating the lead by wrapping it in insulating tape or placing it in a plastic bag.

Reconnecting

6 Ensure that no passengers are in the vehicle and then reconnect the earth (negative) lead to the battery.

7 Where possible reach through the driver's window and turn on the vehicle's sidelights – this will help stabilise the battery voltage and reduce any chance of transient voltage spikes damaging electronic components. Wait two minutes and then start the vehicle.

8 Where necessary enter the radio key code and initialise the power windows – see the general information at the beginning of this section.

Window initialisation

9 Where single touch power windows are

fitted, press the switch to lower the window. With the window fully down hold the switch in the down position for 5 seconds. Raise the window and repeat the procedure with the switch held in the up position.

3 Battery - testing and charging

Testing

Standard and low-maintenance battery

1 If the car covers a small annual mileage, it is worthwhile checking the specific gravity of the electrolyte every three months to determine the state of charge of the battery. Use a hydrometer to make the check and compare the results with the following table. Note that the specific gravity readings assume an electrolyte temperature of 15°C; for every 10°C below 15°C subtract 0.007. For every 10°C above 15°C add 0.007.

	Ambient temperature	
	Above 25°C	**Below 25°C**
Fully-charged	*1.210 to 1.230*	*1.270 to 1.290*
70% charged	*1.170 to 1.190*	*1.230 to 1.250*
Discharged	*1.050 to 1.070*	*1.110 to 1.130*

2 If the battery condition is suspect, first check the specific gravity of electrolyte in each cell. A variation of 0.040 or more between any cells indicates loss of electrolyte or deterioration of the internal plates.

3 If the specific gravity variation is 0.040 or more, the battery should be renewed. If the cell variation is satisfactory but the battery is discharged, it should be charged as described later in this Section.

Maintenance-free battery

4 In cases where a 'sealed for life' maintenance-free battery is fitted, topping-up and testing of the electrolyte in each cell is not possible. The condition of the battery can therefore only be tested using a battery condition indicator or a voltmeter.

All battery types

5 If testing the battery using a voltmeter, connect the voltmeter across the battery and compare the result with those given in the Specifications under 'charge condition'. The test is only accurate if the battery has not been subjected to any kind of charge for the previous six hours. If this is not the case, switch on the headlights for 30 seconds, then wait four to five minutes before testing the battery after switching off the headlights. All other electrical circuits must be switched off, so check that the doors and tailgate are fully shut when making the test.

6 If the voltage reading is less than 12.0 volts, then the battery is discharged.

7 If the battery is to be charged, remove it from the car (Section 4) and charge it as described later in this Section.

4.2 Loosen the clamp nut, and disconnect the battery negative lead ...

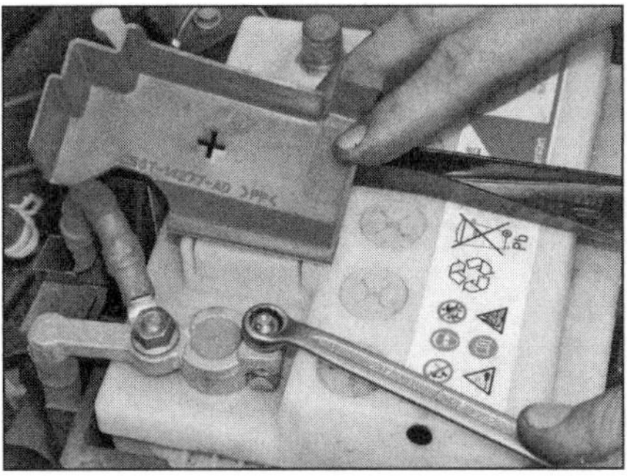

4.3 ... and similarly, the positive lead

Charging

Note: *The following is intended as a guide only. Always refer to the manufacturer's recommendations (often printed on a label attached to the battery), and always disconnect both terminal leads before charging a battery.*

Standard and low-maintenance battery

8 Charge the battery at a rate of 3.5 to 4 amps and continue to charge the battery at this rate until no further rise in specific gravity is noted over a four hour period.

9 Alternatively, a trickle charger charging at the rate of 1.5 amps can safely be used overnight.

10 Specially rapid 'boost' charges which are claimed to restore the power of the battery in 1 to 2 hours are not recommended, as they can cause serious damage to the battery plates through overheating.

11 While charging the battery, note that the temperature of the electrolyte should never exceed 38°C.

Maintenance-free battery

12 This battery type takes considerably longer to fully recharge than the standard type, the time taken being dependent on the extent of discharge, but it can take anything up to three days.

13 A constant voltage type charger is required, to be set, when connected, to 13.9 to 14.9 volts with a charger current below 25 amps. Using this method, the battery should be usable within three hours, giving a voltage reading of 12.5 volts, but this is for a partially-discharged battery and, as mentioned, full charging can take considerably longer.

14 If the battery is to be charged from a fully-discharged state (condition reading less than 12.2 volts), have it recharged by your Ford dealer or local automotive electrician, as the charge rate is higher and constant supervision during charging is necessary.

4 Battery - removal and refitting

Note: *Refer to the warnings given in 'Safety first!' and in Section 1 before starting work.*

Battery

1 The battery is located on the left-hand side of the engine compartment, on a platform above the transmission.

2 Loosen the clamp nut, then detach the earth lead from the battery negative (earth) terminal post **(see illustration)**. This is the terminal to disconnect before working on, or disconnecting, any electrical component on the car. Position the lead away from the battery.

3 Pivot up the plastic cover from the positive terminal, then loosen the positive lead clamp nut **(see illustration)**. Detach the positive lead from the terminal, and position it away from the battery.

4 Undo the two nuts securing the battery top clamp bar, and lift it off **(see illustrations)**. On certain models, two vacuum hoses may be clipped to the clamp bar – if so, detach them before removal.

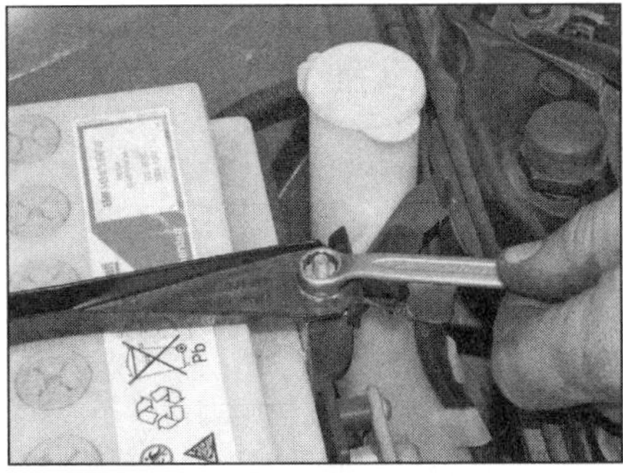

4.4a Undo the two nuts ...

4.4b ... and lift off the battery top clamp

4.5 Lift out the battery

4.9a Working through the headlight aperture, remove the upper ...

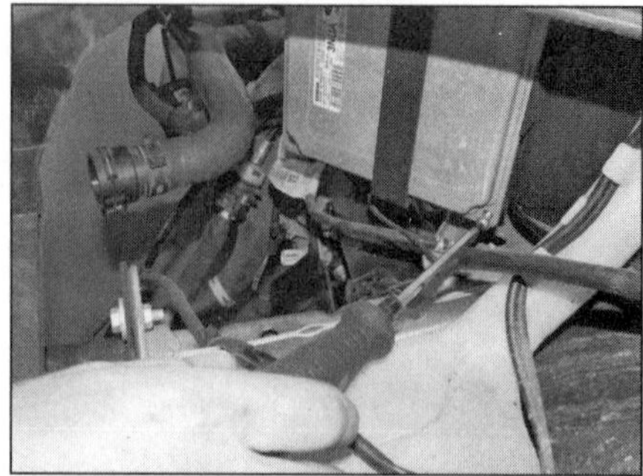
4.9b ... and lower PCM securing screws ...

4.9c ... then unclip and slide the module forwards

4.10a Unclip and lift out the battery junction box ...

4.10b ... if required, the box can be unplugged and removed

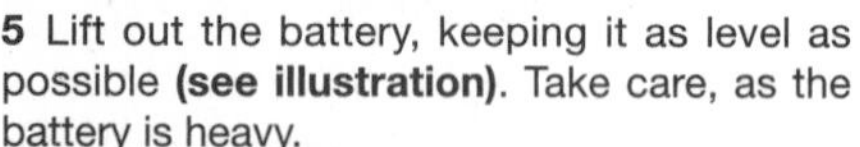
5 Lift out the battery, keeping it as level as possible **(see illustration)**. Take care, as the battery is heavy.

6 Refitting is a reversal of removal. Reconnect the battery negative lead last. Make sure the battery terminals and clamps are clean before refitting, and that the clamp nuts are tightened securely.

Battery tray

7 If required, once the battery has been removed, the battery tray and its support bracket can also be removed, as follows.

Petrol models

8 Remove the left-hand headlight (left as seen from the driver's seat) as described in Chapter 12, Section 7.

9 Remove the two screws securing the powertrain control module (PCM) to its mounting bracket, then slide the module forwards and free it – there is no need to disconnect the wiring connector from it **(see illustrations)**.

All models

10 Unclip and slide the battery junction box upwards out of the slot on the back of the battery tray. There is no need to disconnect any wiring from it, just lay it to one side. If required, however, the box can be unplugged and removed completely, if the main wire to the battery terminal is also disconnected **(see illustrations)**.

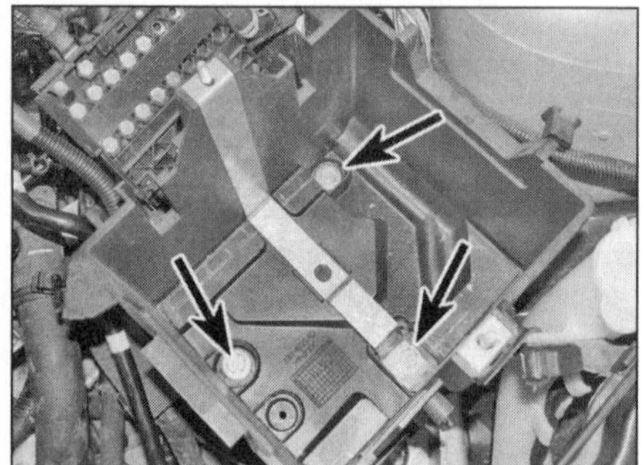
4.11a Remove the three bolts in the base of the battery tray ...

4.11b ... and lift the tray out

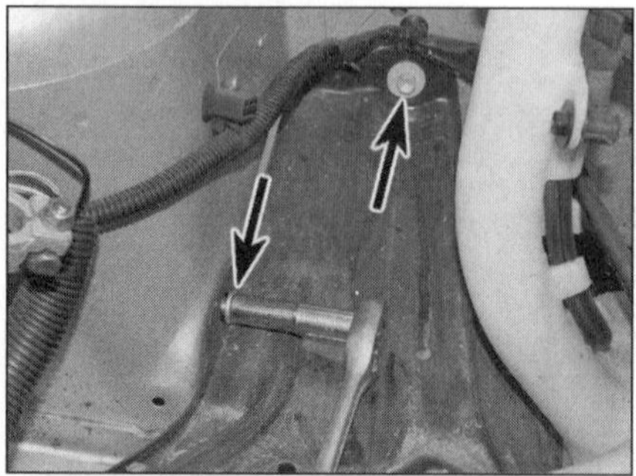
4.12a Two of the battery tray support bracket bolts go into the inner wing ...

4.12b ... while the third is hidden under the junction box wiring

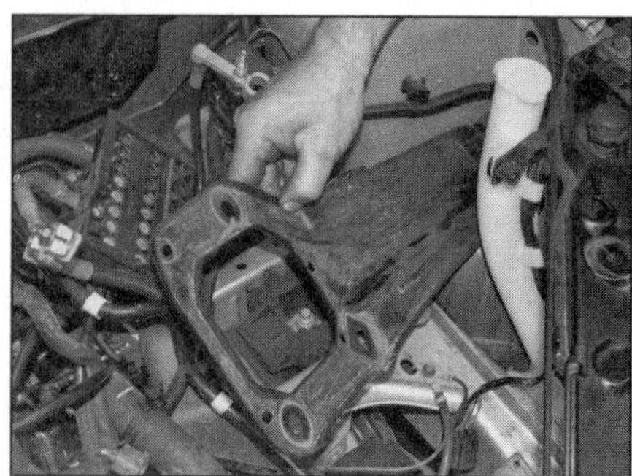
4.12c Removing the battery tray support bracket

11 The battery tray is secured by three bolts at the base. Undo the bolts, and lift the battery tray off its support bracket **(see illustrations)**.

12 The battery tray support bracket is secured by three bolts in total – two into the inner wing, and a third hidden under the junction box wiring. Remove the bolts, and lift out the support bracket **(see illustrations)**.

13 Refitting is a reversal of removal.

5 Electrical fault finding – general information

Refer to Chapter 12, Section 2.

6 Charging system – testing

Note: *Refer to the warnings given in 'Safety first!' and in Section 1 before starting work.*

1 The charging system uses Ford's smart charge technology. The output of the alternator is controlled by the main engine electronic control unit (ECU) in conjunction with the electronics incorporated in the alternator itself. 'Smart' charge has several advantages over a traditional alternator system:

a) *There will be no output from the alternator until the ECU sees an engine running condition. This leaves more battery power available for the starter motor.*
b) *All batteries can be charged more efficiently when cold. By monitoring the air temperature and coolant temperature the ECU can calculate the battery temperature and adjust the alternator output accordingly. This allows for higher charge rates than those associated with a traditional system.*
c) *Idle speed and output can be controlled when the electrical demand is high.*
d) *Heavy electrical consumers, eg, screen heaters can be turned off, or their output reduced when a low battery charge is detected by the ECU.*
e) *In the event of a failure of the smart charge electronics the alternator will operate in the traditional manner.*

2 If the charge warning light fails to illuminate when the ignition is switched on, first check the 7.5 amp fuse in the fusebox (marked with a 'battery' symbol on the back of the glovebox). This is normally fuse number 38 **(see illustration)**. If satisfactory, check the continuity of the wiring between the fuse and the instrument panel. If the wiring is intact and the light fails still fails to illuminate it is more than likely that the LED in the instrument panel is faulty.

3 To check the wiring at the alternator remove the 3 pin multiplug and check for battery voltage at the outer pin. Do this with the ignition on, but the engine not running. If battery voltage is not available check the 3 amp fuse (normally number 28) in the fusebox. If this is intact check for continuity between the fuse and the alternator electrical connector.

4 The other two wires at the multiplug are the control system from the ECU. These can only be tested with an oscilloscope since they are a modulated square wave. However continuity between these wires and the ECU can be checked. Disconnect the battery negative lead, and position the lead away from the battery before checking for continuity.

5 If the ignition warning light illuminates when the engine is running, stop the engine and check that the drivebelt is intact and correctly tensioned (see Chapter 1A, Section 6 or Chapter 1B, Section 7) and that the alternator connections are secure.

6 If the alternator output is suspect even though the warning light functions correctly, the regulated voltage may be checked as follows:

7 Connect a voltmeter across the battery terminals and note the battery voltage. Start the engine.

8 Increase the engine speed to 1500 rpm. The voltmeter should read 2.5 volts above the starting voltage. The reading should be within the range of 14.1 volts to 15.1 volts. The standard output for a 'smart' alternator system is 14.8 volts, but this will vary depending on ambient temperature, electrical demand and battery voltage.

9 Switch on as many electrical accessories (eg, the headlights, heated rear window and heater blower) as possible and increase the engine speed to approximately 2000 rpm. Check that the alternator maintains the regulated voltage between 14.1 and 15.1 volts. Repeat this test at the main (B+) wire at the alternator. This will eliminate a wiring fault between the alternator and battery.

10 If the regulated voltage is not as stated, and all other tests have proved satisfactory, the fault may be due to worn brushes, weak brush springs, a faulty voltage regulator, a faulty diode, a severed phase winding or worn or damaged slip-rings. The alternator should be renewed or taken to an auto-electrician for testing and repair.

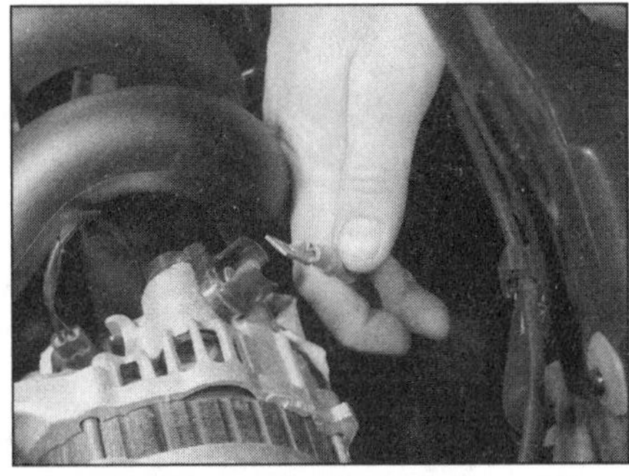

8.5a Disconnecting the battery positive cable from the alternator terminal

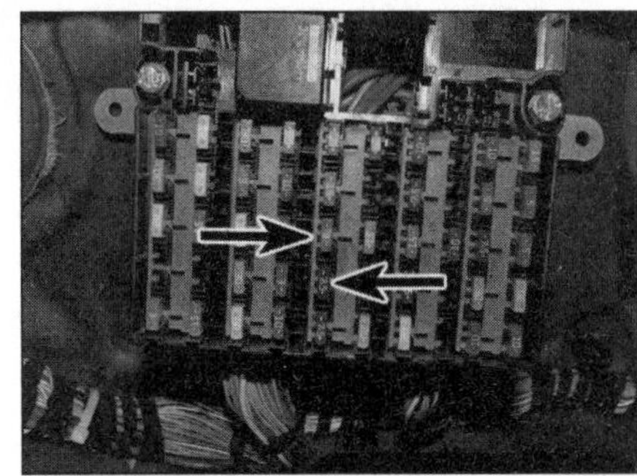

6.2 Typical locations for the alternator fuses

7 Alternator drivebelt – removal, refitting and tensioning

Refer to the procedure given for the auxiliary drivebelt in Chapter 1A, Section 23 or Chapter 1B, Section 22, as applicable.

8 Alternator – removal and refitting

Note: *Refer to the warnings given in 'Safety first!' and in Section 1 before starting work.*

1 Loosen the clamp nut, then detach the earth lead from the battery negative (earth) terminal post. Position the lead well away from the battery.

Petrol engine

Removal

2 Remove the auxiliary drivebelt as described in Chapter 1A, Section 23.

3 Remove the radiator grille as described in Chapter 11, Section 7.

4 Remove the right-hand headlight as described in Chapter 12, Section 7.

5 Prise up the plastic cap and disconnect the alternator battery cable, then disconnect the field wiring multiplug behind it **(see illustrations)**. Note the fitted positions and routing of the wiring.

6 Lift the power steering fluid reservoir off its mounting clips on the inner wing, and place it to one side without disconnecting any hoses.

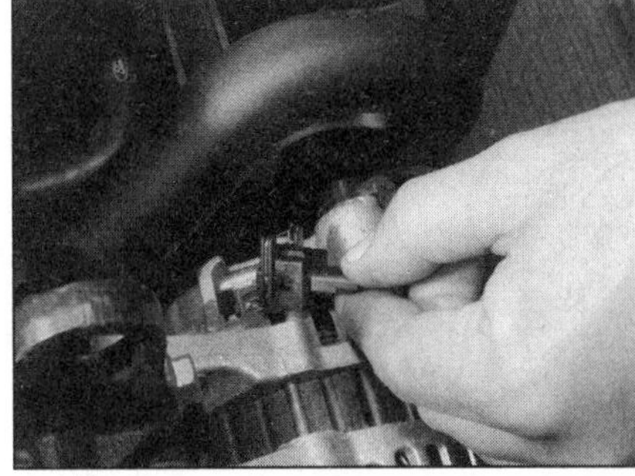

8.5b Disconnecting the field winding wiring

8.8 Alternator lower mounting bolt

8.12 Prise out the cover, then disconnect the alternator wiring and plug

8.14 Alternator left-hand mounting bolts

7 Remove the alternator upper mounting nut and stud, and loosen the upper mounting bolt next to it as far as possible – the bolt cannot be removed at this stage.

8 Support the alternator, remove the alternator lower mounting bolt **(see illustration)**, then twist the alternator so that the upper bolt can be removed, and manoeuvre the alternator out through the headlight aperture.

Refitting

9 Refitting is a reversal of removal, noting the following points:

a) *Fit the upper mounting bolt before offering the alternator in through the headlight aperture.*
b) *Only fit the mounting bolts/stud and nut hand-tight to begin with.*
c) *Tighten the lower mounting bolt to the specified torque, followed by the upper nut and bolt.*
d) *Ensure that the wiring is reconnected correctly, and that the retaining nuts are tight.*
e) *Fit a new auxiliary drivebelt as described in Chapter 1A, Section 23.*

Diesel engine

Removal

10 The alternator is located on the left-hand rear of the engine. First, remove the auxiliary drivebelt as described in Chapter 1B, Section 22.

11 On the 1.6 litre engine, carry out the following:

a) *Loosen the clip and disconnect the intercooler-to-inlet manifold air hose from the inlet air shutoff throttle housing. Position the hose to one side.*
b) *Loosen the clips and remove the intercooler inlet air hose from the turbo air cooler and transfer pipe.*
c) *Unbolt and remove the turbocharger heat shield.*
d) *Unbolt and remove the auxiliary drivebelt tensioner.*

12 Prise up the plastic cap and disconnect the alternator battery cable, then disconnect the field wiring multiplug next to it **(see illustration)**. Note the fitted positions and routing of the wiring.

13 Where applicable, disconnect the wiring plug from the air conditioning compressor, then remove the four mounting bolts and tie the compressor to one side, without disturbing any of the hose connections.

14 Remove the alternator left-hand mounting bolts **(see illustration)**.

15 Support the alternator, then remove the right-hand mounting bolts **(see illustrations)**. On some 1.4 litre models, one of the right-hand bolts is shared with one of the auxiliary drivebelt idler pulleys – if it's the lower one, the idler pulley bolt is hidden under a plastic cover, which must be prised off. Undo the bolts, and remove the alternator from the engine.

Refitting

16 Refitting is a reversal of removal, noting the following points:

a) *Tighten the mounting bolts to the specified torque, including those for the air conditioning compressor, where applicable.*
b) *Ensure that the wiring is reconnected correctly, and that the retaining nuts are tight.*
c) *Refit the auxiliary drivebelt as described in Chapter 1B, Section 22.*

8.15a Alternator right-hand mounting bolt locations ...

8.15b ... one of the bolts will be shared with a drivebelt pulley

9 Alternator – testing and overhaul

If the alternator is thought to be suspect, it should be removed from the car and taken to an auto-electrician for testing. Most auto-electricians will be able to supply and fit brushes at a reasonable cost. However, check on the cost of repairs before proceeding, as it may prove more economical to obtain a new or exchange alternator.

10 Starting system – testing

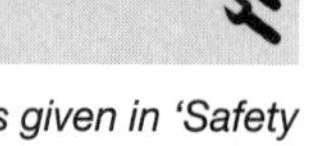

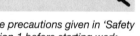

Note: *Refer to the precautions given in 'Safety first!' and in Section 1 before starting work.*

1 If the starter motor fails to operate when the ignition key is turned to the appropriate position, the following possible causes may be to blame.

a) *The battery is faulty.*
b) *The electrical connections between the switch, solenoid, battery and starter motor are somewhere failing to pass the necessary current from the battery through the starter to earth.*
c) *The solenoid is faulty.*
d) *The starter motor is mechanically or electrically defective.*

2 To check the battery, switch on the headlights. If they dim after a few seconds, this indicates that the battery is discharged – recharge (see Section 3) or renew the battery. If the headlights glow brightly, operate the ignition switch and observe the lights. If they dim, then this indicates that current is reaching the starter motor, therefore the fault must lie in the starter motor. If the lights continue to glow brightly (and no clicking sound can be heard from the starter motor solenoid), this indicates that there is a fault in the circuit or solenoid – see

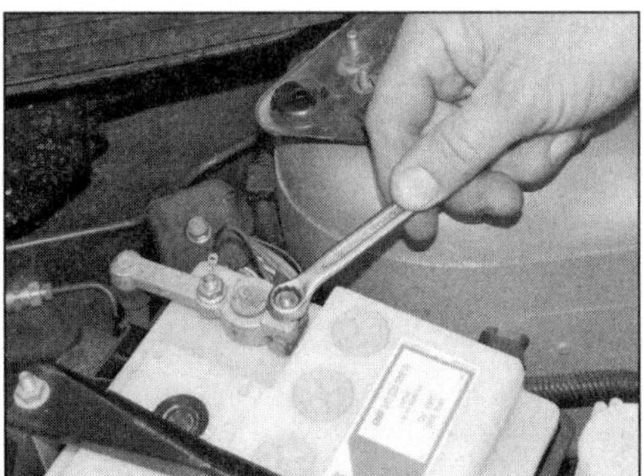

11.1 Disconnect the battery negative lead before starting

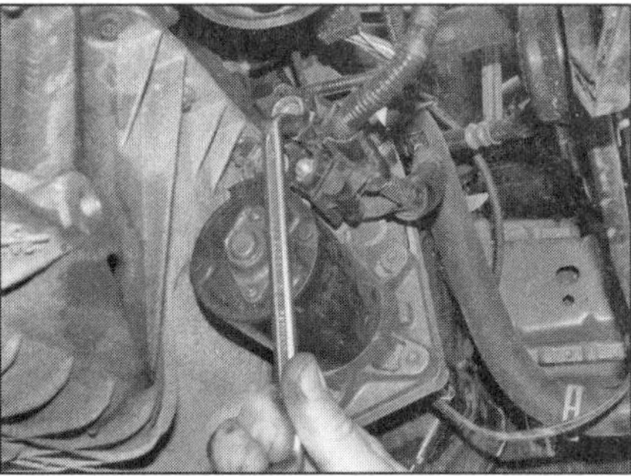

11.3a Unscrew the two nuts ...

11.3b ... and disconnect the starter motor wiring

following paragraphs. If the starter motor turns slowly when operated, but the battery is in good condition, then this indicates that either the starter motor is faulty, or there is considerable resistance somewhere in the circuit.

3 If a fault in the circuit is suspected, disconnect the battery leads (including the earth connection to the body), the starter/solenoid wiring and the engine/transmission earth strap. Thoroughly clean the connections, and reconnect the leads and wiring, then use a voltmeter or test lamp to check that full battery voltage is available at the battery positive lead connection to the solenoid, and that the earth is sound. Smear petroleum jelly around the battery terminals to prevent corrosion – corroded connections are amongst the most frequent causes of electrical system faults.

4 If the battery and all connections are in good condition, check the circuit by disconnecting the wire from the solenoid terminal. Connect a voltmeter or test lamp between the wire end and a good earth (such as the battery negative terminal), and check that the wire is live when the ignition switch is turned to the 'start' position. If it is, then the circuit is sound – if not, the circuit wiring can be checked as described in Chapter 12, Section 2.

5 The solenoid contacts can be checked by connecting a voltmeter or test lamp between the battery positive feed connection on the starter side of the solenoid, and earth. When the ignition switch is turned to the 'start' position, there should be a reading or lighted bulb, as applicable. If there is no reading or lighted bulb, the solenoid is faulty and should be renewed.

6 If the circuit and solenoid are proved sound, the fault must lie in the starter motor. In this event, it may be possible to have the starter motor overhauled by a specialist, but check on the cost of spares before proceeding, as it may prove more economical to obtain a new or exchange motor.

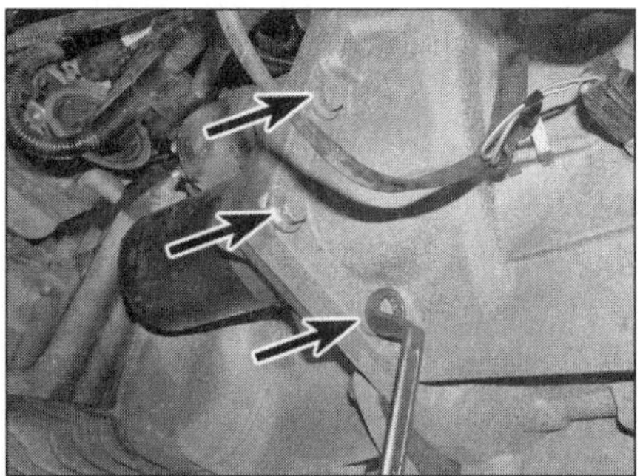

11.4a Unscrew the three bolts ...

11.4b ... and withdraw the starter motor

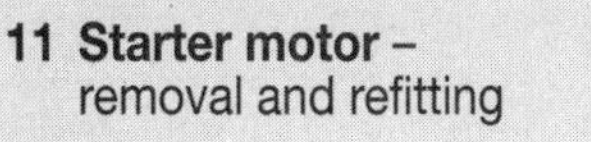

11 Starter motor – removal and refitting

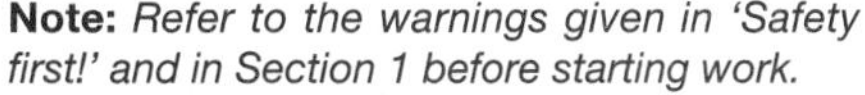

Note: *Refer to the warnings given in 'Safety first!' and in Section 1 before starting work.*

Removal

1 Loosen the clamp nut, then detach the earth lead from the battery negative (earth) terminal. Position the lead away from the battery **(see illustration)**.

Petrol models

2 Apply the handbrake, then jack up the front of the car and support on axle stands (see *Jacking and vehicle support*).

3 Working beneath the left-hand front of the engine, unscrew the two nuts and disconnect the wiring assembly from the starter motor **(see illustration)**. Note the location of each wire, for refitting.

4 Support the starter motor, then unscrew and remove the three starter mounting bolts from the transmission bellhousing, and withdraw the motor **(see illustrations)**.

Diesel models

5 The starter motor is located on the left-hand rear of the engine. First, remove the battery and the battery tray as described on Section 4.

6 Unscrew and remove the two starter motor upper retaining bolts.

7 Apply the handbrake, then jack up the front of the car and support on axle stands (see *Jacking and vehicle support*).

8 Working beneath the front of the engine, unscrew the two nuts and disconnect the wiring from the starter motor. Note the location of each wire, for refitting.

9 Support the starter motor, then unscrew and remove the lower mounting bolt, and withdraw the motor.

Refitting

10 Refitting is a reversal of removal, but tighten the mounting bolts to the specified torque.

12 Starter motor – testing and overhaul

If the starter motor is thought to be suspect, it should be removed from the car and taken to an auto-electrician for testing. Most auto-electricians will be able to supply and fit brushes at a reasonable cost. However, check on the cost of repairs before proceeding as it may prove more economical to obtain a new or exchange motor.

Notes

Chapter 5 Part B:
Ignition system – petrol models

Contents

Degrees of difficulty

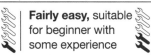

Easy, suitable for novice with little experience	**Fairly easy,** suitable for beginner with some experience	**Fairly difficult,** suitable for competent DIY mechanic	**Difficult,** suitable for experienced DIY mechanic	**Very difficult,** suitable for expert DIY or professional

Specifications

General

System type	Electronic distributorless ignition system (DIS) with ignition module controlled by engine management system (powertrain control module)
Firing order	1-3-4-2
Location of No 1 cylinder	Timing belt end

Ignition system data

Ignition timing	Controlled by the powertrain control module (PCM)
Ignition coil resistances (typical):	
Primary windings	0.4 to 0.6 ohms
Secondary windings	10 500 to 16 500 ohms

Torque wrench settings

	Nm	lbf ft
Ignition coil	6	4
Spark plugs	15	11

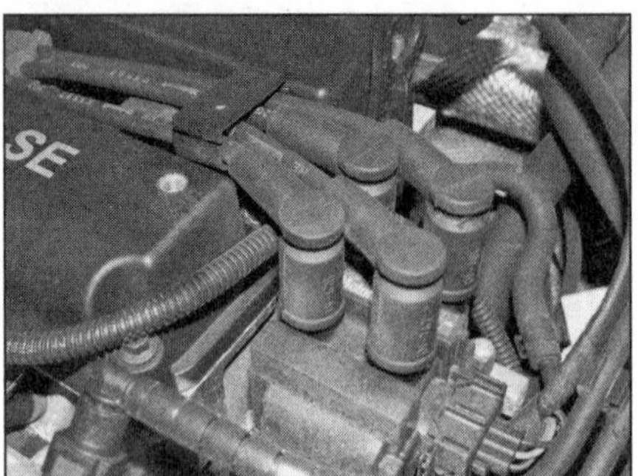

3.1 The ignition coil pack

3.2 Disconnecting the coil wiring plug

3.3 Make sure the HT lead positions are marked on the coil before disconnecting

1 Ignition system – general information and precautions

General information

The ignition system is integrated with the fuel injection system to form a combined engine management system under the control of the powertrain control module (PCM) (see Chapter 4A, Section 1 for further information). The main ignition system components include the ignition switch, the battery, the crankshaft speed/position sensor, the ignition coil, and the spark plugs.

A distributorless ignition system (DIS) is fitted where the main functions of the conventional distributor are superseded by a computerised module within the powertrain control module. The remote ignition coil unit combines a double-ended pair of coils – each time a coil receives an ignition signal, two sparks are produced, one at each end of the secondary windings. One spark goes to a cylinder on its compression stroke and the other goes to the corresponding cylinder on its exhaust stroke. The first will give the correct power stroke, but the second spark will have no effect (a 'wasted spark'), occurring as it does during exhaust conditions.

The information contained in this Chapter concentrates on the ignition-related components of the engine management system. Information covering the fuel, exhaust and emission control components can be found in Chapter 4A and 4C.

Precautions

The following precautions must be observed, to prevent damage to the ignition system components and to reduce risk of personal injury.

a) Do not keep the ignition on for more than 10 seconds if the engine will not start.
b) Ensure that the ignition is switched off before disconnecting any of the ignition wiring.
c) Ensure that the ignition is switched off before connecting or disconnecting any ignition test equipment, such as a timing light.
d) Do not earth the coil primary or secondary circuits.

Warning: Voltages produced by an electronic ignition system are considerably higher than those produced by conventional ignition systems. Extreme care must be taken when working on the system with the ignition switched on. Persons with surgically-implanted cardiac pacemaker devices should keep well clear of the ignition circuits, components and test equipment.

2 Ignition system – testing

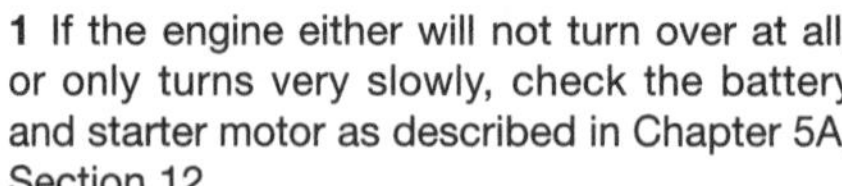

1 If the engine either will not turn over at all, or only turns very slowly, check the battery and starter motor as described in Chapter 5A, Section 12.

2 If the engine turns over at normal speed but will not start, check the HT circuit by connecting a timing light (following the timing light manufacturer's instructions) and turning the engine over on the starter motor; if the light flashes, voltage is reaching the spark plugs, so these should be checked first. If the light does not flash, check the HT leads themselves using the information given in Chapter 1A, Section 16.

3 If there is still no spark, check the coil's primary and secondary winding resistance as described in Section 3; renew the coil if faulty, but be careful to check carefully the wiring connections themselves before doing so, to ensure that the fault is not due to dirty or poorly-fastened connectors.

4 If these checks fail to reveal the cause of the problem, the car should be taken to a suitably-equipped Ford dealer for testing. A wiring block connector is incorporated in the engine management circuit into which a special electronic diagnostic tester can be plugged. The tester will locate the fault quickly and simply, alleviating the need to test all the system components individually which is a time consuming operation that carries a high risk of damaging the PCM. If necessary, the system wiring and wiring connectors can be checked as described in Chapter 12, Section 2.

5 If the engine runs but has an irregular misfire, check the low tension wiring on the ignition coil ensuring that all connections are clean and securely fastened.

6 Check that the coil HT leads are clean and dry. Check the leads themselves and the spark plugs (by substitution, if necessary).

7 Regular misfiring is probably due to a fault in the HT leads or spark plugs. Use a timing light (as described above) to check whether HT voltage is present at all leads.

8 If HT voltage is not present on any particular lead, the fault will be in that lead or in the ignition coil. If HT is present on all leads, the fault will be in the spark plugs; check and renew them if there is any doubt about their condition.

9 If no HT is present, check the coil; its secondary windings may be breaking down under load.

3.4a Unscrew the four mounting bolts ...

3 Electronic ignition HT coil – removal, testing and refitting

Removal

1 The ignition coil is bolted to the coolant outlet elbow on the left-hand end of the cylinder head **(see illustration)**.

2 Make sure the ignition is switched off, then disconnect the main wiring plug from the coil **(see illustration)**.

3 Identify the HT leads for position (mark the leads **and** the coil terminals) then carefully pull them from the terminals on the coil **(see illustration)**.

4 Unscrew the four mounting bolts and remove the ignition coil from the engine compartment. Where applicable, recover the heat shield/mounting plate **(see illustrations)**.

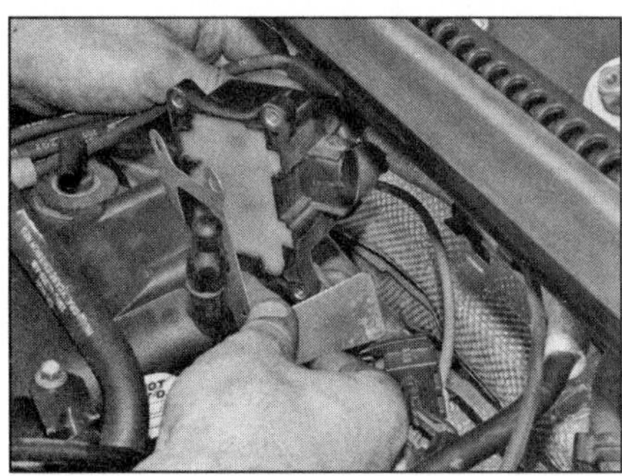

3.4b ... then remove the ignition coil and heat shield/mounting plate from the engine

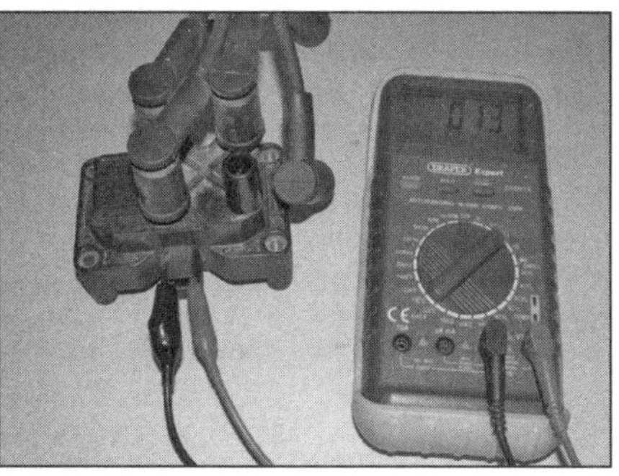

3.5a Checking the coil primary resistance (1.3 ohms) ...

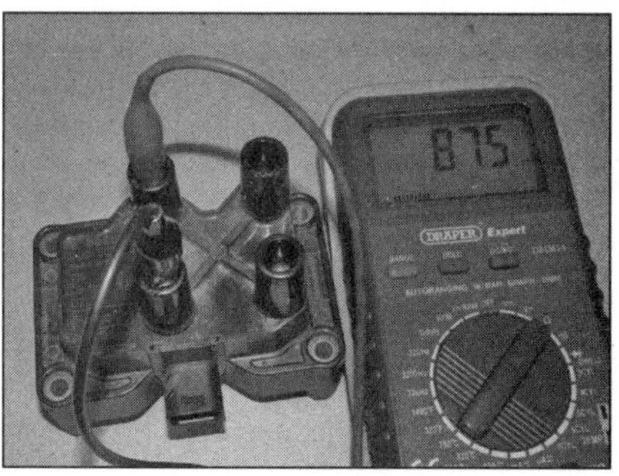

3.5b ... and the secondary (8.75 k ohms)

Testing

5 Using an ohmmeter, measure the resistances of the ignition coil's primary and secondary windings, and compare with the information given in the Specifications **(see illustrations)**. Note that the specification given at the start of the Chapter should only be used as a guide. Our sample coil had a greater primary resistance and lower secondary resistance than that specified, but the ignition system had no faults.

Refitting

6 Refitting is a reversal of removal.

4 Crankshaft position sensor – removal and refitting

Refer to Chapter 4A, Section 14.

5 Ignition timing – checking and adjustment

Due to the nature of the ignition system, the ignition timing is constantly being monitored and adjusted by the engine management PCM, and nominal values cannot be given. Therefore, it is not possible for the home mechanic to check the ignition timing.

The only way in which the ignition timing can be checked is using special electronic test equipment, connected to the engine management system diagnostic connector (refer to Chapter 4A, Section 13). No adjustment of the ignition timing is possible. Should the ignition timing be incorrect, then a fault must be present in the engine management system.

Notes

Chapter 5 Part C: Preheating system – diesel models

Contents

Degrees of difficulty

Easy, suitable for novice with little experience 	**Fairly easy,** suitable for beginner with some experience	**Fairly difficult,** suitable for competent DIY mechanic 	**Difficult,** suitable for experienced DIY mechanic	**Very difficult,** suitable for expert DIY or professional 

Specifications

Glow plugs

Resistance (typical)	1 ohm approximately

Torque wrench setting

	Nm	lbf ft
Glow plugs	8	6

1 Preheating system – description and testing

Description

1 To assist cold starting, diesel engines are fitted with a preheating system, which consists of four glow plugs (one per cylinder), a glow plug module, a facia-mounted warning light, the engine management PCM, and the associated electrical wiring.

2 The glow plugs are miniature electric heating elements, encapsulated in a metal case with a probe at one end and electrical connection at the other. Each combustion chamber has one glow plug threaded into it, with the tip of the glow plug probe positioned directly in line with incoming spray of fuel from the injectors. When the glow plug is energised, it heats up rapidly, causing the fuel passing over the glow plug probe to be heated to its optimum temperature, ready for combustion. In addition, some of the fuel passing over the glow plugs is ignited and this helps to trigger the combustion process.

3 The preheating system begins to operate as soon as the ignition key is switched to the second position, but only if the engine coolant temperature is below 20°C and the engine is turned at more than 70 rpm for 0.2 seconds. A facia-mounted warning light informs the driver that preheating is taking place. The light extinguishes when sufficient preheating has taken place to allow the engine to be started, but power will still be supplied to the glow plugs for a further period until the engine is started. If no attempt is made to start the engine, the power supply to the glow plugs is switched off after 10 seconds, to prevent battery drain and glow plug burn-out.

4 With the electronically-controlled diesel injection system fitted to models in this manual, the glow plug module is controlled by the engine management system PCM, which determines the necessary preheating time based on inputs from the various system sensors. The system monitors the temperature of the inlet air, then alters the preheating time (the length for which the glow plugs are supplied with current) to suit the conditions.

5 Post-heating takes place after the ignition key has been released from the 'start' position, but only if the engine coolant temperature is below 20°C, the injected fuel flow is less than a certain rate, and the engine speed is less than 2000 rpm (1.4 litre engine) or 2500 rpm (1.6 litre engine). The glow plugs continue to operate for a maximum of 60 seconds (1.4 litre engine) or 30 seconds (1.6 litre engine), helping to improve fuel combustion whilst the engine is warming-up, resulting in quieter, smoother running and reduced exhaust emissions.

Testing

6 If the system malfunctions, testing is ultimately by substitution of known good units, but some preliminary checks may be made as follows.

7 Connect a voltmeter or 12 volt test light between the glow plug supply cable and earth (engine or car body). Make sure that the live connection is kept clear of the engine and bodywork.

8 Have an assistant switch on the ignition, and check that voltage is applied to the glow plugs. Note the time for which the warning light is lit, and the total time for which voltage is applied before the system cuts out. Switch off the ignition.

9 Warning light time will increase with lower temperatures and decrease with higher temperatures.

10 If there is no supply at all, the module or associated wiring is at fault.

11 To gain access to the glow plugs for further testing, remove the air cleaner as described in Chapter 4B, Section 4. For the best access, also remove the inlet manifold (which is integral with the cylinder head cover – see Chapter 2B, Section 4 or Chapter 2C, Section 4).

12 Disconnect the main supply cable (behind the fuel filter) and the interconnecting wire from the top of the glow plugs. Be careful not to drop the nuts and washers.

13 Use a continuity tester, or a 12 volt test light connected to the battery positive terminal, to check for continuity between each glow plug terminal and earth. The resistance of a glow plug in good condition is very low (less than 1 ohm), so if the test light does not light or the continuity tester shows a high resistance, the glow plug is certainly defective.

14 If an ammeter is available, the current draw of each glow plug can be checked. After an initial surge of 15 to 20 amps, each plug should draw 12 amps. Any plug which draws much more or less than this is probably defective.

15 As a final check, the glow plugs can be removed and inspected as described in the following Section. On completion, refit any components removed for access.

2.1 Removing the glow plug support bracket (1.6 litre engine)

2.2 Undo the nuts securing the glow plug connections

2.4a Glow plugs (arrowed) on the 1.6 litre engine

2.4b Removing a glow plug (1.6 litre engine)

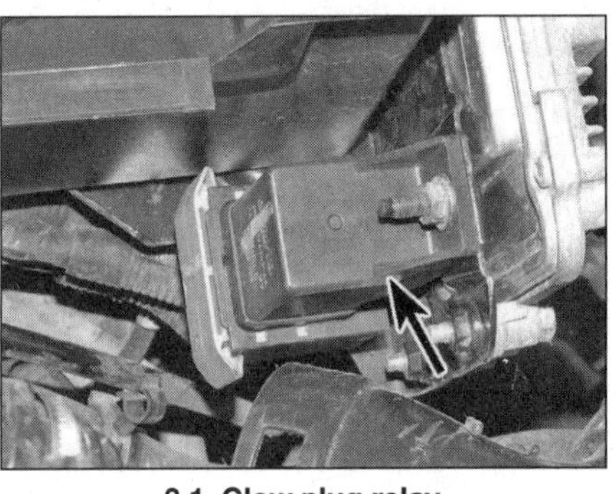

3.1 Glow plug relay

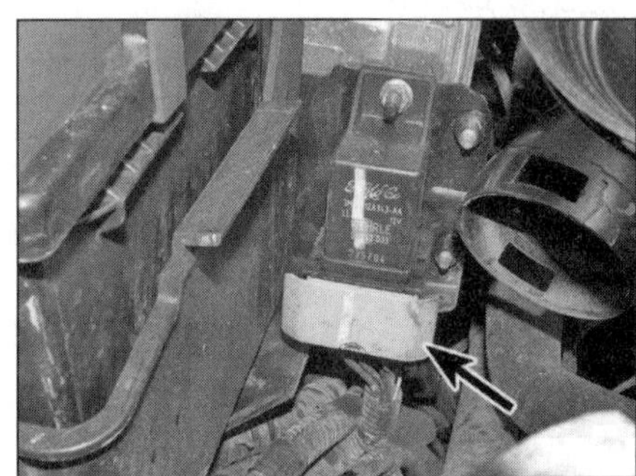

3.2 Disconnect the wiring from the glow plug relay

2 Glow plugs – removal, inspection and refitting

Caution: If the preheating system has just been energised, or if the engine has been running, the glow plugs will be very hot.

Removal

1 Ensure the ignition is turned off. To gain access to the glow plugs, remove the air cleaner as described in Chapter 4B, Section 4. For the best access on 1.4 litre models, also remove the inlet manifold (which is integral with the cylinder head cover – see Chapter 2B, Section 4). It is also possible to access the glow plug with a suitable combination of sockets, extensions and a universal joint, but it is a difficult task. On 1.6 litre models, unbolt and remove the glow plug wiring support bracket **(see illustration)**.

2 On early models (up to 01/2005) unscrew the nuts from the glow plug terminals, and recover the washers, then disconnect the wires **(see illustration)**. On later models release the push-on connector.

3 Where applicable, carefully move any obstructing pipes or wires to one side to enable access to the relevant glow plug(s).

4 Unscrew the glow plug(s) and remove from the cylinder head **(see illustrations). Note:** *On 1.6 litre models, access to No 4 glow plug is difficult.*

Inspection

5 Inspect each glow plug for physical damage. Burnt or eroded glow plug tips can be caused by a bad injector spray pattern. Have the injectors checked if this sort of damage is found.

6 If the glow plugs are in good physical condition, check them electrically using a 12 volt test light or continuity tester as described in the previous Section.

7 The glow plugs can be energised by applying 12 volts to them, to verify that they heat up evenly and in approximately the same time. Observe the following precautions.

a) Support the glow plug by clamping it carefully in a vice or self-locking pliers. Remember, it will become red-hot.

b) Make sure that the power supply or test lead incorporates a fuse or overload trip to protect against damage from a short-circuit.

c) After testing, allow the glow plug to cool for several minutes before attempting to handle it.

8 A glow plug in good condition will start to glow red at the tip after drawing current for 5 seconds or so. Any plug which takes much longer to start glowing, or which starts glowing in the middle instead of at the tip, is defective.

Refitting

9 Refit by reversing the removal operations. Apply a smear of copper-based anti-seize compound to the plug threads, and tighten the glow plugs to the specified torque. Do not overtighten, as this can damage the glow plug element.

10 Refit any components removed for access.

3 Glow plug relay – removal and refitting

Removal

1 The glow plug relay is located in the engine compartment, behind the left-hand headlight **(see illustration)**. It shares a mounting bracket with the engine management PCM.

2 Disconnect the wiring from the glow plug relay **(see illustration)**, then unscrew the mounting nut and remove the relay from the bracket.

Refitting

3 Refitting is a reversal of removal.

Chapter 6
Clutch

Contents

Degrees of difficulty

Easy, suitable for novice with little experience 	**Fairly easy,** suitable for beginner with some experience	**Fairly difficult,** suitable for competent DIY mechanic	**Difficult,** suitable for experienced DIY mechanic	**Very difficult,** suitable for expert DIY or professional 

Specifications

General

Clutch type	Single dry plate, diaphragm spring, hydraulically-operated release mechanism

Friction disc

Diameter:	
All except diesel and 1.6 litre petrol models	180.0 mm
Diesel and 1.6 litre petrol models	210.0 mm
Friction material thickness (minimum)	7.0 mm (approximate)

Clutch pedal

Pedal travel	135.0 ± 5.0 mm

Torque wrench settings

Torque wrench settings	Nm	lbf ft
Clutch slave cylinder	10	7
Pedal pivot shaft nut	25	18
Pressure plate-to-flywheel bolts*	29	21

* *Use new bolts*

1 General information

The clutch consists of a friction disc, a pressure plate assembly, a release bearing and hydraulic slave cylinder; all of these components are contained in the large cast-aluminium alloy bellhousing, sandwiched between the engine and the transmission.

The hydraulic master cylinder is located in the pedal bracket on the bulkhead, and the clutch fluid reservoir is shared with the brake fluid reservoir on the top of the brake master cylinder. Inside the reservoir each circuit has its own compartment, so that in the event of fluid loss in the clutch circuit, the brake circuit remains fully operational.

The clutch disc (friction disc) is fitted between the engine flywheel and the clutch pressure plate, and is allowed to slide on the transmission input shaft splines.

The pressure plate assembly is bolted to the engine flywheel. When the engine is running, drive is transmitted from the crankshaft, via the flywheel, to the friction disc (these components being clamped securely together by the pressure plate assembly) and from the friction disc to the transmission input shaft.

To interrupt the drive, the spring pressure must be relaxed by the hydraulically-operated release mechanism. Depressing the clutch pedal operates the master cylinder which in turn operates the slave cylinder and presses the release bearing against the pressure plate spring fingers. This causes the springs to deform and releases the clamping force on the friction disc.

When the pedal is released, the diaphragm spring forces the pressure plate into contact with the friction linings on the friction disc. The disc is now firmly sandwiched between the pressure plate and the flywheel, thus transmitting engine power to the transmission. When the clutch pedal is released, excess fluid is expelled through the master cylinder into the fluid reservoir.

Wear of the friction material on the friction disc is automatically compensated for by the operation of the hydraulic system. As the friction material on the disc wears, the pressure plate moves towards the flywheel causing the clutch diaphragm spring inner fingers to move outwards.

Durashift (EST) models

Models with the EST transmission system use clutch components which differ only in detail to those fitted to conventional manual transmission models. Although the Durashift-specific components cannot be substituted for normal ones, the removal and refitting procedures are generally identical. For more information on the Durashift system, refer to Chapter 7B, Section 1.

2.4 Hose connections to the master cylinder on the bulkhead

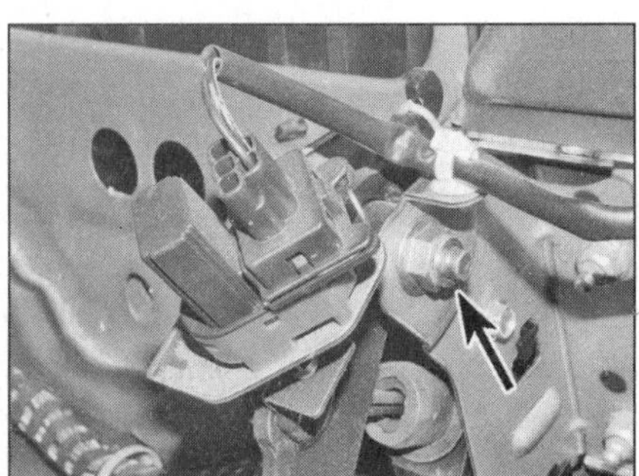

2.7 Unscrew the pedal pivot shaft nut

2 Clutch master cylinder – removal and refitting

Removal

1 Remove the filler cap from the brake master cylinder reservoir on top of the brake master cylinder, and siphon the hydraulic fluid from the reservoir until it is at the MIN mark (below the outlet to the clutch master cylinder). Alternatively, open the slave cylinder bleed screw, and gently pump the clutch pedal to expel the fluid through a plastic tube connected to the screw; tighten the screw when all the fluid has been removed.

Warning: Do not siphon the fluid by mouth, as it is poisonous; use a syringe or an old poultry baster.

2 Remove the air cleaner as described in Chapter 4A, Section 5 or Chapter 4B, Section 4, as applicable. On left-hand-drive models, remove the battery and battery tray as described in Chapter 5A, Section 4.

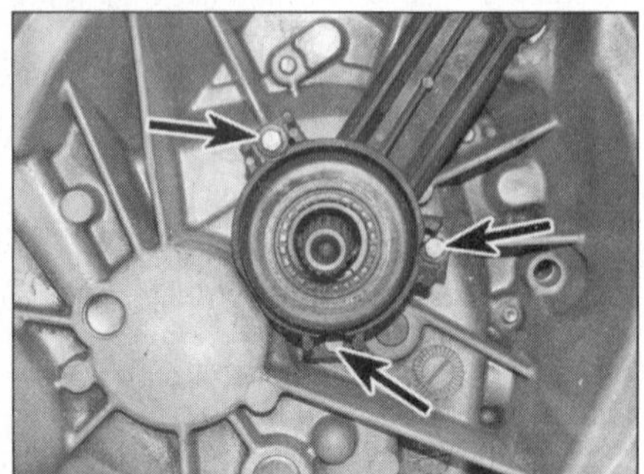

3.2 Slave cylinder and mounting bolts

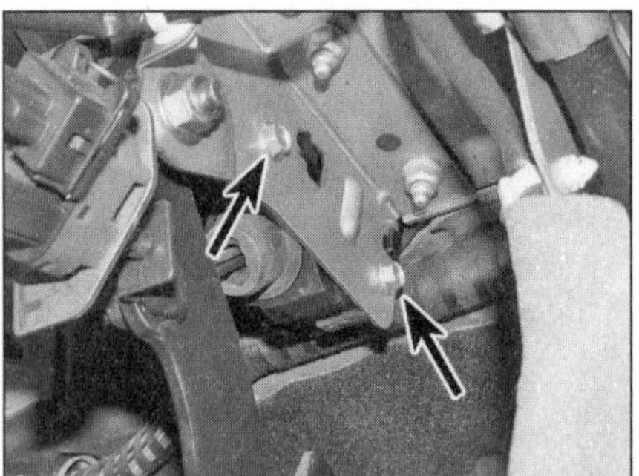

2.6 Loosen the two clutch master cylinder retaining bolts

2.9 Clutch pedal return spring (A) and master cylinder actuating rod connection (B)

3 Have ready a plug of some kind, to fit to the brake fluid reservoir once the clutch master cylinder supply hose is disconnected. Press the clip on the supply hose connector to release it, and take off the hose. Plug the fluid reservoir connection to prevent fluid loss or dirt entry.

4 Trace the clutch master cylinder supply hose to the bulkhead connection, and release it by pulling out the connection retaining clip to the side, towards the transmission **(see illustration)**. Remove the supply hose from the engine bay. There will be some loss of fluid as the hose is removed – wipe up any spillage, and rinse any painted surfaces with water (avoid getting water inside the clutch master cylinder, however).

5 Similarly, disconnect the supply pipe to the clutch slave cylinder from the bulkhead (this is the connection below the one just removed).

6 The master cylinder is removed complete with the clutch pedal. Inside the car, remove the facia lower trim panel (five screws and one clip, top left) to gain clear access to the pedals. Loosen the two bolts to the right of the clutch pedal, securing the master cylinder **(see illustration)**.

7 Unscrew the nut at the top of the clutch pedal which secures the pedal pivot shaft, and withdraw the shaft **(see illustration)**.

8 Remove the two master cylinder bolts, then lift the clutch pedal up to release the assembly from the pedal box, and remove the assembly from the car.

9 To separate the master cylinder from the pedal, unhook the pedal return spring, then detach the master cylinder actuating rod from the peg on the pedal **(see illustration)**.

10 If the master cylinder is faulty it must be renewed – at the time of writing, Ford do not supply a repair kit. Check, however, on parts availability from other sources before purchasing a new unit.

Refitting

11 Refitting is a reversal of removal, noting the following points:

a) *Once the pedal return spring has been hooked on, it may be helpful to hold it in place with a little tape as the pedal and master cylinder assembly is fitted.*
b) *Tighten the pedal pivot shaft nut to the specified torque.*
c) *Ensure that all fluid hose connections are clean, and are securely made.*
d) *Bleed the clutch on completion, as described in Section 5.*

3 Clutch slave cylinder – removal and refitting

Removal

1 Remove the transmission as described in Chapter 7A, Section 7 or Chapter 7B, Section 7.

2 Inside the bellhousing, unscrew and remove the three mounting bolts, then withdraw the slave cylinder over the transmission input shaft **(see illustration)**.

3 With the slave cylinder removed, it is recommended that the transmission input shaft oil seal is renewed. Use a suitable tool to hook it out of the transmission casing and over the input shaft. Refer to Chapter 7A, Section 6 or Chapter 7B, Section 6 if necessary.

4 The release bearing is an interference fit in the slave cylinder, and cannot be renewed separately.

5 If the slave cylinder is faulty it must be renewed, as the manufacturers do not supply repair kits.

Refitting

6 Do not apply grease to any part of the slave cylinder or release bearing.

7 Locate a new oil seal over the input shaft and into the transmission housing, then slide the slave cylinder onto the shaft.

8 Insert the mounting bolts and tighten them progressively to the specified torque. As the bolts are tightened, make sure that the oil seal enters the transmission housing correctly.

9 Refit the transmission as described in Chapter 7A, Section 7 or Chapter 7B, Section 7.

10 Refill the master cylinder reservoir with fresh fluid, then bleed the hydraulic system as described in Section 5.

4 Clutch hydraulic hoses – removal and refitting

Caution: Hydraulic fluid can damage vehicle paintwork. Take the necessary precautions to prevent spillage of fluid.

Removal

1 Remove the filler cap from the brake master cylinder reservoir on top of the brake master cylinder, and siphon the hydraulic fluid from the reservoir until it is down to the MIN mark (below the outlet to the clutch master cylinder). Alternatively, open the slave cylinder bleed screw, and gently pump the clutch pedal to expel the fluid through a plastic tube connected to the screw; tighten the screw when all the fluid has been removed.

2 Remove the air cleaner as described in Chapter 4A, Section 5 or Chapter 4B, Section 4, as applicable. On left-hand-drive models, remove the battery and battery tray as described in Chapter 5A, Section 4.

3 To remove the supply hose, remove the clips then disconnect the hose from the reservoir and master cylinder.

4 To remove the pressure hose, first wipe all traces of dirt from the master cylinder and slave cylinder. Extract the clip from the quick-release connections on the master cylinder and slave cylinder, then remove the hose **(see illustrations)**.

Refitting

5 Refitting is a reversal of removal, but on completion bleed the hydraulic system as described in Section 5.

5 Clutch hydraulic system – bleeding

Warning: Hydraulic fluid is poisonous; wash off immediately and thoroughly in the case of skin contact, and seek immediate medical advice if any fluid is swallowed or gets into the eyes. Certain types of hydraulic fluid are flammable, and may ignite when allowed into contact with hot components; when servicing any hydraulic system, it is safest to assume that the fluid is flammable, and to take precautions against the risk of fire as though it is petrol that is being handled. Hydraulic fluid is also an effective paint stripper, and will attack plastics; if any is spilt, it should be washed off immediately, using copious quantities of fresh water. Finally, it is hygroscopic (it absorbs moisture from the air) – old fluid may be contaminated and unfit for further use. When topping-up or renewing the fluid, always use the recommended type, and ensure that it comes from a freshly-opened sealed container.

4.4a Use a small screwdriver to prise up the spring clip ...

4.4b ... then pull out the hose from the slave cylinder connection on the transmission

1 The correct operation of any hydraulic system is only possible after removing all air from the components and circuit; this is achieved by bleeding the system.

2 During the bleeding procedure, add only clean, unused hydraulic fluid of the recommended type; never re-use fluid that has already been bled from the system. Ensure that sufficient fluid is available before starting work.

3 If there is any possibility of incorrect fluid being already in the system, the hydraulic circuit must be flushed completely with uncontaminated, correct fluid.

4 If hydraulic fluid has been lost from the system, or air has entered because of a leak, ensure that the fault is cured before continuing further.

5 The bleed screw is screwed into the slave cylinder extension which is positioned on the top of the transmission bellhousing – the bleed screw is behind the fluid supply pipe. Access to the screw is difficult, but may be improved by removing the left-hand headlight (left as seen from the driver's seat), as described in Chapter 12, Section 7.

6 First check that all the hydraulic hoses are securely fitted to the master and slave cylinders. Clean any dirt from around the bleed screw.

7 Unscrew the brake master cylinder fluid reservoir cap, and top-up the fluid level to the upper (MAX) level line; refit the cap loosely, and remember to maintain the fluid level at least above the lower (MIN) level line throughout the procedure, or there is a risk of further air entering the system.

8 There is a number of one-man, do-it-yourself bleeding kits currently available from motor accessory shops. It is recommended that one of these kits is used whenever possible, as they greatly simplify the bleeding operation, and reduce the risk of expelled air and fluid being drawn back into the system. If such a kit is not available, the basic (two-man) method must be used, which is described in detail below.

9 If a kit is to be used, prepare the vehicle as described previously, and follow the kit manufacturer's instructions, as the procedure may vary slightly according to the type being used; generally, they are as outlined below in the relevant sub-section.

Bleeding

Ford method

10 The Ford method for bleeding is to attach a hand vacuum pump and a container of fluid to the slave cylinder bleed screw (in front of the fluid supply pipe on top of the gearbox). Open the bleed screw, and then suck the fluid out of the system until no air bubbles are visible in the connecting tubing (the brake fluid reservoir must be kept topped-up with fluid the whole time). On completion, and before removing the vacuum, close the bleed screw. This is obviously the preferred method if suitable tools are available – if not, the more conventional methods described below should also be successful.

Basic (two-man) method

11 Collect a clean glass jar, a suitable length of plastic or rubber tubing which is a tight fit over the bleed screw. The help of an assistant will also be required. Ensure that the fluid level is maintained at least above the outlet to the clutch master cylinder in the reservoir throughout the procedure.

12 Remove the protective cap from the slave cylinder bleed screw. Fit the tube to the screw, place the other end of the tube in the jar, and pour in sufficient fluid to cover the end of the tube.

13 Loosen the bleed screw (this should be possible by hand) half a turn, then have the assistant slowly depress and release the clutch pedal several times until fluid free of air bubbles emerges. On the final stroke, have the assistant hold the pedal fully depressed. Note that the pedal must be fully depressed and fully released each time.

14 With the pedal held down, tighten the bleed screw and have the assistant fully release the pedal slowly. Check the reservoir fluid level and top-up if necessary, then check the operation of the pedal. After the initial free movement, increased pressure should be felt as the clutch pressure plate diaphragm spring is operated.

15 If the pedal feels spongy, air still remains in the hydraulic system and the bleeding operation must be repeated as described in the previous paragraphs.

16 With the hydraulic system bled, tighten the bleed screw securely, then remove the

5.18 Bleeding the clutch – remove the left-hand headlight, and attach the pipe to the bleed screw (arrowed)

tube and spanner and refit the dust cap. Do not overtighten the bleed screw.

Using a one-way valve kit

17 As the name implies, these kits consist of a length of tubing with a one-way valve fitted, to prevent expelled air and fluid being drawn back into the system; some kits include a translucent container, which can be positioned so that the air bubbles can be more easily seen flowing from the end of the tube.

18 The kit is connected to the bleed screw, which is then opened **(see illustration)**. The user returns to the driver's seat, depresses the clutch pedal with a smooth, steady stroke, and slowly releases it; this is repeated until the expelled fluid is clear of air bubbles.

19 Note that these kits simplify work so much that it is easy to forget the fluid reservoir level; ensure that this is maintained at least above the outlet to the clutch master cylinder at all times.

Using a pressure-bleeding kit

20 These kits are usually operated by the reservoir of pressurised air contained in the spare tyre. However, note that it will probably be necessary to reduce the pressure to a lower level than normal; refer to the instructions supplied with the kit.

21 By connecting a pressurised, fluid-filled container to the fluid reservoir, bleeding can be carried out simply by opening the bleed screw and allowing the fluid to flow out until no more air bubbles can be seen in the expelled fluid.

22 This method has the advantage that the large reservoir of fluid provides an additional safeguard against air being drawn into the system during bleeding.

All methods

23 When bleeding is complete, and correct pedal feel is restored, check that the bleed screw is securely tightened and wash off any spilt fluid. Refit the dust cap to the bleed screw.

24 Check the hydraulic fluid level in the reservoir, and top-up if necessary.

25 Discard any hydraulic fluid that has been bled from the system; it will not be fit for re-use.

26 If the clutch is not operating correctly after carrying out the bleeding procedure, the master cylinder or slave cylinder may be faulty.

6 Clutch pedal – removal and refitting

The clutch pedal is removed as an assembly with the clutch master cylinder – refer to Section 2.

7 Clutch assembly – removal, inspection and refitting

Warning: Dust created by clutch wear and deposited on the clutch components may contain asbestos, which is a health hazard. DO NOT blow it out with compressed air, or inhale any of it. DO NOT use petrol or petroleum-based solvents to clean off the dust. Brake system cleaner or methylated spirit should be used to flush the dust into a suitable receptacle. After the clutch components are wiped clean with rags, dispose of the contaminated rags and cleaner in a sealed, marked container.

Note: *Although some friction materials may no longer contain asbestos, it is safest to assume that they do, and to take precautions accordingly.*

Removal

1 Unless the complete engine/transmission unit has to be removed from the car (see Chapter 2D, Section 4 or 5), the clutch can be reached by removing the transmission as described in Chapter 7A, Section 7 or Chapter 7B, Section 7, as applicable.

2 Before disturbing the clutch, use chalk or a marker pen to mark the relationship of the pressure plate assembly to the flywheel.

3 Hold the flywheel stationary using a suitable tool engaged with the starter ring gear teeth – a piece of metal can be tightened to one of the bolt holes, or alternatively an assistant can use a wide-bladed screwdriver engaged with the teeth **(see illustration)**.

4 Working in a diagonal sequence, slacken the pressure plate bolts by half a turn at a time, until spring pressure is released and the bolts can be unscrewed by hand **(see illustration)**. Discard the bolts – new ones should be used when refitting.

5 Prise the pressure plate assembly off its locating dowels, and collect the friction disc, noting which way round the disc is fitted **(see illustration)**.

Inspection

Note: *Due to the amount of work necessary to remove and refit clutch components, it is usually considered good practice to renew the clutch friction disc, pressure plate assembly and release bearing (slave cylinder) as a matched set, even if only one of these is actually worn enough to require renewal. It is also worth considering the renewal of the clutch components on a preventive basis if the engine and/or transmission have been removed for some other reason.*

6 When cleaning clutch components, read first the warning at the beginning of this Section; remove the dust using a clean, dry cloth, and working in a well-ventilated atmosphere.

7 Check the friction disc linings for signs of wear, damage or oil contamination. If the friction material is cracked, burnt, scored or damaged, or if it is contaminated with oil or grease (shown by shiny black patches), the friction disc must be renewed. Check the depth of the rivets below the friction material surface. If any are at or near the surface of the friction material, then the friction disc must be renewed.

7.3 Home-made tool for holding the flywheel stationary

7.4 Slacken and remove the pressure plate bolts

7.5 Prise the pressure plate off its dowels and remove it with the friction disc

8 If the friction material is still serviceable, check that the centre boss splines are unworn, that the torsion springs are in good condition and securely fastened, and that all the rivets are tight. If any wear or damage is found, the friction disc must be renewed.

9 If the friction material is fouled with oil, this must be due to an oil leak from the crankshaft oil seal, from the sump-to-cylinder block joint, or from the transmission input shaft. Renew the seal or repair the joint, as appropriate, as described in Chapter 2A, 2B, 2C, 7A or 7B, before installing the new friction disc.

10 Check the pressure plate assembly for obvious signs of wear or damage; shake it to check for loose rivets or worn or damaged fulcrum rings, and check that the drive straps securing the pressure plate to the cover do not show signs of overheating (such as a deep yellow or blue discoloration). If the diaphragm spring is worn or damaged, or if its pressure is in any way suspect, the pressure plate assembly should be renewed.

11 Examine the machined bearing surfaces of the pressure plate and of the flywheel; they should be clean, completely flat, and free from scratches or scoring. If either is discoloured from excessive heat, or shows signs of cracks, it should be renewed – although minor damage of this nature can sometimes be polished away using emery paper.

12 Check that the release bearing contact surface rotates smoothly and easily, with no sign of noise or roughness. Also check that the surface itself is smooth and unworn, with no signs of cracks, pitting or scoring. If there is any doubt about its condition, the bearing (and slave cylinder) must be renewed.

Refitting

Note: *Self-adjusting clutches (fitted to models with the Durashift EST transmission only) must not be refitted. They must be renewed if removed.*

13 On reassembly, ensure that the disc contact surfaces of the flywheel and pressure plate are completely clean, smooth, and free from oil or grease. Use solvent to remove any protective grease from new components.

14 Fit the friction disc so that its spring hub assembly faces away from the flywheel; there may also be a marking showing which way round the plate is to be refitted. Depending on the type of centralising tool being used, the friction disc may be held in position at this stage **(see illustrations)**.

15 Refit the pressure plate assembly, aligning the marks made on dismantling (if the original pressure plate is re-used), and locating the pressure plate on its locating dowels **(see illustration)**. Fit the pressure plate bolts, but tighten them only finger-tight, so that the friction disc can still be moved.

16 The friction disc must now be centralised, so that when the transmission is refitted, its input shaft will pass through the splines at the centre of the friction disc.

7.14a Clutch friction disc FLYWHEEL SIDE markings should face the flywheel

7.14b Fit the friction disc, then use a centralising tool to align it

7.15 Fit the pressure plate onto its dowels

7.18 Tighten the pressure plate bolts to the specified torque

17 Centralisation can be achieved by passing a screwdriver or other long bar through the friction disc and into the hole in the crankshaft; the friction disc can then be moved around until it is centred on the crankshaft hole. Alternatively, a clutch aligning tool can be used to eliminate the guesswork; these can be obtained from most accessory shops. The normal type consists of a spigot bar with several different adapters, but a more recent type consists of a tool which clamps the friction disc to the pressure plate before locating the two items on the flywheel. A home-made aligning tool can be fabricated from a length of metal rod or wooden dowel which fits closely inside the crankshaft hole, and has insulating tape wound around it to match the diameter of the friction disc splined hole.

18 When the friction disc is centralised, tighten the pressure plate bolts evenly and in a diagonal sequence to the specified torque setting **(see illustration)**.

19 Apply a light coating of oil to the splines of the friction disc and the transmission input shaft. Note that some clutch kits may contain a suitable lubricant as part of the kit.

20 Refit the transmission as described in Chapter 7A, Section 7 or Chapter 7B, Section 7, as applicable.

8 Clutch release bearing – removal, inspection and refitting

Removal

1 For access to the clutch release bearing, the transmission must be removed as described in Chapter 7A, Section 7 or Chapter 7B, Section 7, as applicable.

2 Remove the slave cylinder as described in Section 3. The release bearing is an interference fit in the slave cylinder, and cannot be renewed separately.

Inspection

3 Note that it is often considered worthwhile to renew the release bearing as a matter of course regardless of its condition, considering the amount of work necessary to access it. Check that the contact surface rotates smoothly and easily, with no sign of noise or roughness, and that the surface itself is smooth and unworn, with no signs of cracks, pitting or scoring. If there is any doubt about its condition, the bearing (and slave cylinder) must be renewed.

Refitting

4 Refit the slave cylinder as described in Section 3.

5 Refit the transmission with reference to Chapter 7A, Section 7 or Chapter 7B, Section 7, as applicable.

Chapter 7 Part A: Manual transmission

Contents

Degrees of difficulty

Easy, suitable for novice with little experience	**Fairly easy,** suitable for beginner with some experience	**Fairly difficult,** suitable for competent DIY mechanic	**Difficult,** suitable for experienced DIY mechanic	**Very difficult,** suitable for expert DIY or professional

Specifications

General

Transmission type	Five forward speeds, one reverse. Synchromesh on all forward gears (1st and 2nd gears double-synchronised). Gearchange linkage operated by twin cables
Transmission code	iB5

Selector cable

Adjustment dimension (see text)	138 ± 2.0 mm

Gear ratios (typical)

1st	3.583:1
2nd	1.926:1
3rd	1.281:1
4th	0.951:1
5th	0.756:1
Reverse	3.615:1

Final drive ratios (typical)

Petrol models	4.06:1 or 4.25:1
Diesel models	3.37:1

Torque wrench settings

	Nm	lbf ft
Engine/transmission left-hand mounting:		
Centre nut*	90	66
Outer nuts*	48	35
Engine/transmission rear mounting through-bolts	48	35
Fluid filler/level plug	35	26
Gearchange cable bracket bolts	20	15
Gearchange cable guide plate	9	7
Gearchange mechanism to floor	9	7
Reversing light switch	18	13
Selector lever securing bolt	25	18
Slave cylinder pressure pipe bracket	28	21
Transmission to engine	48	35

** Use new nuts.*

2.3 Unclip the cover from the front of the transmission

2.4 Measure the cable from the upper mounting clip to the centre of the end fitting

2.5 Press the cable insert inwards to release it

1 General information

The models covered by this manual are all equipped with the same 5-speed transmission, but differ in their method of clutch operation. This Chapter contains information on the manual transmission. Service procedures for the Durashift transmission system are contained in Chapter 7B.

The transmission is contained in a cast-aluminium alloy casing bolted to the engine's left-hand end, and consists of the gearbox and final drive differential – often called a transaxle. The transmission unit type is stamped on a plate attached to the transmission.

The iB5 unit is identical to that used in previous Fiesta ranges, with the exception that it is newly-equipped with a cable-actuated gearchange linkage. The transmission is intended to be sealed for life – no oil changes are required, and no drain plug is fitted. Provided that the oil level is maintained as described in Chapter 1A, Section 18 or Chapter 1B, Section 19, no routine maintenance is necessary.

Drive is transmitted from the crankshaft via the clutch to the input shaft, which has a splined extension to accept the clutch friction disc. From the input shaft, drive is transmitted to the output shaft, from where the drive is transmitted to the differential crownwheel, which rotates with the differential and planetary gears, thus driving the sun gears and driveshafts. The rotation of the planetary gears on their shaft allows the inner roadwheel to rotate at a slower speed than the outer roadwheel when the car is cornering.

The input and output shafts are arranged side by side, parallel to the crankshaft and driveshafts, so that their gear pinion teeth are in constant mesh. In the neutral position, the output shaft gear pinions rotate freely, so that drive cannot be transmitted to the crownwheel.

Gear selection is via a floor-mounted lever and selector cable mechanism.

The transmission selector mechanism causes the appropriate selector fork to move its respective synchro-sleeve along the output shaft, to lock the gear pinion to the synchro-hub. Since the synchro-hubs are splined to the output shaft, this locks the pinion to the shaft, so that drive can be transmitted. To ensure that gearchanging can be made quickly and quietly, a synchromesh system is fitted to all forward gears, consisting of baulk rings and spring-loaded fingers, as well as the gear pinions and synchro-hubs. The synchromesh cones are formed on the mating faces of the baulk rings and gear pinions. The new iB5 unit has dual synchromesh on 1st and 2nd gears, for even smoother gearchanging.

Transmission overhaul

Because of the complexity of the assembly, possible unavailability of new parts and special tools necessary, internal repair procedures for the transmission are not recommended for the home mechanic. The bulk of the information in this Chapter is devoted to removal and refitting procedures.

2 Gearchange cables – adjustment

1 Inside the car, move the gear lever to neutral.

2 Apply the handbrake, then jack up the front of the car, supporting it on axle stands (see *Jacking and vehicle support).*

3 At the front face of the transmission, remove the selector mechanism cover by working around the edge, releasing a total of seven clips **(see illustration)**.

4 Measure the selector cable between the upper mounting clip (approximately the centre of the adjuster section) and the end fitting on the transmission **(see illustration)**.

5 If the dimension is not as specified at the start of this Chapter, unlock the (vertical) selector cable by pressing the orange-coloured insert towards the engine – the insert should lock in the retracted position **(see illustration)**. Move the cable's sliding end fitting up or down until the dimension is correct.

6 When adjustment is complete, press inwards on the catch above the selector cable's orange insert to release the insert and lock the cable end fitting **(see illustration)**.

7 Refit the selector mechanism cover, making sure it is fully clipped into place, then lower the car to the ground.

8 Start the engine with the clutch pedal depressed, and check for correct gear selection.

3 Gearchange cables and gear lever – removal and refitting

Removal

Gear lever

1 Disconnect the battery negative (earth) lead (see Chapter 5A, Section 2).

2 Inside the car, place the gear lever in neutral.

3 Carefully prise up the plastic trim ring at the base of the gear lever, and remove it over the gear lever (the rubber gaiter stays behind) **(see illustration)**.

2.6 To release the insert (and relock the cable), press this small catch

3.3 Remove the plastic trim ring from the gear lever

3.4 Lift off the gear lever trim panel

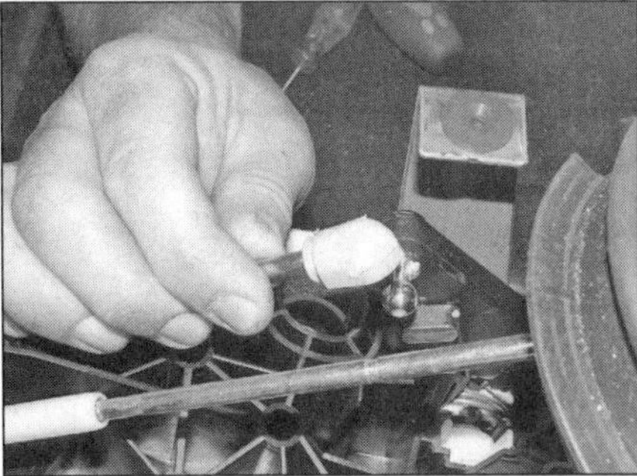
3.5 Prise off the inner cable plastic end fittings

3.6 Use a small screwdriver to turn the cable outer locking collar clockwise

4 Unclip the gear lever trim panel from the top of the centre console by carefully prising it up to release the clips. Once the panel has been lifted, disconnect the wiring plugs from the cigar lighter and/or power outlet socket, as applicable, then remove the panel over the gear lever **(see illustration)**.
5 Disconnect the shift (white) and selector (black) inner cables from the gear lever by prising off the end fittings **(see illustration)**.
6 Disconnect the cable outers from the floor brackets by twisting the collars clockwise **(see illustration)**.
7 Remove the four nuts securing the gear lever to the floor, and lift it out **(see illustration)**.

Cables

8 Remove the gear lever as described previously in this Section.
9 Remove the air cleaner as described in Chapter 4A, Section 5 or Chapter 4B, Section 4, as applicable.
10 Jack up the front of the car, and support it on axle stands (see *Jacking and vehicle support*).
11 Unhook the exhaust system front mounting rubber from its floor mounting.
12 Remove the nuts and slide out the section of exhaust heat from shield under the gear lever.
13 At the front face of the transmission, remove the selector mechanism cover by working around the edge, releasing a total of seven clips.
14 Remove the cables from the support brackets by twisting the spring-loaded knurled collars clockwise. Release the coloured plastic clips which secure the cable adjuster(s), and prise the cable end fittings from the transmission levers – note their fitted locations **(see illustrations)**.
15 Withdraw the cables downwards from the engine compartment, releasing them from their retaining clips, and noting how they are routed. Take care not to kink or bend the cables during removal. Lower the car to the ground.
16 Remove the passenger-side footwell trim panel from the front of the centre console. The panel is secured by a screw at the front, and is clipped to the console at the rear.
17 The cable entry point into the car should now be visible, but the cables themselves are hidden under the carpet. To gain access to them, it will be necessary to cut the carpet and sound-deadening material.
18 Undo the nuts securing the cable guide plate from the floor, and withdraw the cables into the car. Again, take care not to kink or bend the cables as they are removed.

Refitting

19 Refitting is a reversal of removal. On completion, adjust the cables as described in Section 2.

4 Vehicle speed sensor – removal and refitting

Refer to Chapter 4A, Section 14, or Chapter 4B, Section 13. Models with ABS do not have a vehicle speed sensor.

5 Reversing light switch – removal and refitting

Removal

1 The switch is located on the front of the transmission, next to the selector cable front cover. To improve access, jack up the front left-hand side of the car (see *Jacking and vehicle support*).
2 Disconnect the wiring plug from the switch **(see illustration)**.
3 Unscrew and remove the switch from the front of the transmission – anticipate a little oil spillage as this is done **(see illustrations)**.

3.7 Three of the four gear lever mounting nuts

3.14a Twist the knurled collars clockwise ...

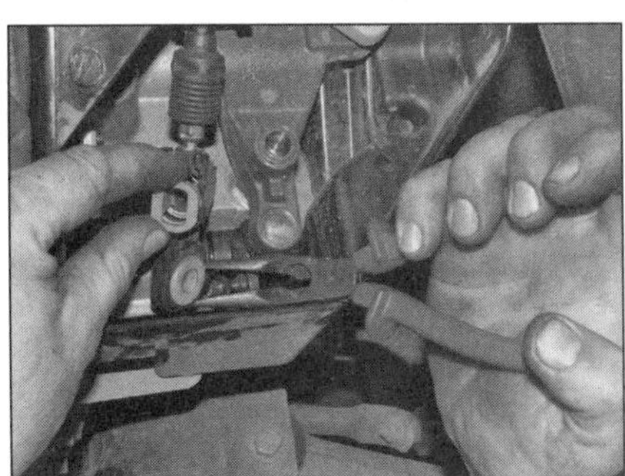
3.14b ... then use a pair of pliers to release the selector ...

3.14c ... and shift cables from the front of the transmission

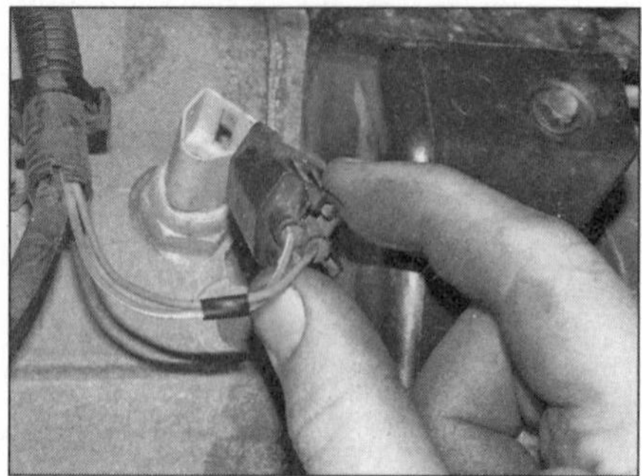

5.2 Disconnect the wiring plug from the reversing light switch

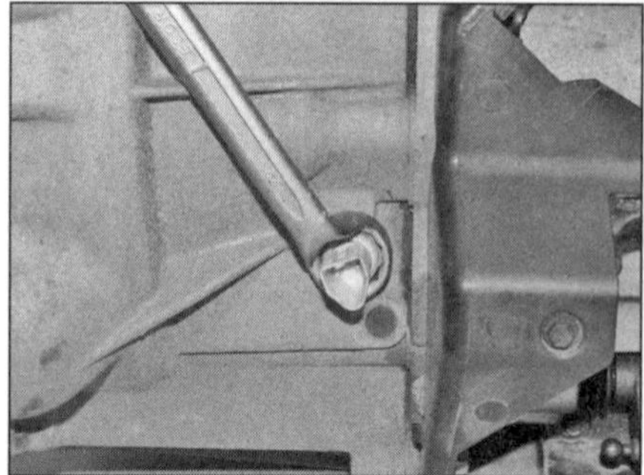

5.3a Unscrew the switch ...

5.3b ... and withdraw it from the front of the transmission

Refitting

4 Refitting is a reversal of removal. Tighten the switch securely.

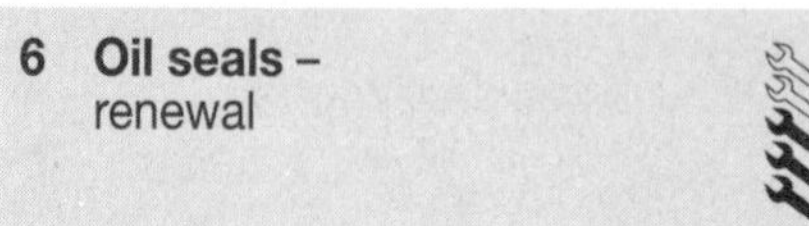

6 Oil seals – renewal

1 Oil leaks frequently occur due to wear or deterioration of the driveshaft oil seals, the selector shaft oil seal, or even the vehicle speed sensor O-ring (where applicable). Renewal of these seals is relatively easy, since the repairs can be performed without removing the transmission from the car.

Driveshaft oil seals

2 The driveshaft oil seals are located at the sides of the transmission, where the driveshafts enter the transmission. If leakage at the seal is suspected, raise the car and support it securely on axle stands. If the seal is leaking, oil will be found on the side of the transmission below the driveshaft.

3 Refer to Chapter 8, Section 2 and remove the appropriate driveshaft.

4 Using a large screwdriver or lever, carefully prise the oil seal out of the transmission casing, taking care not to damage the transmission casing **(see illustration)**.

5 Wipe clean the oil seal seating in the transmission casing.

6 Dip the new oil seal in clean oil, then press it a little way into the casing by hand, making sure that it is square to its seating.

7 Using suitable tubing or a large socket, carefully drive the oil seal fully into the casing until it contacts the seating **(see illustration)**.

8 When refitting the left-hand driveshaft, use the protective sleeve which should be provided with genuine parts. The sleeve is fitted into the seal, and the driveshaft is then fitted through it – the sleeve is then withdrawn and cut free.

9 Refit the driveshaft with reference to Chapter 8, Section 2.

Vehicle speed sensor oil seal

10 Refer to Chapter 4A, Section 14, or Chapter 4B, Section 13. Models with ABS do not have a vehicle speed sensor.

Selector shaft oil seal

11 Apply the handbrake, then jack up the front of the car, supporting it on axle stands (see *Jacking and vehicle support)*.

12 At the front face of the transmission housing, remove the selector mechanism cover by working around the edge, releasing a total of seven clips.

13 Prise off the retaining clips, then pull the shift and selector cables from the transmission levers, and detach them from the cable support brackets by turning the knurled collars clockwise.

14 Unscrew and remove the four bolts securing the selector mechanism rear cover to the transmission housing.

15 Remove the gear shift lever by prising off the protective cap and extracting the retaining clip.

16 With the shift lever removed, unscrew the securing bolt and take off the selector lever and dust cover.

17 The selector shaft oil seal can now be prised out of its location. If using a screwdriver or similar sharp tool, take great care not to mark or gouge the selector shaft or the seal housing as this is done, or the new seal will also leak.

18 Before fitting the new oil seal, carefully clean the visible part of the selector shaft, and the oil seal housing. Wrap a little tape around the end of the shaft, to protect the seal lips as they pass over it.

19 Smear the new oil seal with a little oil, then carefully fit it over the end of the selector shaft, lips facing inwards (towards the transmission).

20 Making sure that the seal stays square to the shaft, press it fully along the shaft (if available, a 16 mm ring spanner is ideal for this).

21 Press the seal fully into its housing, again using the ring spanner or perhaps a deep socket. Remove the tape from the end of the shaft.

22 Further refitting is a reversal of removal. Tighten the selector lever securing bolt to the specified torque, and use new clips when reconnecting the gearchange cables.

23 On completion, check and if necessary adjust the cables as described in Section 2.

7 Transmission – removal and refitting

Warning: The hydraulic fluid used in the clutch system is brake fluid, which is poisonous. Take care to keep it off bare skin, and in particular out of your eyes. The fluid also attacks paintwork, and may discolour carpets, etc – keep spillages to a minimum, and wash any off immediately with cold water. Finally, brake fluid is highly inflammable, and should be handled with the same care as petrol.

Note: *Read through this procedure before starting work to see what is involved, particularly in terms of lifting equipment. Depending on the facilities available, the home mechanic may prefer to remove the engine and transmission together, then separate them on the bench, as described in Chapter 2D, Section 4 or 5. The help of an assistant is highly recommended if the transmission is to be removed (and later refitted) on its own.*

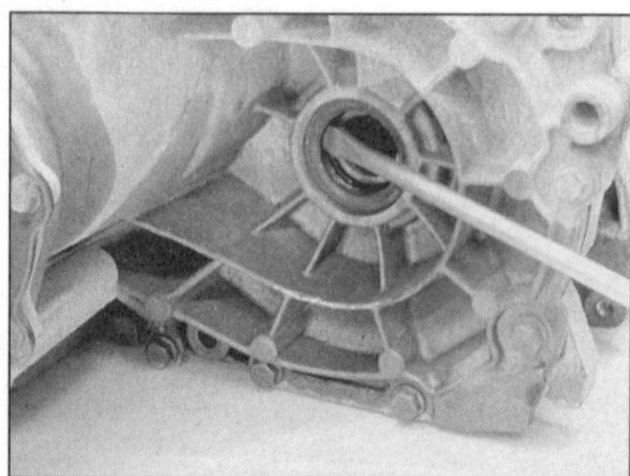

6.4 Prise out the oil seal with a suitable lever

6.7 Drive in the new seal using a socket

Removal

Petrol models

1 Remove the air cleaner as described in Chapter 4A, Section 5.

2 Remove the battery, battery tray and support bracket as described in Chapter 5A, Section 4.

3 Disconnect the PCM wiring plug, or tie it up clear of the working area.

4 Remove the transmission-to-engine bolts which are accessible from above. On some models, at least one of the upper bolts/studs is used to secure a bracket for the engine wiring harness – note its fitted position for use when refitting **(see illustration)**.

5 Remove the starter motor as described in Chapter 5A, Section 11.

6 Disconnect the reversing light switch wiring plug, and also the vehicle speed sensor, where applicable – refer to Section 4 and 5 if necessary.

7 Where fitted, at the rear of the transmission, remove the nut securing the heat shield for the catalytic converter sensor wiring plug **(see illustration)**.

8 Unbolt the engine rear mounting completely from under the car, referring to Chapter 2A, Section 18 if necessary.

9 Disconnect the small upper hose from the coolant expansion tank, then unbolt it from the inner wing and move it to one side, without removing any further hoses.

10 Make sure that the gear lever is in neutral. Taking adequate precautions against fluid spillage (refer to the ***Warning*** at the start of this Section), lift up the securing clip with a small screwdriver, then pull the pipe fitting out of the clutch slave cylinder at the top of the transmission **(see illustrations)**. Unclip the pipe from the battery tray, and raise it to the base of the windscreen, where it can be cable-tied up. Plug or tape over the pipe end, to avoid losing fluid, and to prevent dirt entry.

Diesel models

11 Remove the air cleaner, turbocharger air duct and intake air resonator as described in Chapter 4B, Section 4.

12 Remove the battery, battery tray and support bracket as described in Chapter 5A, Section 4.

13 Unbolt the engine earth strap from the inner wing next to the screen washer filler neck.

14 Disconnect the following wiring (all in the battery tray area):

a) Starting with the one nearest the rear of the car, release the three wiring plugs from the engine management ECU by turning their locking collars anti-clockwise, then pulling towards you.

b) Disconnect the multiplug from the glow plug relay.

c) Unbolt the two glow plug relay power supply cables.

15 Make sure that the gear lever is in neutral. Taking adequate precautions against fluid spillage (refer to the ***Warning*** at the start of this Section), lift up the securing clip with a small screwdriver, then pull the pipe fitting out of the clutch slave cylinder at the top of the transmission. Unclip the pipe from the battery tray, and raise it to the base of the windscreen, where it can be cable-tied up. Plug or tape over the pipe end, to avoid losing fluid, and to prevent dirt entry.

7.4 Some of the transmission-to-engine upper bolts have wiring brackets attached

7.10a Use a small screwdriver to prise up the spring clip ...

16 Remove the transmission-to-engine bolts which are accessible from above, noting that some of them are used to secure wiring harness brackets – note their locations for refitting. Unclip the engine wiring harness from the transmission.

17 On models with air conditioning, remove the single bolt securing the pressure hose bracket to the transmission.

18 Using the information in Chapter 5A, Section 11, remove the three starter motor bolts, and tie it up to one side – there is no need to disconnect the wiring if this approach is taken.

All models

19 To prevent damage to the exhaust flexible section, support it by attaching a pair of splints either side (two scrap strips of wood, plant canes, etc) using some cable-ties. Undo the nuts securing the flexible section to the exhaust manifold, and separate the joint. Recover the gasket, and discard it.

20 Disconnect the shift and selector cables from the front of the transmission, using the information in Section 3 – there is no need to remove the gear lever, nor to remove the cables completely.

21 Using the information in Chapter 8, Section 2, disconnect both driveshafts from the transmission, and also remove the intermediate shaft. There is no need to remove the driveshafts from the hubs, providing they can be supported clear so that the transmission can drop down. The inner and outer joints should not be bent through more than 18° and 45° respectively.

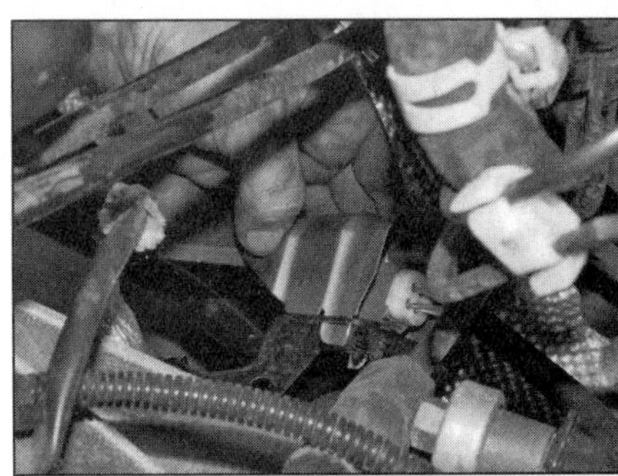

7.7 Remove the converter sensor wiring plug's heat shield

7.10b ... then pull out the hose from the slave cylinder connection on the transmission

22 On diesel models, remove the radiator cooling fan and frame as described in Chapter 3, Section 5. Petrol models may also benefit from the increase in working room this allows.

23 Where applicable, unbolt the power steering fluid hose bracket from the top of the transmission **(see illustration)**.

24 Make a final check round the transmission, to make sure nothing (apart from the left-hand mounting) remains attached or in the way which will prevent it from being lowered out. Also make sure there is enough room under the front of the car for the transmission to be lowered out and withdrawn.

25 Securely attach the engine/transmission

7.23 Unbolt and remove the power steering fluid hose from the top of the transmission

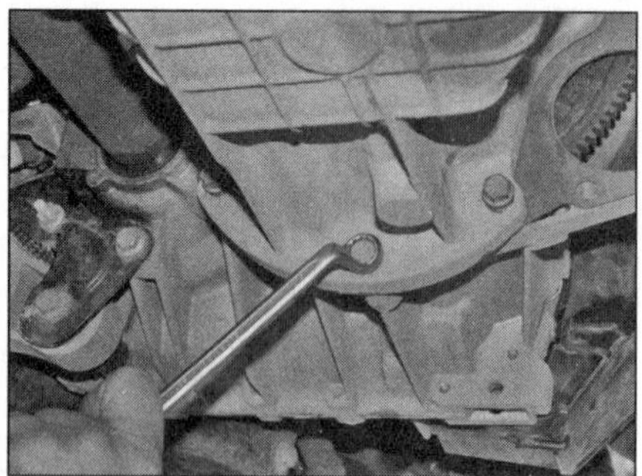

7.29 The three lowest engine-to-transmission bolts go through the sump

7.31 If necessary, prise the transmission off the engine

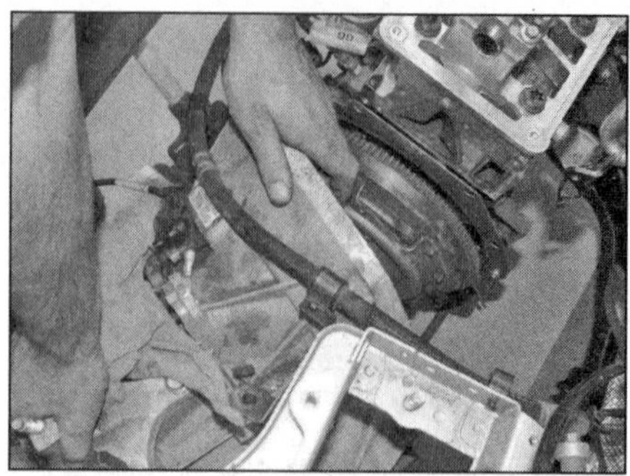

7.33 Move the transmission clear of the engine, then lower it to the ground

unit to a suitable engine crane or hoist (or to an engine support bar), and raise it so that the weight is just taken off the engine left-hand mounting (on top of the transmission). The transmission end of the engine must be supported before the transmission itself can be removed. It is helpful at this stage to have an assistant available, either to work the crane or to guide the transmission out.

26 Supporting the engine and transmission from below should be considered a last resort, and should only be done if a heavy-duty hydraulic ('trolley') jack is used, with a large, flat piece of wood on the jack head to spread the load and avoid damage to the sump. A further jack will be needed to lower the transmission out. **Note:** *Always take care when using a hydraulic jack, as it is possible for this type to collapse under load – generally, a scissor-type jack avoids this problem, but is also less stable, and offers no manoeuvrability.*

27 With the engine/transmission securely supported, remove the three nuts from the engine left-hand mounting (on top of the transmission). Discard the nuts – new ones must be used when refitting.

28 Carefully lower the transmission, checking all the time that nothing is getting caught or stretched. Also take care that the engine right-hand mounting is not being too distorted, or placed under excess strain.

29 Remove the lowest transmission-to-engine bolts now, leaving only the easily-accessed bolts still securing the unit. Note that, on petrol models, the lowest bolts are actually through the sump **(see illustration)**.

30 Support the transmission from below, using a trolley jack, a large piece of board, and several smaller pieces of wood to block-up the transmission. Note that this method carries a risk of the transmission toppling, so have an assistant available to steady it.

31 Unscrew the remaining transmission-to-engine bolts. If the transmission does not separate on its own, it must be prised apart, to free it from the locating dowels **(see illustration)**.

32 As the transmission is withdrawn from the engine, make sure its weight is supported at all times – the transmission input shaft (or the clutch) may otherwise be damaged as it is withdrawn through the clutch assembly bolted to the engine flywheel. Recover the adapter plate fitted between the engine and transmission, as it may fall out when the two are separated.

33 Keeping the transmission steady on the jack head, carefully lower it down and remove it from under the car **(see illustration)**.

34 The clutch components can now be inspected with reference to Chapter 6, Section 7, and renewed if necessary. Unless they are virtually new, it is worth renewing the clutch components as a matter of course, even if the transmission has been removed for some other reason.

Refitting

35 If removed, refit the clutch components (see Chapter 6, Section 7). Also ensure that the engine-to-transmission adapter plates are in position on the engine.

36 With the transmission secured to the trolley jack as on removal, raise it into position, and then carefully slide it onto the engine, at the same time engaging the input shaft with the clutch friction disc splines. If marks were made between the transmission and engine on removal, these can be used as a guide to correct alignment.

37 Do not use excessive force to refit the transmission – if the input shaft does not slide into place easily, readjust the angle of the transmission so that it is level, and/or turn the input shaft so that the splines engage properly with the disc. If problems are still experienced, check that the clutch friction disc is correctly centred (Chapter 6, Section 7).

38 Once the transmission is successfully mated to the engine, insert as many of the transmission-to-engine bolts as possible, and tighten them progressively, to draw the transmission fully onto the locating dowels.

39 Raise the transmission into position, then refit the upper section of the engine left-hand mounting. Tighten the new nuts hand-tight only at this stage, but sufficiently to support the transmission so that the support bar, engine hoist or supporting jack can be removed.

40 Refit the remaining transmission-to-engine bolts, and tighten all of them to the specified torque.

41 Refit the engine rear mounting to the subframe, and tighten the through-bolts to the specified torque.

42 Further refitting is a reversal of removal, noting the following points:

a) Refit the starter motor as described in Chapter 5A, Section 11.

b) Refit the driveshafts as described in Chapter 8, Section 2.

c) Once the driveshafts have been refitted, the three left-hand mounting nuts can be tightened to the specified torque, with the larger centre nut being done up last.

d) On completion, adjust the gear cables as described in Section 2.

8 Transmission overhaul – general information

The overhaul of a manual transmission is a complex (and often expensive) engineering task for the DIY home mechanic to undertake, which requires access to specialist equipment. It involves dismantling and reassembly of many small components, measuring clearances precisely and if necessary, adjusting them by the selection shims and spacers. Internal transmission components are also often difficult to obtain and in many instances, extremely expensive. Because of this, if the transmission develops a fault or becomes noisy, the best course of action is to have the unit overhauled by a specialist repairer or to obtain an exchange reconditioned unit.

Nevertheless, it is not impossible for the more experienced mechanic to overhaul the transmission if the special tools are available and the job is carried out in a deliberate step-by-step manner, to ensure that nothing is overlooked.

The tools necessary for an overhaul include internal and external circlip pliers, bearing pullers, a slide hammer, a set of pin punches, a dial test indicator, and possibly, a hydraulic press. In addition, a large, sturdy workbench and a vice will be required.

During dismantling of the transmission, make careful notes of how each component is fitted to make reassembly easier and accurate.

Before dismantling the transmission, it will help if you have some idea of where the problem lies. Certain problems can be closely related to specific areas in the transmission which can make component examination and renewal easier. Refer to *Fault diagnosis* at the end of this manual for more information.

Chapter 7 Part B: Durashift EST transmission

Contents

Degrees of difficulty

Easy, suitable for novice with little experience	**Fairly easy,** suitable for beginner with some experience	**Fairly difficult,** suitable for competent DIY mechanic	**Difficult,** suitable for experienced DIY mechanic	**Very difficult,** suitable for expert DIY or professional 

Specifications

General

Type	Automated manual transmission system
Designation	Durashift EST

Torque wrench settings

	Nm	lbf ft
Clutch actuator bolt	20	15
Gearshift actuator mounting bolts:		
All except lowest mounting bolt	23	17
Lowest mounting bolt (near transmission selector shaft)	16	12
Gearshift actuator-to-selector shaft bolt	23	17

1 General information

The Durashift electronic shift technology (EST) transmission is unusual in being a manual transmission which offers full automatic operation. The system uses virtually the same 5-speed iB5 manual transmission and hydraulic clutch as normal Fusion models, but has two major electronic and electro-hydraulic units bolted on (the gearshift and clutch actuators) to enable automatic operation **(see illustration)**. Note however that it is not possible to use a standard iB5 transmission in place of the specific Durashift transmission, as the Durashift version uses different gear ratios and has a fine tolerance gear shift system fitted. A clutch pedal is not fitted, and the cable-operated gearchange system used on other Fusions is superseded by an entirely electronic gear lever assembly, which could be said to be a fly-by-wire gearchange system.

The clutch actuator is the heart of the system. Mounted in front of the transmission in the engine compartment, the actuator contains a motor which is used to control the pressure of the hydraulic fluid (supplied from the brake fluid reservoir). A master cylinder is built into the actuator, and the otherwise-conventional clutch is finally operated via a slave cylinder very similar to the one fitted to normal Fusion models. Note that whilst very similar to the standard concentric slave cylinder fitted to manual transmission models the slave cylinder is unique to Durashift models (see Chapter 6, Section 3). By regulating the fluid pressure, the clutch actuator controls all the normal clutch functions, from measured engagement when starting off, to complete disengagement when stopping with a gear selected, as well as the clutch actions required for changing gear. The clutch will engage automatically when the engine is switched off, so that the car can be left 'in-gear' if wished, as a parking aid (the selector must be moved back to N for starting, however). As with the hydraulic clutch fitted to conventional Fusion models, the Durashift clutch is self-adjusting.

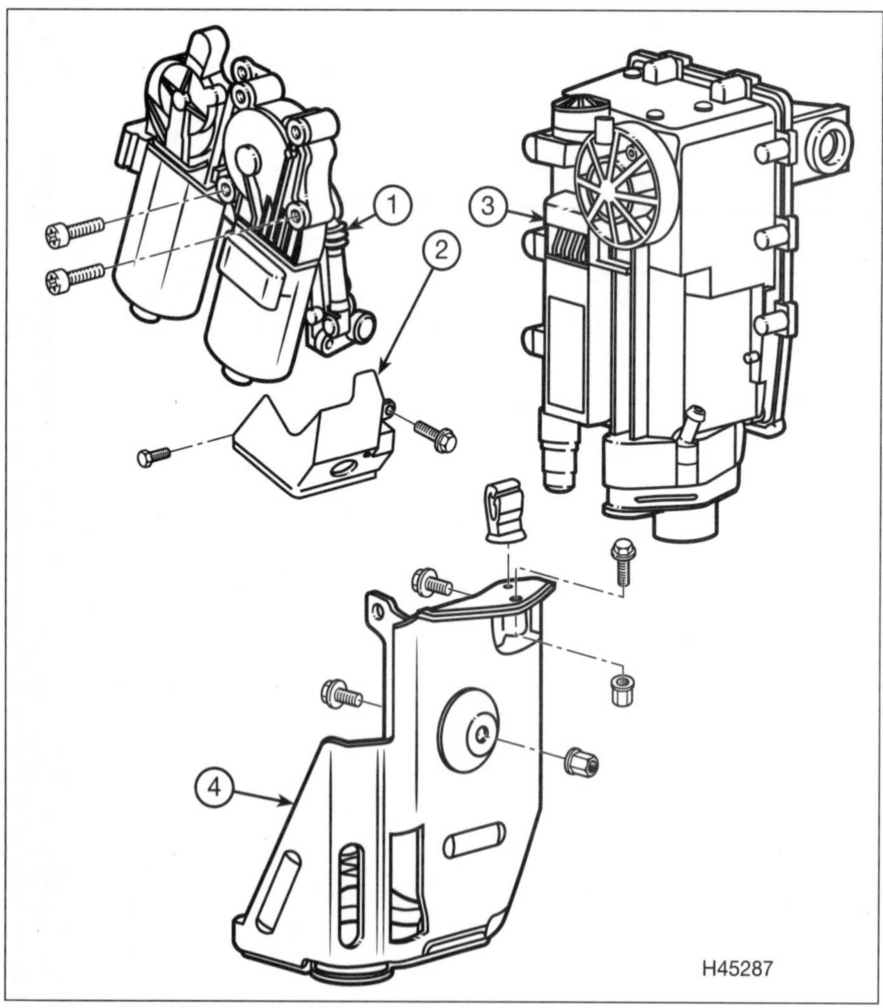

1.1 Durashift EST transmission external components

1 Gearshift actuator
2 Lower cover
3 Clutch actuator
4 Mounting bracket

A degree of transmission 'creep' is built into the system, with the engine management system providing a greater degree of anti-stall control on these models. This only works when the handbrake is released – the handbrake warning light switch signal determines when the handbrake is applied.

Contained within the clutch actuator is the transmission control unit, which evaluates incoming signals from the gear lever inside the car, and information such as engine speed, vehicle speed (from the car's ABS wheel sensors), throttle position, and brake pedal position. From this information, the control unit signals the clutch and/or gearshift actuators as appropriate. The control unit also performs functions such as switching on the reversing lights when R is selected inside the car.

The gearshift actuator is mounted on the front of the transmission, where the gearchange cables would be connected on the normal version of the iB5 unit. The gearshift actuator uses electric motors to operate the shift and selector functions, when signalled by the transmission control unit.

The gear lever inside the car is effectively a complex switch, used by the driver to indicate to the system which mode of operation, or which gear, is required. The system offers the choice of fully-automatic gearchanging (A), or sequential manual operation (using the + or - positions) in D. The only other options which can be selected are N for neutral, and R for reverse. Gear lever movement is detected by electromagnetic Hall sensors, and the signals from these sensors are then processed using electronics contained inside the gear lever assembly, before being sent to the transmission control unit under the bonnet. An instrument panel display indicates to the driver which mode of operation, and which gear, has been selected.

Precautions

Various safeguards are built into the system, to prevent accidents or damage. In common with more conventional automatic transmissions, the Durashift system will only allow the engine to be started in position N, and the footbrake has to be applied (the system uses the brake light switch signal to determine this). The brakes also have to be applied to move the gear lever from N to D. If the driver's door is opened with the engine running and a gear selected, a warning will sound and the instrument panel display will flash. The transmission control unit will not allow manual gearchanges to be made if the engine or roadspeeds are inappropriate.

If a Durashift-equipped car needs to be towed, this must only be done with neutral (N) selected, but there are no other restrictions.

Durashift models can be push- or tow-started from cold if necessary – with the ignition on and N selected, push or tow the car, then slowly move the gear lever from N to D. This method of starting will not work if the battery is completely flat. The engine must be cold before even attempting this, as damage could be caused to the catalytic converter if the engine was hot.

2 Clutch actuator – removal and refitting

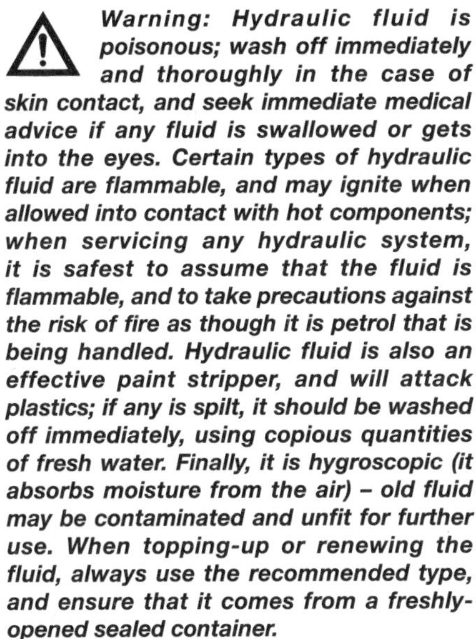

Warning: Hydraulic fluid is poisonous; wash off immediately and thoroughly in the case of skin contact, and seek immediate medical advice if any fluid is swallowed or gets into the eyes. Certain types of hydraulic fluid are flammable, and may ignite when allowed into contact with hot components; when servicing any hydraulic system, it is safest to assume that the fluid is flammable, and to take precautions against the risk of fire as though it is petrol that is being handled. Hydraulic fluid is also an effective paint stripper, and will attack plastics; if any is spilt, it should be washed off immediately, using copious quantities of fresh water. Finally, it is hygroscopic (it absorbs moisture from the air) – old fluid may be contaminated and unfit for further use. When topping-up or renewing the fluid, always use the recommended type, and ensure that it comes from a freshly-opened sealed container.

Note: *It may be necessary on completion to have the Durashift system reprogrammed using Ford diagnostic equipment, to ensure proper operation. To reduce the need for this, keep the loss of fluid from the system to a minimum, as this will reduce the need for bleeding.*

Removal

1 Disconnect the battery negative lead, and position the lead away from the battery.

2 Press the quick-release connector to disconnect the low-pressure fluid supply hose at the top of the actuator. Be prepared for fluid spillage – wipe up any excess fluid, and wash down any painted surfaces (without getting any water inside the actuator). Cap or cover the actuator fluid hose, to prevent further fluid loss or the entry of dirt into the system.

3 Release the locking rings used at the top and bottom of the actuator wiring connector, and disconnect the wiring plug **(see illustration)**.

4 Remove the clips fitted at either end of the high-pressure fluid pipe, and disconnect the pipe from the base of the actuator, and from the slave cylinder on the transmission itself. Again, be prepared for fluid spillage, and take steps to reduce loss of fluid or dirt entry.

5 Remove the bolt securing the actuator, and remove it from under the car.

Refitting

6 Refitting is a reversal of removal, noting the following points:

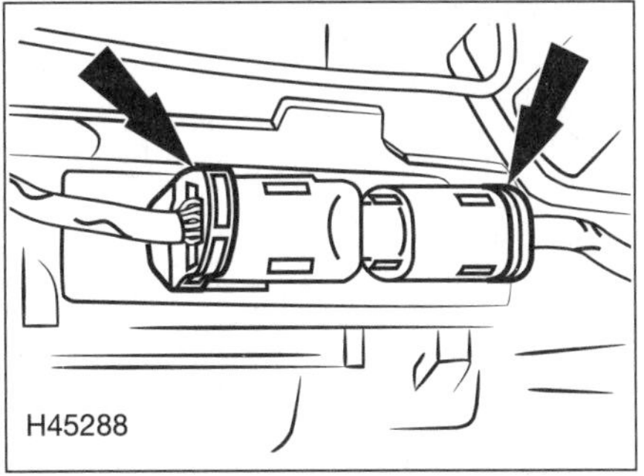

2.3 Disconnect the clutch actuator wiring plug locking rings

a) Tighten the mounting bolt to the specified torque.

b) Ensure that the wiring and fluid connections are securely remade.

c) On completion, the system must be bled to ensure correct operation (see Chapter 6, Section 5). With Durashift, there is no clutch pedal to pump out the fluid, and it is not clear whether bleeding by switching on the ignition and opening the slave cylinder bleed screw would work, or would even be advisable (the actuator may produce a significant fluid pressure, which could be high enough to be hazardous). A pressure-bleeding kit would be the next-best solution, if the Ford method described in Chapter 6, Section 5 is not an option. Seek the advice of a Ford dealer in the first instance, as it may be necessary to have the system reprogrammed using diagnostic equipment, in order to restore correct operation.

3 Gearshift actuator – removal and refitting

Removal

1 Disconnect the battery negative lead, and position the lead away from the battery.

2 Jack up the front of the car, and support it on axle stands (see *Jacking and vehicle support*).

3 The gearshift actuator is fitted to the front face of the transmission. To gain access to it, remove the two cover retaining bolts, and take off the cover.

4 Remove the two wiring plugs, noting their fitted positions – the black one is nearest the front of the car **(see illustration)**.

5 Remove the bolt securing the actuator to the transmission selector shaft, and the bolt at the top securing the actuator to its mounting bracket.

6 Remove the three further actuator mounting bolts, prise off the actuator joint, and lift the actuator off the transmission selector shaft **(see illustration)**.

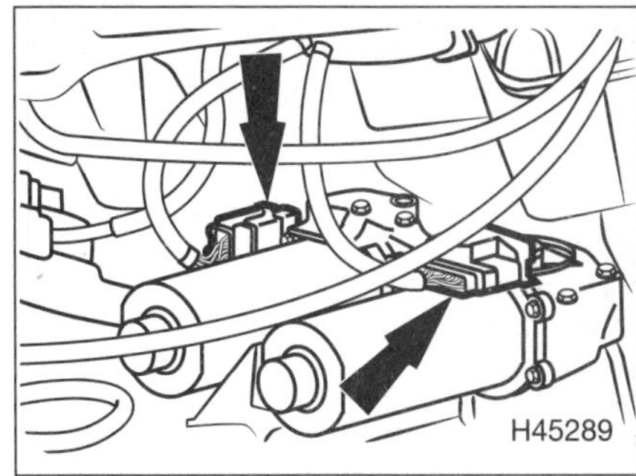

3.4 Disconnect the gearshift actuator wiring plugs

Refitting

7 Refitting is a reversal of removal. Tighten the bolts to the specified torque – note that the actuator mounting bolt nearest the transmission selector shaft is tightened to a lower torque than the others. If a new actuator has been fitted, it may be necessary to have the system reprogrammed using Ford diagnostic equipment before it will work properly.

4 Reversing light/ inhibitor switches – removal and refitting

The reversing light switch and starter inhibitor switch functions are contained within the transmission control unit, which itself is an integral part of the clutch actuator.

5 Gear lever assembly – removal and refitting

Removal

1 Disconnect the battery negative (earth) lead.

2 Carefully prise up the plastic trim ring at the base of the gear lever, and remove it over the gear lever (the rubber gaiter stays behind).

3 Unclip the gear lever trim panel from the top of the centre console by carefully prising

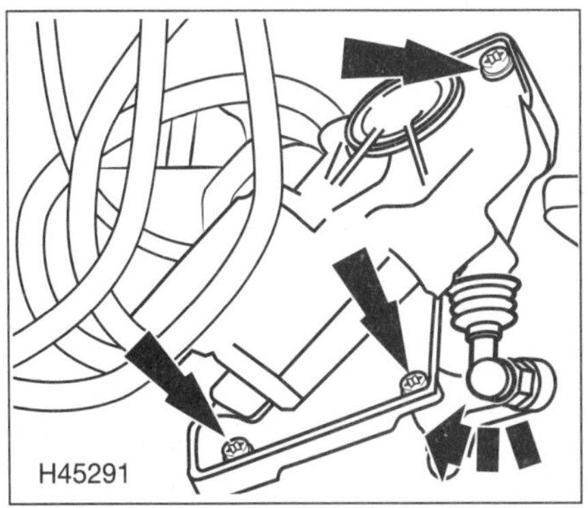

3.6 Remove the three remaining bolts, prise off the selector joint, and remove the gearshift actuator

it up to release the clips. Once the panel has been lifted, disconnect the wiring plugs from the cigar lighter and/or power outlet socket, as applicable, then remove the panel over the gear lever.

4 Disconnect the wiring plug from the gear lever.

5 Remove the four nuts securing the gear lever to the floor, and lift it out.

Refitting

6 Refitting is a reversal of removal. If a new gear lever has been fitted, it may have to be programmed-in using Ford diagnostic equipment before it will work properly. Switch on the ignition, and check the operation of the gearshift instrument display.

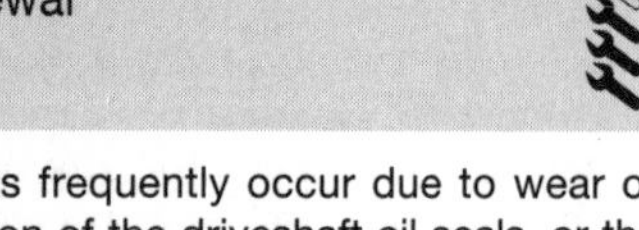

6 Oil seals - renewal

1 Oil leaks frequently occur due to wear or deterioration of the driveshaft oil seals, or the selector shaft oil seal. Renewal of these seals is relatively easy, since the repairs can be performed without removing the transmission from the car.

Driveshaft oil seals

2 Refer to Chapter 7A, Section 6.

Selector shaft oil seal

3 Remove the gearshift actuator as described in Section 3.

4 With the shift lever removed, unscrew the securing bolt and take off the selector lever and dust cover.

5 The selector shaft oil seal can now be prised out of its location. If using a screwdriver or similar sharp tool, take great care not to mark or gouge the selector shaft or the seal housing as this is done, or the new seal will also leak.

6 Before fitting the new oil seal, carefully clean the visible part of the selector shaft, and the oil seal housing. Wrap a little tape around the end of the shaft, to protect the seal lips as they pass over it.

7 Smear the new oil seal with a little oil, then carefully fit it over the end of the selector shaft, lips facing inwards (towards the transmission).

8 Making sure that the seal stays square to the shaft, press it fully along the shaft (if available, a 16 mm ring spanner is ideal for this).

9 Press the seal fully into its housing, again using the ring spanner or perhaps a deep socket. Remove the tape from the end of the shaft.

10 Further refitting is a reversal of removal. Tighten the selector lever securing bolt to the specified torque, and refit the gearshift actuator as described in Section 3.

7 Transmission - removal and refitting

Refer to Chapter 7A, Section 7. Removal and refitting procedures for the Durashift transmission are almost identical to the conventional iB5 unit, with the exception that any references to gearchange cables should be ignored. At the relevant point in the procedure, instead of unclipping the gearchange cables cover and disconnecting the cables, the gearshift actuator cover is removed (two bolts) and the actuator wiring plugs are disconnected (refer to Section 3). Greater working room may be achieved by removing the clutch actuator as described in Section 2, although this is not strictly necessary.

8 Transmission overhaul - general

Refer to Chapter 7A, Section 8. Although the Durashift transmission is extremely similar to the standard iB5 unit, if obtaining any transmission internal parts, or even a complete reconditioned unit, make sure to specify that it's for a Durashift model, as there are significant detail differences.

Chapter 8
Driveshafts

Contents

Degrees of difficulty

Easy, suitable for novice with little experience	**Fairly easy,** suitable for beginner with some experience 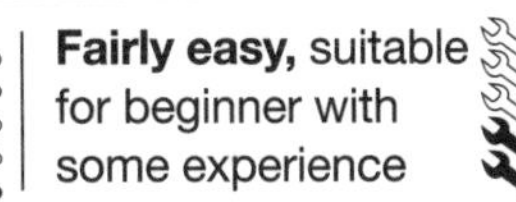	**Fairly difficult,** suitable for competent DIY mechanic	**Difficult,** suitable for experienced DIY mechanic	**Very difficult,** suitable for expert DIY or professional 

Specifications

General

Driveshaft type	Solid steel shafts with inner and outer constant velocity (CV) joints, both outer joints are of the ball-and-cage type and the inner joints of the tripod (spider-and-yoke) type. Right-hand driveshaft is fitted with a support bearing

Lubricant

Type/specification	Special grease (Ford specification WSS-M1C259-A1) supplied in sachets with gaiter kits – joints are otherwise prepacked with grease and sealed
Quantity (per joint):	
Inner joint	100 g
Outer joint	90 g

Torque wrench settings	**Nm**	**lbf ft**
Front hub nut*	290	214
Lower arm balljoint clamp bolt nut	48	35
Right-hand driveshaft support bearing cap nuts*	25	18
Roadwheel nuts	110	81
Suspension strut top mounting nuts	25	18

** Use new nuts*

2.2 Loosen the driveshaft/hub nut with the wheel firmly on the ground

2.3 Loosen the three suspension strut nuts by three turns

1 General information

Drive is transmitted from the differential to the front wheels by means of two, unequal-length driveshafts.

Each driveshaft is fitted with an inner and outer constant velocity (CV) joint. The inner constant velocity joint is of the spider-and-yoke type and the outer joint is of the ball-and-cage type. Each outer joint is splined to engage with the wheel hub, and is threaded so that it can be fastened to the hub by a large nut. The inner joint is also splined to engage with the differential sunwheel (left-hand side) or the intermediate shaft (right-hand side).

On the right-hand driveshaft, the inner constant velocity (CV) joint is located approximately halfway along the shaft length, and the joint outer member is supported by the rear of the cylinder block via a support bearing and bracket.

2 Driveshafts - removal and refitting

Note: *The driveshaft outer joint splines may be a tight fit in the hub, and it is possible that a puller/extractor will be required to draw the hub assembly off of the driveshaft during removal.*

Removal

1 Remove the relevant wheel trim, or the wheel centre cover (alloy wheels) for access to the front hub nut.

2 Ensure that the handbrake is applied (ideally, have an assistant apply the footbrake), then slacken the hub nut using a suitable socket and extension bar **(see illustration)**. Loosen the hub nut almost to the end of its threads, but do not remove it at this stage.

⚠ ***Warning: The driveshaft nut is done up extremely tight, and considerable effort will be required to loosen it. Do not use poor-quality, badly-fitting tools for this task, due to the risk of personal injury.***

3 Working in the engine compartment, loosen the three suspension strut top mounting nuts by three turns each, on the side concerned **(see illustration)**. Do not loosen the centre nut.

4 Slacken the relevant front wheel nuts, then jack up the front of the car, and support securely on axle stands (see *Jacking and vehicle support*). Remove the roadwheel.

5 Remove the lower arm balljoint clamp bolt from the swivel hub (note which way round it fits), and lever down the lower arm to separate it – if necessary, prise the clamp open carefully using a large flat-bladed tool. Take care not to damage the balljoint rubber during the separation procedure. Unclip the balljoint heat shield, and retain it for refitting **(see illustrations)**.

6 The splined end of the driveshaft now has to be released from its location in the hub. It's likely that the splines will be very tight (corrosion may even be a factor, if the driveshaft has not been disturbed for some time), and considerable force may be needed to push the driveshaft out. Ford recommend using a four-legged puller for this, but if one is not available, the shaft will have to be tapped out with a hammer. If a hammer is used, place a small piece of wood over the end of the driveshaft – in addition to the loosened hub nut, this will protect the threads from damage.

7 Once the splines have been released, remove the hub nut and discard it – the nut will probably be of the new 'laminated' type, and is only designed to be used once **(see illustration)**.

8 The driveshaft can be separated from the hub by having an assistant pull the base of the suspension strut outwards, while the splined

2.5a Loosen the lower arm balljoint clamp bolt nut (hold the bolt with a second spanner/socket) ...

2.5b ... then remove the bolt, noting that it fits from the back

2.5c Home-made method of releasing the lower arm – wood block, long pole and length of chain

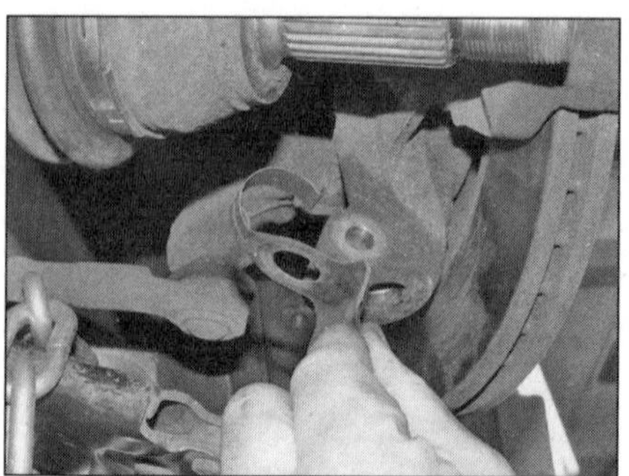
2.5d Unclip and remove the balljoint heat shield

2.7 Remove the hub nut, and get a new one for refitting – laminated nuts can split open if retightened

2.8 Pull the base of the strut outwards, and pull the driveshaft splines through to the inside

2.10a Use a lever to prise the driveshaft out – this may take some time and effort

2.10b Once the driveshaft comes free, support the inner joint and remove the shaft completely

end of the shaft is pulled clear of the hub **(see illustration)**. Do not bend the driveshaft excessively at any stage, or the joints may be damaged – the inner and outer joints should not be bent through more than 18° and 45° respectively. Do not let the driveshaft hang down under its own weight – tie it up level if necessary.

9 Proceed as follows, according to which driveshaft is being removed.

Left-hand driveshaft

10 Insert a lever between the driveshaft inner joint and the transmission housing, positioning a thin piece of wood between the lever and housing to protect it. Also position a container below the inner joint, to catch the transmission oil which will be lost as the driveshaft is removed. Carefully lever the driveshaft inner joint out of the differential, taking great care not to damage the transmission housing or the oil seal **(see illustrations)**.

11 Manoeuvre the driveshaft out of position, ensuring that the constant velocity joints are not placed under excessive strain, and remove the driveshaft from underneath the car. Whilst the driveshaft is removed, plug the differential aperture with a clean, lint-free cloth to prevent dirt getting in.

12 Extract the circlip from the groove on the inner end of the driveshaft, and obtain a new one.

Right-hand driveshaft

13 The right-hand driveshaft may either be removed complete with the intermediate shaft from the transmission, or it may be disconnected from the outer end of the intermediate shaft.

14 If the latter course of action is taken, remove the retaining clip from around the larger end of the inner gaiter, and withdraw the inner tripod joint from the intermediate shaft.

15 If the complete driveshaft is to be removed, proceed as follows. Unscrew the nuts securing the driveshaft support bearing cap to the rear of the cylinder block, and release the heat shield from the studs **(see illustration)**. A new bearing cap and nuts must be used when refitting.

16 Position a container below the transmission, to catch the oil which will be lost as the driveshaft is removed. Withdraw the complete driveshaft from the transmission and from the bearing bracket, and remove it from under the car **(see illustration)**. If necessary, slide the heat shield off the intermediate shaft.

Both driveshafts

17 Check the condition of the differential oil seals, and if necessary renew them as described in Chapter 7A, Section 6.

Refitting

Right-hand driveshaft

18 If the intermediate shaft has not been removed, proceed to paragraph 21. Otherwise, proceed as follows.

19 Carefully refit the complete driveshaft in the support bearing and into the transmission, taking care not to damage the oil seal. Turn the driveshaft until it engages the splines on the differential gears.

20 Tighten the new nuts securing the new support bearing cap to the cylinder block to the specified torque. Proceed to paragraph 26.

21 Locate the inner tripod joint of the driveshaft into the intermediate shaft.

22 After packing the joint with new grease (see Specifications at the beginning of this Chapter), refit the gaiter and tighten its retaining clip.

Left-hand driveshaft

23 Locate the new circlip in the groove on the inner end of the driveshaft **(see illustration)**.

24 Use a special sleeve to protect the differential oil seal as the driveshaft is inserted. If the sleeve is not used, take great care to avoid damaging the seal. (Installation sleeves are supplied with new oil seals, where required.)

25 Insert the driveshaft into the transmission, and push it fully home. Try pulling the shaft out, to make sure the circlip is fully engaged.

Both driveshafts

26 Pull the suspension strut outwards, and insert the outer end of the driveshaft through the hub. Turn the driveshaft to engage the splines in the hub, and fully push on the hub. Ford use a special tool to draw the driveshaft into the hub, but it is unlikely that the splines will be tight. However, if they are, it will be necessary to obtain the tool, or to use a similar home-made tool.

27 Screw on the new driveshaft nut, and use it to draw the driveshaft fully through the hub. Delay fully tightening the nut until the wheel is back on, and the car has been lowered to the ground.

2.15 Unscrew the driveshaft bearing cap nuts

2.16 Withdrawing the right-hand driveshaft

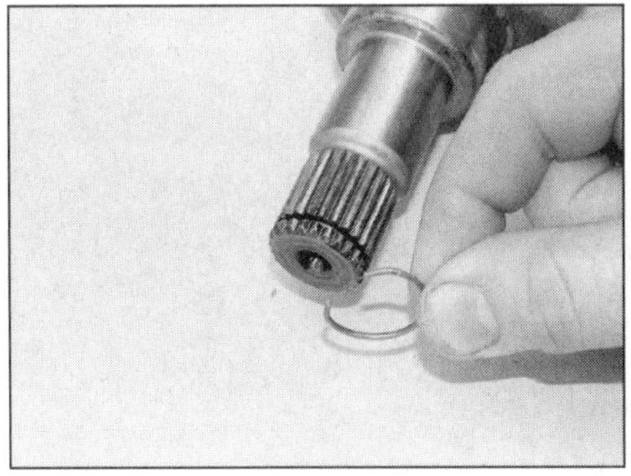

2.23 Fit a new circlip to the driveshaft groove

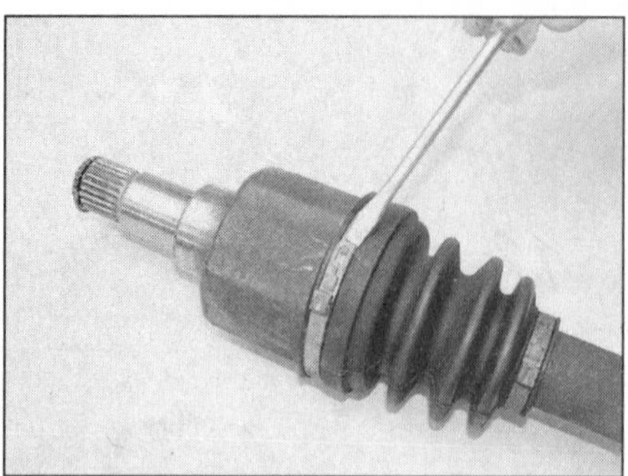

3.22 Remove the gaiter securing clips

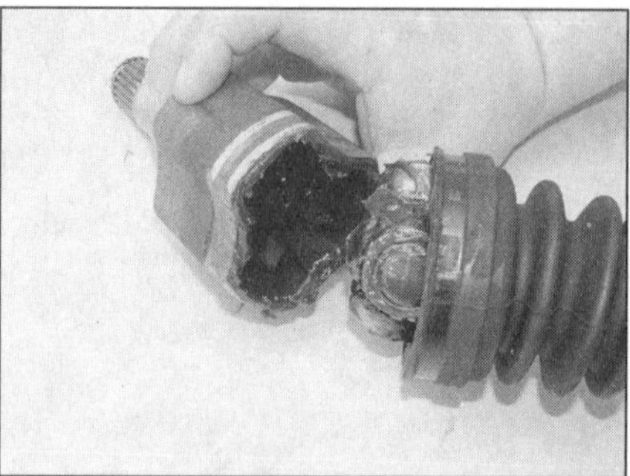

3.23 Withdrawing the joint housing from the tripod joint

28 Locate the front suspension lower arm balljoint stub in the bottom of the swivel hub, making sure the balljoint shield is in place. Insert the clamp bolt in the previously-noted position, screw on the nut, and tighten it to the specified torque.

29 Tighten the suspension strut upper mounting nuts to the specified torque.

30 Fill the transmission, and check the level as described in Chapter 1A, Section 18 or Chapter 1B, Section 19.

31 Refit the wheel, and lower the car to the ground. Tighten the wheel nuts to the specified torque.

32 Fully tighten the driveshaft nut to the specified torque. Finally, refit the wheel trim (or centre cover).

3 Driveshaft inner joint gaiter – renewal

1 The inner joint gaiter can be renewed either with the driveshaft removed from the car, or with it *in situ*. If it is wished to fully remove the driveshaft, refer to Section 2 first. Note that if both the inner and outer gaiters are being renewed at the same time, the outer gaiter can be removed from the inner end of the driveshaft.

Driveshaft fitted

2 Remove the relevant wheel trim or the wheel centre cover (alloy wheels), then slacken the relevant front wheel nuts. Apply the handbrake, then jack up the front of the car, and support securely on axle stands (see *Jacking and vehicle support*). Remove the roadwheel.

3 Remove the lower arm balljoint clamp bolt from the swivel hub (note which way round it fits), and lever down the lower arm to separate it – if necessary, prise the clamp open carefully using a large flat-bladed tool. Take care not to damage the balljoint rubber during the separation procedure. Unclip the balljoint heat shield, and retain it for refitting.

4 Mark the driveshaft in relation to the joint housing, to ensure correct refitting.

5 Note the fitted location of both of the inner joint gaiter retaining clips. Release the clips from the gaiter, and slide the gaiter back along the driveshaft (away from the transmission) a little way.

6 Pull the front suspension strut outwards, while guiding the tripod joint out of the joint housing. Support the inner end of the driveshaft on an axle stand.

7 Check that the inner end of the driveshaft is marked in relation to the splined tripod hub. If not, carefully centre-punch the two items, to ensure correct refitting. Alternatively, use dabs of paint on the driveshaft and one end of the tripod.

8 Extract the circlip retaining the tripod on the driveshaft.

9 Using a suitable puller, remove the tripod from the end of the driveshaft, and slide off the gaiter.

10 If the outer gaiter is also to be renewed, remove it with reference to Section 4.

11 Clean the driveshaft, and obtain a new tripod retaining circlip. New gaiter retaining clips must also be fitted.

3.25 Using circlip pliers to remove the circlip from the shaft

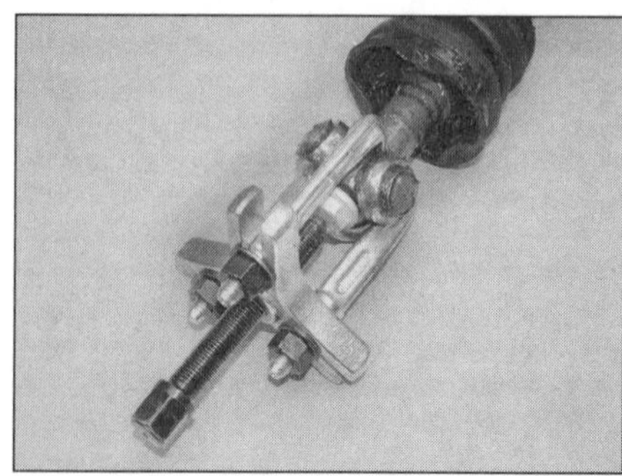

3.26 Using a puller to remove the tripod

12 Slide the new gaiter on the driveshaft, together with new clips.

13 Refit the tripod on the driveshaft splines, if necessary using a soft-faced mallet to drive it fully onto the splines. It must be fitted with the chamfered edge leading (towards the driveshaft), and with the previously-made marks aligned. Secure it in position using the new circlip. Ensure that the circlip is fully engaged in its groove.

14 With the front suspension strut pulled outwards, guide the tripod joint into the joint housing, making sure that the previously-made marks are aligned. Pack the joint with new grease (see Specifications at the beginning of this Chapter).

15 Slide the gaiter along the driveshaft, and locate it on the joint housing. The small-diameter end of the gaiter must be located in the groove on the driveshaft.

16 Ensure that the gaiter is not twisted or distorted, then insert a small screwdriver under the lip of the gaiter at the housing end. This will allow trapped air to escape during the next step.

17 Push the tripod fully into the housing, then pull it out by 20 mm. Remove the screwdriver, then fit the retaining clips and tighten them.

18 Reconnect the front suspension lower arm balljoint to the swivel hub. Refit and tighten the clamp nut and bolt to its specified torque.

19 Refit the wheel, and lower the car to the ground. Tighten the wheel nuts to their specified torque.

Driveshaft removed

20 Mount the driveshaft in a vice.

21 Mark the driveshaft in relation to the joint housing, to ensure correct refitting.

22 Note the fitted location of both of the inner joint gaiter retaining clips, then release the clips from the gaiter **(see illustration)**, and slide the gaiter back along the driveshaft a little way.

23 Remove the inner joint housing from the tripod **(see illustration)**.

24 Check that the inner end of the driveshaft is marked in relation to the splined tripod hub. If not, carefully centre-punch the two items, to ensure correct refitting. Alternatively, use dabs of paint on the driveshaft and one end of the tripod.

25 Extract the circlip retaining the tripod on the driveshaft **(see illustration)**.

26 Using a puller, remove the tripod from the end of the driveshaft **(see illustration)**, and slide off the gaiter.

27 If the outer gaiter is also to be renewed, remove it with reference to Section 4.

28 Clean the driveshaft, and obtain a new joint retaining circlip. The gaiter retaining clips must also be renewed.

29 Slide the new gaiter on the driveshaft, together with new clips **(see illustration)**.

30 Refit the tripod on the driveshaft splines, if necessary using a soft-faced mallet and a suitable socket to drive it fully onto the splines. It must be fitted with the chamfered

3.29 Slide the gaiter and the clips onto the shaft

edge leading (towards the driveshaft), and with the previously-made marks aligned **(see illustration)**. Secure it in position using a new circlip. Ensure that the circlip is fully engaged in its groove.

31 Scoop out all of the old grease from the joint housing, then pack the joint with new grease (see Specifications at the beginning of this Chapter). Guide the joint housing onto the tripod joint, making sure that the previously-made marks are aligned.

32 Slide the gaiter along the driveshaft, and locate it on the tripod joint housing. The small-diameter end of the gaiter must be located in the groove on the driveshaft.

33 Ensure that the gaiter is not twisted or distorted, then insert a small screwdriver under the lip of the gaiter at the housing end. This will allow trapped air to escape during the next step.

34 Push the housing fully on the tripod, then pull it out by 20 mm. Remove the screwdriver, then fit the retaining clips and tighten them **(see illustration)**.

4 Driveshaft outer joint gaiter – renewal

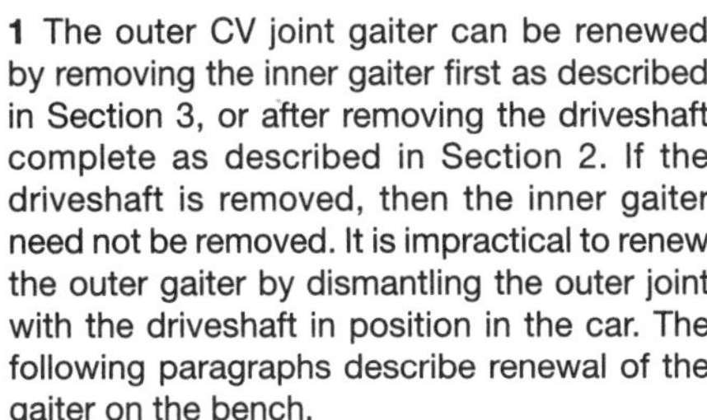

1 The outer CV joint gaiter can be renewed by removing the inner gaiter first as described in Section 3, or after removing the driveshaft complete as described in Section 2. If the driveshaft is removed, then the inner gaiter need not be removed. It is impractical to renew the outer gaiter by dismantling the outer joint with the driveshaft in position in the car. The following paragraphs describe renewal of the gaiter on the bench.

2 If required, mount the driveshaft in a vice.

3 Mark the driveshaft in relation to the CV joint housing, to ensure correct refitting.

4 Note the fitted location of both of the outer joint gaiter retaining clips, then release the clips from the gaiter, and slide the gaiter back along the driveshaft a little way.

5 Using a brass drift or a copper hammer, carefully drive the outer CV joint hub from the splines on the driveshaft **(see illustration)**. Initial resistance will be felt until the internal circlips are released. Take care not to damage the bearing cage.

3.30 Align the marks when refitting the tripod

6 Extract the circlip from the end of the driveshaft **(see illustration)**.

7 Slide the gaiter, and remove it from the driveshaft together with the clips.

8 Clean the driveshaft, and obtain a new joint retaining circlip. The gaiter retaining clips must also be renewed.

9 Slide the new gaiter (together with new clips) onto the driveshaft.

10 Fit a new circlip to the groove in the end of the driveshaft.

11 Scoop out all of the old grease, then pack the joint with new grease (see Specifications at the beginning of this Chapter). Take care that the fresh grease does not become contaminated with dirt or grit as it is being applied.

12 Locate the CV joint on the driveshaft so that the splines are aligned, then push the joint until the internal circlip is fully engaged **(see illustration)**.

4.5 Using a copper hammer to remove the outer CV joint

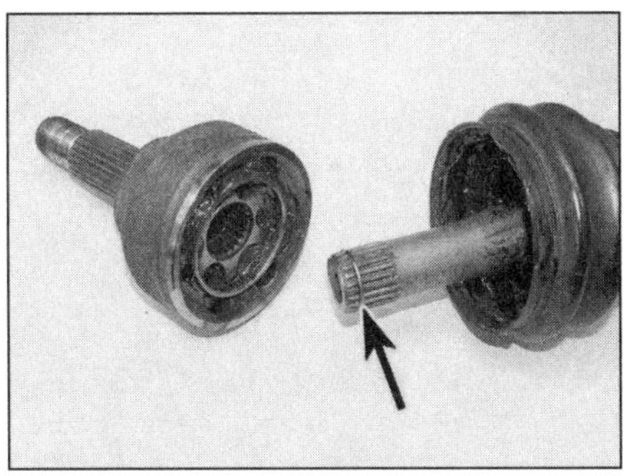
4.12 Make sure the clip (arrowed) engages fully when CV joint is refitted

3.34 Using pincers/pliers to tighten the securing clips

13 Move the gaiter along the driveshaft, and locate it over the joint and onto the outer CV joint housing. The small-diameter end of the gaiter must be located in the groove on the driveshaft.

14 Ensure that the gaiter is not twisted or distorted, then insert a small screwdriver under the lip of the gaiter at the housing end, to allow any trapped air to escape.

15 Remove the screwdriver, fit the retaining clips in their previously-noted positions, and tighten them **(see illustration)**.

5 Driveshafts – inspection and joint renewal

1 If any of the checks described in Chapter 1A, Section 13 or Chapter 1B, Section 14 reveal apparent excessive wear or play in any

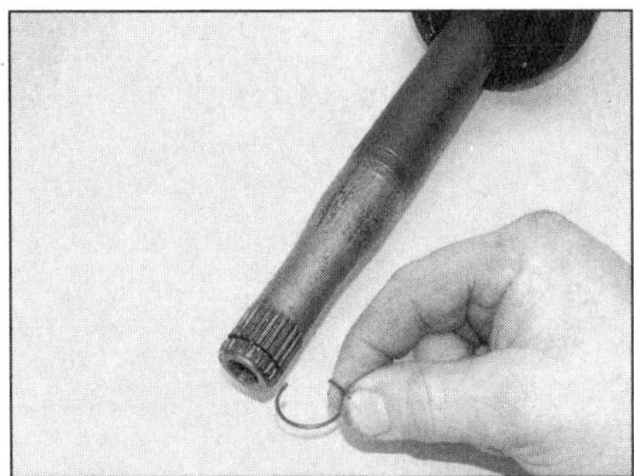
4.6 Renew the retaining clip on the driveshaft

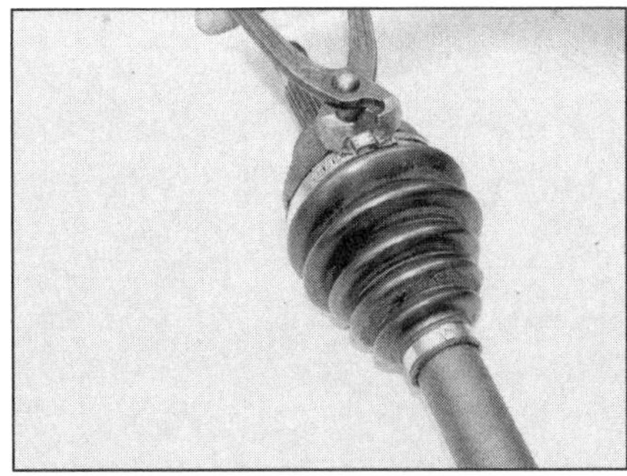
4.15 Using pincers/pliers to tighten the securing clips

driveshaft joint, first remove the wheel trim (or centre cover), and check that the driveshaft nut is tightened to the specified torque. Repeat this check on the other side of the car.

2 Road test the car, and listen for a metallic clicking from the front as the car is driven slowly in a circle on full-lock. If a clicking noise is heard, this indicates wear in the outer constant velocity joint, which means that the joint must be renewed; reconditioning is not possible.

3 To renew an outer CV joint, remove the driveshaft as described in Section 2, then separate the joint from the driveshaft with reference to Section 4. In principle, the gaiter can be left on the driveshaft, provided that it is in good condition; in practice, it makes sense to renew the gaiter in any case, having got this far.

4 If vibration, consistent with roadspeed, is felt through the car when accelerating, there is a possibility of wear in the inner tripod joints.

5 To renew an inner tripod joint, remove the driveshaft as described in Section 2, then separate the joint from the driveshaft with reference to Section 3.

6 Continual noise from the right-hand driveshaft, increasing with roadspeed, may indicate wear in the support bearing. To renew this bearing, the driveshaft and intermediate shaft must be removed, and the bearing extracted using a puller.

7 Remove the bearing dust cover, and obtain a new one.

8 Drive or press on the new bearing, applying the pressure to the inner race only. Similarly drive or press on the new dust cover.

Chapter 9
Braking system

Contents

Degrees of difficulty

Easy, suitable for novice with little experience 	**Fairly easy,** suitable for beginner with some experience	**Fairly difficult,** suitable for competent DIY mechanic	**Difficult,** suitable for experienced DIY mechanic	**Very difficult,** suitable for expert DIY or professional

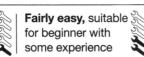

Specifications

Front brakes

Type	Ventilated disc, with single sliding-piston caliper
Disc diameter	258.0 mm
Disc thickness:	
New	22.0 mm
Minimum	20.0 mm
Maximum disc thickness variation	0.025 mm
Maximum disc/hub run-out (installed)	0.050 mm

Rear drum brakes

Type	Leading and trailing shoes, with automatic adjusters
Drum internal diameter:	
New	203.0 mm
Maximum	204.0 mm
Shoe width	36.0 mm
Shoe friction material minimum thickness	1.0 mm

Torque wrench settings

	Nm	lbf ft
ABS hydraulic unit:		
Bracket to body	23	17
Fluid unions	13	10
To bracket	10	7
To control unit	5	4
ABS wheel sensor securing bolts	9	7
Brake hose unions	17	13
Brake pedal cross-shaft nuts	25	18
Front caliper:		
Carrier bracket bolts	70	52
Guide pins	30	22
Handbrake lever mountings	25	18
Master cylinder-to-servo mountings	25	18
PCRV unions	26	19
Rear spindle bolts	70	52
Rear hub nut*	235	173
Roadwheel nuts	110	81
Wheel cylinder bolts	10	7
Vacuum pump mounting bolts (diesel models):		
1.4 litre engine	20	15
1.6 litre engine	18	13
Vacuum servo mounting nuts	25	18

** Use new nut*

1 General information

The braking system is of diagonally-split, dual-circuit design, with ventilated discs at the front, and drum brakes at the rear. Most Fusions covered by this manual have an anti-lock braking system (ABS) as standard. The front calipers are of single sliding-piston design, using asbestos-free pads. The rear drum brakes are of the leading and trailing shoe type, and are self-adjusting. The rear brake shoe linings are of different thicknesses, to allow for the different proportional rates of wear.

The vacuum servo unit uses inlet manifold depression generated when a petrol engine is running to boost the effort applied by the driver at the brake pedal and transmits this increased effort to the master cylinder pistons. Because there is no throttling of the inlet manifold on a diesel engine, it is not a suitable source of vacuum for brake servo operation. Vacuum is therefore derived from a separate vacuum pump, driven from the end of the camshaft.

2.2 Prise the pad retaining clip from the caliper

Pressure-conscious regulator valves (PCRVs) are fitted to the rear brakes on models without ABS, to prevent rear wheel lock-up under hard braking by limiting the flow of fluid to the rear wheel cylinders. The valves, sometimes referred to as pressure control relief valves, are fitted in the master cylinder rear brake outlet ports.

Models with ABS are equipped with electronic brake force distribution (EBD). Simply, this is an electronically-managed version of the rear brake regulator valves fitted to non-ABS models – to prevent rear wheel lock-up, the ABS unit software limits the brake fluid pressure supplied to the rear wheels.

The handbrake is cable-operated, and acts on the rear brakes. The cables operate on the rear trailing brake shoe operating levers. The handbrake lever incorporates an automatic adjuster, which will adjust the cable when the handbrake is operated several times.

Models with ABS have a conventional brake system, together with an ABS hydraulic unit fitted between the master cylinder and the four brake units at each wheel. For more information on the system, refer to Section 15.

Precautions

The car's braking system is one of its most important safety features. When working on the brakes, there are a number of points to be aware of, to ensure that your health (or even your life) is not being put at risk.

- When servicing any part of the system, work carefully and methodically – do not take short-cuts; also observe scrupulous cleanliness when overhauling any part of the hydraulic system.
- Always renew components in axle sets, where applicable – this means renewing brake pads, shoes, etc, on BOTH sides, even if only one set of pads is worn, or one wheel cylinder is leaking (for example). In the instance of uneven brake wear, the cause should be investigated and fixed (on front brakes, sticking caliper pistons is a likely problem).
- Use only genuine Ford parts, or at least those of known good quality.
- Although genuine Ford brake pads and shoes are asbestos-free, the dust created by wear of non-genuine parts may contain asbestos, which is a health hazard. Never blow it out with compressed air, and don't inhale any of it.
- DO NOT use petroleum-based solvents to clean brake parts; use brake cleaner or methylated spirit only.
- DO NOT allow any brake fluid, oil or grease to contact the brake pads or disc.

Warning: Brake fluid is poisonous. Take care to keep it off bare skin, and in particular not to get splashes in your eyes. The fluid also attacks paintwork and plastics – wash off spillages immediately with cold water. Finally, brake fluid is highly inflammable, and should be handled with the same care as petrol.

2 Front brake pads – renewal

Note: *Refer to the precautions in Section 1 before proceeding.*

1 Apply the handbrake. Loosen the front wheel nuts, then jack up the front of the car and support it on axle stands (see *Jacking and vehicle support*). Remove the front wheels. Work on one brake assembly at a time, using the assembled brake for reference if necessary.

2 Using a flat-bladed screwdriver, prise the outer brake pad retaining clip from the caliper **(see illustration)**. Hold the clip with a pair of pliers as this is done, to avoid personal injury.

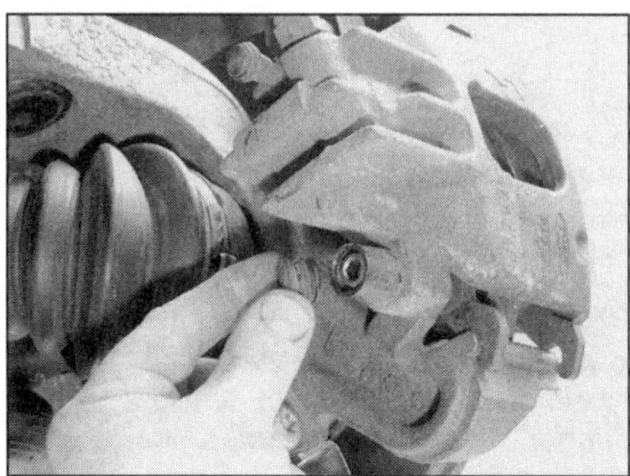

2.3a Prise the covers off to locate the caliper guide pins ...

2.3b ... then slacken and remove the pins

2.4 Withdraw the caliper, complete with brake pads

2.5a Unclip the inner pad from the piston ...

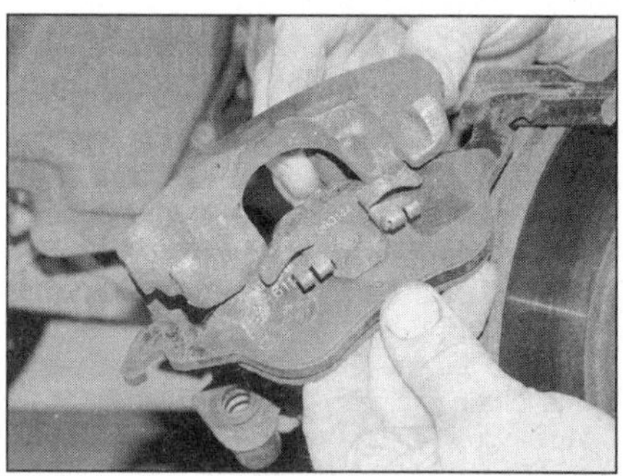

2.5b ... then unclip the outer pad from the caliper

3 Prise the plastic covers from the ends of the two guide pins then, using a 7 mm Allen key, unscrew the guide pins securing the caliper to the carrier bracket **(see illustrations)**.

4 Withdraw the caliper from the disc **(see illustration)**, and support it on an axle stand to avoid straining the hydraulic hose.

5 Pull the inner pad from the piston in the caliper, then remove the outer pad from the caliper by sliding the pad out of the caliper with its securing clip, noting their fitted positions **(see illustrations)**.

6 Brush all dust and dirt from the caliper, pads and disc, but do not inhale it, as it may be harmful to health. Scrape any corrosion from the edge of the disc, taking care not to damage the friction surface.

7 Inspect the front brake disc for scoring and cracks. If a detailed inspection is necessary, refer to Section 4.

8 The caliper piston must be pushed back into the caliper to make room for the new pads – this may require considerable effort. Either use a G-clamp, sliding-jaw (water pump) pliers, or suitable pieces of wood as levers.

Caution: Pushing back the piston causes a reverse-flow of brake fluid, which has been known to 'flip' the master cylinder rubber seals, resulting in a total loss of braking. To avoid this, clamp the caliper flexible hose and open the bleed screw – as the piston is pushed back, the fluid can be directed into a suitable container using a hose attached to the bleed screw. Close the screw just before the piston is pushed fully back, to ensure no air enters the system.

9 If the recommended method of opening a bleed screw before pushing back the piston is not used, the fluid level in the reservoir will rise, and possibly overflow. Make sure that there is sufficient space in the brake fluid reservoir to accept the displaced fluid, and if necessary, siphon some off first. Any brake fluid spilt on paintwork should be washed off with clean water without delay – brake fluid is also a highly-effective paint-stripper.

10 Fit the new pads using a reversal of the removal procedure, and tighten the guide pins to the torque wrench setting given in the Specifications at the beginning of this Chapter.

11 On completion, firmly depress the brake pedal a few times, to bring the pads to their normal working position. Check the level of the brake fluid in the reservoir, and top-up if necessary.

12 Give the car a short road test, to make sure that the brakes are functioning correctly, and to bed-in the new linings to the contours of the disc. New linings will not provide maximum braking efficiency until they have bedded-in; avoid heavy braking as far as possible for the first hundred miles or so.

3 Front brake caliper – removal, overhaul and refitting

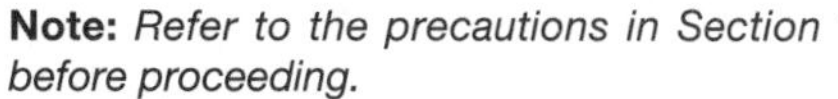

Note: *Refer to the precautions in Section 1 before proceeding.*

Removal

1 Apply the handbrake. Loosen the front wheel nuts, then jack up the front of the car and support it on axle stands (see *Jacking and vehicle support*). Remove the appropriate front wheel.

2 Fit a brake hose clamp to the flexible hose leading to the caliper **(see illustration)**. This will minimise brake fluid loss during subsequent operations.

3 Loosen the union on the caliper end of the flexible brake hose **(see illustration)**. Once loosened, do not try to unscrew the hose at this stage.

4 Remove the brake pads as described in Section 2.

5 Support the caliper in one hand, and prevent the hydraulic hose from turning with the other hand. Unscrew the caliper from the hose, making sure that the hose is not twisted unduly or strained. Once the caliper is detached, plug the open hydraulic unions in the caliper and hose, to keep out dust and dirt.

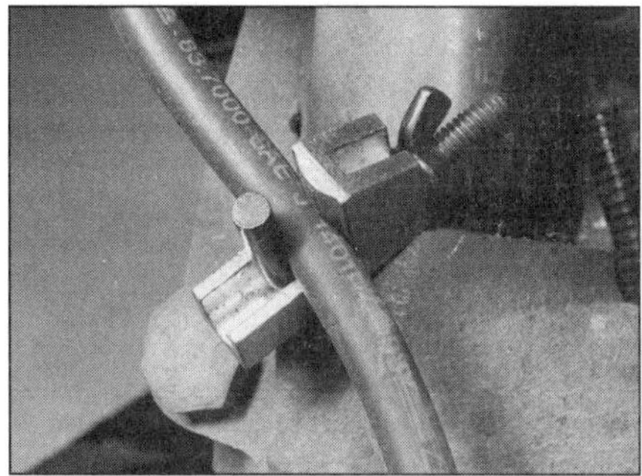

3.2 Brake hose clamp fitted to the front flexible brake hose

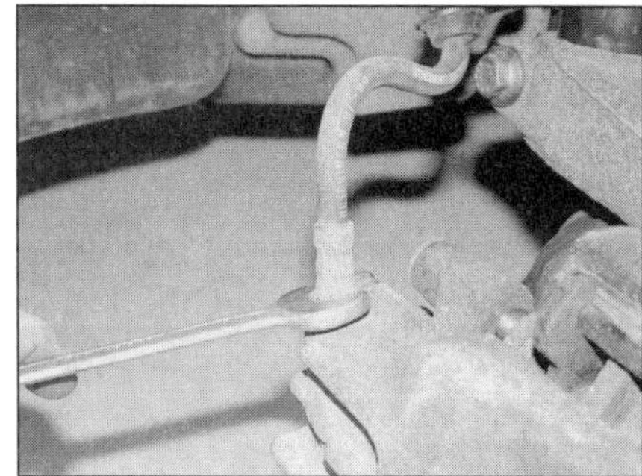

3.3 Slacken the brake hose at the caliper

3.15 Tightening the carrier bracket mounting bolts

6 If required, the caliper carrier bracket can be unbolted from the hub carrier.

Overhaul

Note: *Before starting work, check on the availability of parts (caliper overhaul kit/seals).*

7 With the caliper on the bench, brush away all traces of dust and dirt, but take care not to inhale any dust, as it may be harmful to your health.

8 Pull the dust cover rubber seal from the end of the piston.

9 Apply low air pressure to the fluid inlet union, to eject the piston. Only low air pressure is required for this, such as is produced by a foot-operated tyre pump.

Caution: The piston may be ejected with some force. Position a thin piece of wood between the piston and the caliper body, to prevent damage to the end face of the piston, in the event of it being ejected suddenly.

10 Using a suitable blunt instrument, prise the piston seal from the groove in the cylinder bore. Take care not to scratch the surface of the bore.

11 Clean the piston and caliper body with methylated spirit, and allow to dry. Examine the surfaces of the piston and cylinder bore for wear, damage and corrosion. If the piston alone is unserviceable, a new piston must be obtained, along with seals. If the cylinder bore is unserviceable, the complete caliper must be renewed. The seals must be renewed, regardless of the condition of the other components.

12 Coat the piston and seals with clean brake fluid, then manipulate the piston seal into the groove in the cylinder bore.

13 Push the piston squarely into its bore, taking care not to damage the seal.

14 Fit the dust cover rubber seal onto the piston and caliper, then depress the piston fully.

Refitting

15 Refit the caliper by reversing the removal operations. Make sure that the flexible brake hose is not twisted. Tighten the mounting bolts and wheel nuts to the specified torque **(see illustration)**.

16 Bleed the brake circuit according to the procedure given in Section 11, remembering to remove the brake hose clamp from the flexible hose. Make sure there are no leaks from the hose connections. Test the brakes carefully before returning the car to normal service.

4.3 Nut holding the disc on firmly (arrowed)

4.4 Using a micrometer to measure the thickness of the brake disc

4.5 Measuring the disc run-out with a dial gauge

4.10 Withdraw the disc from the hub

4 Front brake disc – inspection, removal and refitting

Note: *Refer to the precautions in Section 1 before proceeding.*

Inspection

1 Apply the handbrake. Loosen the relevant wheel nuts, jack up the front of the car and support it on axle stands. Remove the appropriate front wheel.

2 Remove the front brake caliper from the disc with reference to Section 2, and undo the two carrier bracket securing bolts. Do not disconnect the flexible hose. Support the caliper on an axle stand, or suspend it out of the way with a piece of wire, taking care to avoid straining the flexible hose.

3 Temporarily refit two of the wheel nuts to diagonally-opposite studs, with the flat sides of the nuts against the disc **(see illustration)**. Tighten the nuts progressively, to hold the disc firmly.

4 Scrape any corrosion from the disc. Rotate the disc, and examine it for deep scoring, grooving or cracks. Using a micrometer, measure the thickness of the disc in several places **(see illustration)**. The minimum thickness is stamped on the disc hub. Light wear and scoring is normal, but if excessive, the disc should be removed, and either reground by a specialist, or renewed. If regrinding is undertaken, the minimum thickness must be maintained. Obviously, if the disc is cracked, it must be renewed.

5 Using a dial gauge or a flat metal block and feeler gauges, check that the disc run-out 10 mm from the outer edge does not exceed the limit given in the Specifications. To do this, fix the measuring equipment, and rotate the disc, noting the variation in measurement as the disc is rotated **(see illustration)**. The difference between the minimum and maximum measurements recorded is the disc run-out.

6 If the run-out is greater than the specified amount, check for variations of the disc thickness as follows. Mark the disc at eight positions 45° apart then, using a micrometer, measure the disc thickness at the eight positions, 15 mm in from the outer edge. If the variation between the minimum and maximum readings is greater than the specified amount, the disc should be renewed.

7 The hub face run-out can also be checked in a similar way. First remove the disc as described later in this Section, fix the measuring equipment, then slowly rotate the hub, and check that the run-out does not exceed the amount given in the Specifications. If the hub face run-out is excessive, this should be corrected (by renewing the hub bearings – see Chapter 10, Section 3) before rechecking the disc run-out.

Removal

8 With the wheel and caliper removed, remove

5.2a Remove the dust cap ...

5.2b ... and undo the hub nut

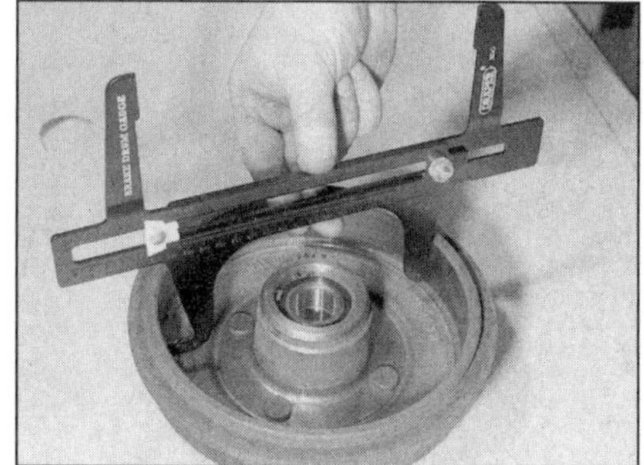
5.5 Checking the drum for wear

the wheel nuts which were temporarily refitted in paragraph 3.

9 Mark the disc in relation to the hub, if it is to be refitted.

10 Remove the washer/retaining clip(s) (where fitted), and withdraw the disc over the wheel studs **(see illustration)**.

Refitting

11 Make sure that the disc and hub mating surfaces are clean, then locate the disc on the wheel studs. Align the previously-made marks if the original disc is being refitted.

12 Refit the washer/retaining clip(s), where fitted.

13 Refit the brake caliper and carrier bracket with reference to Section 2.

14 Refit the wheel, and lower the car to the ground. Tighten wheel nuts to their specified torque.

15 Test the brakes carefully before returning the car to normal service.

5 Rear brake drum - removal, inspection and refitting

Note: *Refer to the precautions in Section 1 before proceeding.*

Removal

1 Chock the front wheels, release the handbrake and engage 1st gear. Loosen the relevant wheel nuts, jack up the rear of the car and support it on axle stands (see *Jacking and vehicle support*). Remove the appropriate rear wheel.

2 Remove the dust cap from the centre of the drum, and remove the retaining nut **(see illustrations)**. This nut is very tight – use only high-quality, close-fitting tools, and take adequate precautions against personal injury when loosening it. **Note:** *The driveshaft/hub nut is of special laminated design, and should not be re-used.*

3 If the drum will not pull off easily, make sure the handbrake is released fully. Inside the car, remove the handbrake lever trim panel, and loosen the handbrake adjuster nut to the end of its thread (refer to Section 19). Ultimately, it may be necessary to use a suitable puller to draw the drum and bearing assembly off the stub axle, but this will almost certainly damage the shoes or springs.

4 With the brake drum removed, clean the dust from the drum, brake shoes, wheel cylinder and backplate, using brake cleaner or methylated spirit. Take care not to inhale the dust, as it may contain asbestos.

Inspection

5 Clean the inside surfaces of the brake drum, then examine the internal friction surface for signs of scoring or cracks. If it is cracked, deeply scored, or has worn to a diameter greater than the maximum given in the Specifications, then it should be renewed, together with the drum on the other side **(see illustration)**.

6 Regrinding of the brake drum is not recommended.

Refitting

7 The wheel bearings may have been damaged on drum removal. If necessary, renew the bearings as described in Chapter 10, Section 9.

8 Refitting is a reversal of removal, noting the following points:

a) *Use a new hub nut.*
b) *When tightening the hub nut to the specified torque, the drum should be spun several times in the opposite direction to tightening, to avoid damaging the wheel bearing.*
c) *If the dust cap was damaged during removal, a new one should be fitted.*
d) *Test the brakes carefully before returning the car to normal service.*

6 Rear brake shoes - renewal

Note: *Refer to the precautions in Section 1 before proceeding.*

1 Chock the front wheels, release the handbrake and engage 1st gear. Loosen the relevant wheel nuts, jack up the rear of the car and support it on axle stands (see *Jacking and vehicle support*). Remove the rear wheels.

2 Where applicable, unscrew the single bolt securing the ABS sensor to the brake backplate.

3 Remove the rear brake drum and hub assembly by unscrewing the four bolts at the rear of the hub assembly **(see illustrations)**. This is to prevent any damage to the wheel bearings on removal of the drum.

4 Note the fitted position of the springs and the brake shoes, then clean the components

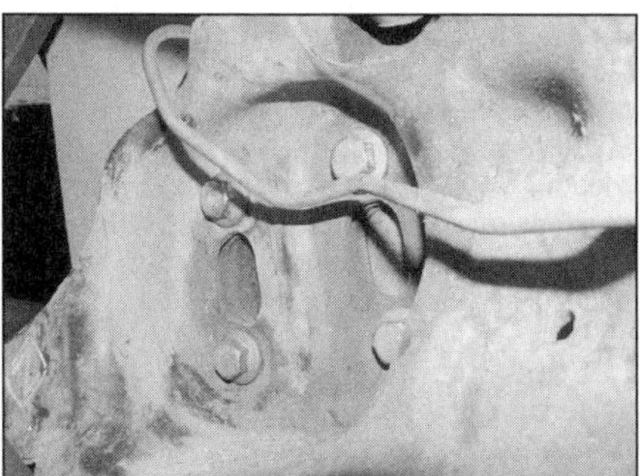
6.3a Undo the four bolts ...

6.3b ... and remove the hub/drum assembly

6.4 Note the position of the springs

6.5a Unclip the brake shoe hold-down springs ...

6.5b ... and pull out the pins from the backplate

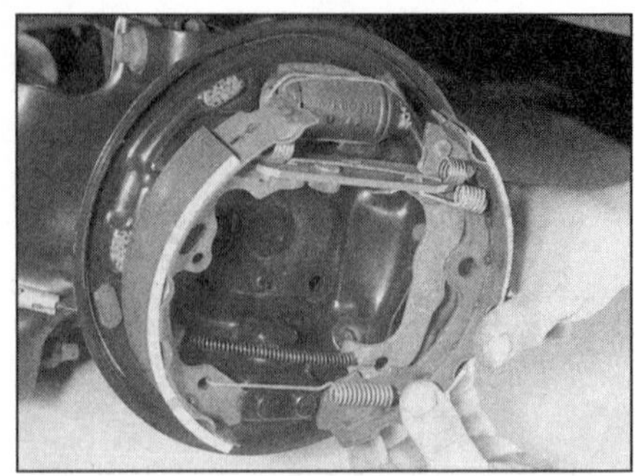
6.8 Pull brake shoe from the bottom anchor

with brake cleaner, and allow to dry **(see illustration)**. Position a tray beneath the backplate, to catch the fluid and residue.

5 Remove the two shoe hold-down springs, use a pair of pliers to depress the ends so that they can be withdrawn off the pins. Remove the hold-down pins from the backplate **(see illustrations)**.

6 Disconnect the top ends of the shoes from the wheel cylinder, taking care not to damage the rubber boots.

7 To prevent the wheel cylinder pistons from being accidentally ejected, fit a suitable elastic band or wire lengthways over the cylinder/ pistons. DO NOT press the brake pedal while the shoes are removed.

8 Pull the bottom end of the brake shoes from the bottom anchor **(see illustration)** (use pliers or an adjustable spanner over the edge of the shoe to lever it away, if required).

9 Pull the handbrake cable spring back from the operating lever on the rear of the trailing shoe. Unhook the cable end from the cut-out in the lever, and remove the brake shoes **(see illustration)**.

10 Working on a clean bench, move the bottom ends of the brake shoes together, and unhook the lower return spring from the shoes, noting the location holes.

11 Pull the leading shoe from the strut and brake shoe adjuster **(see illustration)**, unhook the upper return spring from the shoes, noting the location holes.

12 Pull the adjustment strut to release from the trailing brake shoe, and remove the strut support spring **(see illustration)**.

13 If the wheel cylinder shows signs of fluid leakage, or if there is any reason to suspect it of being defective, inspect it now, as described in the next Section.

14 Clean the backplate, and apply small amounts of high melting-point brake grease to the brake shoe contact points. Be careful not to get grease on any friction surfaces **(see illustration)**.

15 Lubricate the sliding components of the brake shoe adjuster with a little high melting-point brake grease, but leave the serrations on the eccentric cam clean.

16 Fit the new brake shoes using a reversal of the removal procedure, but set the eccentric cam at its lowest position before assembling it to the trailing shoe.

17 Carry out the renewal procedures on the remaining rear brake.

18 Before refitting the drum, check its condition as described in Section 5.

19 With the drum in position and all the securing bolts and nuts tightened to their specified torque, refit the wheel.

20 Lower the car to the ground, and tighten the wheel nuts to the specified torque.

21 Depress the brake pedal several times, in order to operate the self-adjusting mechanism and set the shoes at their normal operating position.

22 Make several forward and reverse stops, and operate the handbrake fully two or three times (adjust the handbrake as required – see Section 19). Give the car a road test, to make sure that the brakes are functioning correctly, and to bed-in the new shoes to the contours of the drum. Remember that the new shoes will not give full braking efficiency until they have bedded-in.

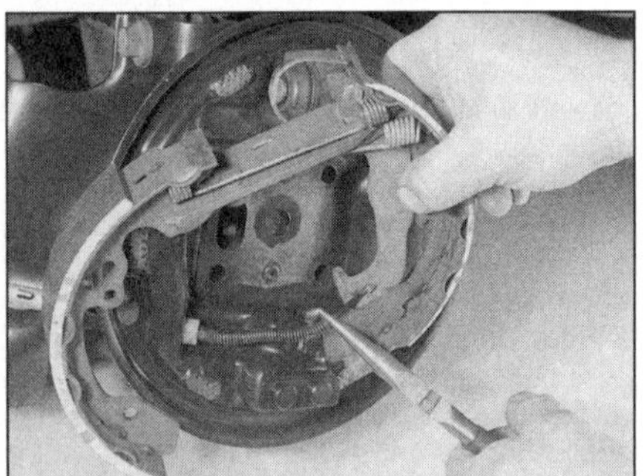
6.9 Use pliers to disengage cable from lever

6.11 Disengage the leading brake shoe

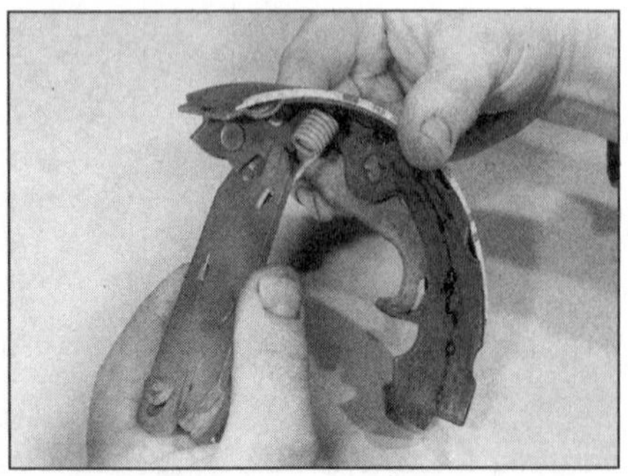
6.12 Disengage the adjustment strut

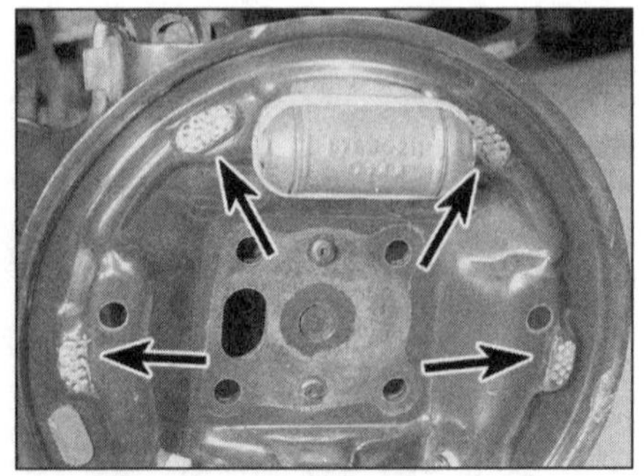
6.14 Grease the brake shoe contact points on the backplate

7 Rear wheel cylinder – removal, overhaul and refitting

Note: *Refer to the precautions in Section 1 before proceeding. Also bear in mind that if the brake shoes have been contaminated by fluid leaking from the wheel cylinder, they must be renewed. The shoes on BOTH sides of the car must be renewed, even if they are only contaminated on one side.*

Removal

1 Remove the brake drum as described in Section 5, paragraphs 1 to 3. If the wheel cylinders have been leaking, there will probably be a significant build-up of brake dust on the failed seals (the dust sticks to the leaking fluid). A leak can be confirmed by carefully prising up the outer lip of the seal – any wetness means a new cylinder will be needed.

2 In recent years, the availability of wheel cylinder repair kits has greatly decreased, but it may still be worth asking. Wheel cylinders do not have to be fitted in pairs (providing they are the same size), but if one is leaking, it's reasonable to assume the other one soon will be too. If the leak has been going on for some time, it may be serious enough to have contaminated the brake shoes, in which case new shoes should be fitted on BOTH sides.

3 Minimise fluid loss either by removing the master cylinder reservoir cap, and then tightening it down onto a piece of polythene to obtain an airtight seal, or by using a brake hose clamp, a G-clamp, or similar tool, to clamp the flexible hose at the nearest convenient point to the wheel cylinder.

4 Pull the brake shoes apart at their top ends, so that they are just clear of the wheel cylinder. The automatic adjuster will hold the shoes in this position, so that the cylinder can be withdrawn.

5 Wipe away all traces of dirt around the hydraulic union at the rear of the wheel cylinder, then undo the union nut.

6 Unscrew the two bolts securing the wheel cylinder to the backplate **(see illustration)**.

7 Withdraw the wheel cylinder from the backplate so that it is clear of the brake shoes. Plug the open hydraulic unions, to prevent the entry of dirt, and to minimise further fluid loss whilst the cylinder is detached.

Overhaul

8 No overhaul procedures or parts were available at the time of writing – check availability of spares before dismantling. Renewing a wheel cylinder as a unit is recommended.

Refitting

9 Wipe clean the backplate and remove the plug from the end of the hydraulic pipe. Fit the cylinder onto the backplate and screw in the hydraulic union nut by hand, being careful not to cross-thread it.

10 Tighten the mounting bolts, then fully tighten the hydraulic union nut.

11 Retract the automatic brake adjuster mechanism, so that the brake shoes engage with the pistons of the wheel cylinder. To do this, prise the shoes apart slightly, turn the automatic adjuster to its minimum position, and release the shoes.

12 Remove the clamp from the flexible brake hose, or the polythene from the master cylinder (as applicable).

13 Refit the brake drum (see Section 5).

14 Bleed the hydraulic system as described in Section 11. Providing suitable precautions were taken to minimise loss of fluid, it should only be necessary to bleed the relevant rear brake.

15 Test the brakes carefully before returning the car to normal service.

8 Master cylinder – removal and refitting

Note: *Refer to the precautions in Section 1 before proceeding.*

Removal

1 Exhaust the vacuum in the servo by pressing the brake pedal a few times, with the engine switched off.

2 Unclip the brake servo vacuum pipe from the servo unit, then disconnect it completely by pulling it free from the rubber grommet. If it is reluctant to move, prise it free, using a screwdriver with its blade inserted under the flange.

3 Disconnect the battery negative lead.

4 Remove the windscreen wiper motor assembly as described in Chapter 12, Section 14.

5 Draw off the hydraulic fluid from the reservoir, using an old battery hydrometer or similar. Alternatively, raise the car, remove the wheels, then slacken the front bleed nipples and drain the fluid from the reservoir.

6 Identify the locations of each brake pipe on the master cylinder. On non-ABS models, there are four pipes; the two rear brake pipes are attached to pressure-control relief valves on the master cylinder **(see illustration)**. On ABS models, there are only two pipes, which lead to the ABS hydraulic unit.

7 Disconnect the clutch master cylinder supply hose at the rear of the master cylinder. Plug or cap the hose, to prevent fluid loss or dirt entry.

8 Undo the master cylinder securing nuts **(see illustration)**, then disconnect the low fluid level wiring plug and withdraw the master cylinder from the studs on the servo unit. Recover the gasket.

9 If the master cylinder is faulty, it must be renewed. At the time of writing, no overhaul kits were available.

Refitting

10 Refitting is a reversal of the removal procedure, noting the following points:

a) *Clean the contact surfaces of the master cylinder and servo, and locate a new gasket on the master cylinder.*

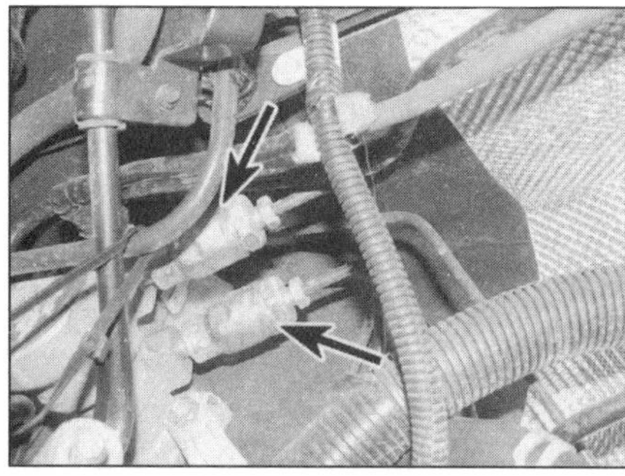

8.6 Pressure-control relief valves on non-ABS models

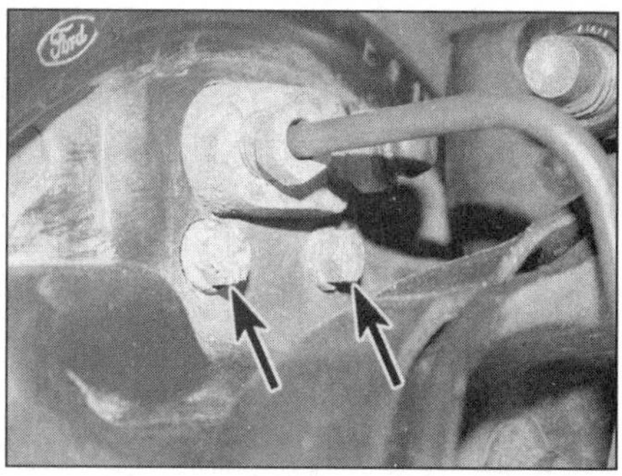

7.6 Loosen the brake pipe union nut, before removing the two securing bolts (arrowed)

b) *Refit and tighten the nuts to the specified torque.*
c) *Carefully insert the brake pipes in the apertures in the master cylinder, then tighten the union nuts. Make sure that the nuts enter their threads correctly.*
d) *Fill the reservoir with fresh brake fluid.*
e) *Bleed the brake hydraulic system as described in Section 11.*
f) *Test the brakes carefully before returning the car to normal service.*

9 Brake pedal – removal and refitting

Note: *Refer to the precautions in Section 1 before proceeding. Take care not to drop or damage the pedal while it is removed, or during removal/refitting. On models manufactured before 02/2004, the pedal has a 'de-coupler' mechanism fitted which is designed to fail in a severe accident – if the pedal is subjected to enough load, the 'de-coupler' pin will break and the pedal will drop to the floor. This mechanism was not fitted to models manufactured from 02/2004-onwards.*

Removal

1 Working inside the car, move the driver's seat fully to the rear, to allow maximum working area.

2 Remove the driver's side lower facia panel, which is secured by five screws (two inside the small storage compartment) and one clip

8.8 Master cylinder securing nuts

9.3 Top of brake pedal, showing brake servo retaining pin (A) and pedal shaft nut (B). Also note the 'de-coupler' mechanism (C) fitted to the top of the pedal on models manufactured before 02/2004

10.2 Check the brake flexible hoses very carefully, especially at the metal end fittings

(at the top left – pull the panel towards you to release it).

3 At the top of the pedal itself, remove the brake servo operating rod by depressing the catch and sliding out the retaining pin to the right **(see illustration)**.

4 Above the pedal, undo the nut on the pivot shaft (bolt), then slide the bolt out to the left. Recover any washers or bushes which may be dislodged as the shaft is withdrawn.

5 Check the condition of the pedal bushes, and renew any that are badly worn.

Refitting

6 Prior to refitting the pedal, apply a little grease to the pivot shaft, pedal bushes and actuator rods.

7 Refitting is a reversal of the removal procedure, but make sure that the pedal bushes and servo operating rod are correctly located.

8 Check the operation of the brake lights on completion.

10 Hydraulic pipes and hoses – inspection, removal and refitting

Note: *Refer to the precautions in Section 1 before proceeding.*

Inspection

1 Jack up the front and rear of the car, and support on axle stands. Making sure the car is safely supported on a level surface.

2 Check for signs of leakage at the pipe unions, then examine the flexible hoses for signs of cracking, chafing and fraying **(see illustration)**.

3 The brake pipes should be examined carefully for signs of dents, corrosion or other damage **(see illustration)**. Corrosion should be scraped off, and if the depth of pitting is significant, the pipes renewed. This is particularly likely in those areas underneath the car body where the pipes are exposed and unprotected.

4 Renew any defective brake pipes and/or hoses.

Removal

5 If a section of pipe or hose is to be removed, loss of brake fluid can be reduced by unscrewing the filler cap, and completely sealing the top of the reservoir with cling film or adhesive tape. Alternatively, the reservoir can be emptied (see Section 11).

6 To remove a section of pipe, hold the adjoining hose union nut with a spanner to prevent it from turning, then unscrew the union nut at the end of the pipe, and release it. Repeat the procedure at the other end of the pipe, then release the pipe by pulling out the clips attaching it to the body.

7 Where the union nuts are exposed to the full force of the weather, they can sometimes be quite tight. If an open-ended spanner is used, burring of the flats on the nuts is not uncommon, and for this reason, it is preferable to use a split ring (brake) spanner **(see illustration)**, which will engage all the flats. If such a spanner is not available, self-locking grips may be used as a last resort; these may well damage the nuts, but if the pipe is to be renewed, this does not matter.

8 To further minimise the loss of fluid when disconnecting a flexible brake line from a rigid pipe, clamp the hose as near as possible to the pipe to be detached, using a brake hose clamp or a pair of self-locking grips with protected jaws.

9 To remove a flexible hose, first clean the ends of the hose and the surrounding area, then unscrew the union nuts from the hose ends. Remove the spring clip, and withdraw the hose from the serrated mounting in the support bracket **(see illustrations)**. Where applicable, unscrew the hose from the caliper.

10 Brake pipes supplied with flared ends and union nuts can be obtained individually or in sets from Ford dealers or accessory shops.

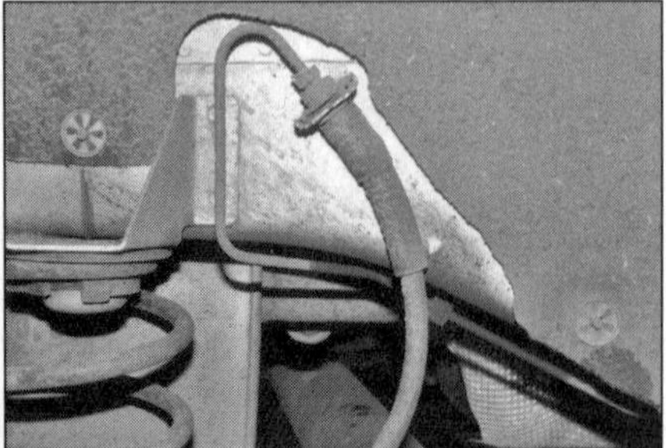

10.3 The rear brake pipes in the wheel arch may be vulnerable to corrosion if dirt builds-up

10.7 Unscrewing a brake pipe union using a split ring spanner

10.9a Pull out the retaining clip ...

The pipe is then bent to shape, using the old pipe as a guide, and is ready for fitting. Be careful not to kink or crimp the pipe when bending it; ideally, a proper pipe-bending tool should be used.

Refitting

11 Refitting of the pipes and hoses is a reversal of removal. Make sure that all brake pipes are securely supported in their clips, and ensure that the hoses are not kinked. Check also that the hoses are clear of all suspension components and underbody fittings, and will remain clear during movement of the suspension and steering.

12 On completion, bleed the hydraulic system as described in Section 11.

11 Hydraulic system - bleeding

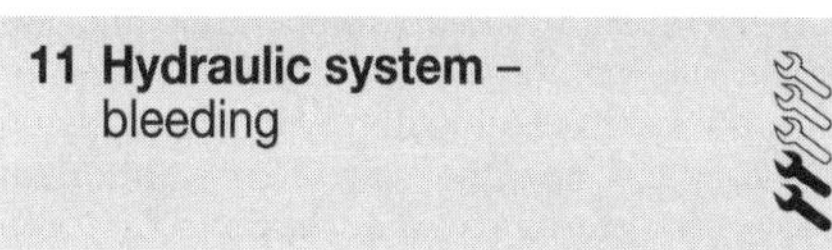

Note: *Refer to the precautions in Section 1 before proceeding.*

1 If the master cylinder has been disconnected and reconnected, then the complete system (all circuits) must be bled of air. If a component of one circuit has been disturbed, then only that particular circuit need be bled.

2 Bleeding should start with the furthest bleed nipple from the master cylinder, followed by the next one until the bleed nipple nearest the master cylinder is bled last.

3 There is a variety of do-it-yourself 'one-man' brake bleeding kits available from motor accessory shops, and it is recommended that one of these kits be used wherever possible, as they greatly simplify the brake bleeding operation. Follow the kit manufacturer's instructions in conjunction with the following procedure. If a pressure-bleeding kit is obtained, then it will not be necessary to depress the brake pedal in the following procedure.

4 During the bleeding operation, do not allow the brake fluid level in the reservoir to drop below the minimum mark. If the level is allowed to fall so far that air is drawn in, the whole procedure will have to be started again from scratch. **Note:** *On models fitted with ABS, if air enters the hydraulic unit, the unit must be bled using special Ford test equipment.* Only use new fluid for topping-up, preferably from a freshly-opened container. Never re-use fluid bled from the system.

5 Before starting, check that all rigid pipes and flexible hoses are in good condition, and that all hydraulic unions are tight. Take great care not to allow hydraulic fluid to come into contact with the car paintwork, otherwise the finish will be seriously damaged. Wash off any spilt fluid immediately with cold water.

6 If a brake bleeding kit is not being used, gather together a clean jar, a length of plastic or rubber tubing which is a tight fit over the bleed screw, and a new container of the specified brake fluid (see *Lubricants and fluids*). The help of an assistant will also be required.

10.9b ... then unhook the brake hose

7 Clean the area around the bleed screw on the rear brake to be bled (it is important that no dirt be allowed to enter the hydraulic system), and remove the dust cap. Connect one end of the tubing to the bleed screw, and immerse the other end in the jar. Ideally, this should be held at least 300 mm above the bleed nipple to maintain fluid pressure to the brake **(see illustrations)**. The jar should be filled with sufficient brake fluid to keep the end of the tube submerged.

8 Open the bleed screw by one or two turns, and have the assistant depress the brake pedal to the floor. Tighten the bleed screw at the end of the downstroke, then have the assistant release the pedal. Continue this procedure until clean brake fluid, free from air bubbles, can be seen flowing into the jar. Finally tighten the bleed screw with the pedal in the fully-depressed position.

9 Remove the tube, and refit the dust cap. Top-up the master cylinder reservoir if necessary, then repeat the procedure on the opposite rear brake.

10 Repeat the procedure on the front brake furthest from the master cylinder, followed by the brake nearest to the master cylinder.

11 Check the feel of the brake pedal – it should be firm. If it is spongy, there is still some air in the system, and the bleeding procedure should be repeated.

12 When bleeding is complete, top-up the master cylinder reservoir and refit the cap.

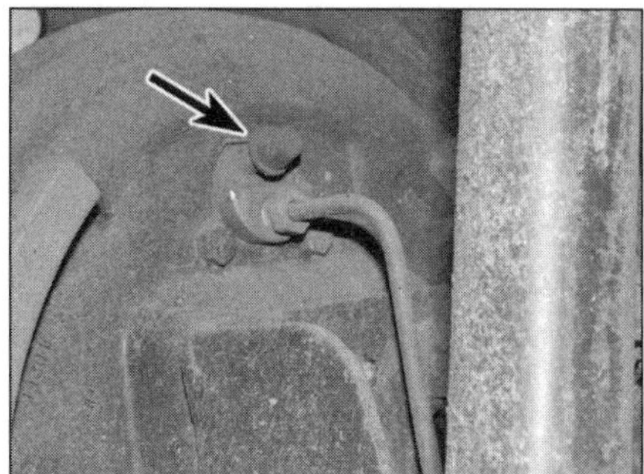

11.7a Remove the rubber dust cap for access to the rear brake bleed screw

13 Check the clutch operation on completion; it may be necessary to bleed the clutch hydraulic system as described in Chapter 6, Section 5.

12 Vacuum servo unit - testing, removal and refitting

Note: *Refer to the precautions in Section 1 before proceeding.*

Testing

1 To test the operation of the servo unit, depress the footbrake four or five times to dissipate the vacuum, then start the engine while keeping the footbrake depressed. As the engine starts, there should be a noticeable give in the brake pedal as vacuum builds-up. Allow the engine to run for at least two minutes, and then switch it off. If the brake pedal is now depressed again, it should be possible to hear a hiss from the servo when the pedal is depressed. After four or five applications, no further hissing should be heard, and the pedal should feel harder.

2 Before assuming that a problem exists in the servo unit itself, inspect the non-return valve as described in the next Section.

Removal

3 Refer to Section 8 and remove the master cylinder.

4 Working inside the car, move the driver's seat fully to the rear, to allow maximum working area.

5 Remove the driver's side facia lower panel, which is secured by a total of five screws.

6 At the top of the brake pedal, remove the brake servo operating rod by depressing the catch and sliding out the retaining peg to the right.

7 Above the pedal, unscrew the four servo mounting nuts **(see illustration)**, then return to the engine compartment and withdraw the servo from the bulkhead. Recover and discard the gasket - a new one should be used when refitting.

8 Note that the servo unit cannot be dismantled for repair or overhaul and, if faulty, must be renewed.

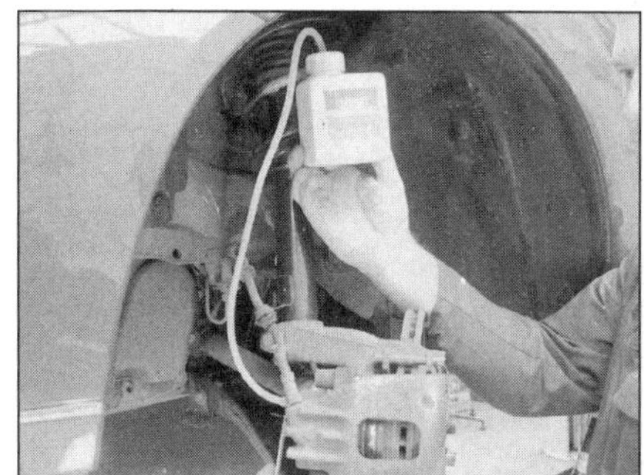

11.7b Hold the fluid container up, to maintain fluid pressure

12.7 Brake servo mounting nuts, above the brake pedal

Refitting

9 Refitting is a reversal of the removal procedure, noting the following points:

a) Make sure the gasket is correctly positioned on the servo.

b) Refit the master cylinder as described in Section 8.

c) Test the brakes carefully before returning the car to normal service.

13 Vacuum servo unit vacuum hose and non-return valve – removal, testing and refitting

Note: *Refer to the precautions in Section 1 before proceeding.*

Removal

1 With the engine switched off, depress the brake pedal four or five times, to dissipate any remaining vacuum from the servo unit.

2 Disconnect the vacuum hose adapter at the servo unit, by pulling it free from the rubber grommet. If it is reluctant to move, prise it free, using a screwdriver with its blade inserted under the flange.

3 Detach the vacuum hose from the inlet manifold connection, pressing in the collar to disengage the tabs, then withdrawing the collar slowly.

4 If the hose or the fixings are damaged or in poor condition, they must be renewed.

Testing

5 Examine the non-return valve **(see illustration)** for damage and signs of deterioration, and renew it if necessary. The valve may be tested by blowing through its connecting hoses in both directions. It should only be possible to blow from the servo end towards the inlet manifold.

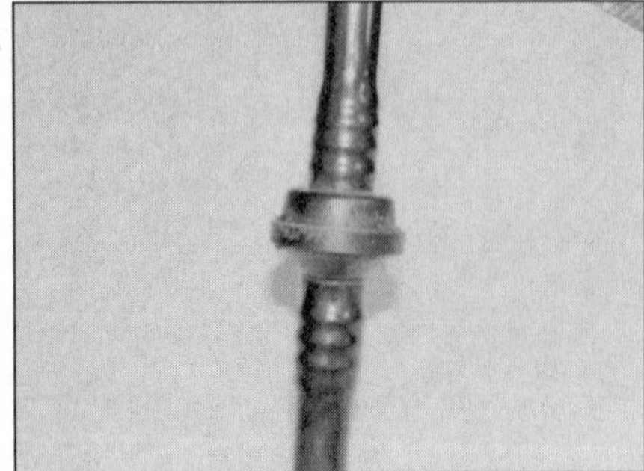

13.5 Non-return valve in brake vacuum hose

Refitting

6 Refitting is a reversal of the removal procedure. If fitting a new non-return valve, ensure that it is fitted the correct way round.

14 Pressure-conscious regulator valve (non-ABS models) – removal and refitting

Note: *Refer to the precautions in Section 1 before proceeding. On models with ABS, the PCRV function is performed by a system known as EBD (electronic brake force distribution) – see Section 15.*

Removal

1 On non-ABS models, the two pressure-conscious regulator valves are located on the master cylinder outlets to the rear brake circuits **(see illustration 8.6)**.

2 Unscrew the fluid reservoir filler cap, and draw off the fluid – see Section 8.

3 Position some rags beneath the master cylinder, to catch any spilled fluid.

4 Clean around the valve to be removed. Hold the valve stationary with one spanner, and unscrew the hydraulic pipe union nut with another spanner. Pull out the pipe, and bend it slightly away from the valve, taking care not to kink the pipe.

5 Unscrew the valve from the master cylinder and plug the master cylinder to prevent dirt contamination.

Refitting

6 Refitting is a reversal of the removal procedure. On completion, bleed the hydraulic system as described in Section 11.

15 Anti-lock braking system (ABS) – general information

ABS is fitted as standard from 2005, and to most earlier models covered by this Manual. The system comprises a hydraulic regulator unit and the four roadwheel sensors. The regulator unit contains the electronic control unit (ECU), the hydraulic solenoid valves and the electrically-driven return pump. The purpose of the system is to prevent the wheel(s) locking during heavy braking. This is achieved by automatic release of the brake on the relevant wheel, followed by re-application of the brake.

The solenoid valves are controlled by the ECU, which itself receives signals from the four wheel sensors (front sensors are fitted to the hubs, and the rear sensors are fitted to the rear brake backplates) which monitor the speed of rotation of each wheel. By comparing these signals, the ECU can determine the speed at which the vehicle is travelling – this information is supplied to the speedometer. It can use this speed to determine when a wheel is decelerating at an abnormal rate, compared to the speed of the vehicle, and therefore predicts when a wheel is about to lock. During normal operation, the system functions in the same way as a non-ABS braking system.

If the ECU senses that a wheel is about to lock, it closes the relevant outlet solenoid valves in the hydraulic unit, which then isolates the relevant brake(s) on the wheel(s) which is/are about to lock from the master cylinder, effectively sealing-in the hydraulic pressure.

If the speed of rotation of the wheel continues to decrease at an abnormal rate, the ECU opens the inlet solenoid valves on the relevant brake(s), and operates the electrically-driven return pump which pumps the hydraulic fluid back into the master cylinder, releasing the brake. Once the speed of rotation of the wheel returns to an acceptable rate, the pump stops; the solenoid valves switch again, allowing the hydraulic master cylinder pressure to return to the caliper, which then re-applies the brake. This cycle can be carried out many times a second.

The action of the solenoid valves and return pump creates pulses in the hydraulic circuit. When the ABS system is functioning, these pulses can be felt through the brake pedal.

The operation of the ABS system is entirely dependent on electrical signals. To prevent the system responding to any inaccurate signals, a built-in safety circuit monitors all signals received by the ECU. If an inaccurate signal or low battery voltage is detected, the ABS system is automatically shut-down, and the warning light on the instrument panel is illuminated, to inform the driver that the ABS system is not operational. Normal braking should still be available, however.

The Fusion is also equipped with an additional safety feature built into the ABS system, called EBD (electronic brake force distribution), which automatically apportions braking effort between the front and rear wheels. The EBD function is built into the system's software, and the intention is to limit braking effort (fluid pressure) to the rear wheels, to prevent them locking-up under heavy braking.

If a fault does develop in the any of these systems, the vehicle must be taken to a Ford dealer or suitably-equipped specialist for fault diagnosis and repair.

16 ABS hydraulic unit – removal and refitting

Note: *Refer to the precautions in Section 1 before proceeding.*

Removal

1 Disconnect the battery negative lead, and position the lead away from the battery.

2 Refer to Section 8 and remove the master cylinder.
3 Unclip and remove the large engine wiring harness multiplug from the left-hand inner wing (left as seen from the driver's seat) – there is no need to separate the two halves of the plug.
4 Undo the six brake pipes to the hydraulic control unit. Cap the end of the pipes and the hydraulic unit to prevent any dirt contamination. Unclip the brake lines from the retaining clips on the bulkhead.
5 Release the cover on the hydraulic control unit and disconnect the electrical connector.
6 Jack up the front of the car, and support it on axle stands (see *Jacking and vehicle support*).
7 Working from underneath, reach up under the left-hand wheel arch and unscrew the single mounting bolt for the ABS unit support bracket.
8 Back in the engine compartment, unscrew the remaining two mounting bolts, then lift out the hydraulic unit.
9 If required, the mounting bracket can be removed by unscrewing the three mounting bolts. Also, the hydraulic unit and control unit can be separated by removing the two Torx bolts on top.

Refitting

10 Refitting is a reversal of removal. Ensure that the multiplug is securely connected, and that the brake pipe unions are tightened to the specified torque. On completion, bleed the hydraulic system as described in Section 11. **Note:** *If air enters the hydraulic unit, the unit must be bled using special Ford test equipment.*

17 ABS wheel sensors – testing, removal and refitting

Note: *Refer to the precautions in Section 1 before proceeding.*

Testing

1 Checking of the sensors is done before removal, connecting a voltmeter to the disconnected sensor multiplug. Using an analogue (moving coil) meter is not practical, since the meter does not respond quickly enough. A digital meter having an ac facility may be used to check that the sensor is operating correctly.
2 To do this, raise the relevant wheel then disconnect the wiring to the ABS sensor and connect the meter to it.
3 Spin the wheel and check that the output voltage is between 1.5 and 2.0 volts, depending on how fast the wheel is spun.
4 Alternatively, an oscilloscope may be used to check the output of the sensor – an alternating current will be traced on the screen, with magnitude depending on the speed of the rotating wheel.

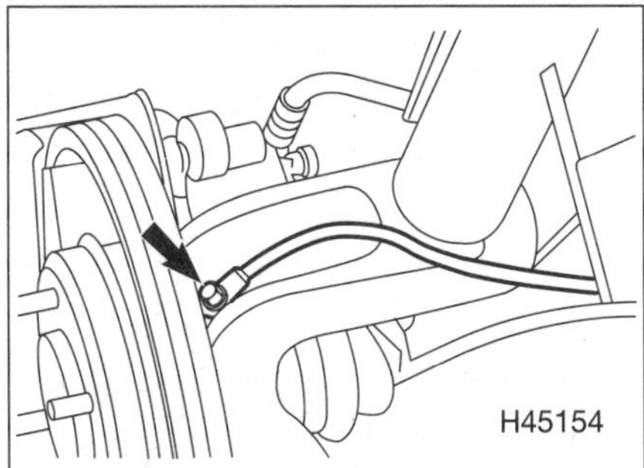

17.7 Unscrew the mounting bolt on the hub carrier to remove the wheel sensor

5 If the sensor output is low or zero, renew the sensor.

Removal

Front wheel sensor

6 Apply the handbrake and loosen the relevant front wheel nuts. Jack up the front of the car and support it on axle stands. Remove the wheel.
7 Unscrew the sensor mounting bolt from the hub carrier and withdraw the sensor **(see illustration)**. The sensors can prove difficult to remove, due to corrosion – try soaking the sensor in maintenance spray (eg, WD-40). Do not use any great force to remove a sensor, or it may be damaged. If the sensor does not have to be removed, unclip and disconnect its wiring instead.
8 Remove the sensor wiring loom from the support brackets on the front suspension strut and wheel arch.
9 Disconnect the multiplug, and withdraw the sensor and wiring loom.

Rear wheel sensor

10 Chock the front wheels, and engage 1st gear. Jack up the rear of the car and support it on axle stands (see *Jacking and vehicle support*). Remove the relevant wheel.
11 Unscrew the sensor mounting bolt, located on the brake backplate, and withdraw the sensor. The sensors can prove difficult to remove, due to corrosion – try soaking the sensor in maintenance spray (eg, WD-40). Do not use any great force to remove a sensor, or it may be damaged. If the sensor does not have to be removed, unclip and disconnect its wiring instead.
12 Disconnect the sensor wiring loom from the supports on the rear suspension arms.
13 Disconnect the multiplug, and withdraw the sensor and wiring loom.

Refitting

14 Refitting is a reversal of the removal procedure.

18 Brake light switch – removal and refitting

Note: *Refer to the precautions in Section 1 before proceeding.*

Removal

1 Disconnect the battery negative lead, and position the lead away from the battery.
2 Working inside the car, move the driver's seat fully to the rear, to allow maximum working area.
3 Remove the driver's side lower facia panel, which is secured by five screws (two inside the small storage compartment) and one clip (at the top left – pull the panel towards you to release it).
4 Disconnect the wiring connector from the brake light switch **(see illustration)**.
5 Rotate the switch by a quarter-turn, and withdraw it from the pedal bracket **(see illustration)**.

Refitting

6 Refitting is a reversal of removal. Check the operation of the switch prior to refitting the facia lower panel.

19 Handbrake lever – removal, refitting and adjustment

Note: *Refer to the precautions in Section 1 before proceeding.*

Removal

1 Chock the front wheels, and engage 1st gear.
2 Though not essential, access to the handbrake lever is greatly improved by

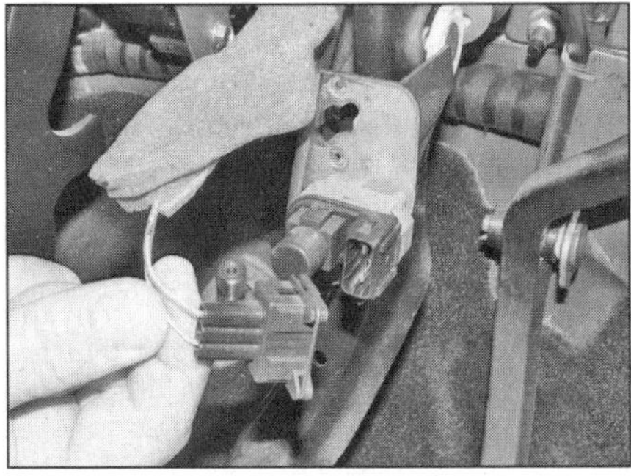
18.4 Disconnect the brake light switch at the top of the pedal ...

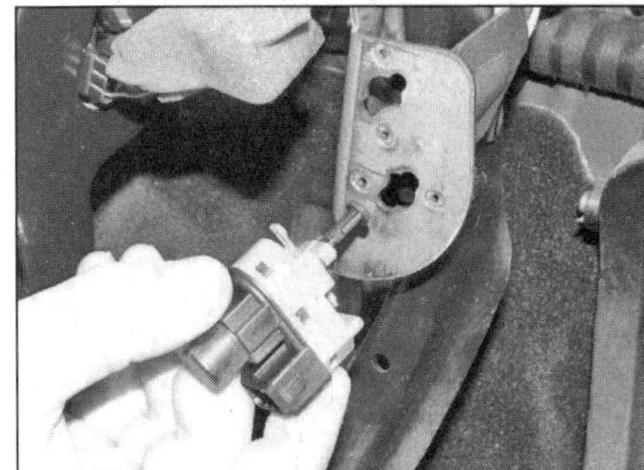
18.5 ... then twist the switch and remove it from the pedal bracket

19.3 Unclip the handbrake lever trim panel, and lift it off

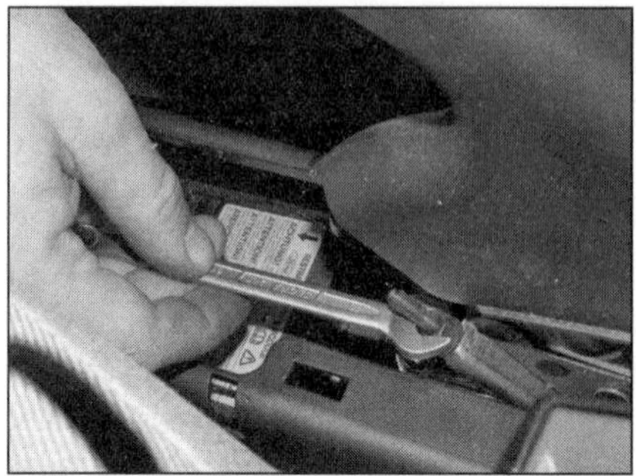
19.4 Unscrew the handbrake adjuster nut and disconnect the cable

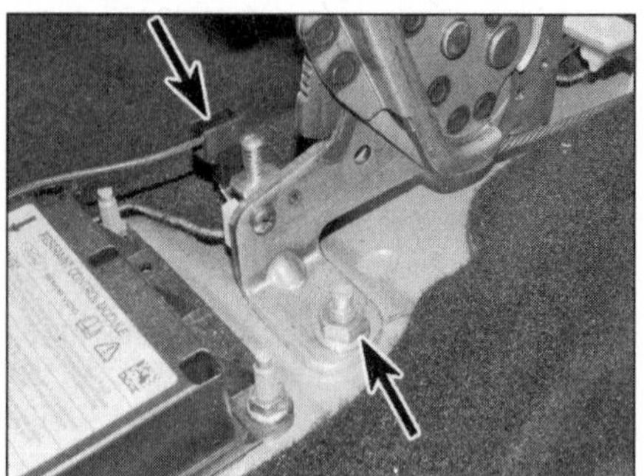
19.5 Handbrake warning light switch connector, and handbrake lever front mounting nut

removing one of the front seats, as described in Chapter 11, Section 23.

3 Where applicable, prise out the power outlet socket fitted into the handbrake trim panel, at the rear, and disconnect the wiring plug beneath it. Unclip the handbrake lever trim panel from the rear of the centre console, and lift it over the handbrake lever **(see illustration)**.

4 Remove the retaining clip from the handbrake adjuster nut, then unscrew the nut completely and disconnect the cable from the lever **(see illustration)**.

5 Disconnect the electrical connector from the handbrake warning light switch **(see illustration)**.

6 Release the handbrake, then remove the two nuts securing it to the floor and remove it from the car.

Refitting

7 Refitting is a reversal of removal.

8 When refitting the lever, it will be necessary to reset and adjust the mechanism, as described below.

Adjustment

9 If the handbrake lever has been removed, or new cables have been fitted, the mechanism must first be settled as follows. Apply the handbrake by four notches, then tighten the adjustment nut until all the slack has been taken up (when the nut starts to feel tight). Apply and release the handbrake firmly ten times, then loosen the adjuster nut to the end of its thread. Finally, depress the footbrake firmly fifteen times.

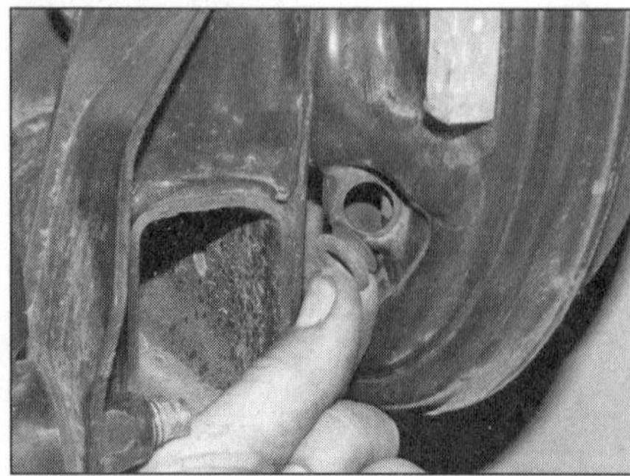
19.14 Remove the rear brake backplate inspection plug

10 If not already done, unclip the handbrake lever trim panel from the rear of the centre console, and lift it over the handbrake lever. Release the handbrake, and check that the cable end is located properly on the lever. Remove the adjuster nut retaining clip – a new one should be fitted on completion.

11 For a quick adjustment, to simply take up any slack in the cable, tighten the adjuster nut by a quarter-turn at a time, then recheck the operation of the handbrake. The handbrake should be fully-applied at four to six notches – do not over-adjust, or the handbrake may not release fully. The full adjustment procedure is as follows:

12 Remove the retaining clip from the handbrake adjuster nut, then unscrew the nut to the end of its thread.

13 Jack up the rear of the car, and support it on axle stands (see *Jacking and vehicle support*).

14 Prise out the rubber inspection plug from each rear brake backplate **(see illustration)**.

15 From the fully-unscrewed position, gradually tighten the adjuster nut inside the car, while an assistant with an electric torch checks for movement on the handbrake lever through the hole in the brake backplate. As soon as movement is seen one side, note the approximate position of the adjuster nut, then have the assistant check that the lever on the other side is also moving. If necessary, slacken the adjuster slightly, then retighten.

16 With the base point for the start of handbrake operation on both sides established, tighten the adjuster nut by two full turns. Refit the inspection plugs to the brake backplates, but do not lower the car yet.

17 Apply and release the handbrake a few times, and check that the lever inside the car returns fully to the released position – if not, repeat the adjustment procedure from the start.

18 With the handbrake released, turn the rear wheels, and check for signs that the handbrake may be dragging. If drag is felt on either wheel, loosen off the adjuster nut at least two full turns, and try again.

19 When handbrake operation is satisfactory, fit a new retaining clip to the adjuster nut, and refit the handbrake lever trim panel. Lower the car to the ground.

20 Check the operation of the handbrake several times before returning the car to normal service.

20 Handbrake cables – removal and refitting

Note: *Refer to the precautions in Section 1 before proceeding.*

Caution: This procedure should only be attempted when the engine and exhaust system are completely cool – the engine should have been switched off for at least a few hours (preferably, after it has been left overnight).

Removal

1 Chock the front wheels, and engage 1st gear. Loosen the wheel nuts on the relevant rear wheel, then jack up the rear of the car and support it on axle stands (see *Jacking and vehicle support*). Fully release the handbrake lever.

2 Unhook the rear silencer from its two rubber mountings, and rest the rear of the exhaust on the rear suspension beam **(see illustration)**.

3 Unscrew the nuts securing the curved centre section of the exhaust heat shield, and remove it from under the car.

4 The cable has a joining sleeve on each side, attached to the rear suspension beam. Lift the securing tang with a small screwdriver, and

20.2 Unhook the rear silencer rubber mountings

20.4a Lift the retaining tang with a small screwdriver ...

20.4b ... and remove the handbrake cable end fitting

20.5a Squeeze the metal clip ...

20.5b ... and pass the cable outer through the lug on the axle

20.7 Unclip the cable grommets from the lugs on the rear axle pivots

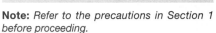

20.8 Unclip the cable from the plastic clips at the back of the floorpan

prise out the inner cable end fitting from the joining sleeve **(see illustrations)**.

5 Trace the cable forwards to the inner mounting lug on top of the rear axle, and release the cable outer by squeezing the metal clip legs together, and passing it back through the lug **(see illustrations)**.

6 Unhook both cables from the equaliser bar at the front, and prise the cable outers from the floor bracket.

7 Back at the pivot points for the rear suspension beam, unclip the handbrake cable from the mounting lugs on the inside **(see illustration)**.

8 Finally, unclip the cables from two clips on the back of the floorpan, and lower them from under the car **(see illustration)**.

Refitting

9 Refitting is a reversal of the removal procedure, noting the following points:

a) *Make sure that the cable end fittings are correctly located, and that the cables are routed as before, without any kinks or sharp bends.*
b) *Adjust the handbrake as described in Section 19.*

21 Vacuum pump (diesel models) – testing, removal and refitting

Note: *Refer to the precautions in Section 1 before proceeding.*

Testing

1 The operation of the vacuum pump can be checked using a vacuum gauge.

2 The vacuum pump is located on the transmission end of the cylinder head **(see illustrations)**. Depress the locking tabs and

21.2a Brake servo vacuum pump location – 1.4 litre diesel models

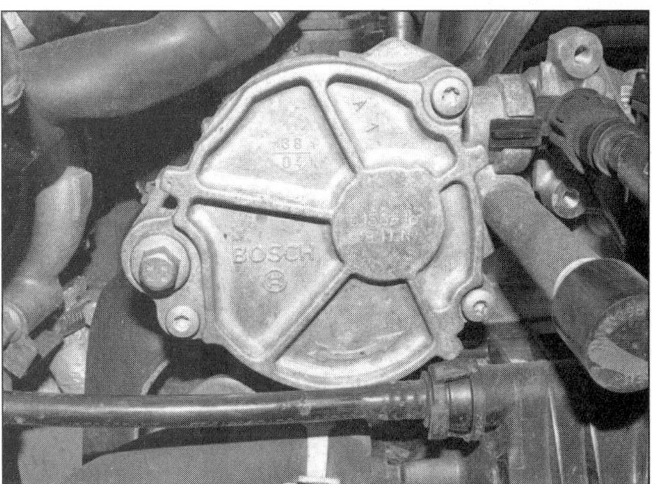

21.2b Brake servo vacuum pump location – 1.6 litre diesel models

21.7 Vacuum pump mounting bolts

release the brake servo vacuum hose from the top of the pump. Connect a suitable vacuum gauge to the pump union using a suitable length of hose.

3 Start the engine and allow it to idle, then measure the vacuum created by the pump. As a guide, after one minute, a minimum of approximately 500 mm Hg should be recorded. If the vacuum registered is significantly less than this, it is likely that the pump is faulty. However, seek the advice of a Ford dealer before condemning the pump.

4 Overhaul of the vacuum pump is not possible, since no components are available separately for it. If faulty, the complete pump assembly must be renewed.

Removal

5 Remove the air cleaner as described in Chapter 4B, Section 4.

6 The vacuum pump is located on the transmission end of the cylinder head. Depress the locking tabs and release the brake servo vacuum hose from the top of the pump.

7 Unscrew the two mounting bolts, and withdraw the pump from the head **(see illustration)**. Recover the O-ring seals – new ones must be used when refitting.

Refitting

8 Refitting is a reversal of removal, noting the following points:

a) Ensure the pump and cylinder head mating surfaces are clean and dry, and fit new seals.

b) Align the pump's drive dog with the slot in the end of the camshaft, and fit it into place, ensuring the seals are not dislodged in the process.

c) Tighten the pump mounting bolts to the specified torque.

d) Make sure the hose connection is securely remade.

e) Start the engine and check the operation of the servo as described in Section 12.

Chapter 10
Suspension and steering

Contents

Degrees of difficulty

Easy, suitable for novice with little experience

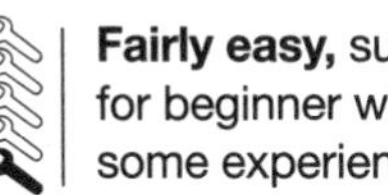

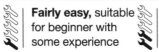

Fairly easy, suitable for beginner with some experience

Fairly difficult, suitable for competent DIY mechanic

Difficult, suitable for experienced DIY mechanic

Very difficult, suitable for expert DIY or professional

Specifications

Wheel alignment and steering angles

Front wheel castor:	
Setting value	+3° 43'
Tolerance range	+4° 43' to +2° 43'
Maximum side-to-side variation	1° 00'
Front wheel camber:	
Setting value	-1° 39'
Tolerance range	+0° 12' to -2°18'
Maximum side-to-side variation	1° 15'
Front wheel toe:	
Setting value	3.3 mm (toe-in) ± 1.1 mm
Tolerance range	3.3 mm (toe-in) ± 2.3 mm
Rear wheel camber:	
Setting value	-1° 09'
Tolerance range	+0° 06' to -2° 24'
Maximum side-to-side variation	1° 15'
Rear wheel toe (check only)	3.9 mm (toe-in) ± 2.3 mm

Torque wrench settings	Nm	lbf ft
Steering		
Power steering fluid pipe bracket bolts	25	18
Power steering gear fluid pipe union	25	18
Power steering pump mounting bolts:		
Petrol models	25	18
Diesel models:		
1.4 litre	23	17
1.6 litre	9	7
Power steering pump high-pressure outlet union:		
Petrol models	40	30
Diesel models:		
1.4 litre	40	30
1.6 litre	33	24
Steering column retaining nuts*	24	18
Steering column shaft-to-rack pinion pinch-bolt*	28	21
Steering rack securing bolts*	48	35
Steering wheel securing bolt	45	33
Track rod end locknuts	63	46
Track rod end-to-swivel hub nuts*	48	35
Front suspension		
Anti-roll bar clamp bolts	55	41
Anti-roll bar drop-link nuts:		
To anti-roll bar	55	41
To suspension strut	48	35
Brake caliper carrier bracket bolts	70	52
Front hub nut*	290	214
Lower arm front bolt:		
Stage 1	80	59
Stage 2	Angle-tighten a further 55°	
Lower arm rear clamp retaining bolts	55	41
Lower arm balljoint pinch-bolt and nut	48	35
Subframe bolts:		
Front bolts	70	52
Inner and outer bolts	175	129
Rear bolts	115	85
Suspension strut piston rod nut	48	35
Suspension strut top mounting nuts	30	22
Swivel hub-to-suspension strut pinch-bolt	85	63
Rear suspension		
Rear axle mounting bolts	115	85
Rear axle pivot through-bolt and nut	125	92
Rear hub spindle retaining bolts	70	52
Rear hub nut*	235	173
Shock absorber lower mounting bolt	115	85
Shock absorber upper mounting bolts	25	18
Roadwheels		
Roadwheel nuts	110	81

** Use new nut/bolt*

1 General information

The front suspension is of independent type, with a subframe, MacPherson struts, lower arms, and an anti-roll bar. The struts, which incorporate coil springs and integral shock absorbers, are attached at their upper ends to the reinforced strut mountings on the body shell. The lower end of each strut is bolted to the top of a cast swivel hub, which carries the hub, and the brake disc and caliper. The hubs run within non-adjustable bearings in the swivel hubs. The lower end of each swivel hub is attached, via a balljoint, to a pressed-steel lower arm assembly. The balljoints are integral with the lower arms. Each lower arm is attached at its inboard end to the subframe, via flexible rubber bushes, and controls both lateral and fore-and-aft movement of the front wheels. An anti-roll bar is fitted to all models. The anti-roll bar is mounted on the subframe, and is connected to the suspension struts via vertical drop-links.

The rear suspension is semi-independent, with an inverted U-section beam welded between tubular trailing arms. This inverted U-section beam allows a limited torsional flexibility, giving each rear wheel a certain degree of independent movement, whilst maintaining optimum track and wheel camber control. This type of arrangement is called a 'twist beam' rear axle. The axle is attached to the body via rubber bushes. The compact springs are mounted under the car, so only the shock absorber housings encroach on the boot area, resulting in more boot space. The shock absorbers are bolted to the trailing arm section of the rear axle at the base, and to the body housings at the top. The rear hubs are integral with the brake drums, and the hub/drums run on stub axles which are bolted to the rear of the trailing arms.

The steering is of conventional rack-and-pinion type, incorporating a collapsible safety column. The column is joined to the steering gear via a flexible coupling. The steering gear is mounted on the front suspension subframe. The steering gear track rods are attached via the track rod ends to the steering arms on the swivel hubs.

All models are equipped with power steering. On all petrol and 1.4 litre diesel models, the power steering pump is belt-driven from the crankshaft pulley. 1.6 litre diesel models are equipped with an electro-hydraulic power steering system, consisting of a variable-speed brush-less electric motor together with a conventional hydraulic power steering gear.

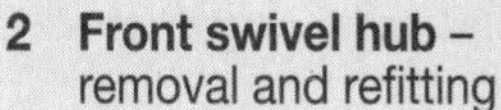

2 Front swivel hub – removal and refitting

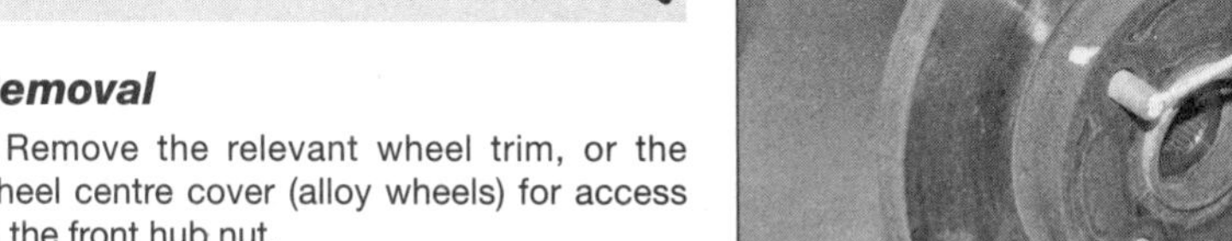

Removal

1 Remove the relevant wheel trim, or the wheel centre cover (alloy wheels) for access to the front hub nut.

2 Ensure that the handbrake is applied (ideally, have an assistant apply the footbrake), then slacken the hub nut using a suitable socket and extension bar. Loosen the hub nut almost to the end of its threads, but do not remove it at this stage.

Warning: The driveshaft nut is done up extremely tight, and considerable effort will be required to loosen it. Do not use poor-quality, badly-fitting tools for this task, due to the risk of personal injury.

3 Working in the engine compartment, loosen the three suspension strut top mounting nuts by three turns each, on the side concerned. Do not loosen the centre nut.

4 Slacken the relevant front wheel nuts, then jack up the front of the car, and support securely on axle stands (see *Jacking and vehicle support*). Remove the roadwheel.

5 Working under the wheel arch, slide out the retaining clip below the brake flexible hose support bracket on the suspension strut, and detach the brake hose **(see illustrations)**.

6 Unscrew the bolts securing the brake caliper carrier bracket to the swivel hub, then slide the caliper/bracket assembly from the swivel hub and brake disc (there is no need to remove the brake pads). Suspend the caliper/bracket assembly from the strut coil spring using wire or string – do not allow the caliper to hang on the brake hose.

7 Mark the brake disc in relation to the hub (assuming it is to be refitted), then remove any retaining clips or washers holding it in place, and withdraw it from the hub **(see illustrations)**.

8 On models with ABS, unscrew the wheel sensor retaining bolt, then withdraw the wheel sensor from the top of the hub. Provided the sensor is placed out of the way, there is no need to disconnect its wiring. **Note:** *The sensors can prove difficult to remove, due to corrosion – try soaking the sensor in maintenance spray (eg, WD-40). Do not use any great force to remove a sensor, or it may be damaged.*

9 Slacken the track rod end balljoint nut, and unscrew it as far as the ends of the threads. Counterhold the balljoint pin using a 5 mm Allen key **(see illustration)**.

10 Disconnect the track rod end balljoint from the swivel hub using a balljoint separator tool (leave the nut fitted to protect the threads), taking care not to damage the balljoint rubber seal **(see illustration)**. Once the balljoint has been released, remove the balljoint nut and discard it – a new one should be used for refitting.

11 Unscrew the pinch-nut and bolt securing the swivel hub to the lower arm balljoint. Push the end of the lower arm down to free the balljoint from the swivel hub. If the balljoint is very tight, it may be necessary to lever down using a large screwdriver, or similar tool, but take care not to damage the balljoint rubber seal. Recover the heat shield from the balljoint **(see illustrations)**.

2.5a Slide out the retaining clip ...

2.5b ... and detach the brake hose

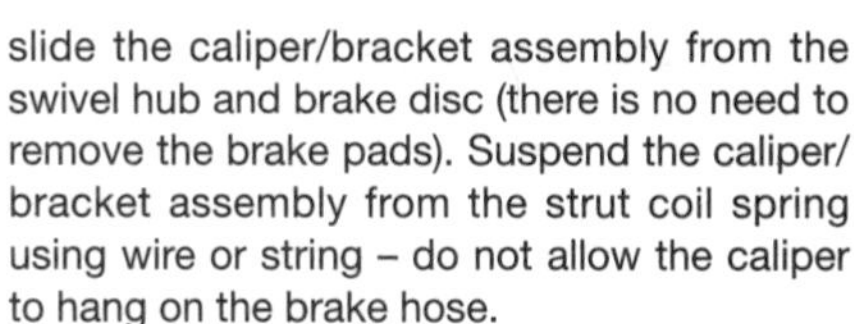

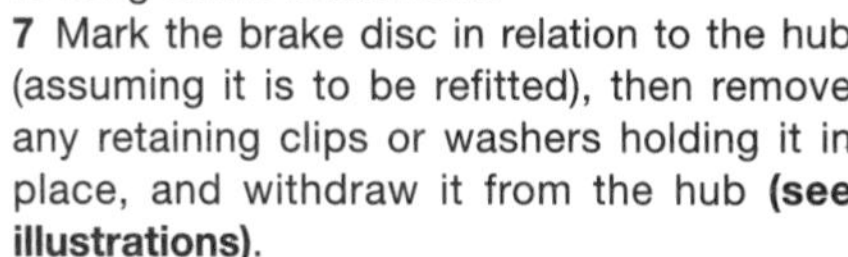

2.7a Mark the disc in relation to the hub ...

2.7b ... then remove it

2.9 Loosen the track rod end balljoint nut, using an Allen key to stop the pin turning

2.10 Using a balljoint separator tool to free the track rod end

2.11a Loosen the lower arm balljoint clamp bolt nut (hold the bolt with a second spanner/socket) ...

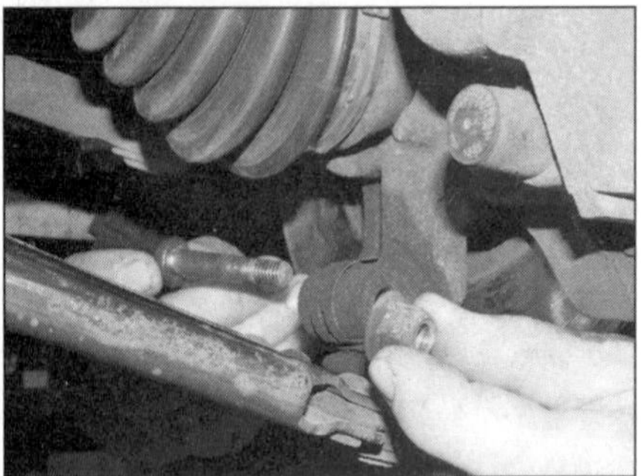

2.11b ... then remove the bolt, noting that it fits from the back

2.11c Home-made method of releasing the lower arm – wood block, long pole and length of chain

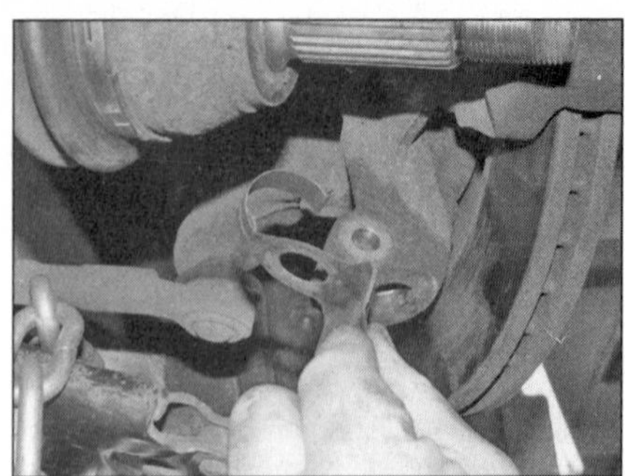

2.11d Unclip and remove the balljoint heat shield

12 The splined end of the driveshaft now has to be released from its location in the hub. It's likely that the splines will be very tight (corrosion may even be a factor, if the driveshaft has not been disturbed for some time), and considerable force may be needed to push the driveshaft out. Ford recommend using a four-legged puller for this, but if one is not available, the shaft will have to be tapped out with a hammer. If a hammer is used, place a small piece of wood over the end of the driveshaft – in addition to the loosened hub nut, this will protect the threads from damage.

13 Once the splines have been released, remove the hub nut and discard it – the nut will probably be of the new 'laminated' type, and is only designed to be used once **(see illustration)**.

14 The driveshaft can be separated from the hub by having an assistant pull the base of the suspension strut outwards, while the splined end of the shaft is pulled clear of the hub **(see illustration)**. Do not bend the driveshaft excessively at any stage, or the joints may be damaged – the inner and outer joints should not be bent through more than 18° and 45° respectively. Do not let the driveshaft hang down under its own weight – tie it up level if necessary.

15 Unscrew the pinch-bolt securing the swivel hub to the lower end of the suspension strut. Using a suitable lever, or a large screwdriver, spread the slot in the top of the swivel hub, until the swivel hub can be pulled from the end of the strut. If necessary, tap the swivel hub down to free it from the strut, using a soft-faced mallet **(see illustrations)**.

Refitting

16 Refitting is a reversal of removal, bearing in mind the following points:

a) Use a new hub nut and track rod end nut.

b) When refitting the swivel hub to the base of the strut, align the slot in the hub with the lug on the strut.

c) Make sure that the slot for the pinch-bolt in the strut aligns with the corresponding holes in the swivel hub.

d) Do not fully-tighten the hub nut until the car is resting on its wheels.

e) Tighten all fixings to the specified torque, including the suspension strut top mounting nuts.

f) Have the front wheel alignment checked on completion.

3 Front hub bearings – renewal

Note: *A press, a suitable puller, or similar improvised tools will be required for this operation. Obtain a bearing overhaul kit before proceeding.*

1 With the swivel hub removed as described in Section 2, proceed as follows.

2 The hub must now be removed from the bearing/swivel hub assembly. It is preferable to use a press to do this, but it is possible to drive out the hub using a metal tube of suitable diameter. Alternatively a suitable puller can be used.

3 Securely support the hub carrier, on two metal bars for instance, with the inner face uppermost then, using a metal bar or tube of suitable diameter, press or drive out the hub flange – we used a bolt and large washer (the same diameter as the end of the hub's splined

2.13 Remove the driveshaft nut, and get a new one for refitting

2.14 Pull the hub outwards, and pull the driveshaft through inside

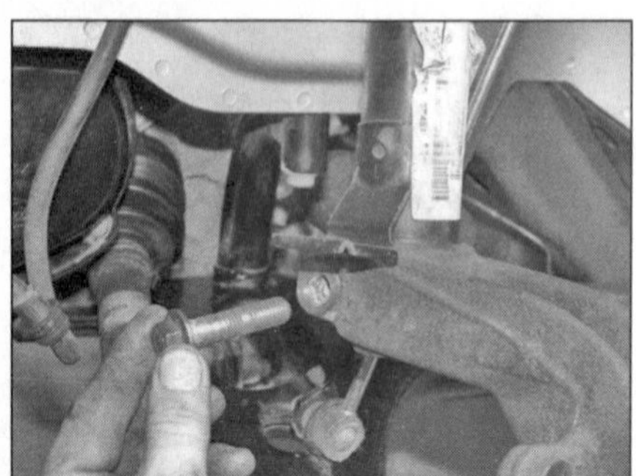

2.15a Unscrew the strut-to-hub pinch-bolt (which fits from the front) ...

2.15b ... then tap the hub downwards to free it from the strut ...

2.15c ... and remove it

3.3a We used a large bolt and washer ...

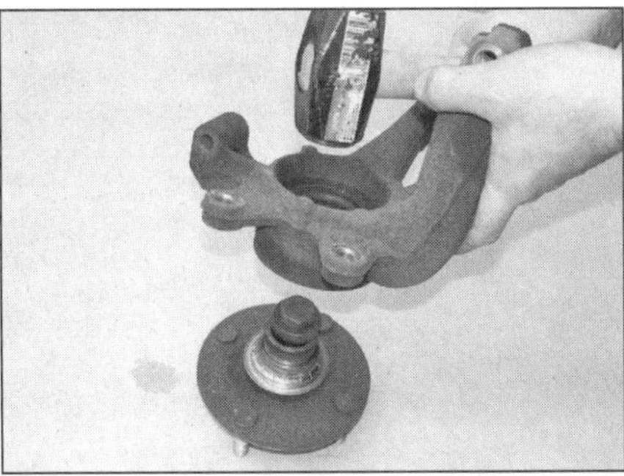

3.3b ... and a large hammer to drive out the hub flange

3.4a Use plenty of maintenance spray ...

3.4b ... then using a suitable drift ...

3.4c ... and several sharp blows from the hammer ...

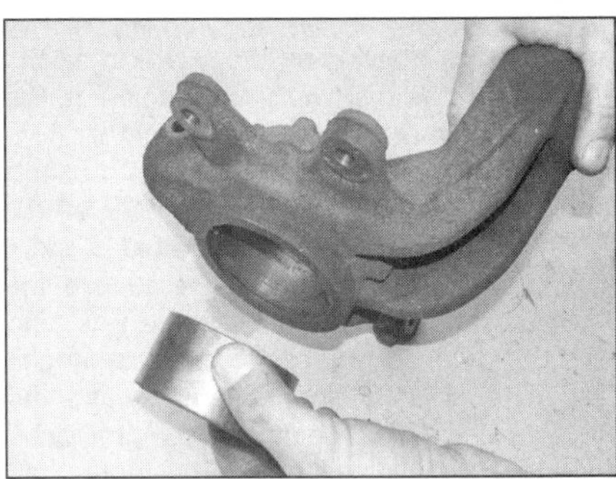

3.4d ... tap out the old bearing

end) **(see illustrations)**. Alternatively, use the puller to separate the hub from the bearing. Note that the bearing inner race will remain on the hub.

4 Now the bearing itself must be removed. After applying a generous amount of spray lubricant, we were able to drive the bearing out, using another old bearing, together with the same large bolt and hammer used previously **(see illustrations)**. Mount the swivel hub across two large blocks of wood (or even bricks) – putting it across the open jaws of a vice might result in damage to the vice, owing to the amount of force which will be necessary.

5 The bearing inner race left on the hub flange must now be removed. To do this, grip the edge of the flange in a vice, and tap the race off with a chisel **(see illustrations)**. Tap the race at the top and both sides (even turn the flange over in the vice) to stop it jamming as it comes off.

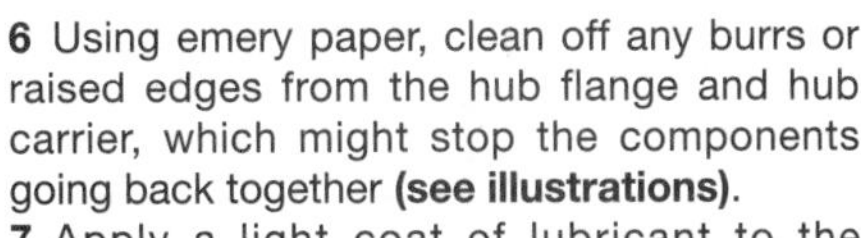

6 Using emery paper, clean off any burrs or raised edges from the hub flange and hub carrier, which might stop the components going back together **(see illustrations)**.

7 Apply a light coat of lubricant to the inside of the hub carrier, and to the outside of the new bearing. Start fitting the bearing by offering it squarely into the carrier, then give it a few light taps with the hammer all round to locate it – keep the bearing square as this is done, or it will jam **(see illustration)**.

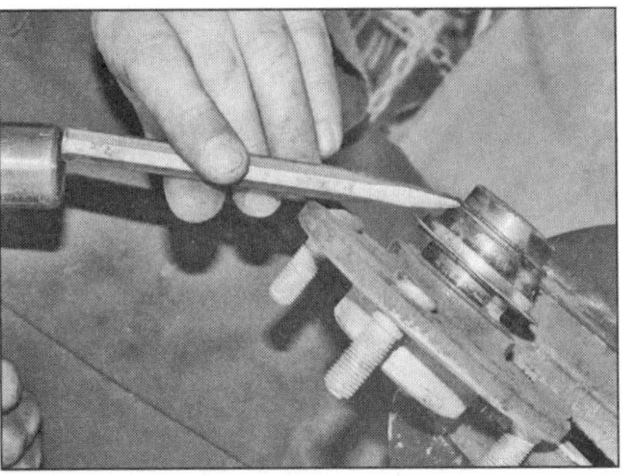

3.5a Mount the hub flange in a vice, and tap the inner race with a chisel ...

3.5b ... until it comes off

3.6a Clean the edges of the hub flange ...

3.6b ... and the hub carrier with emery paper

3.7 Locate the new bearing squarely in the hub carrier with a few light taps from the hammer

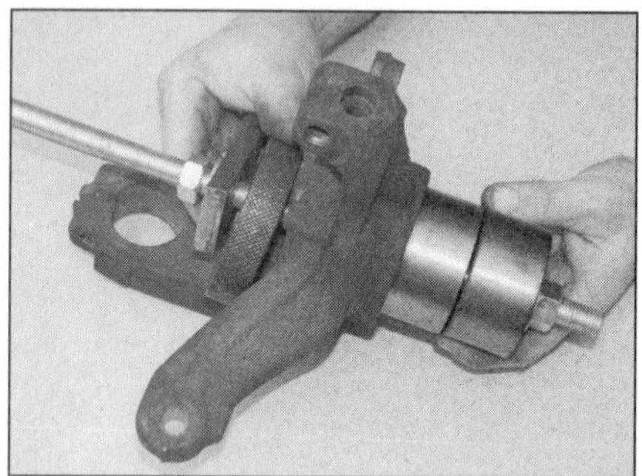
3.8a Home-made arrangement of threaded rod, nuts, washers and the old bearing ...

3.8b ... used to gradually press the new bearing into place

3.9 The same arrangement and method can be used to refit the hub flange

8 Fitting the bearing by tapping it in all the way with a hammer will likely damage it. We used a length of threaded bar (available from motor factors, DIY stores, etc) with a nut, some large washers and a drilled plate on the inside of the hub carrier. With the old bearing, another washer, and a nut on the outside, the whole assembly was mounted in a vice, and the nut tightened to press the new bearing in place. The actual method is to tighten the nut slightly, give the old bearing a few taps round its edge, tighten the nut some more, and so on until the bearing was fully home **(see illustrations)**.

9 The hub flange can be pressed into the new bearing using a very similar method to the one just used **(see illustration)**.

10 On completion, refit the swivel hub as described in Section 2.

4 Front strut – removal, overhaul and refitting

Removal

1 Working in the engine compartment, loosen the three suspension strut top mounting nuts by three turns each, on the side concerned. Do not loosen the centre nut.

2 Slacken the relevant front wheel nuts, then jack up the front of the car, and support securely on axle stands (see *Jacking and vehicle support*). Remove the roadwheel.

3 Working under the wheel arch, slide out the retaining clip below the brake flexible hose support bracket on the suspension strut, and detach the brake hose.

4 Unscrew the nut securing the anti-roll bar drop-link to the suspension strut. If necessary, counterhold the drop-link pin using a 5 mm Allen key **(see illustrations)**.

5 Unscrew the bolts securing the brake caliper carrier bracket to the swivel hub, then slide the caliper/bracket assembly from the swivel hub and brake disc (there is no need to remove the brake pads). Suspend the caliper/bracket assembly using wire or string – do not allow the caliper to hang on the brake hose **(see illustration)**.

6 Mark the brake disc in relation to the hub (assuming it is to be refitted), then remove any retaining clips or washers holding it in place, and withdraw it from the hub.

7 Unscrew the pinch-nut and bolt securing the swivel hub to the lower arm balljoint. Push the end of the lower arm down to free the balljoint from the swivel hub. If the balljoint is very tight, it may be necessary to lever down using a large screwdriver, or similar tool, but take care not to damage the balljoint rubber seal. Recover the heat shield from the balljoint **(see illustrations 2.11a to 2.11d)**.

8 Unscrew and remove the strut-to-hub pinch-bolt (noting that it is fitted from in front), then tap the hub downwards to free it from the base of the strut. Once the base of the strut has been separated from it, hook the hub back onto the lower arm balljoint to support it **(see illustration)**.

9 Support the strut from under the wheel arch then, working in the engine compartment, unscrew the suspension strut top mounting nuts. Lower the strut out, and remove it under the wheel arch **(see illustrations)**.

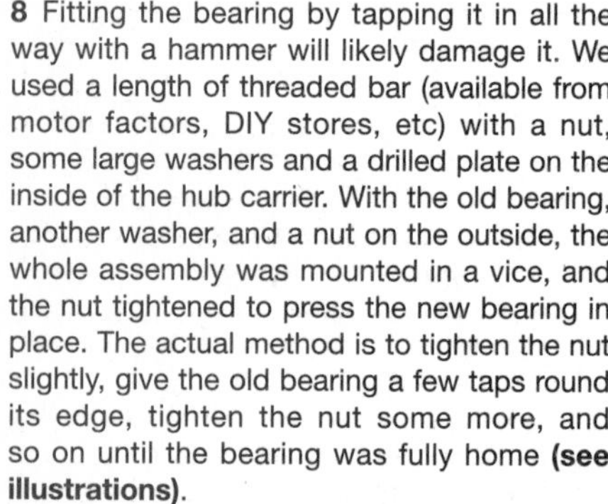
4.4a Unscrew the drop-link nut, using an Allen key to stop the pin turning ...

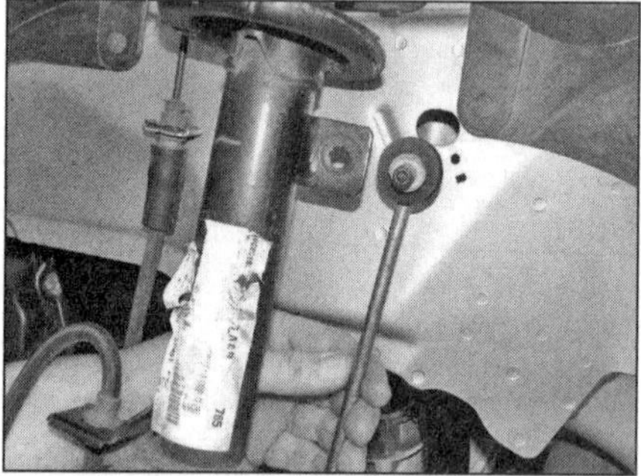
4.4b ... and separate the top of the drop-link from the strut

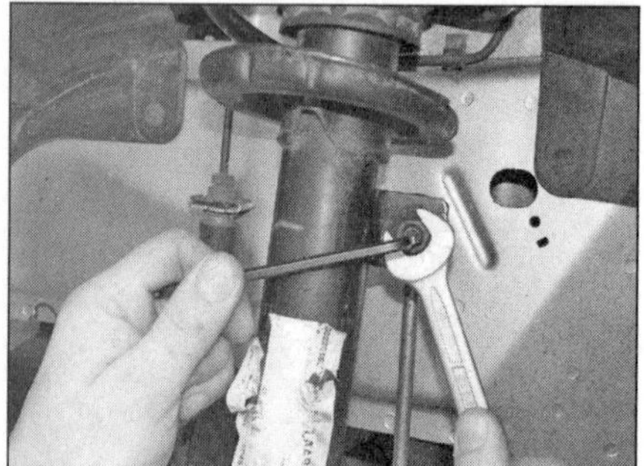

4.5 Hang the brake caliper up from a suitable point to avoid straining the brake hose

4.8 Lift the hub back onto the lower arm balljoint for now

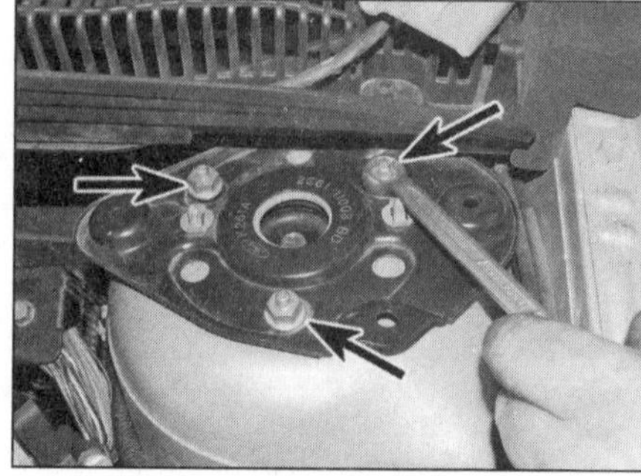
4.9a Fully unscrew the three upper mounting nuts ...

4.9b ... then remove the strut from under the wheel arch

4.10 Make sure spring compressor tool is on securely

4.11 Slacken and remove the retaining nut

Overhaul

Note: *A spring compressor tool will be required for this operation.*

10 With the suspension strut resting on a bench, or clamped in a vice, fit a spring compressor tool, and compress the coil spring to relieve the pressure on the spring seats. Ensure that the compressor tool is securely located on the spring, in accordance with the tool manufacturer's instructions **(see illustration)**.

11 Counterhold the strut piston rod with the Allen key or hexagon bit used during removal, and unscrew the piston rod nut **(see illustration)**.

12 Remove the piston rod nut, followed by the top mounting, strut bearing and upper spring seat, the spring (with compressor tool still fitted), the rubber bump stop, and the dust cover **(see illustrations)**.

13 With the strut assembly now completely dismantled, examine all the components for wear, damage or deformation, and check the thrust bearing for smoothness of operation. Renew any of the components as necessary.

14 Examine the strut for signs of fluid leakage. Check the strut piston for signs of pitting along its entire length, and check the strut body for signs of damage. While holding it in an upright position, test the operation of the strut by moving the piston through a full stroke, and then through short strokes of 50 to 100 mm. In both cases, the resistance felt should be smooth and continuous. If the resistance is jerky or uneven or if there is any visible sign of wear or damage to the strut, renewal is necessary.

15 If any doubt exists as to the condition of the coil spring, carefully remove the spring compressors and check the spring for distortion and signs of cracking. Renew the spring if it is damaged or distorted, or if there is any doubt as to its condition.

16 Inspect all other components for damage or deterioration, and renew any that are suspect.

17 Slide the dust cover, followed by rubber bump stop onto the strut piston.

18 If the spring compressor tool has been removed from the spring, refit it and compress the spring sufficiently to enable it to be refitted to the strut.

19 Slide the spring over the strut, and position it so that the lower end of the spring is resting against the stop on the lower seat **(see illustration)**.

20 Refit the upper spring seat/strut bearing, and rotate it as necessary to position the stop against the upper end of the spring.

21 Refit the top mounting plate, then refit the piston rod nut, and tighten to the specified torque. Counterhold the piston rod using an Allen key or hexagon bit as during removal.

22 Slowly slacken the spring compressor tool to relieve the tension in the spring. Check that the ends of the spring locate correctly against the stops on the spring seats. If necessary, turn the spring and the upper seat so that the components locate correctly before the compressor tool is removed. Remove the compressor tool when the spring is fully seated.

Refitting

23 Refitting is a reversal of removal, bearing in mind the following points:

a) When refitting the strut into the swivel hub, align the lug on the strut with the slot in the hub.

b) Make sure that the slot for the pinch-bolt in the strut aligns with the corresponding holes in the swivel hub.

c) Tighten all fixings to the specified torque.

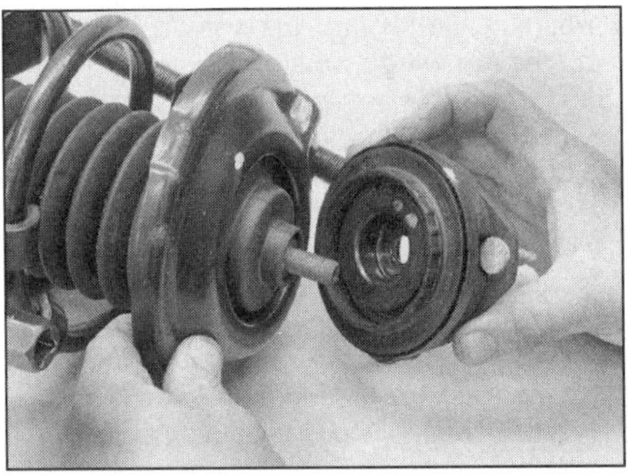
4.12a Remove the upper bearing and spring seat ...

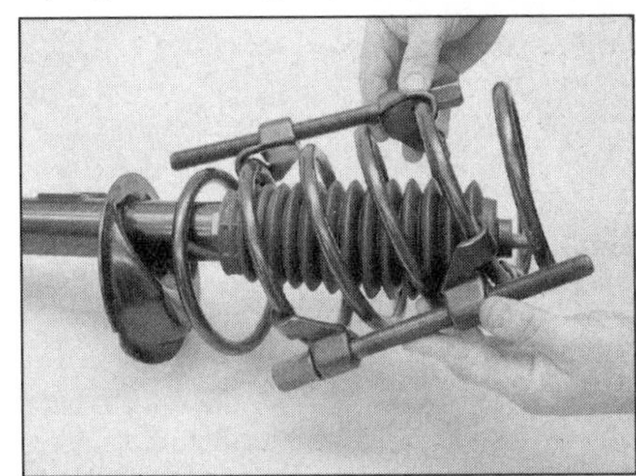
4.12b ... then carefully remove the spring ...

4.12c ... followed by the gaiter ...

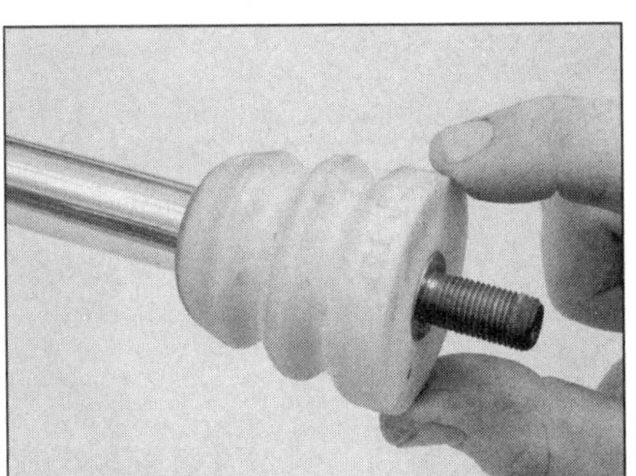
4.12d ... and the bump stop

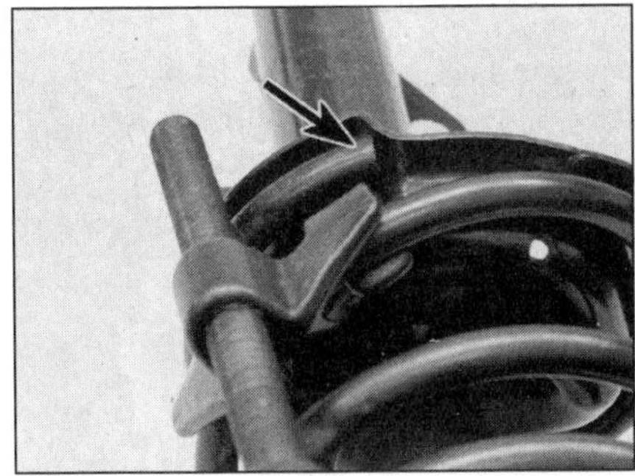
4.19 Spring located in the lower seat (arrowed)

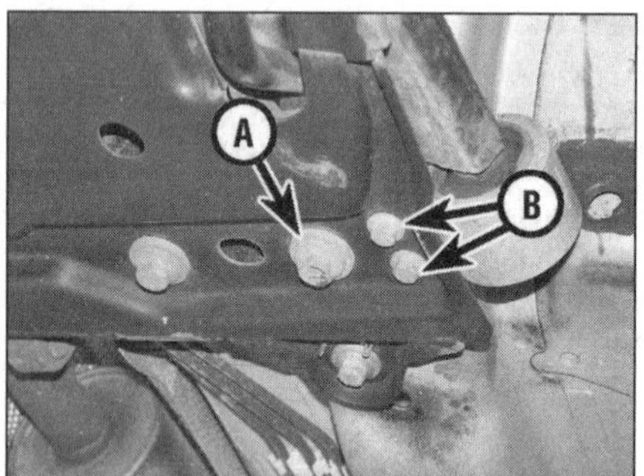

6.3 Subframe outer bolt (A) and the two smaller clamp bolts (B)

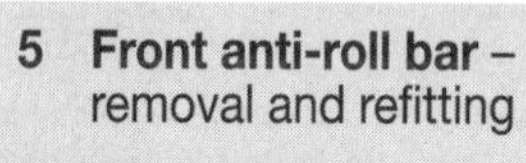

5 Front anti-roll bar – removal and refitting

Removal

1 Remove the front suspension subframe as described in Section 8.

2 Unscrew the bolts securing the anti-roll bar mounting clamps to the subframe, then carefully manipulate the anti-roll bar assembly out from under the car.

3 If desired, the drop-links can be removed from the anti-roll bar after unscrewing the securing nuts. If necessary, counterhold the drop-link pins using a spanner on the flats provided.

Refitting

4 Refitting is a reversal of removal, bearing in mind the following points:

a) *Tighten all fixings to the specified torque.*
b) *Refit the front suspension subframe as described in Section 8.*

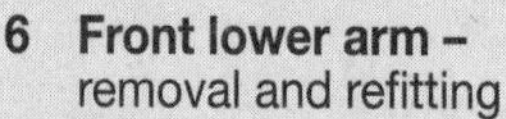

6 Front lower arm – removal and refitting

Removal

1 Slacken the front wheel nuts on the side concerned, then apply the handbrake, jack up the front of the car, and support securely on axle stands (see *Jacking and vehicle support*). Remove the roadwheel.

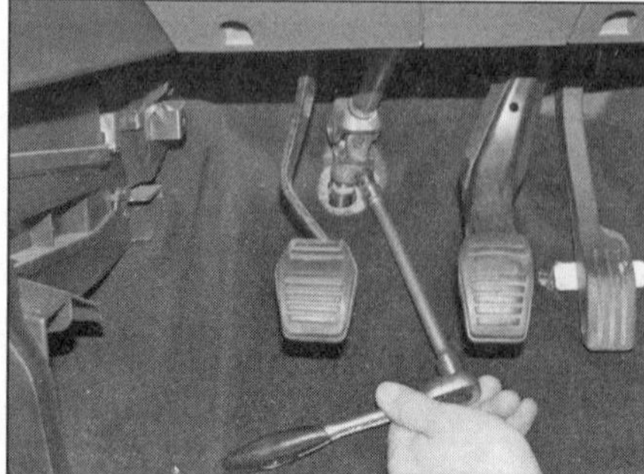
8.3a In the driver's footwell, unscrew ...

6.4 Lower arm front mounting bolt

2 Unscrew the pinch-nut and bolt securing the swivel hub to the lower arm balljoint. Push the end of the lower arm down to free the balljoint from the swivel hub. If the balljoint is very tight, it may be necessary to lever down using a large screwdriver, or similar tool, but take care not to damage the balljoint rubber seal. Recover the heat shield from the balljoint **(see illustrations 2.11a to 2.11d)**.

3 Unscrew and remove the outer of the two subframe rear bolts **(see illustration)**.

4 Remove the lower arm front mounting bolt, then take out the two rear clamp bolts and remove the lower arm from under the car **(see illustration)**.

Overhaul

5 Examine the rubber bushes and the suspension lower balljoint for wear and damage. See Section 7.

Refitting

6 Refitting is a reversal of removal, bearing in mind the following points:

a) *Tighten all fixings to the specified torque.*
b) *The lower arm front bolt and clamp bolts should be tightened firmly by hand initially. When the wheels are refitted and the car is lowered so the weight is fully on the suspension, tighten the three lower arm bolts to the specified torque.*
c) *The lower arm front bolt is tightened in two stages, as quoted in the Specifications. Once the bolt has been tightened to the Stage 1 torque, tighten the bolt further through the specified angle – use an angle gauge (available from tool suppliers, and commonly used for cylinder head tightening) to ensure accuracy.*

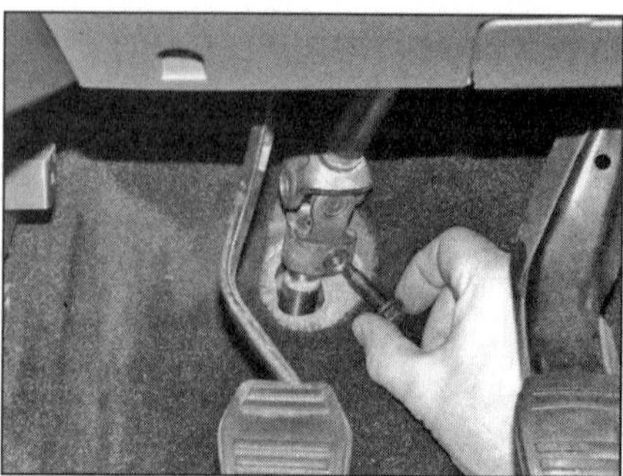
8.3b ... and remove the steering column lower pinch-bolt

7 Front lower arm balljoint – renewal

If the lower arm balljoint is worn, or the rubber seal is damaged, the complete lower arm must be renewed. At the time of writing, the balljoint could not be renewed separately from the lower arm, as it is riveted in place during manufacture. However, balljoint repair kits have become available over time for other similarly-affected models – with these, the original rivets are drilled out, and the new balljoint is bolted onto the arm using the original rivet holes. Check the latest parts availability situation with Ford, and with reputable motor factors, before deciding.

8 Front subframe – removal and refitting

Note: *Special tools (Ford Tool No 205-524) will be required to align the subframe with the body when refitting (see text).*

Removal

1 Disconnect the battery negative lead, and position the lead away from the battery (see Chapter 5A, Section 2).

2 Make sure the front wheels (and steering wheel) are in the straight-ahead position. Lock the steering in this position using the steering column lock.

3 Working in the driver's footwell, behind the pedals, unscrew the pinch-bolt securing the lower end of the steering column shaft to the steering gear pinion **(see illustrations)**. Discard the bolt – a new one should be used when refitting.

4 Remove the wheel trims or the wheel centre plates (alloy wheels), then slacken the front wheel nuts. Apply the handbrake, then jack up the front of the car, and support securely on axle stands (see *Jacking and vehicle support*). Remove the roadwheels.

5 Unscrew the pinch-nut and bolt securing each swivel hub to the lower arm balljoint. Push the end of the lower arm down to free the balljoint from the swivel hub. If the balljoint is very tight, it may be necessary to lever down using a large screwdriver, or similar tool, but take care not to damage the balljoint rubber seal. Recover the heat shield from the balljoint **(see illustrations 2.11a to 2.11d)**.

6 Working on each side of the car in turn, unscrew the nut securing the anti-roll bar drop-link to the anti-roll bar. If necessary, counterhold the drop-link pin using a 5 mm Allen key **(see illustration)**.

7 Unscrew and remove the engine lower mounting link through-bolt **(see illustration)**.

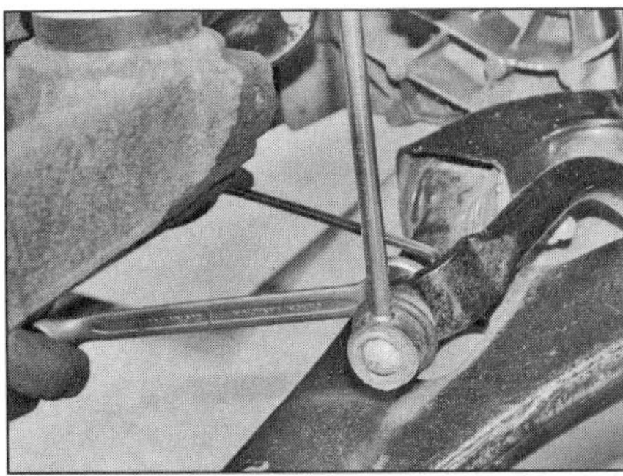

8.6 Loosening the drop-link lower nut

8.7 Remove the engine lower mounting through-bolt

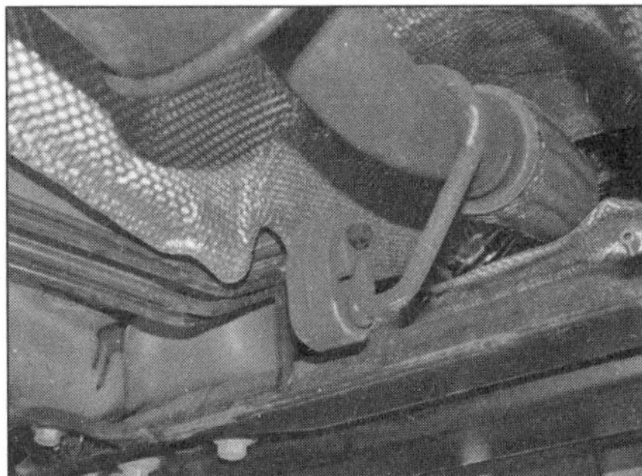

8.8 The exhaust front mounting is on the subframe

8.9 One of the steering gear mounting bolts on the subframe

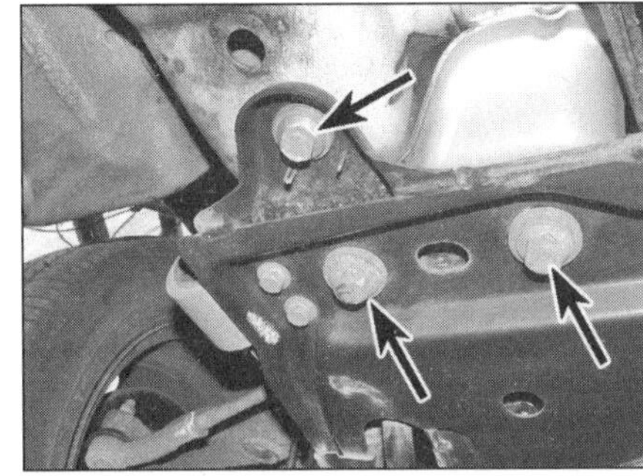

8.12a There are three subframe mounting bolts each side at floorpan level ...

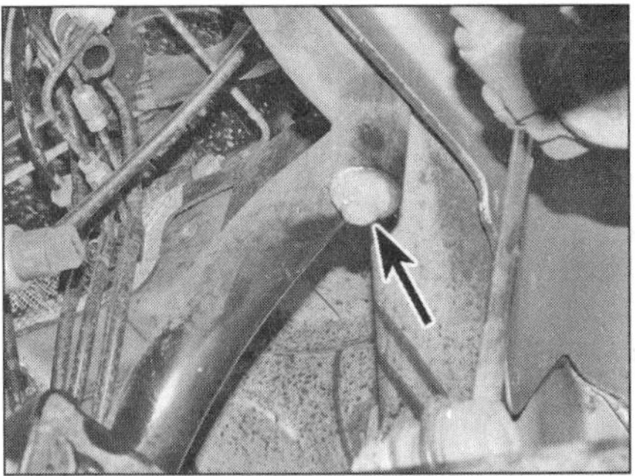

8.12b ... and a fourth on a curved spur up to the chassis leg

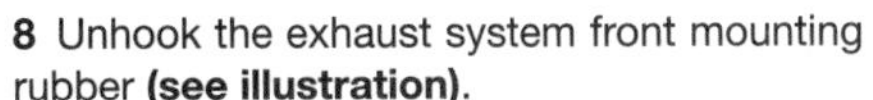

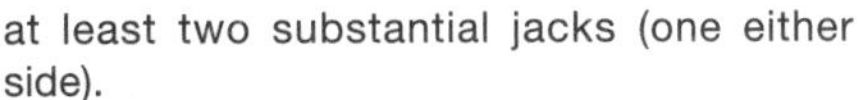

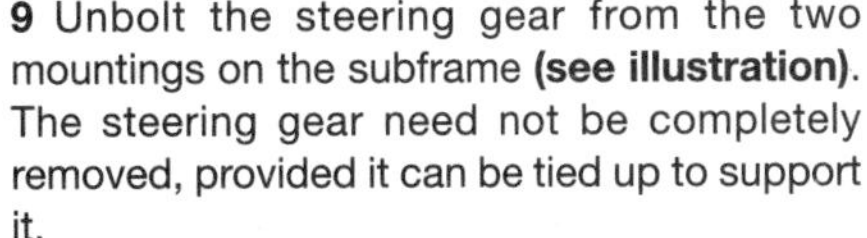

8 Unhook the exhaust system front mounting rubber **(see illustration)**.

9 Unbolt the steering gear from the two mountings on the subframe **(see illustration)**. The steering gear need not be completely removed, provided it can be tied up to support it.

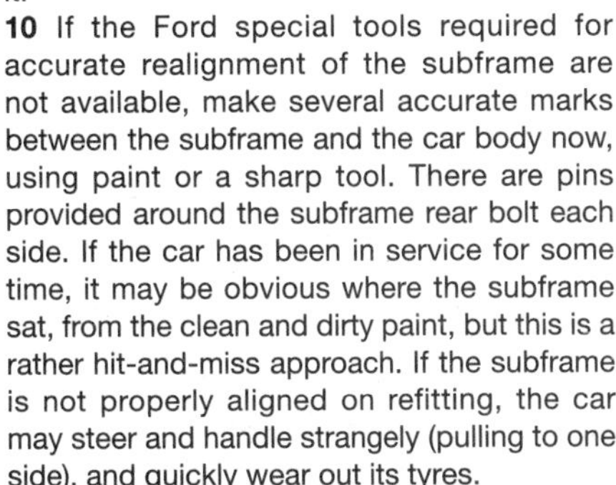

10 If the Ford special tools required for accurate realignment of the subframe are not available, make several accurate marks between the subframe and the car body now, using paint or a sharp tool. There are pins provided around the subframe rear bolt each side. If the car has been in service for some time, it may be obvious where the subframe sat, from the clean and dirty paint, but this is a rather hit-and-miss approach. If the subframe is not properly aligned on refitting, the car may steer and handle strangely (pulling to one side), and quickly wear out its tyres.

11 Support the subframe from below, using at least two substantial jacks (one either side).

12 With the subframe securely supported, progressively loosen the eight mounting bolts. There are four each side – three large ones around the lower arm (inner, outer and rear), and a smaller fourth (front) on a curved spur up to the base of the chassis leg **(see illustrations)**.

13 When all the bolts have been removed, check once more that nothing is still attached to the subframe, and that nothing is still fitted which would hinder it from being lowered. With the help of an assistant, lower the subframe and remove it from under the car.

Refitting

14 With the help of an assistant, position the subframe on the jacks, then raise the subframe into position under the car. Ensure that the subframe is securely supported.

15 If available, fit the Ford alignment pins through the subframe inner and outer bolt holes. If not, align the marks made prior to removal. Fit and tighten the front and rear subframe bolts, ensuring that the subframe does not move, and tighten them all to their specified torques. Remove the tools (if used), fit the inner and outer bolts, and tighten these also.

16 The remainder of refitting is a reversal of removal, noting the following points:

a) *Tighten all fixings to the specified torque.*
b) *Have the front wheel alignment checked on completion.*

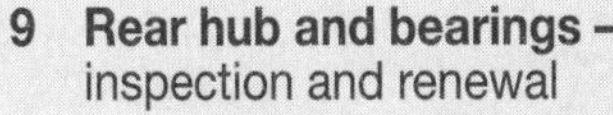

9 Rear hub and bearings – inspection and renewal

Inspection

1 The rear hub bearings are non-adjustable **(see illustration)**.

2 To check the bearings for excessive wear, chock the front wheels, then jack up the rear of the vehicle and support it on axle stands. Fully release the handbrake.

3 Grip the rear wheel at the top and bottom, and attempt to rock it. If excessive movement is noted, or if there is any roughness or vibration felt when the wheel is spun, it is indicative that the hub bearings are worn.

Renewal

4 Remove the rear wheel.

5 Tap off the dust cap and unscrew the hub nut **(see illustration)**. Discard the nut – it is of laminated design, and must not be re-used.

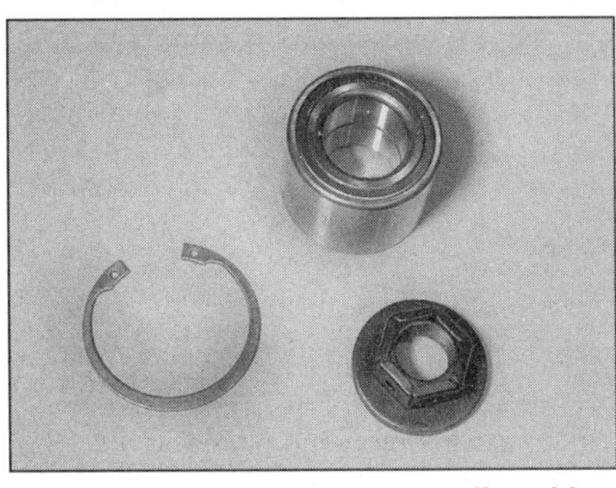

9.1 The wheel bearing is not adjustable

9.5 Remove the dust cap and take off the rear hub nut

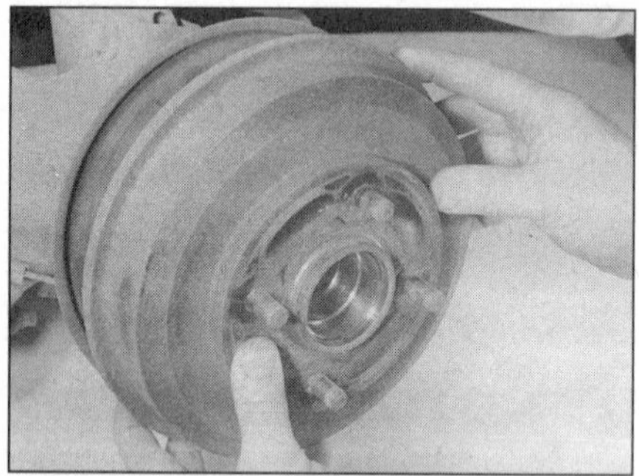
9.6 Pull the brake drum from the stub axle

9.9 Removing the circlip

9.12 Using a tube to press the bearing in

9.15 Fitting the new hub nut

6 Remove the rear brake drum **(see illustration).** If the drum will not pull off easily, use a suitable puller to draw the drum and bearing assembly off the stub axle.
7 Part of the inner race may remain on the stub axle – this should be removed using a puller.
8 Remove the ABS sensor ring from the hub/drum assembly (where fitted). This must be renewed when refitting.

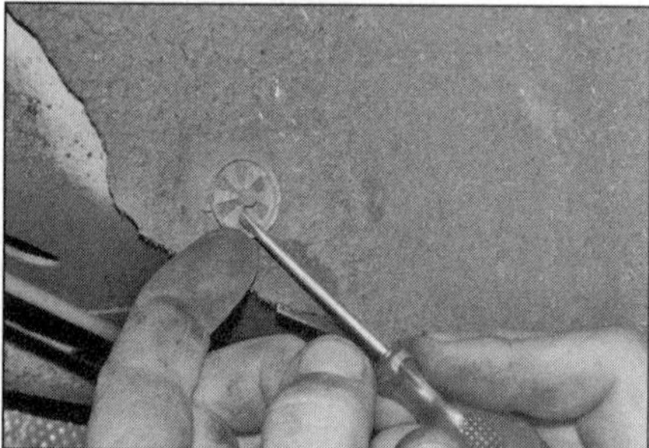
10.2 A typical wheel arch liner clip – unlike earlier types, this is not unscrewed – prise it off

10.3a With the 'trailing arm' supported, unscrew and remove the lower bolt ...

10.3b ... and free the lower end of the shock absorber

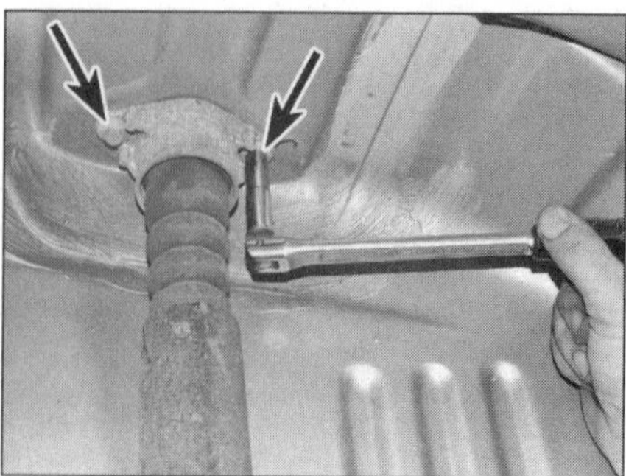
10.4 Undo the two upper mounting bolts, and remove the shock absorber

9 Using circlip pliers, extract the circlip securing the bearing in the hub/drum **(see illustration).**
10 Press or drive out the bearing, using a length of metal tubing of diameter slightly less than the bearing outer race.
11 Clean the bearing seating faces in the hub/drum.
12 Using the length of metal tubing, Press or drive the new bearing into the hub/drum until it is fully located **(see illustration).** Do not apply any pressure to the inner race.
13 Locate the circlip into the groove in the hub/drum to secure the bearing in place.
14 Press the new ABS sensor ring onto the hub assembly slowly and squarely, as damage to the new ring will cause failure of the ABS system (where fitted).
15 Locate the rear hub/drum and bearing assembly on the stub axle, then fit the new hub nut and tighten it to the specified torque **(see illustration).** Rotate the hub assembly in the opposite direction when tightening the hub retaining nut to prevent damage to the bearing.
16 Tap the dust cap fully onto the hub. If the dust cap was damaged on removal, a new one must be fitted.
17 Refit the rear wheel, and lower the vehicle to the ground.

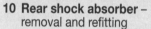

10 Rear shock absorber – removal and refitting

Removal

1 Slacken the relevant rear wheel nuts. Chock the front wheels, select 1st gear, then jack up the rear of the car, and support securely on axle stands (see *Jacking and vehicle support*). Remove the rear roadwheel.
2 Remove the plastic wheel arch liner for access to the shock absorber upper mounting bolts. The liner is secured by a combination of screws and clips (five altogether) **(see illustration).**
3 Support the 'trailing arm' section of the beam axle using a trolley jack, then unscrew the shock absorber lower mounting nut and bolt. Counterhold the bolt using a second spanner as the nut is unscrewed. Withdraw (or tap out) the bolt, then lower the jack supporting the trailing arm. Slide the bottom end of the shock absorber out of its mounting **(see illustrations).**
4 Support the shock absorber, remove the two upper mounting bolts inside the wheel arch, and remove the unit **(see illustration).**

Refitting

5 Refitting is a reversal of removal, noting the following points:
a) *Fit the upper mounting bolts first, and tighten them to the specified torque.*
b) *The lower mounting nut and bolt should be fitted hand-tight only, then tightened fully once the wheel has been refitted and the car is back on the ground.*

11 Rear spring – removal and refitting

Note: *A spring compressor tool will be required for this operation.*

Removal

1 Slacken the rear wheel nuts. Chock the front wheels, select 1st gear, then jack up the rear of the car, and support securely on axle stands (see *Jacking and vehicle support*). Remove the rear roadwheels.

2 Compress the spring using the spring compressor tool.

3 Place a substantial jack under the end of the 'trailing arm' section of the axle, and lift it slightly, so the shock absorber is just compressed.

4 Unbolt the rear shock absorber lower mounting, and detach the shock absorber from the rear axle (see Section 10).

5 Lower the jack slightly, then lift the (compressed) rear spring off its lower mounting, and remove it from under the car. Recover the rubber top mounting if it sticks to the car **(see illustrations)**.

6 If a new spring is being fitted, carefully release the spring compressors, and transfer to the new spring, which should be compressed prior to fitting.

Refitting

7 Refitting is a reversal of removal, noting the following points:

a) Make sure the spring is properly engaged in the upper and lower mounts.

b) Delay fully tightening the shock absorber lower mounting to its specified torque until the car is resting on its wheels.

12 Rear axle assembly – removal and refitting

Removal

1 Slacken the rear wheel nuts. Chock the front wheels, select 1st gear, then jack up the rear of the car, and support securely on axle stands (see *Jacking and vehicle support*). Remove the rear roadwheels.

2 Remove the nut and bolt securing the brake pipe and wheel sensor wiring support bracket, inboard of the brake backplate on each side.

3 Unclip the handbrake cables from the rear axle, with reference to Chapter 9, Section 20.

4 On models with ABS, remove the rear wheel sensors and detach the wiring from the axle as described in Chapter 9, Section 17.

5 Remove the four bolts securing the brake drum and hub on each side, and withdraw the hubs/drums from the axle.

6 Drill out the two rivets securing the brake backplate on each side, and remove the backplates from the axle. Suspend the backplates to avoid placing strain on the brake hoses.

11.5a Lift the compressed spring off its lower mounting ...

7 Support the rear axle using two substantial jacks, one at each end. Raise the jacks just sufficiently to start compressing the shock absorbers.

8 Unbolt the rear shock absorber lower mountings on either side, and detach the shock absorbers from the rear axle.

9 Lower the rear axle on the jacks to relieve the tension on the springs, then lift the rear springs up over their lower mountings, and remove them.

10 The rear axle is secured by three bolts each side, around the pivot points **(see illustration)**. Make sure the axle is well-supported (have an assistant on hand to keep the axle steady), then start loosening the bolts. Leave one bolt loosely in place each side until the axle is ready to come down, then support the axle, remove the last bolt each side, and let the axle rest on the jacks. Lower the jacks equally until the axle can be lifted out from under the car.

Refitting

11 Refitting of the axle assembly is a reversal of removal, bearing in mind the following points:

a) Do not fully-tighten the axle mounting bolts, or the shock absorber lower mounting bolts, until the weight of the car is resting on its wheels.

b) Tighten all fixings to the specified torque.

c) A blind rivet gun will be needed to resecure the brake backplates.

d) Check the operation of the handbrake, and adjust if necessary as described in Chapter 9, Section 19.

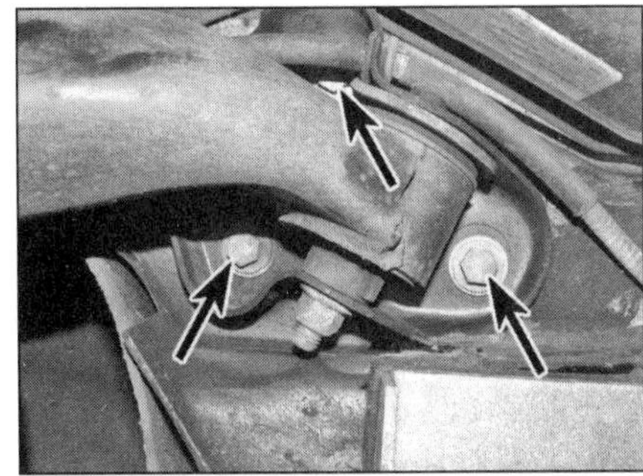

12.10 Rear axle mounting bolts

11.5b ... and check that the rubber top mounting comes away with it

13 Rear axle pivot bushes – renewal

1 Slacken the rear wheel nuts. Chock the front wheels, select 1st gear, then jack up the rear of the car, and support securely on axle stands (see *Jacking and vehicle support*). Remove the rear roadwheels.

2 Support the rear axle assembly using a jack positioned beneath the axle beam. Use a block of wood between the jack and the axle beam to spread the load.

3 Working on each side of the car in turn, release the handbrake outer cable from the clips on the axle – there is no need to unclip the inner cable from the joining link.

4 The rear axle is secured by three bolts each side, around the pivot points. Make sure the axle is well-supported (have an assistant on hand to keep the axle steady), then start loosening the bolts. Leave one bolt loosely in place each side until the axle is ready to come down, then support the axle, remove the last bolt each side, and let the axle rest on the jacks. Lower the jacks equally to gain access to the pivot bushes, but take care that the brake flexible hoses are not put under strain.

5 Make an alignment mark on the bush housing on the trailing arm corresponding to the position of the alignment arrow on the end of the bush.

6 Unscrew the through-bolt and nut and withdraw it through the pivot bush. Recover any washers used, noting their fitted positions.

7 Carefully prise the pivot bush outer dust cover from the relevant trailing arm. Using a metal tube of suitable diameter, flat washers and a long bolt and nut, draw the bush out of its location in the trailing arm.

8 Thoroughly clean the bush housing in the trailing arm.

9 Carefully prise the outer dust cover from the new bush, then mark a line along the side of the bush, corresponding with the alignment arrow on the end of the bush.

10 Lubricate the bush housing, and the new bush, with a soapy solution (eg, washing-up liquid) to aid fitting.

11 Locate the new bush in position against

14.4 Hold the wheel rim with one hand, and undo the bolt with the other

14.5b ... then remove the bolt completely, and take the wheel off

the housing, together with the metal tube, washers, bolt and nut used for removal. Align the line made on the side of the bush with the alignment mark made before removal on the trailing arm, then draw the bush into the housing until it is fully engaged.

15.4 Driver's lower facia panel screws (arrowed)

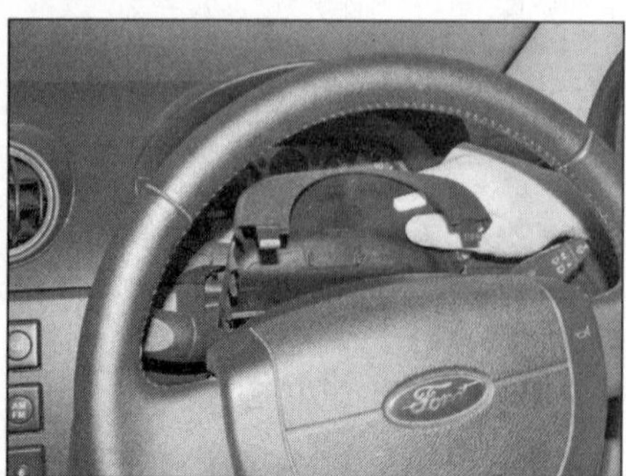
15.6 The shroud can be lifted up, but will not come out

14.5a Leave the steering wheel bolt in place while pulling the wheel off its splines ...

12 Fit the outer dust cover to the bush.

13 Refit the pivot through-bolt and nut, and tighten by hand only at this stage.

14 If desired, repeat the procedure given in paragraphs 5 to 13 for the remaining bush.

15 Further refitting is a reversal of removal, noting the following points:

a) Do not fully-tighten the pivot through-bolts, or the axle mounting bolts, until the weight of the car is resting on its wheels.

b) Tighten all fixings to the specified torque.

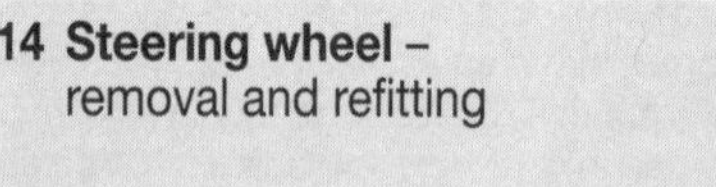

14 Steering wheel – removal and refitting

Removal

1 Disconnect the battery negative lead, and position the lead away from the battery (see Chapter 5A, Section 2). Wait at least one minute before proceeding. If this waiting period is not observed, there is a danger of accidentally activating the airbag(s).

2 Remove the airbag unit from the steering wheel as described in Chapter 12, Section 22.

3 Ensure that the front wheels are pointing in the straight-ahead position, and check that the steering lock is engaged.

4 Prevent the steering wheel turning by grasping the rim firmly, then unscrew and remove the steering wheel securing bolt **(see illustration)**. Do not rely on the steering column lock to prevent the wheel turning, as this may damage the lock.

5 Grip the steering wheel on each side (or top and bottom), then pull and release it from the splines on the end of the column. Remove the securing bolt completely followed by the wheel **(see illustrations)**.

Refitting

6 Make sure that the front wheels are pointing in the straight-ahead position, then fit the steering wheel to the column.

7 Refit the steering wheel securing bolt, and tighten to the specified torque – again, do not rely on the steering column lock to hold the wheel as the bolt is tightened.

8 The remainder of the refitting procedure is a reversal of removal. Refit the airbag unit as described in Chapter 12, Section 22.

15 Steering column – removal and refitting

Removal

1 Disconnect the battery negative lead, and position the lead away from the battery (see Chapter 5A, Section 2). Wait at least one minute before proceeding. If this waiting period is not observed, there is a danger of accidentally activating the airbag(s).

2 Remove the airbag unit from the steering wheel as described in Chapter 12, Section 22.

3 Move the driver's seat fully to the rear, to allow maximum working area.

4 Remove the driver's side lower facia panel, which is secured by five screws (two inside the small storage compartment) and one clip (at the top left – pull the panel towards you to release it) **(see illustration)**.

5 Turn the steering wheel to the side to access the prising point, then use a screwdriver to prise up the upper shroud **(see illustration)**. Turn the wheel to the other side, and release the second clip.

6 The shroud can now be lifted up, but it will still be attached by a rubber 'gaiter' to the base of the instrument panel, and cannot be removed **(see illustration)**.

7 Carefully unclip the hood/surround panel from the instrument cluster, and remove it **(see illustration)**.

15.5 Turn the wheel to one side, and prise up the upper shroud

15.7 Unclip the instrument cluster hood, and lift it away

15.8a Use a small screwdriver to prise down the pegs on the rubber gaiter ...

15.8b ... and the steering column upper shroud can be removed

15.8c On later models there is no need to remove the instrument panel shroud

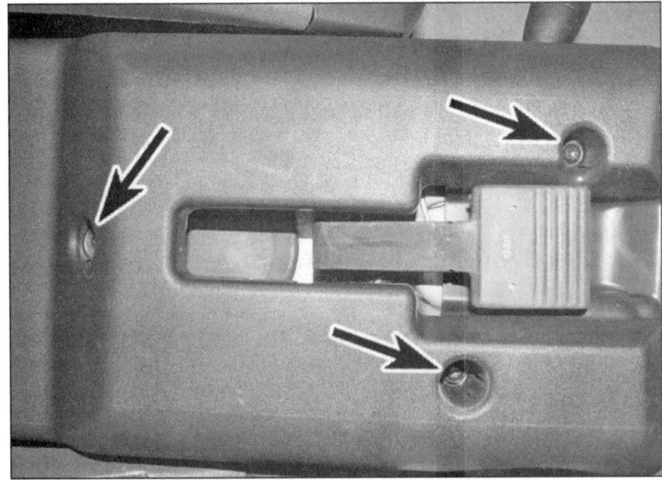
15.9 Steering column lower shroud screws – seen from below

15.10 Lower the height adjuster lever when removing the lower shroud

8 Using a screwdriver, carefully prise down the rubber gaiter to release the securing tabs from the base of the instrument cluster. Now the upper shroud can be removed completely **(see illustrations)**.

9 The lower shroud is secured by three screws underneath **(see illustration)**. On models with remote audio controls on the lower shroud, use a small screwdriver to release the locking tang at the back of the switch, then remove the switch and disconnect the wiring.

10 Remove the three screws, then lower the steering column height adjuster lever, and remove the lower shroud **(see illustration)**.

11 Ensure that the front wheels are pointing in the straight-ahead position, and check that the steering lock is engaged.

12 Working in the footwell, unscrew the pinch-bolt securing the column shaft to the rack pinion **(see illustration)**. Discard the bolt – a new one should be fitted on reassembly.

13 Working around the steering column, disconnect the following wiring plugs **(see illustrations)**:

- *a) Airbag clockspring wiring connector (black, at the bottom).*
- *b) Anti-theft immobiliser transceiver unit wiring connector (unclip the whole unit from the column).*
- *c) Steering column stalk switch wiring connectors.*

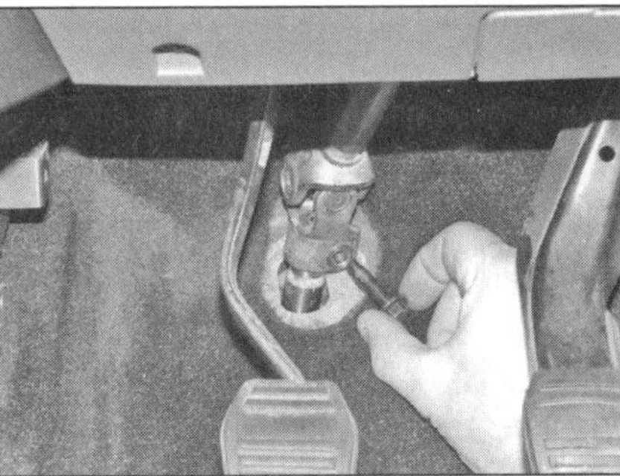
15.12 Removing the column lower pinch-bolt

15.13a Disconnect the airbag clockspring ...

15.13b ... the immobiliser unit ...

15.13c ... column switches (one plug each side) ...

15.13d ... and the ignition switch

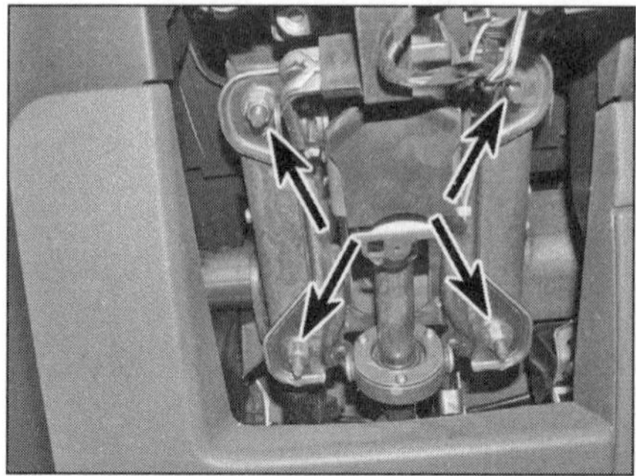
15.14a Unscrew the four nuts ...

15.14b ... and withdraw the column into the car

d) Ignition switch wiring connector (release the tab at the back).

14 Unscrew the four steering column securing nuts, and withdraw the column assembly from inside the car **(see illustrations)**. Discard the nuts – new ones must be used when refitting.

Refitting

15 Refitting is a reversal of removal, bearing in mind the following points:

a) Use new steering column securing nuts, and a new column-to-rack pinion pinch-bolt.

b) Tighten all fixings to the specified torque.

c) Refit the driver's airbag as described in Chapter 12, Section 22.

16 Steering gear rubber gaiters – renewal

1 Remove the relevant track rod end as described in Section 22.

2 Remove the inboard and outboard securing clips, then slide the gaiter off the end of the track rod.

3 Thoroughly clean the track rod, then slide the new gaiter into position.

4 Fit the gaiter securing clips, using new clips if necessary, making sure that the gaiter is not twisted.

5 Refit the track rod end as described in Section 22.

17 Steering gear – removal and refitting

Removal

1 Using the information in Section 8, lower the front subframe to access the steering gear. There is no need to disconnect the lower arm balljoints, and the subframe only needs to be lowered, not removed completely.

2 Disconnect the power steering fluid reservoir return hose by squeezing and releasing the quick-release connector. Anticipate some fluid spillage as this is done – cap or plug the open fluid lines to reduce further spillage and prevent dirt entry.

3 Slacken the track rod end balljoint nut each side, and unscrew it as far as the ends of the threads. Counterhold the balljoint pin using a 5 mm Allen key **(see illustration 2.9)**.

4 Disconnect the track rod end balljoint from the swivel hub using a balljoint separator tool (leave the nut fitted to protect the threads), taking care not to damage the balljoint rubber seal **(see illustration 2.10)**. Once the balljoint has been released, remove the balljoint nut and discard it – a new one should be used for refitting.

5 Unbolt the power steering fluid pipe mounting brackets from the steering gear. Unclip the protective cover fitted over the fluid connection plate at the valve body.

6 Remove the single retaining bolt from the steering gear fluid pipe connection plate, and twist the plate upwards to free it from the steering gear. Anticipate some fluid spillage as this is done – recover the O-ring seals (obtain new ones for reassembly). Cover the open unions, to reduce further fluid loss, and to keep dirt out.

7 Unbolt the steering gear from the two mountings on the subframe, and lower it out **(see illustration 8.9)**. Recover the rubber seal from the bulkhead. If a new unit is to be fitted, remove the three bolts securing the steering gear heat shield, and transfer it to the new unit.

Refitting

8 Refitting is a reversal of removal, noting the following points:

a) Use new O-rings when refitting the fluid pipes.

b) Tighten all fixings to the specified torque.

c) Refit the subframe as described in Section 8.

d) On completion, fill and bleed the power steering system as described in Section 19.

18 Power steering pump – removal and refitting

Petrol models

Removal

1 Remove the auxiliary drivebelt as described in Chapter 1A, Section 23.

2 Under the car, disconnect the power steering fluid reservoir return hose by squeezing and releasing the quick-release connector. Anticipate some fluid spillage as this is done – cap or plug the open fluid lines to reduce further spillage and prevent dirt entry.

3 To create more working room, unbolt the coolant expansion tank and lift it from its rear locating lug, without disconnecting any hoses. Similarly, lift the power steering fluid reservoir off its inner wing mountings, and move it to one side.

4 Unbolt the power steering fluid pipe securing brackets from the power steering pump mounting bracket and from the engine block.

5 Release the spring clip and disconnect the low-pressure fluid hose from the power steering pump – anticipate some loss of fluid as this is done. Plug or cover the pipe ends.

6 Unscrew the high-pressure union nut and disconnect the remaining fluid pipe from the top of the pump. Recover the O-ring seals – new ones should be fitted on reassembly.

7 Remove the four mounting bolts, and remove the pump from the front of the engine.

Refitting

8 Further refitting is a reversal of removal, bearing in mind the following points:

a) Use new O-rings when refitting the high-pressure pipe, and tighten the union nut to the specified torque.

b) Tighten all fixings to the specified torque.

c) Fit a new auxiliary drivebelt as described in Chapter 1A, Section 23.

d) On completion, fill and bleed the power steering system as described in Section 19.

1.4 litre diesel models

Removal

9 Remove the auxiliary drivebelt as described in Chapter 1B, Section 22.

10 Under the car, disconnect the power steering fluid reservoir return hose by squeezing and releasing the quick-release connector. Anticipate some fluid spillage as this is done – cap or plug the open fluid lines to reduce further spillage and prevent dirt entry.

11 Unbolt the power steering fluid pipe securing bracket from the air conditioning compressor.

12 Remove the right-hand headlight as described in Chapter 12, Section 7.

13 Detach the power steering fluid pipe securing bracket from the power steering pump.

14 Unscrew the high-pressure union nut and disconnect the remaining fluid pipe from the top of the pump. Recover the O-ring seals – new ones should be fitted on reassembly.

15 Remove the power steering pump rear mounting bolt.

16 Lift the power steering fluid reservoir off its inner wing mountings, and move it to one side.

17 Release the spring clip and disconnect the low-pressure fluid hose from the power steering pump – anticipate some loss of fluid as this is done. Plug or cover the pipe ends.

18 Turn the power steering pump pulley so that the two front mounting bolts are accessible, then unscrew and remove them. Lift the power steering pump off, and remove it from the engine.

Refitting

19 Further refitting is a reversal of removal, bearing in mind the following points:

a) *Use new O-rings when refitting the high-pressure pipe, and tighten the union nut to the specified torque.*

b) *Tighten all fixings to the specified torque.*

c) *Refit the auxiliary drivebelt as described in Chapter 1B, Section 22.*

d) *On completion, fill and bleed the power steering system as described in Section 19.*

1.6 litre diesel models

Removal

20 Remove the left-hand headlight assembly as described in Chapter 12, Section 7 for access to the power steering pump **(see illustration)**.

21 Disconnect the two wiring plugs from the pump **(see illustration)**.

22 Jack up the front of the car, and support it on axle stands (see *Jacking and vehicle support*). Remove the roadwheel.

23 Undo the fasteners and remove the left-hand wheel arch liner.

24 Position a suitable container beneath the power steering pump.

25 Unscrew the cap from the pump reservoir and siphon the fluid into the container **(see illustration)**.

26 Note the location and routing of the high-pressure hydraulic outlet hose then unscrew the union, disconnect the hose, and drain the fluid.

27 Release the spring clip and disconnect the low-pressure return hose from the pump. If available, use a special tool obtainable from car accessory shops to release the clip, otherwise careful use of large adjustable grips will be sufficient.

28 Unscrew and remove the mounting nuts and rubber pads, then withdraw the pump from the wheel arch **(see illustration)**.

Refitting

29 Refitting is a reversal of removal, but fill and bleed the hydraulic system as described in Section 19.

19 Power steering hydraulic system – bleeding

Note: *For all petrol and 1.4 litre diesel models, Ford recommend that the power steering system is bled using a hand-operated vacuum pump connected to the reservoir filler neck. However, this should only be necessary if persistent problems are experienced with air in the hydraulic system.*

Conventional bleeding

1 On 1.6 litre diesel models only, remove the left-hand headlight as described in Chapter 12, Section 7 for access to the fluid reservoir.

2 Check the power steering fluid level and top up as necessary. If the system has been drained, fill the reservoir very slowly with clean fluid, until the level reaches the MAX line. Make sure the fluid is agitated as little as possible, to reduce aeration.

3 Ensure that the fluid level does not drop below the MIN line during the following procedure. If the system is completely empty, the fluid in the reservoir will disappear very quickly when the engine is started.

4 Jack up the front of the car (see *Jacking and vehicle support*) until the front wheels are clear of the ground. Turn the steering wheel from lock-to-lock several times, then recheck the fluid level and top-up if necessary.

18.20 Electro-hydraulic power steering pump on the 1.6 litre diesel (viewed with front bumper removed)

5 Start the engine and allow it to idle, then slowly turn the steering wheel from lock-to-lock several times – do not hold the steering wheel on full lock for more than 15 seconds at a time. Check for air bubbles in the fluid reservoir – if air bubbles are visible, the system requires further bleeding.

6 Stop the engine, then lower the car to the ground, and recheck the fluid level.

7 If air bubbles appear in the reservoir when the system is operated, or if the pump is noisy in operation, repeat the bleeding procedure. If necessary, leave the car overnight, then repeat the bleeding procedure.

8 On 1.6 litre diesel models only, refit the left-hand headlight with reference to Chapter 12, Section 7.

Bleeding using a vacuum pump

Note: *During the bleeding procedure, the pressure will drop, so adequate pressure should be maintained using the vacuum pump. If the pressure drops by more than 70 mbar in 5 minutes, the system should be checked for leaks. Note that this method must not be used on 1.6 litre diesel models.*

9 Connect a vacuum pump to the fluid reservoir filler neck using a suitable adapter (Ford Tool 211-189 is available for this purpose).

10 Start the engine, and slowly turn the steering from lock-to-lock once, then turn it almost fully to the right, just off full-lock.

11 Stop the engine, and apply a vacuum of 500 mbar, using the vacuum pump, until the

18.21 Power steering pump wiring plugs (1.6 litre diesel)

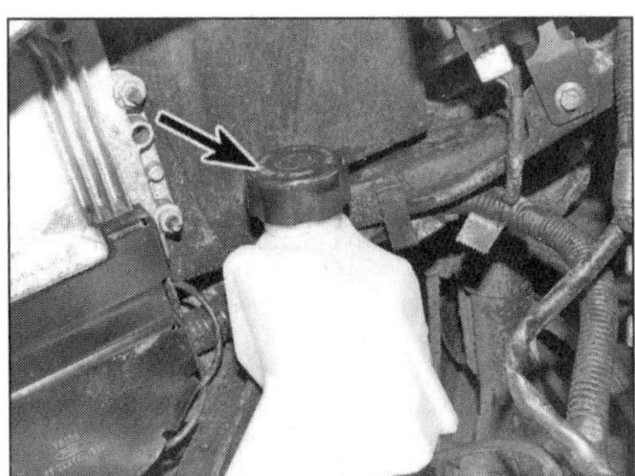

18.25 Power steering pump reservoir filler cap (1.6 litre diesel)

18.28 Power steering pump mounting (1.6 litre diesel)

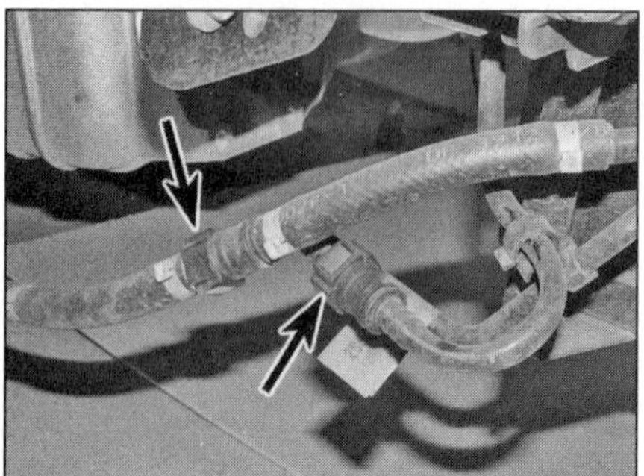

20.3 Squeeze the quick-release connectors to detach the fluid cooler hoses

20.4a Unscrew the mounting bolt on the left ...

20.4b ... and right-hand side, and remove the cooler

air is purged from the system (this will take at least 5 minutes).

12 Depressurise the system using the vacuum pump.

13 Repeat the procedure given in paragraphs 10 to 12 with the steering turned to just off full left lock.

14 Disconnect the vacuum pump from the fluid reservoir, and top-up the fluid level if necessary.

15 Start the engine, and turn the steering wheel from lock-to-lock. If the system is excessively noisy in operation, repeat the bleeding procedure.

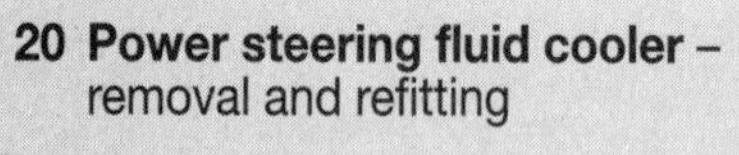

20 Power steering fluid cooler – removal and refitting

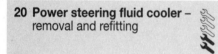

Note: *This Section does not apply to 1.6 litre diesel models.*

Removal

1 Jack up the front of the car, and support it on axle stands (see *Jacking and vehicle support*).

2 This operation is made a great deal easier by removing the front bumper as described in Chapter 11, Section 6. However, this is not absolutely essential.

3 Under the car, disconnect the fluid cooler hoses by squeezing and releasing the quick-release connectors **(see illustration)**. Anticipate some fluid spillage as this is done – cap or plug the open fluid lines to reduce further spillage and prevent dirt entry.

4 Working through the lower grille in the front bumper, unscrew the fluid cooler retaining bolts at each end, and lower the cooler out of position **(see illustrations)**. Try to keep it as level as possible, to reduce the chance of further fluid spillage.

Refitting

5 Refitting is a reversal of removal. On completion, fill and bleed the power steering system as described in Section 19.

21 Power steering fluid pressure switch – removal and refitting

Note: *This Section does not apply to 1.6 litre diesel models.*

Removal

1 The power steering fluid pressure switch provides a signal to the engine management electronic control unit, which is used to increase the engine idle speed during parking, to compensate for the extra drag placed on the engine by the pump when the steering is at or near full-lock.

2 The switch is located in the high-pressure fluid pipe leading down to the steering gear, at the rear of the engine compartment **(see illustration)**.

3 Disconnect the battery negative lead, with reference to Chapter 5A, Section 2.

4 Place a container beneath the switch location to catch any escaping fluid.

5 Disconnect the wiring plug from the switch, then unscrew the switch from the fluid pipe.

6 Be prepared for fluid spillage, and plug or cover the orifice in the pipe to prevent dirt entry and further fluid loss.

Refitting

7 Refitting is a reversal of removal, but tighten the switch securely, and on completion bleed the power steering hydraulic circuit as described in Section 19.

22 Track rod end – removal and refitting

Note: *A balljoint separator tool will be required for this operation. Where applicable, Nyloc-type self-locking nuts must be renewed on refitting.*

Removal

1 Slacken the relevant front wheel nuts. Apply the handbrake, then jack up the front of the car, and support securely on axle stands (see *Jacking and vehicle support*). Remove the roadwheel.

2 Slacken the track rod end balljoint nut, and unscrew it as far as the ends of the threads. Counterhold the balljoint pin using a 5 mm Allen key **(see illustration 2.9)**.

3 Disconnect the track rod end balljoint from the swivel hub using a balljoint separator tool (leave the nut fitted to protect the threads), taking care not to damage the balljoint rubber seal **(see illustration 2.10)**. Once the balljoint has been released, remove the balljoint nut and discard it – a new one should be used when refitting.

4 Slacken the track rod end locknut, then unscrew the track rod end from the track rod, counting the number of turns necessary to remove it **(see illustration)**.

Refitting

5 Screw the track rod end onto the track rod the number of turns noted during removal, then tighten the locknut while holding the balljoint in position.

6 Engage the track rod end balljoint pin with the swivel hub, then fit a new securing nut. Tighten the nut to the specified torque, while counterholding the balljoint pin as during removal.

21.2 Power steering pressure switch

22.4 Slacken the track rod end locknut, and unscrew the track rod end

7 Refit the roadwheel, then lower the car to the ground, and tighten the wheel nuts.
8 Check the front wheel alignment (see Section 23) at the earliest opportunity.

23 Wheel alignment and steering angles – general information

1 Accurate front wheel alignment is essential to good steering and for even tyre wear. Before considering the steering angles, check that the tyres are correctly inflated, that the front wheels are not buckled, the hub bearings are not worn, and that the steering linkage and front suspension are in good order, without slackness or wear at the joints.
2 Wheel alignment consists of four factors:

Camber

- Camber is the angle at which the roadwheels are set from the vertical when viewed from the front or rear of the car. Positive camber is the angle (in degrees) that the wheels are tilted outwards at the top from the vertical. The camber angle is given for reference only, and cannot be adjusted.

Castor

- Castor is the angle between the steering axis and a vertical line when viewed from each side of the car. Positive castor is indicated when the steering axis is inclined towards the rear of the car at its upper end. This angle is not adjustable.

Steering axis inclination

- Steering axis inclination (kingpin inclination) is the angle, when viewed from the front or rear of the car, between the vertical and an imaginary line drawn between the upper and lower front suspension strut mountings. This angle is not adjustable.

Toe

- Toe is the amount by which the distance between the front inside edges of the roadwheel rim differs from that between the rear inside edges. If the distance between the front edges is less than that at the rear, the wheels are said to toe-in. If the distance between the front inside edges is greater than that at the rear, the wheels toe-out.

Front wheel alignment

3 Owing to the need for precision gauges to measure the small angles of the steering and suspension settings, it is preferable that checking of camber and castor is left to a service station having the necessary equipment. Camber and castor is set during production of the car, and any deviation from the specified angle will be due to accident damage or gross wear in the suspension mountings.
4 To check the front wheel alignment, first make sure that the lengths of both track rods are equal when the steering is in the straight-ahead position. The track rod lengths can be adjusted if necessary by releasing the locknuts from the track rod ends and rotating the track rods. If necessary, self-locking grips can be used to rotate the track rods.
5 Obtain a tracking gauge. These are available in various forms from accessory stores, or one can be fabricated from a length of steel tubing suitably cranked to clear the sump and transmission, and having a setscrew and locknut at one end.
6 With the gauge, measure the distances between the two wheel inner rims (at hub height) at the rear of the wheel. Push the car forward to rotate the wheel through 180° (half a turn) and measure the distance between the wheel inner rims, again at hub height, at the front of the wheel. This last measurement should differ from the first by the appropriate toe-in which is given in the Specifications. The car must be on level ground.
7 If the toe-in is found to be incorrect, release the track rod end locknuts and turn both track rods equally. Only turn them a quarter-of-a-turn at a time before rechecking the alignment. If necessary use self-locking grips to turn the track rods – do not grip the threaded part of the track rod during adjustment. It is important not to allow the track rods to become unequal in length during adjustment, otherwise the alignment of the steering wheel will become incorrect and tyre scrubbing will occur on turns.
8 On completion tighten the locknuts without disturbing the setting. Check that the balljoint is at the centre of its arc of travel.

Rear wheel alignment

9 Figures are provided in the Specifications for rear wheel camber and toe-setting for reference only. No adjustment is possible, so any significant deviation from the quoted figures is likely to be due to accident damage, or possibly to poor reassembly. Refer to paragraph 2 for a description of the settings.

Chapter 11
Bodywork and fittings

Contents

Degrees of difficulty

Easy, suitable for novice with little experience

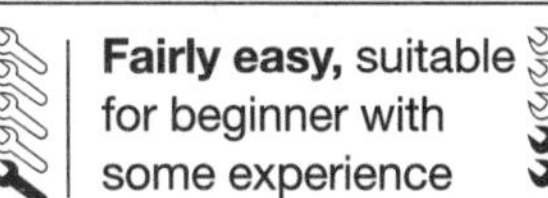

Fairly easy, suitable for beginner with some experience

Fairly difficult, suitable for competent DIY mechanic

Difficult, suitable for experienced DIY mechanic

Very difficult, suitable for expert DIY or professional

Specifications

Torque wrench settings	**Nm**	**lbf ft**
Bonnet:		
Catch bolts	20	15
Hinge bolts	23	17
Bumper retaining bolts:		
Front bumper	25	18
Rear bumper	20	15
Doors:		
Check strap:		
To door pillar	23	17
To door	6	4
Hinge bolts	25	18
Striker plate bolts	14	10
Exterior mirror	11	8
Seat belts:		
Front seat belt height adjuster securing bolts	40	30
Front seat belt sliding rail bolt	40	30
Front seat belt stalk/tensioner assembly securing bolt	47	35
Inertia reel mounting:		
Front seat belt*	35	26
Rear centre seat belt	47	35
Rear side seat belt	40	30
Rear seat belt buckle bolts	55	41
Seat belt buckle securing bolt	47	35
Seat belt upper/lower anchor bolts	40	30
Seats:		
Front seat bolts	48	35
Front seat back rest bolts	48	35
Rear seat backrest catch bolts	27	20
Rear seat backrest/cushion bolts	25	18
Tailgate:		
Bolts	11	8
Nuts	18	13
Striker plate bolts	14	10

** The bolt can only be re-used a maximum of 5 times*

1 General information

The bodyshell is a five-door Hatchback, manufactured from pressed-steel sections. Most components are welded together, but some use is made of structural adhesives. The front wings are bolted on. A plastic front crossmember is fitted, onto which are mounted the radiator, radiator cooling fan and the bonnet lock – the intention is that this section can be easily renewed in the event of a front-end collision.

The bonnet, doors and some other vulnerable panels are made of zinc-coated metal, and are further protected by being coated with an anti-chip primer prior to being sprayed.

Extensive use is made of plastic materials, mainly in the interior, but also in exterior components. The front and rear bumpers and the front grille are injection-moulded from a synthetic material which is very strong, and yet light. Plastic components such as wheel arch liners are fitted to the underside of the car, to improve the body's resistance to corrosion.

2 Maintenance – bodywork and underframe

The general condition of a car's bodywork is the one thing that significantly affects its value. Maintenance is easy, but needs to be regular. Neglect, particularly after minor damage, can lead quickly to further deterioration and costly repair bills. It is important also to keep watch on those parts of the car not immediately visible, for instance the underside, inside all the wheel arches, and the lower part of the engine compartment.

The basic maintenance routine for the bodywork is washing – preferably with a lot of water, from a hose. This will remove all the loose solids which may have stuck to the car. It is important to flush these off in such a way as to prevent grit from scratching the finish. The wheel arches and underframe need washing in the same way, to remove any accumulated mud which will retain moisture and tend to encourage rust. Paradoxically enough, the best time to clean the underframe and wheel arches is in wet weather, when the mud is thoroughly wet and soft. In very wet weather, the underframe is usually cleaned of large accumulations automatically, and this is a good time for inspection.

Periodically, except on models with a wax-based underbody protective coating, it is a good idea to have the whole of the underframe of the car steam-cleaned, engine compartment included, so that a thorough inspection can be carried out to see what minor repairs and renovations are necessary. Steam-cleaning is available at many garages, and is necessary for the removal of the accumulation of oily grime, which sometimes is allowed to become thick in certain areas. If steam-cleaning facilities are not available, there are one or two excellent grease solvents available, which can be brush-applied; the dirt can then be simply hosed off. Note that these methods should not be used on cars with wax-based underbody protective coating, or the coating will be removed. Such cars should be inspected annually, preferably just prior to Winter, when the underbody should be washed down, and any damage to the wax coating repaired. Ideally, a completely fresh coat should be applied. It would also be worth considering the use of such wax-based protection for injection into door panels, sills, box sections, etc, as an additional safeguard against rust damage, where such protection is not provided by the manufacturer.

After washing paintwork, wipe off with a chamois leather to give an unspotted clear finish. A coat of clear protective wax polish will give added protection against chemical pollutants in the air. If the paintwork sheen has dulled or oxidised, use a cleaner/polisher combination to restore the brilliance of the shine. This requires a little effort, but such dulling is usually caused because regular washing has been neglected. Care needs to be taken with metallic paintwork, as special non-abrasive cleaner/polisher is required to avoid damage to the finish. Always check that the door and ventilator opening drain holes and pipes are completely clear, so that water can be drained out. Brightwork should be treated in the same way as paintwork. Windscreens and windows can be kept clear of the smeary film which often appears, by the use of proprietary glass cleaner. Never use any form of wax, or other body or chromium polish, on glass.

3 Maintenance – upholstery and carpets

Mats and carpets should be brushed or vacuum-cleaned regularly, to keep them free of grit. If they are badly stained, remove them from the car for scrubbing or sponging, and make quite sure they are dry before refitting. Seats and interior trim panels can be kept clean by wiping with a damp cloth. If they do become stained (which can be more apparent on light-coloured upholstery), use a little liquid detergent and a soft nail brush to scour the grime out of the grain of the material. Do not forget to keep the headlining clean in the same way as the upholstery. When using liquid cleaners inside the car, do not over-wet the surfaces being cleaned. Excessive damp could get into the seams and padded interior, causing stains, offensive odours or even rot. If the inside of the car gets wet accidentally, it is worthwhile taking some trouble to dry it out properly, particularly where carpets are involved. *Do not leave oil or electric heaters inside the car for this purpose.*

4 Minor body damage – repair

Minor scratches

If the scratch is very superficial, and does not penetrate to the metal of the bodywork, repair is very simple. Lightly rub the area of the scratch with a paintwork renovator, or a very fine cutting paste, to remove loose paint from the scratch, and to clear the surrounding bodywork of wax polish. Rinse the area with clean water.

In the case of metallic paint, the most commonly-found scratches are not in the paint, but in the lacquer top coat, and appear white. If care is taken , these can sometimes be rendered less obvious by very careful use of paintwork renovator (which would other-wise not be used on metallic paintwork); otherwise, repair of these scratches can be achieved by applying lacquer with a fine brush.

Apply touch-up paint to the scratch using a fine paint brush; continue to apply fine layers of paint until the surface of the paint in the scratch is level with the surrounding paintwork. Allow the new paint at least two weeks to harden, then blend it into the surrounding paintwork by rubbing the scratch area with a paintwork renovator or a very fine cutting paste. Finally, apply wax polish.

Where the scratch has penetrated right through to the metal of the bodywork, causing the metal to rust, a different repair technique is required. Remove any loose rust from the bottom of the scratch with a penknife, then apply rust-inhibiting paint, to prevent the formation of rust in the future. Using a rubber or nylon applicator, fill the scratch with bodystopper paste. If required, this paste can be mixed with cellulose thinners, to provide a very thin paste which is ideal for filling narrow scratches. Before the stopper-paste in the scratch hardens, wrap a piece of smooth cotton rag around the top of a finger. Dip the finger in cellulose thinners, and quickly sweep it across the surface of the stopper-paste in the scratch; this will ensure that the surface of the stopper-paste is slightly hollowed. The scratch can now be painted over as described earlier in this Section.

Dents

When deep denting of the bodywork has taken place, the first task is to pull the dent out, until the affected bodywork almost attains its original shape. There is little point in trying to restore the original shape completely, as the metal in the damaged area will have stretched on impact, and cannot be reshaped fully to its original contour. It is better to bring the level of the dent up to a point which is about 3 mm below the level of the surrounding bodywork. In cases where the dent is very shallow anyway, it is not worth trying to pull it out at all. If the underside of the dent is accessible, it can be hammered out gently from behind, using a mallet with a wooden or plastic head. Whilst doing this, hold a suitable block of wood firmly against the outside of the panel, to absorb the impact from the hammer blows and thus prevent a large area of the bodywork from being 'belled-out'.

Should the dent be in a section of the bodywork which has a double skin, or some other factor making it inaccessible from behind, a different technique is called for. Drill several small holes through the metal inside the area – particularly in the deeper section. Then screw long self-tapping screws into the holes, just sufficiently for them to gain a good purchase in the metal. Now the dent can be pulled out by pulling on the protruding heads of the screws with a pair of pliers.

The next stage of the repair is the removal of the paint from the damaged area, and from an inch or so of the surrounding 'sound' bodywork. This is accomplished most easily by using a wire brush or abrasive pad on a power drill, although it can be done just as effectively by hand, using sheets of abrasive paper. To complete the preparation for filling, score the surface of the bare metal with a screwdriver or the tang of a file, or alternatively, drill small holes in the affected area. This will provide a really good 'key' for the filler paste.

To complete the repair, see the Section on filling and respraying.

Rust holes or gashes

Remove all paint from the affected area, and from an inch or so of the surrounding 'sound' bodywork, using an abrasive pad or a wire brush on a power drill. If these are not available, a few sheets of abrasive paper will do the job most effectively. With the paint removed, you will be able to judge the severity of the corrosion, and therefore decide whether to renew the whole panel (if this is possible) or to repair the affected area. New body panels are not as expensive as most people think, and it is often quicker and more satisfactory to fit a new panel than to attempt to repair large areas of corrosion.

Remove all fittings from the affected area, except those which will act as a guide to the original shape of the damaged bodywork (eg body side mouldings etc). Then, using tin snips or a hacksaw blade, remove all loose metal and any other metal badly affected by corrosion. Hammer the edges of the hole inwards, in order to create a slight depression for the filler paste.

Wire-brush the affected area to remove the powdery rust from the surface of the remaining metal. Paint the affected area with rust-inhibiting paint; if the back of the rusted area is accessible, treat this also.

Before filling can take place, it will be necessary to block the hole in some way. This can be achieved by the use of aluminium or plastic mesh, or aluminium tape.

Aluminium or plastic mesh, or glass-fibre matting, is probably the best material to use for a large hole. Cut a piece to the approximate size and shape of the hole to be filled, then position it in the hole so that its edges are below the level of the surrounding bodywork. It can be retained in position by several blobs of filler paste around its periphery.

Aluminium tape should be used for small or very narrow holes. Pull a piece off the roll, trim it to the approximate size and shape required, then pull off the backing paper (if used) and stick the tape over the hole; it can be overlapped if the thickness of one piece is insufficient. Burnish down the edges of the tape with the handle of a screwdriver or similar, to ensure that the tape is securely attached to the metal underneath.

Filling and respraying

Before using this Section, see the Sections on dent, deep scratch, rust holes and gash repairs.

Many types of bodyfiller are available, but generally speaking, those proprietary kits which contain a tin of filler paste and a tube of resin hardener are best for this type of repair. A wide, flexible plastic or nylon applicator will be found invaluable for imparting a smooth and well-contoured finish to the surface of the filler.

Mix up a little filler on a clean piece of card or board – measure the hardener carefully (follow the maker's instructions on the pack), otherwise the filler will set too rapidly or too slowly. Using the applicator, apply the filler paste to the prepared area; draw the applicator across the surface of the filler to achieve the correct contour and to level the surface. As soon as a contour that approximates to the correct one is achieved, stop working the paste – if you carry on too long, the paste will become sticky and begin to 'pick-up' on the applicator. Continue to add thin layers of filler paste at 20-minute intervals, until the level of the filler is just proud of the surrounding bodywork.

Once the filler has hardened, the excess can be removed using a metal plane or file. From then on, progressively-finer grades of abrasive paper should be used, starting with a 40-grade production paper, and finishing with a 400-grade wet-and-dry paper. Always wrap the abrasive paper around a flat rubber, cork, or wooden block – otherwise the surface of the filler will not be completely flat. During the smoothing of the filler surface, the wet-and-dry paper should be periodically rinsed in water. This will ensure that a very smooth finish is imparted to the filler at the final stage.

At this stage, the 'dent' should be surrounded by a ring of bare metal, which in turn should be encircled by the finely 'feathered' edge of the good paintwork. Rinse the repair area with clean water, until all of the dust produced by the rubbing-down operation has gone.

Spray the whole area with a light coat of – this will show up any imperfections in the surface of the filler. Repair these imperfections with fresh filler paste or bodystopper, and once more smooth the surface with abrasive paper. If bodystopper is used, it can be mixed with cellulose thinners, to form a really thin paste which is ideal for filling small holes. Repeat this spray-and-repair procedure until you are satisfied that the surface of the filler, and the feathered edge of the paintwork, are perfect. Clean the repair area with clean water, and allow to dry fully.

The repair area is now ready for final spraying. Paint spraying must be carried out in a warm, dry, windless and dust-free atmosphere. This condition can be created artificially if you have access to a large indoor working area, but if you are forced to work in the open, you will have to pick your day very carefully. If you are working indoors, dousing the floor in the work area with water will help to settle the dust which would otherwise be in the atmosphere. If the repair area is confined to one body panel, mask off the surrounding panels; this will help to minimise the effects of a slight mis-match in paint colours. Bodywork fittings (eg chrome strips, door handles etc) will also need to be masked off. Use genuine masking tape, and several thicknesses of newspaper, for the masking operations.

Before commencing to spray, agitate the aerosol can thoroughly, then spray a test area (an old tin, or similar) until the technique is mastered. Cover the repair area with a thick coat of primer; the thickness should be built up using several thin layers of paint, rather than one thick one. Using 400 grade wet-and-dry paper, rub down the surface of the primer until it is really smooth. While doing this, the work area should be thoroughly doused with water, and the wet-and-dry paper periodically rinsed in water. Allow to dry before spraying on more paint.

Spray on the top coat, again building up the thickness by using several thin layers of paint. Start spraying at the top of the repair area, and then, using a side-to-side motion, work downwards until the whole repair area and about 2 inches of the surrounding original paintwork is covered. Remove all masking material 10 to 15 minutes after spraying on the final coat of paint.

Allow the new paint at least two weeks to harden, then, using a paintwork renovator or a very fine cutting paste, blend the edges of the paint into the existing paintwork. Finally, apply wax polish.

Plastic components

With the use of more and more plastic body components by the car manufacturers (eg bumpers. spoilers, and in some cases major body panels), rectification of more serious damage to such items has become a matter of either entrusting repair work to a specialist in this field, or renewing complete components. Repair of such damage by the DIY owner is not really feasible, owing to the cost of the equipment and materials required for effecting such repairs. The basic technique

6.3 Remove the screw

6.4a Release the plastic clip ...

6.4b ... and prise out the tab

involves making a groove along the line of the crack in the plastic, using a rotary burr in a power drill. The damaged part is then welded back together, using a hot air gun to heat up and fuse a plastic filler rod into the groove. Any excess plastic is then removed, and the area rubbed down to a smooth finish. It is important that a filler rod of the correct plastic is used, as body components can be made of a variety of different types (eg polycarbonate, ABS, polypropylene).

Damage of a less serious nature (abrasions, minor cracks etc) can be repaired by the DIY owner using a two-part epoxy filler repair. Once mixed in equal, this is used in similar fashion to the bodywork filler used on metal panels. The filler is usually cured in twenty to thirty minutes, ready for sanding and painting.

If the owner is renewing a complete component himself, or if he has repaired it with epoxy filler, he will be left with the problem of finding a suitable paint for finishing which is compatible with the type of plastic used. At one time, the use of a universal paint was not possible, owing to the complex range of plastics encountered in body component applications. Standard paints, generally speaking, will not bond to plastic or rubber satisfactorily, but suitable paints to match any plastic or rubber finish, can be obtained from dealers. However, it is now possible to obtain a plastic body parts finishing kit which consists of a preprimer treatment, a primer and coloured top coat. Full instructions are normally supplied with a kit, but basically, the method of use is to first apply the preprimer to the component concerned, and allow it to dry for up to 30 minutes. Then the primer is applied, and left to dry for about an hour before finally applying the special-coloured top coat. The result is a correctly-coloured component, where the paint will flex with the plastic or rubber, a property that standard paint does not normally posses.

6.5 Disconnect the foglight wiring plugs

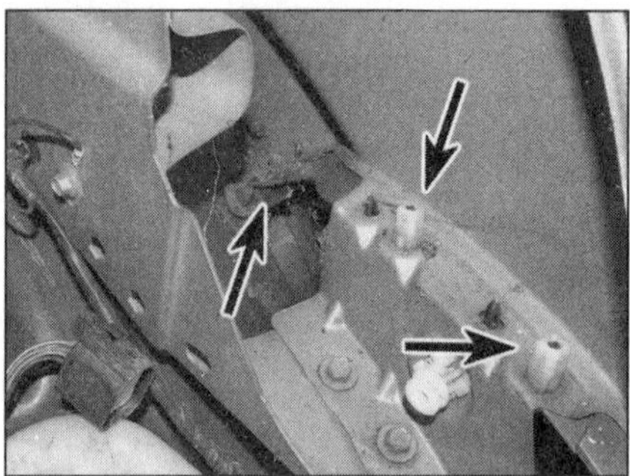

6.6 Remove the bolts (arrowed)

6.7 Release the locking tabs ...

6.8 ... and remove the bumper

5 Major body damage – repair

Where serious damage has occurred, or large areas need renewal due to neglect, it means that complete new panels will need welding-in, and this is best left to professionals. If the damage is due to impact, it will also be necessary to check completely the alignment of the bodyshell, and this can only be carried out accurately by a Ford dealer using special jigs. If the body is left misaligned, it is primarily dangerous, as the car will not handle properly, and secondly, uneven stresses will be imposed on the steering, suspension and possibly transmission, causing abnormal wear, or complete failure, particularly to such items as the tyres.

6 Bumpers – removal and refitting

Front bumper

Removal

1 Remove the headlights as described in Chapter 12, Section 7.

2 Jack up the front of the car, and support it on axle stands (see *Jacking and vehicle support*).

3 Rotate the steering wheel to access the single screw securing the wheel arch liner to the bumper **(see illustration)**. Repeat the procedure on the opposite side.

4 From below release the plastic clips at each end of the bumper **(see illustrations)**.

5 Where applicable, disconnect the wiring plugs from the front foglights **(see illustration)**.

6 Remove the three mounting bolts each side, and release the bumper end locating pegs **(see illustration)**. The bolts are all accessible from the inner wing, but it is also possible to remove the wing liner and access them from below.

7 Release the top edge of the bumper cover from the radiator support panel **(see illustration)**.

8 With the help of an assistant, pull the bumper forwards, and lower it to the ground **(see illustration)**.

6.10 Drill out the large rivets

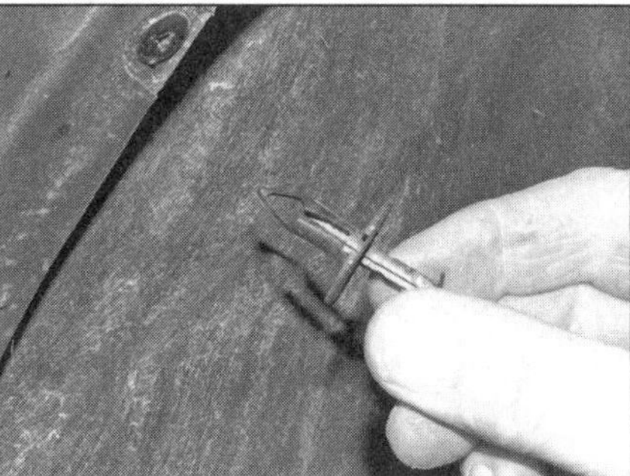

6.12a Remove the fixings from the wing liner rear ...

6.12b ... and bottom edge

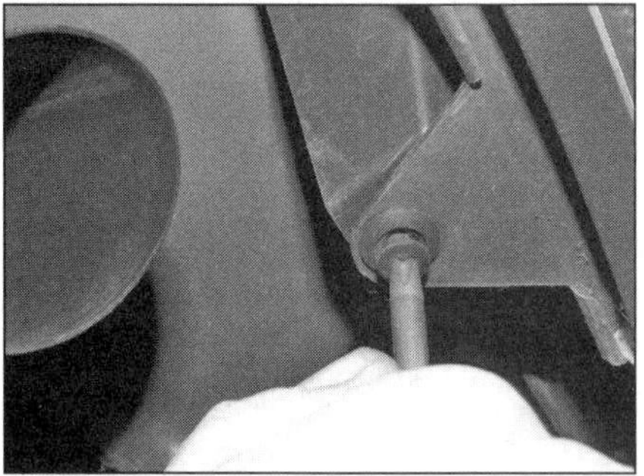

6.14 Remove the 'scrivets'

6.16a Unclip the bumper from the rear wing ...

6.16b ... and remove the bumper

Refitting

9 Refitting is a reversal of removal. Have an assistant available to help align the bumper with the push-in clips, and tighten the mounting bolts to the specified torque.

Rear bumper

Removal

10 Open the tailgate and, using a 5 mm drill bit, drill out the two large rivets at the top corners of the bumper **(see illustration)**.

11 Jack up the rear of the car, and support it on axle stands (see *Jacking and vehicle support*).

12 Working from below, prise out the two clips used to secure the rear edge of the wheel arch liner to the bumper **(see illustration)**.

13 Unscrew and remove the upper retaining bolt inside the wheel arch each side.

14 Unscrew and remove the two screw in retainers used along the bottom edge of the bumper **(see illustration)**.

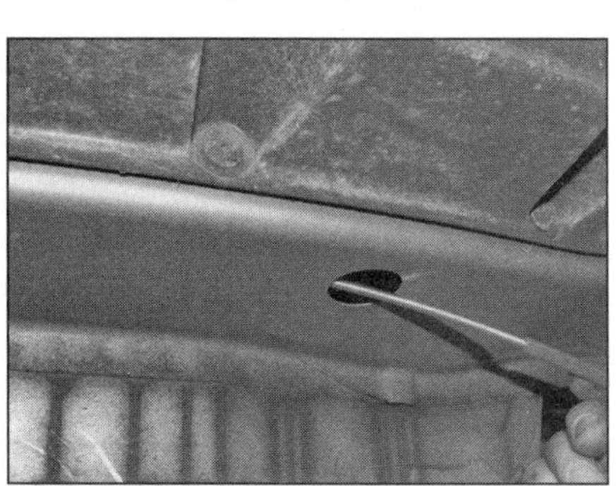

6.17 Recover the remains of the rivets

15 On models with rear parking sensors fitted to the bumper, have an assistant support the bumper, then reach inside and disconnect the wiring plug from each sensor.

16 With the help of an assistant unclip the bumper from the corner brackets and then withdraw the bumper from the car **(see illustrations)**.

17 Recover the remains of the drilled out rivets by removing the blanking plug and 'fishing' for them with a magnetic pick up tool **(see illustration)**.

Refitting

18 Refitting is a reversal of removal, noting the following points:

a) *On models with rear parking sensors, if a new bumper is being fitted, these are supplied without the holes for the sensors. New Ford bumpers are supplied with a template to mark the location of the parking sensors. If you are fitting a second-hand bumper the old bumper will have to be used as a template and suitable holes cut. A 29 mm hole cutter will be required.*

b) *New rivets should be used when refitting.*

7 Radiator grille – removal and refitting

Removal

1 Open the bonnet and remove the grille retaining nuts **(see illustration)**. If necessary apply a liberal dose of penetrating fluid to the nuts.

Refitting

2 Refitting is a reversal of removal.

8 Bonnet – removal, refitting and adjustment

Removal

1 Open the bonnet, and support it on its stay.

2 Using a marker pen or paint, mark around the hinge positions on the bonnet.

3 Disconnect the windscreen washer fluid hose from the T-piece connector on the passenger-side washer jet, then feed the washer hose back to the passenger-side

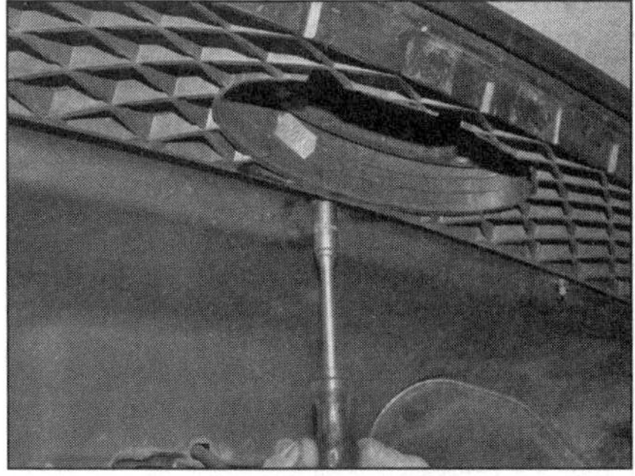

7.1 Remove the nuts

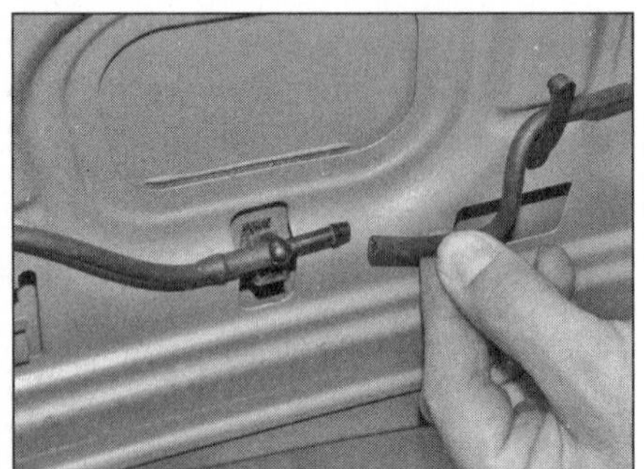
8.3a Pull the washer hose off its T-piece ...

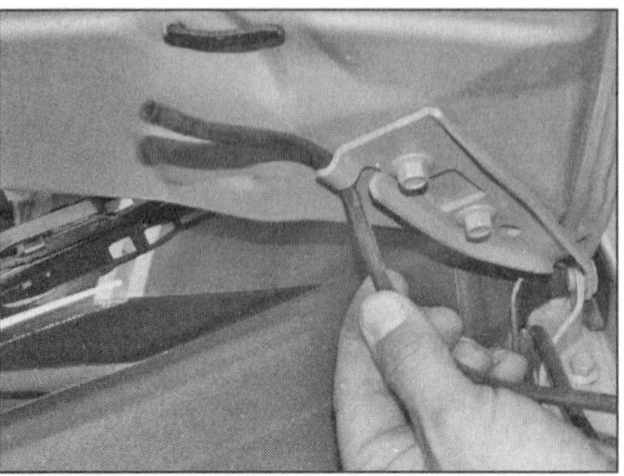
8.3b ... and unclip the main supply hose from the bonnet

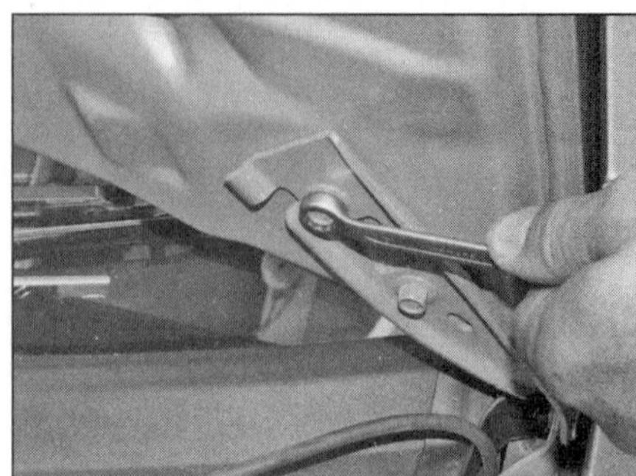
8.4 Unbolt the bonnet hinges, and remove the bonnet

corner of the bonnet, releasing it from the securing clips **(see illustrations)**.

4 With the aid of an assistant, support the bonnet, and unscrew the four bolts securing the bonnet to the hinges **(see illustration)**.

5 Lift off the bonnet.

Refitting

6 Align the marks made on the bonnet before removal with the hinges, then refit and tighten the bonnet securing bolts.

7 Feed the washer hose back across the bonnet, and reconnect it to the washer jet T-piece.

8 Check the bonnet adjustment as follows.

Adjustment

9 Close the bonnet, and check that there is an equal gap at each side, between the bonnet and the wing panels. Check also that the bonnet sits flush in relation to the surrounding body panels.

10 The bonnet should close smoothly and positively without excessive pressure. If this is not the case, adjustment will be required.

11 To adjust the bonnet alignment, slacken the bonnet securing bolts, and move the bonnet on the bolts as required (the bolt holes in the hinges are elongated). To adjust the bonnet closure, adjustable bump stops are fitted to the body front panel. These may be raised or lowered by screwing in or out as necessary. If desired, the bonnet lock can be adjusted as described in Section 10.

9 Bonnet release cable – removal and refitting

Note: *If the cable has broken, use the information in this Section to establish which end of the cable has failed – if the break is inside the car, it may be possible to remove the release lever as described below, and operate the remains of the cable to get the bonnet open. If the break is under the bonnet, there are two ways the bonnet may be opened – through the radiator grille aperture, or from underneath. Even with the bonnet shut, it may still be possible to unclip and remove the grille with minimal damage, though access to the cable will be poor. From underneath, with the car jacked up and supported on axle stands, access to the bonnet lock operating lever may be a little better.*

Removal

1 The bonnet release lever is located to the left of the passenger footwell. Referring to Section 25, remove the trim panels from the passenger-side B-pillar and door sill.

2 Unscrew the two retaining bolts, and withdraw the release lever and its mounting panel **(see illustration)**.

3 Turn the panel over, and release the outer cable from the back of the panel **(see illustration)**.

4 Operate the release lever, and unhook the inner cable from it. Free the cable from its guide, noting how it is routed **(see illustrations)**.

5 Under the bonnet, prise out the outer cable end fitting from its slot in the bonnet lock, then unhook the inner cable from the lock operating lever **(see illustration)**.

6 Release the cable from the clips and brackets in the engine compartment, noting its routing.

7 Tie a length of string to the end of the

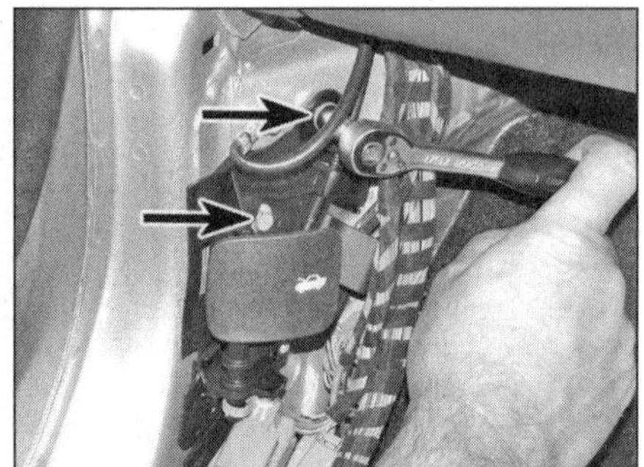
9.2 Unbolt the bonnet lock release lever assembly from the passenger footwell

9.3 Unclip the lock release cable from the back of the assembly

9.4a Operate the lever, and unhook the inner cable end fitting ...

9.4b ... then feed the cable back along its guide channel, and remove it

9.5 Unhook the bonnet cable from the lock

cable at the release lever inside the car, then carefully pull the cable through the bulkhead grommet into the engine compartment.

8 Untie the string from the end of the cable, and leave it in position to aid refitting.

Refitting

9 Refitting is a reversal of removal, but tie the string to the release lever end of the cable, and use the string to pull the cable into position. Ensure that the cable is routed as noted before removal, and make sure that the bulkhead grommet is correctly seated.

10 Bonnet lock – removal and refitting

Removal

1 Open the bonnet, then prise out the outer cable end fitting from its slot in the bonnet lock, then unhook the inner cable from the lock operating lever **(see illustration 9.5)**.

2 Unscrew the securing bolts, and remove the lock assembly **(see illustration)**.

Refitting

3 Refitting is a reversal of removal. If necessary, the position of the lock can be altered to adjust the lock operation, by moving the lock within the elongated holes.

11 Door – removal and refitting

Removal

1 Disconnect the wiring plug from the door to be removed. On front doors, the wiring plug is round, and disconnects by twisting anti-clockwise. For rear doors, open the front door, pull the plug out of the B-pillar, then disconnect the plug using a small screwdriver **(see illustrations)**.

2 Unbolt the door check strap from the door **(see illustration)**.

3 Ensure that the door is adequately supported with the aid of an assistant, or using wooden blocks or similar under the bottom edge of the door (take care not to damage the paintwork).

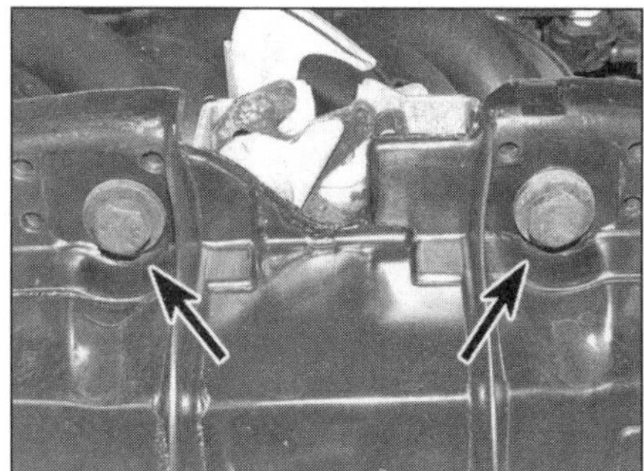

10.2 Bonnet lock securing bolts

4 Mark the position of the hinges on the body or on the door, then unscrew the bolts and remove the door from the car **(see illustration)**.

Refitting

5 Refitting is a reversal of removal.

12 Door inner trim panel – removal and refitting

Front door

Removal

1 Prise off the door mirror trim panel from the front of the door – this panel is secured by two (stiff) clips at the front, which should be released first, before unhooking the panel clips at the back edge. Disconnect the mirror switch wiring plug, and remove the panel completely **(see illustrations)**.

2 Prise the cover plug from the door lock

11.1a On front doors, the wiring harness connector unscrews

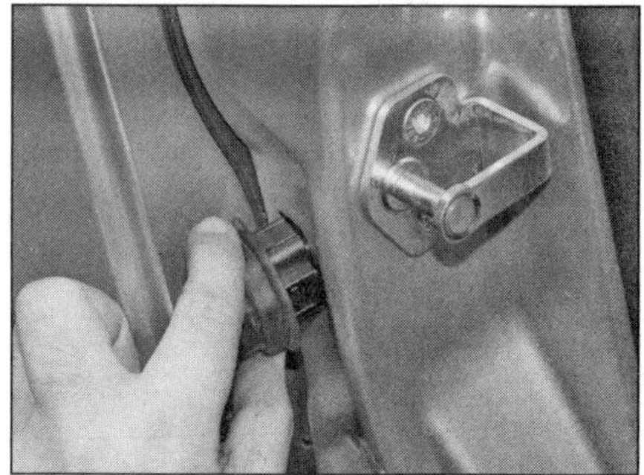

11.1b On rear doors, pull the wiring plug out ...

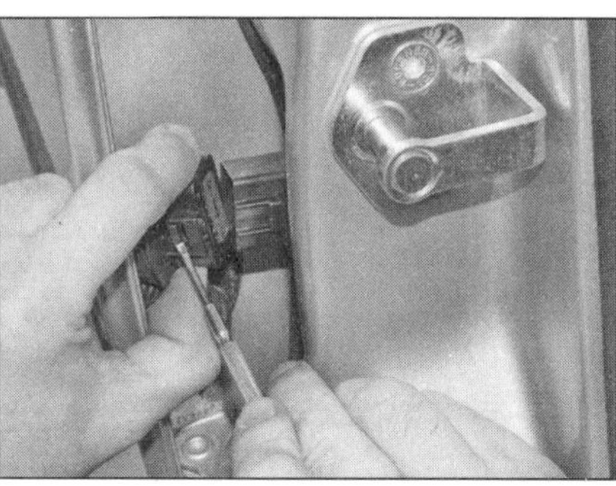

11.1c ... then release the two halves using a small screwdriver

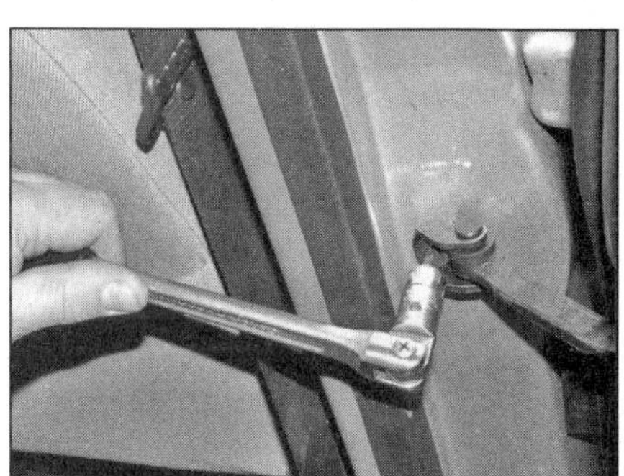

11.2 Undo one bolt and remove the check strap from the door pillar

11.4 Unbolt the door hinges, and remove the door

12.1a Prise off the door mirror trim panel at the front edge first ...

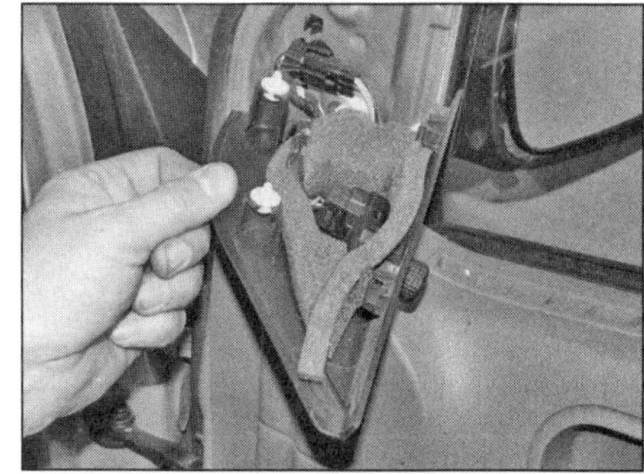

12.1b ... then unhook it at the back edge ...

12.1c ... and remove it completely, after disconnecting the mirror wiring plug

12.2a Prise out the cover plug ...

12.2b ... then remove the screw from the door lock handle (arrowed)

12.4a Lift the door handle trim panel ...

12.4b ... and then prise the panel off ...

12.4c ... and where applicable, disconnect the window switch wiring plugs

handle trim panel, then remove the screw beneath it **(see illustrations)**.

3 On models with manual front windows, remove the winder handle as described in paragraph 12.

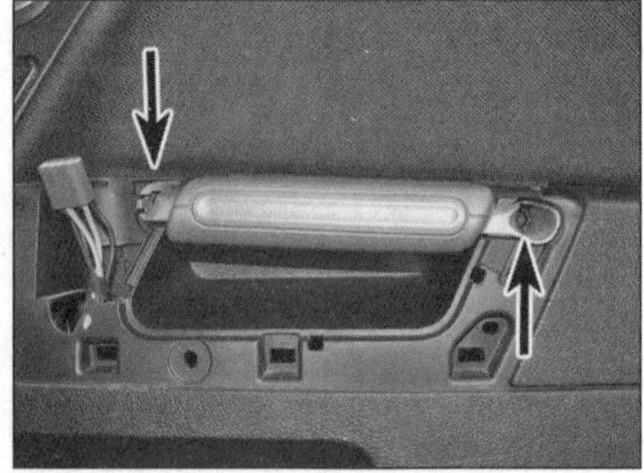

12.5a Remove the two screws behind the handle trim panel ...

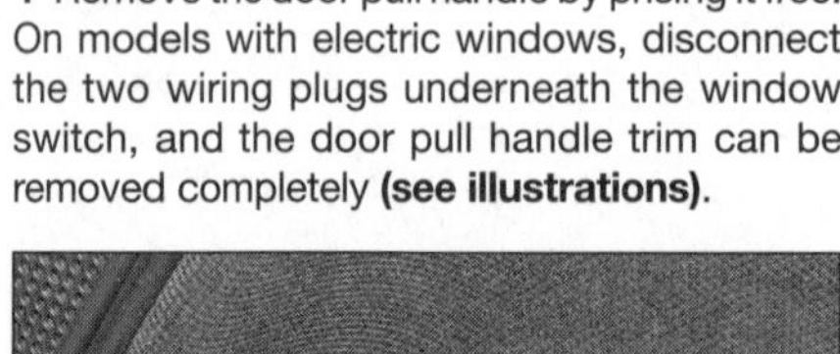

4 Remove the door pull handle by prising it free. On models with electric windows, disconnect the two wiring plugs underneath the window switch, and the door pull handle trim can be removed completely **(see illustrations)**.

12.5b ... and if required remove the handle from the panel

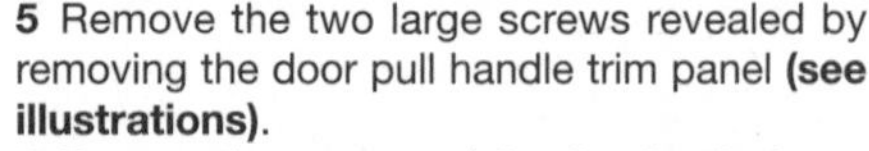

5 Remove the two large screws revealed by removing the door pull handle trim panel **(see illustrations)**.

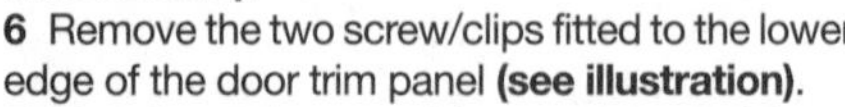

6 Remove the two screw/clips fitted to the lower edge of the door trim panel **(see illustration)**.

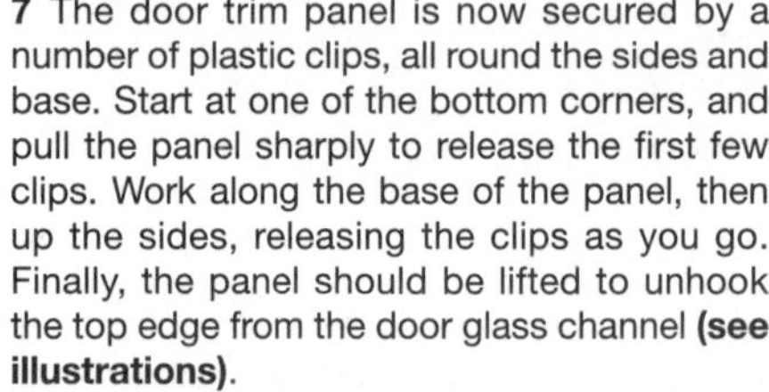

7 The door trim panel is now secured by a number of plastic clips, all round the sides and base. Start at one of the bottom corners, and pull the panel sharply to release the first few clips. Work along the base of the panel, then up the sides, releasing the clips as you go. Finally, the panel should be lifted to unhook the top edge from the door glass channel **(see illustrations)**.

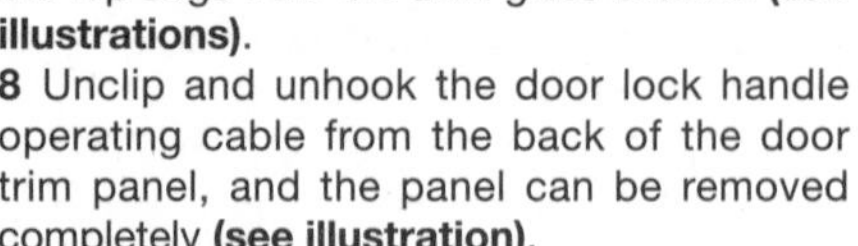

8 Unclip and unhook the door lock handle operating cable from the back of the door trim panel, and the panel can be removed completely **(see illustration)**.

Refitting

9 Refitting is a reversal of removal. Before

12.6 On early models, remove the two screw/clips from the base of the door

12.7a Use a plastic trim to release the clips

12.7b With all the clips released, lift off the panel

12.8 Unclip the door lock handle cable from the back of the panel

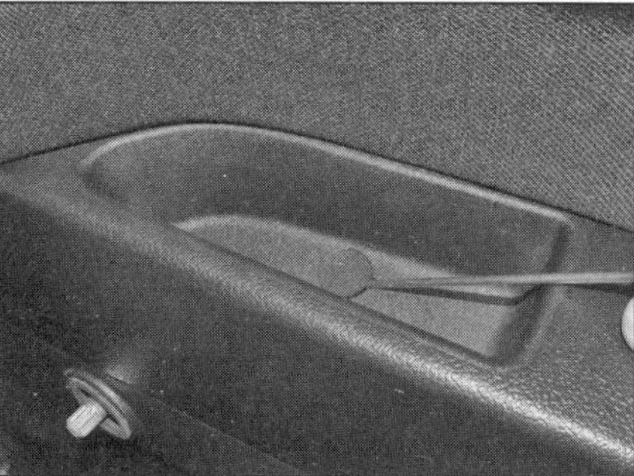

12.10a Prise out the cover plug ...

12.10b ... and remove the screw down inside the door pull

12.11a Remove the screw cover ...

12.11b ... and remove the screw from the door handle trim panel

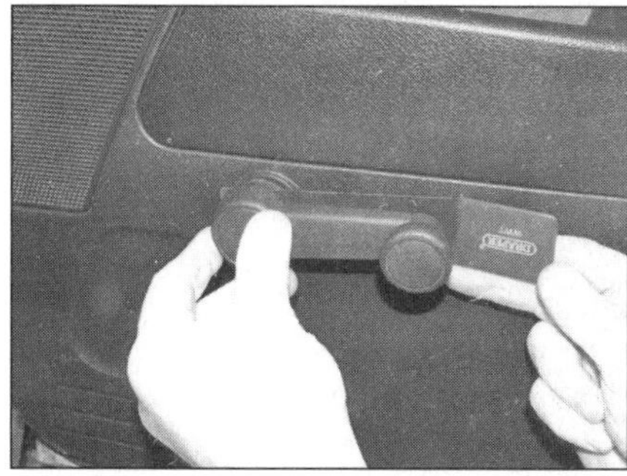

12.12a Special tools are available for pushing out the window handle retaining spring ...

12.12b ... which clips into a groove in the back of the handle

starting, check to see whether any trim clips have been left on the door, and transfer them to the trim panel.

Rear door

Removal

10 Prise the cover plug from inside the door pull, then remove the screw beneath it **(see illustrations)**.

11 Similarly, remove the cover plug and screw from the door lock handle trim panel **(see illustrations)**. We used a piece of very sticky tape to grab hold of the cover and pull it free.

12 Use a hooked piece of wire or a similar tool to release the window regulator handle securing clip from the shaft – if neither of these is available, see the **Haynes Hint**. Pull off the regulator handle, and recover the spring clip and the trim disc **(see illustrations)**.

HAYNES HiNT *Prise the winder handle to open a gap between it and the circular disc behind. Work the edge of a piece of (clean) cloth/rag into the gap behind the handle, either from the top or underneath. Using a 'sawing' action, work the cloth side-to-side, and also pull the ends of the cloth up (or down). It may take some time, but what you're trying to do is snag the ends of the spring clip holding the handle in place – when you do, the sawing action should work the clip off, allowing the handle to be pulled from the splines. A little patience is required, but it will work. Keep an eye on where the spring clip goes, though.*

13 The door trim panel is now secured by a number of plastic clips, all round the sides and base **(see illustration)**. Start at one of the bottom corners, and pull the panel sharply to release the first few clips. Work along the base of the panel, then up the sides, releasing the clips as you go. Finally, the panel should be lifted to unhook the top edge from the door glass channel.

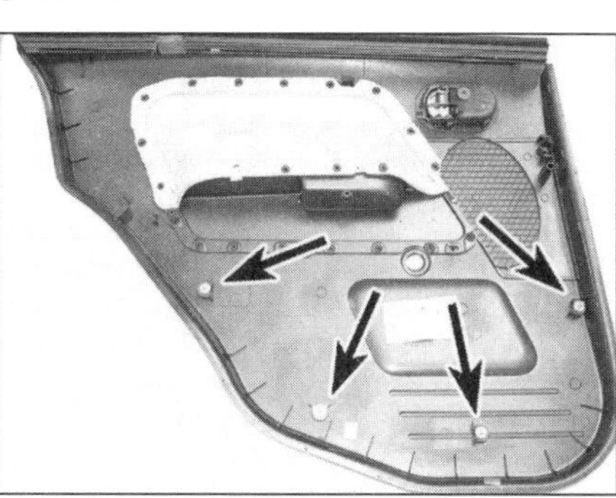

12.13 The panel removed to show the location of the retaining clips (arrowed)

14 Unclip and unhook the door lock handle operating cable from the back of the door trim panel, and the panel can be removed completely **(see illustration)**.

Refitting

15 Refitting is a reversal of removal. Before starting, check to see whether any trim clips have been left on the door, and transfer them to the trim panel.

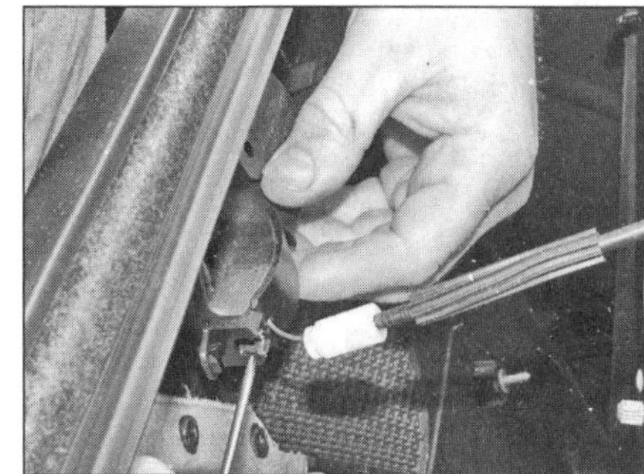

12.14 Unclip the door lock cable fitting from the back of the trim panel

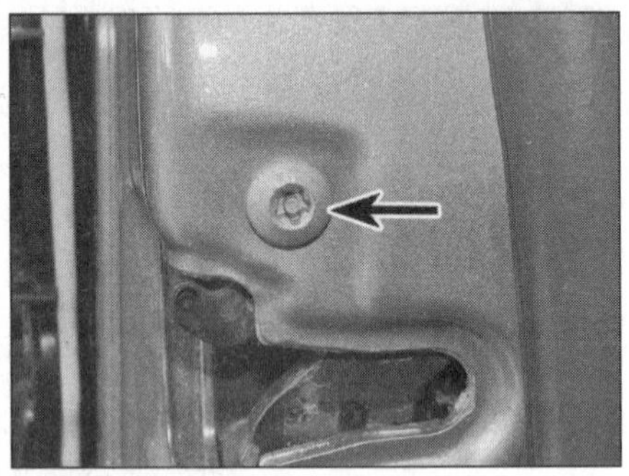

13.4 Remove the handle support screw at the back edge of the door (arrowed)

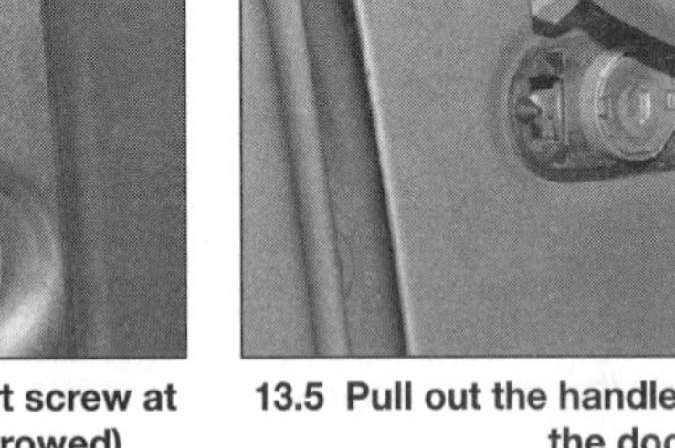

13.5 Pull out the handle rear section from the door

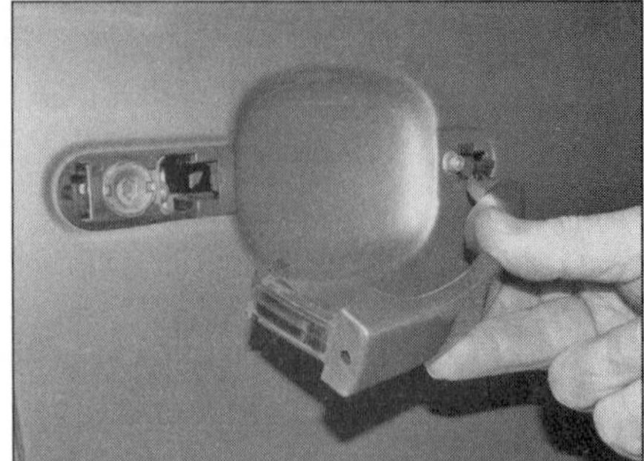

13.6a Pull the handle out at the rear, unhook it at the front, remove it ...

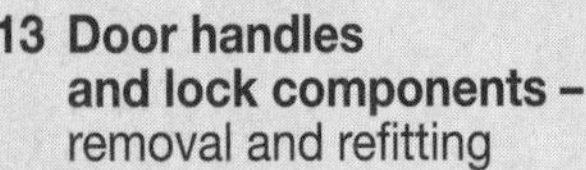

13 Door handles and lock components – removal and refitting

Interior handle

Removal

1 Remove the door inner trim panel as described in Section 12.

2 Once the door lock operating cable has been released from the handle, the handle can be unclipped from the door trim panel and removed.

Refitting

3 Refitting is a reversal of removal. Refit the door trim panel with reference to Section 12.

Exterior handle

Removal

4 Open the door, and remove the handle support screw from the rear edge of the door. A tamperproof Torx type screwdriver bit or socket will be required **(see illustration)**.

5 Pull the handle rear section from the door **(see illustration)**.

6 Pull the main handle outwards at the rear, unhook it at the front. Remove it and then recover the gasket **(see illustrations)**.

Refitting

7 Refitting is a reversal of removal. When refitting a front door handle, especially if the main lock assembly has been disturbed, check that the handle catch (just visible in front of the lock barrel) is positioned vertically before offering the handle into place – if not, it can be flicked out with a small screwdriver **(see illustration)**.

Front lock

Removal

8 Remove the door trim panel as described in Section 12, and the exterior handle as described previously in this Section.

9 The front door glass must be disconnected from the regulator mechanism as described in Section 14 – the glass does not have to be completely removed from the door, and can be taped up to the door frame to support it.

10 Unscrew the plastic locking collar which joins the door wiring harness to the connector on the A-pillar. Push the harness plug into the door **(see illustration)**.

11 Unclip the door mirror wiring plug from the door, and separate the connector **(see illustrations)**.

12 On the outside of the door, unscrew the nut from the front of the door handle location, then squeeze the plastic clips at either side, and push them back inside the door **(see illustrations)**.

13 Remove the three lock assembly screws at the rear edge of the door **(see illustration)**.

13.6b ... and recover the gasket

13.7 On front doors, this small lever must be vertical before refitting the handle

13.10 Unscrew the door wiring harness connector, and push the plug into the door

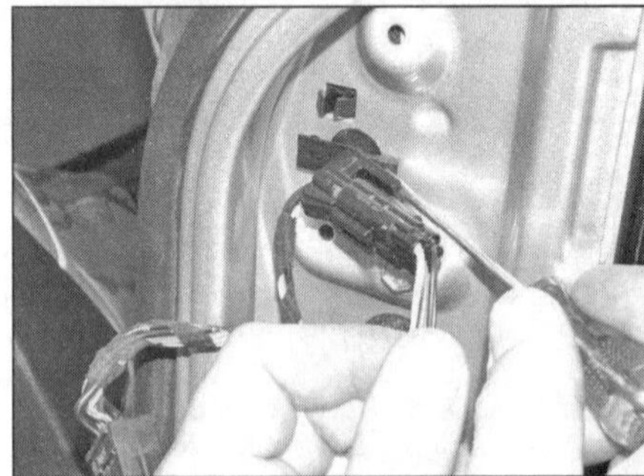

13.11a Unclip the mirror wiring plug ...

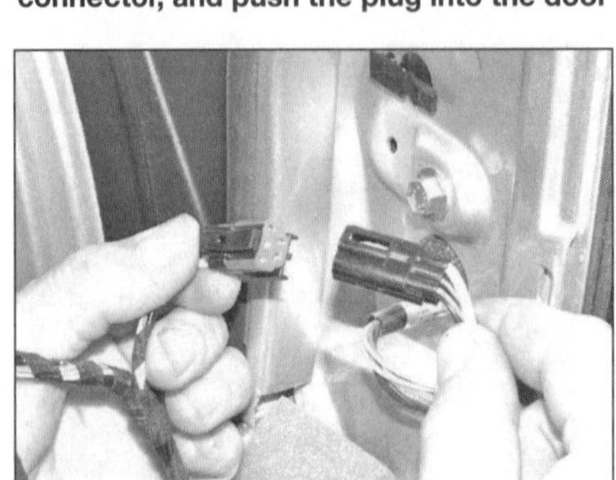

13.11b ... and disconnect it

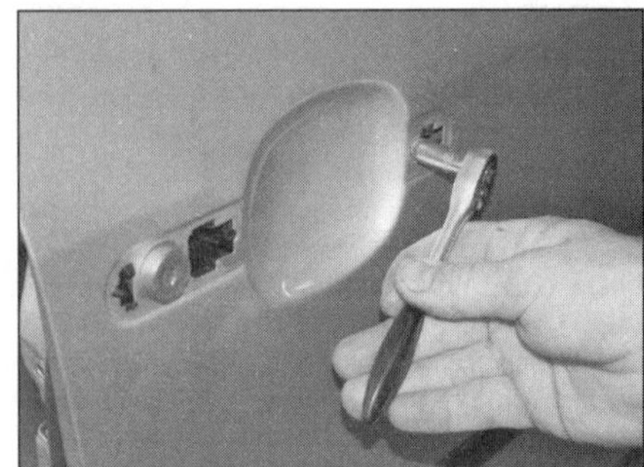

13.12a Unscrew the nut in front of the door handle ...

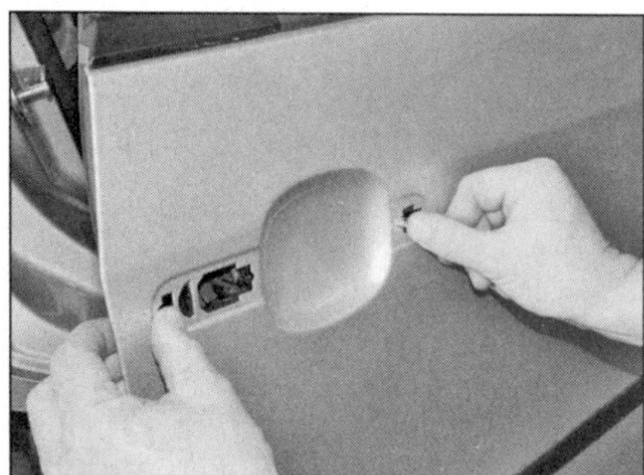
13.12b ... then squeeze the end clips together and in through the door

13.13 Unscrew the three door lock screws at the back edge of the door (arrowed)

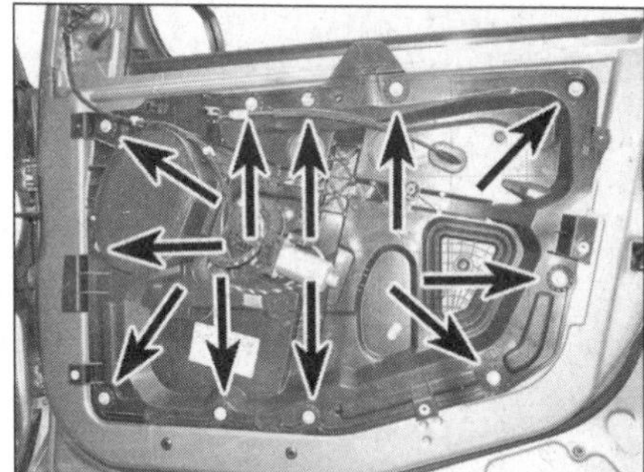
13.14 Remove the eleven bolts around the door inner panel (arrowed)

13.16 Removing the door inner panel

13.17a Unclip the front section of wiring harness from the door ...

13.17b ... and pull it off to the inside

On later models a tamperproof Torx bit will be required to remove these.

14 Work around the edge of the door inner panel, and remove the eleven securing bolts **(see illustration)**.

15 On the outside of the door, check that the lock barrel has been pushed into the door sufficiently so that the inner panel can drop down.

16 First lift the inner panel to release the catch in the centre at the top, then pull the panel down at the rear, and slide it forwards, keeping the base of the panel pulled out. The panel is quite a tight fit in the door, and it can get jammed if not dropped enough at the rear edge, which will cause the lock barrel to catch on the dished-in section of the door panel around the exterior handle **(see illustration)**.

17 Once the panel is essentially free, unclip the wiring harness from inside the front of the door, and the inner panel can then be removed **(see illustrations)**.

18 To remove the lock assembly, first disconnect the large wiring connector. The lock assembly is clipped to the back of the inner panel – release the clips with a screwdriver, and slide the assembly rearwards to remove it **(see illustrations)**. It appears that, with the exception of the lock barrel and link rods, the lock assembly is only available as a complete assembly.

Refitting

19 Refitting is a reversal of removal, bearing in mind the following points:

a) Check the operation of the lock mechanism before refitting the door inner trim panel.

b) Refit the door trim panel with reference to Section 12.

Front lock cylinder

Removal

20 Remove the door inner panel as described for removing the lock assembly (paragraphs 8 to 17). The lock assembly itself does not have to be unclipped from the inner panel.

21 The lock barrel may be removed from the lock assembly by simply prising it out with a small screwdriver **(see illustrations)**.

13.18a Disconnect the wiring plug ...

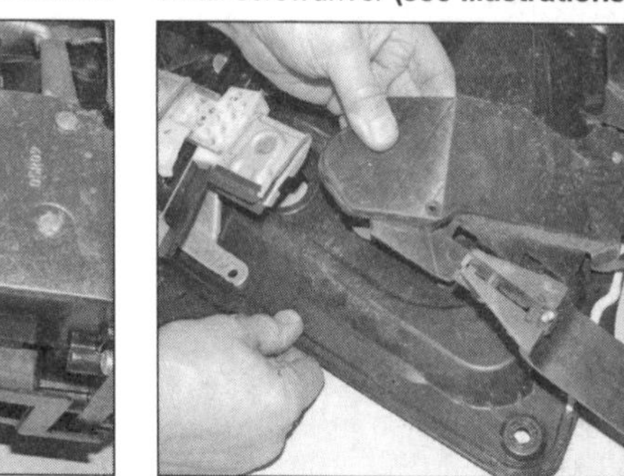
13.18b ... then release the plastic clips, and pull the lock assembly rearwards

13.21a The lock barrel is simply prised out of the lock assembly ...

13.21b ... to remove it completely

13.25a Release the rear door wiring plug ...

13.25b ... separate the connector using a screwdriver if necessary ...

13.25c ... then push the door half of the plug into the door

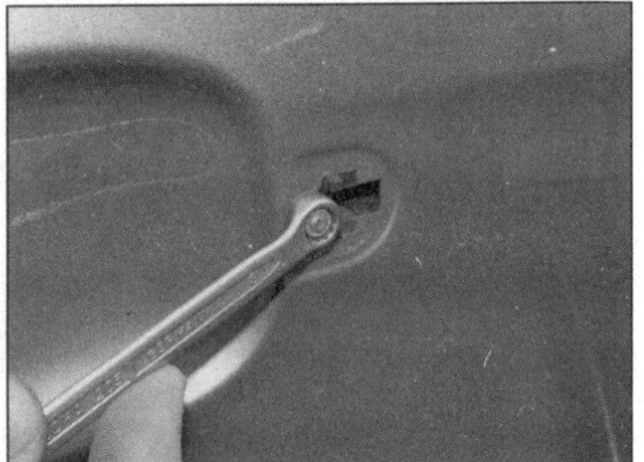
13.26a Unscrew the nut in front of the door handle ...

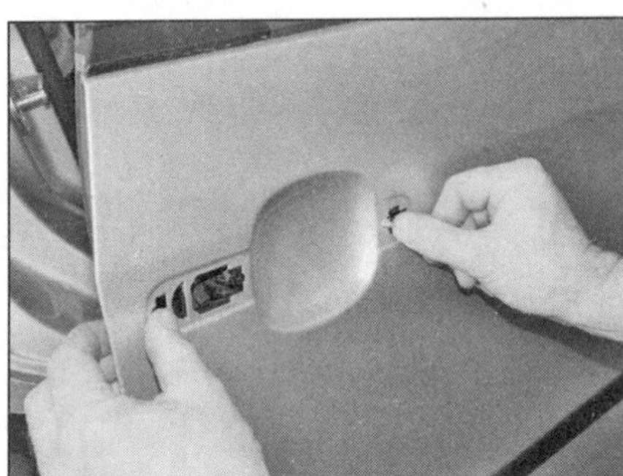
13.26b ... then squeeze the two end clips together and in through the door

Refitting

22 Refitting is a reversal of removal, bearing in mind the following points:

a) Check the operation of the lock mechanism before refitting the door inner trim panel.

b) Refit the door trim panel with reference to Section 12.

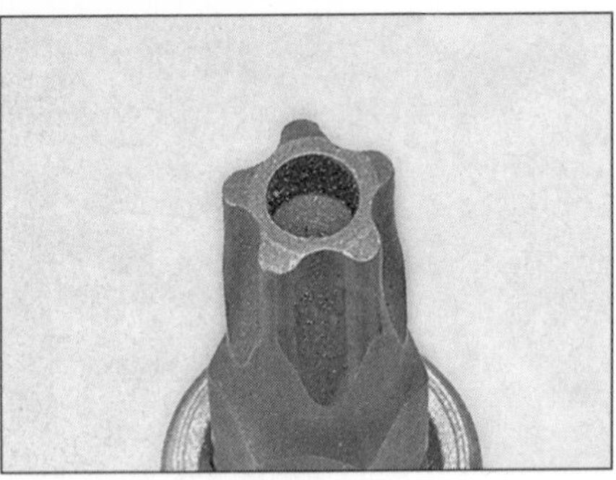
13.27a A tamperproof Torx bit maybe required ...

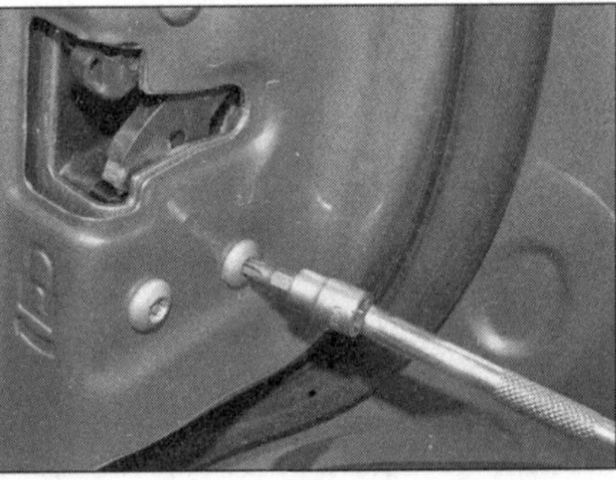
13.27b ... to remove the three lock screws

Rear lock

Removal

23 Remove the door trim panel as described in Section 12, and the exterior handle as described previously in this Section.

24 The front door glass must be disconnected from the regulator mechanism as described in Section 14 – the glass does not have to be completely removed from the door, and can be taped up to the door frame to support it.

25 Open the front door, and separate the rear door wiring connector on the B-pillar by pulling it back (use a small screwdriver if necessary, to lift the connector's rubber boot). Try not to lose the B-pillar half of the connector, or the B-pillar and door sill trim panels inside the car may have to be removed to retrieve it. The rear door half of the wiring can be pushed back inside the rear door **(see illustrations)**.

26 On the outside of the door, unscrew the nut from the front of the door handle location, then squeeze the plastic clips at either side, and push them back inside the door **(see illustrations)**.

27 Remove the three lock assembly screws at the rear edge of the door **(see illustrations)**.

28 Work around the edge of the door inner panel, and remove the nine securing bolts **(see illustration)**.

29 First lift the inner panel to release the catch in the centre at the top, then pull the panel down at the rear, and slide it forwards, keeping the base of the panel pulled out. The panel is quite a tight fit in the door, and careful manipulation will be needed to successfully remove it **(see illustrations)**. Make sure the

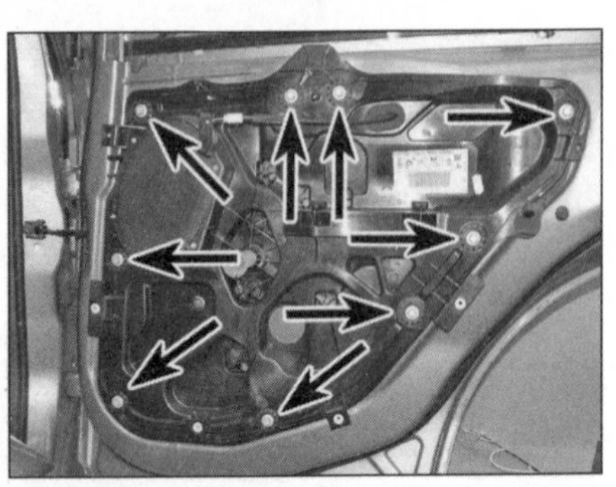
13.28 On rear doors, there are nine inner panel bolts to remove (arrowed)

13.29a Lift the inner panel off the top catch, then lower it ...

13.29b ... and slide forwards to remove the panel and lock assembly

door wiring harness does not become trapped, and is free to be removed with the inner panel.

30 To remove the lock assembly, first disconnect the large wiring connector. The lock assembly is clipped to the back of the inner panel – release the clips with a screwdriver, and slide the assembly rearwards to remove it **(see illustration)**. It appears that the lock assembly is only available complete.

Refitting

31 Refitting is a reversal of removal, bearing in mind the following points:

a) *Check the operation of the lock mechanism before refitting the door inner trim panel.*
b) *Refit the door trim panel with reference to Section 12.*

14 Door window glass and regulator – removal and refitting

Front door window

Removal

1 Remove the door trim panel as described in Section 12.

2 Prise out the two large rubber grommets (or self adhesive pads on later models) from the door inner panel – these provide access to the door glass retaining bolts **(see illustration)**.

3 Reconnect the electric window switch (or window winder handle), and lower the glass until the door glass retaining bolts are visible in the grommet holes in the inner panel **(see illustration)**.

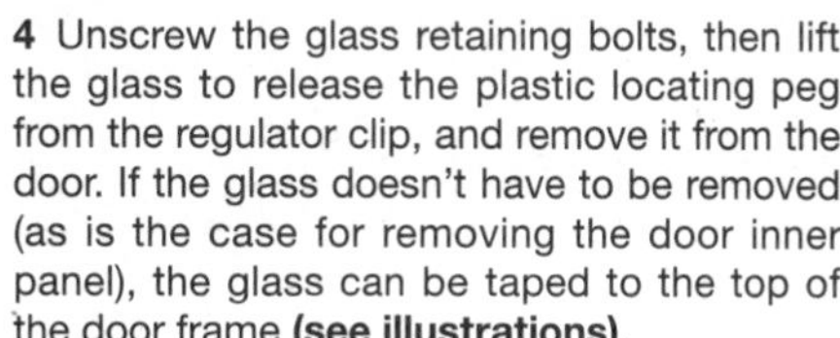

4 Unscrew the glass retaining bolts, then lift the glass to release the plastic locating peg from the regulator clip, and remove it from the door. If the glass doesn't have to be removed (as is the case for removing the door inner panel), the glass can be taped to the top of the door frame **(see illustrations)**.

Refitting

5 Refitting is a reversal of removal, noting the following points:

a) *Line up the plastic locating peg in the centre of the regulator guide clip, and push down to locate it* ***(see illustration)****.*
b) *Tighten the glass retaining bolts securely.*
c) *Refit the door trim panel as described in Section 12.*

Front regulator

Removal

6 Remove the door window glass as described previously in this Section – the glass can be taped to the door frame, as it does not have to be removed completely.

7 Unscrew the plastic locking collar which joins the door wiring harness to the connector on the A-pillar. Push the harness plug into the door.

8 Unclip the door mirror wiring plug from the door, and separate the connector.

9 On the outside of the door, unscrew the nut from the front of the door handle location, then squeeze the plastic clips at either side, and push them back inside the door.

10 Remove the three lock assembly screws at the rear edge of the door.

11 Work around the edge of the door inner panel, and remove the eleven securing bolts.

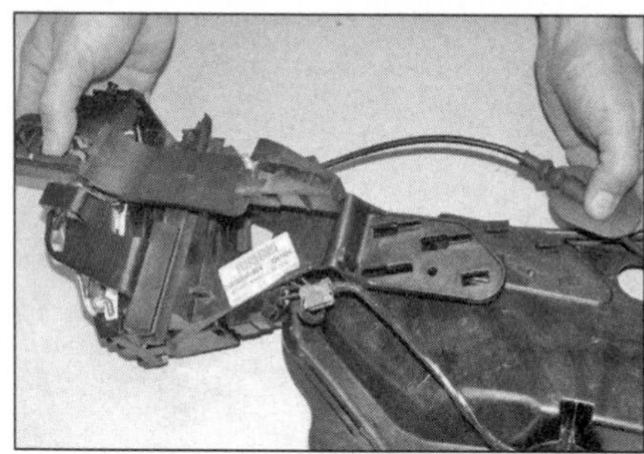

13.30 Disconnect the wiring plug, then unclip the lock assembly from the inner panel

12 On the outside of the door, check that the lock barrel has been pushed into the door sufficiently so that the inner panel can drop down.

13 First lift the inner panel to release the catch in the centre at the top, then pull the panel down at the rear, and slide it forwards, keeping the base of the panel pulled out. The panel is quite a tight fit in the door, and it can get jammed if not dropped enough at the rear edge, which will cause the lock barrel to catch on the dished-in section of the door panel around the exterior handle.

14 Once the panel is essentially free, unclip the wiring harness from inside the front of the door, and the inner panel can then be removed.

15 To remove the regulator assembly, release the plastic clips securing the cable guide to the door inner panel, and lift it away **(see illustration)**.

14.2 Prise out the large rubber grommets

14.3 Lower the window until the two bolts are visible

14.4a Unscrew the bolts ...

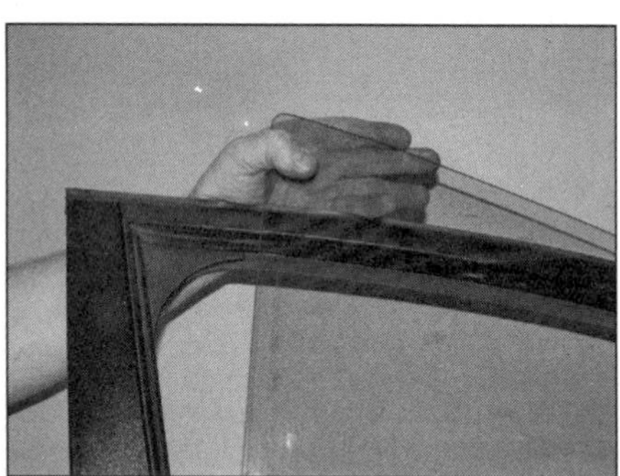

14.4b ... then either lift the glass out completely, or tape it to the door frame

14.5 Locate the plastic peg at the base of the glass into the guide clip

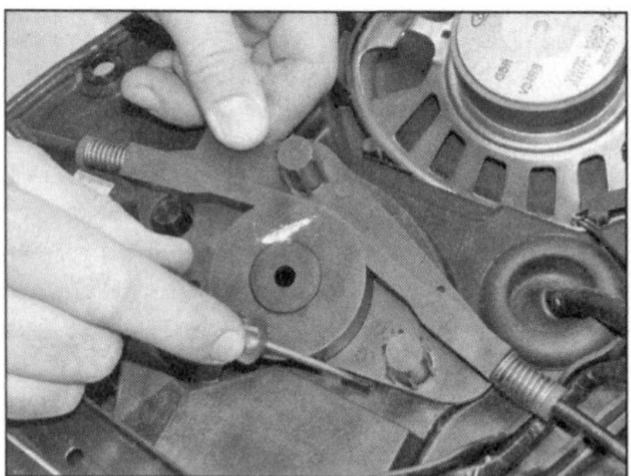

14.15 Unclip the regulator cable guide from the inner panel

14.16 Undo the four regulator bolts, and remove the regulator

14.19 Disconnect the window motor wiring plug

14.20a Unscrew the three Torx screws ...

14.20b ... and lift out the window motor

14.23a Prise out the door inner panel rubber grommet ...

14.23b ... or peel off the self-adhesive pad

16 Undo the four (or two on later models) regulator retaining bolts on the door inner panel, and withdraw the regulator from the panel **(see illustration)**.

Refitting

17 Refitting is a reversal of removal, but check the operation of the window regulator mechanism before refitting the door trim panel.

Front window motor

Removal

18 Refer to paragraphs 6 to 14, and remove the door inner panel.

19 Disconnect the wiring plug from the motor **(see illustration)**.

20 Remove the three Torx screws securing the motor to the door inner panel, and remove it **(see illustrations)**.

Refitting

21 Refitting is a reversal of removal, but check the operation of the motor before refitting the door trim panel.

Rear window

Removal

22 Remove the door trim panel (Section 12).

23 Prise out the large rubber grommet from the door inner panel. Later models have a self-adhesive pad fitted. Peel this back **(see illustrations)**.

24 Refit the window winder handle, and lower the glass until the glass retaining peg is visible in the grommet hole **(see illustration)**.

25 With one hand to support the glass in case it suddenly drops, use a screwdriver to firmly push the regulator locating peg through the glass. Lift the glass up in the frame, and tape it in place. If the glass doesn't have to be removed (as is the case for removing the door inner panel), the glass can be left here **(see illustrations)**.

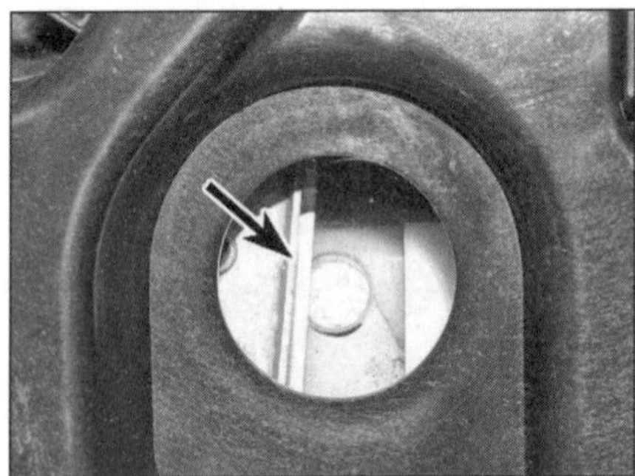

14.24 Lower the glass until the locating peg is visible (arrowed)

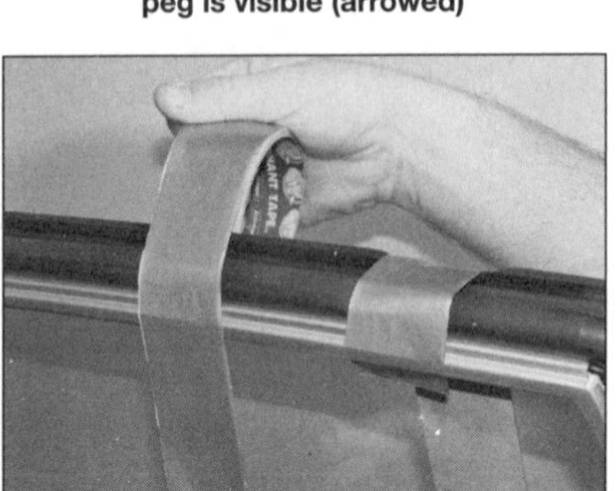

14.25b ... then tape the glass to the door frame

26 To remove the glass completely, the door inner panel has to be removed as described in paragraphs 29 to 33. Lower the glass into the door frame and remove the guide rail. Remove the quarter glass and then remove the glass **(see illustrations)**.

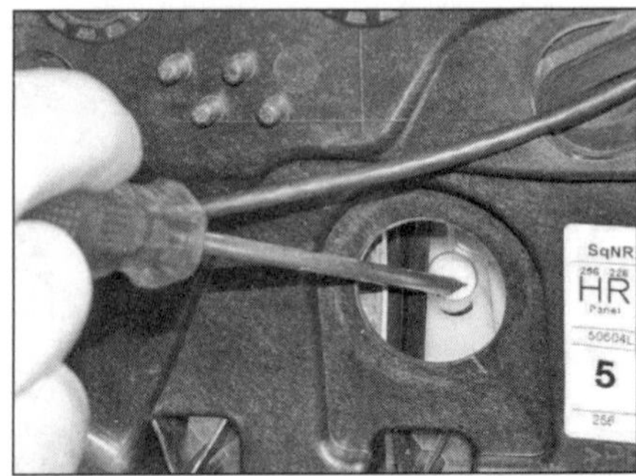

14.25a Push the regulator peg firmly through the glass ...

14.26a Unbolt the guide rail ...

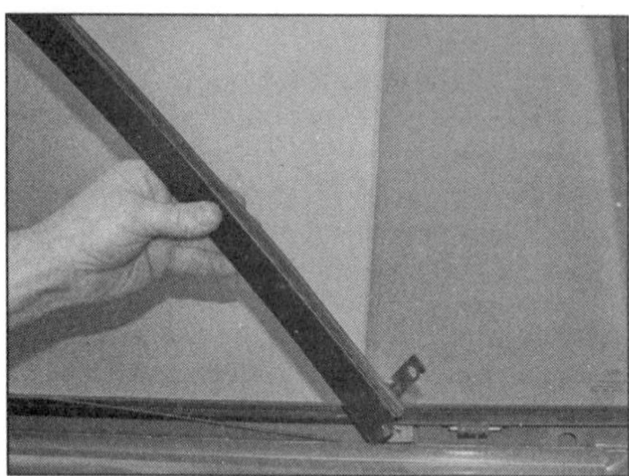

14.26b ... pull it down and remove it

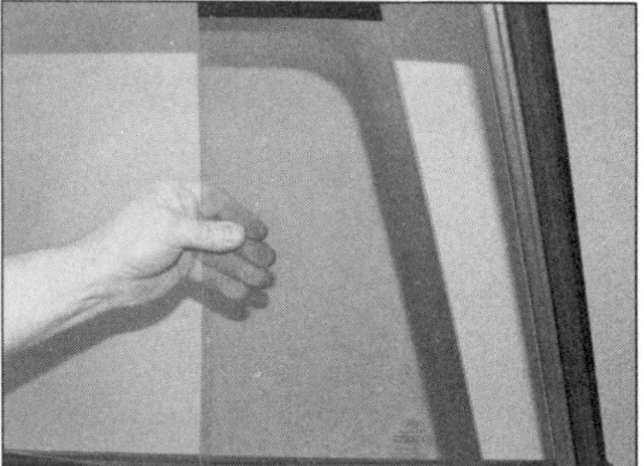

14.26c Remove the quarter light glass ...

14.26d ... and then the main glass panel can be removed

14.34 Remove the two screws from the cable guide

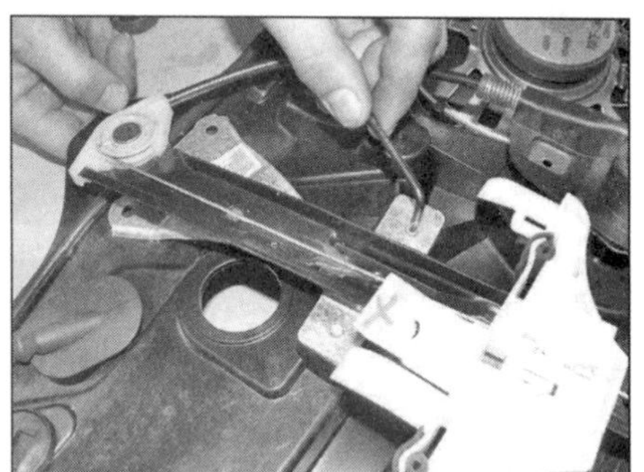

14.35a Undo the regulator screws ...

14.35b ... then lift it off the door inner panel

Refitting

27 Refitting is a reversal of removal, noting the following points:

a) Line up the glass over the regulator plastic peg, and push the glass firmly onto it.

b) Check the operation of the window by temporarily refitting the handle.

c) Refit the door trim panel (see Section 12).

Rear regulator

Removal

28 Remove the door window glass as described previously in this Section – the glass can be taped to the door frame, as it does not have to be removed completely.

29 Open the front door, and separate the rear door wiring connector on the B-pillar by pulling it back (use a small screwdriver if necessary, to lift the connector's rubber boot). Try not to lose the B-pillar half of the connector, or the B-pillar and door sill trim panels inside the car may have to be removed to retrieve it. The rear door half of the wiring can be pushed back inside the rear door.

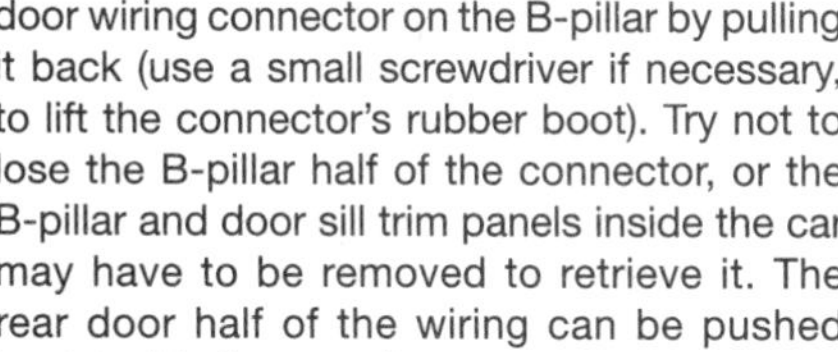

30 On the outside of the door, unscrew the nut from the front of the door handle location, then squeeze the plastic clips at either side, and push them back inside the door.

31 Remove the three lock assembly screws at the rear edge of the door.

32 Work around the edge of the door inner panel, and remove the nine securing bolts.

33 First lift the inner panel to release the catch in the centre at the top, then pull the panel down at the rear, and slide it forwards, keeping the base of the panel pulled out. The panel is quite a tight fit in the door, and careful manipulation will be needed to successfully remove it. Make sure the door wiring harness does not become trapped, and is free to be removed with the inner panel.

34 To remove the regulator assembly, remove the two screws securing the cable guide to the door inner panel, and lift it away **(see illustration)**.

35 Undo the regulator retaining screws on the door inner panel, and withdraw the regulator from the panel **(see illustrations)**.

Refitting

36 Refitting is a reversal of removal, but check the operation of the window regulator mechanism before refitting the door trim panel.

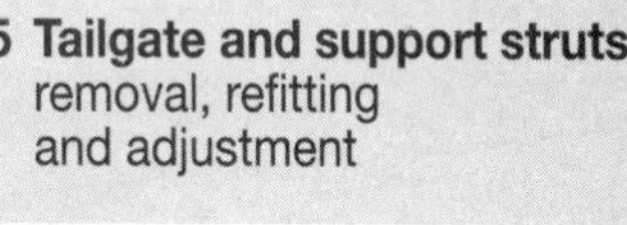

15 Tailgate and support struts – removal, refitting and adjustment

Tailgate

Removal

1 Remove the high-level brake light and number plate light unit as described in Chapter 12, Section 7.

2 Also with reference to Chapter 12, Section 15, disconnect the wiring from the rear wiper motor.

3 Refer to Section 16 and disconnect the wiring from the tailgate lock.

4 As far as possible, release all the tailgate wiring from any clips or ties, as it must all be fed back through the top of the tailgate and removed.

5 Using a pencil or marker pen, mark the position of the hinges on the tailgate to aid refitting.

6 Support the tailgate, and disconnect the support struts as described later in this Section.

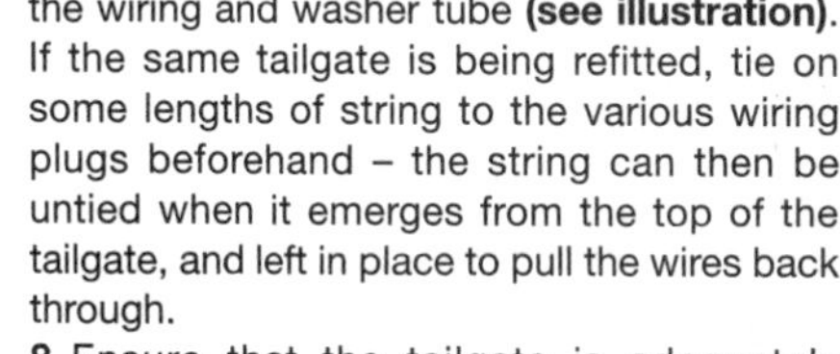

7 Prise out the rubber gaiters at the top of the tailgate, and carefully start to pull through the wiring and washer tube **(see illustration)**. If the same tailgate is being refitted, tie on some lengths of string to the various wiring plugs beforehand – the string can then be untied when it emerges from the top of the tailgate, and left in place to pull the wires back through.

8 Ensure that the tailgate is adequately supported, ideally with the aid of an assistant, then unscrew the bolts securing the hinges

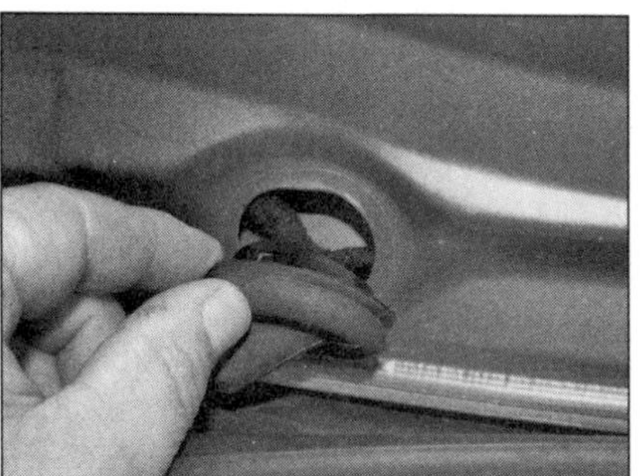

15.7 Prise out the rubber grommets for the wiring at the top of the tailgate

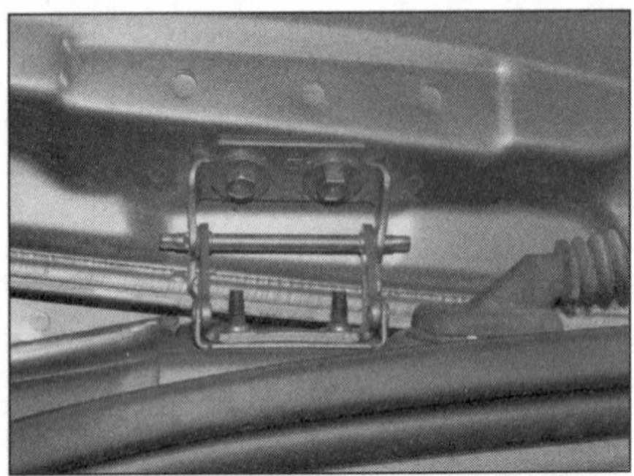

15.8 Tailgate hinge bolts

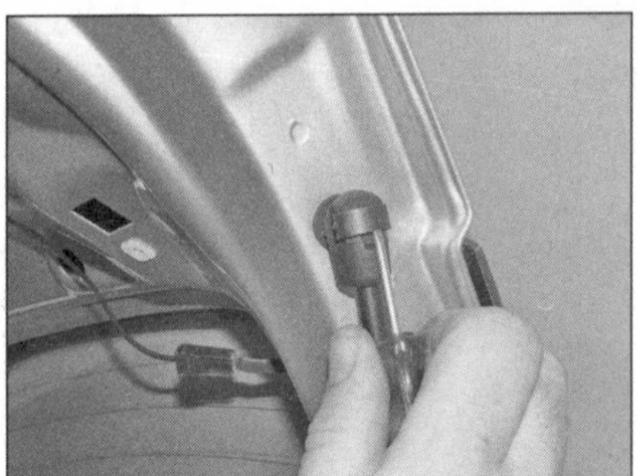

15.11a Lever out the metal clip ...

15.11b ... and prise off the strut

to the tailgate **(see illustration)**, and lift the tailgate from the car.

Refitting

9 Refitting is a reversal of removal, bearing in mind the following points:

a) Make sure that the hinges are aligned with the marks made before removal.

b) Where applicable, use the string to pull the wiring harness and the washer fluid hose into position in the tailgate.

c) On completion, check the alignment of the tailgate with the surrounding body panels and, if necessary, adjust the position of the tailgate hinges within the elongated holes until satisfactory alignment is achieved.

Support struts

Removal

10 Open the tailgate, and support it in the open position, using a wooden prop or similar tool. Note that the tailgate is heavy, and will fall closed if either of the support struts are disconnected.

11 Working at the top end of the strut, lever off the retaining clip, and prise off the end of the strut from the lug on the tailgate **(see illustrations)**.

12 Repeat the procedure at the bottom end of the strut, and withdraw the strut.

Refitting

13 Refitting is a reversal of removal.

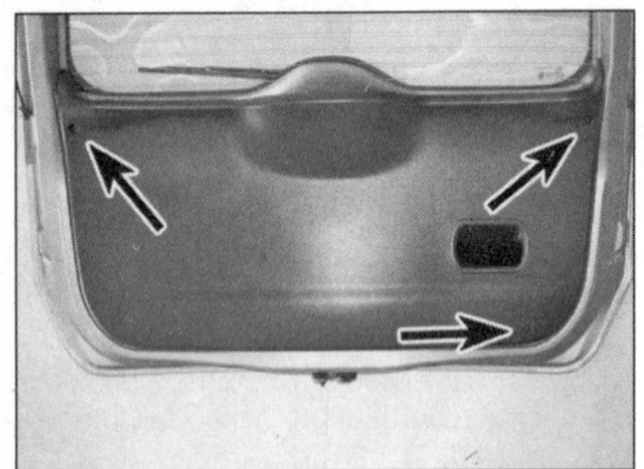

16.1a Remove the screws (arrowed) ...

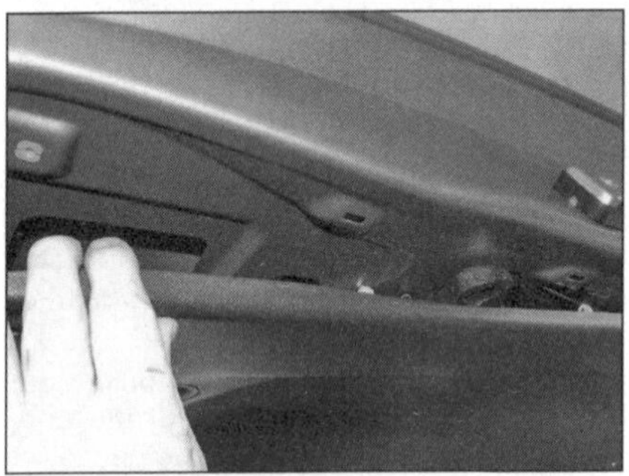

16.1b ... then unclip and remove the tailgate trim panel

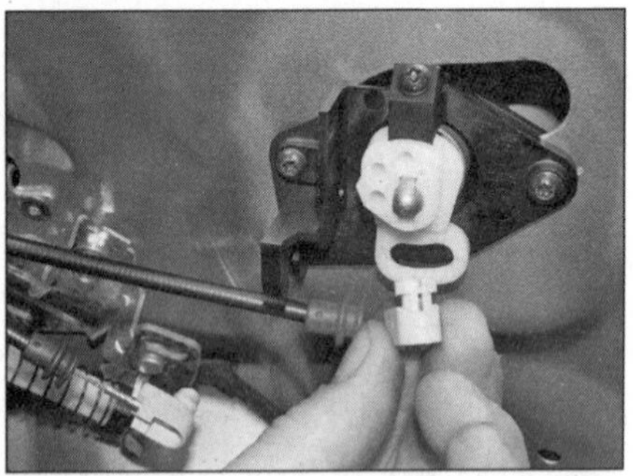

16.2 Unclip the lock barrel operating cable

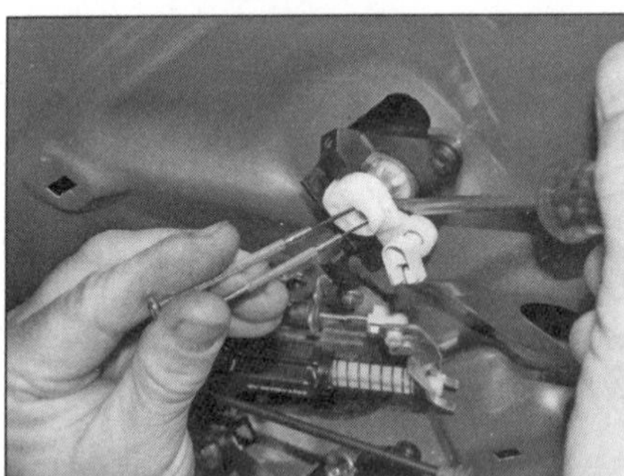

16.3 Removing the lock operating quadrant, using three screwdrivers

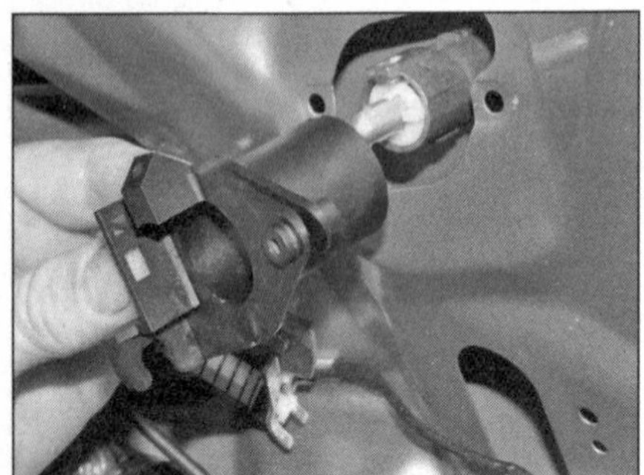

16.4 Removing the lock barrel surround

16.5 Push out the lock barrel

16 Tailgate lock components - removal and refitting

Lock barrel

Removal

1 Open the tailgate, and remove the inner trim panel, which is secured by three cross-head screws and several clips **(see illustration)**.

2 Unclip the lock barrel operating cable collar (red plastic on our project car) from the mounting clip on the barrel surround, then release the cable end fitting by squeezing the lugs together behind the lock quadrant **(see illustration)**.

3 Removing the lock operating quadrant is tricky – there are two small plastic lugs which hold it onto the lock barrel shaft, and these can only be released using two very small (precision) screwdrivers, or possibly, using two pieces of stiff wire. At the same time, prise the quadrant off with another screwdriver from behind **(see illustration)**.

4 Remove the two screws securing the lock barrel surround, then twist it anti-clockwise and withdraw it from the tailgate **(see illustration)**.

5 The lock barrel can now be removed by pushing it through to the outside of the tailgate **(see illustration)**.

16.8 Unclip the tailgate lock operating cable

16.9a Disconnect the lock wiring plug inside the tailgate

16.9b Undo the two lock securing screws ...

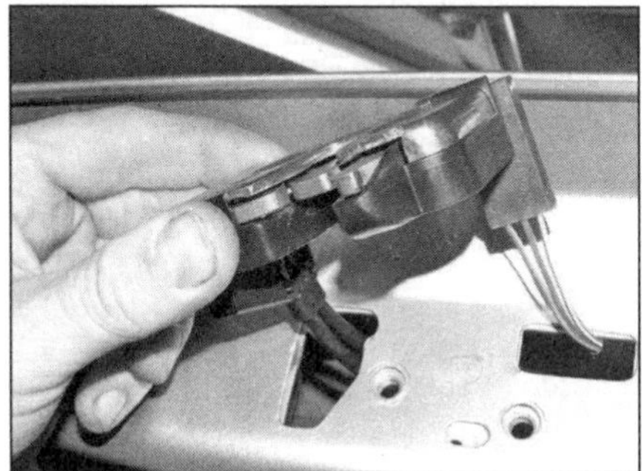

16.9c ... then lift out the lock

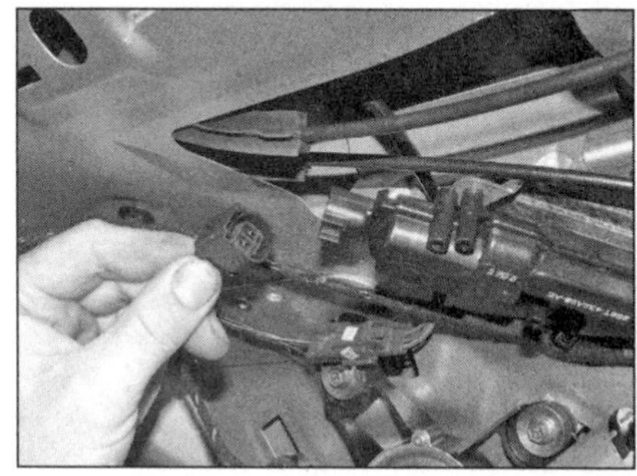

16.13 Disconnect the actuator wiring plug

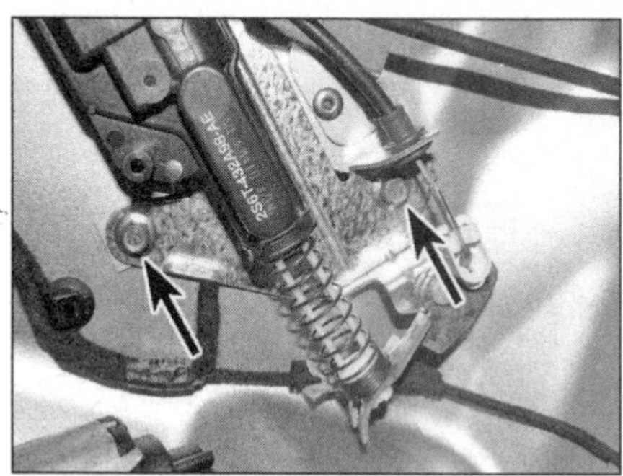

16.14 Remove the actuator mounting bolts

Refitting

6 Refitting is a reversal of removal, bearing in mind the following points:

a) *Make sure the lock quadrant is fully located by pressing it firmly onto the lock barrel shaft, so that both lugs are felt to engage.*

b) *Check the operation of the lock mechanism before refitting the tailgate trim panel.*

Lock assembly

Removal

7 Open the tailgate, and remove the inner trim panel, which is secured by three cross-head screws and several clips.

8 Unclip the lock operating cable collar (green plastic on our project car) from the mounting clip on the actuator, then release the cable end fitting **(see illustration)**.

9 Disconnect the anti-theft alarm switch wiring plug. Unscrew the two lock securing screws, and manipulate the lock out from the tailgate **(see illustrations)**. Feed the operating cable out, and remove the lock completely.

Refitting

10 Refitting is a reversal of removal, but check the operation of the lock mechanism before refitting the tailgate trim panel.

Lock actuator

Removal

11 Open the tailgate, and remove the inner trim panel, which is secured by three cross-head screws and several clips.

12 Unclip the lock operating cable collar (green plastic on our project car) from the mounting clip on the actuator. Release the cable end fitting by pulling the cable out to get some slack, then unhooking it **(see illustration 16.8)**.

13 Disconnect the actuator wiring connector **(see illustration)**.

14 Remove the two actuator securing bolts, then withdraw the actuator from the tailgate **(see illustration)**.

Refitting

15 Refitting is a reversal of removal, but check the operation of the mechanism before refitting the tailgate trim panel.

17 Central locking system components – general information

Door lock motor

1 The door lock motors are an integral part of the lock assemblies. Removal and refitting is part of the door lock removal and refitting procedure in Section 13.

Door lock microswitch

2 The door lock microswitches (fitted to the front doors) are an integral part of the lock assemblies. Removal and refitting is part of the door lock removal and refitting procedure in Section 13.

Remote control battery renewal

3 Refer to Chapter 1A, Section 25 or Chapter 1B, Section 24.

Door lock control unit (GEM)

Note: *If a new GEM is fitted, it must be programmed using Ford's IDS diagnostic system, otherwise various systems on the car, including the central locking, may not work properly.*

4 The central locking control function is incorporated in an ECU behind the driver's side of the facia, which also controls the alarm, wipers, lighting and heated rear window. This unit is known by Ford as the generic electronic module, or GEM.

5 To remove the unit, remove the panel below the steering column. Remove the panel retaining screws, pull the panel towards you and remove it.

6 The unit has a total of five wiring plugs fitted – these are disconnected by swinging down the hinged locking bar fitted to each one, using a small screwdriver **(see illustrations)**. The plugs will only fit one of the unit's sockets, so there is no need to mark their positions.

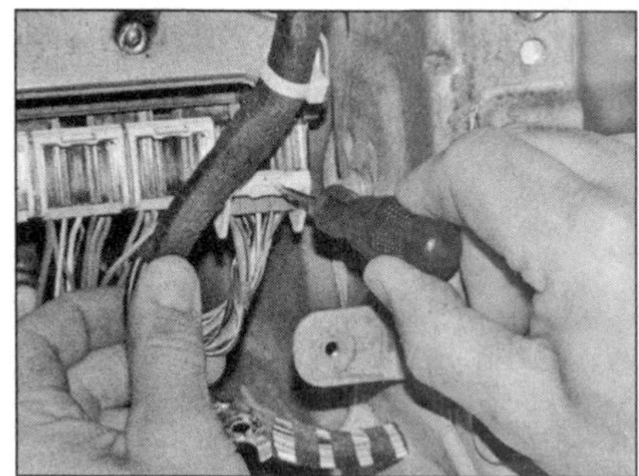

17.6a Use a screwdriver to swing down the locking bar ...

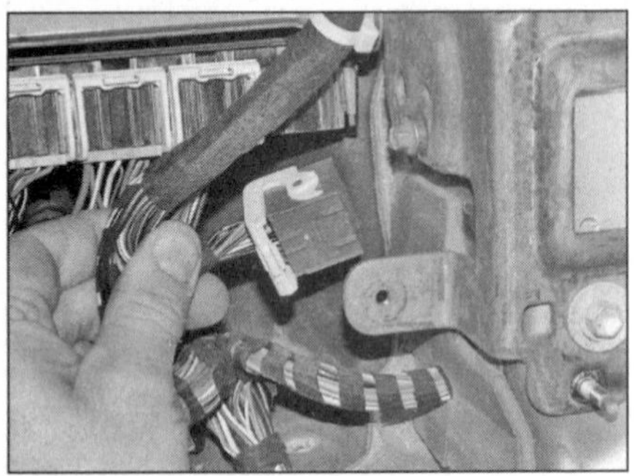
17.6b ... and disconnect the GEM unit wiring plugs

7 Remove the two screws securing the unit, and lower it out from under the facia **(see illustration)**. Note the warning label on the unit, which states that the unit is scrap if dropped – treat it with care.

8 Refitting is a reversal of removal.

9 For more information on the other functions controlled by the GEM, and information on the module's self-test facility, refer to Chapter 12, Section 3.

18 Electric window components - removal and refitting

Window switches

1 Refer to Chapter 12, Section 4.

Window regulator motors

2 The motors are integral with the regulator assemblies, and if faulty, the complete regulator assembly must be renewed. Removal and refitting of the regulator assemblies is described in Section 14.

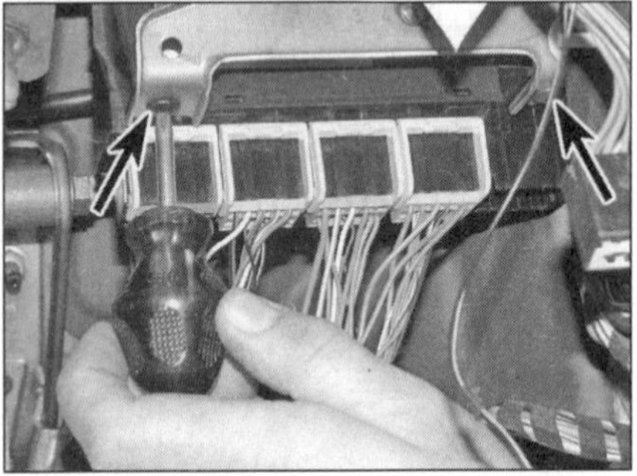
17.7 Remove the two screws, and lower the unit out

19 Exterior mirrors and associated components - removal and refitting

Mirror

Removal

1 On models with manual mirrors, remove the sleeve fitted to the manual adjuster knob by twisting anti-clockwise and pulling it off **(see illustration)**.

2 Remove the door mirror inner trim panel. On models with manual mirrors, first squeeze together the clips located each side of the adjuster knob, then move the panel slightly to the rear to release it from the front clips. On models with electric mirrors, the panel is secured by two (stiff) clips at the front, which should be released first, before unhooking the panel clips at the back edge **(see illustrations)**.

3 On models with electric mirrors, disconnect the mirror switch wiring plug, and remove the panel completely **(see illustration)**.

4 Where applicable, use a small screwdriver to release the mirror wiring from the clip on the door, then separate the two halves of the wiring connector **(see illustrations)**.

5 On models manufactured before 10/2005, remove the single bolt in the centre of the mirror mounting panel. On models manufactured after 10/2005, undo the two screws **(see illustrations)**.

6 Support the mirror, then release the front mounting peg, and withdraw the mirror (and its wiring where applicable) from the outside of the door **(see illustrations)**. On models manufactured before 10/2005, use pliers to squeeze together the securing lugs; on later models, use a small screwdriver to release the peg.

Refitting

7 Refitting is a reversal of removal, noting the following points:

a) Press the mirror firmly onto the door to engage the front mounting peg.

b) On models manufactured before 10/2005, check the condition of the top mounting peg's securing clip, and use a new one if necessary.

c) Tighten the mirror mounting bolt/screws securely.

19.1 Twist and pull to remove the mirror knob cover

19.2a Prise off the door mirror trim panel at the front edge first ...

19.2b ... then unhook it at the back edge

19.3 On models with electric mirrors, disconnect the mirror wiring plug

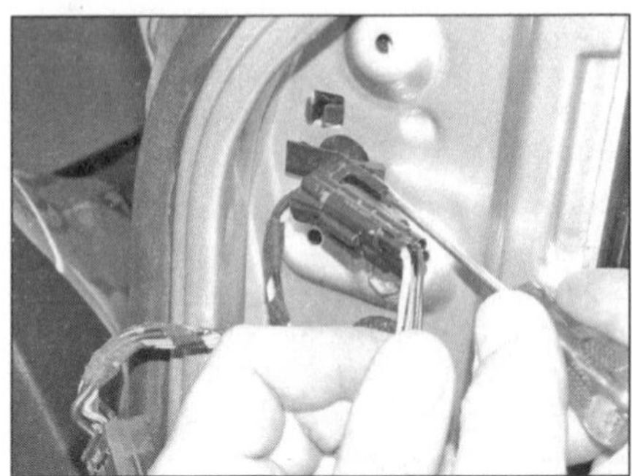
19.4a Unclip the mirror wiring plug ...

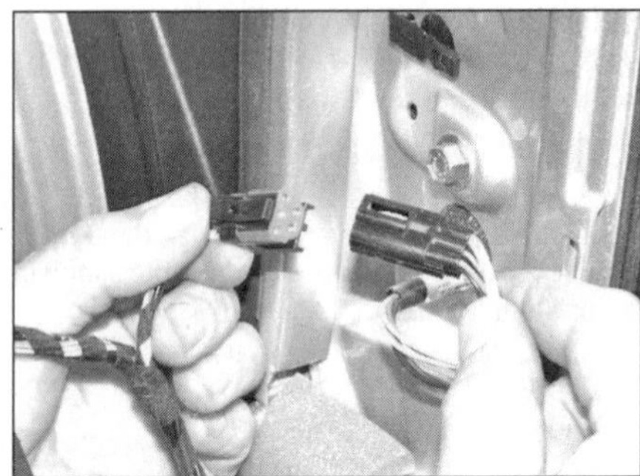
19.4b ... and disconnect it

19.5a Remove the mirror mounting bolt

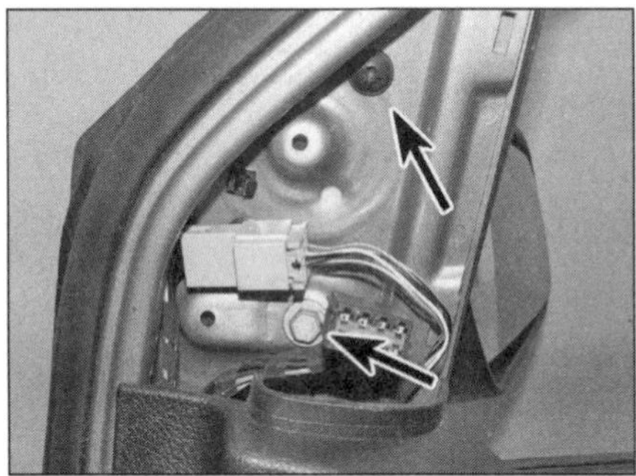
19.5b On later models (10/2005 onwards) undo the two fixings (arrowed)

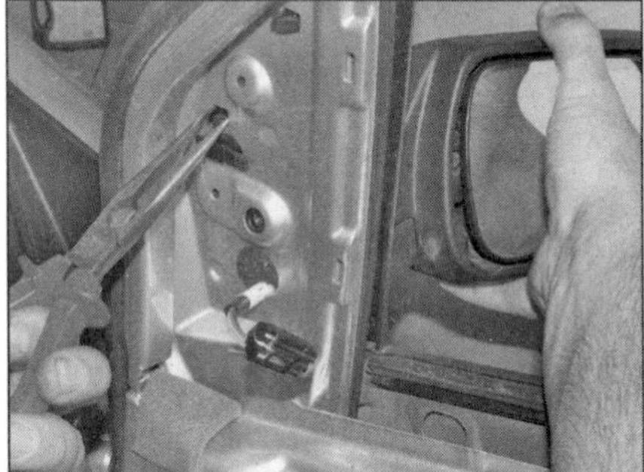
19.6a Squeeze the mirror mounting peg ...

19.6b ... and withdraw the mirror from the door

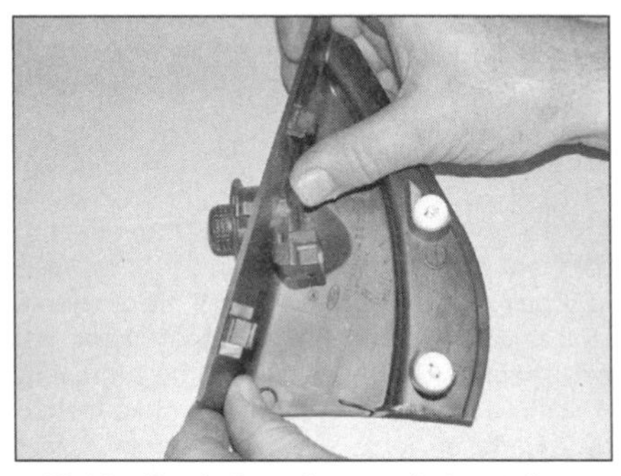
19.11a Push the mirror switch out from behind ...

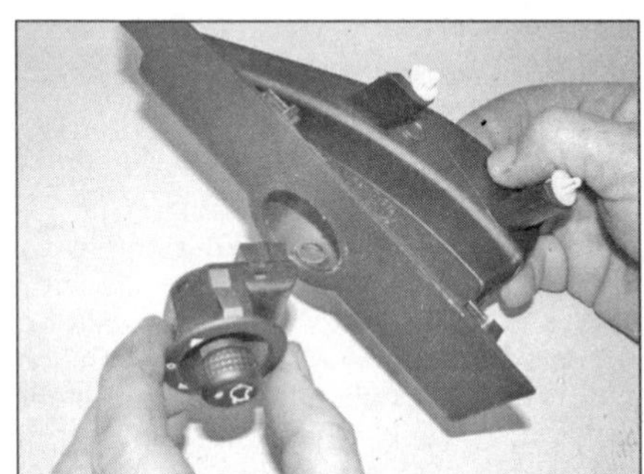
19.11b ... to remove it from the panel

Mirror motor

8 The motor is integral with the mirror, and cannot be renewed separately. If faulty, the complete mirror assembly must be renewed.

Mirror switch

Removal

9 Prise off the door mirror trim panel from the front of the door – this panel is secured by two (stiff) clips at the front, which should be released first, before unhooking the panel clips at the back edge.

10 Disconnect the mirror switch wiring plug, and remove the panel completely.

11 Press the mirror switch out of the mirror trim panel from behind to remove it **(see illustrations)**.

Refitting

12 Refitting is a reversal of removal. Check the operation of the switch before clipping the mirror trim panel back into place.

Mirror glass

Warning: If the mirror glass is broken, wear gloves to protect your hands.

Removal

13 Remove the mirror as described previously in this Section.

14 Press the mirror glass fully in at the inside edge (nearest the car).

15 The glass is hooked over its backplate at the inner edge, with a large clip at the outer edge. Wearing gloves and protecting the surface of the glass with a clean rag, use a broad-bladed

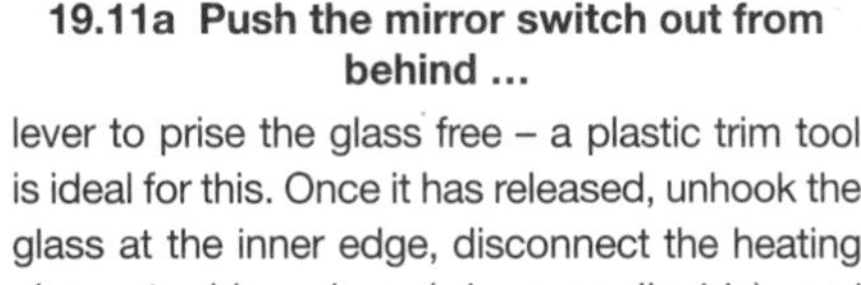
lever to prise the glass free – a plastic trim tool is ideal for this. Once it has released, unhook the glass at the inner edge, disconnect the heating element wiring plugs (where applicable), and remove it **(see illustrations)**.

Refitting

16 Refitting is a reversal of removal. Hook the glass on at the inner edge, then press it firmly on the outer edge until an audible click is heard and the glass locks in position **(see illustrations)**.

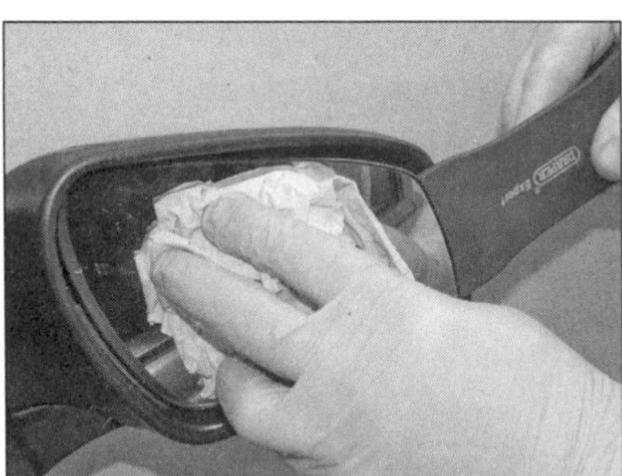
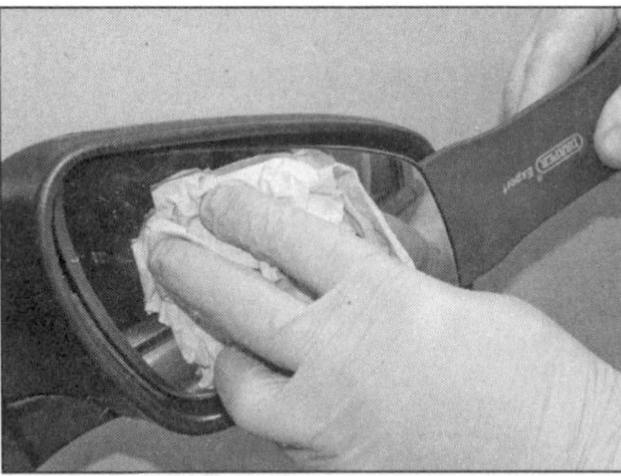
19.15a Prise the outer edge of the mirror glass to unclip it from the backplate

19.15b Once removed, disconnect the heating element wires

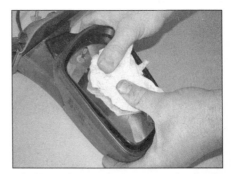

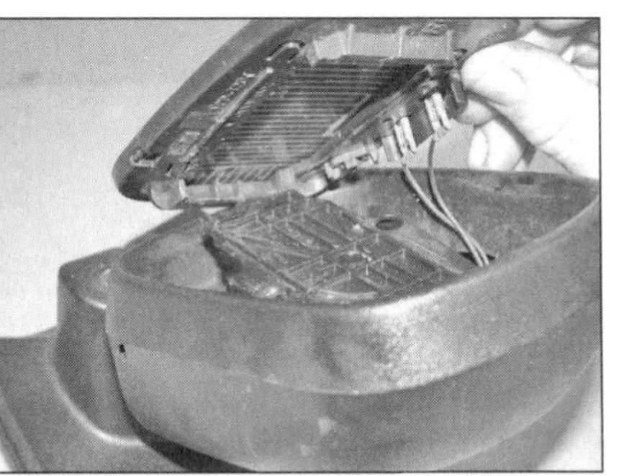
19.16a Hook the glass on at the inner edge ...

19.16b ... then press the outer edge firmly to engage it

22.3a Prise the securing clips with a screwdriver ...

22.3b ... to release the fuel filler lock barrel

20 Windscreen, tailgate and fixed window glass - general information

These areas of glass are secured by the tight fit of the weatherseal in the body aperture, and are bonded in position with a special adhesive. Renewal of such fixed glass is a difficult, messy and time-consuming task, which is considered beyond the scope of the home mechanic. It is difficult, unless one has plenty of practice, to obtain a secure, waterproof fit. Furthermore, the task carries a high risk of breakage; this applies especially to the laminated glass windscreen. In view of this, owners are strongly advised to have this sort of work carried out by one of the many specialist windscreen fitters.

21 Sunroof - general information and adjustment

1 Due to the complexity of the sunroof mechanism, considerable expertise is required to repair and renew the sunroof components successfully. Removal of the roof mechanism first requires the headlining to be removed, which is a tedious operation, and not a task to be undertaken lightly. Therefore, any problems with the sunroof should be referred to a Ford dealer. However adjustment of the sunroof panel is a straightforward operation.

2 To adjust the panel close the sunroof and loosen the adjustment screws on both sides. Place a 1.0 to 1.2 mm thick spacer between the rear edge of the glass and the roof panel. The spacer should be at least 150 mm in length.

3 Push the rear edge up or down so that it lies flush with the roof panel and lightly tighten the rear adjustment screws. Check that the sunroof is located centrally in the roof panel.

4 Adjust the front edge so that it lies flush with the roof panel. Tighten the front adjustment screws and then fully-tighten the rear and centre screws.

5 Remove the spacer and check the operation of the sunroof. Adjust again if necessary.

6 Finally check the sunroof for leaks. If the roof leaks carry out the adjustment procedure and then check that the drain holes (in each corner of the roof opening panel) are clear of debris. If necessary they can be cleared with an airline or with the careful use of a jet of water from a hose pipe.

22 Body exterior fittings - removal and refitting

Radiator grille panel

1 Refer to Section 7.

Bumpers

2 Refer to Section 6.

Fuel filler flap

Removal

3 If required, the filler flap lock barrel can be removed by prising the barrel's securing clips with a small screwdriver **(see illustrations)**.

4 To remove the flap completely, proceed as follows. Loosen the left-hand rear wheel nuts, then jack up the left-hand rear corner of the car, and support it on an axle stand (see *Jacking and vehicle support*). Remove the rear wheel.

5 Prise off the clips securing the wheel arch liner, and pull it down to remove it from under the car.

6 Trace the fuel filler pipe from the flap down inside the wheel arch, and under the car. Remove the screw securing the pipe mounting bracket to the inner wheel arch, and also detach the bracket where the pipe bends to go under the car **(see illustrations)**.

7 Open the fuel filler flap, and remove the filler cap.

8 Inside the wheel arch, gently pull the fuel filler pipe downwards to detach it from the filler flap **(see illustration)**.

9 Twist the filler flap anti-clockwise, until it can be withdrawn from outside the rear wing **(see illustration)**.

Refitting

10 Refitting is a reversal of removal.

Wheel arch liners

11 The wheel arch liners are secured by a combination of self-tapping screws and push-pin clips.

12 The push-pin clips are removed by prising out the centre expanding pin, then prising out the main clip body **(see illustrations)**.

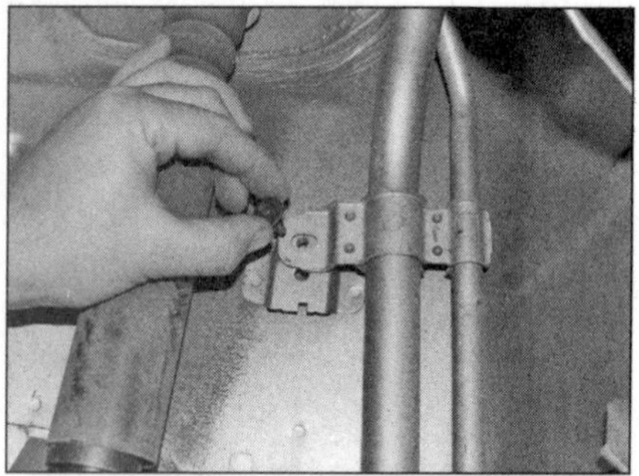
22.6a Remove the filler pipe bracket bolt inside the wheel arch ...

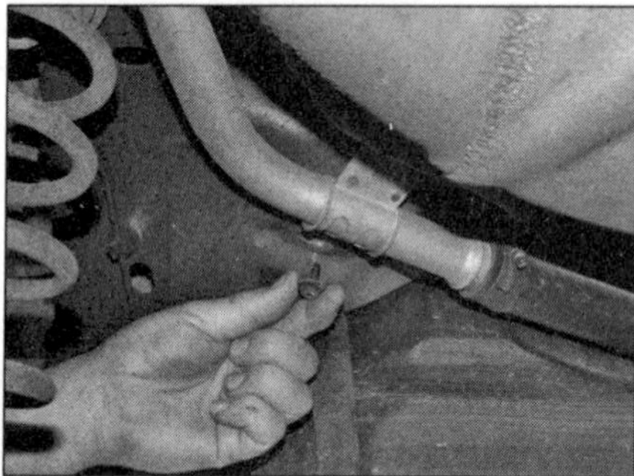
22.6b ... and just under the car

22.8 Pull the filler pipe down so the neck detaches from the filler flap

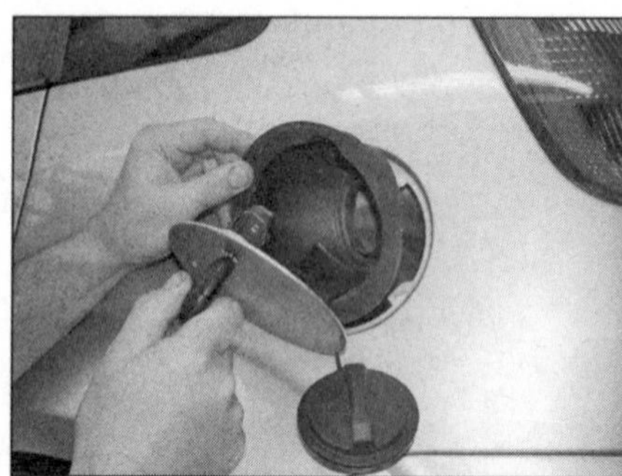
22.9 Twist the filler flap assembly anti-clockwise, and withdraw it

13 The metal star clips used to unscrew from their mounting studs – now the metal tabs have to be prised up at the centre with a small screwdriver to release them **(see illustration)**.

14 With all the fasteners removed, pull the liner down from the arch and remove it **(see illustration)**.

Body trim strips and badges

15 The various body trim strips and badges are held in position with a special adhesive. Removal requires the trim/badge to be heated, to soften the adhesive, and then cut away from the surface. Due to the high risk of damage to the paintwork during this operation, it is recommended that this task should be entrusted to a Ford dealer.

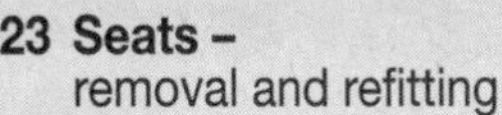

23 Seats – removal and refitting

Front seat

Warning: If removing the passenger seat, disconnect the battery negative lead (see Chapter 5A, Section 2), then wait for two minutes before proceeding. If this waiting period is not observed, there is danger of activating the seat belt tensioner. On models with side airbags (denoted by labels on the sides of the seats), this warning applies when removing either front seat.

1 Slide the seat fully rearwards, then unscrew the two front Torx bolts securing the seat rails to the floor **(see illustrations)**.

2 Slide the seat fully forwards, then unscrew the two rear Torx bolts **(see illustration)**.

3 If the passenger seat (or a driver's seat equipped with side airbag) is being removed, tilt it backwards and disconnect the wiring plug from under the seat **(see illustration)**.

4 Lift the seat, complete with mounting rails, and remove it from the car **(see illustration)**.

5 Refitting is a reversal of removal, but tighten the seat mounting bolts to the specified torque.

Seat back release cable

6 The passenger seat folds flat to allow the transport of long loads. The mechanism is cable-operated and renewal requires a full stripdown of the seat. This is a complex and difficult job.

7 Remove the seat from the vehicle as described in paragraphs 1 to 4 of this Section.

8 Unclip and remove the side panel trims from the seat **(see illustrations)**.

9 Remove the headrest and then remove the

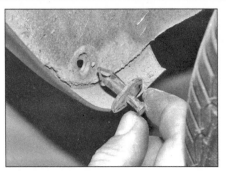

22.12a Prise out the centre pins ...

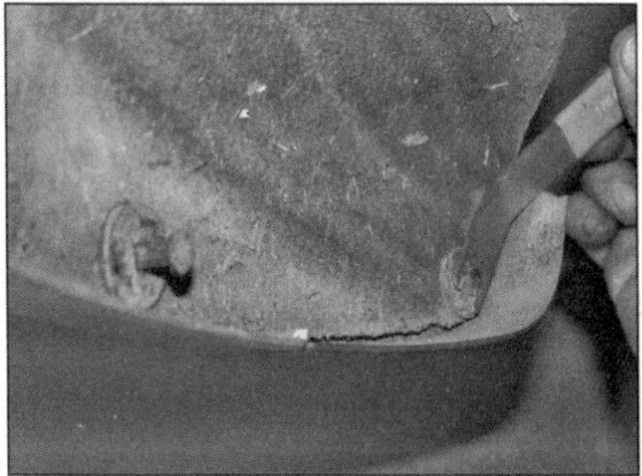

22.12b ... then lever out the main part of the push-pin clips

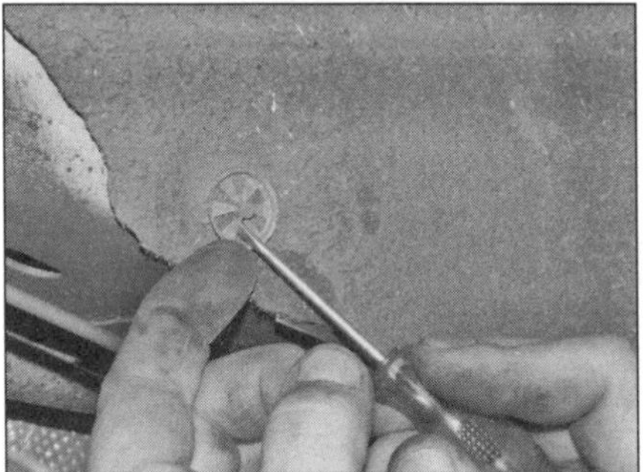

22.13 The star clips are removed by prising with a screwdriver

22.14 Removing a typical arch liner

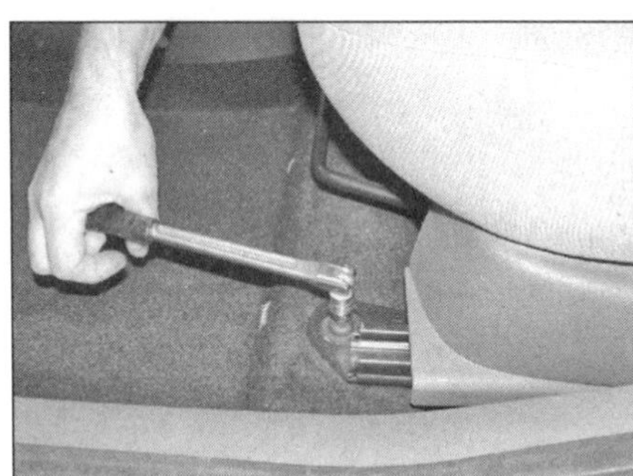

23.1a With the seat slid back, unscrew ...

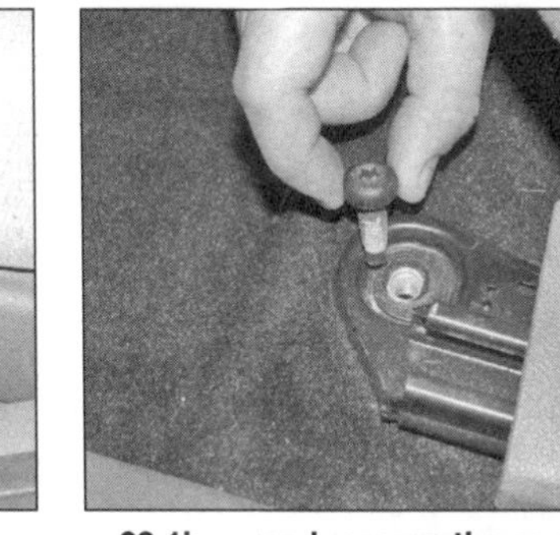

23.1b ... and remove the seat rail front Torx bolt

23.2 Remove the seat rail rear mounting bolts

23.3 Tilt the seat backwards and disconnect any wiring plugs underneath

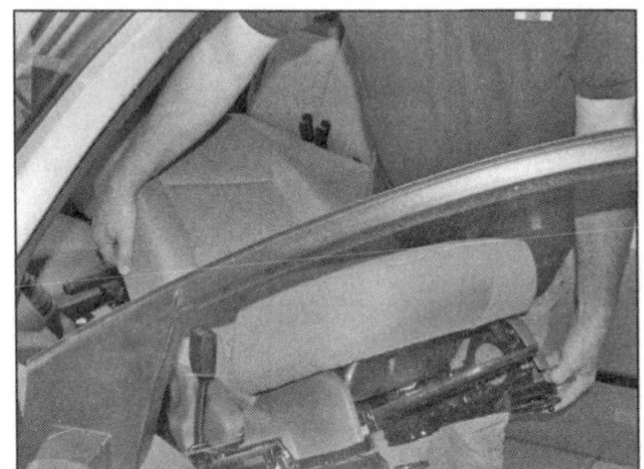

23.4 Lift the seat out of the car

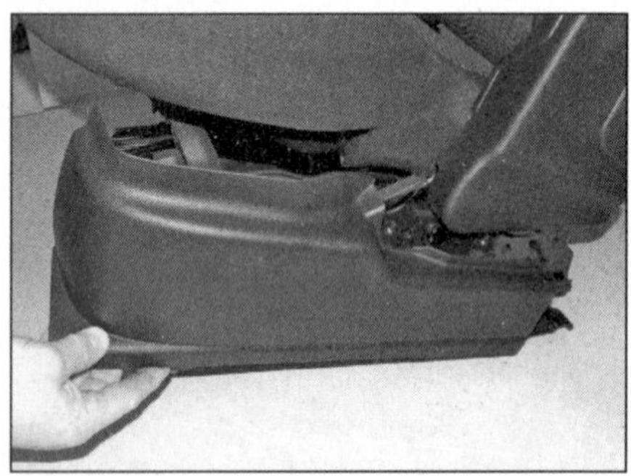

23.8a Remove the side panels ...

23.8b ... and prise off the seat back adjuster knob

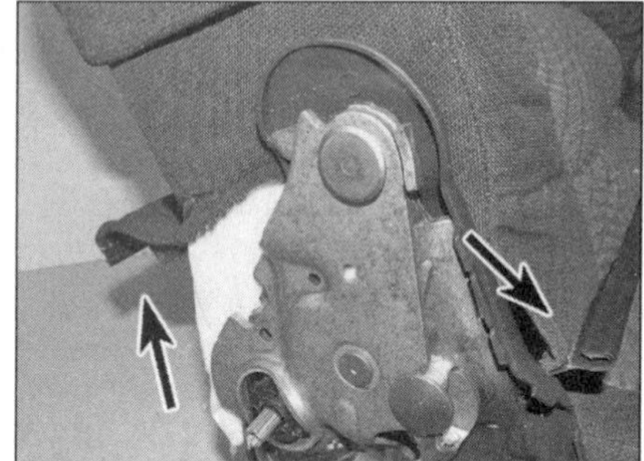

23.10a Unhook the locking strips (arrowed) ...

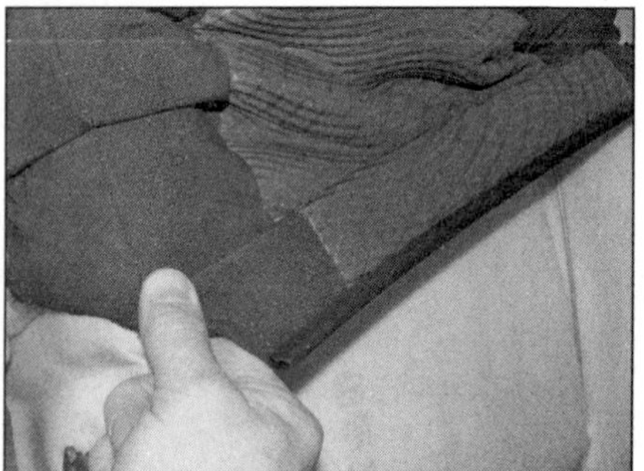

23.10b ... and work the cover up the seat back

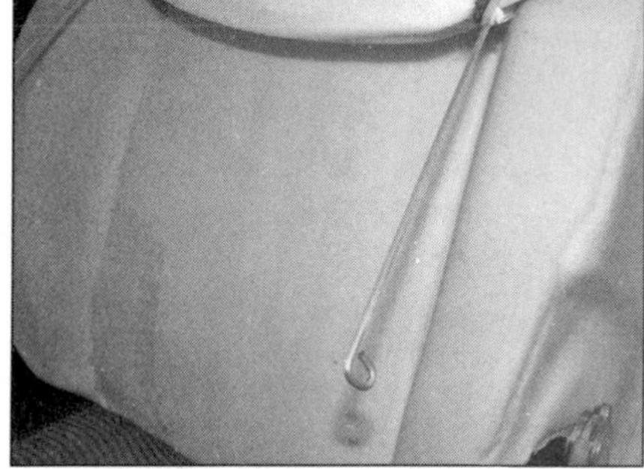

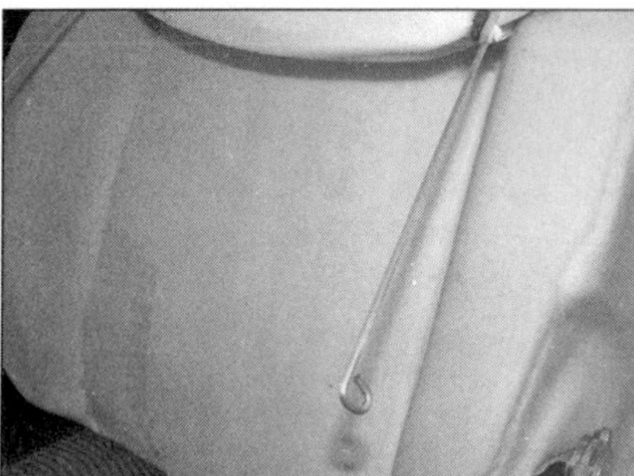

23.11a Release the vertical struts ...

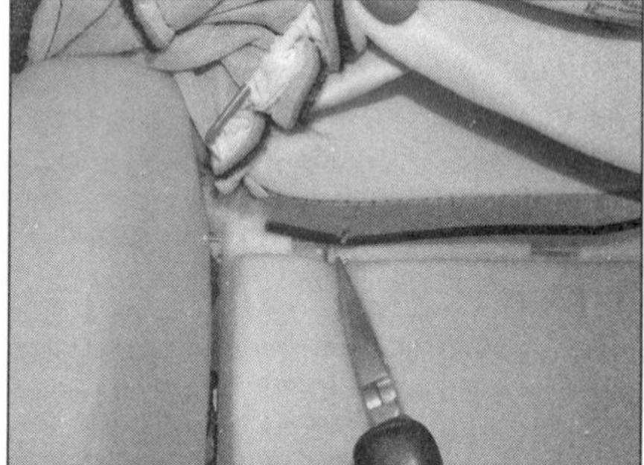

23.11b ... and work the hog rings free from the horizontal strut

blanking plugs from the tray fitted to the seat back. Remove the fixing screws and remove the tray.

10 Unhook the front and rear seat cover locking strips and work the cover up the seat back **(see illustrations)**.

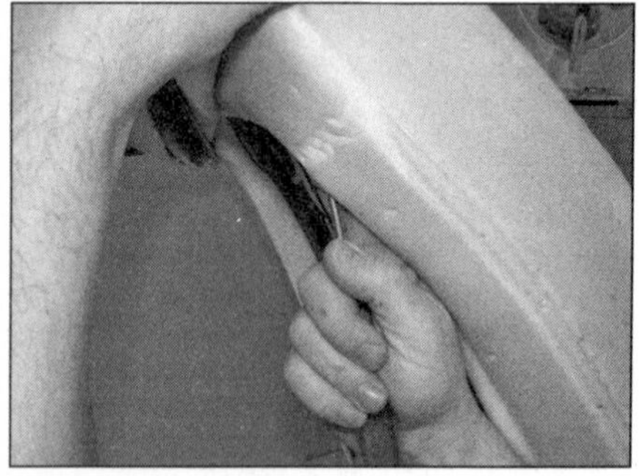

23.12a With difficulty release the handle from the inside ...

11 Unhook the support struts as the cover is removed and then remove the 'hog rings' from the horizontal strut at the top of the seat back **(see illustrations)**.

12 At this point the headrest guides and the release handle should be removed. It is worth attempting to remove them from the outside, but we found this impossible, so we released them from the inside **(see illustrations)**. This proved to be a difficult procedure, with every chance of causing damage to the upholstery, so take your time.

23.12b ... and remove it

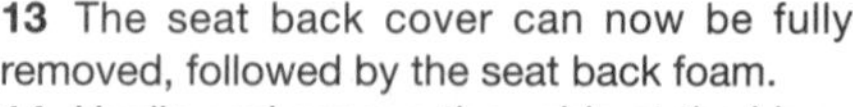

13 The seat back cover can now be fully removed, followed by the seat back foam.

14 Unclip and remove the cable at the hinge and then remove it from seat back **(see illustrations)**.

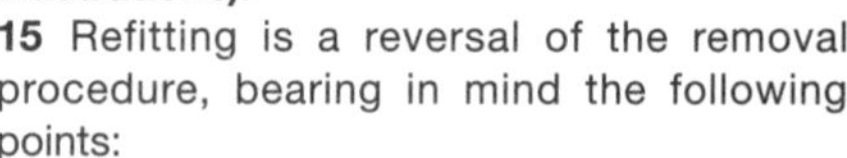

15 Refitting is a reversal of the removal procedure, bearing in mind the following points:

a) *Orientate the inner section of the release handle correctly **(see illustrations)**.*
b) *Ensure the headrest guides are fitted correctly.*
c) *After crimping the hog rings, rotate them so that the ends of the ring are towards the inside of the seat back.*

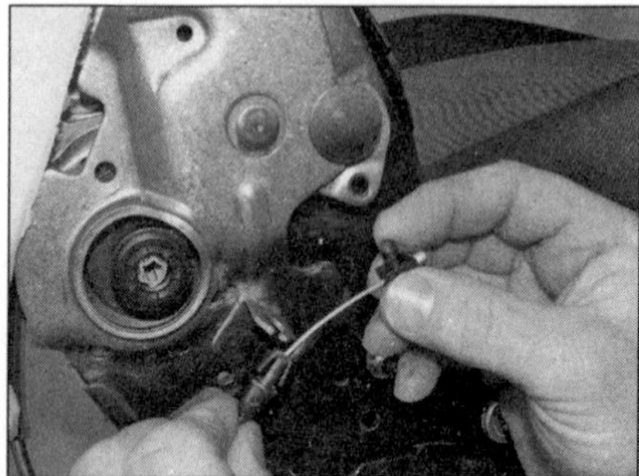

23.14a Release the cable at both sides ...

23.14b ... and remove the cable

23.15a The tabs (arrowed) must interlock correctly

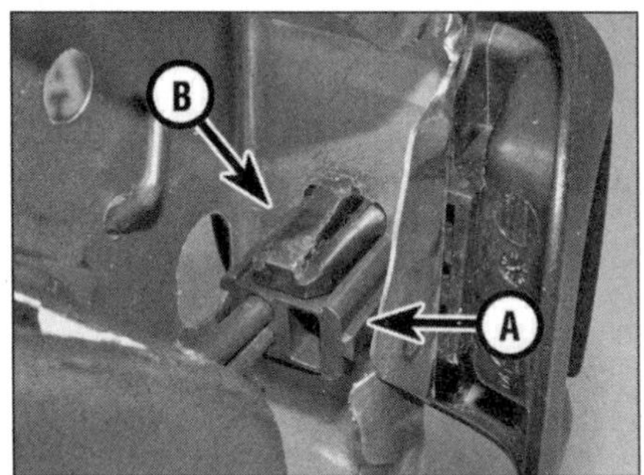

23.15b The release cable housing (A) correctly locked with the handle tabs (B)

23.16 Remove the two rear seat cushion front screws (arrowed)

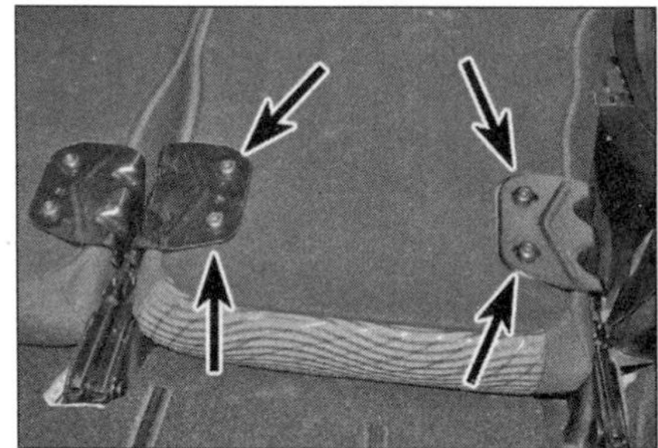

23.20 The seat backs can be removed most easily by unbolting them from the side and centre hinges (arrowed)

Rear seat

Cushion

16 Working at the front lower edge of the seat cushion, remove the two screws securing the seat cushion to the floor **(see illustration)**. Repeat the procedure for the other seat.

17 Lift up the rear of the cushion, and withdraw it from the car.

18 Refitting is a reversal of removal.

Seat back

19 Release the catch, and fold the rear seat back down on top of the cushion.

20 Unscrew the bolts securing the seat back to the hinges, then remove the seat back **(see illustration)**. Repeat the procedure for the other seat.

21 If required the hinge section can now be removed from the floor

22 Refitting is a reversal of removal.

24 Seat belt components – removal and refitting

Front belt

Warning: If removing the driver's seat belt, disconnect the battery negative lead (see Chapter 5A, Section 2), then wait for two minutes before proceeding. If this waiting period is not observed, there is danger of activating the seat belt tensioner.

Removal

1 Move the seat belt height adjuster to its lowest position.

2 Remove the upper and lower B-pillar trim panel(s) as described in Section 25.

3 Hold onto the belt webbing, and unscrew the seat belt lower anchor bolt. Recover the bolt and its spacer, noting how they are fitted **(see illustrations)**.

4 Feed the end of the seat belt through the B-pillar trim panel **(see illustration)**.

5 Unscrew the seat belt upper anchor bolt, and withdraw the upper anchor from the car **(see illustration)**. Ensure that the bolt is removed together with its spacer and washer, and that these components remain together until they are refitted.

6 Detach the seat belt guide loop from the B-pillar by twisting it clockwise, then sliding it downwards.

7 Where fitted, disconnect the wiring plug from the inertia reel pretensioner.

8 Unscrew the inertia reel anchor bolt, then lift the inertia reel out from the door pillar, and withdraw the seat belt assembly **(see illustration)**.

Refitting

9 Refitting is a reversal of removal, but tighten the seat belt bolts to the specified torque. Note that the inertia reel mounting bolt should only be re-used a maximum of five times – stamp the bolt with a centre punch to indicate how many times it has been re-used.

Front belt stalk

Note: *The front seats have a seat belt tensioner system fitted, which is a combination of a regular seat belt stalk and a gas cylinder. Note the routing of the tensioner wiring harness*

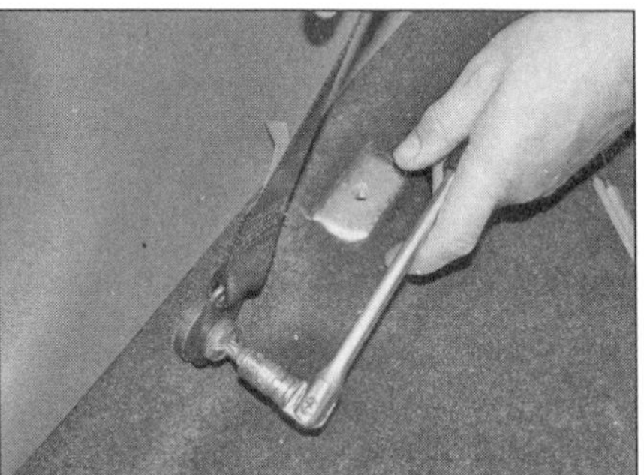

24.3a Unscrew and remove the lower anchor bolt ...

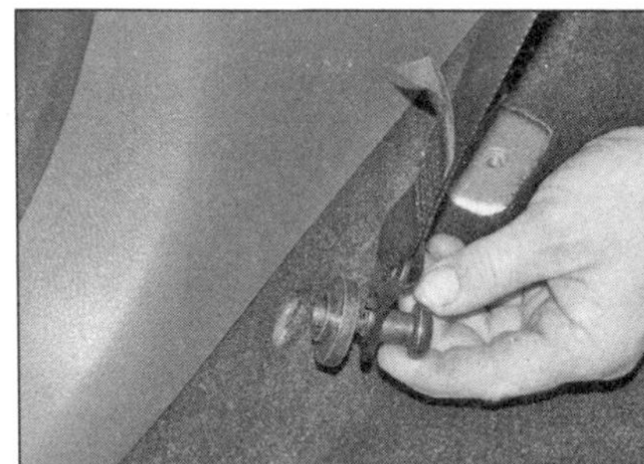

24.3b ... noting how the washers and spacers are fitted

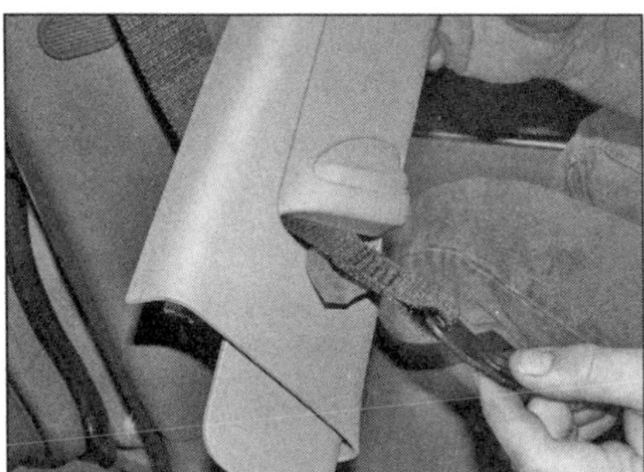

24.4 Feeding the end of the belt through the B-pillar trim panel

24.5 Seat belt upper anchor bolt

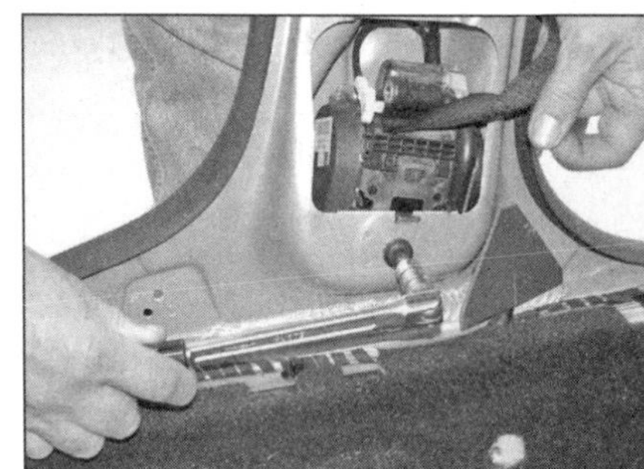

24.8 Unscrew the inertia reel bolt, and remove the seat belt

24.12 Remove the bolt

24.18 Seat belt height adjuster upper bolt

before removal. Handle the tensioner with care once it has been removed.

Removal

10 Remove the front seat (see Section 23) and remove the trim panel from the side of the seat frame.

11 Disconnect the wiring plug at the front of the seat belt tensioner.

12 Unscrew the bolt securing the stalk assembly to the seat frame. Note that the bolt is held captive in the stalk assembly by a paper washer **(see illustration)**.

13 Withdraw the assembly from the seat. On the passenger side seat belt tensioner, handle the assembly by the tensioner barrel, or the buckle – **do not** hold the assembly by the stalk.

Refitting

14 Refitting is a reversal of removal, bearing in mind the following points:

a) Make sure that the stalk is angled towards the seat.
b) Ensure that the passenger seat belt tensioner wiring is routed as noted prior to removal, and cannot become damaged.
c) Tighten the securing bolt to the specified torque.
d) Refit the seat with reference to Section 23.

Front belt height adjuster

Removal

15 Remove the B-pillar trim panel as described in Section 25.

16 Set the height adjuster to its lowest position (it may have to be re-adjusted later, to access the lower mounting bolt – this is a precaution against personal injury, as the adjuster drops down suddenly when triggered).

17 Unscrew the seat belt upper anchor bolt, and withdraw the upper anchor from the car. Ensure that the bolt is removed together with its spacer and washer, and that these components remain together until they are refitted.

18 The height adjuster is secured by two further bolts, one top and one bottom **(see illustration)**. Remove the bolts and withdraw the adjuster from the car.

Refitting

19 Refitting is a reversal of removal. Tighten the bolts to the specified torque.

Rear side belt

Removal

20 With reference to Section 25, remove the parcel shelf, parcel shelf the boot side trim panel and the D- pillar lower scuff panel.

21 Remove the cover and then unbolt the seat belt upper anchor **(see illustrations)**. Ensure that the bolt is removed together with its spacer and washer, and that these components remain together until they are refitted.

22 Unbolt and remove the lower mounting point.

23 Remove the rear seat latch assembly **(see illustrations)**.

24 Undo the bolt and unhook the inertia reel from the locating tangs. Remove the inertia reel from the vehicle.

Refitting

25 Refitting is a reversal of removal. Tighten the bolts to the specified torque.

Rear centre belt

Removal

26 Detach the back rest cover. Discard the carpet cover from the seat back. Remove the two screws and take out the access cover from the backrest **(see illustrations)**.

27 At the top of the seat, unclip the seat belt trim panel, and feed the webbing through the side **(see illustration)**.

28 Unscrew the inertia reel mounting nut, and turn the reel slightly, for access to the backrest interlock cable **(see illustrations)**. The interlock cable prevents the seat belt operating unless the backrest is locked in the upright position.

24.21a Remove the cover ...

24.21b ... and then remove the bolt

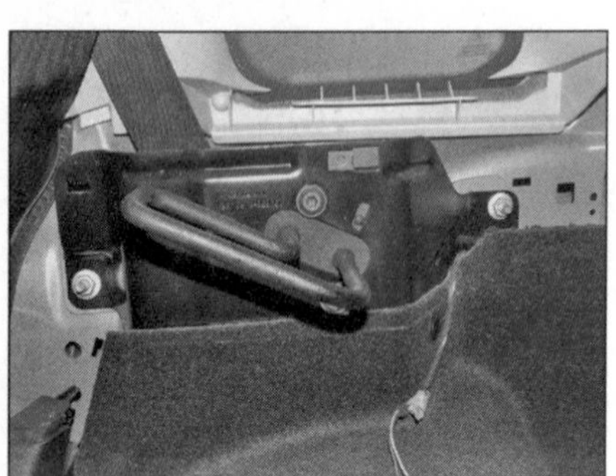
24.23a Unbolt and remove ...

24.23b ... the latch assembly

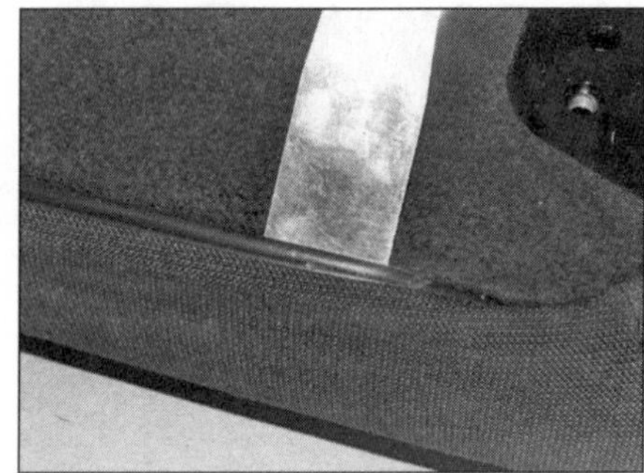
24.26a Release the rear seat back cover

24.26b Remove the two cross-head screws ...

24.26c ... and remove the backrest access cover

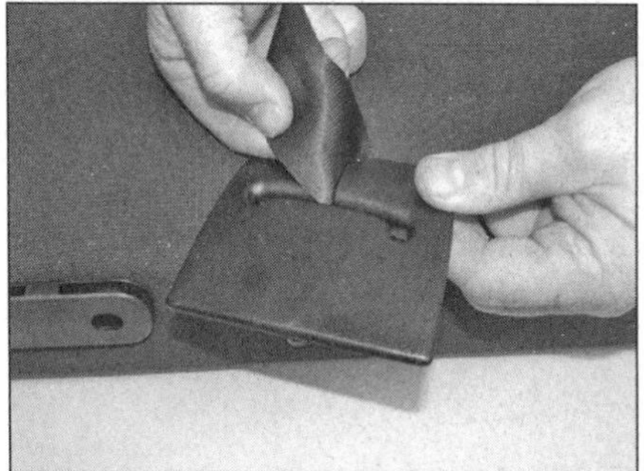
24.27 Unclip the top trim panel from the seat, and feed the seat belt through

24.28a Remove the inertia reel mounting nut ...

24.28b ... and turn it sideways to access the interlock cable

24.29 Unhook the inner cable, then unclip the outer cable

29 Unhook the inner cable end fitting from the side of the inertia reel, then unclip the outer cable **(see illustration)**.

30 Unbolt the lower anchor, unclip the seat belt buckles, and the inertia reel can be removed from the car **(see illustrations)**.

Refitting

31 Refitting is a reversal of removal, but note that the seat back cover will require renewal. Tighten the bolts to the specified torque.

Rear buckles

Removal

32 With the rear seat cushion tipped forwards, the rear seat belt buckles can be unbolted from the floor and removed **(see illustrations)**.

Refitting

33 Refitting is a reversal of removal. Tighten the bolts to the specified torque.

25 Interior trim and fittings - removal and refitting

General

1 The interior trim panels are secured by a combination of clips and screws, with easily-broken plastic clips featuring heavily. Removal and refitting is generally self-explanatory, noting that it may be necessary to remove or loosen surrounding panels to allow a particular panel to be removed. The following paragraphs describe the removal and refitting of the major panels in more detail.

Door inner trim panels

2 Refer to Section 12.

Steering column shrouds

Upper shroud

3 From the straight-ahead position, turn the steering wheel to the side to access the prising point, then use a screwdriver (or suitable trim tool) to prise up the upper shroud **(see illustration)**. Turn the wheel to the other side, and release the second clip.

4 The shroud can now be lifted up, but it will still be attached by a rubber 'gaiter' to the base of the instrument panel, and cannot be removed.

5 On early models (up to 10/2005) carefully unclip the hood/surround panel from the instrument cluster, and remove it **(see illustration)**.

6 Using a screwdriver, carefully prise down the rubber gaiter to release the securing tabs from the base of the instrument cluster. Now

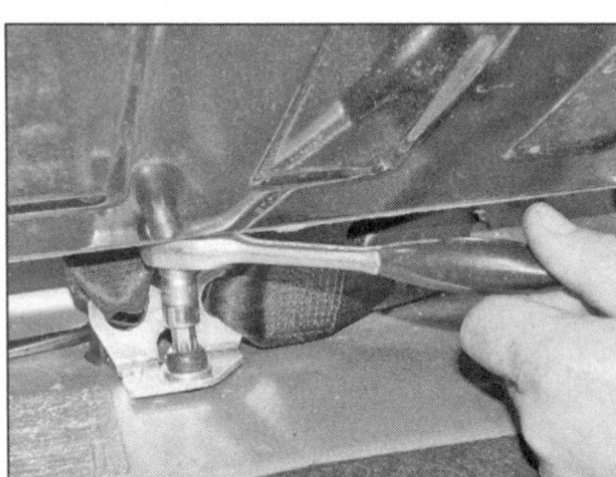
24.30a Unbolt the lower anchor plate

24.30b Removing the centre inertia reel

24.32 The rear seat belt buckles can be unbolted with the seat cushion tipped forwards

25.3 Turn the wheel to one side, and release the upper shroud

25.5 Remove the shroud from the instrument panel

25.6a Unclip the gaiter ...

25.6b ... and remove the upper shroud

the upper shroud can be removed completely **(see illustrations)**.

7 Refitting is a reversal of removal.

Lower shroud

8 The lower shroud is clipped to the upper

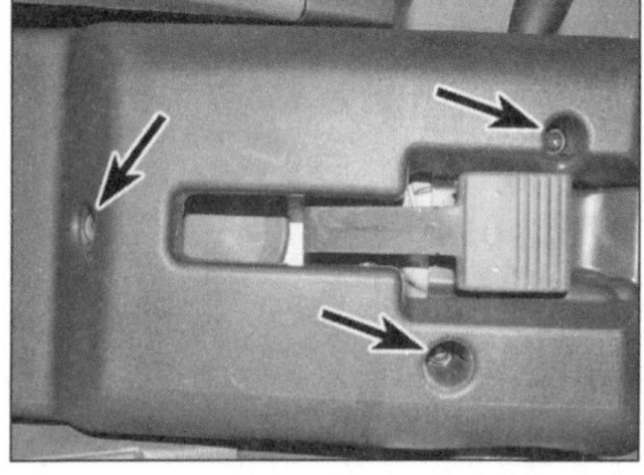
25.8 Steering column lower shroud screws – seen from below

shroud at the top, at either side, and is further secured by three screws underneath **(see illustration)**. On models with remote audio controls on the lower shroud, use a small screwdriver to release the locking tang at the back of the switch, then remove the switch and disconnect the wiring.

9 Remove the three screws, then lower the steering column height adjuster lever, and remove the lower shroud. If the upper shroud is still in place, the lower shroud will have to be unclipped from it during removal.

10 Refitting is a reversal of removal.

Driver's lower facia trim panel

11 The panel is secured by five screws (two inside the small storage compartment) and one clip (at the top left – pull the panel towards you to release it) **(see illustration)**.

12 Refitting is a reversal of removal.

Sill trim panels

13 Pull away the rubber door seals, and remove the B-pillar lower trim panel **(see illustration)**. It may be necessary to partly remove the B-pillar upper trim panel, which is also clipped in place at the bottom.

14 The sill trim panels are clipped in place. Several clips are used, and some are quite stiff to release – start at one end of the panel, and pull the panel back as it is released. Check whether any of the clips pull out of the panel, to be left on the car – transfer them back to the panel before refitting **(see illustrations)**.

15 Refitting is a reversal of removal.

A-pillar trim panel

16 Open the door, and carefully prise the rubber door seal from the edge of the door aperture.

17 The A-pillar trim panels are clipped in place. Several clips are used, and some

25.11 Driver's lower facia panel screws (arrowed)

25.13 Unclip the B-pillar lower trim panel

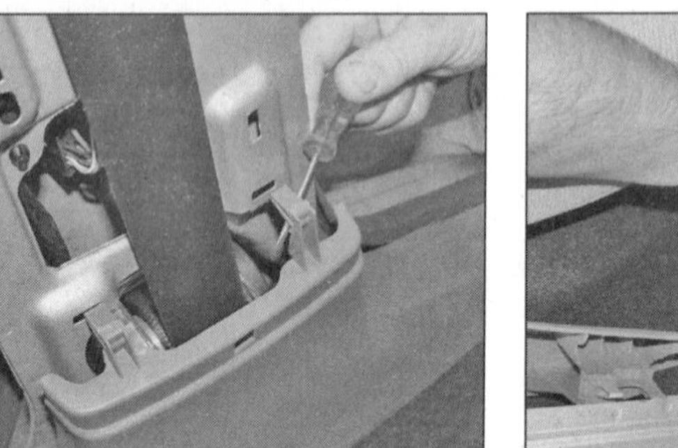
25.14a Start by removing the sill trim panels by unhooking two clips by the seat belt reel

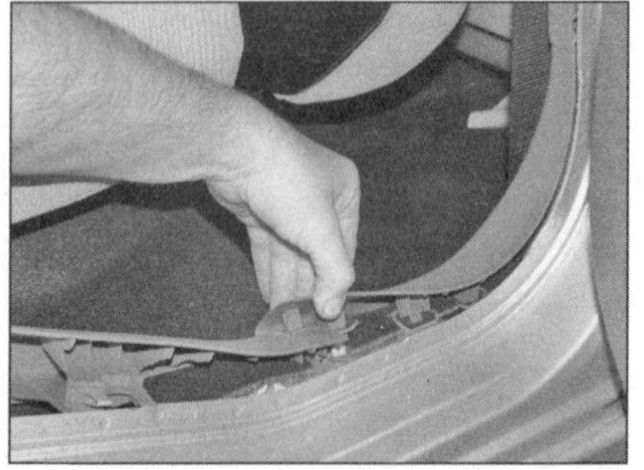
25.14b Lift the back end of the sill trim panel to release the locating pegs

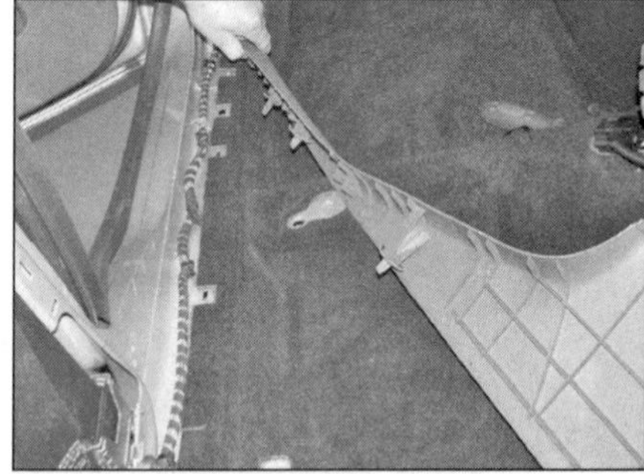
25.14c The sill trim panel is secured by many clips ...

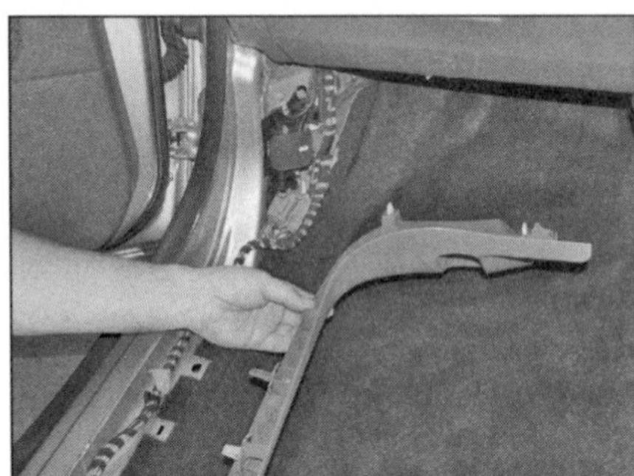
25.14d ... which extend all the way to the front footwells

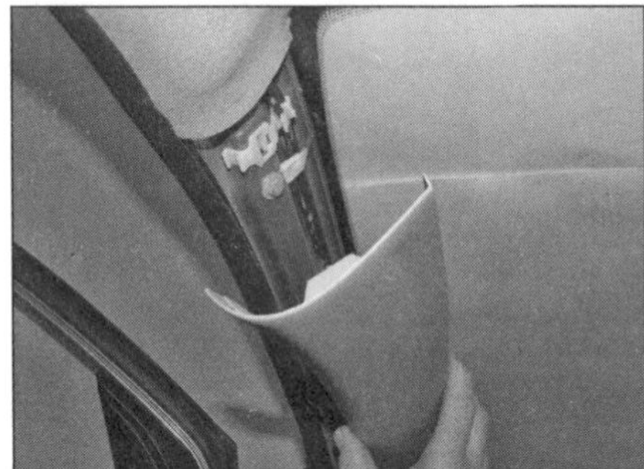
25.17a The A-pillar trim panels are best released from the top

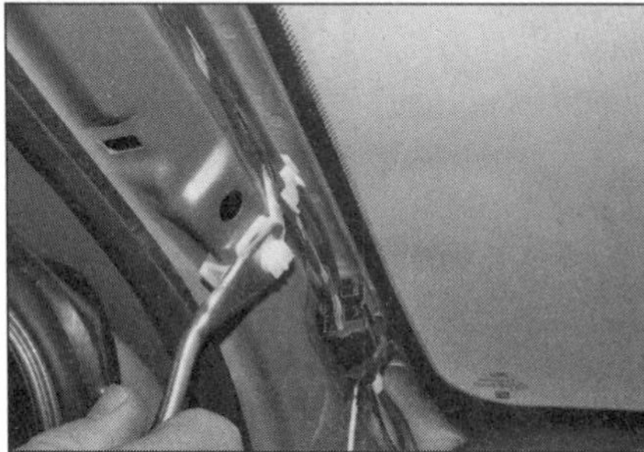
25.17b Remove any clips which stay in the pillar, and put them back in the trim panel mounts

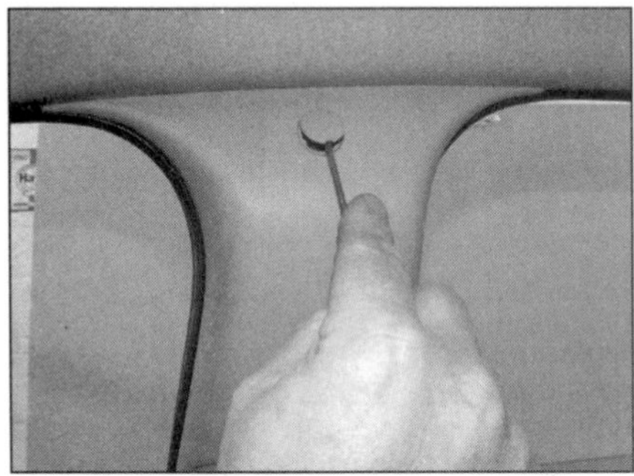
25.21a Remove the upper screw cover ...

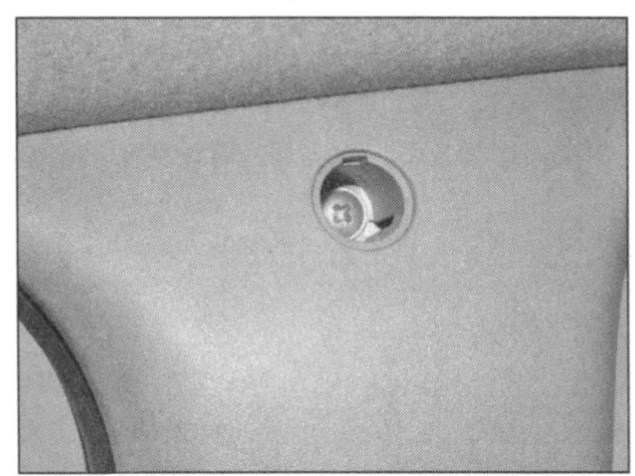
25.21b ... remove the screw ...

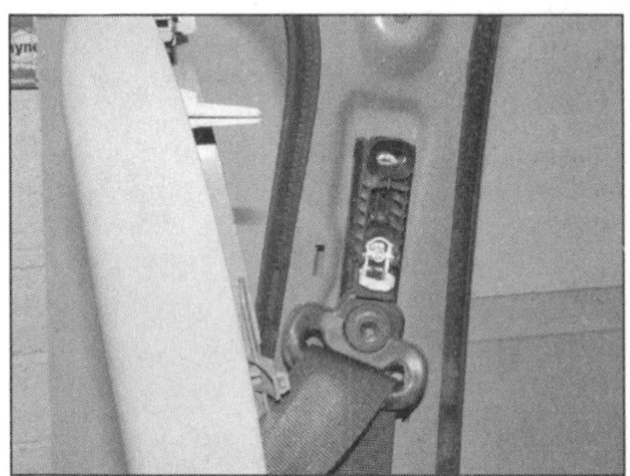
25.21c ... and then unclip the B-pillar upper trim panel

are quite stiff to release – start at the top of the panel, and pull the panel back as it is released. Check whether any of the clips pull out of the panel, to be left on the car – transfer them back to the panel before refitting **(see illustrations)**.

18 Refitting is a reversal of removal.

B-pillar trim panels

19 Detach the rubber weatherstrip from the B-pillar as necessary to free the edges of the trim panel.

20 Hold onto the belt webbing, and unscrew the seat belt lower anchor bolt. Recover the bolt and its spacer, noting how they are fitted.

21 Prise out the trim cap and remove the trim panel upper screw, then release the upper panel from the clip at the front and rear **(see illustrations)**. Pass the seat belt through the panel, and remove it.

22 If required, remove the B-pillar lower trim panel, which is secured by a total of four clips **(see illustration 25.13)**.

23 Refitting is a reversal of removal.

Rear trim panels

C-pillar trim panel

24 Pull off the rubber seals from the rear door and tailgate apertures, in the area adjoining the trim panel.

25 Remove the parcel shelf support panel on the side concerned, as described later in this Section.

26 Remove the rear seat belt upper mounting **(see illustration 24.21b)**.

27 Prise out the trim panel retaining clip at the top rear of the panel **(see illustration)**.

28 Prise off the screw cover and remove the single screw at the top of the panel, just inside the rear door **(see illustration)**.

29 Unclip the C-pillar trim panel **(see illustration)**.

30 If required the lower section of the panel can now be removed. These panels are just an extension of the door sill trims, and are easily unclipped.

31 Refitting is a reversal of removal. Tighten the rear seat belt lower anchor bolt to the specified torque.

Parcel shelf support

32 Detach the rubber weatherstrip from the tailgate and rear door aperture as necessary to free the edges of the trim panel.

33 Remove the parcel shelf.

34 Remove the two cross-head screws, then unclip the parcel shelf support at the front and remove it**(see illustrations)**. On the right-hand

25.27 Remove the clip

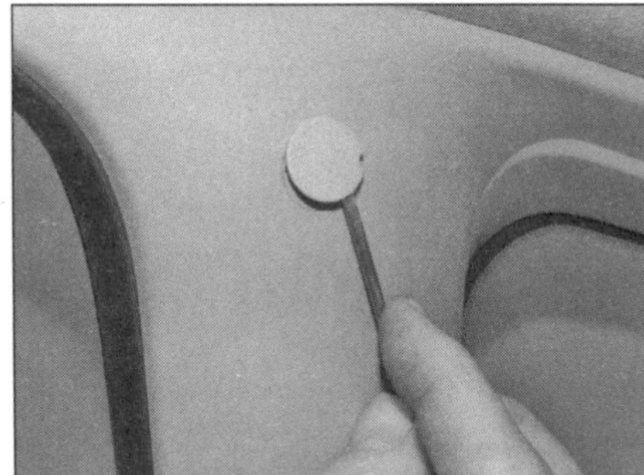
25.28 Remove the screw cover

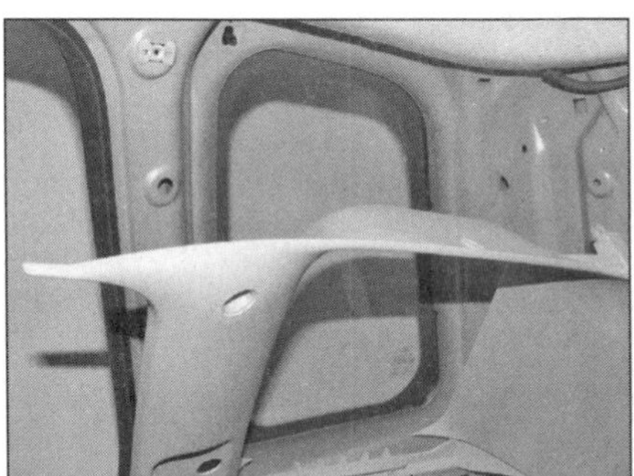
25.29 Remove the trim

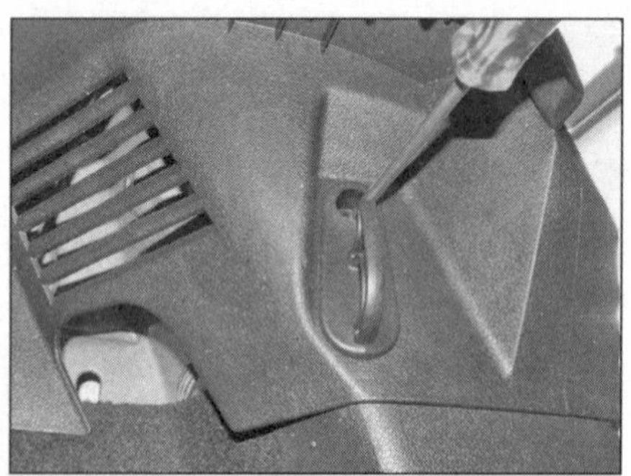
25.34a Remove the rear fixing ...

25.34b ... and the front fixing

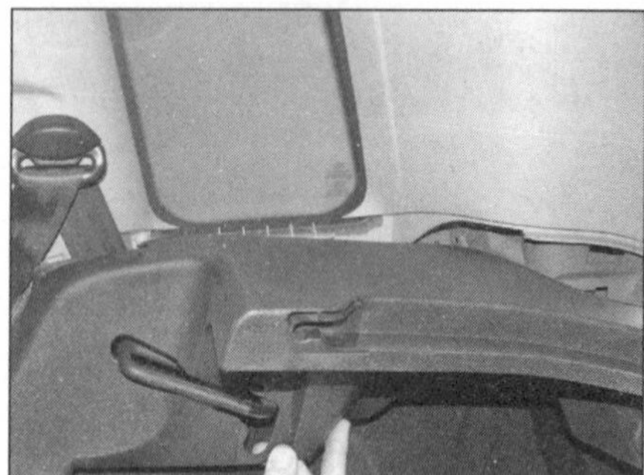
25.34c Remove the panel

25.36 Remove the scuff panel

25.38 Prise the panel free

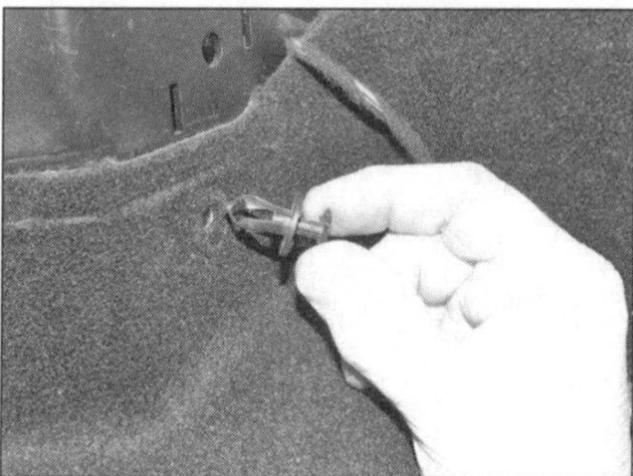
28.41 Remove the trim clips

panel, disconnect the boot light wiring plug as the panel is withdrawn.

35 Refitting is a reversal of removal.

Load area panels

Tailgate scuff panel

36 Prise up the panel and remove it **(see illustration)**.

37 Refitting is a reversal of removal.

D-pillar trim panels

38 Remove the tailgate scuff panel (as described above) and then prise free the trim panel **(see illustration)**.

39 Refitting is a reversal of removal.

Load area side panels

40 The side panels are held in place by several trim clips. They are also partially trapped in position by the shelf support panel and the D-pillar trim panels.

41 Prise free and remove the trim clips **(see illustration)**. The panel can now be released from the adjoining trim panels.

42 Refitting is a reversal of removal, but it may be necessary to remove the parcel shelf support to refit the panel.

Carpets

43 The passenger compartment floor carpet is in several pieces, and is secured along the edges by various types of clips.

44 Carpet removal and refitting is reasonably straightforward, but time-consuming, due to the fact that all adjoining trim panels must be released, and the seats and centre console must be removed.

Headlining

45 The headlining is clipped to the roof, and can be withdrawn only once all fittings such as the grab handles, sunvisors, sunroof, front, centre and rear pillar trim panels, and associated components have been removed **(see illustrations)**. The door, tailgate and sunroof aperture weatherseals will also have to be prised clear.

46 Note that headlining removal requires considerable skill and experience if it is to be carried out without damage, and is therefore best entrusted to an expert.

47 On models equipped with side curtain airbags, note that the curtain airbag units are contained within the headlining, and it may therefore be dangerous to proceed with removing the headlining unless the battery is first disconnected (see Chapter 12, Section 21).

Roof console

48 Prise out the interior light, then disconnect the wiring and remove it.

49 On models with an electric sunroof, prise out the sunroof switch surround panel from the console, then disconnect the wiring from the switch, and remove the panel from the car.

50 On models with a manual sunroof, remove the sunroof operating handle by opening it out and removing the single securing screw from the handle. Prise out and remove the handle surround panel from the roof console.

51 The roof console is now secured by two screws above the interior light location, two central clips inside the sunroof switch/handle trim panel, and a further clip at the rear. Remove the screws, release the clips, and remove the roof console.

52 Refitting is a reversal of removal.

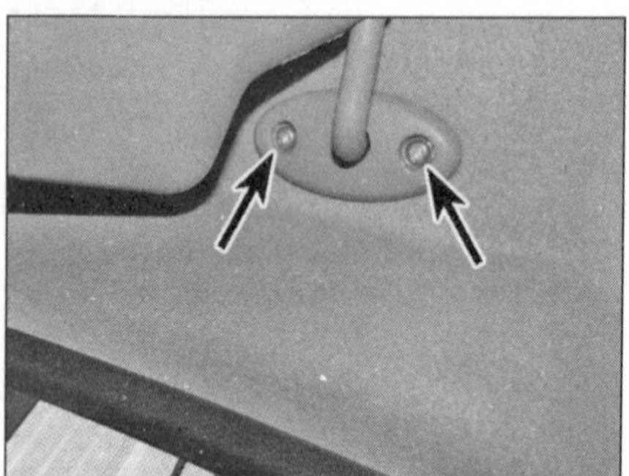
25.45a Sunvisor mounting screws

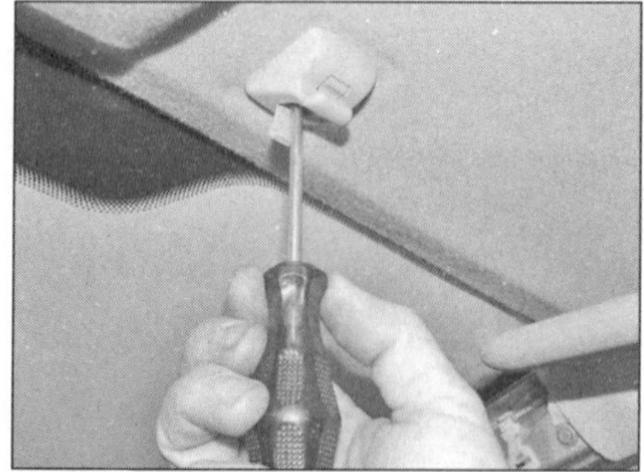
25.45b Removing the screw from the sunvisor mounting clip

25.53a Press the side stops inwards to fully lower the glovebox

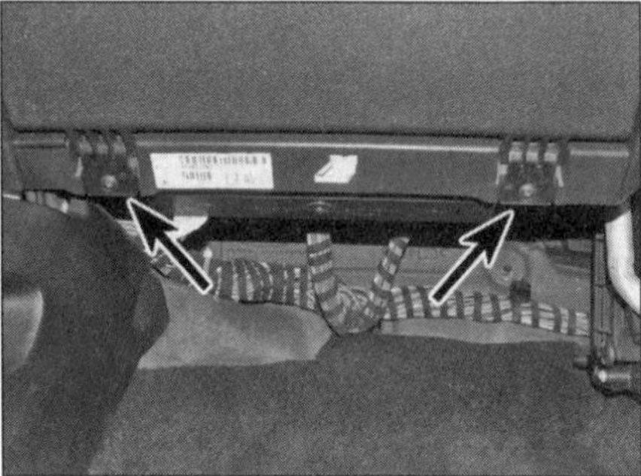
25.53b On early models remove the screws (arrowed) ...

25.53c ... on later models pull the glovebox free ...

25.53d ... and remove it

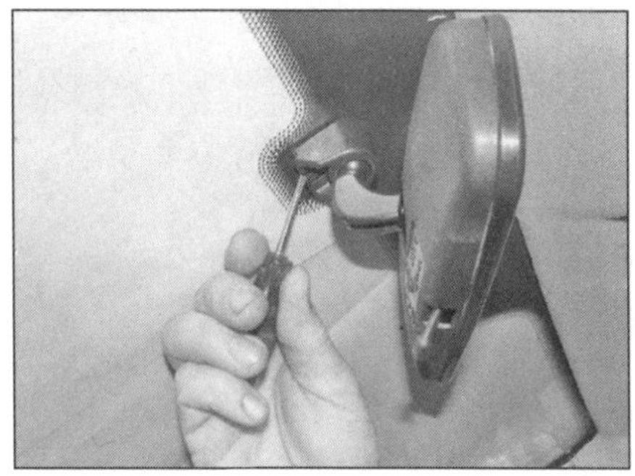
25.55 Release the mirror retaining tab ...

25.56 ... and remove it from the windscreen

Glovebox

53 Open the glovebox, and press the sides inwards to release the stops, which allows the glovebox to be opened further than normal. On models built up to 10/2005 remove the screw from each hinge at the base of the glovebox, and slide it out of the facia completely. On later models the glovebox can be pulled free from the lower hinge **(see illustrations)**.

54 Refitting is a reversal of removal.

Interior mirror

55 Support the mirror then, using a small screwdriver, release the retaining tab at the front of the mirror mounting **(see illustration)**.

56 Remove the mirror from the windscreen **(see illustration)**.

57 Refitting is a reversal of removal. Ensure that the mirror is firmly clipped back into place.

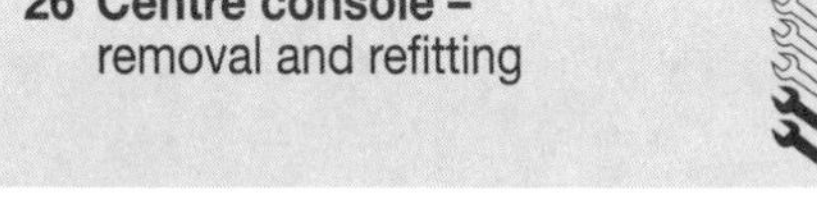

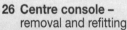

26 Centre console – removal and refitting

Removal

1 Where applicable, prise out the power outlet socket fitted into the handbrake trim panel, at the rear, and disconnect the wiring plug beneath it.

2 Unclip the handbrake lever trim panel first at the rear, and remove it over the handbrake lever **(see illustration)**.

3 Carefully prise up the plastic trim ring at the base of the gear lever, and remove it over the gear lever (the rubber gaiter stays behind) **(see illustrations)**.

4 Unclip the gear lever trim panel from the top of the centre console by carefully prising it up to release the clips. Once the panel has been lifted, disconnect the wiring plugs from the cigar lighter and/or power outlet socket, as applicable, then remove the panel over the gear lever **(see illustrations)**. On later models disconnect the audio unit auxiliary input socket.

5 Remove the single screw fitted at the front

26.2 Unclip the handbrake lever trim panel, then lift it off

26.3a Taking care not to mark the trim, prise up ...

26.3b ... and remove the gear lever trim ring

26.4a Unclip and lift up the gear lever trim panel ...

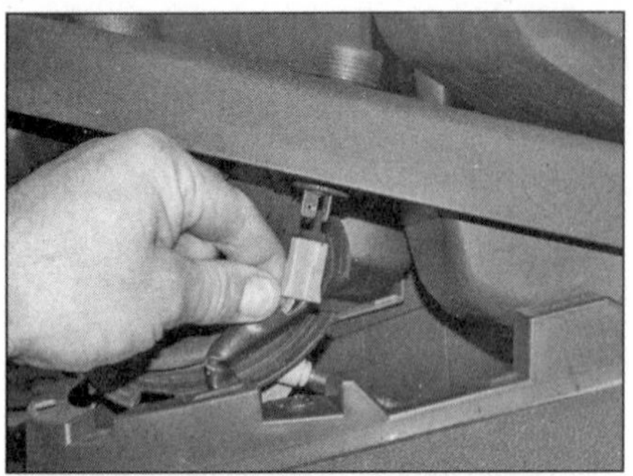
26.4b ... disconnecting the cigar lighter wiring as it becomes accessible

26.5a Remove the single screw at the front ...

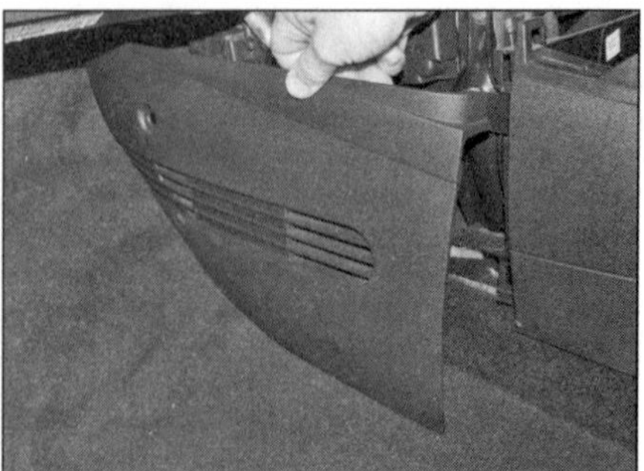
26.5b ... then unhook the console side panels at the rear edges

26.6a Remove the screw each side at the front ...

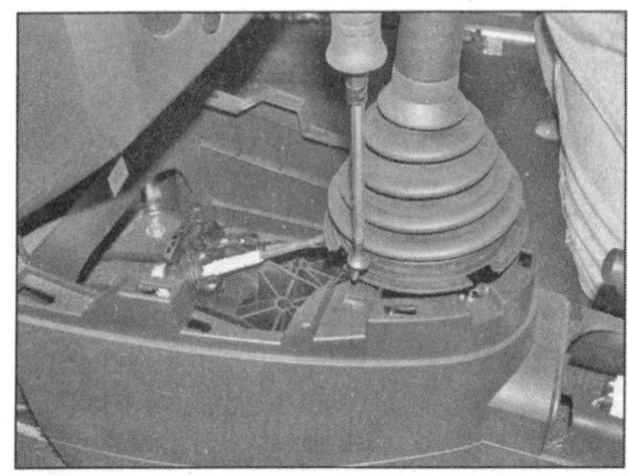
26.6b ... one screw either side of the gear lever ...

26.6c ... and one behind the handbrake ...

of the console front side panels, and remove the panels on both sides **(see illustrations)**.

6 The centre console is now secured by a total of five screws – one either side at the front, at floor level, one either side of the gear lever, and one at the rear, behind the handbrake. Remove the screws, then slide the console back and upwards to remove it **(see illustrations)**.

Refitting

7 Refitting is a reversal of removal.

27 Facia assembly – removal and refitting

Note: *This is a difficult procedure, carried out in two stages – removing the plastic facia panel, and then the large metal crossmember underneath it, which involves disconnecting large sections of the car's wiring loom. Both facia sections have to be removed, for example, to gain access to the heater assembly. It is strongly recommended that this Section is read through thoroughly before starting the procedure.*

Models made before 10/2005

Removal

1 Disconnect the battery negative lead, with reference to Chapter 5A, Section 2 then wait for two minutes before proceeding. If this waiting period is not observed, there is danger of activating the airbags.

2 Remove the passenger airbag as described in Chapter 12, Section 22.

3 Remove the centre console as described in Section 26.

4 Remove the steering column assembly as described in Chapter 10, Section 15.

5 Remove the radio/CD player as described in Chapter 12, Section 17.

6 Remove the instrument panel as described in Chapter 12, Section 11.

7 Remove the A-pillar trim panels as described in Section 25.

8 Release the diagnostic connector plug fitted below the steering column location, by pivoting down the locking collar and removing the wiring plug **(see illustration)**.

9 Remove the hazard warning light switch, passenger airbag deactivation switch (where applicable) and tailgate release button, as described in Chapter 12, Section 4.

10 At either end of the facia, remove the outer side trim panels, which are secured by a single cross-head screw **(see illustrations)**.

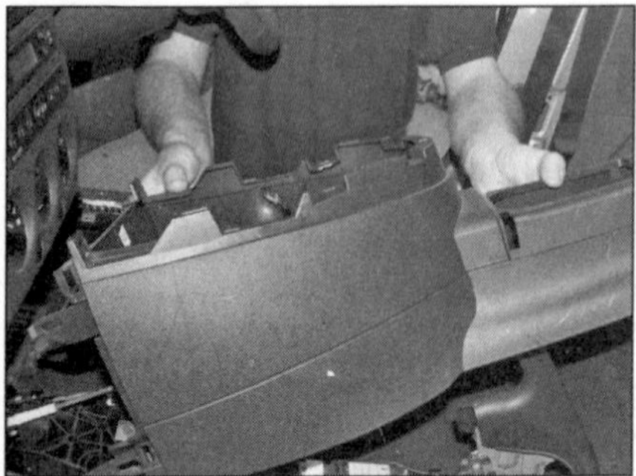
26.6d ... then slide the console back and lift it out

27.8 Pivot down the plastic locking collar and detach the diagnostic plug

27.10a Remove the single screw at the top ...

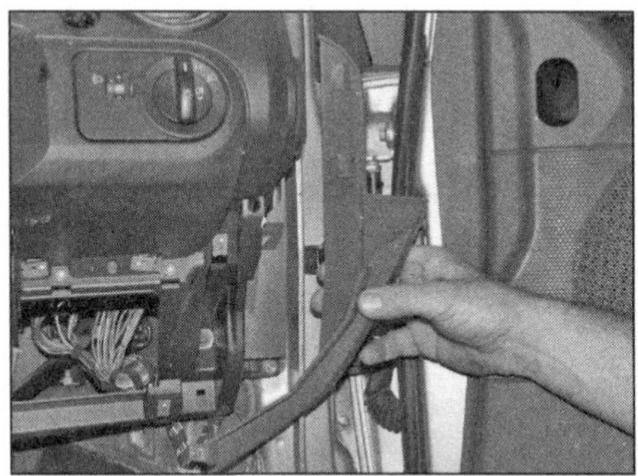
27.10b ... then unclip and remove the outer side panels

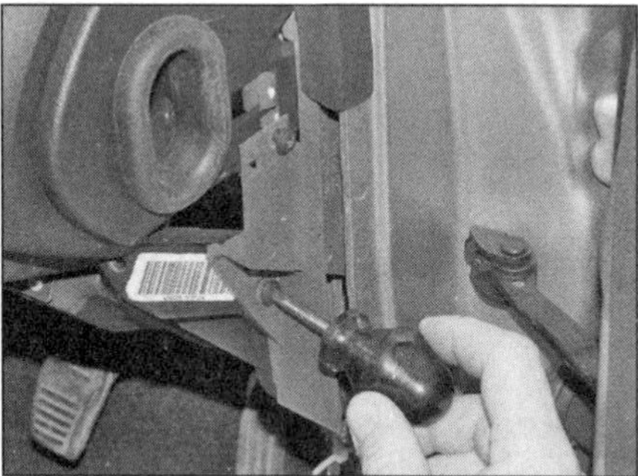
27.11a Remove the two screws ...

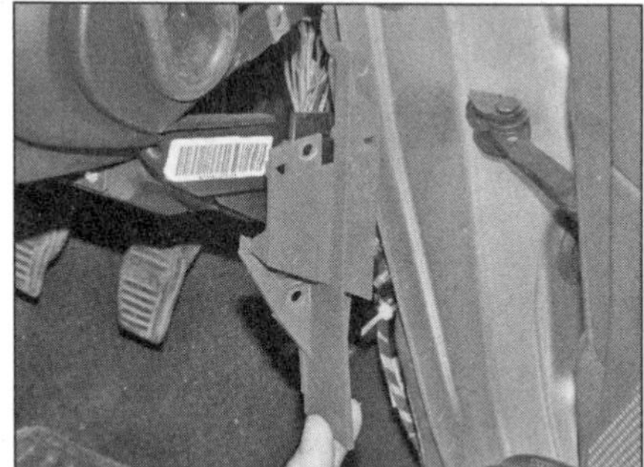
27.11b ... and unclip the inner side panels

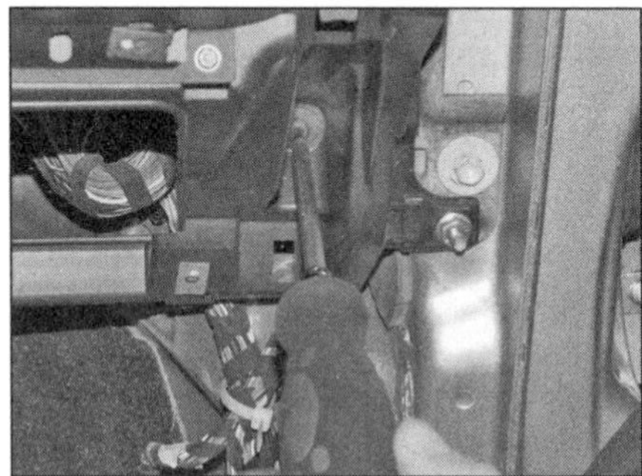
27.12a Remove the single screw ...

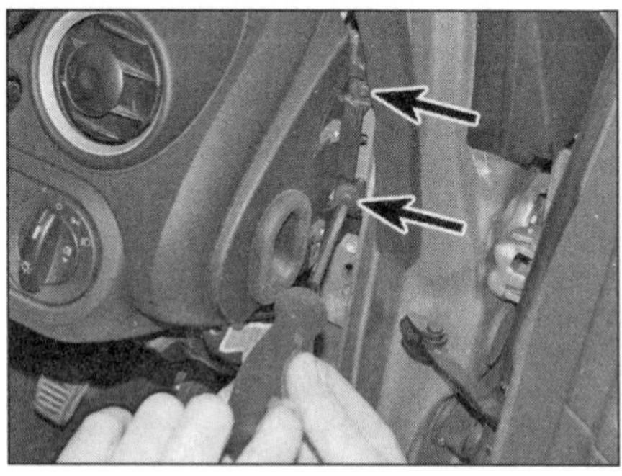
27.12b ... followed by two outer screws ...

27.12c ... and a nut underneath

11 Similarly, with the outer side trim panels removed, remove the inner side trim panels at either end, which are secured by two screws **(see illustrations)**.

12 Remove the various screws and nuts at each end of the facia – there's a single screw to the inside, then two screws and a nut below at the outer edge **(see illustrations)**.

13 Remove three nuts from the centre of the facia – one either side, approximately where the heater controls were, and a further nut inside the instrument panel location **(see illustrations)**.

14 Remove the two bolts securing the audio unit support bracket, and withdraw the bracket from the facia. Unclip the radio aerial lead from the clip in the radio aperture **(see illustrations)**.

27.13a Remove the nut in the centre of the facia on the right ...

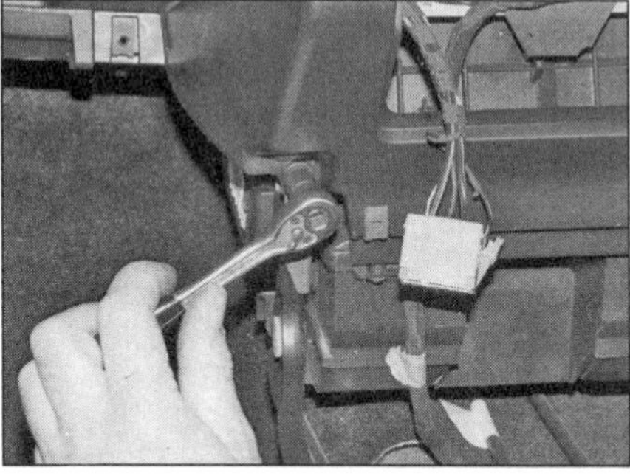
27.13b ... and on the left-hand side ...

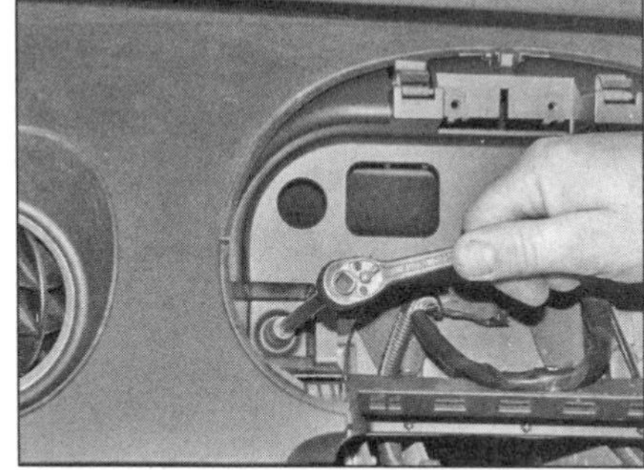
27.13c ... and a further nut inside the instrument panel location

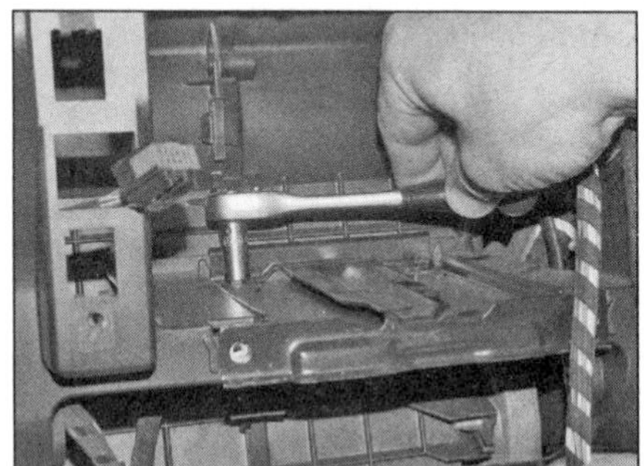
27.14a Remove the two bolts ...

27.14b ... and withdraw the audio unit support bracket

27.14c Unclip the aerial lead from the radio aperture

27.15 Remove the Torx screw securing the glovebox striker to the crossmember

27.16 Reach in behind the light switch, and disconnect the wiring plug

27.17 Removing the facia panel

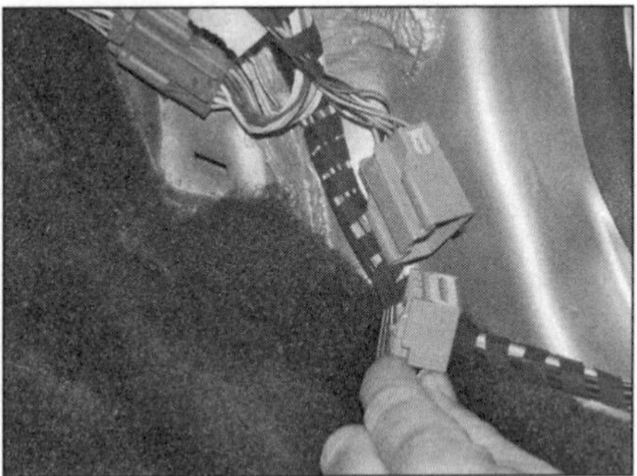
27.20 Disconnect the wiring plugs to the right of the driver's footwell

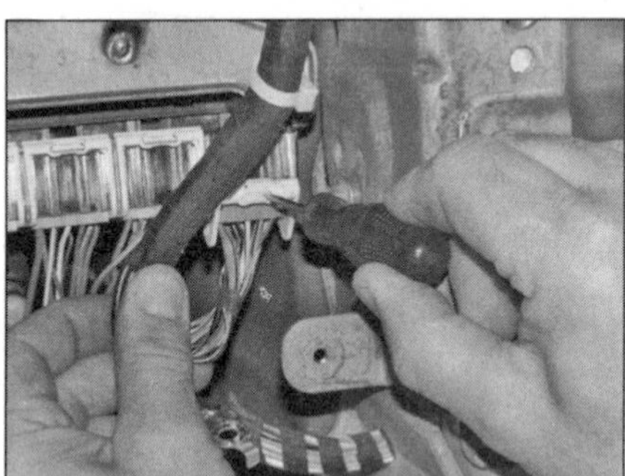
27.21a Use a small screwdriver to hinge down the locking bar ...

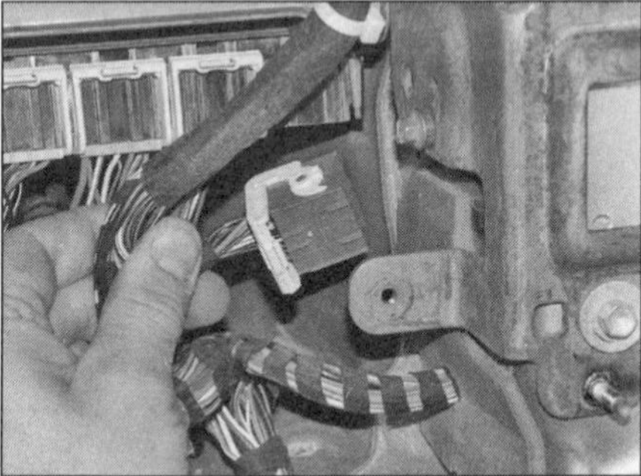
27.21b ... then disconnect the end wiring plug

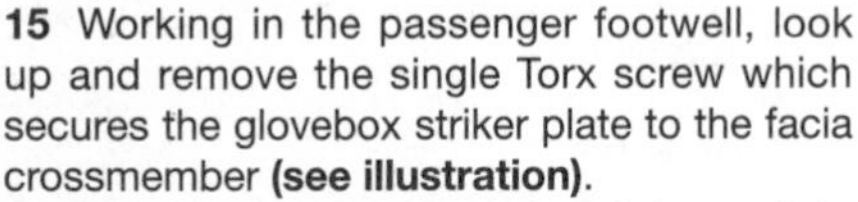
15 Working in the passenger footwell, look up and remove the single Torx screw which secures the glovebox striker plate to the facia crossmember **(see illustration)**.

16 Reach in behind the main lighting switch, and disconnect the large wiring plug on the back. This is not as simple as it sounds, and it may be necessary to pull the facia panel out slightly to gain better access **(see illustration)**.

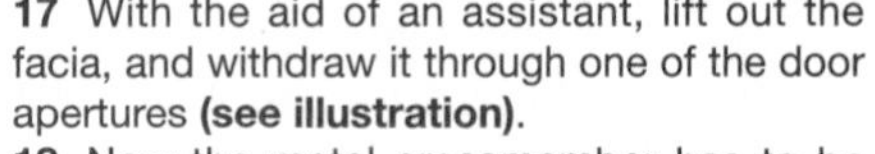
17 With the aid of an assistant, lift out the facia, and withdraw it through one of the door apertures **(see illustration)**.

18 Now the metal crossmember has to be removed – this requires some studying of the wiring harness, to decide which plugs need to be disconnected, as much of the wiring is removed with the crossmember.

19 Unclip the front sections of the door sill trim panels, using the information in Section 25.

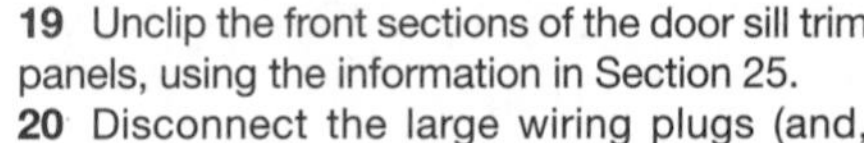
20 Disconnect the large wiring plugs (and, where applicable, unbolt the earth strap) to the right of the driver's footwell **(see illustration)**.

21 Also on the driver's side, reach up and disconnect the right-hand plug from the central locking/alarm module (GEM), which has five wiring plugs altogether (only the right-hand one has to be disconnected). Using a small screwdriver, hinge down the locking bar (yellow on our project car), then pull off the plug **(see illustrations)**.

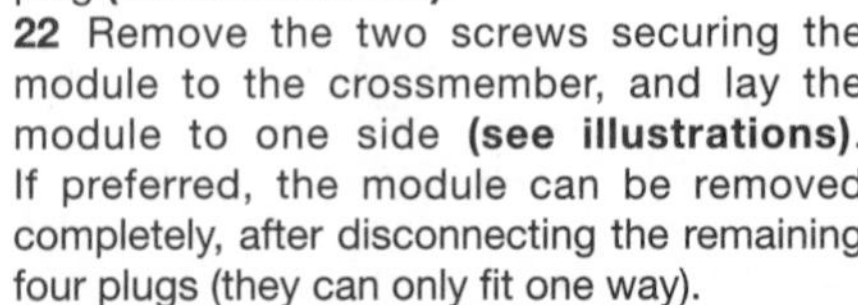
22 Remove the two screws securing the module to the crossmember, and lay the module to one side **(see illustrations)**. If preferred, the module can be removed completely, after disconnecting the remaining four plugs (they can only fit one way).

23 The radio aerial lead is clipped to the crossmember in several places. Work back along the lead, unclipping and feeding it through **(see illustration)**. Note how the lead is routed, for refitting (taking a few digital pictures for reference might be useful here).

24 In the passenger footwell, unbolt the earth strap and disconnect the large wiring plugs below the bonnet release lever **(see illustrations)**.

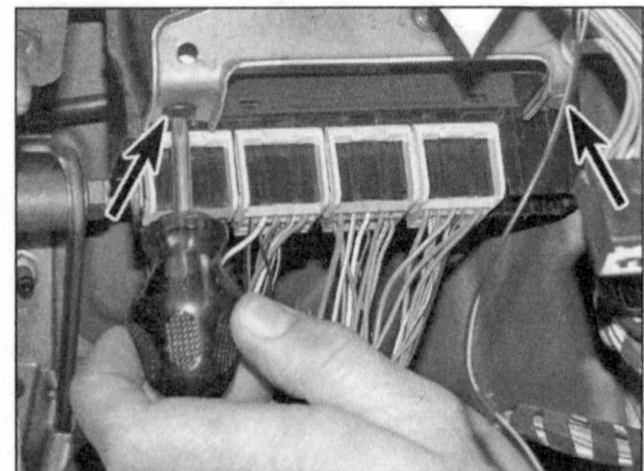
27.22a Remove the two securing screws ...

27.22b ... and lower out the module

27.23 Unclip and feed through the aerial lead, noting its routing

27.24a Unbolt the earth strap ...

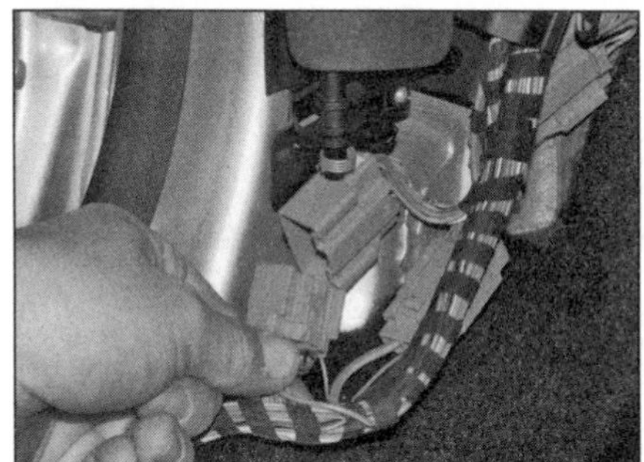

27.24b ... and disconnect the various wiring plugs around the bonnet release lever

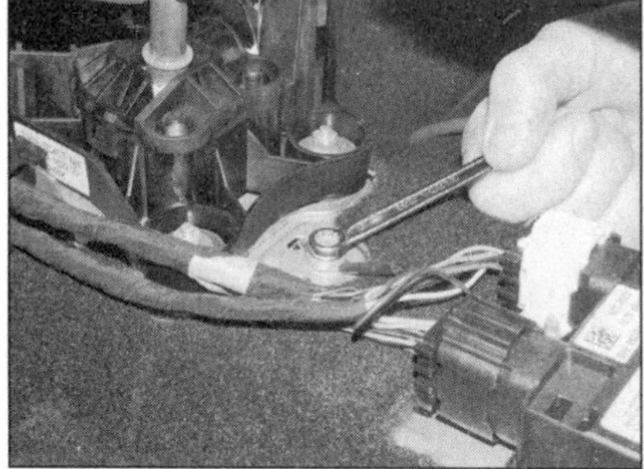

27.25 Unbolt the earth strap in front of the airbag module

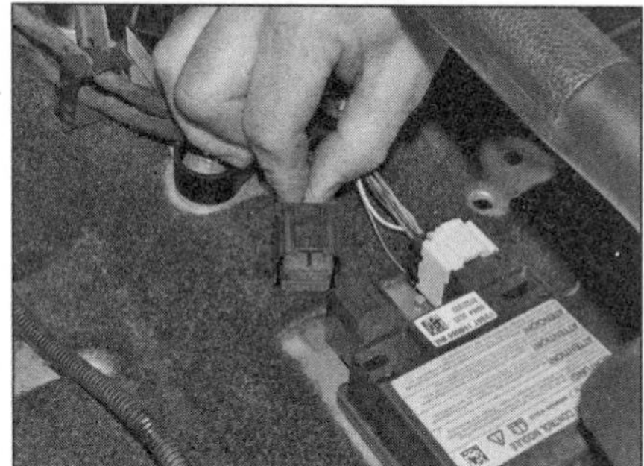

27.26 Disconnect the left-hand plug from the airbag module

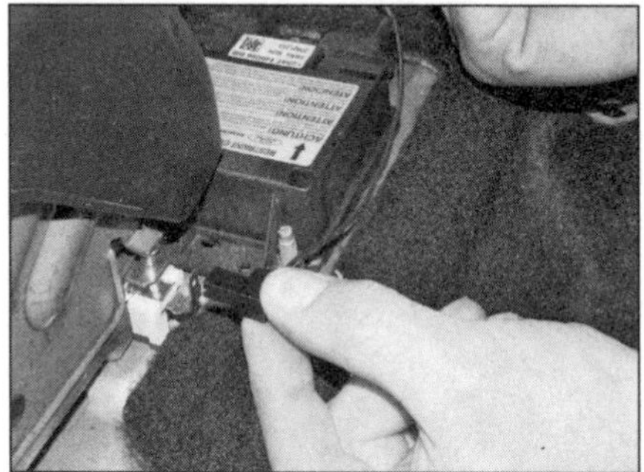

27.27 Disconnect the handbrake warning light switch

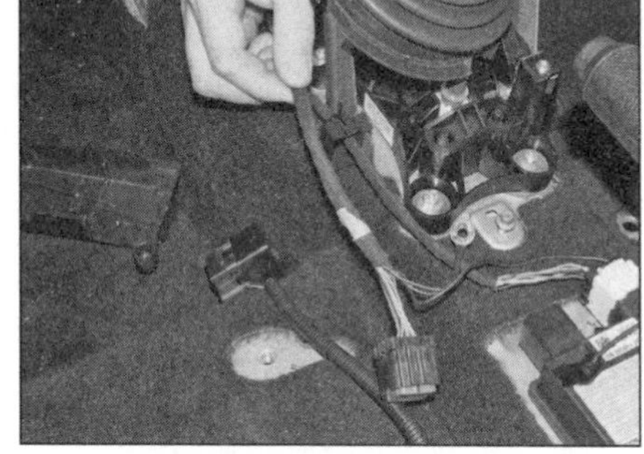

27.28 Unclip the airbag and handbrake wiring harness from the gear lever mounting

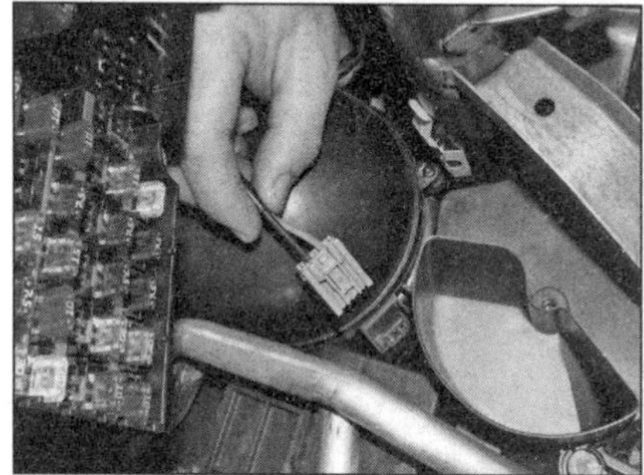

27.29 Disconnect the blower motor wiring plug

25 Unbolt the earth strap in the centre of the car, situated in front of the airbag control module **(see illustration)**.

26 Disconnect the left-hand plug from the airbag module – the right-hand plug is not part of the harness attached to the crossmember, and can be left connected **(see illustration)**.

27 Disconnect the wiring from the handbrake warning light switch **(see illustration)**.

28 Unclip the airbag and handbrake warning light switch wiring from the gear lever mounting **(see illustration)**.

29 Reach up on the left-hand side of the heater housing, and disconnect the wiring plug from the blower motor **(see illustration)**.

30 On the right-hand side of the heater housing, disconnect the wiring from the blower motor resistor pack, and also from the air inlet flap actuator (models with air conditioning only) **(see illustration)**.

31 Now the windscreen air ducts have to be unscrewed from the crossmember – the single screw securing each windscreen duct is one of the trickiest to reach. Once the screws are undone, pull each vent upwards to remove **(see illustrations)**.

32 Using paint or a marker pen, make alignment marks between the crossmember and the A-pillars **(see illustration)**.

33 Now the triangular trim panels on the outside of the car, in front of the door mirrors, have to be prised off for access to the crossmember mounting bolts. These trim panels are held on by the stiffest plastic clips you'll ever find, and damaging something during removal is highly likely. Prise the panel from the rear corner to start, and protect the paint from damage, as considerable effort will be required **(see illustrations)**. If any of the clips stay on the car, transfer them back to the trim panel for refitting.

34 With the trim panels removed, prise off the circular trim cap underneath, then unscrew the long bolt each side **(see illustrations)**.

35 Inside the car, remove the two bolts on top of the heater housing **(see illustration)**.

27.30 Disconnect the blower motor resistor pack wiring plug

27.31a Remove the hard-to-reach screw...

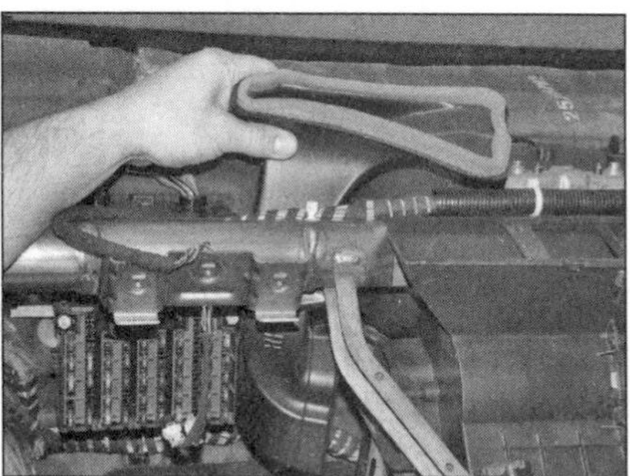

27.31b ... then lift out the windscreen vent

27.32 Make alignment marks between the crossmember and A-pillars

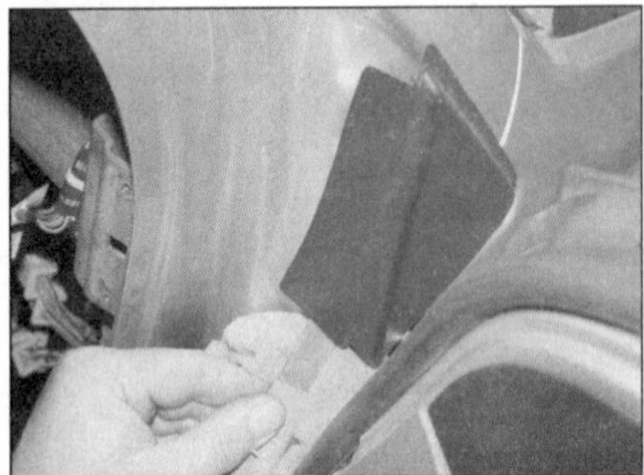

27.33a Prise the panels at the rear (note the cloth pad behind the tool) ...

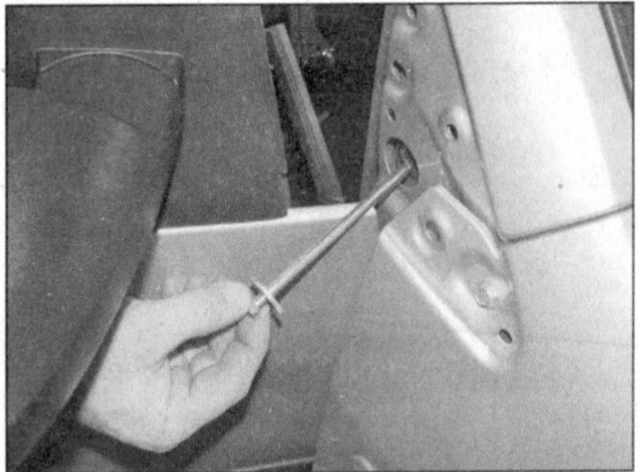

27.34b ... then unscrew and remove the long crossmember bolts

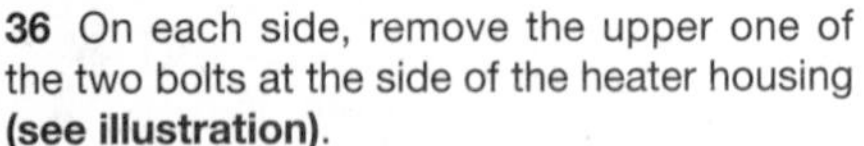

36 On each side, remove the upper one of the two bolts at the side of the heater housing **(see illustration)**.

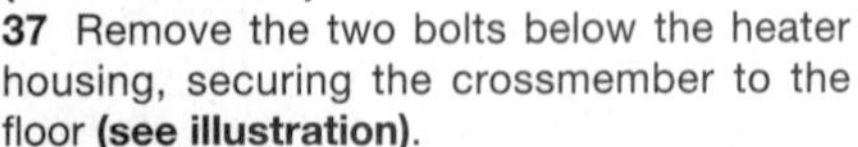

37 Remove the two bolts below the heater housing, securing the crossmember to the floor **(see illustration)**.

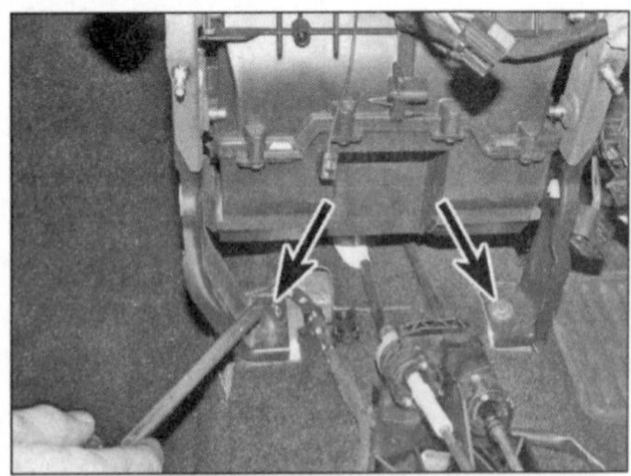

27.37 Remove the two crossmember-to-floor bolts

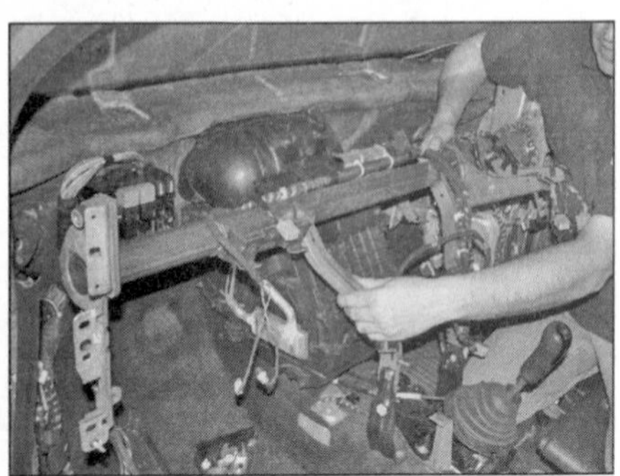

27.39 ... and remove the crossmember from the car

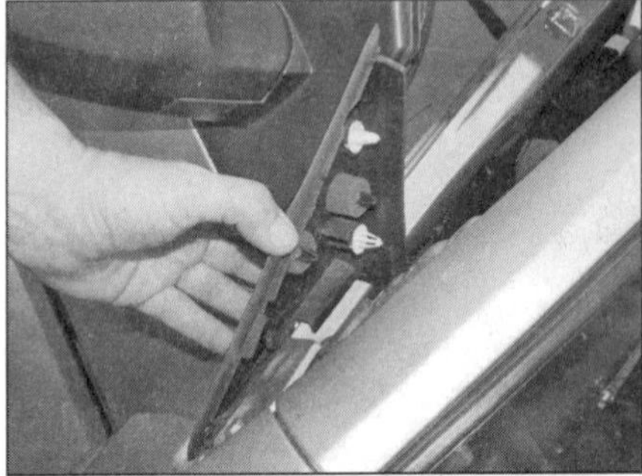

27.33b ... and remove the triangular trim panels

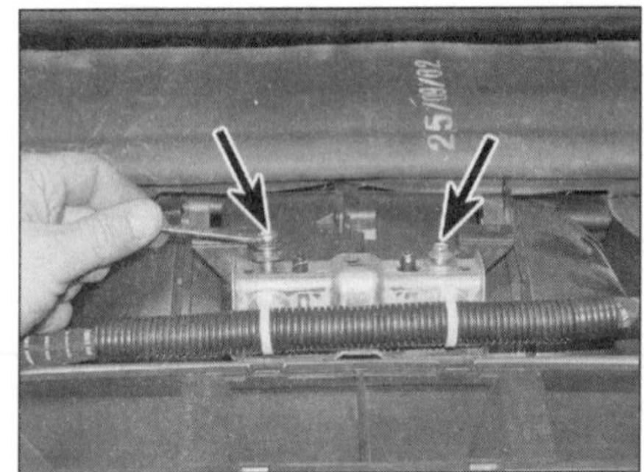

27.35 Remove the two bolts from the heater housing

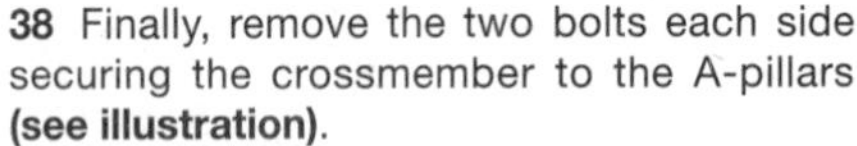

38 Finally, remove the two bolts each side securing the crossmember to the A-pillars **(see illustration)**.

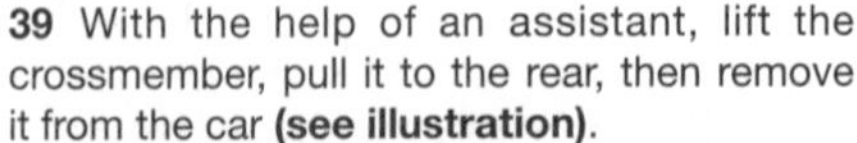

39 With the help of an assistant, lift the crossmember, pull it to the rear, then remove it from the car **(see illustration)**.

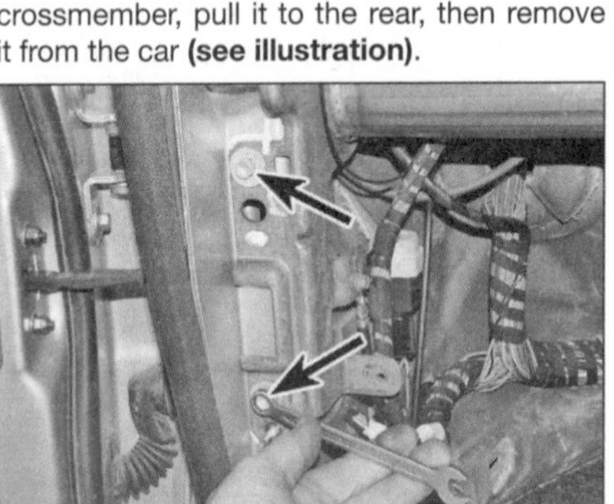

27.38 Remove the two outer bolts ...

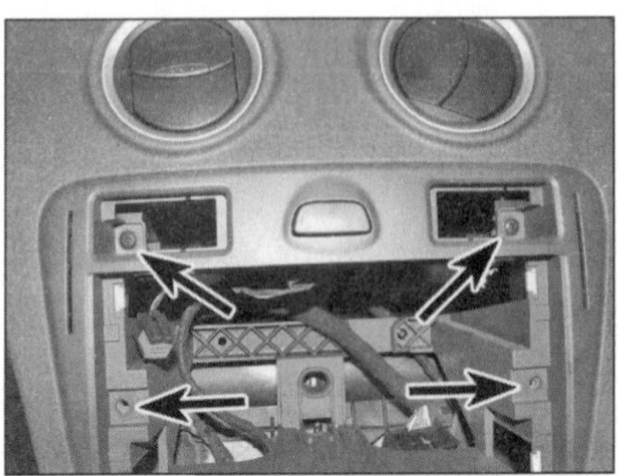

27.45 Remove the heater control panel screws (arrowed)

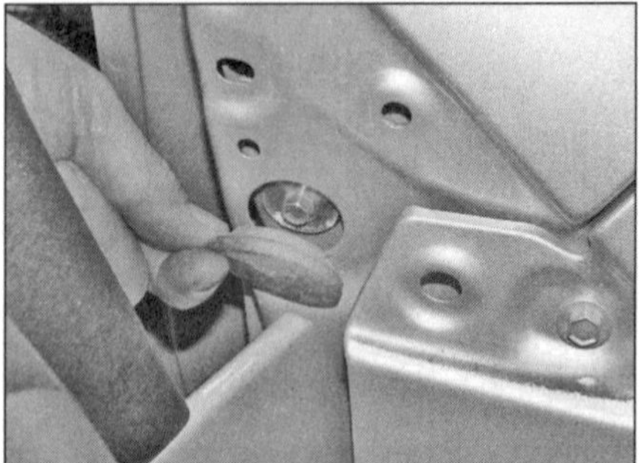

27.34a Prise off the cap behind the panels ...

27.36 Remove the top bolt each side of the heater housing

Refitting

40 Refitting is a reversal of removal, bearing in mind the following points:

a) If the facia is to be refitted at a later date, ensure that the battery is disconnected before starting. It is dangerous, for example, to reconnect the airbag wiring with the battery connected.

b) Offer in the facia crossmember, and locate it by fitting the long side bolts in from the outside of the car first. Align the marks made between the crossmember and the A-pillars before continuing.

c) Ensure that the wiring harnesses, aerial lead, etc, are routed as noted before removal.

d) Tighten all bolts securely.

Models made after 10/2005

Removal

41 Disconnect the battery negative lead (see Chapter 5A, Section 2) then wait for two minutes before proceeding. If this waiting period is not observed, there is danger of activating the airbags.

42 Remove the centre console as described in Section 26.

43 Remove the steering column assembly as described in Chapter 10, Section 15.

44 Remove the audio unit as described in Chapter 12, Section 17.

45 Remove the climate control panel as described in Chapter 3, Section 9 **(see illustration)**.

46 Remove the instrument panel as described in Chapter 12, Section 11.

27.51a Remove the fixings ...

27.51b ... and remove the storage compartment

27.54 Remove the support bracket fixing

27.55 Remove the end panels

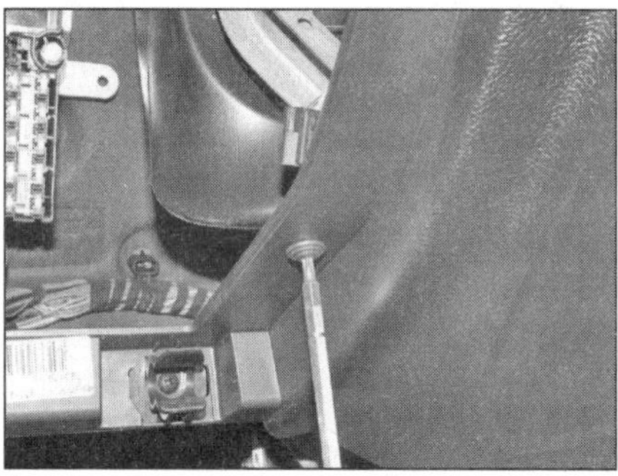
27.57a Remove the various screws ...

27.57b ... and nuts that secure the facia to the support bar

47 Remove the A-pillar trim panels as described in Section 25.

48 Release the diagnostic connector plug from the lower facia panel by pivoting down the locking collar and removing the wiring plug.

49 Remove the tailgate remote release switch from the facia panel with reference to Chapter 12, Section 4.

50 Where fitted, remove the passenger airbag deactivation switch from inside the glovebox with reference to Chapter 12, Section 4.

51 Remove storage compartment from the centre of the facia **(see illustration)** and where fitted remove the air temperature sensor

52 Unfasten the noise insulation from below the glovebox.

53 Remove the glovebox as described in Section 25.

54 Unbolt and remove the passenger airbag support bracket **(see illustration)** then disconnect the wiring from the airbag.

55 At each end of the facia, remove the outer side trim panels, which are secured by a single cross-head screw **(see illustration)**.

56 Similarly, with the outer side trim panels removed, remove the inner side trim panels at each end, which are secured by two screws.

57 Work along the facia and remove the various screws and nuts from the facia **(see illustration)**.

58 Remove three nuts from the centre of the facia – one either side, approximately where the heater controls were, and a further nut inside the instrument panel location.

59 Reach in behind the main lighting switch, and disconnect the large wiring plug on the back. This is not as simple as it sounds, and it may be necessary to pull the facia panel out slightly to gain better access.

60 With the aid of an assistant, lift out the facia, and withdraw it through one of the door apertures **(see illustration)**.

61 If necessary, remove the metal crossmember as described for earlier models in paragraphs 18 to 39. Note however that removal of the outer triangular trim panel is not required on later models **(see illustrations)**.

27.60 Remove the facia

27.61a Remove the blanking plug from below the trim piece ...

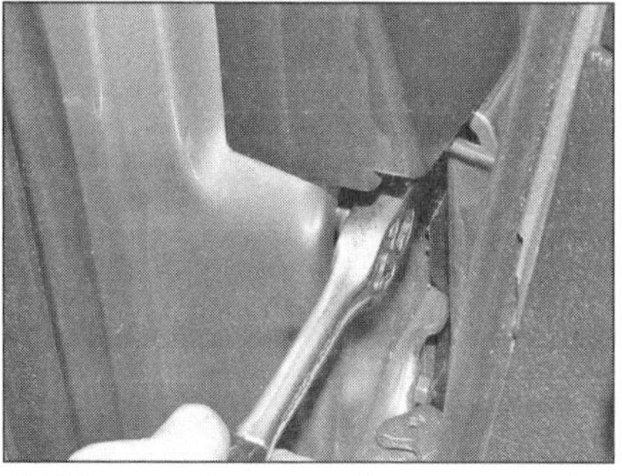
27.61b ... and use a socket to remove the bolt

27.61c Mark the position of the crossmember ...

27.61d ... and remove it

Refitting

62 Refitting is a reversal of removal, bearing in mind the following points:

a) *Ensure that the wiring harnesses, etc, are routed as noted before removal.*

b) *Tighten all bolts securely.*

Chapter 12
Body electrical system

Contents

Degrees of difficulty

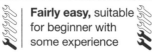

Easy, suitable for novice with little experience 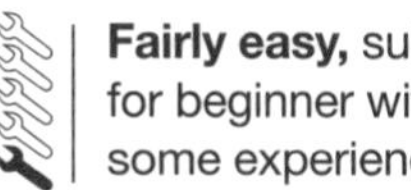	**Fairly easy,** suitable for beginner with some experience	**Fairly difficult,** suitable for competent DIY mechanic	**Difficult,** suitable for experienced DIY mechanic	**Very difficult,** suitable for expert DIY or professional 

Specifications

General

System type	12 volt, negative earth

Fuses

Refer to label on back of glovebox

Bulbs	**Type**	**Wattage**
Brake light (high-level)	Push-fit	16
Brake/tail light	P21/5	21/5
Courtesy light	Festoon	10
Direction indicator light:		
Front	PY21W/P21W	21
Side repeater light	WY5W	5
Rear	P21W	21
Foglight:		
Front	H11	55
Rear	P21W	21
Glovebox light	Push-fit	5
Headlight	H4	55/60
Luggage compartment light	W5W	5
Map reading lights	Spherical	5
Number plate light	ZW5	5
Reversing light	P21W	21
Sidelight	W5W	5

Torque wrench settings	**Nm**	**lbf ft**
Airbag:		
Control unit mounting nuts	9	6
Passenger airbag mounting bolts/nuts	10	7
Side impact sensor bolt	9	6
Wiper arm nuts:		
Front	18	13
Rear	15	11
Wiper motor bolts:		
Front	12	9
Rear	7	5

1 General information and precautions

Warning: Before carrying out any work on the electrical system, read through the precautions given in 'Safety first!' at the beginning of this manual, and in Chapter 5A, Section 1.

The electrical system is of 12 volt negative earth type. Power for the lights and all electrical accessories is supplied by a lead-acid type battery, which is charged by the alternator.

Certain models manufactured from 08/2005 are equipped with an autolamp system. When the lighting switch is positioned on Auto, low beam headlights and sidelights will be switched on automatically by the general electronic module (see Section 3) provided the following conditions are satisfied:

a) The ignition switch is in position II or III.
b) Ambient light is below the stored threshold value.

The autolamp system includes a combined rain sensor/light sensor located on the windscreen, near the interior rear view mirror. There are two specific sensors in the light sensor, one determines the 'general' light intensity, and the other determines the light intensity 'directly in front of the vehicle'. If both sensors detect a sudden reduction in light intensity, the system determines that the vehicle has entered a tunnel and the lights will be switched on. However, if the sun is shining and the vehicle is thrown into shade from a large truck, the two sensors will detect different light intensities, and the lights will not be switched on.

This Chapter covers repair and service procedures for the various electrical components not associated with engine. Information on the battery, alternator and starter motor can be found in Chapter 5A.

It should be noted that, prior to working on any component in the electrical system, the battery negative terminal should first be disconnected, to prevent the possibility of electrical short-circuits and/or fires. Refer to Chapter 5A, Section 2.

2 Electrical fault finding – general information

Note: *Refer to the precautions given in 'Safety first!' and Chapter 5A, Section 1 before starting work. The following tests relate to testing of the main electrical circuits, and should not be used to test delicate electronic circuits (such as anti-lock braking systems), particularly where an electronic control module is used.*

General

1 A typical electrical circuit consists of an electrical component, any switches, relays, motors, fuses, fusible links or circuit breakers related to that component, and the wiring and connectors which link the component to both the battery and the chassis. To help to pinpoint a problem in an electrical circuit, wiring diagrams are included at the end of this Chapter.

2 Before attempting to diagnose an electrical fault, first study the appropriate wiring diagram, to obtain a more complete understanding of the components included in the particular circuit concerned. The possible sources of a fault can be narrowed down by noting whether other components related to the circuit are operating properly. If several components or circuits fail at one time, the problem is likely to be related to a shared fuse or earth connection.

3 Electrical problems usually stem from simple causes, such as loose or corroded connections, a faulty earth connection, a blown fuse, a melted fusible link, or a faulty relay (refer to Section 3 for details of testing relays). Visually inspect the condition of all fuses, wires and connections in a problem circuit before testing the components. Use the wiring diagrams to determine which terminal connections will need to be checked, in order to pinpoint the trouble-spot.

4 The basic tools required for electrical fault finding include a circuit tester or voltmeter (a 12 volt bulb with a set of test leads can also be used for certain tests); a self-powered test light (sometimes known as a continuity tester); an ohmmeter (to measure resistance); a battery and set of test leads; and a jumper wire, preferably with a circuit breaker or fuse incorporated, which can be used to bypass suspect wires or electrical components. Before attempting to locate a problem with test instruments, use the wiring diagram to determine where to make the connections.

5 To find the source of an intermittent wiring fault (usually due to a poor or dirty connection, or damaged wiring insulation), a 'wiggle' test can be performed on the wiring. This involves wiggling the wiring by hand, to see if the fault occurs as the wiring is moved. It should be possible to narrow down the source of the fault to a particular section of wiring. This method of testing can be used in conjunction with any of the tests described in the following sub-Sections.

6 Apart from problems due to poor connections, two basic types of fault can occur in an electrical circuit – open-circuit, or short-circuit.

7 Open-circuit faults are caused by a break somewhere in the circuit, which prevents current from flowing. An open-circuit fault will prevent a component from working, but will not cause the relevant circuit fuse to blow.

8 Short-circuit faults are caused by a 'short' somewhere in the circuit, which allows the current flowing in the circuit to 'escape' along an alternative route, usually to earth. Short-circuit faults are normally caused by a breakdown in wiring insulation, which allows a feed wire to touch either another wire, or an earthed component such as the bodyshell. A short-circuit fault will normally cause the relevant circuit fuse to blow.

Finding an open-circuit

9 To check for an open-circuit, connect one lead of a circuit tester or voltmeter to either the negative battery terminal or a known good earth.

10 Connect the other lead to a connector in the circuit being tested, preferably nearest to the battery or fuse.

11 Switch on the circuit, bearing in mind that some circuits are live only when the ignition switch is moved to a particular position.

12 If voltage is present (indicated either by the tester bulb lighting or a voltmeter reading, as applicable), this means that the section of the circuit between the relevant connector and the battery is problem-free.

13 Continue to check the remainder of the circuit in the same fashion.

14 When a point is reached at which no voltage is present, the problem must lie between that point and the previous test point with voltage. Most problems can be traced to a broken, corroded or loose connection.

Finding a short-circuit

15 To check for a short-circuit, first disconnect the load(s) from the circuit (loads are the components which draw current from a circuit, such as bulbs, motors, heating elements, etc).

16 Remove the relevant fuse from the circuit, and connect a circuit tester or voltmeter to the fuse connections.

17 Switch on the circuit, bearing in mind that some circuits are live only when the ignition switch is moved to a particular position.

18 If voltage is present (indicated either by the tester bulb lighting or a voltmeter reading, as applicable), this means that there is a short-circuit.

19 If no voltage is present, but the fuse still blows with the load(s) connected, this indicates an internal fault in the load(s).

Finding an earth fault

20 The battery negative terminal is connected to 'earth' – the metal of the engine/transmission unit and the car body – and most systems are wired so that they only receive a positive feed, the current returning via the metal of the car body. This means that the component mounting and the body form part of that circuit. Loose or corroded mountings can therefore cause a range of electrical faults, ranging from total failure of a circuit, to a puzzling partial fault.

21 In particular, lights may shine dimly (especially when another circuit sharing the same earth point is in operation), motors (eg, wiper motors or the radiator cooling fan motor) may run slowly, and the operation of one circuit may have an apparently-unrelated effect on another.

22 Note that on many vehicles, earth straps

are used between certain components, such as the engine/transmission and the body, usually where there is no metal-to-metal contact between components, due to flexible rubber mountings, etc.

23 To check whether a component is properly earthed, disconnect the battery, and connect one lead of an ohmmeter to a known good earth point. Connect the other lead to the wire or earth connection being tested. The resistance reading should be zero; if not, check the connection as follows.

24 If an earth connection is thought to be faulty, dismantle the connection, and clean back to bare metal both the bodyshell and the wire terminal or the component earth connection mating surface. Be careful to remove all traces of dirt and corrosion, then use a knife to trim away any paint, so that a clean metal-to-metal joint is made.

25 On reassembly, tighten the joint fasteners securely; if a wire terminal is being refitted, use serrated washers between the terminal and the bodyshell, to ensure a clean and secure connection.

26 When the connection is remade, prevent the onset of corrosion in the future by applying a coat of petroleum jelly or silicone-based grease, or by spraying on (at regular intervals) a proprietary ignition sealer.

3 Fuses, relays and generic electronic module (GEM) – general information

Fuses

1 Fuses are designed to break a circuit when a predetermined current is reached, in order to protect the components and wiring which could be damaged by excessive current flow. Any excessive current flow will be due to a fault in the circuit, usually a short-circuit (see Section 2).

2 The main fuses are located in the fusebox, behind the glovebox.

3 Open the glovebox, and press the sides inwards to release the stops, which allows the glovebox to be opened further than normal. Alternatively (and preferably), remove the screw from each hinge at the base of the glovebox, and slide it out of the facia completely **(see illustrations)**.

4 A blown fuse can be recognised from its melted or broken wire **(see illustration)**.

5 To remove a fuse, first ensure that the relevant circuit is switched off – for maximum safety, disconnect the battery (see Chapter 5A, Section 2).

6 Pull the fuse from its location, using thin-nosed pliers if necessary **(see illustration)**.

7 Before renewing a blown fuse, trace and rectify the cause, and always use a fuse of the correct rating. Never substitute a fuse of a higher rating, or make temporary repairs using wire or metal foil; more serious damage, or even fire, could result.

3.3a Depress the arm inwards to release it

3.3b On early models remove the glovebox hinge screws ...

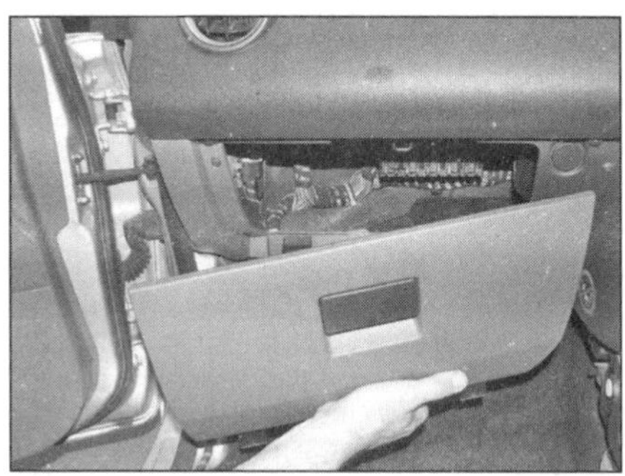

3.3c ... and slide the glovebox out of the facia

3.3d On later models the glovebox can be pulled from the lower mounting (arrowed)

8 Note that the fuses are colour-coded as follows. Refer to the markings on the back of the glovebox for details of the circuits protected. Also note that the Fusion uses the later-type 'mini' fuses.

Colour	Rating
Orange	5A
Red	10A
Blue	15A
Yellow	20A
Clear or white	25A
Green	30A

9 Additional 'midi' fuses are located the engine fusebox, at the rear of the battery box in the engine compartment. Since many of these are rated at 60 amps, if any of these is found to have blown, it indicates a serious wiring fault, which should be investigated – just fitting a new fuse may cause further problems.

Relays

10 A relay is an electrically-operated switch, which is used for the following reasons:

a) A relay can switch a heavy current remotely from the circuit in which the current is flowing, allowing the use of lighter-gauge wiring and switch contacts.

b) A relay can receive more than one control input, unlike a mechanical switch.

c) A relay can have a timer function – for example, the intermittent wiper relay.

11 Most of the relays are located under the facia, above the main fusebox **(see illustration)**. On diesel models, or those with air conditioning, additional relays are located next to the engine fusebox, at the rear of the battery box in the engine compartment.

12 Access to the relays in the fusebox can be obtained by removing the glovebox as described in paragraph 3.

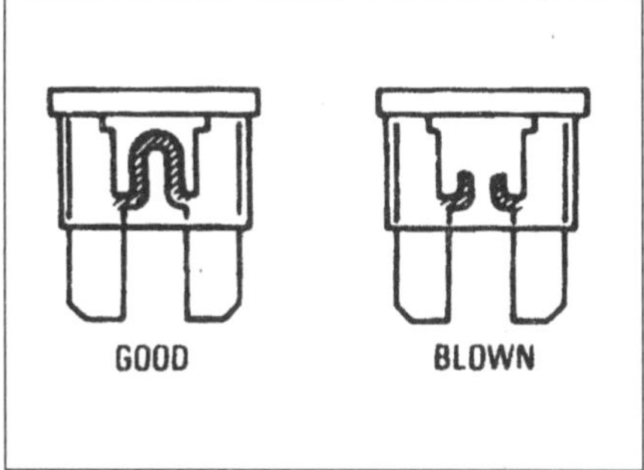

3.4 The fuses can be checked visually to determine if they have blown

3.6 Pull the fuses out for inspection

3.11 Most of the relays are located at the top of the fusebox

3.14 The relays can be pulled out of their sockets

13 If a circuit or system controlled by a relay develops a fault, and the relay is suspect, operate the system. If the relay is functioning, it should be possible to hear it 'click' as it is energised. If this is the case, the fault lies with the components or wiring of the system. If the relay is not being energised, then either the relay is not receiving a main supply or a switching voltage, or the relay itself is faulty. Testing is by the substitution of a known good unit, but be careful – while some relays are identical in appearance and in operation, others look similar but perform different functions.

14 To remove a relay, first ensure that the relevant circuit is switched off. The relay can then simply be pulled out from the socket, and pushed back into position **(see illustration)**.

Generic electronic module (GEM)

15 This module, which is fitted high up behind the facia, to the right of the steering wheel, controls many of the car's electrical functions:

- *Direction indicators and hazard lights.*
- *Interior lighting, including battery saver function (the interior lights and chimes are automatically shut off after a predetermined period of inactivity).*
- *Heated windscreen and rear window.*
- *Electric mirrors.*
- *Wipers and washers.*
- *Lights-on and door-ajar warnings.*
- *Central locking.*
- *Tailgate release.*
- *Alarm system.*
- *Autolamp system.*

16 Removal of the module is described in Chapter 11, Section 17.

17 The module has a self-test facility (service mode), which can be used without specialist diagnostic equipment. Although ultimately, any problem with the GEM may have to be referred to a Ford dealer, this procedure may help in tracking down the cause of any particular problem. For instance, in the event of a fault with the wipers, if they 'pass' the GEM test, the switch and the GEM are proved okay, and the fault must lie elsewhere.

18 Before starting the test, switch off the ignition and all electrical equipment. The handbrake should be applied, the gear lever in neutral, and all doors closed.

19 To activate the service mode, press and hold the heated rear window switch (on models with a heated windscreen, the rear window switch is the lower of the two). Turn the ignition to position II, release the heated rear window switch, then operate the switch 8 times within 6 seconds. A signal should sound, and the indicators will flash. If the car's alarm sounds, service mode cannot be activated.

20 Except when testing the wipers, make sure the wiper switch is in the 'off' position to test the input signals listed below. Operate each item in turn, and a signal should sound, together with a flash of the indicators.

1) *Direction indicators (right, left, hazard lights).*
2) *Lights-on warning.*
3) *Windscreen wipers (intermittent).*
4) *Windscreen washers.*
5) *Rear wiper.*
6) *Rear washer.*
7) *Doors open/closed.*
8) *Central locking.*
9) *Bonnet open/closed.*
10) *Heated rear window.*
11) *Heated windscreen.*

21 Now move the wiper switch to the 'intermittent' position to test the output signals listed below. Pressing the heated rear window switch activates each of the following signals, in the following order:

1) *Windscreen wipers (a signal sounds and direction indicators flash when the wiper 'park' position is reached).*
2) *Heated rear window.*
3) *Interior lights (switches must be on).*
4) *Rear wiper.*
5) *Heated windscreen (only with the engine running).*

22 The GEM will automatically end the service mode after 20 seconds. To end the service mode manually, press and hold the heated rear window switch, switch off the ignition, and release the heated rear window switch. There will be three sound signals, and the direction indicators will flash, to confirm the end of the service mode.

4 Switches – removal and refitting

Note: *Before removing any switch, disconnect the battery negative lead, and position the lead away from the battery (see Chapter 5A, Section 2).*

Ignition switch/steering lock

Steering column lock cylinder

1 Remove the steering column shrouds as described in Chapter 11, Section 25.

2 Disconnect the wiring plug, then unclip and withdraw the anti-theft immobiliser transceiver unit from the ignition switch/steering lock assembly **(see illustration)**.

3 Insert the ignition key, and turn it to position I.

4 Using a small screwdriver, depress the locking pins at the front, then at the rear, of the lock housing, and pull out the lock cylinder using the key **(see illustrations)**.

5 To refit the lock cylinder, push the assembly into the lock housing, until the locking pins

4.2 Disconnect the plug and unclip the key reader

4.4a Push in the locking pin at the front ...

4.4b ... and from behind ...

4.4c ... and withdraw the lock cylinder

4.7 Use a screwdriver to release the wiring plug tab

4.8a Release the switch assembly's retaining tabs top and bottom ...

4.8b ... then withdraw the switch from the column

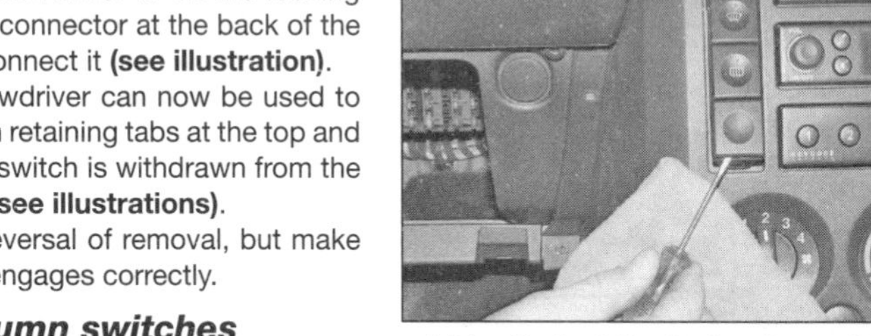
4.11 Disconnect the switch wiring plug

4.12 Release the catch at the top, and slide the switch upwards

engage, then turn the ignition key to position 0 and withdraw the key.

Ignition switch

Caution: Do not remove the ignition switch whilst the steering column lock cylinder is removed.

6 Remove the steering column shrouds as described in Chapter 11, Section 25.

7 Use a small screwdriver to lift the locking tab on the wiring connector at the back of the switch, then disconnect it **(see illustration)**.

8 The same screwdriver can now be used to release the switch retaining tabs at the top and bottom, then the switch is withdrawn from the steering column **(see illustrations)**.

9 Refitting is a reversal of removal, but make sure that switch engages correctly.

Steering column switches

10 Remove the steering column shrouds as described in Chapter 11, Section 25.

11 Use a small screwdriver to release the wiring plug from the back of the relevant switch **(see illustration)**.

12 Using a screwdriver if necessary, release the plastic catch at the top of the relevant switch, then slide the switch upwards to remove it **(see illustration)**.

13 Refitting is a reversal of removal.

Heated rear window and windscreen switches

14 On early models prise out the switch panel. On later models the switches can be pushed out from the rear after the audio unit has been removed (as described in Section 17). Note that it is possible to remove the switches with the audio unit fitted, but the switch covers may be damaged in the process **(see illustrations)**.

15 Disconnect the wiring plug from the switch panel, and remove it **(see illustration)**.

16 Refitting is a reversal of removal.

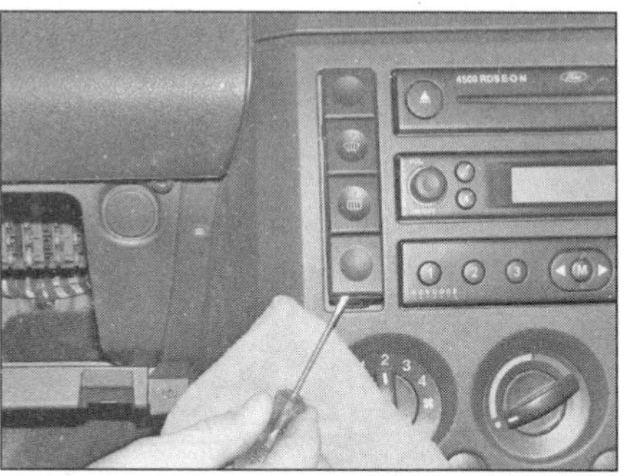
4.14a Protect the facia when prising out the switch panel

4.15 Disconnect the wiring plug, and remove the switches

Hazard warning light switch

17 On early models it is almost impossible to remove the switch without damaging it. If the switch is faulty this is not an issue, however if you wish to remove the switch for testing then

4.14b Push the switches out from the rear

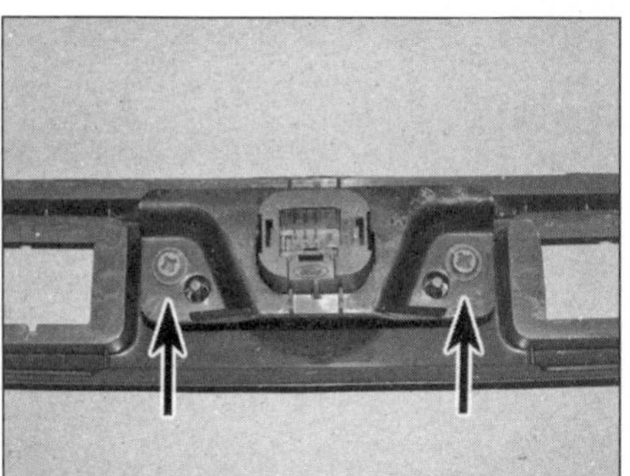
4.17 Remove the screws (arrowed) to release the switch

4.18a Prise out the hazard warning light switch (early model shown) ...

4.18b ... and use a screwdriver to disconnect the wiring plug

4.20 Prise out the switch

4.21 Disconnecting the tailgate release wiring plug

remove the heater control panel (as described in Chapter 3, Section 9) and push the switch from the rear of the panel. On later models the heater control panel must be removed to access the switch **(see illustration)**.

18 Protect the facia panel from damage using a piece of cloth or tape, then prise out the switch. Disconnect the wiring plug from the switch, and remove it **(see illustrations)**.

19 Refitting is a reversal of removal.

4.33a Prise up the door pull handle trim ...

4.33b ... then remove the trim and disconnect the switch wiring plugs underneath

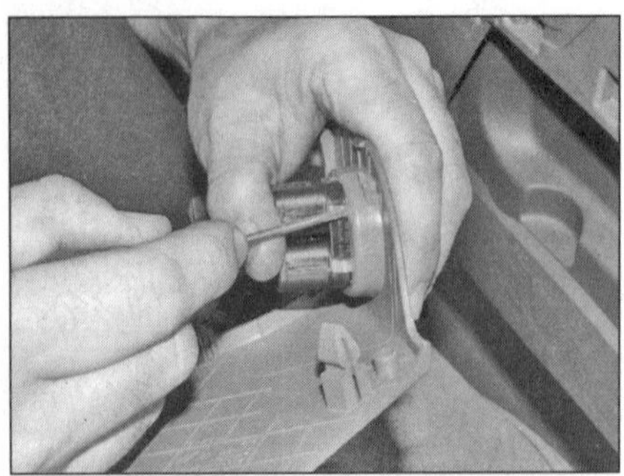

4.34a Release the switch retaining tabs ...

4.34b ... and withdraw the switch from the panel

Tailgate release button

20 Protect the facia panel from damage using a piece of cloth or tape, then prise out the button **(see illustration)**.

21 Disconnect the wiring plug from the switch and remove it **(see illustration)**.

22 Refitting is a reversal of removal.

Airbag deactivation switch

23 The switch is an optional accessory that can be fitted by a Ford dealer. Where fitted the switch is located in the facia left hand end panel. The switch warning light is located in the instrument panel.

Warning: If the battery is not disconnected before starting this procedure, the airbag could be activated.

24 Disconnect the battery negative lead, and position the lead away from the battery (see Chapter 5A, Section 2). Wait at least one minute before proceeding.

25 Lower the glovebox and push the switch free from the rear.

26 Disconnect the wiring plug from the switch, and remove it.

27 Refitting is a reversal of removal.

Air conditioning and recirculation switches

28 The switches are part of the heater control panel, which is removed as described in Chapter 3, Section 9.

Blower motor switch

29 The switch can only be removed from the back of the heater control panel, which is removed as described in Chapter 3, Section 9.

Electric sunroof switch

30 Prise the switch out of the roof console using a small screwdriver.

31 Disconnect the wiring plug from the rear of the switch, and remove it.

32 Refitting is a reversal of removal.

Electric window switches

33 Taking care not to mark the trim, prise off the section of the door trim panel surrounding the door pull handle, which is secured by several plastic clips. Start from the base of the panel, and work round until it is free **(see illustrations)**.

34 Disconnect the wiring plug(s) from the window switch assembly, then use a small screwdriver to release the switch retaining tabs, and withdraw the assembly from the panel **(see illustrations)**.

35 Refitting is a reversal of removal.

Electric mirror switch

36 Prise off the door mirror trim panel from the front of the door – this panel is secured by two (stiff) clips at the front, which should be released first, before unhooking the panel clips at the back edge. Disconnect the mirror switch wiring plug, and remove the panel completely **(see illustrations)**.

4.36a Prise off the mirror panel at the front, then unhook it at the rear

4.36b Disconnect the mirror switch wiring plug

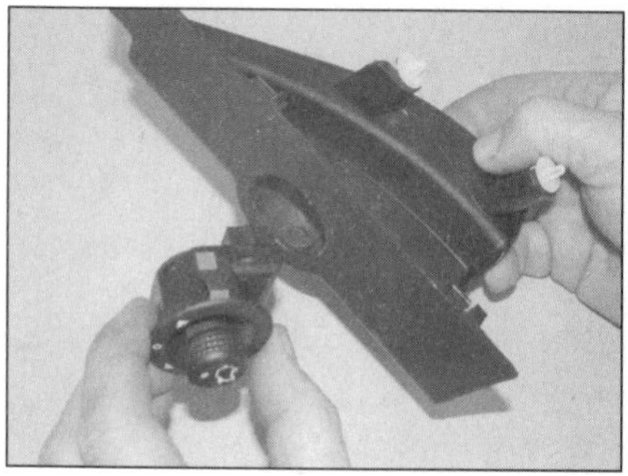
4.37 Push the mirror switch out of the panel from behind

37 The mirror switch can now be pushed out of the trim panel from behind, and removed **(see illustration)**.

38 Refitting is a reversal of removal.

Handbrake-on warning switch

Note: *Although not absolutely necessary, access to the handbrake switch is greatly improved if the driver's seat is removed as described in Chapter 11, Section 23.*

39 Where applicable, prise out the power outlet socket fitted into the handbrake trim panel, at the rear, and disconnect the wiring plug beneath it.

40 Unclip the handbrake lever trim panel first at the rear, and remove it over the handbrake lever **(see illustration)**.

41 Disconnect the wiring plug from the switch, then remove the securing screw and withdraw the switch **(see illustration)**.

42 Refitting is a reversal of removal.

Fuel cut-off (inertia) switch

43 The inertia switch is located on the left-hand side of the passenger footwell.

44 Open the glovebox, and press the sides inwards to release the stops, which allows the glovebox to be opened further than normal. Alternatively (and preferably), remove the glovebox, and slide it out of the facia completely **(see illustrations 3.3b, 3.3c and 3.3d)**.

45 Disconnect the wiring plug from the base of the switch, then remove the mounting bolt and withdraw the switch from the car **(see illustration)**.

46 Refitting is a reversal of removal.

Exterior light switch

47 Remove the lower trim panel from below the steering column.

48 Reach up behind the facia panel squeeze the upper and lower retaining tabs and push the switch from the panel **(see illustrations)**.

49 Disconnect the large wiring plug from the rear of the switch **(see illustration)**.

50 Refitting is a reversal of removal.

Interior (courtesy) light switch

51 The interior light switches are built into the individual door lock assemblies, which are removed as described in Chapter 11, Section 13. Note that the interior light switches itself off after a time, to save the battery – it will only 'reset' once the doors have been shut.

Luggage compartment light switch

52 The boot light switch is built into the tailgate lock assembly, which is removed as described in Chapter 11, Section 16. Note that the boot light switches itself off after a time, to save the battery – it will only 'reset' once the tailgate has been shut.

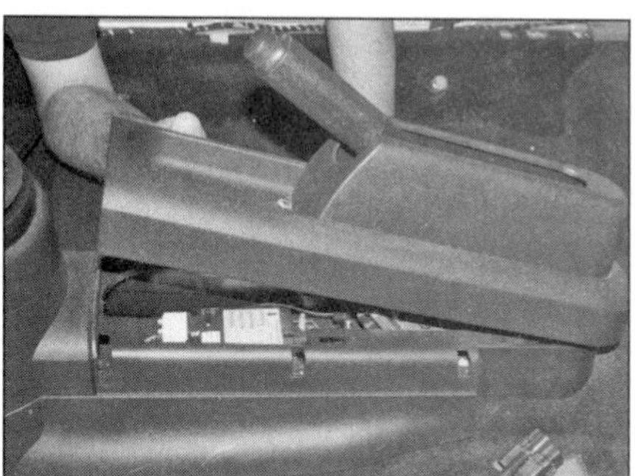
4.40 Unclip and lift off the handbrake lever trim panel

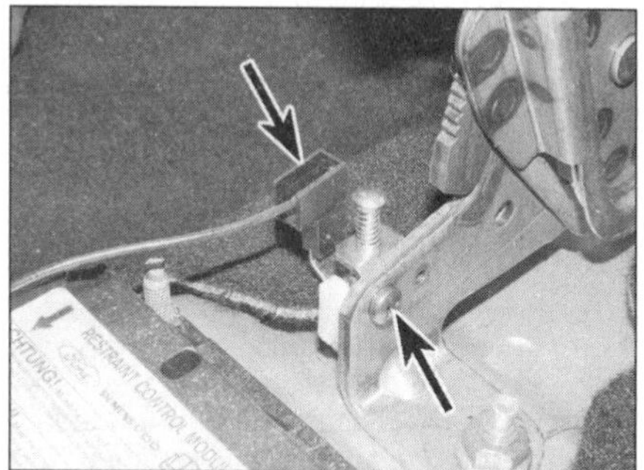
4.41 Handbrake warning light switch and mounting screw (arrowed)

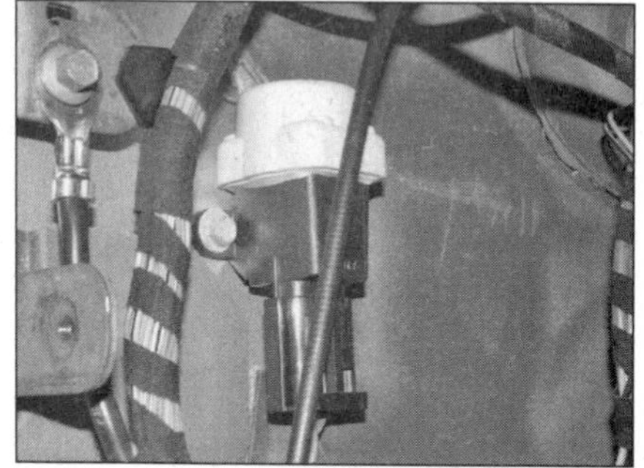
4.45 Remove the inertia switch mounting bolt

4.48a Push the switch free

4.48b The location of the locking tabs (arrowed)

4.49 Disconnect the wiring plug from the back of the light switch

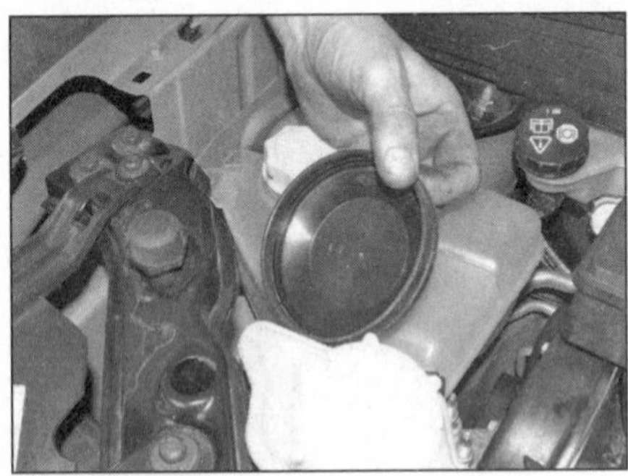
5.3 Remove the cover

5.5a Unhook the wire clip (arrowed) ...

Brake light switch

53 Refer to Chapter 9, Section 18.

Clutch pedal switch

54 Refer to Chapter 4A, Section 14.

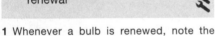

5 Bulbs (exterior lights) – renewal

1 Whenever a bulb is renewed, note the following points:

a) Disconnect the battery negative lead before starting work (see Chapter 5A, Section 2).
b) Remember that, if the light has just been in use, the bulb may be extremely hot.
c) Always check the bulb contacts and holder, ensuring that there is clean metal-to metal contact between the bulb and its live(s) and earth. Clean off any corrosion or dirt before fitting a new bulb.
d) Wherever bayonet-type bulbs are fitted (see Specifications), ensure that the live contact(s) bear firmly against the bulb contact.
e) Always ensure that the new bulb is of the correct rating, and that it is completely clean before fitting it; this applies particularly to headlight/foglight bulbs (see below).

5.4 Pull off the headlight bulb wiring plug

5.5b ... and withdraw the bulb

Headlight

2 Remove the headlight (see Section 7). Removing the headlight is a simple job, and it makes bulb renewal much easier. It is possible to change a headlight bulb with the unit in place but working room is limited. If you have no tools available, the bulb will have to be renewed with the headlight *in situ*.

3 Pull the headlight rear cover free and remove it **(see illustration)**.

4 Pull the wiring plug from the rear of the bulb **(see illustration)**.

5 Release the bulb's wire retaining clip by unhooking it and releasing the clip. Withdraw the bulb **(see illustrations)**.

6 When handling the new bulb, use a tissue or clean cloth, to avoid touching the glass with the fingers; moisture and grease from the skin can cause blackening and rapid failure of this type of bulb. If the glass is accidentally touched, wipe it clean using methylated spirit.

7 Install the new bulb, ensuring that its locating tabs are correctly seated in the light cut-outs. Secure the bulb in position with the spring clip, and reconnect the wiring plug.

8 Refit the cover, making sure the seal inside is not damaged.

9 If the headlight was removed refit it as described in Section 7.

Sidelight

10 It is possible to remove the bulb with the headlight *in situ*, however the task is simpler with the headlight removed (as described in Section 7).

11 Pull off the rear cover from the headlight **(see illustration 5.3)**.

12 Twist and pull the bulbholder to release it from the headlight **(see illustration)**.

13 Pull out the wedge-base bulb from the holder, and fit a new one firmly into place **(see illustration)**.

14 Refit the bulbholder and rear cover, then refit the headlight (if removed) as described in Section 7.

Front indicator light

Note: *Colourless front direction indicator light bulbs are fitted to models manufactured from 08/2005. Previous models are fitted with amber bulbs with a special fitting to avoid confusion with the main light bulb.*

15 It is possible to remove the bulb with the headlight *in situ*, however the task is simpler with the headlight removed (as described in Section 7).

16 Using the raised rib on the back of the indicator bulbholder, twist the holder anti-clockwise and withdraw it from the headlight **(see illustration)**.

5.12 The sidelight bulb (arrowed) is located below the headlight bulb

5.13 Pull out the sidelight bulb

5.16 Twist and remove the bulbholder

5.17 Remove the bayonet-fit bulb

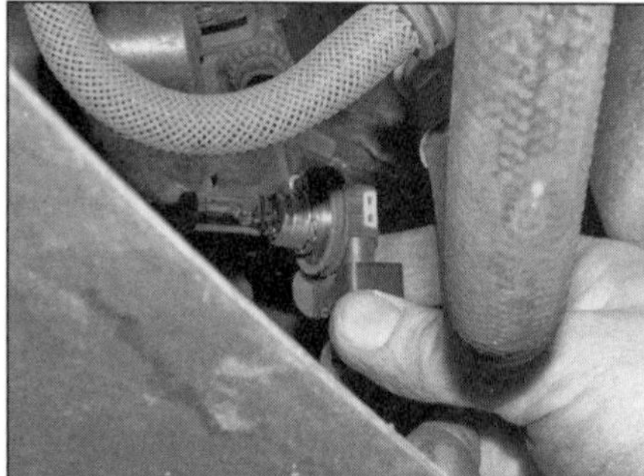
5.21 Twist and remove the combined bulb and plug socket from the light

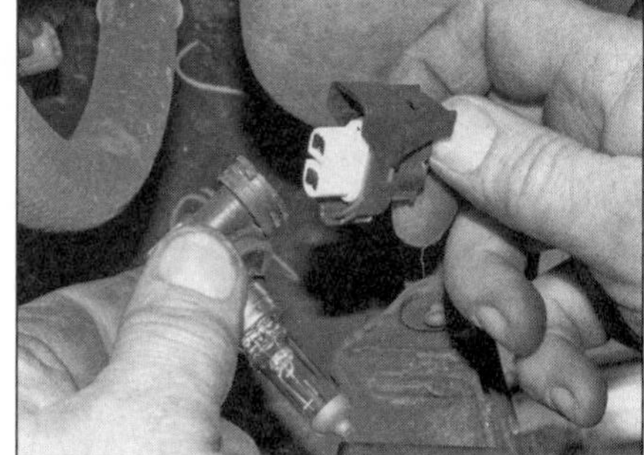
5.22 Pull the wiring plug from the back of the light

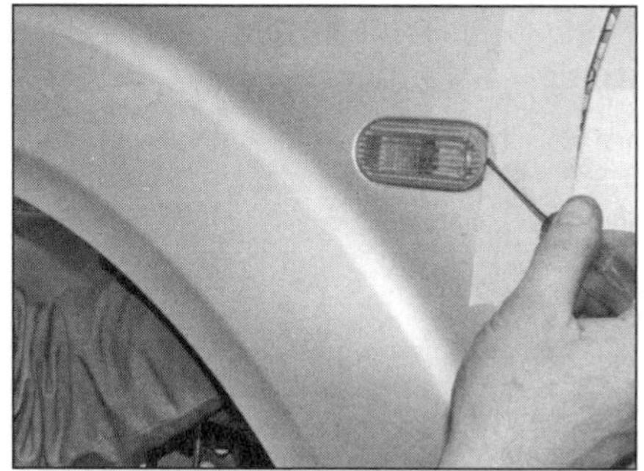
5.28 Push the light unit and unhook the edge – note the masking tape

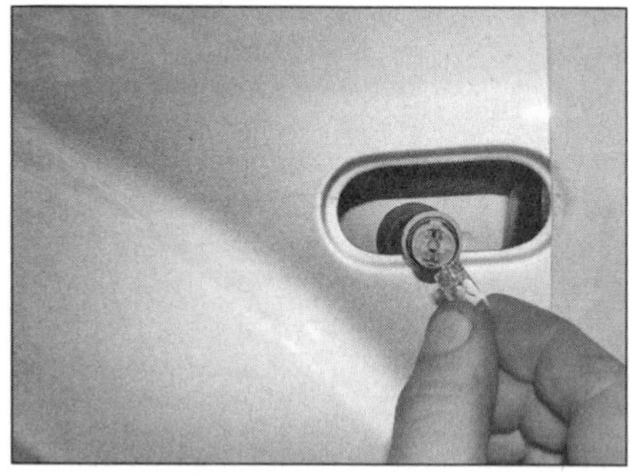
5.29 Pull out the side repeater light bulb

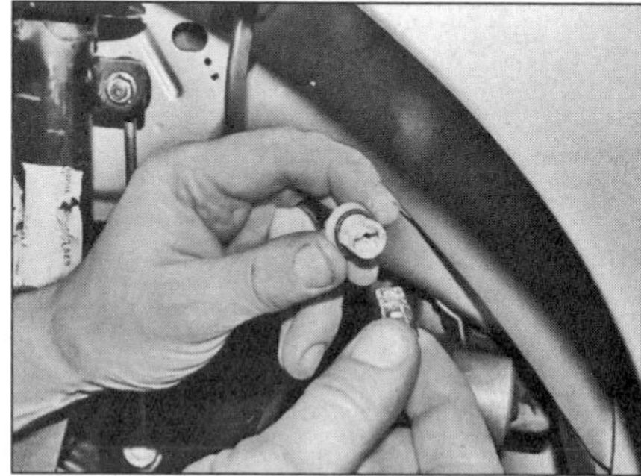
5.33 With the wheel arch liner removed, the bulbholder can be taken out to the front

17 Depress and twist the bulb anti-clockwise to remove it **(see illustration)**.
18 Fit the new bulb, then twist the bulbholder clockwise into the back of the headlight – the raised rib should be vertical when the bulbholder is fully located.
19 If removed, refit the headlight as described in Section 7.

Front foglight

20 Jack up the front corner of the car on the side concerned, and support it on axle stands (see *Jacking and vehicle support*).
21 Twist the bulb anti-clockwise to remove it from the back of the light unit **(see illustration)**.
22 With the bulb removed disconnect the wiring plug from the base of the light unit **(see illustration)**.
23 The H11 bulb is unusual in having its wiring socket integrated with it.
24 When handling the new bulb, use a tissue or clean cloth, to avoid touching the glass with the fingers; moisture and grease from the skin can cause blackening and rapid failure of this type of bulb. If the glass is accidentally touched, wipe it clean using methylated spirit.
25 Reconnect the wiring plug and then fit the new bulb, twisting it clockwise into the back of the light unit to secure. Lower the car to the ground.

Indicator side repeater light

26 There are two ways to change the side repeater light bulb. The first, which involves removing the light unit, appears to be the easier option, but carries a high risk of damage to the light unit and paintwork. The second option is to remove the wheel arch liner, which gives access to the light from behind – a longer process, but safer.

Method 1

27 To remove the light, first check which way round it has previously been fitted. The light has to be slid in the direction of the Ford logo embossed on the light lens – if the Ford logo is to the front, slide the light forwards; to the rear, press it backwards. As a small screwdriver will be needed to apply enough force, protect the paintwork with some masking tape (or similar).
28 Slide the light unit in the appropriate direction. Once the light has moved slightly, keep pressure on it, and use the screwdriver to unhook the end of the light which is being pushed – ie, if the light is being pushed forwards, unhook it at the rear edge **(see illustration)**. This operation requires surprising amounts of force, and carries a high risk of breaking the light (or scratching the paint if the screwdriver slips).
29 When the light unit has been removed, twist the bulbholder anti-clockwise to release it, and pull out the wedge-base bulb **(see illustration)**.
30 Refitting is a reversal of removal.

Method 2

31 To remove the wheel arch liner, first loosen the front wheel nuts, then jack up the corner of the car and support it on axle stands (see *Jacking and vehicle support*). Take off the wheel.
32 The wheel arch liner is secured with a combination of screws and clips, and removal is self-evident (once any accumulated dirt has first been removed). It may be sufficient to release the liner fasteners at the rear, to allow a hand to be slid up inside.
33 Once access to the back of the light is achieved, the bulbholder can be twisted off anti-clockwise, then the bulb can be pulled out and changed, without even removing the light itself **(see illustration)**.
34 If required, or preferred, the light can be removed by pushing it out from inside, helped if necessary by squeezing the retaining catch (which will be at the front or rear, depending on how the light was fitted) **(see illustration)**.
35 Refitting is a reversal of removal.

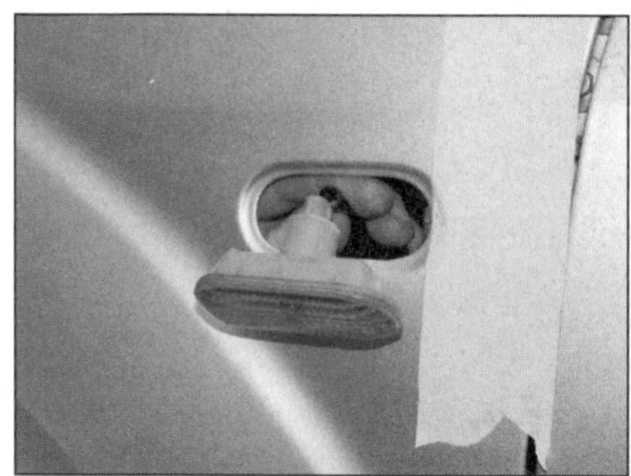
5.34 If preferred, the light can be removed from behind

5.36 Remove the rear light cluster upper and lower screws

5.37 Remove the plastic wing nut

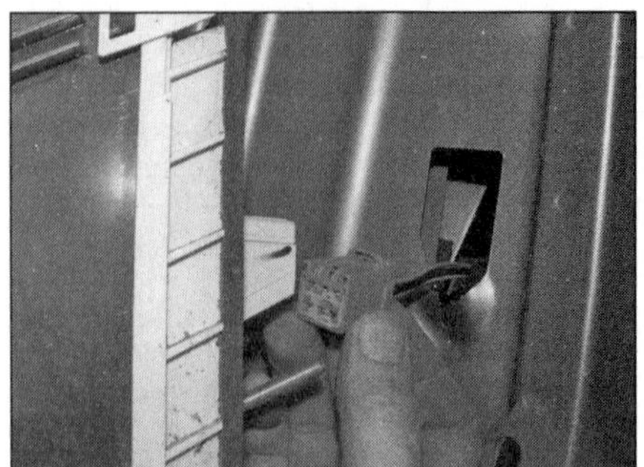
5.38 Disconnect the light unit wiring plug

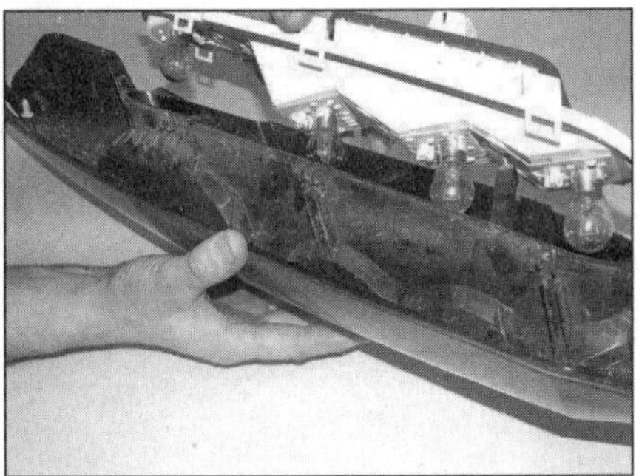
5.39a Unclip and remove the bulbholder ...

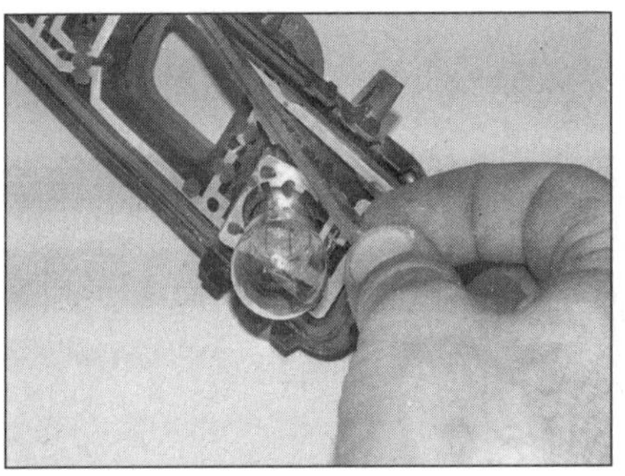
5.39b ... taking care not to damage the rubber seal

5.40 Press and turn the bayonet-fit bulbs to remove them

Rear lights

36 Open the tailgate, and remove the two cross-head screws in the tailgate aperture securing the light unit **(see illustration)**.

37 Inside the boot, fold back the small section of carpet at the rear of the light for access to the plastic wingnut which retains the light unit in position. Support the light unit with one hand outside, then remove the wing nut anti-clockwise **(see illustration)**.

38 On early models, disconnect the wiring plug from the back of the light unit, then remove it from the outside. On later models, remove the light unit then disconnect the wiring **(see illustration)**.

39 The bulbholder is retained by three sets of two clips along its length – pull the clips apart to release the bulbholder, noting that it has a rubber seal fitted **(see illustrations)**.

40 Any of the bayonet-fitting bulbs can now be removed by pressing and turning them anti-clockwise **(see illustration)**.

41 Fit the new bulb(s), then clip the bulbholder back onto the light unit, making sure the seal is correctly located and not damaged, and that the clips engage securely.

42 On early models, offer the light unit back into place, engaging the peg on the rear with the hole in the car, then secure inside with the wingnut and reconnect the wiring plug. On later models, reconnect the wiring plug, then refit the light unit, engaging the peg with the hole. On all models, refit the two screws outside, and tighten them securely.

Number plate light

43 To make access easier, open the tailgate and hold it approximately half-open.

44 Each of the two lights is secured by two torx screws – remove the screws and prise down the light lens **(see illustration)**.

45 Prise out the festoon-type bulb from the two spring contacts, and remove it **(see illustration)**.

46 When fitting the new bulb, ensure that the contacts are holding the bulb securely – if not, careful bending may be necessary, but take care not to fracture the metal.

47 Refitting is a reversal of removal.

High-level brake light

48 Open the tailgate, and prise out the two small rubber covers at the top **(see illustration)**.

49 Using a small screwdriver, release the two catches accessible through the two holes, and free the light unit from the tailgate **(see illustrations)**.

5.44 Remove the two screws from the number plate light lens

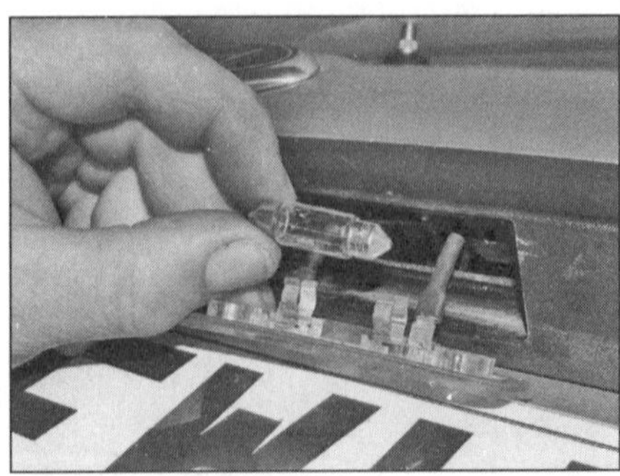
5.45 Prise out the number plate light bulb

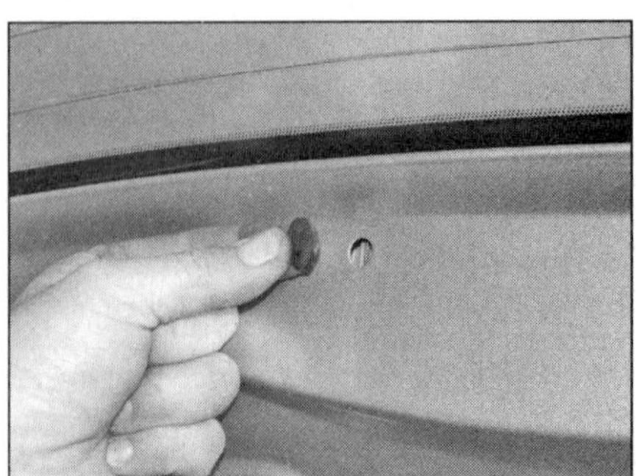
5.48 Prise out the rubber covers at the top of the tailgate

50 Taking care not to pull off the washer hose, disconnect the wiring plug from the light **(see illustration)**.

51 Pull out the wedge-base bulb, and press a new one into place **(see illustration)**.

52 Reconnect the wiring plug, then clip the light unit into position. Refit the rubber covers to the tailgate.

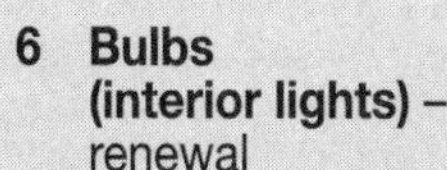

6 Bulbs (interior lights) – renewal

General

1 Refer to Section 5, paragraph 1.

Interior and map reading lights

2 Several different types of interior light assemblies are fitted depending on the trim level and the year of production. All the units and bulbs are renewed in a similar manner.

3 Carefully prise the light unit down at the front, using a small screwdriver **(see illustrations)**.

4 Prise the festoon-type bulb free **(see illustration)**.

5 On higher specification models remove the cover to access the wedge-type bulbs **(see illustrations)**.

6 Fit the new bulb(s) using a reversal of the removal procedure.

Luggage compartment light

7 Carefully prise the light unit out from the trim panel **(see illustration)**.

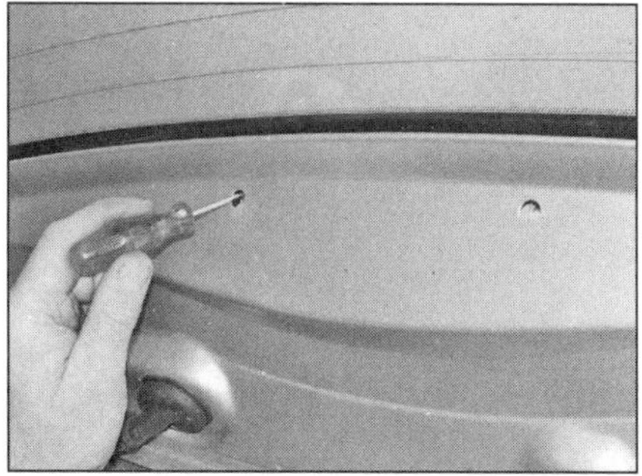

5.49a Release the light unit catches using a screwdriver ...

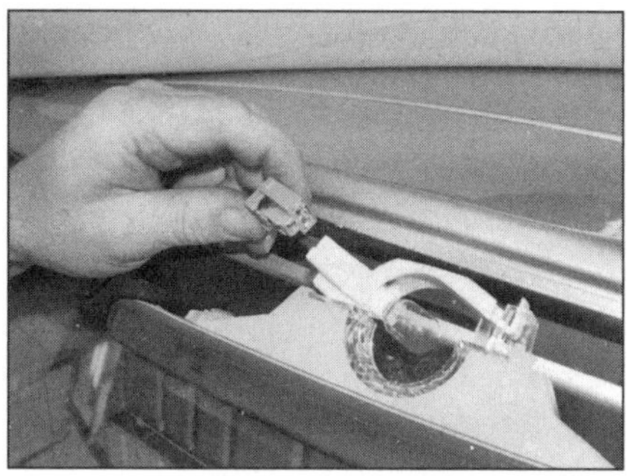

5.50 Disconnect the wiring plug from the high-level brake light

8 Pull out the wedge-type bulb **(see illustration)**.

9 Fit the new bulb using a reversal of the removal procedure.

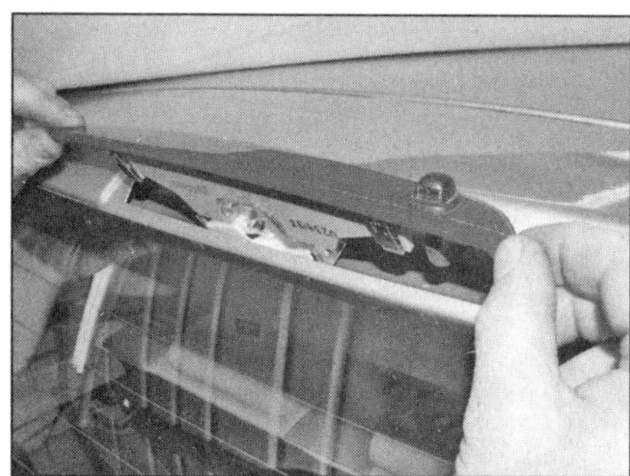

5.49b ... and withdraw the light unit

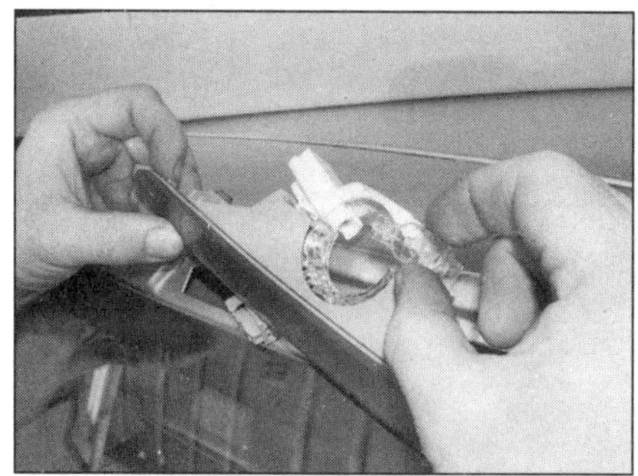

5.51 Pull out the high-level brake light bulb

Instrument panel illumination

10 Conventional bulbs are not fitted to the instrument panel. Illumination is provided by a series of LEDs (light emitting

6.3a Prise down the interior light ...

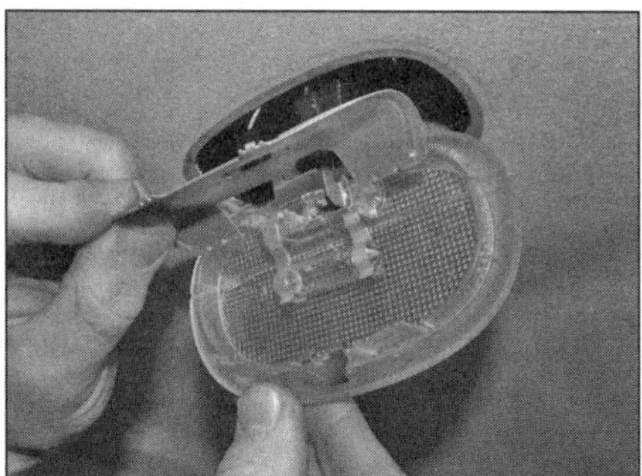

6.3b ... and on some models open the reflector

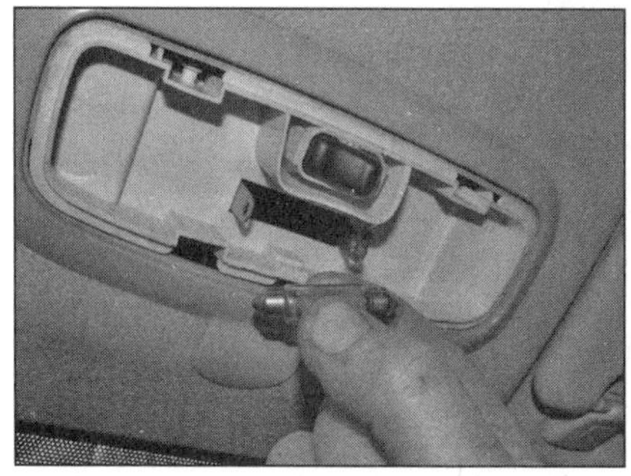

6.4 Remove the bulb

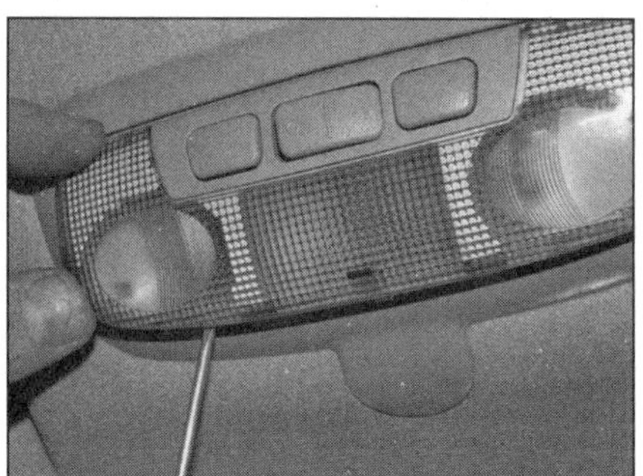

6.5a Remove the cover ...

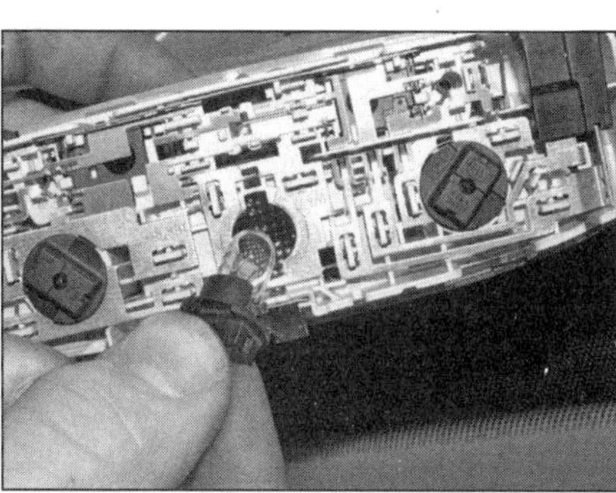

6.5b ... remove the bulbholder ...

6.5c ... and pull the wedge-type bulb free

6.7 Prise the lamp free

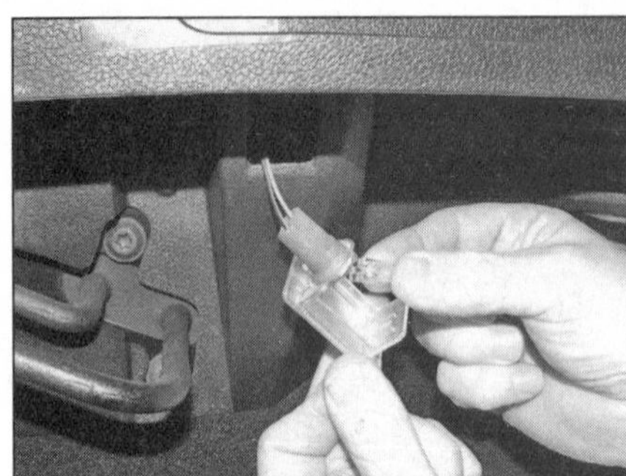
6.8 Pull out the bulb

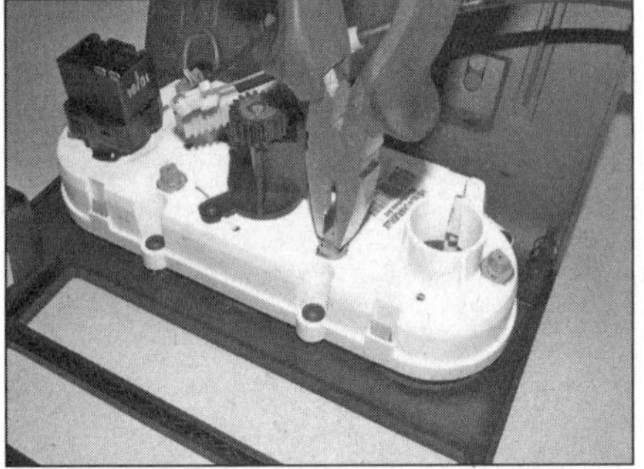
6.13a Twist and pull out the bulbholders ...

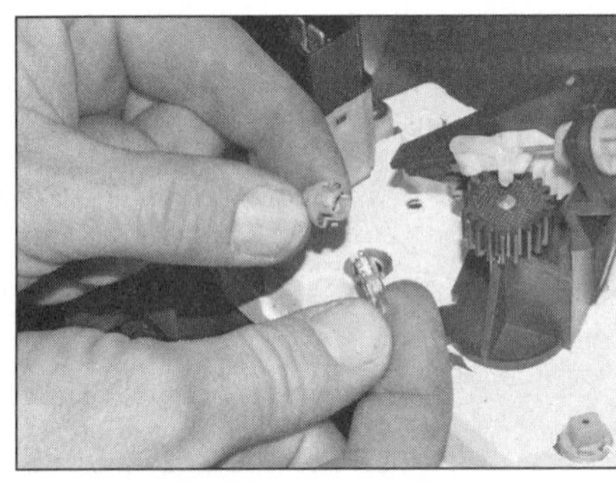
6.13b ... and pull out the wedge-base bulb

diodes). If a fault develops with the panel illumination then carry out the self-test procedure described in Section 10. If the results are inconclusive consult a Ford dealer or suitably-equipped specialist. If a new instrument panel is required, it must be programmed to the vehicle using suitable diagnostic equipment.

Switch illumination

11 The bulbs are integral with the switches, and cannot be renewed separately.

Heater control unit illumination

12 Remove the heater control unit as described in Chapter 3, Section 9.

13 Twist the relevant bulbholder anti-clockwise and remove it from the rear of the panel. Pull out the wedge-base bulb, and fit a new one firmly into place **(see illustrations)**.

14 Refit the heater control unit as described in Chapter 3, Section 9.

7 Exterior light units – removal and refitting

Note: *Before removing any light unit, disconnect the battery negative lead, and position the lead away from the battery (see Chapter 5A, Section 2).*

Headlight

1 Open the bonnet.

2 Remove the three headlight securing screws **(see illustration)**.

3 Pull the unit forwards slightly, disconnect the wiring plug from the side, and remove the unit completely **(see illustration)**.

4 To refit the headlight hook the upper rear under the inner wing and locate the lower edge correctly in the retaining clip **(see illustration)**. Refit the mounting screws and reconnect the wiring plug.

Front indicator light

5 The front indicator is integral with the headlight.

Front foglight

Models made before 10/2005

6 Jack up the front corner of the car, and support it on an axle stand (see *Jacking and vehicle support*).

7 Remove the bulb and wiring pug from the rear of the lamp **(see illustration 5.21)**.

8 Unscrew and remove the two cross-head screws on top of the light, then lift it to unhook the lower mounting lug, and withdraw the light from the rear of the bumper **(see illustrations)**.

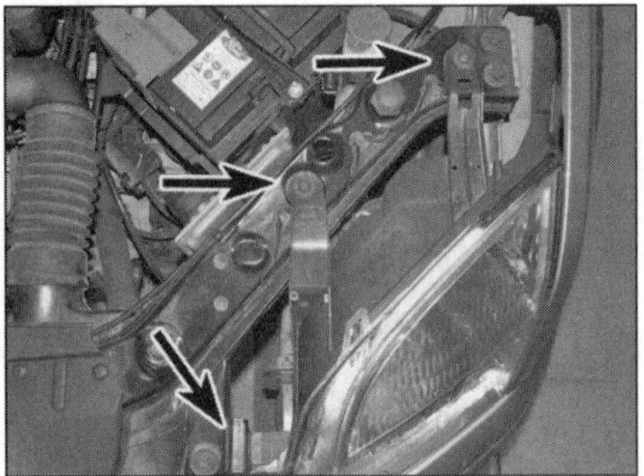
7.2 Remove the three headlight screws (arrowed)

7.3 Disconnect the wiring plug at the side

7.4 The headlamp must engage correctly with the retaining clip (arrowed)

7.8a Remove the two screws on top...

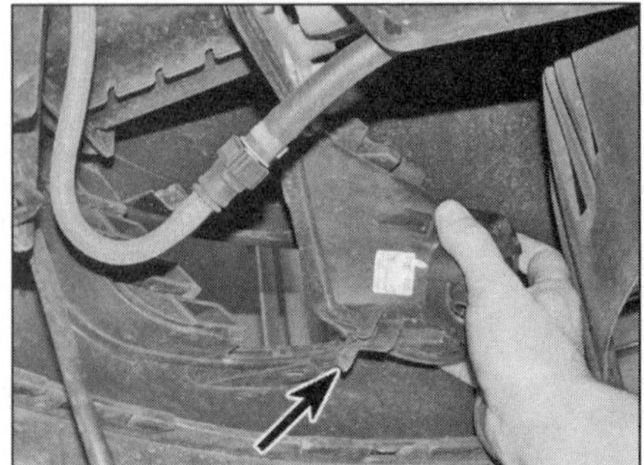
7.8b ... then unhook the light at the bottom to remove it

7.9a Use a plastic trim tool ...

7.9b ... and remove the trim

7.10 Front foglight mounting bolts (arrowed)

Models made after 10/2005

9 Remove the foglight bezel from the front bumper **(see illustrations)**.

10 Undo the two mounting bolts and withdraw the foglight far enough to disconnect the wiring plug **(see illustration)**.

All models

11 Refitting is a reversal of removal, but if necessary check the beam alignment and adjust by turning the screw provided on the bottom of the foglight with a 6.0 mm Allen key.

Indicator side repeater light

12 The procedure is described as part of the bulb renewal procedure in Section 5.

Rear lights

13 The procedure is described as part of the bulb renewal procedure in Section 5.

Number plate light

14 The procedure for removing the light alone is described as part of the bulb renewal procedure in Section 5. If required, once the lens securing screws have been removed, the light unit itself can be removed complete by disconnecting the spade terminals at either end **(see illustration)**.

High-level brake light

15 Remove the light as described in Section 5.

16 Pull off the washer hose, and tape the end of the hose up to the tailgate, end upwards, to reduce fluid spillage **(see illustration)**.

17 Refitting is a reversal of removal. To secure the light, press it in, then upwards, until the retaining catches click home.

8 Headlight adjuster components – removal and refitting

Adjuster switch

1 Refer to Section 4, paragraphs 47 to 50.

Adjuster motor

2 The motor is integral with the headlight, and is not available separately. The headlight is removed as described in Section 7.

7.14 If required, disconnect the spade terminals and remove the light

9 Headlight beam alignment – general information

1 All models are equipped with an electrical vertical beam adjuster unit – this can be used to adjust the headlight beam, to compensate for the load which the car is carrying. An adjuster switch is provided on the facia. Refer to the car's handbook for further information.

2 Accurate adjustment of the headlight beam is only possible using optical beam-setting equipment, and this work should therefore be carried out by a Ford dealer or suitably-equipped workshop.

3 For reference, the headlights can be finely adjusted by rotating the adjuster screws fitted to the top of each light unit. The vertical adjustment screw is mounted at the inner end of the headlight. The horizontal adjustment screw is mounted at the outer end of the headlight **(see illustration)**. Note if the vertical adjustment is altered, this will affect the horizontal adjustment, which will have to be adjusted too.

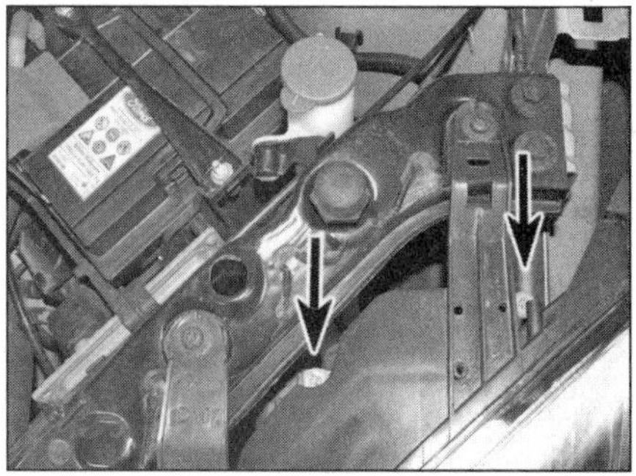
9.3 The headlight beam adjustment screws

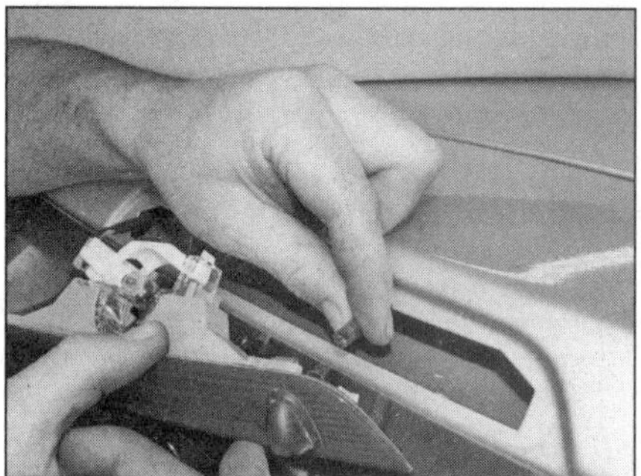
7.16 Disconnect the washer hose from the top of the high-level brake light

10 Instrument panel – general information and testing

1 The instrument panel appears to be a solid-state item, with no parts shown as being available separately. There are some illumination bulbs on the rear of the panel which can be renewed, but that appears to be all that's within the scope of the DIY owner.

2 There is, however, a self-test facility for the instrument cluster, which can be performed without any diagnostic equipment. Thirty separate tests are carried out on the instrument cluster and related circuits as part of this. As with the self-test facility on the GEM (see Section 3), this instrument cluster test can really only be used as part of the fault diagnosis process, and ultimately, a Ford dealer's services will be required if a problem is evident.

Self-test mode

3 To enter the instrument cluster self-test mode, proceed as follows.

4 Press and hold the trip meter reset button (the right-hand one), and turn the ignition to position II (ignition on).

5 When TEST is displayed on the LCD panel, release the trip meter button.

Test	Display	Item Tested	Description
1. Gauge drive	GAGE	Tachometer, Speedometer, Temperature and Fuel	All pointers activated. All LCD segments illuminated for Temperature and Fuel level
2. LCD segments	All segments illuminated	Odometer LCD	Illuminated all Odometer LCD segments
3. Indicator LED	bulb	Indicators and warning lights	All cluster warning lights illuminated
4. ROM Level	rXXX/Fail	Cluster ROM	ROM (Read Only Memory) level and type
5. Non-volatile Memory level	nrXXXX	Cluster NVM	NVM (Non-Volatile Memory) type and level stored in cluster ROM
6. None	EE XX/FAIL	Checksum fault	Unavailable
7. None	CF1 XX	Configuration	Unavailable
8. None	CF2 XX	Configuration	Unavailable
9. None	CF3 XX	Configuration	Unavailable
10. DTC (Diagnostic Trouble Code)	dtc XXXX/NONE	DTCs	DTCs stored in cluster
11. Vehicle speed (m.p.h)	E XXXX	Speedometer	Displays miles per hour. Dashes shown if no signal available
12. Vehicle speed (k.p.h)	XXXX	Speedometer	Displays kilometres per hour. Dashes shown if no signal available
13. None	SGXXXX	Speedometer	Speedometer driver gauge count
14. Engine speed	T XXXX	Tachometer	Displays the engine RPM. Dashes shown if no signal available
15. None	tGXXXX	Tachometer	Tachometer driver gauge count
16. Fuel volume	F1 XXX	Fuel sender	Displays the volume: 000-009 = Short circuit, 010-254 = Normal and 255 = open circuit
17. None	FP1 XXX	Input	Unavailable
18. None	FPt XXX	Input	Unavailable
19. Fuel level	FGXXXX	Fuel LCD	Illuminates LCD segments in the gauge
20. Engine coolant temperature	XXX C	Coolant temperature	Displays the last coolant temperature
21. Engine temperature	CGXXXX	Temperature LCD	Illuminates the segments in the temperature LCD
22. Odometer input	odoXXX	Odometer display	Displays the odometer input: 0-254 = valid, 255 = invalid input
23. None	Trn -X	Input	Unavailable
24. None	IUd XX	Input	Unavailable
25. Battery voltage	bAtXXX	Voltage	Displays battery voltage
26. Brake fluid	Bf -x	Fluid level	Good level = -O. Low level = -G
27. Handbrake	Hb -X	Handbrake input	Handbrake on = -G. Handbrake off = -O
28. Illumination	SLP -X	Sidelight	Sidelight on = -b. Sidelight off = -O
29. None	LCXXXX	LCD duty cycle	Unavailable
30. Crank sensor	Cr -X	Crank sensor circuit	Displays the sensor input to the cluster. –b = Input high, -O = Input low

10.7 Instrument cluster self test. X represents a numerical value

11.2 Remove the shroud

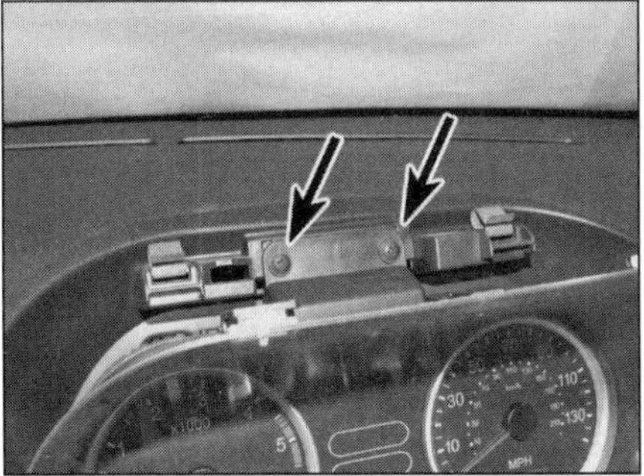
11.3a Remove the two screws (arrowed) ...

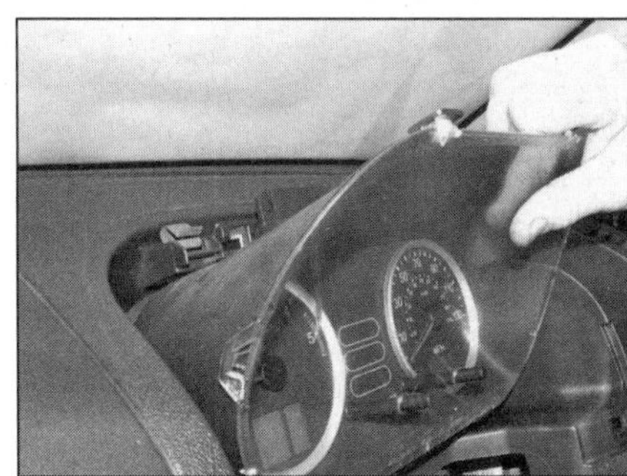
11.3b ... and lift out the instrument panel

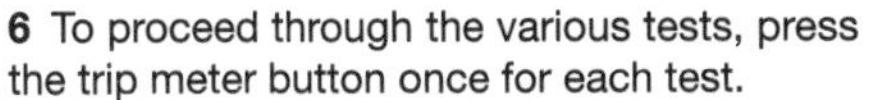
6 To proceed through the various tests, press the trip meter button once for each test.

7 A certain amount of interpretation **(see illustration)** will be required to decipher the meaning of the results which will be displayed on the LCD panel – some tests will produce no reading (- - - -), for instance, and this doesn't necessarily indicate a fault. Any serious concerns, especially associated with a warning light or gauge which does not seem to be working in normal use, should be referred to a Ford dealer.

8 To exit the test mode, press the trip meter button for more than 3 seconds, or turn off the ignition.

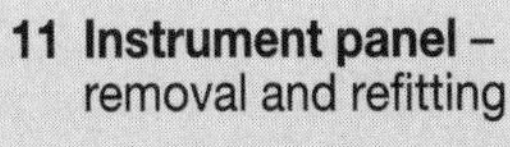
11 Instrument panel – removal and refitting

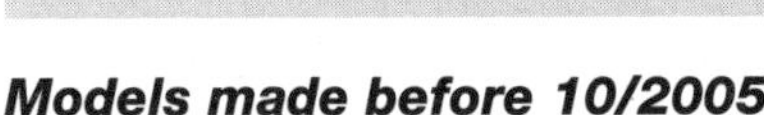
Models made before 10/2005

Removal

1 Disconnect the battery negative lead, and position the lead away from the battery (see Chapter 5A, Section 2).

2 Remove the instrument panel shroud **(see illustration)**. This is slightly easier if the upper column shroud is removed first (as described in Chapter 11, Section 25).

3 Remove the two Torx screws at the top of the instrument panel, then withdraw it from the facia **(see illustrations)**.

4 Release the hinged locking catch on the single wiring plug at the rear, disconnect the plug, and remove the instrument panel **(see illustrations)**.

Refitting

5 Refitting is a reversal of removal. If a new instrument panel is fitted, it will have to be programmed using Ford's IDS diagnostic equipment before it will work properly.

Models made after 10/2005

Removal

6 Disconnect the battery negative lead, and position the lead away from the battery (see Chapter 5A, Section 2).

7 Adjust the steering column to its lowest position, then turn the steering wheel to give access to the upper shroud. Using a small screwdriver remove the steering column upper shroud by depressing the two clips **(see illustrations)**.

8 Remove the lower facia panel beneath the steering wheel. To do this, undo the lower screws, then undo the upper screws located in the stowage compartment, release the clip and withdraw the panel

9 Undo the two lower screws and remove the instrument panel finishing panel **(see illustrations)**.

11.4a Slide the wiring plug locking catch to the side ...

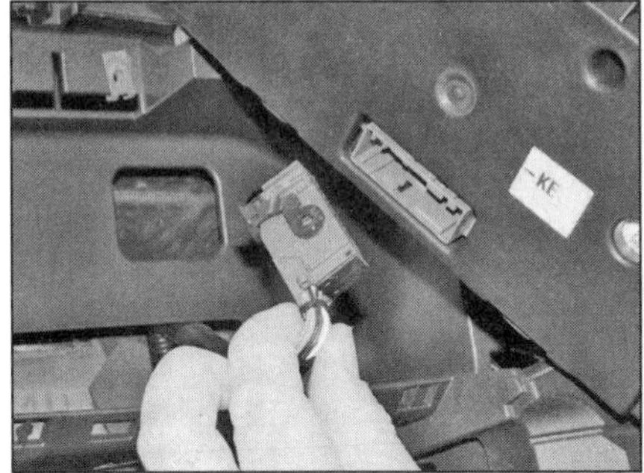
11.4b ... then disconnect the plug and remove the panel

11.7a Remove the upper shroud ...

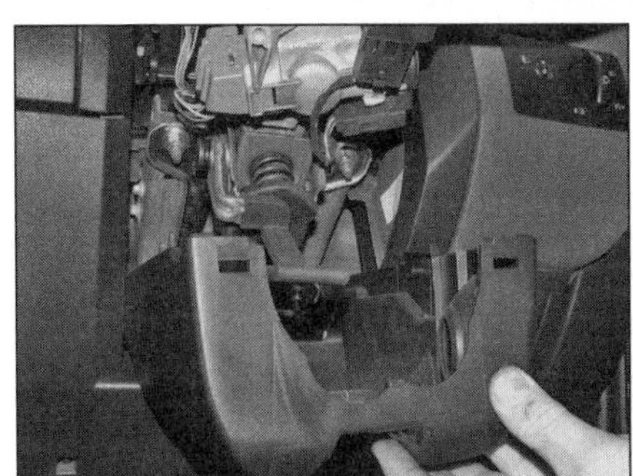
11.7b ... and the lower shroud

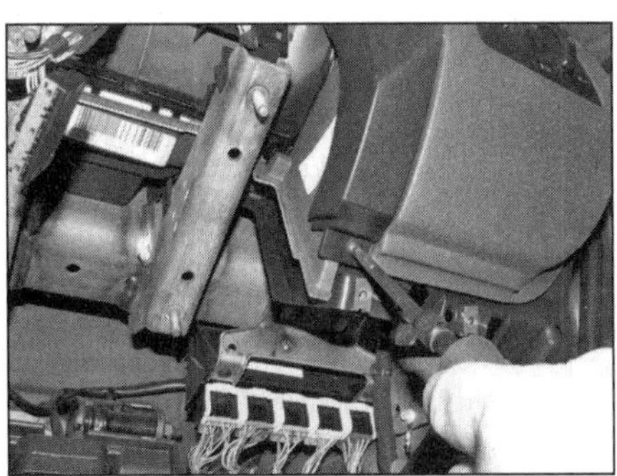
11.9a Remove the screws (column removed for clarity) ...

11.9b ... and release the panel

11.10 Remove the screws (arrowed)

11.11b This is the locking tab (arrowed) that must be released

10 Undo the retaining screws located on the bottom of the instrument panel **(see illustration)**.
11 Release the top of the instrument panel from the facia by carefully inserting a round-ended steel rule or thin plastic trim tool at the apex of the panel to depress the retaining clip **(see illustrations)**. We found it impossible to reach the clip without pulling the panel partially forward first. Please note this is a difficult procedure with a high chance of damaging the instrument panel glass, so proceed with caution.

12.4 The horn on early models

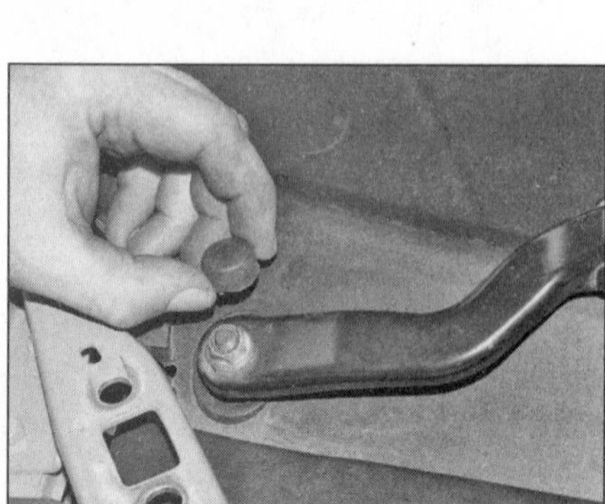
13.2 Prise off the cover for access to the wiper arm nut

11.11a Release the panel

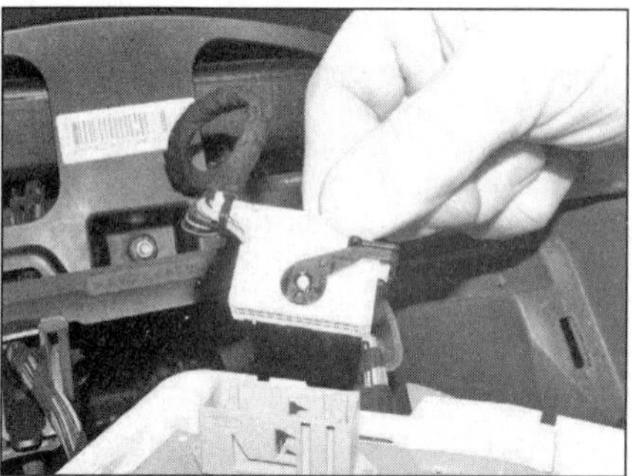
11.12 Release the wiring plug

12.6 The horn on later models

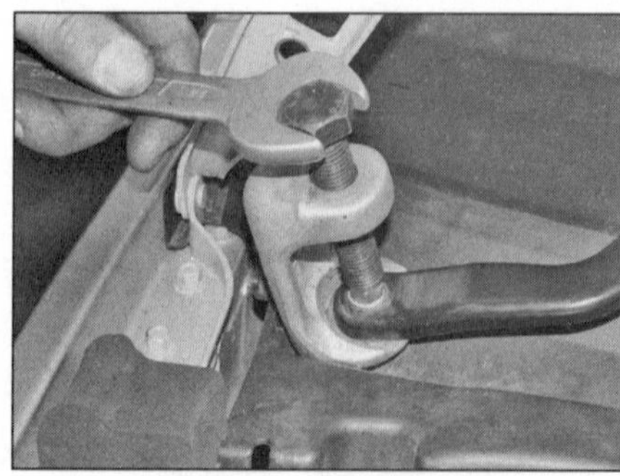
13.3a If necessary a suitable puller can be used ...

12 Release the hinged locking catch on the single wiring plug at the rear, disconnect the plug, and remove the instrument panel **(see illustration)**.

Refitting

13 Refitting is a reversal of removal. If a new instrument panel is fitted, it will have to be programmed using Ford's IDS diagnostic equipment. The vehicle will not start until the instrument panel has been programmed to the vehicle.

12 Horn – removal and refitting

Removal

Early models

1 On early models the horn is located under the left-hand headlight (left as seen from the driver's seat).
2 To improve access, remove the left-hand headlight as described in Section 7.
3 Disconnect the wiring plug from the horn.
4 Unscrew the securing nut, and remove the horn from its mounting bracket **(see illustration)**.

Later models

5 On later models the horn is mounted behind the front bumper. Remove the front bumper as described in Chapter 11, Section 6.
6 Disconnect the wiring plug and unbolt the horn **(see illustration)**.

Refitting

7 Refitting is a reversal of removal.

13 Wiper arm – removal and refitting

Removal

1 Operate the wiper motor, then switch it off so that the wiper arm returns to the park position. Mark the resting position of the wiper blade on the windscreen with masking tape.
2 Prise up the wiper arm spindle nut cover, then slacken and remove the spindle nut **(see illustration)**. Recover the washer.
3 Lift the blade off the glass, and pull the wiper arm off its spindle. Note that on some models, the wiper arms may be very tight on the spindle splines – it should be possible to lever the arm off the spindle, using a flat-bladed screwdriver (take care not to damage the scuttle cover panel). In extreme cases, it may even be necessary to use a small puller to free the arm **(see illustrations)**.

Refitting

4 Ensure that the wiper arm and spindle splines are clean and dry, then refit the arm to the spindle. Where applicable, align the

wiper blade with the tape fitted on removal. Note that index marks are provided on some factory-fitted windscreens for precise wiper blade alignment.

5 Refit the spindle nut, tightening it securely, and clip the nut cover back into position.

14 Windscreen wiper motor and linkage – removal and refitting

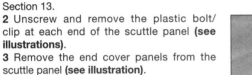

Removal

1 Remove the wiper arms as described in Section 13.

2 Unscrew and remove the plastic bolt/ clip at each end of the scuttle panel **(see illustrations)**.

3 Remove the end cover panels from the scuttle panel **(see illustration)**.

4 The scuttle panel is clipped into a plastic channel running the full width of the windscreen – prise it gently at the rear, at one end, to start it. The channel may stay in place or it will come off with the panel. Remove the panel from the car **(see illustrations)**.

5 Remove the three screws at the top of the wiper motor cover panel **(see illustration)**. Do not remove the single bolt lower down, between the wiper spindles.

6 **Do not** at any point raise the front of the vehicle. The tyres must remain in contact with the ground at all times

7 Remove the three nuts from the suspension strut tower **(see illustration)**.

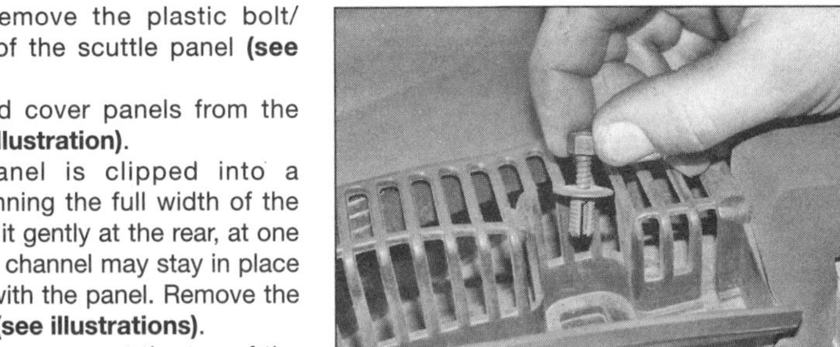

13.3b ... to remove the wiper arm

14.2b ... and remove the plastic bolt/clip

14.2a At each end of the scuttle, unscrew ...

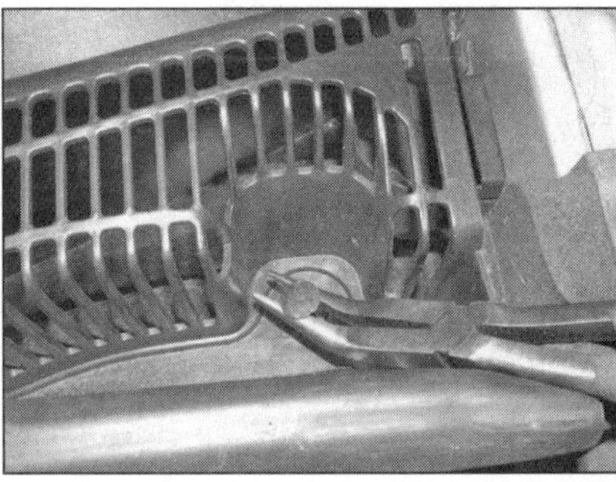

14.2c On later models prise out the trim clip

8 Where fitted detach the cross-brace from motor support panel.

9 Lift the cover panel out, together with the attached motor and linkage. Turn the panel over and disconnect the wiper motor wiring plug **(see illustration)**.

14.3 Remove the rain channels

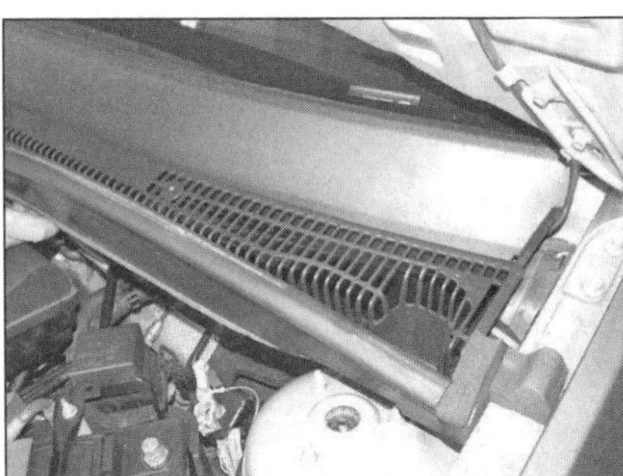

14.4a Remove the panel ...

14.4b ... and recover the plastic channel if necessary

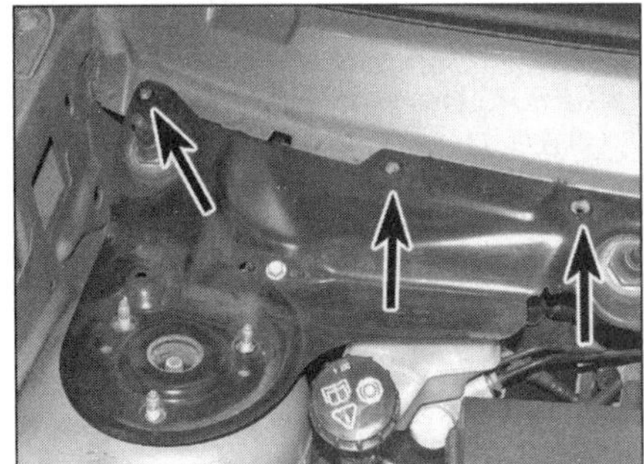

14.5 Remove the Torx head screws (arrowed)

14.7 Remove the three suspension strut nuts (arrowed)

14.9 Disconnect the wiper motor wiring plug

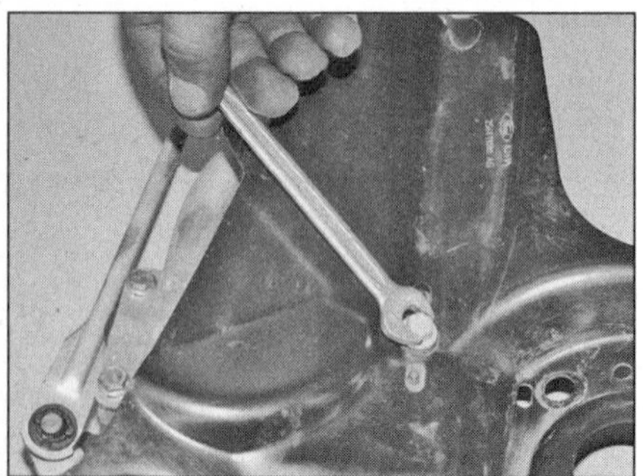

14.10 Remove the motor mounting bolt

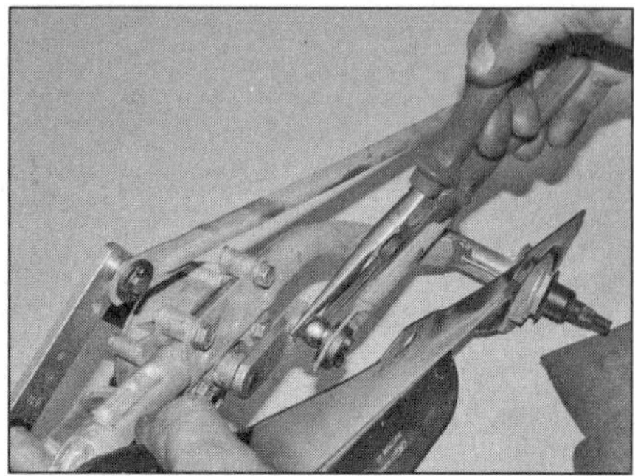

14.11 Prise off the motor arm

14.12a Turn the motor arm slightly clockwise ...

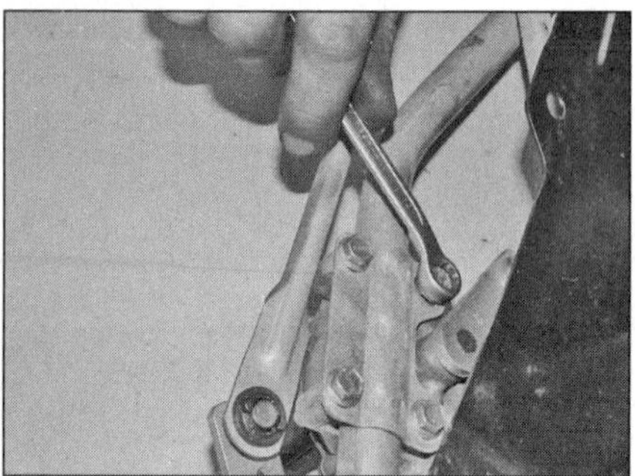

14.12b ... to access all four motor mounting bolts ...

14.12c ... and remove the wiper motor

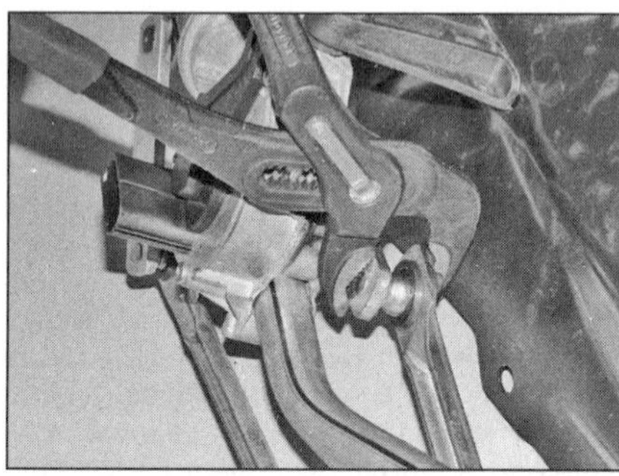

14.13 Using a pair of slip-joint ('water pump') pliers to reconnect the wiper motor arm

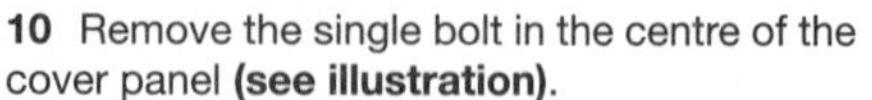

10 Remove the single bolt in the centre of the cover panel **(see illustration)**.

11 Note the fitted position of the wiper motor arm (typically, it will be horizontally aligned, along the axis of the motor frame), then prise off the ball fitting using a pair of pliers **(see illustration)**.

12 Turn the wiper motor arm slightly clockwise, to access all four of the wiper motor mounting bolts. Use paint to mark the positions of the bolts, as they are in slotted holes. Remove the four bolts, and remove the wiper motor **(see illustrations)**.

Refitting

13 Refitting is a reversal of removal, bearing in mind the following points:

a) Ensure that the motor is in the 'parked' position before refitting.

*b) Reset the motor arm to the position noted prior to removal, then press on the ball fitting using a pair of pliers **(see illustration)**.*

c) Refit the wiper arms with reference to Section 13.

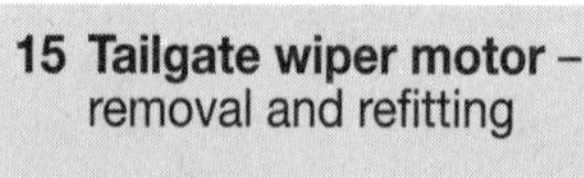

15 Tailgate wiper motor – removal and refitting

Removal

1 Open the tailgate, and remove the inner trim panel, which is secured by three cross-head screws and several clips.

2 Remove the wiper arm as described in Section 13 **(see illustrations)**.

3 Disconnect the wiper motor wiring plug **(see illustration)**.

4 Remove the three motor mounting bolts, recover the washers, and withdraw the motor from the tailgate **(see illustration)**.

Refitting

5 Refitting is a reversal of removal. Ensure that the wiper motor spindle grommet stays in place in the tailgate glass as the spindle is fitted back through.

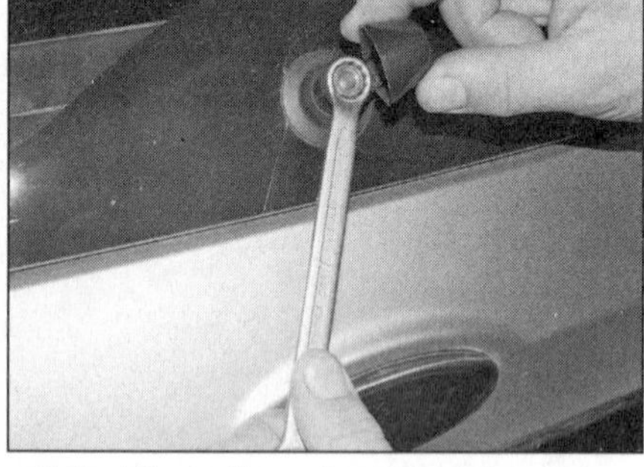

15.2a Flip up the nut cover, and unscrew the wiper arm nut ...

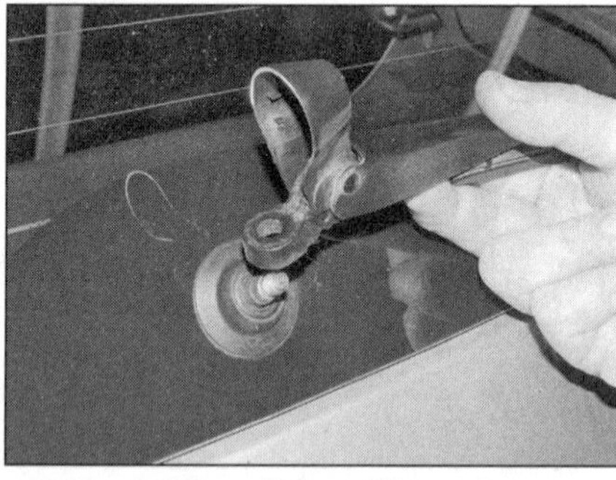

15.2b ... then pull the tailgate wiper arm from its splines

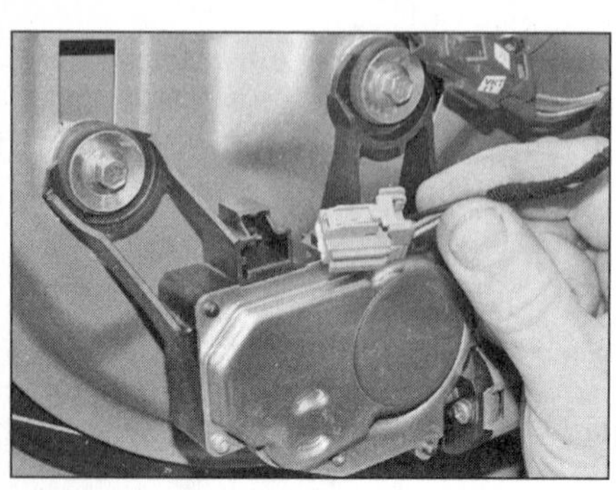

15.3 Disconnect the tailgate wiper wiring plug

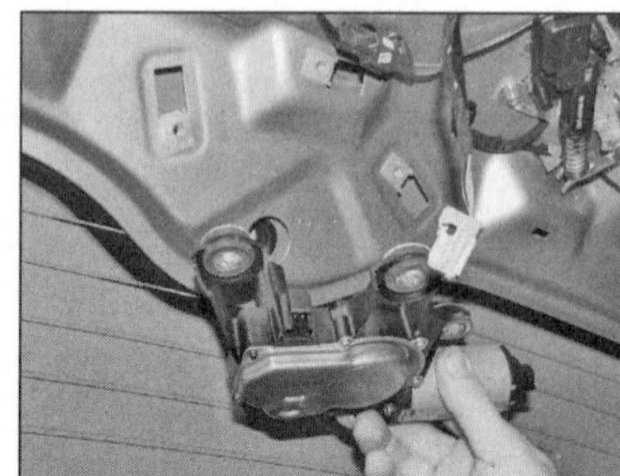

15.4 Undo the three bolts and remove the tailgate wiper motor

16.1 Reservoir upper mounting bolt location

16 Windscreen/tailgate washer system components – removal and refitting

Washer fluid reservoir

Except later 1.6 litre diesel models

1 The windscreen washer fluid reservoir is located on the left-hand side of the engine compartment, next to the battery. First, remove the bolt from the mounting bracket at the top of the reservoir filler neck **(see illustration)**.

2 Remove the left-hand headlight (left as seen from the driver's seat) as described in Section 7.

3 Remove the centre bolt securing the reservoir to the chassis leg **(see illustration)**.

4 Loosen the left-hand front wheel nuts, then raise the front corner of the car and support it on an axle stand (see *Jacking and vehicle support*). Remove the wheel.

5 Remove the wheel arch liner, which is secured by a combination of screws and clips **(see illustration)**.

6 Disconnect the wiring plug from the washer pump. Where applicable, also disconnect the wiring from the low-level warning switch which may also be fitted to the reservoir.

7 Anticipate some spillage of washer fluid (have a suitable container ready), then disconnect the washer hoses, noting their fitted locations. Alternatively, siphon out the fluid using a long tube inserted through the filler neck.

8 Remove the lower mounting bolt from the reservoir **(see illustration)**, and manoeuvre it out from its location, taking care not to damage the filler neck.

9 Refitting is a reversal of removal. Make sure the washer hoses are securely reconnected to their original positions.

Later 1.6 litre diesel models

10 The windscreen washer fluid reservoir is located on the right-hand side of the engine compartment, next to the engine coolant expansion tank. In order to remove the reservoir, it is necessary to remove the air conditioning dehydrator which involves having the air conditioning system evacuated by a Ford dealer or air conditioning specialist. Refer to Chapter 3, Section 11 for details of the removal procedure.

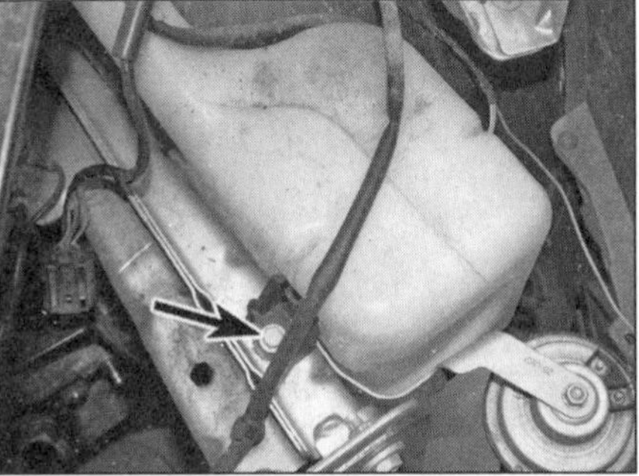

16.3 Washer reservoir middle mounting bolt (headlight removed)

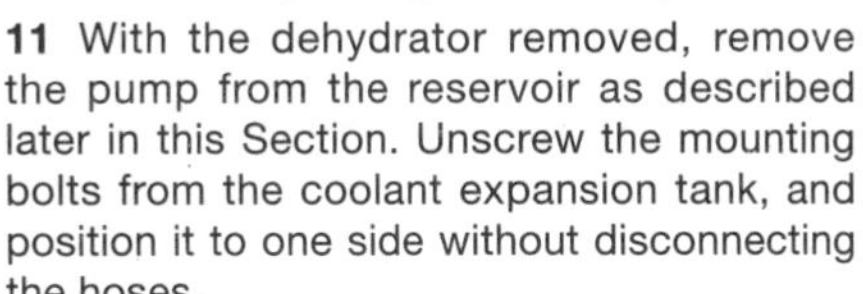

11 With the dehydrator removed, remove the pump from the reservoir as described later in this Section. Unscrew the mounting bolts from the coolant expansion tank, and position it to one side without disconnecting the hoses.

12 Unscrew the three mounting bolts and withdraw the washer fluid reservoir so that the hoses can be disconnected. Manoeuvre the reservoir out from its location, taking care not to damage the filler neck

13 Refitting is a reversal of removal. Make sure the washer hoses are securely reconnected to their original positions.

Washer fluid pump

14 If possible, siphon the fluid from the reservoir into a suitable container using a long tube inserted through the filler neck.

15 Refer to the previous sub-Section and carry out the relevant work to gain access to the fluid reservoir.

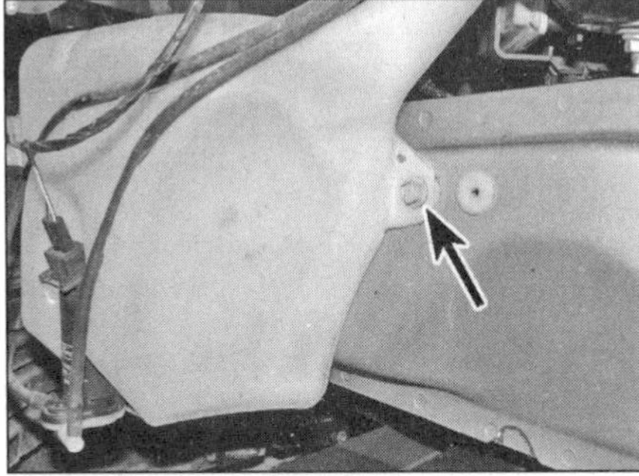

16.8 Reservoir lower mounting bolt on the inside of the wheel arch

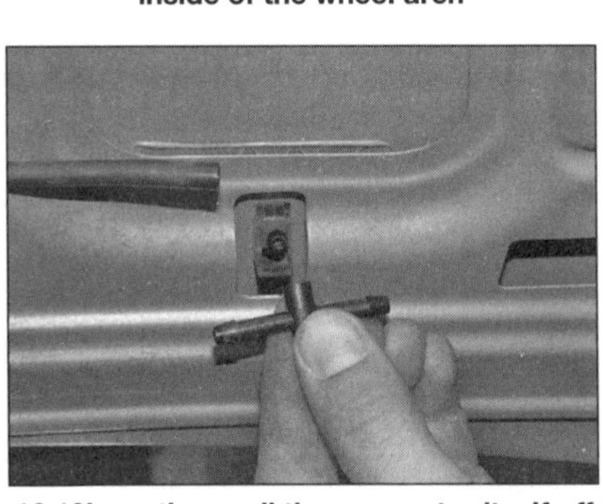

16.19b ... then pull the connector itself off the base of the washer jet

16.5 Removing the front wheel arch liner

16 Prise the pump from the reservoir, and recover the rubber sealing grommet. If all the fluid was not removed, position a container beneath the reservoir.

17 Examine the rubber sealing grommet, and renew if necessary.

18 Refitting is a reversal of removal, but take care not to push the grommet into the reservoir when refitting the pump. Make sure that the pump is securely fitted in its sealing grommet, and make sure that the fluid hose(s) are securely reconnected.

Windscreen washer jet

19 Working under the bonnet, disconnect the washer hoses as necessary, then carefully pull the fluid hose T-piece from the washer jet **(see illustrations)**.

20 Carefully prise the washer jet from the outside of the bonnet – push it forwards slightly against the clip, then unhook it at the rear **(see illustration)**.

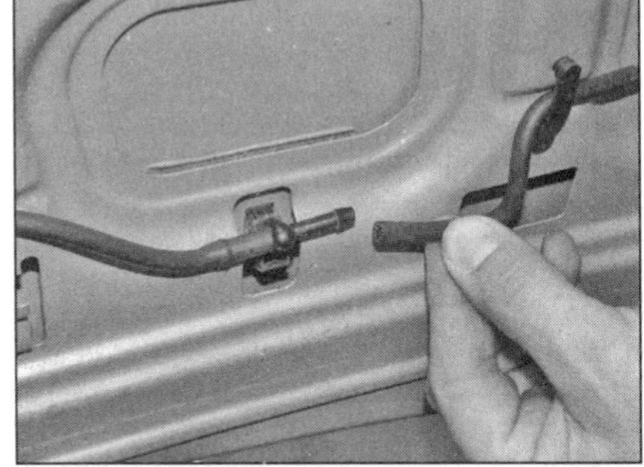

16.19a Pull the washer hoses off the T-piece connector ...

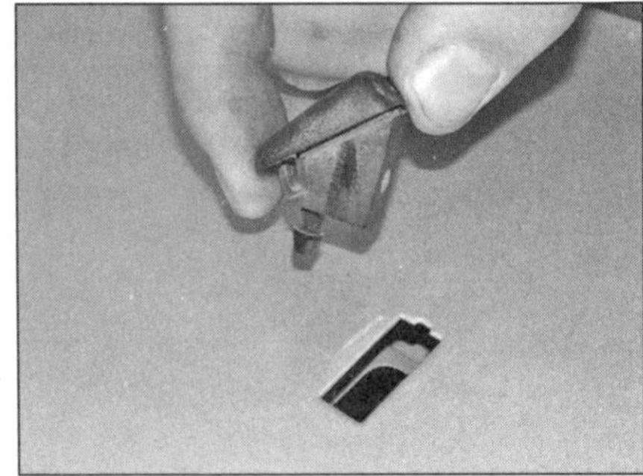

16.20 Removing the washer jet from the bonnet – note the clip at the front

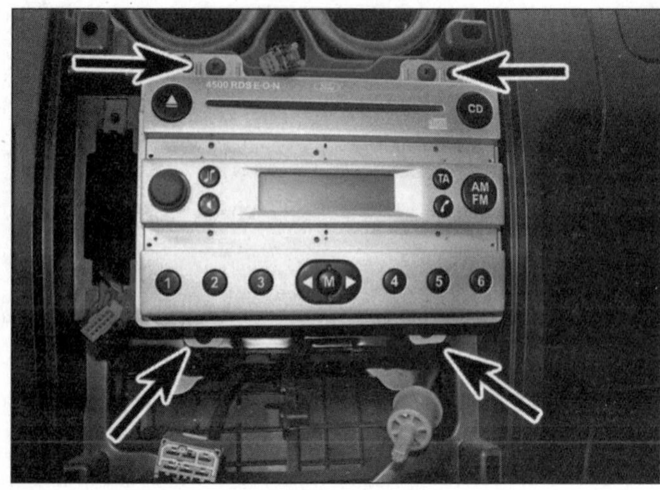

17.2a Remove the four screws (arrowed) ...

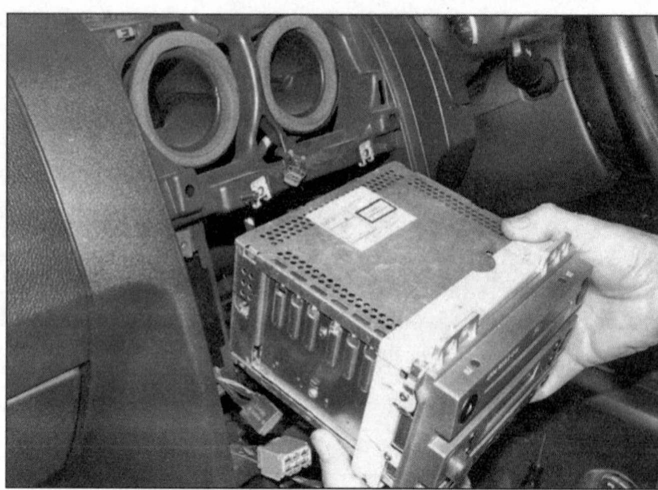
17.2b ... and withdraw the radio from the facia

21 Refitting is a reversal of removal, but make sure that the fluid hose connections are securely remade.

Tailgate washer jet

22 The washer jet is fitted to the high-level brake light. Remove the light as described in Section 7.

23 Carefully prise the jet out of the light unit, taking care not to damage either component.

24 Refitting is a reversal of removal. Refit the light unit as described in Section 7.

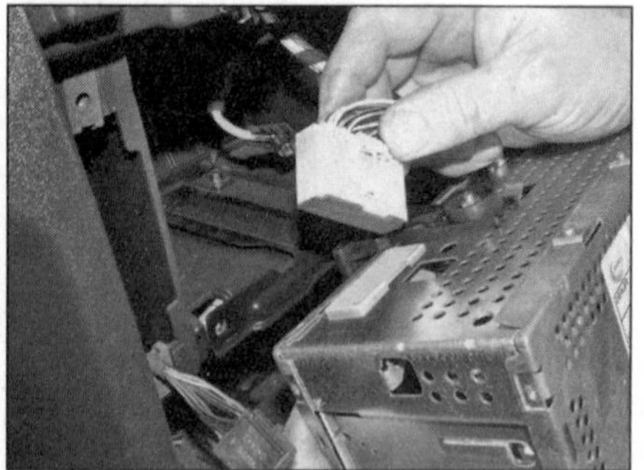
17.3 Disconnect the power/speaker wiring plug and aerial lead

17.6b ... and withdraw the radio/CD player from the facia

17 Audio unit – removal and refitting

Models made before 10/2005

Note: *If a Ford 'Keycode' unit is fitted, and the battery is disconnected, the unit will not function again on reconnection until the correct security code has been entered.*

Removal

1 Remove the heater control panel as described in Chapter 3, Section 9.

17.6a Insert the keys and push them keys sideways...

17.7 Remove the wiring plug

2 Remove the four screws (two above, two below) securing the radio/CD player to the facia, and withdraw it **(see illustrations)**.

3 Disconnect the wiring plug and the aerial lead, and remove the unit **(see illustration)**.

Refitting

4 Refitting is a reversal of removal. Refit the heater control panel as described in Chapter 3, Section 9.

Models made after 10/2005

Removal

5 Four special removal keys are required to remove the audio unit on models manufactured from 10/2005. Ford technicians use Ford tool set number GV3301 inserted at the four corners of the unit, however, suitable alternative tools may be available from car accessory shops. The keys are marked for position – eg, TOP L is the top left-hand key – and the markings should face upwards when in position. It is not possible to use feeler blades, as the special tools have contours which engage with internal spring clips.

6 Insert the keys (with their flat edges facing outwards) in the slots provided at each corner of the unit, then push all four keys sideways at the same time, away from the unit – this has the effect of releasing the internal clips. Withdraw the unit from the facia for access to the rear wiring and aerial **(see illustrations)**.

7 Disconnect the wiring plug by pulling the locking lever open **(see illustration)**, then disconnect the aerial. Remove the unit then remove the keys from each corner by depressing the side clips.

Refitting

8 Refitting is a reversal of removal – with the wiring and aerial reconnected, press the unit into position until the retaining clips engage. If a new audio unit is fitted, it will have to be programmed using Ford's IDS diagnostic equipment before it will work properly.

18.2a Remove the four Torx screws (arrowed) ...

18.2b ... withdraw the speaker ...

18.2c ... and disconnect the wiring plug

18 Loudspeakers - removal and refitting

Removal

1 Remove the relevant door inner trim panel (or rear side trim panel), as described in Chapter 11, Section 12 or 25.

2 Unscrew the four loudspeaker securing screws, then withdraw the loudspeaker and disconnect the wiring plug **(see illustrations)**.

Refitting

3 Refitting is a reversal of removal.

19 Radio aerial - removal and refitting

Removal

1 If only the aerial mast is to be removed, this can be unscrewed from the aerial base. To remove the base, proceed as follows.

2 On models without a sunroof, remove the interior light as described in Section 6 **(see illustration)**. On models with a sunroof, remove the roof console as described in Chapter 11, Section 25.

3 To remove the cable first remove the sunvisors **(see illustration)**.

4 Remove the sunvisor clips by prising out the cover flaps, and unscrewing the single screw inside **(see illustration)**.

5 Carefully unclip the front edge of the headlining panel to gain access to the cable.

6 Remove the right-hand A-pillar trim panel as described in Chapter 11, Section 25.

7 Unscrew the bolt, and disconnect the cable.

8 Partially lower the headlining and release the cable. Disconnect the wiring plug from the heated screen and then unclip the cable from the A-pillar.

9 With reference to Chapter 11, Section 25, remove the driver's side lower panel and the column shrouds.

10 Remove the audio unit (as described in Section 17) and release the aerial cable.

11 Detach the cable from the clips located on the crossmember **(see illustration)**.

12 Attach a length of stout cord to the end of the cable and with care pull the cable out from the facia.

Refitting

13 Attach the end of the cord to the new cable and use the cord to aid pulling the cable under and through the facia.

14 Refitting the rest of the cable is a reversal of the removal procedure.

20 Anti-theft alarm system and engine immobiliser - general information

Certain models are equipped with an anti-theft alarm system, in addition to the engine immobiliser fitted to all models. Various types of system may be fitted, depending on specification and market.

The anti-theft alarm system is automatically activated by the central locking system (manually, or via the remote control, where applicable). The engine immobiliser system is operated by a coded unit in the ignition key – the engine can only be started using one of the ignition keys originally supplied with the car when new.

The alarm system uses the courtesy light switches built into the door lock assemblies.

Any faults with the system should be referred to a Ford dealer or suitably-equipped garage.

Immobiliser system

An engine immobiliser system is fitted as standard to all models, and the system is operated automatically every time the ignition key is inserted/removed.

The immobiliser system ensures that the car can only be started using the original Ford

19.2 With the lamp removed the aerial base can be accessed (arrowed)

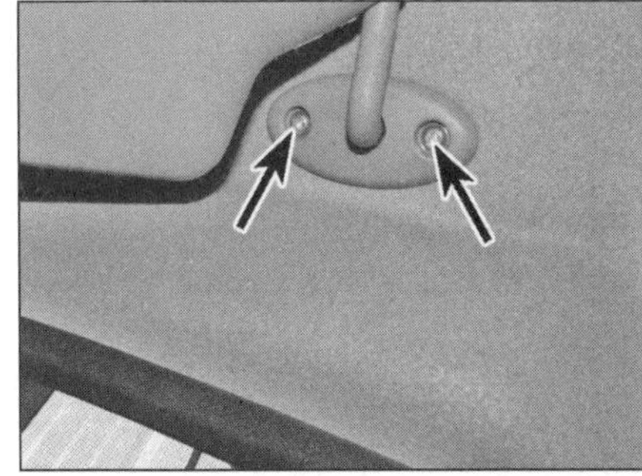
19.3 The sunvisor hinges are secured by two screws ...

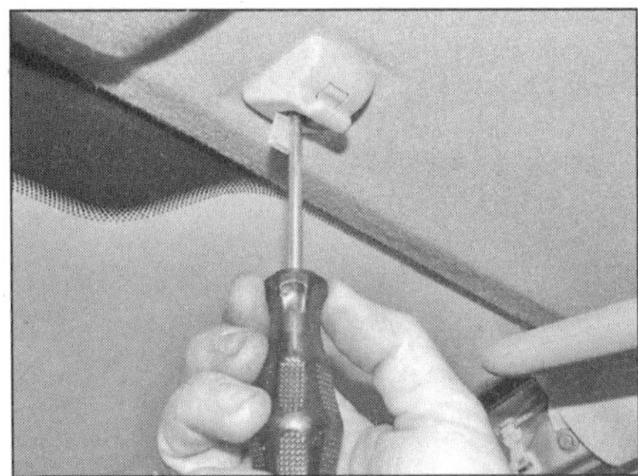
19.4 ... while the visor clips have one, under a covering flap

19.11 The route of the cable (arrowed). Facia removed for clarity

ignition key. The key contains an electronic chip (transponder) which is programmed with a code. When the key is inserted into the ignition switch, it uses the current present in the sensor coil (which is fitted to the switch housing) to send a signal to the immobiliser electronic control unit (ECU). The ECU checks this code every time the ignition is switched on. If the key code does not match the ECU code, the ECU will disable the starter circuit to prevent the engine being started.

If the ignition key is lost, a new one can be obtained from a Ford dealer. They have access to the correct key code for the immobiliser system of your car, and will be able to supply a new coded key.

If you have any spare keys cut, they will only open the doors, etc, if they are not coded correctly, and will not be capable of starting the engine. For this reason, it may be best to have any spare keys supplied by your Ford dealer, who will also be able to advise you on coding the keys. Providing the function has not been disabled with Ford's diagnostic equipment it is possible for the owner to programme new keys, providing that at least two fully-functioning keys are available. To programme a new key proceed as follows:

1) *Insert the first programmed key into the ignition.*
2) *Turn the key to position II and hold in this position for one second.*
3) *Remove the key and within five seconds insert the second programmed key.*
4) *Turn the second key to position II and hold it there for one second.*
5) *Remove the key and within ten seconds insert the unprogrammed key into the ignition.*
6) *Turn the key to position II and hold it there for one second.*
7) *Remove the key.*
8) *To programme additional keys repeat the procedure from stage 1 to 7.*

If the new key does not start the vehicle, repeat the procedure. If this method fails it is more than likely that the vehicle has been programmed with diagnostic equipment to disable this function. This is a common feature on cars originally supplied to hire fleets and company cars. Another possible reason is that the key limit of eight programmed keys has been exceeded.

21 Airbag system – general information, precautions and system de-activation

General information

Driver's and front seat passenger's airbags are fitted as standard equipment on all models. The driver's airbag is fitted to the steering wheel centre pad, while the passenger's unit is fitted to the top of the facia.

Higher specification models also have side airbags, which fire from modules built into the front seats, and side curtain airbags, which are deployed from modules in the headlining.

The system is armed only when the ignition is switched on, however, a reserve power source maintains a power supply to the system in the event of a break in the main electrical supply. The system is activated by a 'g' sensor (deceleration sensor), incorporated in the electronic control unit. Note that the electronic control unit also controls the front seat belt tensioners, fitted to all models.

The airbags are inflated by gas generators, which force the bags out from their locations. Although these are safety items, their deployment is violently rapid, and this may cause injury if they are triggered unintentionally.

Precautions

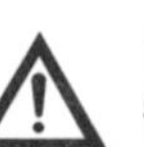

Warning: The following precautions must be observed when working on vehicles equipped with an airbag system, to prevent the possibility of personal injury.

General precautions

The following precautions must be observed when carrying out work on a vehicle equipped with an airbag:

a) *Do not disconnect the battery with the engine running.*
b) *Before carrying out any work in the vicinity of the airbag, removal of any of the airbag components, or any welding work on the car, de-activate the system as described in the following sub-Section.*
c) *Do not attempt to test any of the airbag system circuits using test meters or any other test equipment.*
d) *If the airbag warning light comes on, or any fault in the system is suspected, consult a Ford dealer without delay. Do not attempt to carry out fault diagnosis, or any dismantling of the components.*

Precautions when handling an airbag

a) *Transport the airbag by itself, bag upward.*
b) *Do not put your arms around the airbag.*
c) *Carry the airbag close to the body, bag outward.*
d) *Do not drop the airbag or expose it to impacts.*
e) *Do not attempt to dismantle the airbag unit.*
f) *Do not connect any form of electrical equipment to any part of the airbag circuit.*

Precautions when storing an airbag

a) *Store the unit in a cupboard with the airbag upward.*
b) *Do not expose the airbag to temperatures above 80ºC.*
c) *Do not expose the airbag to flames.*
d) *Do not attempt to dispose of the airbag – consult a Ford dealer.*
e) *Never refit an airbag which is known to be faulty or damaged.*

De-activation of airbag system

Before carrying out any work on the airbag components or surrounding area the system must be de-activated as follows.

1) *Switch off the ignition.*
2) *Remove the ignition key.*
3) *Switch off all electrical equipment.*
4) *Disconnect the battery negative lead (see Chapter 5A, Section 2).*
5) *Insulate the battery negative terminal and the end of the battery negative lead to prevent any possibility of contact.*
6) ***Wait for at least a minute** before carrying out any further work.*

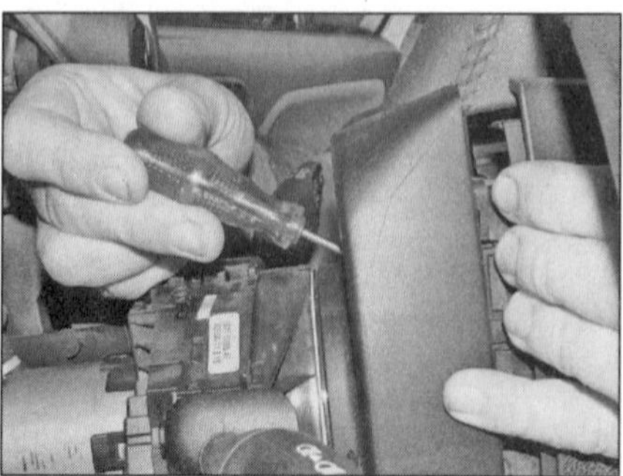

22.3 Prise the ends of the airbag spring clips, and pull the centre pad gently

22 Airbag system components – removal and refitting

Warning: Refer to the precautions given in Section 21 before attempting to carry out work on the airbag components.

Driver's airbag unit

1 De-activate the airbag system as described in Section 21. The airbag unit is an integral part of the steering wheel centre pad.

2 Remove the steering column upper shroud as described in Chapter 11, Section 25.

3 Turn the steering wheel through 90° from the straight-ahead position (to the side) to access the first of the airbag retaining clips. Use a small screwdriver in the hole provided at the back of the wheel, to prise the end of the spring clip used to retain the airbag – as this is done, pull gently on the steering wheel centre pad to release it **(see illustration)**.

4 Turn the wheel through 180° (to the other side), and repeat the process to free the airbag unit completely.

5 Withdraw the unit from the wheel by tilting it back from the top, then lifting it to release the lower clips. Disconnect the wiring plug, and remove the unit **(see illustrations)**. Store it in a safe place, with reference to the precautions in Section 21.

6 Refitting is a reversal of removal, noting the following points:

a) *The battery must still be disconnected when reconnecting the airbag wiring.*
b) *Ensure that the airbag wiring plug is securely reconnected.*

22.5a Tilt the airbag unit back, and lift at the base ...

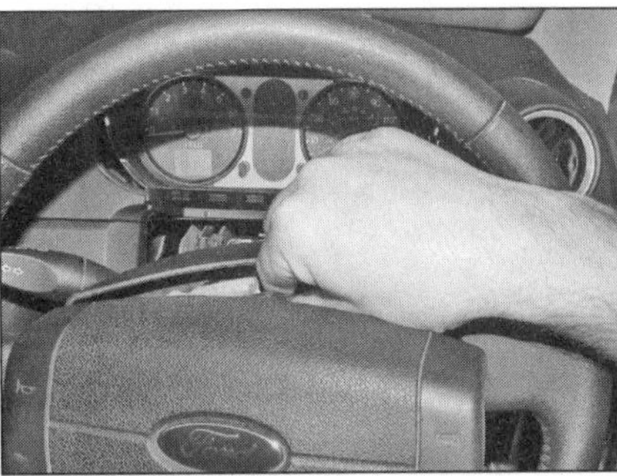

22.5b ... then reach in behind at the top, and disconnect the airbag wiring plug

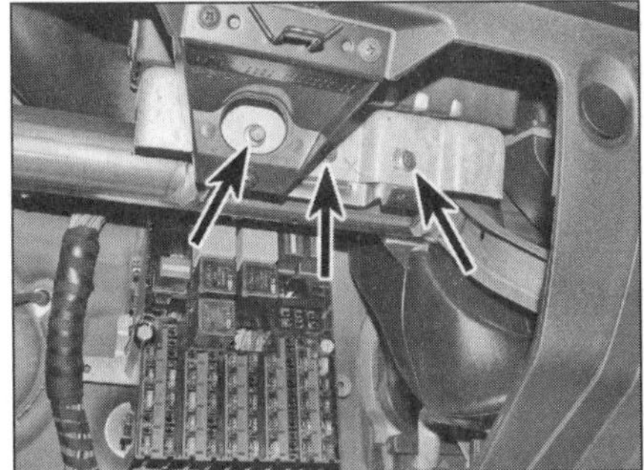

22.8 Passenger airbag mounting bolts

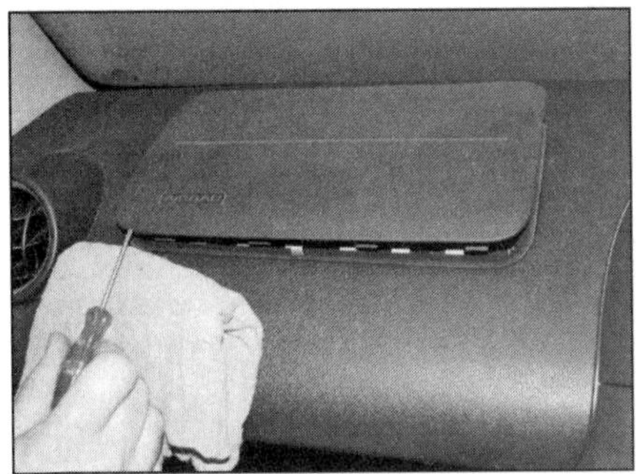

22.9a Protect the facia, then prise up the passenger airbag ...

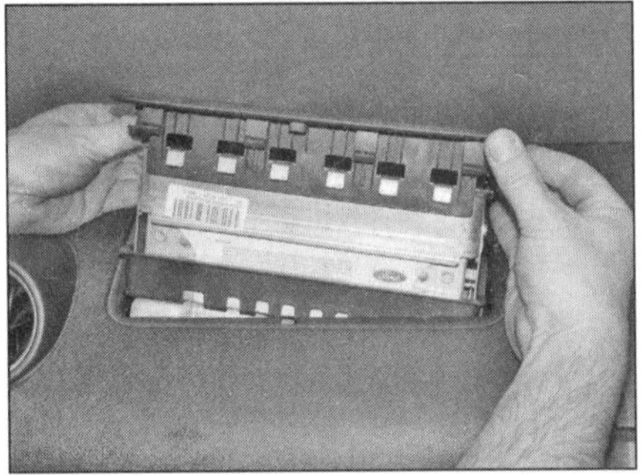

22.9b ... and lift it out

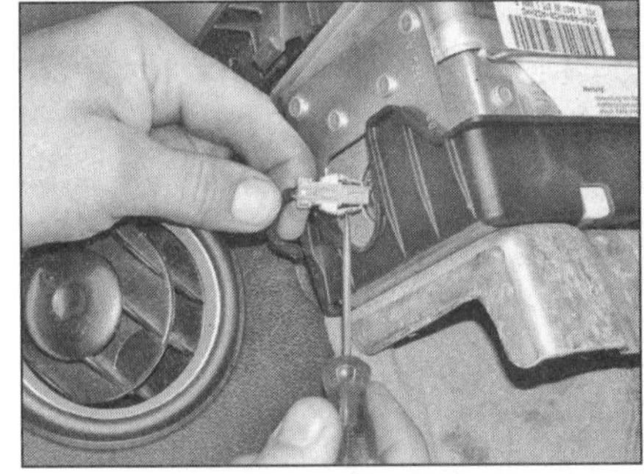

22.10 Press in the airbag wiring plug tabs with a small screwdriver

c) *The airbag must be firmly pressed into place to secure the spring clips.*

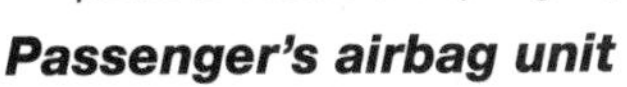

Passenger's airbag unit

Models made before 10/2005

7 De-activate the airbag system as described in Section 21.

8 Remove the glovebox as described in Chapter 11, Section 25, then remove the three bolts which secure the airbag to the facia crossmember **(see illustration)**.

9 Protect the facia with a layer of cloth around the front of the airbag location, then carefully prise up the airbag unit, and lift it out of the facia **(see illustrations)**.

10 Use a small screwdriver to help release the airbag wiring plugs **(see illustration)**. On models manufactured before 11/2004 there are two – one each side – and they're colour-coded (the yellow/brown plug on the left fits into a brown socket, while the right-hand yellow/black plug fits a black one). On models manufactured from 11/2004-onwards, there is just one wiring plug.

11 Unclip the airbag wiring from the front of the unit, and remove it completely **(see illustration)**. Take care not to scratch the facia as the unit is removed – the metal edges on the base are sharp.

12 Refitting is a reversal of removal, bearing in mind the following points:

a) *The battery must still be disconnected when reconnecting the airbag wiring.*

b) *Make sure that the wiring harness is routed as noted before removal, and that the connectors are reconnected to their original positions.*

c) *Make sure that the wiring connectors are securely reconnected.*

d) *Tighten the airbag mounting bolts to the specified torque.*

Models made after 10/2005

13 Remove the facia assembly as described in Chapter 11, Section 27. Unscrew the six mounting nuts and remove the airbag unit from the facia **(see illustration)**.

14 Refitting is a reversal of removal, bearing in mind the following points:

a) *The battery must still be disconnected when reconnecting the airbag wiring.*

b) *Make sure that the wiring harness is routed as noted before removal, and that the connectors are reconnected to their original positions.*

c) *Make sure that the wiring connectors are securely reconnected.*

d) *Tighten the airbag mounting nuts to the specified torque.*

Airbag control unit

15 Where applicable, prise out the power outlet socket fitted into the handbrake trim panel, at the rear, and disconnect the wiring plug beneath it.

16 Unclip the handbrake lever trim panel first at the rear, and remove it over the handbrake lever **(see illustration)**.

17 Disconnect the two wiring plugs at the front of the control unit **(see illustrations)**.

18 Remove the three mounting nuts, and lift the unit out of the centre console **(see illustration)**.

19 Refitting is a reversal of removal, bearing in mind the following points:

a) *The battery must still be disconnected when reconnecting the airbag wiring.*

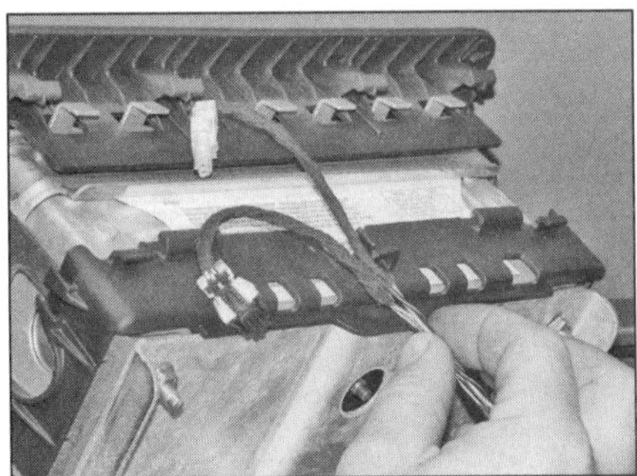

22.11 Unclip the airbag wiring at the front

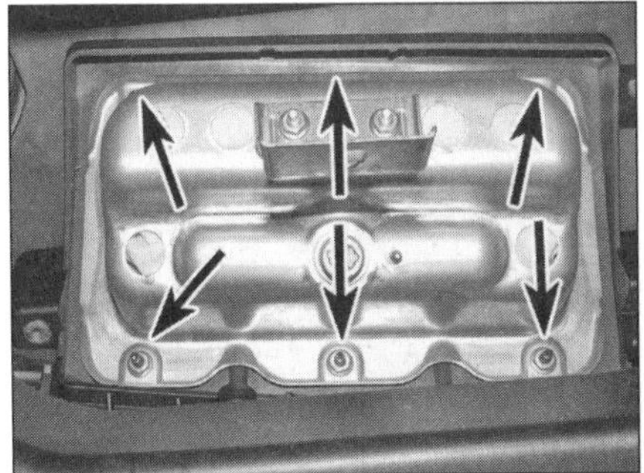

22.13 Remove the mounting nuts (arrowed – three visible and three hidden)

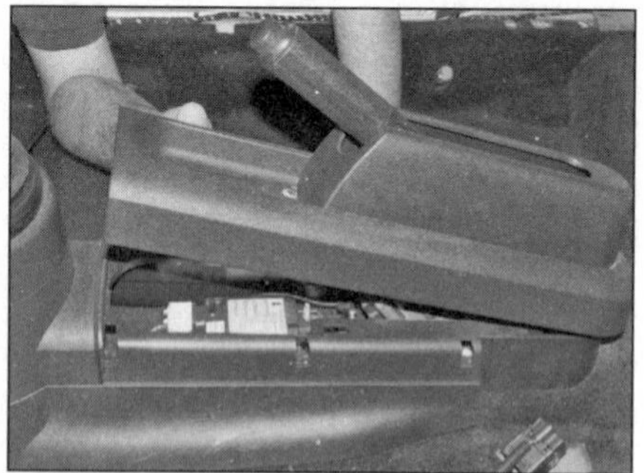
22.16 Unclip and lift off the handbrake lever trim panel

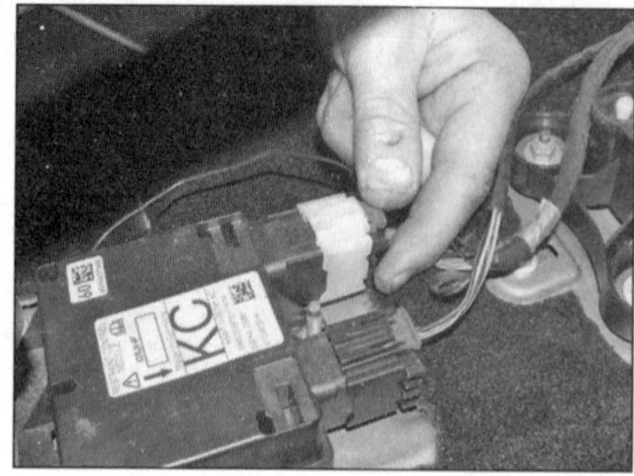
22.17a Lift up the locking tab ...

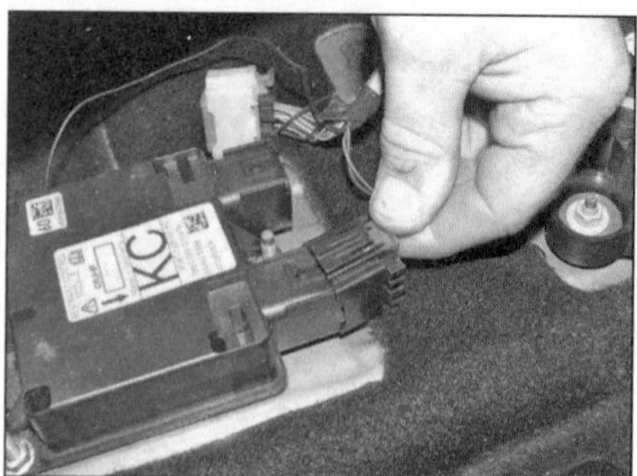
22.17b ... and remove the wiring plugs

b) *Make sure that the wiring connectors are securely reconnected.*

c) *Tighten the mounting nuts securely.*

Airbag clockspring (rotary connector)

20 Remove the driver's airbag unit as described previously in this Section.

21 Remove the steering wheel as described in Chapter 10, Section 14.

22 Remove the large coil spring from the centre of the clockspring **(see illustration)**.

23 Remove the steering column lower shroud, with reference to Chapter 11, Section 25.

24 Remove the steering column switches by squeezing the locking tab at the top of each switch, then sliding them upwards. There is no need to disconnect the switch wiring.

25 Disconnect the clockspring wiring plug at the base of the unit **(see illustration)**.

26 Unscrew the single screw on top of the unit **(see illustration)**.

27 Use a small screwdriver to prise up the four locking tangs (two either side) and withdraw the clockspring assembly from the steering column, if possible without turning it **(see illustrations)**.

28 Refitting is a reversal of removal.

29 Before refitting the coil spring and steering wheel, the clockspring unit should be centralised (unless it is known absolutely that the steering wheel was centralised before removal, and that the clockspring has not been turned during or since its removal).

30 The procedure for centralising should be written on the clockspring itself. If this procedure conflicts significantly with what appears here, consult a Ford dealer for the latest information.

31 First, turn the clockspring anti-clockwise gently, until resistance is felt. Now turn the clockspring about two turns clockwise, until the arrow marking on the front face aligns with the raised V marking at the 12 o'clock position on the clockspring's outer cover.

32 Refit the coil spring, then refit the steering wheel as described in Chapter 10, Section 14.

Side airbags

33 The side airbags are located internally within the front seat backrest, and no attempt should be made to remove them. Any suspected problems with the side airbag system should be referred to a Ford dealer.

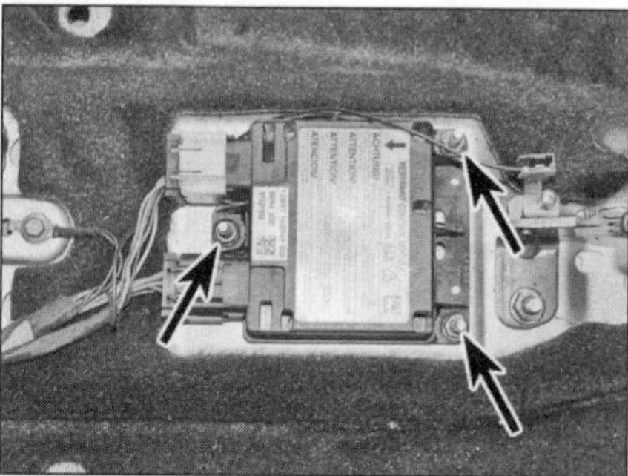
22.18 Airbag unit mounting nuts – seen with centre console removed

22.22 Remove the coil spring at the centre

22.25 Disconnect the clockspring wiring plug

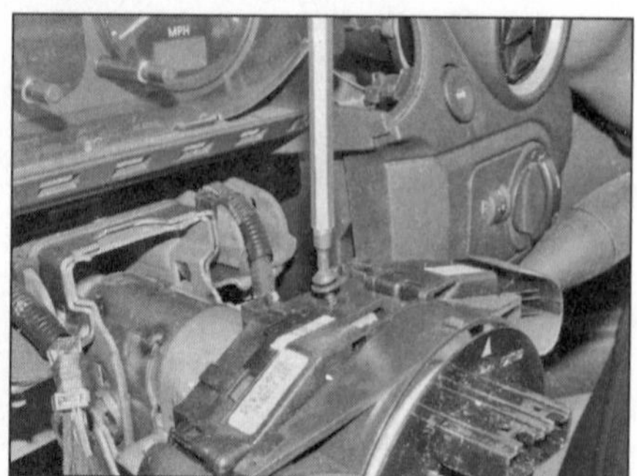
22.26 Remove the single screw on top ...

22.27a ... then release the two tangs each side ...

22.27b ... and withdraw the clockspring from the column

Side curtain airbags

34 The modules for the side curtain airbags are located at the sides of the headlining. It is strongly recommended that any work which requires even just the removal of the headlining, never mind any work on the side curtain airbags, be referred to a Ford dealer.

Crash sensor

Note: *The remote crash sensor is only fitted to models built before 11/2004. On later models, it is incorporated into the airbag control unit.*

35 De-activate the airbag system as described in Section 21.

36 Remove the radiator grille as described in Chapter 11, Section 7.

37 Mark the position of the bonnet lock on the cross panel, then unscrew the mounting bolts and move the lock to one side.

38 Unscrew the bolt and withdraw the crash sensor, then disconnect the wiring plug by sliding the cover to the rear.

39 Refitting is a reversal of removal, but make sure the locating tang is correctly located in the cross panel.

FORD FUSION wiring diagrams

Diagram 1

Key to symbols

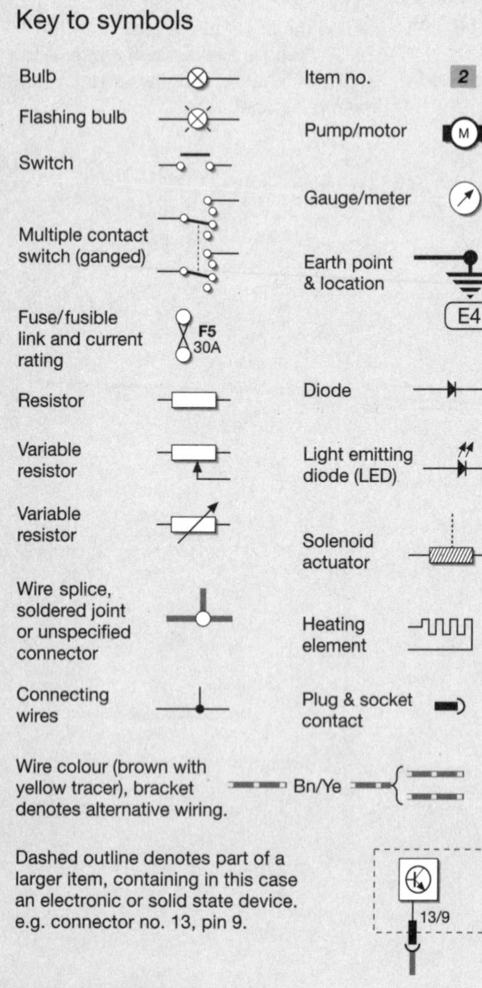

Earth locations

E1 Near battery -ve terminal
E2 On clutch bell housing
E3 Behind LH headlight, on inner wing
E4 Base of strut tower, RH inner wing
E5 On LH inner sill, behind floor cross member, in front of E15
E6 On RH inner sill, behind floor cross member, in front of E8
E7 At base of RH 'A' pillar at dashboard cross member
E8 On RH inner sill, behind E6
E9 At base of LH 'A' pillar above dashboard cross member
E10 On RH side of steering column bracket above E23
E11 At base of LH 'D' pillar below LH rear light unit
E12 At base of RH 'D' pillar below RH rear light unit
E13 On transmission tunnel, behind gearchange
E14 LH inner wing, in front of strut tower
E15 On LH inner sill, behind E5
E16 LH side engine compartment
E17 On LH side of steering column bracket, above E19
E18 At base of LH 'A' pillar below dashboard cross member
E19 On LH side of steering column bracket, below E17
E20 On centre of engine bulkhead
E21 On LH 'A' pillar
E22 At base of RH 'A' pillar below dashboard cross member
E23 On RH side of steering column bracket, below E10

H32983

Passenger compartment fuses 6

Fuse	Rating	Circuit protected
F1	-	Not used
F2	-	Not used
F3	7.5A	Trailer battery charging (before 09/2002)
F4	10A	Heater control module, A/C wide open throttle relay
F5	20A	ABS control unit
F6	30A	ABS control unit
F7	15A	Gearshift lever unit (Durashift EST)
F8	7.5A	Electric mirrors
F9	10A	LH dipped beam headlight
F10	10A	RH dipped beam headlight
F11	15A	Daytime running lights
F12	15A	Engine cooling fan, fuel injectors, engine electronics
F13	20A	Engine electronics
F14	30A	Starter inhibitor relay
F15	20A	Fuel pump relay
F16	3A	Engine management control unit
F17	15A	Light switch
F18	15A	Radio, navigation, DVD player
F19	15A	Daytime running lights
F20	7.5A	Instrument cluster, generic electronic module (GEM)
F21	-	Not used
F22	7.5A	LH sidelight
F23	7.5A	RH sidelight
F24	20A	Generic electronic module (GEM)
F25	15A	Generic electronic module (GEM)
F26	20A	Generic electronic module (GEM)
F27	10/15A	Generic electronic module (GEM)
F28	3A	Alternator
F29	15A	Cigar lighter
F30	15A	Ignition switch
F31	20A	Trailer control unit (before 09/2002)
F32	7.5A	Heated mirrors
F33	7.5A	GEM, number plate lights, interior lighting
F34	20A	Sunroof switch
F35	7.5A	Heated seats
F36	30A	Electric windows
F37	3A	ABS control unit
F38	7.5A	Generic electronic module (GEM), instrument cluster
F39	7.5A	SRS control unit
F40	10A	Light switch
F41	7.5A	Gearshift lever unit, transmission control unit (Durashift EST)
F42	30A	LH heated screen element
F43	30A	RH heated screen element
F44	3A	Instrument cluster, radio, navigation, DVD player
F45	15A	Stop lights
F46	20A	Front wiper motor, wash/wipe switch, GEM
F47	10A	Rear wiper motor, generic electronic module (GEM)
F48	7.5A	Transmission switch, reversing lights
F49	30A	Heater blower motor
F50	20A	Light switch
F51	15A	Battery saving relay
F52	10A	LH main beam headlight
F53	10A	RH main beam headlight
F54	7.5A	Trailer battery charger (from 09/2002)
F55	-	Not used
F56	20A	Trailer control unit (from 09/2002)

Engine fusebox

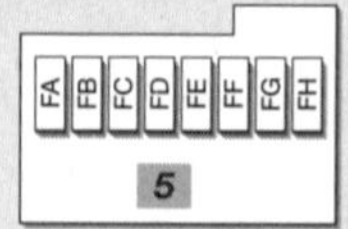

Engine relay box

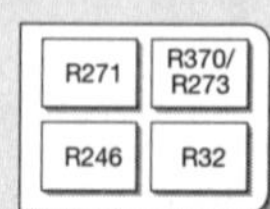

Passenger fusebox

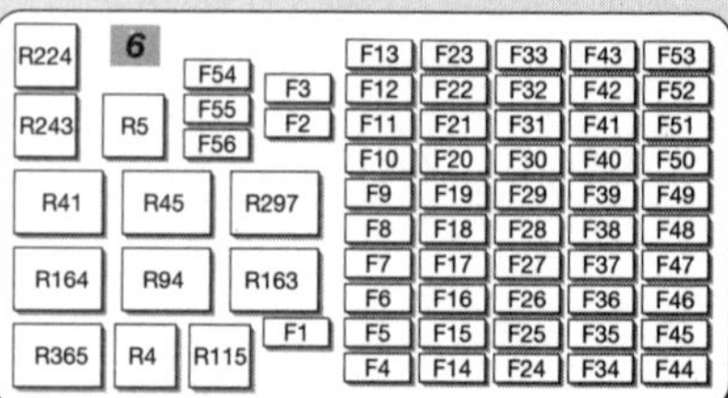

Diagram 2

Wire colours

Bk	Black	**Vt**	Violet
Gn	Green	**Rd**	Red
Pk	Pink	**Gy**	Grey
Lg	Light green	**Bu**	Blue
Bn	Brown	**Wh**	White
Og	Orange	**Ye**	Yellow
Na	Natural	**Sr**	Silver

* red sleeve at ends

Key to items

1 Battery
2 Starter motor
3 Alternator
4 Ignition switch
5 Engine fusebox
6 Passenger fusebox
R45 = fan relay
R94 = starter relay
R163 = engine management relay
7 Engine cooling fan
8 Engine cooling fan resistor
9 Steering wheel clock springs
10 General electronic module (GEM)
11 Horn switch
12 Horn
13 Engine relay box
R46 = high speed fan relay

H32984/a

Starting & charging system

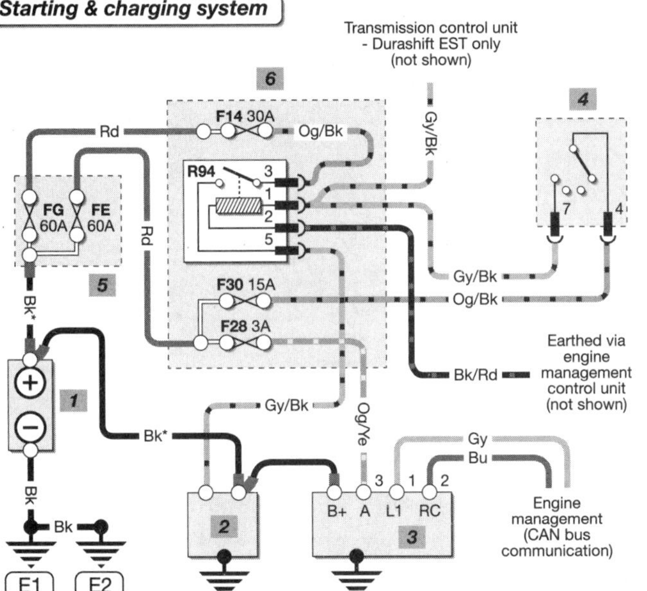

Engine cooling fan - with A/C

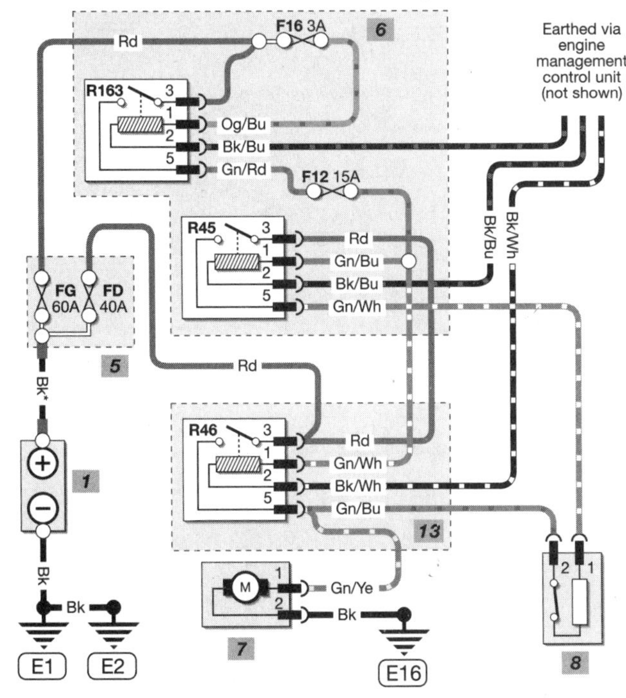

Engine cooling fan - without A/C

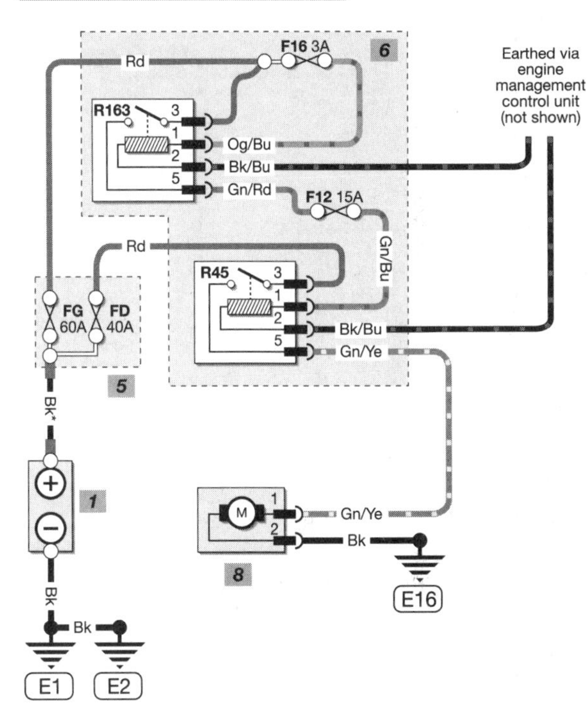

Horn

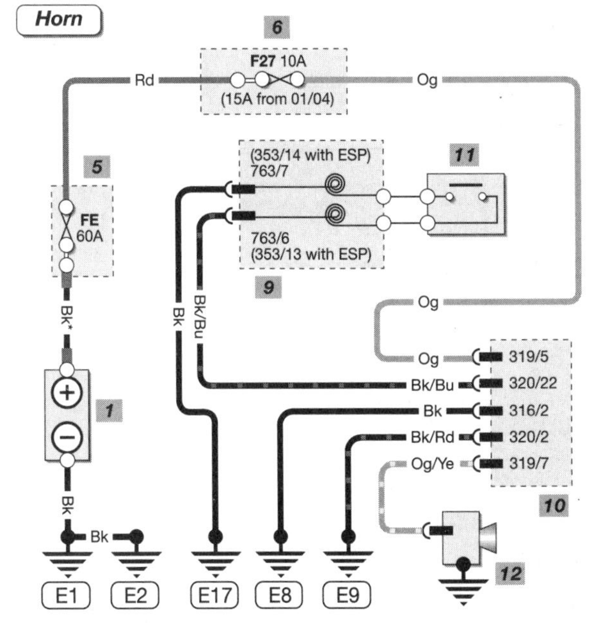

Diagram 3

Wire colours

Bk	Black	**Vt**	Violet
Gn	Green	**Rd**	Red
Pk	Pink	**Gy**	Grey
Lg	Light green	**Bu**	Blue
Bn	Brown	**Wh**	White
Og	Orange	**Ye**	Yellow
Na	Natural	**Sr**	Silver

* red sleeve at ends

Key to items

1 Battery
4 Ignition switch
5 Engine fusebox
6 Passenger fusebox
  R9 = ignition relay
  R243 = dip beam relay
  R244 = main beam relay
15 Light switch
  a = off
  b = sidelight
  c = side/headlight
16 LH headlight unit
  a = sidelight
  b = dip beam
  c = main beam
17 RH headlight unit
  a = sidelight
  b = dip beam
  c = main beam
18 LH number plate light
19 RH number plate light
20 LH rear light unit
  a = stop/tail light
  b = reversing light
21 RH rear light unit (as item 21)
22 Multifunction switch
  a = dip beam
  b = flasher
  c = main beam
23 High level brake light
24 Stop light switch
25 Reversing light switch

H32985

Side, tail & number plate lights

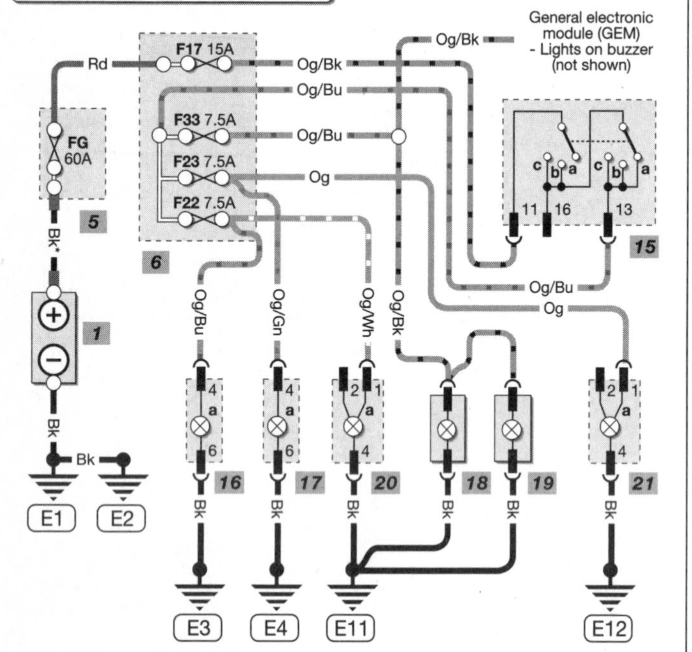

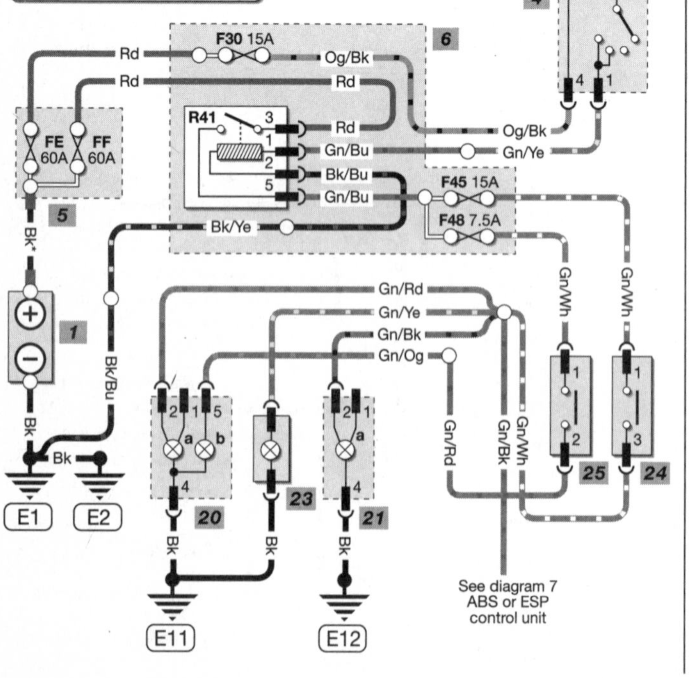

Headlights

Stop & reversing lights

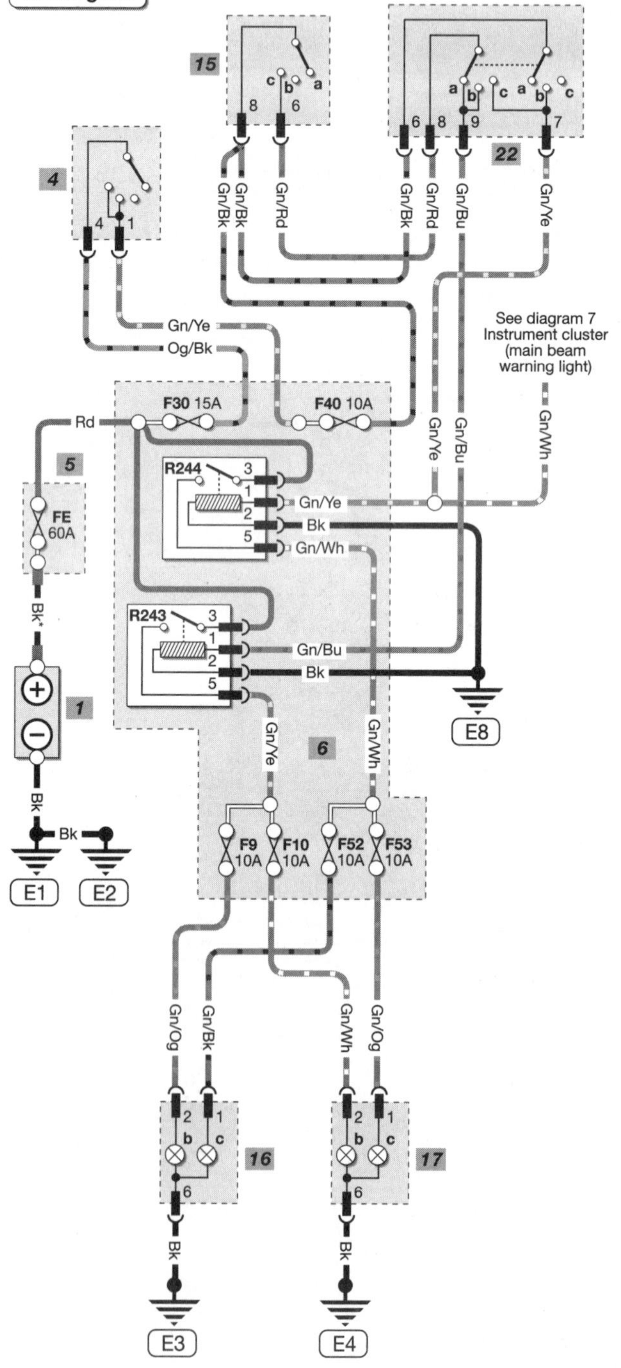

Diagram 4

Wire colours

Bk	Black	**Vt**	Violet
Gn	Green	**Rd**	Red
Pk	Pink	**Gy**	Grey
Lg	Light green	**Bu**	Blue
Bn	Brown	**Wh**	White
Og	Orange	**Ye**	Yellow
Na	Natural	**Sr**	Silver

* red sleeve at ends

Key to items

1 Battery
4 Ignition switch
5 Engine fusebox
6 Passenger fusebox
  R41 = ignition relay
10 General electronic module (GEM)
15 Light switch
  a = off
  b = sidelight
  c = side/headlight
  d = front foglight
  e = front/rear foglight
  f = headlight levelling adjuster
16 LH headlight unit
  b = dip beam
  d = direction indicator
  e = headlight levelling unit
17 RH headlight unit
  b = dip beam
  d = direction indicator
  e = headlight levelling unit
20 LH rear light unit
  d = direction indicator
21 RH rear light unit
  b = foglight
  c = direction indicator
22 Multifunction switch
  d = direction indicator
  e = buzzer
28 LH front foglight
29 RH front foglight
30 LH direction indicator side repeater
31 RH direction indicator side repeater
32 Hazard warning switch

H32986

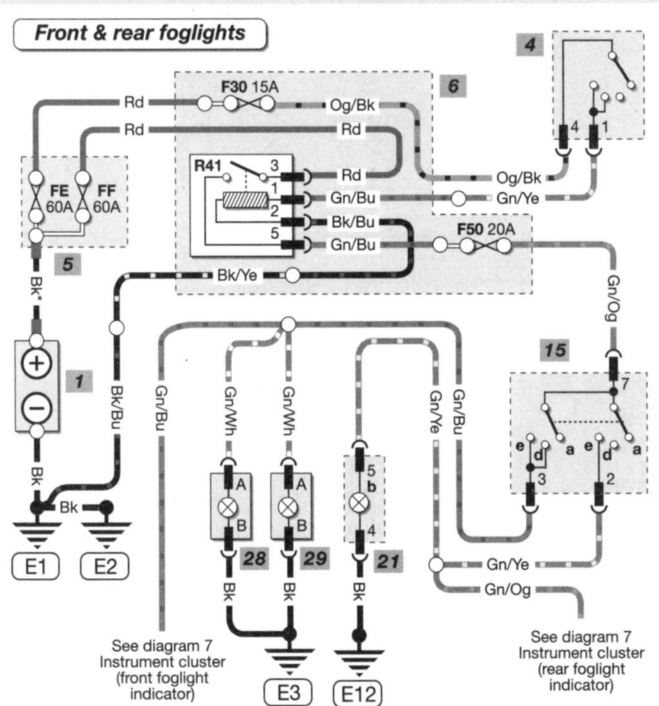

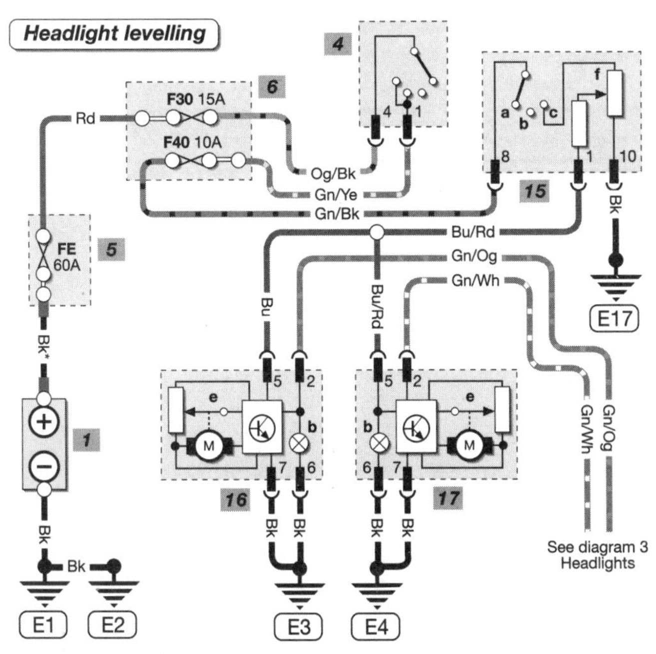

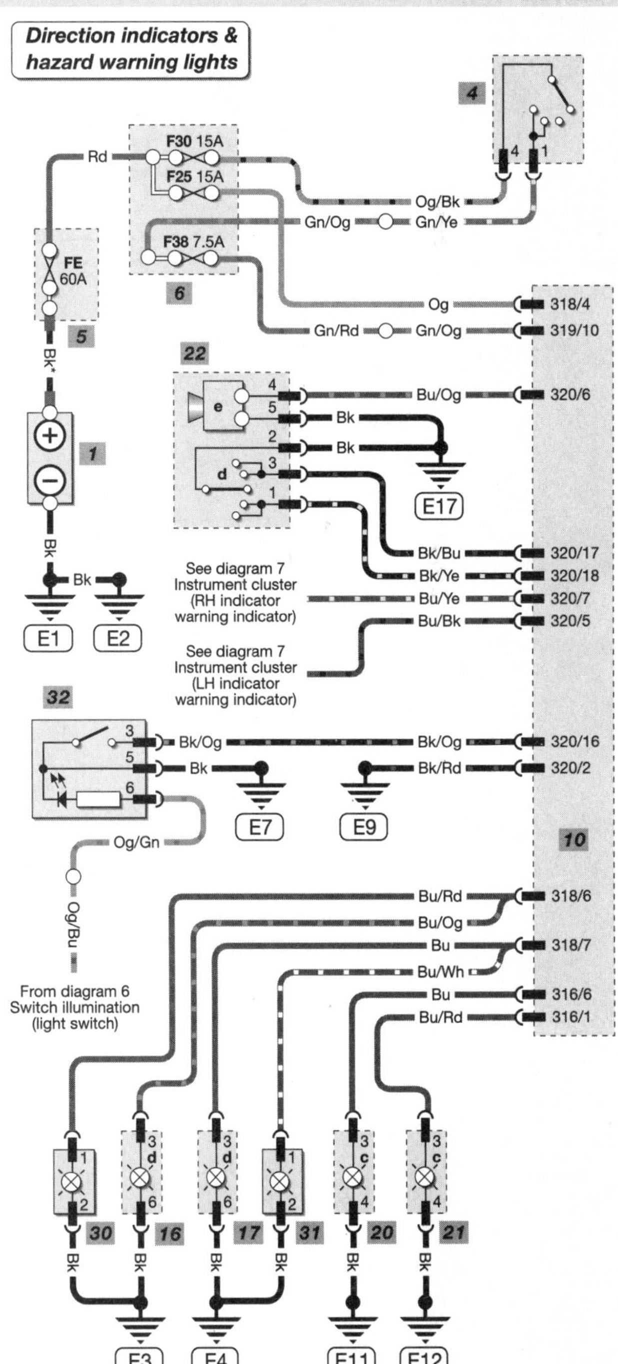

Wire colours

Bk Black
Gn Green
Pk Pink
Lg Light green
Bn Brown
Og Orange
Na Natural
Vt Violet
Rd Red
Gy Grey
Bu Blue
Wh White
Ye Yellow
Sr Silver

* red sleeve at ends
** with 13 pin socket

Key to items

1 Battery
4 Ignition switch
5 Engine fusebox
6 Passenger fusebox
   R41 = ignition relay
15 Light switch
   a = off
   b = sidelight
   c = side/headlight
20 LH rear light unit
   a = stop/tail
   b = reversing light
   c = direction indicator
21 RH rear light unit
   a = stop/tail
   b = foglight
   c = direction indicator
24 Stop light switch
25 Reversing light switch
35 7 or 13 pin trailer socket
36 Trailer control unit

Diagram 5

H32987

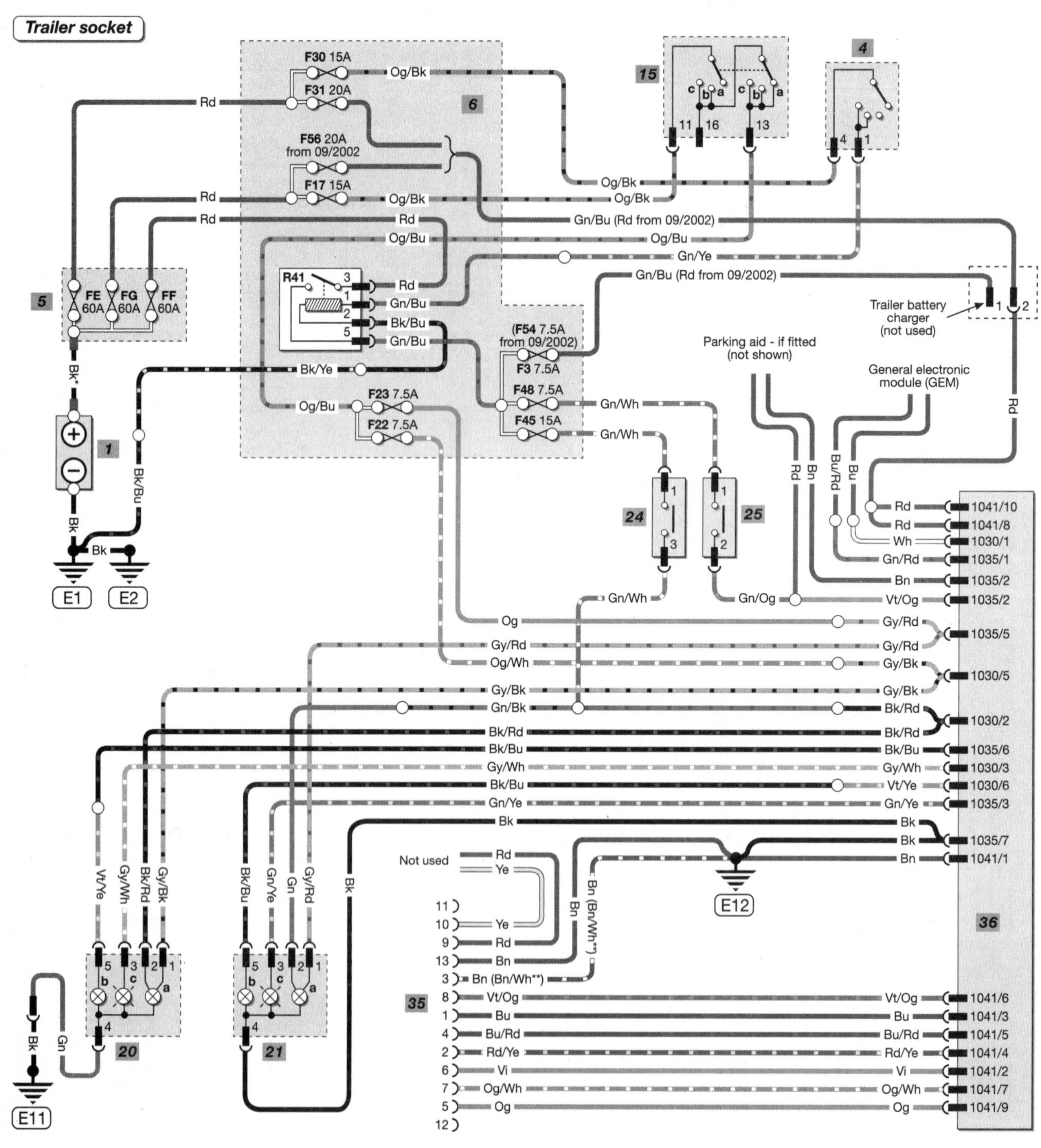

Wire colours

Bk	Black	**Vt**	Violet
Gn	Green	**Rd**	Red
Pk	Pink	**Gy**	Grey
Lg	Light green	**Bu**	Blue
Bn	Brown	**Wh**	White
Og	Orange	**Ye**	Yellow
Na	Natural	**Sr**	Silver

* red sleeve at ends

Key to items

Diagram 6

1 Battery
4 Ignition switch
5 Engine fusebox
6 Passenger fusebox
R41 = ignition relay
10 General electronic module (GEM)
a = battery saving relay
b = microprocessor
15 Light switch
a = off
b = sidelight
c = side/headlight
g = lights on indicator
h = switch illumination
40 Tailgate switch
41 Luggage compartment light
42 Front interior light
43 Rear interior light (if fitted)
44 LH rear map light (if fitted)
45 RH rear map light (if fitted)
46 Driver's door lock assembly
47 Passenger's door lock assembly
48 LH rear door lock assembly
49 RH rear door lock assembly
50 LH heated seat switch
51 RH heated seat switch
52 LH heated seat
53 RH heated seat
54 Gearshift lever illumination

H32988

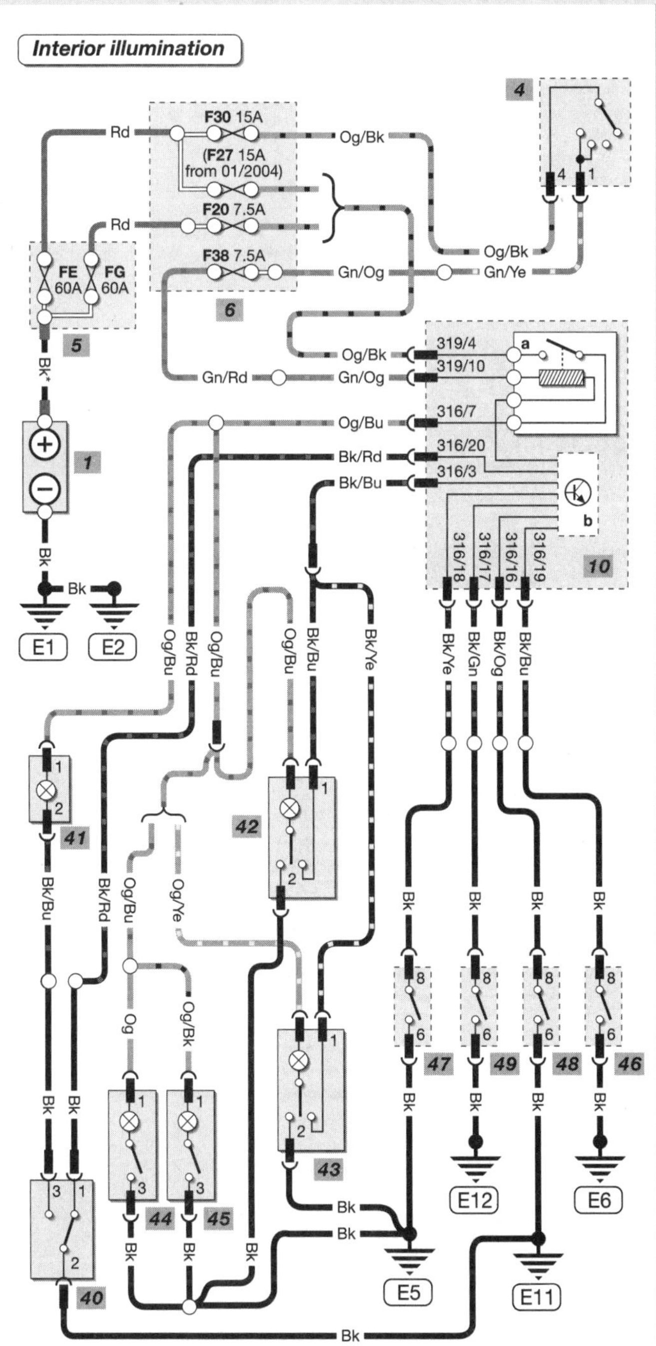

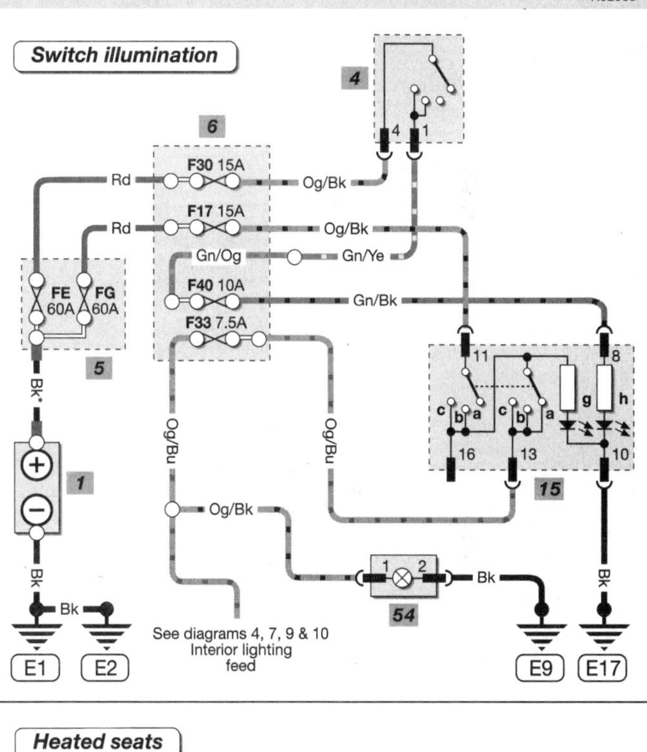

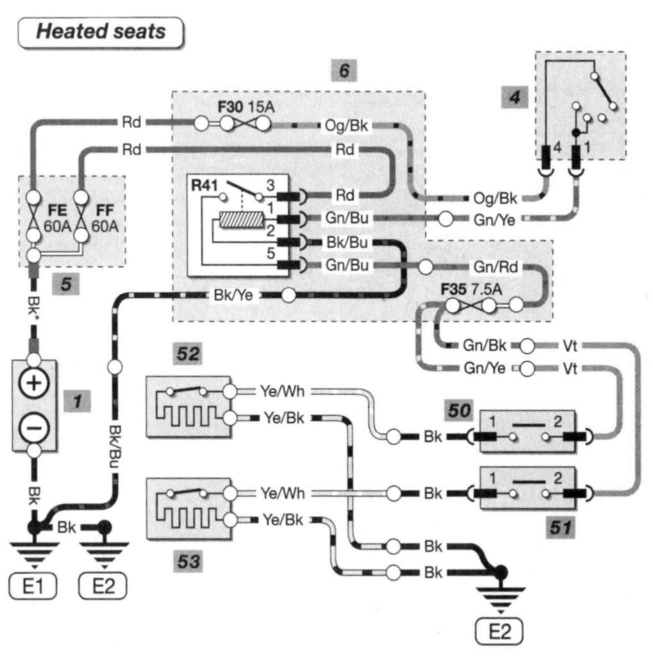

Diagram 7

Wire colours

Bk Black	**Vt** Violet		
Gn Green	**Rd** Red		
Pk Pink	**Gy** Grey		
Lg Light green	**Bu** Blue		
Bn Brown	**Wh** White		
Og Orange	**Ye** Yellow		
Na Natural	**Sr** Silver		

* red sleeve at ends
** from 01/2004

Key to items

1 Battery
4 Ignition switch
5 Engine fusebox
6 Passenger fusebox
R41 = ignition relay
9 Steering wheel clock springs
a = steering position sensor
55 Instrument cluster
a = clock/odometer
b = microprocessor
c = LCD display
d = coolant temp. gauge
e = fuel gauge
f = instrument illumination
g = gear position indicator (Durashift EST)
h = low fuel indicator
i = engine management fault indicator
j = high coolant temp. indicator
k = O/D off indicator
l = no charge indicator
m = ABS fault indicator
n = glow plug indicator
o = ESP indicator
p = immobiliser indicator
q = low brake fluid/ handbrake indicator
r = speedometer
s = tachometer
t = low oil pressure indicator
u = door ajar indicator
v = airbag fault indicator
w = front foglight indicator
x = rear foglight indicator
y = main beam indicator
z = LH direction indicator
a1 = RH direction indicator
56 Low brake fluid switch
57 Handbrake switch
58 Fuel gauge sender unit/fuel pump
59 Low oil pressure switch
60 ABS or ESP control unit
61 Integrated control panel
a = ESP deactivation switch & indicator
b = panel illumination
62 Yaw rate acceleration sensor (ESP only)
63 Primary brake pressure sensor (ESP only)
64 Wheel sensor

H32989

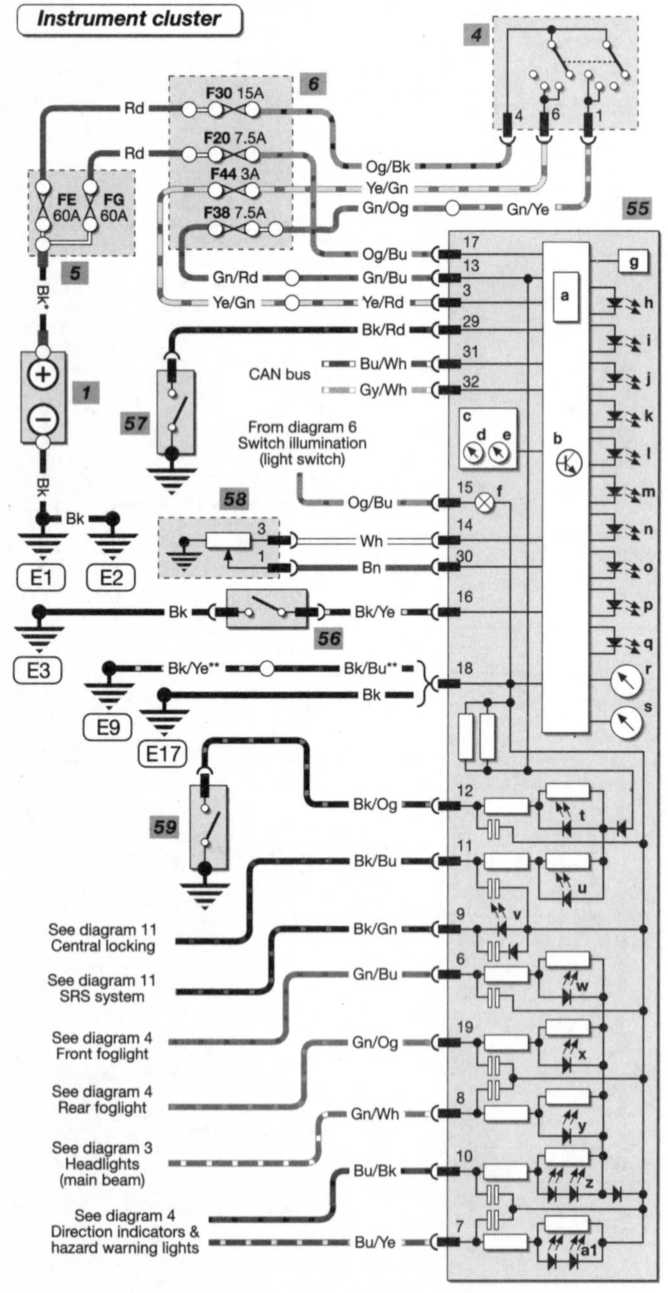

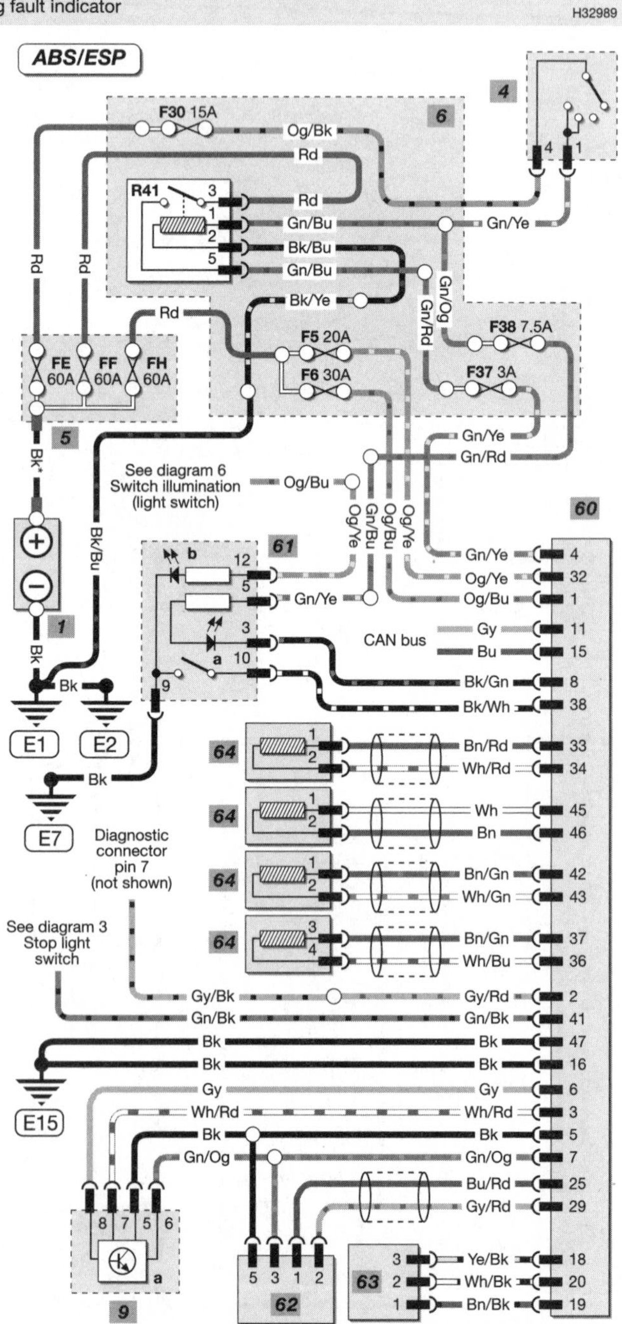

Wire colours

Bk	Black	**Vt**	Violet
Gn	Green	**Rd**	Red
Pk	Pink	**Gy**	Grey
Lg	Light green	**Bu**	Blue
Bn	Brown	**Wh**	White
Og	Orange	**Ye**	Yellow
Na	Natural	**Sr**	Silver

* red sleeve at ends

Key to items

Diagram 8

1 Battery
4 Ignition switch
5 Engine fusebox
6 Passenger fusebox
  R41 = ignition relay
  R115 = battery saving relay
10 General electronic module (GEM)
  a = battery saving relay
  b = microprocessor
  c = front wiper relay
  d = rear wiper relay
68 Front wiper motor
69 Wash/wipe switch
  a = front flick wipe
  b = off
  c = front intermittent
  d = front normal wipe
  e = front fast wipe
  f = rear wipe
  g = rear wash
  h = front wash
70 Front & rear washer pump
71 Rear wiper motor
72 Cigar lighter
73 Accessory socket

H32990

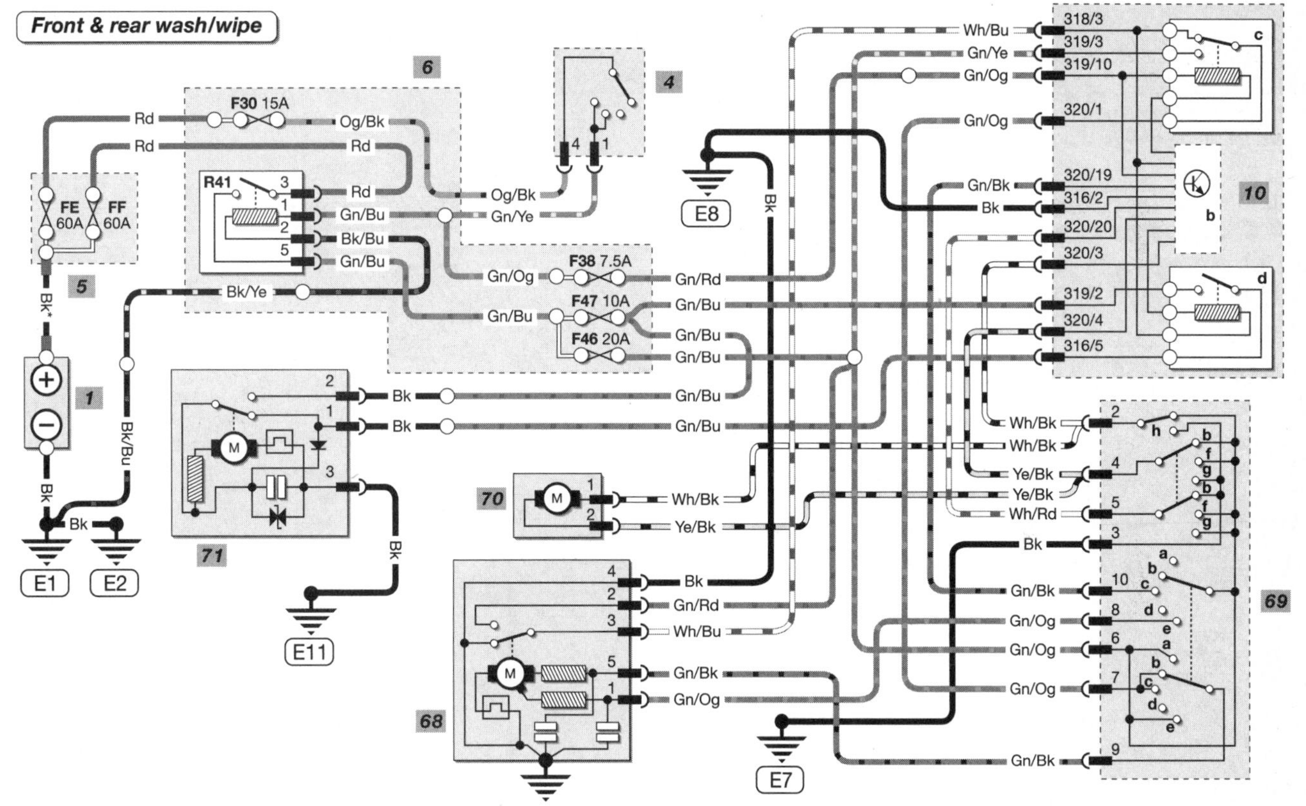

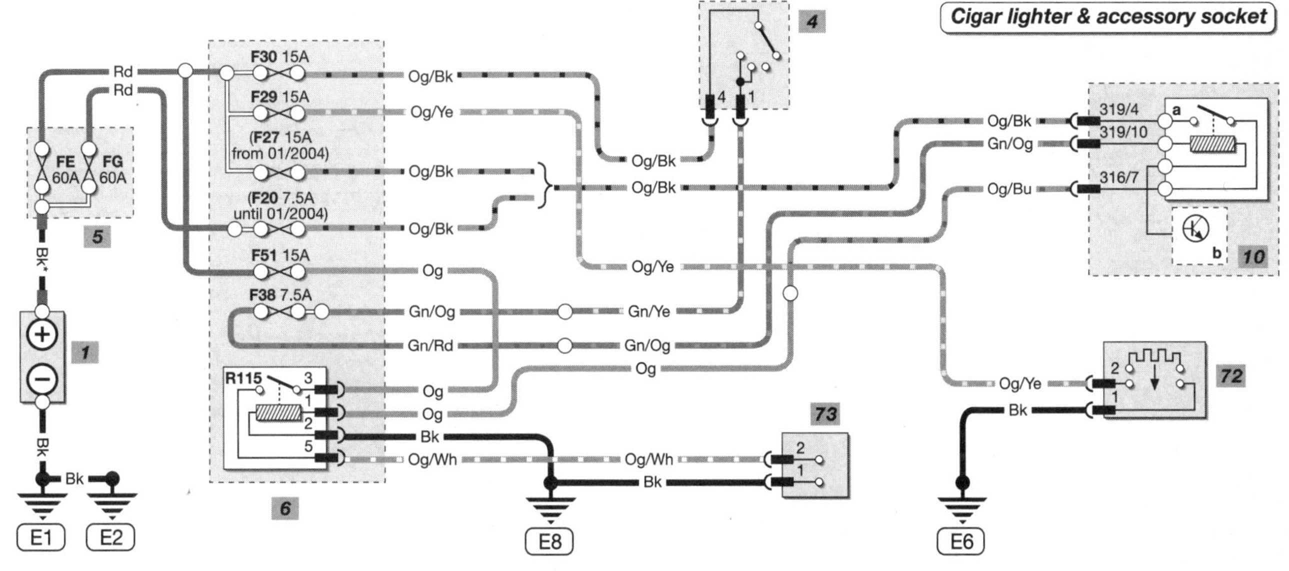

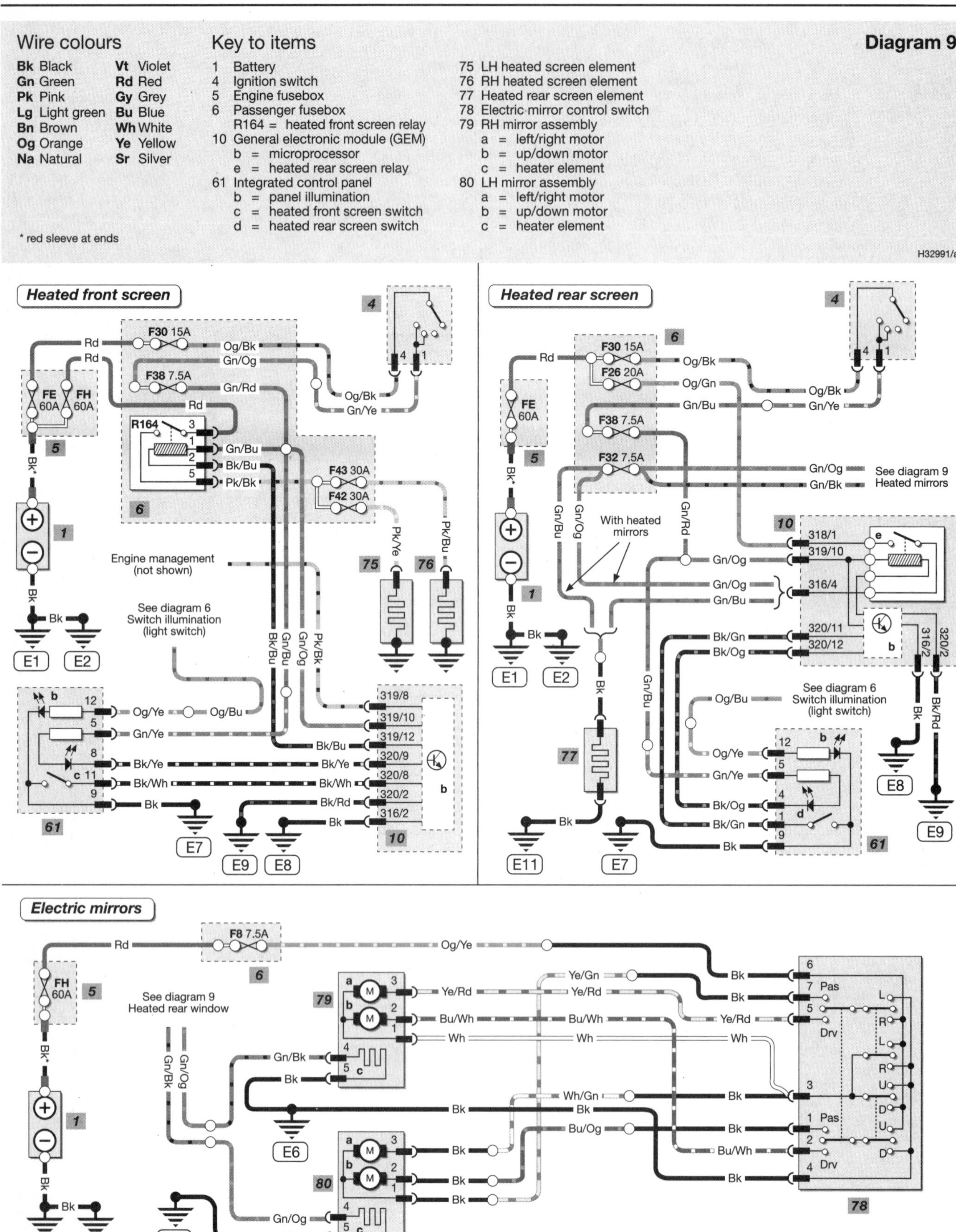
Wire colours
Bk Black
Gn Green
Pk Pink
Lg Light green
Bn Brown
Og Orange
Na Natural
Vt Violet
Rd Red
Gy Grey
Bu Blue
Wh White
Ye Yellow
Sr Silver
* red sleeve at ends
Key to items
1 Battery
4 Ignition switch
5 Engine fusebox
6 Passenger fusebox
R164 = heated front screen relay
10 General electronic module (GEM)
b = microprocessor
e = heated rear screen relay
61 Integrated control panel
b = panel illumination
c = heated front screen switch
d = heated rear screen switch
75 LH heated screen element
76 RH heated screen element
77 Heated rear screen element
78 Electric mirror control switch
79 RH mirror assembly
a = left/right motor
b = up/down motor
c = heater element
80 LH mirror assembly
a = left/right motor
b = up/down motor
c = heater element
Diagram 9
H32991/a
Heated front screen
F30 15A
F38 7.5A
FE 60A
FH 60A
F43 30A
F42 30A
Engine management (not shown)
See diagram 6 Switch illumination (light switch)
Heated rear screen
F30 15A
F26 20A
F38 7.5A
F32 7.5A
FE 60A
See diagram 9 Heated mirrors
With heated mirrors
See diagram 6 Switch illumination (light switch)
Electric mirrors
F8 7.5A
FH 60A
See diagram 9 Heated rear window
Pas
Drv
E1
E2
E5
E6
E7
E8
E9
E11

Wire colours

Bk	Black	**Vt**	Violet
Gn	Green	**Rd**	Red
Pk	Pink	**Gy**	Grey
Lg	Light green	**Bu**	Blue
Bn	Brown	**Wh**	White
Og	Orange	**Ye**	Yellow
Na	Natural	**Sr**	Silver

* red sleeve at ends

Key to items

1 Battery
4 Ignition switch
5 Engine fusebox
6 Passenger fusebox
R41 = ignition relay
83 Sunroof switch
84 Sunroof motor
85 Heater blower motor
86 Heater blower switch
87 Heater blower resistors
88 Remote audio controls
89 LH front speaker
90 LH rear speaker
91 RH front speaker
92 RH rear speaker
93 Audio unit
94 Driver's window switch
95 Passenger's window switch
96 Driver's window motor
97 Passenger's window motor
98 Heater panel illumination

Diagram 10

H32992

Sunroof

6 F30 15A Rd Og/Bk
4
Rd Rd
FE 60A FF 60A
R41 3 1 2 5
Rd Og/Bk
Gn/Bu Gn/Ye
Bk/Bu Gn/Rd
Gn/Bu
F34 20A
Bk/Ye
5
Bk*
83
1
Gn/Bu
Bk
Ye
Wh
Bk
84
Bk/Bu
Bk
Bk
E1 E2 E5

Heater blower

6 F30 15A Rd Og/Bk
4
Rd Rd
FE 60A FF 60A
R41 3 1 2 5
Rd Og/Bk
Gn/Bu Gn/Ye
Bk/Bu
Gn/Bu
F49 30A
Bk/Ye
5
Bk*
85
Gn/Og
Bk/Rd
See diagram 6 Switch illumination (light switch)
Og/Bu Og/Gn
98
1
87
Bk/Bu Bk/Og
Bk/Bu
Bk/Ye
Bk/Wh
Bk
86
Bk/Bu
Bk
Bk
E1 E2 E22 E7

Audio system

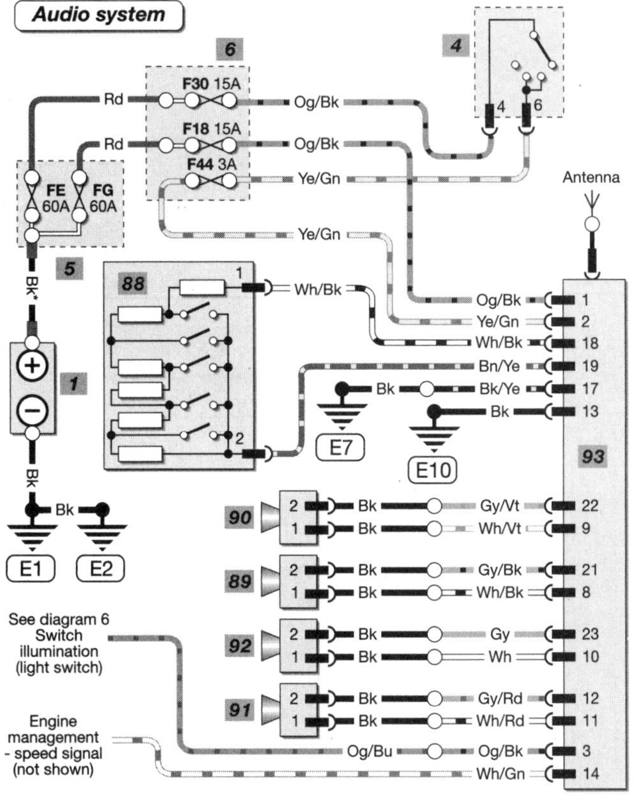

Electric windows

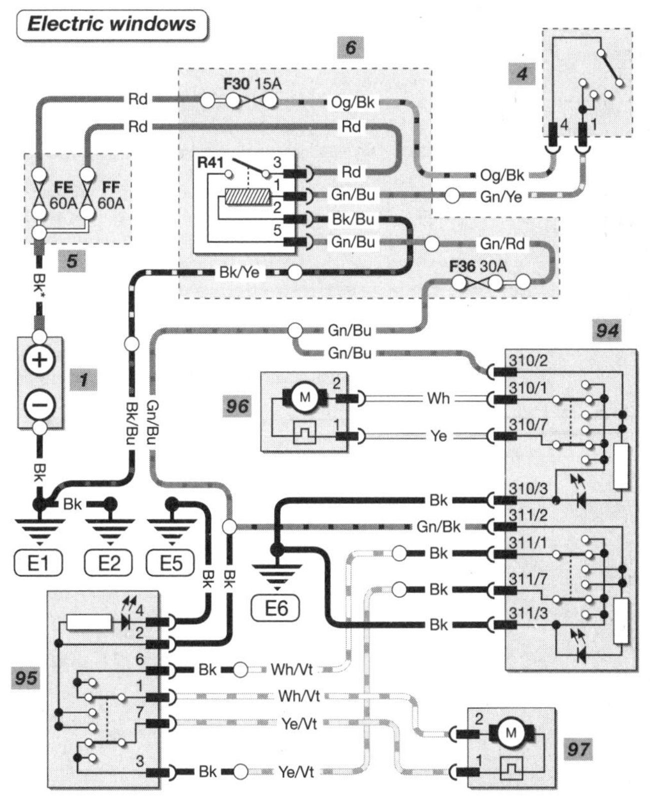

Wire colours

Bk Black
Gn Green
Pk Pink
Lg Light green
Bn Brown
Og Orange
Na Natural
Vt Violet
Rd Red
Gy Grey
Bu Blue
Wh White
Ye Yellow
Sr Silver

* red sleeve at ends
** only with double locking

Key to items

Diagram 11

1 Battery
4 Ignition switch
5 Engine fusebox
6 Passenger fusebox
9 Steering wheel clock springs
10 General electronic module (GEM)
40 Tailgate switch
46 Driver's door lock assembly
- a = lock motor
- b = lock/unlock
- c = door ajar
- d = double lock**

47 Passenger's door lock assembly (as item 46)
48 LH rear door lock assembly
- a = lock motor
- b = door ajar

49 RH rear door lock assembly (as item 48)
61 Integrated control panel
- e = airbag deactivation indicator

100 Tailgate lock motor
101 Tailgate release switch
107 SRS control unit
108 Driver's side airbag
109 Passenger's side airbag
110 Driver's curtain airbag
111 Passenger's curtain airbag
112 Driver's front airbag
113 Passenger's front airbag
114 Driver's seatbelt pretensioner
115 Passenger's seatbelt pretensionner
116 Driver's side airbag sensor
117 Passenger's side airbag sensor
118 Crash sensor
119 Passenger's airbag deactivation switch

H32993

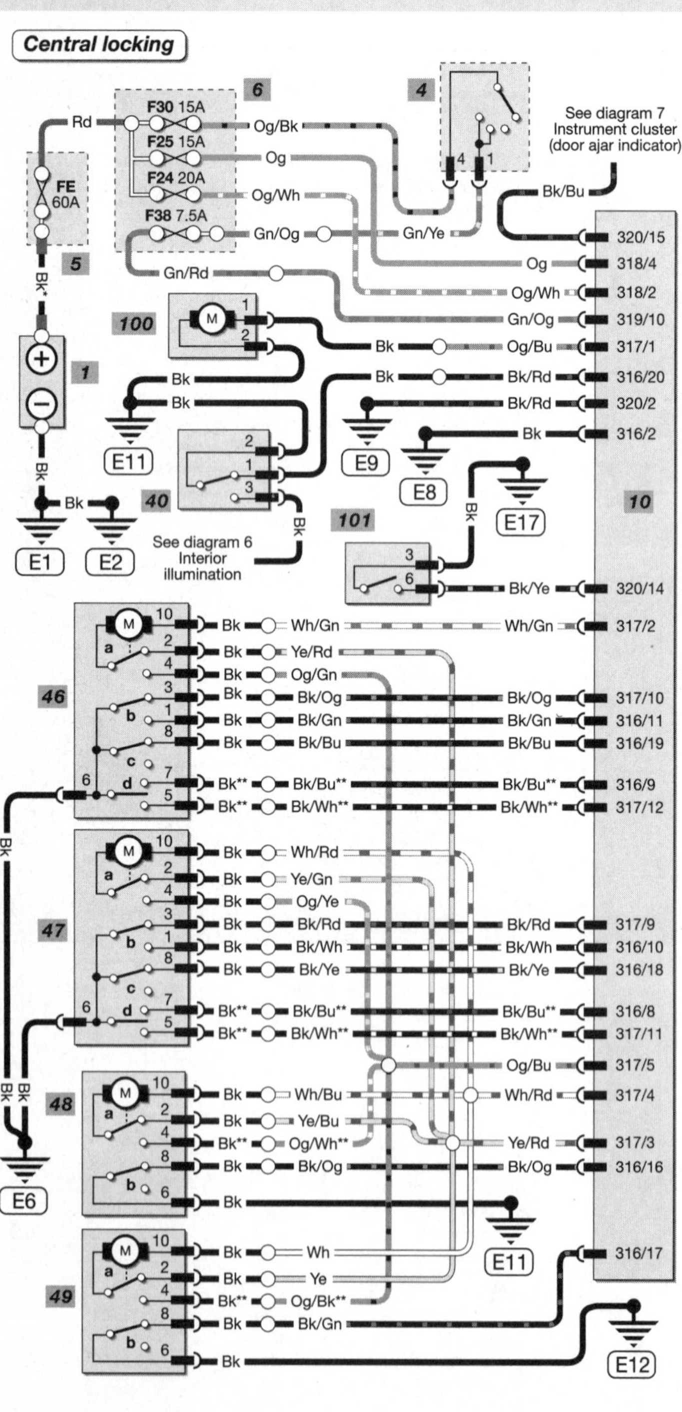

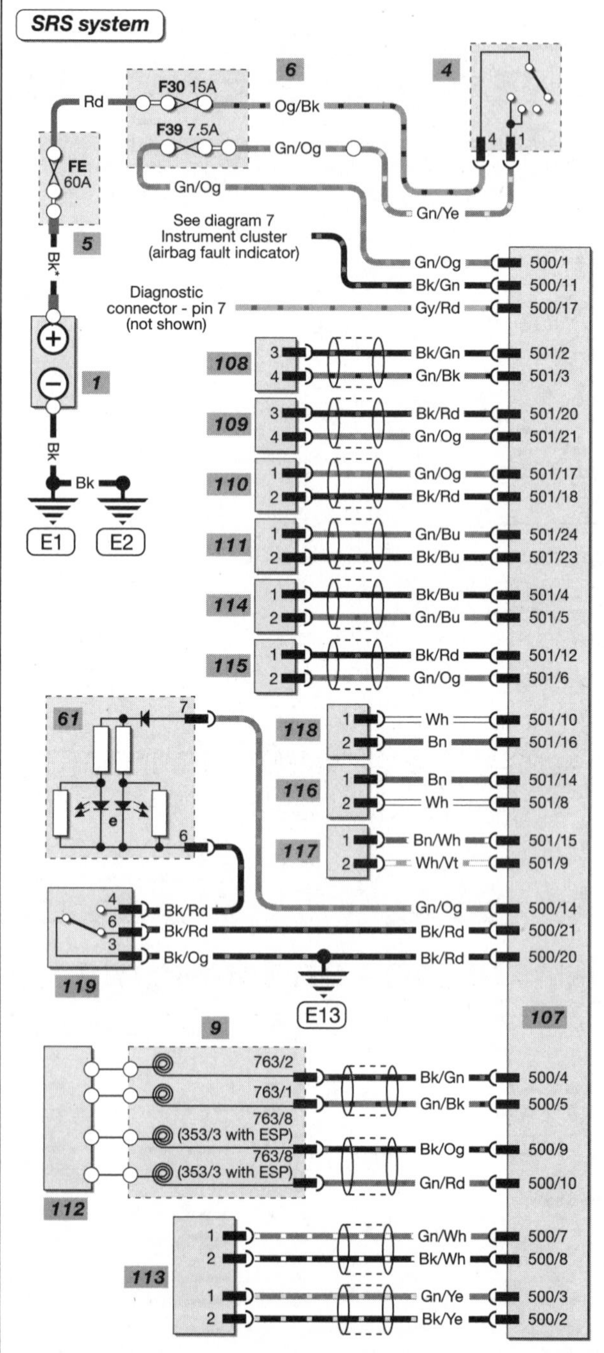

Dimensions and weights

Note: *All figures are approximate, and may vary according to model. Refer to manufacturer's data for exact figures.*

Dimensions

Overall length	4013 mm
Overall width (with electric mirrors)	1963 mm
Overall height (unladen)	1512 to 1543 mm

Weights

Kerb weight:	
Petrol engine models	1156 to 1162 kg
Diesel engine models	1157 to 1165 kg
Permissible gross weight:	
Petrol engine models	1600 to 1630 kg
Diesel engine models	1635 to 1675 kg
Maximum roof rack load	25 kg (75 kg for models with ESP)

Fuel economy

Although depreciation is still the biggest part of the cost of motoring for most car owners, the cost of fuel is more immediately noticeable. These pages give some tips on how to get the best fuel economy.

Working it out

Manufacturer's figures

Car manufacturers are required by law to provide fuel consumption information on all new vehicles sold. These 'official' figures are obtained by simulating various driving conditions on a rolling road or a test track. Real life conditions are different, so the fuel consumption actually achieved may not bear much resemblance to the quoted figures.

How to calculate it

Many cars now have trip computers which will display fuel consumption, both instantaneous and average. Refer to the owner's handbook for details of how to use these.

To calculate consumption yourself (and maybe to check that the trip computer is accurate), proceed as follows.

1. Fill up with fuel and note the mileage, or zero the trip recorder.
2. Drive as usual until you need to fill up again.
3. Note the amount of fuel required to refill the tank, and the mileage covered since the previous fill-up.
4. Divide the mileage by the amount of fuel used to obtain the consumption figure.

For example:

Mileage at first fill-up (a) = 27,903
Mileage at second fill-up (b) = 28,346
Mileage covered (b - a) = 443
Fuel required at second fill-up = 48.6 litres

The half-completed changeover to metric units in the UK means that we buy our fuel in litres, measure distances in miles and talk about fuel consumption in miles per gallon. There are two ways round this: the first is to convert the litres to gallons before doing the calculation (by dividing by 4.546, or see Table 1). So in the example:

48.6 litres ÷ 4.546 = 10.69 gallons
443 miles ÷ 10.69 gallons = 41.4 mpg

The second way is to calculate the consumption in miles per litre, then multiply that figure by 4.546 (or see Table 2).

So in the example, fuel consumption is:

443 miles ÷ 48.6 litres = 9.1 mpl
9.1 mpl x 4.546 = 41.4 mpg

The rest of Europe expresses fuel consumption in litres of fuel required to travel 100 km (l/100 km). For interest, the conversions are given in Table 3. In practice it doesn't matter what units you use, provided you know what your normal consumption is and can spot if it's getting better or worse.

Table 1: conversion of litres to Imperial gallons

litres	1	2	3	4	5	10	20	30	40	50	60	70
gallons	0.22	0.44	0.66	0.88	1.10	2.24	4.49	6.73	8.98	11.22	13.47	15.71

Table 2: conversion of miles per litre to miles per gallon

miles per litre	5	6	7	8	9	10	11	12	13	14
miles per gallon	23	27	32	36	41	46	50	55	59	64

Table 3: conversion of litres per 100 km to miles per gallon

litres per 100 km	4	4.5	5	5.5	6	6.5	7	8	9	10
miles per gallon	71	63	56	51	47	43	40	35	31	28

Maintenance

A well-maintained car uses less fuel and creates less pollution. In particular:

Filters

Change air and fuel filters at the specified intervals.

Oil

Use a good quality oil of the lowest viscosity specified by the vehicle manufacturer (see *Lubricants and fluids*). Check the level often and be careful not to overfill.

Spark plugs

When applicable, renew at the specified intervals.

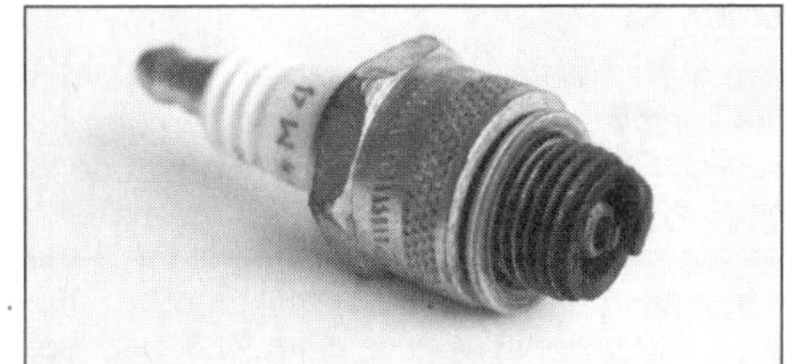

Tyres

Check tyre pressures regularly. Under-inflated tyres have an increased rolling resistance. It is generally safe to use the higher pressures specified for full load conditions even when not fully laden, but keep an eye on the centre band of tread for signs of wear due to over-inflation.

When buying new tyres, consider the 'fuel saving' models which most manufacturers include in their ranges.

Driving style

Acceleration

Acceleration uses more fuel than driving at a steady speed. The best technique with modern cars is to accelerate reasonably briskly to the desired speed, changing up through the gears as soon as possible without making the engine labour.

Air conditioning

Air conditioning absorbs quite a bit of energy from the engine – typically 3 kW (4 hp) or so. The effect on fuel consumption is at its worst in slow traffic. Switch it off when not required.

Anticipation

Drive smoothly and try to read the traffic flow so as to avoid unnecessary acceleration and braking.

Automatic transmission

When accelerating in an automatic, avoid depressing the throttle so far as to make the transmission hold onto lower gears at higher speeds. Don't use the 'Sport' setting, if applicable.

When stationary with the engine running, select 'N' or 'P'. When moving, keep your left foot away from the brake.

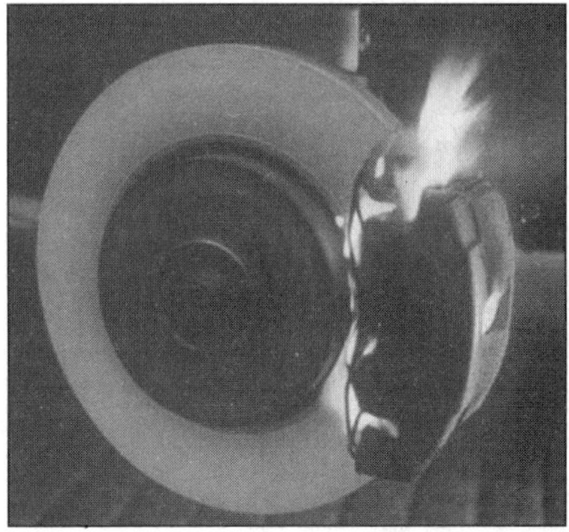

Braking

Braking converts the car's energy of motion into heat – essentially, it is wasted. Obviously some braking is always going to be necessary, but with good anticipation it is surprising how much can be avoided, especially on routes that you know well.

Carshare

Consider sharing lifts to work or to the shops. Even once a week will make a difference.

Electrical loads

Electricity is 'fuel' too; the alternator which charges the battery does so by converting some of the engine's energy of motion into electrical energy. The more electrical accessories are in use, the greater the load on the alternator. Switch off big consumers like the heated rear window when not required.

Freewheeling

Freewheeling (coasting) in neutral with the engine switched off is dangerous. The effort required to operate power-assisted brakes and steering increases when the engine is not running, with a potential lack of control in emergency situations.

In any case, modern fuel injection systems automatically cut off the engine's fuel supply on the overrun (moving and in gear, but with the accelerator pedal released).

Gadgets

Bolt-on devices claiming to save fuel have been around for nearly as long as the motor car itself. Those which worked were rapidly adopted as standard equipment by the vehicle manufacturers. Others worked only in certain situations, or saved fuel only at the expense of unacceptable effects on performance, driveability or the life of engine components.

The most effective fuel saving gadget is the driver's right foot.

Journey planning

Combine (eg) a trip to the supermarket with a visit to the recycling centre and the DIY store, rather than making separate journeys.

When possible choose a travelling time outside rush hours.

Load

The more heavily a car is laden, the greater the energy required to accelerate it to a given speed. Remove heavy items which you don't need to carry.

One load which is often overlooked is the contents of the fuel tank. A tankful of fuel (55 litres / 12 gallons) weighs 45 kg (100 lb) or so. Just half filling it may be worthwhile.

Lost?

At the risk of stating the obvious, if you're going somewhere new, have details of the route to hand. There's not much point in achieving record mpg if you also go miles out of your way.

Parking

If possible, carry out any reversing or turning manoeuvres when you arrive at a parking space so that you can drive straight out when you leave. Manoeuvering when the engine is cold uses a lot more fuel.

Driving around looking for free on-street parking may cost more in fuel than buying a car park ticket.

Premium fuel

Most major oil companies (and some supermarkets) have premium grades of fuel which are several pence a litre dearer than the standard grades. Reports vary, but the consensus seems to be that if these fuels improve economy at all, they do not do so by enough to justify their extra cost.

Roof rack

When loading a roof rack, try to produce a wedge shape with the narrow end at the front. Any cover should be securely fastened – if it flaps it's creating turbulence and absorbing energy.

Remove roof racks and boxes when not in use – they increase air resistance and can create a surprising amount of noise.

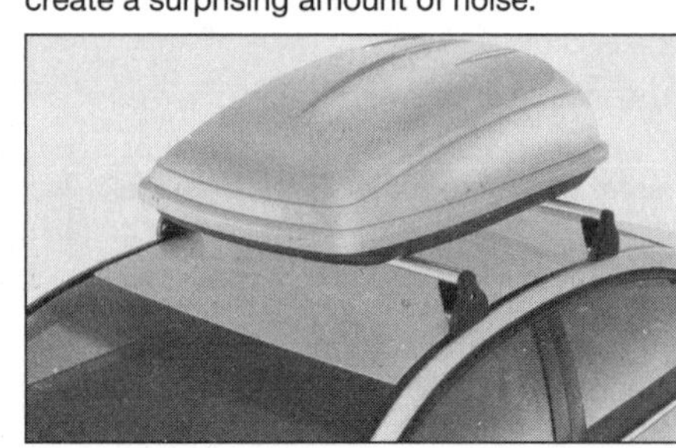

Short journeys

The engine is at its least efficient, and wear is highest, during the first few miles after a cold start. Consider walking, cycling or using public transport.

Speed

The engine is at its most efficient when running at a steady speed and load at the rpm where it develops maximum torque. (You can find this figure in the car's handbook.) For most cars this corresponds to between 55 and 65 mph in top gear.

Above the optimum cruising speed, fuel consumption starts to rise quite sharply. A car travelling at 80 mph will typically be using 30% more fuel than at 60 mph.

Supermarket fuel

It may be cheap but is it any good? In the UK all supermarket fuel must meet the relevant British Standard. The major oil companies will say that their branded fuels have better additive packages which may stop carbon and other deposits building up. A reasonable compromise might be to use one tank of branded fuel to three or four from the supermarket.

Switch off when stationary

Switch off the engine if you look like being stationary for more than 30 seconds or so. This is good for the environment as well as for your pocket. Be aware though that frequent restarts are hard on the battery and the starter motor.

Windows

Driving with the windows open increases air turbulence around the vehicle. Closing the windows promotes smooth airflow and

reduced resistance. The faster you go, the more significant this is.

And finally . . .

Driving techniques associated with good fuel economy tend to involve moderate acceleration and low top speeds. Be considerate to the needs of other road users who may need to make brisker progress; even if you do not agree with them this is not an excuse to be obstructive.

Safety must always take precedence over economy, whether it is a question of accelerating hard to complete an overtaking manoeuvre, killing your speed when confronted with a potential hazard or switching the lights on when it starts to get dark.

Conversion factors

Length (distance)

Inches (in)	x 25.4	= Millimetres (mm)	x 0.0394	= Inches (in)
Feet (ft)	x 0.305	= Metres (m)	x 3.281	= Feet (ft)
Miles	x 1.609	= Kilometres (km)	x 0.621	= Miles

Volume (capacity)

Cubic inches (cu in; in^3)	x 16.387	= Cubic centimetres (cc; cm^3)	x 0.061	= Cubic inches (cu in; in^3)
Imperial pints (Imp pt)	x 0.568	= Litres (l)	x 1.76	= Imperial pints (Imp pt)
Imperial quarts (Imp qt)	x 1.137	= Litres (l)	x 0.88	= Imperial quarts (Imp qt)
Imperial quarts (Imp qt)	x 1.201	= US quarts (US qt)	x 0.833	= Imperial quarts (Imp qt)
US quarts (US qt)	x 0.946	= Litres (l)	x 1.057	= US quarts (US qt)
Imperial gallons (Imp gal)	x 4.546	= Litres (l)	x 0.22	= Imperial gallons (Imp gal)
Imperial gallons (Imp gal)	x 1.201	= US gallons (US gal)	x 0.833	= Imperial gallons (Imp gal)
US gallons (US gal)	x 3.785	= Litres (l)	x 0.264	= US gallons (US gal)

Mass (weight)

Ounces (oz)	x 28.35	= Grams (g)	x 0.035	= Ounces (oz)
Pounds (lb)	x 0.454	= Kilograms (kg)	x 2.205	= Pounds (lb)

Force

Ounces-force (ozf; oz)	x 0.278	= Newtons (N)	x 3.6	= Ounces-force (ozf; oz)
Pounds-force (lbf; lb)	x 4.448	= Newtons (N)	x 0.225	= Pounds-force (lbf; lb)
Newtons (N)	x 0.1	= Kilograms-force (kgf; kg)	x 9.81	= Newtons (N)

Pressure

Pounds-force per square inch (psi; lbf/in^2; lb/in^2)	x 0.070	= Kilograms-force per square centimetre (kgf/cm^2; kg/cm^2)	x 14.223	= Pounds-force per square inch (psi; lbf/in^2; lb/in^2)
Pounds-force per square inch (psi; lbf/in^2; lb/in^2)	x 0.068	= Atmospheres (atm)	x 14.696	= Pounds-force per square inch (psi; lbf/in^2; lb/in^2)
Pounds-force per square inch (psi; lbf/in^2; lb/in^2)	x 0.069	= Bars	x 14.5	= Pounds-force per square inch (psi; lbf/in^2; lb/in^2)
Pounds-force per square inch (psi; lbf/in^2; lb/in^2)	x 6.895	= Kilopascals (kPa)	x 0.145	= Pounds-force per square inch (psi; lbf/in^2; lb/in^2)
Kilopascals (kPa)	x 0.01	= Kilograms-force per square centimetre (kgf/cm^2; kg/cm^2)	x 98.1	= Kilopascals (kPa)
Millibar (mbar)	x 100	= Pascals (Pa)	x 0.01	= Millibar (mbar)
Millibar (mbar)	x 0.0145	= Pounds-force per square inch (psi; lbf/in^2; lb/in^2)	x 68.947	= Millibar (mbar)
Millibar (mbar)	x 0.75	= Millimetres of mercury (mmHg)	x 1.333	= Millibar (mbar)
Millibar (mbar)	x 0.401	= Inches of water (inH_2O)	x 2.491	= Millibar (mbar)
Millimetres of mercury (mmHg)	x 0.535	= Inches of water (inH_2O)	x 1.868	= Millimetres of mercury (mmHg)
Inches of water (inH_2O)	x 0.036	= Pounds-force per square inch (psi; lbf/in^2; lb/in^2)	x 27.68	= Inches of water (inH_2O)

Torque (moment of force)

Pounds-force inches (lbf in; lb in)	x 1.152	= Kilograms-force centimetre (kgf cm; kg cm)	x 0.868	= Pounds-force inches (lbf in; lb in)
Pounds-force inches (lbf in; lb in)	x 0.113	= Newton metres (Nm)	x 8.85	= Pounds-force inches (lbf in; lb in)
Pounds-force inches (lbf in; lb in)	x 0.083	= Pounds-force feet (lbf ft; lb ft)	x 12	= Pounds-force inches (lbf in; lb in)
Pounds-force feet (lbf ft; lb ft)	x 0.138	= Kilograms-force metres (kgf m; kg m)	x 7.233	= Pounds-force feet (lbf ft; lb ft)
Pounds-force feet (lbf ft; lb ft)	x 1.356	= Newton metres (Nm)	x 0.738	= Pounds-force feet (lbf ft; lb ft)
Newton metres (Nm)	x 0.102	= Kilograms-force metres (kgf m; kg m)	x 9.804	= Newton metres (Nm)

Power

Horsepower (hp)	x 745.7	= Watts (W)	x 0.0013	= Horsepower (hp)

Velocity (speed)

Miles per hour (miles/hr; mph)	x 1.609	= Kilometres per hour (km/hr; kph)	x 0.621	= Miles per hour (miles/hr; mph)

Fuel consumption*

Miles per gallon, Imperial (mpg)	x 0.354	= Kilometres per litre (km/l)	x 2.825	= Miles per gallon, Imperial (mpg)
Miles per gallon, US (mpg)	x 0.425	= Kilometres per litre (km/l)	x 2.352	= Miles per gallon, US (mpg)

Temperature

Degrees Fahrenheit = (°C x 1.8) + 32

Degrees Celsius (Degrees Centigrade; °C) = (°F - 32) x 0.56

** It is common practice to convert from miles per gallon (mpg) to litres/100 kilometres (l/100km), where mpg x l/100 km = 282*

Buying spare parts

Spare parts are available from many sources, including maker's appointed garages, accessory shops, and motor factors. To be sure of obtaining the correct parts, it will sometimes be necessary to quote the vehicle identification number. If possible, it can also be useful to take the old parts along for positive identification. Items such as starter motors and alternators may be available under a service exchange scheme – any parts returned should be clean.

Our advice regarding spare parts is as follows.

Officially appointed garages

This is the best source of parts which are peculiar to your car, and which are not otherwise generally available (eg, badges, interior trim, certain body panels, etc). It is also the only place at which you should buy parts if the car is still under warranty.

Accessory shops

These are very good places to buy materials and components needed for the maintenance of your car (oil, air and fuel filters, light bulbs, drivebelts, greases, brake pads, touch-up paint, etc). Components of this nature sold by a reputable shop are usually of the same standard as those used by the car manufacturer.

Besides components, these shops also sell tools and general accessories, usually have convenient opening hours, charge lower prices, and can often be found close to home. Some accessory shops have parts counters where components needed for almost any repair job can be purchased or ordered.

Motor factors

Good factors will stock all the more important components which wear out comparatively quickly, and can sometimes supply individual components needed for the overhaul of a larger assembly (eg, brake seals and hydraulic parts, bearing shells, pistons, valves). They may also handle work such as cylinder block reboring, crankshaft regrinding, etc.

Engine reconditioners

These specialise in engine overhaul and can also supply components. It is recommended that the establishment is a member of the Federation of Engine Re-Manufacturers, or a similar society.

Tyre and exhaust specialists

These outlets may be independent, or members of a local or national chain. They frequently offer competitive prices when compared with a main dealer or local garage, but it will pay to obtain several quotes before making a decision. When researching prices, also ask what extras may be added – for instance fitting a new valve, balancing the wheel and tyre disposal all both commonly charged on top of the price of a new tyre.

Other sources

Beware of parts or materials obtained from market stalls, car boot sales, on-line auctions or similar outlets. Such items are not invariably sub-standard, but there is little chance of compensation if they do prove unsatisfactory. In the case of safety-critical components such as brake pads, there is the risk not only of financial loss, but also of an accident causing injury or death.

Second-hand components or assemblies obtained from a car breaker can be a good buy in some circumstances, but this sort of purchase is best made by the experienced DIY mechanic.

Jacking and vehicle support

The jack supplied with the car's tool kit should only be used for changing the roadwheels – see *Wheel changing* at the front of this book. When carrying out any other kind of work, raise the car using a hydraulic (or 'trolley') jack, and always supplement the jack with axle stands positioned under the jacking/support points **(see illustration)**. If the roadwheels do not have to be removed, consider using wheel ramps – if wished, these can be placed under the wheels once the car has been raised using a hydraulic jack, and then lowered onto the ramps so that it is resting on its wheels.

Only ever jack the car up on a solid, level surface. If there is even a slight slope, take great care that the car cannot move as the wheels are lifted off the ground. Jacking up on an uneven or gravelled surface is not recommended, as the weight of the car will not be evenly distributed, and the jack may slip as the car is raised.

As far as possible, do not leave the car unattended once it has been raised, particularly if children are playing nearby.

Before jacking up the front of the car, ensure that the handbrake is firmly applied. When jacking up the rear of the car, place wooden chocks in front of the front wheels, and engage first gear.

To raise the front and/or rear of the car, use the jacking/support points at the front and rear ends of the door sills, which are located at the places marked by a notch in the sill's lower flange. Position a block of wood with a groove cut in it on the jack head to prevent the car's weight resting on the sill edge; align the sill edge with the groove in the wood so that the car's weight is spread evenly over the surface of the block. Supplement the jack with axle stands (also with slotted blocks of wood) positioned as close as possible to the jacking points.

When using a hydraulic jack or axle stands, always try to position the jack head or axle stand head under one of the relevant jacking points.

Providing care is taken (and a block of wood is used to spread the load), the centre of the front subframe and centre of the rear axle beam, may be used as support points. It may be safe also to use reinforced areas of the floor pan ('chassis legs'), particularly those in the region of suspension mountings, as support points – consult a Ford dealer for advice before using anything other than the approved jacking points, however.

Do not jack the car under any other part of the sill, sump, floor pan, or directly under any of the steering or suspension components.

Never work under, around, or near a raised vehicle, unless it is adequately supported on stands. Do not rely on a jack alone, as even a hydraulic jack could fail under load.

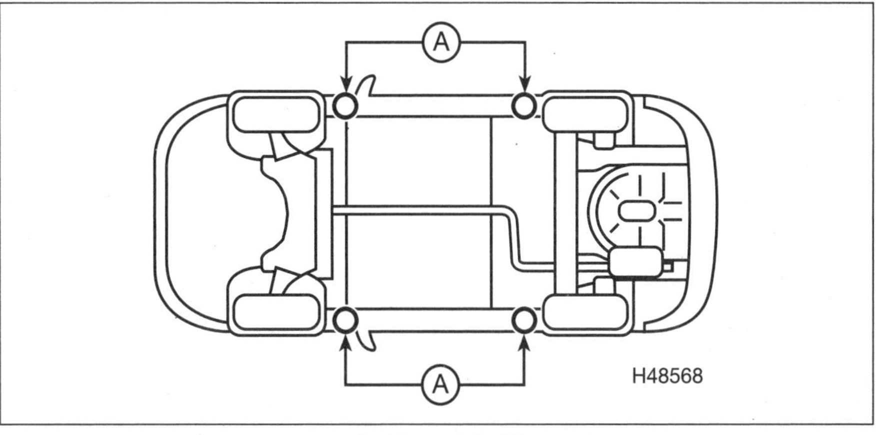

Jacking points (A)

General repair procedures

Whenever servicing, repair or overhaul work is carried out on the car or its components, observe the following procedures and instructions. This will assist in carrying out the operation efficiently and to a professional standard of workmanship.

Joint mating faces and gaskets

When separating components at their mating faces, never insert screwdrivers or similar implements into the joint between the faces in order to prise them apart. This can cause severe damage which results in oil leaks, coolant leaks, etc upon reassembly. Separation is usually achieved by tapping along the joint with a soft-faced hammer in order to break the seal. However, note that this method may not be suitable where dowels are used for component location.

Where a gasket is used between the mating faces of two components, a new one must be fitted on reassembly; fit it dry unless otherwise stated in the repair procedure. Make sure that the mating faces are clean and dry, with all traces of old gasket removed. When cleaning a joint face, use a tool which is unlikely to score or damage the face, and remove any burrs or nicks with an oilstone or fine file.

Make sure that tapped holes are cleaned with a pipe cleaner, and keep them free of jointing compound, if this is being used, unless specifically instructed otherwise.

Ensure that all orifices, channels or pipes are clear, and blow through them, preferably using compressed air.

Oil seals

Oil seals can be removed by levering them out with a wide flat-bladed screwdriver or similar implement. Alternatively, a number of self-tapping screws may be screwed into the seal, and these used as a purchase for pliers or some similar device in order to pull the seal free.

Whenever an oil seal is removed from its working location, either individually or as part of an assembly, it should be renewed.

The very fine sealing lip of the seal is easily damaged, and will not seal if the surface it contacts is not completely clean and free from scratches, nicks or grooves. If the original sealing surface of the component cannot be restored, and the manufacturer has not made provision for slight relocation of the seal relative to the sealing surface, the component should be renewed.

Protect the lips of the seal from any surface which may damage them in the course of fitting. Use tape or a conical sleeve where possible. Where indicated, lubricate the seal lips with oil before fitting and, on dual-lipped seals, fill the space between the lips with grease.

Unless otherwise stated, oil seals must be fitted with their sealing lips toward the lubricant to be sealed.

Use a tubular drift or block of wood of the appropriate size to install the seal and, if the seal housing is shouldered, drive the seal down to the shoulder. If the seal housing is unshouldered, the seal should be fitted with its face flush with the housing top face (unless otherwise instructed).

Screw threads and fastenings

Seized nuts, bolts and screws are quite a common occurrence where corrosion has set in, and the use of penetrating oil or releasing fluid will often overcome this problem if the offending item is soaked for a while before attempting to release it. The use of an impact driver may also provide a means of releasing such stubborn fastening devices, when used in conjunction with the appropriate screwdriver bit or socket. If none of these methods works, it may be necessary to resort to the careful application of heat, or the use of a hacksaw or nut splitter device. Before resorting to extreme methods, check that you are not dealing with a left-hand thread!

Studs are usually removed by locking two nuts together on the threaded part, and then using a spanner on the lower nut to unscrew the stud. Studs or bolts which have broken off below the surface of the component in which they are mounted can sometimes be removed using a stud extractor.

Always ensure that a blind tapped hole is completely free from oil, grease, water or other fluid before installing the bolt or stud. Failure to do this could cause the housing to crack due to the hydraulic action of the bolt or stud as it is screwed in.

For some screw fastenings, notably cylinder head bolts or nuts, torque wrench settings are no longer specified for the latter stages of tightening, "angle-tightening" being called up instead. Typically, a fairly low torque wrench setting will be applied to the bolts/nuts in the correct sequence, followed by one or more stages of tightening through specified angles.

When checking or retightening a nut or bolt to a specified torque setting, slacken the nut or bolt by a quarter of a turn, and then retighten to the specified setting. However, this should not be attempted where angular tightening has been used.

Locknuts, locktabs and washers

Any fastening which will rotate against a component or housing during tightening should always have a washer between it and the relevant component or housing.

Spring or split washers should always be renewed when they are used to lock a critical component such as a big-end bearing retaining bolt or nut. Locktabs which are folded over to retain a nut or bolt should always be renewed.

Self-locking nuts can be re-used in non-critical areas, providing resistance can be felt when the locking portion passes over the bolt or stud thread. However, it should be noted that self-locking stiffnuts tend to lose their effectiveness after long periods of use, and should then be renewed as a matter of course.

Split pins must always be replaced with new ones of the correct size for the hole.

When thread-locking compound is found on the threads of a fastener which is to be re-used, it should be cleaned off with a wire brush and solvent, and fresh compound applied on reassembly.

Special tools

Some repair procedures in this manual entail the use of special tools such as a press, two or three-legged pullers, spring compressors, etc. Wherever possible, suitable readily-available alternatives to the manufacturer's special tools are described, and are shown in use. In some instances, where no alternative is possible, it has been necessary to resort to the use of a manufacturer's tool, and this has been done for reasons of safety as well as the efficient completion of the repair operation. Unless you are highly-skilled and have a thorough understanding of the procedures described, never attempt to bypass the use of any special tool when the procedure described specifies its use. Not only is there a very great risk of personal injury, but expensive damage could be caused to the components involved.

Environmental considerations

When disposing of used engine oil, brake fluid, antifreeze, etc, give due consideration to any detrimental environmental effects. Do not, for instance, pour any of the above liquids down drains into the general sewage system, or onto the ground to soak away. Many local council refuse tips provide a facility for waste oil disposal, as do some garages. You can find your nearest disposal point by calling the Environment Agency on 08708 506 506 or by visiting www.oilbankline.org.uk.

Note: It is illegal and anti-social to dump oil down the drain. To find the location of your local oil recycling bank, call 08708 506 506 or visit www.oilbankline.org.uk.

Modifications are a continuing and unpublicised process in car manufacture, quite apart from major model changes. Spare parts manuals and lists are compiled upon a numerical basis, the individual vehicle identification numbers being essential to correct identification of the component concerned.

When ordering spare parts, always give as much information as possible. Quote the car model, year of manufacture, body and engine numbers as appropriate.

The *vehicle identification plate* is located at the base of the driver's door B-pillar, and can be viewed with the door open. In addition to many other details, it carries the vehicle identification number (VIN), maximum vehicle weight information, and codes for interior trim and body colours **(see illustration)**.

The VIN is also stamped into the driver's-side front suspension strut mounting in the engine compartment and may also be viewed through the base of the windscreen on the passenger's side **(see illustrations)**.

The *engine number* is stamped in the following locations, according to engine type:

a) On petrol engines it appears at the transmission end of the engine, below the throttle body ***(see illustration).***

b) On diesel engines, the number is stamped at the top of the engine, below and in line with the oil filler cap ***(see illustration).***

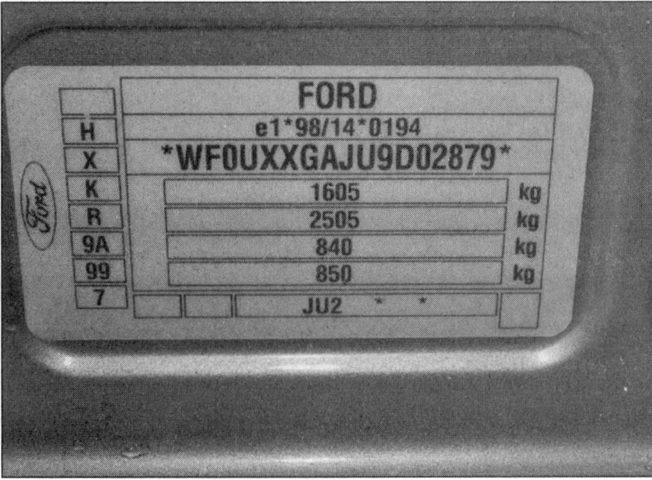

VIN plate at the base of right-hand door pillar

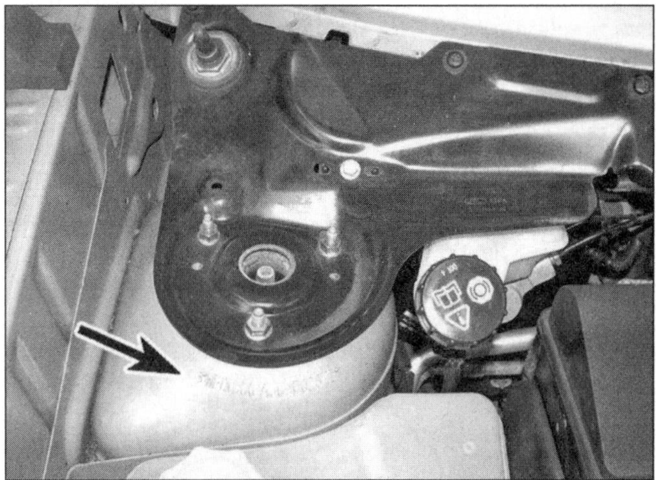

VIN number stamped into the right-hand strut tower

VIN visible through the left-hand side of the windscreen

On petrol engines the engine number is located below the throttle body

The engine number on diesel engines

Introduction

A selection of good tools is a fundamental requirement for anyone contemplating the maintenance and repair of a motor vehicle. For the owner who does not possess any, their purchase will prove a considerable expense, offsetting some of the savings made by doing-it-yourself. However, provided that the tools purchased meet the relevant national safety standards and are of good quality, they will last for many years and prove an extremely worthwhile investment.

To help the average owner to decide which tools are needed to carry out the various tasks detailed in this manual, we have compiled three lists of tools under the following headings: *Maintenance and minor repair, Repair and overhaul*, and *Special*. Newcomers to practical mechanics should start off with the *Maintenance and minor repair* tool kit, and confine themselves to the simpler jobs around the vehicle. Then, as confidence and experience grow, more difficult tasks can be undertaken, with extra tools being purchased as, and when, they are needed. In this way, a *Maintenance and minor repair* tool kit can be built up into a *Repair and overhaul* tool kit over a considerable period of time, without any major cash outlays. The experienced do-it-yourselfer will have a tool kit good enough for most repair and overhaul procedures, and will add tools from the *Special* category when it is felt that the expense is justified by the amount of use to which these tools will be put.

Maintenance and minor repair tool kit

The tools given in this list should be considered as a minimum requirement if routine maintenance, servicing and minor repair operations are to be undertaken. We recommend the purchase of combination spanners (ring one end, open-ended the other); although more expensive than open-ended ones, they do give the advantages of both types of spanner.

- ☐ *Combination spanners:*
  Metric - 8 to 19 mm inclusive
- ☐ *Adjustable spanner - 35 mm jaw (approx.)*
- ☐ *Spark plug spanner (with rubber insert) - petrol models*
- ☐ *Spark plug gap adjustment tool - petrol models*
- ☐ *Set of feeler gauges*
- ☐ *Brake bleed nipple spanner*
- ☐ *Screwdrivers:*
  Flat blade - 100 mm long x 6 mm dia
  Cross blade - 100 mm long x 6 mm dia
  Torx - various sizes (not all vehicles)
- ☐ *Combination pliers*
- ☐ *Hacksaw (junior)*
- ☐ *Tyre pump*
- ☐ *Tyre pressure gauge*
- ☐ *Oil can*
- ☐ *Oil filter removal tool (if applicable)*
- ☐ *Fine emery cloth*
- ☐ *Wire brush (small)*
- ☐ *Funnel (medium size)*
- ☐ *Sump drain plug key (not all vehicles)*

Repair and overhaul tool kit

These tools are virtually essential for anyone undertaking any major repairs to a motor vehicle, and are additional to those given in the *Maintenance and minor repair* list. Included in this list is a comprehensive set of sockets. Although these are expensive, they will be found invaluable as they are so versatile - particularly if various drives are included in the set. We recommend the half-inch square-drive type, as this can be used with most proprietary torque wrenches.

The tools in this list will sometimes need to be supplemented by tools from the *Special* list:

- ☐ *Sockets to cover range in previous list (including Torx sockets)*
- ☐ *Reversible ratchet drive (for use with sockets)*
- ☐ *Extension piece, 250 mm (for use with sockets)*
- ☐ *Universal joint (for use with sockets)*
- ☐ *Flexible handle or sliding T "breaker bar" (for use with sockets)*
- ☐ *Torque wrench (for use with sockets)*
- ☐ *Self-locking grips*
- ☐ *Ball pein hammer*
- ☐ *Soft-faced mallet (plastic or rubber)*
- ☐ *Screwdrivers:*
  Flat blade - long & sturdy, short (chubby), and narrow (electrician's) types
  Cross blade – long & sturdy, and short (chubby) types
- ☐ *Pliers:*
  Long-nosed
  Side cutters (electrician's)
  Circlip (internal and external)
- ☐ *Cold chisel - 25 mm*
- ☐ *Scriber*
- ☐ *Scraper*
- ☐ *Centre-punch*
- ☐ *Pin punch*
- ☐ *Hacksaw*
- ☐ *Brake hose clamp*
- ☐ *Brake/clutch bleeding kit*
- ☐ *Selection of twist drills*
- ☐ *Steel rule/straight-edge*
- ☐ *Allen keys (inc. splined/Torx type)*
- ☐ *Selection of files*
- ☐ *Wire brush*
- ☐ *Axle stands*
- ☐ *Jack (strong trolley or hydraulic type)*
- ☐ *Light with extension lead*
- ☐ *Universal electrical multi-meter*

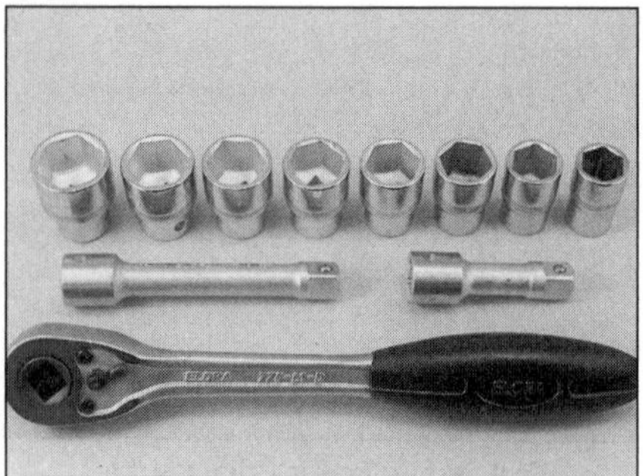

Sockets and reversible ratchet drive

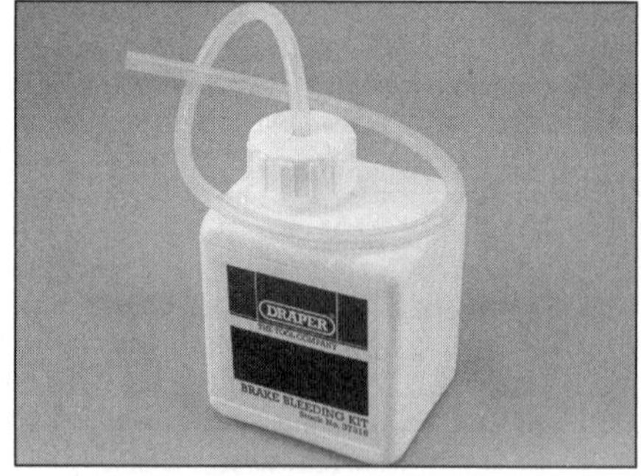

Brake bleeding kit

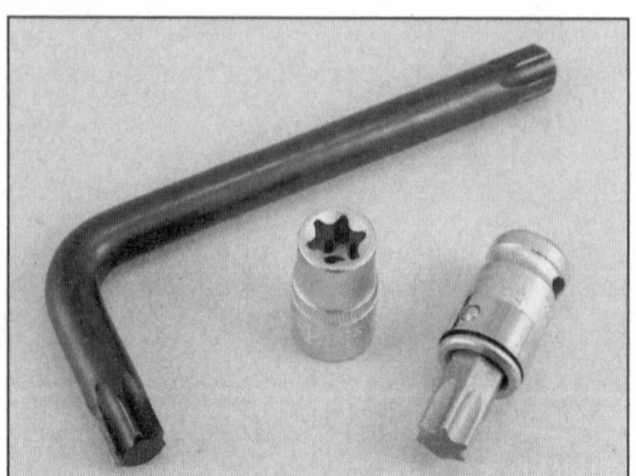

Torx key, socket and bit

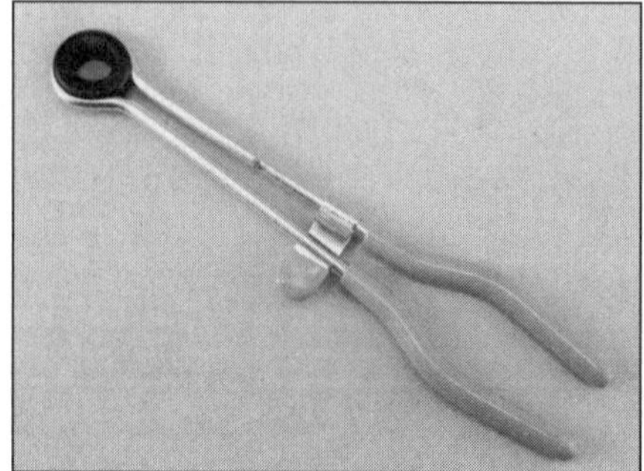

Hose clamp

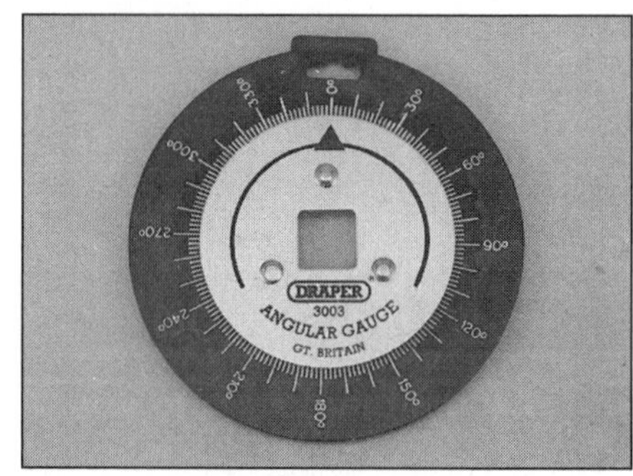

Angular-tightening gauge

Special tools

The tools in this list are those which are not used regularly, are expensive to buy, or which need to be used in accordance with their manufacturers' instructions. Unless relatively difficult mechanical jobs are undertaken frequently, it will not be economic to buy many of these tools. Where this is the case, you could consider clubbing together with friends (or joining a motorists' club) to make a joint purchase, or borrowing the tools against a deposit from a local garage or tool hire specialist.

The following list contains only those tools and instruments freely available to the public, and not those special tools produced by the vehicle manufacturer specifically for its dealer network. You will find occasional references to these manufacturers' special tools in the text of this manual. Generally, an alternative method of doing the job without the vehicle manufacturers' special tool is given. However, sometimes there is no alternative to using them. Where this is the case and the relevant tool cannot be bought or borrowed, you will have to entrust the work to a dealer.

- ☐ *Angular-tightening gauge*
- ☐ *Valve spring compressor*
- ☐ *Valve grinding tool*
- ☐ *Piston ring compressor*
- ☐ *Piston ring removal/installation tool*
- ☐ *Cylinder bore hone*
- ☐ *Balljoint separator*
- ☐ *Coil spring compressors (where applicable)*
- ☐ *Two/three-legged hub and bearing puller*
- ☐ *Impact screwdriver*
- ☐ *Micrometer and/or vernier calipers*
- ☐ *Dial gauge*
- ☐ *Tachometer*
- ☐ *Fault code reader*
- ☐ *Cylinder compression gauge*
- ☐ *Hand-operated vacuum pump and gauge*
- ☐ *Clutch plate alignment set*
- ☐ *Brake shoe steady spring cup removal tool*
- ☐ *Bush and bearing removal/installation set*
- ☐ *Stud extractors*
- ☐ *Tap and die set*
- ☐ *Lifting tackle*

Buying tools

Reputable motor accessory shops and superstores often offer excellent quality tools at discount prices, so it pays to shop around.

Remember, you don't have to buy the most expensive items on the shelf, but it is always advisable to steer clear of the very cheap tools. Beware of 'bargains' offered on market stalls, on-line or at car boot sales. There are plenty of good tools around at reasonable prices, but always aim to purchase items which meet the relevant national safety standards. If in doubt, ask the proprietor or manager of the shop for advice before making a purchase.

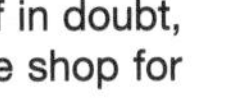

Care and maintenance of tools

Having purchased a reasonable tool kit, it is necessary to keep the tools in a clean and serviceable condition. After use, always wipe off any dirt, grease and metal particles using a clean, dry cloth, before putting the tools away. Never leave them lying around after they have been used. A simple tool rack on the garage or workshop wall for items such as screwdrivers and pliers is a good idea. Store all normal spanners and sockets in a metal box. Any measuring instruments, gauges, meters, etc, must be carefully stored where they cannot be damaged or become rusty.

Take a little care when tools are used. Hammer heads inevitably become marked, and screwdrivers lose the keen edge on their blades from time to time. A little timely attention with emery cloth or a file will soon restore items like this to a good finish.

Working facilities

Not to be forgotten when discussing tools is the workshop itself. If anything more than routine maintenance is to be carried out, a suitable working area becomes essential.

It is appreciated that many an owner-mechanic is forced by circumstances to remove an engine or similar item without the benefit of a garage or workshop. Having done this, any repairs should always be done under the cover of a roof.

Wherever possible, any dismantling should be done on a clean, flat workbench or table at a suitable working height.

Any workbench needs a vice; one with a jaw opening of 100 mm is suitable for most jobs. As mentioned previously, some clean dry storage space is also required for tools, as well as for any lubricants, cleaning fluids, touch-up paints etc, which become necessary.

Another item which may be required, and which has a much more general usage, is an electric drill with a chuck capacity of at least 8 mm. This, together with a good range of twist drills, is virtually essential for fitting accessories.

Last, but not least, always keep a supply of old newspapers and clean, lint-free rags available, and try to keep any working area as clean as possible.

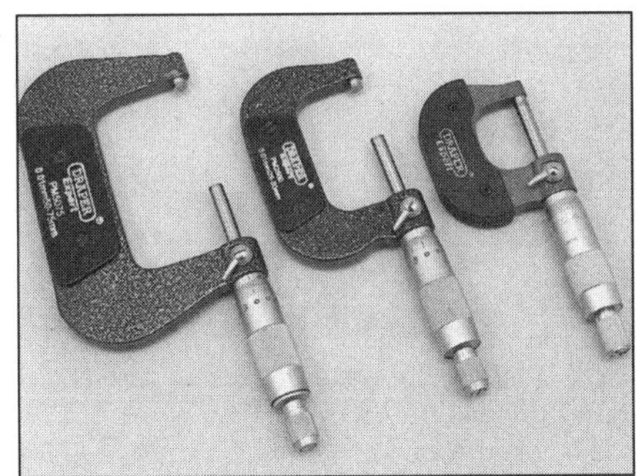

Micrometers

Dial test indicator ("dial gauge")

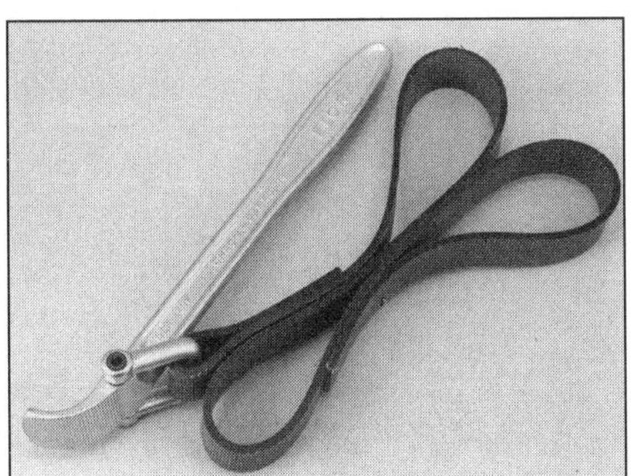

Oil filter removal tool (strap wrench type)

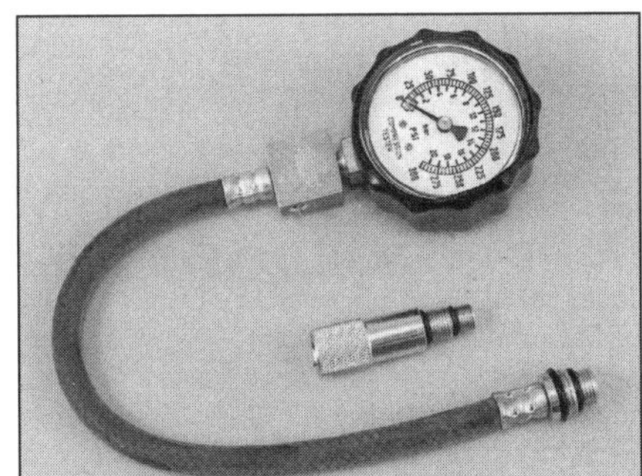

Compression tester

Bearing puller

This is a guide to getting your vehicle through the MOT test. Obviously it will not be possible to examine the vehicle to the same standard as the professional MOT tester. However, working through the following checks will enable you to identify any problem areas before submitting the vehicle for the test.

It has only been possible to summarise the test requirements here, based on the regulations in force at the time of printing. Test standards are becoming increasingly stringent, although there are some exemptions for older vehicles.

An assistant will be needed to help carry out some of these checks.

The checks have been sub-divided into four categories, as follows:

1 Checks carried out **FROM THE DRIVER'S SEAT**

2 Checks carried out **WITH THE VEHICLE ON THE GROUND**

3 Checks carried out **WITH THE VEHICLE RAISED AND THE WHEELS FREE TO TURN**

4 Checks carried out on **YOUR VEHICLE'S EXHAUST EMISSION SYSTEM**

1 Checks carried out FROM THE DRIVER'S SEAT

Handbrake (parking brake)

☐ Test the operation of the handbrake. Excessive travel (too many clicks) indicates incorrect brake or cable adjustment.

☐ Check that the handbrake cannot be released by tapping the lever sideways. Check the security of the lever mountings.

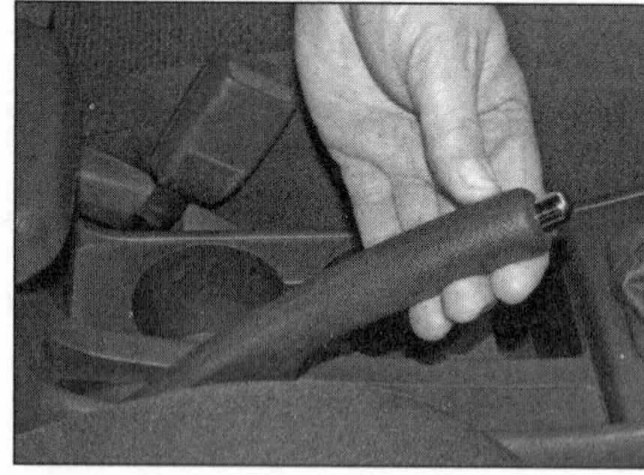

☐ If the parking brake is foot-operated, check that the pedal is secure and without excessive travel, and that the release mechanism operates correctly.

☐ Where applicable, test the operation of the electronic handbrake. The brake should engage and disengage without excessive delay. If the warning light does not extinguish when the brake is disengaged, this could indicate a fault which will need further investigation.

Footbrake

☐ Depress the brake pedal and check that it does not creep down to the floor, indicating a master cylinder fault. Release the pedal, wait a few seconds, then depress it again. If the pedal travels nearly to the floor before firm resistance is felt, brake adjustment or repair is necessary. If the pedal feels spongy, there is air in the hydraulic system which must be removed by bleeding.

☐ Check that the brake pedal is secure and in good condition. Check also for signs of fluid leaks on the pedal, floor or carpets, which would indicate failed seals in the brake master cylinder.

☐ Check the servo unit (when applicable) by operating the brake pedal several times, then keeping the pedal depressed and starting the engine. As the engine starts, the pedal will move down slightly. If not, the vacuum hose or the servo itself may be faulty.

Steering wheel and column

☐ Examine the steering wheel for fractures or looseness of the hub, spokes or rim.

☐ Move the steering wheel from side to side and then up and down. Check that the steering wheel is not loose on the column, indicating wear or a loose retaining nut. Continue moving the steering wheel as before, but also turn it slightly from left to right.

☐ Check that the steering wheel is not loose on the column, and that there is no abnormal movement of the steering wheel, indicating wear in the column support bearings or couplings.

☐ Check that the ignition lock (where fitted) engages and disengages correctly.

☐ Steering column adjustment mechanisms (where fitted) must be able to lock the column securely in place with no play evident.

Windscreen, mirrors and sunvisor

☐ The windscreen must be free of cracks or other significant damage within the driver's field of view. (Small stone chips are acceptable.) Rear view mirrors must be secure, intact, and capable of being adjusted.

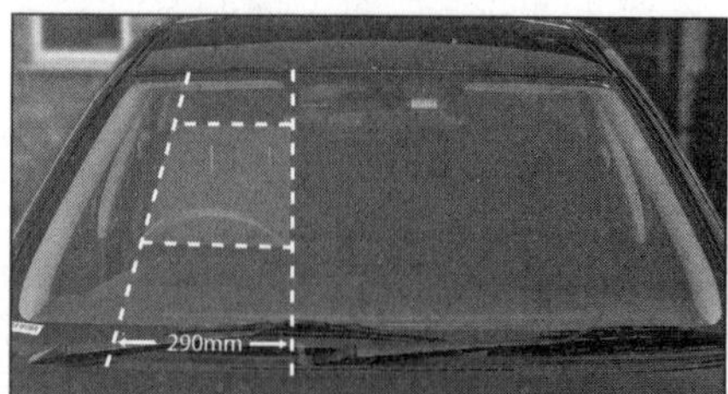

☐ The driver's sunvisor must be capable of being stored in the "up" position.

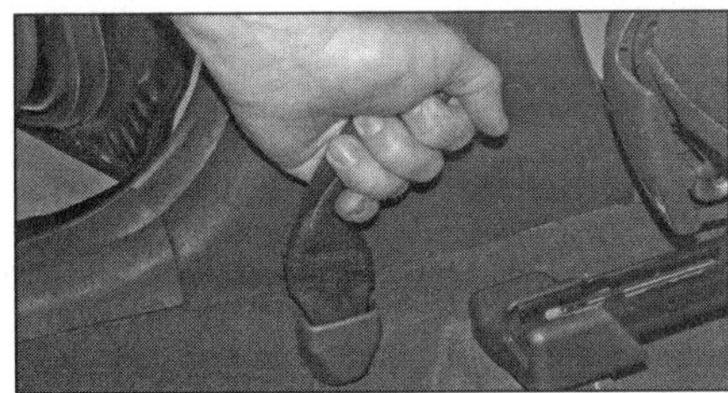

Seat belts and seats

Note: *The following checks are applicable to all seat belts, front and rear.*

☐ Examine the webbing of all the belts (including rear belts if fitted) for cuts, serious fraying or deterioration. Fasten and unfasten each belt to check the buckles. If applicable, check the retracting mechanism. Check the security of all seat belt mountings accessible from inside the vehicle, ensuring any height adjustable mountings lock securely in place.

☐ Seat belts with pre-tensioners, once activated, have a "flag" or similar showing on the seat belt stalk. This, in itself, is not a reason for test failure.

☐ The front seats themselves must be securely attached and the backrests must lock in the upright position.

Doors

☐ Both front doors must be able to be opened and closed from outside and inside, and must latch securely when closed.

Bonnet and boot/tailgate

☐ The bonnet and boot/tailgate must latch securely when closed.

2 Checks carried out WITH THE VEHICLE ON THE GROUND

Vehicle identification

☐ Number plates must be in good condition, secure and legible, with letters and numbers correctly spaced – spacing at (A) should be 33 mm and at (B) 11 mm. At the front, digits must be black on a white background and at the rear black on a yellow background. Other background designs (such as honeycomb) are not permitted.

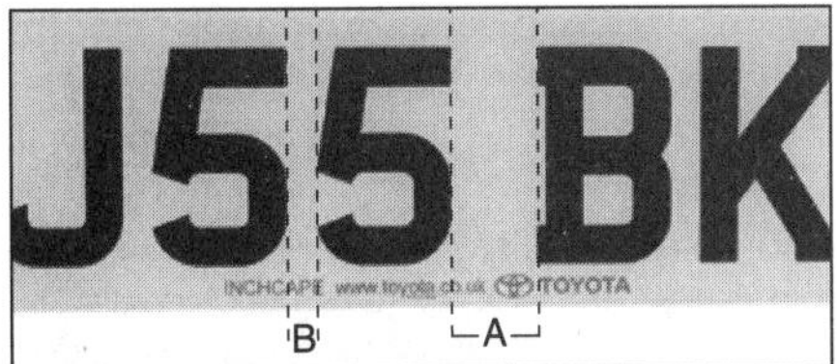

☐ The VIN plate and/or homologation plate must be permanently displayed and legible.

Electrical equipment

☐ Switch on the ignition and check the operation of the horn.

☐ Check the windscreen washers and wipers, examining the wiper blades; renew damaged or perished blades. Also check the operation of the stop-lights.

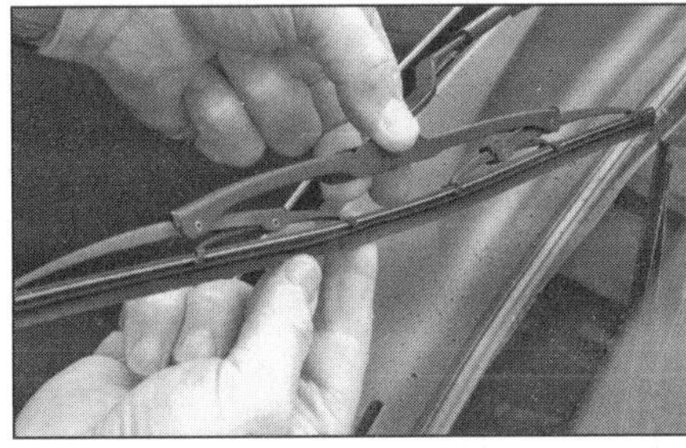

☐ Check the operation of the sidelights and number plate lights. The lenses and reflectors must be secure, clean and undamaged.

☐ Check the operation and alignment of the headlights. The headlight reflectors must not be tarnished and the lenses must be undamaged.

☐ Switch on the ignition and check the operation of the direction indicators (including the instrument panel tell-tale) and the hazard warning lights. Operation of the sidelights and stop-lights must not affect the indicators - if it does, the cause is usually a bad earth at the rear light cluster. Indicators should flash at a rate of between 60 and 120 times per minute – faster or slower than this could indicate a fault with the flasher unit or a bad earth at one of the light units.

☐ Check the operation of the rear foglight(s), including the warning light on the instrument panel or in the switch.

☐ The ABS warning light must illuminate in accordance with the manufacturers' design. For most vehicles, the ABS warning light should illuminate when the ignition is switched on, and (if the system is operating properly) extinguish after a few seconds. Refer to the owner's handbook.

Footbrake

☐ Examine the master cylinder, brake pipes and servo unit for leaks, loose mountings, corrosion or other damage. If ABS is fitted, this unit should also be examined for signs of leaks or corrosion.

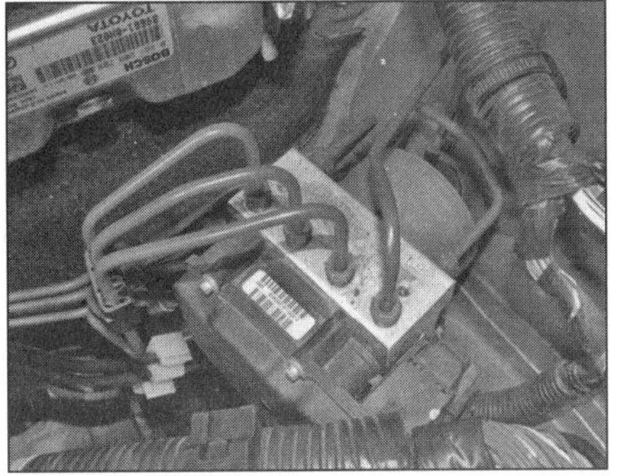

☐ The fluid reservoir must be secure and the fluid level must be between the upper (**A**) and lower (**B**) markings.

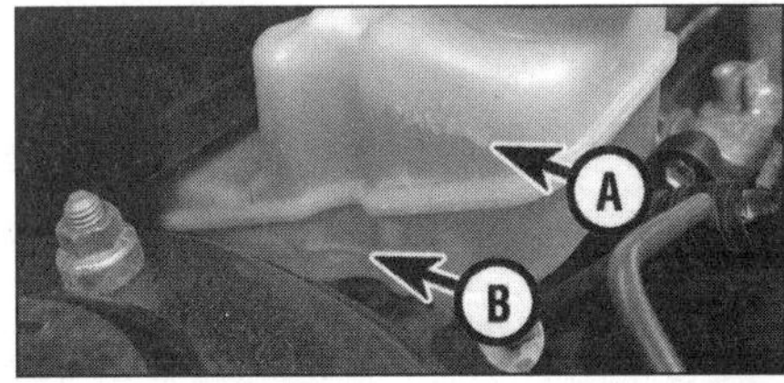

☐ Inspect both front brake flexible hoses for cracks or deterioration of the rubber. Turn the steering from lock to lock, and ensure that the hoses do not contact the wheel, tyre, or any part of the steering or suspension mechanism. With the brake pedal firmly depressed, check the hoses for bulges or leaks under pressure.

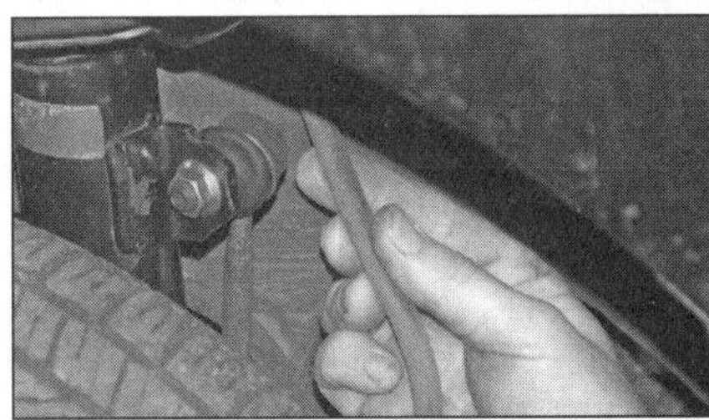

Steering and suspension

☐ Have your assistant turn the steering wheel from side to side slightly, up to the point where the steering gear just begins to transmit this movement to the roadwheels. Check for excessive free play between the steering wheel and the steering gear, indicating wear or insecurity of the steering column joints, the column-to-steering gear coupling, or the steering gear itself.

☐ Have your assistant turn the steering wheel more vigorously in each direction, so that the roadwheels just begin to turn. As this is done, examine all the steering joints, linkages, fittings and attachments. Renew any component that shows signs of wear or damage. On vehicles with power steering, check the security and condition of the steering pump, drivebelt and hoses.

☐ Check that the vehicle is standing level, and at approximately the correct ride height.

Shock absorbers

☐ Depress each corner of the vehicle in turn, then release it. The vehicle should rise and then settle in its normal position. If the vehicle continues to rise and fall, the shock absorber is defective. A shock absorber which has seized will also cause the vehicle to fail.

Exhaust system

☐Start the engine. With your assistant holding a rag over the tailpipe, check the entire system for leaks. Repair or renew leaking sections.

3 Checks carried out WITH THE VEHICLE RAISED AND THE WHEELS FREE TO TURN

Jack up the front and rear of the vehicle, and securely support it on axle stands. Position the stands clear of the suspension assemblies. Ensure that the wheels are clear of the ground and that the steering can be turned from lock to lock.

Steering mechanism

☐Have your assistant turn the steering from lock to lock. Check that the steering turns smoothly, and that no part of the steering mechanism, including a wheel or tyre, fouls any brake hose or pipe or any part of the body structure.

☐ Examine the steering rack rubber gaiters for damage or insecurity of the retaining clips. If power steering is fitted, check for signs of damage or leakage of the fluid hoses, pipes or connections. Also check for excessive stiffness or binding of the steering, a missing split pin or locking device, or severe corrosion of the body structure within 30 cm of any steering component attachment point.

Front and rear suspension and wheel bearings

☐Starting at the front right-hand side, grasp the roadwheel at the 3 o'clock and 9 o'clock positions and rock gently but firmly. Check for free play or insecurity at the wheel bearings, suspension balljoints, or suspension mount-ings, pivots and attachments.

☐Now grasp the wheel at the 12 o'clock and 6 o'clock positions and repeat the previous inspection. Spin the wheel, and check for roughness or tightness of the front wheel bearing.

☐If excess free play is suspected at a component pivot point, this can be confirmed by using a large screwdriver or similar tool and levering between the mounting and the component attachment. This will confirm whether the wear is in the pivot bush, its retaining bolt, or in the mounting itself (the bolt holes can often become elongated).

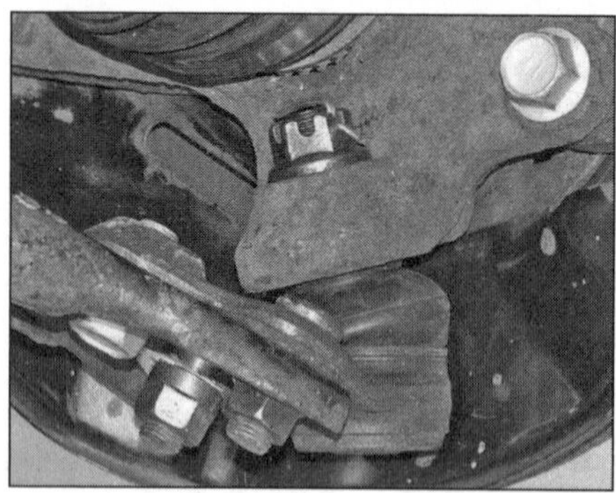

☐Carry out all the above checks at the other front wheel, and then at both rear wheels.

Springs and shock absorbers

☐Examine the suspension struts (when applicable) for serious fluid leakage, corrosion, or damage to the casing. Also check the security of the mounting points.

☐If coil springs are fitted, check that the spring ends locate in their seats, and that the spring is not corroded, cracked or broken.

☐If leaf springs are fitted, check that all leaves are intact, that the axle is securely attached to each spring, and that there is no deterioration of the spring eye mountings, bushes, and shackles.

☐The same general checks apply to vehicles fitted with other suspension types, such as torsion bars, hydraulic displacer units, etc. Ensure that all mountings and attachments are secure, that there are no signs of excessive wear, corrosion or damage, and (on hydraulic types) that there are no fluid leaks or damaged pipes.

☐Inspect the shock absorbers for signs of serious fluid leakage. Check for wear of the mounting bushes or attachments, or damage to the body of the unit.

Driveshafts (fwd vehicles only)

☐Rotate each front wheel in turn and inspect the constant velocity joint gaiters for splits or damage. Also check that each driveshaft is straight and undamaged.

Braking system

☐If possible without dismantling, check brake pad wear and disc condition. Ensure that the friction lining material has not worn excessively, (A) and that the discs are not fractured, pitted, scored or badly worn (B).

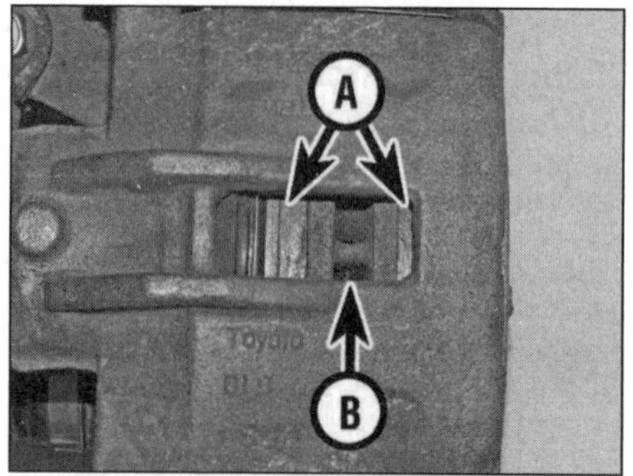

☐Examine all the rigid brake pipes underneath the vehicle, and the flexible hose(s) at the rear. Look for corrosion, chafing or insecurity of the pipes, and for signs of bulging under pressure, chafing, splits or deterioration of the flexible hoses.

☐Look for signs of fluid leaks at the brake calipers or on the brake backplates. Repair or renew leaking components.

☐Slowly spin each wheel, while your assistant depresses and releases the footbrake. Ensure that each brake is operating and does not bind when the pedal is released.

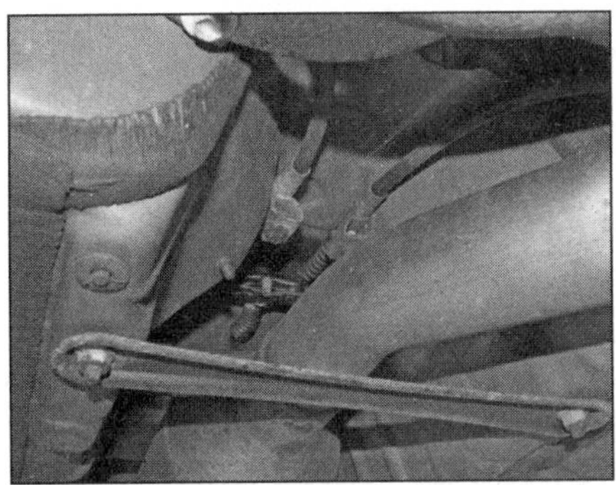

□Examine the handbrake mechanism, checking for frayed or broken cables, excessive corrosion, or wear or insecurity of the linkage. Check that the mechanism works on each relevant wheel, and releases fully, without binding.

□It is not possible to test brake efficiency without special equipment, but a road test can be carried out later to check that the vehicle pulls up in a straight line.

Fuel and exhaust systems

□Inspect the fuel tank (including the filler cap), fuel pipes, hoses and unions. All components must be secure and free from leaks. Locking fuel caps must lock securely and the key must be provided for the MOT test.

□Examine the exhaust system over its entire length, checking for any damaged, broken or missing mountings, security of the retaining clamps and rust or corrosion.

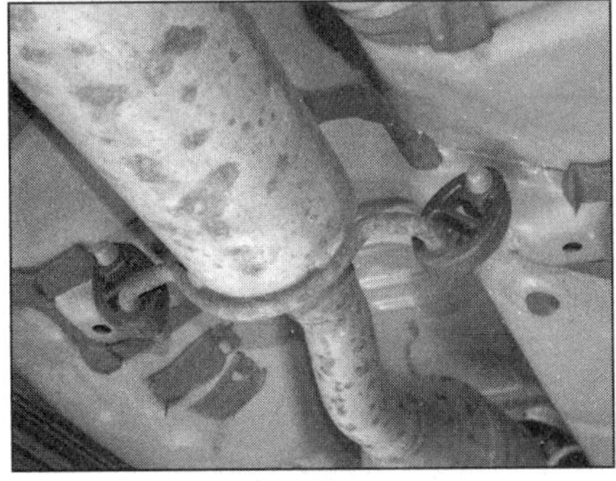

Wheels and tyres

□Examine the sidewalls and tread area of each tyre in turn. Check for cuts, tears, lumps, bulges, separation of the tread, and exposure of the ply or cord due to wear or damage. Check that the tyre bead is correctly seated on the wheel rim, that the valve is sound and properly seated, and that the wheel is not distorted or damaged.

□Check that the tyres are of the correct size for the vehicle, that they are of the same size and type on each axle, and that the pressures are correct.

□Check the tyre tread depth. The legal minimum at the time of writing is 1.6 mm over the central three-quarters of the tread width. Abnormal tread wear may indicate incorrect front wheel alignment or wear in steering or suspension components.

□If the spare wheel is fitted externally or in a separate carrier beneath the vehicle, check that mountings are secure and free of excessive corrosion.

Body corrosion

□Check the condition of the entire vehicle structure for signs of corrosion in load-bearing areas. (These include chassis box sections, side sills, cross-members, pillars, and all suspension, steering, braking system and seat belt mountings and anchorages.) Any corrosion which has seriously reduced the thickness of a load-bearing area (or is within 30 cm of safety-related components such as steering or suspension) is likely to cause the vehicle to fail. In this case professional repairs are likely to be needed.

□Damage or corrosion which causes sharp or otherwise dangerous edges to be exposed will also cause the vehicle to fail.

Towbars

□Check the condition of mounting points (both beneath the vehicle and within boot/hatchback areas) for signs of corrosion, ensuring that all fixings are secure and not worn or damaged. There must be no excessive play in detachable tow ball arms or quick-release mechanisms.

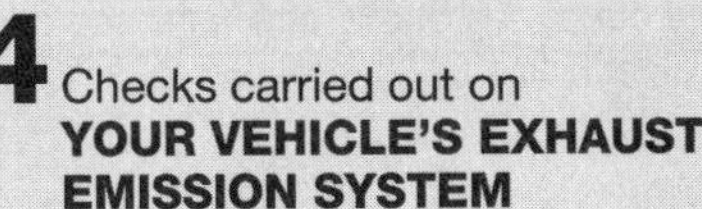

4 Checks carried out on **YOUR VEHICLE'S EXHAUST EMISSION SYSTEM**

Petrol models

□The engine should be warmed up, and running well (ignition system in good order, air filter element clean, etc).

□Before testing, run the engine at around 2500 rpm for 20 seconds. Let the engine drop to idle, and watch for smoke from the exhaust. If the idle speed is too high, or if dense blue or black smoke emerges for more than 5 seconds, the vehicle will fail. Typically, blue smoke signifies oil burning (engine wear); black smoke means unburnt fuel (dirty air cleaner element, or other fuel system fault).

□An exhaust gas analyser for measuring carbon monoxide (CO) and hydrocarbons (HC) is now needed. If one cannot be hired or borrowed, have a local garage perform the check.

CO emissions (mixture)

□The MOT tester has access to the CO limits for all vehicles. The CO level is measured at idle speed, and at 'fast idle' (2500 to 3000 rpm). The following limits are given as a general guide:

At idle speed – Less than 0.5% CO
At 'fast idle' – Less than 0.3% CO
Lambda reading – 0.97 to 1.03

□If the CO level is too high, this may point to poor maintenance, a fuel injection system problem, faulty lambda (oxygen) sensor or catalytic converter. Try an injector cleaning treatment, and check the vehicle's ECU for fault codes.

HC emissions

□The MOT tester has access to HC limits for all vehicles. The HC level is measured at 'fast idle' (2500 to 3000 rpm). The following limits are given as a general guide:

At 'fast idle' – Less then 200 ppm

□Excessive HC emissions are typically caused by oil being burnt (worn engine), or by a blocked crankcase ventilation system ('breather'). If the engine oil is old and thin, an oil change may help. If the engine is running badly, check the vehicle's ECU for fault codes.

Diesel models

□The only emission test for diesel engines is measuring exhaust smoke density, using a calibrated smoke meter. The test involves accelerating the engine at least 3 times to its maximum unloaded speed.

Note: *On engines with a timing belt, it is VITAL that the belt is in good condition before the test is carried out.*

□With the engine warmed up, it is first purged by running at around 2500 rpm for 20 seconds. A governor check is then carried out, by slowly accelerating the engine to its maximum speed. After this, the smoke meter is connected, and the engine is accelerated quickly to maximum speed three times. If the smoke density is less than the limits given below, the vehicle will pass:

Non-turbo vehicles: 2.5m-1
Turbocharged vehicles: 3.0m-1

□If excess smoke is produced, try fitting a new air cleaner element, or using an injector cleaning treatment. If the engine is running badly, where applicable, check the vehicle's ECU for fault codes. Also check the vehicle's EGR system, where applicable. At high mileages, the injectors may require professional attention.

Engine

- ☐ Engine fails to rotate when attempting to start
- ☐ Engine rotates, but will not start
- ☐ Engine difficult to start when cold
- ☐ Engine difficult to start when hot
- ☐ Starter motor noisy or excessively-rough in engagement
- ☐ Engine starts, but stops immediately
- ☐ Engine misfires, or idles unevenly
- ☐ Engine stalls, or lacks power
- ☐ Engine backfires
- ☐ Engine noises
- ☐ Oil consumption excessive
- ☐ Oil pressure warning light illuminated with engine running

Cooling system

- ☐ Overheating
- ☐ Overcooling
- ☐ External coolant leakage
- ☐ Internal coolant leakage
- ☐ Corrosion

Fuel and exhaust systems

- ☐ Fuel consumption excessive
- ☐ Fuel leakage and/or fuel odour
- ☐ Black smoke in exhaust
- ☐ Blue or white smoke in exhaust
- ☐ Excessive noise or fumes from exhaust system

Clutch

- ☐ Pedal travels to floor – no pressure or very little resistance
- ☐ Clutch fails to disengage (unable to select gears)
- ☐ Clutch slips (engine speed increases, with no increase in vehicle speed)
- ☐ Judder as clutch is engaged
- ☐ Noise when depressing or releasing clutch pedal

Durashift EST transmission

- ☐ Noisy in neutral with engine running
- ☐ Noisy in one particular gear
- ☐ Difficulty engaging gears
- ☐ Jumps out of gear
- ☐ No drive, or poor operation
- ☐ Vibration
- ☐ Lubricant leaks

Manual transmission

- ☐ Noisy in neutral with engine running
- ☐ Noisy in one particular gear
- ☐ Difficulty engaging gears
- ☐ Jumps out of gear
- ☐ Vibration
- ☐ Lubricant leaks

Driveshafts

- ☐ Vibration when accelerating or decelerating
- ☐ Clicking or knocking noise on turns (at slow speed on full-lock)

Braking system

- ☐ Car pulls to one side under braking
- ☐ Noise (grinding or high-pitched squeal) when brakes applied
- ☐ Excessive brake pedal travel
- ☐ Brake pedal feels spongy when depressed
- ☐ Excessive brake pedal effort required to stop vehicle
- ☐ Judder felt through brake pedal or steering wheel when braking
- ☐ Brakes binding
- ☐ Rear wheels locking under normal braking

Suspension and steering

- ☐ Car pulls to one side
- ☐ Wheel wobble and vibration
- ☐ Excessive pitching and/or rolling around corners, or during braking
- ☐ Wandering or general instability
- ☐ Excessively-stiff steering
- ☐ Excessive play in steering
- ☐ Lack of power assistance
- ☐ Tyre wear excessive

Electrical system

- ☐ Battery will only hold a charge for a few days
- ☐ Ignition (no-charge) warning light remains illuminated with engine running
- ☐ Ignition (no-charge) warning light fails to come on
- ☐ Lights inoperative
- ☐ Instrument readings inaccurate or erratic
- ☐ Horn faults
- ☐ Windscreen/tailgate wiper faults
- ☐ Windscreen/tailgate washer faults
- ☐ Electric window faults
- ☐ Central locking system faults

Introduction

The car owner who does his or her own maintenance according to the recommended service schedules should not have to use this section of the manual very often. Modern component reliability is such that, provided those items subject to wear or deterioration are inspected or renewed at the specified intervals, sudden failure is comparatively rare. Faults do not usually just happen as a result of sudden failure, but develop over a period of time. Major mechanical failures in particular are usually preceded by characteristic symptoms over hundreds or even thousands of miles. Those components which do occasionally fail without warning are often small and easily carried in the car.

With any fault-finding, the first step is to decide where to begin investigations. Sometimes this is obvious, but on other occasions, a little detective work will be necessary. The owner who makes half a dozen haphazard adjustments or replacements may be successful in curing a fault (or its symptoms), but will be none the wiser if the fault recurs, and ultimately may have spent more time and money than was necessary. A calm and logical approach will be found to be more satisfactory in the long run. Always take into account any warning signs or abnormalities that may have been noticed in the period preceding the fault – power loss, high or low gauge readings, unusual smells, etc – and remember that failure of components such as fuses may only be pointers to some underlying fault.

The pages which follow provide an easy reference guide to the more common problems which may occur during the operation of the car. These problems and their possible causes are grouped under headings denoting various components or systems, such as Engine, Cooling system, etc. The Chapter and/or Section which deals with the problem is also shown in brackets. Whatever the fault, certain basic principles apply. These are as follows:

Verify the fault. This is simply a matter of being sure that you know what the symptoms are before starting work. This is particularly important if you are investigating a fault for someone else, who may not have described it very accurately.

Donít overlook the obvious. For example, if the car won't start, is there fuel in the tank? (Don't take anyone else's word on this particular point, and don't trust the fuel gauge either!) If an electrical fault is indicated, look for loose or broken wires before using the test gear.

Cure the disease, not the symptom. Substituting a flat battery with a fully-charged one will get you off the hard shoulder, but if the underlying cause is not attended to, the new battery will go the same way.

Donít take anything for granted. Particularly, don't forget that a 'new' component may itself be defective (especially if it's been rattling around in the boot for months), and don't leave components out of a fault diagnosis sequence just because they are new or recently fitted. When you do finally diagnose a difficult fault, you'll probably realise that all the evidence was there from the start.

Consider what work, if any, has recently been carried out. Many faults arise through careless or hurried work. For instance, if any work has been performed under the bonnet, could some of the wiring have been dislodged or incorrectly routed, or a hose trapped? Have all the fasteners been properly tightened? Were new, genuine parts and new gaskets used? There is often a certain amount of detective work to be done in this case, as an apparently-unrelated task can have far-reaching consequences.

Diesel engine fault diagnosis

The majority of starting problems on small diesel engines are electrical in origin. The mechanic who is familiar with petrol engines but less so with diesel may be inclined to view the diesel's injectors and pump in the same light as the spark plugs and distributor, but this is generally a mistake.

When investigating complaints of difficult starting for someone else, make sure that the correct starting procedure is understood and is being followed. Some drivers are unaware of the significance of the preheating warning light – many modern engines are sufficiently forgiving for this not to matter in mild weather, but with the onset of winter problems begin.

As a rule of thumb, if the engine is difficult to start but runs well when it has finally got going, the problem is electrical (battery, starter motor or preheating system). If poor performance is combined with difficult starting, the problem is likely to be in the fuel system. The low pressure (supply) side of the fuel system should be checked before suspecting the injectors and injection pump. The most common fuel supply problem is air getting into the system, and any pipe from the fuel tank forwards must be scrutinised if air leakage is suspected. Normally the pump is the last item to suspect, since unless it has been tampered with there is no reason for it to be at fault.

Engine

Engine fails to rotate when attempting to start

- ☐ Battery terminal connections loose or corroded (*Weekly checks*).
- ☐ Battery discharged or faulty (Chapter 5A).
- ☐ Broken, loose or disconnected wiring in the starting circuit (Chapter 5A).
- ☐ Defective starter solenoid or ignition switch (Chapter 5A or 12).
- ☐ Defective starter motor (Chapter 5A).
- ☐ Flywheel ring gear or starter pinion teeth loose or broken (Chapter 2A, 2B, 2C or 5A).
- ☐ Engine earth strap broken or disconnected.
- ☐ Engine suffering 'hydraulic lock' (eg from water ingested after traversing flooded roads, or from a serious internal coolant leak) – consult a Ford dealer for advice.
- ☐ EST transmission not in position N, or footbrake not depressed, or faulty brake light switch (Chapter 7B or 9).

Engine rotates, but will not start

- ☐ Fuel tank empty.
- ☐ Battery discharged or inadequate capacity (engine rotates slowly) (Chapter 5A).
- ☐ Battery terminal connections loose or corroded (*Weekly checks*).
- ☐ Ignition components damp or damaged – petrol engines (Chapter 1A or 5B)
- ☐ Worn, faulty or incorrectly-gapped spark plugs – petrol engines (Chapter 1A)
- ☐ Incorrect use of diesel preheating system, or preheating system fault (Chapter 5B).
- ☐ Diesel fuel waxing (in very cold weather).
- ☐ Immobiliser or anti-theft alarm faulty or incorrectly used, or 'uncoded' ignition key being used (Chapter 12).
- ☐ Crankshaft sensor, or other engine management system sensor, fault (Chapter 4A or 4B)
- ☐ Air filter element dirty or clogged (Chapter 1A or 1B).
- ☐ Blockage in exhaust system (Chapter 4A or 4B).
- ☐ Poor compressions (Chapter 2A, 2B or 2C).
- ☐ Air in diesel fuel system (Chapter 4B).
- ☐ Valve timing incorrect, possibly through a poorly-fitted timing belt (Chapter 2A, 2B or 2C).
- ☐ Major mechanical failure (eg camshaft drive) (Chapter 2A, 2B or 2C).

Engine difficult to start when cold

- ☐ Battery discharged (Chapter 5A).
- ☐ Battery terminal connections loose or corroded (see *Weekly checks*).
- ☐ Worn, faulty or incorrectly-gapped spark plugs – petrol models (Chapter 1A).
- ☐ Other ignition system fault – petrol models (Chapter 5B).
- ☐ Fuel system fault (Chapter 4A or 4B).
- ☐ Diesel glow plug(s) defective (Chapter 5C).
- ☐ Wrong grade of engine oil used (*Weekly checks* or Chapter 1A or 1B).
- ☐ Low cylinder compressions (Chapter 2A, 2B or 2C)

Engine difficult to start when hot

- ☐ Air filter element dirty or clogged (Chapter 1A or 1B).
- ☐ Fuel system fault (Chapter 4A or 4B).
- ☐ Low cylinder compressions (Chapter 2A, 2B or 2C).

Starter motor noisy or excessively-rough

- ☐ Starter pinion or flywheel ring gear teeth loose or broken (Chapter 2A, 2B, 2C or 5A).
- ☐ Starter motor mounting bolts loose or missing (Chapter 5A).
- ☐ Starter motor internal components worn or damaged (Chapter 5A).

Engine starts, but stops immediately

- ☐ Loose or faulty electrical connections in the ignition circuit – petrol models (Chapter 1A or 5B).
- ☐ Vacuum leak at the throttle body, inlet manifold or associated hoses – petrol models (Chapter 4A).
- ☐ Blocked injectors/fuel system fault (Chapter 4A or 4B).
- ☐ Fuel very low in tank.
- ☐ Restriction in fuel feed or return.
- ☐ Air in diesel fuel system (Chapter 4B).
- ☐ Air cleaner dirty or blockage in air intake system (Chapter 1A, 1B, 4A or 4B).
- ☐ Blockage in exhaust system (Chapter 4A or 4B).

Engine (continued)

Engine misfires, or idles unevenly

- ☐ Air cleaner dirty or blockage in air intake system (Chapter 1A, 1B, 4A or 4B).
- ☐ Vacuum leak at the throttle body, inlet manifold or associated hoses – petrol models (Chapter 4A).
- ☐ Worn, faulty or incorrectly-gapped spark plugs – petrol models (Chapter 1A).
- ☐ Blocked or defective hydraulic tappets – diesel engines (Chapter 2B or 2C).
- ☐ Valve clearances incorrect – valve petrol engines (Chapter 2A).
- ☐ Uneven or low cylinder compressions (Chapter 2A, 2B or 2C)
- ☐ Camshaft lobes worn (Chapter 2A, 2B or 2C).
- ☐ Timing belt incorrectly fitted (Chapter 2A, 2B or 2C).
- ☐ Blocked injectors/fuel injection system fault (Chapter 4A or 4B).
- ☐ Valve(s) sticking, valve spring(s) weak or broken, or poor compressions (Chapter 2A, 2B or 2C).
- ☐ Overheating (Chapter 3).
- ☐ Cylinder head gasket blown (Chapter 2A, 2B or 2C).

Engine stalls, or lacks power

- ☐ Fuel filter choked (Chapter 1A or 1B).
- ☐ Petrol fuel pump faulty, or delivery pressure low (Chapter 4A).
- ☐ Air in diesel fuel system (Chapter 4B).
- ☐ Blocked or defective hydraulic tappets – diesel engines (Chapter 2B or 2C).
- ☐ Valve clearances incorrect – petrol engines (Chapter 2A).
- ☐ Vacuum leak at the throttle body, inlet manifold or associated hoses – petrol models (Chapter 4A).
- ☐ Worn, faulty or incorrectly-gapped spark plugs – petrol models (Chapter 1A).
- ☐ Faulty spark plug HT leads – petrol models (Chapter 1A).
- ☐ Faulty ignition coil – petrol models (Chapter 5B).
- ☐ Uneven or low cylinder compressions (Chapter 2A, 2B or 2C).
- ☐ Blocked injector/fuel system fault (Chapter 4A or 4B).
- ☐ Blocked catalytic converter (Chapter 4A or 4B).
- ☐ Engine overheating (Chapter 3).
- ☐ Air filter element blocked (Chapter 1).
- ☐ Throttle position sensor fault (Chapter 4A or 4B).
- ☐ Engine warning light on (fault code in system) (Chapter 4A or 4B).
- ☐ Timing belt worn, or incorrectly fitted (Chapter 2A, 2B, 2C or 2D).
- ☐ Turbo boost pressure inadequate – diesel models (Chapter 4B).
- ☐ Brakes binding (Chapter 1 or 9).
- ☐ Clutch slipping (Chapter 6).

Engine backfires

- ☐ Timing belt incorrectly fitted (Chapter 2A, 2B, 2C or 2D).
- ☐ Spark plug HT leads incorrectly fitted – petrol models (Chapter 1A or 5B).
- ☐ Vacuum leak at the throttle body, inlet manifold or associated hoses – petrol models (Chapter 4A).
- ☐ Blocked catalytic converter (Chapter 4A or 4B).
- ☐ Ignition coil unit faulty – petrol models (Chapter 5B).

Engine noises

Pre-ignition (pinking) or knocking during acceleration or under load

- ☐ Ignition system fault – petrol models (Chapter 1A or 5B).
- ☐ Incorrect grade of spark plug – petrol models (Chapter 1A).
- ☐ Incorrect grade (or type) of fuel used (Chapter 4A or 4B).
- ☐ Vacuum leak at the throttle body, inlet manifold or associated hoses – petrol models (Chapter 4A).
- ☐ Excessive carbon build-up in cylinder head/pistons (Chapter 2A, 2B, 2C or 2D).
- ☐ Blocked injector/fuel injection system fault (Chapter 4A or 4B).

Whistling or wheezing noises

- ☐ Leaking inlet manifold or throttle body gasket – petrol models (Chapter 4A or 4B).
- ☐ Leaking exhaust manifold gasket, or pipe-to-manifold joint (Chapter 4A or 4B).
- ☐ Leaking vacuum hose (Chapter 4 or 9).
- ☐ Blowing cylinder head gasket (Chapter 2A, 2B or 2C).
- ☐ Partially blocked or leaking crankcase ventilation system (Chapter 4C).

Tapping or rattling noises

- ☐ Blocked or defective hydraulic tappets – diesel engines (Chapter 2B or 2C).
- ☐ Worn camshaft (Chapter 2A, 2B or 2C)
- ☐ Ancillary component fault (coolant pump, alternator, etc) (Chapter 3, 5A, etc).
- ☐ Air in diesel fuel system (Chapter 4B).
- ☐ Valve clearances incorrect – petrol engines (Chapter 2A).

Knocking or thumping noises

- ☐ Worn big-end bearings (regular heavy knocking, perhaps less under load) (Chapter 2D).
- ☐ Worn main bearings (rumbling and knocking, perhaps worsening under load) (Chapter 2D).
- ☐ Piston slap – most noticeable when cold, caused by piston/bore wear (Chapter 2D).
- ☐ Ancillary component fault (coolant pump, alternator, etc) (Chapter 3, 5A, etc).
- ☐ Engine mountings worn or defective (Chapter 2A, 2B or 2C).
- ☐ Front suspension or steering components worn (Chapter 10).

Oil consumption excessive

- ☐ External leakage (standing or running) – eg sump gasket, crankshaft oil seals (Chapter 2A, 2B or 2C).
- ☐ New engine not yet run-in.
- ☐ Engine oil incorrect grade/poor quality, or oil level too high (*Weekly checks*).
- ☐ Crankcase ventilation system obstructed (Chapter 1A, 1B or 4C).
- ☐ Burning oil due to general engine wear – pistons and/or bores, valve stem oil seals, etc (Chapter 2D).

Oil pressure warning light illuminated with engine running

- ☐ Low oil level or incorrect oil grade (*Weekly checks*).
- ☐ Faulty oil pressure warning light switch (Chapter 2A, 2B or 2C).
- ☐ Worn engine bearings and/or oil pump (Chapter 2A, 2B or 2C).
- ☐ High engine operating temperature (Chapter 3).
- ☐ Oil pick-up strainer clogged – remove sump to check (Chapter 2A, 2B or 2C).

Cooling system

Overheating

- ☐ Insufficient coolant in system (*Weekly checks*).
- ☐ Thermostat faulty (Chapter 3).
- ☐ Radiator core blocked or grille restricted (Chapter 3).
- ☐ Radiator electric cooling fan(s) or coolant temperature sensor faulty (Chapter 3).
- ☐ Pressure cap faulty (Chapter 3).
- ☐ Inaccurate coolant temperature gauge sender (Chapter 3).
- ☐ Airlock in cooling system (Chapter 1A or 1B).
- ☐ Engine management system fault (Chapter 4A or 4B).
- ☐ Blockage in exhaust system (Chapter 4B).
- ☐ Cylinder head gasket blown (Chapter 2A, 2B or 2C).

Overcooling

- ☐ Thermostat faulty (Chapter 3).
- ☐ Inaccurate coolant temperature gauge sender (Chapter 3).

External coolant leakage

- ☐ Deteriorated or damaged hoses or hose clips (Chapter 1A or 1B).
- ☐ Radiator core or heater matrix leaking (Chapter 3).
- ☐ Pressure cap faulty (Chapter 1A or 1B).
- ☐ Water pump or thermostat housing leaking (Chapter 3).
- ☐ Boiling due to overheating (Chapter 3).
- ☐ Core plug leaking (Chapter 2D).

Internal coolant leakage

- ☐ Leaking cylinder head gasket (Chapter 2A, 2B or 2C).
- ☐ Cracked cylinder head or cylinder bore (Chapter 2D).

Corrosion

- ☐ Infrequent draining and flushing (Chapter 1A or 1B).
- ☐ Incorrect antifreeze mixture, or inappropriate antifreeze type (*Weekly checks* and Chapter 1A or 1B).

Fuel and exhaust systems

Fuel consumption excessive

- ☐ New engine not yet run-in.
- ☐ Air cleaner element dirty, or blockage in air intake system (Chapter 1A, 1B, 4A, or 4B).
- ☐ Fuel system fault (Chapter 4A or 4B).
- ☐ Crankcase ventilation system blocked (Chapter 4C).
- ☐ Unsympathetic driving style, or adverse conditions.
- ☐ Tyres under-inflated (see Weekly checks).
- ☐ Brakes binding (Chapter 1 or 9).
- ☐ Fuel leak, causing apparent high consumption (Chapter 1A, 1B, 4A, or 4B).
- ☐ Valve timing incorrect, possibly through a poorly-fitted timing belt (Chapter 2A, 2B or 2C).

Fuel leakage and/or fuel odour

- ☐ Damaged or corroded fuel tank, pipes or connections (Chapter 1A or 1B).
- ☐ Evaporative emissions system fault – petrol models (Chapter 4C).

Black smoke in exhaust

- ☐ Air cleaner element dirty, or blockage in air intake system (Chapter 1A, 1B, 4A, or 4B).
- ☐ Turbo boost pressure inadequate – diesel models (Chapter 4B).
- ☐ Exhaust gas recirculation system fault – diesel models (Chapter 4C).
- ☐ Fuel system fault (Chapter 4A or 4B).

Blue or white smoke in exhaust

- ☐ Engine oil incorrect grade or poor quality, or fuel passing into sump (worn piston rings/bores).
- ☐ Diesel glow plug(s) defective (white smoke at start-up only) (Chapter 5C).
- ☐ Air cleaner element dirty, or blockage in air intake system (Chapter 1A, 1B, 4A, or 4B).
- ☐ Injector(s) faulty (Chapter 4A or 4B).
- ☐ Blocked or damaged emissions system hoses or components (Chapter 4C).
- ☐ General engine wear – pistons and/or bores, valve stem oil seals, etc (Chapter 2D).

Excessive noise or fumes from exhaust system

- ☐ Leaking exhaust system or manifold joints (Chapter 1A, 1B, 4A, or 4B).
- ☐ Leaking, corroded or damaged silencers or pipe (Chapter 1A, 1B, 4A, or 4B).
- ☐ Exhaust gas recirculation system fault – diesel models (Chapter 4C).
- ☐ Oxygen sensors loose or damaged – petrol models (Chapter 4C).
- ☐ Broken mountings, causing body or suspension contact (Chapter 1A, 1B, 4A, or 4B).

Clutch

Note: *This section also applies to models with the Durashift transmission, with the exception of problems relating to the clutch pedal.*

Pedal travels to floor – no pressure or very little resistance

- ☐ Air in hydraulic system/faulty master or slave cylinder (Chapter 6).
- ☐ Faulty hydraulic release system (Chapter 6).
- ☐ Clutch pedal return spring detached or broken (Chapter 6).
- ☐ Broken clutch release bearing or fork (Chapter 6).
- ☐ Broken diaphragm spring in clutch pressure plate (Chapter 6).

Clutch fails to disengage (unable to select gears)

- ☐ Air in hydraulic system/faulty master or slave cylinder (Chapter 6).
- ☐ Faulty hydraulic release system (Chapter 6).
- ☐ Clutch disc sticking on transmission input shaft splines (Chapter 6).
- ☐ Clutch disc sticking to flywheel or pressure plate (Chapter 6).
- ☐ Faulty pressure plate assembly (Chapter 6).
- ☐ Clutch release mechanism worn or incorrectly assembled (Chapter 6).

Clutch slips (engine speed increases, with no increase in vehicle speed)

- ☐ Faulty hydraulic release system (Chapter 6).
- ☐ Clutch disc linings excessively worn (Chapter 6).
- ☐ Clutch disc linings contaminated with oil or grease (Chapter 6).
- ☐ Faulty pressure plate or weak diaphragm spring (Chapter 6).

Judder as clutch is engaged

- ☐ Clutch disc linings contaminated with oil or grease (Chapter 6).
- ☐ Clutch disc linings excessively worn (Chapter 6).
- ☐ Faulty or distorted pressure plate or diaphragm spring (Chapter 6).
- ☐ Worn or loose engine/transmission mountings (Chapter 2A, 2B or 2C).
- ☐ Clutch disc hub or transmission input shaft splines worn (Chapter 6 or 7).

Noise when depressing or releasing clutch pedal

- ☐ Worn clutch release bearing (Chapter 6).
- ☐ Worn or dry clutch pedal bushes (Chapter 6).
- ☐ Worn or dry clutch master cylinder piston (Chapter 6).
- ☐ Faulty pressure plate assembly (Chapter 6).
- ☐ Pressure plate diaphragm spring broken (Chapter 6).
- ☐ Broken clutch disc cushioning springs (Chapter 6).

Durashift EST transmission

Note: *Though the Durashift EST transmission is inherently simpler and more durable than a normal automatic transmission, in the event of a problem arising with the system, it is advisable to consult a Ford dealer in the first instance. It may be possible to have the problem accurately traced using the Ford IDS diagnostic equipment, for example.*

Noisy in neutral with engine running

- ☐ Lack of oil (Chapter 1A).
- ☐ Input shaft bearings worn (noise apparent in N) (Chapter 7B).*
- ☐ Clutch release bearing worn (noise apparent when stationary, with gear selected) (Chapter 6).

Noisy in one particular gear

- ☐ Worn, damaged or chipped gear teeth (Chapter 7B).*

Difficulty engaging gears

- ☐ Clutch fault (Chapter 6).
- ☐ Clutch actuator, transmission control unit or gearshift actuator fault (Chapter 7B).
- ☐ Engine management system fault – eg crankshaft sensor or throttle position sensor (Chapter 4A).
- ☐ ABS wheel sensor fault – provides vehicle speed information (Chapter 9).
- ☐ Gear lever fault (Chapter 7B).
- ☐ Worn synchroniser assemblies (Chapter 7B).*

Jumps out of gear

- ☐ Gearshift actuator fault (Chapter 7B).
- ☐ Gear lever fault (Chapter 7B).
- ☐ Engine management system fault – eg crankshaft sensor or throttle position sensor (Chapter 4A).
- ☐ ABS wheel sensor fault – provides vehicle speed information (Chapter 9).
- ☐ Worn synchroniser assemblies (Chapter 7B).*
- ☐ Worn selector forks (Chapter 7B).*

No drive, or poor operation

- ☐ Clutch fault (Chapter 6).
- ☐ Clutch actuator, transmission control unit or gearshift actuator fault (Chapter 7B).
- ☐ Engine management system fault – eg crankshaft sensor or throttle position sensor (Chapter 4A).
- ☐ ABS wheel sensor fault – provides vehicle speed information (Chapter 9).
- ☐ Gear lever fault (Chapter 7B).
- ☐ Brake light switch or handbrake warning light switch fault (Chapter 9).

Vibration

- ☐ Lack of oil (Chapter 1A).
- ☐ Worn bearings (Chapter 7B).*

Lubricant leaks

- ☐ Leaking differential side gear oil seal (Chapter 7B).
- ☐ Leaking housing joint (Chapter 7B).*
- ☐ Leaking input shaft oil seal (Chapter 7B).*
- ☐ Leaking selector shaft oil seal (Chapter 7B).

** Although the corrective action necessary to remedy the symptoms described is beyond the scope of the home mechanic, the above information should be helpful in isolating the cause of the condition, so that the owner can communicate clearly with a professional mechanic.*

Manual transmission

Noisy in neutral with engine running

- ☐ Lack of oil (Chapter 1A or 1B).
- ☐ Input shaft bearings worn (noise apparent with clutch pedal released, but not when depressed) (Chapter 7A).*
- ☐ Clutch release bearing worn (noise apparent with clutch pedal depressed, possibly less when released) (Chapter 6).

Noisy in one particular gear

- ☐ Worn, damaged or chipped gear teeth (Chapter 7A).*

Difficulty engaging gears

- ☐ Clutch fault (Chapter 6).
- ☐ Worn or damaged gear cables (Chapter 7A).
- ☐ Incorrectly-adjusted gear cables (Chapter 7A).
- ☐ Worn synchroniser assemblies (Chapter 7A).*

Jumps out of gear

- ☐ Worn or damaged gear cables (Chapter 7A).
- ☐ Incorrectly-adjusted gear cables (Chapter 7A).
- ☐ Worn synchroniser assemblies (Chapter 7A).*
- ☐ Worn selector forks (Chapter 7A).*

Vibration

- ☐ Lack of oil (Chapter 1).
- ☐ Worn bearings (Chapter 7A).*

Lubricant leaks

- ☐ Leaking differential side gear oil seal (Chapter 7A).
- ☐ Leaking housing joint (Chapter 7A).*
- ☐ Leaking input shaft oil seal (Chapter 7A).*
- ☐ Leaking selector shaft oil seal (Chapter 7A).

** Although the corrective action necessary to remedy the symptoms described is beyond the scope of the home mechanic, the above information should be helpful in isolating the cause of the condition, so that the owner can communicate clearly with a professional mechanic.*

Driveshafts

Vibration when accelerating or decelerating

- ☐ Worn inner constant velocity joint (Chapter 1A, 1B, or 8).
- ☐ Bent or distorted driveshaft (Chapter 8).
- ☐ Worn intermediate bearing (Chapter 8).
- ☐ Loose or damaged driveshaft nut (Chapter 1A, 1B, or 8).

Clicking or knocking noise on turns (at slow speed on full-lock)

- ☐ Lack of constant velocity joint lubricant (Chapter 8).
- ☐ Worn outer constant velocity joint (Chapter 1A, 1B, or 8).
- ☐ Worn intermediate bearing (Chapter 8).
- ☐ Loose or damaged driveshaft nut (Chapter 1A, 1B, or 8).

Braking system

Note: *Before assuming that a brake problem exists, make sure that the tyres are in good condition and correctly inflated, that the front wheel alignment is correct, and that the car is not loaded with weight in an unequal manner. Apart from checking the condition of all pipe and hose connections, any faults occurring on the Anti-lock Braking System (ABS) should be referred to a Ford dealer for diagnosis.*

Car pulls to one side under braking

- ☐ Worn, defective, damaged or contaminated front or rear brake pads/shoes on one side (Chapter 1A or 1B).
- ☐ Seized or partially-seized front caliper/wheel cylinder piston (Chapter 9).
- ☐ A mixture of brake pad/shoe lining materials fitted between sides (Chapter 1A or 1B).
- ☐ Brake caliper mounting bolts loose (Chapter 9).
- ☐ Rear brake backplate mounting bolts loose (Chapter 9).
- ☐ Worn or damaged steering or suspension components (Chapter 10).

Noise (grinding or high-pitched squeal) when brakes applied

- ☐ Brake pad or shoe friction lining material worn down to metal backing (Chapter 1A or 1B).
- ☐ Excessive corrosion of brake disc or drum (may be apparent after the car has been standing for some time) (Chapter 1A or 1B).

Excessive brake pedal travel

- ☐ Inoperative rear brake self-adjust mechanism (Chapter 9).
- ☐ Rear wheel cylinders leaking (Chapter 9).
- ☐ Faulty master cylinder (Chapter 9).
- ☐ Air in hydraulic system (Chapter 9).

Brake pedal feels spongy when depressed

- ☐ Air in hydraulic system (Chapter 9).
- ☐ Rear wheel cylinders leaking (Chapter 9).
- ☐ Deteriorated flexible rubber brake hoses (Chapter 9).
- ☐ Master cylinder mounting nuts loose (Chapter 9).
- ☐ Faulty master cylinder (Chapter 9).

Excessive brake pedal effort required to stop car

- ☐ Faulty vacuum servo unit (Chapter 9).
- ☐ Disconnected, damaged or insecure brake servo vacuum hoses (Chapter 9).
- ☐ Brake vacuum pump leaking or faulty (Chapter 9).
- ☐ Primary or secondary hydraulic circuit failure (Chapter 9).
- ☐ Seized brake caliper or wheel cylinder piston(s) (Chapter 9).
- ☐ Brake pads or brake shoes incorrectly fitted (Chapter 9).
- ☐ Incorrect grade of brake pads or brake shoes fitted (Chapter 1A or 1B).
- ☐ Brake pads or brake shoe linings contaminated (Chapter 1A or 1B).

Judder felt through brake pedal or steering wheel when braking

- ☐ Excessive run-out or distortion of front discs or rear discs/drums (Chapter 9).
- ☐ Brake pad or brake shoe linings worn (Chapter 1A or 1B).
- ☐ Brake caliper or rear brake backplate mounting bolts loose (Chapter 9).
- ☐ Wear in suspension or steering components or mountings (Chapter 10).

Brakes binding

- ☐ Seized brake caliper or wheel cylinder piston(s) (Chapter 9).
- ☐ Faulty handbrake mechanism (Chapter 9).
- ☐ Faulty master cylinder (Chapter 9).

Rear wheels locking under normal braking

- ☐ Rear brake pad/shoe linings contaminated (Chapter 1A or 1B).
- ☐ Faulty brake pressure regulator valves, or ABS unit (Chapter 9).

Suspension and steering

Note: *Before diagnosing suspension or steering faults, be sure that the trouble is not due to incorrect tyre pressures, mixtures of tyre types, or binding brakes.*

Car pulls to one side

- ☐ Defective tyre (Chapter 1A or 1B).
- ☐ Excessive wear in suspension or steering components (Chapter 10).
- ☐ Incorrect front wheel alignment (Chapter 10).
- ☐ Accident damage to steering or suspension components (Chapter 10).

Wheel wobble and vibration

- ☐ Front roadwheels out of balance (vibration felt mainly through the steering wheel) (Chapter 1A or 1B).
- ☐ Rear roadwheels out of balance (vibration felt throughout the car) (Chapter 1A or 1B).
- ☐ Roadwheels damaged or distorted (Chapter 1A or 1B).
- ☐ Faulty or damaged tyre (*Weekly checks*).
- ☐ Worn steering or suspension joints, bushes or components (Chapter 10).
- ☐ Roadwheel nuts loose (Chapter 1A or 1B).
- ☐ Wear in driveshaft joint, or loose driveshaft nut (vibration worst when under load) (Chapter 1A, 1B, or 8).

Excessive pitching and/or rolling around corners, or during braking

- ☐ Defective shock absorbers (Chapter 10).
- ☐ Broken or weak coil spring and/or suspension components (Chapter 10).
- ☐ Worn or damaged anti-roll bar or mountings (Chapter 10).

Wandering or general instability

- ☐ Incorrect front wheel alignment (Chapter 10).
- ☐ Worn steering or suspension joints, bushes or components (Chapter 10).
- ☐ Tyres out of balance (*Weekly checks*).
- ☐ Faulty or damaged tyre (*Weekly checks*).
- ☐ Roadwheel nuts loose (Chapter 1A or 1B).
- ☐ Defective shock absorbers (Chapter 10).

Excessively-stiff steering

- ☐ Lack of steering gear lubricant (Chapter 10).
- ☐ Seized track-rod end balljoint or suspension balljoint (Chapter 10).
- ☐ Broken or slipping auxiliary drivebelt (Chapter 1A or 1B).
- ☐ Incorrect front wheel alignment (Chapter 10).
- ☐ Steering rack or column bent or damaged (Chapter 10).

Excessive play in steering

- ☐ Worn steering column universal joint (Chapter 10).
- ☐ Worn steering track-rod end balljoints (Chapter 10).
- ☐ Worn rack-and-pinion steering gear (Chapter 10).
- ☐ Worn steering or suspension joints, bushes or components (Chapter 10).

Lack of power assistance

- ☐ Broken or slipping auxiliary drivebelt (Chapter 1A or 1B).
- ☐ Incorrect power steering fluid level (*Weekly checks*).
- ☐ Restriction in power steering fluid hoses (Chapter 10).
- ☐ Faulty power steering pump (Chapter 10).
- ☐ Faulty rack-and-pinion steering gear (Chapter 10).

Tyre wear excessive

Tyres worn on inside or outside edges

- ☐ Tyres under-inflated (wear on both edges) (*Weekly checks*).
- ☐ Incorrect camber or castor angles (wear on one edge only) (Chapter 10).
- ☐ Worn steering or suspension joints, bushes or components (Chapter 10).
- ☐ Excessively-hard cornering.
- ☐ Accident damage.

Tyre treads exhibit feathered edges

- ☐ Incorrect toe setting (Chapter 10).

Tyres worn in centre of tread

- ☐ Tyres over-inflated (*Weekly checks*).

Tyres worn on inside and outside edges

- ☐ Tyres under-inflated (*Weekly checks*).

Tyres worn unevenly

- ☐ Tyres out of balance (*Weekly checks*).
- ☐ Excessive wheel or tyre run-out (Chapter 1A or 1B).
- ☐ Worn shock absorbers (Chapter 10).
- ☐ Faulty tyre (*Weekly checks*).

Electrical system

Note: *For problems associated with the starting system, refer to the faults listed under 'Engine' earlier in this Section.*

Battery will only hold a charge for a few days

- ☐ Battery defective internally (Chapter 5A).
- ☐ Battery electrolyte level low (Chapter 5A).
- ☐ Battery terminal connections loose or corroded (*Weekly checks*).
- ☐ Auxiliary drivebelt worn or slipping (Chapter 1A or 1B).
- ☐ Alternator not charging at correct output (Chapter 5A).
- ☐ Alternator or voltage regulator faulty (Chapter 5A).
- ☐ Short-circuit causing continual battery drain (Chapters 5A and 12).

Ignition (no-charge) warning light remains illuminated with engine running

- ☐ Auxiliary drivebelt broken, worn, or slipping (Chapter 1A or 1B).
- ☐ Alternator brushes worn, sticking, or dirty (Chapter 5A).
- ☐ Alternator brush springs weak or broken (Chapter 5A).
- ☐ Internal fault in alternator or voltage regulator (Chapter 5A).
- ☐ Disconnected or loose wiring in charging circuit (Chapter 5A).

Ignition (no-charge) warning light fails to come on

- ☐ Warning light bulb blown (Chapter 12).
- ☐ Broken, disconnected, or loose wiring in warning light circuit (Chapters 5A and 12).
- ☐ Alternator faulty (Chapter 5A).

Lights inoperative

- ☐ Bulb blown (Chapter 12).
- ☐ Corrosion of bulb or bulbholder contacts (Chapter 12).
- ☐ Blown fuse (Chapter 12).
- ☐ Faulty relay (Chapter 12).
- ☐ Broken, loose, or disconnected wiring (Chapter 12).
- ☐ Generic Electronic Module fault (Chapter 12).
- ☐ Faulty switch (Chapter 12).

Instrument readings inaccurate or erratic

Gauges give no reading

- ☐ Faulty gauge sender unit (Chapter 3 or 4A).
- ☐ Wiring open-circuit (Chapter 12).
- ☐ Faulty gauge (Chapter 12).

Gauges give continuous maximum reading

- ☐ Faulty gauge sender unit (Chapter 3 or 4A).
- ☐ Wiring short-circuit (Chapter 12).
- ☐ Faulty gauge (Chapter 12).

Horn faults

Horn fails to operate

- ☐ Blown fuse (Chapter 12).
- ☐ Cable or cable connections loose or disconnected (Chapter 12).
- ☐ Faulty horn (Chapter 12).

Horn emits intermittent or unsatisfactory sound

- ☐ Cable connections loose (Chapter 12).
- ☐ Horn mountings loose (Chapter 12).
- ☐ Faulty horn (Chapter 12).

Horn operates all the time

- ☐ Horn push either earthed or stuck down (Chapter 12).
- ☐ Horn cable to horn push earthed (Chapter 12).

Windscreen/tailgate wiper faults

Wipers fail to operate, or operate very slowly

- ☐ Wiper blades stuck to screen, or linkage seized (Chapter 12).
- ☐ Blown fuse (Chapter 12).
- ☐ Cable or cable connections loose or disconnected (Chapter 12).
- ☐ Faulty relay (Chapter 12).
- ☐ Faulty wiper motor (Chapter 12).
- ☐ Generic electronic module fault (Chapter 12).

Wiper blades sweep over the wrong area of glass

- ☐ Wiper arms incorrectly-positioned on spindles (Chapter 12).
- ☐ Excessive wear of wiper linkage (Chapter 12).
- ☐ Wiper motor or linkage mountings loose or insecure (Chapter 12).

Wiper blades fail to clean the glass effectively

- ☐ Wiper blade rubbers worn or perished (Weekly checks).
- ☐ Wiper arm tension springs broken, or arm pivots seized (Chapter 12).
- ☐ Insufficient windscreen washer additive to adequately remove road film (*Weekly checks*).

Windscreen/tailgate washer faults

One or more washer jets inoperative

- ☐ Blocked washer jet (Weekly checks or Chapter 12).
- ☐ Disconnected, kinked or restricted fluid hose (Chapter 12).
- ☐ Insufficient fluid in washer reservoir (*Weekly checks*).

Washer pump fails to operate

- ☐ Broken or disconnected wiring or connections (Chapter 12).
- ☐ Blown fuse (Chapter 12).
- ☐ Faulty washer switch (Chapter 12).
- ☐ Faulty washer pump (Chapter 12).

Washer pump runs for some time before fluid is emitted from jets

- ☐ Faulty one-way valve in fluid supply hose (Chapter 12).

Electric window faults

Window glass will only move in one direction

- ☐ Faulty switch (Chapter 12).

Window glass slow to move

- ☐ Regulator seized or damaged, or lack of lubrication (Chapter 11).
- ☐ Door internal components or trim fouling regulator (Chapter 11).
- ☐ Faulty motor (Chapter 12).

Window glass fails to move

- ☐ Blown fuse (Chapter 12).
- ☐ Faulty relay (Chapter 12).
- ☐ Broken or disconnected wiring or connections (Chapter 12).
- ☐ Faulty motor (Chapter 12).

Central locking system faults

Complete system failure

- ☐ Blown fuse (Chapter 12).
- ☐ Faulty relay (Chapter 12).
- ☐ Broken or disconnected wiring or connections (Chapter 12).
- ☐ Generic Electronic Module fault (Chapter 12).

Latch locks but will not unlock, or unlocks but will not lock

- ☐ Faulty master switch (Chapter 11).
- ☐ Faulty lock (Chapter 11).
- ☐ Faulty relay (Chapter 12).

One lock motor fails to operate

- ☐ Broken or disconnected wiring or connections (Chapter 12).
- ☐ Faulty lock motor (Chapter 11).
- ☐ Fault in door latch (Chapter 11).

Glossary of technical terms

A

ABS (Anti-lock brake system) A system, usually electronically controlled, that senses incipient wheel lockup during braking and relieves hydraulic pressure at wheels that are about to skid.

Air bag An inflatable bag hidden in the steering wheel (driver's side) or the dash or glovebox (passenger side). In a head-on collision, the bags inflate, preventing the driver and front passenger from being thrown forward into the steering wheel or windscreen.

Air cleaner A metal or plastic housing, containing a filter element, which removes dust and dirt from the air being drawn into the engine.

Air filter element The actual filter in an air cleaner system, usually manufactured from pleated paper and requiring renewal at regular intervals.

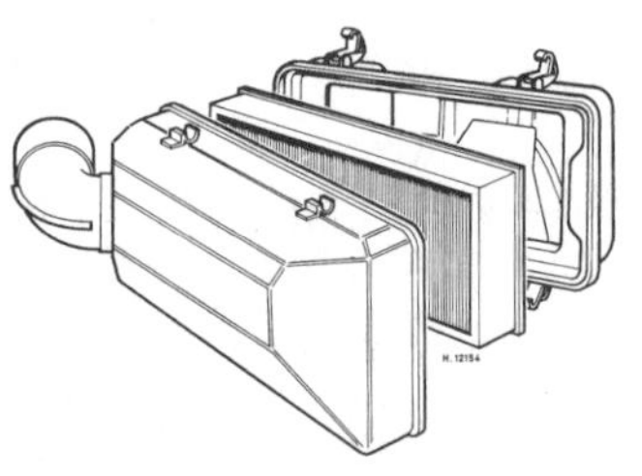

Air filter

Allen key A hexagonal wrench which fits into a recessed hexagonal hole.

Alligator clip A long-nosed spring-loaded metal clip with meshing teeth. Used to make temporary electrical connections.

Alternator A component in the electrical system which converts mechanical energy from a drivebelt into electrical energy to charge the battery and to operate the starting system, ignition system and electrical accessories.

Ampere (amp) A unit of measurement for the flow of electric current. One amp is the amount of current produced by one volt acting through a resistance of one ohm.

Anaerobic sealer A substance used to prevent bolts and screws from loosening. Anaerobic means that it does not require oxygen for activation. The Loctite brand is widely used.

Antifreeze A substance (usually ethylene glycol) mixed with water, and added to a vehicle's cooling system, to prevent freezing of the coolant in winter. Antifreeze also contains chemicals to inhibit corrosion and the formation of rust and other deposits that would tend to clog the radiator and coolant passages and reduce cooling efficiency.

Anti-seize compound A coating that reduces the risk of seizing on fasteners that are subjected to high temperatures, such as exhaust manifold bolts and nuts.

Asbestos A natural fibrous mineral with great heat resistance, commonly used in the composition of brake friction materials. Asbestos is a health hazard and the dust created by brake systems should never be inhaled or ingested.

Axle A shaft on which a wheel revolves, or which revolves with a wheel. Also, a solid beam that connects the two wheels at one end of the vehicle. An axle which also transmits power to the wheels is known as a live axle.

Axleshaft A single rotating shaft, on either side of the differential, which delivers power from the final drive assembly to the drive wheels. Also called a driveshaft or a halfshaft.

B

Ball bearing An anti-friction bearing consisting of a hardened inner and outer race with hardened steel balls between two races.

Bearing The curved surface on a shaft or in a bore, or the part assembled into either, that permits relative motion between them with minimum wear and friction.

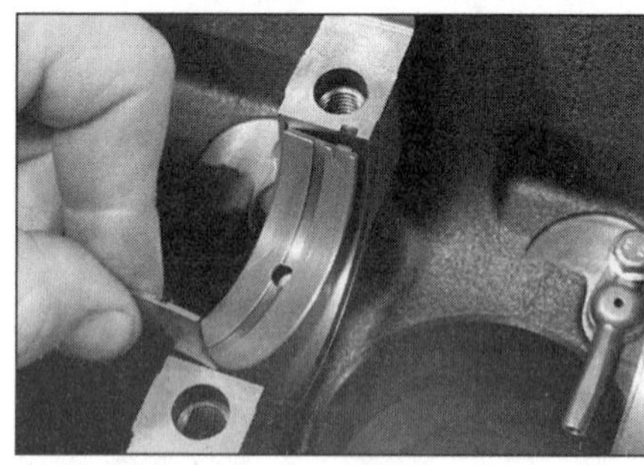

Bearing

Big-end bearing The bearing in the end of the connecting rod that's attached to the crankshaft.

Bleed nipple A valve on a brake wheel cylinder, caliper or other hydraulic component that is opened to purge the hydraulic system of air. Also called a bleed screw.

Brake bleeding Procedure for removing air from lines of a hydraulic brake system.

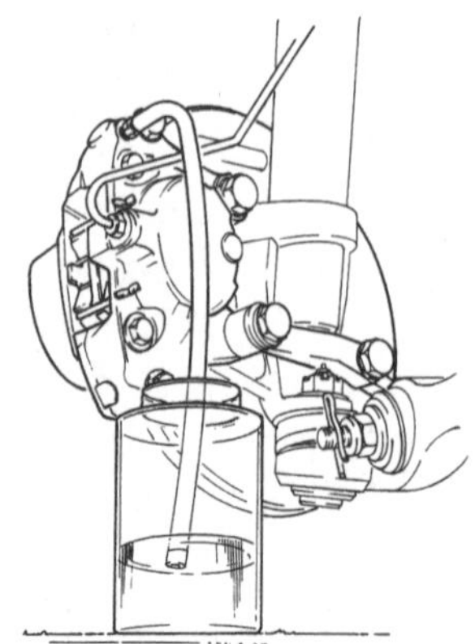

Brake bleeding

Brake disc The component of a disc brake that rotates with the wheels.

Brake drum The component of a drum brake that rotates with the wheels.

Brake linings The friction material which contacts the brake disc or drum to retard the vehicle's speed. The linings are bonded or riveted to the brake pads or shoes.

Brake pads The replaceable friction pads that pinch the brake disc when the brakes are applied. Brake pads consist of a friction material bonded or riveted to a rigid backing plate.

Brake shoe The crescent-shaped carrier to which the brake linings are mounted and which forces the lining against the rotating drum during braking.

Braking systems For more information on braking systems, consult the *Haynes Automotive Brake Manual*.

Breaker bar A long socket wrench handle providing greater leverage.

Bulkhead The insulated partition between the engine and the passenger compartment.

C

Caliper The non-rotating part of a disc-brake assembly that straddles the disc and carries the brake pads. The caliper also contains the hydraulic components that cause the pads to pinch the disc when the brakes are applied. A caliper is also a measuring tool that can be set to measure inside or outside dimensions of an object.

Camshaft A rotating shaft on which a series of cam lobes operate the valve mechanisms. The camshaft may be driven by gears, by sprockets and chain or by sprockets and a belt.

Canister A container in an evaporative emission control system; contains activated charcoal granules to trap vapours from the fuel system.

Canister

Carburettor A device which mixes fuel with air in the proper proportions to provide a desired power output from a spark ignition internal combustion engine.

Castellated Resembling the parapets along the top of a castle wall. For example, a castellated balljoint stud nut.

Castor In wheel alignment, the backward or forward tilt of the steering axis. Castor is positive when the steering axis is inclined rearward at the top.

Catalytic converter A silencer-like device in the exhaust system which converts certain pollutants in the exhaust gases into less harmful substances.

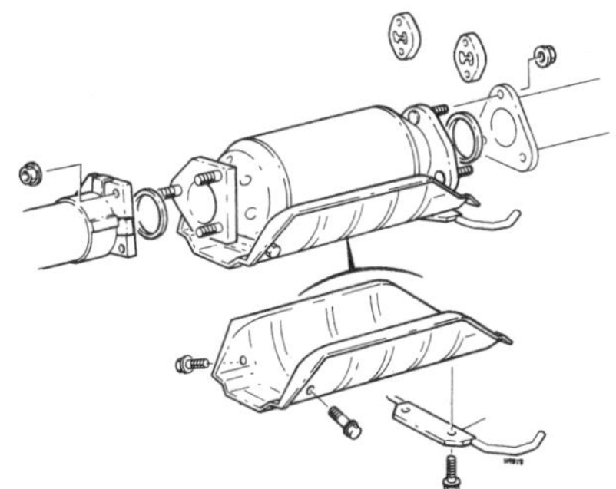

Catalytic converter

Circlip A ring-shaped clip used to prevent endwise movement of cylindrical parts and shafts. An internal circlip is installed in a groove in a housing; an external circlip fits into a groove on the outside of a cylindrical piece such as a shaft.

Clearance The amount of space between two parts. For example, between a piston and a cylinder, between a bearing and a journal, etc.

Coil spring A spiral of elastic steel found in various sizes throughout a vehicle, for example as a springing medium in the suspension and in the valve train.

Compression Reduction in volume, and increase in pressure and temperature, of a gas, caused by squeezing it into a smaller space.

Compression ratio The relationship between cylinder volume when the piston is at top dead centre and cylinder volume when the piston is at bottom dead centre.

Constant velocity (CV) joint A type of universal joint that cancels out vibrations caused by driving power being transmitted through an angle.

Core plug A disc or cup-shaped metal device inserted in a hole in a casting through which core was removed when the casting was formed. Also known as a freeze plug or expansion plug.

Crankcase The lower part of the engine block in which the crankshaft rotates.

Crankshaft The main rotating member, or shaft, running the length of the crankcase, with offset "throws" to which the connecting rods are attached.

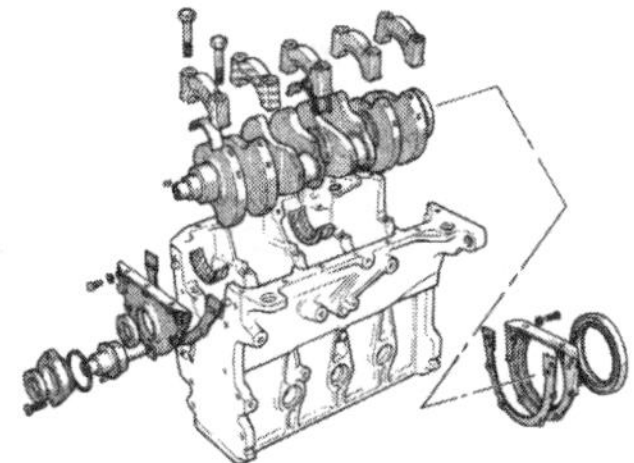

Crankshaft assembly

Crocodile clip See Alligator clip

D

Diagnostic code Code numbers obtained by accessing the diagnostic mode of an engine management computer. This code can be used to determine the area in the system where a malfunction may be located.

Disc brake A brake design incorporating a rotating disc onto which brake pads are squeezed. The resulting friction converts the energy of a moving vehicle into heat.

Double-overhead cam (DOHC) An engine that uses two overhead camshafts, usually one for the intake valves and one for the exhaust valves.

Drivebelt(s) The belt(s) used to drive accessories such as the alternator, water pump, power steering pump, air conditioning compressor, etc. off the crankshaft pulley.

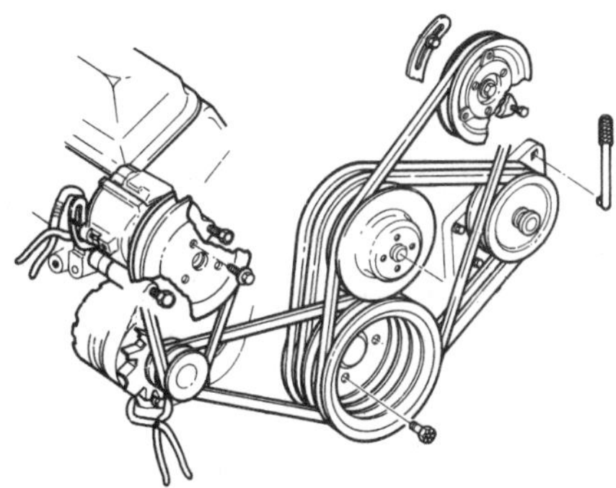

Accessory drivebelts

Driveshaft Any shaft used to transmit motion. Commonly used when referring to the axleshafts on a front wheel drive vehicle.

Drum brake A type of brake using a drum-shaped metal cylinder attached to the inner surface of the wheel. When the brake pedal is pressed, curved brake shoes with friction linings press against the inside of the drum to slow or stop the vehicle.

E

EGR valve A valve used to introduce exhaust gases into the intake air stream.

Electronic control unit (ECU) A computer which controls (for instance) ignition and fuel injection systems, or an anti-lock braking system. For more information refer to the *Haynes Automotive Electrical and Electronic Systems Manual.*

Electronic Fuel Injection (EFI) A computer controlled fuel system that distributes fuel through an injector located in each intake port of the engine.

Emergency brake A braking system, independent of the main hydraulic system, that can be used to slow or stop the vehicle if the primary brakes fail, or to hold the vehicle stationary even though the brake pedal isn't depressed. It usually consists of a hand lever that actuates either front or rear brakes mechanically through a series of cables and linkages. Also known as a handbrake or parking brake.

Endfloat The amount of lengthwise movement between two parts. As applied to a crankshaft, the distance that the crankshaft can move forward and back in the cylinder block.

Engine management system (EMS) A computer controlled system which manages the fuel injection and the ignition systems in an integrated fashion.

Exhaust manifold A part with several passages through which exhaust gases leave the engine combustion chambers and enter the exhaust pipe.

F

Fan clutch A viscous (fluid) drive coupling device which permits variable engine fan speeds in relation to engine speeds.

Feeler blade A thin strip or blade of hardened steel, ground to an exact thickness, used to check or measure clearances between parts.

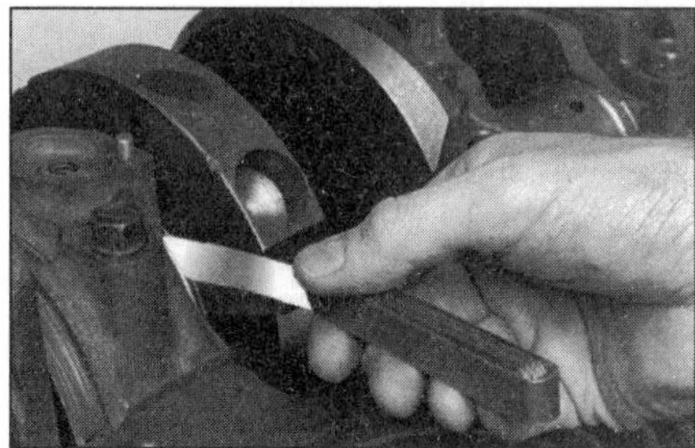

Feeler blade

Firing order The order in which the engine cylinders fire, or deliver their power strokes, beginning with the number one cylinder.

Flywheel A heavy spinning wheel in which energy is absorbed and stored by means of momentum. On cars, the flywheel is attached to the crankshaft to smooth out firing impulses.

Free play The amount of travel before any action takes place. The "looseness" in a linkage, or an assembly of parts, between the initial application of force and actual movement. For example, the distance the brake pedal moves before the pistons in the master cylinder are actuated.

Fuse An electrical device which protects a circuit against accidental overload. The typical fuse contains a soft piece of metal which is calibrated to melt at a predetermined current flow (expressed as amps) and break the circuit.

Fusible link A circuit protection device consisting of a conductor surrounded by heat-resistant insulation. The conductor is smaller than the wire it protects, so it acts as the weakest link in the circuit. Unlike a blown fuse, a failed fusible link must frequently be cut from the wire for replacement.

G

Gap The distance the spark must travel in jumping from the centre electrode to the side electrode in a spark plug. Also refers to the spacing between the points in a contact breaker assembly in a conventional points-type ignition, or to the distance between the reluctor or rotor and the pickup coil in an electronic ignition.

Adjusting spark plug gap

Gasket Any thin, soft material - usually cork, cardboard, asbestos or soft metal - installed between two metal surfaces to ensure a good seal. For instance, the cylinder head gasket seals the joint between the block and the cylinder head.

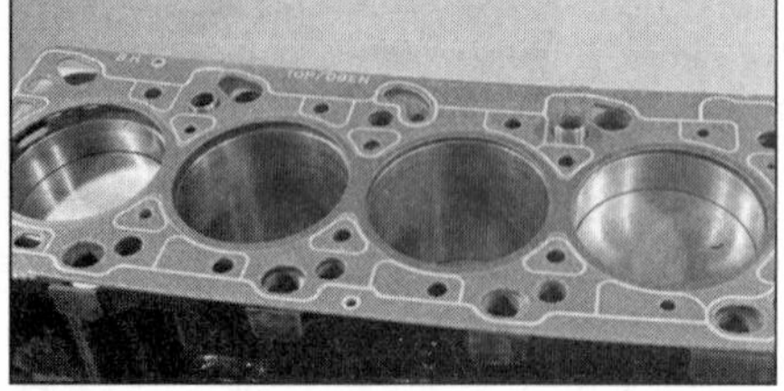

Gasket

Gauge An instrument panel display used to monitor engine conditions. A gauge with a movable pointer on a dial or a fixed scale is an analogue gauge. A gauge with a numerical readout is called a digital gauge.

H

Halfshaft A rotating shaft that transmits power from the final drive unit to a drive wheel, usually when referring to a live rear axle.

Harmonic balancer A device designed to reduce torsion or twisting vibration in the crankshaft. May be incorporated in the crankshaft pulley. Also known as a vibration damper.

Hone An abrasive tool for correcting small irregularities or differences in diameter in an engine cylinder, brake cylinder, etc.

Hydraulic tappet A tappet that utilises hydraulic pressure from the engine's lubrication system to maintain zero clearance (constant contact with both camshaft and valve stem). Automatically adjusts to variation in valve stem length. Hydraulic tappets also reduce valve noise.

I

Ignition timing The moment at which the spark plug fires, usually expressed in the number of crankshaft degrees before the piston reaches the top of its stroke.

Inlet manifold A tube or housing with passages through which flows the air-fuel mixture (carburettor vehicles and vehicles with throttle body injection) or air only (port fuel-injected vehicles) to the port openings in the cylinder head.

J

Jump start Starting the engine of a vehicle with a discharged or weak battery by attaching jump leads from the weak battery to a charged or helper battery.

L

Load Sensing Proportioning Valve (LSPV) A brake hydraulic system control valve that works like a proportioning valve, but also takes into consideration the amount of weight carried by the rear axle.

Locknut A nut used to lock an adjustment nut, or other threaded component, in place. For example, a locknut is employed to keep the adjusting nut on the rocker arm in position.

Lockwasher A form of washer designed to prevent an attaching nut from working loose.

M

MacPherson strut A type of front suspension system devised by Earle MacPherson at Ford of England. In its original form, a simple lateral link with the anti-roll bar creates the lower control arm. A long strut - an integral coil spring and shock absorber - is mounted between the body and the steering knuckle. Many modern so-called MacPherson strut systems use a conventional lower A-arm and don't rely on the anti-roll bar for location.

Multimeter An electrical test instrument with the capability to measure voltage, current and resistance.

N

NOx Oxides of Nitrogen. A common toxic pollutant emitted by petrol and diesel engines at higher temperatures.

O

Ohm The unit of electrical resistance. One volt applied to a resistance of one ohm will produce a current of one amp.

Ohmmeter An instrument for measuring electrical resistance.

O-ring A type of sealing ring made of a special rubber-like material; in use, the O-ring is compressed into a groove to provide the sealing action.

Overhead cam (ohc) engine An engine with the camshaft(s) located on top of the cylinder head(s).

Overhead valve (ohv) engine An engine with the valves located in the cylinder head, but with the camshaft located in the engine block.

Oxygen sensor A device installed in the engine exhaust manifold, which senses the oxygen content in the exhaust and converts this information into an electric current. Also called a Lambda sensor.

P

Phillips screw A type of screw head having a cross instead of a slot for a corresponding type of screwdriver.

Plastigage A thin strip of plastic thread, available in different sizes, used for measuring clearances. For example, a strip of Plastigage is laid across a bearing journal. The parts are assembled and dismantled; the width of the crushed strip indicates the clearance between journal and bearing.

Plastigage

Propeller shaft The long hollow tube with universal joints at both ends that carries power from the transmission to the differential on front-engined rear wheel drive vehicles.

Proportioning valve A hydraulic control valve which limits the amount of pressure to the rear brakes during panic stops to prevent wheel lock-up.

R

Rack-and-pinion steering A steering system with a pinion gear on the end of the steering shaft that mates with a rack (think of a geared wheel opened up and laid flat). When the steering wheel is turned, the pinion turns, moving the rack to the left or right. This movement is transmitted through the track rods to the steering arms at the wheels.

Radiator A liquid-to-air heat transfer device designed to reduce the temperature of the coolant in an internal combustion engine cooling system.

Refrigerant Any substance used as a heat transfer agent in an air-conditioning system. R-12 has been the principle refrigerant for many years; recently, however, manufacturers have begun using R-134a, a non-CFC substance that is considered less harmful to the ozone in the upper atmosphere.

Rocker arm A lever arm that rocks on a shaft or pivots on a stud. In an overhead valve engine, the rocker arm converts the upward movement of the pushrod into a downward movement to open a valve.

Rotor In a distributor, the rotating device inside the cap that connects the centre electrode and the outer terminals as it turns, distributing the high voltage from the coil secondary winding to the proper spark plug. Also, that part of an alternator which rotates inside the stator. Also, the rotating assembly of a turbocharger, including the compressor wheel, shaft and turbine wheel.
Runout The amount of wobble (in-and-out movement) of a gear or wheel as it's rotated. The amount a shaft rotates "out-of-true." The out-of-round condition of a rotating part.

S

Sealant A liquid or paste used to prevent leakage at a joint. Sometimes used in conjunction with a gasket.
Sealed beam lamp An older headlight design which integrates the reflector, lens and filaments into a hermetically-sealed one-piece unit. When a filament burns out or the lens cracks, the entire unit is simply replaced.
Serpentine drivebelt A single, long, wide accessory drivebelt that's used on some newer vehicles to drive all the accessories, instead of a series of smaller, shorter belts. Serpentine drivebelts are usually tensioned by an automatic tensioner.

Serpentine drivebelt

Shim Thin spacer, commonly used to adjust the clearance or relative positions between two parts. For example, shims inserted into or under bucket tappets control valve clearances. Clearance is adjusted by changing the thickness of the shim.
Slide hammer A special puller that screws into or hooks onto a component such as a shaft or bearing; a heavy sliding handle on the shaft bottoms against the end of the shaft to knock the component free.
Sprocket A tooth or projection on the periphery of a wheel, shaped to engage with a chain or drivebelt. Commonly used to refer to the sprocket wheel itself.
Starter inhibitor switch On vehicles with an automatic transmission, a switch that prevents starting if the vehicle is not in Neutral or Park.
Strut See MacPherson strut.

T

Tappet A cylindrical component which transmits motion from the cam to the valve stem, either directly or via a pushrod and rocker arm. Also called a cam follower.
Thermostat A heat-controlled valve that regulates the flow of coolant between the cylinder block and the radiator, so maintaining optimum engine operating temperature. A thermostat is also used in some air cleaners in which the temperature is regulated.
Thrust bearing The bearing in the clutch assembly that is moved in to the release levers by clutch pedal action to disengage the clutch. Also referred to as a release bearing.
Timing belt A toothed belt which drives the camshaft. Serious engine damage may result if it breaks in service.
Timing chain A chain which drives the camshaft.
Toe-in The amount the front wheels are closer together at the front than at the rear. On rear wheel drive vehicles, a slight amount of toe-in is usually specified to keep the front wheels running parallel on the road by offsetting other forces that tend to spread the wheels apart.
Toe-out The amount the front wheels are closer together at the rear than at the front. On front wheel drive vehicles, a slight amount of toe-out is usually specified.
Tools For full information on choosing and using tools, refer to the *Haynes Automotive Tools Manual.*
Tracer A stripe of a second colour applied to a wire insulator to distinguish that wire from another one with the same colour insulator.
Tune-up A process of accurate and careful adjustments and parts replacement to obtain the best possible engine performance.
Turbocharger A centrifugal device, driven by exhaust gases, that pressurises the intake air. Normally used to increase the power output from a given engine displacement, but can also be used primarily to reduce exhaust emissions (as on VW's "Umwelt" Diesel engine).

U

Universal joint or U-joint A double-pivoted connection for transmitting power from a driving to a driven shaft through an angle. A U-joint consists of two Y-shaped yokes and a cross-shaped member called the spider.

V

Valve A device through which the flow of liquid, gas, vacuum, or loose material in bulk may be started, stopped, or regulated by a movable part that opens, shuts, or partially obstructs one or more ports or passageways. A valve is also the movable part of such a device.
Valve clearance The clearance between the valve tip (the end of the valve stem) and the rocker arm or tappet. The valve clearance is measured when the valve is closed.
Vernier caliper A precision measuring instrument that measures inside and outside dimensions. Not quite as accurate as a micrometer, but more convenient.
Viscosity The thickness of a liquid or its resistance to flow.
Volt A unit for expressing electrical "pressure" in a circuit. One volt that will produce a current of one ampere through a resistance of one ohm.

W

Welding Various processes used to join metal items by heating the areas to be joined to a molten state and fusing them together. For more information refer to the *Haynes Automotive Welding Manual.*
Wiring diagram A drawing portraying the components and wires in a vehicle's electrical system, using standardised symbols. For more information refer to the *Haynes Automotive Electrical and Electronic Systems Manual.*

Note: *References throughout this index are in the form* **"Chapter number" • "Page number"**. *So, for example, 2C•15 refers to page 15 of Chapter 2C.*

A

B

C

D

Note: *References throughout this index are in the form* **"Chapter number" • "Page number"**. *So, for example, 2C•15 refers to page 15 of Chapter 2C.*

Note: *References throughout this index are in the form* **"Chapter number" • "Page number"**. *So, for example, 2C•15 refers to page 15 of Chapter 2C.*

Note: *References throughout this index are in the form* **"Chapter number" • "Page number"**. *So, for example, 2C•15 refers to page 15 of Chapter 2C.*

Haynes Manuals – The Complete **UK Car** List

Title	Book No.
ALFA ROMEO Alfasud/Sprint (74 - 88) up to F *	**0292**
Alfa Romeo Alfetta (73 - 87) up to E *	**0531**
AUDI 80, 90 & Coupe Petrol (79 - Nov 88) up to F	**0605**
Audi 80, 90 & Coupe Petrol (Oct 86 - 90) D to H	**1491**
Audi 100 & 200 Petrol (Oct 82 - 90) up to H	**0907**
Audi 100 & A6 Petrol & Diesel (May 91 - May 97) H to P	**3504**
Audi A3 Petrol & Diesel (96 - May 03) P to 03	**4253**
Audi A4 Petrol & Diesel (95 - 00) M to X	**3575**
Audi A4 Petrol & Diesel (01 - 04) X to 54	**4609**
AUSTIN A35 & A40 (56 - 67) up to F *	**0118**
Austin/MG/Rover Maestro 1.3 & 1.6 Petrol (83 - 95) up to M	**0922**
Austin/MG Metro (80 - May 90) up to G	**0718**
Austin/Rover Montego 1.3 & 1.6 Petrol (84 - 94) A to L	**1066**
Austin/MG/Rover Montego 2.0 Petrol (84 - 95) A to M	**1067**
Mini (59 - 69) up to H *	**0527**
Mini (69 - 01) up to X	**0646**
Austin/Rover 2.0 litre Diesel Engine (86 - 93) C to L	**1857**
Austin Healey 100/6 & 3000 (56 - 68) up to G *	**0049**
BEDFORD CF Petrol (69 - 87) up to E	**0163**
Bedford/Vauxhall Rascal & Suzuki Supercarry (86 - Oct 94) C to M	**3015**
BMW 316, 320 & 320i (4-cyl) (75 - Feb 83) up to Y *	**0276**
BMW 320, 320i, 323i & 325i (6-cyl) (Oct 77 - Sept 87) up to E	**0815**
BMW 3- & 5-Series Petrol (81 - 91) up to J	**1948**
BMW 3-Series Petrol (Apr 91 - 99) H to V	**3210**
BMW 3-Series Petrol (Sept 98 - 03) S to 53	**4067**
BMW 520i & 525e (Oct 81 - June 88) up to E	**1560**
BMW 525, 528 & 528i (73 - Sept 81) up to X *	**0632**
BMW 5-Series 6-cyl Petrol (April 96 - Aug 03) N to 03	**4151**
BMW 1500, 1502, 1600, 1602, 2000 & 2002 (59 - 77) up to S *	**0240**
CHRYSLER PT Cruiser Petrol (00 - 03) W to 53	**4058**
CITROËN 2CV, Ami & Dyane (67 - 90) up to H	**0196**
Citroën AX Petrol & Diesel (87 - 97) D to P	**3014**
Citroën Berlingo & Peugeot Partner Petrol & Diesel (96 - 05) P to 55	**4281**
Citroën BX Petrol (83 - 94) A to L	**0908**
Citroën C15 Van Petrol & Diesel (89 - Oct 98) F to S	**3509**
Citroën C3 Petrol & Diesel (02 - 05) 51 to 05	**4197**
Citroen C5 Petrol & Diesel (01-08) Y to 08	**4745**
Citroën CX Petrol (75 - 88) up to F	**0528**
Citroën Saxo Petrol & Diesel (96 - 04) N to 54	**3506**
Citroën Visa Petrol (79 - 88) up to F	**0620**
Citroën Xantia Petrol & Diesel (93 - 01) K to Y	**3082**
Citroën XM Petrol & Diesel (89 - 00) G to X	**3451**
Citroën Xsara Petrol & Diesel (97 - Sept 00) R to W	**3751**
Citroën Xsara Picasso Petrol & Diesel (00 - 02) W to 52	**3944**
Citroen Xsara Picasso (03-08)	**4784**
Citroën ZX Diesel (91 - 98) J to S	**1922**
Citroën ZX Petrol (91 - 98) H to S	**1881**
Citroën 1.7 & 1.9 litre Diesel Engine (84 - 96) A to N	**1379**
FIAT 126 (73 - 87) up to E *	**0305**
Fiat 500 (57 - 73) up to M *	**0090**
Fiat Bravo & Brava Petrol (95 - 00) N to W	**3572**
Fiat Cinquecento (93 - 98) K to R	**3501**
Fiat Panda (81 - 95) up to M	**0793**
Fiat Punto Petrol & Diesel (94 - Oct 99) L to V	**3251**
Fiat Punto Petrol (Oct 99 - July 03) V to 03	**4066**
Fiat Punto Petrol (03-07) 03 to 07	**4746**
Fiat Regata Petrol (84 - 88) A to F	**1167**
Fiat Tipo Petrol (88 - 91) E to J	**1625**
Fiat Uno Petrol (83 - 95) up to M	**0923**
Fiat X1/9 (74 - 89) up to G *	**0273**
FORD Anglia (59 - 68) up to G *	**0001**

Title	Book No.
Ford Capri II (& III) 1.6 & 2.0 (74 - 87) up to E *	**0283**
Ford Capri II (& III) 2.8 & 3.0 V6 (74 - 87) up to E	**1309**
Ford Cortina Mk I & Corsair 1500 ('62 - '66) up to D*	**0214**
Ford Cortina Mk III 1300 & 1600 (70 - 76) up to P *	**0070**
Ford Escort Mk I 1100 & 1300 (68 - 74) up to N *	**0171**
Ford Escort Mk I Mexico, RS 1600 & RS 2000 (70 - 74) up to N *	**0139**
Ford Escort Mk II Mexico, RS 1800 & RS 2000 (75 - 80) up to W *	**0735**
Ford Escort (75 - Aug 80) up to V *	**0280**
Ford Escort Petrol (Sept 80 - Sept 90) up to H	**0686**
Ford Escort & Orion Petrol (Sept 90 - 00) H to X	**1737**
Ford Escort & Orion Diesel (Sept 90 - 00) H to X	**4081**
Ford Fiesta (76 - Aug 83) up to Y	**0334**
Ford Fiesta Petrol (Aug 83 - Feb 89) A to F	**1030**
Ford Fiesta Petrol (Feb 89 - Oct 95) F to N	**1595**
Ford Fiesta Petrol & Diesel (Oct 95 - Mar 02) N to 02	**3397**
Ford Fiesta Petrol & Diesel (Apr 02 - 07) 02 to 57	**4170**
Ford Focus Petrol & Diesel (98 - 01) S to Y	**3759**
Ford Focus Petrol & Diesel (Oct 01 - 05) 51 to 05	**4167**
Ford Galaxy Petrol & Diesel (95 - Aug 00) M to W	**3984**
Ford Granada Petrol (Sept 77 - Feb 85) up to B *	**0481**
Ford Granada & Scorpio Petrol (Mar 85 - 94) B to M	**1245**
Ford Ka (96 - 02) P to 52	**3570**
Ford Mondeo Petrol (93 - Sept 00) K to X	**1923**
Ford Mondeo Petrol & Diesel (Oct 00 - Jul 03) X to 03	**3990**
Ford Mondeo Petrol & Diesel (July 03 - 07) 03 to 56	**4619**
Ford Mondeo Diesel (93 - 96) L to N	**3465**
Ford Orion Petrol (83 - Sept 90) up to H	**1009**
Ford Sierra 4-cyl Petrol (82 - 93) up to K	**0903**
Ford Sierra V6 Petrol (82 - 91) up to J	**0904**
Ford Transit Petrol (Mk 2) (78 - Jan 86) up to C	**0719**
Ford Transit Petrol (Mk 3) (Feb 86 - 89) C to G	**1468**
Ford Transit Diesel (Feb 86 - 99) C to T	**3019**
Ford Transit Diesel (00-06)	**4775**
Ford 1.6 & 1.8 litre Diesel Engine (84 - 96) A to N	**1172**
Ford 2.1, 2.3 & 2.5 litre Diesel Engine (77 - 90) up to H	**1606**
FREIGHT ROVER Sherpa Petrol (74 - 87) up to E	**0463**
HILLMAN Avenger (70 - 82) up to Y	**0037**
Hillman Imp (63 - 76) up to R *	**0022**
HONDA Civic (Feb 84 - Oct 87) A to E	**1226**
Honda Civic (Nov 91 - 96) J to N	**3199**
Honda Civic Petrol (Mar 95 - 00) M to X	**4050**
Honda Civic Petrol & Diesel (01 - 05) X to 55	**4611**
Honda CR-V Petrol & Diesel (01-06)	**4747**
Honda Jazz (01 - Feb 08) 51 - 57	**4735**
HYUNDAI Pony (85 - 94) C to M	**3398**
JAGUAR E Type (61 - 72) up to L *	**0140**
Jaguar MkI & II, 240 & 340 (55 - 69) up to H *	**0098**
Jaguar XJ6, XJ & Sovereign; Daimler Sovereign (68 - Oct 86) up to D	**0242**
Jaguar XJ6 & Sovereign (Oct 86 - Sept 94) D to M	**3261**
Jaguar XJ12, XJS & Sovereign; Daimler Double Six (72 - 88) up to F	**0478**
JEEP Cherokee Petrol (93 - 96) K to N	**1943**
LADA 1200, 1300, 1500 & 1600 (74 - 91) up to J	**0413**
Lada Samara (87 - 91) D to J	**1610**
LAND ROVER 90, 110 & Defender Diesel (83 - 07) up to 56	**3017**
Land Rover Discovery Petrol & Diesel (89 - 98) G to S	**3016**
Land Rover Discovery Diesel (Nov 98 - Jul 04) S to 04	**4606**
Land Rover Freelander Petrol & Diesel (97 - Sept 03) R to 53	**3929**
Land Rover Freelander Petrol & Diesel (Oct 03 - Oct 06) 53 to 56	**4623**

Title	Book No.
Land Rover Series IIA & III Diesel (58 - 85) up to C	**0529**
Land Rover Series II, IIA & III 4-cyl Petrol (58 - 85) up to C	**0314**
MAZDA 323 (Mar 81 - Oct 89) up to G	**1608**
Mazda 323 (Oct 89 - 98) G to R	**3455**
Mazda 626 (May 83 - Sept 87) up to E	**0929**
Mazda B1600, B1800 & B2000 Pick-up Petrol (72 - 88) up to F	**0267**
Mazda RX-7 (79 - 85) up to C *	**0460**
MERCEDES-BENZ 190, 190E & 190D Petrol & Diesel (83 - 93) A to L	**3450**
Mercedes-Benz 200D, 240D, 240TD, 300D & 300TD 123 Series Diesel (Oct 76 - 85)	**1114**
Mercedes-Benz 250 & 280 (68 - 72) up to L *	**0346**
Mercedes-Benz 250 & 280 123 Series Petrol (Oct 76 - 84) up to B *	**0677**
Mercedes-Benz 124 Series Petrol & Diesel (85 - Aug 93) C to K	**3253**
Mercedes-Benz A-Class Petrol & Diesel (98-04) S to 54)	**4748**
Mercedes-Benz C-Class Petrol & Diesel (93 - Aug 00) L to W	**3511**
Mercedes-Benz C-Class (00-06)	**4780**
MGA (55 - 62) *	**0475**
MGB (62 - 80) up to W	**0111**
MG Midget & Austin-Healey Sprite (58 - 80) up to W *	**0265**
MINI Petrol (July 01 - 05) Y to 05	**4273**
MITSUBISHI Shogun & L200 Pick-Ups Petrol (83 - 94) up to M	**1944**
MORRIS Ital 1.3 (80 - 84) up to B	**0705**
Morris Minor 1000 (56 - 71) up to K	**0024**
NISSAN Almera Petrol (95 - Feb 00) N to V	**4053**
Nissan Almera & Tino Petrol (Feb 00 - 07) V to 56	**4612**
Nissan Bluebird (May 84 - Mar 86) A to C	**1223**
Nissan Bluebird Petrol (Mar 86 - 90) C to H	**1473**
Nissan Cherry (Sept 82 - 86) up to D	**1031**
Nissan Micra (83 - Jan 93) up to K	**0931**
Nissan Micra (93 - 02) K to 52	**3254**
Nissan Micra Petrol (03-07) 52 to 57	**4734**
Nissan Primera Petrol (90 - Aug 99) H to T	**1851**
Nissan Stanza (82 - 86) up to D	**0824**
Nissan Sunny Petrol (May 82 - Oct 86) up to D	**0895**
Nissan Sunny Petrol (Oct 86 - Mar 91) D to H	**1378**
Nissan Sunny Petrol (Apr 91 - 95) H to N	**3219**
OPEL Ascona & Manta (B Series) (Sept 75 - 88) up to F *	**0316**
Opel Ascona Petrol (81 - 88)	**3215**
Opel Astra Petrol (Oct 91 - Feb 98)	**3156**
Opel Corsa Petrol (83 - Mar 93)	**3160**
Opel Corsa Petrol (Mar 93 - 97)	**3159**
Opel Kadett Petrol (Nov 79 - Oct 84) up to B	**0634**
Opel Kadett Petrol (Oct 84 - Oct 91)	**3196**
Opel Omega & Senator Petrol (Nov 86 - 94)	**3157**
Opel Rekord Petrol (Feb 78 - Oct 86) up to D	**0543**
Opel Vectra Petrol (Oct 88 - Oct 95)	**3158**
PEUGEOT 106 Petrol & Diesel (91 - 04) J to 53	**1882**
Peugeot 205 Petrol (83 - 97) A to P	**0932**
Peugeot 206 Petrol & Diesel (98 - 01) S to X	**3757**
Peugeot 206 Petrol & Diesel (02 - 06) 51 to 06	**4613**
Peugeot 306 Petrol & Diesel (93 - 02) K to 02	**3073**
Peugeot 307 Petrol & Diesel (01 - 04) Y to 54	**4147**
Peugeot 309 Petrol (86 - 93) C to K	**1266**
Peugeot 405 Petrol (88 - 97) E to P	**1559**
Peugeot 405 Diesel (88 - 97) E to P	**3198**
Peugeot 406 Petrol & Diesel (96 - Mar 99) N to T	**3394**
Peugeot 406 Petrol & Diesel (Mar 99 - 02) T to 52	**3982**

* Classic reprint

Title	Book No.
Peugeot 505 Petrol (79 - 89) up to G	**0762**
Peugeot 1.7/1.8 & 1.9 litre Diesel Engine (82 - 96) up to N	**0950**
Peugeot 2.0, 2.1, 2.3 & 2.5 litre Diesel Engines (74 - 90) up to H	**1607**
PORSCHE 911 (65 - 85) up to C	**0264**
Porsche 924 & 924 Turbo (76 - 85) up to C	**0397**
PROTON (89 - 97) F to P	**3255**
RANGE ROVER V8 Petrol (70 - Oct 92) up to K	**0606**
RELIANT Robin & Kitten (73 - 83) up to A *	**0436**
RENAULT 4 (61 - 86) up to D *	**0072**
Renault 5 Petrol (Feb 85 - 96) B to N	**1219**
Renault 9 & 11 Petrol (82 - 89) up to F	**0822**
Renault 18 Petrol (79 - 86) up to D	**0598**
Renault 19 Petrol (89 - 96) F to N	**1646**
Renault 19 Diesel (89 - 96) F to N	**1946**
Renault 21 Petrol (86 - 94) C to M	**1397**
Renault 25 Petrol & Diesel (84 - 92) B to K	**1228**
Renault Clio Petrol (91 - May 98) H to R	**1853**
Renault Clio Diesel (91 - June 96) H to N	**3031**
Renault Clio Petrol & Diesel (May 98 - May 01) R to Y	**3906**
Renault Clio Petrol & Diesel (June '01 - '05) Y to 55	**4168**
Renault Espace Petrol & Diesel (85 - 96) C to N	**3197**
Renault Laguna Petrol & Diesel (94 - 00) L to W	**3252**
Renault Laguna Petrol & Diesel (Feb 01 - Feb 05) X to 54	**4283**
Renault Mégane & Scénic Petrol & Diesel (96 - 99) N to T	**3395**
Renault Mégane & Scénic Petrol & Diesel (Apr 99 - 02) T to 52	**3916**
Renault Megane Petrol & Diesel (Oct 02 - 05) 52 to 55	**4284**
Renault Scenic Petrol & Diesel (Sept 03 - 06) 53 to 06	**4297**
ROVER 213 & 216 (84 - 89) A to G	**1116**
Rover 214 & 414 Petrol (89 - 96) G to N	**1689**
Rover 216 & 416 Petrol (89 - 96) G to N	**1830**
Rover 211, 214, 216, 218 & 220 Petrol & Diesel (Dec 95 - 99) N to V	**3399**
Rover 25 & MG ZR Petrol & Diesel (Oct 99 - 04) V to 54	**4145**
Rover 414, 416 & 420 Petrol & Diesel (May 95 - 98) M to R	**3453**
Rover 45 / MG ZS Petrol & Diesel (99 - 05) V to 55	**4384**
Rover 618, 620 & 623 Petrol (93 - 97) K to P	**3257**
Rover 75 / MG ZT Petrol & Diesel (99 - 06) S to 06	**4292**
Rover 820, 825 & 827 Petrol (86 - 95) D to N	**1380**
Rover 3500 (76 - 87) up to E *	**0365**
Rover Metro, 111 & 114 Petrol (May 90 - 98) G to S	**1711**
SAAB 95 & 96 (66 - 76) up to R *	**0198**
Saab 90, 99 & 900 (79 - Oct 93) up to L	**0765**
Saab 900 (Oct 93 - 98) L to R	**3512**
Saab 9000 (4-cyl) (85 - 98) C to S	**1686**
Saab 9-3 Petrol & Diesel (98 - Aug 02) R to 02	**4614**
Saab 9-3 Petrol & Diesel (02-07) 52 to 57	**4749**
Saab 9-5 4-cyl Petrol (97 - 04) R to 54	**4156**
SEAT Ibiza & Cordoba Petrol & Diesel (Oct 93 - Oct 99) L to V	**3571**
Seat Ibiza & Malaga Petrol (85 - 92) B to K	**1609**
SKODA Estelle (77 - 89) up to G	**0604**
Skoda Fabia Petrol & Diesel (00 - 06) W to 06	**4376**
Skoda Favorit (89 - 96) F to N	**1801**
Skoda Felicia Petrol & Diesel (95 - 01) M to X	**3505**
Skoda Octavia Petrol & Diesel (98 - Apr 04) R to 04	**4285**
SUBARU 1600 & 1800 (Nov 79 - 90) up to H *	**0995**

Title	Book No.
SUNBEAM Alpine, Rapier & H120 (67 - 74) up to N *	**0051**
SUZUKI SJ Series, Samurai & Vitara (4-cyl) Petrol (82 - 97) up to P	**1942**
Suzuki Supercarry & Bedford/Vauxhall Rascal (86 - Oct 94) C to M	**3015**
TALBOT Alpine, Solara, Minx & Rapier (75 - 86) up to D	**0337**
Talbot Horizon Petrol (78 - 86) up to D	**0473**
Talbot Samba (82 - 86) up to D	**0823**
TOYOTA Avensis Petrol (98 - Jan 03) R to 52	**4264**
Toyota Carina E Petrol (May 92 - 97) J to P	**3256**
Toyota Corolla (80 - 85) up to C	**0683**
Toyota Corolla (Sept 83 - Sept 87) A to E	**1024**
Toyota Corolla (Sept 87 - Aug 92) E to K	**1683**
Toyota Corolla Petrol (Aug 92 - 97) K to P	**3259**
Toyota Corolla Petrol (July 97 - Feb 02) P to 51	**4286**
Toyota Hi-Ace & Hi-Lux Petrol (69 - Oct 83) up to A	**0304**
Toyota RAV4 Petrol & Diesel (94-06) L to 55	**4750**
Toyota Yaris Petrol (99 - 05) T to 05	**4265**
TRIUMPH GT6 & Vitesse (62 - 74) up to N *	**0112**
Triumph Herald (59 - 71) up to K *	**0010**
Triumph Spitfire (62 - 81) up to X	**0113**
Triumph Stag (70 - 78) up to T *	**0441**
Triumph TR2, TR3, TR3A, TR4 & TR4A (52 - 67) up to F *	**0028**
Triumph TR5 & 6 (67 - 75) up to P *	**0031**
Triumph TR7 (75 - 82) up to Y *	**0322**
VAUXHALL Astra Petrol (80 - Oct 84) up to B	**0635**
Vauxhall Astra & Belmont Petrol (Oct 84 - Oct 91) B to J	**1136**
Vauxhall Astra Petrol (Oct 91 - Feb 98) J to R	**1832**
Vauxhall/Opel Astra & Zafira Petrol (Feb 98 - Apr 04) R to 04	**3758**
Vauxhall/Opel Astra & Zafira Diesel (Feb 98 - Apr 04) R to 04	**3797**
Vauxhall/Opel Astra Petrol (04 - 08)	**4732**
Vauxhall/Opel Astra Diesel (04 - 08)	**4733**
Vauxhall/Opel Calibra (90 - 98) G to S	**3502**
Vauxhall Carlton Petrol (Oct 78 - Oct 86) up to D	**0480**
Vauxhall Carlton & Senator Petrol (Nov 86 - 94) D to L	**1469**
Vauxhall Cavalier Petrol (81 - Oct 88) up to F	**0812**
Vauxhall Cavalier Petrol (Oct 88 - 95) F to N	**1570**
Vauxhall Chevette (75 - 84) up to B	**0285**
Vauxhall/Opel Corsa Diesel (Mar 93 - Oct 00) K to X	**4087**
Vauxhall Corsa Petrol (Mar 93 - 97) K to R	**1985**
Vauxhall/Opel Corsa Petrol (Apr 97 - Oct 00) P to X	**3921**
Vauxhall/Opel Corsa Petrol & Diesel (Oct 00 - Sept 03) X to 53	**4079**
Vauxhall/Opel Corsa Petrol & Diesel (Oct 03 - Aug 06) 53 to 06	**4617**
Vauxhall/Opel Frontera Petrol & Diesel (91 - Sept 98) J to S	**3454**
Vauxhall Nova Petrol (83 - 93) up to K	**0909**
Vauxhall/Opel Omega Petrol (94 - 99) L to T	**3510**
Vauxhall/Opel Vectra Petrol & Diesel (95 - Feb 99) N to S	**3396**
Vauxhall/Opel Vectra Petrol & Diesel (Mar 99 - May 02) T to 02	**3930**
Vauxhall/Opel Vectra Petrol & Diesel (June 02 - Sept 05) 02 to 55	**4618**
Vauxhall/Opel 1.5, 1.6 & 1.7 litre Diesel Engine (82 - 96) up to N	**1222**
VW 411 & 412 (68 - 75) up to P *	**0091**
VW Beetle 1200 (54 - 77) up to S	**0036**
VW Beetle 1300 & 1500 (65 - 75) up to P	**0039**

Title	Book No.
VW 1302 & 1302S (70 - 72) up to L *	**0110**
VW Beetle 1303, 1303S & GT (72 - 75) up to P	**0159**
VW Beetle Petrol & Diesel (Apr 99 - 07) T to 57	**3798**
VW Golf & Jetta Mk 1 Petrol 1.1 & 1.3 (74 - 84) up to A	**0716**
VW Golf, Jetta & Scirocco Mk 1 Petrol 1.5, 1.6 & 1.8 (74 - 84) up to A	**0726**
VW Golf & Jetta Mk 1 Diesel (78 - 84) up to A	**0451**
VW Golf & Jetta Mk 2 Petrol (Mar 84 - Feb 92) A to J	**1081**
VW Golf & Vento Petrol & Diesel (Feb 92 - Mar 98) J to R	**3097**
VW Golf & Bora Petrol & Diesel (April 98 - 00) R to X	**3727**
VW Golf & Bora 4-cyl Petrol & Diesel (01 - 03) X to 53	**4169**
VW Golf & Jetta Petrol & Diesel (04 - 07) 53 to 07	**4610**
VW LT Petrol Vans & Light Trucks (76 - 87) up to E	**0637**
VW Passat & Santana Petrol (Sept 81 - May 88) up to E	**0814**
VW Passat 4-cyl Petrol & Diesel (May 88 - 96) E to P	**3498**
VW Passat 4-cyl Petrol & Diesel (Dec 96 - Nov 00) P to X	**3917**
VW Passat Petrol & Diesel (Dec 00 - May 05) X to 05	**4279**
VW Polo & Derby (76 - Jan 82) up to X	**0335**
VW Polo (82 - Oct 90) up to H	**0813**
VW Polo Petrol (Nov 90 - Aug 94) H to L	**3245**
VW Polo Hatchback Petrol & Diesel (94 - 99) M to S	**3500**
VW Polo Hatchback Petrol (00 - Jan 02) V to 51	**4150**
VW Polo Petrol & Diesel (02 - May 05) 51 to 05	**4608**
VW Scirocco (82 - 90) up to H *	**1224**
VW Transporter 1600 (68 - 79) up to V	**0082**
VW Transporter 1700, 1800 & 2000 (72 - 79) up to V *	**0226**
VW Transporter (air-cooled) Petrol (79 - 82) up to Y *	**0638**
VW Transporter (water-cooled) Petrol (82 - 90) up to H	**3452**
VW Type 3 (63 - 73) up to M *	**0084**
VOLVO 120 & 130 Series (& P1800) (61 - 73) up to M *	**0203**
Volvo 142, 144 & 145 (66 - 74) up to N *	**0129**
Volvo 240 Series Petrol (74 - 93) up to K	**0270**
Volvo 262, 264 & 260/265 (75 - 85) up to C *	**0400**
Volvo 340, 343, 345 & 360 (76 - 91) up to J	**0715**
Volvo 440, 460 & 480 Petrol (87 - 97) D to P	**1691**
Volvo 740 & 760 Petrol (82 - 91) up to J	**1258**
Volvo 850 Petrol (92 - 96) J to P	**3260**
Volvo 940 petrol (90 - 98) H to R	**3249**
Volvo S40 & V40 Petrol (96 - Mar 04) N to 04	**3569**
Volvo S40 & V50 Petrol & Diesel (Mar 04 - Jun 07) 04 to 07	**4731**
Volvo S60 Petrol & Diesel (01-08)	**4793**
Volvo S70, V70 & C70 Petrol (96 - 99) P to V	**3573**
Volvo V70 / S80 Petrol & Diesel (98 - 05) S to 55	**4263**

DIY MANUAL SERIES

Title	Book No.
The Haynes Air Conditioning Manual	**4192**
The Haynes Car Electrical Systems Manual	**4251**
The Haynes Manual on Bodywork	**4198**
The Haynes Manual on Brakes	**4178**
The Haynes Manual on Carburettors	**4177**
The Haynes Manual on Diesel Engines	**4174**
The Haynes Manual on Engine Management	**4199**
The Haynes Manual on Fault Codes	**4175**
The Haynes Manual on Practical Electrical Systems	**4267**
The Haynes Manual on Small Engines	**4250**
The Haynes Manual on Welding	**4176**

* Classic reprint

Preserving Our Motoring Heritage

< *The Model J Duesenberg Derham Tourster. Only eight of these magnificent cars were ever built – this is the only example to be found outside the United States of America*

Almost every car you've ever loved, loathed or desired is gathered under one roof at the Haynes Motor Museum. Over 300 immaculately presented cars and motorbikes represent every aspect of our motoring heritage, from elegant reminders of bygone days, such as the superb Model J Duesenberg to curiosities like the bug-eyed BMW Isetta. There are also many old friends and flames. Perhaps you remember the 1959 Ford Popular that you did your courting in? The magnificent 'Red Collection' is a spectacle of classic sports cars including AC, Alfa Romeo, Austin Healey, Ferrari, Lamborghini, Maserati, MG, Riley, Porsche and Triumph.

A Perfect Day Out

Each and every vehicle at the Haynes Motor Museum has played its part in the history and culture of Motoring. Today, they make a wonderful spectacle and a great day out for all the family. Bring the kids, bring Mum and Dad, but above all bring your camera to capture those golden memories for ever. You will also find an impressive array of motoring memorabilia, a comfortable 70 seat video cinema and one of the most extensive transport book shops in Britain. The Pit Stop Cafe serves everything from a cup of tea to wholesome, home-made meals or, if you prefer, you can enjoy the large picnic area nestled in the beautiful rural surroundings of Somerset.

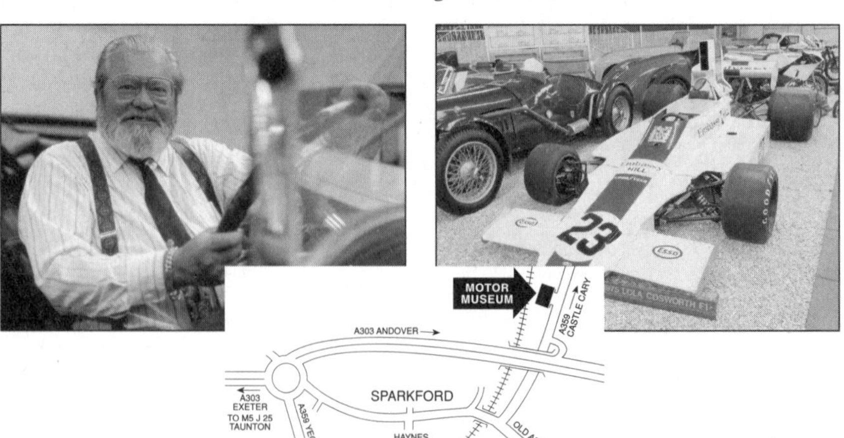

> *John Haynes O.B.E., Founder and Chairman of the museum at the wheel of a Haynes Light 12.*

< *Graham Hill's Lola Cosworth Formula 1 car next to a 1934 Riley Sports.*

The Museum is situated on the A359 Yeovil to Frome road at Sparkford, just off the A303 in Somerset. It is about 40 miles south of Bristol, and 25 minutes drive from the M5 intersection at Taunton.

Open 9.30am - 5.30pm (10.00am - 4.00pm Winter) 7 days a week, *except Christmas Day, Boxing Day and New Years Day*

Special rates available for schools, coach parties and outings Charitable Trust No. 292048